OXFORD HISTORY OF
MODERN EUROPE

General Editors
LORD BULLOCK *and* SIR WILLIAM DEAKIN

Oxford History of Modern Europe

THE STRUGGLE FOR MASTERY
IN EUROPE 1848–1918   *Available in paperback*
By A. J. P. TAYLOR

THE RUSSIAN EMPIRE 1801–1917
By HUGH SETON-WATSON

A HISTORY OF FRENCH PASSIONS
By THEODORE ZELDIN   *Available in paperback in two volumes:*

AMBITION, LOVE, AND POLITICS
INTELLECT, TASTE, AND ANXIETY

GERMANY 1866–1945
By GORDON A. CRAIG   *Available in paperback*

THE LOW COUNTRIES 1780–1940
By E. H. KOSSMANN

SPAIN 1808–1975   *Available in paperback*
By RAYMOND CARR

GERMAN HISTORY 1770–1866   *Available in paperback*
By JAMES J. SHEEHAN

THE TRANSFORMATION OF EUROPEAN POLITICS 1763–1848

BY

PAUL W. SCHROEDER

CLARENDON PRESS · OXFORD
1994

Oxford University Press, Walton Street, Oxford OX2 6DP
Oxford New York Toronto
Delhi Bombay Calcutta Madras Karachi
Kuala Lumpur Singapore Hong Kong Tokyo
Nairobi Dar es Salaam Cape Town
Melbourne Auckland Madrid
and associated companies in
Berlin Ibadan

Oxford is a trade mark of Oxford University Press

Published in the United States
by Oxford University Press Inc., New York

British Library Cataloguing in Publication Data
Data available

Library of Congress Cataloging in Publication Data
The transformation of European politics 1763–1848.
p. cm.
1. Europe—Politics and government—1648–1789. 2. Europe—
Politics and government—1789–1815. 3. Europe—Politics and
government—1815–1848.
D295.T73 1994 93–26439 940—dc20
ISBN 0-19-822119-3

1 3 5 7 9 10 8 6 4 2

Typeset by Best-set Typesetter Ltd., Hong Kong
Printed in Great Britain
on acid free paper by
Bookcraft (Bath) Ltd.
Midsomer Norton, Avon

*To friends made years ago in Vienna,
and especially to the memory of
Drs. Gertrud Morauf and Karl Schuster*

PREFACE

THIS book has a simple central theme: European international politics was transformed between 1763 and 1848, with the decisive turning-point coming in 1813–15. A fundamental change occurred in the governing rules, norms, and practices of international politics. Those of the eighteenth century, with its competitive and conflictual balance of power, gave way to those of a nineteenth-century concert and political equilibrium. This change led to striking results. The most obvious and demonstrable was a dramatic decline in the incidence, scope, length, and violence of wars in the nineteenth century as compared to the eighteenth. (Overall, the ratio of battlefield deaths to the total population of Europe was about seven times as great in the eighteenth as in the nineteenth century.)[1] Just as important were the problems solved and crises peacefully managed by nineteenth-century methods that had been insoluble without war by eighteenth-century ones. The devices of international diplomacy—alliances, treaties, conferences, even the language of diplomacy itself—changed significantly in form and intent. So did the spirit and goals of international politics. Aims considered normal and permissible in the eighteenth century were banned in the nineteenth, practices once routinely sanctioned or prescribed were proscribed. One dramatic illustration of the change, frequently illustrated in the narrative to follow, is the frequency and normality of partition schemes in the eighteenth century—plans devised and efforts made to partition various states, either eliminating them completely or reducing them to impotence or dependent status, and the disappearance of these schemes in the post-Vienna era, to be replaced by norms, rules, and efforts devoted precisely to preserving the existence and guaranteeing the independence of the actors most threatened within the system. Many more signs of a dramatic shift in the purposes and goals

---

[1] For the statistics, see J. S. Levy (1983); for this particular calculation, Schroeder (1986: 11).

of international politics, some obvious, others more subtle, will emerge as the story unfolds.[2]

The change could be called a revolution. This book, in fact, will argue that in this era more real change occurred in the arena of international politics than can be demonstrated in other areas of politics and society from other more celebrated revolutions—the French, the so-called Atlantic, the Industrial, the Napoleonic, or those of 1830 and 1848. 'Transformation', however, is a more accurate and useful word for what happened, less over-used and abused than 'revolution' and without its excess baggage of emotion. Though the transforming process involved much violence and force, certain characteristics usually considered essential to great political revolutions (the violent overthrow of an existing political and social order, the destruction and replacement of the ruling class, the imposition of new political principles by force) were not present here.

Moreover, while violence on a grand and in some respects unprecedented scale—twenty-eight years of almost unbroken large-scale international war and upheaval—proved to be one necessary condition of the transition from eighteenth- to nineteenth century international politics, it was not really its main cause. International violence on a similar or greater scale had occurred before, in the Thirty Years War or the wars of Louis XIV, without producing analogous results. The vastly greater violence of the twentieth century would not do so either, at least for a long time after the two world wars. The transformation was not simply or mainly the product of war, or of one side's victory and imposition of its will and ideas in the peace, but of Europe's finding a way beyond war, transcending violence, changing the previous goals and limits of power politics. The transformation occurred first and above all in the field of ideas, collective mentalities, and outlooks. A religious or theological analogy may in today's world hinder rather than aid understanding. None the less, the best clue to the heart of this transformation is the New Testament term for repentance, the Greek *metanoia*, a turning around of the mind. What happened, in the last analysis, was a general recognition by the states of Europe that they could not pursue the old politics any longer and had to try something new and different. This book attempts to describe how that happened, and what it led to; to explain the process by which European statesmen, taught slowly

[2] For brief analyses of the changes in the structure and language of international politics after 1815, see Schroeder (1986; 1989).

and painfully by repeated defeats and disaster, finally and suddenly succeeded in learning how to conduct international politics differently and better. J. H. Plumb has argued that political stability need not always develop slowly by a gradual accretion of changes, but can form quickly at particular moments.[3] The insight fits this particular story of the long gestation and sudden birth of a new international system.

If this book succeeds at all in making the case for this transformation, it could have certain implications for historiography in general. One is that historians of this era will no longer, while routinely acknowledging and/or endlessly debating and analysing other supposed revolutions (French, industrial, bourgeois, radical, Jacobin, liberal, democratic, socialist, and even Napoleonic or aristocratic), describe even greater, more drastic, and more palpable changes in international politics in such terms as 'a restoration of the old order', a 'renewal of the balance of power', a 'return to stability and monarchic solidarity', or even 'an era of reaction and repression'.

The work also aims to bring international politics back into the centre of this era of European history, where it once was and where it still belongs. The goal is not, of course, to return international politics to the position of primacy it had for Leopold von Ranke and a host of nineteenth- and early twentieth-century historians, as the central driving force of history and chief motor of change and progress. That kind of *Primat der Aussenpolitik* is gone, and no one wants it back. But international politics does belong in history on its own terms, as an equal and autonomous element, inextricably interwoven, naturally, with other parts of the collective human endeavour, but to be understood and approached primarily from the standpoint of its own system and structure, and not as a dependent variable of any other systems or structures in society.

This book aims, among other things, to offer a concrete refutation of the view, not uncommon in recent decades, that so-called diplomatic history is superficial event history, meaningless if not attached to an analysis of the real forces shaping history and society and forming only a small part of them, the kind of history which, pursued for its own sake, gets nowhere and misses the forest for the trees. It will try, by detailed historical exposition rather than theoretical argument, to meet the view of Marxists that international history without a Marxist perspective misses

[3] (1966: introd.).

the roots of international politics lying in socio-economic conditions, class structures, and relations of production; of *Annales*
historians that it misses the essential framework of history, the
deeper structures and conjunctures of serial and total history; of
Gesellschaftsgeschichte that it misses the driving force of modern
history, the transformations wrought by industrialization and
modernization. I do not doubt that traditional diplomatic history often misses the forest for the trees. I am also convinced,
however, that Marxists usually miss the forest for the roots; that
Annalistes, if they pay any attention to international politics at
all, miss the forest for the total global landscape; and that the
Gesellschaftsgeschichtler miss the forest for the lumber industry.

Above all, I believe that there is a way of conceiving and doing
international history that offers the possibility of avoiding all these
misdirections. It is to see and understand the forest of international
politics as a professional forester would do, with knowledge of
and respect for scientific forestry as an autonomous discipline,
closely related to others and drawing on them, but also possessing
its own rules and system. It means deliberately studying forests as
forests, as entities important in their own right and not simply
as the key to something else (climate, ecology, the economy
of forest products, the social organization of forest animals and
dwellers, or what have you). It requires posing as one's central
questions the issues of what makes forests grow or die, what role
chance and necessity, contingent events and deep organic developments, play in their growth or decline, what different forms
and structures forests may take, how they gradually change over
time, and what is required to keep forests from giving way to
desert. In short, international history must be done systemically
and ecologically, and must be done as international history, not
primarily as a branch of or contribution to anything else.

It is important, I believe, that this be done precisely for this
era of history, one treated intensively in the late nineteenth and
earlier twentieth century by many historians, including some of
the greatest, from Leopold von Ranke to Georges LeFebvre and
Charles K. Webster, but one which in recent decades, despite
individual works of real merit, has lain largely fallow. There is no
better example of its neglect or fall from favour in recent years
than the flood of publications accompanying the bicentenary of
the French Revolution in 1989. Though much of what appeared
was fluff, *pièces d'occasion*, the occasion also produced much serious
scholarship and some major historiographical results. Among other
things, the reigning Marxist 'bourgeois revolution' paradigm was

dethroned and a new political-cultural one erected in its stead. Yet this revival of the politics of the French Revolution occurred without reconsideration of, almost without reference to, the international developments of the era—despite the undisputed and decisive importance of international politics in the course and fate of the French Revolution itself from at least early 1791.[4] To use Theda Skocpol's phrase,[5] we have now brought the state back into society for the revolutionary era; but we have not brought international politics back into the state, society, and human affairs in general, or on the right terms. The task is worth doing not just in this era, but in history and politics in general.

I have tried in researching and writing this book to take relevant international-relations theory into account; it is a field I find fascinating and valuable, though I am far from expert in it. Readers may detect from time to time the influence of regime theory, hegemony theory, coalition theory, theories of perception and misperception, political economy, and game theory, and should have no difficulty seeing where the book stands on the idea of balance of power and on realist political theory, both classical and structural. The book is written, however, in what political scientists call the historiographical mode, with theory used only to illuminate particular developments rather than the other way round. Still, certain assumptions are important. The first is an agreement, for once, with Kenneth N. Waltz[6] on the superiority of system-level explanation and structural analysis over unit-level explanations of international politics. Explanations of outcomes in international politics based simply on studying the policies of individual actors and how they clashed or interwove are inadequate; it is vital also to show how systemic rules and structural limits influenced and shaped these outcomes. Hence I consciously attempt in this book to go beyond unit-level to systemic analysis, though my understanding of 'system' and 'structure' differs from that of Waltz and realist theory, and rejects the balance of power as a necessary conceptual basis for that dimension.

Friendly critics have charged that, while attacking the familiar omnibus phrase 'balance of power' as often useless and misleading for analysis and dangerous and unworkable in practice, I replace it by another phrase as protean and meaningless or worse, 'the

---

[4] Blanning (1991) discusses this phenomenon; his book (1986) is one of the major exceptions to the general neglect of international politics in the era.

[5] (1979).

[6] (1979).

international system'. The charge is plausible, the danger real and
to an extent unavoidable. The term 'system' is inherently elastic
and slippery; it can apply equally to things precisely defined ('solar
system', 'cardio-vascular system') or broad and vague ('business
system', 'social system'). 'International system' obviously belongs
more in the latter category. A careful definition may help, but
nothing is easier in history and other disciplines than to start with
a reasonably precise definition and then gradually expand or alter
it in practice. Let me therefore offer a definition of what is meant
by 'system' and 'systemic analysis' in this book, not with the idea
of making the term fully precise or eliminating all ambiguity, but
in the hope of explaining what is meant by 'system' here, and
helping readers judge whether the concept has real content, makes
sense, and is used hereafter with reasonable consistency.

By 'international system' I do not mean what is usually meant
by political scientists, i.e. the number of major international actors
in permanent, regular contact and interaction with each other, and
the distribution of power among them.[7] This is a perfectly good
definition for many purposes, but not for analysing the process of change described in this book. Instead, 'system' in international politics means here essentially what I understand Michael
Oakeshott to mean by the constituent rules of a practice or a civic
association:[8] the understandings, assumptions, learned skills and
responses, rules, norms, procedures, etc. which agents acquire
and use in pursuing their individual divergent aims within the
framework of a shared practice. Examples of a 'system' in this
sense are the structure, grammar, and rules of a common language;
the rules and understandings involved in playing a game or practising a profession; and, in this case, the rules and understandings
underlying the practice of international politics. 'Systemic analysis'
means simply a consistent attempt to determine not only how the
game of international politics turned out and how the decisions,
policies, and actions of individual states led to that outcome, but
also how these individual policies and actions were shaped and
limited by these shared rules and understandings, and how these
collective understandings were in turn challenged and altered,
sometimes violently, by violations or different versions of the
rules. The idea, though simple, is easily ignored or forgotten and
its importance overlooked. The rules of the game in international
politics, as in many games, are not simply restraining, but also
empowering; one set of rules permits outcomes that under another

[7] e.g. Snyder and Diesing (1977: 28).
[8] (1972).

are impossible or unthinkable. No amount of analysis of internal foreign policy-making or the decision-making process in particular states, vital though this is, can substitute for this kind of systemic analysis, because it cannot take into account, or even see, the restraints and possibilities which only the prevailing 'system' imposes. If this book succeeds, it will illustrate the point time and again.

A further assumption is that the history of international politics is not one of an essentially unchanging, cyclical struggle for power or of the shifting play of the balance of power, but a history of systemic institutional change—change essentially linear, moving overall in the direction of greater complexity, subtlety, and capacity for order and problem-solving. In other words, the history of international politics is essentially like the history of capitalism, parliamentary government, or business—a history of change and even, in a certain sense, of progress. Once again, the exposition is supposed to back up this assertion.

I hope one day to try to show how this is true for the longer period in which one can speak of a European states system, 1648–1945. This book will not attempt to sketch that development, but will start abruptly in 1763, at the close of the Seven Years' War. This date marks in a sense the high point of the eighteenth-century balance of power system, the end of its most exhausting and decisive war. If ever eighteenth-century balance-of-power politics was capable of producing stability, it should have done so in the period after 1763; many scholars have supposed that this happened. The year, therefore, marks a good place to begin the story of how this did not happen, and why systemically it could not.

I owe an apology for the length of time it took me to research and write this book, and thanks to those who helped me in it, supported the research, and waited patiently for it. I admire historians who can write history quickly and beautifully, like an artist painting a landscape; others who, like sculptors, take longer, but produce work smooth, polished, and massive; and still others whose history impresses one as architecture, bold and imposing in design. The only way I know to do history resembles working in wrought iron. It requires gathering and combining an intractable mass of raw materials, and then endlessly refining, heating, and beating them into the shape one feels ought to emerge. The end-product may not be beautiful, possibly not even graceful; the marks of the hammer will never be polished out. But wrought iron has one virtue: if made well, it can bear considerable weight.

Many persons have helped me gather the raw materials and do the heating and beating; not all can be mentioned here. The greatest debt is owed to the University of Illinois—the Library and its staff, the Research Board, the Center for Advanced Study, the former School of Humanities, the Program for Arms Control, Disarmament, and International Security, and the Department of History, for various kinds of assistance and support. A number of able graduate students have worked as research assistants, among them Sina Dubowoj, David Murphy, Katherine Aaslestad, Loyal Cowles, John Moser, and Jonathan Huener. Other libraries have been very helpful, especially the Library of Congress, the British Library, the Bodleian, and the *Nationalbibliothek* and *Universitätsbibliothek* in Vienna. A Fellowship at the Woodrow Wilson International Center for Scholars in Washington and a Visiting Research Fellowship at Merton College in Oxford combined to make 1983–4 one of the most rewarding and enjoyable years of my life. While most of this book is not based upon archival research, the researches I was able to do were made pleasant and fruitful by the directors and staffs of the Public Record Office and Historical Manuscripts Commission in London, the British Library, the *Haus-Hof-und Staatsarchiv* in Vienna, the City archives at Leeds, the County and University archives at Durham, and the Public Record Office of Northern Ireland. Some of the materials gathered for earlier projects under fellowships from the American Council of Learned Societies and the National Endowment for the Humanities have found their way into this book. Several friends— Professors Barbara Jelavich, Alan Reinermann, Karl Roider, James Sheehan, and Robert Jervis—did me an enormous favour in reading and commenting on the huge manuscript. Their suggestions were invariably pertinent and helpful, even if I did not always follow them. In fact, the suggestion I finally took most to heart was that, though any book can always be made better, there comes a time when one has to pronounce it good enough and quit. Lord Bullock was invariably patient, encouraging, and helpful while waiting for the book, and made valuable suggestions for its improvement.

Finally, my wife. She was not heavily involved in the scholarship, but she bore patiently for many years the noise, heat, curses, and groans from the forge.

P. W. S.

Urbana, Illinois
July 1992

CONTENTS

LIST OF MAPS

AN EXPLANATION OF THE
FOOTNOTES
AND BIBLIOGRAPHY

H AVING originally intended to have very few footnotes in the book, discussing the main sources in a bibliographical essay instead, I have been persuaded by readers that footnotes and a formal Bibliography would be helpful to other scholars and students. I also became convinced that, having offered controversial interpretations, I ought to indicate as clearly as possible the evidence on which they are based.

This is not easy to do, given the scope of the book and the volume of relevant literature and published documents. To avoid overburdening the reader, I have chosen to support only certain specific points with precise citations, otherwise indicating in each paragraph or section the general sources on which I have relied.

To save space, I have also adapted a form of citation common among political scientists, citing works in the footnotes only by the last name of the author and the year of publication, followed by the relevant page numbers, or document numbers in the case of some documentary publications. These footnote citations correspond to the works listed alphabetically and cited in full in the Bibliography. For example: Schroeder (1962: 55–67) refers to pp. 55–67 of P. W. Schroeder, *Metternich's Diplomacy at its Zenith 1820–1823* (Austin, Texas, 1962). A list of the abbreviations used in both the footnotes and the Bibliography, chiefly of the titles of journals, follows this explanation.

The system has the disadvantage of requiring the reader to refer to the Bibliography for information on the works cited in the notes. It also requires sources of all types—documentary publications, secondary works, memoirs, articles—to be listed without classification other than the alphabet. I regret the inconvenience of an arrangement dictated by reasons of space, but remain convinced, as one reader wrote, that the only thing worse than a burdensome set of footnotes and scholarly apparatus is none at all.

ABBREVIATIONS

AHR	*American Historical Review*
AHRF	*Annales historiques de la Révolution Française*
AOG	*Archiv für österreichische Geschichte*
BIHR	*Bulletin of the Institute for Historical Research* (University of London)
BL, Add. MSS	British Library, Additional Manuscripts
CASS	*Canadian-American Slavonic Studies*
CEH	*Central European History*
CHR	*Catholic Historical Review*
EEQ	*East European Quarterly*
EHQ	*European History Quarterly*
EHR	*English Historical Review*
FBPG	*Forschungen zur brandenburgischen und preussischen Geschichte*
FHS	*French Historical Studies*
GG	*Geschichte und Gesellschaft*
GWU	*Geschichte in Wissenschaft und Unterricht*
HHStA	Haus- Hof- und Staatsarchiv (Vienna)
HJ	*Historical Journal*
HZ	*Historische Zeitschrift*
IHR	*International History Review*
ISIEMC	Istituto storico italiano per l'età moderna e contemporanea (Rome)
JAH	*Journal of Asian History*
JBS	*Journal of British Studies*
JCEA	*Journal of Central European Affairs*
JEH	*Journal of Economic History*
JG	*Jahrbuch für Geschichte*
JGMOD	*Jahrbücher für die Geschichte Mittel- und Ostdeutschlands*
JGO	*Jahrbücher für die Geschichte Osteuropas*
JIH	*Journal of Interdisciplinary History*
JMH	*Journal of Modern History*
MES	*Middle Eastern Studies*
MIOG	*Mitteilungen des Instituts fur österreichische Geschichtsforschung*
MOS	*Mitteilungen des Österreichischen Staatsarchivs*

NRS	*Nuova rivista storica*
PCRE	*Proceedings, Consortium on Revolutionary Europe*
PP	*Past and Present*
PRO, FO	Public Record Office, Foreign Office (London)
RBPH	*Revue belge de philologie et d'histoire*
Rel. dipl.	*Relazioni diplomatiche* (see Bibliography)
RESEE	*Revue des études sud-est européennes*
RH	*Revue historique*
RHD	*Revue d'histoire diplomatique*
RHMC	*Revue d'histoire moderne et contemporaine*
RSI	*Rivista storica italiana*
RSR	*Rassegna storica del Risorgimento*
SEER	*Slavonic and East European Review*
SR	*Slavic Review*
TRHS	*Transactions of the Royal Historical Society*
WP	*World Politics*
ZBLG	*Zeitschrift für bayerische Landesgeschichte*
ZGW	*Zeitschrift für Geschichtswissenschaft*

PART I

The Destruction of Eighteenth-Century Politics

1
The European System, 1763–1787

The period after the Peace of Paris which concluded the Seven Years' War (1756–63) has often been described as one of relative stability. Certainly this is what many Europeans needed and wanted. The great world war of fifty years before, the War of the Spanish Succession (1702–14), had ended the threat of the hegemony of Louis XIV's France in Europe and had established a recognizable balance of power. Despite the efforts of some British and French statesmen to establish a durable peace by a system of collective security, however, old contests had continued after the Peace of Utrecht-Rastatt and new ones developed in the succeeding decades, involving Northern Europe, Italy, Germany, the Near East, the Polish succession, the Austrian succession, India, and the New World. A climax to forty years of indecisive balance-of-power struggle was reached in the Seven Years' War of 1756–63. Even wider and bloodier than the War of the Spanish Succession, it ended with all the belligerents tired of fighting and some of them exhausted. The outcome was decisive in both the maritime and Continental theatres, though in different ways. Britain clearly defeated France and Spain in the contest for colonies and control of the seas. The Continental struggle ended in a general military stalemate, but the political results were equally decisive and should have been more conducive to durable peace than clear-cut victory for one side or the other. France was defeated by Prussia on land as well by Britain at sea, and financially exhausted by the war. Prussia survived the war, but barely, and the aggressive spirit of King Frederick the Great was broken by it. Russia retired from the war into a profitable neutrality before it ended. This compelled Austria to abandon its central aims, to recover the province of Silesia, which Frederick had seized and held since 1740, and to reduce Prussia to second-rank status in Germany and Central Europe. The European post-war balance in 1763 looks like the one that characterized Europe after 1815. Britain was victorious and invulnerable on the seas, France defeated and weakened, Austria and Prussia worn out by war, Russia secure and dominant in the east and north.

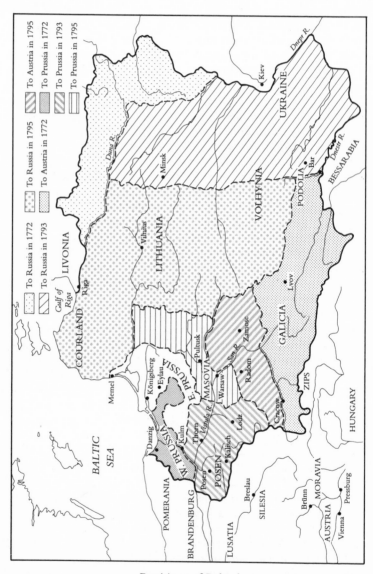

Partitions of Poland

1763–87, however, proved to be more like 1919–39 than 1815–48. Once again, on the Continent peace proved to be only a truce marred by constant crises and smaller wars threatening to spread and become general. Overseas, Britain's victory over France in North America would soon promote a revolt in its colonies which would turn into an international war, pitting Britain against its European foes in North America, the West Indies, India, and the high seas. If actual fighting failed to spread to the Continent as it had in 1756, it was only because this time Britain could not secure allies in Europe, and because the war in America had been preceded by crises in Poland and by a great Russo-Turkish war. These would not only preoccupy the Eastern powers, but also change the map of Europe, yielding Russia greater direct and indirect gains in Europe than it would ever make again before 1945. The 'peace' after 1763 also featured a new war between the German great powers, which ended inconclusively only because both were still too exhausted to fight effectively; the undermining of several lesser powers vital to the system; and the partial destruction of one of them. Finally, just twenty-four years after the Peace of Paris, another world war would begin which ultimately dwarfed the Seven Years' War far more dramatically than it had the War of the Spanish Succession. Overall, the late eighteenth-century trend was toward escalation, not diminution, of conflict.

Why did statesmen, genuinely desirous of peace and stability, fail so strikingly to achieve them in the late eighteenth-century? Why (still more strikingly) did they succeed at this same task a generation later? The questions are relevant not merely to this book or history in general, but also to the theory of international politics, and possibly even to its practice.

I. THE BALANCE OF POWER AND ITS RULES

An easy answer to the first question is that the 1763 settlement broke down because it failed to establish a stable balance of power. Britain had not intended in 1763 to make the peace too harsh for France and Spain to live with. Nonetheless, the terms destroyed any colonial and maritime balance against Britain; here the British insisted on supremacy. Naturally, then, Britain's European enemies would take advantage of the American rebellion to try to correct the imbalance, while Britain would be unable to find Continental allies. Meanwhile the balance of power had also been upset on the Continent. With France weakened and the German powers, paralysed by their stalemated rivalry, both competing for an alliance with Russia, Russia was free to pursue aggressive policies toward Poland and the Ottoman Empire.

The 'defective balance of power' argument obviously has something to it. The difficulty is that, like balance-of-power arguments generally, it explains any outcome equally well. War or peace can be accounted for either by a balance or by an imbalance of power. Wars arise because conflicts end too indecisively, like the War of the Austrian Succession (1740–8), or because they end too decisively, like the Seven Years' War; because one side gains a dangerous superiority, like Britain on the high seas, or because neither has the upper hand, like Austria and Prussia in Germany. Thus the balance-of-power argument fails really to explain anything and begs the question. Worse, it conceals the main fact: balance-of-power rules and practices were not a solution to war in the eighteenth century (if they ever have been) but a major part of the problem.

This assertion demands some explanation of what the rules were—a slippery subject. They were never written down like the Ten Commandments; as M. S. Anderson has remarked, often the phrase 'balance of power' served as a substitute for thought (as, one might add, it still does).[1] Discussing the rules means examining unarticulated premisses, making unspoken assumptions explicit, inferring rules and mutual understandings from common practices, and deducing logical consequences sometimes not seen or acknowledged by the players themselves. Yet at the same time balance-of-power language and doctrine was often used and sometimes discussed in explicit terms. By and large, statesmen in the late eighteenth-century understood the rules, presuppositions, and practices of international politics quite well. These governed conduct in the sense that statesmen accepted them as the way politics had to work; those who operated according to them were playing the game and those who did not were not. The code can be summarized under a few simple headings: compensations; indemnities; alliances as instruments for accruing power and capability; *raison d'état*; honour and prestige; Europe as a family of states; and finally, the principle or goal of balance of power itself.

The rule of compensations is perhaps the easiest to understand: basically, it meant keeping up with the Joneses. One's own state must have compensation for gains made by any other state

[1] Anderson (1970).

important to oneself; failure to get this signified defeat. The right to compensation applied not merely to gains in territory and wealth from aggression or war, but also to gains acquired legally (e.g. by dynastic inheritance or marriage) or from natural growth and development, and even to gains in honour, prestige, and standing in the international community.

Almost as important was the rule of indemnities, i.e. payments for services or losses. If the shorthand for the rule of compensations was 'keeping up with the Joneses', for indemnities it was 'nothing for nothing'. Naturally, this meant that one would try to exact the costs of war from the enemy wherever possible, but states also expected their allies to indemnify them for aid they supplied, either by direct payments or by sharing the spoils of war. The principle was further applied to 'losses' incurred by forgoing potential gains and possible claims or rights; the loss of status and prestige; and running risks or assuming obligations even if no concrete loss resulted.

These rules regularly helped make eighteenth-century alliances, whether defensive or offensive, into power-political instruments designed for capability aggregation, normally intended for expansion and acquisitions as well as mutual security. Alliances were usually specifically limited in respect to their duration, the *casus foederis* (the situation which would bring the alliance into play), and the attendant obligations. Commonly, treaties would specify the exact numbers and categories of armed forces to be supplied, or their equivalent in subsidies; often they also stipulated in advance the alliance goals and rewards (compensations and indemnities), usually in secret clauses or additional protocols. The reigning assumption was that the ally which was directly attacked or which chose to launch the war, as the principal, was expected to bear the brunt of the fighting. Its ally, the auxiliary, was obliged to render only the services specified in the alliance treaty, and was entitled to appropriate compensations and indemnities; if it did not receive them, its alliance obligations lapsed. This understanding naturally promoted the evasions of alliance commitments and sudden reversals of alliances for which the eighteenth-century was famous. Alliance flexibility of this sort was not merely considered normal, so that statesmen, when concluding alliances, regularly tried to calculate at what point their ally was likely to defect, but was even considered to a degree necessary, as one means of maintaining an overall balance. A common excuse for betraying an ally was the claim that it now represented the real danger to the balance of power. The principle *pacta sunt servanda rebus sic stantibus* (treaties are to be observed, so long as conditions remain the same), though seldom acknowledged, governed most commitments.

All this was part of the doctrine of *raison d'état*, and derived from it. The motive and rule of all action was to advance the interests of the state—meaning first of all its power, security, and wealth, but also, almost equally, its monarch's honour and prestige (*considération*) and rank among other princes. Reason of state thus closely linked the state with its monarch and dynasty, but not with its people or nationality; that link was only beginning to emerge in some countries. Louis XIV's idea of the state as dynastic patrimony (*L'état, c'est moi*) still prevailed in much of Europe, and if the Enlightenment notion of the monarch as the first servant rather than the owner of the state was beginning to make headway, the distinction made little difference in practice, especially in foreign policy. An enlightened ruler might acknowledge his/her responsibility to work for the state and promote the welfare of its subjects, but not to share his/her responsibility and power with them, and certainly not to carry on foreign policy for their welfare rather than for the glory of the state and its monarch. The welfare of subjects was a means to the power and glory of the state and its monarch more than the reverse, and enlightened despots tended to be more warlike and expansionist than old-fashioned paternalist monarchs. As for nationality, even where a monarch was linked to the state's dominant nationality, language, and culture (as in France, Spain, England, or Sweden), that monarch did not depend on this to sustain princely authority and ensure the loyalty of his or her subjects. Traditional dynastic, religious, and local attachments remained more important. Multinational empires were still common, and it was still considered a special jewel in a monarch's crown to rule over a number of different peoples.

In all these respects international politics, if not quite a pure zero-sum game, approached it; a rival's loss usually meant one's own gain, and vice versa. The rationality underlying reason of state was strictly limited, applying only to the means rather than the ends of international politics, and its moral constraints even more limited. Human and divine law, treaty commitments, and scruples about others' rights or human suffering were not supposed to interfere with the state's right and duty to pursue its interests and glory, especially the right to wage war, the *ultima ratio regum*. Religious ties, feelings, and ambitions, though still prominent in international politics, were more servants of reason of state than serious limits on it.

Yet the system was not quite without moral guidelines and principles. One was the concept of a European family of states. Even while pursuing their own interest in a competitive, often ruthless way, governments still saw themselves as forming a rudimentary community of juridically equal partners. Along with this went the abstract notion of balance of power, which may perhaps have had a certain restraining effect, though this is difficult to establish. The assumption was that the game of international politics, even if pursued competitively for individual state interests, was supposed to promote an overall general interest, the independence and security of individual states, or of most states, or of at least the most important ones. European empire, the domination of the whole family of states by one or two powers, was bad; a balance of power was good, and necessary to prevent the former. Fundamental to balance-of-power theory, then as now, was the belief (as in classical liberal economic theory) that the play of forces arising from each power's pursuing its own interest would ensure the preservation of an overall balance and thereby prevent empire. This prescriptive, moral side to balance-of-power doctrine, the idea that in international politics the vicious practices of individual states actually promoted international virtue and that the supposed outcome, a balance of power, made the pursuit of self-interest morally justified and socially useful, helps explain not merely why balance-of-power doctrine was so often invoked but also how it could serve as the basis for many arguments, filled with strange mixtures of sincere conviction, sophistry, cynicism, and hypocrisy, which served to justify open breaches of faith, naked aggression, and obvious imbalances of power.[2]

Not everyone, of course, believed in this code of international conduct. Certain eighteenth-century jurists and publicists saw through it and denounced it.[3] As will be seen, some leaders of smaller states saw from the outset that the system was rigged against them, and tried to hide from it, drop out of it, or somehow erect defences against it; the same insight would ultimately spread to leaders of some great powers as well, and lead to similar reactions. Yet as a belief system, an ideology, eighteenth-century balance-of-power doctrine was durable and powerful not merely

---

[2] For classic accounts of balance-of-power theory, see M. A. Kaplan (1957); Morgenthau (1967); Waltz (1979). For recent discussions, see the special issue of the *Review of International Studies*, 15(2) (Apr. 1989). For an excellent brief account of why balance of power should in theory produce stability (but does not always), see Jervis (1992). Good descriptions of eighteenth-c. international politics are in McKay and Scott (1983) and J. Black (1990).

[3] A good example is Justi (1763).

because of its surface plausibility and consistency, and its utility in sanctioning actions and policies statesmen wanted to follow in any case; not even because the eighteenth century, though riddled with dangerous conflict, was less murderous under the sway of a balance-of-power system than the sixteenth and seventeenth had been with their religious wars and bids for universal empire. The chief attractive power of this balance-of-power doctrine, then as now, was its apparent inescapability, the absence of a practical alternative. Anyone who tried to follow other rules of conduct than these, before these had been universally abandoned and a general consensus reached on new ones, would at best fail, or indulge in useless self-sacrifice, and at worst be destroyed by the attempt. The system always offered each state the hope that it could work the rules for its individual benefit while somehow the system would automatically produce the necessary public or collective goods, i.e. a minimum of general stability and individual security, a tolerable level of overall conflict and violence. As a result, eighteenth-century statesmen by and large accepted this system, more or less believed in it, operated by its rules, and were thus trapped by it.

Trapped because the promise of stability and security, for most states at least, was illusory. Seeking durable peace through a balance of power was futile first because there never was or could be any general consensus on what a suitable balance was; almost every individual state had a concept of a European balance which contradicted the concepts envisioned and pursued by others. Secondly, the assumptions, methods, and devices required by balance-of-power politics and actually used to achieve and maintain the supposed desirable balance blocked the peaceful resolution of conflicts except in temporary, unstable ways, directly promoted conflict, and made the periodic escalation of particular conflicts into general systemic wars more likely. Thirdly, the size, structure, power, and geographical position of the various European states virtually guaranteed that the free play of competitive forces among them would not result in a general stability, independence, and balance, but in destruction for some, mutilation for others, dependence for still others, and hegemony, if not outright empire, for one or two.

These truths could be illustrated time and again, and will be: how these lessons were driven home to Europe is the main theme of this book, or at least of its entire first half. In this chapter, the two most important international developments of the period are instances of it: the first partition of Poland (1772) and the

War of the American Revolution (1775–83). Their significance from the standpoint of world history is obvious. One gained independence for the American colonists and broke up a great overseas empire; the other undermined the independence of one major state, Poland, and promoted the drive of another, Russia, toward Continental hegemony. Great forces of history can be seen at work in them—political and social emancipation, moderniz-ation, and nation-building—as well as the forces of resistance. Both events point to the great revolutions and conflicts which we know lay ahead in the late eighteenth and early nineteenth centuries, whose consequences are still being worked out in the late twentieth century.

To dwell on the world-historical importance of the partition of Poland and the American Revolution, however, is a good way to miss what they did and meant in eighteenth-century international politics. For within the eighteenth-century system these were not particularly sensational or important events. For European international politics, the Dutch revolt in the 1780s was at least as important as the American Revolution, and the decay of the Ottoman Empire and the German Empire threatened the system more than the decline of Poland. Moreover, neither of these developments was revolutionary in systemic terms; both of them, along with many others, were instead natural outcomes of eighteenth-century rules and practices.

II. THE FIRST PARTITION OF POLAND

By the mid-eighteenth century, internal anarchy and decay had cost the Polish Republic most of the power, cohesion, and inde-pendence it had once enjoyed. It was dominated by a large noble class (szlachta) very diverse in wealth and culture but fairly united in defending its extensive privileges and effectively unchallenged by other classes or élites. The king, elected by the nobles and having no power over taxation, no effective administration, and no sizeable standing army, was helpless to control the noble-dominated Polish Diet (Sejm), itself riddled with factions and paralyzed by the right of each member to veto any decision (the liberum veto) and even to organize a rebellion against it (the right of confederation).

Under this political system, Poland from the late seventeenth century on regressed socially, economically, and culturally com-pared to other parts of Europe, and increasingly lost the ability to defend its own frontiers and independence. Other states, especially Russia, assembled armies on Polish soil, marched troops across it, and even conducted military campaigns in Polish territory. The climax was reached in the Seven Years' War. Poland, though neutral, was a principal theatre of the fighting and a virtual puppet of the belligerents, again especially Russia. Poles could no longer freely choose their own sovereign, preserve or alter their constitution, prevent neighbouring powers from intervening in their internal affairs on other questions, or conduct their own foreign policy. This condition was sealed in 1764 when Russia, aided by Prussia and working with a faction in Poland led by two powerful families, the Poniatowskis and Czartoryskis, secured the election of Stanislas Poniatowski, Tsarina Catherine II's favourite, as King Stanislas Augustus. Through her minister to Poland, Prince Nikolai Repnin, Catherine became the real ruler of Poland.[4]

Thus Poland's weakness, combined with Russia's growing power and invulnerability and the rivalry between Prussia and Austria, which made both of them seek an alliance with Russia, laid the groundwork for the first partition of Poland. They did not, however, make it inevitable or even probable. Catherine and her advisers would have preferred to maintain Poland outwardly intact under Russian domination. The Poniatowski–Czartoryski faction and Stanislas Augustus pinned their hopes for Polish reform on Russia; Prussia and Austria could not break the connection between the Polish government and Russia, and did not plan to try. Though Prussia's drive to great power status included expansion at Poland's expense, Frederick the Great had other more immediate ambitions at this time, and Poland was not Austria's target at all.

Partition instead came about mainly as a by-product of events, a means to other ends. After 1764 Catherine, who was not wholly hostile to reform in Poland within certain limits, decided to exercise a right Russia claimed to protect Polish religious dissidents, both Orthodox and Protestant, against Roman Catholic discrimination. She wished thus to demonstrate her enlightened principles to Europe, her power to the Poles, and her zeal for Orthodoxy to the Russians (an important concern for a German princess baptized a Lutheran and become a sceptic who had gained the throne in 1762 through conniving at the assassination of her husband Peter III). Her programme at first seemed to succeed. Despite some

[4] M. G. Müller (1983; 1984: 28–9; 1986: 279–95); Lukowski (1990: 178–81); Zernack (1981: 4–20).

opposition, a Polish Confederation (assembly of nobles) held at Radom in 1767 supported her religious-political demands, and even expanded Russia's right to maintain the existing anarchic Polish constitution. But in reaction a Confederation of Bar in 1768, inspired by Polish-Catholic patriotism, set off a widespread brushfire insurgency against King Stanislas Augustus and his Russian supporters. In the course of suppressing this insurrection, Cossack units from Russia operating in south Poland crossed over into the Ottoman Empire, attacking the town of Balta-Liman. The Porte (the government of the Sultan at Constantinople), Russia's traditional enemy now especially aroused by Russia's encroachments against Poland and itself, took the occasion to declare war.[5]

Russo-Turkish wars usually started slowly and indecisively. This one, however, led quickly to major Russian victories on land and sea, raising the danger of a Turkish collapse and of large-scale Russian expansion. The threat to Europe in general and the two German powers in particular was grave. Frederick the Great of Prussia found himself in a painful position. His alliance with Russia of 1764, concluded on a one-sided basis for protection against Austria, not only required Prussia to support Russia's war effort with subsidies, but also threatened to drag it into the conflict if Austria came to Turkey's defence. If that happened, Prussia would face the stronger enemy and bear the brunt of a war Russia had provoked. Austria's dilemma was even worse. Russia's victories and its prospective gains in the Black Sea and the Balkans endangered Austria strategically almost as much as they did the Turks, but an Austrian intervention to stop Russia would bring Prussia into the war and force Austria to fight the main battle in Germany, while freeing Russia to concentrate on the Turks.[6]

Recognizing their joint interest in ending the war quickly and limiting Russia's gains, Frederick and Joseph II, who was both Holy Roman Emperor (i.e. Emperor of Germany) and co-regent of the Habsburg monarchy together with his mother, the Empress Maria Theresa, met to discuss a joint plan of action in 1769 and again in 1770. Joseph sought a lasting Austro-Prussian partnership; Frederick and Maria Theresa, much as they hated each other, were willing to entertain a temporary one. But at Vienna the Chancellor and Foreign Minister Prince Wenzel von Kaunitz insisted

---

[5] Hoensch (1973: esp. 286–307); Cegielski (1982: 21–7); Lukowski (1990: 186–203); Zernack (1967); M. G. Müller (1984: 30–3).
[6] Stribrny (1966); Roider (1982: 109–17); Beales (1987: 272–9).

that Prussia was the main threat to Austria and an irreconcilable foe, while at Berlin Frederick's brother Prince Henry, like many Prussians, argued the same case against Austria. Henry was willing to join the Habsburgs for the purpose of partitioning Germany, but not for any other reason. This rivalry between the German powers, here represented by Kaunitz and Henry, helps explain the failure of the Austro-Prussian talks.[7] Yet if their mutual distrust made a long-range partnership impossible, it need not have kept them from a temporary alliance to end the war and limit Russia's gains. Balance-of-power thinking called for just such a move; their failure to act according to balance-of-power principles reflects, not a lack of alliance flexibility arising from mutual hatred and suspicion, but the inherent contradictions and deficiencies of balance theory and practice. First of all, both powers, as was usual in the eighteenth century and as the rule of indemnities prescribed, expected side-payments for their alliance co-operation, and had incompatible expectations on this score. Prussia insisted that if it restrained Russia for Austria's sake and thus alienated its ally, it must be compensated in Germany. The prime requirement of the balance of power for Austria, however, was to prevent Prussia from growing in power relative to itself, especially in Germany. It could agree to Prussia's demands, therefore, only if it made at least equivalent gains in Germany for itself, which Prussia was determined to prevent. The impasse reflected contradictory definitions of a tolerable balance of power in Germany and Europe. For Prussia it meant equality with Austria, for Austria superiority over Prussia.

This was not the only difficulty. A basic security problem made any partnership between Austria and Prussia against Russia brittle and unreliable: the fact that Russia, though not intrinsically too strong for them to defeat in alliance, none the less enjoyed a geographical advantage which made a joint Austro-Prussian war against her impracticable under eighteenth-century political and military conditions. The two German powers, which combined undoubtedly possessed more military power than Russia, lacked a secure position from which to exert it. Russia not only had the advantage of great, thinly populated, ill-developed spaces in which invading armies could be swallowed up, but was open to attack only on its western borders. These were covered by weaker states (Sweden, Poland, and the Ottoman Empire), the first two

---

[7] Schlitter (1907: pp. x–xiii); Easum (1942: 254–8); Beales (1987: 285–93); Gembruch (1988).

of which were largely under Russia's thumb. Thus Austria and Prussia would have to fight Russia in what would almost certainly be long, exhausting campaigns while watching out for possible foes on other fronts, including France and, most particularly, each other. Whichever one of them took the initiative in confronting or attacking Russia would automatically make itself the principal in the conflict, thus reducing its partner's role to that of an auxiliary free to exploit its predicament; other neighbours could be expected to do the same. Eighteenth-century alliances could offer no protection against this possibility of defection; balance-of-power doctrine even encouraged and sanctioned it. Thus the distrust which kept Austria and Prussia from combining against the common Russian threat arose not merely from personal animosity between their rulers or statesmen, nor even from their historic enmity and rival ambitions, but from their geographical position in Europe and the rules of the prevailing system. No amount of goodwill and sweet reason could have overcome this organic, systemically rooted mistrust.

The Habsburg monarchy had another possible response: to persuade France, its ally since 1756, to help defend its old eastern allies, the Ottoman Empire and Poland. This choice also was less viable than it appeared. True, France traditionally had used these states as a barrier against Russia in the East, but the Austro-French alliance was of little use for this purpose. The alliance made strategic sense only against Prussia, which suited Austria but not France, and even for this purpose it had disappointed both powers in the Seven Years' War. France could not help Austria much against Russia, and considered Austria almost as dangerous to Turkey as Russia was. Nor did the French see any use in their helping Austria to become dominant over Prussia in Germany— quite the contrary. Similarly, Austria could not help France fight Britain at sea or overseas, and France was the main threat to the Austrian Netherlands (Belgium). Besides, both powers were still fiscally too weakened by the Seven Years' War to co-operate militarily, and French policy was in disarray following the Duc de Choiseul's fall from power in December 1770.

Austria had a final option, the most risky of all: to ally with the Ottoman Empire and force Russia to accept a moderate peace. This was the one it seemed to adopt. Baron Johann Thugut was sent on a special mission to Constantinople, and when he succeeded in negotiating an alliance in the summer of 1771 he supposed that he had fulfilled its real purpose. But Kaunitz actually intended to bluff Russia with an alliance Austria never proposed to put into effect, while swindling the Turks into paying for it. Yet Austria's move, really a feint, aroused fears of a general war in Russia and Prussia, especially in Frederick. These fears, along with the fact that Austria had earlier occupied a certain territory in Poland to which it had old claims, the county of Zips, prompted Frederick now to propose something he had long been contemplating, a joint partition of Poland.

Frederick sent Prince Henry to Russia with two partition schemes. Henry's own, the more radical one, was directed more against Turkey and Austria than against Poland. It proposed that Prussia take certain small but strategic pieces of western Poland while Russia seized the northern coast of the Black Sea and the Danubian Principalities of Moldavia and Wallachia from Turkey. If Austria objected, Russia and Prussia would offer her Ottoman territory in the western Balkans as compensation; but if Austria tried to stop the plan, Russia and Prussia would declare war. Frederick's proposal called for Russia to conclude a moderate peace with the Ottoman Empire, compensating Austria for its gains with Turkish territory as well. Prussia and Russia would then reward themselves for their moderation with pieces of Poland. If Austria insisted, she would be allowed to share in the partition of Poland, but Russia and Prussia should fight if she tried to stop it entirely.

Only Frederick's proposal had any chance for acceptance at St Petersburg, but the vital fact was that Prussia made the offers at all. It assured Russians that the combined Austro-Prussian threat had disappeared, and that Russia controlled the situation. Though Catherine did not object to partitioning Poland in principle, she first tried to use Prussia's proposals to make Austria accept Russia's gains in the Ottoman Empire while Poland remained nominally intact under Russian tutelage. When Austria balked at this, Russia concluded a bilateral convention with Prussia in January 1772 for the partition of Poland.

Austria protested violently. Frederick's later gibe that Maria Theresa wept in taking her share of Poland, and that the more she wept the more she took, is better proof of Frederick's cynicism than of her alleged hypocrisy. Not only did she have genuine moral scruples about the transaction, but she also realized that a partition of Poland inherently hurt Austria (as other Austrians did, then and later). A partition was certain to strengthen Austria's great power rivals while weakening a valuable and inoffensive intermediary state. But it was better to weaken Poland than to let the Ottoman Empire be destroyed, and Joseph and Kaunitz, especially the latter, argued that if such an evil as a partition of Poland could not be prevented, Austria must at least be compensated for it. The more the transaction damaged Austria's interests, of course, the more compensation in territory, population, and revenues it must receive. It was therefore true, instead, of Kaunitz that the more he wept the more he took, for systemic reasons.

Austria's protest, whether genuine or tactical, had the practical effect of widening the Russo-Prussian scheme of partition and cutting Austria in for the largest share. Under a three-power agreement reached in principle by March 1772 and confirmed in treaties at St Petersburg on 5 August, Russia gained the most territory (92,000 square kilometres with 1.3 million inhabitants, mainly Ukrainians and White Russians), Austria almost as much territory and the most subjects (83,000 square kilometres in East Galicia and south of the Vistula containing 2.1 million Poles and Ukrainians), and Prussia a smaller but strategically and commercially important slice of north-west Poland (36,000 square kilometres with 600,000 inhabitants). Occupying these territories and forcing Poland to accept its losses proved no serious problem for the three powers, though considerable time was required to overcome the passive resistance in the Polish Diet. On the other hand, disputes between the partitioning powers over boundary issues and port, trade, and customs questions took years to resolve.[8]

The common verdict that the partition paved the way for Poland's extinction later is certainly true,[9] but not exactly in the ways one might suppose. The amputation of 1772 did not destroy the Polish state, and even seemed for a time to spur Poland to reform and renewal. Nor is it true, as is often said, that the partition set a dangerous precedent in international affairs and marked a decline in international morality. If it was a crime, it was a commonplace one, one of many seventeenth- and eighteenth-century proposals and efforts to divide up states, including major international actors. To take only the more prominent examples, the Netherlands were targeted in the latter seventeenth century,

[8] On the partition in general, see H. H. Kaplan (1962); Cegielski (1988); M. G. Müller (1983: 12–43); Davies (1982: i. 510–27); Jablonowski (1972: 222–61); Kaiser and Stasiewski (1974); G. Zeller (1953–5: ii. 249–62). Important documents are in Martens (1874–1905: ii. 12–61; vii. 11–81); Lutostanski (1918). On Catherine's policy, see Madariaga (1981: 187–205); Lord (1915: 47–63). On Austria, see Roider (1982: 119–39; 1987: 29–36); Beales (1987: 294–305). On Prussia, see also Moritz (1968: 16–19).

[9] For some divergent appraisals, see M. G. Müller (1984: 7–11); Cegielski (1982: 24–7); Topolski (1973; 1981). On the contemporary reactions in Britain and France, see Horn (1945); Venturi (1989: ch. 7).

Sweden in the Northern War of 1701–21, the Spanish Empire in the War of the Spanish Succession, the Habsburg monarchy in 1740, Prussia in 1756–63, and the Ottoman Empire repeatedly from the late seventeenth to the early nineteenth centuries, including at this very moment in 1772. The same was true of various smaller German and Italian states.

It could even be argued that the first partition of Poland was in some ways less criminal and dangerous than most such projects. The others generally were aims of war, and often they directly caused wars or created grave risks of them. This partition was carried out fairly peacefully and co-operatively, and served to keep a war already under way from spreading. Most partitions were intended to destroy or drastically weaken the target state, and to shift the general balance of power in favour of the partitioning state or states. Poland, already wholly under Russia's thumb, was considered little or no factor in the general balance before the partition, and emerged merely reduced in size while its existing status and functions as a buffer state were preserved. The partitioning powers could even claim to have improved the balance of power, because Russia had shared its former exclusive preserve in Poland with its neighbours.

Thus it is not cynical or sarcastic to call this partition an example of system-conforming behaviour, an instance of eighteenth-century international co-operation. It made the existing Russian protectorate over Poland somewhat less overt and oppressive. The great-power bargaining involved was not cut-throat or greedy by eighteenth-century standards. Each power involved gave up something—Prussia the territorial prizes it most coveted, Danzig and Thorn, Austria its objections to any partition at all, Russia its exclusive political monopoly.

This is not a whitewash of the first partition of Poland, only an analysis of it. The same things which made it better in some respects than other partition schemes made it worse in another. Poland was here not even treated like a European state, but like colonial territory. Just as the Congo Basin or West Africa in the late nineteenth century became targets for imperialist partition, not because they posed a danger to European governments or were even especially coveted by them, but because a peaceful division of them would avoid trouble among European governments and promote the smoother functioning of the European system, so Poland was sliced up in 1772 not mainly because it was a tempting prize or a danger to European stability (these would be major factors in the second and third partitions), but as a device to avoid a wider conflict and help settle more important questions.

This in turn says something profound about the eighteenth-century system. Like late nineteenth-century imperialism outside Europe, its rules made co-operative system-conforming conduct indistinguishable from naked aggression, at least from the point of view of the victims. Three great powers, perceiving their shared interest in the maintenance of general peace, discovered the best way to do so: to aggrandize themselves at the expense of a helpless third party. All, especially Austria, felt some regrets, but all said, and really believed, that the system's requirements and rules permitted this. And they were right. The arguments they used conformed to all the eighteenth-century balance-of-power assumptions—indeed, to realist assumptions in any age. All three powers, again especially Austria, continued to consider Poland a buffer state useful for separating them and helping to preserve peace. To Austria's qualms about whether Poland could survive the amputation, the Russians replied that Austria could ensure this by co-operating in a peaceful partition. The 'crime' of the first Polish partition rose directly from the rules and needs of standard eighteenth-century politics.

III. RUSSIA AND THE OTTOMAN EMPIRE

The partition failed, of course, to have the promised benign effects on Poland or to yield equal advantages to the three partitioning powers. Economic exploitation of Poland, especially by Prussia and Austria, followed the territorial seizure, while Russia reached the limits of the constitutional reform it would tolerate in Poland by about 1776 (though the 1780s did see an educational and cultural flowering of the Polish Enlightenment).[10] The international consequences were more decisive. The partition made Russia territorially even more invulnerable, deepened the rivalry between Austria and Prussia, and generally reinforced the other conditions (the exclusion of French influence, weak dependent neighbours, Swedish–Danish rivalry in the Baltic, and Russian dynastic connections in Germany) which brought Russia close to achieving its vision of a satisfactory European balance of power, i.e. Russian hegemony. More concretely, with its position in the north secure, Russia could shift its attention later in the 1770s to the south, where major gains were still to be made. The Foreign Minister, Count Nikita I. Panin, whose policy was an essentially defensive Northern System (an alliance with Prussia to help

[10] M. G. Müller (1984: 39–43); Lukowski (1990: 204–38).

control Poland and Sweden and restrain Austria), steadily lost favour as the star of Catherine's current favourite, Prince Grigori Potemkin, rose.

How seriously Catherine took Potemkin's Greek Project, which proposed the overthrow of the Ottoman Empire and the establishment of a Greek–Byzantine kingdom as a Russian apanage in its stead, is hard to say. Various signs (Panin's fall and Potemkin's rise, the christening of Catherine's second grandson as 'Constantine', her turn from Prussia to Austria) prove that she was certainly interested. Yet Catherine's expansionism was always opportunistic, she knew that Potemkin had his own personal agenda in the south, and though she was an absolute monarch she did not ignore advice from her counsellors. Nor was she unaware of the considerable opposition to an adventurous policy which existed within the Russian government.[11] In any case, a change in the focus of Russian policy in the late 1770s was unmistakeable, as were its wider implications. Russian expansion in the south would not only require that Austria be gained as an ally while Prussia became superfluous; it would mean that the tide of Russian expansion, engulfing the Ottoman Empire, would thereby isolate Austria.

All this made the Russo-Turkish War of 1768–74 of greater immediate importance in eighteenth-century international politics than the partition of Poland. Russia's military triumphs on land and sea, especially its great naval victory at Çesme in 1770, seemed to force the Ottoman Empire to the brink of collapse and bring political gains in Europe in their wake. Russia not only was able to renew its alliance with Prussia in 1769, but also secured a Prussian guarantee of the existing Swedish constitution, which helped to keep Sweden weak and under Russian influence and to control Swedish–Danish rivalry in the Baltic. The one minor concession Catherine made to Frederick in return, a promise to support Prussia's eventual acquisition of Ansbach and Bayreuth against possible Austrian or Bavarian opposition, gave her an additional useful lever in German politics.

Dangers, however, began to cloud the picture. Frederick hated the humiliating role to which the Russian alliance consigned him, while the Austrians, having earlier in the century viewed Russia as

---

[11] On Panin's Northern System and its decline, see Griffiths (1967; 1970); Rahbek-Schmidt (1957); Ransel (1975: 236–53). On the roots of Russian expansionism earlier in the eighteenth c. and its acceleration under Catherine, see Mediger (1952: esp. 690–3). On the Greek Project and opposition within Russia, see Hösch (1964); Ragsdale (1988a); R. E. Jones (1984).

a useful junior partner against the Ottoman Empire, now saw Russia as a serious rival. Even without a genuine alliance, the two German powers could cause Russia trouble by diplomatic co-operation. Far greater was the danger of an Austro-Turkish alli-ance, with Austria mobilizing or attacking Russia's exposed flank in the Balkans. The French represented another potential threat and might actually have tried to help the Turks, had not confusion and divisions followed the fall of Choiseul in 1770. In Sweden, Gustavus III's coup to regain effective royal power in 1772 sud-denly turned Sweden from a client of Russia and Britain once again into a potential opponent of Russia in the Baltic. The Turkish war took an indecisive military turn in 1771, and its fiscal burdens exerted mounting pressure on Russia's ever-precarious state finances. Worse yet, the great Pugachev Revolt of 1773, not so much a peasant rising as a proto-nationalist, anti-modern rebel-lion of the Cossacks against the Russian state, caught fire in much of south-east Russia and seriously threatened the regime. Mean-while, Russia's efforts to raise Christian revolutions against the Turks in the Balkans failed.

Russia's 'natural ally' in Europe at this time was Britain; British naval officers contributed heavily to Russia's success at sea. Yet even London disapproved of Russia's war, though not for the reasons that in the nineteenth century would make Britain and Russia rivals in the Near East—British concern for the Ottoman Empire, trade, the routes to India, and the European balance of power. At this time the British welcomed Russia's navy into the Mediterranean as a check on France, and cared little about what the war did to the Ottoman Empire or Central Europe. What Britain feared was the outbreak of general war in Europe while it faced mounting problems in America, plus the prospect that France, its East European positions destroyed, might turn its attention wholly to the Low Countries and the Atlantic. For these reasons Britain supported an Austro-Prussian offer of mediation for peace between Russia and the Ottomans.

Catherine showed great political skill in 1770–4 in meeting these dangers, seizing opportunities, exploiting divisions among her opponents, and neutralizing one threat with another. She ac-cepted a temporary loss of control over Swedish internal politics, and came to terms with Gustavus in order to keep peace in the Baltic. Concealing her anger at the Austro-Prussian offer of medi-ation in the Russo-Turkish war, she responded by continuing the war while offering a peace based on Russia's maximum aims (territorial expansion to the Black Sea, independence for the

Crimea, and a Russian occupation of the Danubian Principalities for twenty-five years), with the intention of reducing her demands if necessary and claiming compensations elsewhere for her moderation. As has been seen, this strategy succeeded when Frederick proposed to compensate Russia for its moderation toward Turkey and secure compensation to Prussia for its subsidies to Russia at Poland's expense.

The partition of Poland ended the worst dangers for Russia, an Austro-Prussian or Austro-Turkish alliance. Still, 1773 proved a difficult year of military set-backs, passive resistance in Poland, and annoying haggling with Russia's partners over details of the Polish settlement, all coinciding with the Pugachev rebellion. But more Russian victories in 1774 forced the Turks to sue for peace and to sign the Treaty of Kuchuk-Kainarji in July.

The treaty was not quite as disastrous and foolish for the Turks as it has sometimes been painted. The Ottoman Empire retained the Danubian Principalities, Bessarabia, and the crucial Black Sea port and fortress of Ozi (Ochakov), and though the Crimean peninsula in the Black Sea became independent from Ottoman rule under Russian protection, the Sultan retained spiritual suzerainty over its Muslim Tatar population. Article VII of the treaty, later expanded and distorted by Russia into a right of protection over all the Orthodox Christian peoples of the Ottoman Empire, actually required that the Sultan, not Russia, protect them. Yet the treaty did seriously increase the threat to Ottoman independence and security. Russia gained most of the northern coast of the Black Sea, from which it could menace Constantinople. The 'independence' of the Crimea was virtually certain to produce conflicts between Russia and Turkey over their respective claims and rights, leading to further Russian interventions and the likelihood of more annexations or another war. Finally, the religious clauses gave Russia a specious legal justification for intervention in the Porte's internal affairs.[12]

Russia quickly exploited these advantages after the war. Russian agents were active in Bessarabia and the Danubian Principalities, and the Russian government exerted pressure at the Porte on behalf of its Christian subjects. In the Crimea, though initially the Russians hoped to control the territory indirectly through khans independent in name and subservient to Russia in fact,

[12] Madariaga (1982: 72–5, 205–36, 270–3); Fisher (1970: 29–57); Saul (1970: 10–15); Gerhard (1933: 104–9); Martens (1874–1905: vii. 51–63); Roider (1987: ch. 2); M. S. Anderson (1954; 1956); Madariaga (1962: 6–7).

such indirect rule proved unworkable. A vicious spiral of half-deliberate, half-involuntary Russian imperialism developed in which clan rivalries and their competition for Russia's support promoted disorders compelling Russia to intervene, creating more instability and dependence which led in turn to still further interventions.

The Russian decision in 1783 to annex the Crimea was therefore not surprising, but the Porte's failure promptly to react to it was. Russia's move clearly violated the treaty of Kuchuk-Kainarji, and increased the threat to Constantinople from Russia's new and growing Black Sea fleet. A further surprise was that Austria, now Russia's ally, supported the Russian annexation without demanding compensations.[13] There seemed no limits in 1783 to what Russia could get away with. In July, by the Treaty of Georgievsk, it established a protectorate over the Christian kingdom of Georgia in the Caucasus, reviving Peter the Great's expansionist policy against Iran as well.[14] Whatever may have been the intrinsic advantages and detriments of Catherine's forced modernization and reorganization of Russia from above (verdicts, as usual, diverge),[15] no one can deny the great boost she gave to Russian expansion.

The limits and dangers, however, were sometimes perceived earlier and more clearly by other Russians. The Porte, though slow to react, was not inert. By 1784 a war party had gained ascendancy at Constantinople, and the Ottoman Empire began seeking European support against Russia, especially from Prussia. Catherine still could have warded off trouble. The Turks were not ready to fight, their diplomatic efforts in Europe proved unsuccessful, and important Turkish leaders opposed war. Russia, however, made no effort to avoid it, and Austria did little to stop Russia in its course.[16] Thus Russia's over-confidence, especially Catherine's, promoted yet another war in the East, and this one began the generation of European wars usually attributed to the French Revolution. Before turning to this war, however, one must see how Russia's expansion in the East and developments in Central Europe were connected.

[13] Fisher (1970: 1–6, 20–5, 57–159); Madariaga (1982: 378–81); Jewsbury (1977: 18–19); Madariaga (1962: 426–9, 436–43); Roider (1982: 151–68).

[14] Madariaga (1982: 368–9); Atkin (1980: 3–25); Gerhard (1933: 398–407).

[15] See e.g. Madariaga (1982: chs. 18–19); Raeff (1983: 224–5, 236–9); LeDonne (1984).

[16] Shaw (1971: 21–7); Zinkeisen (1840–63: vi. 592–611); Roider (1982: 168–74).

IV. THE GERMAN QUESTION, 1763–1787:
AUSTRIA, PRUSSIA, RUSSIA,
AND THE REICH

The only consistent factor among the innumerable complications of the German question in this era was Austro-Prussian enmity. Both Kaunitz and Frederick believed this was not accidental, the result of particular policies or leaders, but organic, due to the very existence and structure of the Prussian monarchy. Only this belief in an unavoidable Austro-Prussian enmity explains Frederick's constant courtship and appeasement of Russia through the last quarter-century of his reign, for privately he considered Russia's expansion and domination the worst long-range danger Prussia faced. But then, fear underlay Prussia's policy and ambitions in general, a consciousness that its power base was fragile and its great-power status marginal. More than once Frederick remarked that Prussia's crest should feature a monkey rather than an eagle, for it could only ape the great powers.

Hence Prussia's membership in the great-power club cost it frequent humiliation. Frederick had to pay for his alliance with Russia in 1764 by sacrificing the Saxon dynasty in Poland for a Russian one, again in 1768 by subsidizing Russia's war against Turkey, and in 1769 by supporting Russian policy in the Baltic. As has been seen, his attempt at a *rapprochement* with Austria broke down; his initiative in partitioning Poland resulted in giving Austria a lion's share of the spoils and Russia a new chance to play Prussia and Austria off against each other. When Berlin complained about Russia's disloyalty, the Russians proposed that Prussia join Russia and Britain in a triple alliance so that the three could ignore Austria (an example of how balance-of-power politics promoted hegemonic alliances to isolate other great powers rather than blocking coalitions to check hegemons). Such an alliance, as both Berlin and St Petersburg knew, would not only make Prussia a still more junior partner, but further threaten it. By targeting France, it would drive the French into Austria's arms against Prussia, leaving Russia secure and helping it make a separate deal with Austria over the Ottoman Empire.[17]

If Frederick hated the way Russia exploited the alliance, he feared losing it even more. Yet from 1774 on, despite his efforts, Russia moved gradually toward Austria. Prussia generally came out worse in the quarrels over the details of the partition of

---

[17] Stribrny (1966: 9–77); H. M. Scott (1977); Nathan (1980); Cegielski (1982).

Poland. Russia allowed Austria to annex the district of Bukovina from the Ottoman Empire in 1775, which Frederick claimed upset the balance of power. The decisive shift came in 1778–81, when Catherine failed to support Prussia in its quarrel and war with Austria over the Bavarian succession, declined to renew the Prusso-Russian alliance, and concluded one with Austria.

Frederick persisted in trying to win Catherine back. He accepted her proposals for joint mediation in the American War of Independence, joined her League of Armed Neutrality against Britain, proposed a triple alliance with France or Britain against Austria like the Russian proposal he had earlier seen as a trap, offered Russia his own proposals for a partition of the Ottoman Empire, encouraged Catherine's Greek Project, and effusively congratulated her on the annexation of the Crimea. It was all useless. Russia took whatever Prussia offered and went its own way.

Even their dynastic relations deteriorated. While Frederick hid his real feelings for Catherine under a layer of flattery and she at least recognized his abilities as a ruler, she openly despised his nephew and heir apparent Frederick William and considered him unfit to rule (a judgement Frederick largely shared). Added to this was her resentment of Frederick William's friendship with her rebellious son Paul. Frederick died in 1786 without illusions about Russo-Prussian relations or the dangers to Prussia from the colossus of the north, and with little confidence in his successor's ability to handle them.[18]

Meanwhile Austro-Russian relations were apparently changing from hostility to close alliance. Russia had dealt Austria one blow after another in the 1760s. Tsar Peter III had defected to Prussia's side in the Seven Years' War in 1762, and Catherine followed this with a neutrality almost as bad, saving Prussia and rendering the whole war worthless for Austria.[19] Then came Russia's alliance with Prussia, the election of Stanislas Augustus, and Russia's virtual take-over of Poland. Worst of all was the Russo-Turkish war. Russia's gains not only ruined Austria's hopes for economic penetration of the Ottoman Empire, but also created a critical strategic threat. If Russian territory once reached the lower Danube or beyond, Austria, surrounded as it was by other threats and security commitments as well, was finished as an independent great power. The diplomatic means Austria had tried first to curb Russia, a 'wait-and-see' neutrality intended to worry the

[18] Stribrny (1966: 85–237); Bissing (1967: 32–3); Kunisch (1988a).
[19] Kunisch (1978); M. G. Müller (1980a).

Russians and an attempted *rapprochement* with Prussia, did not work. Extending Austria's southern military frontier into Transylvania helped protect Austria from the fighting, but similarly failed to check Russia. The proposal of Joseph and some Austrian generals to join Russia in partitioning the Ottoman Empire was rejected by Maria Theresa on religious and political grounds. Kaunitz's suggestion of combining a military demonstration in Transylvania with a diplomatic approach to Turkey to check Russia and gain compensations from Turkey led to the Austrian manœuvre in 1771 described earlier: a defensive alliance with Turkey which Kaunitz never intended to honour, while trying to get Turkish payment for it in cash and territory.

Austria's final decision, as already seen, was to join Russia for a price; Poland paid it in 1772, the Ottoman Empire in 1775 with Bukovina. Maria Theresa objected that Austria's amoral flexibility was only making the Russian threat worse by undermining vital buffer states protecting Austria against it. Kaunitz admitted as much; Austria's interests called for maintaining Poland and Turkey intact as long as possible. But this could not be done, he insisted, so long as Austria was isolated over against Prussia and Russia. His only practical answer was more underhand and ineffective manœuvre, a suggestion in 1777 that Austria woo Russia by pretending to support Catherine's Greek Project while secretly encouraging France and the Venetian Republic to help Turkey block it. His reply to the Empress's renewed objections was that Austria had to replace Prussia as Russia's main ally now, while Russia still needed its help in the south; once that game was over, Austria's chance would be gone.[20]

This was more than just greedy expediency; behind it was Kaunitz's shrewd and pessimistic analysis of the source of Austria's dilemma, which was forcing her to help Russia destroy states Austria wished preserved. The problem, Kaunitz insisted, was not Russia's power; Austria was actually stronger in purely military terms. It was the fact that Russia was strategically invulnerable while Austria was exposed and over-committed, above all in Germany; only after that problem was solved could Austria stand up to Russia as it should. One normal eighteenth-century method of solving the difficulty, reducing Prussia to harmless proportions, had been tried and had failed. Already in 1764 Austrians had begun thinking of another standard device; security through *arrondissement* by territorial exchanges—in this case trad-

[20] Dyck (1980; 1981); McGill (1971); Roider (1982: 109–50); Plaschka (1975).

ing Austrian Belgium, wealthy but distant, exposed, and difficult to govern, for Bavaria, poorer but contiguous. This would eliminate a direct threat from France and make Austria stronger and more secure in Germany. Certain Habsburg claims, hereditary and imperial, on particular Bavarian territories made the idea still more attractive. If Russia helped Austria bring off this exchange, it would repay Austria somewhat for the costs of its alliance in the East.

Joseph II favoured the idea, being willing to get rid of the scattered Habsburg territories in south-west Germany as well, for the right price. He tried without success to persuade Frederick II and the French foreign minister Charles Gravier, Count Vergennes, to accept it. The actual proposal, however, originated from Elector Karl Theodor of Bavaria rather than from Austria, and out of it developed, in ways too complicated to trace fully here, a major constitutional crisis in the Holy Roman Empire and an Austro-Prussian war. Though much of the trouble stemmed from faulty Austrian tactics in pursuing the exchange, it is once again vital to see how individual errors were not the whole story, and were not just fortuitous but deeply rooted in the eighteenth-century system.

Joseph, hoping to improve long-term Austro-Prussian relations, proposed that Austria let Prussia acquire the Margravates of Ansbach and Bayreuth in southern Germany, which Prussia coveted, in exchange for its acquisition of Bavaria, compensating Karl Theodor in Belgium. By eighteenth-century standards this was a fair deal, not especially selfish in goals or aggressive and treacherous in tactics. But Austria launched it without attempting to consult and satisfy all the interested parties in advance—Karl Theodor, Prussia, the future heir to Bavaria the Duke of Zweibrücken, the other estates (i.e. constituent members) of the German Reich, and France, which since the Treaties of Westphalia in 1648 had enjoyed a right of protection over the Reich constitution. Instead, Austria first claimed part of Bavaria as a reversion of a feudal fief. Then it attempted to give Karl Theodor other compensations instead of Belgium, which he wanted. Next, Vienna tried to bypass the Reich through a complicated compensations scheme worked out directly with Prussia; and finally, Austria occupied certain Bavarian territories in advance to ensure that it would not come away empty-handed. All this not only alienated Karl Theodor and the Reich estates, but also convinced Frederick that the deal would probably not go through and that Prussia would gain more ground territorially and politically by opposing it, by force if necessary. The decision to oppose Austria did not come about automatically. Prince Henry, usually Austria's enemy, favoured a bargain with her at this point, mainly because the deal would promote his goal of dividing Germany up between Prussia and Austria. But when Joseph insisted that Austria must get something more than the straight exchange of Belgium for Bavaria which Karl Theodor demanded, Frederick decided to challenge Austria under the plausible pretext that he was defending the Reich constitution. Maria Theresa, who opposed the exchange, and Kaunitz, who favoured it but was critical of Joseph's tactics, made last-ditch efforts to avoid war but were unsuccessful; in July 1778 Prussian troops marched into Bohemia, and war was declared in August.[21]

Yet even if the proximate cause of the crisis and war was Austria's (especially Joseph's) ineptitude and miscalculation, behind this were deeper systemic factors. One reason for Austria's use of stealth, surprise, and pressure was long experience that straightforward multilateral negotiation did not pay off under eighteenth-century conditions, for structural reasons. Most states were dynastic states, living and dying by the principle that the ruler's legitimate title and authority derived from dynastic succession and that its territories were ruled and passed on as patrimony. This meant that succession questions were the most numerous, bitterly contested, and critical issues in European high politics. If wars over them were to be avoided, territorial exchanges like this one were necessary or at least desirable. At the same time, they were almost inevitably complicated, dangerous, and extremely difficult to bring off peacefully.[22] Every actor with any shadow of a legal claim would press it and demand satisfaction for it, while those without such claims would try to prevent any bargain profitable to their neighbour, or at least demand payment for their consent—not simply out of greed or bloody-mindedness, but out of the principle of compensations: any gain for a neighbour without an equivalent gain for oneself was a defeat, and undermined the balance of power. The combination of the principles of dynastic rights and balance of power, each itself conflictual to the core, created boundless possibilities for conflict, and fatally narrowed the room for peaceful compromise and harmonious settlement.

For this reason, even reasonable transactions in the eighteenth

---

[21] Aretin (1967: i. 62–5, 110–17; 1976: 64–5, 73–87); Zeller (1953–5: ii. 290–2); Roider (1982: 151–7); B. P. Bernard (1965a); Beales (1987: 367–8, 375–6, 388–403).

[22] See esp. Kunisch (1979).

century usually required finding an outside party like Poland or the Ottoman Empire to pay the transaction costs, i.e. serve as a sacrificial lamb. Germany, with its small, weak states, offered many such potential victims, but to this point they were protected by residual German loyalty to the Reich constitution, the fear of outside intervention (France, Russia, even Sweden and Denmark), and the competition between Austria and Prussia for clients. Austria, therefore, could have carried through this exchange, at this time or later, only by agreeing to pay the transaction costs—to accept a deal more favourable to others in terms of compensations and indemnities than to itself, simply to improve its overall position within Germany. Austrian generosity in some such form might theoretically have been a good idea. Leading historians have suggested that Austria would have done better to claim only its rights under the Reich constitution, thus defending the Reich per se.[23] Political economists and regime theorists point out that hegemonic powers need to pay a disproportionate share for the public goods of a system if that system and their leading role in it is to be preserved.[24] But this kind of course is hard to imagine in the cut-throat late eighteenth century, especially for Austria, whose hegemony in Germany was anything but secure and which had no resources to spare.

The fact that the War of the Bavarian Succession ended with little fighting had nothing to do with moderate aims of the belligerents. Prussia opened the war with an all-out offensive intended to drive Austria back to the Danube. It failed (though not before bringing Joseph to the brink of panic) on account of logistical problems, weather, and a defensive Austrian strategy adopted out of sheer necessity. By mid-September Prussia had to retreat without the decisive battle it had sought, and by November Russian mediation solicited by Austria brought operations to an end. The war cost both powers heavily in money and damage to their military and political reputations. Each alienated other German states, Prussia by asking Russia to intervene on its side, Austria by trying to enlist the Reich estates in an anti-Prussian crusade. Concretely, neither gained or lost anything important by the Peace of Teschen in May 1779. Prussia temporarily blocked the Bavarian–Belgian exchange while keeping its own claim to Ansbach and Bayreuth out of imperial jurisdiction, where Austria

---

[23] e.g. Beales (1987: 394–5). Aretin (1967) is especially critical of Joseph's policy toward the Empire, e.g. i. 62–4.

[24] e.g. Gilpin (1987); Oye (1986); Krasner (1983).

had an advantage; Austria gained the Inn district (*Innviertel*) from Bavaria without having to renounce its larger exchange project.

But there was a winner, Russia, and a loser, the Reich. Catherine was again dealt good cards and played them well. Her promise to support her ally Prussia had helped ensure that the two German powers would come to blows; her refusal to give Prussia any actual military help promoted a stalemate; and her mediation of peace gained Russia a legal status in Germany equal to that of France as a protector of German 'liberties' and guarantor of the Treaty of Teschen. As for the Reich, its individual estates were dragged still deeper into the great-power competition threatening their independence, while the Empire itself, a traditional political order based on law trying to survive in a European states system based on power, gained a new lawless great-power 'protector' working to undermine its constitution while pretending to save it.[25]

Both German powers, knowing and hating what Russia was doing, continued after the war to compete for a Russian alliance. Austria won, but only because Russia had already collected the profits from its ties with Prussia, and what Prussia now offered, a defensive Russo-Prussian–Turkish alliance, had less appeal to Catherine than Austrian help in partitioning the Ottoman Empire. In the ensuing alliance negotiations, Catherine did not get everything she wanted. Austria refused to guarantee the Russo-Swedish border or promise naval help against Turkey in the Black Sea, and stubbornly defended the Habsburg Emperor's traditional right of formal precedence in treaties. Since Catherine demanded equal status, the alliance had to be concluded in 1781 by an exchange of letters rather than a formal treaty. The main Russian goal of an offensive alliance against the Ottoman Empire, however, was achieved.

Joseph and Kaunitz managed to dodge a prompt joint execution of the Greek Project, which the alliance implied. By early 1783, however, Russia was obviously bent on at least annexing the Crimea, which was likely to provoke a Russo-Turkish war and made an Austrian decision on whether to join Russia in destroying the Ottoman Empire virtually unavoidable. Joseph, at least sometimes, was willing to do so, provided Russia guaranteed Austria

---

[25] Aretin (1967: i. 117–27; 1976: 90–3); Stribrny (1966: 98–115); Madariaga (1962: 98–101); Moritz (1968: 21–2); Martens (1874–1905: ii. 61–96); Easum (1942: 296–308); Beales (1987: 404–31). For thorough discussions of the Reich's constitutional weaknesses, various ideas and efforts at reform, and the damaging effects of Austro-Prussian rivalry, see Aretin (1967: i. 13–103); Cegielski (1988).

sufficient compensations in Turkish and other territory, supported the Bavarian exchange, allowed compensations to France and Venice, agreed to return the Saxon dynasty to Poland, and promised to weaken or destroy Prussia if it intervened. Austria's ambassador to Russia, Count Ludwig Cobenzl, urged a bargain with Russia now, while it still was interested in one. Kaunitz, however, opposed the idea, convinced that, once Russia got Austria to agree to a partition scheme, Catherine, exploiting Austria's strategic vulnerability, would collect her gains while reneging on her part of the bargain. Kaunitz was right, as the Russian response to Austrian hints about the price for its co-operation showed. Catherine, irritated at Vienna's terms and annoyed that Turkey tacitly accepted the annexation of the Crimea, robbing her of an excuse for war, announced that Russia would stop with this for the moment. Adding insult to injury, she promised Austria help in finding compensations for Russia's acquisition of the Crimea— provided these were outside the Near East.[26]

Stymied, Austria turned again to Germany, where Kaunitz's first moves after Teschen had been defensive. He had organized a league of Catholic princes (*Corpus Catholicorum*) to counter the Prussian-led *Corpus Evangelicorum*, and got Austrian candidates, especially Habsburg archdukes, elected to key ecclesiastical positions within the Reich. But even when the Austro-Prussian competition for clients was fairly restrained as this was, it proved unstable, tending to escalate as the clients pursued their own interests and resisted great-power control. By 1783 several lesser princes had begun trying to form a League of Princes (*Fürstenbund*) to constitute a Third Germany that would be free of Austrian or Prussian domination.

Frederick promptly decided to take this League over for his purposes, and Joseph II played into his hands. In his determination to reform and control the Catholic Church in Austria, the Emperor set out to realign episcopal boundaries in Germany so as to conform to Austria's territorial limits. This involved Austria in a quarrel with both the Pope and Austria's clients and allies within the German Church. Joseph, since his mother's death in 1780 sole ruler of the Monarchy, also chose to renew the Bavarian exchange project, this time being ready to sacrifice all of Belgium for Bavaria, but still demanding additional compensations elsewhere

[26] For the origins and aftermath of the alliance of 1781, see Roider (1982: 160–8); Madariaga (1981: 382–9; 1959); Glassl (1969); Martens (1874–1905: ii. 98–101, 116–31). Sources showing Austrian attitudes are Joseph (1901: pp. viii–ix, Nos. 38–131; 1871: Nos. 3–4, 11). See also Dyck (1980: 456–61, 468–9).

for Austria. In order to increase the value of Belgium as an object of exchange, he attempted to open the Scheldt River to commerce, provoking Dutch and British protests based on the old treaties closing the Scheldt.

These moves, which took little account of the likely reactions in the Reich and Europe, led to another set-back for Austria worse than 1778–9. One ally, France, gave Austria no support on the Belgian–Bavarian exchange at all; the other, Russia, offered its usual diplomatic but not military support, tied to conditions which made it useless. While Prussia gained control of the *Fürstenbund* and used it against the Emperor, the British and Dutch opposed the exchange on strategic and commercial grounds, arguing that a Belgium ruled by a small German prince would be an easy prey for France. Even Britain's King George III, as Elector of Hanover, joined his old enemy Frederick of Prussia against Austria, Joseph, outmanœuvred, suffered a further loss of prestige, and Frederick gained undeserved laurels as the saviour of German constitutional liberties.[27] But if Austria lost the power-political game, the Reich and its smaller members lost the more important legal-constitutional one. The original purpose of the *Fürstenbund* had been to reform and revitalize the decaying Reich constitution and its institutions, so that what some princes correctly termed the real German 'balance' could be restored, i.e. the rule of law under the old German constitution, to protect the rights and independence of individual estates and check the sway of power politics. Now the *Fürstenbund* itself had been turned into a lawless balance-of-power weapon.[28]

Joseph, chastened, turned eastward again in his search for compensations for the Crimea, seeking something small that the Turks might surrender without war. He and Kaunitz disagreed, however, on which Turkish territories along Austria's south-eastern frontier would be most valuable, or whether any of them would be. Indeed, as Joseph constantly complained, expansion southward would not break the vicious circle in which Austria was trapped, but strengthen it, increasing its insecurity *vis-à-vis* Prussia, making it more dependent on Russia, and undermining the Ottoman Empire, which was no longer the dangerous enemy of old.

---

[27] General discussions in Aretin (1967: i. 128–98; 1976: 96–119); important articles by Kohler (1975: 71–96); Wangermann (1982). On the German confessions, see Aretin (1958). On British policy, Ehrman (1969: 472–6); Blanning (1977). For useful documents on the exchange project and its aftermath, see Aretin (1967: ii. Nos. 18, 21, 24–5, 27); Joseph (1873: 168–83).

[28] Aretin (1967: i. 238–41); Kohler (1975).

The Emperor pleaded with Catherine, predictably in vain, either to bring about a reconciliation between Austria and Prussia or else help Austria destroy Prussia, so that Austria could become a useful ally for Russia.[29]

Thus both Joseph and Kaunitz knew how unenviable Austria's position was in early 1787: Russia deliberately steering toward another war with Turkey against Austria's interests; France paralyzed by internal unrest; Austria's policy in Germany unpopular, its position threatened by Prussia and other opponents; rebellion brewing in Belgium, discontent rising in the rest of the monarchy over the precipitate pace and centralizing tendencies of Joseph II's internal reforms. The only apparent choices Austria had in foreign policy were to join Russia in an undesirable and dangerous war against the Ottoman Empire so as to preserve a balance of conquests, or to stay out and watch Russia become totally dominant in the East.

Austria's situation could be traced to a number of obvious factors—internal weaknesses, indecision and blunders in policy, a central geographical position and strategic vulnerability, and so on. But to stop with these is to commit the grave fault for historians generally of contenting oneself with half-truths and surface explanation, and the special one for international historians of stopping at the unit level and ignoring systemic components. Austria's central problem would have persisted even had all these other weaknesses somehow (impossibly) been taken care of: it was inextricably involved as a great power in a game whose rules made it almost impossible for Austria to win, and guaranteed that even a victory would finally prove counter-productive. The eighteenth-century balance-of-power game had become, as it often tends to do, one of pure balance of conquests. Yet the Habsburg monarchy had arisen only partly through conquest, and could not survive by it. It was a *Hausmacht*, a multi-ethnic, patrimonial state *par excellence*, based far more on tradition, dynastic succession, successful marriage, and territorial compromise. Its monarch exercised authority over his/her hereditary lands through a host of diverse legal and traditional claims and titles far more than by naked power, and presided over Germany as a traditional elected leader, not as sovereign at all.

Balance-of-power rules therefore militated against the Habsburg

---

[29] Roider (1982: 172–9); Madariaga (1981: 392–5); Stefanovic-Vilovsky (1909: 132–3). Much documentary evidence on Austria's internal debate and how Catherine exploited it can be found in Joseph (1901: vols. i, ii; 1873); Martens (1874–1905: vol. vii).

monarchy in two ways. One was obvious: a state so centrally located but ethnically and politically diverse, with territories stretched over Europe from the Ottoman Empire and Poland across northern Italy and Germany to the Low Countries, could not possibly develop the kind of military power it needed for adequate security against its numerous neighbours and potential foes without calling into being a great counter-coalition against itself. The fairly modest and inept attempts Austria made at this time merely to achieve a certain improvement in its strategic position demonstrate this. Here, at least, balance-of-power theory is helpful; Austria illustrates in classic fashion the security dilemma various scholars have discussed,[30] in which the very efforts of one state to achieve military security provoke counter-measures from opponents, leading to greater individual and general insecurity. The other crucial disadvantage of balance-of-power rules for Austria is more subtle. It depended for its independence and security as a great power upon the survival of elements of tradition and international law, and on certain moral and legal norms and rules, which balance-of-power politics was steadily undermining and would continue to undermine even if Austria, by some improbable chance, succeeded in winning the power-political competition. Thus to save Austria by a successful balance-of-power policy was in some sense to destroy it.

There were other units in Europe, it is true, even more dependent for survival than Austria on conditions and restraints being destroyed by the *realpolitik* of the late eighteenth century— Poland, the German Empire, the Ottoman Empire, and many small states. But these, not being great powers, could at least try to hide from the cut-throat competition of great-power politics. King Stanislas Augustus of Poland wished to hide under the protection of Russia; many German principalities tried to hide behind Austria or Prussia, or to find or create a niche to hide in between them. The Dutch and the Swiss hoped to hide in neutrality. The Habsburg monarchy could not hide; more than any other great power, it was forced to play the balance-of-power game, and to lose.

This insight was not entirely hidden from Austrian eyes. Maria Theresa and Joseph both sensed it, she instinctively, he more intellectually. Kaunitz thought his way through to it, though only near the end of his career; Leopold II would not only see the dilemma but attempt to transcend it with a new kind of politics.

[30] Herz (1950); Jervis (1978).

The contradiction between the Habsburg monarchy's nature and needs as a political organism and the demands placed on it as a great power by the prevailing international system, between the rules and practices needed for its survival and the rules and practices it had to follow, helps us understand many puzzling characteristics of Habsburg policy: its constant hesitations and half-measures, its pleas to enemies and rivals for help and understanding, its attempts to win gambles without really betting and to outmanœuvre unscrupulous opponents without really breaking the law. This is what would make Austria in this era pursue for so long, with consistently negative results, a policy half of legality and half of piracy; not 'à corsaire, corsaire et demi' but 'à corsaire, demi-corsaire'.

V. FRANCE, BRITAIN, AND WESTERN EUROPE

France, though considerably stronger and more advanced than Austria, experienced similar defeats and problems after 1763. The minister of war, Choiseul, immediately began rebuilding the French navy, only soon to abandon the programme as too expensive. Efforts to revive French trade enjoyed moderate success at best; attempts to limit France's commitments on the Continent and free its hands for action against Britain none at all. Both the official diplomacy of the foreign ministry and the private diplomacy of Louis XV failed to prevent France's defeat in the Polish election of 1764, allowing a key member of France's old barrier system in the East to slide into Russia's orbit and encouraging Austria and Prussia to drift toward it. Choiseul, on becoming foreign minister in 1766, encouraged the Ottoman Empire to resist Russia, and then had to stand by impotently while France's old ally was defeated in the ensuing war. France succeeded in 1772 in helping Gustavus III restore the power of the Crown in Sweden against opposition parties backed by Britain and Russia, but this gain was temporary and considerably outweighed by the first partition of Poland. Besides further weakening Poland, it proved that Austria was useless as an ally against Russia and dangerous in its own right. France's failure to support its old ally Spain against Britain in 1770 over the Falkland Islands made Spaniards feel much the same way about France. Even the French acquisition of Corsica from Genoa in 1768 was a mixed gain at best, strengthening French control of the western Mediterranean but also saddling France with a rebellious province whose discontent Britain could exploit in time of war, and drawing British attention to the one sea-coast where France was still secure.[31]

Louis XVI's accession to the throne in 1774 brought a long-overdue reappraisal of France's position and policy. The new foreign minister, Count Vergennes, saw that, while France's problems over the past decade derived partly from contingent, potentially remediable factors such as shortages of money, trained seamen, and naval stores and timber, most of them derived from France's unalterable strategic position. Choiseul's belief that France could somehow limit its Continental commitments and concentrate on the British challenge overseas had proved wrong; it could not escape its Continental position or gain reliable allies. The Austrian alliance, in Vergennes's view, was useful only for restraining Austria itself, and might not even do this after Maria Theresa died; Kaunitz and Joseph only wanted to exploit it for Austrian ends. Prussia, though it wanted better relations with France, would never stand up to Russia. France, Vergennes concluded, must stop seeking major victories and try for security and prosperity through peace and balance of power. This was prudence, not pacifism or resignation. He still felt duty-bound to enhance his king's honour and his country's glory above all else, and morally obliged to undertake any war that would advance these ends. Yet among the leading statesmen of his period, Vergennes had the most rational, moderate concept of politics and was most interested in maintaining the European equilibrium. His reward would be to die in 1787 in disgrace, with France's power and influence at a new nadir—a good commentary on late eighteenth-century politics.[32]

France's political failures after 1763 were even more galling because they came when Britain seemed to be vulnerable. It was diplomatically isolated after 1763, at a time when political instability at home, growing difficulties with its American colonies and India, and a popular reaction against expensive foreign and colonial wars heightened the risks of isolation. After Britain's abandonment of Prussia in 1762, Frederick would never consider another British alliance so long as he lived. Kaunitz was anti-British and, as will be seen, Russia did not respond to British

---

[31] H. M. Scott (1975; 1975–6; 1979); Jarrett (1973: 74–5, 89–91); Zeller (1953–5: ii. 264–6, 269); Bitterauf (1905: 3–7); Murphy (1982: 151–61).

[32] Ibid. pp. x–xi, 212–31; Murphy (1981); Madariaga (1962: 12–15); Fagniez (1922: 1–25, 161–207); Vergennes's instructions to Count Breteuil, 9 Mar. 1777, in *France: Recueil* (1884: 502–22); Contamine (1970: 11).

courtship. French enmity was taken for granted, and there were the usual British imperial quarrels with Spain. The results of these were mixed for Britain, failure over the so-called Manila Ransom issue in 1766 and inconclusive success over the Falkland Islands in 1770. All this caused Britain no great immediate danger, given its naval superiority, but eighteenth-century Britain was not equipped to enjoy a splendid isolation in international affairs. Its systems of taxation, finance, and administration were superior to France's and its governmental finances far sounder, but British policy-making was still hampered by fiscal and parliamentary restraints and ministerial instability. Neither France nor Britain seemed in the 1770s to have a clear edge over the other in terms of domestic political and social stability, and the margin of superiority of Britain's navy over its Bourbon rivals was not insuperable, while its army did not remotely compare to France's. France clearly excelled in the size, organization, training, and direction of its foreign service.[33] Just as Austria tried to compensate for Russia's greater invulnerability and freedom of action toward the Ottoman Empire by developing a more skilled, professional corps of diplomats,[34] so France tried to compensate for Britain's greater freedom of action by a better trained and organized foreign ministry. In economic power and resources the rivals seemed well matched. Growth trends in trade and industry favoured Britain, but the two countries' total wealth and production remained comparable, and Britain's home territories were far smaller in size and population.

Yet France, far from catching up in the international competition, fell further behind—once again mainly because of geography. Britain's insular position not only gave it greater security from attack and enabled it to concentrate its resources on one main theatre and one branch of its armed forces, but also enabled it, like Russia, to isolate its foreign policy from its domestic problems far better than others could. A Belgian or Hungarian

[33] For general developments in Britain after 1763, see Watson (1960); Christie (1982: chs. 1–4). The standard work on British foreign policy is now H. M. Scott (1990). For comparisons of parallel development patterns in France and Britain, see Jarrett (1973); Christie (1984); for their international rivalry, Black (1986); on the effects of the Peace of Paris, Hyam (1975); Langford (1976: 153–9, 162–4). On their respective administrative, tax, and fiscal systems, see Brewer (1989; 1988); Bosher (1970); Mathias and O'Brien (1976); Riley (1986). On their foreign services, see Horn (1961), Middleton (1977), Langford (1976: 3–15); Sallet (1953); Masson (1903). On the British–Spanish disputes, see Rice (1980); Langford (1976: 159–62).

[34] Roider (1980); Heppner (1982). On the Prussian, Austrian, and Russian foreign services and ministries, see Lauren (1979b: 14–23); Matsch (1980); and Altbauer (1980).

revolt could paralyse Austria's policy, internal problems could cripple France's; but the Pugachev Revolt in Russia, a rebellion in Ireland, or the great anti-Catholic Gordon Riots in London might affect Russian or British foreign policy little or not at all.

This seemed, however, not to apply to Britain's troubles with its American colonies, leading to revolution and war in 1775. It gave France an apparent golden opportunity to recoup its losses in the Seven Years' War and since. Vergennes thought otherwise. He feared instead a pre-emptive British attack on France. His policy was a cautious, essentially defensive one aimed at checking British expansion and saving the threatened French and Spanish colonies rather than destroying the British Empire, erecting a maritime balance rather than achieving French naval supremacy, and gaining France recognition as the arbiter of the struggle, indeed—but arbiter of peace. In short, he genuinely worked for the balance of power that others talked so much about.

This policy reaped the rewards of moderation in an immoderate world. His goal for the British–American struggle, a draw leaving both sides exhausted and eager for peace, was inherently difficult to achieve, and the premiss of his policy, that France could limit its involvement and withstand the financial and political strains of war better than its enemy, was doubtful from the outset. To organize and lead the anti-British coalition, moreover, France was compelled to make side-payments to its allies and auxiliaries, and defend their interests and aims as well as its own. While trying to restore a balance of power overseas and in Western Europe, Vergennes had to tolerate a Russo-Prussian–Austrian destruction of the balance in Central and Eastern Europe, indirectly at France's expense. Most of this was beyond his control, but some baneful effects stemmed from eighteenth-century limitations in outlook he also shared, especially the conviction that a war, even if dangerous and expensive, had to be waged if the king's honour and France's glory was at stake.[35]

This helps explain the long-range outcome of the American war for Britain and France: that Britain lost the war and France lost the peace. Vergennes brought France into the war in 1778 only when it was clear that Britain was mired in a long hard struggle. Then Britain helped him form a great coalition. Spain came in as France's ally, the British forced the Dutch to fight, and Catherine's League of Armed Neutrality menaced Britain in the Baltic. The French

[35] Murphy (1982: 234–5, 252–60); Gerhard (1932–3: 21–31); Crout (1983).

army then decided the land war in North America with a victory the French navy made possible.

But it yielded France few gains or laurels. Against the decisive Battle of Yorktown in 1781 the British could set their naval victory in the Antilles the next year, and against the loss of Minorca in the Mediterranean their successful defence of Gibraltar. Against British victories in India the French had no offset at all. In the peace negotiations Vergennes, loyal to France's allies, ended up working primarily for them, especially for Spain, making it easier for Britain under Lord Shelburne to divide the coalition and give the Spanish and Americans generous terms while France got little. This largely frustrated Vergennes's main aim, to tie the balances in the New World and Europe together. The Americans, Benjamin Franklin in particular, followed their republican principles, first exploiting France and then forsaking her. The war failed to revive France's overseas empire (it may have actually discouraged French belief and interest in it) and ultimately worsened France's naval position while restoring Britain's. Both countries seemed to be in serious financial straits when it was over, but France's weakness was structural, Britain's only temporary.[36] Spain also really profited little, though it emerged from the war with its position in the Americas apparently improved and its prestige in Europe renewed. Gibraltar, the key to Spanish security in the Mediterranean, remained in British hands, and the weakening of France's position in Europe automatically weakened Spain. The territorial gains Spain made in North America meant little alongside the persistent British commercial and naval threat to the Spanish empire, now augmented by the existence of an independent American republic dangerous both politically and commercially.[37]

Britain achieved its post-war recovery more rapidly in trade, finance, and domestic politics than in international politics. Nonetheless, the recovery underlined the failure of French strategy.

[36] Murphy (1982: 261–88, 321–6, 360–7, 382–94); Zeller, (1953–5: ii. 278–84); Langford (1976: 169–85); Watson (1960: 252–7); Ritcheson (1983); Dull (1983); Schama (1977: 60–3); Gerhard (1933: 152–61); Madariaga (1962); Misra (1963: ch. 1); Lokke (1932: 112–16); Bamford (1956: 206–11); P. M. Kennedy (1987: ch. 4). For British foreign policy during the war, see H. M. Scott (1990); for an argument that Britain could have won the war in North America militarily, see Mackesy (1976); for an argument that it never really lost command of the sea, see Baugh (1988).

[37] Hull (1980: 245–52, 265–97); Hargreaves-Mawdsley (1979: 131–9); Liss (1983: 26–30, 46–9, 108–11, 136–47).

The British soon recaptured the American market even while preserving and strengthening the mercantilist system against which the colonies had revolted. The government, though it tolerated American treaty violations, also did not have to concede the Americans much politically. Moderate reforms under William Pitt the Younger promoted economic and political recovery at home. Even during the war, Britain's insular security and the underlying strength of its economy had enabled it to handle domestic crises like the Gordon Riots of 1780 or the Irish Rebellion of 1781–2 without serious effects on its war effort or international standing.

The Eden Treaty concluded by Britain and France in 1786 signalled their reversal of fortunes. Commercially it favoured Britain in moving the two countries somewhat closer to free trade; politically it meant that Vergennes was ready to make commercial concessions for the sake of peace and *détente*, despite heated objections from French merchants and industrialists.[38] This concealed British victory in the Eden Treaty, however, would pale alongside an open and humiliating French defeat in the Dutch United Provinces that followed it.

A long period of Dutch economic, social, and political decline, aggravated by the naval defeats and devastation of trade in the Fourth Anglo-Dutch War, had given rise in the 1780s to a patriotic reform movement which issued in a revolt against the Stadholder, traditionally leader of the House of Orange. The reform movement, petty bourgeois in its social base with specific local roots and a specifically Dutch, largely religious, character and inspiration, had mainly internal goals. The only important connection with foreign policy was the Patriots' impatience with the passivity of Orangist policy, especially toward Britain, and their desire to reassert Dutch power at sea. Yet the struggle for power between moderate and radical reformers gained international significance because of the country's key geographical position, and when it led in 1787 to a deadlocked civil war between the democratic Patriots and the patrician Orangists, foreign intervention became virtually inevitable. The French were first drawn in when Vergennes, yielding to repeated requests for help from the Hague and to pressure at home, granted the Dutch government a defensive alliance in November 1785. Since only the Patriot party backed the French alliance, this tended to make France's position dependent upon a Patriot triumph. Vergennes was reluctant to tie France to one faction, but in 1787 the French minister to the Hague persuaded him that the Patriots would win, that the Stadholder Prince William and his party could be overthrown, that Prussia's new King Frederick William II (Frederick II had died in 1786) would not intervene in favour of his brother-in-law the Stadholder, and that the influence exerted at the Hague by the able British minister Sir James Harris, later the Earl of Malmesbury, could be undermined.

Vergennes accepted the gamble, and died before it failed. Frederick William, having reached agreement with Britain, decided after some hesitation to intervene. France, by this time nearly bankrupt and torn by internal dissent in the early stages of its pre-revolution, had to watch helplessly while Prussian troops in September 1787 marched in to overthrow the Patriots, restore the Stadholder, and establish Anglo-Prussian ascendancy.[39] The triumph owed far more to Prussian force than British diplomacy. Nonetheless, it enhanced Britain's position in Europe while France's precipitously declined, led to a Triple Alliance between Britain, Prussia, and Holland, encouraged the foreign secretary, the Marquis of Carmarthen, to seek a general British-led alliance system in Europe, and promoted Pitt's long-standing hopes of gaining a larger share in Far Eastern commerce. The British tried hard, though unsuccessfully, to make the Dutch pay for their rescue by compensations, territorial exchanges, and mutual trade concessions uniting the British and Dutch against other competitors.[40]

While France's position in Western Europe thus deteriorated, it declined also in Central and Eastern Europe. The Franco-Austrian alliance was a major but little-noted factor in both developments, as well as in the evolution of the system as a whole. Various explanations, some plausible, have been advanced as to why war was so much more extensive in Europe between 1790 and 1815 than in the decades before, which had been far from peaceful. The answers always include the French Revolution, for obvious reasons, and almost always stress French expansion in general and Napoleonic imperialism in particular. They usually include the age-old struggle between Britain and France for hegemony or

[39] Schama (1977: 25–46, 64–75, 79–135); Sas (1985: 31–5); Murphy (1982: 459–72); Langford (1976: 194–7); Ehrman (1969: 534–7); Te Brake (1985); Rowen (1988: 222–7); Venturi (1991: ii. ch. 7).

[40] Harlow (1952–64: ii. 329–418); Ehrman (1969: 416–33); J. Black (1984); R. D. Harris (1986: 228–9).

balance of power; sometimes the growth of Russian power; occasionally the struggle between Austria and Prussia over Germany. The most obvious difference in international politics between the two generations is never mentioned. From 1763 to 1790 France and Austria were allies and never went to war with each other; after 1790 they were never allies and almost constantly at war. Until 1809, moreover, when Austria was finally beaten into submission, it was their wars that were the really big, serious ones. These facts are not coincidental; they point to the root cause of the expansion of war. The explanation is not simply or mainly that after 1790 the old Habsburg–Bourbon rivalry in Europe, temporarily and rather artificially interrupted in 1756, revived. It is rather (to oversimplify) that an alliance which since 1763 had worked to sustain the European system while doing little or nothing for the power and security of the two partners finally broke down. With its disappearance went a vital dike against general war as well.

The Austro-French alliance obviously never worked as most balance theory and alliance theory would suggest it should have done, and as statesmen in both states would have liked it to have done. For purposes of controlling European politics, resisting hegemonic threats, and preserving a general balance of power it was a flat failure. The reason is that it was really a kind of alliance more common in the nineteenth century and more suited to it, a pact for management and mutual restraint of one's partner, not for capability aggregation and aggrandizement. It served the cause of general peace by restraining the alliance partners themselves, partly against their will, and thereby helped their chief opponents, Britain and Russia, grow as hegemonic threats. Both powers had entered the alliance on the eve of the Seven Years' War for ordinary security and power-political reasons; both emerged disillusioned with it for these purposes. Both decided none the less to maintain the alliance, mainly because it gave each a means of controlling the other's policy, and because without it they would probably fall into war with each other again, as they had so often in the past. The alliance served in every crisis from 1763 to 1790 to inhibit dangerous French or Austrian initiatives, while at the same time reducing the risks of predatory policies for their rivals, especially Britain and Russia. Thus it was simultaneously good for peace and bad for France and Austria; it both enabled the system to last longer and increased the likelihood of extensive violence at its ultimate demise.

All the French and Austrian efforts to co-ordinate their policies and theatres of action proved unsuccessful. At the time after 1763 when Kaunitz wanted to base a genuine, though still anti-Prussian, system of European peace on the alliance, Choiseul was busy preparing for a new war with Britain. By the time Vergennes and Louis XVI reversed France's direction, Joseph II had reversed Austria's. The French consistently opposed his efforts after 1774 to use the alliance for Austrian gains in Germany, the Ottoman Empire, or Belgium (e.g. Joseph's attempt to open the Scheldt for commerce in 1785) as dangerous for general peace or particular French interests, or both.[41] The beneficial effects for Europe of this alliance of restraint between two historic enemies show up clearly in Switzerland and Italy, where France's leading influence in Switzerland counterbalanced Austria's in northern Italy, and both areas were spared the balance-of-power, Habsburg–Bourbon conflicts common to earlier eras.[42]

Had Britain and Russia ever reached a real alliance, this also might have helped the late eighteenth-century system last longer, though not to work less rapaciously. Many Britons and some Russians thought of each other as natural allies. There were close commercial ties between the two countries, with Russia enjoying a favourable balance of trade. Britain depended on Russia for naval stores, Russia bought British finished goods and needed British ships and merchants for its carrying trade. They had a common opponent in France, kindred interests in the Baltic, and no apparent conflict of aims anywhere. After the Seven Years' War, moreover, Russia was Britain's only possible great power ally.

But this put Catherine in a position to exploit Britain's quest for an alliance, which she did. Russia's response to British offers of a trade treaty and political alliance in 1763–6 was to demand British subsidies in peacetime, a British guarantee of Poland, and a *casus foederis* directed against the Ottoman Empire. Britain rejected these conditions, not because they were arrogant, involved huge British Continental commitments, and threatened the balance of power, peace, and international law (though they did), but because they violated British traditions of not giving peacetime subsidies or

[41] Beer (1872: 63–74); Murphy (1982: 292–300, 306–19, 336–44, 405–16); Sorel (1884: i. 26–9, 524–35); R. D. Harris (1986: 90, 145–6, 210).

[42] Bonjour (1965: ii. 104–20); Woolf (1979: 40–1); Valsecchi (1974: 222–3, 228). For Vergennes's attempts to cultivate ties with Russia as a supplement to the Austrian alliance, see Murphy (1982: 447–58); Fox (1971); for Austrian fears of French instability and attempts to form a French–Russian–Austrian coalition or secure Spain as a substitute ally, see Kleinmann (1967: 354–69).

making unilateral concessions. In any case, the trade treaty the two powers concluded in 1766, with its implied British consent to Russia's take-over in Poland, gave Russia all the political help it needed from Britain at this time. When Britain offered its good offices for peace during the Russo-Turkish War, Catherine concealed her annoyance and went her way. Meanwhile British naval officers and advisers helped Russia defeat Turkey at sea. Russia's victory and territorial expansion at Turkey's expense failed seriously to alarm the British government. British trade in the area was not yet very important, and Russia's advance toward the Mediterranean and apparently imminent overthrow of the Ottoman Empire seemed to threaten France rather than Britain. Besides, Britain's vision of a desirable European balance of power was in a way similar to Russia's, and like it hegemonic. It involved forming a Russo-British–Prussian coalition against France which would either leave Austria isolated or force it also to follow the British–Russian lead.[43]

This great coalition remained a dream; though their interests seemed mutual and their aims similar, Britain and Russia had trouble collaborating under eighteenth-century rules. The process by which great powers undermined smaller and weaker states in the latter eighteenth-century is best illustrated by what happened to Poland, the Ottoman Empire, and the German Reich; on the other hand, the way in which great powers could make fools of themselves over smaller ones is illustrated by Sweden and Denmark. Russia's goal was a balance of power in Scandinavia, Russian-style—meaning that Sweden and Denmark, paralyzed by their individual internal difficulties and locked in their mutual rivalry, should balance each other while Russia controlled both, settled their quarrels, and excluded France. British policy in Scandinavia, mainly concerned with promoting trade, combating French influence, and preserving the 1720 Swedish constitution with its restrictions on royal authority, harmonized fairly well with Russia's. Both powers supported the same Swedish party, the Caps, against its rival, the Hats. After 1763 Choiseul made Britain's and Russia's task easier by failing to maintain the French subsidy to Sweden while simultaneously trying to promote a stronger Swedish and Danish stand against Russia and Britain. This alienated Sweden, and Choiseul's attempt to promote a palace revolution in favour of the King failed, helping

[43] H. H. Kaplan (1981); Gerhard (1933: 17–23, 26–9, 36–73, 77–80); H. M. Scott (1975–6); Martens (1874–1905: x. 220–42, 280–7).

Russia secure an alliance with Denmark while Britain's able minister at Stockholm, Sir John Goodricke, obtained one with Sweden.[44]

These gains, however, proved ephemeral. First, Britain and Russia failed to agree on who benefited most from gaining Sweden and therefore should pay the Swedes the required bribes. Then Russia's actions in Poland and Turkey from the mid-1760s on frightened Sweden, causing the Russophile Cap party gradually to lose its ascendancy, while the Swedish heir apparent Gustavus concluded that only constitutional reform to create a stronger monarchy could save Sweden from the fate of Poland. Against British and Russian opposition, Gustavus resolved on a royal coup. With help supplied by the French foreign minister, the Duc d'Aiguillon, through Vergennes, then minister at Stockholm, Gustavus III shortly after his coronation carried out a bloodless coup in August 1772, strengthening royal authority though not restoring absolutism. The next year he renewed Sweden's traditional alliance with France and survived the crisis it occasioned. This French victory, however, proved as ephemeral as Britain's had earlier. The British quickly regained their position at Stockholm and Russia continued to profit from Danish–Swedish rivalry, now intensified by Gustavus's desire to take Norway from Denmark.[45]

Fifteen years of great-power intervention had thus left Sweden by the late 1770s about where it had been before, to no one's gain. The episode could have taught useful lessons to eighteenth-century statesmen, had anyone been interested. Statesmen and parties, once bought, frequently fail to stay bought, and bribing one tends to necessitate bribing them all. Able men on the spot like Sir John Goodricke can contribute greatly to diplomatic success, but only if their governments are willing to back them up. Once powers commit themselves to competition for a particular prize, the game is likely to be played out regardless of its original rationale and far beyond the value of the stakes. An alliance between dominant powers like Britain and Russia may not work even where their interests are congruent, because they fall out over who should lead the alliance and how its benefits and costs should be shared. But the late eighteenth century was a poor time for learning such lessons, and a worse one for applying them.

Britain's troubles in America made an Anglo-Russian alliance still more unlikely. Catherine was delighted at the war, expecting

[44] M. Roberts (1980: 7–211).
[45] Ibid. 213–409; id. (1964); Murphy (1982: 180–201); Barton (1986: 133–7); Nordmann (1971: 358–67).

it to help her make Russia independent of Britain in trade and on the seas—besides which, she entertained the same disdain for George III as for most of her fellow monarchs. But she managed to conceal this well enough to keep the beleaguered British courting her. Even clearly anti-British policies (Russia's *rapprochement* with France in 1779–80, Catherine's creation of a League of Armed Neutrality in 1780, and a Russian proposal for joint Austro-Russian mediation to end the war in 1781–82) failed to stop British appeasement. Britain offered Russia the island of Minorca in the western Mediterranean for a permanent alliance. In 1782 Foreign Secretary Charles James Fox, a naïve Russophile, expressed a willingness to adopt Catherine's principles on neutral rights at sea. The British welcomed Russian predominance over Central Europe; it meant that if Russia became Britain's ally it could bring at least one of the German great powers over to Britain's side for nothing.[46]

Foiled during the war, Britain continued to seek a Russian alliance after 1783, though less ardently. Fox accepted Russia's annexation of the Crimea without protest, and his rival and successor Pitt maintained the courtship, though with fewer illusions and partly in order to prevent an alliance between Russia, Austria, and France. But by 1787 Anglo-Russian relations had cooled. Catherine resented George III's joining the *Fürstenbund* and helping Frederick defeat the Bavarian exchange project, on which she at least verbally supported Austria. Negotiations to renew the Anglo-Russian trade treaty broke down in 1786, and with the outbreak of another Russo-Turkish war British began to be concerned about Russia's Eastern policy. Still, these two flank powers, each on its way to achieving hegemony in its sphere, were not thereby destined to fall out between themselves. They continued to co-operate in the Baltic, Britain focusing on Denmark and the west, Russia on Sweden and Finland.[47]

VI. THE OUTLOOK

It is time to draw together the threads of international politics from 1763 to 1787, just sketched in oversimplified fashion. The pattern shows four main features: dominant flanks, a vulnerable centre, threatened intermediaries, and a general crisis in status and

[46] Madariaga (1962); Gerhard (1933: 112–35); Martens (1874–1905: x. 319–26).
[47] Gerhard (1933: 146–51, 172–83); Ehrman (1969: 470–1, 502–9); Martens (1874–1905: x. 324–36).

security. During this period Britain and Russia, rendered relatively invulnerable by geography, were able to widen this advantage and increase the vulnerability of the other great powers. All the great powers, whether rivals or allies, ate away at the existence and independence of vital intermediary states—Poland, the Ottoman Empire, Bavaria, the German Empire. Balance-of-power practices had led to a general security crisis on the Continent, worst for France, Austria, Prussia, Poland, Turkey, and Germany, and continued to undermine the devices which to some small degree had confined conflict earlier in the eighteenth century—the legal restraints of the Treaties of Westphalia, the imperial constitution, the Austro-French restraining alliance, Russia's defensive Northern System, the French–Spanish Family Compact as a check on Britain in the west and overseas, France's barrier in the East against Russia. As was predictable under balance-of-power rules, the aim and goal of international politics was to lead a dominant winning coalition or at least be part of one, not a defensive blocking one. By 1787 Russia and Austria were allied for aggressive purposes against Turkey; Russia, Austria, and Prussia had already cooperated for aggression against Poland. Prussia wanted a dominant Anglo-Russian–Prussian alliance against Austria, Austria a similar coalition against Prussia, Britain a kindred one against France. Russia had the widest choices, and would choose whichever combination would provide it the clearest hegemony and greatest profit at a given time.

The general security crisis Europe faced was clearly seen, especially by statesmen of the European center. Before Vergennes died, he and his critics recognized that his moderate, pacific policy had failed and left France in grave danger. German statesmen and publicists repeatedly warned that the current balance-of-power competition was destroying the German Empire, and that the smaller states and ecclesiastical principalities of Germany could not survive without its protection. Frederick II died believing that a new general war was coming which might mean the end of Prussia as a major power.

The most convincing testimony comes from Austria. For years Kaunitz had been warning that, although the monarchy possessed impressive size and substantial resources, the challenges and threats surrounding it on all sides made it weak rather than strong. Prussia's rivalry, Russia's encroachments, and the general lawlessness of European politics were gradually destroying Austria's independence. Having said this, however, Kaunitz had only a lawless remedy to offer—an all-out alliance with Russia for the sake of immediate security and territorial gains at Turkey's and Prussia's expense. The imminent prospect of a new Russo-Turkish war in 1787 compelled the usually optimistic Count Ludwig Cobenzl, Austrian ambassador at Petersburg, to share Kaunitz's pessimism. He could not decide which of three possibilities was worst— that Russia would again proceed, as in 1774 and 1783, to dismember Turkey without compensating Austria, or that Russia would ignore Turkey and fall on Austria in alliance with Prussia, or that a general war would break out whose main burdens would fall on Austria. He was sure that Austria needed a conservative alternative to the reigning balance-of-power system in order to survive as a great power, but recognized at the same time that no such system could be created except by common consent, and that unilateral restraint on Austria's part would simply hasten its decline. Therefore he agreed with Kaunitz: Austria had to cling to Russia and pin its hopes on the possibility of a war between Prussia and France or Britain and France over the Netherlands. Such a war in the west would afford Austria and Russia a chance to fall on Prussia and Turkey together and destroy them both, giving Austria some temporary, partial relief. It made no sense, he admitted, to look to more and bigger war for salvation—but what choice did Austria have?

But, one will say to me, always more war, always more conquests! This language breathes the politics of the last 34 years. Do we not have enough with what we already possess? Must we run the risks inevitable in such enterprises, even when they are the best arranged and the most advantageously formed? No doubt we could be content with what we have, if all the other powers were willing to do likewise. But we have already been made to see the inconveniences of the expansion of Russia.[48]

Here, from one of its leading practitioners, was as convincing a refutation of balance-of-power theory and exposé of the effects of its practice as one could hope for. The story of European international politics from 1763 to 1787, as in other periods, refutes the notion that balancing practices and techniques promote equilibrium, limit conflict, and preserve the independence of essential actors, or can do so. Instead, they naturally tend to produce imbalance, hegemony, and systemic conflict. Only actual or aspiring hegemonic powers can consistently practise balance of power techniques, and only fundamentalists can really believe the doctrine.

[48] Cobenzl's *Denkschrift* of Aug. 1787 is in Joseph (1901: ii. 462–7). For Kaunitz's earlier warnings, see Beer (1872: 4–17, 19–38, 74–98, and *passim*).

Yet even if the picture of eighteenth-century practices depicted by Cobenzl and others is true and damning, it could be that his *cri de cœur* gives too pessimistic and determinist a picture of the whole eighteenth-century system, ignoring countervailing forces, opportunities, and programmes for useful change. One might want to call attention to the political philosophers, theorists, and publicists who argued for a more rational international system.[49] The cosmopolitan ideals and reform impulses of the Enlightenment seemed to point in the same general direction. Eighteenth-century developments in military tactics, strategy, and organization had apparently made possible a more limited, rational conduct of war. Growth in international trade and communications had made states somewhat more interdependent within the world economy, and might in time have constituted an incentive for avoiding conflict or keeping it confined. Most governments knew that they faced unsolved problems and strains at home, and that a war, especially an unsuccessful one, might push them over the edge into revolution.

This is true, and means that certain ideas and movements current in the late eighteenth century, had they been adopted and supported generally by rulers and statesmen, could have helped keep a defective international system going and possibly even reform it. But that proves nothing. Undoubtedly, many factors within state and society—domestic politics, economic trends, social change, intellectual currents, what have you—influence the course of international politics, sometimes decisively. Their impact on international politics, however, is indirect, indeterminate, unpredictable, and often ironical. The effects they actually have depend less on their intrinsic nature and purpose than on how they enter into the processes of decision-making and policy formation, how statesmen and publics react to them, and what influence they exert when filtered through the policy process and mixed in with the other ingredients of international politics. When one applies this general rule of thumb to the late eighteenth century, one sees that even the more hopeful and progressive trends did not work for peace, stability, and reform in international politics. In fact, they

[49] See Hinsley (1963: 62–6, 72–9, 175–81); Rein (1927: 58–73); Heinz Gollwitzer (1972: 218–21, 274–5, 282–3, 298–305; 1964: 66–77, 84–7); Bonjour (1956: 527–47); Sorel (1969: 348–51). The decisive point, in my view, is that while there was much eighteenth-c. criticism of balance-of-power practices (e.g. Justi, 1763), there were no practical ideas for reforming or replacing them, and some like Immanuel Kant considered a balance of power system, with its incurable conflictual competition, a necessary stage in the ultimate evolution of a peaceful confederation of states.

probably did the opposite—heightened its potential for conflict and increased the structural instability of the system.

This was clearly the case with the leading political doctrine of the eighteenth-century Enlightenment, enlightened absolutism. Historians have argued for decades over the term, and the nature and aims of the movement it designates.[50] There is no serious doubt, however, concerning the main impact of enlightened absolutism on international politics. It was a doctrine and method for increasing the power of the ruler and his bureaucratic servants over the state machine, his subjects, the economy, and the social groups resisting central authority. As such, enlightened absolutism directly increased the war-making potential of states (often its explicit purpose) and indirectly weakened traditional norms and restraints in international politics. It is no accident that enlightened absolutists ruled the most expansionist, aggressive great powers in the latter half of the eighteenth century, Russia, Prussia, and Austria, or that France, the great power with the most moderate foreign policy, also had the least success with enlightened centralizing reforms at home.

Much the same holds for the military reforms of the late eighteenth century. The progress made in the training, discipline, equipment, and support of armies, together with advances in strategy and tactics, weaponry, the professional training of officers, and the organization of general staffs and special services, all tended to make warfare to some extent more rational and efficient. They

---

[50] Three points seem to emerge clearly from the welter of divergent views on many questions. First, the central target and opponent of enlightened absolutism was the traditional society of orders still persisting in varying degrees throughout most of Europe. The attack by enlightened absolutism on the society of orders and the attendant secularization of the basis of princely rule helped pave the way for revolution. Second, though the reform programmes of enlightened absolutism were everywhere riddled with contradictions and tensions, they succeeded well enough in certain countries (e.g. Prussia, Tuscany, and Spain) in averting the danger of revolution. They created a danger of revolution, however, either where reform efforts failed (France) or where they were precipitously applied to governments and societies where the orders were strong enough to resist (e.g. the Habsburg monarchy and Württemberg). Third, whatever the intentions of reformers might have been, in practice enlightened absolutism always tended to promote the primacy of the state over society and of state power over the welfare of its subjects. This was the case not merely because means tend to dominate ends or because rulers and state officials thirsted for power and glory, but in part because of the eighteenth-c. international system. Only states strong enough to survive ruthless international competition could expect to live and prosper. Among the immense literature, works I have found especially helpful are: Aretin (1974); Behrens (1985); Rosenberg (1968); Raeff (1983); Raumer (1957); Oestreich (1969).

were not intended to reduce its incidence or scope, and did not.[51]

Increased international trade, improved communications, expanded contacts among European states, and the opening up of more of the world to Europeans did not serve to diminish interstate rivalry, but provided more arenas for it. Wherever trade expanded outside Europe (the Western Hemisphere, India, the Far East, the Levant) it involved fierce competition and frequent conflict. Even close and mutually beneficial trade relationships, like Britain's with Russia or with the United States after 1783, allowed political rivalry to continue below the surface.[52]

Finally, even had the effects of these societal trends on international politics been more benign than they were, they still would have made no real difference. They did not address the central security crisis in Europe which was destroying the international system, and nothing which failed to meet this issue could save the system or produce a substitute for it.

This suggests a different way for historians and social scientists to look at late eighteenth-century Europe. Its social movements and revolutions are usually seen as great structural developments with profound organic causes and consequences; its events and developments in foreign policy as surface phenomena, the result of contingency, chance, and individual wills and choices. This is dangerously one-sided. No one would deny that the late eighteenth-century revolutions ultimately had profound structural effects on Europe and the world, however diverse and contradictory those results may have been. Yet at the same time, in a certain way the outbreak of the French Revolution was a contingent event, and the great systemic wars which began in 1787 were not. The French Revolution, considered as an event which occurred in 1789, was not inevitable; it came about because reform programmes

[51] See Parker (1990); Best (1982: 22-59); Paret et al. (1986: 32-122); Kunisch (1978: 83-9); S. F. Scott (1973: 26-33); Bien (1979). This is not to deny that there were some attempts during the Enlightenment to make the conduct of war more humane; see Best (1980: ch. 1).

[52] On the foreign-policy implications of Europe's economic penetration of the wider world in the latter eighteenth c., see Rein (1927); Heinz Gollwitzer (1972: 222-53); Gerhard (1933: 30-3); Fugier (1954: 1-7). On the specific importance of economic expansion overseas for Britain, see Schumpeter and Ahston (1960: 10-12); Knick (1982: 280-5); Ehrman (1969: 161-5, 332-5, 412-13); Calder (1981: 784-9); on French overseas commerce, Stein (1983). On the growth of Anglo-French trade rivalry in the late eighteenth c. even in the Levant, once unimportant to England, and on Anglo-Russian competition, see Gerhard (1933: 82-101, 125-9, 391-8).

designed to avoid it happened to fail.[53] Other states threatened by revolutions avoided or controlled them in this same period—Britain, Russia, some German and Italian states, above all Austria; it is possible to construct a reasonable scenario by which France might have done so as well. During the same period, no state seriously threatened by war avoided it in the long run, including many who tried very hard to do so. The explanation is structural, not contingent. The reigning European domestic order gave states fairly effective weapons to use against revolution—standing armies and police forces, bureaucratic state machines, systems of law and taxation, class structures, religious and social traditions and sanctions, constitutions, etc. Against war the eighteenth-century international system offered states and leaders only the very weapons and methods of balance-of-power politics which caused and exacerbated the problem.

Once again Austria offers a simple, convincing illustration. As will be seen, when Leopold II ascended the Habsburg throne in early 1790, he faced actual revolution and threats of revolution far worse than those Louis XVI had faced in France a year earlier. Within a year, by great skill, prudence, and effort, Leopold defeated the revolutionary threat; it never really revived again in Austria throughout the generation of wars, invasions, and upheavals that followed. But that same remarkable skill, prudence, and tireless effort did Leopold no good in fending off war. All he could do was delay it for a time; his efforts may even conceivably have made it worse; and once it started nobody could stop it.

Pace R. R. Palmer, Jacques Godechot, Franco Venturi, and other distinguished historians of this era, Europe in the 1780s was not heading inexorably toward revolution, but toward war, whether or not there was revolution. Revolution was contingent; war systemic and structural.

[53] See esp. Egret (1978). For an argument that the Revolution was 'unnecessary', see W. G. Runciman (1983).

2
War and Revolution, 1787–1792

THOUGH the wars of the French Revolutionary era pre-
dated the Revolution and were not caused by it, there is a
certain parallel between the Revolution and the wars in
terms of origins and results. The French Revolution arose from
the failure of a patriotic reform movement—that is, various efforts
by enlightened rulers and ministers, aristocrats, and liberal reformers to make the old regime work better.[1] Once started, however, the Revolution in France quickly became a movement for
something different and bigger than reform: a powerful, confused,
and incoherent effort to replace the old aristocratic-monarchic
political order with a new democratic one. In the traditional
society of orders, law and governing authority came from the top
down, based on tradition, prescription, and religious sanctions,
and liberties and rights were corporate privileges based on one's
particular status in society. In the new democratic society, the
state and the political and social order was to spring from below,
from the whole people conceived as a body of free and equal
citizens endowed with natural rights; political authority and governmental decisions would rest on the people's will. The concept,
though not new, was genuinely revolutionary, particularly for
old-regime France and Europe, and, as recent historians have emphasized, the attempt to create new institutions, a new language,
and a new political culture embodying the democratic ideal would,
more than anything else, make 1789 a memorable turning-point
for posterity.[2]

The quest for democracy, however, quickly became a disastrous
failure, producing not liberty, equality, and fraternity, a stable
polity, viable institutions, and a durable new political culture, but
divisions, disillusionment, chaos, civil war, and rule by force and

---

[1] 'It is the failure of patriotism, rather than the search for democracy, that is the
key to the revolutions of the late eighteenth century' (Jarrett, 1973: 93). For further
arguments in this general direction, see Doyle (1976: esp. 204–13); Gruder (1984);
Lucas (1976); Eisenstein (1965–6).

[2] For major recent discussions along these lines, see Furet (1978); Hunt (1984);
Baker (1987a; 1990); Doyle (1980). An interesting comparison between the
American Revolution as the natural culmination of American colonial history and
the French Revolution as a fiery break with France's is in L. S. Kaplan (1979:
422–5).

France and South-West Germany, 1790

terror. These results had begun to emerge even before France went to war with much of Europe; the war both heightened these trends within France and turned most of Europe against the Revolution and its ideals. As a result, a revolution originating in patriotic reform and fought in the name of democracy came to discredit revolution and democracy for many Europeans for two generations to come, and to discourage for a considerable time the very idea of political reform and popular participation in politics of any kind. Yet the seed of the democratic ideal would survive and ultimately revive, so that all later democracies would stand to some extent in the French Revolution's debt.

The wars of the French Revolution show an analogous pattern. They too sprang from the breakdown of the old regime, i.e. the eighteenth-century international system, and the failure of various efforts to reform it and make it work. Like the Revolution, the wars resulting from the collapse of the old international politics went farther than anyone had anticipated, vastly exceeding previous general wars in the scale of violence and destruction. Here, too, ideas sprang up for a new international order and attempts were made to create a new and better basis for international politics. Most would be as futile, self-contradictory, and utopian as efforts in the French Revolution to create freedom and democracy through terror. Yet one serious, non-utopian vision of a new international order emerged during this period. Though it had no chance to be realized then, it also left behind the seeds of something a future generation would pick up.

I. WAR AND CRISIS IN THE EAST, 1787–1790

The Russo-Turkish war arose in August 1787, as many wars do, from the decision of a threatened defensive power to halt its decline and regain security by violence.[3] The Ottoman Empire declared war on Russia out of the conviction that its previous acceptance of Russian expansion, especially the annexation of the Crimea in 1783, only encouraged further Russian pressure and subversion. The Porte's decision seemed to give Russia another great opportunity. It was unprepared for war, but so were the Turks, and Russia's political situation was much improved over that of 1768. Austria, then a potential foe, was now an ally, and

---

[3] For a general discussion of this recurrent phenomenon, see J. S. Levy (1987).

the *casus foederis* clearly applied to this war. Poland, in revolt against Russia in 1768, seemed under control. France was distracted by its internal troubles and its defeat in the Low Countries; Britain and Prussia, similarly occupied there, were eager for an alliance with Russia. Even France wooed Russia in hopes of preventing a war and saving Turkey, proposing a quadruple alliance (France, Spain, Russia, and Austria) against Britain. The British, on balance, considered a Russo–Turkish war useful as a way to distract and weaken France.

As for Catherine, though she was not eager at this time to fight a war or carry through the Greek Project, she expected more victories and conquests, helped by Christian revolts in the Balkans. This time, however, victories proved elusive. A storm wrecked much of Russia's Black Sea fleet, while on land Prince Potemkin proved an irresolute army commander, even proposing to evacuate the Crimea in the face of a Turkish threat. Though Marshal Suvorov managed to defend the Crimea, Russia's only success in the first year's campaigns was the siege and capture of Ochakov on the Black Sea in December 1788.

The Tsarina could not be blamed for the military set-backs. Some of Russia's other troubles, however, arose from her one weakness in foreign policy, a disdain for other players that sometimes made her overreach. After initial success in evading France's offers of mediation and alliance and getting Austria to join the war in February 1788, she then miscalculated in dealing with Prussia and Poland. Both were courting Russia. Prussia offered to mediate in the war and to renew the old alliance and subsidy arrangement of 1764, even hinting that it would allow Prussian volunteers to fight on Russia's side. The Polish King, hoping to strengthen his crown under Russian protection, offered direct Polish participation in the war in exchange for Russian subsidies and Russia's consent to an expansion of the Polish army, some territorial acquisitions for Poland, and internal reforms. Catherine, influenced by Potemkin who had personal ambitions in Poland, rejected Prussia's offer and secretly promised to help Austria resist any Prussian aggrandizement. She might have got away with spurning Prussia, which was a necessary price for the Austrian alliance. In June 1788, however, she also chose to accept Stanislas's alliance offer on her own terms, which required Poland to supply 12,000 cavalrymen to fight under Russian command, without payment in additional territories or reforms and with Polish foreign policy turned over to direct Russian management. This alienated the

King and his party, and worse still convinced Prussia that the proposed Russo-Polish alliance would be directed against her, thus changing Prussia from a suitor into an opponent.

At this same time Britain, now an ally of Prussia and the Dutch United Provinces, adopted a policy of strict neutrality, denying Russia the facilities needed to bring the Russian Baltic fleet into the Mediterranean. Gustavus III of Sweden, tired of Russia's intrigues with restive Swedish nobles and Finnish dissidents, decided to use this opportunity to relieve Sweden of Russia's pressure and possibly recapture some past losses. After a war of words with Catherine, Gustavus declared war in July 1788. At first the move backfired on him. A Swedish offensive failed, the Russians managed to raise an insurgent movement in Finland (this tactic had failed in the Balkans against the Turks), and Denmark came into the war against Sweden, threatening it with invasion. But diplomatic intervention by Britain and a warning from Prussia forced the Danes to retire and revived the Swedish war effort. Thus by early 1789 Russia was at war with Sweden in the north and the Ottoman Empire in the south, while Prussia was hostile, Poland becoming uncontrollable, and Britain no longer friendly.[4]

In reality, however, the situation threatened Austria more than Russia. For some Russians a war in the Near East was welcome; not for Austrians. Kaunitz, who recommended joining Russia in it, did so not because he thought Austria could make useful gains at Ottoman expense but because he saw this as the only way to maintain the Russian alliance and a balance of conquests, and hoped to turn the war against Austria's real foe, Prussia. Joseph not only feared that, while Austria was fighting in the south, revolution would erupt in Belgium and Prussia aggrandize itself in Poland or Germany, but also considered conquests in the Balkans, especially the Danubian Principalities, as worse than useless, increasing Austria's vulnerability *vis-à-vis* Russia and Turkey and adding nothing to its security elsewhere. The vice-chancellor Philipp Cobenzl's standpoint was even simpler: any war with its attendant financial strains would ruin the monarchy. True, Austria had a better chance than Russia to use the weapon of popular revolution against the Turks and so make gains without formally going to war. A 5,000-strong Serbian Free Corps had been formed by refugees from earlier risings in the Ottoman Empire now living in the Banat (southern Hungary), ready to fight under Austrian leadership for Serbian liberation and unification under Habsburg rule. But two Austrian attempts to use this weapon by seizing Belgrade in late 1787 and early 1788 failed; by the time Austria reluctantly entered the war in February, it had lost its best chance for a quick victory.

Worse still, all its efforts to limit its participation in the war to that of an auxiliary and tie it to strict conditions broke down. For the obvious strategic, geographical, and systemic reasons already discussed, after Austria's entry Russia was able to limit its war effort, while Austria ended up mobilizing 245,000 men and 37,000 officers, more than in the Seven Years' War. Still, only about half of these could be deployed against Turkey, and various factors—irresolute Austrian generals, disease, Joseph's shortcomings as a field commander, and the failure of the allies to co-ordinate their strategies and take the offensive—combined to yield Austria few successes and some humiliating if inconclusive defeats in its first campaign. By autumn 1788 Philipp Cobenzl was urging peace at any price and Joseph pleading for Kaunitz to end the war quickly. The Emperor could not advise Kaunitz just how to do this, or decide himself which was better—to make a separate peace, persuade Russia to accept a joint peace on the status quo ante bellum, or go for a military victory so that Austria's gains would match Russia's. After Russia captured the first major prize in Ochakov in December 1788, Catherine agreed to make peace for Austria's sake, on condition that Austria first capture the fortress of Chotin and Russia retain Ochakov. These conditions, as intended, made the peace talks opened with Turkey through France in early 1789 useless. A new sultan, Selim III, took the throne in April vowing to reform his empire and renew the war effort.[5]

This showed again that Austria's worst problem was with its ally Russia, but its enemy Prussia also presented dangers, prominent among them its new king Frederick William II. He was a religious mystic devoid of piety, self-willed, gullible, dissolute, greedy for quick victories, and thoroughly anti-Austrian. Prussia's Foreign Minister Ewald Friedrich Count Hertzberg, though not especially hostile to Austria by Prussian standards, also had ideas that were as dangerous as the King's or worse. His reaction to the Eastern war, which he expected Russia and Austria to win fairly quickly, was to concoct a Grand Design for a peace settlement in January 1788. It called for Russia to keep the Crimea and acquire

---

[5] Roider (1982: 180–8; 1976: 538–56); Stefanovic-Vilovsky (1909: 138–42). The best documentary source for the internal debate in Austria is Joseph (1901: ii); but see also Joseph (1873: 286–329; 1869: 326–50).

Ochakov and Bessarabia; Austria would return Galicia to Poland and get Moldavia and Wallachia in exchange; and Poland in exchange for regaining Galicia would cede Danzig, Thorn, and the palatinates of Posen and Kalisch to Prussia.

This was a normal late eighteenth-century arrangement for international peace and co-operation, and represented one of several contemporary efforts to make the eighteenth-century system work better. Hertzberg sincerely considered his plan a way to preserve general peace, reconcile the three Northern Courts, and satisfy everyone's interests, including Poland's (naturally at Ottoman expense—someone had to pay). The Austrians, learning of it through intercepted dispatches, saw it differently, as a scheme calling for Austria to fight a major war to destroy a state, the Ottoman Empire, it preferred to preserve, in order to acquire territories which would be difficult and expensive to rule and develop, would make Austria's ethnic and nationality problems still worse, and would worsen its strategic vulnerability *vis-à-vis* Turkey and Russia. For the sake of these poisoned gains, Austria was supposed to sacrifice a province it already owned and wished to keep, Galicia, so that its rival Prussia could acquire vital strategic territory and greater influence in Poland, with no exertion or costs on its part.

Hertzberg's Grand Design represented almost as bad a fool's deal for Russia. It would have limited the gains Russia hoped to make in Turkey and established Austria in the Danubian Principalities as a permanent territorial barrier to any possible future Russian expansion in the Balkans and a rival to Russian influence there, while expanding Prussia's territory and influence at Russia's expense in Poland. Even Frederick William could see that only military failure would make Russia and Austria accept this plan. If that happened, he argued, Prussia could take what it wanted without compensating them at all. Britain's minister at Berlin, Joseph Ewart, also opposed Hertzberg's plan because its aim, to reconcile the three Northern Courts, was opposed to Britain's desire to isolate Austria, forcing it to break with France and Russia and support British interests on the continent.[6] Hertzberg

[6] On Hertzberg's Grand Design, see Klueting (1986: 257–9, 267–73; 1988: 146–51); Bissing (1967: 32–3); F. K. Wittichen (1905: 20–3); Schlitter (1907: 24–5); Gerhard (1933: 270–3). Scholars have rehabilitated certain of Frederick William's advisers somewhat, especially his minister for education and public worship, Johann Christian Woellner. See e.g. Aretin (1967: ii. 60–1); Bissing (1967: 42–5); Epstein (1966: 354–69). On the King himself, his foreign policy, and the general character of his reign, however, no rescue is possible; see Real (1958: 1–10); Bissing (1967: 36–9, 46–61, 78–81).

stuck to his proposal none the less, and developments in the West seemed to give it a chance for success.

II. AUSTRIA'S CRISES IN WEST AND EAST

The revolutionary events which shook France from May to August 1789 (the meeting of the Estates General, the Tennis Court Oath, the triumph of the Third Estate, the fall of the Bastille, the forced move of the Court from Versailles to Paris, the Great Fear and the abolition of feudal privilege) captured the attention of Europe, but had little impact on international politics. The Belgian revolution had a far more direct effect on the international scene. Russia and Austria had begun to win their war against the Ottoman Empire in the summer and autumn of 1789. Selim III's new army suffered shattering defeats in the Danubian Principalities; Austria took Belgrade in October and occupied Bucharest in November, while Potemkin captured key fortresses on the Dnestr. These victories, however, only gave Austria prizes to retain or exchange, not the peace she needed and craved. Selim, trusting in European complications to aid him, decided to fight on,[7] and military success made Catherine more determined to win the war. Meanwhile the long-smouldering resistance in Brabant to Joseph's centralizing and innovating 'reforms' had burst into open flame in June 1789, when Joseph abrogated the old Belgian constitution. Despite its surface resemblances to the American and French revolutions, the Belgian movement was at bottom conservative, a revolt in favour of old Belgian privileges and autonomy against Joseph's innovations. Secretly encouraged by Prussia, the Belgians declared war in October, defeated and expelled the Austrian army and government in November, and proclaimed a United States of Belgium in January 1790. Once the Austrians were expelled, the movement turned more radical, an open split developing between traditional conservatives and reformist democrats; populist radicalism became important when France invaded Belgium two years later.

Whatever the domestic character of the revolt, the overthrow of Austrian rule in Belgium had revolutionary implications for international politics. Combined with a host of other troubles— the war against Turkey, a brewing revolt in Hungary, serious troubles in the Tyrol, Bohemia, Galicia, and Lombardy, stirrings

[7] Shaw (1971: 32–45).

in Transylvania, and the imminent death of Emperor Joseph—it confronted the Habsburg monarchy with one of the worst crises in its long crisis-ridden history.[8]

This crisis provides a further test of balance-of-power theory, according to which the central purpose and function of a balance of power is to preserve the independence of member states—if not all of them, at least all major or essential actors (the theory is ambiguous on this score, as on many others). The ways Prussia and Britain reacted to the threat to Austria's survival say much both about their policies and about how balance-of-power politics actually works.

Hertzberg's ideas were, once again, fairly moderate, if impractical: to use the Belgian revolution to promote his Grand Design. Austria should be forced to cede Galicia to Poland and make peace with the Ottoman Empire, gaining compensation for Galicia from the Turks, so that Prussia could have Danzig and Thorn. Beyond this, he hoped to bring Austria to abandon Russia and join Prussia in backing Poland against it. Frederick William wanted even bigger gains at no cost. Uncertain just where and how to get them, he toyed with various possibilities: taking Belgium away from Austria and giving it to the Dutch, or allying with the Ottoman Empire in war against Austria, or breaking up the monarchy by war and thus making Prussia once again Russia's main ally. Meanwhile the Prussian minister at Vienna, Baron Constans Jacobi, following the King's orders, encouraged Hungarian dissidents to rise, offering the hope of a Prussian guarantee of the traditional Hungarian constitution against Vienna, or even support of an independent Hungary to be ruled by a Prussian or Saxon prince. Meanwhile Prussian troops occupied the Bishopric of Liège adjacent to Belgium, whose prince-bishop had also been overthrown by revolution, allegedly to restore the old order on behalf of the Empire, actually to protect the revolution and work against Austria. Even the aristocratic *émigrés* who had fled France to launch a counter-revolution entered the act, Louis XVI's brother, the Count of Artois, urging Prussia to overthrow the French revolution by armed force and promising a Franco-Prussian alliance against Austria as the reward.

British policy was less greedy and reckless. Pitt and his foreign secretary, the Duke of Leeds (formerly the Marquis of Carmarthen), though little concerned at this time about the Ottoman Empire or

[8] Polasky (1987: 9–34; 1984); Dunk (1966: 16–17); Wandruszka (1963–5: ii. 186–90, 202–25); F. K. Wittichen (1905: 1–11); M. J. Levy (1988); Epstein (1966: 404–13); Hitchins (1987: 111–20); Venturi (1991: ii. 605–98).

the French threat to the Low Countries, were involved in a quarrel with Spain over Nootka Sound on the north-west coast of North America, and did not want to see Belgium ultimately fall from Austria's hands into France's. Therefore they did not want the war or the revolution to spread, or the monarchy to break up. Their goal instead was a standard British one: to get Austria to return to its position as Britain's 'natural ally' on the Continent, which involved depriving Austria of allies (currently Russia, since Austria's other ally, France, was already crippled by revolution) so that it would have to join Britain and its allies and serve British Continental purposes gratis. The British therefore agreed with Hertzberg that Britain and Prussia should ensure that Austria kept Belgium and continued to defend it against France, while imposing restrictions on Austrian rule, making it rely on British and Prussian support to retain Belgium.

Thus neither acted to prevent the collapse of a threatened major actor (in this case, some Prussians wanted to promote it); both tried to capitalize on its peril to undermine it further or make it still more dependent—the normal aim and outcome of balance-of-power politics. The anti-Austrian aspect of Prussian policy, however, was the only thing clear in Berlin's manœuvres, otherwise almost unintelligible. One move was apparently pro-Austrian, a secret mission to Vienna in October 1789 offering Austria a joint guarantee of both states' territories and other inducements if it would accept Hertzberg's Grand Design; but at the same time Prussia encouraged the rebels in Belgium and occupied the Bishopric of Liège to forestall action by Catholic Reich estates sympathetic to Austria. Hertzberg, Jacobi, and others urged the King to order immediate mobilization and threaten Austria with war; Frederick William was greedier than Hertzberg or Jacobi and ready to foment revolution in Hungary, but he declined to mobilize or move until the next spring.[9]

Indecision at Berlin coincided with growing panic in Vienna. Joseph, ignoring Kaunitz's advice to stand firm, pleaded with Catherine to make peace quickly to save Austria. Catherine, ready with a cup of water for a drowning man, offered more war instead, promising to give Austria additional aid should the war spread and suggesting that the two empires assume the defensive against Turkey and attack Prussia. Prince Potemkin, engaged in peace talks with the Turks at Shumla, exploited Austria's plight

[9] Schlitter (1907: 26–79); F. K. Wittichen (1905: 25–69); Bissing (1967: 64–8); Polasky (1987: 115–29); Silagi (1961: 6–9, 22–8); Neugebauer-Wölk (1991: 59–76); Ehrman (1969).

more openly, offering to reduce Russia's territorial demands and secretly support Turkey if it would support Russia's position in Poland and reject all of Austria's territorial claims. By the end of 1789 Kaunitz, an Anglophobe of long standing, was reduced to seeking an alliance with Britain simply to ensure its benevolent neutrality in Belgium. By January 1790, shortly before he died, Joseph was ready to accept Russia's idea of defensive war against the Turks and offensive war against Prussia, which he had earlier rightly denounced as a crude trap.[10]

What saved Austria in early 1790 was the accession of one of the most shrewd and sensible monarchs ever to wear a crown, Joseph's brother Leopold II. As Grand Duke of Tuscany, he had long warned Joseph that only gradual reforms based on the monarchy's historic traditions could succeed. Now he used this principle, his own reforming experience, and his considerable gifts of persuasion and manipulation to quell revolts and conciliate the nobles and other alienated groups in Belgium, Hungary, Bohemia, Galicia, Transylvania, and the Tyrol. Certain factors helped him. Joseph had reversed some of his own measures before his death to make things easier for his successor. Prussia's attempt to exploit the revolt at Liège against Austria had backfired when some smaller German estates, acting through the Westphalian Reich circle, limited the intervention to the restoration of the legal status quo ante and ultimately forced Prussia to remove its troops and withdraw its concessions to the rebels. This was a small triumph for law over power politics within the Reich and a hopeful omen for Austria's cause in Belgium.[11] Leopold was lucky, moreover, to face an opponent like Frederick William at Berlin, rather than his formidable uncle.

Still, Leopold's skill was indispensable in his success—his sense of priorities and timing, his willingness to compromise on everything but what was essential, and his combination of flexibility in means with steadfastness in goals. He was willing to use remarkably liberal means to preserve the integrity of the Empire, not merely accepting the idea of constitutional monarchy but actually aiming for one in the long run. To solidify Austria's traditional leadership in the Reich, he would if necessary have joined the *Fürstenbund* which Prussia led. He was a master at political manœuvres, employing disadvantaged groups in particular

---

[10] Kramer and McGrew (1974); Roider (1987: ch. 3); Shaw (1971: 46–9); F. K. Wittichen (1905: 58–61); Joseph (1901: ii. Nos. 285–96; 1873: 331–55); Vivenot and Zeissberg (1873–90: i. No. 335).

[11] Aretin (1967: i. 218–25); Real (1958: 16–19).

provinces to counter the pressure from a dominant group or nationality, knowing which problem among various pressing ones to meet first, and using that step to help solve others. By midsummer he had basically managed to appease Hungary, and this became the basis for his dealings with reactionary nobles in Bohemia and restive estates elsewhere (Galicia, the Tyrol, and Lombardy).[12]

He had even clearer priorities in foreign policy: first to escape from the Eastern war with a whole skin, and then to restore Austrian authority in Belgium. It was easier said than done. Though Leopold succeeded in initiating talks between Austria and Prussia in the spring, the danger from the war party in Berlin continued to grow. The Turks also were a major obstacle to peace, especially after a final Austrian offensive designed to pave the way for a more favourable settlement failed in May. Leopold faced opposition at home. Kaunitz, still fighting to control foreign policy as he had done for decades under Leopold's predecessors, argued against a peace with Turkey restoring the status quo ante as destructive of Austria's prestige and great-power status, denouncing Leopold's offer of reconciliation with Frederick William as absurd and dangerous and the Emperor's approach to Britain as little better. But none of his arguments and devices, including threats to resign, worked with Leopold. It was hard to quarrel with so reasonable and patient a monarch or abandon his service in a crisis, just as Frederick William found it difficult to fight someone who insisted on offering him peace and friendship. Besides, mistaking conciliation for weakness, the King thought he might talk Leopold into surrendering Galicia, enabling Prussia to get Danzig and Thorn for nothing. If this did not work, war was always available. This was the opposite of Leopold's outlook. The Emperor's regular reply to Kaunitz was that he was willing to try for limited gains from the Turks, but that Austria's real goal had to be an end to war—not merely the present war against the Ottoman Empire or a wider war with Prussia at this particular time, but a complete and durable escape from war in general. The monarchy could not survive, much less thrive, under conditions of constant war and preparation for war. Moreover, even if Britain was unfriendly, it was at least not an enemy, and could be used to help restrain Prussia and pacify Belgium.

Leopold proved the better judge of realities during the long,

[12] The best account of Leopold's character and policy is Wandruszka (1963–5); for the particular points made here, see ii. 197, 199–200, 232–8, 250–1, 260–1. Cf. also Epstein (1966: 413–28); M. J. Levy (1988).

tense Austro-Prussian negotiations at Reichenbach in the spring and early summer of 1790. At times an agreement on some form of Hertzberg's exchange programme seemed possible; at others, everything pointed to war. Finally Frederick William, to Hertzberg's dismay, gave Austria an ultimative choice: either peace with Turkey on the status quo ante bellum or war with Prussia. Austria accepted the former, with reservations on possible border rectifications with Turkey, while Prussia agreed that the Triple Alliance would help restore Belgium to Austrian rule under its ancient constitution guaranteed by Prussia.

The two powers signed the Convention of Reichenbach on this basis on 27 July. It was like the 'humiliation of Olmütz' which Austria supposedly inflicted on Prussia sixty years later: apparently a shameful retreat, actually a lucky escape. By promising to abandon its war with Turkey with little or no gains, Austria avoided a potentially disastrous general war and secured the chance to recover more important territories in the West and to put down revolts at home. In promising to restore the ancient Belgian constitution, Leopold made no concession; he had always intended to do so, and Prussia, by guaranteeing this constitution, turned its back on the Belgian revolutionaries who were counting on Prussian support for their independence. The consent of Prussia's allies Britain and Holland to the restoration of Austrian rule, even if that consent involved conditions, strengthened Leopold's hand in Belgium and restricted their freedom of action more than Austria's. Reichenbach did require Austria to surrender Belgrade, and thus betrayed the hopes of Austrian Serbs for Serbian union under the Habsburgs. But fateful as this concession might appear in the light of 1914, in 1790 it was unavoidable, not only because of Turkish and Prussian attitudes but also because of Hungarian and Russian ones. The Hungarians wanted no more Serbs in the monarchy, and the Russians needed to be persuaded that Austria in making peace was not betraying them for selfish gains but yielding to necessity. For Prussia, meanwhile, Reichenbach was really a defeat. By mobilizing at great expense and then failing to act, it had let down the Turks, betrayed the Poles, irritated the Russians, worried its English and Dutch allies, and finally let its opponent off the hook, all for an ephemeral gain in prestige.[13]

Yet Reichenbach, like Leopold's domestic moves, was at best a

[13] Wandruszka (1963–5: ii. 264–73); F. K. Wittichen (1905: 72–84); Joseph (1873: 361–79); Vivenot and Zeissberg (1873–90: i. Nos. 344, 371–2); P. Wittichen (1899: 37–9); Stefanovic-Vilovsky (1909: 163–75); Silagi (1961: 30–7); Shaw (1971: 52–7); Kaunitz to Potemkin, 7 Mar., 2 May 1790, HHStA, *Russland II Correspondenz* 217, fos. 66–71.

skilful retreat, and Leopold's aim was not *reculer pour mieux sauter* but *reculer pour mieux construire*. Whether he could build anything upon this retreat would depend in good part on how he met another challenge from the West.

III. STORM IN THE WEST: THE REVOLUTION IN FRANCE

The French Revolution poses an obvious question for international historians: at first so marginal a factor in international politics, why then did it suddenly became central? Revolutions are often closely connected with international affairs. War, foreign-policy failure, and national humiliation frequently help to bring on revolution; Russia in 1905 and 1917, Germany in 1918 and 1933, China in 1911, and France in 1848 and 1870–1 are a few examples. Frenchmen could have blamed France's domestic troubles in the late 1780s in part on its problems and failures in international politics—its fiscal problems provoked by the war in America, the economic troubles of the late 1780s on the Eden Treaty. True, scholars have largely discredited both these notions, arguing that the real cause of the deficit was the vicious French system of taxation and tax collection,[14] and that the problems of the French economy likewise lay deeper,[15] but public perceptions at the time are what count. The regime's foreign-policy record offered ample grounds for attack—huge expense, failed wars, useless and unpopular alliances, a hated foreign queen, defeats and failures for France in Poland, the East, and the Low Countries, and the concurrent successes of the great enemy, Britain. And if critics had plausible grounds to attack the regime for its foreign policy, the King's supporters should have been alarmed at the decline in his prestige and France's power and influence in a Europe as dangerously competitive as that of 1790. Yet foreign-policy issues played no great role in the pre-revolution or its early stages. Only from about mid-1791 did the spirit of nationalism, aroused and mobilized by the revolution, become clearly visible, initially more in domestic affairs. Even the way Britain exploited France's weakness and undermined its alliances in 1788–91 produced no widespread reaction.

There is no real puzzle here, however. Revolutions tend at first

[14] Bosher (1970: 276–313); Harris (1976).
[15] On economic conditions in the 1780s generally as a factor in the Revolution, see Kemp (1971: 14–79); on the effects of the Eden Treaty, see Donaghay (1984; 1978).

to intensify most peoples' normal preoccupation with immediate domestic concerns; foreign policy becomes important only if and when it affects them directly in terms of foreign threat, war, taxes, or economic distress. Alongside this general tendency went the idealistic naïvety of early revolutionary thinking about international politics: the belief that new democratic principles would somehow produce a natural harmony between France and its neighbours, just as they were supposed to do among Frenchmen. Thus it was understandable that Frenchmen at first would fail to take seriously what was happening to France in the international arena, and then react violently when they caught on.

It is actually harder to answer certain questions about Europe's reaction to the Revolution. Did the fears of governments and elites in Europe that it threatened their authority and the existing social-political order plant the seeds which ultimately ripened into war? Clearly such fears developed over the course of time. Initially, however, it is hard to show a connection between the way the governments and educated publics of Europe reacted to the Revolution and actions these governments took in their foreign policies, at least toward France. In Germany, only a narrow literary-intellectual élite paid much attention to the Revolution, and its reactions, divergent in any case, lacked political significance. Those who favoured political reform in Germany looked mostly to other models than France, in Britain, Prussia, and America. Most German thinkers in any case concerned themselves more with abstract political principles than concrete programmes for action. The approval a good many German intellectuals showed for the Revolution derived from the way it confirmed their Enlightenment ideas and attitudes without involving them. Those who later came into actual contact with the Revolution, through the war or by travelling in France, tended to receive a quite different impression about it—favourable regarding France and the French people, unfavourable toward Jacobinism and the Revolution itself.[16]

Even in Britain, despite a wider and more lively debate over developments in France which had a greater impact on domestic party politics (it was one cause of a split in the Whig party), the Revolution remained mainly a subject for observation and speculation. If it made the Irish problem slightly harder to handle and encouraged political radicalism to some degree, it created no

[16] Dippel (1977: 332–64); Real (1958: 10–12); Vierhaus (1983); Raumer (1957b: 60–3); Schneider (1980); Weis (1991); Fink (1983: 299–301); Möller (1983: 71–81); Wegert (1981; 1987).

serious internal threat.[17] Certain small principalities and free cities in Germany, especially in the Rhineland, faced more real revolutionary danger. Yet the threat became serious only where, as in Belgium, the governments themselves provoked unrest by assaults on traditional privileges. Most German regimes felt confident that they could handle their domestic unrest without help, or with only that of the Empire. Even where they felt inclined to use force against movements the French Revolution supposedly touched off, they did not propose to strike at the supposed root of the evil in France.[18]

The counter-revolutionary activities of French émigrés abroad make more sense as seeds of future war. The agitation and plots of the early high-aristocratic émigrés were certainly provocative, and clearly helped radicalize developments within France. But the émigrés aroused little sympathy and much irritation in Europe, especially from the major governments. Their influence on international politics, such as it was, became felt only after a serious threat of war arose, and never became crucial. As for the revolutionary agents France allegedly sent out to stir up revolution abroad, in this early period there were none, only travellers returning from France with accounts, largely favourable, of what was happening there.[19]

In fact, the direct effect of the first years of the Revolution in international politics was to isolate France, making both the French and other powers act as if it was not part of the system. The Anglo-Prussian–Dutch Triple Alliance was originally concluded in 1788 principally to bar France from the Low Countries, but by 1790 this aim hardly counted. The British tried to use the alliance to extract trade concessions from the Dutch[20] and worried more

[17] In general, see McDowell (1979); Elliott (1982); Dickinson (1989); Goodwin (1979); Ehrman (1969: 42–9); L. G. Mitchell (1971: 160–4, 192, 200–5); Christie (1984: 3–53).
[18] Blanning (1983: 12–58); Molitor (1980: 158–69); Braubach (1976: ii. 322–4); Reichardt (1981); Epstein (1966: 250–3, 285–9); Press (1989).
[19] Vidalenc (1983b); Godechot (1981: chs. 1–4); Ruiz (1983). While certain scholars have argued that a real potential for Jacobin-inspired movements existed in Germany and Austria (e.g. W. Grab (1967) and Reinalter (1983)), a sounder picture emerges from Blanning (1983); Molitor (1980); Weis (1975); Droz (1983; 1949: 476–81). A sample of a good Tory's views of the émigrés can be found in notes by Robert Stewart, later Viscount Castlereagh, evidently written in late 1791 or early 1792, blaming the anarchy and violence in France largely on their folly and provocations. Durham County Archives, D/Lo/F 418 (14–15).
[20] Harlow (1952–64: ii. 392–418); Grenville (1892–1927: vol. ii, pp. xi–xii, Nos. 23, 61). For British motives in the original alliance, see ibid. iii. 438–42; for French reactions to the defeat, see Egret (1978: 40–2).

about Austrian influence in the United Provinces than French,[21] while Prussia quickly ceased to fear French revenge and wanted to use the Triple Alliance against Austria. Except for Frederick William's briefly thinking of a French alliance as a possible fall-back position against Austria, France never entered seriously into Prussia's calculations in 1789–90.[22]

The clash between Britain and Spain, France's ally, over Nootka Sound in 1790 illustrates the same point. The dispute, involving Spain's claim to exclusive sovereignty on the western coast of North America up to 60° N (the southern boundary of Russia's claim), threatened to erupt into war when the Spanish seized a British vessel, the *Princess Royal*, for illegal fur-trading. Spain appealed to its ally, and France again proved a negligible quantity; the French National Assembly refused even to consider the use of force. This enabled Britain to take revenge on Spain for its role during the American Revolution, forcing it to release the ship and retreat on the issue of sovereignty. The humiliation, a severe blow to the Spanish government and empire, compelled even the strongest advocates of the French alliance to give up on France and look elsewhere for support.[23] Austria also gave up on France as an ally after it proved useless over Belgium in 1789, trying in vain to recruit Spain as an ally against Prussia.[24] Vergennes's successor as foreign minister, Charles-Marc Count Montmorin, until he was replaced in late 1791, could do little more than watch France's alliances crumble and the finest diplomatic machine in Europe be ruined by the National Assembly.[25] As for the Revolution itself, only Sweden did any more than watch it unfold. The quixotic crusade launched by Gustavus III and his envoy to France, Count Axel Fersen, for a European intervention to rescue the French royal family proved in the end no help to Louis XVI and Marie Antoinette, but helped lead instead to Gustavus's assassination in March 1792.[26]

In these respects, then, the Revolution and international politics went their separate ways, only tenuously linked by contingent events and developments. There is another way, however, in which they were organically connected from the outset. Just as

[21] Grenville (1892–1927: ii. 1–2, Nos. 217, 251, 270, 286, 287; vol. iii, p. xvi).

[22] Bissing (1967: 62–3); Ludtke (1929); Bourel (1991: 43–9).

[23] Harlow (1952–64: ii. 419–48); Ehrman (1969: 551–71); Norris (1955: 562–80); Cook (1973: 212, 217, 226–31, 249, 270); Konetzke (1929); Auckland (1861: ii. 373–8).

[24] Joseph (1873: 349–50); Kleinmann (1967: 362–78).

[25] Masson (1903: 55–110); Rain (1950: 1–15); Harris (1986: 303–6).

[26] Nordmann (1971: 431–51); Sorel (1893–1912: ii. 378–82).

the Revolution fundamentally changed domestic politics, so it changed the nature and rules of the international game. Its new revolutionary political language and culture, in defining the state as the highest incorporation of the popular will, as noted, dramatically raised the stakes of domestic politics, making the central issue that of who truly represented the people's will and had the right to govern by its name and authority. Those who fought and lost in this contest for representing the popular will, or who refused to support the winners, were by implication (and, increasingly, by explicit doctrine and decree) not part of the people but its enemies, traitors to the Revolution and the fatherland. In a similar way, the Revolution presented a challenge to the whole legal and conceptual basis of international politics. Instead of international claims and transactions being argued and fought out on the basis of treaties and legal rights, the popular will was now to be the decisive factor. This vastly increased the potential for international conflict, magnified uncertainties, and elevated quarrels over concrete interests into struggles over fundamental principles and world-views.[27]

The first concrete international disputes to arise out of the Revolution, between France and various German estates and the German Empire, illustrate this. They need not be described in detail; they concerned the feudal and ecclesiastical rights of German princes within French territory, the revolutionary Civil Constitution of the Clergy promulgated in France, France's claim to exclusive power and rights in Alsace-Lorraine on the basis of popular sovereignty, and the counter-revolutionary activities of French émigrés in Germany versus the agitation of German collaborators with the revolution in Paris. The quarrels were not simply petty ones; concrete interests were involved on both sides, and together with other factors they contributed finally to the outbreak of general war. Yet in so far as material interests were at stake, the disputes could have been settled by compromise, and probably would have been. The German princes whose traditional and legal rights were being usurped by France could not defend them by force, and the French were not inherently eager to quarrel or averse to a deal. The deeper problem was the conflict of principles. The French claim that rights based upon popular sover-

[27] For discussions of the political culture of the Revolution, see Furet (1978); Hunt (1984); on the changing concept of the state itself, see Skocpol (1979). For discussions of how 3 crucial political concepts, legitimacy, lèse-majesté, and freedom, were altered by the Revolution, see Applewhite (1978); Kelly (1981); Erdmann (1981).

eignty transcended those based upon treaties, a position endorsed early on by the National Assembly, denied that German rights had any legal basis, and made any French negotiation with the German princes a matter of gracious concession. Similarly, the French Civil Constitution of the Clergy in July 1790 unilaterally cancelled the diocesan rights of German bishops in Alsace-Lorraine. Ecclesiastical princes like the Bishops of Speyer and Trier who fought this were not simply defending their privileged places in an outworn and irrational order (though it has to be remembered that they were already threatened by Josephist and Erastian attacks on the Church in Germany) but correctly saw that their existence and that of the Empire was at stake. The French concept of an exclusive sovereign authority exercised by a single government over a clearly defined territory clashed directly with their life-principle, that of *Landeshoheit* (territorial supremacy rather than sovereignty). According to this principle, a prince of the Empire enjoyed supremacy within his territories according to established right and custom, but had to share the exercise of governmental authority in varying degrees with other holders of authority (*Herrschaften*) within his domains and beyond them—the Emperor and the Imperial Court Chamber, the Imperial Diet, the Church and its bishops, the immediate princes of the Empire, even Imperial knights. Sweeping away feudalism might be the way to consolidate revolutionary France; it would destroy Germany, and could undermine much of the rest of Europe.

At first the new French doctrine of state hit hardest at smaller states unable and unwilling to fight, especially the Papal State. Its French enclaves of Avignon and Venaissin were incorporated into France on the basis of popular sovereignty, and its control of the Church was undermined by the Civil Constitution of the Clergy. But quarrels with greater powers were bound to arise, for France's new principles gave it new powerful weapons of territorial expansion. Louis XIV had had to find or invent legal justifications for his annexations; France now could claim any territory where the people, or any group it chose to regard as the people, proclaimed its allegiance. Old-regime France had exploited its right to defend German liberties under the Imperial constitution; revolutionary France could now claim the right to defend the 'people's' liberties in any of the innumerable contests between princes and estates or oligarchs and democrats in Europe. France's eighteenth-century policy of pragmatic, piecemeal expansion to the north and north-east for strategic security would give way to an essentially new doctrine that France must attain its so-called natural frontiers, foreshadowed earlier but never before central in French policy. The idea of popular sovereignty would help one revolutionary faction, the Girondins, to provoke war abroad for domestic-revolutionary purposes, and then aid another party, the Montagnards, to demonize their enemies, domestic and foreign.[28]

All this would come later, to be sure, as the new concept of the state developed, not as a necessary or inevitable consequence of it. Still, the fact remains that by its doctrines the French Revolution challenged every state in Europe whose existence rested less on power than on the old traditional legal order, most of whom (the Low Countries, Germany, Switzerland, and Italy) were France's neighbours. The new French challenge to their existence was rendered doubly dangerous by what Austria, Prussia, and Russia had already done and were doing to undermine that legal order. The French Revolution was not, as often supposed, a threat to the international system mainly because its example and doctrines incited neighbouring peoples to revolution, and thereby spurred neighbouring governments to counter-revolution. By and large this never happened. The states to the north and east of France, especially in the German Rhineland, were too small, divided, and diverse in character, and the lines of authority and fealty within them were too loose and intertwined, for any general revolutionary movement to take hold. The trouble was rather that the same loose, traditional character of these regimes which kept them from being likely objects of revolution also made them incapable of defending themselves against French revolutionary attack and subversion. They could not unite for defence without threatening their individual existence and *raison d'être*, or call on their peoples for great sacrifices without undermining their allegiance, and they dared not rely on other great powers for protection because these powers were in some respects more dangerous to them than France itself.

Thus the Revolution did not really pit France against the great monarchies of Europe—at least not at first. Instead, Revolutionary France joined an attack already being waged by other great powers against what remained of the legal international order in Europe and the smaller intermediary bodies dependent upon it. Only later, when threatened itself, did France turn its revolutionary

[28] Voss (1983); Braubach (1976: ii. 324); Raumer (1952b: 88–9, 96–7, 99); Sorel (1893–1912: ii. 306–9); Blanning (1983: 60–3); Bitterauf (1905: 12–13); Aretin (1967: i. 251–8); Fugier (1954: 22–5); DeClercq (1880–1917: i. 213–15). For the natural frontiers, see Zeller (1933: 1936); Sahlins (1990). For the Jacobin demonization of the enemy, esp. Austria, see M. L. Kennedy (1982: 224 ff.).

forces mainly against great powers. But to understand how this happened, one must turn from France to a revolution more important at this time in international politics, the one in Poland.

IV. POLAND AND THE EASTERN POWERS, 1790–1792

The Polish revolution, unlike the French, was always integrally linked to international politics. Even after the first partition, different factions within Poland continued to look outside it for support against their rivals, especially to Russia. Patriotism and/or self-interest made some Poles lean toward Prussia or Austria (many leading magnates, for example, owned estates in Galicia making them simultaneously Polish citizens and Austrian subjects), but the German powers were not inclined to challenge Russia's position. At the same time in 1787–8 as Stanislas Augustus, hoping to strengthen his authority internally, offered Catherine an alliance and a Polish contingent for war against the Turks, leaders of the opposition to Stanislas were intriguing with Potemkin.[29]

Catherine, as noted, ruined Russia's favourable position in the summer of 1788 by a response to Stanislas's alliance offer which humiliated the King, encouraged his opponents, and angered Prussia. Prussia's reply when the Polish Diet opened in Warsaw in October was to have its minister, Count August von der Goltz, denounce the proposed Russian alliance and offer Poland a Prussian alliance instead. The offer released a wave of pent-up anti-Russian feeling, leading to a take-over of the Diet by a Patriot party led by Ignacy Potocki, opposed to Stanislas as well as Russia. Trusting Prussia's promises and assuming that its aims were compatible with Poland's, the Diet, in defiance of warnings from the Russian minister, Count Stackelberg, proceeded first to dismantle the structure of Russian control within Poland (the Military Department and the King's Permanent Council) and then in May 1789 to demand and secure the removal of Russian troops.[30]

The Prussians by this time were embarrassed by their victory. Instead of gaining them the Polish territories they coveted, it had created a threat of war with Russia. But Catherine, pressed by Austria and involved in other conflicts, decided to swallow her

[29] Michalski and Senkowska-Glück (1981: 35–47); Lojek (1975: 1–7); Zernack (1991: 24–8).
[30] Michalski and Senkowska-Glück (1981: 47–50); Lojek (1975: 7–9); Moritz (1968: 22–3); Lord (1915: 82–111).

defeat in Poland for the time being. This decision relieved Austria of the threat of a general war, but raised the danger that the Tsarina, disgusted with Austria's timidity, might decide to renew her lapsed alliance with Prussia by means of a second Polish partition, which some of her advisers advocated. Kaunitz, after trying vainly to get France and Spain to prevent this by guaranteeing Poland, began urging Russia to end the war with Turkey and, in alliance with Austria, turn to stopping Prussia and preserving Poland, either as a reformed monarchy or in its old unregenerated state. At this point in 1789, each of the three powers was still interested in saving Poland, but in different ways and for different purposes. Prussia was willing to support Polish reforms if it were paid with a Polish–Prussian alliance, territorial concessions, and a commercial agreement. Russia wanted to preserve an unreformed Poland under its thumb. Austria wanted to preserve Poland, whether reformed or unreformed, as an intermediary body under joint Russian and Austrian control, serving to separate them territorially, link them politically, and help frustrate Prussia. Each of these programmes had some supporters within Poland, though Austria's less than the others.

The Polish patriots decided to cast in their lot with Prussia. In response to Prussia's alliance offer of 1788, the Diet in July 1789 proposed a direct alliance with Prussia, with Poland becoming a member of the Triple Alliance, and to make the Polish Crown hereditary in the Wettin house of Saxony. Hertzberg denounced these terms of alliance as absurd, but some at Berlin, especially Frederick William, wanted a Polish alliance as part of Prussia's extensive preparations for the war contemplated against Austria the next spring. Hertzberg and Stanislas therefore entered into negotiations in December, neither of them eager for an alliance. Both raised new demands, Stanislas that Polish trade be freed from Prussian tolls and Hertzberg that Danzig and Thorn be ceded to Prussia. Nonetheless, an alliance, defensive in words but offensive and anti-Austrian in spirit, was concluded 29 March 1790 and unanimously ratified by the Diet.[31]

Leopold II had just taken power at this time. He first tried to extricate Austria from its Turkish war by offering the Turks peace on the basis of the Peace of Passarowitz of 1718, with Austria retaining Belgrade. His move encouraged the British to urge Prussia not to go to war with Austria but to force it to make peace on the basis of the status quo ante. It also revived Hertzberg's hopes

[31] Ibid. 78–81, 112–27; Lojek (1975: 9–15).

for his exchange scheme—Danzig and Thorn for Prussia, Galicia for Poland, Belgrade for Austria. Thus Prussia went into the Reichenbach negotiations with at least three possible programmes— war against Austria in alliance with Poland, a status quo ante peace in the East, and an exchange settlement along the lines of Hertzberg's Grand Design. The Reichenbach Convention, already described, settled for the second of these. An inconclusive draw for Prussia, Austria and the Ottoman Empire, it was for Poland a disaster. It ended Polish hopes of forming a great league with the Triple Alliance and the Ottoman Empire for purposes of war on Austria and the recovery of its independence and territory, and it left Poland dependent on support from a greedy, unsatisfied, un-reliable Prussia against the inevitable future challenge from Russia. Any prospect of Turkish help for Poland, moreover, vanished when Prussia repudiated an alliance it had negotiated in January 1790 with the Ottoman Empire (the Prussian minister Heinrich Diez had exceeded his instructions by promising Turkey the re-covery of the Crimea). Finally, any prospect that Prussia would actually fulfil its alliance obligations to Poland was greatly dim-inished when the Polish Diet in September forbade any alienation or exchange of Polish land, thus dashing Prussian expectations of payment in Polish territory.[32]

No doubt Poland's policy was unrealistic. It defied Russia, trusting in a Prussian commitment which was never wholehearted and after Reichenbach had no foundation; it ruled out payment for the Prussian support on which it depended; and (less obviously) it failed to distinguish between its essential and accidental enemies. Prussia and Russia were essential enemies of Polish independence— the former because of its commercial, territorial, and political ambitions, the latter by virtue of its concept of Russian security.[33] Austria was opportunistic and unreliable, but it was the one par-titioning state that recognized its vital interest in the republic's survival. Yet Poland in the recent crisis had come close to joining Prussia in a war to destroy or paralyse Austria.

This Polish unrealism, however, was not just accidental, the product of the Poles' inexperience, romantic illusions, and fac-tional struggles. It was organic, part of a deeper dilemma, a wider

[32] Lord (1915: 127–52); Michalski and Senkowska-Glück (1981: 50–2); Lojek (1975: 15–23).

[33] Both worked to strangle Poland's economic development, Prussia by divert-ing Polish trade to its own Baltic ports and by duties on transit trade, Russia by its tariffs and by cutting the Polish access through Turkey to the Black Sea. Gerhard (1933; 286–7).

unrealism, and profound contradictions integral to the whole European international system, shared by Poland's enemies as well as the Poles themselves. In any European system based on a competitive balance of power, whether in 1790, 1919, or 1939, Poland, if it hoped to survive as an independent state, had to develop into at least a substantial regional power in Eastern Europe, possessing alliance capability. The rules of late eighteenth-century international politics, like those of the twentieth, had the effect of giving Poland apparent opportunities to achieve this goal and powerful motives to exploit them, while at the same time virtually guaranteeing that its efforts to do so would fail. A still worse contradiction: the eighteenth-century system needed Poland and other intermediary bodies for stability, yet it worked to prevent Poland either from surviving as a useful intermediary state or from developing into a great power. To explain: the two central requirements for Poland's survival and independence were internal reforms to strengthen the state and external support against an eventual Russian counter-attack. Prussia seemed in 1790 to offer Poland help in achieving both these ends. It has been suggested that the Poles should have done everything necessary to ensure its support, including ceding Prussia some Polish territory.[34] Yet such territorial cessions would have ruined the cause of internal reform by discrediting the Patriot party and its programme, and would not at all have guaranteed Prussia's reliability. First of all, it was commonplace in the eighteenth century for a state, after accepting payment for its services, not to render them. Second, Russia could always outbid Poland in any competition for Prussian support, offering Prussia more Polish territory at less risk and a lower price than the Poles could. The first partition had already proved this, and the second would prove it again. Finally, the central aim of Prussian policy was never a permanent alliance with Poland to stop Russian expansion; there were always influential Prussians strongly opposed to this. The main Prussian aim was to weaken Austria and make gains in both of Prussia's traditional areas of expansion, Poland and Germany; an alliance with Poland would serve this Prussian aim only if it got into a war against Austria, a war which Prussia's other allies opposed and which held its own dangers for Poland.

In short, there was no way Poland could have played the current game of international politics successfully, even had it been endowed with greater strength, skill, and realism; the game itself

[34] Lojek (1975) makes this argument.

was stacked against Poland and other intermediary bodies. More than a stronger, more faithful ally, it needed a different, better international system—one which sustained Poland and other intermediary bodies for their own sake, as requirements for a stable, peaceful Europe. To ask for this in 1790 was to ask for the moon, not because no one wanted a new system—some did—but because no one, or almost no one, knew how to define or construct it, or would pay for it. The old system would muddle on, with great powers and smaller ones alike ensnared in tortuous efforts, more or less clever on the surface, stupid at bottom, to survive and win by its rules.

Prussia promptly illustrated this after Reichenbach by trying to secure other prizes on the cheap to substitute for those which had just eluded it—the cession of Swedish Pomerania as a reward for rescuing Sweden from Denmark, or Austria's consent to Prussia's acquisition of Berg and Jülich in western Germany. In the summer of 1790 the Prussians unofficially contacted moderate leaders in revolutionary France (the Feuillants) in the interest of a possible alliance against Austria; later that year they tried to prevent Austria from finally putting down the revolt in Belgium so that Vienna would be more amenable to a deal over Poland. At one point Prussia even tried to help Austria acquire some territory from the Turks in their peace talks at Sistova, so as to revive the Galicia–Danzig–Thorn exchange scheme.

Yet while everyone at Berlin wanted territorial gains, some were also interested in a new relationship with Austria. This was the motive for a secret mission to Vienna by the King's adviser Johann Bischoffwerder in February 1791. His proposed alliance, which would have required Austria to defend Poland and Prussia against a revival of Russian domination in Poland, looked like the usual Prussian snare. He hoped as well to tie Austria's hands in regard to Bavaria and block Austria's claims to the reversion of Saxon Lusatia, while paving the way for Prussia's acquisition of Danzig and Thorn. But this was normal eighteenth-century bargaining. Bischoffwerder wanted something in addition to one-sided Prussian gains—an alliance to guarantee both powers' possessions, avoid further quarrels, and free them from mutual paralysis and dependence on Russia. So did Frederick William, in his fashion. Kaunitz saw only the impudence in the Prussian offer; Leopold recognized the underlying desire for an Austrian connection, and was prepared to use it.[35]

---

[35] Lord (1915: 158–61, 172–7); Bissing (1967: 72–5); Möller (1983: 65–71); Holzapfel (1977: 794–7). The Bischoffwerder mission and Austria's reaction are fully documented in Vivenot and Zeissberg (1873–90: i. Nos. 47–78).

At this same time another move to 'reform' the international system, more ambitious and complicated, was under way, Pitt's so-called Federative (i.e. alliance) System. So far the Triple Alliance had served Britain splendidly. Prussia's land forces combined with the threat of British sea power had rescued Holland from France in 1787, Sweden from Denmark in 1788, Belgium from Austrian despotism and French-inspired revolution in 1790, Turkey from Austrian conquest, and Poland from Russian domination—all without involving Britain too deeply on the Continent or encouraging dangerous Prussian ambitions. Two British goals remained unfulfilled, however: bringing Russia like Austria to the peace table with Turkey on the basis of the status quo ante, and breaking up the unnatural Austro-Russian alliance so that Austria would again be available for Britain's purposes on the Continent.[36]

Pursuing these goals brought Pitt his first foreign-policy defeat— the Ochakov Affair. The main story is quickly told. In January 1791 Pitt, adopting a plan urged by Joseph Ewart at Berlin and supported by his Foreign Secretary Leeds, demanded that Russia agree to end its war with the Ottoman Empire on the basis of the status quo ante, surrendering the fortress and town of Ochakov on the Black Sea, near present-day Odessa. Catherine flatly refused. Thereupon in March Britain reached an agreement with Prussia to enforce the demand by war if necessary, with the Prussian army and the British fleet co-operating in the Baltic. Denmark agreed to benevolent neutrality, while subsidies were supposed to gain Sweden's support. Before the plan could be carried out, however, Pitt's old rival Charles James Fox, an admirer of Catherine, denounced it as a plan for war against a friendly power where no British interests were involved. Prince Semyon Vorontsov, the Russian ambassador at London, helped promote an outcry against it in Parliament and the British press, raising doubts among Pitt's followers about his brinkmanship. Under this pressure, the government first retreated, dropping its plans for military action, and then gave up the whole effort, leaving Catherine to make peace with Turkey on her own terms.

Commercial reasons were probably uppermost in prompting Pitt's challenge to Russia. Dissatisfaction over Russia's refusal to renew the Anglo-Russian commercial treaty; fear that it might

[36] Gerhard (1933: 216–21, 264–9); Ehrman (1969: 542–51); P. Wittichen (1899: 12–15, 42–7); E. Herrmann (1867: 4–12); Carter (1968: 130–4). Documents on the sea powers' mediation of the Austro-Belgian dispute in the latter half of 1790 are in Vivenot and Zeissberg (1873–90: i. Nos. 7–44).

emancipate itself commercially from Britain and reach closer ties with France, expanding southwards and eventually acquiring an outlet to the Mediterranean; and hopes that, through ties with Prussia and Poland, Britain could expand its trade, end its dependence on Russia for naval stores, and gain access to the Russian market all played a role. Political and strategic aims were also involved: splitting Austria from Russia, bludgeoning the Russians into a more friendly attitude, stabilizing Eastern Europe, and, by attaching Poland and possibly Turkey to the Triple Alliance, constructing a broad Federative System to protect the smaller powers of Europe. The scheme failed because Pitt overestimated Russia's difficulties and underestimated Catherine's nerve, relied too much on Ewart's judgement and Prussia's resolve, ignored the limits to British sea power, and prepared insufficiently for various contingencies in an elaborate scheme where many things could go wrong. Over-confidence born of Britain's earlier easy victories contributed to these miscalculations.

The immediate results were not earth-shaking—a set-back for Pitt and triumph for Catherine, the replacement of Leeds by Lord William Grenville as foreign secretary, and Britain's withdrawal to relative isolation from Continental affairs. The crisis did not seriously affect the Eastern war, the ultimate Russo-Turkish peace, the French revolution and its impact on Europe, or even the basic pattern of Anglo-Russian relations. Nor does this represent an early British attempt to defend the Ottoman Empire against Russian expansion, or foreshadow the Anglo-Russian rivalry of the nineteenth century. The restoration of Ochakov and the preservation of the Ottoman Empire were more pretexts than motives for Pitt's actions, and while this initiative was certainly anti-Russian, Pitt's overall policy was not. Britain continued to seek an alliance with Russia on its terms and Catherine to reject one except on hers.

Yet this account of the affair and its results fails to indicate its real significance in systemic terms. First, Samuel Johnson's dictum about women preaching and elephants dancing applies here: whether this British attempt to organize Europe for peace, its only one prior to the revolutionary and Napoleonic wars, was done well is less important than that it was done at all. It was uncommon for British statesmen to conceive of any kind of general organization of Europe for its own sake, rather than simply for purposes of a British-orientated 'balance of power'. The failure of this scheme and the subsequent British retirement from European politics, moreover, had a considerable impact on Prussia and

Poland,[37] and some connection with the origins of war on the Continent in 1792.

The main point, however, concerns what this crisis represented. It was not just a clash over peace terms with Turkey or a contest of wills between Pitt and Catherine, but a wider contest between the two relatively invulnerable flank powers over which of them would lead Europe and control the balance of power. The Ochakov affair was not a sign of a future Anglo-Russian world rivalry, but the beginning of an ongoing Anglo-Russian competition (often mixed with co-operation) over hegemony in Europe. The lesson for Pitt here was that his way of exercising hegemony would not be as easy and profitable as it had seemed. Britain's strategy failed not merely because it met too much domestic opposition or because its navy could not get at Russia effectively, but because Britain proved unable to do what Ewart and Pitt had wished— use various states on the Continent (Prussia, Holland, Poland, Sweden, Turkey, Denmark, and, it was hoped, Austria) to force Russia into line. William Eden, Lord Auckland, Britain's minister at the Hague and one of its best diplomats, had doubts about this from the beginning, and events confirmed them. The Prussians developed cold feet, the Dutch were apathetic, the Danes wanted to be left alone, the Turks suffered disastrous defeats, and Gustavus, angry over Britain's refusal to support his earlier war effort against Russia, demanded extortionate payment for Sweden's services. As for Austria, Leopold wished the British success in ending a war he also wanted ended, but declined to join them if it meant antagonizing Russia.[38]

Britons therefore drew an important lesson from Ochakov for the future: Britain could not organize the intermediary states of Europe against Russia at all, nor could it organize them against France without Russia's help. This lesson had vital importance for the central issue of European politics (until overtaken by French imperialism under Napoleon), the question of Anglo-Russian relations. Would the two flank great powers, growing more invulnerable as others grew more insecure and as the international system broke down, fight, or compete, or co-operate with each other in their efforts to control and use the states in between?

[37] E. Hermann (1867: 19–25); Lojek (1975: 36–52).
[38] For general accounts, see Ehrman (1983: 3–41); Webb (1980: 13–33); Cunningham (1964–5: 209–37). Useful points are added by Lord (1915: 153–5, 162–5); Horn (1961: 196–7); Langford (1976: 200–5); Gerhard (1933: 206–11, 326–30, 354–5). For the Russian side, see Madariaga (1981: 414–19); D. M. Griffiths (1979); Marcum (1973); Martens (1874–1905: x. 341–54).

Ochakov made a difference on this crucial question. For the next twenty-three years, when Britain wanted to gain help from some power or powers in Central or Eastern Europe, it looked first to Russia to secure it, either directly or through its influence.

Ochakov thus also served to increase the burdens, pressures, and dangers of international politics for the intermediary states—a factor which discussions of the crisis regularly ignore. Sweden and Denmark, to be sure, escaped lightly and Sweden was left free to pursue a *rapprochement* and possible marriage alliance with Russia.[39] But the Turks ended up worse off; having abandoned their cause, Britain now urged them to make peace with Russia at any price.[40] Poland also lost, for the crisis left its enemy Russia more free to take revenge and its ally Prussia more frustrated, greedy, and unreliable.

Austria, apparently little affected by the crisis, actually had much at risk. Under strong pressure from the allies to support their ultimatum, especially as Prussia grew more afraid of fighting Russia alone on land, Austria faced an impossible choice. If it joined Britain and Prussia in trying to force Russia to back down, it would betray its only ally. Should the joint pressure succeed, Russia would blame Austria for its humiliation; should it fail and lead to war, Austria, because of its geographical position, would have to do the main fighting against Russia. Or Austria could resist the British and Prussian pressure. If they then went ahead with their plan and war ensued, Russia could invoke the casus foederis of their alliance and make Austria again do the main fighting, this time against Prussia. As a reward for its services Britain offered Austria an alliance with Austria's enemy Prussia and a British version of a 'balance of power' which Kaunitz rightly labelled a chimera. Most Austrians understandably viewed this scheme as one more Prussian swindle and British attempt to force Austria into dependence. Yet in contrast to Kaunitz, who wanted to reject it out of hand, Leopold characteristically wanted to use it to draw the British and Prussians into some kind of joint European mediation between Russia and Turkey. However the mediation turned out, it would help promote the general peace Austria and Europe needed.

---

[39] Madariaga (1981: 414–15); Barton (1976). For the projected and finally abortive marriage alliance, see the private correspondence between Catherine and the Russian ambassador to Sweden, General Budberg, in *Sbornik* (1867–1916: ix. 195–384).

[40] For Pitt's urging this on Grenville, see BL Add. MS 58906, fos. 98–9, 108–10.

Britain's retreat relieved Austria of these dangers, but not of some after-effects on Anglo-Austrian relations. Coming on top of British dissatisfaction over the way Austria conducted its peace negotiations with the Turks at Sistova, and added to British suspicions that Austria was trying to gain influence in Holland, it promoted an anti-Austrian bias in the minds of British leaders, especially Grenville and Auckland.[41]

V. RUSSIAN AND AUSTRIAN PEACE PROGRAMMES, 1790–1792

The end of the Ochakov affair eliminated the Prussian and British programmes for bringing order and stability to Central and Eastern Europe and reforming the European system, leaving the field to the states with serious ideas on the subject, Russia and Austria.

Catherine's triumph in 1791 owed more to strength and nerve than skill and subtlety. Russian policy had involved some shrewd moves—making peace with Sweden in August 1790 on the basis of non-interference in Swedish domestic politics, using Pitt's domestic opponents to defeat him, reacting prudently to Austria's defection from the war at Reichenbach and to events in Poland. But at the same time some Russian political initiatives had failed (attempts to win over Denmark and Sweden to its side and to rally France and Spain against Britain, for example). The main reasons Catherine won were that in late 1790 and early 1791 Russia defeated the Turkish forces decisively everywhere, forcing the Sultan in July to sue for peace, and that she refused to give way to outside pressure even when most of her advisers believed Russia would be lucky to escape with peace on the status quo ante.[42]

Just when she was celebrating her victory over 'Gegu' (her contemptuous joint nickname for George III and Frederick William (Guillaume)), Catherine's will and nerve were tested again by news of a new challenge from Warsaw. On 3 May 1791, an unlikely alliance between Potocki and his Patriot party and the

---

[41] For Austrian policy, see Vivenot and Zeissberg (1873–90: i. 45–8, No. 45); Joseph (1873: 386–7, 395). For samples of the Anglo-Prussian pressure on Austria and British resentment of Austrian conduct, see Joseph Ewart to Pitt, Berlin, 30 Apr. 1791, BL Add. MS 58906, fos. 102–7; Grenville (1892–1927: ii. 59–63, 80–5, 94–5, 113–14, 129–30, 139–42, 216–18, 251–2).

[42] Madariaga (1981: 417–20); Shaw (1971: 58–62). For eloquent testimony on the crisis atmosphere in Petersburg in late 1790 and the first half of 1791, see Vorontsov (1870–95: xx. 15–22, xxvi. 405–83).

King enabled them to push a new constitution through the Diet, transforming Poland from an anarchic republic of nobles into a reasonably modern constitutional monarchy. It provided for a hereditary Saxon dynasty to succeed Stanislas, a sizeable standing army, and a central government with considerable authority, and it laid at least some of the foundations for social and economic reform and modernization. Townspeople were admitted to citizenship and political participation, though little was done for the peasants. The new constitution came as an unwelcome surprise to the Prussians; hereditary Saxon rule in Poland would be one more barrier to Prussian ambitions. Yet the wave of patriotic enthusiasm in Poland forced them to accept it, and at least the real target of the new constitution was St Petersburg rather than Berlin. If it remained in force, the days when Russia could rule Poland as its satellite were over.[43]

Catherine's response seemed clearly spelled out in rescripts prepared for Potemkin in late May and July (or perhaps prepared by him for her). They called for restoring the old Polish constitution and Polish liberties under Russia's control as soon as the Turkish problem was finally settled (Russo-Turkish preliminaries of peace were signed at Galaţi in August). The details of how to achieve this (under whose auspices Russia should intervene, whether to keep Poland united or divide it into four hetmanates, as one of the Poles conspiring with Potemkin wanted, and whether to appease Prussia and/or Austria by a second partition) were left to be decided according to circumstances. But military and political preparations for restoring the 1775 constitution and Russian control were to start forthwith.[44]

This looked like a clear blueprint for intervention and possible partition. Actually it was neither. For one thing, Potemkin, whose increasingly erratic conduct led to fears that he was going insane (he died of syphilis in October 1791), was given only a sham permission to intervene in Poland, tied to conditions unlikely to be fulfilled. For another, Catherine did not make vital foreign-policy decisions by herself or solely on the basis of *raison d'état*, and rival groups in Russia disagreed over policy. Potemkin, who advocated partitioning Poland for personal reasons, was losing favour. One group of prominent counsellors (Aleksandr Bezborodko, Ivan Ostermann, Aleksandr Vorontsov) opposed it on various grounds, while another, including Platon Zubov and

[43] Lukowski (1990: 239–52); Russocki (1979: 28–33); M. G. Müller (1986).
[44] Madariaga (1981: 420–5); Moritz (1968: 26–7); Lord (1915: 243–7); Davies (1982: i. 528–35).

A. I. Morkov, though Potemkin's rivals for influence, favoured acquisitions of Polish territory in the Ukraine. Besides, though the worst foreign threats to Russia were past, it did not yet have a free hand. The Prusso-Polish alliance still existed; Austria constantly urged Russia to accept the Polish constitution with some revisions as a way of preserving Poland; and the relative strengths of Russia's opponents and potential collaborators in Poland had to be considered.[45]

Thus the Russian response to the Polish constitutional revolution was not predetermined. A genuine acceptance of it, however, was never among the possible choices. Had Leopold succeeded in creating a European concert to defend Poland, this might have forced Russia to tolerate the revolution for a while; other conceivable contingencies could have compelled Russia to delay its overthrow. Nothing would have made Catherine or most Russians live with it willingly. Besides, Russia seemed to face a choice not between two evils but between two goods. After restoring the old order, Russia could either keep Poland intact as a Russian satellite or promote another partition and take the lion's share, whichever turned out to be better and safer at the time.

One important reason for Russia's confidence was the conviction that what it was contemplating broke no rules but represented normal, system-conforming, eighteenth-century balance-of-power conduct. A Russian intervention to restore the old legal order in Poland in no way differed in principle from the Anglo-Prussian intervention in the United Provinces in 1788 to crush the Dutch revolt and restore the Stadholder, or Prussia's and the Westphalian Circle's restoration of the Prince-Bishop of Liège, or the kind of intervention to restore order in France that émigrés and some European princes were calling for. Russia was thinking of another possible partition, true, but was not bent on it, and definitely wanted to avoid a war or other dangerous complications. While Catherine intended to keep Prussia and Austria from interfering with her plans, she did not intend to violate their rights and interests, as she and other Russians understood them. From 1764 to 1788 they both had accepted Russia's political monopoly in Poland. Should they now insist on compensation for Russia's regaining that monopoly, the Tsarina was willing to consider a standard eighteenth-century kind of transaction.

As for Russia's propaganda line, that the reform movement in Poland had to be crushed because it was part and parcel of French

[45] Madariaga (1981: 428–31); Lojek (1970: 570–82); Zernack (1991: 29–33); R. E. Jones (1984); Ragsdale (1988a).

revolutionary radicalism and subversion, this must not be dismissed as a cynical pretext. Even the most ruthless power politics usually rests on a substratum of principle and conviction, and this was Catherine's. The argument that a reformed independent Poland menaced European peace and balance just as a radical republican France did grew logically from the Russian concept of balance of power, according to which the other European powers, especially in Central and East-Central Europe, were supposed to balance each other, while Russia held the balance. This was exactly parallel to Britain's concept of a good European balance, above all in Western and Central Europe, and was just as defensible a definition as any other. According to the Russian view, the French revolution had ruined France for its proper balancing role in Europe, which was to check Britain on the sea and Prussia and Austria on land, and the revolution in Warsaw ruined Poland for its proper balancing role, which was to be the keystone of Russia's defensive glacis against the West. In defending its vital, legitimate interest in this balance, Russia intended to use traditional, time-honoured means, could expect considerable Polish help and collaboration, and was reasonably confident that no serious fighting or other trouble would occur.

In other words, this was a serious, middle-of-the-road kind of programme for dealing with the Polish problem, stabilizing Central and Eastern Europe, and making the European system work—about as good a one as the eighteenth century could offer. Only Leopold II had a genuine alternative, and he started from a position far weaker than Catherine's. His defensive successes in his first year had hardly reduced Austria's international problems at all. Peace still had to be negotiated with the stubborn Turks at Sistova, and the British government, while pressing Turkey to make peace with Russia at any price, joined Prussia at the same time in warning the Turks against any concessions to Austria. Meanwhile Britain's minister at Vienna, Lord Elgin, was still trying to pull Austria away from its alliance with Russia and urging Vienna to support Prussia's claim to Danzig. For Kaunitz and Philipp Cobenzl, this was one more British effort to make Austria a British dependency like Holland; and to use the monarchy to cover Britain's retreat from its Ochakov fiasco now and promote a British alliance with Russia later—a perceptive interpretation. Prussia was even more importunate and slippery. The King's emissary Bischoffwerder returned in June and July to urge an Austro-Prussian alliance, now to stop the revolutionary menace from France. While insisting that Prussia was supporting Austria's claims at Sistova (in fact, the Prussian representative, Marchese Girolamo Lucchesini, a notorious Austrophobe, did his best to frustrate them), Bischoffwerder argued that, if Austria actually gained anything from Turkey, Prussia must be compensated with Danzig, which he claimed was only a commercial port of no strategic significance.[46]

Meanwhile, in June 1791, the revolution in France took a critical turn. Louis XVI and Marie Antoinette, ignoring Leopold's warnings but encouraged and helped by Russia,[47] attempted to escape the country for the purpose of organizing a counter-revolution from abroad. Their capture at Varennes on June 21 and their return to Paris as virtual prisoners put them in grave personal danger, compromised the monarchy, radicalized the Revolution in France, and lent new urgency to the stream of appeals from Marie Antoinette and the royalist *émigrés* that Austria lead an anti-revolutionary crusade. Russia, Prussia, and other states also pressed Leopold to act. At the same time many Reich estates, including the Electors of Mainz and Köln, important clients of the monarchy, called on Austria to defend the German rights being violated by France in Alsace-Lorraine. Worst of all was the dark cloud threatening Poland.

In this critical situation, Leopold did what he always did and what any shrewd statesman will do: he tried to use one pressure and danger to neutralize another. His difficulties with the British, Prussians, and Turks at Sistova helped him fend off the *émigrés* and the Reich estates demanding action in the West, while Britain's pressure for an alliance against Russia helped him handle Prussia and the Belgians and manage Russia. He assured Elgin and Bischoffwerder that Austria was willing to join the Triple Alliance, but to avoid provoking further radicalism in France the alliance must be a purely defensive one, which Russia could also join and which would promote peace in the East. To bring Kaunitz to accept a quick peace with the Ottoman Empire on the status quo ante, he argued that only a general peace would check the revolutionary danger from France. To draw Russia toward a quick peace with Turkey and a union with Austria and Prussia over Poland, he urged the need for a European concert to confront

---

[46] Vivenot and Zeissberg (1873–90: i. Nos. 86–90, 95–7, 105–9, 131, 132).

[47] The Russian minister at Paris supplied the necessary passports for the flight, and Catherine fanned the flames of counter-revolution before and after the attempted escape with anti-revolutionary proclamations. Masson (1903: 95); E. Herrmann (1867: 117–27). For Austria's warnings, see Vivenot and Zeissberg (1873–90: i. No. 378); Wandruszka (1963–5: ii. 358–9).

France. At the same time he warned Marie Antoinette that until peace was achieved in the East and European unity forged in regard to the French Revolution he could do nothing concrete, and that any attempt by the French court or the *émigrés* to precipitate European action would ruin everything. In a similar way he fended off the restless Reich estates, shunting their quarrels with France into the tortuous legal channels of the German Empire.[48]

All this can be interpreted as merely a skilful juggling act dictated by Austria's many interests and weaknesses and designed to avoid dangers and commitments. Leopold's detractors at the time denounced these tactics as Machiavellian; an historian today might describe them as Metternichian. The disputes between Kaunitz and Leopold also can be seen as a reflection, not of differences in policy, but only of Kaunitz's concern for his authority and resentment of his rivals, his more doctrinaire Prussophobia, and his conviction that Austria ought to try to make gains rather than simply survive.

But this would be too narrow a view. Leopold resembled Metternich in some ways, especially in his flexibility and tactical skill, but excelled him in other, more important respects, and lacked only the longevity and luck to which Metternich would owe his fame. Metternich was a skilful diplomat; Leopold was a great statesman. A generation before the Congress of Vienna, long before successive wars and disasters finally converted Metternich for a few years from a clever but shallow diplomat and *grand seigneur* into something of a statesman, Leopold anticipated him in breaking with eighteenth-century politics and trying to create a new international system. Only thus, and not just as expedients to get Austria out of trouble or to manage an increasingly chaotic situation, must Leopold's actions in the summer of 1791 and later be understood. His dispute with Kaunitz was not over tactics; Kaunitz understood Leopold's manœuvres and endorsed them. They diverged on what Austria's basic goals should be, what alliances should be used for, how stability and peace should be achieved. Later—too late—Kaunitz would be converted to Leopold's views.[49]

The key to understanding the Emperor's policy lies in an area

[48] Vivenot and Zeissberg (1873–90: i. Nos. 86–133); Joseph (1873: 380–420); Aretin (1967: ii. Akt 38); Roider (1987: 81–8).

[49] For Kaunitz's analysis, which approved Leopold's tactics but criticized his limited goals, see Vivenot and Zeissberg (1873–90: i. Nos. 138–9); for an argument that Kaunitz had already abandoned the balance-of-power doctrine as a chimera, see Szabo (1979: 398–408).

where he and Kaunitz always agreed: how to handle the French and Polish revolutions. Historians have often described how Leopold tried to form a European concert to manage the French Revolution, not by forcible intervention but by moral and political pressure. He hoped to use the Eastern crisis and the danger of general war which it and the Revolution created to unite the European powers in jointly restraining anyone, whether radicals and royalists within France or *émigrés* and German or other European princes outside it, from provoking war. If peace were preserved, the Revolution would have a chance to settle down along moderate constitutional lines and France to become a normal country.[50]

The interpretation is sound enough in regard to France and the Revolution, but not for Leopold's policy as a whole; it reverses his priorities. He was not trying to use the crisis over Poland and the danger of war in Eastern Europe to manage the dangers of the French Revolution and war in the West, but the other way round— to use the French revolutionary danger to solve the Polish–East European crisis. He was more concerned about saving Poland not because the Polish reform movement was more conservative and monarchic or Poland intrinsically a more important state than France, but because Poland was the key to Austria's relations with Prussia and Russia and therefore to the structure of European politics and peace. The French Revolution needed to be checked, the French problem managed; the Polish revolution and the Polish state had to be saved, the Polish problem solved. His policy never had much chance of succeeding on either front; that has to be said at the outset. At the same time, it represented the only faint hope of avoiding the generation of European war and five generations of Polish captivity that ensued.

The French Revolution, of course, could not be ignored for many reasons—Austria's prestige, the security of Belgium, the interests of the Reich, and the danger to the royal family and the institution of monarchy. At one moment in June, reacting to a false report that the King and Queen had successfully fled France and reached safety in Luxemburg, Leopold seems to have considered some sort of intervention to restore order in France under their auspices, though not to restore the old regime.[51] But at no other time did he contemplate direct intervention in France. Those

---

[50] For judgements of Leopold's policy along these lines, see Sorel (1893–1912: ii. 224–33); Godechot (1981: 154–7); Wandruszka (1963–5: ii. 356–63, 378–81); Real (1958: 30–1, 34–5); Chaumié (1965:, 145–50); Silagi (1961: 20–1, 86–7).

[51] Vivenot and Zeissberg (1873–90: i. No. 386).

pushing Austria to do this were the French royal family, especially Marie Antoinette, the *émigrés*, the Russians and Swedes, and above all the Prussians. Having failed to reach an agreement with the Feuillants directed against Austria in late 1790, Frederick William switched to insisting that war with France was inevitable. Bischoffwerder on his first mission had proposed an alliance against France as well as Russia, and with Hertzberg's fall and the second Bischoffwerder mission in June and July 1791 the pressure from Berlin to act against France became intense. The ill-concealed hope at Berlin was that a joint war against France in which Austria was the principal and Prussia the auxiliary would yield Prussia the territorial gains in the east that had eluded it till now.

Leopold played along with Prussia, but for opposite purposes. The circular he issued at Padua on 6 July, the Vienna Convention signed on 25 July which laid the basis for an Austro-Prussian alliance, and the declaration he made jointly with Frederick William at Pillnitz on 27 August were all intended not only to calm Marie Antoinette, curb the *émigrés*, warn the French radicals, and re-assure Austria's German clients, but above all to tie Prussia's hands in a general alliance designed for mutual restraint rather than military action and territorial acquisition. It was part of what Kaunitz called an Austrian programme of counter-reform instead of counter-revolution, and for a moment it seemed it might work. Louis XVI accepted the new constitution drawn up by the Constituent Assembly on 13 September. Kaunitz considered the danger of war over; Louis had surrendered and Austria had united Europe in masterly inactivity. Leopold and several Prussian leaders agreed.[52]

This hope quickly faded. Austria reinforced its troops in Belgium and south-west Germany in the autumn, partly for security reasons but mainly to reassure the German princes.[53] But the danger in the east arising from the Polish revolution was also growing, and more ominously. Both Kaunitz and Leopold favoured the 3 May constitution, but with different ends in mind. Kaunitz, insisting that Prussia only pretended to be in favour of it, argued that, if Austria and Russia joined to support the new constitution, it would make Poland more useful to Russia, block Prussia's search for compensations, frustrate Britain's efforts to split the Imperial alliance, and give Russia and Austria preponderance in

[52] Ibid. Nos. 146–8, 167–74, 176, 197; Wandruszka (1963–5: ii. 368–9); E. Herrmann (1867: 70–82, 89–94, 99). For Prussian policy, see esp. Real (1958: 26–9, 32–3); Vivenot and Zeissberg (1873–90: i. Nos. 154, 166).

[53] Ibid. Nos. 182, 188, 189.

Europe.[54] This strategy, though favourable to Poland, was at bottom a competitive balance-of-power one, pitting Austria and Russia against Prussia; in addition, it was unrealistic in expecting Russia to share its control of Poland with Austria and help Austria defeat Prussia rather than exploit their rivalry. Leopold had a different aim. He wished to combine the alliance Prussia was now offering Austria with the existing Austro-Russian one, thus creating a general alliance of the three Northern Courts designed not for capability aggregation and territorial gain but for mutual restraint and the preservation of peace, especially in Poland. He even hoped eventually to bring Britain, Holland, and other states into this alliance for peace, expanding it into a general European Concert. Here, in 1791–2, was the germ of the Holy Alliance and the European Concert of 1815.

Though at first afraid that the Polish revolution would ruin his proposed alliance of restraint by stimulating Prussia's appetites and inciting Russia to reprisal, Leopold saw fairly quickly how to use the Polish problem to advantage. In the preliminary alliance convention of Vienna signed on 25 July, Prussia had originally proposed including a separate, secret guarantee of the new Polish constitution, clearly in order to split Austria from Russia and make Austria share the burdens of Prussia's alliance with Poland. Austria's negotiator, Baron Anton Spielmann, watered this Prussian proposal down to a self-denying ordinance. Both powers pledged not to act against the Polish constitution or place a prince of their houses on the Polish throne, and invited Russia to accede to it. Again the tactical aim was obvious—to bring Russia into the concert and help control Prussia—but more than tactics was involved. R. H. Lord, in his classic study of the Second Partition of Poland, states that this secret article was useful, although it failed explicitly to guarantee Poland's independence and existing constitution.[55] One could put it differently: this article was potentially valuable for Poland precisely *because* it did not guarantee Poland's complete independence and its current constitution, and was not intended to do so. Leopold hoped instead to place Poland under the joint protection of its three great neighbours, allied in a commitment to preserve its existence and autonomy and ready if possible to share that commitment with a general European concert.

This kind of joint protectorate, not a guarantee of the Polish constitution, represented the best practical hope for Poland. No

---

[54] Ibid. Nos. 102, 378.   [55] Lord (1915: 202–15).

amount of political and military reform, economic growth, and alliances could have given eighteenth-century Poland, vulnerable as it was, the capacity to survive independently and to play the great-power game. However natural the aspiration, the quest for that kind of independence would prove futile at best and suicidal at worst; this kind of competitive politics in Europe was exactly what was killing Poland. Poland's hope of survival, like that of the German Empire or the Republic of Venice, lay in a special agreement among its great neighbours to preserve it as a vital *corps intermédiaire*, backed by Europe as a whole. Russia in Leopold's scheme would still have played the leading role in Poland, but no power would have a free hand or exclusive control. Once again Leopold anticipated 1815 and the nineteenth century, proposing for Poland precisely the devices that would preserve the Ottoman Empire for a century after it seemed doomed.

Kaunitz, apparently converted to Leopold's goal, worked hard to achieve this kind of concert with Prussia and Russia and to persuade the Elector of Saxony to accept the Polish throne. In a plea to Prussia in early January 1792 he assured Berlin that 'the permanent preservation of the general peace based on a genuine indestructible harmony between our court and that of Berlin is the main goal of the political system of the Emperor'. But, said Kaunitz, this was possible only if the two powers brought Russia into their system and shared Russia's friendship rather than trying to monopolize it, as each had been doing for decades. This in turn required the partners to stabilize Poland through its new constitution and the Saxon dynasty. Without these reforms, Poland would continue to breed revolution and foment discord between the three allies. With them, Poland would settle down internally and would unite the allies in their common purpose and interest of keeping Poland from causing trouble in international politics while preserving it as a *corps intermédiaire* useful for each of them. At the same time, Kaunitz constantly assured the Russians that Austria's aim was not to challenge Russia's preponderance in Poland, or even get a share of it, but to preserve a peaceful Poland under Russian influence against Prussia's greed. Only a reformed, satisfied Poland, however, could survive and promote peace rather than revolution. Obviously, tactical purposes were involved in these arguments, but so also was a core of conviction and good sense, the recognition that Austrian security, tolerable Austro-Prussian–Russian relations, and stability and peace in Central and Eastern Europe all depended on a general alliance to preserve Poland as a shared interest and sphere of influence. Russian primacy in Poland was not a problem *per se*; Austria had accepted Russian preponderance over Poland before, and would do so again. What Austria could not stand, Leopold insisted, was the renewal of all-out international rivalry over Poland.[56]

To succeed, Leopold's peace campaign needed to do three main things: tie Prussia to Austria in a restraining alliance, bring Russia into it, especially in regard to Poland, and curb France without war. If these vital requirements were met, other troublesome factors—the *émigrés*, the Reich princes, the Elector of Saxony's reluctance to accept the Polish throne, the divisions within Poland, the pressure from Sweden, Spain, and other states for action against the revolution, etc.—could be managed.

The French problem was the first to prove unmanageable. Between November 1791 and April 1792 Austro-French relations spiralled downward into war. Already, in May 1790, the Constituent Assembly had vested the power of peace and war in the nation rather than the king, instituting the reign of diplomacy supervised by legislative committee. In November and December the Legislative Assembly, even less experienced and more radical than its predecessor, committed France in a series of debates and resolutions to encouraging revolution abroad and supporting the activities of foreign 'patriots' within France—this at the same time as France demanded that the activities of French *émigrés* in the German Rhineland and elsewhere be curbed. Still worse, a propaganda campaign in favour of war was launched by influential members of the republican Girondin party, and gained strength despite opposition from both the fading constitutional monarchists on the right and the rising Paris Jacobins on the left. A reshuffled ministry formed in November, though still dominated by moderates (the Feuillants), made the mistake of assigning foreign affairs to an indecisive mediocrity, Jean Marie de Lessart, while entrusting the war ministry to an enthusiastically patriotic *grand seigneur*, the Duc de Narbonne. Narbonne, quickly becoming a leading force in the ministry, undercut the Feuillant programme of peace and compromise with his own plans for regenerating the demoralized French army and monarchy through a war with France's hereditary Continental enemy, Austria. Louis XVI, having failed to secure help from Europe or to curb the provocations of the *émigrés* under the leadership of his brothers, the Counts of Provence and Artois, now played into the hands of Narbonne and the Girondins.

[56] The quotation is in Vivenot and Zeissberg (1873–90: i. No. 221); cf. also Nos. 206–9 and Lord (1915: 219–28).

Assuming the role of patriot, he announced on 14 December that he would demand that the Elector of Trier disperse the *émigrés* by January 15.

The French government's attempted diplomatic preparations for war with Austria got nowhere. Two French missions to Prussia in January to secure a Prussian alliance failed. The renegade Bishop of Autun, Prince Charles Maurice de Talleyrand-Périgord, received a friendlier reception in his special missions to London in January and March 1792, but secured no British commitment to neutrality. Though these diplomatic failures briefly slowed France's slide into war, the illusion persisted in Paris that France could fight Austria in single combat, or even gain allies against her. France's career diplomats knew better. While de Lessart did his best to reassure Vienna about France's contacts with Berlin, both Count Ségur at Berlin and the Duc de Noailles at Vienna warned that the Austro-Prussian alliance was too far advanced to be stopped, and pleaded that France avoid war by paying some attention to its problems with the Empire. In the Assembly's debates of 5–25 January, however, the Girondins deliberately swept prudential calculations aside by appeals to revolutionary chauvinism and hatred of the court and the *émigrés*. On 25 January the Assembly passed a decree giving Leopold until 1 March to renounce all acts hostile to France and any intervention in French affairs, on penalty of war.

Though by this time Austria's own stance had hardened, it failed to respond as the war party expected and wanted. Kaunitz's reply of 17 February took an uncompromising, haughty line on the legal issues, but at the same time Austria satisfied the concrete French demands by curbing Trier and the *émigrés*. A chance for conciliation and compromise arose when in early March the moderates succeeded in ousting Narbonne for collaborating with the Girondins against them. But this was immediately followed by a Girondin attack on de Lessart for his alleged conspiracy with the so-called 'Austrian committee' connected with the court. When the Assembly voted a decree of accusation against de Lessart, the ministry resigned.

A Girondin one succeeded it with an ambitious general, Charles François Dumouriez, in charge of the foreign ministry. This added a further set of motives for war. The Girondins wanted war because it would help them overthrow the monarchy by revealing how the court had plotted with foreign powers. The court in desperation had also begun seeing war as its only chance of salvation; the country, faced with defeat and foreign invasion, would turn to its king to save it. Dumouriez had a third rationale for war: to save France and the revolution from their destructive internal conflicts by diverting French energies to foreign conquest. A war declared against the Habsburg monarchy, the foe of France by tradition and of Dumouriez by personal sentiment, and fought to gain territories France had long sought, especially in Belgium, would unite Frenchmen, revitalize the army and the government, promote a more practical constitution, and furnish France with a new hero, Dumouriez himself.

Dumouriez launched his diplomatic career with renewed French demands on Austria, further efforts to keep the Empire neutral, especially Bavaria, more offers of alliance to Prussia, and another attempt through Talleyrand to secure Britain's neutrality by an alliance or a formal *entente* and mutual guarantee. None of this succeeded, but Dumouriez was not deterred. By early and mid-April, France and Austria were both convinced that war was inevitable. Though the French ambassador to Vienna, Noailles, tried to stop the slide by threatening to resign, at Dumouriez's urging the Assembly declared war against the Emperor on 20 April.[57]

During the whole preceding exchange of hostile notes and propaganda, Austria's basic outlook and goals had not really changed. Even those who felt about Jacobin democracy the way conservatives felt about Bolshevism in 1919 were still convinced that the French sickness could be cured only from within, that foreign intervention would merely make it worse, and that left to itself the Revolution was unlikely to infect its neighbors. Kaunitz sharply criticized Edmund Burke's anti-revolutionary propaganda in Britain, and the Austrian government flatly opposed any restoration of the old regime in France, insisting that a constitutional government along British lines would make France inherently less dangerous.[58] Nonetheless, Austria's tone and tactics hardened markedly as the crisis developed. While meeting French grievances in mid-January by forcing the *émigrés* to disperse their forces at

[57] The fullest account, still indispensable, is Sorel (1893-1912: ii. 312-434); but see also Rain (1950: 16-41); Lefebvre (1962-4: i. 179-226); Fugier (1954); Masson (1903: 74-83, 111-81); Blanning (1986: chs. 3-4). For French attitudes toward Prussia, see Kerautret (1991: 279-85). For the war of notes between Austria and France, see Vivenot and Zeissberg (1873-90: i. Nos. 259-60, 287, 293, 295). For examples and analysis of Girondist propaganda and Dumouriez's tactics, see Biro (1957: i. 46-61); Goetz-Bernstein (1912); on the role of the radical Jacobin press in inciting chauvinism, panic, and war, see Michon (1941).

[58] Vivenot and Zeissberg (1873-90: i. Nos. 211-13, 217, 559, 560); Roider (1987: 84-93); E. Herrmann (1867: 128-64).

Trier and in Baden, Austria also proposed that three joint Austro-Prussian armies of observation be drawn up along the German frontier. At the same time, the two allies would propose a European concert to demand that France restore German rights in Alsace or pay compensation for their loss, return Avignon and Venaissin to papal rule, and assure Europe that the monarchy would be preserved and the French royal family kept free and safe. The object of this plan was doubtless peace; the supposition was that France, faced by an armed, united Europe when its own army was in disarray, would allow Louis XVI to save it by mediating with the European powers, with the points in conflict being negotiated at an international congress.[59] The armies of observation were intended not only to intimidate France but also to control the *émigrés* and reassure the nervous small German princes. The proposed European concert was once again a clarion call to inaction—or better, it was supposed to make Spain, Sweden, and Russia, vocal critics of Austria for failing to act, either do something concrete themselves—which Austria knew they would not—or keep quiet. At the same time, the concert was supposed to supply a plausible European menace from which Louis could save France.

Thus the plan, abstractly viewed, made some sense—but not in the practical terms of the prevailing revolutionary mentality in France, which the Austrians, like other European governments, almost totally misunderstood. For example, Vienna considered its demand that France return Avignon and Venaissin to the Pope a minor matter, and included it in the plan to appease the clergy in Belgium and to anticipate Spain's raising it at the proposed congress. In the same way, the demands for assurances about the royal family and a monarchic constitution completely ignored French thinking about popular and national sovereignty.

Thus Austria's proposal waved a red flag before the Gallic bull and, by making war more imminent, also changed the character of the alliance Austria and Prussia were then negotiating and finally concluded on 7 February. Leopold, who had wanted an alliance for management and restraint, obtained one for joint military action instead. Under eighteenth-century rules such an alliance was inconceivable without compensations, which France would have to supply. The provisional scheme called for conquering Alsace, with Austria keeping part of it and giving the rest to the Elector Palatine so that Prussia could acquire Jülich and Berg. This made Austria, the principal in the anticipated war, de-

[59] Vivenot and Zeissberg (1873–90: i. Nos. 231–6).

pendent on Prussia as its auxiliary, and compromised any chances for ending that war quickly, involving Austria in the very scramble for compensations and indemnities which Leopold had wanted to escape. Alsace, Jülich, and Berg were up for grabs now; Belgium, Bavaria, and Poland could not be far behind.[60]

Thus Leopold by early February, mainly by force of circumstances but partly by his own doing, had almost certainly lost the chance to control France and prevent a war in the West, and was rapidly losing control of Prussia and their joint war aims. On another crucial front, Russia and its attitude toward Poland, he never had anything to lose. Catherine simply bided her time, brushed aside Austria's pleas and arguments in favour of supporting the constitution and conservative reforms in Poland, and pushed Austria and Prussia as hard as she could to intervene in France. Her answer to Austria's call for a three-power Eastern alliance to preserve Poland was to propose to the Elector of Mainz that Austria, Prussia, and Russia ally to guarantee the Peace of Teschen and preserve German liberties against France—with the German powers doing the fighting, needless to say.

In early February, Count Goltz, now Prussian minister to Russia, reported to Berlin that Catherine had decided to intervene in Poland but would, if necessary, offer the German powers compensations or a second partition. The report was basically true; Russia had already laid the groundwork for an intervention in discussions with die-hard Polish defenders of the old anarchic constitution. Russia's hint about compensations, as intended, aroused Prussia's greed. Berlin now seized its chance to link spoils in Poland to the coming war in the West. The Russian minister at Berlin, Maksim Alopeus, was informed that Prussia would probably support whatever Russia was planning in Poland, while Bischoffwerder, scheduled to return to Vienna, was instructed to work out more detailed arrangements with Austria for territorial compensations from the war. His instructions mentioned the Alsace–Jülich–Berg scheme for form's sake, but clearly implied Poland. On 28 February, the day Bischoffwerder arrived in Vienna, Catherine gave Goltz and Austria's ambassador, Count Ludwig Cobenzl, a perfunctory notice of Russia's intent to intervene in Poland. Prussia's eagerness to share in the spoils encouraged Catherine to ignore Cobenzl's protests and proceed with the intervention without offering the German powers anything for their consent.[61]

[60] Ibid. Nos. 243, 250, 251; Bissing (1967: 81–3).
[61] Lord (1915: 228–42, 248–55).

On 1 March, Leopold II died suddenly from an illness, apparently viral pneumonia, which, had he not received medical treatment (mainly bleeding), he might well have survived. Had he done so, could he somehow have prevented war with France? The answer is almost certainly, 'No'.[62] His efforts to avoid war and create an Eastern alliance to save Poland were both essentially wrecked before he died. That does not mean, however, that his death made no difference. Given Leopold's realism and his skill in cutting losses and beating retreats, it is hard to imagine Austria under his rule throwing good money after bad in repeated disastrous wars against France, as happened under his mediocre son and successor Francis II.

Nor, after his policy suffered shipwreck, would he have jumped overboard clinging to the anchor. This is what Francis promptly did, ignoring Kaunitz's advice and listening to Spielmann and Philipp Cobenzl. When Prussia rejected Austria's proposal that the two powers and Saxony jointly protest against the Russian intervention in Poland (another defeat for Leopold's policy of mutual restraint), Spielmann, encouraged by hints of territorial gains from Bischoffwerder and the Russian ambassador to Austria, Count Andrei Razumovski, decided that now was the time for a large-scale territorial transaction to solve Austria's security problem and seal its alliance with Prussia. On 21 March he suggested to the Prussian minister at Vienna, Jacobi, that the question of compensations might best be handled if Austria acquired hers through the exchange of Belgium for Bavaria while Prussia gained hers in Poland. This was egregious folly. It first of all undercut Kaunitz's efforts to dissuade Catherine from intervening in Poland and to persuade Elector Frederick August to take the Polish throne, and helped wreck his last hopes of avoiding or delaying the war against France which Frederick William was eager to start. Still worse, it linked the war in the West to the further subjugation of Poland, and helped ensure that the war would aggrandize Austria's main rivals there, at the expense of an intermediary state which Austria needed. Thus Spielmann's move virtually guaranteed, before war even started, that Russia would win the first French Revolutionary war without fighting it, and that Poland would be its chief victim.[63]

Britain played no role in this. The government declined to be goaded into action by the increasing violence of the Revolution in

[62] See e.g. Aretin (1967: i. 260–1).
[63] Lord (1915: 255–61, 263–6); Vivenot and Zeissberg (1873–90: i. Nos. 262, 264, 265, 279).

France and the mounting public indignation over it, or lured by Talleyrand's offers of a 'natural alliance' with France. They were pleased to be well out of the affair. Now that the German powers were at war, France posed no danger, and though the British understood fairly well what was happening in Eastern Europe, this situation did not concern them. Auckland, perhaps the ablest of British diplomats, advised his brother, Morton Eden, sent to Berlin as British minister, to stay on good terms with the Prussians but commit himself to nothing. Closer British relations with Russia might be helpful, Auckland remarked to Grenville, but not with the Prussian government in its present state. Britain currently had no allies 'and, perhaps, *so much the better*'.[64] Thus the two flank powers could observe the outbreak of war in Western Europe with a certain satisfaction: Russia very much involved, but seeing everything going its way, Britain uninvolved and convinced that nothing that could happen would affect it.

[64] On British policy generally, see Ehrman (1983: 196–9); on Talleyrand's mission, see Sorel (1893–1912: ii. 387–93); Lacour-Gayet (1928–30: i. 147–53); documentation in Talleyrand (1891). Auckland's advice to Morton Eden is in Auckland (1861: ii. 392–4); the quotation is in Grenville (1892–1927: ii. 261–2).

3
The First Coalition, 1792–1797

ONE might expect that the outbreak of war would at least restore France's importance in international politics.[1] Ultimately this happened with a vengeance, but not for a while; both France and the war against France continued for some time to be international sideshows. One reason for this, as will be seen, was that at first, despite the radical Revolution, France's foreign policy continued along traditional lines. A more important reason was that none of the members of the first coalition fought mainly to overthrow the Revolution, and some were loath to fight at all. Their main reaction to the discovery that it would be more difficult than expected to defeat France and restore order was not to fight harder, but to attempt to end the war, coexist with Revolutionary France, and pursue other goals—which some found possible, others not. The problem is not to explain how the War of the First Coalition started, which is fairly easy, but why it persisted and proved difficult or impossible to end. The basic answer is that the same kind of traditional politics that got both sides into war also kept them from ending it.

I. THE DEFEAT OF THE AUSTRO-PRUSSIAN COALITION, 1792

It may seem odd to characterize the war begun in April 1792 as a minor affair undertaken without serious thought. Goethe, seeing the French win the Battle of Valmy on 20 September, predicted that it would change the course of history, and he was proved right. The struggle between France and Europe begun in 1792 and continuing almost unbroken for twenty-three years would ultimately become the third largest conflict ever in European history, and by far the greatest to that time. Yet neither side was prepared for war at the outset or took it seriously.

One can hardly talk of France's policy at all. Much of what passed for it was the product of confused struggles within the

---

[1] For the collapse of French influence in the Near East (at the Porte and on the Turkish peace treaties with Austria and Russia at Sistova and Iaşi) at the same time as it was reduced to nullity in Europe, see Lebel (1955: 58–60).

The Low Countries, 1790

Assembly, the Paris Commune, and the sections, clubs, and streets of Paris. The definable war programs (those of the Girondins, the court, and Dumouriez) all clashed with each other, and none correlated means with ends. For reasons of internal mobilization and propaganda, the government early on proclaimed the war to be revolutionary ('war against kings, peace to the nations'). Yet it actually intended to wage an ordinary limited war against the hereditary enemy, Austria, in the traditional theater, Belgium, while expecting other states (Prussia, Bavaria, Sardinia, Turkey) to remain neutral or come in as French allies or satellites. France, moreover, was in no way prepared to fight even this traditional kind of war. The royal army was near dissolution from revolutionary indiscipline, the resignation or flight of noble officers, and general neglect. The initial French invasion of Belgium failed completely, despite the use of revolutionary propaganda, support from Belgian and Liégois *émigrés* in France, and some sympathy among the Belgian people.[2] The French army would at first offer almost no resistance to the allied forces when they in turn invaded France. Financially the government was equally unprepared; the war turned the fall in value of the revolutionary currency, the *assignat*, into a runaway inflation.

Just as striking was the lack of political and diplomatic preparation for war. Besides clinging to the delusion that Prussia would not honour its unnatural alliance with Austria, the regime tried sending a special mission to Constantinople to lure Turkey into alliance and war against Russia, and called on Britain to help break up the Austro-Prussian alliance. These actions were only futile; others, like trying to undermine the coalition through propaganda and subversion, urging Belgians to rise and desert the Austrian army, supporting committees of Belgian and Dutch 'patriots' at Paris and encouraging their revolutionary aims, and proclaiming the principles of revolutionary liberty and popular sovereignty, were dangerous as well, undermining France's attempts to reassure small neighbouring governments. By June, Dumouriez's failure was obvious even to him; he declared the fatherland in danger and laid down the foreign ministry for the command of the Army of the North. While French radicals were losing touch with reality, the moderate royalists, though more sensible, were no more successful in trying to set up a mediation between Louis and the invading powers.

Fortunately for France, its enemies gave it time to reorganize its army, radicalize the government, and inspire a national revolutionary resistance. After an attempt to overawe the Assembly and the King failed on 20 June, radicals seized power in Paris on 10 August, overthrowing the monarchy and proclaiming a republic. Massacres of alleged counter-revolutionaries followed in early

September, ushering in a period of terror and revolutionary dictatorship by committee. This helped to galvanize the war effort and save France, at the cost of raising the ideological stakes of the struggle and making it more difficult for France to end the conflict and easier and more tempting to expand it.[3]

Austria and Prussia, not handicapped by revolutionary passions and confusion, did no better than France; they merely lost control of the war in a more complicated way. While they had to respond to the French declaration of war, both powers gravely underestimated the difficulties of invading France, overthrowing the Revolution, restoring Louis, and collecting compensations, and made their task worse by blunders like publishing the Brunswick Manifesto (of which more later) and allowing the *émigrés* to accompany the allied army into France.[4] Warnings from Kaunitz and others about the dangers and counter-productive effects of intervention went unheeded.

Greed for conquests lay behind this allied recklessness, as is well known,[5] but it was greed of a complicated sort. All Prussia's leaders were determined not to pass up this opportunity for territorial gains as they had others in recent years, but they diverged on the means to be used and on their overall priorities. The King's closest adviser at the time, Cabinet Minister Count Gebhard von der Schulenburg, believed that an Austrian alliance was the best means to meet Prussia's security problems and territorial ambitions. Prussia's main goal, therefore, should be to secure this alliance, and a joint war fought with Austria would help cement it. The King and some other leaders considered territorial gains, especially in Poland, their most important goal, but accepted an alliance with Austria and a joint war with equal compensations as the necessary price to pay. There were others, however, who considered Austria Prussia's real enemy. They included the new envoy to Austria, Count Christian Haugwitz, Marquis Lucchesini, Prince Henry, and General Wichard Möllendorff, in charge of Prussia's contingent in the allied army commanded by Karl Wilhelm Ferdinand, Duke of Brunswick. For them, Prussia's main goal should be acquiring territories and allies, including France, strengthening it against Austria. Each of these views would dominate Prussian

[3] Sorel (1893–1912: ii. 435–515; iii. 1–20); Lefebvre (1962–4: i. 228–47); Talleyrand (1891a: Nos. 99 and 104). On the French army, see Scott (1973); Bertaud (1988); Lynn (1984).

[4] On the inglorious fate of the *émigré* forces during the allied advance and after, see Godechot (1971: 162–72); Vidalenc (1963: 129–62).

[5] e.g. Aretin (1967: i. 262–5).

policy at different times: Schulenburg's when the alliance was concluded, the King's when the war was being prepared, and Haugwitz's and Möllendorff's when it was actually fought.

Austrian leaders were agreed on Austria's main goal, to solve its security dilemma, but not on the means. After Leopold's death, Kaunitz resigned himself to fighting France, but grimly predicted that the French would rally and fight desperately behind democratic slogans, overthrow the monarchy for a republic, and destroy the aristocracy in a wave of terror; and worse still, that Catherine would use the invasion of France to destroy Poland's independence, thus further menacing Austria where it was most vulnerable. His advice in regard to the war was to expand the anti-French concert as much as possible, bringing in Russia, Britain, and Holland, so as to end the intervention quickly with as much equality of sacrifice as possible and as few allied demands on France as necessary. Meanwhile he clung to Leopold's programme on Poland: an independent neutralized state with an army of 50,000 men under Saxon rule, with Austria, Prussia, and Saxony first guaranteeing its constitution and then persuading Russia to accept it also. Such a Poland would be 'a secure, peaceful *Puissance intermédiaire et de convenance* under all its immediate neighbours'.[6]

Kaunitz's forecast of imminent disaster unless everyone, including Austria, exercised restraint, made sacrifices, and gave up the idea of concrete gains went unheeded. Francis's new advisers, Baron Spielmann and Philipp Cobenzl, were sure Austria could do better than that. Specifically, it could use the Prussian alliance and the war to forge a permanent Austro-Prussian partnership, ending Austria's vulnerability *vis-à-vis* Russia and France, above all by reviving and carrying through the Belgian–Bavarian exchange project. Other Austrians joined Kaunitz in opposing this scheme, for different reasons—doubts as to the value of the exchange, suspicions of Prussia as an ally, and in some cases a belief that the most important threat was the French Revolution itself.

By mid-1792 Kaunitz's policy had obviously failed, winning no support on Poland either from Prussia or from the Elector of Saxony. In May Catherine launched the intervention announced in late February. After a group of Polish reactionaries had worked out plans with Russia at St Petersburg, they convoked a Confederation at the eastern Polish town of Targowica and appealed

---

[6] For documents illustrating Kaunitz's views on France, see Vivenot (1873–90: i. Nos. 276, 301, 311, 404–5); on Poland, ibid. Nos. 289, 290, 293 (the passage quoted is from No. 290); on Russia, ibid. Nos. 312–13; cf. also Kaunitz (1899: pp. xxxviii–xxxix, 58–9, 62–3).

to the Empress to restore Poland's liberties. She responded by sending in 90–100,000 men. The Polish army resisted and even won an initial success, but the final outcome was never in doubt. Russia had a threefold military superiority, Prussia refused to honour its alliance commitments, some Poles and Lithuanians rallied to the Targowicans, and King Stanislas defected to Russia's side. By the end of July official Polish resistance was abandoned.

Russia's take-over ended any hope of reform in Poland, but not quite all hope of preserving an unreformed Poland as an intermediary state. Toward the end of the brief civil war, Stanislas and others tried to negotiate with Catherine for an autonomous Poland whose territorial integrity would be guaranteed by Russia (always the King's goal). Though Catherine demanded total submission, such a plan was in line with her announced policy; Kaunitz immediately supported the idea. But Austria's failure to stop the Russian intervention had proved that it could be ignored. At the same time the intervention had enflamed hatred within Poland for Russia and its Polish allies, promoting Polish radicalism and leading to a breakdown of order. This gave Russia a plausible justification not only for its intervention, but also for expanding its control and possibly for a new partition.[7]

Kaunitz's efforts to widen the coalition against France proved equally fruitless. Britain, which had never urged a European intervention, declined to join one now; but neither would any of the states which had loudly called for it (Russia, Sweden, Spain, Sardinia). The Reich and the German princes, whose quarrels with France had contributed heavily to the war, also responded with apathy, for understandable reasons. For one thing, the Austro-Prussian alliance posed almost as great a threat to their independence as the French Revolution, especially since Austria and Prussia made it clear that they expected the Reich to supply men and money but to have no voice in running the war. For another, the best way for a German prince to promote revolution at home was to impose war taxes and conscription on his subjects. Germany's apathy, in any case, made Austria more dependent on Prussia, more reliant on indemnities and compensations to support its own exertions, and less able to resist Prussian pressure for a deal to cover the costs of war.

Not outsiders but other Austrians, however, finally killed off Leopold's and Kaunitz's policy. Kaunitz had been trying to hold

[7] Lojek (1970: 582–93); Lukowski (1990: 252–5); Madariaga (1981: 429–33); Davies (1982: i. 535–6).

off the nervous and greedy Prussians on the question of indemnities by offering them various choices (including the unheard-of suggestion that the allies assume the costs of war themselves and not try to collect them from France), while carefully omitting Poland from the list. Schulenburg, negotiating with Spielmann behind Kaunitz's back, suggested that the allies establish a joint observation corps on the Polish frontier, set to enter Poland as soon as the Russians did to guarantee the German powers' interests. Then if Russia proposed to annex the Polish Ukraine, Prussia could seize its indemnities in western Poland while Austria took its from France along the Rhine. Spielmann, with Philipp Cobenzl's backing and Francis's approval, did worse than step into this obvious trap; he helped Prussia to lay it, and dug it deeper. He rejected the idea of a joint observation army on the Polish frontier (which might have given Austria some control over developments) on the ground that it would arouse Russian and British suspicions, but accepted what was most dangerous in the Prussian proposal, that the Ukraine and western Poland serve as areas for Russia's and Prussia's acquisitions. Even this was not all. Asking, 'What good is expansion without *arrondissement?*', he rejected Alsace as Austria's compensation and proposed the Belgian–Bavarian exchange instead. An unofficial agreement was reached on this basis—Austrian consent to Prussian gains in Poland for Prussian consent to the exchange.

The deal, supposed to provide equal compensations and sacrifices for both partners, did nothing of the sort. Even had it promised the two sides equivalent gains according to the normal eighteenth-century criteria of territory, population, and revenues (and it did not—Prussia would gain new acquisitions, Austria would exchange wealthier old lands for poorer new ones), it offered the two parties wholly unequal prospects and guarantees of actually acquiring their respective compensations. Given Russia's previous hints on the subject, all Prussia still needed to assure its territorial gains in Poland was Austria's consent, which here it got. But for Austria to collect its part of the bargain, Prussia would have to support the exchange actively in the Reich and exert pressure on the Elector of Bavaria and his successors to accept it, which Prussia did not commit itself to do. In other words, Austria gave hard cash to a notorious swindler in exchange for his conditional promissory note. The side-effects of the deal were potentially just as bad. By compelling Prussia to collaborate with Russia in order to collect its gains in Poland, the agreement delivered Prussia into Russia's hands and ended any Austrian hope of restraining Russia. It also made the war against France even more difficult to control or change into a joint Concert enterprise; it gave Prussia a further incentive to desert the war; and it directly encouraged a new partition of Poland.

It is hard to imagine a worse fool's deal; but also hard to see how a different policy by Austria could have done much better. The Leopold–Kaunitz policy of mutual restraint was dead, Poland. helpless, Russia in the saddle, Austria caught in a useless war, and Prussia bent on profiting from it. Spielmann was simply trying to use normal balance-of-power tactics and rules to turn a modest profit for Austria under these circumstances, or avoid a loss.[8]

From June to September the consequences of this bargain worked themselves out. Kaunitz, calling the policy dishonorable and disastrous, offered his resignation, and though at first persuaded by Francis to stay on, quit for good when the Emperor failed to reverse it. This left Austria's foreign policy in charge of Philipp Cobenzl. It quickly became obvious that the agreement reached with Prussia was very shaky, denounced in each camp as too favourable to the other side and dangerous for themselves. Schulenburg and Spielmann, professing their devotion to the alliance, each asked the other to solve its difficulties. Schulenburg, insisting that Frederick William could not possibly put any pressure on the Elector of Bavaria or his successor the Duke of Zweibrücken to agree to the exchange, proposed that Austria make the proposal more attractive by conquering the French province of Hainaut and using it as additional compensation to them for Bavaria. Spielmann replied that Prussia need only point out the obvious advantages of the exchange to get it accepted at Munich, while to ensure the necessary and promised equality of compensations, Prussia must turn the Margravates of Ansbach and Bayreuth, which it had recently occupied, over to Austria. On 17 July an Austrian state conference held at Frankfurt in conjunction with Francis's coronation as German Emperor endorsed the exchange as a goal vital for Austria's security and independence. But to satisfy those who opposed it, the conference, against the advice of Spielmann and Cobenzl, insisted on absolute

[8] For Austrian and Prussian policy in general, see Lord (1915: 300–12); Real (1958: 45–54); for its consequences for the Reich, see Aretin (1967: i. 249–51, 266–8). For Kaunitz's efforts to create a concert, see Vivenot and Zeissberg (1873–90: i. Nos. 317–318, 324–5, 413, 422, 436); for Austria's unpreparedness, ibid. Nos. 410–11; for the critical exchanges with Prussia, ibid. Nos. 419, 443, 451.

equality of compensations, and demanded Ansbach and Bayreuth as a supplement to the exchange.[9]

As ever, Russia used an Austro-Prussian quarrel as its opportunity. By hinting at a separate alliance with Prussia, it frightened Austria in July into renewing the Austro-Russian alliance, including an Austrian guarantee of the old Polish constitution.[10] Then it insisted on being compensated in the Ukraine for any Austrian and Prussian gains in the West. Philipp Cobenzl, though he instructed his cousin Ludwig in St Petersburg to work for Poland's survival, revealed the Austro-Prussian agreement over Poland to the Russian ambassador at Vienna, Count Andrei Razumovski. The Russians, who already knew about the agreement from other sources and had quietly encouraged Prussia's ambitions, protested loudly against it to Austria. Since a Russian veto on Prussia's aims on Poland would jeopardize the Bavarian exchange project, Cobenzl felt impelled to devise another expedient to save it. Austria had long been appealing to Russia to fulfil its clear treaty obligations to Austria by sending troops to help in the fight against France, an appeal which Russia evaded by claiming that it was fighting the Jacobins in Poland. Cobenzl now suggested to Prussia that Russia would consent to Prussia's acquisitions in Poland if both powers agreed to corresponding Russian gains in Poland, and if Austria absolved Russia of its obligation to support the war against France. As payment for Austria's sacrifice in doing this, Cobenzl stipulated, Prussia should add Ansbach and Bayreuth to Austria's compensations. Instead of appeasing the Prussians, this offer made them suspect that Austria was reneging on its original promises about Poland, when Austria was in fact proposing to bribe Russia into consenting to them.

In attempting to clarify its policy, Vienna only made the confusion worse. A state conference on 3 September decided to maintain the exchange project, but to take Galicia in Poland as Austria's supplemental compensation if Prussia would not cede the Margravates. This decision, however, was quickly reversed after strong protests from the opposition. A few days later the Emperor decided to seek the supplement from France in Alsace, to consolidate Austria's supremacy in South Germany.[11] This

[9] Lord (1915: 310–33); Real (1958: 46–8). On the Austro-Prussian exchanges over compensations, see Vivenot and Zeissberg (1873–90: i. Nos. 456, 461, 486); for Kaunitz's initial and final resignations, ibid. Nos. 480–3, 521, 526, 528; for the conference of 17 July, ibid. Nos. 497–501.

[10] Martens (1874–1905: ii. 196–7, 211–12).

[11] Lord (1915: 332–47); Real (1958: 54–7); Vivenot and Zeissberg (1873–90: i. Nos. 514–15, 525, 533–40, 549, 551, 562); Aretin (1967: ii. *Akt* 42).

made Austria's compensations even more dependent on the fortunes of war and the war even more one of conquest, at a time when Philipp Cobenzl and other Austrians were already convinced that even the fall of Paris would not bring military victory over France, and that only a political settlement was possible.[12]

The same kind of confusion and mistrust pervaded the allied preparations for war, which occupied far less attention at the highest levels than disputes over compensations. The Duke of Brunswick and the Austrian commander Prince Hohenlohe agreed on 12 May to raise 100,000 men to march on Paris from three directions. But this bold decision bore no relation to Brunswick's mood or the armies' morale. A meeting between Francis and Frederick William in Frankfurt in July failed to galvanize the military preparations, producing instead another proof of allied confusion and cross-purposes, the notorious Brunswick Manifesto. Published to accompany the allied invasion, it threatened the French people with the destruction of Paris if the royal couple were harmed. Such appeals to peoples over the heads of their governments were normal eighteenth-century practice. Prussia had been ready to use this weapon against Austria in 1790, to the extent of promoting an anti-Habsburg revolution in Hungary,[13] and the French were already using it at this time by summoning the Belgians to rise. Austria's response to French revolutionary propaganda was fairly mild compared to Prussia's. The Brunswick Manifesto, moreover, did not mean that the allies were planning a war of revenge against France. In an Austrian state conference at Frankfurt on 17 July, virtually everyone agreed that the allied armies should enter France as 'tutelary angels', not avenging ones. Louis XVI, Marie Antoinette, and their advisers, Baron Louis-Auguste Breteuil and Count Axel Fersen of Sweden, similarly favoured a moderate proclamation of allied aims. Yet none of this kept a draft drawn up by bloodthirsty émigrés led by the King's brother, the Count of Artois, from being adopted, mainly because the Austrians and Prussians, too distracted to consider it carefully, considered it a compromise containing both stick and carrot for the French people—another sign of their total misunderstanding of the revolutionary spirit in France. In a phrase coined twelve years later, it was worse than a crime; it was a blunder.[14]

All this leaves no doubt that greed, bad faith, and folly reigned among the allies; but it is worth remarking that this was *systemic*,

---

[12] Vivenot and Zeissberg (1873-90: i. Nos. 548, 561).

[13] Andreas (1956); Wangermann (1982).

[14] Bissing (1967: 84-91); Sorel (1893-1912: iii. 43-7); Barton (1967); Vivenot and Zeissberg (1873-90: i. Nos. 447-9, 455, 505).

not individual or accidental, greed, bad faith, and folly. The main goal pursued by both German powers, even Prussia, was security and independence, not territorial expansion *per se*. Both, especially Austria, were not simply trying to grab all they could from their neighbours, but floundering in quicksand and trying to reach solid ground by scrambling on the backs of others even more mired than they. Moreover, at least some of their leaders saw that the way to independence and security was not for each to acquire sufficient power and resources to defy their enemies or dominate Europe, but to form an Austro-Prussian alliance solid enough to prevent the rest of Europe from dominating them. Though operating by the tactics and assumptions of the eighteenth century, they were pursuing the nineteenth- and twentieth-century goal of *Mitteleuropa*, a united Central Europe. The specific gains they sought reflect this aim, or at least were compatible with it. A Belgian–Bavarian exchange would clearly have made Austria more compact and less vulnerable; gaining Danzig and Thorn would have strengthened Prussia *vis-à-vis* Russia. Even their quarrels over respective sacrifices and advantages were derived not simply from greed and pride, but also from the belief that the Austro-Prussian union could only work and endure on a basis of equality.

This does not mean that they had defensible goals but used faulty means and tactics to achieve them; quite the contrary. The concept of *Mitteleuropa*, of achieving German and European security by uniting Germany and putting it in control of all of Central and much of Eastern Europe, was as wrong and dangerous an idea at this time as it would be later. This bad idea was, however, a natural successor of a failed good one. Leopold had sought security through a different kind of politics, promoting a general European solidarity based on the recognition of common dangers and sustained by mutual restraint rather than competitive balance of power. Following Leopold's failure, Schulenburg, Spielmann, Philipp Cobenzl, and Francis tried old means, balance-of-power politics, to achieve something half-new, a permanent Austro-Prussian alliance for mutual security.[15] No one, save perhaps Kaunitz, saw the hopeless contradictions in this quest.[16]

[15] Ibid. ii. Nos. 541, 547.

[16] P. Cobenzl, it is true, dimly recognized that Austria and Europe needed some common ground of solidarity so as to transcend the reigning balance-of-power competition. He argued that the Belgian–Bavarian exchange would provide it by creating a new intermediary body in Belgium which everyone would value and support. To Prince Reuss, 8 Aug. 1792, ibid. 517–18. What Cobenzl advocated

II. THE WAR AND THE COALITION
EXPANDED, 1792–1793

The allied drive into north-eastern France was stopped on 20 September at the Battle of Valmy, which, though mainly an artillery duel, proved that French forces would stand and fight. The French victory led to an almost unopposed French advance which by late 1792 had expelled the allied armies from France. Instead of helping end the war, this served to make it for the first time general and serious.

The explanation of this on the French side is easy: France moved quickly from national defence to revolutionary conquest. Even before Valmy the French had sought separate negotiations with Prussia. After the battle the Duke of Brunswick, never keen to fight, ignored Austrian wishes and began to withdraw his mainly Prussian army under the cover of Franco-Prussian negotiations. Bad weather, disease, and lack of supplies turned the retreat into something like a rout. After French soil was evacuated by 25 October, the French army under General Adam-Philippe Custine proceeded almost automatically to invade the German Rhineland. Speyer, Worms, Mainz, Coblenz, Mannheim, Homburg, and Frankfurt quickly fell; ruling princes fled, French propaganda and revolutionary symbols spread, and a small but noisy group of Germans emerged as partisans of the revolution. Both the French conquest and French revolutionary influence proved superficial. Hessian troops soon retook Coblenz and occupied the fortress of Ehrenbreitstein. The Prussian army stopped its retreat and prepared to return, while French military rule and heavy contributions soon dissipated any initial sympathy for the occupiers. Nevertheless, the conquest had revived old ambitions and created new ones in France.

Other intoxicating conquests came just as easily. Savoy was liberated by General Anne-Pierre Montesquiou-Fézensac in late September. A revolution in October ended the old regime fairly peacefully, leading to Savoy's annexation to France by plebiscite. In contrast, when Nice, also belonging to the House of Savoy, rulers of Sardinia-Piedmont, was conquered by General Anselme, the victory was followed by considerable anarchy and pillage and the installation of a Jacobin regime. Anselme and others urged

would actually come to pass after 1830. He failed to explain, however, why Europe should unite behind a new intermediary body at a time when 3 of its great powers were uniting to destroy an old one, Poland.

the further conquest of northern Italy and Rome to overthrow the main enemies of the revolution, Austria and the Church. Already potent factors old and new were combining to fuel French expansion—revolutionary anticlericalism, traditional anti-Habsburg feelings, military ambition, the need for contributions and desire for loot, and France's tradition of seeking security through satellites.

But the temptations were not yet irresistible. In Switzerland a prudent general, Montesquiou, and a sensible minister to Switzerland, François Barthélemy, kept a dangerous situation under control. The newly elected French National Convention called for war on the canton of Bern if it failed promptly to withdraw its troops from Geneva, a city on the French frontier allied to the Swiss Confederation but not part of it. French and Genevan radicals were eager for war to help revolutionize Geneva and annex it to France. Montesquiou, however, ignoring orders from the Convention's executive council, negotiated a treaty which removed the Bernese troops without violating Genevan independence or overthrowing its aristocratic constitution.[17]

None of these victories had needed serious fighting. In the north, however, Dumouriez invaded Belgium and defeated the Austrians at Jemappes in a hard-fought battle on 6 November. With this battle and Austria's retreat, the old order in Belgium collapsed. The way was open to French control of Belgium either as a sister republic, as Dumouriez and the Girondins who still dominated the executive council and its diplomatic committee preferred, or by annexation, increasingly the preference of their Paris-based Montagnard rivals.

The French advance did not stop with Belgium. Though aware of the importance of Dutch independence to Britain, the Executive Council ordered Dumouriez to pursue the fleeing Austrians onto Dutch soil and liberate Holland, and followed this with a decree opening the Scheldt River to commerce. On 19 November the Convention declared France the protector of liberated peoples everywhere. Even in Belgium, where the army, neglected by Paris, was hard-pressed to feed itself, this declaration rang hollow. None the less, it expressed the Girondin ideal in foreign policy, and could easily serve the more realistic purposes of the Montag-

[17] Sorel (1893–1912: iii. 99–127). On French activities in Italy, see Cleyet-Michaud (1972); on the conquest of Belgium, Verhaegen (1929: i. 90–5); Polasky (1987: 217). On French conquests in the Rhineland, and especially the formation of the Republic of Mainz, see Blanning (1974); Biro (1957: i. 110–44); Dumont (1983).

nards who would soon take control. Even Dumouriez, though increasingly alienated from the government at Paris, wanted to conquer and revolutionize the United Provinces to give France security behind its so-called natural frontiers, enabling it either to defeat Britain with the aid of the Dutch navy or to force Britain to become France's partner in Europe. What most impelled France toward revolutionary expansion, however, was not territorial greed, military strategy, or ideology, but simple economic necessity—the need for conquests to prop up the government and the revolution in France, where inflation and economic distress were feeding a vicious cycle of growing radicalism, counter-revolution, and civil conflict. The ancient principle that war should feed war became official revolutionary policy in a decree of 15 December authorizing the confiscation of the goods of the privileged and the imposition of contributions on conquered territory (meaning especially Belgium).[18]

It was French expansion in the Low Countries which ultimately prompted Britain in February 1793 to break relations with France and declare war. Many other factors played a part, either accelerating the slide into war or slowing it down: the growing violence and factional conflicts of the Revolution, culminating in the trial of Louis XVI for treason and his execution on 21 January; the proclamation of France's war aim of the 'natural frontiers' (the Rhine, the Alps, and the Pyrenees) by the revolutionary tribune Jacques Danton; Danton's secret efforts at the same time to save Louis XVI's life and avoid war with Britain; an Anglo-French war of diplomatic notes waged on the surface and a web of secret contacts woven beneath it; a propaganda war fought before the public, highlighted by the anti-revolutionary crusade of Edmund Burke and other conservatives in Britain. But the crucial factor was France's expansion in the Low Countries, and this was driven by the internal struggles of the revolution, traditional Anglo-French rivalry, military momentum, and the army's and regime's need for spoils and contributions.[19]

Britain's official policy toward France remained essentially defensive almost to the end. From April to August 1792 it had watched the war passively, expecting the allies to win easily and worried only that Holland might be dragged into the war. Some

[18] Sorel (1893–1912: iii. 159–75, 197–209, 233–7); Reinhard (1950–2: ii. 28–36); Verhaegen (1929: i. 96–9).

[19] The best account for France remains Sorel (1893–1912: iii. 144–297), and for Britain Ehrman (1983: 206–63); there are important arguments and material also in Lefebvre (1962–4: i. 265–84); Blanning (1986: 131–72); Masson (1903: 237–84).

British secret-service activity was carried on in France, but of a sporadic and unimportant kind. The French representatives in Britain, Talleyrand acting unofficially and Chauvelin as France's official envoy, obtained informal British assurances of its neutrality, though Grenville refused French requests for a formal assurance or an alliance.[20] The French advance into Germany created little anxiety in London, much less than the overthrow of the French monarchy and the mounting threat to the royal family. George Canning, Pitt's disciple and under-secretary at the foreign office, was glad to see the Prussians beaten, though he allowed that France's immorality made it unfit for liberty. Pitt's government on the whole considered the radical trend in France useful for Britain, weakening France and dividing and discrediting the opposition Whigs, one wing of which sympathized with the Revolution. The ministry refused to intervene in French politics, even to help save the King's life.[21]

All this changed with the invasion of Belgium and the November decrees. Britain began warning France to stop while urging the Dutch, fearful, divided, and eager for neutrality, to prepare to defend themselves. British measures to bolster their own defenses and guard against subversion, the Militia Bill of 19 December and the Alien Bill of 8 January, were, like earlier acts in May, designed mainly to deal with internal concerns, especially food shortages and the danger of riots. None the less, by rallying the public against the traditional enemy, France, and linking native reformers and radicals to the foreign threat, they increased the danger of war and the public readiness for it. Yet the government in December and January neither pushed for war nor tried strenuously to avoid it. It treated the unofficial French peace feelers with a certain diffidence, and made tepid proposals of its own to mediate peace on the Continent. Grenville, who generally took a harder line than Pitt, became convinced by early January that war was inevitable; yet he was still willing to recognize a republican regime in France if a stable one emerged. The French threat to Holland was decisive in prompting the British to expel Chauvelin; this led to a French declaration of war on Britain on 1 February and the invasion of Holland two weeks later. With

[20] Auckland (1861: ii. 419, 422–32); Grenville (1892–1927: ii. 281); Cobban (1968: 192–227). On the Talleyrand and Chauvelin missions, see Talleyrand (1891c).

[21] Auckland (1861: ii. 464–70); Grenville (1892–1927: ii. 342–43; iii. 458–61); Canning to Granville Leveson-Gower, 13 Dec. 1792, PRO 30/29/8/1, fos. 14–16. For a convincing argument that the French Revolution discredited the Enlightenment in Britain and thus played into the hands of British conservatives, see Deane (1988: esp. 1–3, 158, 169–70).

such *légèreté* began this last and greatest chapter of the secular Anglo-French struggle.[22]

Recounting how the war started, however, is less important than seeing what lay behind the French challenge and the British response. Albert Sorel's answer to this question in his classic and still indispensable nineteenth-century study of the French Revolution and Europe was that the decisive factors were revolutionary France's determination to follow Louis XIV and Henry IV in seeking France's natural frontiers, and Britain's and Europe's refusal to let France have them.[23] There is something to Sorel's argument, though it cannot be sustained in its original form. The idea of the 'natural frontiers', though not new, was a revolutionary development more than France's traditional policy. Moreover, it functioned, not as a clear goal to unite Frenchmen, but as an ambiguous slogan to help conceal how divergent their aims were. From the beginning it was unclear both what France's 'natural frontiers' exactly were, and whether they were to be gained and held through annexations or satellite republics or in some other way. This confusion and disagreement would persist even after the natural frontiers had been annexed. Moreover, as will be seen later, Britain and Europe did not consistently try to deny France the natural frontiers, but sometimes conceded them. Yet if Sorel's thesis as stated was wrong, his instincts, master historian that he was, were right. The root cause of Anglo-French conflict lay in something France sought, symbolized by the slogan of the natural frontiers, which Britain resisted at this time and most others: not the natural frontiers *per se*, but security through hegemony in Western Europe, acquired by French influence and control over the smaller states surrounding it from the Low Countries through western Germany, Switzerland, and northern Italy to Spain. This goal was common to many divergent French war aims and programs, whose differences were often concealed or blurred by the slogan 'natural frontiers': to create for France a protective glacis out of its neighbours and compel its enemies to recognize its due status in European affairs. This would make the revolution as well as the state secure—not a revolutionary but a normal goal.

---

[22] Ehrman (1983: 91–3, 157–8, 206–24, 238–48). On the last-minute efforts to avoid war, see Grenville (1892–1927: vol. iii, pp. xviii–xix; ii. 356–7, 372–9); useful materials also in PRO 30/8/333 (Pitt Papers) and BL Add. MS 34446 (Auckland Papers).

[23] Sorel (1893–1912: iii. 144–53, 278–9). It is important to note that Sorel was not an apologist for France here; he considered the quest for the natural frontiers foolish and dangerous.

Security always means more than safety against military threats, and includes protection for a state's and people's values, status, and way of life.

Naturally, almost automatically, the British with their concept of the balance of power saw this French goal as aggressive and dangerous, and portrayed Britain's resistance to it as self-defence, essential for preserving British and European independence and peace. Precisely because the British would naturally think this way, scholars must not, but turn a critical eye on the British balance-of-power view of European politics, still the dominant one. France's so-called 'natural frontiers' were not natural. In some places, the mouth of the Rhine or some portions of the Alps and Pyrenees, there was no natural geographical frontier; in other places, along most of the Rhine, the 'natural' frontier defied economic, military, and ethnic realities. (Sorel, incidentally, recognized all this clearly.) The French aspiration to hegemony in Western Europe, on the other hand, was entirely natural. France was by far the leading state in the area, in terms of military power, wealth, economic development, and cultural influence. The natural, legitimate way for France to seek security, as great powers always do, was through a sphere of influence. What was unnatural and needed to be reversed in the current situation was France's steep decline in influence in the last half of the eighteenth century, culminating in its humiliating impotence in 1787–91.

Thus, while France clearly provoked war with Britain just as it had with Austria, both powers' fundamental drives were equally natural, neither inherently aggressive and imperialist nor inherently defensive and peaceful, though both could become either. One could go further: if anything was 'unnatural', it was Britain's effort most of the time over the next twenty years to keep France weak and insecure, denying it its natural weight in Europe. Both powers' policies reflect a common phenomenon, a security dilemma in which one power's security equals the other's insecurity, or is believed to, and when each sees the only means to obtain security in measures which increase the other's insecurity. In such cases conflict is virtually inevitable unless the two sides can work out a bargain, usually either by one of them tacitly acknowledging the other's superiority and accepting relative insecurity, or by both accepting a mutual relative insecurity and agreeing to divide or share the area in dispute. (The United States and Canada illustrate the former; Austria and Russia in the Balkans from the late 1880s to 1907 the latter.)

These are all truisms, almost clichés. None the less, they say something useful about the character of the Anglo-French war, and why it was so difficult to end. From the outset, it was not just a duel in single combat between these two powers, but a struggle over who would control Europe, especially Western Europe. France would always necessarily try to organize Europe so that it could be secure and have its hands free against Britain; Britain would always necessarily try to organize Europe to achieve the opposite end. The struggle was intractable not merely because of geography, the stand-off between land and sea power, tiger and shark, but also the fact that both powers entered the war without a concept of peace—an idea of a Europe in which their opposed security drives might both be realized. Both proposed to use Europe for their individual ends; neither gave serious consideration to what kind of Europe it wanted, or what kind would work, or what kind of settlement other European states, including its rival, could be brought to accept and live with. Thus they fought over Europe and, to a considerable extent, at the expense of Europe without really thinking about Europe. They would over the next two decades often consider making peace between themselves, sometimes try seriously to achieve it, and once temporarily succeed, but never come even close to creating European peace.

The expansionist dynamics which drove France into war with Britain also kept it from exploiting potential openings for peace on the Continent. The National Convention's executive council was aware that many in Prussia opposed the war and that the allies were at odds over compensations, war aims, and strategy, and had hints from Tuscany that Austria wanted peace. But it wanted peace and alliance with Prussia only in order to fight Austria more effectively, creating a French-led coalition to fight for goals of conquering Belgium, restoring Poland, breaking up the Habsburg monarchy into three separate kingdoms, reviving the Ottoman Empire, and pushing back Russia. Here too revolutionary France, knowingly or not, followed traditional aims and methods; the partition scheme for Austria resembled the Franco-Prussian–Bavarian one of 1740–41. (Dumouriez also had a partition scheme for the Spanish Empire, and considered offering Britain a partnership in it.)[24]

Britain would of course have rejected any such French pro-

---

[24] Ibid. 21–5, 52–4, 77–96, 128–31, 175–82, 301–6. There were exceptions to the rule; Barthélemy in Switzerland showed a concern and facility for making French hegemony tolerable, and Talleyrand, escaping from the early Terror by another mission to London, developed his ideas for a French policy of liberation but not aggrandizement (see Lacour-Gayet 1928–30: i. 157–66).

posal. It expected to make colonial gains in the West Indies at France's expense, exerting its main military effort there while giving its Dutch allies only naval help and a token land force.[25] Austria also soon discovered that Britain intended not to lighten its military burdens but increase them. Prince Philipp Stadion, Austria's minister at London, had repeatedly sought without success to gain British diplomatic co-operation in 1792 in ending the war or saving Louis XVI. Then, in early December, Grenville suddenly began preaching to Austria the same message Stadion had urged for months, the need for European unity against the French threat. Philipp Cobenzl optimistically detected a possible change in Britain's policy of trying to keep Austria vulnerable and dependent, and suggested that Austria should refuse to reconquer Belgium unless the British consented in advance to the Bavarian exchange. Grenville, however, who, along with other Britons, deeply distrusted Austria, especially on account of Poland, quickly made clear what his concept of 'European unity' meant: that Austria should expand its war effort, working for Europe instead of merely for itself, by defending the Pope, saving Sardinia-Piedmont, supporting Spain, and above all reconquering Belgium.[26]

Vexatious as the British pressure on Austria was, Prussian extortions were much more dangerous. After Valmy, Frederick William demanded a steep price for another campaign: the Reich, England, and Russia must be brought into the war and Prussia must receive its Polish indemnity now. This was not an attempt to get out of the war (at least not yet) but an effort to satisfy the demands of wounded prestige, territorial appetite, and poverty (the war chest Frederick the Great had left behind was already depleted). Spielmann, while angrily rejecting Prussia's claim that it was in the war solely as Austria's auxiliary, accepted these demands on certain conditions: Prussia must guarantee the Belgian–Bavarian exchange, get the Duke of Zweibrücken to consent to it, and agree that Austria could occupy part of Poland as a pledge for the acquisitions promised Austria in Alsace. With Haugwitz at Vienna personally conceding all these points save the last, an agreement seemed possible.

But the King, persuaded by Lucchesini that Austria was respon-

[25] J. Ehrman (1983: ii. 262–3); Auckland (1861: ii. 439–520); M. Duffy (1987: 5–6, 25). For the general reliance on the navy and expectations about sea warfare, see Black and Woodfine (1988: esp. 7).
[26] Vivenot and Zeissberg (1873–90: ii. Nos. 681–4, 692, 696–7, 712–18, 724, 730); BL Add. MS 34446, fos. 457, 525–6.

sible for Prussia's military failure, invited Austrian representatives to his military headquarters at Merle, and presented them with a note flatly repudiating the basis previously accepted for their alliance and joint war, a complete equality in efforts and advantages. Austria was the principal in the war, Prussia only its auxiliary. Prussia would therefore help Austria only as a member of a general European concert (impossible to form) or with the forces it was obliged to provide as an estate of the Reich (absurdly inadequate). Any Prussian effort beyond this would have to be compensated immediately by an Austro-Russian guarantee of territorial gains in Poland, said gains to be occupied by Prussia now regardless of whether Austria ultimately gained anything elsewhere or not.

This was a normal eighteenth-century instance of defection from an alliance, distinguished only by somewhat more hypocrisy and mendacity than usual. Spielmann, shocked but aware that Austria could not sustain the war without Prussian help, again tried to link Prussia's demands to his own on the exchange project. Haugwitz, who was now foreign minister, still seemed willing to guarantee it and to concede an interim Austrian occupation of Poland. More tempting still, the Prussians suggested that Austria might occupy part of Bavaria now, especially the crucial Palatinate, to prevent the Elector from collaborating with France. In exchange Austria must help make Russia consent to Prussia's immediate entry into Poland. Spielmann, still hopeful that the alliance could be restored on its original basis, joined Haugwitz in advocating these propositions at Vienna. On 29-30 November the Austrian State Conference, after deliberation, resolved on two actions: to offer Prussia and Russia the choice either of permitting an interim Austrian occupation of Poland or guaranteeing the Belgian-Bavarian exchange, and also to inform Britain of the exchange project. This became the basis of Austria's reply to Prussia's Merle note.

This was a remarkable decision. Austria, wishing to stop Prussia's defection from the alliance and the war and to gain Russian and British support for Austria in it, decided to achieve these ends by ignoring Prussia's principal demands, pressing its own claims on Prussia and Russia, and informing the British of an exchange project which Britain was known to oppose, while also hinting at Austrian actions in Poland which the British wanted to discourage. If this were not enough, Ludwig Cobenzl was also instructed immediately to seek an anti-Prussian agreement with Russia endorsing an interim Austrian occupation of Polish territory, drastically reducing Prussia's gains in Poland (gains to which Austria had already agreed), and preventing Prussia from receiving even these gains until the Belgian exchange project was carried out. To cap the comedy, Haugwitz left Vienna claiming that Emperor Francis had verbally agreed to let Prussia take immediate possession of its indemnity in Poland, while the government continued to insist that any occupation was contingent on the execution of the exchange project.[27]

These strange manœuvres make Austria seem driven purely by greed for territory; actually it was scrambling to ward off unacceptable losses in security, honour, and status. Unlike its partners, Austria was caught in a real war and faced genuine threats. By the end of 1792 the French had overrun Belgium and the Rhineland, captured Villafranca, Nice, and Savoy, invaded Piedmont, and were threatening Milan and Switzerland, forcing Austria to put its whole army on a war footing. It was bad enough that Austria should have to fight France virtually alone while one ally, Russia, refused to help, another ally, Prussia, threatened to defect, and a new partner, Britain, merely urged Austria to greater exertions. The really intolerable aspect of this was that Russia would grow stronger by abstention and Prussia by defection while Austria exhausted itself. Austria's insistence on equality of compensations and sacrifices and its frantic efforts to enforce it, impractical though they were, were intended to prevent this; so were its arguments to justify its territorial demands on European grounds—for example, the claim that the Belgian exchange and Austria's acquisition of Alsace-Lorraine would benefit Europe more than Austria.[28] Nothing helped; like Brer Rabbit fighting the Tar Baby, the more Austria struggled, the more it ensnared itself.

An alternative policy would have required either great boldness or resignation. From his retirement in late 1792 Kaunitz urged the latter. Austria should forget all about compensations and concentrate on getting out of the war as honorably as possible, asking France only to take back the *émigrés* and allow the royal family to escape France in safety. This was too much for Philipp Cobenzl, though he also wanted peace and expected no more success in a second campaign than in the first. He insisted on peace conditions which only a military victory could secure, and the Emperor

[27] Lord (1915: 348–76); Vivenot and Zeissberg (1873–90: ii. Nos. 661–2, 720, 722–3).

[28] Ibid. Nos. 568, 593, 635, 647–60, 674, 677; Thugut (1872: i. No. 3).

backed him up.[29] Theoretically this left a bold alternative: to recognize frankly that, at least so far as Austria's principal war aim, the Bavarian exchange, was concerned, its allies and supposed friends were its real opponents. They either opposed it outright (the British, many Prussians, the Duke of Zweibrücken, most Reich estates, and many Bavarians) or would passively consent to it only at the price of active Austrian support for their interests, which were contrary to Austria's (other Prussians, Russia, and the Elector of Bavaria). With such partners, Austria would get no real help in the war, and would either have to pay far more than the exchange was worth, or by refusing to pay would fail to achieve it, or, worst and most likely of all, would end up paying the transaction costs and still not getting the transaction—all entirely in accord with eighteenth-century system rules.

What Austria needed, then, was a partner interested in the exchange for its own sake and ready to help promote it. One other great power in Europe stood to profit from the exchange as much as Austria did, and would repeatedly propose it over the next four years: France. At this very time, in negotiating with Prussia for peace, France made one of its terms the execution of the Belgian–Bavarian exchange, with the Elector of Bavaria becoming Stadholder of Belgium (an old eighteenth-century French idea).[30] A bold Austrian reply to Prussia's extortions, Russia's refusal to fulfil its alliance obligations, and Britain's demands for more Austrian sacrifices would therefore have been simply to defect from the war, either by trying to negotiate peace with France on the basis of the formal exchange or by simply ceding Belgium to France and seizing Austria's compensations in Germany. That too would have been in accord with eighteenth-century rules.

This was not a practical possibility, of course. Austria was politically and psychologically incapable of playing such a game of *à corsaire, corsaire et demi*, especially against its supposed allies. Moreover, the Austro-French struggle had become too bitter by this time, more because of tradition and emotion than genuine interests, to be broken off so quickly. Yet if this counter-factual speculation cannot tell us what else might have happened (it seldom can), it illuminates what did happen. Austria and France both faced similar security dilemmas, insoluble by normal means

---

[29] Vivenot and Zeissberg (1873–90: ii. Nos. 616–17, 629–30, 650).
[30] Bissing (1967: 98–9); Biro (1957: i. 85–6).

because neither could bring its power to bear effectively against its respective main opponent, Russia or Britain, and neither could escape from ancillary security threats on other fronts. Though theoretically this should have brought them into a mutual defensive alliance, this solution had been tried after 1756 and found wanting. They might at least, however, have recognized a mutual interest in limiting their rivalry and avoiding fighting each other for the benefit of their respective foes. Yet this last is precisely what they actually did. Each, moreover, compounded the error by trying to bribe Prussia into co-operation; and each succeeded, in the course of fighting, in making the other a real enemy.

No changed Austrian policy, in any case, could have saved Poland from a second partition. Catherine, though she probably considered one inevitable, did not wish to rush things or, originally, to exclude Austria from it. A further partition at this time did not even necessarily contradict the long-range Russian goal of controlling all of Poland, for in the eighteenth century even partitions were provisional. The Tsarina gave way in mid-December to Prussia's pleas for prompt action out of various concerns—that Prussia would make peace with France, that Russia's occupation of Poland might become untenable because it was so unpopular and her Targowica allies so ineffective, and that Austria might try to compensate itself in Poland for its defeat in the West and the failure of the exchange project. For many leading Russians the goal was a positive one—seizing the Polish Ukraine.

Hence on 16 December Vice-Chancellor Ostermann announced to the Prussian envoy Buchholtz that Russia would permit Prussia to occupy its coveted indemnity in Poland, but only on Russia's terms. These were reflected in the treaty of St Petersburg, signed on 23 January 1793 after Russia had brushed aside a number of Prussian requests. It gave Russia almost the whole eastern half of Poland, while Prussia got only a slice of territory connecting East Prussia with Brandenburg and Silesia, one-quarter Russia's in area and one-third in population. Other provisions made the treaty even more unequal, committing Prussia to continue to fight France while Russia stood by. Yet the treaty was still so valuable for Prussia and disastrous for Austria that Berlin readily closed on Russia's terms. While a pitiful slice of Poland still separated Russia and Prussia, Russia and Austria now had reached Austrian Galicia. This violated all previous Austro-Russian understandings and destroyed Poland's value for Austria as an intermediary state. Adding hypocrisy and insult to injury, Prussia and Russia pledged to help Austria gain compensations for their acquisitions—but only through the exchange project and from France, and by actions within their means.

A week before the treaty was signed, Prussia informed the Polish government that it intended to occupy western Poland to suppress disorder and revolution. On 24 January the Prussian occupation was launched, the Russian one soon followed, and Polish resistance was broken by a combination of force and guile. In July, the Diet confirmed the second partition.

The excuse the two powers gave the world, that they were helping save European civilization from Jacobinism, seems, like so much else in this era, pure hypocrisy. To believe this is to underestimate the need of even the most Machiavellian power-politicians for self-justifying moral and ideological universes, and their capacity to construct and adopt them and believe in them. Few mortals entirely escape this need; in this era Napoleon was the only one to do so. Of course 'Polish Jacobinism' was a pretext, and the whole transaction reeks with hypocrisy, toward Austria and the Confederation of Targowica as much as toward the Poles. (For cynicism, nothing can match Catherine's reply to the protests of her Polish allies at the destruction of their country: Russia had to be compensated for the great sacrifices it had made on their behalf.) But (to repeat a vital point) even such cynical transactions as this one were normal and within the eighteenth-century system's rules, though here, perhaps, reaching its outer limits.

Moreover, this particular claim by Catherine that she was hereby fighting the Jacobins at Warsaw is not really an instance of the patriotism which is the last refuge of a scoundrel. (Her boast to the Russian people that she was gathering in Russian lands is a good example of this.) It represents, rather, the anti-Jacobinism which was in that era (like anti-Communism in much of ours) the first resort of the fanatic. In fact, one is tempted to say that it was the most sincere thing about the whole business. The differences between Polish reformers and French Jacobins had no more importance for Catherine than the distinction between democratic socialists and Bolsheviks has for many twentieth-century conservatives; like them, she was determined to deny any real distinction. Catherine believed profoundly, as other monarchs did, that rebels against authority anywhere threatened all thrones and the whole social order everywhere, and that only armed force and repression could answer the threat.[31] To prove this, she and others

[31] On this point, see Marcum (1974); Madariaga (1981: 441–3). For good expressions of the combined cynicism and anti-revolutionary fervour of Catherine's *realpolitik*, see Vorontsov (1870–95: xx. 23–4, 27–33, 37–40, 56–8).

could point to the progress revolution and terror had made within France, the advances French arms were making in Europe, and the assassination in March 1792 of Gustavus III of Sweden, the would-be organizer and leader of a counter-revolutionary crusade. The grains of truth in this counter-revolutionary doctrine helped make it plausible; actions like the second partition of Poland helped make it a self-fulfilling prophecy. In Poland, as over much of Europe, reformers were being turned into radicals by the actions of counter-revolutionary governments, and into conservatives or reactionaries by the course of the Revolution. The vital centre was being destroyed in domestic politics and ideology, just like the vital intermediary bodies in international politics.[32]

Only Austria could have offered any effective opposition to the second partition of Poland, as Russia and Prussia knew. Though Vienna had indications of what was happening, Ludwig Cobenzl was not told of the Russo-Prussian treaty's existence until 5 March, after it had been ratified. Confronted with a *fait accompli* and paralyzed by differences within the ministry, Austria failed to seize part of Poland or Bavaria as its own *gage matériel*. The revelation of the treaty's terms on 23 March forced Philipp Cobenzl to resign in favour of Baron Johann Thugut. The change gave Austrian foreign policy greater competence and determination, but not necessarily better vision or political realism, and did nothing for Poland. Thugut's memorandum to the Emperor on 4 April recognized the partition as irreversible, only urging that Austria hold out for absolute equality of compensations as the price of accession. He hoped that Britain might support the Polish resistance to the partition and delay its execution, which would give Austria time to win its compensations from France, achieve true equality, and sustain the balance of power. The war with France, once clearly seen by Austria as at best a necessary evil, was now becoming a source of its salvation.[33]

Poles found no comfort in British or French policy either. Britain's protests against the partition were largely pro forma. Its main interest in Poland was trade, while its chief political aims, to keep Prussia in the war against France and to gain Russia as an ally, prompted it to appease the partitioners. France attempted to revive its old pro-Polish policy in late 1792 and early 1793; a leading Polish patriot, Tadeusz Kosciusko, went to France in

[32] Lord (1915: 377–97); Moritz (1968: 28–35); Lukowski (1990: 252–6); Davies (1982: i. 535–8); Madariaga (1981: 434–8). On events in Sweden and its counter-revolutionary crusade, see Barton (1975: 60–154).

[33] Lord (1915: 398–439).

January and February to promote this. But soon French defeats in early 1793 and Danton's 'peace' policy would lead France to approach Prussia for a separate peace.[34]

III. THE WAR IN THE WEST, 1793

France's strategy in 1793 had called for a rapid conquest of Holland, which would confront the British with the amassed financial and naval resources of Belgium, Holland, and France; together with the spectre of revolution at home, this would force Britain to peace. Nothing in France's situation and little in Britain's justified such hopes. The Army of the North, ill-fed and near mutiny, could barely hold onto Belgium, where the populace was in incipient revolt against French rule and its annexations, forced contributions, and anticlericalism. Dumouriez fought bitterly with the government at Paris over its neglect of supplies and interference with his plans and operations. Serious revolts broke out in the Vendée in France in the winter of 1792–3. In the Rhineland Custine had to retreat before the forces of Prussia and the Reich, while a reorganized Austrian army under Prince Coburg prepared to retake the Netherlands. Meanwhile the Convention resolved the growing tension between France and Bourbon Spain over French propaganda and subversion by declaring war on Spain on 7 March.

Disaster seemed ready to overwhelm France after the Austrians defeated Dumouriez at Neerwinden on 18 March. Virtually in revolt against the executive council and its commissioners even before the battle, Dumouriez now concluded two agreements with the Austrian commanders designed to enable him, under cover of a truce, to march his army south and restore order at Paris. Most of his troops and officers refused to follow him, and the Austrian government, under British pressure, repudiated the promises its commanders gave to respect France's territorial integrity, so that Dumouriez's proposed coup ended in failure; only he and a handful of supporters defected to the enemy. None the less, Belgium was lost, the Austrians were welcomed back as liberators, and the road to Paris seemed open.[35]

[34] Ibid. 440–53; Horn (1945: 78–86).
[35] Sorel (1893–1912: iii. 310–14, 338–49, 353–65); Polasky (1987: 260–2). On Naples, see Acton (1956: 245–53); on Spain, Fugier (1954: 72–5), Konetzke (1929: 189–97), Hyslop (1950: 208–11); on the Spanish reaction to the Revolution, Herr (1958: 239–68, 272–86, 297–315); Wohlfeil (1965: 4–7).

Where the French foreign minister, Lebrun, had once dreamed of matching the expanded allied coalition with an even greater one led by France, the allied military threat now promoted French moves that seemed to prepare the way for a negotiated peace. On 13 April the decrees of 19 November and 15 December, calling for the liberation of foreign peoples and the forcible spread of revolution abroad, were virtually revoked. Movements for further annexations, as in Geneva, were discouraged, and compensations suggested for states which had lost by earlier ones (e.g. Sardinia-Piedmont). The foreign ministry in May urged exploiting divergent aims within the coalition, to break it up and induce its members to peace. Other signs of normal diplomacy appeared. The French tried to regain their old alliance with the Ottoman Empire, renewed their ties to Sweden, sent a mission to Tuscany to gain the diplomatic co-operation of Archduke Ferdinand III and his chief minister, Manfredini, continued previous efforts to lure Prussia into peace, and, at least briefly, thought of concluding peace with Austria and England. Even the coup carried out by the armed forces of the radical Paris sections against the Convention on 22 June, leading to the imprisonment and ultimate execution of twenty-two Girondin members including Lebrun, played a part in this. Danton, who organized the coup and temporarily took command of the committee of public safety after it, hoped by crushing the federalist party to repress a latent civil war and organize the nation for an effort at peace.

Things turned out differently. Danton soon gave way to Maximilien Robespierre, and the coup of 22 June only accelerated France's slide into civil war, a more radical Terror, and a more unrestrained war effort.[36] Danton's underground quest for peace is supposed to have failed because it did not fit the dynamics of the revolution and the kind of image and rhetoric a French leader needed to stay in power. This accurately describes its defects in terms of French domestic politics, but not what ruined it as a move for international peace. Rather than being a real try for peace, it was an attempt to avoid defeat by turning from revolutionary to normal international politics and a different kind of war. The offers of peace, alliance, and compensations to Prussia, Piedmont, Tuscany, Switzerland, and other states were made so that France could continue the war against Austria and/or Britain and put together a hegemonic alliance system in Western Europe

---

[36] Sorel (1893–1912: iii. 373–429); Lebel (1955: 66–70); Biro (1957: i. 92, 152–65); Aulard (1902: 54–65, 87–137); Kerautret (1991: 287–92).

with the help of territories wrested from Austria, the ecclesiastical princes of Germany, and the Pope. True, Danton wanted to end the fighting now, Robespierre had opposed war earlier, and both feared the impact of the war on the Revolution. What matters, however, is that even they and others who wanted peace had no concept of peace, neither understood nor accepted its requirements; and they could not have carried out a real peace programme even if they had had one.

Britain was no different. The government, distracted by internal concerns—growing unrest in Ireland, reform agitation in England, fiscal problems, cabinet and parliamentary divisions—sought victories and gains at France's expense to help solve them. Since these appeared easiest in the West Indies, it promptly became the main focus of the British war effort and remained so for years. British leaders did not expect victories there to bring France down, only to help pay for the war and make it popular, and exhaust and demoralize the enemy. But given Britain's small army and its inefficient military administration,[37] the war in the decisive Continental theatre had to be fought and won and the Low Countries defended mainly by Britain's allies, with British aid in the form of naval action, subsidies, and mercenaries. Sardinia-Piedmont was brought in with subsidies for 50,000 men in April; Naples, frightened by a war scare in November and incidents arising over French revolutionary activity since, joined the British camp in June. A convention was signed with Spain, already at war; Britain's ally Portugal closed its ports to France; and during the spring and fall, 17,000 German troops were hired as mercenaries, mainly from Electoral Hesse.[38]

Building and leading an effective coalition in this way, insisting on full military value for every pound, was not easy. Russia asked an impossible price for sending even a token force to the battlefield, and none of the smaller allies were worth much.[39] Fortunately, Austria, France's most powerful enemy by far, was already in the war and so did not require subsidies, only encouragement and prodding. Unfortunately, Austria tended to fight ineffectively and for the wrong cause, the Belgian–Bavarian ex-

[37] On British strategy and military problems, M. Duffy (1987 *passim*; 1983); Watson (1960: 363–71); Ehrman (1983: 477–81); Mackesy (1978). On Britain's internal problems, see Ehrman (1983: 385–440); Emsley (1979: 5–21; 1981).

[38] Sherwig (1969: 17–27); Ehrman (1983: 278–82). For an example of unsuccessful British alliance diplomacy, in this case with Tuscany, see Moloney (1968).

[39] For expressions of British dissatisfaction, see Auckland (1861: iii. 144–6, 149–50, 161–7).

change. Britain therefore centred its political strategy on getting Austria to fight the war properly, which meant several things: more Austrian effort, an Austrian renunciation of the exchange and a commitment to retain and defend Belgium, and an Austrian bribe to the Dutch to fight harder in their own defence by promising to cede them northern Belgium. All this should be gained without British subsidies or other concrete help.

To impress Austria with the efficacy of British leadership of the coalition, the British kept some of their forces in the Low Countries and reinforced them there even after the French had left Belgium, and planned expeditions for themselves and their allies in Flanders, the French Atlantic coast, and the Mediterranean. At an allied war-aims conference at Antwerp on 8–9 April, the British and Dutch pressed Austria into denouncing the commitments the Austrian commander Friedrich Prince of Coburg had given Dumouriez and later published, that the allies would hold French fortresses and territory only as a pledge for the restoration of constitutional monarchy in France. Austria agreed to make conquests in northern France instead, to weaken France and compensate itself for the proposed cession of northern Belgium to the Dutch.[40]

The conference at Antwerp led to a summer campaign in which the allies attempted to capture fortresses in northern France, ultimately without success. This makes it appear that they wasted a golden opportunity while France was weak to drive on to Paris, win a decisive victory, and restore the monarchy—an understandable but misleading impression. No Austrian or Prussian commander seriously considered driving on to Paris, and no British or other allied army could have dreamed of it. The allies had no plans for restoring the Bourbons, Austria opposed the idea, and it is hard to see how a foreign intervention could have done so, or why even the capture of Paris would necessarily have won the war. But besides these factual objections, there is a deeper one: the underlying assumption that military victory and the restoration of order in France were, or should have been, the real aims of the war, as well as the notion that Britain wished to keep these goals uppermost but was repeatedly frustrated by other coalition members seeking particular gains instead, is unsound. Not only does this view ignore certain British aims as self-centred as anyone's,

[40] Ehrman (1983: 264–5, 270–3); Sorel (1893–1912: iii. 366–7); Verhaegen (1929: i. 104–8, 190–5); Vivenot and Zeissberg (1873–90: iii. Nos. 4, 20; Auckland (1861: 4–17, 23–31, 41–6, 62–8); Hüffer and Luckwaldt (1907: pp. xxxiv–v, xliv–v).

but, more importantly, it assumes that the defeat of France should have been the primary goal of the coalition, because all the other allied aims depended on it and could be expected to flow from it—an assumption which turns out on examination to be wrong. By normal eighteenth-century rules, a victorious war waged for this end would have failed fully to satisfy the primary interests of any of the major powers, and would have been useless or actually harmful to some of them. Any state, therefore, which operated on this assumption, making a joint allied victory its main goal and expecting this outcome to satisfy its vital interests, would set itself up for frustration, manipulation, and exploitation by other members of the coalition.

The best proof of this crucial fact is the relationship in the coalition between Britain and Austria. Britain, of course, wanted France defeated and monarchic order restored at Paris, but these results alone would not nearly have satisfied its purposes. France had to be kept permanently in check, which required seizing French territory and fortresses, not solely to weaken France, but even more to strengthen the Low Countries and to force Austria to defend them. A central requirement of the British concept of a stable balance of power, it must be understood, was that one of the German great powers stand guard against France in the Low Countries. Prussia would have done as well as Austria, but the British never could get it to do this and mainly looked to Austria. This did not mean that the British wanted Austria and France constantly to fight, which would disturb commerce and normal relations; it only required a certain natural, salutary tension and conflict of interests between them, which the British, as holders of the balance, expected to use and manage.

Austria's interests and desires were entirely opposed to this. Austria's military leaders feared the French fortress system; most Austrians did not want either to keep Belgium or to acquire the French territory adjacent to it—only at most Alsace, which served no British purpose. It was no secret that even Thugut, very anti-French and pro-war, still hoped some day to exchange Belgium for Bavaria, and considered the competition with Prussia and Russia over Germany and Eastern Europe far more important to Austria than reducing French power. The only way in which defeating France could help Austria, Austrians saw, was if it ended their confrontation once for all. The British knew all this, but never mind: the balance of power required a Continental great power to defend the Low Countries; Prussia would not, and so Austria must. Moreover, since by eighteenth-century rules Austria had a right to expect payment for the exertions the British were demanding that it make against France and the concessions that it give the Dutch, and since Britain and the Dutch had no intention of paying anything themselves, the obvious answer was that Austria should collect its compensations, or Britain's idea of its proper compensations, along the Belgian frontier of France.

In other words, the strategy adopted at Antwerp of conquering fortresses in northern France was not an aberration from sound military strategy resulting from individual territorial greed, but the product of the normal rules of eighteenth-century politics and the traditional British attitudes towards Austria, the Continent in general, and the balance of power. The problem with British policy, especially toward Austria, was not British ignorance, insularity, prejudice, and selfishness; these were all present, but not worse at this time or later than they normally were in the earlier eighteenth century. The problem was that while in earlier wars Britain and Austria had shared at least some common aims and Britain had contributed substantially to Austria's war effort, here Britain depended almost entirely for the success of its war strategy upon a partner to whose fundamental aims and interests it was as hostile as it was to those of their common enemy, France.

The realities of British policy toward Austria were concealed from many contemporaries (and most historians); the confusion pervading Austria's dealings with Britain was obvious. Already at the end of 1792, at the same time as Philipp Cobenzl instructed Count Florimond Mercy d'Argenteau, Austria's ambassador at London, to warn the British that Austria would not reconquer the Netherlands unless Britain agreed in advance to the Belgian–Bavarian exchange, Austrian military leaders were agreeing, in a military council at Frankfurt led by the Duke of Brunswick, to make the reconquest of the Netherlands the chief goal of the next campaign. When, a few days later, the news arrived that Russia had given Prussia permission to move into Poland, Cobenzl wanted Austria quickly to seize Polish territory to protect its interests. Other advisers, however, persuaded Francis that Austria must meet the military and revolutionary threat in the Netherlands instead, and that, in reconquering them, Austria could secure British and Dutch help to carry through the exchange. There was no basis for this hope, or for other Austrian ideas of somehow making the Netherlands useful for Austria or getting Russia and Prussia to fulfil their promises to help effect the exchange. When Britain proposed the Antwerp conference on war aims, an Austrian ministerial conference called to prepare for it split hopelessly over what Austria's priority should be—securing an alliance with Britain, upholding the principle of equal compensations with Prussia, or effecting the exchange—and further disagreed on how to achieve any of these ends. Thugut proposed squaring the circle. Since the exchange for the time being was impractical, Austria should tell Britain that it would take Britain's objections to it into account and would consider compensations from France instead, but that Britain must designate now the compensations it had in mind for Austria, and show how these balanced the sacrifice Austria would make in retaining the Netherlands. The conference decided to outdo Thugut in cleverness. Austria should demand that Britain endorse both the exchange and additional gains for Austria in Alsace; if, as seemed likely, Britain rejected this, Austria could then get London to promise Austria compensations elsewhere fully equal to Prussia's and Russia's in Poland.

The Austrian decision, confused though it was, none the less meant something—a decision to rely on Britain rather than Prussia for Austria's main support in the war, and to make conquests in France, rather than the Belgian–Bavarian exchange, the main goal. This change was reflected in the instructions Thugut drew up and Francis originally approved for Count Mercy. Philipp Cobenzl, fighting to retain his post against Thugut, managed to alter them, ordering Mercy to seek all the British and Dutch help possible for Austria's reconquest of the Netherlands, but at the same time to persuade the British that the exchange, coupled with French losses in Alsace-Lorraine, would serve British interests, by forming the cornerstone of a system of barrier states against France from the North Sea to Switzerland. (Here Cobenzl tied into plans by Thugut for a territorial and political reconstruction of the Reich.)[41]

The Antwerp conference revealed how futile all these notions were. Britain flatly rejected the exchange, the British and the Dutch refused to give Austria any help in recovering the Netherlands, and the prospect of an Anglo-Austrian alliance did less than nothing to make Russia and Prussia respect Austrian interests in Poland.[42] The most unreal idea of all was that Mercy or his partner, Prince Ludwig Starhemberg, could persuade the British that the Belgian–Bavarian exchange would make Austria strong and independent and thus a better ally for Britain. Britain did not

[41] Vivenot and Zeissberg (1873–90: ii. Nos. 730, 733–4, 738, 756, 758–60, 767, 769–74, 776, 781–2, 788, 790); Roider (1987: 103–26); Real (1958: 64–73).
[42] Vivenot and Zeissberg (1873–90: iii. Nos. 2, 6, 7, 9–11, 21, 23); Vivenot (1870: 378–83).

want a strong, independent Austria; only a dependent, threatened one would fight for British interests fundamentally contrary to its own.

It is easy—too easy—to explain Austria's confusion and illusions as the product of the typical Viennese bureaucratic muddle and *Schlamperei*, so well portrayed by the popular Austrian playwright Johann Nestroy. Franz Kafka, however, rather than Nestroy, could best depict Austria's situation. It was less greedy than it was trapped; behind its confused policy lay a tortuous rationale, a Weberian *Zweckvernunft*. It went without saying that it had to make good its defeat and humiliation in the second partition of Poland. Its lost power and security could be restored only by the Belgian–Bavarian exchange; its lost prestige and honour only by enforcing the principle of equal compensations against Prussia and Russia. Since Austria was not strong enough to achieve these aims or end the war with France on tolerable terms alone, it needed help from the British and Dutch. Securing this meant accepting the Anglo-Dutch programme of conquests in northern France; but this programme *per se* would further undermine Austria's security and independence. If, however, Austria expanded the programme to include more gains from France in Alsace, these might be used to reorganize Germany and strengthen Austrian influence there, enabling Austria at some future date to carry out its real aim, the Belgian–Bavarian exchange.

This logic, to be sure, was implied rather than explicitly stated in various Austrian arguments and positions, and is therefore clearer in this exposition than it was in any Austrian's mind. None the less, it represents normal eighteenth-century thinking and action; many states, then and now, follow one failed gamble by an even riskier one at higher stakes. Moreover, it alone explains why Austria would respond to Prussia's defection and Russia's exploitation by seeking an alliance with a power, Britain, which all Austrians considered selfish and unreliable and many considered an enemy; or why Austria, to gain this British alliance, would commit itself to conquering the strongest fortresses in France, not in order to retain and defend the Netherlands, but with an eye to getting rid of them; or why Austria, in return for fighting for British war aims in the Low Countries, would expect the British to endorse Austria's and other German states' aims in Alsace, and expect this to make the Reich estates and Prussia accept an Austrian reorganization of Germany they opposed, so that Austria finally could carry through the exchange Britain opposed. Meanwhile, the practical result of this scheme was to commit

Austria more deeply to all-out war against France, the only other state favouring the Belgian–Bavarian exchange, and thereby to heighten the worst dangers Austria faced, from militant French nationalism, French revolutionary doctrines, and war itself.

Austria's situation was to some degree unique, to be sure, though other smaller states faced problems as bad or worse. Certain aspects of Vienna's decision-making process contributed to its dilemma. Yet Austria's statesmen were not fools, or at least not more so than most. They were among the first to be trapped, as everyone would be sooner or later, in a vicious, self-destructive system.

Prussia and Russia, far from being intimidated by an Austro-British alliance as Vienna hoped, saw that it would help them by dragging Austria deeper into the war, promoting Prussia's claim that it was only Austria's auxiliary and had to be paid to fight, adding Britain's and Holland's open opposition to the exchange to Prussia's secret one, and allowing Russia to pose as Austria's only friend while doing nothing for her in Germany and ignoring her complaints about Poland. If Austria wanted compensations, its friends in St Petersburg urged, it had to be more energetic and ruthless; it should conquer Alsace-Lorraine and exchange it for Bavaria, or simply seize Bavaria.[43]

The Anglo-Austrian negotiations for a formal alliance at London fulfilled Prussia's and Russia's hopes. Grenville, besides insisting as usual that Austria decisively defeat and weaken France, give Belgian territory to the Dutch, and irrevocably renounce the exchange, demanded that Austria patch up relations with Prussia for the sake of what Britons often referred to as the 'good cause' or 'common cause'. He refused to guarantee Austria any particular gains, and answered its worries about Russo-Prussian domination of Poland and south-east Europe with the wonderfully British observation that, since British influence would replace French influence at the Porte, this would ensure a balance of power. British leaders disagreed over their own war aims and priorities, with Grenville stressing the Low Countries, Henry Dundas emphasizing the West Indies and popular support for the war, Auckland underlining the revolutionary danger from France, and Pitt most concerned with financing the war. But a united front toward Austria presented no problem.[44]

[43] On Prussia, see Vivenot and Zeissberg (1873–90: iii. Nos. 32, 50, 73, 82, 205, 212); on Russia, ibid. Nos. 44–6, 62–6, 153, 219.

[44] Ibid. Nos. 26, 34, 58, 77, 89, 91, 140–2; BL Add. MSS 59061, fos. 3–11; 58906, fos. 185–8; PRO 30/8/334, fos. 183–202; Ehrman (1983: 282–6).

Throughout the summer, alliance negotiations went nowhere, while the Austrians besieged fortresses in northern France, capturing Condé and Valenciennes, and the British, over Austria's objections, marched off to besiege Dunkirk to gain a prize of their own to exchange at the peace. The French, given time to reorganize their war effort, first defeated the Duke of York at Dunkirk, forcing Austria to come to the rescue, and then forced Austria back onto the defensive in northern France and Belgium. A half-hearted Austrian offensive into Alsace was also halted and forced into retreat, so that by the fall the allies retained only Condé and Valenciennes. Having failed to exploit the rising in the Vendée in the spring, the British perceived new opportunities rising from the civil war in France in the autumn, but these also ended in failure and mutual recrimination. In Toulon, where royalists temporarily seized control of the city, the British landed Spanish soldiers, organized the city's defences under Admiral Lord Hood, and called on their allies for troops, especially Austria. Austria reluctantly promised help and then failed to send it because the military and political conditions it specified were not met. The French, with a young artillery officer named Napoleon Bonaparte playing an important role, recaptured Toulon. In this same period, an expedition under Lord Moira arrived before Nantes to support the royalists in the Vendée, only to discover that they had already been crushed.

The military set-backs, rather than leading to an attempt at negotiated peace, turned the war more overtly into a counter-revolutionary crusade. Britain formally committed itself during the siege of Toulon to restoring the French monarchy. Austria would not go that far, but became more fearful of Jacobinism, more for the military power it generated than the revolutionary doctrines it spread. Austrians had earlier expected the revolution so to weaken France that it would collapse with a little external pressure; they now feared that unless the revolution was destroyed quickly it would make France invincible.[45]

The defeats also radicalized intra-coalition diplomacy. Britain's answer to the coalition's failure was to lure new partners in with promises of maximum gains at minimal investment, while demanding that Austria devote more resources to the war and carry its main costs. After their defeat at Dunkirk the British held more

[45] Vivenot and Zeissberg (1873–90: iii. Nos. 161, 184, 187, 216, 249–50); Grenville (1892–1927: ii. 428–30, 438–9, 443, 450–1, 464); Auckland (1861: 68, 79–81, 137–43); M. Duffy (1987: 53–4; 1976); Crook (1980); Ehrman (1983: 286–326).

inconclusive talks with Austria on a formal alliance and plans for the next campaigns, while they simultaneously negotiated with Russia and Prussia. To Russia, which had consistently refused to honour its existing alliance commitments to Austria, they offered subsidies and a guarantee of the status quo in Poland, in exchange for some kind of auxiliary land or naval help for Britain. In late September, Prussia announced that it would drop out of the war unless it received payment in full for its services from Austria, the Reich, and Britain, along with a guarantee of its acquisitions in Poland. The British declined to give Prussia the guarantee, but responded to the demand for money by urging Austria to conciliate Prussia, drop the Polish issue, and help raise a subsidy to keep Prussia fighting. In December, Lord Malmesbury was brought out of semi-retirement to go to Berlin to keep Prussia in the war. Meanwhile Grenville devised more tasks for Austria in the common cause. It should help persuade Bavaria to supply troops if Prussia defected, support Sardinia's territorial ambitions in south-eastern France, make its Belgian lands after their reconquest into a transit zone for British goods entering the Continent, and grant Britain the commercial privileges Britain had enjoyed with France under the Eden Treaty of 1786 in any French territories Austria would conquer and retain. Grenville never accompanied these demands with any British concessions or inducements. He ignored or rejected claims and principles advanced by Austria, and routinely expected it to supply the great majority of the forces fighting France without British financial aid.[46]

Thus the picture sometimes drawn of Grenville's trying loyally to pull Britain's fractious allies together in a common cause will not do. Neither will it do, however, to portray Austria as the innocent victim of British exploitation. Though some of its statesmen, particularly Thugut and Mercy, saw Britain's tactics clearly and bitterly resented them, they were too anti-Prussian, anti-revolutionary, and eager for territorial gains themselves to do anything about it. By late 1793 and early 1794 Thugut was talking of pushing the French frontier back to the Somme, or to that of the Peace of the Pyrenees in 1659, contemplated possible Austrian compensations from Venice, and like Britain, only less successfully, was trying to shift the burdens of war on to others, notably the Reich and Sardinia-Piedmont.[47]

This indicates who were the real victims of this ruthlessly

[46] Grenville (1892–1927: ii. 399–400, 408, 434–5, 441–3); Sherwig (1969: 27–32); Vivenot and Zeissberg (1873–90: iii. Nos. 161, 196, 216).
[47] See e.g. ibid. Nos. 249–50; Vivenot (1870: 383–91, 399–403).

competitive system—the small intermediary states. Austria, to be sure, had grounds to complain about its smaller allies. The Imperial Diet's response to Austrian appeals was weak and tardy. It voted to raise an Imperial army in November 1792 only under the impact of French invasion, and when it finally proclaimed a state of war and actually armed in March 1793, this was solely to defend the Empire rather than to support Austria against France. Some important estates, notably Bavaria, remained neutral except for their Reich contributions. Yet the German response was not worthless even in military terms, and the fear of many German estates that Austria and Prussia would use them for their rival purposes was justified. Thugut, for example, had a secret plan for reconstructing the Reich which called for conquering Alsace-Lorraine, transferring the ecclesiastical princes from the Rhineland into the interior of Germany, and making their territories and Alsace into a strong military barrier against France built around expanded Austrian holdings in south-west Germany. Austria never adopted this proposal; Thugut knew that it would cause trouble in the Reich and that Prussia would surely obstruct it. But along with the exchange project and other Austrian ideas, it illustrates why the Reich estates were right to be fearful. No territorial quarrels had yet arisen between Austria and Sardinia-Piedmont, but there was already much rivalry and suspicion, and Thugut made clear that he expected Piedmont and Tuscany to follow the orders of the great powers and pay for any help they received.[48]

IV. FRENCH VICTORIES AND THE THIRD PARTITION OF POLAND

France found its key to salvation and victory in 1793: revolutionary *élan*. Drastic internal measures—a *levée en masse* proclaimed in August, full Terror decreed in September, the constitution suspended in October, campaigns waged against suspects in Paris and the provinces thereafter—coincided with victories won by new revolutionary generals (Jean-Baptiste Jourdan, Louis-Lazare

---

[48] On Reich politics, Aretin (1967: i. 270–86); Real (1958: 48–9); Bitterauf (1905: 18–22). On the basic defects of the Reich's military organization, see Schmidt (1984: 228–9); Neuhaus (1986); Schulze (1987). Numerous documents in Vivenot and Zeissberg (1873–90: iii) and Thugut (1872: i) illustrate the Austro-Prussian struggle over the Reich and its war effort. For typical expressions of Thugut's attitude toward Sardinia and Tuscany, see ibid., Nos. 34, 105, 107.

Hoche, and Jean-Charles Pichegru of the Armies of the North, Mosel, and Rhine respectively) over the British at Dunkirk, the Austrians at Wattignies, and the Prussians and Austrians along the Rhine and in Alsace.

It was not entirely clear, to be sure, how domestic terror and military success were connected. The Revolution by late 1793 had succeeded in defeating its internal foes more decisively than the foreign armies. Jourdan was surprised by his victory over Austria at Wattignies; the Prussians managed to repulse the French with heavy losses at Kaiserslautern. Besides, it was organizers like Lazare Carnot and Jean-Bon St André who did the real work of promoting France's national defence, not leaders of the Terror like Robespierre and Louis-Antoine Saint-Just. Danton had, in fact, continued to work for a negotiated peace with England through much of this period; his rivals in control of the government had apparently known about it and had not tried to stop him.[49]

Yet late 1793 clearly marked a point where France surpassed its rivals in its ability to recruit and train large masses of men and organize its economy for war. Both achievements proved two-edged swords for the Republic in the longer run. The *levée en masse* promoted desertion, resistance, and counter-revolution as well as the national defence; the demands of war worsened France's runaway inflation and its other fiscal and economic problems. But in the short run its measures worked. Even St André's rebuilding of the navy, though it proved abortive, was an impressive effort.

The most important changes came in the French army. The disintegration of the royal army was reversed and old professional soldiers successfully amalgamated with revolutionary recruits in 1792–3. This amalgamation, laying the basis for a rapid expansion in numbers, together with the development of effective small-group ties and of new bases for discipline, *esprit de corps*, and promotion, gave France an army admirably suited for the kind of warfare it needed to wage. It could disorganize the enemy with light troops and rout him with mass attacks; could live off enemy country and make the war nourish the war; could employ large numbers of relatively raw recruits and still survive defeat and heavy losses. Its success, moreover, made some revolutionary ideals (fraternity, nationalism, social equality, careers open to talents, and sacrifice for the general will) take root more deeply

---

[49] Sorel (1893–1912: iii. 507–41); Dupré (1940: 122–5, 130–4); Biro (1957: i. 176–209); M. Reinhard (1953). On the connection between the Terror and the war, see also Fehrenbach (1989).

and durably in the new army than anywhere else in French political and social life.

But while giving the Revolution and French foreign policy a weapon of great power and flexibility, this army also posed threats. It is easy to exaggerate some of the dangers it created— militarism, a national addiction to military glory and foreign conquest, military dictatorship. While the French people grew fond of victories and wanted a glorious peace, they also quickly tired of war like everyone else. The Revolution did eventually lead to military dictatorship, but only after a long decay of civilian rule had created a power vacuum something had to fill. The new army did, however, engender a grave problem directly affecting foreign policy: it promoted a strong vested interest in continued war. Unlike the other new élites created by the Revolution, army officers were bound to fear peace. It would threaten rather than consolidate their careers, the military reforms and gains of the revolution, and their new status in society.

Nor were army officers the only ones to fear peace; so might the government. The new army had been built without a long-term reorganization of the national economy, state finances, and other infrastructure to sustain it. Yet one regime after another relied on it not only for security against foreign and domestic enemies, but even more for the contributions and loot from abroad to sustain it financially at home. Coinciding with the expansion of the army, at once indispensable and unsustainable, was the long-term decline of the navy and the loss of France's overseas trade and imperial position. These further reduced the resources available to support the army, increased its political influence and the government's dependence on it, and made Continental gains even more necessary to compensate for losses overseas.[50] Thus the French victories in Belgium and the Rhineland in 1793–4, while marking the beginning of two decades of French military superiority in Europe, also made the war harder to end, especially for France.

The allied coalition, however, was wrecked more by internal divisions than French victories. Prussia's threat to leave the war had prompted the Malmesbury mission to Berlin in December. For three months Malmesbury tried to arrange a subsidy of £2 million to hire the main Prussian army, with Britain to supply

[50] The basic works on the army are Lynn (1984); S. F. Scott (1973), 117–209; Bertaud (1988: ch. 5); see also Fugier (1954: 82–7); Best (1982: 84–9, 92–8); Bouloiseau (1984: 151–2, 230–1); Gembruch (1968: 10–12); J. Meyer (1980: 150–3, 156–63); McElwee (1975: 18–21); and G. Parker (1988: 151–3).

half and Austria, the Reich, the Dutch, and Prussia itself to contribute the rest (the Prussians would collect their share from France
after victory). The effort broke down mainly because Austria
refused to subsidize Prussia. With the Prussian army actually
under orders to break off and march east, Malmesbury seized the
occasion to get control of at least a major portion of it for Anglo-
Dutch purposes. Two treaties signed on 19 April at The Hague
provided that an army of 62,000 Prussians, under Prussian command but subsidized by the British and the Dutch (the British
actually paying most of the Dutch share as well), would campaign
in the Netherlands, with all conquests to be at British and Dutch
disposal.

The agreement was severely criticized from the outset. Prussian
opponents argued that it made Prussia's soldiers virtual mercenaries and kept Prussia in a useless war far from the important
theater, Poland. British critics said it was too expensive, allowed
Prussia to evade its obligations to Britain and Holland under the
1788 Triple Alliance, and failed to give Britain clear control of the
Prussian forces it was paying for. Austria and other opponents of
Prussia in the Reich unanimously condemned it for rewarding
the Prussians for their previous broken promises, supporting a
Prussian army that would be an enemy within their ranks, and
encouraging Prussia to fight only so long as it profited from the
war. All the criticisms were sound, all the critics' dire predictions
would come true. Yet one still encounters efforts to explain the
treaties as the outcome of well-intentioned British efforts to hold
its quarrelling partners together in the common cause of winning
the war.[51]

This interpretation, for one thing, ignores salient facts. Britain
launched its negotiations with Prussia without even notifying
Austria and while trying its best to make Austria and the Reich,
already bearing the heaviest burdens in the war, pay for Prussia's
army as well as their own. Malmesbury himself provoked the
Prussian military order in March that would have pulled Prussia's
troops out of the western theatre, leaving Austria in an untenable
position. More important, however, is the simple fact that this
agreement put Britain squarely on Prussia's side against Austria

[51] Real (1958: 94–7); Ehrman (1983: 332–7); Sherwig (1969: 33–43); Malmesbury
(1844: iii. 1–91); Auckland (1861: iii. 170–3); Grenville (1892–1927: ii. 494–7);
Vivenot and Zeissberg (1873–90: iv. Nos. 10, 13, 19, 22, 70–5, 77, 80, 88, 91–2,
128–9). For accounts of Grenville's policy as a valiant struggle to keep the coalition
going against incorrigible Austro-Prussian rivalry and selfishness, see Ehrman
(1983: 537–41); Jupp (1985: 152–84).

on the most vital issues dividing them. In agreeing to subsidize a Prussian army to fight for Anglo-Dutch purposes and accepting this as Prussia's main contribution to the war, Britain concretely endorsed Prussia's view of the war, that Austria was the principal and Prussia only an auxiliary: Prussia must be paid for its limited exertions while Austria, fighting for its life, had no right to any compensations save those it could conquer from France. This was a vital issue for Austria, even if British statesmen at that time failed or refused to see it. Still worse, by paying a large Prussian army to remain in the main theatre, operating under its own officers and only nominally under Anglo-Dutch control, Britain handed Prussia the ideal means by which to destroy Austria's position in Germany and promote its own. Austria repeatedly told the British this, warning them that Prussian forces, to be of any use against France, must be under allied command; otherwise the Prussian army would operate more to frustrate Austria and promote Prussian aims in Germany than to defeat France.[52]

The Austrians were proved right. Almost immediately Britain and Prussia began to quarrel over the control and deployment of the army. Though the Prussian commander Möllendorf did not flatly refuse to fight, he urged his king to make peace with France and fought only for Prussia's interests, which, like Haugwitz, Lucchesini, and another rising Prussian statesman from Hanover, Prince Karl August von Hardenberg, he defined mainly in terms of weakening Austria's position in Germany. Hence Möllendorf refused to follow up the Prussian victory at Kaiserslautern or to assist the Austrians, British, and Dutch in their ill-fated offensive in Belgium. While Emperor Francis and Thugut went west to the front to oversee the allied effort against France, Frederick William left for the east to inspect his gains in Poland. A Polish rising under the leadership of Thadeusz Kosciusko gave Möllendorf more excuses for keeping his subsidized forces inactive in the west, while affording Berlin an excuse to order the Prussian auxiliary corps under Austrian command to prepare to break off and march east. The British repeatedly failed in their efforts to gain control of the subsidized army, efforts complicated by delays

---

[52] To reply that the British did not understand this and were concentrating on other goals is true, but misses the point. History is about what really happened, not what actors wanted to happen or perceived as happening. An analogy: American leaders during the Second World War did not think their policies were objectively anti-British. Many British leaders did, some British historians such as Christopher Thorne have pointed it out, and some American historians have changed their verdicts as a result.

in the subsidy payments. After the French defeat of Austria at Fleurus in mid-July 1794, with the Austrian army collapsing and retreating to the Rhine, all hope of making Prussia fight disappeared. Britain suspended its subsidy payments, Prussia responded by denouncing the alliance, and Britain cancelled the subsidy entirely in October. By this time Prussia was wholly preoccupied with Poland and actively negotiating for peace with France.[53]

Britain had assumed throughout in dealing with Prussia that it had to be paid to fight, since it could defect and wanted to do so. A corollary principle was applied to Austria: it should not be paid, because it was fighting for its life and could not defect. For a long time the assumption seemed to work. Austria planned a great offensive for 1794 under new commanders, mobilizing 315,000 men. Of these, 170,000, aided by 40,000 men in British pay, mainly German mercenaries, were to invade France from Belgium, capture the French fortresses, and drive on Paris. Even this Austrian proposal did not entirely satisfy Grenville. Insisting that Austria was not doing its share or appreciating Britain's sacrifices for Austria, and warning that Britain might pull out of the Continent and fight a separate war, Grenville supplemented his usual demands for Austrian concessions to Prussia and the Dutch with new calls for Austrian help to the Italian states and the British in the Mediterranean (where, having taken Corsica, the British navy was supporting Genoa against France). Austria's defeat and collapse in Belgium in May and June confirmed British suspicions about Austrian cowardice and bad faith, without diminishing British demands and expectations. In July Pitt still demanded that Austria revive its war effort in the Low Countries and take on commitments to the Dutch and others, with its only reward the possibility of an alliance with Britain and some undefined financial assistance.[54]

Austria's reverses had a greater effect at home, strengthening the peace party, which included Archduke Carl, the Emperor's brother and Austria's best commander. Thugut, though no Anglophile—he complained bitterly about the sorry British and Dutch military performance (on the latter score the British agreed), and characterized Britain's negotiating procedures as 'revolting'—

[53] Real (1958: 100–7); Bissing (1967: 122–5); Sherwig (1969: 43–53); Grenville (1892–1927: ii. 564–92); Malmesbury (1844: iii. 142–3).
[54] Ehrman (1983: 328–32, 337–40, 344–50); Thugut (1872: i. No. 95; Vivenot and Zeissberg (1873–90: iv. Nos. 25, 43, 56, 69); Grenville (1892–1927: ii. 558–60, 593–4, 612–14, 617–20); BL Add. MS 58907, fos. 46–9.

continued to advocate war for the common cause.[55] Count Mercy, Austria's most distinguished diplomat, sent to London in August to try once more for an alliance, died before achieving anything. A British mission to Vienna in the fall by Grenville's brother Thomas and Lord Spencer also failed, mainly because Grenville and Spencer, insisting that Austria had ample resources and lacked only leadership and will, pressed for an immediate offensive; after Austria's defeats, even Thugut could not commit Austria to this but sought instead a large loan guarantee for the next year. The mission's failure brought Austro-British relations to a new low. Pitt and the secretary for war, William Windham, deliberated whether Britain should not ignore Austria and Prussia and spend £2 million recruiting soldiers elsewhere in Europe. Poland, Pitt reflected, was probably too distant to acquire troops there in time for next year's campaign. He seems to have been unaware that by this time Poland had almost disappeared from the map, and that what was left of it was entirely occupied by Russia and Prussia.[56]

Britain's disappointments with the German powers only encouraged its courtship of Russia. The quest for a commercial treaty had been renewed soon after Ochakov, and once Britain was fighting France it actively sought to engage Russia. The Anglo-Russian treaty of 25 March 1793, binding Britain to prosecute the war to victory while committing Russia only to commercial warfare and limited naval co-operation against France, did little to this end; its main effect was further to free Russia's hands in Poland. Though disappointed, the British continued to woo Russia all through 1794, seeking, besides soldiers and warships, an increase in trade, a mutual guarantee of possessions, Russia's use of its influence with Sweden and Denmark in Britain's favour, and, above all, Russian help in gaining Austria and Prussia as Britain's allies. Catherine answered all British inducements and pleas by insisting that Russia could not act in Western Europe until the Polish question was settled. Accepting this, the British swallowed and even welcomed the final suppression of the Kosciusko revolt and the Austro-Russian agreement in January 1795 for a third

[55] For arguments and evidence that Austria fought hard to defend Belgium and that Thugut genuinely sought an alliance despite his feelings about Britain, see Roider (1987: 140–61); Verhaegen (1929: i. 196–260, 386–9); Real (1958: 107–15); Thugut (1872: Nos. 146–7); Vivenot and Zeissberg (1873–90: vol. iv, pp. v–xiii, Nos. 198–246); for Carl's plea for peace to save the army, see ibid. No. 261; Grenville (1892–1927: iii. 510–20).

[56] Ehrman (1983: 362–7); Grenville (1892–1927: ii. 614–15, 626–8); BL Add. MS 59061, fos. 34–59; Thugut (1872: i. Nos. 162–4, 177, 184); Windham (1913: i. 231–2).

partition of Poland (to be discussed later), because it helped pave the way to an Anglo-Russian alliance on 18 February 1795.[57]

For military purposes this treaty also was little use. It offered Britain only what it least needed, twelve ships of the line and six frigates, in exchange for a British pledge of no separate peace and other commitments. Grenville's hope that it might draw Russia further into war took little account of Catherine's personality and her real feelings about the British. But his further expectation that the alliance would at least compel Austria to do its duty was more realistic, and indicates the real significance of the alliance for Britain and Russia alike. It helped Russia continue to evade its long-standing alliance obligations to Austria, while increasing Russia's invulnerability and Austria's dependence. For Britain it ensured Russia's help in compelling Austria to continue to fight without concrete British aid. Symbolically, it united Russia and Britain in a joint programme, followed, despite their latent differences and rivalry, for most of the next twelve years: to defeat France, overthrow Jacobinism, and establish their versions of a European 'balance of power' not primarily by their own exertions, but by proxy.

While Russia and Britain moved closer toward joint exercise of hegemony in Europe, Austria and Prussia were struggling for control of Germany. In this contest, as critical and bitter as the one over Poland, the Reich constitution and the Reich estates were turned into mere objects and the war against France became a subordinate issue. Prussia's call in October 1793 for the Reich to supply 10 millions of the 22 million taler subsidy it demanded to stay in the war arose partly from real financial distress but mainly from the desire to create a second Reich army, led by itself and independent of Austrian control. The Reich estates, shocked, readily followed Austria in rejecting it. But Thugut met almost as much resistance with his call in January 1794 for a general arming of the German populace and a massive increase in the Reich war effort, which he hoped would let Austria dispense with Prussian troops except for its auxiliary corps and Reich contingent. Neither power succeeded in exploiting the Reich's war potential; instead, the Diet resolved in May to reject general mobilization but authorize subsidies for an extra 20,000 Prussians to be used solely for Reich purposes. To be sure, great-power ambitions were

[57] Ehrman (1983: 274–7); Allardt (1976: 7–11); Martens (1874–1905: x. 360–85); Grenville Papers, BL Add. MSS 59191, fos. 2–4, 22–31, 33–8, 45–52, 58–62; 59192, fos. 1–28, 31–65, 71–3 (dispatches of Grenville in 1791–5 to Sir Charles Whitworth, ambassador to Russia).

matched by small-state indifference and selfishness; great and lesser powers alike coveted ecclesiastical territory. Yet the Reich war effort was not worthless; it reached about three-quarters of its proclaimed goals in men and money, and Reich troops fought decently if unheroically under Austrian command for much of 1794.

By that autumn, however, military failures and Prussia's obvious intent to defect from the war made the pressure for peace within Germany irresistible. Various small and middle-sized estates met at Wilhelmsbad and proposed to revive the League of Princes, establishing an independent League army to fight alongside Austria, but solely for the purpose of a negotiated peace and the defence of the Reich and its estates. On 13 October Germany's most important ecclesiastical prince, the Archbishop Elector of Mainz, Karl von Dalberg, also called for peace. Prussia, still formally Austria's ally in the war with France, now proposed itself as a mediator. The fact that Berlin openly endorsed peace with France, a power Hardenberg described as 'a useful element in the balance for Prussia', and that it supported a League of Princes as a weapon against Austria, gave Prussia advantages more than balancing Austria's traditional leadership in the Reich and Prussia's worse recent record of treachery and greed. None the less, Thugut and his colleague Prince Franz Colloredo-Mansfeld, in charge of Reich affairs for Austria, managed to hold off the peace party both at Vienna and in Germany. The initiatives for a League of Princes and a League army were defeated, though a Reich peace resolution passed in December. The victory, however, cost Austria something. Prussia's reputation was somewhat rehabilitated, it gained the lead in the peace movement, and more estates were induced to abandon Austria in order to escape the war.[58]

Through it all Poland remained the chief subversive factor in the coalition. Valuable as the second partition was for Prussia, the task of occupying and administering its new Polish lands against underground resistance took its toll. The occupation costs, combined with the war and Frederick William's extravagance and inefficiency, compelled Prussia to demand massive subsidies from its allies. Help for Prussia came in the spring of 1794 in two forms: the British subsidy treaty and the outbreak of a revolt in Poland under Kosciusko's leadership, initially directed primarily against Russia in rump Poland. Prussia, with almost half its forces

[58] Real (1958: 89–93); Aretin (1967: i. 286–318; ii. *Akten* 46, 50); Bitterauf (1905: 22–7); Hölzle (1931: 124–9); Dorda (1969).

already in Poland and eastern Prussia, saw a chance for more gains. By suppressing the revolt in rump Poland, it could crush the opposition in its own Polish lands, establish itself as an equal to Russia, and steal another march on Austria. At first things went well. Prussian troops defeated the Polish forces, occupied much of rump Poland, including the key fortress of Cracow on the Vistula, beating the Austrians to it, and even captured Warsaw. But soon the task of suppressing the revolt outgrew Prussia's resources. By September it had to evacuate Warsaw and retreat, calling on Russia for help.[59]

This gave Russia back the upper hand politically, if not yet militarily. Austria had finally agreed in February 1794 to accede to the Russo-Prussian partition of Poland of January 1793. Russia gave nothing in return but a promise to renew the Russo-Austrian alliance of 1781 and extend its *casus foederis* against Prussia, ignoring Austria's other requests—alliance help in the war, a commitment to equality of compensations, a guarantee of Austrian compensations either in France or in Poland, and a promise to sustain Austria's lead over Prussia in Germany. Austria dared not press its demands out of fear that Russia might decide to conquer Turkey and exclude Austria from the spoils. Thugut pleaded with Russia at least to postpone any such projects until Austria was better able to check Prussia and join in the partition of the Ottoman Empire. Privately, Russians expected both German powers to exhaust themselves in fighting France, leaving Russia all-powerful, as Morkov explained to S. Vorontsov in London in phrases that capture both the essence of Russian policy and the real import of balance of power language:

The present war, despite the laxity with which Prussia wages it, continues to exhaust it, and depending on how long it lasts its means will be considerably diminished. You will say that this will be as much the case with Austria, but imagine how we will remain fresh and intact, and how we will set a weight in the balance which will carry everything before it.[60]

Though niggardly with help for Austria, Russia was free with advice. Razumovski and Morkov, more pro-Austrian than most Russians, suggested to Thugut that, if Austria could not obtain its compensations from France, it might take them from the Venetian Republic. Thugut, though preferring to await the outcome of the

[59] Moritz (1968: 36–7, 42–4, 64–7, 85–147); Bissing (1967: 126–7); Madariaga (1981: 444–51); Lukowski (1990: 256–61); Davies (1982: i. 538–41).
[60] Vorontsov (1870–95: xx. 44).

war with France, welcomed the Russian suggestion, but pointed out that if the Republic was to supply all or most of Austria's indemnity, the portion to which Austria had old claims, Istria and Dalmatia, would not be nearly enough.

Having Austria's promised accession to the Second Partition safely in its pocket, Russia used the Kosciusko rising once more to play the German powers off against each other. It allowed Prussian troops to enter Poland to suppress it, but in order to curb Prussia's pretensions (Morkov remarked that his heart bled at the size of Prussia's gains in 1793) it prepared for a final partition, this time with Austria.[61]

Once more Austria, had it been bolder or less paralyzed, might have seen the Kosciusko rising as an opportunity. For various reasons, leaders of the Polish insurrection sought Austria's support, appealing to Vienna's old desire for a Polish *corps intermédiaire* and even offering the Polish throne to an Austrian archduke, preferably Carl. Austria could conceivably have tried to save Poland as a client state, to mediate, to revise the Second Partition, or at least to carry out its own occupation, preventing Prussia from taking anything important to Austria. Russia would have supported this last move, which was actively debated at Vienna. Having steadily insisted that it had no troops available to help Austria fight France, St Petersburg now offered 10,000 men to help Austria protect Galicia and occupy southern Poland. However, Austria remained stuck in half-measures and indecision for various reasons: military weakness, defeats in Belgium, fears for Austria's internal security, especially in Galicia and in Hungary, where a so-called Jacobin conspiracy was being suppressed, and above all fear of losing the Russian alliance to Prussia. It lost a race with Prussia to occupy Cracow, the key to Galicia, managing only to lock the stable door after the horse was stolen by occupying the adjoining Cracow and Sandomir districts. Had it come to blows, Austria could not have fought even the Prussians, much less Russia.

The Kosciusko rising ended Austria's paralysis, but in a wrong direction: it gave Thugut the excuse finally to abandon the long-standing principle of preserving Poland and to agree with Russia on a final partition. This was supposed to do three things for Austria: acquire Russian help in restoring the German balance upset by Prussia's gains; get Austria compensation in Poland for its exertions in the West and for the Second Partition and thus

[61] Vivenot (1870: 378–81, 383–98, 403–5); Vivenot and Zeissberg (1873–90: iv. Nos. 36, 37, 127); HHStA, *Russland II Correspondenz* 217, fos. 1–4.

preserve the general balance of power (which Thugut defined as Russia's and Austria's each being stronger than Prussia by a ratio of three to two); and eliminate rump Poland as Prussia's buffer against Russia, since Austria's was already gone. All three aims exemplified how balance-of-power thinking escalates conflicts, and all made Russia's game easier. Austria's pleas that Russia use its preponderant power against Prussia helped Russia get more concessions from Austria on the proposed lines of partition. While the Russian army was crushing Kosciusko's forces in October and November, Austria continued to lose the war in the West. Meanwhile, Prussia and other states (the Reich, Sardinia, Tuscany, Naples, Holland) were defecting from the war or threatening to, and the Austro-British alliance negotiations were foundering.[62]

The Austro-Russian treaty of 5 January 1795 for the final partition of Poland thus only appeared on the surface an alliance against Prussia, and Austria's revenge for January 1793. In reality it was another defeat and fool's deal for Austria. Russia and Austria did not exclude Prussia from the partition, as Russia and Prussia had done to Austria in 1793. The Prussians had already suggested a final one to Russia in July 1794, though wishing to delay it and carry it through without Austria. Catherine simply brought the idea out into the open in September, forcing Prussia into trilateral negotiations in which the Russians used their whip hand and their partners' rivalry to the disadvantage of both. The Prussian negotiator Tauentzien tried to fight this, attempting to retain the city of Cracow while wresting the palatinates of Cracow and Sandomir from Austria. It was only because, after failing in this, he rashly decided to break off negotiations on the Cracow question that Austria and Russia decided on a separate treaty in January.

In any case, Austria and Prussia were really quarrelling less over who would get Cracow than over who would have Russia as an ally, just as their broader quarrel was not over Poland, but over Germany and the general competition for compensations. Prussia would if necessary have given Cracow to Russia to keep Austria from having it. As for Thugut, the thought that Austria might somehow alienate Russia in a quarrel over Poland nearly drove him to despair.[63] Russia answered the question of which German power it would support and at what price by supporting Austria

---

[62] Moritz (1968: 157–62); Thugut (1872: i. Nos. 124–5, 137, 140–3, 158, 165, 169); Vivenot and Zeissberg (1873–90: iv. Nos. 95–6, 105–8, 110, 121, 123, 155, 159, 164–9, 176–8, 182, 236, 310–11; v. Nos. 2–4, 11–21).

[63] For a typical expression of this fear, see Thugut (1872: i. No. 186).

as a rope supports a hanging man, making Austria pay for the rope. The Third Partition did not advance Russia's main aim in regard to Prussia, to force it to remain in the war against France; it actually encouraged Prussia to make a separate peace. It did, however, promote Russia's main aim with Austria, to make it still weaker and more dependent and keep it mired in a war which served Russia's purposes. Prussia eventually would receive a generous share of Polish territory from the third partition; Austria, so long as Catherine lived, never received one man of the 30,000 men the Empress had promised would fight at Austria's side against France as soon as the Polish business was settled. Prussia made no side-payments to Russia for the partition, though it served Prussia's purposes. Austria, as payment for the final destruction of a state which Austrians continued privately to insist was important to them, secretly gave its formal consent to Catherine's Greek Project and the creation of a Russian satellite kingdom of Dacia in the Danubian Principalities. Thus it accepted in advance its own further encirclement by Russia and the further destruction of the Ottoman Empire, which, with Poland gone, represented the last dike against the Russian tide.[64]

Little need be said about the nine months of acrid negotiations required in 1795 before Prussia would agree to disgorge Cracow, accede to the Austro-Russian convention, and conclude the partition. The only noteworthy point is that, faced by a threat of an Austro-Prussian war, Austria for the first time compromised its war effort in the West in order to amass forces in Poland and Bohemia-Moravia. Otherwise the pattern was predictable— bluster and bluff by Prussia, pleas for Russia's help by Austria, and calls for more Austrian concessions from St Petersburg. In the end Austria gained Cracow at the price of territorial concessions to Prussia in Masovia and to Russia in Volhynia.[65]

The conventional verdict on the Third Partition as another tragedy and crime is certainly true, especially from the Polish standpoint. It is also easy and, to an extent, legitimate to blame

---

[64] Moritz (1968: 167–79); Martens (1874–1905: ii. 221–48); Vivenot (1870: 406–83); Vivenot and Zeissberg (1873–90: v. 33, 38–9). This was not the limit of Russian pretensions. At a time when Austria was losing the war, Prussia and other allies were defecting, and Russia doing nothing to help, Catherine asked Austria to recognize Monsieur (the Count of Provence, Louis XVI's brother and later Louis XVIII) as Regent of France and pledge to fight until the Bourbons were restored. This at least Austria refused. HHStA, *Russland II Correspondenz* 217, fos. 9–10.

[65] Moritz (1968: 186–9); see the vast documentation in Vivenot and Zeissberg (1873–90: v. Nos. 137–336); also Vivenot (1870: 105–15); Martens (1874–1905: 249–59); and Vorontsov (1870–95: xviii. 97–100).

Austria for its own plight. Thugut in particular let his hatred of Prussia, fear of France, abhorrence of the revolution, and greed for territory lead Austria into complete dependence on Russia. But one must again ask what the alternatives were. Austria leaned on Russia, not blindly, but by conscious choice out of perceived necessity. Thugut operated from three assumptions which he considered axiomatic: Austria must stop France, or European civilization would be destroyed. Austria must check Prussia, or the Central European balance and Austria's security in Germany would be destroyed. Austria must gain compensations so as emerge from this contest stronger compared to other great powers, or at least not weaker, or Austria's general security, rank, and prestige in Europe would be destroyed. These three premises were all either objectively true (if one accepts balance-of-power doctrine) or at least so widely believed in the eighteenth century as to be almost unchallengeable. Grant these premises; grant further the fact that no serious help was available for Austria anywhere else; and the conclusion that Austria must have Russian help at any cost became inescapable. Thugut's opponents argued correctly that the war was ruining Austria and that Russia, Britain, and other states were exploiting Austria's efforts for their own purposes. Thugut, however, knew this just as well, and the knowledge did not help to suggest an alternative policy.

Only if and when Thugut's basic assumptions could be successfully challenged; only when someone could show that Austria did not have to fight France, stop the advance of democracy and revolution, check Prussia, or gain security by compensations and *arrondissement* in order to remain an independent great power; only when someone could demonstrate how, in abandoning these goals, Austria could find peace, reasonable security, and a decent status in Europe; only then would there be a serious alternative policy for Austria to consider. Leopold and Kaunitz had proposed one, and it had failed. No one would do so again for a long time.

This meant that Austria would suffer even more defeats before seeing that it could not continue the course it was pursuing. Russians would need still more victories to learn the same lesson. Nothing indicated to them in 1795 that they were approaching their limit in possible gains. The Polish problem was now settled, though many Russians, including Catherine, still expected to recover all of Poland some day; but the Turkish question remained, and was on the agenda. Besides, certain neighbours needed more of the tutelage and discipline only Russia could supply, especially Prussia. As Russians repeatedly told Austria and Britain, Russia's contribution to their war effort consisted in watching Prussia and preparing to crush it if necessary, thus freeing them to defeat France. Or as Morkov put it (in a mirror image of Grenville's attitude), the rivalries and bad faith of other European powers compelled Russia to force them to serve the good of the whole.[66]

Few Russians feared that a nemesis would attend Russia's current hubris. Its size, isolation, and self-sufficiency made it secure it against the power and subversive principles of France, and it had no threats in its immediate neighbourhood. There was some concern at St Petersburg about the aggressive immorality of Catherine's policy, and occasional worries that Russia's success, carried too far, might strain the international system and eventually bring it down. But the real danger went unnoticed: that Russia, the overgrown spoiled adolescent of Europe, would fail to see how little real power backed up its commanding position, and that Catherine's successors would continue her ruthless expansion and imperialism without her luck and skill.[67]

For Prussia, in contrast, 1794–5 was something of a watershed. In trying to take over Poland in the summer of 1794, while at the same time the King still wished to control the outcome of the war against France, Prussia made the last in a long series of efforts to become a full-fledged great power and act as one. The attempt failed in both East and West; Prussia had to be rescued by Russia in Poland and was forced to drop out of the war against France. Its defeat over Cracow merely underlined a fact Prussia was more or less forced to recognize: it was a second-rank power. While maintaining its ambitions and anti-Austrian aims in Poland and Germany, it concentrated now on consolidating its gains in peace and neutrality.

V. THE COALITION RESHAPED, 1795

By early spring 1795 France had won the war, having driven Britain's forces from the Continent, overrun Belgium, Holland, and the Rhineland, and sent Austria's armies reeling in retreat. Prussia had already stopped fighting and was about to sign a peace treaty, and most smaller states in the coalition wished to follow its example. The story of 1795–7, however, is one of French failure

[66] Ibid. 46–55, 60–5; Martens (1874–1905: ii. 273, 275–80).

[67] For some Russian expressions of concern over the gangrenous condition of Europe, but conviction that Russia was immune to infection, see Lord (1915: 322); Vorontsov (1870–95: x. Nos. 13–14, 18; xviii. 124–7; xx. 31–2, 71–3).

to translate its military victories into peace or durable political advantages, while Austria and Britain proved unable to deal effectively either with France or with each other. This meant that the coalition, near collapse in 1795, would be rebuilt; the fighting would go indecisively for two more years in the old theatres, to be ended only by spectacular French successes in a new one. Even these decisive French victories and a peace treaty would not end the war.

France and Prussia by late 1794 shared the desire for a separate peace. It would help the French government finish some important conquests (Holland, part of the left bank of the Rhine, and the key fortress of Mainz) and thus help it survive at home. Though Robespierre had been overthrown and the Terror ended by the so-called Thermidorean Reaction in July, the new Committee of Public Safety continued to need military victory, loot, and contributions. In Prussia the King protested loudly against a separate peace, but this was mainly show and self-deception; he was averse not so much to making a separate peace *per se* as to taking the blame for it in Europe. In any case, Prussia needed peace more than France. Its treasury was exhausted, revolutionary unrest threatened its western provinces, France's conquest of Holland in late 1794 and early 1795 threatened all of North Germany, and Prussia wanted its hands free in Poland (the best argument of all).[68]

Thus the peace talks, unofficial since the autumn and official from January to April, were not about whether there would be peace, but on what terms. Once the Prussians had discarded some naïve or unworkable ideas (that France should renounce the left bank and any further conquests, or that the King might mediate a general European peace, or that Prussia could become France's ally against Austria, as Prince Henry and Lucchesini urged), two basic options were left. The first, favoured by most Prussians, called for following Frederick's tradition by subordinating general German to particular Prussian interests, i.e. leaving the war, taking compensations on the right bank of the Rhine for Prussia's losses on the left, pursuing territorial gains in Poland, and not worrying too much about Germany. The second, advocated by Prussia's chief negotiator in the latter phase of the talks, Prince Hardenberg, proposed to combine Prussia's eastern aims with anti-Austrian

---

[68] Biro (1958: i. 316–19); Real (1951–2: 27–112); Real (1958: 117–25); Stine (1980: 210–18); Moritz (1968: 145–55); Haussherr (1957: 298–307); Holzapfel (1984).

goals in Germany. Prussia should try to make peace with France both on its own behalf and on that of the Reich, bringing all the German territories save Austria's into a neutral zone recognized by France and protected by Prussia. This would give Prussia the leadership of Germany.

Neither Hardenberg's compatriots nor the French went along with his ideas. The treaty which he and the French minister to Switzerland, Barthélemy, signed at Basel on 5 April basically satisfied France and the old-line Prussians, though certain provisions were designed to save Prussia's reputation in Europe and keep Hardenberg's German ambitions alive. *De facto* the German left bank of the Rhine was surrendered to France, but the cession was disguised by making French occupation provisional until peace was concluded with the Reich. Similarly, France guaranteed Prussia compensation on the right bank for its losses on the left, but kept the guarantee secret. France recognized a neutrality zone under Prussian leadership in Northern Germany, though with a restricted demarcation line, and granted a three-month armistice to the Reich estates fighting on Austria's side, so that Prussia could offer them its mediation for peace.[69]

None of these fig-leaves could disguise the fact that Prussia was abandoning its allies or save its reputation in Germany and Europe. None the less, the Peace of Basel was not a short-sighted act of appeasement, for which Prussia would be punished in 1806. Prussia had played for high stakes in the great-power game ever since 1787, never winning a big prize but making some major gains and escaping disaster more by luck than skill. Now, in the Peace of Basel, Prussia decided to quit while it was ahead. Its decision to preserve peace for itself and the rest of North Germany was as sensible a choice as eighteenth-century rules allowed, one denied many other states; the other North German states endorsed it, and it proved fairly durable. It even had a certain value for Europe as a whole. From 1795 to 1806 a neutral North Germany, led by Prussia, served as a useful, viable *corps intermédiaire* separating the real great powers in Europe and limiting the war. What ultimately ruined it was not Prussia's cowardice and folly, but the fatal combination of an unstable eighteenth-century system and Napoleon's ambition. There is a general point to be drawn from this for the nineteenth-century German question as a whole.

---

[69] Real (1951–2: 115–87; 1958: 126–31); Aretin (1967: i. 312–33); Haussherr (1957: 308–29); Thielen (1967: 76–7); Bailleu (1881–7: vol. i, pp. ix–xv, xviii–xxi); Biro (1957: i. 324–6); Gembruch (1988: 110–13); Easum (1942: ch. 26).

North Germany under Prussian leadership as a *corps intermédiaire* was fine; Prussia using its position in North Germany to become and act like a real great power in Europe was inherently dangerous.

Austria, Britain, Russia, and the Reich estates immediately denounced Prussia's defection, but others accompanied and followed it. Tuscany had already escaped from the war on 9 February; the Dutch, conquered in December and January, made peace with France on 16 May and Spain on 22 July. Holland's fate was especially harsh; France occupied strategic Dutch territory, took direct control of the Dutch navy, and turned the United Provinces into a satellite state as the Batavian Republic. Easy treatment for Tuscany, on the other hand, helped France split this Habsburg secundogeniture further away from Austria, while Spain, with whom France hoped to renew its traditional alliance, only had to give up its half of the isle of Santo Domingo. French revolutionary diplomacy, though not generous, was skilful in exploiting opportunities and rifts in the coalition.[70]

More states would have liked to leave the coalition (Naples, Sardinia, and especially various German states and the Reich), but could not do so because Britain and Austria decided to continue the war. This was not an easy decision for Vienna. In early 1795 Emperor Francis approved an anonymous memoir from the peace party arguing that Austria must get out. Even Thugut repeatedly warned Russia and Britain that Austria might be forced to quit. But the peace alternative was specious. The leader of the peace party, Count Ferdinand Trauttmansdorff, advocated ceding the Netherlands, Luxemburg, and part of the Rhineland to France, neutralizing the four western Reich circles, and allying Austria with France, so that, while France fought Britain, Austria could retake Silesia from Prussia and reconstitute the Poland of 1792. In other words, Trauttmansdorff recognized who Austria's real foes were, but his policy was a recipe for more war, not peace. No real chances for peace came from France, which, despite considerable internal debate and some hesitations over policy, still saw Austria as its main Continental enemy. A French feeler in mid-1795 for peace based on the Belgian–Bavarian exchange was probably a trap, as Thugut claimed.

[70] For the various treaties, see DeClercq (1880–1917: i. 245–7, 321–42); Guyot (1912: 103–7). For the futile allied efforts to keep Prussia and other states from defecting, see Thugut (1872: i. Nos. 153–4); Vivenot and Zeissberg (1873–90: v *passim*); Windham (1913: i. 235–56); Auckland (1861: iii. 202–7); Ehrman (1983: 373–9). On Spain, see Herr (1958: 285–96, 321–37).

Most important, a separate peace, even were it possible, would not have done Austria much good. Its fiscal situation was as desperate as Prussia's, but peace would ruin rather than improve it, at least in the short run. Austria currently hoped to avoid bankruptcy by negotiating a huge war loan guaranteed by Britain, and its hopes of repaying the loan rested on either collecting the money from a defeated France or getting the debt forgiven by Britain after a victorious war. France was avoiding fiscal collapse by continuing to fight and win; Austria by continuing to fight and lose. The Peace of Basel assured Prussia of compensations in Germany, helped improve its position in Poland, and enhanced its general security. A similar separate peace would have had just the opposite effects for Austria, endangering its gains in Poland, undermining its German position, ruining the all-important alliance with Russia, and destroying any hope of gaining one with Britain, without rendering Austria more secure against either its open opponent, France, or its secret enemy, Prussia.

In short, Austria would once more have had to decide for peace out of despair—an acknowledgment that accepting defeat, though terrible, was better than continuing the war. Archduke Carl, to his credit, openly drew this conclusion. Thugut refused to, and plodded on, openly fighting strictly for Austrian interests, criticizing the Imperial vice-chancellor, Prince Colloredo-Mansfeld, for putting Reich interests ahead of Austria's, and using extreme pressure and deceptive promises to keep the Reich estates in the war.[71]

Thugut still hoped, however, that Britain and Russia would assume the main burden of the war. This seemed possible when Britain, after allying with Russia in February 1795, finally concluded a formal alliance with Austria in May, after more than two years of fighting on the same side. It included a British guarantee of a £4,600,000 Austrian war loan, for which Austria was to keep 170,000 men in the field against France. The apparent solidarity was deceptive. Not only were the British still very distrustful of Austria; more fundamentally, Austria was Britain's third and last choice as its main ally, distinctly a *pis aller*. The British would have much preferred a real alliance with Russia for various reasons, among them that this would be the best and cheapest way of

---

[71] On French policy during this period, see esp. Sorel (1881–2); also Biro (1957: i. 386–414). For Austria, see Roider (1987: ch. 7); Hüffer and Luckwaldt (1907: vol. i, pp. liv–ix; Vivenot and Zeissberg (1873–90: v. Nos. 69–136; for Francis's approval of the peace memorandum, No. 119); Thugut (1872: i. Nos. 282, 285–6, 299, 310, 316, 320–1, 326).

making Austria fight. Even Prussia remained more desirable as a partner. Over Grenville's objections, Pitt had insisted in early 1795 on one more effort to lure Berlin back into the war by a massive subsidy. Only after learning of the impending Peace of Basel did the British turn to Austria, with grave reservations. Windham and others were convinced that supporting royalist insurrections in France would pay off better than helping the greedy and lethargic Austrians; Dundas continued to hope for conquests in the West Indies and fiscal collapse in France; Grenville, though more Continental on strategy, was incensed at Austria for doing too little to help Sardinia, conciliate Prussia, and support the Prince of Condé's *émigré* army.[72]

The loan also produced angry quarrels in which Thugut denounced 'those devils of the English' for usury. Each power criticized the other for fighting badly and shirking its responsibilities, and each took its complaints to Russia as arbiter. This was to cast Shylock in the role of Solomon,[73] and Russia exploited the opportunity, giving no help to either ally while seeking more commercial concessions from Britain and military-political ones from Austria. All Russia's forces, it claimed, were needed to defend itself against a French–Prussian–Swedish–Turkish threat created by the Peace of Basel.[74]

The plausible explanation of why the Anglo-Austrian alliance failed to work here and later is that their objective congruence of interests was spoiled by mutual distrust and the failure of one or the other to concentrate on defeating the common enemy. Once again, this interpretation has things backwards. Because leaders in both countries believed that they were natural allies against a common enemy, and because each government in different ways fixed its attention mainly on winning the war, neither was able to see that their alliance was unnatural because their interests and policies clashed. Instead of facing and working out these

[72] Ehrman (1983: 516–28, 548–59); Sherwig (1969: 56–75); Grenville (1893–1927: iii. 25–30, 57–8); Windham (1913: i. 281–5); Wickham (1870: 25–30, 34–9).

[73] Morkov illustrated the Russian attitude well in complaining to S. Vorontsov about Britain's foolish persistence in bringing up Russia's verbal promises rather than relying only on the letter of treaties. Russia's alliance with Britain did not oblige it to do one thing more than it was already doing for the good cause, Morkov insisted; except in terms of principles, the war had nothing to do with Russia. Austria, he said, had learned to be more sensible, to stop asking for troops and to accept that Russia's proper role in the war was to watch Prussia. 19 Apr. 1796, Vorontsov (1870–95: xx. No. 31).

[74] Martens (1874–1905: x. 388–408); Grenville (1892–1927: iii. 21–5, 45, 74–5); Guyot (1912: 100–2); Vivenot and Zeissberg (1873–90: v. Nos. 309, 318, 321); Thugut (1872: i. No. 290).

differences, each denounced the other for failure to do its duty to the common cause. Their conflicts of interests and policies, already discussed, were sharpened by their competition to be Russia's prime ally. Britain wished to supplant Austria, for whom the Russian alliance was all-important, in order to manage Continental affairs in an Anglo-Russian partnership, possibly including Prussia. This strategy, obvious enough in Britain's previous policy toward Prussia and Russia and the way it used its naval and financial resources in the war, showed up also in the alliance convention and loan agreement with Austria. The source of the problem, to repeat, was not that British feelings were anti-Austrian, or vice versa; it was that the British concept of European balance and peace was anti-Austrian, and vice versa.

While the allied coalition was superficially consolidated, the French were following up the Peace of Basel with persistent efforts to get Prussia to join the war on their side. This appeared to have a chance of success when Hardenberg quit the ministry, having failed to save part of the left bank from France and mediate peace for the Reich. His successor, Count Alvensleben, favoured co-operating with France. But a series of developments—French and Austrian violations of the neutral demarcation line in Germany, France's *de facto* annexation of the left bank and much of Holland, and a French invasion of southern Germany and northern Italy in the summer of 1796—made Prussia retreat into isolation and the defence of purely Prussian interests. In August 1796, Haugwitz and the French minister, Antoine-Bernard Caillard, signed a convention at Berlin in which France formally recognized Prussia as the protector of a smaller North German neutral zone, while Prussia formally ceded the left bank to France in exchange for compensations on the right bank for itself, the two Hesses, and the House of Orange (Nassau). By this convention Prussia became France's passive partner in the destruction of the Reich, but still avoided being its active ally. Thus it worked neither to end the war, as French moderates like Barthélemy hoped, nor to reorganize Germany under French and Prussian leadership, as other more radical French leaders urged; nor did it follow a co-ordinated anti-Austrian strategy, as some Prussians wanted.[75] Meanwhile Austria retained its control of the Reich and kept it in the war.[76]

Thus the coalition survived and the war continued, both sides

[75] Real (1951–2: 188–99; 1958: 134–7); Bailleu (1881–7: i *passim*); Haussherr (1957: 330–5); DeClercq (1880–1917: i. 279–83); Biro (1957: 348–53, 364, 366–7); Sorel (1881–2 *passim*).
[76] Aretin (1967: i. 332–44); Hölzle (1931: 136–9); Bitterauf (1905: 30–1).

still hoping for victory and neither worrying overmuch about the kind of peace it should bring. For a moment, however, a change in France's collective outlook seemed possible. A new constitution was adopted in 1795 establishing a conservative republican government with a five-man executive Directory and two elected legislative councils, the Ancients and the Five Hundred.

The Directory (1795–9) has gone down in history as an unstable, corrupt regime leading France from Jacobin revolution to military dictatorship. Though this was how things ultimately turned out, the Directory tried to do something else: to overcome terror and war, the great obstacles to stable government at home and to peace abroad. From early on revolutionary leaders had used coercion of various kinds—in the broadest sense, terror—to compel the people to support and participate in the Revolution. Its use and intensity had risen almost continuously; even the surface calm between August 1789 and June 1791 was deceptive. What mainly necessitated and promoted the use of terror, moreover, was not the organized counter-revolution, but a broader, more diffuse popular reaction to the Revolution which may be termed anti-terror. Despite the real grievances which brought on the Revolution and the genuine popularity of many of its early slogans, ideals, and measures, prolonged experience with it soon led the majority of Frenchmen, and far larger majorities of the peoples it affected outside France, to reject the changes and uncertainty it brought into their daily lives and to resist being coerced into them. Anti-terror resistance, ranging all the way from non-participation and non-compliance to violent armed struggle, represented the broad groundswell behind the more organized forms of the counter-revolution—emigration, non-juring priests and their supporters, local struggles, great risings in the Vendée, and drawn-out guerilla warfare in Brittany and Normandy. These more organized responses evoked further terror, fed the spiral of violence, and in many instances readily became terrorist in methods themselves.

The parallel to terror as a revolutionary means of combating internal insecurity was war as the means of combating external insecurity. In both cases the problems were real and serious, the methods natural and almost inescapable, but self-defeating. Widening the use of terror was intended to produce a genuine, unforced revolutionary consensus within France; expanding French power and influence by war was intended to end encirclement and hostility on the part of Europe. Both attempted to solve intractable problems by trying harder, by overcoming reality instead of facing it: the natural resort of sincere second-rate minds like that of Robespierre—and of his contemporaries, Thugut, Pitt, Grenville, and many more.[77]

Scholars have recently emphasized the Directory's efforts to break the vicious cycle of internal resistance and terror in France, and to restore consensus, community, and real freedom by returning to limited government and the rule of law.[78] Generations ago, historians discussed analogous French efforts just before and during the Directory to end the war, consolidate France's gains, and find durable security and peace.[79] The Directory failed in both efforts; whether external or internal factors were more to blame is almost impossible to decide. In any case, by the time it fell, the government of France had become even weaker, more arbitrary, and more discredited, and the war had grown wider and more expansionist, than during the Revolution. So far as France is concerned, moreover, one vital factor is common to the failure in both arenas. Frenchmen may sincerely have wanted stability and peace, but too many of them failed to understand the requirements of either. Even where they did, they chose to ignore them on the ground that these requirements were unrealistic, unattainable in the real world of politics. This is another sign of the ultimate utopianism of *realpolitik*.

France's internal troubles were, as ever, Britain's opportunity. It sought to exploit them by a war of internal subversion, a struggle in which the British anticipated and outstripped France. The Vendée was now quiescent, but the Chouan rebels in Brittany still raised hopes of an armed insurrection. In late 1794 William Wickham, minister to Switzerland, began developing other forms of secret war, gathering intelligence, organizing espionage, promoting conspiracies, supporting Condé's *émigré* forces, recruiting mercenaries in Switzerland and elsewhere, and working to get Austria and Sardinia to launch military offensives in co-ordination with the British strategy of overthrow. Lord MacArtney undertook a mission to the Count of Provence in Italy, who now claimed the French throne as Louis XVIII following the death of Louis XVI's son. Through MacArtney, Britain offered to recognize Louis if he would proclaim an amnesty and announce a

---

[77] See in general Hampson (1988); Schama (1989); for particular points, Godechot (1981: 214–47); Cobb (1972: 26–7, 128–31; 1987: esp. 1–16); LeGoff and Sutherland (1983); H. Mitchell (1968; 1974; 1965: 1–12); Vidalenc (1963: 34–56); Ozouf (1984); G. A. Kelly (1980); Cobban (1968: 136–57); Berce (1987: 198–222).

[78] e.g. Lucas (1978); Sutherland (1986); Woronoff (1984); Hunt *et al.* (1979).

[79] For the last months of the Convention, see Sorel (1881–2), still fascinating in its eloquence and insights, and for the Directory, Guyot (1912).

programme suitable for uniting moderate constitutional royalists and other monarchists inside and outside France against the Directory.

All these efforts broke down in mid- and late 1795. The Count of Provence responded to MacArtney's mission by issuing a Declaration at Verona so intransigent as to make a united monarchist opposition in France impossible. The disastrous outcome in July of a British expedition to aid the Chouans was followed by a humiliating failure to hold the isle of Yeu off the coast of France as a base for French *émigré* forces. Meanwhile the chances of a constitutionalist-royalist overthrow of the Directory were destroyed in October when units of the French army, with Napoleon Bonaparte again playing a key role, crushed a royalist-inspired rising of the Paris sections.[80]

These set-backs, plus British disappointment at Austria's failure to support these ventures as it should have,[81] forced the British to think about ending the war before resistance on the Continent collapsed. They still needed time, however, for victories in the West Indies to give Britain good cards in the negotiations. Hence Pitt sent Francis Jackson on a special mission to Vienna in October 1795, with instructions to get Austria to launch a major offensive the next year, mainly to retake and defend the Netherlands. Thugut, at that moment emboldened by the success of an Austrian counter-offensive in Germany, the conclusion of the Polish partition, and reports of internal anarchy in France, asked for another large British loan to Austria and troop subsidies for the Reich and Russia, but declined to be pinned down to retaking Belgium. The British, ready as usual to subsidize Russia but not Austria, ignored Austria's financial and strategic wishes, but, encouraged by the signs that Austria would continue to fight, pursued their plans for a major expedition to the West Indies under Lord Abercromby. The military story in 1796 unfortunately repeated that of 1795. Abercromby's expedition, delayed and weakened by storms in the Atlantic, arrived in the West Indies too late to have much chance for success, while Austria, having refused British demands to reconquer Belgium, later in 1796 suffered major defeats, especially in Italy. Catherine once more evaded her promises to join the war

---

[80] Ehrman (1983: 368–73, 567–87); Hutt (1983); Fryer (1965: 9–78); H. Mitchell (1965: 40–69); Fryer (1979–80); Mansel (1981: 111–15); Godechot (1949–50); Tulard (1977: 74–7). Many examples of wild counter-revolutionary military schemes cooked up by *émigrés* in England are preserved in Pitt's papers (PRO 30/8/334).

[81] Wickham (1870: i. 40–172); Hutt (1983: i. 204–6, 210–11, 229–37).

actively, and when her son Paul succeeded her on her death in October 1796 he repudiated them. By December 1796 Britain and Austria were agreed on only two points: they had to have help from Russia, and they had to deal with the Republic in France. Even these insights, however, did no good; Russia, while refusing to help them, insisted at the same time that the Republic must be overthrown and Louis XVIII restored.

Meanwhile Pitt and Grenville, hearing reports of Austro-French negotiations, had decided early in 1796 to launch their own peace move through Pitt's secret contacts with French agents. They still, against all experience and evidence, hoped for Russian and Prussian help to force France to the peace table. When Russia suggested that Britain subsidize another Prussian army for this purpose, Grenville explained that this was impossible, since Britain had just refused a subsidy to Austria. However, the difficulty could be overcome, Grenville suggested, if Russia would persuade Prussia merely to make an armed demonstration on the borders of Holland. This would force France to pull out just as it had in 1787; Britain would guarantee that Prussia would be fully indemnified for its expenses, either by the Dutch Stadholder himself or by Britain, out of revenues from Dutch colonies Britain intended to keep after the peace.[82]

Both this proposal and Britain's approach to France through underground contacts between Wickham and the French minister Barthélemy in Switzerland met the fate they deserved. Britain's stiff manner of negotiating (it tried to learn France's peace terms without even calling the Republic by its name, much less recognizing it formally) no doubt influenced the Directory's equally stiff reply, that the French constitution forbade the alienation of any territory France had annexed, including the Low Countries. But even a more flexible British approach would probably have met the same fate. The Directors, though not locked into an expansionist programme like the former Convention, were constantly divided on personal and substantive grounds, including the question of whether Britain or Austria was France's main enemy. Besides, no French government would have met Britain's demand that it surrender its main military conquests.[83]

The British were justified in suspecting Austrian–French con-

---

[82] Ehrman (1983: 588–99); Guyot (1912: 96–8, 145–51); Rose (1903); Wickham (1870: i. 321–35 and *passim*); Hüffer (1900–1: vol. i, pp. lxxxiv–v); Grenville (1892–1927: iii. 173); Grenville to Whitworth, 9 Feb. 1796, BL Add. MS 59193, fos. 3–12.

[83] Guyot (1912: 151–6).

tacts in late 1795 and early 1796, but no serious negotiation went on. Thugut continued to fight the domestic opposition to the war, and to resist French pressure and attempted blackmail with equal stubbornness.[84] Even the spectacular victories which the new commander of the Army of Italy, Napoleon Bonaparte, won in northern Italy in April and May 1796 in splitting apart and defeating the Sardinian and Austrian armies, forcing Sardinia to make peace, and driving the Austrians from Milan, made no real difference.[85] Thugut attributed the defeats to French luck, Sardinian treachery, and Austrian incompetence, and resolved to fight harder.

The Austro-French talks, therefore, simply demonstrate how once again each power, in speaking of peace and balance of power, meant victory and hegemony. The French at least had a general plan for achieving this in Western Europe: to force Austria to break with Britain, recognize French conquests on the left bank of the Rhine, and accept territorial losses in Germany or Italy compensated through wide-scale secularizations within the Reich. Such a settlement would not only make France secure but also give it Austria's place as leader of Germany. There were persistent divisions among the Directors over whether France's primary goals should be continental or maritime-colonial, and whether France had to gain its natural frontiers, especially on the Rhine, or be satisfied with an improved strategic frontier. The divergences, however, actually affected policy toward Austria little: in either case, Austria was an obstacle to be overcome or an opponent to be pushed away to a safe distance. It was not, like Britain, a mortal enemy or, like Prussia, a possible ally. Two other points about French war aims are interesting. First, almost every peace feeler or plan up to 1797 conceded or stipulated the Belgian–Bavarian exchange for Austria. Second, France also argued, quite effectively, on the basis of balance of power. France had to make territorial gains, it claimed, to restore the Continental balance destroyed by the partitions of Poland and by Russia's expansion at the expense of the Ottoman Empire. Furthermore, no European balance

---

[84] A special French peace emissary, the Marquis de Poteratz, was instructed to remind Thugut that France had proof that prior to the Revolution he had supplied the French government with information for pay. Thugut seems to have shrugged the matter off, which indicates that he had probably sold the French only what his own government allowed him to. Roider (1987: 42–4). On the negotiations, see Biro (1957: ii. 680–9); Guyot (1912: 98–9, 119–23); Hüffer (1900–1: i. Nos. 1–29).

[85] Fugier (1930: 8–37); Guyot (1912: ch. 5); Ferrero (1961: 26–63).

of power was worth anything so long as Britain remained unchallenged on the seas and in the colonial world. Obviously, these
were self-serving arguments for French imperialism—but irrefutable on the basis of balance-of-power reasoning or evidence.[86]

Austria, though more pessimistic about the war and more defensively orientated than France, paradoxically was more committed than France or any other power to carrying it on. The
reason should be by now familiar: a separate peace would not only
cost Austria territory vis-à-vis France, but would alienate it from
Britain and Russia and isolate it in the face of France and Prussia.
The only alteration in Thugut's strategy at this time was to switch
his search for compensations from Germany (Bavaria, Swabia,
Alsace) to northern Italy, especially Venetia and the Papal Legations. The reason was not that Italian territory was more desirable
or easier to get, but that any Austrian gains in Germany at this
time would set off a general scramble, ruining Austria's position
and aiding France and Prussia. This change of target helps explain
why Thugut denounced Sardinia, Tuscany, Genoa, and the Pope
for their cowardice and treachery, though his charges were not
always unfounded.[87]

In the summer of 1796, French armies in Germany under Moreau
and Jourdan forced the Austrian army under Archduke Carl,
weakened by having to send reinforcements to Italy, to retreat
almost to the Austrian frontier. The French victories knocked
the south German states out of the war, and, combined with
Bonaparte's in Italy, convinced the British that Austria was about
to make peace. Fearing the exhaustion of Britain's credit and
reserves of specie in addition, Pitt suspended Britain's loan payments to Austria. At the same time the British again tried to get
Russia and Prussia to replace Austria in the coalition, offering
Prussia territorial gains from a general reshuffle in Germany to get
it to assume the defence of the Netherlands.[88] This failed, and on
top of it came news of a Franco-Spanish offensive alliance signed
on 19 August at San Ildefonso, directed squarely at Britain and its
ally Portugal. The treaty served to heighten Britain's fear of

[86] Biro (1957: i. 378–81; ii. 501–13).
[87] Roider (1987: 197–8); Hüffer (1900–1: i. Nos. 34–8); Thugut (1872: i. Nos.
452–60, 472–4, 479–80).
[88] Ehrman (1983: 624–9); Sherwig (1969: 76–82); Grenville (1892–1927: iii.
186–92, 206–7, 214–15, 227–30); Guyot (1911: 261–7); Bailleu (1881–7: i. 532–4).
As part of the reshuffle, the British proposed to let Austria have Bavaria, but
neglected to make any provision for the Elector. Thugut later inquired what the
British had in mind for him—perhaps strangling, or exile in Australia? Hüffer
(1868: 224–5).

invasion or loss of its maritime supremacy, and marked the beginning of a long period in which France would enjoy more success overall than Britain in coalition-building.[89] When Spain declared war on 5 October, Britain's first thought was to abandon Corsica, the only prize in Europe it had wrested from France, so as to concentrate its fleet closer to home; its second was to offer the island to Russia as a bribe for entering the war. But Catherine's death in October killed any hopes for this; her son Paul I had long opposed her foreign policy as aggressive and immoral.[90]

Britain's troubles continued to mount. Austria, to Britain's surprise, stayed in the war and continued to fight hard, driving the French back in south Germany in the late summer and fall. But Carl's success was outstripped by Bonaparte's astonishing successes in Italy, which among other things ruined British hopes of France's collapse from financial exhaustion. Imposing truces on the Papal State, Parma-Piacenza, and Modena and then peace treaties on Genoa, Naples, and Parma in October and November, Bonaparte provided France vital infusions of cash, contributions, and services. Neutrals also were forced into line; Bonaparte occupied the Tuscan port of Livorno and closed it to the British, while Hamburg had to ransom its ships held in French ports in order to regain its French trade. Even French influence in the Near East seemed to revive with victory; in late 1796 the Ottoman Empire appeared about to ally with France against Russia and Austria.[91] Britain found itself unable to defend its ally Portugal against the French and Spanish threat. Abercromby's lack of success in the West Indies added to a general discouragement and disaffection at home.

The British government therefore asked France in the fall of 1796 to receive Lord Malmesbury at Lille for direct peace talks. The Directory, preparing new blows against Britain at the time, initially refused, but then decided to let Malmesbury come. Archduke Carl's offensive in Germany had raised a threat on the Rhine, and a single defeat might still overturn Bonaparte's victories in northern Italy. Peace talks with Britain would serve to frighten Austria and encourage the British peace party, while a refusal

[89] DeClercq (1880–1917: i. 287–91); Lyon (1934: 88–97); Guyot (1912: 231–46); Fugier (1930: 2–30); Herr (1958: 358–61).

[90] Martens (1874–1905: x. 409–18); Ehrman (1983: 630–3); Grenville (1892–1927: iii. 261–2); various letters of Grenville to Whitworth, Aug.–Nov. 1796, BL Add. MS 59193, fos. 16–56.

[91] DeClercq (1880–1917: i. 271–9, 300–11); Biro (1957: ii. 817–25); Testa (1864–1911: ii. 208–21, 233–41, 244–7); Fugier (1954: 92–9).

to treat would give the British ministry a propaganda weapon against France at home and abroad.[92]

The Malmesbury mission, therefore, made sense for both powers; the way it was conducted did not. The British, having launched the move without Austria and over its protests, then tried to persuade Austria to join it. In the meantime Malmesbury was instructed to defend Austria's interests, negotiate jointly with the Austrian representative if one appeared, and reject any separate peace. The terms Malmesbury was given were unrealistic (a mutual restoration of conquests, by which Britain still hoped to wrest Belgium from French control); worse still, he was instructed not to reveal them, but to induce the French instead to state theirs. When Austria refused to join the negotiations, Malmesbury got permission to disclose his terms, which, as he had predicted, were rejected. Thereupon Grenville drew up even stiffer ones for him to present, and the French in late December ended the talks and expelled the mission.

This makes the initiative appear insincere. The real problem, however, was not insincerity about peace, but internal divisions within both powers, especially Britain. While Malmesbury tried hard for peace and Pitt and Canning were interested in a compromise, Grenville remained intransigent on the question of Belgium, and George III always opposed any negotiation with France at all. Yet even if Britain was primarily responsible for the failure, this is not very important, for the talks at Lille could not have produced a European peace, only at best an unstable Anglo-French truce like the Peace of Amiens in 1802. Only a narrow range of issues was considered, from exclusively British and French points of view. Germany and Italy figured mainly as places to find compensations, and the problems of Central and Eastern Europe (Prussia, Austria, Poland, Russia, the Ottoman Empire) were not addressed at all. The British (at least those Britons willing to think about it) were not unaware that there was a connection between their negotiations and the interests of other powers, especially their ally Austria, but they knew nothing could be done about the divergence. George Canning expressed this clearly to his close friend Granville Leveson-Gower after the negotiations had failed. Noting that Britain knew that Emperor Francis did not want Belgium, he discussed the clash of Austro-British interests with philosophical detachment:

---

[92] Ehrman (1983: 603–50); Guyot (1912: 280–7); Grenville (1892–1927: iii. 235–6, 239–42, 256); BL Add. MS 58907, fos. 101–6.

The Netherlands, though they may not be worth his keeping, are worth our gaining for him:——placed as we are by treaty, + by the necessity either of negotiating some creditable peace, or of breaking off the negotiation upon some simple + intelligible ground—in the singular situation of having to wrest from our enemy what of all things they are least willing to give up, + to obtain for our ally what he is of all things the least anxious to acquire. But so it is.[93]

After Lille, the question was which of the two main belligerents, France or Austria, would crack first. Though Austria was in worse straits, France also was under serious strain. War-weariness, inadequate pay and provisions, and widespread draft-dodging had reduced the army from 800,000 to 450,000 men. The state's finances remained ruinous, and while Italy could still be exploited, France had lost south Germany's resources to Austria, which now used its opportunity to make war nourish war in ways somewhat less arbitrary than the French but hardly less destructive. Carl's victories also, ironically, helped Thugut stay in power and prolong the war Carl was eager to end. Even in Italy, where Bonaparte continued to defeat one Austrian army and general after another, the French position remained exposed and potentially vulnerable.

Bonaparte's victory at Rivoli in January 1797 and the subsequent fall of the great fortress of Mantua finally removed that danger. Carl, who had captured the last French positions on the right bank of the Rhine, was sent to Italy to reorganize the shattered remnants of the Austrian army, and immediately pleaded with Vienna for an armistice and peace. Even so, only Bonaparte's bold march across the Alps and into Austria to within sixty miles of Vienna ended Thugut's resistance, and it took equally bold diplomatic moves by Bonaparte to get Austria to sign the Truce of Leoben in April.[94]

This military victory and armistice, Bonaparte's personal achievements, had major domestic- and foreign-policy consequences. In the long run, they helped discredit the civilian Directory and Bonaparte's military rivals, paving the way for Bonaparte's mili-

[93] Guyot (1912: 287–304); Malmesbury (1844: iii. 260–365); Grenville (1892–1927: iii. 276, 278–80, 282–4). The quotation is in PRO 30/29/8/1, fos. 66–7; other letters on the negotiations are in fos. 51–5, 60–1, 64–6.

[94] For the problems Lazare Carnot, organizer of France's war effort, had with the army and Bonaparte, see Reinhard (1950–2: ii. 191–211). For Austria's victories and defeats, see Roider (1987: ch. 8); Hüffer (1900–1: vol. i, pp. cxiv–xxiii); Rössler (1940: i. 110–11). For the sufferings of the s. German states from both camps, and Thugut's attitudes, see Hölzle (1931: 154–9, 162–4); Blanning (1988); Thugut (1872: i, pp. 345–55, 360–76); Thugut to Cobenzl, 13 Jan. 1797, HHStA, *Russland II Correspondenz* 217, fos. 19–20.

tary dictatorship. More immediately, they meant that Bonaparte, who had already seized control of French foreign policy in regard to Italy, could now ensure that no real peace issued from the truce he had imposed on Austria. How this happened needs some explaining.

In its plans to force Austria to peace in the summer and autumn of 1796, the Directory had wavered between either expelling Austria from Italy and compensating it in Germany or the reverse strategy, usually favouring the latter. Driving Austria from both theatres seemed out of reach, especially after Carl reversed Moreau's and Jourdan's initial gains in Germany. In November General Henri Clarke, a personal friend of the Director Lazare Carnot, was sent to seek a direct peace negotiation with Thugut, based on Austria's ceding Belgium and the whole German left bank for compensations in Italy. Thugut tried to fend off Clarke, posing unrealistic demands and negotiating with him only through a subordinate in Turin. In mid-January the Directory resolved to issue an ultimatum to Vienna through Clarke demanding its minimum terms, the cession of Belgium and of Austria's Rhenish territories (i.e. not the whole left bank) for the return of Austrian territories in Italy. Clarke, however, was told to secure Bonaparte's consent. Bonaparte, who had no intention of allowing his authority in Italy to be challenged or his conquests sacrificed, settled the issue by his victories at Rivoli and Favorite and the conquest of Mantua. These scuttled the Directory's proposal and Clarke's mission and aroused such enthusiasm in the Directory and the nation that no French government could henceforth defy Bonaparte.

Bonaparte himself launched the next French peace initiative after he had driven deep into Lower Austria, offering Archduke Carl an armistice and negotiations. Thugut, unable to stem the panic in Vienna, reluctantly sent General Count Merveldt and a Neapolitan statesman, Marzio Nostrilli, Duke of Gallo, to negotiate with Clarke and Bonaparte.[95] It took Bonaparte just four days to hustle Merveldt and Gallo into the Truce of Leoben on 18 April. Outwardly, considering Austria's defeat, the terms were favourable, especially on Germany. Austria had to cede Belgium and its own left-bank territories, but recognize French ownership of only those territories France had constitutionally annexed

[95] Thugut chose Gallo partly to please the Empress, a member of the peace party and the daughter of the Neapolitan Queen, Maria Carolina, partly because he did not trust any other Austrian to negotiate, and partly to have a non-Austrian upon whom to blame an unsatisfactory peace. Roider (1987: 241–3).

(Belgium, Luxemburg, Nice, and Savoy), leaving the left-bank issue to be settled at a future peace congress on the basis of the integrity of the Reich. The main provision of Leoben was that Austria would surrender Lombardy, which would become a French-style republic, and would receive the mainland territories of the Republic of Venice in return. Venice would be compensated with the Papal Legations, which France had taken from the Pope in the Treaty of Tolentino in February. The details of execution were deliberately left vague, but the Austrians knew the answer to the main problem well enough, i.e. how France would get possession of the Venetian terra firma to deliver to Austria. With Bonaparte's troops already occupying much of Venetia, the French would provoke a revolution, overthrow the Venetian government when it tried to intervene, and install a new government which would put the territories at France's disposal.[96]

This was another normal eighteenth-century partition scheme like Poland, except that this partition would occur in one blow rather than three and that the revolution serving as its excuse needed to be arranged instead of happening spontaneously. The Austrians were at first willing co-conspirators, aware that agitation by French-sponsored radicals in Venetia had already led before Leoben to clashes between French soldiers and the inhabitants, climaxing in a serious anti-French rising at Verona on Easter Monday, 17 April. Austria had claims and aspirations to certain Venetian territories dating back to Joseph's time; Thugut had formally gained Russia's consent to compensations from Venice in their Polish partition treaty of January 1795. His insistence that Venice must be compensated with the Legations, without specifying how this would be carried out, makes Austria look like a would-be respectable businessman averting his gaze while his criminal partner starts the fire to enable the firm to collect on its insurance.

Yet there is clear evidence that Thugut did not want the Republic of Venice destroyed, just as Austria had not wanted Poland destroyed. Before Leoben he constantly tried to keep the proposed compensation deals limited and reciprocal, refusing, for example, to take Bavaria as Austria's compensation unless the Elector was compensated. He denounced the Truce of Leoben as criminal folly and advised Francis not to ratify it. Though he had no serious

---

[96] Guyot (1912: 312–15, 323–63); Biro (1957: ii. 704–29); Hüffer (1900–1: vol. i, pp. ccxxiv–ccxxxix, Nos. 46, 51–2, 72, 77–8, 81–94); Roider (1987: 229–48); DeClercq (1880–1917: i. 319–22); Zimmermann (1965: i. 114–19).

moral scruples about Venice's rights or partitions *per se*, he realized that, much as Austria needed compensations, it also needed the intermediary states which schemes like this were destroying. Venice was not as important as Poland had been or as the Reich and the German states now were, but it was still a useful aristocratic *corps intermédiaire*. Merveldt hoped that it, Sardinia, and the new north Italian republic would form a chain of buffer states separating Austria and France. In other words, Thugut's scheme was a typically Austrian piece of half-piracy in an increasingly piratical world—a territorial shuffle to strengthen Austria without further undermining the system, using the Legations which the Pope had already lost to keep the conservative Venetian Republic alive and France at bay.[97]

By the Truce of Leoben, Bonaparte overthrew the Directory's programme, which called for forcing Austria to recognize the French annexation of the left bank and promoting French goals in Germany without committing France deeply in Italy. Yet the Directors promptly voted 4–1 to ratify it. This decision was not produced by Bonaparte's arguments (that it would give France control of Italy and might lead to revolutions in Germany and Hungary worse for Austria than his victories had been), or simply by his popularity and power and the general enthusiasm for a glorious peace. The decisive factor was Bonaparte's assurance that the whole agreement was provisional; France could have the Rhine along with much of Italy.[98] With this in view the Directory instructed Clarke to improve on Leoben, which gave Austria too much of the spoils of Venice. In addition, the final peace should remove Austria entirely from the right bank of the Rhine as well as the left and give France a permanent occupation of Mainz; until then it should occupy four other right-bank fortresses. Bonaparte, though more interested in Italy, approved the offensive spirit the Directory was showing.

The stage was thus set for six months of Austro-French wrangl-

---

[97] Hüffer (1900–1: vol. i, pp. cxliii–cli, Nos. 100, 124, 129); on Austro-Papal and Franco-Papal relations and the Treaty of Tolentino, see Reinerman (1990); Hales (1961: 100–11); Guyot (1912: 344–7); on the Veronese and other anti-French risings in Italy and Bonaparte's use of them, Godechot (1981: 309–11); Zaghi (1986: 74–97); Guyot (1912: 476–85).

[98] For Bonaparte's cynical arguments for his revolutionary policy in Italy, see Napoleon (1858–70: ii. 342–6, 501–3, iii. No. 1811); for the treaties he imposed on Tuscany, the Pope, and Sardinia, DeClercq (1880–1917: i. 312–19, 322–4); for the measures he contemplated to promote revolution in Austria, Lebel (1955: 71–4); for evidence that the Directors, whatever other differences some of them had with Bonaparte, encouraged this, Homan (1971: 134–5); Ferrero (1961: 158–61).

ing between Leoben and the final peace, itself ultimately only a truce. The problem was not, as has been argued, that the Directory, by surrendering to Bonaparte, sacrificed a rational, self-limiting policy of the natural frontiers for an unlimited programme of revolutionary propaganda and expansion. The natural frontiers were anything but a clear, self-limiting goal, as Clarke's instructions to secure the Rhine frontier by acquiring strong points and a defensive glacis on the right bank demonstrate. The Directory's programme of compensations, secularizations, and French satellites in Germany, all supposed to protect the natural frontier, was at least as revolutionary as Bonaparte's programme for Italy, and dragged France deep into the bottomless mire of German politics. There were other, more important ways in which Leoben and the subsequent compromise between Bonaparte and the Directory were obstacles to a stable settlement. Bonaparte's control over French policy meant the further degradation of the French foreign ministry and subordination of civil to military power. The destruction of Venice was destabilizing in itself, and made doubly so by the manner in which it would be carried out. Bonaparte's determination to take Venetia's Ionian Isles in the Adriatic territories brought France closer to a collision with Russia in the Near East.[99] Above all, while it was not critical for purposes of a stable peace between France and Austria whether France chose Germany or Italy as its main area for expansion, it was critical that France choose one or the other, rather than threatening Austria in both theatres at once. Leoben represented a choice, the Bonaparte–Directory compromise a decision to go for both.[100]

The simultaneous threat to Austria in both spheres rapidly emerged. Taking the Veronese Easter rising as his pretext, Bonaparte overthrew the Doge's government, installed his own puppet municipal regime, occupied the city of Venice, and radicalized the country while stripping it of its wealth (among much else, the treasures of the Cathedral of San Marco). This greatly reduced the value of the Venetian territory Austria was to receive,

[99] Masson (1903: 357–96); Guyot (1911: 364–71); Hüffer (1900–1: vol. i, pp. clxii–clxvii, No. 134); Napoleon (1858–70: ii. Nos. 1748, 1756).

[100] A sign of this is the disappearance after Leoben of the idea France had constantly pushed in all its peace feelers with Austria, the Belgian–Bavarian exchange. Now the French assured Prussia that it would never happen. Biro (1957: ii. 832–3). Both Bonaparte and Thugut used balance language to discuss Leoben, with diametrically opposed meanings. Napoleon justified it because it enabled France to 'hold the balance' in Germany and Italy; Thugut denounced it because it further destroyed the old balance of possessions Russia and Prussia had already upset. See Thugut (1872: ii. No. 617; Vivenot 1870: 125–35).

raised a new revolutionary danger for Austria, and destroyed any motive for Austria to insist on compensating the new radical Venetian government with the Legations. While Thugut protested, Gallo, though unable to get Bonaparte to fulfil the terms of Leoben, signed a convention pledging Austria to conclude a final peace within two months.

Thugut tried for months to escape from this trap, proposing that France and Austria either strike a new and better deal, or return to the strict terms of Leoben, or accept a general congress. He appealed to Tsar Paul for help, and even tried to communicate with moderates at Paris behind the back of Bonaparte and the Directory.[101] Bonaparte was surprisingly patient, knowing that the longer Austria waited the worse he could make things for her. By combining the former Lombard and Cispadane Republics into the Cisalpine Republic, he turned what Austria had hoped would be a small, independent, intermediary body in northern Italy into a sizeable territorial rival occupied by 20,000 French troops, France's pressure on what was left of the Papal State suggested that it would be next to be revolutionized and partitioned, without Austrian participation, and Pius VI's death while a prisoner of France at Valence raised the spectre of a French puppet becoming the new Pope. France outflanked Austria to the south-east by taking the Ionian Isles from Venice, ignoring Thugut's complaint that, if the Mediterranean was to be a French lake, Austria should at least have the Adriatic.

The French not only ignored Austria's protests in action, but sometimes answered them by pointing to Austria's own conduct. When Austria called for the general congress which France had promised, the French asked how a congress could approve the destruction of Venice. Bonaparte readily admitted that he intended to bleed Venetia white before turning it over, but pointed out that this was the usual eighteenth-century practice, and claimed that Joseph II would have gladly accepted his peace terms—which Gallo, Merveldt, and others also believed. His most persuasive argument, however, was a warning that, if Austria would not sign a final peace, France would keep what it had, grant no compensations, and renew the war.[102]

[101] Guyot (1912: 485–91, 509–21); Biro (1957: ii. 780–2, 813–15); Fournier (1930: 114–19); Hüffer (1900–1: i. Nos. 175–221); Vivenot (1870: 135–47).

[102] Hüffer (1900–1: i. Nos. 152, 165, 167, 203, 274, 279); Napoleon (1858–70: iii. Nos. 1937, 2033, 2050–2, 2220–1, 2224). For widely divergent interpretations of Napoleon's policy in the Cispadane and Cisalpine Republics, see Zaghi (1986: 29–31, 99–229) and Ferrero (1961: 114–17, 184–9, 198–207).

Any hope that the monarchy might be restored in France or that civilians would exercise control over Bonaparte disappeared on 18 Fructidor (4 September) when three of the Directors, Paul-François Barras, Louis-Marie La Révellière, and Jean-François Reubell, aided by troops sent by Bonaparte, ousted the two moderate Directors, Carnot and Barthélemy, and purged the Assembly. The coup of Fructidor increased popular support for Bonaparte's policy of expansion in Italy and the East, a course encouraged by France's new foreign minister, Talleyrand.[103] Fructidor made Thugut give up trying to avoid a separate peace. Austria's ablest negotiator, the ambassador to Russia, Ludwig Cobenzl, was sent to deal with Bonaparte on the major unsettled territorial and strategic issues, including Mainz, Cattaro, and the Ionian Isles in the Adriatic, compensation for the Duke of Modena, the coming settlement in Germany, and above all the Austro-Cisalpine frontier in Italy. All Cobenzl's arguments and delaying tactics proved futile. Bonaparte stood fast on the issue of the Italian frontier, and even forced new concessions on Austria before the Treaty of Campo Formio was signed October 18.[104]

Territorially the treaty was still surprisingly favourable for Austria. It gave her most of Venice's former territory (the mainland up to the Adige, the city of Venice itself, Istria, and Dalmatia) in exchange for Belgium and Lombardy, and exchanged minor Austrian holdings in south-west Germany for the Archbishopric of Salzburg and the Bavarian Inn quarter, which rounded out the Austrian heartland. Austria did not have to give formal recognition to the French annexation of the entire Rhine frontier, and could thus claim to be trying to defend the Reich's independence and integrity. Though the treaty opened the floodgates to a territorial scramble in Germany by stipulating that those who lost territory on the left bank had a right to compensations on the right, France declared itself willing to return Prussia's left-bank territories, thus excluding her from compensations. The mildness of the treaty angered all the Directors. Even Bonaparte, though he was too popular and powerful to be challenged openly, defended it on grounds of expediency, arguing that it was too late in the year to resume the war and that it would give France a chance to finish with Britain.

[103] On Fructidor, see H. Mitchell (1965: 158–61, 211–13); Godechot (1981: 284–95); M. Reinhard (1950–2: ii. 225–38); Tulard (1977: 86–7). For its effects on French policy, see Guyot (1912: 522–5); Talleyrand (1891a *passim*); Biro (1957: ii. 783–6).

[104] Hüffer (1900–1: vol. i, pp. cxci–cxcix, Nos. 230–98).

Yet the treaty was a grave defeat for Austria, as Thugut saw, though he was right for the wrong reasons. Militarily and strategically, France secured the keys to Germany, northern Italy, and the Near East by acquiring Mainz, Mantua, and the Ionian Isles and Venetian Albania. Austria's attempt to save the integrity of the Empire and to score against Prussia in Germany by recognizing French acquisitions only on the upper Rhine, thus shutting Prussia out of compensations, was too clever by half. France had already made its deal with Prussia on this score. Campo Formio now gave France the opportunity to play Austria, Prussia, and the smaller German states off against each other and to be arbiter of the final German settlement, to be negotiated at Rastatt. Moreover, Austria had implicitly sanctioned the fatal principle of secularizations in the Reich by accepting the Bishopric of Salzburg in exchange for its losses in southwest Germany, and its attempt to hide this exchange and the French acquisition of Mainz in secret articles of the treaty, when these arrangements were bound to become public, further ruined Austria's reputation. Worst of all, with the timing and execution of almost every major provision left up in the air, the treaty gave Bonaparte and the Directory more opportunities to exploit—the French evacuation of Venetian territory and its transfer to Austria, the final German settlement, and the delineation and evacuation of the Cisalpine–Austrian frontier.[105] This all meant more grounds for ambitious princes and ministers in south Germany, especially Duke Frederick of Württemberg and Elector Maximilian of Bavaria and his minister, Count Maximilian Montgelas, to break away from Austria and gravitate toward France.[106]

Prussia had already done this two years before, and, given the tenacious indecision of its new king, Frederick William III (1797–1840), nothing could have brought it over to Austria's side. Yet French–Prussian relations since their treaty of August 1796 had been far from smooth, and not a few Prussians were now worried by French expansion and by the fall of Barthélemy, the trusted architect of the Peace of Basel. Campo Formio made sure that even those would co-operate with France rather than Austria at Rastatt.[107]

As for Britain, Leoben and the subsequent Austro-French nego-

---

[105] DeClercq (1880–1917: i. 335–44); Biro (1957: ii. 937–9, 945–9); Fournier (1930: 128–30); Zaghi (1956: 7–11); Napoleon (1858–70: iii. No. 2307). For Thugut's cries of despair, see Thugut (1872: ii. Nos. 671, 678, 694, 696).

[106] Aretin (1967: i. 344–5); Weis (1971: 324–32).

[107] Bailleu (1881–7: i. Nos. 79–148); Wollstein (1978).

tiations dealt further blows to a ministry already deep in trouble. Repeated British attempts to gain support from Tsar Paul I or to prevent a separate Austro-French peace by getting Russia and Prussia to arrange a general congress failed.[108] The underground war against France went badly; one spy ring in Paris was broken up in early 1797 and in May a wider royalist conspiracy with British connections was discovered, to be crushed later.[109] Defeats on the Continent coincided with relative failure and high casualties in the West Indies, while naval mutinies, financial troubles, and radical agitation threatened the war effort in England, and latent rebellion in Ireland was made more dangerous by the active conspiracy of *émigré* United Irish leaders with the Directory.[110] All this moved Pitt, despite the resistance of Grenville and George III, to another try for peace. The French government agreed to receive Malmesbury once more, though insisting that this time he must be authorized to sign a definitive treaty.

Not much need be said of the second round of desultory Anglo-French negotiations at Lille from mid-June to late September. The initial French demands for the restitution of all Britain's colonial conquests from France, Spain, and Holland, plus a series of other substantive and symbolic concessions, nearly wrecked the talks in late June. But Talleyrand, who replaced Charles Delacroix as foreign minister in July, genuinely wanted peace, as did Malmesbury and the chief French negotiators Hugues Maret and C.-L. Le Tourneur. Malmesbury, lacking political room for manœuvre, succeeded by secret negotiations in narrowing the differences down to the question of whether Britain would have to restore all its colonial conquests or could retain some as compensation for French Continental gains, especially the Dutch colonies of the Cape of Good Hope and Ceylon. An internal struggle within both governments proved the decisive factor. Grenville, Windham, the King, and others resisted what they termed a humiliating surrender, while in France three Directors opposed peace and some military leaders backed them. Talleyrand's only hope was to carry through a peace agreement in Paris by surprise; this disappeared when Pitt, facing opposition in Britain and hoping

[108] Guyot (1912: 372–97); Grenville (1892–1927: iii. 296–301, 307–13, 315–21, 328–33); various dispatches, Grenville to Whitworth, Nov. 1796 to June 1797, BL Add. MS 59193, fos. 57–79.

[109] On the general failure of the underground war in late 1796 and 1797, see H. Mitchell (1965: 103–99, 254–5); Fryer (1965: 90–117, 198–230, 249–68).

[110] M. Elliott (1982: 26–145); McDowell (1979: 351–89, 486–90, 500–21); M. Duffy (1987: 295, 330–4).

for French concessions, flatly rejected a return to the colonial status quo ante. The coup of 18 Fructidor put the French war party clearly in charge, and France's new negotiators essentially returned to the original hard line, leading to Malmesbury's requesting and receiving his passports. Despite shadowy efforts to rescue the peace effort through offers of massive bribes to leading French politicians, especially the Director Barras, the initiative finally collapsed in early October.[111]

The question most historians have asked about these negotiations, whether some kind of peace treaty could have been reached in 1797 and who was responsible for frustrating it, is legitimate; the answers naturally vary. It makes more sense, however, to ask whether France and Britain really wanted peace, or understood what it meant. Did they believe that their war, having become futile and counter-productive, should be ended once for all? Did they understand that peace meant replacing their secular struggle for supremacy by some structure for coexistence between themselves and with the rest of Europe?

These questions answer themselves. France and Britain in 1797 were still miles away from any such notions. Britain's current problems, serious though not crippling, made many Britons want to end this particular war, but not the long-term struggle with France. Some difficulties, like early industrial unrest or discontent with an unreformed semi-parliamentary system, were actually easier to manage during a war against the traditional enemy. The British economy was not really vulnerable to French economic warfare, at least not yet. War increased the danger of rebellion in Ireland, but also helped justify the drastic measures taken to suppress it. Anyway, in late 1797 the immediate dangers from the bank crisis, the Irish problem, English radicalism, and the Nore and Spithead naval mutinies were fairly well under control.[112] The British had not lost the war militarily, or lost hope of gains from it; plenty of colonial and world positions remained to be conquered. They had only temporarily lost their heart for it; the more the French perceived this, the more bellicose and demanding they became, and the more this helped to revive flagging British spirits.[113] The same points held even more true for France. There

[111] Guyot (1912: 400–11, 422–56): Malmesbury (1844: iii. 369–569); Rose (1911: 322–7); Grenville (1892–1927: vol. iii, pp. xlvi–li, 377–82).

[112] Emsley (1979: 41–64); Rose (1911: 304–16); Crouzet (1958: i. 39–90, 102–7).

[113] For British colonial and commercial gains to 1797 and their continued hopes and undertakings in this arena, see Fugier (1954: 102–3); Parkinson (1954: 59–149); Ehrman (1983: 500–7, 566–7); Geggus (1983). For samples of the British debate

the government was winning the war, not losing it, and internal troubles pushed it more toward war than peace. The lesson of Fructidor was that, even if peace might promote political stability and the rule of law in the long term, only military victory and the use of force would enable the regime to survive right now.

More important still, even those who favoured a peace treaty at this time did not want it for the purpose of ending the Anglo-French struggle for power, or altering its character decisively, but in order to improve their side's long-range prospects in it. Malmesbury, urging his colleagues to accept the colonial status quo ante, argued that peace would cause France to sink into chaos. Frenchmen expected peace to promote revolution in England and Ireland. The British anticipated that peaceful commerce would widen the industrial and commercial lead they had opened up over France, and many Frenchmen agreed with them. This was one reason Reubell wanted to continue the war, and why the Directory demanded that Britain formally renounce the Eden Treaty. France was already organizing itself and its dependencies for a protectionist economic campaign against Britain which it would have waged regardless of any peace treaty; Napoleon's Continental blockade would later develop from it. From a military standpoint, each side, while negotiating for peace, constantly worried about its position in the next round of war. Pitt, for example, was worried about a treaty France negotiated with Portugal, later rejected by Lisbon.[114]

Thus neither power wanted to conceal the hatchet, much less bury it. And even had they wanted peace, could they have constructed it? On what basis could they have overcome their hostility and lived in coexistence, involving what general system for themselves and Europe? The peace they later reached at Amiens provides no answer: it would fail almost immediately. A more plausible model for an Anglo-French peace is the one France and Russia reached at Tilsit in 1807: a division of the areas over which Britain and France were fighting into their respective spheres of influence and/or control. This is not conjecture. The actual negotiations show that those who advocated peace implicitly recognized that a divided hegemony was the only way peace could be reached or could work.

over peace, see Malmesbury (1844: iii. 396–9); Grenville (1892–1927: iii. 368–9, 378–9, 381–2); Windham to Canning, 21 Sept. 1797, Canning Papers (Leeds), 34a.

[114] Fugier (1954: 108–11); Bruguière (1973: 468–75); Groote (1969: 120–3); Malmesbury (1844: iii. 524–7); Guyot (1912: 456–75); Nabonne (1951: 52–61).

Yet such schemes for peace, often proposed and sometimes tried, seldom prove stable, for two main reasons. The first is that the two sides either cannot agree on a division of the respective spheres (as was the case here) or quickly fall out over it after the agreement is reached (as happened after Tilsit). The other is that, even when they do agree, their joint hegemony proves unacceptable to other major and minor players, provoking conflict and systemic breakdown. In other words, hegemonic partners need not merely to satisfy each other, but also to provide a minimum of satisfaction for other actors; their shared hegemony has to be benign or at least tolerable for the other players.

There is plenty of evidence that, in 1797, the kind of peace based on shared hegemony which a few Britons and Frenchmen dimly and fitfully envisioned would not have been benign or tolerable, but exploitative. Malmesbury repeatedly urged the French to make the Dutch and Spanish pay for an Anglo-French peace, and the French advocates of peace echoed his advice; the fact that the French government declined to do so proved a major stumbling-block in the negotiations. Malmesbury was openly contemptuous of Austria and willing to let France impose any terms on Austria it wanted to, and was as indifferent as other Britons to the fate of Germany, Italy, and other intermediary bodies. His only Continental concern was for good Anglo-Russian relations; Britain might need Russia in the future.

In the face of this, the recognition of a few statesmen (Talleyrand, for example) that Britain and France needed to stay out of each other's way for peace to endure[115] is largely meaningless. Neither state had any serious ideas for a general system of European peace in 1797, or would have for a long time to come.

[115] On Talleyrand's role, see Lacour-Gayet (1928–30: i. 215–19, 235–40, 244–57, 280–3); Talleyrand (1891*b*).

4
The Second Coalition, 1798–1802

A FTER Campo Formio and the breakdown of Anglo-French negotiations, the war could have simmered on inconclusively between Britain and France. Instead, it flared up quickly into another great Continental struggle. The reasons begin with one of the strangest episodes of the era.

I. EGYPT AND THE MEDITERRANEAN

Behind the French expedition to Egypt lay the difficulty France had in getting at England. Following the collapse of the peace talks at Lille, the Directors, particularly Reubell, again took up the idea of a cross-Channel invasion, despite the failure of an earlier effort and the fact that France did little to support the insurrectionary plans of the United Irishmen led by Wolfe Tone. But Bonaparte, given command of the proposed invasion force, soon decided that he would not sacrifice his popularity in this hopeless enterprise. With invasion infeasible and revolutionary subversion and raids on British commerce clearly inadequate, the idea of undermining Britain's will and capacity to fight by seizing Egypt and threatening the route to India seemed more attractive.[1] Other purposes, however, were at least as important. The Directors wanted Bonaparte out of France, while Bonaparte was eager for

---

[1] Nabonne (1951: ch. 7); Lean (1970: 6–7); M. Elliott (1982; 1989: 202–15); Bertaud (1988: 225–8). Historians still debate whether the expedition was seriously intended to threaten the British in India or presented an actual threat. Edward Ingram (1981: 42–52, 292–303, 312–13, and *passim*) defends the view of Henry Dundas that it genuinely menaced India, arguing that the French could have advanced on India from Egypt and that Egypt could have become a base for French domination of the Arab world, which would threaten the routes to India even though Britain controlled the seas. This certainly has some validity; the British were bound to consider the French move a threat and to tighten their hold on India in response, as actually happened. However, Ingram's impressive body of evidence seems to me on the whole to support Grenville's view that the expedition was a strategic blunder and that the French army should be trapped in Egypt and allowed to die on the vine. Arthur Wellesley, the British commander in India, believed that France's position in Egypt was too weak and risky to endanger India or to serve in the long run as a base for any other conquests.

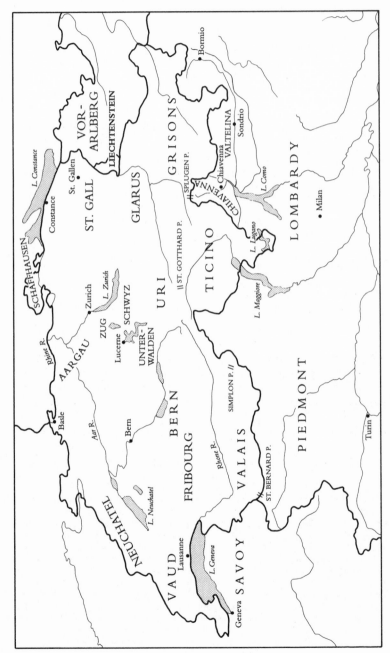

Switzerland

action and hoped to see the government decay further in his absence.[2] The expedition also intrinsically appealed to his sense of destiny and desire to emulate the military heroes of antiquity. He already possessed stepping-stones to the East in the Ionian Isles and Venetian Albania; now Egypt beckoned, ancient, mysterious, and vulnerable.[3]

Talleyrand also argued that Egypt would replace France's lost colonies in terms of colonial goods, maritime and commercial development, international prestige, and domestic morale. The Levant, especially Egypt, was an area of traditional French trade and influence not yet deeply penetrated by Britain, in easy contact with France via the Mediterranean. Talleyrand may have hoped that France could expand here without colliding head-on with Britain, and that a move into Egypt would prevent more dangerous French actions in Europe; and he certainly argued that the Ottoman Porte, once again friendly to France, might consent to a peaceful take-over of Egypt and become a useful military ally for France against Russia now and against Austria in the future.[4] Yet even these superficially rational arguments should not be seen as decisive. Talleyrand was in the same chauvinist mood as most Frenchmen; the expedition was fundamentally an aggressive impulse followed by a weak divided government for domestic more than foreign-policy reasons, without serious calculation of its feasibility and likely results.[5]

However reckless the thinking behind the expedition, it was carefully prepared and started out brilliantly in mid-1798, with Bonaparte managing to seize Malta quickly, evade Admiral Horatio Nelson's fleet, land in Egypt, and destroy the armies of its Mameluke rulers. Then luck ran out. Nelson almost wiped out the French fleet at Aboukir Bay near Alexandria in August, cutting the army's communications with France. The British commander in India, Arthur Wellesley, supported by his brother Richard as Governor-General and Henry Dundas as President of the Board of Control, exploited the putative French threat to India to wage a campaign against Tipu Sultan of Mysore and the Mahrattas Confederacy. Wellesley's victories, if they did not entirely end the threat to British control of India, did establish

[2] Zaghi (1969: 182-5); Tulard (1977: 95-6); Groote and Müller (1968: 16-17).

[3] Napoleon (1858-70: iii. Nos. 2103-7); J. Howard (1961: No. 258); H. Parker (1979: 72-88); Dard (1937: 21-5); Fournier (1930: i. 111).

[4] Talleyrand (1891a: 254-9, 272-3, 337-41); Lacour-Gayet (1928-30: i. ch. 17); Lokke (1932: 166-75, 182-203); Silvera (1974); Naff (1960: 172-4, 180-1).

[5] Zaghi (1969: 175-9, 189-200, 210-16); Rodger (1964: 18-27).

British paramountcy more openly and permanently and launched Britain on its Great Game in Asia, the drive to secure the land and sea routes to India—a game already competing with the Great Game in America and soon to overshadow it.[6]

More immediately, the expedition galvanized Britain's whole war effort. Seeing the French prepare at Toulon for an expedition against an unknown target, the British took defensive measures in the Mediterranean, the Indian Ocean, the Red Sea, the Channel, Portugal, and Ireland—every theatre but the actual one. Just as the French left Toulon, rebellion broke out in Ireland, but by July the Irish movement, never formidable, was brutally crushed, along with two small expeditions France sent to support it. These events, linking the foreign and domestic threats in the public mind, helped to popularize the war, strengthen the government, and make Britons accept the higher taxes and prices, recruitment, and labour shortages it caused. They also prompted the government to de-emphasize the West Indies in favour of the European theatre. Then Nelson's victory at Aboukir Bay gave Britain a new national hero, and changed danger into triumph.[7] Britain was still not fully secure. Bonaparte's army remained a menace, invading Syria after Turkey's declaration of war and threatening to march on Constantinople. While the British fleet besieged Malta, a French fleet escaped from Brest in April 1799, underlining the ever-present danger that the French and Spanish fleets would break out and combine to attack the divided and overstretched British forces in the Mediterranean or Atlantic.[8] None the less, Aboukir Bay gave Britain a great morale and military boost, put the French on the defensive, and brought home more clearly to the British the strategic and commercial importance of the eastern Mediterranean for Europe and India alike. If the Royal Navy now had more to attack and defend (Naples, Syria, Malta, Egypt), it also had more bases from which to operate and to harass France.[9]

The expedition had consequences even worse for France on the Continent, first in Russia. Catherine's death in late 1796 had undone all Britain's and Austria's Sisyphean labours to bring it into the war. Paul I ascended the throne determined to pursue

[6] Ibid. 41–53; Ingram (1981: 115–53, 166–77, 188–9); Butler (1973: 122–91, 242–50); Alder (1972: 18–22); Auckland (1861: vi. 68–70); Huttenback (1961); Förster (1988).

[7] Zaghi (1969: 188, 222–3); Rodger (1964: 38–41); M. Elliott (1982: ch. 6); McDowell (1979: ch. 17); Rose (1911: i. ch. 16); Emsley (1979: 65–73); Dickinson (1985); S. Palmer (1988: 140–3); M. Duffy (1987: 319).

[8] Rodger (1964: 78–84, 96–117); Ingram (1981: 262–6).

[9] Ibid. 36–42, 54–7, 62–7; Crimmins (1988: 221–36).

peace and domestic reform. Though his earlier ideas about constitutional changes to turn Russia into a *Rechtsstaat* soon disappeared and his reign would become more violent and despotic than any since Peter the Great, he remained determined that his foreign policy must be more peaceful and moral than his mother's. His chief minister, Chancellor Aleksandr Bezborodko, supported this. Yet neither of them was indifferent to Russia's national interests, especially in the Near East. France's seizure of the Ionian Isles in June 1797 had put Russia on the alert; in February 1798 Russia began arming to defend the Black Sea against a French fleet, and considering how to get the Ionian Isles away from France into safer hands. (Characteristically, Russia proposed that Austria should take them and compensate France in Germany.) Poland also caused Russia constant, if little-publicized, anxiety, especially the thought that Austria might join France in restoring Poland's independence. Paul also opposed France out of a strong belief in monarchic legitimacy; in March he invited Louis XVIII to take up residence in Russia, and began supporting Condé's *émigré* forces.

Still, it took Bonaparte's seizure of Malta on the way to Egypt to move Paul to an active anti-French policy. The Tsar took a strong personal interest in the Maltese Order, and considered himself and Russia the protectors of small states in Europe against great-power predators. Endorsing Neapolitan and Sardinian protests against the French seizure of Malta, he moved an army of observation to the Turkish frontier on the Dnestr, began promising aid to Austria, and ordered the Black Sea fleet, under Admiral Fedor Ushakov, to cruise near the Bosporus ready to aid Turkey if needed.[10]

Not content with alienating the new Tsar, France forced the Ottoman Empire into war. No ruler had less reason or desire to join the European conflict than Sultan Selim III, and particularly to fight his old ally France in alliance with his old enemy Russia. He needed peace to carry on his military and administrative reforms, already blighted by the war with Russia in 1787–92 and by his struggles with rebellious pashas and subjects in various parts of his empire, especially the Balkans. The French Revolution and the wars attending it had prompted the Porte to seek new openings in Europe for information and diplomatic relations, but the struggle

[10] Saul (1970: 52–68); Zaghi (1956: 306–11); Rodger (1964: 88); *Sbornik* (1867–1916: ii. 166–73); Vorontsov (1870–95: x. 249–50). On Paul's education and aims, see Ransel (1979: 1–16; 1975: chs. 8, 10).

itself left the Ottoman government cold, or, if anything, mildly sympathetic towards France. Yet just when France, by defeating Austria, had revived its old influence at Constantinople, it destroyed this by a series of overt challenges—the seizure of the Ionian Isles and Venetian Albania, a French war of propaganda and subversion among the Greeks, French encouragement to rebels against the Sultan, especially Ali Pasha of Janina in Albania and Epirus and Pasvan Oglu in Little Wallachia, and, topping it all, the invasion of Egypt. The folly of Talleyrand's belief that he could persuade or bribe the Turks to give up Egypt was matched by the arrogance of Bonaparte in thinking that he could break Ottoman resistance as easily as he had broken Egypt's, through military force, selective terror, and promises of protection for Islam.

The Sultan and his Grand Council, having no choice, declared war on France and accepted a Russian alliance in September 1798. The Turkish forces defending Syria, supplied and stiffened by the British navy and troops led by Sir Sidney Smith, stopped Bonaparte in the spring of 1799, forcing him to lift the siege of Acre and return to Egypt. Worse still, a Russo-Turkish naval expedition moved through the Straits and captured the Ionian Isles, whose occupation by France had started the whole Eastern adventure and whose strategic value Bonaparte rated higher than that of Italy. Meanwhile the Kingdom of Naples, reacting to the seizure of Malta, the French threat to its commerce, and the anti-revolutionary zeal of its Queen Maria Carolina, welcomed Nelson's fleet and gave it a base from which to control the central Mediterranean.[11]

II. THE SLIDE INTO CONTINENTAL WAR

The Egyptian expedition thus proved a political and strategic disaster for France in the Near East and Mediterranean. It would not seriously affect France's hold on Western Europe, however, unless Austria rejoined the war, which France had the means of preventing. True, Thugut soon after the Treaty of Campo Formio began seeking support for Austria in case of a new war, especially from Russia. Yet even he realized that Austria had compelling

---

[11] Guyot (1912: 832–53); Clogg (1969: 87–94); Shaw (1971: 71–127, 248–63); Naff (1960: 117–97, 228–48); Rodger (1964: 88–91); Saul (1970: 80–92); Napoleon (1858–70: iv. Nos. 2662, 2683).

reasons for peace. A powerful party in Vienna argued that another war would destroy Austria, and that the terms of Campo Formio were acceptable. Thugut, though he disagreed, was determined not to let Austria again be exploited and abandoned by its allies as it had been in the First Coalition. Only one thing could bring Austria back into the war, French provocations and threats—and they did.

The French challenge to Austria was most obvious in Italy. In February 1798 the Cisalpine Republic, whose independence was guaranteed by the Treaty of Campo Formio, was turned into a French satellite by an offensive–defensive alliance imposed by Bonaparte. The treaty required the Republic automatically to join any war declared by France, forced it to maintain 25,000 French soldiers at its own expense, and delivered the fortresses of Mantua, Peschiera, and Ferrara into French hands. A related commercial treaty deprived the Republic of control over its own commerce.[12]

French treatment of the Papal State was less directly threatening to Austria but even more ruthless and illegal. The failure of the royalist coup of Fructidor in September 1797 had revived French Jacobinism at home and French anticlericalism abroad. Rome wanted reconciliation and peace with France, but its accumulated wealth made it a tempting target. The Directory applied strong internal and external pressure on the Papal State, among other things permitting the Cisalpine Republic to occupy papal territory. France's opportunity to move in came in late December 1797, when, in the course of a riot in Rome, papal police invaded the French embassy and a French general was killed in a mêlée. The Directory, working closely with Bonaparte, recalled the French envoy, Bonaparte's brother Joseph, and ordered General Alexandre Berthier, in command of French forces already occupying the papal port of Ancona on the Adriatic, to occupy Rome and establish a Roman Republic. Talleyrand warned Austria and Naples that any interference or protest from them would bring a French declaration of war or French occupation of still more Italian territory. Berthier, setting off for Rome in early February, sent ahead severe demands on the Pope, expecting them to be rejected; the papal government disappointed him by accepting them. This momentary obstacle to a French take-over disappeared when, on 15 February, revolutionaries who had been released from Roman jails proclaimed a Roman Republic, thus saving Berthier the trouble of doing so as his troops occupied Rome.

[12] Guyot (1912: 598–600); DeClercq (1880–1917: i. 350–4).

France's seizure of Rome, among other things, frustrated the Cisalpine Republic's territorial ambitions in the Papal State, as it was intended to do. It also led to an orgy of depredations by French soldiers, collaborators, and army provisioners, in which Berthier's successor, General André Masséna, cheerfully joined. Pius VI, meanwhile, was exiled as a French prisoner, first in Florence and later in Valence in France.[13]

The Kingdom of Sardinia-Piedmont, caught between France and the Cisalpine Republic, escaped Rome's fate, but not by much. In June the French commander in northern Italy, General Guillaume Brune, the Cisalpine government, and the French ministers to Piedmont and the Ligurian Republic (Genoa), acting without authorization by Paris, joined in attempting to overthrow the government at Turin and establish a republic. The move failed, but Piedmont was forced to accept French protection and the occupation of Turin, and to pay heavily for them. Genoa was also squeezed ruthlessly for contributions. Tuscany escaped fairly lightly through careful appeasement of France, while Naples managed to get away with open hostility for the time being under the protection of the British navy.[14]

Internally, France's peacetime rule over Italy resembled its general foreign policy, a continuation of war by other means. Bitter quarrels raged between civil and military authorities, with civil commissaires sent from Paris regularly proving unable to control massive corruption and abuses by the army and its generals. Local radicals fought for power with aristocrats and moderate reformers. *Pace* Jacques Godechot, the problem was basically not that the army defied the civil authorities, nor was it, *pace* Carlo Zaghi, that Bonaparte's moderate, rational policy was being supplanted by the senselessly provocative one of the Directory. The Directors' policies may have differed from Bonaparte's in form and efficiency, but their goals and directives were equally cynical and exploitative. Raymond Guyot's verdict is better: under the late Directory, saved once more by a coup in May 1798, this time against the left, French policy went out of control, becoming revolutionary in the most primitive sense.[15] This not only alien-

[13] Guyot (1912: 601–24); Hales (1961: 112–15); Napoleon (1858–70: iii. No. 2404); Godechot (1937: ii. 11–41).
[14] Guyot (1912: 785–828); Zaghi (1956: 44–6, 80–91); Troisi (1979); Napoleon (1858–70: iv. No. 2502).
[15] Godechot (1937: ii. 160–294); Zaghi (1956: 141–84); Guyot (1912: 784–5). Zaghi's more recent work (1986) maintains his earlier favourable verdict on Bonaparte's Italian policy before Campo Formio.

ated the peoples France ruled, discouraged potential allies, and provoked Austria into war, but also cost France a good chance to organize northern and central Italy into useful intermediary bodies under its leadership. The Prussian minister at Paris, Sandoz-Rollin, repeatedly reported that France was throwing away a historic opportunity for the sake of direct control and loot.[16]

Austria's policy in Italy may not have been much more far-sighted; it was certainly less effective. It tried repeatedly to gain compensations and an improved strategic frontier, more from the Cisalpine Republic and Piedmont than from France, and always failed. Nor could it stop France from turning its smaller neighbours into puppets. The Cisalpine Republic's vice-president, Melzi d'Eril, disillusioned with France, turned to Austria for help in forming an independent north Italian buffer state between France and Austria; Vienna turned him down.[17]

Meanwhile French policy made Switzerland almost as great a menace to Austria as Italy. France's earlier restraint (it had expanded in Switzerland only by annexing parts of the Prince-Bishopric of Basel in 1793 on popular initiative) was due both to the skill and moderation of French representatives like Barthélemy and to the obvious value of Swiss neutrality for a beleaguered France. During the previous war the allies, especially Britain, had abused Swiss neutrality more than the French had. But Bonaparte's conquests and ambitions in Italy had raised the strategic value of Switzerland for the control of vital passes connecting Germany and Italy. The Swiss cantons, despite the modest prosperity they enjoyed, had internal problems which France could easily exploit—conflicts between oligarchs and democrats, interventionists and neutralists, unitarists and defenders of cantonal independence, Bern and its dependency the Vaud, and other socioeconomic, linguistic, and religious tensions.

The idea of French intervention in Switzerland arose late in the first war, the product of collaboration between the Director Reubell and certain émigré Swiss radicals, notably Peter Ochs and the philosophe Frédéric-César La Harpe. Ochs and La Harpe wanted to create a democratic united Switzerland; Reubell wanted to punish France's enemies and establish French domination; Bonaparte wanted the Valais and the Simplon Pass for the Cisalpine Republic, to which he had already attached the Grison dependencies of Valtelina, Chiavenna, and Bormio. The Treaty of

---

[16] Bailleu (1881–7: i. 178–81, 214–18).
[17] Zaghi (1956: 28–39, 48, 54–7, 60–5, 272–5).

Campo Formio, by requiring Austria to cede France the Frickthal in southern Germany to give to Switzerland, laid the basis for a possible Franco-Swiss exchange of territory and alliances. The Swiss Diet (*Tagsatzung*) at Bern might under pressure have accepted an alliance with France. Ochs, La Harpe, Reubell and Bonaparte, however, decided on wider goals at Paris in December 1797. France should intervene to support a revolution in the Vaud against its overlords at Bern, out of which they expected a French annexation of the Valais and a unitary constitution for Switzerland to follow.

Like most such conspiracies, this one failed to proceed according to plan, but France went ahead anyway, declaring the Vaud under its protection. The failure of the Swiss Diet to organize any common defence against the French enabled local radicals and French leaders on the spot, especially the French chargé d'affaires and Generals J.-F.-Xavier Ménard and Brune, to carry the plan further. In February the French army invaded Switzerland. The Vaud and lower Valais were occupied, Bern's resistance was broken, and a unitary constitution drawn up by Ochs and patterned after that of France was proclaimed for Switzerland. It soon became obvious that few Swiss liked it, but only the five forest cantons of eastern Switzerland organized a stubborn resistance, and this was crushed by late summer.

In the mean time, the French annexed Geneva and imposed contributions on Bern and other cantons, ostensibly to cover the costs of liberation, actually to pay the Army of Italy and to support French generals in the style to which they were accustomed. In August an offensive-defensive alliance was imposed on Switzerland which put it under French guarantee and promised it some commercial advantages, while pledging the Swiss to supply France an indefinite number of auxiliaries and giving France control of two vital military and commercial routes between France and northern Italy. While the Swiss suffered less under French control than other peoples, the same struggles for control between French civil and military authorities went on here as elsewhere, along with the contest between Swiss radicals and conservatives over the new, unworkable constitution.[18] Here too France sacrificed a valuable *corps intermédiaire* for direct military and fiscal gains.

Though France's take-over in Switzerland threatened Austria in

---

[18] Bonjour (1965: i. 121–55); Guyot (1912: 624–69, 740–7, 772–7, 782–3); Godechot (1937: ii. chs. 2–4); Oechsli (1903–13: i. 113–19, 145–208); Pfulg (1961).

southern Germany, Italy, and its hereditary domains (in fact, Austria's province of Vorarlberg was mentioned in French–Swiss discussions of territorial exchanges), Austria's response was again feeble. It had a bad reputation itself in Switzerland, and felt the French menace more directly in Germany. The main danger there was no longer French revolutionary subversion, if it ever had been. The Revolution's initial impact had quickly dissipated; Germany was nowhere ripe for revolution. Broadly speaking, Prussia was too progressive and well governed; German Austria too loyal; much of North Germany too backward; and most of the rest, including the Hanseatic towns, the Rhineland, and the south, too fragmented, diverse in its discontents, and set in its local loyalties. There was considerable political discontent, aroused by the slow decay of the Reich and breakdown of the old legal and moral order, incessant political, dynastic, and territorial quarrels, the Reich's blurred lines of legal authority and sovereignty, and the inability of the smaller states to organize themselves for reform or common defense. Modernizing reformers clashed in various principalities with traditional élites, princes with estate assemblies, privileged classes and status groups with the unprivileged. Germany's social and economic development was very diverse and uneven, ranging from deep agrarian poverty and feudalism in some areas to a relatively free and prosperous peasantry and commercial prosperity and nascent industrialization in others. But all these conditions, if they made Germany ripe for change, served to inhibit a general revolution or a common reaction to French events or ideas.

They also helped make and keep Germany a power vacuum inviting foreign intervention, the likely arena and major prize of any general war. This promoted what ultimately happened, a German revolution of sorts deriving, not from French revolutionary ideas or propaganda, but from France's military power and foreign policy. Here too a familiar pattern emerged, in which 'liberation' almost immediately gave way to exploitation, and conquest replaced and wrecked French influence and various French ideas for a new Germany. The idea, repeatedly promoted by some Frenchmen, of neutralizing the Reich, confining it to a Third Germany separate from Austria and Prussia, and putting it under French protection, was nullified in order to gain territory or court Prussia. A persistent debate went on between annexationists and anti-annexationists at Paris, but ultimately the need for military victory and fiscal survival would decide the case for the former. The Rhine, adopted as France's natural frontier in the course of this debate, served to draw France beyond it for security, while the Rhine made little sense as an economic, linguistic, ethnic, or political frontier. By 1795 at the latest, support for France from German revolutionary collaborators had disappeared; not a little of later anti-French hostility in Germany, as elsewhere, came from disillusioned Jacobins. This was no great loss for France. More important was the sacrifice of the chance to build up a French clientele among the smaller German states, especially in south-west Germany, offering them neutrality and protection and mediating various disputes between estates and princes—also discarded at this time in favour of direct control and contributions. Yet French leaders did not especially regret these lost opportunities. For republican France, like other great powers, cash, control, and power were more important than influence, sympathy, or ideological principle.[19]

Even if French occupation and annexation of the left bank may over the long term have favourably affected German economic development, the immediate effects were to divide a natural economic unit along the Rhine and dislocate its growing trade. Repeated military campaigns, by overthrowing governments and ousting princes and their courts, further ruined local economies on the right bank already damaged by French levies, requisitioning, and looting. Though Germany would eventually recover economically under French rule (German trade with France, especially between the two halves of the divided Rhineland, actually grew in the latter 1790's, much of it in the form of smuggling), economic independence was ruled out. The annexed territories were quickly incorporated into France's protectionist system, while the rest of Germany within France's reach became the target of a French economic imperialism ostensibly designed to defeat Britain, actually intended to ruin or subjugate France's economic rivals.[20]

Thus by 1797 France was overtaking Austria and Prussia as the leader in undermining the Reich and the old corporate German liberties (*Libertät*) which it represented. In the process it also discredited French *liberté* as a replacement.[21] The other French revolutionary slogans, equality and fraternity, never figured seriously in French policy toward Germany. This left modernity as the legacy of the French Revolution to Germany. It would receive this from Bonaparte, as a poisoned gift.

[19] Blanning (1983: 72–7 and *passim*; 1974: 273–334); Dufraisse (1973a: 103–25); Dumont (1983); Bitterauf (1905: 15–17, 38–44, 68–71).

[20] Blanning (1983: ch. 4); Dufraisse (1973a: 508–13; 1983).

[21] Dumont (1978); Raumer (1957).

Campo Formio had no effect on France's occupation policies or the civil–military struggle in the Rhineland.[22] It did, however, require France somehow to bring its treaty with Austria into line with its earlier conflicting agreements with Prussia and other states, and to secure the Reich's formal consent to its losses at a Congress at Rastatt. French policy-makers, undisturbed by these problems, expected Rastatt to improve upon Campo Formio, enabling France to keep the whole left bank plus bridgeheads on the right bank, to construct a glacis of independent states under French influence beyond the Rhine, and to push Prussia and Austria eastward. They differed only on how extensive the German territorial changes should be, whether the independent states under France's wing should be ruled by their traditional princes or by 'free peoples', and how aggressive a character to give their proposed alliance with Prussia against Austria. On these points Talleyrand held views more moderate than those of the Abbe Siéyès and Bonaparte, who during his brief appearance at Rastatt urged Prussia to join France in despoiling Austria. He was not alone in this; another French diplomat urged Prussia to ally with Bavaria to divide up Bohemia.

In mid-April, the possibility of a Franco-Austrian war arose over an incident at Vienna in which a mob insulted the flag of the French embassy. The French ambassador, General Bernadotte, threatened to break relations, and Bonaparte, who had left Rastatt, was ordered to return to demand satisfaction from Austria. But with the Congress going extremely well for France (after the Rhine frontier was conceded and the principle of compensations through secularizations adopted, a general scramble for territories ensued in which everyone sought France's help), war with Austria would have been an unnecessary distraction. Bonaparte left for the Egyptian expedition, while Talleyrand, no friend of Austria's but in favour of peace on the Continent, offered to negotiate the embassy incident, hinting that other subjects such as Italy and Switzerland might be discussed as well.[23]

This sealed an easy victory for France at Rastatt, more the result of German disunity and weakness than French power. Only a feeble resistance was put up, by Austria as leader of the Reich and by the Elector of Mainz as leader of the ecclesiastical

[22] Bitterauf (1905: 36–63); Blanning (1983 passim); Dufraisse (1973b: 125–32; 1964); Godechot (1937: ii. 327–43).

[23] Zaghi (1956: 13–29, 121–39); Bitterauf (1905: 56–7, 73–82); Bailleu (1881–7: vol. i, pp. xl–xliii, 35–7); Guyot (1912: 667–82); Adler-Bresse (1976: vol. i, pp. xxxi, cxvii–cxviii).

estates. Austria and Prussia were unable to co-operate, though neither really wanted a territorial revolution or to be blamed for permitting one; the ecclesiastical estates were easy targets, the other estates were war-weary and greedy, and the most important south German states, Bavaria and Württemberg, feared and admired France, Prussia, and Russia while hating Austria. As usual, balance-of-power arguments were used to justify anything and everything. Bavaria, Württemberg, and other states who attached their wagons to France's star could claim, as Bavaria's Montgelas did, that, with the Reich dying and Austria and Prussia fighting over its remains, their aggrandizement as independent states and alliance with France would re-establish the German balance.[24]

Establishing a new French-led system in Germany would prove more difficult than undermining the old, however. Siéyès, sent on special mission to Berlin in mid-1798 to negotiate an alliance, came back empty-handed. Some Prussians supported his proposals, but more feared entanglement, all resented his arrogant style, and some, including the King, were becoming nervous at France's rapid growth in power and Austria's decline.[25] The Congress of Rastatt dragged on indecisively into 1799, bringing France potential clients in Third Germany but not the general protectorate over the smaller states earlier envisioned, and further convincing Thugut that only another coalition, this time formed by Russia and including Prussia, could check French expansion. Though he accepted Bonaparte's and Talleyrand's offers of negotiations in the forlorn hope of making gains in Italy that would render Austria's position there defensible, the actual negotiations in mid-1798 at Seltz in Alsace convinced Austria's negotiator, Ludwig Cobenzl, normally an optimist, that another war was unavoidable.[26]

Both powers slid toward war in a manner which makes their conflict look inevitable; they doubtless felt that it was. Yet each would really have preferred a mutually profitable peace, and such a peace was at least theoretically possible. In mid-1798 no great gap existed between France's basic aims in Germany and

[24] Aretin (1967: i. 346–52, 361–71; ii. *Akten* 57, 60); Weis (1971: 344–403); Gagliardo (1980: 187–91); Hölzle (1931: 200–41); Thugut (1872: ii, 73–6, 165); Thugut's *Vorträge*, 26 Jan. and 27 Feb. 1798, HHStA, StK *Vorträge* 158.

[25] Bailleu (1881–7: i. 202–497); Adler-Bresse (1976: pp. xxxvi–lxix).

[26] Zaghi (1956: 216–58); Thugut (1872: ii. 104–12); Roider (1987: ch. 10); various letters of Thugut and Cobenzl in July–Aug. 1798 in HHStA, StK *Vorträge* 158.

those of Austria, Prussia, and some German states, especially Bavaria. Everyone now accepted France's Rhine frontier; Austria and Prussia were essentially willing to be moved east in Germany and rounded out there; the states of Third Germany were ready to provide a buffer zone between France and the German great powers; both of these in turn wanted to preserve what was left of the Reich, which the French were not yet bent on destroying and did not know how to replace. The end of the Polish question and Prussia's retreat into passive neutrality had at least lowered the temperature of Austro-Prussian rivalry over Germany, and Austria had plenty else to worry about. With Austria's ambitions switched to Italy, Austro-Bavarian enmity became less acute. The Austro-French slide toward war, in other words, was not the result of irreconcilable aims but of old assumptions and entrenched patterns of thought and action. France did not really try for a negotiated settlement at all, and Austria did not try hard; Prussia and the German states tried only to avoid trouble and to profit where they could. Fundamental conflicts of interest did not make an Austro-French armed struggle inevitable; the belief in an inevitable armed struggle created a conflict of interests.

French control of the Low Countries affected Britain and, less directly, Russia rather than Austria. In early 1798 France tightened its control on the Batavian Republic, forcing the Dutch to carry out their own Fructidor and tie themselves even closer to Paris. This made Britain still more determined to continue and expand the war—which in turn helped make Russia, least European among the great powers, and Paul I, the most incalculable of its monarchs, arbiters of Europe.

The questions of whether Paul was mad, and whether personal whim or rational calculation were more important in his actions, are good questions *per se*, but answering them does not necessarily explain his policy. Paul was probably never mad in a clinical sense, but he grew so increasingly violent, brutal, and unpredictable in his conduct that at the end one could say that, if he was not mad, he might as well have been. A similar observation applies to his foreign policy: derived both from Russian interests and his particular impulses, it was at once highly personal and traditionally Russian in unique, unpredictable ways.

Paul, having been educated under the supervision of enlightened nobles, came to the throne with a sober appraisal of Russia's needs and interests in regard to Poland, the Ottoman Empire, Persia, and Germany. He favoured Nikita P. Panin's defensively orien-tated northern system, and wanted peace in order to develop

Russia's commerce and improve its finances. He also, however, felt a personal and national mission to defend the smaller states of Europe against great-power predators. This feeling, more than Russia's concrete interests or Paul's religious convictions, explains his decision first to assume the role of protector of the Maltese Knights and then to accept being elected (illegally) as Grand Master of the Order, moves with important European implications. Even if he did not solicit these roles or the patronage over smaller states in Italy and Germany which others offered him, the opportunities they offered fitted his convictions like a glove. He could seek to increase Russia's power and influence by the normal methods of *realpolitik*, genuinely convinced that he was working for peace, legitimacy, and the independence of smaller states. Russian imperialism has sometimes been more dangerous, but never more high-principled.[27]

The critical question for the powers of the nascent anti-French coalition, however, was not what motivated Paul. It was whether his policies and ideas about Russia's role and those of the other main players in Europe would fit more with Austrian ideas or British, for the coalition's Achilles' heel lay in their differences. British leaders disagreed on certain points of strategy, but their underlying consensus was more important. The debate at London over a maritime versus a Continental strategy, for example, concerned priorities and allocation of resources rather than basic goals, and disputes were usually resolved by trying both strategies, with the one that seemed more promising at a given time getting more support. The disagreement at London over whether the French monarchy should be restored was even more superficial. Even advocates of a negotiated peace felt that this would require a stable government at Paris, usually taken to be a monarchy of some sort; even the most ardent counter-revolutionaries knew that they could not bring back the old regime. Similarly superficial was the disagreement between Pitt and Grenville over whether Prussia and Austria was a better partner. Neither power was Britain's first choice; real partnership and an equal voice in strategy were offered only to Russia.

Meanwhile an unspoken harmony prevailed over questions of central British interests and aims. It is useless to try to distinguish among the war aims of the various European powers on the score

---

[27] See Ragsdale (1988*a*: esp. 79–88, 202–3); also various essays, esp. by N. Saul and R. McGrew, in Ragsdale (1979*a*); Atkin (1980: 52–60); Feldbaek (1982: 18–39). For a good expression of Russian hubris, see N. P. Panin to Paul, 10 Dec. 1797, Panin (1888–92: ii. 256–7).

of how greedy or moderate, selfish or unselfish, they were. If one had to render a judgement, it would be the Old Testament one: 'They are all gone astray, they have all become as an unclean thing; there is none that doeth good, no, not one.' But a useful distinction can be drawn among them on the score of their breadth—how much of Europe and how many of its problems their programmes seriously dealt with. On this score, it is clear that beneath British rhetoric about the common cause was a set of war aims distinctly narrower and less European than those of any other great power. France and the Low Countries came first in importance, well behind these came the Iberian Peninsula and the Baltic, and the Mediterranean and the Near East after that, mainly for reasons of trade and the routes to India. Interests outside Europe—the West Indies, India, other colonies, trade, maritime rights—rivalled these European concerns in importance. But most of the main issues of European stability and peace—Germany, Italy, Poland, the Balkans, and relations between Russia, Austria, and Prussia—concerned Britain only to the extent that they affected its particular interests and the war against France.

   Hence the question of whether British policy was centred on Europe or the British Empire loses significance alongside the fact that the British had no serious concept of Europe or disposition to understand and take seriously those of others, and that this governed their military strategy and search for allies. Russia was Britain's 'natural ally' not so much because of its disposable military power, which was neither very great nor easily available, nor for its trade, which was important to Britain but not directly at stake in the war, but because Russia in some vital respects was, like Britain, a half-European, half-world power. This fact would eventually, later in the nineteenth century, make them rivals (though never as much as is often supposed); during much of this era it tended to make them friends. Together they could impose solutions to various European problems (or thought they could) with an urbane impartiality born of their own invulnerability and relative indifference to the outcome. This is what British and Russian talk of their being natural allies with many common interests and none in conflict really meant. The great virtue of Russia in British eyes was that, unlike Austria or Prussia, it would not try to make Britain act in areas or solve problems Britain wanted nothing to do with, but could essentially take care of those areas and problems itself. Best of all, it could force Austria and/or Prussia to bear the main brunt of fighting France. Austria sought Russian help as an ally in solving Austria's problems in Central and Eastern Europe; Britain wanted Russia as its ally to help Britain ignore them.

This same mind-set explains Britain's paradoxical attitude toward the two German powers. The evidence since 1794 proved overwhelmingly that Austria could fight France and would, Prussia could not and would not. Yet time and again Britain was willing to do and pay more to get Prussia into alliance and action than it would for Austria.[28] The reasons were simple and by now familiar: Austria had to fight for its survival anyway and so need not be paid, and the arenas vital to it, southern Germany and Italy, were not vital to British interests. Prussia had to be bribed or pressured into fighting, but if it did it might serve British purposes, especially in the Low Countries. Moreover, Britain could use Prussia for particular purposes on the Continent and then withdraw; the history of the Seven Years' War and the Triple Alliance had shown that. If Britain once became genuinely involved in supporting Austria, with its many interests and problems, it might be entangled on the Continent permanently.

All this augured ill for Austrian hopes of a new defensive coalition. By fervent courtship it succeeded in August 1798 in renewing its old defensive alliance with Russia, but this meant little—the alliance had done nothing for Austria in the five previous years of war.[29] At the same time its hopes were dashed that Paul could either bring Prussia into the coalition or neutralize Prussia in Germany. Frederick William stubbornly refused to make any commitment that might conceivably lead to war. The only war other Prussians would consider entering was one which made Austria the principal and paid Prussia to keep Austria from really winning it.[30]

This was predictable; more serious was Vienna's failure to renew the Austro-British alliance. The apparent obstacle was Austria's refusal to ratify a loan agreement which the Austrian ambassador Prince Starhemberg had signed in May 1796, pledging Austria to repay that portion of the British-guaranteed loan of 1795 actually advanced to Austria. Thugut insisted that Starhemberg had not

[28] Note e.g. British efforts to bring Prussia back into the alliance in late 1797 and early 1798, while pressing Austria for concessions to make this possible. Grenville (1892–1927: iv. 8–10, 41–3, 56–60, 71–7, 80–5, 89–91, 160–6, 172–7, 209–13); BL Add. MS 59161, fos. 1–3.

[29] This is best shown by the extensive correspondence between Thugut and Austrian emissaries in Russia in HHStA, StK *Weisungen* 181, 182.

[30] Steffens (1943–52: 155–81); Bailleu (1881–7: i. 266–71); Mackesy (1974: 28–31); Panin (1888–92: ii. 196–384); Michailowski-Danilevsky and Miliutin (1856–8: i. 342–51).

been authorized to negotiate this kind of agreement, and that its terms would destroy what remained of Austria's credit, making it impossible for her to raise money for a new war. The British government denounced Thugut's action as an outrageous breach of faith, and made Austrian ratification of the loan agreement a pre-condition for any alliance. The loan issue had importance symbolically in British domestic politics, with the ministry under attack for throwing money away on faithless allies. The real problem, however, was not the loan, but the two powers' divergent views of their roles in the previous coalition and the proposed one. Austrians argued that they had borne the brunt of the last war, that Britain had given them far less help than other states like Prussia who did little or nothing, and that Austria's exertions and ruined finances entitled it to generous British support. The British replied that Austria had fought only because it had to and had finally defected from the war for its own selfish interests, that Britain had other allies to support and interests to protect, and that any British help for Austria now would be an act of pure generosity tailored to Britain's resources and needs.[31]

When Paul I offered to mediate at Vienna's request, the British used this to seek a special Anglo-Russian alliance through which Britain could force Austria into war and control its war policy, with British aid to Austria funnelled through Russia. Even if the alliance failed to bring Austria under control, Britain would still gain Russian forces to use for its special interests at sea, in the Low Countries, or even, as Dundas dreamed, in India. Meanwhile, French aggression or Austria's other commitments and interests might force Austria to re-enter the war on its own. A defensive treaty Austria had signed with Naples in May gave the British a chance to promote this outcome. In November 1798 the Neapolitan government, with strong encouragement from Admiral Nelson but against Austria's wishes, attacked the French at Rome. It proved a military and political disaster. The Neapolitan army collapsed under a French counter-attack, the court had to flee to Sicily under the protection of the British fleet, and the French, after breaking some popular resistance, occupied Naples and set up still another satellite regime called the Parthenopean Republic. Austria accused Naples and Britain of trying to trap it in

---

[31] Helleiner (1965: 1–123); Sherwig (1969: 83–93); Mackesy (1974: 10–14); Beer (1877a: 5–9); Otruba (1965: 84–7). For Anglo-Austrian exchanges over the loan agreement, see Grenville (1892–1927: iv. 92–5, 99–100, 150–2, 154–9, 170–2, 250–2); Grenville Papers, BL Add. MS 59100, fos. 1–28; Thugut to Emperor Francis, 4 Mar. 1798, HHStA, StK *Vorträge* 158.

war before it was ready; the British denounced Austria for cowardice and bad faith in refusing to recognize the *casus foederis*.[32]

Meanwhile negotiations at St Petersburg failed to settle the loan issue and bring Britain and Austria into alliance. The usual explanation, that Grenville tried hard to create a great four-power coalition in the autumn of 1798, but was frustrated by Prussia's resistance and Austria's evasions and trickery, will not do.[33] The Tsar wanted a four-power coalition (indeed, an all-European one, with the small states of Europe enjoying his special protection), and so did Thugut; but the British, including Grenville and Pitt, wanted no such thing. Grenville constantly told the Russians that Britain would not become Austria's ally until after Britain and Russia had concluded their own alliance and Austria had met Britain's conditions. The main condition, far more important than ratification of the loan convention, was that Austria commit itself in advance of an alliance to a war strategy and war aims determined by Britain and Russia. Britain was already helping Austria generously, Grenville claimed, by aiding Portugal and Naples, promoting an anti-French revolt in Switzerland, and keeping its navy in the Mediterranean.[34] Without a prior Austrian commitment to Anglo-Russian aims, any more British aid would only mean more sacrifices to Austria's selfish purposes.

For a moment, Russian mediation at St Petersburg seemed to succeed; Cobenzl and the British ambassador, Sir Charles Whitworth, reached an agreement in December on the loan convention, to serve as the basis for an Anglo-Austrian alliance. But Grenville, in angrily rejecting it, berated Whitworth privately for completely misunderstanding the purpose of his mission. He was not supposed to reach an Anglo-Austrian alliance through Russia's mediation, but to conclude a direct Anglo-Russian alliance so that the two of them could control Austria's war effort and war aims. Instead of reaching agreement with Cobenzl, Grenville said, Whitworth should have committed the Tsar to an Anglo-Russian expedition to liberate Holland, which they could launch as soon as Austria was fully engaged in war with France in Central Europe.[35]

---

[32] Zaghi (1956: 213); Acton (1956: 308–34); Mackesy (1974: 51–7); HHStA, StK *Weisungen* 182, fos. 400–9.

[33] Mackesy (1974: 2–9); Sherwig (1969: 97–115); Sherwig (1962); Jupp (1985: 209–22). For different views, see Ingram (1981: 28–9); Schroeder (1987).

[34] Grenville had a simple answer to the question that has been raised by historians, whether Britain's Mediterranean fleet was there mainly to serve its European or its Near Eastern and imperial purposes. As Grenville repeatedly insisted to Vienna, the Royal Navy was there solely to help Austria.

[35] For a detailed summary of the evidence, see Schroeder (1987: 260–6).

What Grenville sought, an Anglo-Russian alliance separate from Austria enabling the two powers to exploit and control Austria's war effort, he partially attained in a treaty of 29 December 1798, in which Russia promised to supply Britain a subsidized auxiliary corps of 45,000 men for the express purposes of restoring the European balance in general and the Stadholder in Holland in particular. The agreement would take effect, however, only if Prussia entered the war; further consultation on how to use the Russian auxiliary corps was called for if Prussia stayed out. Britain and Russia also concluded separate alliances with the Ottoman Empire in December and early January, the Russian alliance being the main one, and reached an agreement with Naples over the ultimate disposition of Malta when it was recaptured. Though Nelson was wary of Russian expansion into the Mediterranean, Pitt and Grenville encouraged it. The two allies agreed to keep up their own pressure on Austria, excluded from all these agreements, but to count on France to force it into war.[36]

Thus Anglo-Russian policy toward Austria could not have succeeded without French help, and the Directory had every motive to make it fail. If another lost war might destroy the Habsburg monarchy, another great war, whether won or lost, was almost sure to destroy the French Republic. At the moment its domestic counter-revolutionary enemies were crushed or disorganized, with neither Chouannerie in the West nor monarchist conspiracy elsewhere any longer a real danger, while the *émigrés* and the Bourbon court dragged out a pitiful existence scattered round Europe. But these victories had only increased France's political instability, drained the regime of credibility, and made it dependent on its military rescuers. War could only worsen these problems, along with the chronic economic and fiscal ones.

Added to France's disincentives for widening the war were the risings that broke out in 1798 and early 1799 in many of its newly annexed territories and satellites, the worst threat of this kind to French imperialism until 1813–14. A peasant revolt expelled the French from southern Italy. Similar risings in Belgium, Luxemburg, and the Helvetic Republic could be contained and finally suppressed only because they were unco-ordinated, broke out prematurely, and were not accompanied by major war elsewhere. Even areas which remained quiet on the surface, like the Batavian Republic and the German Rhineland, seethed with discontent and

[36] Martens (1874–1905: x. 418–25); Naff (1960: 249–74, 298–316); Shaw (1971: 264–7); Rodger (1964: 68–73).

passive resistance. The risings reflected, not failed policies or wrong individual actions by French political and military leaders, but a spontaneous, widespread aversion to the practical effects of French rule.[37] The erstwhile sympathy for French leadership and protection in Belgium was long gone, the patriotic-national reformers who had once collaborated with France in the Batavian Republic, and to some extent in the Cisalpine, were disillusioned and discredited.[38]

Nor could France rely on its alliance with Spain. Resentful of the negotiations at Lille, the economic effects of the maritime war against England, and French pressure to hand over the Louisiana Territory without the promised French compensations, the Spaniards were in no mood for an expanded war, though they did not defect as the French feared. The British fleet's seizure of Port Mahon in November temporarily drove Godoy from office. To counteract French domination and the Anglo-Russian threat, Spain even tried drawing closer to the United States, as surprising a move as the Turkish approach to Russia.[39]

The French government made diplomatic efforts to avert a new coalition and a widened war, but they were feeble and sporadic. Besides its essentially meaningless negotiations with Austria at Seltz, it tried to win over Prussia and to woo Third Germany. The only significant proposal France made, however, was Talleyrand's offer in September to conclude treaties of mutual guarantee with Prussia and Austria. It quickly broke down (partly because Siéyès sabotaged it at Berlin), and the French returned to promoting secularizations and territorial revolution in Germany and Italy.[40]

This was the familiar republican strategy of a flight forward—an attempt to break up the nascent coalition and avert general war by taking the offensive. The response to the threat by Naples in 1798 was to seize Piedmont to force it into war on France's side. After the Neapolitan attack was crushed, the Directory overthrew

[37] Godechot (1956: ii. 500–697; 1981: 296–335, 384–7); Verhaegen (1929: iii. 274–586); Zaghi (1956: 152–9); Chadwick (1981: 462–71); Blanning (1983: 302–4; 1980: 1000–1).

[38] Schama (1977: esp. 321–84); Colenbrander (1905–22: ii. Nos. 129, 147, 149, 162, 168, 173–5, 193, 201).

[39] Nabonne (1951: 91–107); Guyot (1912: 723–32); Fugier (1930: i. 78–89); Liss (1983: 172–3).

[40] Guyot (1912: 860–6). Lacour-Gayet (1928–30: i. 292–5) sees this as a typical move by Talleyrand in favour of moderation and peace. I see it as his typical scrambling for cover when the disastrous results of his previous advice became apparent. See Zaghi (1956: 346–8); Talleyrand (1891b: 165–86, 243–345, 364–5).

the regime, set up the Parthenopean Republic, and began milking it for contributions, with General Championnet outdoing Bonaparte's record of 1796 in extortions. In answer to the defeat in Aboukir Bay, the Turkish declaration of war, and the imminent threat of Russo-Turkish co-operation, the Directory gave Bonaparte authorization either to restrict his operations or to expand them as he wished, possibly driving toward Constantinople or India, overthrowing the Sultan, seizing strong points in the Ottoman Empire, and raising revolution in the Balkans and Poland with the aid of the Orthodox Christians and Kosciusko—all this supposedly to deter Russia or Austria from joining Britain. To counter the threat of an Anglo-Russian descent on Holland or the French coast, the French contemplated more raids on the Irish coast in support of an Irish uprising (already suppressed).[41] France planned for the Continental war in the same spirit, resolving on offensives everywhere and ignoring the rampant corruption, indiscipline, and war-weariness in the army and the dispersal of French forces in Egypt and other theatres. Conscription under the new Loi Jourdan of 1798 was expected to refill the army's ranks, while France's satellites replenished its coffers and French *élan* made up for the army's numerical inferiority.[42]

The long-awaited Austro-French war was touched off by a French offensive under Masséna into eastern Switzerland in March, but it would have come soon anyway: a Russian reserve army had been on Austrian soil since January, and Austria had intended to fight when ready. Even where France's offensives in Italy, on the Rhine, and in Switzerland succeeded at first (Switzerland and southern Germany), they were politically counter-productive, driving many Swiss and South Germans who only wanted to be neutral into the allied camp.

Thus France and Austria had both come to the same decision, France recklessly, Austria with dogged resignation: to take arms against a sea of troubles and by opposing end them. Both took each other seriously as military foes, but would not deal seriously with each other politically. They fought each other not because they were really mortal enemies, but because, in the general security crisis they both faced, the other was the only enemy each could get at, and each convinced itself that defeating the other would somehow solve its general problems. Thus, despite everything that had changed since 1792, the War of the Second Coalition

[41] Guyot (1912: 829–32, 868–99); W. Kennedy (1972).
[42] Forrest (1990: 20–37); Ross (1967; 1969: 179–87).

began like the first, as essentially an Austro-French war, and would remain so. The only differences this time were that Russia joined Britain as Austria's auxiliary and Prussia replaced Russia as the laughing third party.

III. ALLIED VICTORY AND DEFEAT, 1799–1800

The military campaign went better for the allies from March to August 1799 than any since early 1793. After the initial French offensive in Switzerland was stopped, Archduke Carl drove the French back beyond Zurich and defeated an attempted offensive in southern Germany. Meanwhile the French tried to retain their hold on central and southern Italy, partly in hopes of staying in contact with Bonaparte in Egypt, while they attacked Austria in the north. The result was French defeat everywhere. While the Austrians repelled them in northern Italy, a popular rising begun in Calabria led by a charismatic cleric, Cardinal Fabrizio Ruffo, threw them out of Naples and Rome.

Even these successes paled, at least in the popular imagination, alongside the exploits of Marshal Aleksandr Suvorov. Paul named him commander of the Russian corps in Italy mainly to get him out of Russia, and Vienna invited him to command the combined Austro-Russian army in Italy chiefly to flatter the Tsar. His strategy and tactics were fairly crude, and he depended on Austria for all his staff and support services, much of his supplies, and more than half his men, all of which the Austrian generals claimed he wasted. None the less, under his bold and charismatic leadership the combined Russo-Austrian army by mid-August had destroyed two French armies and bottled a third up in Genoa. Virtually all of Italy had been retaken, and France seemed open to invasion from the south-east.[43]

The victories were deceptive, however. France's defeats, like its fiasco in Egypt, were mainly the result of its own ill-considered offensives. The closer the allies drew to France, the more France's strategic and logistic position improved and their own worsened. Though valuable parts of France's empire had been captured, its territory and resources were intact. It still held the key passes in Switzerland and the fortresses of the upper Rhine, while on the

    [43] Hüffer (1904: i. 10–16); Guyot (1912: 900–2); Ross (1969: 170–87); Rothenberg (1982b: 54–9); Keep (1980: 505–6, 509–10); Hölzle (1931: 242–9).

middle Rhine its positions threatened Austria and south Germany, and Prussian neutrality gave France security along the lower Rhine. British hopes and plans for risings in the Low Countries in support of their proposed Anglo-Russian expedition were unfounded. The Dutch, though discontented, were unable and unwilling to rise, and the Belgian rising of 1798 had already failed for lack of external support. The chances that France would collapse internally, regularly overestimated in London, actually dimmed as the regime improved in its conduct of the war. The Loi Jourdan of 1798, instituting conscription, was initially not very effective owing to large-scale evasion, but by calling five classes to the colours at once the government raised 400,000 new men, something the allies could not hope to match. By mid-1799 the strategic errors of 1798 had been corrected and the revolts in the satellites were under control, the allies having spoiled their chances to exploit popular discontent by their conduct in liberated territory, especially Switzerland and Italy.[44] The allies' victories had also cost them heavily in manpower and resources, especially Austria, whose army constituted three-quarters of the allied forces. Russia and Britain, unable and unwilling to make good these losses, instead called on Austria to fill every imaginable fiscal, supply, and manpower need of their own. Finally, the French army was still qualitatively superior to Austria's, and far better than Russia's or Britain's.

In short, the Anglo-Russian notion that the coalition could quickly invade France and overthrow the Republic was completely unrealistic. A compromise peace, which Thugut favoured, might have been within reach, but the British and Russians flatly ruled it out. Paul was determined to reduce France to its ancient limits, restore the monarchy, and protect Italy, Switzerland, and Germany from Austria's selfish greed. The British, while endorsing all these aims, fixed their sights on liberating and protecting the Low Countries.

Hence Grenville worked out a strategy with Paul, accepted by Thugut in order to appease the Tsar and keep the coalition together, which called for winning the war in 1799 by an all-out offensive. Suvorov was to break off his conquest of Italy and move his Russian corps to Switzerland, where it would join another Russian corps under General Korsakov, which Britain would subsidize but which Austria was supposed to staff, supply,

[44] Rodger (1964: 204-7); Godechot (1981: 327-55); Mackesy (1974: 72-5). For the similarity between French and allied conduct in Switzerland, see Godechot (1937: ii. 294-326); Dunant (1901: 203-49); Oechsli (1903-13: i. 210-76).

and support. This Russian army, to be commanded by Suvorov and reinforced with Swiss recruits and German mercenaries, would march on Paris over Lyons, inspiring a royalist rising under the Bourbon standard *en route*. Supporting this main thrust would be an Austro-Sardinian invasion of France from northern Italy and an offensive by Archduke Carl's army on the upper Rhine. Meanwhile Britain and Russia, joined (it was hoped) by Prussia, would land an army in Holland, liberate the Low Countries, and drive on Paris from the North.

Two things inspired this plan: British ideological zeal and military amateurism, especially on the part of Grenville and Windham, and distrust and dislike of Austria. The main offensive from Switzerland was assigned to a Russian army under Suvorov, while Austria's much larger forces were confined to supporting roles, specifically to prevent Vienna from controlling operations or hampering the offensive. This also points to the reason why a plan based on such amazingly optimistic military assumptions could be adopted: those calling the tune were not paying the piper. Throughout the entire span of the revolutionary and Napoleonic wars, Britain and Russia never gambled with the British navy or the Russian army in a high-risk offensive strategy like this. When their backs were against the wall, their strategy was always defensive. They were ready to play *va banque* here because not their forces but the survival of the Habsburg army and monarchy would be at stake.[45]

The Anglo-Russian strategy of overthrow, however, would fail politically before collapsing militarily, and Prussia made it do so. Basically, Russia and Britain were trying to get Austria to do two things: exert all its strength under Anglo-Russian direction in bringing France down, and at the same time accept British and Russian war aims which diverged sharply from Austria's and were in some ways harmful to its interests. In accepting the Anglo-Russian war plan, Thugut seemed to ensure the first, military half of this programme; by bringing Prussia into the coalition, Britain and Russia would ensure above all the second, political half. Of course the British and Russians wanted Prussian military help, believing that it might make a critical difference in their proposed campaign in the Low Countries and discourage the French while encouraging dissidents in France and its satellites. But they did not expect the Prussian army to help win the war in the decisive

[45] Best (1982: 90–1); Mackesy (1974: 76–87, 136–57); Rodger (1964: 154–7); Allardt (1976: 38–43); Schroeder (1987: 252–66).

theaters, Germany, Switzerland, Italy, and France itself; they knew Prussia would never consider playing more than a very limited military role, and never asked more than this. The great advantage of gaining Prussia would be political: it would compel Austria to fight an all-out war, because Prussia would also be in the coalition competing for gains at Austria's expense in Germany, while Russia and Britain, as leaders and arbiters of the coalition, decided which rewards each of the subordinate partners would get. This motivation and reasoning is crystal-clear in the bid Britain and Russia made in early and mid-1799 for a separate alliance with Prussia, and the kind of alliance they offered Berlin. It was one in which Prussia would be subsidized (while Austria was not), would be asked only for a strictly limited war effort (while Austria's was unlimited), and would be included as a full partner in an allied agreement on war aims (while Austria was excluded).

The special envoys negotiating with Haugwitz, Russia's foreign minister, N. P. Panin, and Grenville's brother Thomas, offered tempting terms. Prussia would be asked only to help Britain and Russia clear the French from Holland and Belgium and then stand guard on the middle and upper Rhine, not to invade France. For this service it would receive a subsidy, preparation money, and a voice in the peace settlement, both in regard to the Low Countries and in Germany and Europe generally. The potential profits for Prussia were dazzling: to preserve and enhance its control of North Germany and its influence in Northern Europe, make decisive gains in Germany as a whole at Austria's expense, and ensure itself a post-war Anglo-Russian alliance to guard against French revenge.

But the risks were also serious, less in the task Prussia was assigned—to fight as a temporary auxiliary in one secondary theatre—than in what might develop from it. If the allied military strategy failed, Britain and Russia could still withdraw from the fighting, formally or *de facto*. Prussia, situated in the heart of Europe, might not be able to. More important still, while the allied offer fully met the conditions Prussia regularly set for participating in the war alongside Austria, namely, that Austria be the principal, Prussia the auxiliary, and Prussia be guaranteed control over Austria's gains, there was no assurance that circumstances might not upset this tidy arrangement. Suppose Prussia entered the war and Austria was subsequently defeated or made a separate peace; might not the main burden of fighting then fall on Prussia? Or suppose Prussia's entrance enabled Austria to win the war decisively; might she not then gain even more out of her victory than Prussia would? All these calculations, and more,[46] were factors in Prussian thinking, but the decisive element was simply Frederick William's aversion to war. He would have liked a defensive alliance with Britain and Russia, especially if he could get paid for it, but rejected any commitment to military action.[47]

With the collapse of the negotiations with Prussia the allies' strategy of overthrow became unworkable. It seemed in the event, however, to break down over a failure of military co-ordination caused mainly by Austria. According to the conventional account, Thugut broke the agreement on a joint strategy by sending Archduke Carl's army from Switzerland not to the upper Rhine, where it could stay in touch with the Russian forces in Switzerland, but to the middle Rhine. Ostensibly this was to guard against a French offensive on the middle Rhine; actually, it is claimed, Thugut did it to pre-empt any Prussian action along the Rhine and to pave the way for Austria to intervene in the Netherlands campaign, once it was under way, to protect Austrian interests.

This Austrian move (still according to the conventional account) left Korsakov's Russian corps in Switzerland facing a much stronger French army with only weak Austrian support. Masséna, seeing his opportunity, attacked and routed the Russians in the second battle of Zurich in September, sending them in disorganized flight eastward. Suvorov, marching from Italy to join Korsakov, was forced to lead his own corps on a brilliant but costly fighting retreat across Switzerland to join them, ending up in eastern Switzerland in late October with his army unfit for further combat. At the same time, an Anglo-Russian expedition launched to liberate Holland failed miserably. The joint army landed successfully, but was first checked, then defeated by French and Dutch forces, and finally forced to evacuate.[48]

As a description of military developments, the conventional story will do; nor is there much to quarrel with in its account of how defeat affected the coalition. Paul, long convinced that the Austrians were greedy ingrates, blamed the Swiss reverses entirely

[46] One other consideration was prominent in both Prussian and Russian thinking, the possibility that Austria might emerge from the war technically victorious over France but exhausted and weakened. On balance, both powers considered this a gain. The British did not worry about such things.

[47] Schroeder (1987: 266–8); Bailleu (1881–7: i. Nos. 248–79); D. Elliot (1954).

[48] On events in Switzerland, see Mackesy (1974: 224–33, 316–19); on the expedition to Holland, ibid. 102–35, 174–7, 184–220, 254–307; Schama (1977: 389–99); Ingram (1981: 343–5); Piechowiak (1962–3).

on Austrian treachery. An Austrian take-over of the papal port of Ancona in November after a Russo-Turkish expedition had captured it further enraged the Tsar, and the fiasco in Holland turned him even against the British. He decided first not to fight any longer on Austria's side, though he still expected Austria to maintain his troops in their winter headquarters and still wanted to direct the policy of the coalition. But by the end of 1799, despite desperate but unco-ordinated Austrian and British efforts to appease him, he took Russia out of the war entirely.

Where the prevailing version goes wrong is not in recounting events, but in explaining them and assessing responsibility. Thugut neither betrayed the allies nor caused the military defeat by sending Carl's army to the middle Rhine. If any particular thing was responsible for the defeat, it was the removal of Carl's army from Switzerland in the first place—a move Britain and Russia insisted on and Thugut accepted for the sake of allied unity. Other factors contributing to the military set-back had nothing to do with Austria—Korsakov's incompetence, the weakness of his corps and Russia's failure to bring it even close to its promised strength, the Russian army's lack of training and equipment for mountain fighting, Suvorov's disobedience of his orders in delaying his departure from Italy, and (the biggest element of all) the French army's energy and skill. In any case, though the allies lost an important defensive postion in Switzerland, it had never been a suitable base for launching a major allied offensive into France; this was part of the unrealism of the Anglo-Russian strategy, resting on the wildly inaccurate belief that France was militarily near collapse. As the equally disastrous failure in Holland proved, the French had actually recovered military superiority.

Besides, military failures only provided the occasion for Paul's defection from the good cause; the real reasons were political. While defeats deepened his long-standing antipathy to Austria and showed their clash of interests, especially over Italy,[49] they more importantly revealed unsuspected differences between him and Britain. Anglo-Russian co-operation had worked thus far because, as noted, the two powers could direct the war in pursuit of apparently harmonious aims without really fighting it themselves. These aims, cloaked in vague rhetoric about 'the common cause', 'the liberation of Europe', and 'the balance of power', involved a

[49] Thugut (1872: ii. Nos. 861–3, 905, 908, 916, 920, 941–2, 946–7); Michailowski-Danilevsky and Miliutin (1856–8: iii. 189–96); Panin (1888–92: iv. No. 849).

tacit division of Europe into two spheres, a Western one under British hegemony and a larger Central and Eastern one under the hegemony of Russia—a division rendered possible by Britain's peculiar concept of a European balance of power, which made the British indifferent to Russian domination over the Ottoman Empire, Germany, much of Italy, and the Baltic, or positively in favour of it. (One is inescapably reminded of American and British attitudes toward Soviet expansion through most of World War II.) The only thing about Russian expansion disturbing to some Britons was Russia's growing presence in the Mediterranean and the Near East, and even this failed to affect official policy. As late as early 1800 the government was still offering Russia Majorca as a naval base in the western Mediterranean to keep it in the war.

It was not the military set-backs *per se* which ruined this harmony between the two flank powers, but the different conclusions they drew from them. Paul blamed Austria and resolved that it had to be punished for its treachery. The British outdid Paul in denouncing Austria, but also concluded that Russian troops were useless or worse unless they were brought under British or Austrian command and discipline and supplied and staffed by Austria. (Some naval officers had already reached similar conclusions about the Russian fleet.) In other words, the British concluded that, though Russia was a desirable political partner and Austria a contemptible one, Russia could not fight, Austria could, and only massive Austrian help would make Russia worth anything militarily. Already in September the British had aroused Paul's suspicions by proposing to use Austria's greed for the sake of the good cause. Austria should be promised major gains in Italy, including all of Piedmont (actually more territories than Austria desired, and different ones) so as keep her in the war, control her conduct, and bring her directly into territorial contact with France.

Had Austria dropped out of the war in the fall of 1799, as everyone in Britain expected, the Anglo-Russian alliance might have been saved. The British would then have had to adopt Dundas's insular–imperial strategy, under which Britain and Russia could still have co-operated against France in political opposition, naval action, and possible small diversions on the periphery of Europe (or even, as Dundas dreamed, in India). But Austria, surprisingly, decided to stay in the war. Given Paul's rage at Vienna, this forced Britain to choose between Russia, the ally it desired but found militarily of little value, and Austria, the non-ally it despised but recognized as the only major power willing and able to fight France.

Grenville concocted several schemes, each more absurd than the last, designed somehow to keep Britain and Russia allied and in control of the war effort while Austria did the fighting—all in vain. In early 1800 Britain decided to go with Austria, and Paul took it as an unpardonable insult. Other issues, especially Malta, widened the breach. The British in December 1798 had promised Russia and Naples to return the island to the Maltese order, but had then received no Russian or Neapolitan help in recapturing it; Nelson and Admiral Ushakov fell out, and Ushakov's Mediterranean squadron was pulled back in late 1799. Many Britons, now aware of Malta's importance as a base, became suspicious of Russia's motives in pressing Britain to give it up. Yet even on the Malta question London refused to do anything to irritate the Tsar until Paul himself broke relations with Britain in a spectacular and wounding way in September 1800. Even after this, London still desired close ties to St Petersburg. For the moment, however, it needed Austria more to fight France.[50]

France was meanwhile being transformed. The Directory's final achievement, military recovery, had exhausted its last reserves of political will and credibility. In July Talleyrand abandoned the sinking ship, like the consummate survivor he was. Further attempted coups and shake-ups among the Directors brought the government even deeper into contempt; every faction looked for a military hero to lead it, while France as a whole sought a savior. When Bonaparte, having abandoned his army in Egypt and evaded Nelson's fleet, landed in France in early October, the crowds that hailed him plainly pictured him in the role. In a conspiracy between Bonaparte and two Directors, Siéyès and Roger Ducos, the Directory was overthrown on 18–19 Brumaire (9–10 November) and authority placed in Bonaparte's hands as First Consul. The coup at one point had nearly failed, and the power he enjoyed was far from total. Nonetheless, France was now ruled by a military dictator.[51]

Bonaparte's reign in Egypt had already shown what kind of

---

[50] For general accounts, see Schroeder (1987: 271–82); Allardt (1976: 103–35); Stanislavskaia (1962: ch. 3). On the internal struggle in Russia, see Saul (1970: 132–43); Hüffer (1904: i. 360–6); Panin (1888–92: iv. 290–8). For evidence that Paul's anti-Austrian feelings and policy antedated the defeats in Switzerland, see Michailowski-Danilevsky and Miliutin (1856–8: iii. 181–9, 206–17, 464–5). Various points about British attitudes are made in Mackesy (1974: 33); Grenville (1892–1927: v. 401–2, 404–5); G. Elliot (1874: iii. 78–89); Wickham (1870: ii. 322–412); BL Add. MSS 58861, fos. 94–9.

[51] Lacour-Gayet (1928–30: i. ch. 19); Hüffer (1904: i. 307–59); Tulard (1977: 28–9, 110–11); Fournier (1930: i. 190–3); Sutherland (1986: 330–5); Thompson (1988: 134–45).

ruler he would be: rational (at least in terms of immediate goals), efficient, authoritarian, centralizing, modernizing, opportunistic, and ruthless. The main question for other governments was how he would use France's power, and that too his Egyptian campaign had foreshadowed. He would always be on the offensive, pausing only to prepare for another leap forward; he would always know his immediate goals, never his ultimate ones; he would be brilliant in playing roles, including that of peacemaker, but poor at sustaining them; and he would always be ready to saddle subordinates with the results of failure while he went on to bigger and better things.[52]

Though he offered Austria peace in February 1800 on the basis of Campo Formio, he did not expect it to accept or want it to. He needed to consolidate his power by military triumphs and was determined to destroy the Austrian army in order to show France's satellites and allies, as his propaganda put it, that they must either be friends of France or slaves of Austria and Britain. Yet the move was not wholly deceptive. Bonaparte did want a victorious Continental peace and a maritime truce so as to organize his rule in France and prepare for further moves in Europe, and Campo Formio could serve as a useful starting point.[53]

The interesting question is why Austria did not follow up the French bid. Thugut in late 1799 once again had many reasons for seriously considering peace. He was disgusted with his allies and despondent over Austria's future, under pressure from the peace party and the army, had no assurances of British support, and faced a Russia growing steadily more hostile and moving toward alliance with Prussia. Bonaparte's seizure of power promised to end the revolution and restore order in France, and though Austria's relations with him had not been pleasant, he was easier to deal with than the Directory. Yet before 1799 was out Thugut had promised both Britain and Russia that Austria would continue the war, concluded a loan convention ending Austria's old quarrel with Britain, and begun seeking a new loan with advances. Talleyrand, once again French foreign minister under Bonaparte, found Austria unwilling to negotiate seriously for peace.[54]

---

[52] Lokke (1932: 209–35); Rodger (1964: 123–31). Some revealing Napoleonic documents on the Egyptian expedition are: Napoleon (1858–70: iv. Nos. 3045, 3259; v. Nos. 3439, 3952, 4035, 4138, 4156, 4225, 4329, 4374).

[53] Rodger (1964: 230–5); Napoleon (1858–70: vi. Nos. 4623, 4649).

[54] Roider (1987: 328–33); Thugut (1872: ii. Nos. 953–64, 1970). The lengthy Thugut–Cobenzl correspondence in HHStA, StK *Russland Weisungen* 184 and *Russland II Correspondenz* 215, 217 constantly demonstrates the same attitudes

The usual explanation of this is that Austria had territorial ambitions in Italy which only a victorious war could satisfy. This is true, but not the real explanation. Austria's territorial ambitions were a means to the goal, not the goal itself; that goal was to remain a great power. For Austria, to quit the war was to surrender its status as a great power *vis-à-vis* France; to abandon the search for territorial compensations was to abdicate its great-power status *vis-à-vis* Russia and Prussia. Thugut considered anything preferable to this, including all the risks of another campaign. His were normal eighteenth-century balance-of-power notions, to which he clung with uncommon determination. At least, he reasoned, Austria could now run its war effort without bullying and interference from its allies, and British gold would be spent on Austria rather than on Russians, Prussians, *émigrés*, and mercenaries.

Austria and Britain, however, still had trouble concluding an alliance. While Vienna demanded major military and financial aid, the British continued to see the Continental war as primarily Austria's responsibility, wanted to curb its appetites, urged Austria to avoid or soften its breach with Russia, and tried to keep most of its help to Austria indirect. British disagreements at home over Continental versus insular–imperial strategies first helped delay a Mediterranean expedition designed to aid Austria in Italy and then rendered it useless. Only when disaster began looming in Italy after Bonaparte's army crossed the Alps in April, catching the Austrian army in Italy in the rear, were the negotiations stepped up, and by the time the alliance was finally signed on 20 June, the Austrian army had already suffered a crushing defeat at Marengo. Yet quicker and better Austro-British co-operation would have made no great difference. Not even an Austrian victory at Marengo, which nearly happened, would have won the campaign or the war. In fact, had Bonaparte earlier been able to make his rival General Moreau follow his strategy in Germany, France might have achieved victory in both theaters more quickly and completely.[55]

---

toward Russia—bitter anger at the treatment Austria was receiving, but determination to appease Paul as long as possible.

[55] On Anglo-Austrian relations, see Helleiner (1965: 122–9); Grenville (1892–1927: vi. 56–7, 72–4, 119, 124–5, 168–9, 242–3, 247, 256, 261–2, 269–72); BL Add. MSS 58861, fos. 61–2, 68–9, 80; 59061, fos. 134–6; 59102–3, fos. 1–46; 59111, fos. 45–6, 63–5, 71–2. For the failures in British and Austrian military co-operation, see Mackesy (1984: 70–91, 95–116); Rodger (1964: 210–18).

IV. PEACE AT LUNÉVILLE AND AMIENS, 1801-1802

Once again, the only surprise is that Austria stayed in the war another six months after Marengo, passing up another chance for a relatively easy escape. Soon after the battle Bonaparte, having granted an armistice to his defeated opponent General Mélas, left Italy to secure his hold on power in Paris, following up the truce with another peace appeal to the Emperor. Francis, shaken by Marengo, forced Thugut to respond; he sent General Count St Julien to Milan and thence to Paris, but with specific orders not to make peace, only to gain time. At Paris, Bonaparte and Talleyrand hustled and wheedled St Julien into violating his instructions and signing a peace treaty on 28 July which generally confirmed Campo Formio with certain changes. The terms, given the circumstances, were not unfavourable, though they contained some 'rubber clauses' of the sort Bonaparte was good at exploiting. In addition, the treaty would have broken Austria's pledge of no separate peace to Britain. Meanwhile, on 15 July General Kray, pushed back by Moreau in Germany, had accepted a truce at Parsdorf which surrendered Bavaria but retained Austrian control of three vital fortresses in southern Germany, Philippsburg, Ingolstadt, and Ulm.

Thugut persuaded Francis not to ratify St Julien's treaty but to call instead for a general peace congress while Austria prepared to renew the war. This irritated Bonaparte, eager for a separate peace with Austria to help him force Britain into one as well, or at least to gain France an armistice on land and sea that would save the French forces besieged in Malta and Egypt. At one time in late summer Pitt was ready to concede France a partial naval armistice, but others in his cabinet prevented it, and the British capture of Malta on 5 September scuttled the idea. Austria, meanwhile, continued to flounder between peace and war. Francis, unwilling to give Carl command of the army in Germany for fear that he would use the position to call for peace, gave nominal command to the eighteen-year-old Archduke John and real authority to General Lauer, an officer with engineering expertise but no capacity for general command. This made Austria even more unready to meet the expected French onslaught when the truce expired, and so the Emperor personally purchased a 45-day extension of the truce in September by surrendering Philippsburg, Ingolstadt, and Ulm to the French.

Thugut resigned, incensed both over the action itself and over the fact that it was done behind his back, but continued to guide policy behind the scenes. The Austrian government, nominally presided over by Franz Colloredo and Ludwig Cobenzl, sent the latter to Lunéville to negotiate for a general peace. Bonaparte tried his usual tactics of surprise and pressure on Cobenzl, luring him to Paris and threatening an immediate resumption of war if he refused to enter direct negotiations. Cobenzl, however, held his ground and left again for Lunéville, where he entered into negotiation with Joseph Bonaparte, hinting clearly that he would sacrifice Austria's alliance with Britain for a price. More than once the two sides seemed close to agreement, but Cobenzl's stubborn pursuit of a better frontier in Italy prevented it.

After the armistice expired in November, disaster quickly followed in the form of Moreau's crushing victory on 3 December at Hohenlinden, followed by more French victories in northern Italy. On 28 December, with French cavalry only forty miles from Vienna, Francis accepted another truce. Thugut was ousted, this time permanently, and after more futile negotiating efforts Cobenzl accepted the French terms at Lunéville in February 1801.[56]

This final result was wholly unsurprising, but the political strategies followed by the two sides repay a little analysis. Bonaparte's was simple: to divide and make peace. A separate peace with Austria was to promote another separate peace or truce with Britain to help him establish peace and stability within France. Each peace was intended to yield immediate gains without tying Bonaparte to a general settlement, and to lay the basis for later moves in any of several possible directions. The technique overall worked well. For example, when Bonaparte sent St Julien back to Vienna demanding that the Emperor promptly ratify the unauthorized treaty St Julien had signed, he also included several new demands St Julien had not agreed to. He used Austria's rejection of that treaty as an excuse to seize and plunder Tuscany; Tuscany served him as compensation to the Duke of Parma so that Spain would turn Louisiana over to France. When Austria protested the seizure of Tuscany, he made this the ground for a harder French line on Austria's Italian frontier, while the need to compensate Grand Duke Ferdinand of Tuscany somewhere in Germany gave Bonaparte more reason to promote a German territorial revolution, which became his means to win over the South German states and draw closer to Prussia and Russia.

[56] Fournier (1930: i. 240–5); Fugier (1954: 124–9); Roider (1987: ch. 12); Aretin (1967: i. 354–60); A. Herrmann (1912: 474–91, 505–23, 544–60, 697–99); Rodger (1964: 246–9); Arneth (1898: i. 21–8).

At Vienna, Thugut was alone in wanting to continue the war, but his opponents were divided over just what to try to preserve through peace, and how. Francis cared only for saving his hereditary domains and the army as the last bastion of his throne; he believed, for example, that he had done well in surrendering the South German fortresses in October because it brought his troops out of Germany and closer home. Thugut tried to save Austria's great-power position by the usual game of half-piracy—to make peace with France and get compensations in Italy without exactly breaking Austria's word or destroying the British alliance. At one point he even thought of reviving the Franco-Austrian alliance of 1756. Cobenzl simply wanted to sell a separate peace for as much as he could get in Italy. Trauttmansdorff dreamed of a common front with Prussia against France. Carl, the one man with a coherent if negative programme—peace pure and simple—sat in Prague, excluded from power by Francis and Thugut and unwilling to take responsibility for more defeats.[57]

British policy was more consistent and loyal to the alliance. Nothing in the Second Coalition became Britain more than the way it helped to end it. After Marengo, the government did not try to prevent Austria from seeking peace or stop the subsidy just agreed on, but only urged joint negotiations, and adhered to the alliance and the joint war until Austria abandoned them. This was mainly prudence, to be sure; the old aversion to Austria repeatedly welled up (Grenville still blamed Austria for the breach with Russia, 'our near and natural ally'), and the British were concerned that a separate peace might be followed by a Franco-Austrian alliance. None the less, the British did not try to exploit Austria's disasters.[58]

The Treaty of Lunéville outwardly changed Campo Formio little. Austria now recognized France's annexation of the whole left bank of the Rhine both on its own behalf and that of the

[57] A. Herrmann (1912: 523–41); Thugut (1872: ii. 234–41, 277–81, 288–351, 449–65); Napoleon (1858–70: vi. Nos. 4914, 5131, 5200); Vivenot (1870: 157–67); Rauchensteiner (1972: 54–7). On how Russia's hostility influenced Austria's decision to make peace, see Ragsdale (1980: 52–64); on Bonaparte's efforts to promote a Hungarian revolt for independence, see Kosary (1979: 7–14).

[58] Mackesy (1984: 138–41); Grenville (1892–1927: vi. 296–301, 306–7, 330–5, 368–70, 374–5, 408); Elliot (1874: iii. 153–78); BL Add. MSS 59102, fos. 51–84; 59103, fos. 1–16. George III remained strongly anti-Austrian to the end; see BL Add. MS 58861, fos. 108–14. For evidence that some Britons began to appreciate Austria's performance and importance to the cause better after Austria had lost, see Grenville (1892–1927: vi. 439–40, 454–6); BL Add. MS 37295 (Wellesley Papers), fos. 1–68.

Reich, accepted the razing of a number of right-bank fortresses, agreed to the Adige frontier in northern Italy, compensated Ferdinand of Tuscany with the Archbishopric of Salzburg, and recognized the independence of France's satellite republics. Still, Lunéville left Austria territorially intact and nominally a great power.[59]

This fact, plus the great changes outside the treaty Bonaparte was already making and would continue to make in France and Europe, seem to make Lunéville insignificant. Yet together with the Treaty of Amiens a year later it has a certain importance. On the surface, the wars of 1792–1815 appear one long, virtually unbroken conflict fought for a single main purpose: to prevent France from dominating Europe. This ignores important differences between distinct phases in the wars. The wars from 1792 to 1802 were not solely or even mainly about French domination of Europe; that became the dominant issue only after 1802, and was not the only one even then. The first decade of war, the result of a general breakdown of the eighteenth-century balance-of-power system rather than a French revolutionary and imperialist challenge to it, was about two broad issues: whether and how far France would recover its lost place in Western Europe and international politics generally, and, even more important, what settlement would emerge from war and revolution in Central and Eastern Europe. Lunéville and Amiens, in ending this phase of the war, seemed also to resolve these problems. They not only restored France to a prominent role in European affairs, but distributed power in Europe in such a way—France dominant in Western Europe, Britain on the seas, and Russia in Eastern Europe—that one could reasonably speak here of a real balance of power, in contrast to most so-called balances, which were plainly code-words and fig-leaves for imbalance and hegemony.

This does not mean that Lunéville–Amiens should have proved durable; no balance-of-power settlement was likely to be, especially under eighteenth-century rules. It does mean that Lunéville–Amiens had important things going for it. First, it was actually accepted by many powers. Austria viewed Lunéville, unlike Campo Formio, as a final settlement rather than a breathing space before the next war, and wanted to live with it. Even Thugut, from retirement, saw Austria's defeat and decline as irreversible and warned against any more war.[60] Prussia after Marengo was

---

[59] Text in DeClercq (1880–1917: i. 424–9) (for the preliminary peace of 28 July 1800, see 395–6).

[60] Roider (1987: 371–3); Vivenot (1870: 180–3).

eager to become France's junior partner.[61] Except for Austria, all the great powers emerged with gains in the form of spheres of influence and reasonable security—Britain in India and overseas, Russia in northern, eastern, and south-eastern Europe, Prussia in North Germany. Even Austria had not lost much absolutely, only relative to the others.

Equally important, French hegemony was widely accepted and supported by the leaders of smaller states in Western Europe—for example, Montgelas in Bavaria, Reitzenstein in Baden, Melzi d'Eril in the Italian Republic, and Grand Duke Ferdinand. Both the peoples and the leaders in Holland, Switzerland, and Belgium, blaming previous French exploitation on the revolutionary Republic, looked to Bonaparte to restore law and order.[62] As for most German and Italian princes, they jumped on the French bandwagon not only out of greed and fear, but because they could see that the old order in Italy and Germany was undermined, that France would lead whatever new order arose, and that only France could provide them with stability and peace.[63]

Sensible Frenchmen were aware that France now had a unique opportunity. On 9 March 1801, the French foreign ministry presented Bonaparte with a plan to reorganize Germany under French hegemony by pushing Austria to the east, confining Prussia to the north, and erecting a glacis of protected states on the right bank. The plan resembles the Confederation of the Rhine set up in 1806, with one vital difference: this Third Germany was to be a true *corps intermédiaire*, leaning on France in foreign policy but internally independent of France as well as of Austria and Prussia. Even Bonaparte saw what was called for: a Europe divided into spheres of influence, with intermediary bodies separating the great powers and France in charge of the best part of Europe and managing the system as a whole. The speech he gave in presenting the Treaty of Lunéville to the French senate, legislative body, and tribunate stressed that it would guarantee permanent peace by creating a wide territorial buffer between France and Austria, giving France its natural frontier on the Rhine, preventing foreign powers from interfering in France's sphere, and guaranteeing the independence

[61] Bailleu (1881–7: i. 369–70, 384–5, 514–25; ii. 4–9).

[62] To be sure, they were quickly undeceived. For samples of how Bonaparte immediately on assuming power began exploiting France's satellites and allies, see Napoleon (1858–70: Nos. 4425, 4518–21, 4600, 4647, 4871, 4958, 5028); Schama (1977: 399–409).

[63] Galasso (1979: 82–5); Zaghi (1969: 439–47); Chroust (1932: 10–13); Huber (1957: i. 38–43); A. Pingaud (1914: i. 272–4, 390–1); Press (1989: 80–1).

of the Cisalpine and Ligurian Republics. This was the devil quoting Scripture, of course; nothing was further from Bonaparte's intentions or actions. But still, the fact that he used this argument means something.[64]

The usual reply is that other European great powers, especially Austria, Britain, and Russia, would not have tolerated French hegemony in Western Europe, at least not for long. In Austria's case that contention is clearly wrong. Not only was Austria after 1801 cured of any disposition to fight; the French foreign ministry's proposed buffer zone between France and Austria in Italy and Germany was basically what Austria wanted. The objection has more force in regard to Britain and Russia. Given their expansionism in the two decades before 1802, more consistent and pronounced overall than France's, and the ambitions and mutual suspicions and hostility all three powers still entertained, they would probably have come into conflict sooner or later; this was almost unavoidable under balance-of-power politics and eighteenth-century rules. But this does not mean either that Russia or Britain in 1800–2 would not have tacitly consented to a peaceful, non-expansionist French hegemony in Western Europe, or that this kind of system could not have lasted as long as any conceivable under eighteenth-century conditions.

In fact, developments in 1800–2 prove the opposite, beginning with Russia. It abandoned the war against France de facto, though not officially, in 1800, and soon started a virtual war against Britain at France's side. This volte-face, to be sure, owed much to Paul's violent and erratic impulses. Yet his basic aims had not changed—to defend Russian interests, control the outcome of the war, and protect the smaller states of Germany and Italy. He simply decided that he could pursue them best first by leaving the war and then by co-operating with France. Already during the autumn campaign in October 1799 he had concluded a treaty with Bavaria which made it a virtual Russian protectorate, a very anti-Austrian move. After finally deciding to leave the war, he first moved, not against Britain or toward France (at this time he still wanted to reduce it to its ancient limits), but toward Prussia and against Austria. These steps, moreover, were in line with Russian tradition and domestic sentiment; many leading Russians were eager not to break with England, but not eager to defend

---

[64] Bitterauf (1905: 88–9); Napoleon (1858–70: vii. No. 5362). For examples of how Bonaparte was already expanding France's sphere far beyond the limits he indicated accepting at Lunéville, see ibid. Nos. 5466–70, 5560.

Austria.[65] N. P. Panin, a moderate, endorsed Paul's policy, tried hard to conclude an anti-Austrian alliance with Prussia, and even hinted at possible mobilization and war; he and others were only concerned that Paul might go too far, endangering Austria's existence and ignoring the longer-range threat from France.[66]

Once again Prussia, though eager to help Russia make peace with France and turn against Austria, refused to take risks for Russia's sake, and especially to supply the military force to enable the Tsar to protect South Germany. The Prussians also asked Russia to guarantee them against France as well as Austria, and wanted gains that Russia could not promise. Russia got only a renewal of their old defensive alliance. This indicated that, though Berlin's policy was opportunistic, it was also becoming aware that it could carry its rivalry with Austria too far; some day Prussia might need Austria against French power and Russian pressure.[67]

The Battle of Marengo in June 1800 brought this same lesson home to Panin: if Austria were destroyed, Russia would be face to face with France. But he could not persuade Paul that Russia should now work with Prussia to save Austria. Paul, by then obsessed with his quarrel with Britain, liked the advice of the sycophantic V. I Kurakin and the isolationist-nationalist Fedor Rostopchin much better.[68] In a famous *mémoire* of 1 October 1800, Rostopchin urged the Tsar to abandon Europe's quarrels and pursue Russia's national interests, specifically by partitioning the Ottoman Empire with France and Austria and forming a Russian-led Continental coalition against Britain. It is still disputed whether Paul approved the *mémoire* and seriously considered partitioning the Ottoman Empire at this time. Obviously Russia always wanted to have the lead at Constantinople, but the ways it contemplated of protecting its interests ranged all the way from a protective alliance with the Ottoman Empire to partition. As for Rostopchin's proposal, it was unmistakably expansionist but not chauvinist. He showed an awareness of Russia's limits in proposing that France and Austria share in the spoils of the Ottoman Empire and recognizing that Russia needed allies in Europe in

---

[65] Hüffer (1904: i. 398–405); Saul (1970: 110–11); Grenville (1892–1927: v. 377–9, 392–3, 402–3, vi. 2–3); Martens (1874–1905: vii. 246–9, 463–89); *Sbornik* (1867–1916: xx. Nos. 26–7).

[66] Panin (1888–92: v. 120–51, 189–301).

[67] Ibid. 311–56; Martens (1874–1905: vii. 264–80); Bailleu (1881–7: i. Nos. 310–12, 333–5, 374–5, 378–9).

[68] On the evolution of Russian policy and Panin's struggle against his rivals, see Panin (1888–992: v. 356–515); Krüger-Löwenstein (1972: 21–7).

order to act effectively against Britain. Even in Russia, the lessons of what had been happening were not completely ignored: Russia's military defeats, its first in some time; Bonaparte's forcing peace on Austria without paying attention to Russia; French control of most of Italy and ability to expand from there into the Levant;[69] France's presence on the Adriatic coast, challenging Russia's position in the 'independent' republic of the Ionian Isles under its protection. All this menaced Austria and the Ottoman Empire more directly than Russia, but the implication that Russia might have passed its peak in expansion and relative power and influence was not lost on St Petersburg.[70]

Spectacular developments in 1800 masked this possible decline, however, at least for Paul. In mid-summer 1800 he expelled the British ambassador Whitworth on a trivial pretext (the failure of Britain's minister at Stockholm to pay a courtesy call on his Russian counterpart at his departure) and ordered the Russian ambassador S. Vorontsov home (he refused to leave London). This was only the beginning. Because Britain, having captured Malta, refused to return it to the Maltese Order, the Tsar embargoed trade with Britain, sequestered British goods, and seized British ships in Russian ports, imprisoning their crews.[71] A trade war and naval conflict would eventually have damaged Russia more than Britain, but at that moment, coming on top of other serious military, political, and economic strains, this was a severe blow to British commercial and industrial interests. In seeking a negotiated peace with France beginning in late 1800, Britain was motivated as much as anything by the danger of sliding into war with Russia.[72]

Bonaparte eagerly exploited the Anglo-Russian rift. In mid-summer he wrote the Tsar offering to re-outfit and repatriate France's Russian prisoners of war, whose gallantry, said Bonaparte, was responsible for whatever military successes Britain and Austria had enjoyed. The flattery was crude but effective.

---

[69] Various discussions of the *mémoire* in Waliszewski (1913: 354–7); Ragsdale (1980: 14–17, 36–9, 109–19); Stanislavskaia (1962: 111–12); Krüger-Löwenstein (1972: 7–15).

[70] Stanislavskaia (1976: chs. 1–3); Saul (1970: 98–9); McKnight (1965); Michailowski-Danilevsky and Miliutin (1856–8: i. 380–3).

[71] Stanislavskaia (1962: 136–77); Ragsdale (1980: 74–5); Saul (1970: 144–9); Rodger (1964: 200–4). Interesting documents in Grenville (1892–1927: vi. 286–7, 449); Vorontsov (1870–95: x. 231–4); Panin (1888–92: v. 154–5, 160–5).

[72] MacMillan (1975); Grenville to his brother Thomas, 28 Nov. 1800, BL Add. MS 48152, fos. 74–5.

Paul fiercely resented Britain's criticism of the Russian army[73] and its refusal to exchange captured French soldiers for Russians. The Tsar responded by sending a diplomatic-military mission to Paris early in 1801, ostensibly to regulate an exchange of prisoners, actually to arrange for Franco-Russian co-operation in Europe. He now dreamed of organizing the Continent for commercial war on Britain, while France also helped Russia fulfil its aims in the Near East, Germany, and the Mediterranean. For a few Frenchmen (such as Baron d'Hauterive, political director at the Quai d'Orsay) the idea of a long-range Franco-Russian condominium in Europe was attractive. But as the Russian envoys, Count Kolichev and General Sprengporten, who began negotiating with Talleyrand and General Clarke in February 1801 quickly found out, Bonaparte's aims were even more self-centred than Paul's: to get Russia immediately to join the war, help France impose its peace terms on the Continent, consent to the French occupation of Naples and French reinforcements at Tarento and Brindisi (jumping-off places for the Near East), help France retain Egypt, and join a Continental system against Britain led by France. Kolichev constantly complained to St Petersburg about French demands and pleaded to be recalled, but managed to avoid any commitments or even signing a formal treaty of peace.[74]

The most spectacular aspect of the Franco-Russian *rapprochement* was unconnected with these negotiations. Paul decided purely on his own to send 22,000 Cossacks into Central Asia in mid-winter to march on India. Though Bonaparte would have tried to exploit the move given the chance, it was not the kind of Russian action he wanted.[75] An assassination plot by a group of nobles in March 1801 put an end, along with Paul's life, to this venture and his almost equally rash idea of an alliance with France.[76]

Meanwhile another of Paul's blows at Britain, a League of Armed Neutrality, caused Britain some anxiety but also ended up revealing the limits to Russia's power. It grew out of a long-standing quarrel between Britain and Denmark. The Danes pursued the typical neutral's policy of avoiding war while exploiting

[73] Dietrich Beyrau's analysis of the Russian army (1984: 1–32) indicates that British and Austrian charges of brutality, corruption, and inefficiency were fully justified.

[74] *Sbornik* (1867–1916: lxx. Nos. 1–49); Napoleon (1858–70: vi. Nos. 5232, 5315, 5327); Manfred (1971).

[75] Strong (1965); Shneidmann (1957).

[76] For a discussion of the specific connection between Paul's foreign policy and the assassination, see Warner (1977: 47–8, 90, 99–100, 112–13); for the domestic causes, see Keep (1979); Kenney (1979).

its commercial opportunities under the cover of neutral rights, opportunities that grew with the expansion of war and the disappearance of their traditional competitor, Holland. The profits more than matched the risks to Danish shipping and goods from French privateering and British searches and seizures, and the Danes deliberately let belligerent vessels sail under their flag and used it to protect enemy goods themselves. Until late 1797 no serious clash developed; the British took the attitude that, though Danish practices helped the French and their Dutch satellites, especially in the Far East, they also helped the British. But in late 1797 the Danish government, acting against the advice of its foreign minister, Count Andreas Peter Bernstorff, resolved to answer Britain's allegedly illegal and arbitrary searches and seizures with naval convoys of its merchant vessels.

Even this precipitated no immediate crisis; the British, concerned to conciliate Russia and keep Denmark out of France's camp, used their right of search cautiously. In July 1800, however, the British warship *Nemesis* stopped and seized a small convoy protected by the Danish frigate *Freya*. Even the prudent Bernstorff felt this as an affront to Denmark's national honour, while the British, less eager by this time to appease Russia, suspected the Danes of deliberately seeking trouble in preparation for another League of Armed Neutrality, which under current conditions would pose a serious threat. A provisional Anglo-Danish convention in late August temporarily defused the crisis, but in the mean time Denmark stood by its principles and appealed to Russia and other neutrals to support her.[77]

The Danish appeal to St Petersburg coincided almost exactly with the news of something more dangerous to Russia than the Anglo-Danish conflict over maritime rights—an apparent Austro-French peace (the abortive St Julien treaty) which might lead to an Austro-French alliance. The Tsar now called on Denmark, Prussia, and Sweden to form a Nordic League, ostensibly to defend their neutral rights jointly against Britain, actually to support Russia in Europe. While Paul began preparing to seize British ships and goods and to defend Russia against a possible British naval attack, he was also amassing two armies on the Austrian frontier. (This is another example of how almost every anti-British move by the Tsar in this period was also an anti-Austrian one, sometimes primarily so.)

Bernstorff reluctantly agreed to a new league, counting on

[77] Feldbaek (1980: 16–24, 210–17).

Prussia's refusal and Sweden's hesitancy to frustrate the scheme. Instead the Tsar began raising the stakes in the conflict, escalating his anti-British campaign and taking a far tougher stand on neutral rights than the Danes wanted. Britain in turn stepped up its measures against the neutrals, which helped Russia compel Denmark and an equally reluctant Sweden to join the league in December (at one point Paul broke relations with Denmark and sent its envoy home). On Rostopchin's advice, Paul also urged Prussia to occupy Hanover and advised the French to do so if the Prussians would not. He further pushed Denmark to seize Hamburg and Sweden Lübeck, and both of them to embargo British shipping, as Russia had already done. Delighted, Bonaparte fanned the flames of conflict, even proposing that he and France's satellites would like to join the league of neutrals themselves. In late January 1801 Britain finally reacted as Bernstorff had feared it would. It embargoed Danish, Swedish, and Russian shipping and recognized a state of war with the League of Armed Neutrality.[78] Prussia now was also forced to join the league and to occupy Hanover— which it had long coveted, but not at the price of open conflict with Britain. Prussia also had to let the Danes occupy Hamburg and Lübeck, cities Prussia was pledged to protect. Its pay-off for giving way to Russia in this way was every Central European statesman's nightmare—a prospective alliance between France and Russia.[79]

Everyone except France stood to lose heavily in this conflict, including Russia, though for a time it could make others pay the costs. By the time Paul was assassinated, he had pushed Russia into open war with Britain, caused Denmark, Sweden, and North Germany to be menaced by the British fleet, brought about the paralysis of Prussian and Russian maritime trade, threatened Russia's own fleet, compromised Russia's moral and political position in Europe, helped Napoleon expand at will in the West and South, and sent Russian troops on a mad expedition into Central Asia—all for no concrete Russian interest. Paul's assassination was connected with foreign policy only in a secondary way, but one can understand why S. Vorontsov called it God's way of saving Russia from revolution at home and disaster abroad.

Paul's son, Alexander I, acted quickly to liquidate Paul's projects

[78] Ibid. 24–137; *Sbornik* (1867–1916: ii. 1–17); Rodger (1964: 276–8). Feldbaek correctly concludes (1980: 100–1) that the League of Armed Neutrality was basically an armed façade for Russia's European great-power politics.

[79] Krauel (1914: 189–228); Ragsdale (1980: 82–8); Feldbaek (1980: 120–7); Grenville (1892–1927: vi. 400–3).

and get Russia back to peace, neutrality, and sanity. Panin was put back in charge of Russian foreign policy, effectively if not officially, and the expedition recalled from Central Asia. Russia ended its co-operation with France, but launched negotiations which led in October 1801 to a formal Russo-French peace treaty (of which more later). Bonaparte, initially devastated by Paul's death, sensibly accepted this as the best he could get.[80]

Meanwhile Britain used drastic action to disperse the storm clouds between it and Russia, with a small power paying the price. Alexander, though respectful of British naval power and ready for normal relations, still hoped to maintain the League of Neutrality and support its principles at London. (Vorontsov, ordered to do so, characteristically disobeyed.) In any case, the time for diplomatic compromise was past; the British had already decided to teach a lesson in naval power directly to the Danes and indirectly to the Russians. After Denmark rejected a British ultimatum to abandon the League and accept a defensive alliance with Britain, a naval squadron under Admirals Parker and Nelson sailed to Copenhagen to enforce the British demands. A hard-fought battle off Copenhagen on 2 April ended with a decisive British victory, somewhat obscured by a truce which saved the Danish fleet from total destruction. Even after this defeat Bernstorff waged a stubborn and supple diplomatic defence, agreeing only to a fourteen-week suspension of Denmark's anti-British measures.

Meanwhile the British fleet moved into the Baltic toward Reval and Kronstadt. Alexander warned the British of dire consequences from an attack on Russia, but he was warning of what Russia's partners might do, and that threat was an empty one. Sweden and Prussia were even less eager for war than Russia, while Denmark, already defeated, did not even want Swedish help because Sweden had its eyes on Norway. When Panin let the new British envoy, St Helens, understand that saving Russia's face was more important than enforcing neutral rights, a compromise Anglo-Russian agreement was reached in July. This agreement was finally imposed on the Danes and Swedes between August and October, and settled the issue of neutral rights for the time being.[81] Prussia, also irritated with Russia, rejected the convention and tried to

[80] Saul (1970: 156–71); Grimsted (1969: 68–80); Tatistcheff (1891: 17–18); Panin (1888–92: vi. No. 305).

[81] Feldbaek (1980: 139–65, 171–89, 194–201); *VPR* (1960–: ser. 1. i. Nos. 2, 5, 9); Martens (1874–1905: xi. 8–11, 14–28, 49–64); Panin (1888–92: vi. 36–105); Vorontsov (1870–95: x. 251–4, 353–67, 389–400, 408–10).

negotiate its own agreement with Britain in the hope of keeping Hanover, but failed, and reluctantly ended the occupation in October. It had damaged Prussia's prestige, created a dangerous precedent for France to exploit, worsened Prussian relations with the Scandinavian states and German free cities, and earned Prussia the resentment of the Hanoverians and the British alike.[82]

The main lesson of the affair for Sweden was that great powers do not always pay their promissory notes, especially to smaller ones; Russia failed to pay its expenses for preparing to defend Denmark as promised. Bernstorff had already learned a more important truth, that receiving support and protection from one great power might be more dangerous than isolation, and could not substitute for an international system guaranteeing the independence of all states.[83] But this lesson would require repeated applications before it would stick, and smaller powers were not the ones who most needed to learn it.

The Russo-British peace treaty of July represented a reasonable compromise; the Franco-Russian peace agreements of 8 and 10 October did not. The French got Russia to accept a series of *faits accomplis* in Italy, including a French–Neapolitan peace treaty making Naples a virtual co-belligerent against Britain and allowing France to occupy it for the duration; the conversion of Tuscany into the Kingdom of Etruria; and the certain prospect that France would annex Piedmont. In addition, Russia endorsed the French position on Malta, Egypt, and the freedom of the seas, and helped France make peace and restore relations with the Ottoman Empire. For all this Russia got nothing more than the end to a state of war more embarrassing and dangerous to France than to Russia, plus the promise of Franco-Russian co-operation in settling the affairs of Germany. The two Russian negotiators at Paris, Kolichev and his successor, A. I. Morkov, repeatedly denounced Bonaparte's tactics and aims in their reports; St Petersburg was worried about his ambitions in the Mediterranean. Morkov condemned the treaty he himself had signed, blaming the outcome on defective instructions and the lack of great-power unity in Europe. France's success showed Bonaparte's and Talleyrand's skill at flattery, pressure, and vague assurances. They were also able to take advantage of Panin's fall and his replacement in October by Rostopchin's follower Kochubei, and to exploit a mutual Russian–French interest in repressing the activities of *émigrés*, Frenchmen in Russia and

---

[82] Krauel (1914: 228–45); Sieske (1959: 27–39); Thielen (1967: 110–13).
[83] Feldbaek (1980: 170–91, 202–9); *Sbornik* (1867–1916: ii. 18–23).

Poles in France. The main thing France exploited in the negotiations, however, was Alexander's inexperience, over-confidence,
and determination to be his own foreign minister. Morkov and
the Russian minister Baron Paul Krüdener from Berlin repeatedly
warned the Tsar that France could not be contained without
European unity, especially between Austria and Prussia. But
Alexander continued to assume that their rivalry was a good
thing, making Russia the arbiter of Central and Eastern Europe
and enabling him to pursue peace, retrenchment, and reform
at home while simultaneously co-operating with Bonaparte and
restraining France.[84]

Alexander was too over-confident to try to stop Bonaparte in
Germany; Prussia was too fearful even to think about it. The
Prussians knew about French ideas of pushing Prussia north and
east out of the heart of Germany. For example, Talleyrand, in
offering Prussia the Mecklenburg duchies as compensation for
French gains, declared South and West Germany off limits to
everyone but France. Even Lucchesini, now minister at Paris, saw
the dangers into which his Machiavellian and Austrophobe advice
had helped lead Prussia, but he had no remedy to recommend.[85]

Bonaparte dealt with Spain in 1800-1 as skilfully as he had with
Russia, managing to keep it in the war against Britain for the
moment, while preparing to conclude peace himself with Britain
and to expand at Spain's expense later. He had long been trying to
make Spain fight harder, especially helping France save Malta and
Egypt. In October 1800 he concluded the Treaty of San Ildefonso,
which gave France Louisiana in exchange for Italian territory for
the Duke of Parma and six ships of the line. The deal not only
gave France enormous colonial territories but also drew Spain
more deeply into the war and made it France's hostage in Italy. In
January 1801 Godoy secured what he had long sought, a secret
Franco-Spanish accord for the conquest and partition of Britain's
ally Portugal if it refused to abandon Britain and join France.
Portugal seemed an easy target, especially after the British pulled
out and left them to their own resources in early 1801. But
Bonaparte initially delayed carrying out his promise to Godoy in

---

[84] Krüger-Löwenstein (1972: 32-84); Schiemann (1904: i. 93-4); Martens (1874-
1905: vii. 295-300). Documents in Napoleon (1858-70: vii. Nos. 5525-6, 5528,
5545, 5588, 5957); *VPR* (1960-: 1. i. Nos. 18, 25, 30; pp. 54-7); *Sbornik* (1867-
1916: lxx. Nos. 50, 56, 62, 92, 93, 95-7, 111, 119, 121, 123); Vorontsov (1870-95:
xx. 78-88); DeClercq (1880-1917: i. 467-75). On Bonaparte's Italian policy, see
Zaghi (1986: 231-91); Fugier (1954: 136-7); Acton (1956: 446-7).
[85] Bailleu (1881-7: ii. 26-63).

hopes of making a quick peace with England while he still held Egypt. Meanwhile he coerced Spain and the Duke of Parma into improving on the treaty of San Ildefonso in regard to Italy.

In April 1801 the invasion of Portugal was launched, and Lisbon quickly sued for peace. Bonaparte, after promising his brother Lucien control of the peace negotiations in Madrid, then tried to undercut him by concluding a harsh peace himself with the Portuguese representative in France. Lucien and Godoy, however, refused to relinquish their opportunity for personal gain (bribes and presents for favourable treaties or successful negotiations were still part of the diplomatic game). Ignoring Bonaparte's instructions, they drew up their own milder peace treaty with Portugal at Badajoz on 6 June, forcing Portugal to break with England, close its ports to British ships, grant France a favourable commercial treaty, and pay a contribution of £15 million. Spain, though it gained nothing, none the less ratified it. Bonaparte responded by ignoring Spain's claim to the return of the island of Trinidad in the Anglo-French negotiations currently going on. In September, Bonaparte consented grudgingly to peace with Portugal at the price of a larger indemnity and greater cessions to France in Guiana. These tricks and manœuvres had no long-range importance for the Iberian peninsula; Bonaparte's later policies would annul them all. They merely illustrate again how he waged diplomacy like war and treated allies as enemies, and thus should help scotch the persistent notion that Bonaparte started out as a normal politician and only later went to extremes. As always, his ruthless short-range tactics had hidden long-range costs. A useful tool in Spain, Godoy, was embittered; Lucien, the most talented of his brothers, quit his service in disgust; Spain's desire to escape from the war and the French alliance grew more intense.[86]

Even certain peaceful measures Bonaparte took had expansionist implications. The best example is his concordat with Pope Pius VII in July 1801. It served him well for purposes of domestic governance, ending the religious schism that had divided Frenchmen and poisoned the Revolution, aligning the Church behind his regime, and helping to pacify the rebellious west of France. No divine-right monarch ever went further than he would go in claiming divine sanction for his throne, or subordinating the altar to the throne. The concordat was also valuable for foreign policy,

[86] Fugier (1930: i. 106–74; 1954: 138–9); Lyon (1934: 101–10); DeClercq (1880–1917: i. 412–13, 420–3, 435–63); Napoleon (1858–70: vi. Nos. 5034, 5120, 5165; vii. 5336–7, 5585–6, 5364–5, 5629–30).

serving as a model for French satellites to imitate (at that moment in Italy, later in Germany) and strengthening France's hold on Belgium and northern Italy. The Pope, eager to end the schism and abolish the Civil Constitution of the Clergy, readily adapted the agreement to Napoleon's wishes.

But soon it became apparent that, for Bonaparte, there was no such thing as enough; trouble arose over the concordat and in French—Papal relations. Bonaparte altered its provisions unilaterally, promoted Gallicanism in France, and encouraged its extension to the Cisalpine Republic without the Pope's consent. At the same time he refused to make any changes in the draconian Treaty of Tolentino imposed on the Papal State in 1797. Pius VII, a genuinely unworldly bishop who throughout his life would consider Bonaparte a wayward son of the Church, was dismayed at the opportunity here being thrown away for a long-term reconciliation between France and the Church. He had no principial or political objections to placing the Church's influence behind French hegemony in Europe, and was eager to co-operate with Bonaparte as a temporal prince so long as his spiritual prerogatives were respected. Nor did he object to Bonaparte's exploiting religion and Christian doctrine for political purposes. As for Bonaparte, he had no specific grounds for not conceding the Church internal autonomy and the Papal State a reasonably independent existence like some other satellites. The problem, as always, lay in Bonaparte's character: his inability to see a jugular without going for it, to forgo short-run opportunities for long-range goods— here, the Church's co-operation over the long run.[87]

He did at this time, however, want peace with Britain, at least temporarily, for the sake of internal consolidation. The British also wanted peace. The war, though not lost, had become useless and dangerous for them, a source of economic strain, mounting debt, and loss of trade. Britain's military prospects were dim. Its navy, though everywhere victorious, was stretched thin; it had no Continental allies or prospects of any, and had just escaped a confrontation with a hostile coalition in the Baltic. A few Britons believed that Bonaparte was interested in peace and stability, more were willing to test him and see, and still more had become highly critical of the government's conduct of the war. In March 1801 Pitt resigned over the question of Catholic Emancipation, to which the King put up an invincible resistance. It was a genuine issue—in fact, domestic questions, especially those affecting

[87] Latreille (1935: 2–21).

Ireland, were always at least as prominent in British politics as the war—but it also gave Pitt a good ground on which to resign and leave the inevitable experiment at peace to his subordinate, Henry Addington.[88] Even for colonial-imperial purposes the war had become redundant. The East India Company had already greatly expanded its territorial base in India and brought the danger from native principalities under control; now both the Company and the government wanted to avoid further expensive conquests and administrative responsibilities. The campaigns in the West Indies had ultimately proved costly and unproductive, with trade seeming more important than new bases or territory. In the Far East and Indian Ocean, Britain had secured a lead over its various colonial rivals which peacetime trade would solidify. The war had aroused greater interest in Malta, Egypt, and the Mediterranean generally, but here too the main goal now was to avoid dangers, not gain new prizes.[89]

The fact that both powers wanted peace for internal consolidation, however, did not make achieving it easy. Both the preliminaries concluded on 1 October 1801 by the French envoy, Otto, and the British foreign secretary, Robert Jenkinson, Lord Hawkesbury, and the final Treaty of Amiens, signed by Lord Charles Cornwallis on 25 March, required long, painful negotiations. The French bargained in the spirit of 'What's mine is mine, what's yours is negotiable'. They banned most Continental questions, especially the provisions of Lunéville, not only from the treaty but also from any discussion now or in the future (though France did agree in the treaty to respect the independence of Naples, Portugal, and the Batavian Republic). Bonaparte had not granted Russia and Prussia a right to discuss the provisions of Lunéville either, but he and Talleyrand had tried to sugar-coat the pill for them; Britain was supposed to swallow it plain. Since the British did not contest the point, the two main results of the war, France's conquest and domination of Western Europe and Britain's conquest of India and maritime supremacy, were tacitly accepted and excluded from the negotiations and the treaty.

This made Egypt, Malta, and the restoration of British colonial conquests from France, Holland, and Spain the key questions. In the fighting still going on in 1801 in Egypt, neither side covered itself with glory. The British government had scuttled a convention reached by France and the Ottoman Empire at El-Arish in early 1800 to allow the French army to evacuate Egypt peacefully, to the anger of the Turks and of Sir Sidney Smith, who had encouraged them to sign it. Marooned in Egypt, the French army inflicted more defeats on the Turks, but Bonaparte's effort to reinforce it by a naval expedition in early 1801 was a costly failure. The British, at considerable risk, then landed their own expedition and conquered Egypt in the autumn of 1801, winning more by good luck and French incompetence than their own prowess. Though the victory helped British morale, it otherwise proved empty. British quarrels with the Sultan over their treatment of the Mamelukes in Egypt helped France regain influence at Constantinople, while Bonaparte and his brother Joseph succeeded in avoiding paying for the French defeat. Both the preliminary treaty and the final one tied the French evacuation of Egypt (already lost by the time of Amiens) to Britain's commitment to evacuate Malta.[90]

The treaty had further defects from Britain's standpoint, resulting from France's skill and persistence in negotiations, the Addington government's distraction and weakness, and Cornwallis's inexperience as a negotiator. Britain agreed to return all its colonial conquests save Trinidad and Ceylon and to evacuate Malta, the latter to be returned to the Order and neutralized under nominal Neapolitan suzerainty. There was no explicit provision to protect British trade interests on the Continent or to guarantee the independence stipulated for the French satellites at Lunéville.

The one-sided character of Amiens, together with the fact that it quickly broke down, justify labelling it historically a mere truce. One should not, however, jump to the conclusions that it contained no possibilities for a stable peace, or that neither side entered into it seriously, intending it to last.[91] The treaty was unsatisfactory not because no workable settlement could possibly develop from it, but because its one-sided provisions made it easy for France, if it chose, to exploit its advantages and promote a new war, and hard for Britain to respond without violating the treaty. Granted, precisely this happened, and given Bonaparte's character it was bound to; but another French leader interested in

[90] Rodger (1964: 219–27, 250–65); Shaw (1971: 268–82); Naff (1960: 316–51, 380–91, 400–31); Testa (1864–1911: ii. 3–25, 135–9); Napoleon (1858–70: vii. 5442–8).
[91] For varying appraisals, see Fournier (1930: i. 254–7); Deutsch (1938: 20–33); Rodger (1964: 282–7); Langford (1976: 215–17); Beer (1877b: 61–3); Geyl (1967: 274–7).

a durable peace would not necessarily have used Amiens and Lunéville in this way.

Nor is it true, as often supposed, that the British went into this settlement with no interest in a durable peace and no willingness to live with the treaty. True, there was considerable criticism of it in Britain, but usually behind the scenes, and even its critics admitted that peace had to be given a chance. Addington's government wanted the settlement to last; Pitt declined to criticize the treaty; even George Canning, the most strident of Addington's foes, attacked it mainly for personal political reasons. Moreover, critics of the treaty chiefly condemned it not for its essence—that it endorsed French domination of the Continent and destroyed the so-called balance of power—but for its details—that it meant too much sacrifice for Britain in commercial and colonial gains and in honour and prestige.

In other words, the British, though wary, were interested in peace, willing to try coexistence with France, and relatively indifferent at this time to the fate of Europe, including even the Low Countries.[92] And if Britain was willing to give Amiens a try, other European countries were ready to do more than that. France's neighbours were surprised that Britain had failed to insist on guarantees of the Continental status quo, an omission that affected them more directly than Britain. Yet the almost universal reaction to the treaty was relief that the war was over. Only a few die-hards like Friedrich von Gentz, a publicist recently switched from Prussian to Austrian service, still urged Britain to restore the European balance against France, and Gentz had a strong personal reason for selling his ideas and services to Britain (his constant need of money). The rival concept of a European balance developed by Baron d'Hauterive had more appeal to most Europeans: French leadership of the Continent to counterbalance Britain's domination of the seas. Even Russia accepted France as the leader of Western and Southern Europe.[93]

In sum, Amiens and Lunéville were bad, technically deficient as treaties—yet not necessarily unworkable in eighteenth-century terms as an overall basis for peace. If a sustainable balance of

[92] For various British reactions, see Ziegler (1965: 124–7); Renier (1930: 25–8); Auckland (1861: iv. 136–8, 143–52, 172–3); Malmesbury (1844: iv. 65, 77, 147, 156–7); Grenville (1892–1927: vii. 112–13, 139–40); BL Add. MS 48152, fos. 109–16; PRO 30/29/8/2, fos. 161–91.

[93] Raumer (1952: 140–1); Heinz Gollwitzer (1964: 105–11); Ragsdale (1980: 46–7); Forsyth (1980). For the ambivalent reactions in Russia, see Stanislavskaia (1962: 221–4); VPR (1960–: 1. i. Nos. 72, 74, 78).

power is important, the settlement was clearly better and potentially more durable on this score than either 1763 or the Anglo-Russian condominium in Europe which the Second Coalition was intended to establish. In fact, it achieved the only sensible balance of power possible: recognizing that there were three real great powers in terms of power and invulnerability, France, Britain, and Russia, assigning each its particular sphere of influence, and separating them either by geographical barriers (the Channel) or by extensive intermediary zones, including Austria and Prussia. The terms offered real advantages to some smaller states, and laid the groundwork for reorganizing Germany and Italy.

Inevitably there were losers and victims—Poland, Venice, Piedmont, the Prince of Orange, the German ecclesiastical princes, and other states and groups. None of these could have overthrown the settlement, however, and in certain remaining troublespots and contested areas, especially the Mediterranean and the Near East, the stipulations of Amiens, if executed, could actually have promoted stability. With France evacuating Naples, Britain evacuating Egypt and Malta while retaining Gibraltar, Russia pulling its squadron from the Mediterranean but retaining a foothold in the Ionian Isles, and Malta neutralized, no one power could dominate the whole region or directly threaten the others.

This is not to argue that Lunéville and Amiens could have led to a really durable, stable peace, only that they might well have been the basis for a normal eighteenth-century general peace, lasting at least a decade or two before more general war. More important still, what kept Europe from enjoying such a normal eighteenth-century respite from general war after Amiens was not the (alleged) absence of a satisfactory balance of power. On that score, 1802 was at least as good as 1763, 1748, 1714, 1697, 1659, 1648, or any other date one could select for comparison—including even 1815.

The point is not an abstract theoretical one, or advanced to promote a particular theory or polemic. It involves understanding the causes of the wars that followed Amiens and the character of the peace finally achieved in 1815. The reason war revived so soon after the peace of Amiens was not that France dominated Western Europe. There is clear evidence that all the other great powers had come to terms with this French hegemony, and that many smaller powers either accepted or welcomed it. To find the proximate cause for the swift renewal of war, we need not look beyond Bonaparte—the way he exercised French hegemony, or better, his refusal to be content with hegemony, his insistence on empire.

Behind this, to be sure, lay his restless drive for glory, his un-satisfied ambitions, his unslaked rage and frustration at Britain[94]— but nothing more than this, nothing deeper in the structure of European international politics. Just as 1939 was Hitler's war, in the sense that only he willed it and made it possible, so all the wars after 1802 were Bonaparte's wars. Yet just as the proximate cause of future wars did not lie in the defects of the Lunéville–Amiens settlement but rather in Bonaparte's personality, so also the deeper causes of the absence and failures of peace did not lie in the defects of the 1802 settlement, but in the tenacious sway of the competitive politics of balance of power, the inability of Europe until 1814–15 to conceive and practise anything better than eighteenth-century schemes of peace. Bonaparte's ambition would cause the next war, and several more after it. The sway of balance-of-power politics would cause the failures of peace.

[94] For a good sample of this anti-British fury, see Napoleon (1858–70: vii. No. 5749).

5
The Third Coalition, 1802–1805

THE quick collapse of the Lunéville–Amiens settlement, though mainly Bonaparte's responsibility, was not his alone. Even he could hardly have done certain things that would have helped make it more durable—for example, opening the French sphere in Europe to British trade. Nor was he the only one in France eager for military glory and expansion; so were many of his troops, other generals, both rivals and followers, and ordinary French civilians.[1] In any case, France had begun to undermine the settlement before the treaties were even signed. The main story in 1802–5, therefore, is not the quick revival of war between France and Britain, but the long, difficult process required to renew it on the Continent.

I. THE RENEWAL OF WAR, 1802–1803

The French government chose first of all not to conceal its overseas ambitions from Britain, but to flaunt them, even where it had no specific plans for expansion. For example, it deliberately created a false impression that it was preparing to reconquer Egypt. Colonel Horace Sébastiani was sent on a special mission to Egypt in 1802, and his enthusiastic report on how easy and valuable a conquest Egypt would be was published in the official *Moniteur*. Talleyrand boasted to the British ambassador, Whitworth, that French recovery of Egypt was only a matter of time. Other French initiatives in Algiers and Muscat reinforced British fears of French expansion in the Mediterranean and Near East.[2]

France's acquisition of Louisiana from Spain in 1801 posed a more concrete challenge to Britain in the New World, underlined by General Charles LeClerc's expedition to Santo Domingo to put down a slave insurrection under Toussaint L'Ouverture. LeClerc's army was eventually destroyed by yellow fever, helping induce France to sell Louisiana to the United States in 1803. In the interim, however, the French attempted repeatedly to acquire

---

[1] Fugier (1954: 160–3); Lefebvre (1969: i. 162–9).
[2] Dard (1937: 56–9); Fugier (1954: 170–7); Testa (1864–1911: ii. 45–62).

other Spanish New World colonies, especially Florida.[3] A change in France's policy toward the United States made these moves even more disturbing. Under the Convention and the Directory, France had played directly into Britain's hands by its arrogant and unrealistic demands on America for preferential treatment or active assistance in the war. These had helped the British regain its American trade and conclude the Jay Treaty with the United States in 1794, which benefited both sides commercially and politically. Later Franco-American quarrels had led to the embarrassing XYZ Affair in 1798, involving efforts by Talleyrand and other officials to collect the usual bribes for helping settle commercial disputes, and issued in a French–American commercial war and naval clashes in the Antilles from 1797 to 1800. Bonaparte solved his American problem through a provisional settlement of the question of neutral rights in the Treaty of Mortefontaine in September 1800, enabling him to begin the policy he would pursue over the next fourteen years, to pit America against Britain.[4] Other actual or potential French challenges to Britain arose in India, where Bonaparte appointed an extreme Anglophobe as Captain-General of France's remaining possessions, and on the seas, where he ordered his minister of marine, Admiral Denis Decrès, to build a French navy that would outstrip Britain's within a few years.[5]

The British were actually less disturbed by these overseas challenges, however, than by one of Bonaparte's most successful and durable acts of statecraft, his Act of Mediation in Switzerland in February 1803. Abolishing the Swiss unitary constitution fashioned by France and its Swiss collaborators in 1798, Bonaparte imposed new constitutions on the nineteen cantons, and provided the necessary federal ties and institutions among them by a Federal Act naming him Mediator of Switzerland. Even anti-French historians agree that until about 1812 the Swiss remained content with this regime and the French hegemony it perpetuated, for good reasons. The Act was sensible, progressive, and compatible with Swiss traditions. French intervention abolished the hated

[3] Lyon (1934: 106–9); Sloane (1899); Napoleon (1858–70: vii. Nos. 5825–7, 5845, 5846, 5863). For background, see Lokke (1932: 119–60).

[4] Fugier (1954: 146–9); Bonnel (1961: 33–42, 58–137); Nabonne (1951: 63–90); Blumenthal (1970: 8–15). For Anglo-American relations, see Ehrman (1983: 509–16); Ritcheson (1969). On the Franco-American quasi-war, the standard work is De Conde (1966).

[5] Parkinson (1954: 187–96); Mackesy (1957: 3–4); A. Herrmann (1912: 732–3); J. Howard (1961: 520–1); Napoleon (1858–70: vii. No. 5968). On the French naval threat in this era and the reasons why, despite French weaknesses, the British did not fully overcome it till 1805, see Arthur (1986).

Helvetic Republic with its confusion and civil conflict, while protecting Switzerland from international wars like that of 1799–1800. The end of the unitary constitution pleased aristocrats and conservatives, cantonal independence and the abolition of privileges and dependencies among the cantons satisfied radicals. Napoleonic rule even promoted a specifically Swiss kind of nationalism, multilingual, multi-ethnic, and confederate.

Yet the British were right to view the Act of Mediation as a dangerous, aggressive move. Bonaparte launched his intervention in 1800 by demanding French control of the Swiss side of the Simplon Pass as the price for permitting the Swiss to be neutral in the war. When the Swiss envoy responded with an offer to cede the Valais in exchange for compensations, Bonaparte took the Valais as a free gift, occupying it and establishing it as an 'independent' republic under virtually total French control. Only Russia's disapproval at that moment in 1802 deterred him from annexing it. He carried out the Act of Mediation itself by summoning Swiss deputies to Paris for consultation and then dictating the solution to them. More important, his purposes in the Act were nakedly power-political, and specifically anti-British and anti-Austrian. Switzerland was to be a 'neutral' under French control, he insisted, and not one undesirable Briton must be allowed to remain there; 'Switzerland, so far as France is concerned, must be entirely French, like all countries on the borders of France.' A subsequent convention, moreover, required the Swiss to provide 16,000 volunteers for the French army, while an offensive–defensive alliance called for an additional 8,000 in wartime. France also published the Act in a way designed to emphasize the point that Britain had no voice whatsoever in European affairs.[6]

As in Switzerland, French intervention in Germany was arguably good for Germany but dangerous for the European system, posing a direct threat to Austria and an indirect one to Britain, Prussia, and Russia. The end-product of French intervention, and of a long series of developments to be described below, was the so-called Imperial Recess of February 1803, a resolution drawn up by a deputation of Reich estates and accepted by the Reich which gave legal form to a massive territorial revolution in Germany already long under way. It eliminated 112 independent estates of the Reich, among them 66 ecclesiastical principalities containing

    [6] DeClercq (1880–1917: 1–82); Napoleon (1858–70: vii. Nos. 5383, 6206, 6207, 6225; viii. Nos. 6480, 6483, 6577, 6600). Oechsli (1903–13: i. 318–25, 428–30); Fournier (1930: i. 304–5); W. Groote (1969: 72–3); Surrateau (1973: 71–83); Roulet (1961); Warburton (1980).

three million inhabitants, plus 41 free cities. The spoils went mainly to the larger and middle-sized princely states, especially Prussia and the South German states; Austria, Hanover, and Saxony received proportionately less. This princely revolution of 1800–3, along with its later developments and consequences, represented in some ways the greatest political revolution Germany has ever experienced. It was also an astonishingly easy revolution for France to effect and direct, with many factors contributing to it and playing into France's hands.

There had been widespread support for secularizations of ecclesiastical principalities within the Reich since the Middle Ages, with the Reformation, enlightened absolutism, the eighteenth century's wars and rivalries, and the French Revolution all helping to promote the idea. Both Austria and Prussia had advocated it in the past. The ecclesiastical principalities and free cities, supported by some intellectual leaders and jurists and by states fearful of Prussia's ambitions, especially Hanover and Saxony, tried to defend themselves and justify their existence, mainly with the argument that an attack on them would destroy the whole German constitution. This was true, but, as their enemies in aspiring princely states like Bavaria pointed out, drawing as ever on balance-of-power doctrine for convenient arguments, the German great powers had already destroyed the constitution, and secularization would restore the balance in Germany by strengthening the middle states. Even the German Church, crippled by the long-standing struggle between the Pope's claims for supreme authority and the rival claims of territorial bishops, put up no determined resistance.[7]

Austria should have led the resistance to large-scale secularizations in its own interest. When in late April 1802 the Diet asked Austria to negotiate on its behalf with France, the monarchy seemed for a moment to rise to the challenge. The election of the Habsburg Archduke Anton to the vacant Archbishopric of Cologne rallied the ecclesiastical princes to its side, and two able Austrian diplomats, Prince Karl Schwarzenberg and Count Philipp Stadion, were sent on special missions to Russia and Prussia seeking support in holding France strictly to the treaties, while at the same time Ludwig Cobenzl tried to work out a deal with Paris.

But this led only to Austria's usual compromises and indecision,

---

[7] Aretin (1967: i. 372–5, 427–47); Lill (1979); Gagliardo (1980: 225–6, 290–305); Oer (1980: 193–228); Huber (1957: 56–9); Weis (1971: 339–40).

born of internal divisions, weakness, mistrust of all its potential partners, and an inability to decide what to sacrifice or to save. Unlike Buridan's ass, Austria starved because it was placed between equally repellent bales of hay. If it accepted Russia's lead, it would have to agree to large gains for Prussia and sacrifice specific Austrian interests without assuring itself of Russian support in the long run. Prussia was obviously no fit partner, and while a partnership with France was potentially attractive and some of the deals Talleyrand wafted before Cobenzl's eyes were tempting, the risks and traps were obvious. In the end, Austria itself suggested that a deputation of estates work out the proposed revisions with France, thus abdicating its leadership and tacitly encouraging individual estates to make separate deals with Paris.[8]

Austria thus failed to check France's tactics of division and manipulation; Prussia actively co-operated in them, to make sure that it got to the trough before others. Lucchesini, urged on by the King's cabinet minister, Johann Lombard, an ardent Francophile, negotiated a separate agreement on compensations with France in May 1802. Frederick William tried to persuade Alexander also to bypass Austria, insisting that separate deals like his with France did not compromise Prussia's or Germany's independence. This was whistling past the graveyard. An awareness of the danger from France was growing at Berlin; for Lucchesini and Lombard it was overcome by hatred of Austria, for Frederick William and Haugwitz by fear of war and eagerness to ascend the victor's bandwagon. The arguments which Haugwitz, already noted for his opportunism, supplied Frederick William to use when he met Alexander at Memel in May 1802 show that he recognized Prussia's long-range dangers as well as its short-run needs and opportunities. Facing the Russian complaint that Prussia had chosen a special deal with France over co-operation with Russia, Haugwitz replied by appealing to fundamental political and moral principles. The real goal of statecraft, he insisted, was not to achieve gains for one's own state, but to preserve the general international peace and order by defending natural and legal rights. Currently the greatest threat to international order, one which menaced Austria and Prussia most immediately, arose from France's power, ambitions, and lack of ties to Europe's traditions and laws. The best way to stop this menace, Haugwitz argued, was to conclude a Russo-Prussian defensive alliance and bring France into it.

[8] Deutsch (1938: 38-55); Beer (1875: 477-504; 1877b: 6-16, 31-40); Aretin (1967: i. 446-7).

This would end France's dangerous isolation and create political equilibrium in Europe. Prussia's separate agreement with France over Germany was a step in this direction, and therefore helped preserve the balance in Germany and the German constitution.

The sophistry is obvious: Haugwitz proposed to check the threat of France's excessive power and its aggression against Germany and Austria by allying with France in Germany and further isolating Austria. Yet accompanying the sophistry was a grain of insight and even (strange as the word sounds in connection with Haugwitz) of conviction. He saw that France's power and aggression was not the whole problem; that a still deeper one was the disappearance of all restraints in international politics. Moreover, he, like some Continental statesmen and unlike others, especially the British, implicitly recognized the difference between a political equilibrium, i.e. a balance of security and satisfactions, and a balance of power, and saw that the former was better. He further saw, at least dimly, that political equilibrium could best be achieved, not by confronting an aggressive state (here, France) with a hostile coalition, but by grouping it within a restraining alliance. Haugwitz's ways of implementing these ideas were patently absurd: to restrain France and promote equilibrium, restraint, and orderly behaviour in international politics by helping France expand territorially and destroy the legal order in Germany. Yet the underlying insights were sound.[9]

Only Russia could have given France serious problems in Germany. Bonaparte avoided them once more by exploiting Alexander's inexperience, ambitions, and particular brand of idealism. Alexander shared Haugwitz's goal, to 'group' France within a larger restraining alliance; but while Haugwitz hoped to make Prussia the tongue on the wagon, Alexander expected to join Bonaparte in steering the wagon while making Prussia and Austria pull it. Both Panin and his rival Kurakin encouraged Alexander to believe that Russia and France could co-operate as 'mediating arbiters' in Germany, and that at the same time Russia could restrain France in Italy and preserve its own monopoly of influence over the Ottoman Empire. Other Russians opposed this idea, but for divergent reasons. Panin's successor as foreign minister, V. P. Kochubei, and some others advocated pulling back from involvements in Europe. The pro-British party at court and some leading Russian diplomats abroad warned that France was bent on ex-

[9] Bailleu (1881–7: vol. ii, pp. xxvi–ix, 76–97; 1900: 11–14, 17–23); Martens (1874–1905: ii. 376–7); VPR (1960–:1. i. 306–8).

clusive control of Germany and Italy, and that no sound Russo-French relationship was possible before the German and Italian questions were settled and a stable European system established. Alexander, however, preferred the flattery and encouragement he received from the French, the Prussians, and certain of his relatives and sycophants surrounding him.[10] He therefore instructed Morkov to conclude a plan with France for territorial changes in Germany, and Morkov did so in June 1802, vigorously protesting all the while. Kurakin assured Alexander that this agreement would make the whole world 'see in you the protector of Germany and the angel of peace for the universe'.[11]

This convention, which the two powers conveyed jointly to the Diet, together with separate agreements France reached with various lesser states in Germany between May and September, served to settle matters in Germany long before the formal resolution of the Imperial Deputation in February 1803.[12] A brief crisis and war scare arose when Prussia decided in August to occupy some of the territories it had been promised without waiting for formal Imperial ratification. Austria, which had earlier tried to gain Bavaria as an ally with promises of territory, now occupied the Bavarian town of Passau as a way of deterring Prussia, ensuring that legal procedures would be followed, and making sure of its own compensations. In response to Prussian and Bavarian protests, France allied with them, guaranteed Bavaria its promised compensations, and threatened Austria with war if it did not pull out. When Russia refused to back Austria, it quickly retreated. The episode taught Austria again what it could expect from an alliance with Russia, and Russia what it should expect from partnership with France. This was a more open and brutal display of France's hegemony in Germany than Catherine's had been a gen-

---

[10] For discussions of Alexander's basic foreign-policy ideas and the situation at the beginning of his reign, see Grimsted (1969: 80–103); Shapiro (1956); Saul (1970: 172–81); Stanislavskaia (1962: 190–203); McConnell (1969); Krüger-Löwenstein (1972: 27–31). For a Russian nationalist attack on Alexander, see Mouraviev (1954: 67–89). Important documents on the debate within Russia are in: Vorontsov (1870–95: x. 93–156, 264–95); Panin (1888–92: vi. Nos. 311–17, 320, 336, 338, 350, 351); *VPR* (1960–: 1. i. 42–9, 59–68).

[11] Krüger-Löwenstein (1972: 97–108). The main documents are in *Sbornik* (1867–1916: lxx. Nos. 125–91); others in Vorontsov (1870–95: xx. 93–105); *VPR* (1960–: 1. i. Nos. 64, 66, 81); Napoleon (1858–70: vii. No. 6019).

[12] For the individual treaties and territorial changes, see DeClercq (1880–1917: i. 397–400, 414–19, 449–52, 580–610); Huber (1957: 46–51). On the French tactics and German reception of them, see Dunan (1961: 7–23); Gmeinwiser (1928: 20–3); Hölzle (1931: 277–302); Napoleon (1858–70: viii. Nos. 6281, 6284, 6297).

eration before at Teschen, yet even St Petersburg did not protest.[13]

Thus no serious challenge arose to French leadership in Germany. Things that would later burn the souls of German patriots— the loss of the Rhineland, French domination and exploitation, Bonaparte's lust for war and conquest—caused hardly a moment's discomfort now. Austria and Britain were more widely hated in the Germany of 1802–3 than France, and would remain so for some time. The dying Reich, if mourned at all by politically active Germans, was regretted chiefly because of the degrading manner in which it was being pushed toward its grave; France was not blamed for that, and the French claim that German liberties would be better protected in its new order was widely accepted. France could even have kept the Reich formally in being and exercised its hegemony within its framework. States like Bavaria were delighted with the French leadership that gave them additional territory, independence, and security against Austria, but would have liked to preserve some links to the past.[14]

The great powers had divergent reactions to Bonaparte's German revolution. The British paid little attention to it and cared less; German developments played no important role in British reasons for renewing the war in 1803. Austria and Prussia learned lessons from it which by this time were becoming redundant: for Austria, the futility of resisting France or relying upon Russia, for Prussia, the fact (of which Talleyrand repeatedly reminded them) that it remained a great power solely by France's permission.[15] The German experience was for Alexander another in a series of blows to his dream of a peaceful, mutually beneficial Russo-French partnership in Europe. Germany showed that Russo-French co-operation would not be easy or glorious; Switzerland, where Russia accepted Bonaparte's *faits accomplis* only to meet French requests for more favours and signals of new moves to come, showed that it would be anything but equal and mutual. The simultaneous increase in French activity in the Levant showed that the partnership would not guarantee Russia's special national interests, and the growing danger of a new Anglo-French war showed that it would probably not work to preserve general

[13] Krüger-Löwenstein (1972: 109–17); Deutsch (1938: 56–67); Panin (1888–92: vi. No. 165).

[14] Raumer (1957b: 126–35); Krüger-Löwenstein (1972: 117–18); Quint (1971: 88–91); Fugier (1954: 166–9); Deutsch (1938: 70–2); Driault (1910: 30–3); Gagliardo (1980: 192–5, 228–31, 246–55).

[15] Bailleu (1881–7: ii. 114–15).

peace.[16] Finally, Bonaparte's flat rejection of Russia's intercession on behalf of the King of Sardinia proved that he would not make even symbolic gestures to preserve Alexander's prestige and soothe his *amour propre*. This prompted Alexander in late 1802 to begin looking for ways to check France, though he was not yet thinking about breaking with France or going to war. The Tsar, like other Russians, believed that Russia could still get other states to resist France on its behalf.[17]

Bonaparte's Italian policy was more important in rekindling war than his German revolution, not because his moves in Italy provoked more resistance from other powers—he got away with them just as easily at first—but because they more clearly violated the treaties and undermined any possible stability in Europe. He imposed a new French-style authoritarian regime on the Cisalpine Republic in December 1801 and January 1802, renamed it the Italian Republic, and had himself elected its president. He also assumed direct power over the Ligurian Republic; reorganized Tuscany into a Kingdom of Etruria, giving Parma to the Cisalpine Republic, annexing Elba to France, and maintaining an occupation force at Tuscan expense; and finally annexed Piedmont in September 1802. All these moves except the last were made before the Treaty of Amiens was signed, and all either directly violated Lunéville or broke promises connected with it. Austria was particularly shocked at the fate of the Cisalpine Republic and Piedmont.

Yet most of these moves did not deter Britain from concluding peace, and by the end of 1802 all the powers had recognized these changes save Britain, Russia, and Denmark. Britain declined to do so on general principles, and because Bonaparte threatened further annexations if it refused to accept them; Russia did so because France refused to compensate the King of Sardinia-Piedmont; and Denmark acted out of fear of Britain and Russia. In contrast, Austria lay low, Prussia appeased France, and the Italians murmured but complied.

---

[16] A conversation between the French ambassador at St Petersburg, General Gabriel d'Hédouville, and General Valentin Zubov illustrates how the French conceived of the Franco-Russian partnership as an instrument of peace. Hédouville claimed that, if France and Russia were united, no cannon could fire in Europe without their permission, to which Zubov raised a question about wars of invasion. Hédouville's answer was that the two powers should come to agreements for these as well. Hédouville to Talleyrand, 25 Aug. 1802, *Sbornik* (1867–1916: lxx. No. 197).

[17] Schaeder (1934: 16–25); documents in *Sbornik* (1867–1916: lxx. Nos. 194–244; lxxvii. 4–35); *VPR* (1960–: 1. i. Nos. 98, 120, 121, 123, 171); Vorontsov (1870–95: x. 307–10; xx. 142–53); Nesselrode (1904–12: ii. 206–8).

War, therefore, did not exactly result from these acts of aggression; instead it represented their purpose. All were designed to expand France's military power. Piedmont was made into four French military districts. Immediately on reorganizing the Italian and Ligurian Republics, Bonaparte ordered them to arm, at the very moment when peace was breaking out in Europe. Under Bonaparte, as earlier under the Republic, France brought to new heights the state-building tradition of the old regime: the art of creating states by and for war, for whose perpetuation war sooner or later would be necessary—all outwardly by 'peaceful' means. Yet Bonaparte's success in getting foreign leaders to help him destroy their own states' independence, and in making these states and others accept the process as voluntary and legal, had some costs and sowed some seeds dangerous for his empire. Beyond a certain point, the domination of force and fraud in international politics may lead some normally opportunistic and unscrupulous actors to discover the practical uses of moderation, persuasion, and consensus. Austria finally showed an example of this in accepting the Italian Republic even though it clearly violated Lunéville. Vienna did so partly out of fear of Bonaparte, but also partly in the hope that the Republic might become more independent and thus serve as a real intermediary body between Austria and France. Furthermore, the name 'Italian Republic' implicitly encouraged a spirit of Italian nationalism which the realities of French exploitation and domination turned against France, leaving in the end no basis for French rule in Italy save force.[18]

In still another violation of Lunéville, France forced the Dutch to write a new constitution modelled on its own, and declared this constitution confirmed by a plebiscite in which only 17,000 voted for it and 52,000 against, by the expedient of counting 400,000 abstentions as votes in its favour.[19] Bonaparte continued to press Spain to cede Florida along with Louisiana, and when war with Britain drew near in early 1803 he immediately demanded more Spanish naval armaments, ignoring the devastating economic effects of the previous war. The once important pro-French party of enlightened reformers in Spain, called *afrancesados* by their opponents, continued to decline in credibility, and France began to replace Britain as Spain's main enemy in the popular mind.[20]

[18] A. Pingaud (1914: i. 378–81, 457–80); Fournier (1930: i. 300–3); Deutsch (1938: 76–7, 82–93); Chroust (1932: 14–21); Napoleon (1858–70: vii. Nos. 5807, 5965, 5970, 5974–5, 5990–1, 6213, 6218).

[19] Schama (1977: 412–43).

[20] Napoleon (1858–70: viii. Nos. 6280, 6455, 6424–9); Vicens Vives (1969:

Despite Bonaparte's ambitions in the East, France's actual policy was much less aggressive and dangerous there. The French intrigues reported by Russian agents in the Balkans had no major goals and accomplished little; rather than challenging Russia, the French twice suggested a possible joint partition of the Ottoman Empire. The Russians easily retained their primacy at Constantinople and in the Principalities, and were at least as active working against the French in the Balkans as vice versa. France's Eastern policy at this time was a greater threat to Austria than to Russia or the Ottoman Empire. In a move more serious and provocative than the Sébastiani mission to Egypt, General P. L. Roederer was sent on a special mission through Austria and Hungary in mid-1802 to gather intelligence on military affairs, potential risings in Hungary or the South Slav provinces, and ways to promote an Austro-Russian confrontation in the Balkans. At the same time Bonaparte was urging Vice-President Melzi of the Italian Republic to menace Vienna with an Austrian Legion created out of deserters from the Austrian army, and trying to lure Austria into a quarrel with Russia by an offer of the Ionian Isles. This would both distract Austria from Italy and Germany and induce Russia to combine with France.[21]

Objectively, therefore, the French were not as yet a menace to Russia in the Near East, just as they were not to Britain in India. Yet Russia perceived a threat, and began an approach to Britain to counter it, first signalled by Russia's advice to the British in February 1803 not to evacuate Malta.[22] Russia's perception of this threat owed much to a traditional security concern; Russians were aware that historically Russia had been vulnerable in the south. The great expansion achieved by Peter and Catherine and maintained by Paul and Alexander had diminished but not yet fully eliminated it. Late in his reign Paul had annexed the Kingdom of Georgia in the Caucasus, and Alexander decided to retain it, despite warnings from subordinates that it would be difficult to rule and defend.

National psychology and a sense of history, however, were also

578–81, 586–7); Herr (1958: 396–7, 438–45); Juretschke (1961: 222–41); Artola (1976); Hyslop (1950: 234–41).

[21] Puryear (1951: 2–15); Lebel (1955: 78–85, 90–2); Krüger-Löwenstein (1972: 120–1); Beer (1877b: 27–30); Napoleon (1858–70: vii. Nos. 6077, 6093, 6152, 6192, 6232); VPR (1960–: 1. i. Nos. 59, 88, 90, 93, 95, 110, 138, 154, 159, 172).

[22] Schaeder (1934: 7–9); Stanislavskaia (1962: 240–6); Fugier (1954: 180–1); Dostian (1974: 12–13). For documents illustrating Russia's changed attitude on Malta and toward Britain, see VPR (1960–: 1. i. Nos. 102, 153–4, 163, pp. 394–7).

involved in Russia's expansion to its south-east, making it in some ways resemble Britain's in India and elsewhere. Neither drive was the product of European politics—indeed, they had little or no direct connection with it—yet both affected Russian and British attitudes toward Europe. The fact that Russia had the now-decayed empires of Turkey and Persia as neighbours, and the smaller states and tribes of the Caucasus served as buffers against them, not only provided Russia with the kind of security, power, influence, and potential for gains in the Middle East comparable to Britain's overseas, but also, Russians believed, enhanced their choices in European politics. Like the British, they could either intervene in European questions to promote their interests or stay out and concentrate on areas where Russia had no competition. Therefore any hint of a French intrusion into their sphere was genuinely perceived as a threat. Thus Russian exceptionalism made Russians react to perceived threats, however remote, much like Britain in its heyday and the United States throughout its national existence. In general, two kinds of state show an inordinate sensitivity to perceived security threats: those really threatened, and those facing the possible loss of a customary or cheap security.[23]

Most of France's moves by early 1803 were provocative; none constituted a *casus belli*, at least not for Britain or Russia. Nor did Bonaparte want a war with Britain or anyone else, at least until he was more ready for it. This forced the British to take the initiative—i.e. first to decide to resist further French expansion at the risk of war, and then to violate the Treaty of Amiens in doing so. After considerable hesitation, Addington refused in late 1802 to evacuate Malta in accordance with the treaty. The British did not really dig in their heels even on this score, however, until Bonaparte, while insisting on a literal fulfilment of Amiens, dismissed British complaints about the violations of Lunéville and France's general expansionism as irrelevant, and flaunted his intervention in Switzerland before the British to emphasize the point. Then Bonaparte, having underestimated Britain's determination to resist, tried to avoid or postpone the conflict. This led to Anglo-French negotiations from November to the final break in May 1803, which seemed at times to have a chance of success. Talleyrand and the British ambassador, Whitworth, genuinely wished to avoid war, and a peace party was active in both countries. But Bonaparte's determination to exclude Britain from the Continent now and bring it to its knees in the future made war, in the last analysis, unavoidable.

Most scholars have recognized this. Another aspect of the failed negotiations has gone largely unnoticed. The terms Britain proposed in November 1802 for a revised settlement are sometimes portrayed as a challenge Bonaparte had to take up. Actually they show the opposite: that the British were coming to terms with French hegemony in Europe and trying to get Bonaparte to exercise it in a somewhat different way. Britain proposed that it should retain Malta, and that France should withdraw its troops from Holland and Switzerland. In exchange, Britain would accept France's annexation of Elba and recognize the Italian and Ligurian Republics and the Kingdom of Etruria, provided some compensation were found for the King of Sardinia. Of course Bonaparte was bound to reject this offer—but because it stemmed from Britain and set some limits on his actions (in other words, because he was Bonaparte), not because the terms were insulting, dangerous, or unreasonable for France. Objectively, this proposal meant British recognition of France's acquisitions and French hegemony in all of Western Europe, formally in Italy, tacitly in Germany. It would not have cost France its political hold over Holland and Switzerland, only direct military control of them. The British did not even raise issues once vital to them, such as the fate of Belgium or commercial access to the Continent.

Thus these terms indicate further who the real aggressor was, but the main thing they prove is less obvious. The root cause widely seen as responsible for the Anglo-French conflict here being renewed is the old struggle since the seventeenth century between France's efforts to dominate the continent of Europe and Britain's determination to maintain a European balance of power against it. In this case, that issue really had nothing to do with it. Britain here would have conceded France a position in Europe which Frenchmen like Talleyrand, Joseph Fouché, and Joseph Bonaparte considered all that France could desire. The British went to war simply because they could not stand being further challenged and humiliated by Bonaparte; France went to war because Bonaparte could not stop doing it.[24]

Yet if this justifies Britain's resort to war, it does not justify

[24] For sensible interpretations of the origins of the war, see Rodger (1964: 288–95); Ziegler (1965: 182–5); Sieburg (1971: 161–70); for an elaborate but unconvincing argument that the Addington government forced Napoleon into it, see Deutsch (1938: 103–47). Details on the negotiations, esp. the Malta issue, are in Schmitt (1971: 60–72); Whitworth (1887).

its policy overall. The Addington government has often been criticized for its inadequate diplomatic and military preparations for war—a criticism possibly warranted, though its defenders cite mitigating circumstances and some achievements.[25] The bigger question is how Britain conceived of this war and intended to fight it, and this question has been largely overlooked. One reason for neglecting it may be the common impression that the key question for international politics is who is responsible for a war— who started or provoked it. Deciding who is the aggressor, and whether the war is just, is vital; once this is determined, it somehow matters less how the war is fought, how long, to what ends, and at whose expense.

This is a dangerous, pernicious illusion. Means make more difference than ends in international politics; the total results of a war usually depend less on its so-called defensive or aggressive character, or even on the goals one is fighting for, than on the means used to win it, the amount and nature of the force employed.

Here lies one of many ironies in this era: France was the real aggressor in this war, Britain the defender; but each intended to fight a similar kind of war, with the same target. Both (Britain even more than France) foresaw that this would be a war of attrition, and both expected the rest of the Continent to suffer for it. The British government under Addington, supplanted by Pitt in 1804, had a strategy like Neville Chamberlain's after September 1939. They expected Britain to win a prolonged war, hoped for a French financial and internal collapse, and looked forward to the time when Bonaparte, defeated in naval and commercial warfare and frustrated in his attempts to invade Britain, would turn and fall on the Continent, thereby creating a great new anti-French coalition. One cannot blame them for this hope and desire, but it is legitimate to ask whether the British had learned anything important from the first two coalitions about forming and leading a new one. The answer is that they had learned nothing, or the wrong things. They wrote Austria and Prussia off, considering only Russia and Sweden worth pursuing and subsidizing as allies. The German powers' armies were critically important, of course; but just as in the first two coalitions, Russian pressure and French aggression were supposed to force Austria and Prussia ultimately to fight—and to fight not merely at Britain's side, but under British and Russian direction. The British gave little thought to

[25] C. D. Hall (1988).

the possibility that these powers and others, rather than hating France for threatening and exploiting them, might instead hate Britain for starting another war and so encouraging France to do it. This means that the Anglo-French war renewed in 1803 offers two lessons, by now predictable. One is that Bonaparte provoked it and the British accepted war on defensible grounds of honour and security. The other is that Britain entered the war ignorant of Europe and indifferent to its interests and its fate.[26]

II. THE ANTI-BRITISH COALITION, 1803–1804

If Britain's strategy involved long-run dangers for the Continent, they were nothing compared to the immediate threat from France. The picture dear to French historians of how British diplomacy and gold repeatedly built new coalitions against France, often misleading, is simply false here. Britain remained isolated for most of this war while Bonaparte fashioned a great coalition of satellites and allies against it. The 'independent' Batavian and Italian Republics were brought into the war automatically, Switzerland by an alliance in September, Spain in October. Neutral status was no defence. Naples and Hanover were supposedly neutral; by June French troops had seized the Neapolitan ports of Tarento, Otranto, and Brindisi and occupied the whole Electorate of Hanover, without serious repercussions in Europe.

Bonaparte's heavy demands on France's allies and on neutrals strained their economies and civic life, wrecking the efforts of loyal followers like Grand Pensionary Schimmelpenninck in Holland and of Melzi and his finance minister, Prina, in the Italian Republic to bring fiscal order out of chaos. Bonaparte knew this, and blamed everything on the British. This would symbolize the impact of Bonapartist rule on Europe. It helped destroy an old order and gave rise to a new generation of leaders, whose efforts to create modern states and new forms of national life under French leadership and protection Bonaparte himself would frustrate. He also showed his skill at making imperialism feed imperialism just

[26] For Britain's strategy, see Ziegler (1965: 198–9); for examples of British attitudes toward the Continent, Allardt (1976: 153–77); Whitworth (1887 passim, esp. 104–5); Malmesbury (1844: iv. 208–9, 246–7, 264–79, 312–13); BL Add. MS 48152, fos. 103–10, 126–31. On the economic, social, fiscal, and military problems the government faced in going to war, see Crouzet (1958: i. 107–25, 150–3); Emsley (1979: 99–112); C. D. Hall (1988); Groote and Müller (1968: 88–91).

as war fed war. For example, he succeeded not only in making other countries contribute troops to the army he gathered at Boulogne to invade Britain but in giving that army a specifically imperial character attached personally to him. By making Europe pay for his wars, moreover, he spared France most of the costs and preserved his popularity at home.[27]

Still, this war came inopportunely for him, before the Continent was fully organized for it. Besides, he wanted at this point to humiliate Britain and exclude it from Europe, but not necessarily conquer it. His momentary unpreparedness, added to a desire to alienate Russia from Britain, explains his conciliatory response to a Russian proposal to mediate the Anglo-French conflict. France offered to accept Russia's arbitration or, alternatively, to allow Russia to garrison Malta while the British moved to the isle of Lampedusa and France withdrew its troops from Holland and Switzerland and assigned some compensation to the King of Sardinia, though not in Piedmont. Bonaparte even agreed in vague terms to some sort of congress on European security, provided France's 1803 borders were not affected.

The reply was shrewdly calculated to appeal to the Tsar, who was dismayed by the outbreak of war and especially by the danger that Bonaparte, unable to attack Britain, would expand it into the Continent—a fear which the French occupation of the Neapolitan ports and Hanover strengthened. Russia's response to these aggressive French moves was, as usual, to push others forward against France. It asked Britain to join Russia in a guarantee of the Ottoman Empire and Naples, and urged Prussia to take the lead in defending Northern Europe, especially the Hansa cities. This was an attempt to make others protect Russian interests, true; but it also involved a broader insight into Europe's problem, and a special conception of Russia's duty in regard to it. Russian statesmen repeatedly insisted during this war, as in the earlier ones, that Russia faced no threat to its own security and interests. The danger instead was the possible overthrow of Europe, described by the chancellor and foreign minister, A. P. Vorontsov, as 'a republic or great society where there were perhaps three or four of influence, but never a single master'. Not only must Russia eventually do something to prevent this; the solution also could no longer be found in individual political and military

[27] A. Pingaud (1914: i. 397–420; ii. 48–287); Deutsch (1938: 148–59); Schama (1977: 446–7, 468–73); Napoleon (1858–70: ix. Nos. 7271, 7311, 7322, 7334–5, 7338, 7362, 7375, 7943, 7946, 7949).

alliances and other arrangements. Only a broad restructuring of Europe to guarantee the independence of all states, large and small, would do.

This was a genuine and important insight; even in Russia there were initial signs of a break with eighteenth-century thinking. But Russians applied this principle of the necessity of preserving smaller states as independent intermediary bodies in a special way. It was important first and foremost for Russia's own defensive glacis in Northern Europe, southern Italy, and the Ottoman Empire, and secondly for Holland, Switzerland, and northern Italy. In western and southern Germany, however, Russia tacitly ignored it, having collaborated with France in undermining the Reich and many intermediary states; its applicability to Austria was doubtful, and to Poland non-existent. Moreover, while the Russian government was eager for partners in the effort to preserve intermediary states (Prussia, Britain, even France), it did not wish to work with Austria.[28]

Bonaparte's request for Russian mediation therefore fell on fertile soil. Even Morkov was momentarily impressed, and pro-British Russians felt that Britain should not have started the war without waiting for Russia's mediation, and ought to accept it now. Alexander promptly produced a peace plan. It called for returning Malta to the Knights of St John, with Russia to garrison it for ten years, Britain to acquire Lampedusa instead, and the King of Sardinia to be compensated somewhere in Italy. All six leading European powers would recognize France's satellite republics as well as Naples, Etruria, Sardinia, and the Ottoman Empire, guaranteeing independence and a right to neutrality to all of them. France would evacuate Hanover, Holland, Switzerland, and all of Italy and give up any right to reoccupy them. England would restore its conquests and maritime prizes and France return the contributions it had taken from Hanover and the prizes it had captured at sea.

Alexander's surprise when Bonaparte angrily rejected his proposal again shows his inexperience and naïvety. Bonaparte's claim that Russia's terms were worse than Britain's and failed to restore a balance in the Mediterranean and overseas was correct—besides which he had to leave an even greater objection unstated: these terms would have reversed France's expansion and destroyed his

---

[28] *VPR* (1960–: 1. i. Nos. 181–3, 192, 196); *Sbornik* (1867–1916: lxxvii. 108–12, 153–64, 180–91, 203–5, 208–13, 217–19, 285) (the letter of A. Vorontsov quoted is on pp. 190–1); Vorontsov (1870–95: xx. 159–67, 170–1).

prestige.[29] The British, having warned Russia when accepting its mediation that, besides Malta, other issues created by France's expansion and violations of treaties would also have to be settled, similarly rejected Russia's proposal. Calling it unfriendly and dangerous, they made clear that they would not give up Malta, and called on Russia to join them in organizing the Continent to resist French aggression. As usual, S. Vorontsov supported Britain against his own government.[30] Britain also could not say openly what it most resented about the mediation, that Russia was trying to shelter itself and the Continent from the war.

Rebuffed, Alexander withdrew in a spirit of 'a plague on both your houses'. He soon re-entered the scene, however, this time taking sides, not because of a major international or military development, but because of actions Bonaparte took to solidify his power at home. In January and February 1804 the French police uncovered a complex conspiracy connected with the British spy network in France and abroad. Involving the old Chouan leader Georges Cadoudal and the former Republican general Pichegru, it was tied in one direction to Bonaparte's rival General Moreau and in another to a group of émigrés living in London, led by Louis XVIII's brother, the Comte d'Artois. The conspirators, though divided over whether to restore a French monarchy and, if so, what kind, were united in wanting to overthrow Bonaparte.

The conspirators caught in France were quickly dealt with, but the leaders elsewhere could not be, especially those in Britain. Across the French border at Ettenheim in Baden, however, lived a Bourbon prince, the Duc d'Enghien, who, though not involved in this plot, was believed to be in English pay and working for an invasion of France and restoration of the Bourbons. Talleyrand helped persuade Bonaparte to order the arrest of Enghien. Kidnapped on Badenese soil by French soldiers, Enghien was brought to Vincennes and there tried and executed on 20–1 March.[31]

For Bonaparte this was a normal, fairly routine act of state serving several purposes: revenge against the Bourbons, a salutary warning to the émigrés and potential conspirators at home, and a further justification for making his rule hereditary to safeguard the

[29] Deutsch (1938: 196–7); *Sbornik* (1867–1916: lxvii. 203–5, 276–85, 321–5, 328–9, 278–81); Napoleon (1858–70: viii. Nos. 7032–5).

[30] Martens (1874–1905: xi. 68–76); *VPR* (1960–: 1. i. Nos. 200, 210); Vorontsov (1870–95: x. 420–6); *Sbornik* (1867–1916: lxxvii. 228–41, 252–63).

[31] Bertaud (1972); Lefebvre (1969: i. 180–5); Godechot (1981: 376–81); Lacour-Gayet (1928–30: ii. 130–42).

regime. The senate proclaimed him Napoleon I, Emperor of the French, on 18 May 1804. The Enghien affair did not keep him from posing, as before, as the defender of international law against the British and their state-sponsored terrorism; he probably believed in the role himself and played it successfully, at least in France.[32]

If Napoleon wished to avoid a break with Russia, however, the Enghien affair was a mistake (though whenever Napoleon sensed that another government would resent some move of his, this encouraged him to do it). Russo-French relations had already degenerated through the fall and winter of 1803-4. Morkov and Talleyrand, personal enemies, bickered constantly over essentially petty questions. Napoleon angrily demanded Morkov's recall, Alexander complied but declined to name a successor, and Morkov delayed his departure to prolong the quarrel. While the main grievance on both sides was injured honour, a substantive issue involved Alexander's use of French *émigrés* in Russian diplomatic positions at Dresden and Rome, where they spied and conspired against Napoleon.

Still, the tension had not made St Petersburg abandon the hope of co-operating with France in Europe, especially over Germany. In January 1804, for example, Chancellor A. Vorontsov, himself an Anglophile, suggested that France and Russia authorize their ministers at Vienna to settle a quarrel brewing between Austria and Bavaria.[33] British and French factions still competed for influence in Russian court and governmental circles, and Russians resented Britain's domination of the seas almost as much as they feared the French menace to Northern Europe and the Levant. Vorontsov's physical decline and loss of influence increased the uncertainty over policy, while opening the door to a man of great personal charm and dangerously superficial ideas: Prince Adam Czartoryski, one of Alexander's youthful intimates and the scion of a great Polish family.

Arnold Toynbee once remarked that Greeks in the Ottoman Empire were torn between two ambitions: to free themselves from Ottoman rule, and to take over the Ottoman Empire and run it themselves. Something similar can be said of Czartoryski as a Pole in Russian service. At this time, as for some time to come, his aim was to restore Poland's greatness by means of expanding

---

[32] Napoleon (1858-70: ix, No. 7799); Deutsch (1938: 190-1); Driault (1912: 64-9).

[33] *Sbornik* (1867-1916: lxxvii. 426-546).

Russia's. He advised Alexander that Russia, invulnerable itself, could and should follow an active policy in Europe. While it needed to manage Britain for a time until Russia's navy and merchant marine could command its respect, otherwise Russia had little to fear. Germany, Austria, and Prussia formed a barrier protecting Russia from France, and at the same time they had to lean on Russia out of fear of France. However, the jealousy and ambitions of the German powers *vis-à-vis* Russia made them potentially dangerous, especially if they allied with Turkey and Sweden; Russia's best ally against them would be an independent Polish kingdom linked to the Russian crown. If this were unacceptable, then Russia should annex all the old Polish territories, or as much of them as possible, partition the Ottoman Empire, liberate the Balkans, and in co-operation with France establish an independent Italy and a federated Germany free of Austrian and Prussian control. This would establish a new peaceful European order under Russian hegemony. Czartoryski at this time more than Alexander represented that combination of philanthropy, ambition, arrogance, and ignorance which made Russia potentially as dangerous to Europe as France. As for the Tsar, though his ideas were still unformed, he conceived of a peaceful Europe divided into British, French, and Russian spheres of influence. (For example, he considered sharing control over the Balkans with Britain, as a counterweight to French gains in Central Europe.)[34]

In this labile situation at St Petersburg, the judicial murder of the Duc d'Enghien, to use Bismarck's phrase, had the effect of beating a drum in a sickroom. The French ambassador, General d'Hédouville, immediately warned of a possible break in relations; Alexander ordered his court into official mourning. The Russian state council resolved on 17 April to lodge a strong protest at Paris and to authorize the Russian chargé, d'Oubril, to leave if the French response was unsatisfactory. Yet this move was not intended as a direct challenge to France. Some council members opposed any serious action on isolationist-nationalist grounds, others for fear of drawing Napoleon's wrath away from Britain toward the Continent. Czartoryski presented arguments for and against a break with France, coming down in favour of strong action basically because he thought Russia could not lose. Britain was always available as an ally, and any French action directed against Russia would drive Austria and Prussia into Russia's arms. Following

[34] Grimsted (1970); Stanislavskaia (1962: 268–73, 381–8); *VPR* (1960–: 1. i. No. 231); Vorontsov (1870–95: xv. 455–80).

this meeting Russia tried, though not very seriously, to organize a united German protest to France through Prussia and the Imperial Diet, and attempted still more feebly to force France to evacuate Hanover and the Neapolitan ports.

France could have evaded Russia's demands easily enough. Since the Margrave of Baden did not dare protest against the French violation of his territory, the Imperial Diet, Prussia, and Austria claimed that they had no grounds for action. This enabled France to tell Russia that it had nothing to answer for in international law. Talleyrand might have finessed his way out of the other Russian demands as well, had he wished. He did talk Oubril out of demanding his passports after the first Russian protest, and Czartoryski told Oubril that Russia's call for the evacuation of Hanover was not a *sine qua non*. But artful dodging was not Napoleon's style, nor at this point Talleyrand's either. Besides, like many bullies and actors, Napoleon when he played the role of the injured party genuinely believed in his own performance. Enraged (as he put it) by the impertinences of Russia on top of the insults of England, he counterattacked. Refusing any explanations, France denounced the protest as an interference in its internal affairs, drew insulting comparisons between the Enghien affair and the assassination of Paul I, and made sneering references to the disparity between Russia's claim to leadership in Europe and its real power. The war of words climaxed in a break in relations in early August.[35]

The break ultimately led to an Anglo-Russian alliance and a third anti-French coalition, but the road to it was long, indirect, and tortuous. No effective coalition was possible without bringing in one or both great powers in Central Europe, and Austria, the more likely candidate, was bent on avoiding trouble and minding its own affairs. The Cobenzl–Colloredo government was only unsure how to do so. Following the Imperial Recess in 1803, it momentarily tried to regain its following among the old Imperial *Herrschaften* in Germany when it moved to stop Bavaria and other estates from confiscating the estates of the imperial knights and mediatizing them (i.e. ending their independence as direct vassals of the Emperor and making them subordinate to the sovereignty of the territorial princes). But at the same time it seemed to seek a

---

[35] Deutsch (1938: 202–7); Driault (1912: 51–64); *VPR* (1960–: 1. i. No. 278; ii. Nos. 3–7, 35); *Sbornik* (1867–1916: lxxvii. 547–686, 745–8); Napoleon (1858–70: ix. Nos. 7745 (this contains the words about the insults of Britain and impertinences of Russia), 7894–5, 7909).

better share for itself out of the general liquidation of the Reich by proposing a territorial exchange with Bavaria and trying to secure the revenues from secularized Church lands through its reversionary rights in the Empire. Whatever it was hoping to do, it failed. The Bavarians protested, Russia, thinking to restore its own German position, proposed a joint Franco-Russian intervention, and Napoleon, turning Russia aside, formed an alliance with Prussia and Bavaria and forced Austria to back down.

Austria showed that it had learned its lesson from this initiative when Napoleon, proclaimed Emperor of the French in May 1804, crowned himself with the crown of Charlemagne, so long associated with the Habsburgs, at his coronation in Paris in December. Francis responded by declaring himself Emperor Francis I of Austria, which meant not only accepting the French title but also preparing to surrender the Imperial German crown. This timid stance was not universally approved at Vienna. Philipp Stadion, ambassador at St Petersburg and an Imperial knight and patriot, urged the formation of a great anti-Napoleonic coalition including Prussia, while Friedrich von Gentz, who had left Prussia's service for Austria's in 1802 in hopes of better pay and a stronger anti-French policy, now bit the hand that fed him, denouncing Austria's cowardice and weakness to the British (also for pay). But Cobenzl insisted on lying low, Francis was tired of war and the threats to his patrimony, and the dominant sentiment at Vienna was that Austria should forget Germany and go it alone.[36]

The German states also generally preferred not to take sides. Some ambitious leaders (e.g. Montgelas in Bavaria and Duke Frederick I of Württemberg) looked for great-power patrons to help them build up and modernize their states, make territorial gains, and play an independent role in European politics; Montgelas leaned toward France, Frederick to Russia. But other German governments were unclear even on what to aim for internally, and no one knew how to provide for German security, individual or collective. The proposals for reform of the Reich still in circulation had no realistic chances of success. Austria was widely considered too weak and/or hostile to help, Prussia unreliable and potentially dangerous, France and Russia potentially useful but either too close and powerful or too remote. If any consensus existed at all, it favoured forming some sort of Third

[36] Aretin (1967: i. 453–69); Driault (1912: 34–45); Deutsch (1938: 214–28); Rössler (1940: i. 75–6, 82–4; 1966: i. 200–5); Hase (1970: 589–92).

Germany, independent of Austria and Prussia and guaranteed jointly by France and Russia.[37]

Russia made a bid at Vienna for an alliance against France in December 1803. The experienced Cobenzl correctly assumed, first, that Russia had already tried and failed at Paris, London, and Berlin, and second, that Russia hoped after getting Austria in the bag then to gain Prussia as well, after which it could either make a profitable deal with France and tyrannize (*déspotiser*) its neighbours, or push Austria forward against France. The alliance offer also rested on Russia's usual premise: that Austria, directly threatened and forced to fight for its life, should be glad to accept any Russian help and allow Russia to control the war effort and its aims in a spirit of disinterested benevolence. Concretely, the Russian proposal called for Austria to mobilize its entire army to stop any further French encroachments, also keeping some forces in reserve to watch Prussia and Turkey, while Russia provided 80,000 men as auxiliaries to create a diversion on Austria's behalf. Cobenzl instructed Stadion to flatter the Russians but say nothing that might involve Austria in war. The same proposal renewed in April 1804, with the Russian contribution raised to 100,000 men, got the same response: Austria would accept only a purely defensive alliance to preserve peace and the status quo. Vienna's first choice would have been an Austro-Russian–French alliance to restore the European balance—meaning the now standard Central European definition of balance, achieved not by building a coalition to block an aggressor or by having two hostile coalitions confront each other, but by fashioning a general restraining alliance within which to group a dangerous state or states.[38]

Prussia's response to renewed war was that of the hedgehog and the possum. The King tried initially to restrain France from occupying Hanover by pleas and assurances of Prussian neutrality, failing because he rejected the advice of his counsellors to arm or prepare to occupy Hanover himself. After accepting Napoleon's occupation of Hanover, Prussia next had to endure a French occupation of the North German ports of Cuxhaven and Ritzebüttel as well, which seriously damaged its trade.

In July 1803, Cabinet Minister Lombard went to Brussels and Paris to seek a defensive alliance with France, hoping thereby

[37] Aretin (1967: i. 474–85, 492–6); Bitterauf (1905: 120–53); Hölzle (1931: 309–26); Quint (1980: 100–35); Jürgens (1976: 21–52); Raumer (1952: 146–7, 294–6).

[38] Beer (1877b: 67–75); *VPR* (1960–: 1. i. Nos. 216, 222–3, 230, 236, 246, 251, 295; 1. ii. Nos. 8, 15); HHStA, *Russland II Correspondenz* 217, fos. 2–3, 10–11.

to protect the neutrality of North Germany and divert French expansion to the south against Austria. This began almost ten months of negotiations. The French used every possible menace and lure to get Prussia to defend their gains in South Germany and Italy, threatening to join Austria in war on Prussia, offering Berlin Hanover and other territorial gains, and even talking of making Frederick William the German Emperor. The tactics only made the King more skittish; he interrupted the negotiations when offered the Emperorship in January 1804, and broke them off completely when France tried in April to compromise Prussia in the Enghien affair by involving it in a joint guarantee of South Germany. Napoleon naturally had no use for the King's assurance of his continued goodwill, but the negotiations themselves had not been useless for France. Without conceding anything, France continued to occupy Hanover and the North German ports, and could be assured that Prussia would offer no resistance to anything short of a direct attack. This success cost something, to be sure; France was using up its supply of useful idiots like Lombard at Berlin. But once manipulation ceased to work for Napoleon, force remained. As for Frederick William, Haugwitz gave an apt summary of his 'policy':

Your Majesty, if I am correct, wishes neither to make war on France, nor to allow its usurpations to continue, nor to resort to armaments to prevent it, nor to make Russia too disgusted to give aid in possible danger, nor none the less to tie your hands on the application of that principle by entering into any fixed concert with the Emperor [Alexander]. This is not the moment to examine if so many delicate conditions can be fulfilled simultaneously. Your servants' duty, Sire, is to try everything to fulfil them in so far as their contradictions will permit.[39]

Haugwitz omitted one item from his long list of the things the King was unwilling to do: join with Austria in mutual defence. But no one at Berlin took this option seriously, less out of Austrophobia or blindness (some Prussians had been calling for a united Austro-Prussian front for years) than from fear of bringing down Napoleon's wrath on Prussia. Napoleon wanted a Prussian alliance which would help him either overawe Austria or destroy it, depending on which course would better help him defeat Britain and neutralize Russia. The King wanted a French alliance

---

[39] Aengeneydt (1922); Sieske (1959: 39–56); Deutsch (1938: 160–71); Bailleu (1881–7: ii. 125–253) (the quotation is from Haugwitz's memorandum of 30 Mar. 1804, p. 253).

which would let France do whatever it wanted to Austria, so long as it left Prussia alone.

Prussia dealt in similar fashion with Russia's repeated efforts to commit it to some kind of stand—an alliance, or an undertaking to force the French to evacuate Hanover and the North German ports, or at least to defend North Germany against further French encroachments. Though the terms Russia offered Prussia were far more generous than those it would later offer Austria, Frederick William held Alexander off as long as he had any hope of an agreement with France, and when this disappeared in the wake of the Enghien affair he threw himself on Alexander's neck for advice and succour. Even then he gave Russia only a secret Prussian declaration in May that it would defend North Germany against French encroachments across the Weser if Russia would aid Prussia with 40,000-50,000 men and help get Denmark, Saxony, and other states (not including Austria) to accede to the cause. The Russians regarded this as a *de facto* defensive alliance—but not so the Prussians.[40]

Up to mid-1804, then, both the large and small German states staved off French and Russian efforts to being them into the war or use them for their policies. This also helped make Russia turn its attention from Germany to the defence of its interests in the Near East. Here Britain, whose commercial and strategic interest in the Mediterranean was growing with the renewal of war and the French occupation of Neapolitan ports, was Russia's natural ally. Sicily had now become a key British base like Gibraltar and Malta, protected by the fleet and an expeditionary force intended to defend the island and to create diversions elsewhere. The British responded eagerly to a Russian proposal in December 1803 for consultations on a possible joint defence of the Ottoman Empire— too eagerly for some Russians, concerned about involvement in the war and the growth of British influence in the Ottoman Empire. Czartoryski advised the Tsar to receive British offers of men and ships with friendly reserve. Russia must not allow any other power to share its protection of the Greeks (i.e. Orthodox Christians) or its special relationship with the Ottoman Empire. On whether the Ottoman Empire should survive or not, Czartoryski's attitude, and that of most leading Russians, was like the modern Christian's version of the Sixth Commandment:

[40] Martens (1874-1905: vii. 314-17, 338-45); *VPR* (1960-: 1. i. Nos. 176, 184-5, 194-5, 198, 234; 1. ii. Nos. 23-4); Bailleu (1900: 30-5, 42-51, 56-7).

> Thou shalt not kill, but needst not strive
> Officiously to keep alive.

Once the Ottoman Empire fell, as it inevitably would, Russia had to prevent its competitors (which meant for Czartoryski France and possibly Britain—he did not take Austria seriously as one) from obtaining crucial areas by occupying them itself. Meanwhile Russia should continue to build up its influence at Constantinople and penetrate the Balkans with Russian agents.

Thus Russia's policy toward the Ottoman Empire remained intrinsically revolutionary and expansionist (though it was not in a hurry) and matter-of-factly anti-Austrian. It took a defensive stance, however, in the Mediterranean, i.e. in regard to Italy, Malta, and to an extent the Ionian Isles, scene of a considerable Russian military and naval build-up. Britain and Russia, therefore, had no serious clash of interests in the Mediterranean or the Near East; the British were not yet thinking of backing the Ottoman Empire against Russian encroachments. The obstacles to a *rapprochement* and alliance lay elsewhere. Both powers wanted to defend the Neapolitan mainland as well as Sicily; Russia promised Naples to do so. But even in alliance they could not achieve this unless Austria and/or Prussia challenged Napoleon in the heart of Europe. Each looked to the other to bring this about—Russia (the British said) by its power and position as arbiter of Europe, Britain (said the Russians) by subsidies. In fact, neither could make Austria or Prussia fight; only France could.[41]

The fact that Britain in 1804 lacked a disposable expeditionary force or a usable Central European ally did more than hamper its quest for a Russian alliance. Spain, near exhaustion, was nursing a growing list of grievances against France, including commercial quarrels, Napoleon's Italian policy in general and his continued occupation of Etruria in particular, French colonial ambitions at Spain's expense, and Napoleon's sale of Louisiana to the United States. The latter deal, carried through by France without consulting Spain or fulfilling its part of the original French–Spanish bargain, put the Spanish Empire at greater risk from America's illegal trade and subversive republican principles. What Spaniards wanted above all, however, was to stay out of the war. Had a sizeable British land force been available to help defend Spain if it were attacked by France or to threaten it if it joined France,

---

[41] Mackesy (1957: 5–17, 32–57); Jelavich (1984: 10–11); Sirotkin (1960); Saul (1970: 184–5); *VPR* (1960–: 1. i. Nos. 233, 256, 260, 265–6, 268). The quotation is from Gerard Manley Hopkins's poem, 'A Modern Decalogue'.

Spain might have tried to turn neutral. As it was, Napoleon only managed to bully Spain into a subsidy treaty in October 1803 similar to Portugal's earlier. Moreover, he was angered by the tepid performance of both Spain and Portugal as his allies in the year that followed. Godoy, under fire in Spain, tried to get France to join in conquering Portugal as the only way for Spain to acquire territory and thus vindicate his pro-French policy. This failing, he appealed secretly to Britain for support.

At this point Pitt, returning to power with a new ministry in May, saved Godoy's position by forcing Spain into active war. Refusing to tolerate Spain's subsidies to Napoleon as Addington had done, his government in October 1804 ordered a British naval squadron to seize three Spanish ships carrying treasure from the New World to Spain. A break in relations was followed by a Spanish declaration of war in early January 1805. The war was almost two years old, and Britain was still isolated against a widening French coalition.[42]

III. THE COALITION AGAINST FRANCE, 1804–1805

Britain's hopes for allies, however, began to revive in late 1804. Having first failed to mediate and then having broken with France, Alexander now turned to Britain for a new effort to restore peace. Historians have seen the ensuing negotiations as crucial for two reasons: because they led to an Anglo-Russian alliance, a third coalition against France, and great battles that decided this war and still rank among the most spectacular in history; and because the peace terms the two powers set down in these negotiations supposedly laid a foundation for the eventual peace settlement in 1814–15. The first reason is correct, the second is not. The long-range significance of these negotiations in the history of international politics, as opposed to military history, lies elsewhere.

Alexander chose Count Novosiltsev for a special alliance mission to London because Vorontsov, the regular ambassador, was too pro-English for the task, and armed him with three sets of instructions from Czartoryski. This was not unusual; envoys commonly had different sets of instructions to serve different purposes, ostensible and secret. These three sets, however, were unusual in

---

[42] Fugier (1930: i. 186–97, 204–47, 294–313); DeClercq (1880–1917: ii. 82–4); Napoleon (1858–70: viii. Nos. 6942, 6978–9, 7007–8; x. No. 8147).

their sharp differences in spirit and aims. The first, stating the broad purposes of the mission and intended for the consumption and edification of Vorontsov and the British, reminds one of Woodrow Wilson; the second, containing secret instructions for Novosiltsev regarding Russia's specific goals and terms, of Franklin Roosevelt; the third, still more secret and intended to guide Novosiltsev in particular contingencies, of Josef Stalin.

According to the first set, Russia, were it to follow only its individual interests, would not involve itself in European entanglements at all. It had already exceeded its duty toward Europe in its efforts to build peace, first in co-operation with France and then, after France became an open aggressor, in support of France's neighbors. Russia, however, remained willing to go yet another mile by discussing with Britain how they together might form a European coalition, defining the goals of the war and establishing the rewards for the various combatants in such a fashion as to end the war and give Europe lasting peace, security, and independence.

The second set of instructions combined concrete Russian proposals for territorial and political changes in Europe with broad schemes for a new world order. Sardinia-Piedmont, Switzerland, and the Netherlands should be restored and enlarged under constitutional rule. The United Provinces should be ruled by an hereditary Stadholder, chosen by Britain and Russia either from some German house or from Prussia or Denmark, as a means of inducing one or the other of these powers to join the coalition. France would have to surrender its conquests and return to monarchic rule; Russia and Britain would decide who should wear the French crown, but would also guarantee France free institutions. Austria and Prussia should be separated from Germany; the remaining German states and Italy should be organized into federations under Anglo-Russian protection. In general, the allied goals should be to promote a sensible liberty in government, form states with natural frontiers and naturally homogeneous populations, establish a league of nations, support the rule of international law, and provide sanctions against aggressors and law-breakers. Guaranteeing these great advances in peace and justice would be a permanent alliance between Russia and Britain, who were incapable of ever becoming rivals or pursuing dangerous interests of their own.

These goals, of course, required certain practical steps. Austria would have to enter the war, driven by its fear of France and lured by British subsidies. Gaining Prussia was more problematic; it would probably not yield to persuasion, and the use of force might be unwise. In any case, Britain and Russia should take care not to reveal their war aims to either German power until it was in the war. As for the Ottoman Empire, the two powers ought to consider whether the continued existence of so despotic a state was compatible with their principles. If it joined France, it would obviously have to be partitioned; if allowed to exist, it must be compelled to treat its subject peoples better. Neither Britain nor Russia would seek special gains for themselves from the war. Russia's profit would be an indirect one—the greater security its neighbours would gain—and both powers would enjoy their preponderant status in Europe and the joint leadership of a peace league of secondary states.

The cloven hoof could already be glimpsed through this second set of instructions; it was naked in the third. Once Austria and Prussia were separated from the German Empire, Czartoryski suggested, the Dutch provinces (possibly ruled by a Russian grand princess as Stadholder) and Switzerland should be added to it, with the whole Reich placed under Anglo-Russian protection. He stressed further that Russia and Britain must refuse to fight on the Continent until and unless Austria had assumed the main burden of an offensive war against France. Then, finally, he explained why Russia did not wish to specify the particular gains it might make. First, it did not want to arouse the same fears in Europe as Bonaparte had, and second:

In speaking of the advantages which the two powers ought to provide themselves at the end of the struggle, no acquisition has been designated more precisely because for Russia it is the conduct of its neighbors and the operations one might be in a position to undertake against them which would produce possibilities and free its hands in this respect.

To this end, Czartoryski noted, Russia intended to reserve most of its forces in the war for possible use against the Ottoman Empire and Prussia. He also sent Novosiltsev a proposed treaty for an alliance between the Ottoman Empire and Russia, but warned him not to show it to the British. It called for introducing Russian garrisons into Turkey, which would help Russia to defend Turkey now and pave the way for erecting later one or two Greek and Slavic satellite republics like the Ionian Isles within Turkey. There was no point, however, in revealing this and arousing British jealousy.

The Russian programme contained three kinds of discourse: first, a Wilsonian internationalist idealism; second, a Rooseveltian, fake-realist, liberal-paternalist new order, intended to concentrate real power and decision in the hands of Two Policemen who would police Europe for peace, concealing this arrangement behind a façade of internationalism; and finally, a fairly naked version of Russian imperialism (Stalinist or Catherinian, as you will). It is tempting and natural to suppose that the first two sets were only fig-leaves for the third, the real Russian programme. The temptation must be resisted. It makes Czartoryski and Alexander into cynics and Machiavellians, when in fact they were the kind of idealists common in international politics, genuinely convinced of the nobility of their own aims and the selfishness of everyone else's. All three sets of instructions were genuine—and therefore all the more dangerous.

The most important point, however, is that this was not a programme for a Russian and British war effort. It was a programme for a Central European, above all an Austrian, war effort; a programme for once again making other powers fight for Russian and British aims, deliberately concealing from them what these aims were; for enabling two hegemonic powers to direct a war effort others would mainly wage and pay for; and for empowering them to organize and manage the peace settlement, and run Europe after it. Britain and Russia would differ sharply, during these negotiations and later, over exactly how this programme should be carried through, and the precise terms of the proposed European settlement. They never disagreed on this hegemonic goal, the central aspect of their alliance.[43]

Following hard bargaining between Pitt and Novosiltsev from November to February 1805, Novosiltsev returned with Pitt's counter-proposal of 19 January to St Petersburg. Still more difficult talks followed there between the British ambassador, Lord Granville Leveson-Gower, and Czartoryski and Alexander, ending when Gower on 11 April signed a compromise treaty *sub spe rati* (i.e. in the hope his government would ratify it). Throughout the negotiations, the Russians took the same superior stance toward Britain as they did toward Austria. Czartoryski praised Novosiltsev for using the Foxite Whigs in Parliament to put pressure on Pitt. He denounced Britain's policy toward Spain, and called on Britain to accept Russian mediation in their war. He laid down strict conditions on how Britain ought to subsidize the coalition and assist Russia's mediation with France; demanded that

[43] Novosiltsev's instructions are in *VPR* (1960–: 1. ii. Nos. 49–51); for further evidence of Czartoryski's aims and style, see ibid., No. 73; Grimsted (1969: 124–33); Martens (1874–1905: xi. 76–89); Vorontsov (1870–95: xv. 254–68, 273–4, 278–9).

Britain support Russia's proposed alliance with Turkey; warned that only Russia could overcome the suspicion and hostility toward Britain widespread on the Continent; and called on Britain to accept a new code of neutral rights at sea—this on top of the most irritating demand of all, that Britain surrender Malta. Even Vorontsov joined the act, criticizing Pitt for his unjust suspicions of Russia's aims toward the Ottoman Empire.

Pitt and his foreign secretary, Lord Harrowby, put up with all this in the hope of achieving the old British goal, a working coalition to win the war and establish a balance of power in Europe, i.e. alliances and barriers against France.[44] Many elements in the Russian schemes suited these British purposes; some did not. Pitt still instinctively favoured Prussia; Czartoryski hated it. Pitt wanted to lure the German powers into war and render them permanent barriers against France by offering territorial expansion to Austria in Italy and to Prussia in north-west Germany, even thinking of giving Prussia a strip of territory reaching to the North Sea between Holland and France. The Russians, especially Czartoryski, did not want to strengthen the German powers. Russia wanted a German confederation separated from Austria and Prussia and put under its protection; Britain wanted a Germany somehow united under Austro-Prussian leadership against France. Friction and uncertainty emerged over how far to reduce France territorially and what kind of post-war government to impose or encourage at Paris, as well as other details of the territorial settlement in Europe. Russia demanded major sacrifices for peace from Britain as well as from other powers. It should restore all its conquests since 1803, support Russia's proposed North German and south Italian expeditions with large subsidies, naval help, and other aid, and surrender Malta and its maritime code.

These issues dominated the negotiation until the alliance was signed, and threatened its survival thereafter, and have naturally led historians to stress the fragility of the alliance. But, once again, these disagreements have served to conceal an underlying unity in the two powers' basic assumptions. Both felt that Europe needed them much more than they needed Europe. They were in agreement on who should decide the question of whether there would be peace or war on the Continent and who should set the war aims and peace terms—themselves; on who should fight the war— mainly Austria; and on who should run Europe after it—again,

---

[44] Ingram (1984: 103–16) argues convincingly that Lord Mulgrave inspired Pitt's plan, a traditional British balance-of-power scheme.

themselves. Russia pronounced its verdict on issues affecting Austria and Sweden in much the same way as the British spoke for the dispossessed House of Orange. In short, on the central issues of who was in charge of Europe, who gave the orders, and who had to follow and obey, Russia and Britain were never anything but full and genuine allies.

For this reason above all it is a great mistake to see the Anglo-Russian programme of 1805 as the forerunner and model for the settlement of 1814–15. Inevitably, the two settlements would resemble each other on certain specific points (discussed below), similarities largely dictated by obvious geographical and strategic factors. A more important similarity in terms of the distribution of power (ignored or denied by balance-of-power theory) is that they both rested and depended on Anglo-Russian hegemony rather than on a balance of power. But there was a decisive difference in the way this joint Anglo-Russian hegemony would be exercised. In 1805, two dominant states, alike half-European and half-world powers, each supposing itself invulnerable, each ignorant of Europe's conditions and needs and armed only with crude notions of possible solutions, proposed to impose upon Europe a settlement they had concocted while making Europe in the main fight and pay for it. In 1815, these same two powers, now (albeit still somewhat superficially) genuinely European in spirit, worked out a settlement in advance with the rest of Europe. Everyone participated, everyone consented to it, everyone (with certain small-power exceptions) fought and paid for it, and the two hegemonic powers themselves were no longer intimate allies, no longer bent on controlling the others.[45]

The treaty of 11 April 1805 was, therefore, not progressive at all, but a backward-looking, eighteenth-century scheme, a reprise of Anglo-Russian attitudes in 1798–9. This showed clearly in the plans for creating a coalition army and starting the war. Of the required 400,000 men (500,000 would be better, both powers agreed, but this assumed Prussia's entry, which was unlikely), 250,000 were to be Austrians, 115,000 Russians, and the rest Neapolitans, Hanoverians, Swedes, Sardinians, and others, to be subsidized by Britain. Novosiltsev was to present peace terms to Napoleon, whereupon the two powers would decide whether his reply made peace possible or a wider war necessary. The treaty

[45] Webster (1921: 190–3; 1931: 53–63); Sherwig (1969: 148–61, 164–5); Renier (1930: 32–5); VPR (1960–: 1. ii. Nos. 79, 87, 103); Martens (1874–1905: xi. 96–100, 104–5).

called for establishing a 'balance' in Europe, meaning a blocking coalition against France and a balance of power between the German powers (Russia was especially interested in the latter). The particular stipulations concerning Italy, the Low Countries, Hanover, Switzerland, and North Germany reflected the familiar glacis policies of the two powers. Pitt's famous 'federative system' meant basically a barrier system against France for Britain and protectorates over Germany and Italy for Russia. The German question, the heart of Austria's concerns and the most important question for Europe as a whole, was referred to only in vague terms. The British may not have known or seriously considered what would become of Austria's great-power position and security if the German Empire were made independent and neutral, like Switzerland, under Anglo-Russian protection; the Russians certainly did. The alliance would be implemented, finally, only if Austria, Sweden, or both went to war with France within four months (later, seven months) after the treaty was signed.[46]

The repetition of the 1798–9 pattern of Anglo-Russian partnership extended to Naples as well. Since late 1804 the Russians had been pressing Britain to enlarge its garrison in Sicily for the purpose of co-operating with a Russian force to be landed in Naples to oust the French and encourage Austria to fight. The British responded in the spring of 1805 by sending 4,000 additional men under Sir James Craig to occupy Sicily, and a Russian military mission under General Lacy would succeed temporarily in September 1805 in bringing mainland Naples wholly under Russia's control. This was not enough for Czartoryski. As he told Dmitri Tatishchev, his envoy to Naples, alliances with individual small states like Naples did not profit Russia. What it wanted, in Italy as well as Germany, was a league of states under Russian protection.[47]

Left to itself, the Anglo-Russian alliance would have rotted before it was ripe, ruined by Russia's arrogance, various differences over terms, especially the Malta issue, and the underlying problem typical of hegemonic partnerships: disputes over sharing the

---

[46] For the last-minute negotiations and the treaty texts, see *VPR* (1960–: 1. ii. Nos. 117, 125); Martens (1874–1905: ii. 428–68; xi. 106–18). For conventional verdicts on Pitt and on the alliance, see Rose (1911: 560–1 and *passim*); Webster (1931: 60–1); Watson (1960: 424–5); Tulard (1977: 182–3); Christie (1982: 268–9); Langford (1976: 222–3). For evidence backing the interpretations given here, see Renier (1930: 32–5); Driault (1912: 196–207); Narochnitskii and Kazakov (1979: 70–2); Arneth (1898: i. 78); Raumer (1957b: 148–9).

[47] *VPR* (1960–: 1. ii. Nos. 72, 105, 108, 179, 188); Mackesy (1957: 58–66); Sirotkin (1960: 220–5).

costs and benefits of hegemony. Pitt refused to ratify the treaty with Gower's unauthorized concessions in it. Alexander not only insisted on them but also raised further demands over Britain's maritime code, the Ottoman Empire, Naples, and Spain.[48] Like Czartoryski, he took every concession as evidence that Britain could not do without Russia, and every resistance as proof that the British were greedy rather than benevolently unselfish like himself. Czartoryski's demand later in the year that Britain begin paying 'the debt of gratitude it had contracted toward the Continent' epitomizes the Russian style. Still worse, Alexander really did not intend to fight. The British had accepted Russia's proposal of a Novosiltsev peace mission to Paris only as the formal prelude to war, while the Tsar envisioned it as a serious effort for peace, and was ready to go well beyond the treaty in concessions to France. A. Vorontsov, Czartoryski's nominal superior, warned him against letting Russia enter the war before it was fully prepared financially and militarily, and urged narrow limits on Russia's involvement, at the same time as he denounced the Austrians for not going to war over Italy long before.[49]

Only Napoleon could have saved the Anglo-Russian alliance, and he obliged. In mid-1805, at a time when Novosiltsev was in Berlin on his way to Paris and when Alexander had virtually decided, like the British, not to ratify the alliance treaty, the news of the French annexation of Genoa reached St Petersburg. The action was a blow to Alexander's pride and ambition more than to Russia's interests, but it led him to suspend the Novosiltsev mission and prompted both powers to ratify the treaty, though in a way that only papered over the cracks.[50] Thus Britain and Russia planned the Third Coalition, but Napoleon really created it. Georges Lefebvre concludes, in his classic account of Napoleon's reign, that the war revived in 1803 was a clash between two imperialisms. This is misleading as to its causes; Napoleon's aggression was responsible both for renewing the war in 1803 and for expanding it in 1805. Nor is there much to Lefebvre's view that the basis for the coalition was aristocratic class bias against Napoleon.[51] Class bias instead made many European aristocrats,

[48] For Alexander's demands in regard to Spain and the British reply, see *VPR* (1960–: 1. ii. Nos. 130, 178).

[49] *Sbornik* (1867–1916: lxxxii. Nos. 16–17, 22–3); Vorontsov (1870–95: x. 429–44; xv. 290–6, 298–321, 351–4); *VPR* (1960–: 1. ii. Nos. 118, 132, 138); PRO 30/8/337, pt. 2, fos. 173–85; Grimsted (1969: 140–1).

[50] *VPR* (1960–: 1. ii. No. 139); *Sbornik* (1867–1916: lxxxii. No. 25); Vorontsov (1870–95: xv. 332–50).

[51] Lefebvre (1969: i. 178–89, 198–99, 212–13).

especially in Austria and Germany, favour Napoleon as a bastion against the Revolution. But Lefebvre's verdict is sound, if in-complete, on the character of the war. It was a clash of three imperialisms, not two, and each of the imperialist powers was fighting not so much against its avowed foe as over the control of the rest of Europe.

The aggressive actions by which Napoleon saved the Anglo-Russian alliance and brought Austria into it were not simply wilful on his part. Although there were always chances for him to consolidate his power by peaceful means to the end of his reign, these chances naturally diminished with time, as his perceived opportunities for glory grew. This happened here. He was more hampered by his inability to attack Britain and Russia than they were by their corresponding difficulties in getting at him. As the Anglo-Russian negotiations illustrated, Britain and Russia each believed that it could retire to defensive positions if it failed to secure the coalition it wanted. For Napoleon this was more difficult, personally and politically. By 1805, colonial expansion and naval and commercial warfare had clearly failed as means to bring Britain to its knees. The sale of Louisiana to the United States in 1803 cut France's potential losses to Britain in the New World and raised money for war, but at the cost of further angering the Spanish and leaving the remaining French colonies in the Antilles vulnerable. Napoleon's control of Europe was still too incomplete and porous to exclude British trade, which actually increased in volume after the outbreak of war in 1803. His naval plans offered little real hope of success, despite the expanded resources at France's disposal and the Emperor's constant demands on his naval minister and his satellites and allies for more naval construction. Ships could be built; trained seamen and gunners could not. Even more important, Napoleon was incompetent at naval war, and refused to recognize it. He made serious and massive plans and preparations at Boulogne for a cross-Channel invasion, but by 1805 the likely results of an attempt were as clear to him as to the British, who hoped he would try it.[52]

Another leader facing this dilemma might have tried for a

---

[52] For Napoleon's naval efforts, see Napoleon (1858–70: x. Nos. 8787, 8794, 8809–11, 8814, 8817, 8836–7; xi. Nos. 9064, 9107–15). For the Louisiana Purchase and Franco-American relations, see DeClercq (1880–1917: ii. 59–63); Lyon (1934: 199, 206–7, 231–3); Bonnel (1961: 187–96); Tucker and Hendrickson (1990: 87–135). For Napoleon's planned invasion, see Lefebvre (1969: i. 186–9), Beaucour (1982). Renn (1974) argues that the British may have been too sanguine about their ability to defeat it.

political solution; Napoleon could only think of expanding the war. Preoccupied with plans for invading England, he had been curiously passive toward Germany in 1803–4. He met with German princes in Mainz in September 1804 only to win them over personally and to counteract the effects of the Enghien affair and his break with Russia. Certain German leaders, in particular the Prince-Primate Karl von Dalberg and the Bavarian premier, Montgelas, launched initiatives for reorganizing Germany into a Confederation of the Rhine or a western–south-western German Republic under French leadership, but Napoleon showed little interest. In the French–Bavarian alliance negotiations started in early 1805, he pursued hard military assets, not influence or hegemony. Montgelas offered a defensive alliance against Austria and an auxiliary army; the French demanded an all-out offensive–defensive alliance, a larger army entirely at France's disposal, a Bavarian guarantee of Napoleon's new acquisitions in Italy, and full Bavarian participation in any war on Austria.[53]

In Italy Napoleon's policy was much more aggressive than in Germany, because the peninsula played a larger role in his war against England, was more exposed to British attack, and intrinsically interested him more, both for its own sake and as a step toward the East. Immediately after being proclaimed Emperor he began pressing the Italian Republic, of which he was president, to change itself into a satellite Kingdom of Italy. The vice-president, Melzi, was willing to do this and also to make Napoleon its hereditary monarch, provided that he remain viceroy, that the kings succeeding Napoleon live in Italy, and that the new kingdom enjoy some internal autonomy and guarantees of its existence. In other words, Melzi was an Italian with some independent spirit; this made him disposable. After the Republic's Consultà was summoned to Paris in November but failed to reach the desired decision, further Napoleonic pressure produced simultaneous French and Italian decrees in March 1805 proclaiming him the hereditary king of Italy. This was a flagrant violation of Lunéville, and the little comedy by which Napoleon first offered the Italian throne to his brother Joseph, who by refusing compelled Napoleon to assume it, was no more convincing than Napoleon's argument that, in taking the Italian throne himself, he ensured its permanent separation from France.

As if to make his challenge to Austria and Europe even more

[53] Deutsch (1938: 238–53); Bitterauf (1905: 161–2); Gmeinwiser (1928: 24–7, 159–61); Quint (1971: 144–54); Dunan (1961: 186–7).

explicit, on 26 May in Milan Napoleon crowned himself with the Iron Crown of Lombardy, companion piece to the Imperial crown of Charlemagne he had worn since the previous December. Other displays of his power over Italy quickly followed: the replacement of Melzi by his stepson, Prince Eugène de Beauharnais, as viceroy of Italy, thus making Eugène eligible to marry Princess Augusta of Bavaria, and the granting of a constitution and guarantee to Lucca and Piombino, ruled by Felix Bacciochi and his wife, Napoleon's sister Elisa. This was capped by a triumphal journey through Italy in June and early July. The step most important in immediate military terms was taken with the least fanfare; in early June an Imperial decree changed the Ligurian Republic (Genoa) into three new districts of metropolitan France. Napoleon's demands on it for ships, seamen, and contributions, already heavy, were stepped up, just as were those on Spain, Portugal, and the Batavian Republic. When his Dutch satellite briefly tried to resist his demands in late 1804, Napoleon reorganized it in March 1805 into a centralized state more responsive to his control.[54]

As usual, in striking at Britain Napoleon hit Austria. Some historians, while recognizing Napoleon's aggressiveness, divide the responsibility for renewed Austro-French hostility and war between the two powers. Austria's military preparations, its persistent territorial ambitions in Italy and Germany, its alliance with Russia in November 1804, and the niggling and grudging attitude it allegedly took in negotiations with France are supposed to show that, if it did not directly provoke a confrontation, it refused to accommodate itself to Napoleon and the new order in Europe.

This kind of case can certainly be argued for the 1790's, but not here. It is like saying that Poland should have found some way of getting along with Hitler's Germany in 1939—worse, in fact, because the Poles refused to compromise in 1939 and Austria was anything but intransigent in 1804–5. The pattern of Austro-French relations until almost the very end was one of constant French menaces, pressure, and *faits accomplis*, to which Austria regularly responded by avoiding a fight and seeking a bargain. It began with Austria's backing down under French threats in its quarrel with Bavaria over the imperial knights. It continued when Austria, seeking to respond in a minimal way to Russian pressure over the Enghien affair without angering France or stirring up trouble,

---

[54] Driault (1912: 76–81, 145–51, 159–71, 178–82, 212–19); Fugier (1954: 186–9); A. Pingaud (1914: ii. 397–481); Napoleon (1858–70: x. Nos. 8261, 8298, 8299, 8336; xi. No. 9226).

made an anodyne declaration to the German Diet, only to produce more angry threats from Napoleon and a rejection of the golden bridges Austria was trying to erect for him. The Austrian response to Napoleon's Emperorship and his coronation, in which he took over Austria's traditional seat of honour in Europe, was, as indicated, another surrender. There was something besides fear and weakness behind Austria's appeasement. Francis I, Ludwig and Philipp Cobenzl, Colloredo, and many other Austrians credited Napoleon with saving France and Europe from the Revolution, and believed that, if he would only be satisfied with Continental hegemony and the establishment of his dynasty, Austria and France could get along well. This collaborationist attitude at Vienna, more than Austria's individual actions, was what enraged enemies of Napoleon like Gentz.

Northern Italy became the touchstone for Austria's hopes of peaceful coexistence with France. In December 1804, worried by the changes evidently brewing there, Austria sent a note to probe France's intentions, pointing out that, while Austria would accept having the Italian Republic changed into a monarchy, it was crucial that the Kingdom remain independent. Uniting Italy to France would not only violate the Treaty of Lunéville but also overthrow France's own policy of interposing intermediary states between itself and Austria. Napoleon denounced this note as an intolerable interference in French internal affairs, accompanying his warning with formidable military preparations, but at the same time Talleyrand insisted that France had no intention of making the Republic into a French province. Francis's weak reply convinced Napoleon that Austria would never fight and that he could do whatever he wished. When rumours began circulating that the Crown of Italy would be given to Joseph Bonaparte, the Austrians tried to sell their consent to this arrangement in exchange for other concessions in Italy. The French response in March was to proclaim the union of the French and Italian Crowns, accompanying it with arguments of insulting mendacity—that the action was the only way to preserve Italy's separate identity, that the British and Russians had forced France into it, and that once the British and Russians were out of Malta and Corfu the status quo ante would be restored. Next followed the coronation at Milan, rich in menacing symbolism, the annexation of Genoa, and other actions, all proving that Napoleon's legend on his new royal insignia, *Rex totius Italiae* (King of all Italy), was no idle boast. Even at this point Ludwig Cobenzl continued to hope for some kind of French concession or compromise that could avoid war, and ardent patriots like Philipp Stadion wished to postpone the war till the next year. The French, however, presented an ultimative demand in August that Austria disarm and formally declare its neutrality. Few confrontations in history display the distinction between aggressor and defender as clearly as this. This does not mean, as has sometimes been said, that Napoleon deliberately provoked Austria into war in order to put to use the army he had gathered at Boulogne. He certainly recognized the opportunities a war in Central Europe would offer him, and had he deliberately intended to provoke Austria into war he would hardly have done anything differently. But in fact he had to improvise his 1805 campaign in important respects, and he probably would have preferred that Austria remain neutral. The trouble lay in Napoleon's conception of neutrality. Being neutral meant for him not that a state stand aside from a conflict as long as its vital interests were unaffected, but that it get out of his way and present no obstacle to his will, regardless of its vital interests.[55]

As for the military reforms and armaments Austria had carried through since 1801 under Archduke Carl as president of the *Hofkriegsrat* (court war council), they were important in their way, but not for encouraging Austria to go to war. Carl, more the spirit and symbol behind the reforms than their driving force, was a strong if somewhat inconsistent opponent of war, partly out of fear and admiration of Napoleon but mainly because he considered Britain weak and treacherous, believed that the best thing for Europe might be a prolonged single duel between Britain and France, and looked on Russia as Austria's real mortal enemy. His councillor, Matthias Fassbender, the main architect and executor of the military reforms, favoured a purely defensive alliance with Prussia. When Ludwig Cobenzl, hitherto a thoroughgoing appeaser of France, changed his mind in late 1804 and began preparing for possible war, he ran into strong military and political opposition to his new stand, which made sustaining his policy a matter of his political survival as well. This encouraged him to look for military advisers (in this case, the over-confident and overrated General Mack) who unlike Carl believed that Austria could get ready to fight. Anyway, Austria's military reforms, while useful, were not far-reaching or effective. Universal military

---

[55] Beer (1877*b*: 43–59, 82–91, 130–5, 453); Deutsch (1938: 208–96); Fournier (1930: i. 345–63); Napoleon (1858–70: ix. Nos. 7900, 7906; x. Nos. 8250, 8282, 8283, 8306–8, 8445–8, 8581, 8590; xi. Nos. 8999, 9000, 9023, 9032, 9038–9, 9055, 9070).

service remained a remote ideal even in Austria's hereditary provinces, to say nothing of Hungary with its special privileges.[56]

Austria, to be sure, concluded a defensive alliance with Russia on 4 November 1804, but not at all with the idea of going to war. Throughout the negotiations Austria was bent on keeping the alliance defensive and provisional. Russia, while it insisted that Austria must launch a war against France before it received any Russian help, pursued its own quarrel with France and broke relations without even consulting Austria. Repeatedly Cobenzl instructed Stadion to curb Russia's bellicosity and moderate its impossible demands on France. The two powers diverged sharply over both the central issues in the alliance—the respective troop contingents, the *casus foederis*, the territories and areas to be guaranteed—and other questions. The Russians were suspicious of Austrian policy toward the Ottoman Empire and Serbia, where a Serb rebellion against the Turks was just breaking out on Austria's frontiers, and demanded that Austria recognize a Russian protectorate over Montenegro. Austria insisted that northern Italy was the prime area of critical concern; Russia was more interested in Naples, the fate of the King of Sardinia, Hanover, and Northern Germany.

The treaty itself offers an ironic commentary on Russia's constant claim that, invulnerable itself, it was acting solely to help others. Not only was Austria required to provide 235,000 troops for the potential coalition to Russia's 115,000; many territories brought under the treaty's *casus foederis* (the Ionian Isles, Hamburg, Bremen, North Germany, the Ottoman Empire, and Naples) represented Russian far more than Austrian interests. Austria, however, clung to its right to decide when the *casus foederis* would arise, and explicitly defended itself against being dragged into war by a Neapolitan attack on France, as the allies had tried to do to Austria in 1798–9. The treaty was therefore defensive not merely in form but, at least for Austria, also in its purpose: to deter France from further encroachments and to secure Russian help if Austria was compelled to fight.[57]

In early 1805 a new envoy, Count Klemens von Metternich, was sent to Berlin to join the regular Russian minister, Alopeus,

---

[56] Rössler (1940: i. 122–49); Rauchensteiner (1972: 58–75); Criste (1912: ii. 308–16); Zimmermann (1965: 120–7); Rothenberg (1982a).

[57] Beer (1877b: 75–81); Deutsch (1938: 267–72); Driault (1912: 122–9); Oer (1965: 10–13); Martens (1874–1905: ii. 406–19); *VPR* (1960–: 1. ii. Nos. 25, 29, 31, 45, 63, 68, 69, 80, 83); Nikitin *et al.* (1980–3: i. Nos. 14, 21, 31–4); HHStA, *Russland II Correspondenz* 217, fos. 8–37, 42–59.

and a special Russian envoy, in an attempt to win Prussia over to the Austro-Russian alliance. The idea was old; the spirit in which Austria pursued it was fairly new. It put aside old quarrels over compensations and leadership in Germany and argued simply for an Austro-Prussian union to preserve the territorial status quo, curb French expansion, and establish a political balance in Europe. Here again one sees the evolution of a concept of political equilibrium decisively different from the British or Russian ideas of a balance of power to be created by weakening France and erecting barriers and coalitions against it. For Austria and other states, the European political equilibrium now called for accepting France's gains, recognizing its hegemony in Western Europe, and seeking general political arrangements simply to curb further French expansion. Though this Austro-Russian effort to win Prussia over failed, it marked another small step from eighteenth-century Austro-Prussian rivalry toward their nineteenth-century partnership.[58]

The failure at Berlin was a disappointment but no surprise for Vienna; the Anglo-Russian alliance of 11 April, in contrast, was a shocking blow. For one thing, Russia deceived Austria throughout the negotiations. Having represented the Novosiltsev mission and the negotiations as an attempt to curb Britain's lust for war, Russia signed a treaty with Britain which called on Austria to start the war and assume its principal burden—this within four months, though the Russians knew that Archduke Carl considered a war suicidal before the following year, and highly risky even then. More important still, as Cobenzl argued passionately to Stadion on 26 May, the British and Russian war aims being forced on Austria were impossible, almost insane. The proposed 400,000-man allied army, predominantly Austrian, might suffice to contain Napoleon and conceivably make him recede from certain of his post-Lunéville usurpations, but anything like the Anglo-Russian programme of returning France to or near its ancient frontiers was absurd. The most the allies should ask was the strict execution of the treaties of 1801–2. To the constant Russian and British warnings that Napoleon's power was growing while Austria dithered, and that Austria's potential allies, especially Russia, might change their minds and leave Austria to its fate, Cobenzl replied that, if the allies were not basing their policy on permanent interests

[58] Beer (1877b: 107–29); Thielen (1967: 130–3); Aretin (1967: ii. 328–31); Oncken (1876: ii. 535–40, 554–8, 570–6); Metternich (1880–4: ii. 33–40); VPR (1960–: 1. ii. No. 76).

harmonious with Austria's, it would be folly for Austria to league
with them. The greatest of all risks for Austria would be to enter
another war with insufficient means and support. Austria could
not and would not fight to reduce France to its ancient limits; it
would only fight to achieve a sensible and durable peace.[59]

Alexander responded to Austria's protests with some concessions (he would raise his own contribution to 180,000 men if the
Austrians would raise theirs proportionately), and his usual vague
assurances and covert threats. He promised to bring Prussia into the coalition one way or another; Denmark, Hesse, Saxony,
Brunswick, and Sweden would also come in, bringing the allied army to 600,000 men. Austria's pleas also played a role in
Alexander's desire to make Novosiltsev's journey to Paris a
genuine peace mission rather than a pretext for war, even though
Austria and Russia remained as far apart as Russia and Britain
were on what to require of France. Along with these concessions
and promises went repeated warnings from St Petersburg that
Russia might still join France or Prussia, that the Tsar might
be permanently alienated from Austria, that he could cancel the
Austro-Russian defensive alliance, and that Russia could revert to
isolation or renew its expansion against the Ottoman Empire.
While exerting this pressure on Austria, Alexander and other
Russian leaders still planned to fight only a limited war themselves,
and debated whether France or Prussia should be its main target.

Austria agonized over whether it should accede to the Anglo-
Russian alliance, thus opting for war, right up to the final decision
on 7 July 1805. Carl argued strongly against it, insisting that the
allied promises and calculations were wholly unreliable. Cobenzl
and Colloredo stressed that war was inevitable and that Austria
had no real choice, that it was losing its only chance for allies, and
that Prussia, Bavaria, Saxony, and Hesse might still come in to
help. All Austrians, especially the Emperor, who simply wanted
peace and quiet, wished to conciliate France by moderating the
terms of Russia's ultimatum. Austria's positive goal in Italy was
not to end French control but to restrain and share it, securing a
better border for Austria and transforming direct French rule into
a system of French satellites as intermediary bodies. If Napoleon
chose to have his relatives rule these satellites, Austria had no
objection. But it was also agreed at Vienna that, if war became
unavoidable, it had to be waged offensively, so as to anticipate the

[59] Beer (1877b: 92–8); HHStA, *Russland II Correspondenz* 217, fos. 60–94.

dreaded French offensive and deny France the resources of South Germany.[60]

The Continental war finally began when Austria acceded on 8 August to a somewhat revised Anglo-Russian alliance, and ignored a subsequent French ultimatum to disarm and declare its neutrality. One needs no detailed account to explain why Austria decided as it did; the reason was simply the desire of a great power to remain independent in the face of an overwhelming challenge and threat.[61] But other questions about the war are more important than 'Who started it?'—questions such as 'Who spoke for Europe? Who had some ideas on how to avert its further dissolution? Who had a defensible concept of peace?' Ludwig Cobenzl, Archduke Carl, and other Austrians were nothing special, as statesmen go. Their minds, however, were dreadfully concentrated by Austria's plight, and their ideas on how to construct European peace were to those of Pitt, Alexander, and Czartoryski (to say nothing of Napoleon) Hyperion to a satyr.

Yet one cannot stop there. The other side is that Austria, having resolved on war, forgot what it had so painfully learned about the limits and dangers of military force as an instrument for constructing a durable peace, and decided to fight this war in the same counter-productive eighteenth-century way as everyone else. It does not matter that the compensations in Italy and Germany which Austria was promised were more Russia's and Britain's ideas than its own; it accepted them, and went beyond them in its own war aims. It does not matter whether Francis I did or did not say, as the French envoy to Bavaria reported, that he wished not to destroy Bavaria but to devour it. It does not even matter that the Bavarians under French pressure had already committed themselves body and soul to France, that they pursued vast anti-Austrian goals themselves, or that Austria decided to launch its pre-emptive invasion and occupation of Bavaria because it believed this the only chance for military success. The fact remains that the one major European power which before the war had shown some recognition that a new durable European order had to be based, not on military victory, but on a general political settlement

[60] Beer (1877b: 100–6); Driault (1912: 208–12); VPR (1960–: 1. i. Nos. 107, 119–22, 124, 133–7); Vorontsov (1870–95: x. 310–14; xv. 323–31).

[61] Driault (1912: 220–3); Beer (1877b: 496–7); VPR (1960–: 1. ii. Nos. 151, 153–6, 158); Sbornik (1867–1916: lxxxii. Nos. 32, 44). Roider (1990) explains Austria's decision much as I have done here.

without victors and vanquished abandoned that insight even before its share in the fighting began.[62]

Other intermediary states were also caught between the upper and nether millstones. Bavaria, motivated by the Austrian threat, French pressure and inducements, and its own ambitions, became France's active ally in late August; Baden and Württemberg followed in September and October after the war was under way. All these states, or at least their princes, would have preferred neutrality; neither Austria nor France would allow them that option. Against the huge advantage Napoleon thus gained in acquiring the South German states and the Danube route for the invasion of Austria, the allied success in getting Naples opened up for Russian troops meant little, and proved worthless in the event.[63] So did Russia's and Britain's earlier success in bringing in Sweden as a subsidized ally. Napoleon again proved better than his opponents at forming effective coalitions for war.[64]

He also succeeded in keeping Prussia neutral, which was as vital as gaining the South German states and closely connected with it, for Bavaria and Württemberg feared Prussia's army more than Austria's. By this time, many in Berlin knew that failure to act at this crucial juncture could prove fatal. Even former Francophiles like Lucchesini now saw Napoleon as the ultimate menace.[65] At the same time they could see that Prussia's waverings were helping Czartoryski promote the Russo-Prussian conflict he wanted for the purpose of uniting the Poles under Russia.[66] The outbreak of war therefore produced another crisis at Berlin. While Austria and Russia tried to pull Prussia over to their side, Marshal Géraud Duroc appeared at Berlin offering Prussia Hanover as the bait for an alliance with France, while at the same time the French seized Cleves as security against Prussia's joining the enemy.

Lucchesini, though aware of the dangers, advised accepting the French offer; the prospect of acquiring Hanover enticed the King. He approached Hardenberg for advice like a nervous parishioner asking a casuistic priest to explain how what he was tempted to

[62] Hölzle (1931: 326–31); Oer (1965: 10–13); Fournier (1903: i. 366–9); Rauchensteiner (1972: 75–7); HHStA, *Russland II Varia* 237, fos. 522–4.

[63] DeClercq (1880–1917: ii. 120–8); Quint (1971: 154–65); Oer (1965: 32–9); Deutsch (1938: 348–58).

[64] Driault (1912: 116–18); *Sbornik* (1867–1916: ii. 23–41); *VPR* (1960–: 1. ii. Nos. 21, 114, 143, 166, 167).

[65] Thielen (1967: 119–23); Haussherr (1957: 270–2); Driault (1912: 173–6). The documents for this period are mainly in Bailleu (1881–7: ii. 255–351).

[66] Grimsted (1969: 134–9); *VPR* (1960–: 1. ii. Nos. 78, 91, 92, 109–16); Griewank (1935: 251–61).

do was not really sinful, and Hardenberg instructed and comforted him with lectures on the higher laws of *raison d'état*. But in the end the fear of war made the King again choose neutrality and isolation, which was all France needed.[67]

At Constantinople the Russians made no pretence of acting disinterestedly for the common cause, but set out openly to destroy French influence and make their own dominant. The struggle between them in 1804 and early 1805 had been indecisive; Russia kept the Porte from granting Napoleon the same honorific title of *Padishah* given the Russian and Austrian emperors, and France kept the Porte from renewing and extending the Russo-Turkish alliance of 1798 and entering the war. But in September Russia won the contest, with a defensive alliance granting its warships special wartime privileges of transit through the Straits.[68]

This contest with France was straightforward; Russia's dealings with its allies in the Near East were much trickier. The problem was how at one and the same time to exclude them from its sphere and use them for Russian interests while retaining their co-operation in Europe. Russia carried off the *tour de force* easily with Britain, gaining assurances of British diplomatic support and possible military help in defending the Ottoman Empire and the Ionian Isles.[69] In the Balkans the involvement of Austria and the native peoples made for greater complications. In 1804 a Serb revolt broke out, initially directed against local oppressors rather than the Sultan, but soon turning against him as well. The Serbs appealed to both Russia and Austria for help; Austria, having a sizeable Serb population in southern Hungary, was better suited to supply it. The revolt, which, along with other unrest, convinced Russians that the chronic crisis facing the Ottoman Empire was now entering an acute stage, posed several tasks simultaneously for Russian policy: (1) to get Austria to provide aid to the Serbs through Russia, so as to preserve Russia's influence and check Austria's; (2) to prevent any Austrian interference in the neighbouring principality of Montenegro, whose prince-bishop was a Russian client; (3) to convince the Serbs and other Christians that only Russia could defend them against Turkish misrule; (4) to

[67] Driault (1912: 238–41); Griewank (1935: 232–3, 264–71); Thielen (1967: 136–41); Bailleu (1881–7: ii. 351–77); Napoleon (1858–70: xi. Nos. 9104, 9116–18, 9126–7).
    [68] Stanislavskaia (1962: 298–319, 343–50); Puryear (1951: 27–38); Driault (1912: 151–6, 230–4); Testa (1864–1911: ii. 254–73); *VPR* (1960–: 1. ii. Nos. 41, 75, 94, 184, 203); Napoleon (1858–70: x. Nos. 8329, 8502).
    [69] Stanislavskaia (1962: 324–8); *VPR* (1960–: 1. ii. No. 90).

convince the Porte that only Russia could help it maintain its rule over its Christian subjects; (5) to lay a foundation for later Russian initiatives in mainland Greece, Albania, Epirus, and the Danubian Principalities; and (6) not to alienate Austria or distract it from fighting France in central Europe.[70]

Though Russia did not entirely succeed in this juggling act—no one could have—it achieved much of its goals, in good part because the Sultan, like Austria, was too threatened and vulnerable to resist Russia effectively.[71] At the same time, Russian expansion continued in the Caucasus and against Iran. The conquest of the khanate of Ganjeh in 1803–5 stored up future trouble for Russia with Persia and Britain, but strengthened the impression at the time that Russia was unstoppable.[72] To what extent Russia consciously intended its European policy to fix its rivals' attention on Europe and assure Russian success elsewhere is hard to say. Russian statesmen certainly knew, as Americans did in both World Wars, that a great war in Europe would serve their world interests, and took advantage of it.

IV. NAPOLEON'S VICTORIES AND EUROPE'S COLLAPSE

The war that took more than two years to develop on the Continent was ended by French arms in four months. Hurling his armies rapidly eastward from France and north-west Germany in a brilliantly improvised campaign, Napoleon caught and surrounded the main Austrian army under General Mack in Bavaria and forced it to surrender at Ulm in mid-October. This disaster effectively ended allied hopes for military victory; the question now became whether the Austrian army and the Habsburg monarchy itself could be saved. Archduke Carl, who had opened his campaign in Italy with an initial success against Masséna, retreated quickly under heavy pressure to protect the hereditary lands, but his effort came too little and too late. By 13 November Napoleon's cavalry had entered an undefended Vienna, while his main army pursued the retreating Austrian and Russian armies into Moravia. The allies were in a critical military situation; demoralization,

---

[70] On the Serb revolt, see Shaw (1971: 318–27); Vucinich (1982a: 23–39, 72–84); on Russian policy, ibid. 41–70; Stanislavskaia (1962: ch. 6; 1976: ch. 5); VPR (1960–: 1. ii. Nos. 43, 52, 56, 74, 101, 204).

[71] Shaw (1971: 286–307, 330–1).

[72] Atkin (1980: 66–91, 98–9, 123–44).

indiscipline, and lack of supplies threatened both armies, and serious rifts between their leaders seemed to paralyse any initiative. But Napoleon's army also appeared to be vulnerable, deep in enemy territory at the onset of winter, with its flanks and lines of communication exposed. The impasse was broken by an allied decision to take the offensive, made by Alexander in a mixture of desperation and bravado. On 2 December the Russo-Austrian army attacked the French army at Austerlitz, where it fell into a French trap and was virtually annihilated. This brought Austria, already seeking peace, to its knees. Russia withdrew its remaining troops behind its frontiers without entering formal negotiations. Meanwhile, almost simultaneously with the surrender at Ulm, the British navy under Lord Nelson had caught and destroyed a combined French-Spanish fleet off Cape Trafalgar in southern Spain. The British victory at sea, which cost Nelson his life, was as complete as France's on land, but the results were unequal. Napoleon's victories won the war on the Continent; Nelson's only ensured Britain's survival to carry on the struggle if it chose.[73]

These military events seem to back the common perception of the War of the Third Coalition as a triumph of Napoleon's sword over Pitt's gold, military power over politics and diplomacy. Pitt died in despair in early January 1806, symbolically confirming the verdict. Yet the war had not rendered politics irrelevant. For one thing, it had a great deal to do with the military outcome. As already noted, Napoleon won a vital political victory prior to his military one in gaining the South German states as allies. Furthermore, as will be shown, his ability to handle Prussia politically helped ensure his survival after Ulm and his ultimate triumph at Austerlitz. Granted, these political factors were not decisive; even under less favourable political conditions Napoleon probably would still have won the war militarily. There remains the central significance of this war: the political possibilities it opened up for France, and what Napoleon decided to do with them.

This was precisely what Talleyrand tried to tell Napoleon in a long memorandum he sent from Strasbourg on 17 October, when Mack was on the point of surrender at Ulm. Generally, Talleyrand was a mere executor of Napoleon's wishes, and a sycophantic one; here, for once, he attempted to persuade Napoleon to accept the ideas of the foreign ministry (technically, the department of external relations—the historic name was not restored officially until 1814). The memorandum proposed fairly harsh territorial

[73] Van Creveld (1977: 42–57, 70–4); Beer (1877a: 142–63).

terms for Austria. It would lose its remaining south-west German lands, the Tirol, Vorarlberg, Venetia, and probably the Adriatic Littoral, rendering it virtually land-locked and expelling it entirely from Italy and Germany. But the memorandum also advised preserving Austria as a state, concluding an alliance with it against Russia, and encouraging Austria's expansion in the Balkans as a bulwark against Russia. The territory taken from Austria would be used to strengthen France's German clients, and to create new small buffer states between it and Austria. France should commit itself not to expand its present frontiers in Germany and Italy; Napoleon should retain his Italian throne but promise to separate the two Crowns under his successors, whom he would name now and compel Europe to recognize.

The Strasbourg memorandum has sometimes been pictured as a moderate programme for a stable peace, in contrast to Napoleon's ambition and lust for war. There is little to this. Here, as throughout his life, Talleyrand demonstrated more opportunism than moderation. He adulated Napoleon, was eager to share his glory, and wanted to weaken France's foes as much as possible. There was nothing in the Strasbourg memorandum to promote reconciliation with Britain, which was Talleyrand's one fairly consistent peaceful aim throughout his career; as for Austria, a proposal to push it into a confrontation and probable war with Russia over the Balkans showed little concern either for Austria's survival or for a stable European peace.

Yet the memorandum is none the less important. Talleyrand and the other foreign-ministry officials who produced it, though as ready as Napoleon to exploit his victory for a glorious peace, also hoped to stabilize and institutionalize French domination in Europe, and saw that this required France to observe certain limits in its expansion and to base its hegemony on buffer states rather than naked power. This distinguished them from Napoleon. Even if it were true, as sometimes claimed, that their programme was unworkable because Britain and Austria would never have genuinely accepted and lived with it (actually this contention is questionable even for Britain and clearly wrong for Austria), the argument misses the point. This was the best plan that French professional diplomats could hope to sell to Napoleon and thus rein him in.[74]

Napoleon's general response to the Strasbourg memorandum became clear only a bit later; he was already acting on one tenet of it, that Prussia was weak and cowardly and could be ignored.

[74] Raumer (1961a); Oer (1965: 18–21); Dard (1937: 95–103); Driault (1912: 252–3).

When Berlin proved impervious to Austro-Russian pleas to join them after the outbreak of war, Czartoryski, more interested in war with Prussia than with France, persuaded Alexander to force the issue by demanding free passage for Russian troops across Prussia so that they could operate against France in North Germany together with the Swedes and the British. Warned of the coming Russian ultimatum by the Russian envoy, M. M. Alopeus, Frederick William responded by partially mobilizing his army to stop a Russian entry. Even Austria pleaded with the Russians not to invade Prussia; it was better to have Prussia neutral than an enemy. Hardenberg, hoping to use the crisis to acquire Hanover from France, offered Alexander a personal meeting with the King to arrange for Prussian mediation with France for peace.

The crisis seemed past when Alexander accepted this and called off his ultimatum. At that moment, the Prussian government learned that, on Napoleon's express orders, Marshal Bernadotte had marched his forces from north-west Germany toward the Danube across Prussian territory at Ansbach and Bayreuth. Napoleon did not do this to challenge Prussia; it was like the Enghien affair or dozens of other Napoleonic actions, a normal specimen of his statecraft. Having earlier violated Prussia's neutrality zone in lesser ways with impunity, he viewed it as a dead letter and intended to follow the usual eighteenth-century rules of passage through neutral territory; it was a matter of principle for him not to let legal scruples or another party's sense of honour get in the way of a military advantage. Such concern for legality, as he remarked early in his career, was for fools like Emperor Francis of Austria. French explanations at Berlin only made the insult worse. At the precise moment that Prussia was risking war with Russia in order to defend its neutrality, a neutrality very valuable to France, Napoleon deliberately treated Prussia as a negligible quantity.[75]

Exploiting this affair during his state visit, Alexander drew Frederick William into the Potsdam Convention of 3 November, to which Austria also acceded. The treaty seemed to offer the coalition a real chance to bring Prussia into the war, thereby rescuing Austria and turning Napoleon's flank with an offensive in the north. Russia and Prussia agreed on peace terms apparently severe enough to ensure that France would reject them (basically,

[75] Deutsch (1938: 361–71); Beer (1877b: 164–80); Grimsted (1969: 134–9); Bitterauf (1914: 459–68); Griewank (1935: 272–6); VPR (1960–: 1. ii. Nos. 159–61, 163, 181, 189–90); Bailleu (1900: 68–78); Napoleon (1858–70: xi. Nos. 9314, 9316, 9319, 9203).

a return to Lunéville plus guarantees of neutrality for the Swiss, the Dutch, and the German Reich), which Prussia was supposed to present to Napoleon, On their rejection, Prussia would enter the coalition.

In reality the Potsdam Convention was not even potentially a turning-point in the war. There was a war party at Berlin—younger officers in the army, Baron Karl vom Stein, Queen Louise, and others—but it had less real influence than the peace party led by the King's adjutant-general, Köckritz, Lombard, Beyme, General Möllendorff, and the commander-in-chief, the Duke of Brunswick. Moreover, the two rivals, Haugwitz and Hardenberg, jointly responsible for foreign policy did not really represent a choice at this juncture between peace and war, but between trying some kind of armed mediation or negotiation for peace now (Haugwitz) and agreeing to some kind of eventual accession to the coalition if the allies met all of Prussia's conditions (Hardenberg). The King, reluctant even to meet the Tsar for fear of being dragged into something dangerous, retained both men in office, not to help him reach a decision but to help him avoid one. Hardenberg, hoping to move the King a step toward the allies, persuaded him to authorize a Prussian occupation of Hanover after the French troops left. Since Frederick William considered his decision to occupy Hanover an adequate response to the French violation of Ansbach, this step became, not an advance toward joining the coalition, but a retreat from it. At the same time, Prussia insisted in a secret article of the Potsdam Convention that Russia must try to persuade Britain to cede Hanover to Prussia, which ruined any chance of an Anglo-Prussian alliance and British subsidies, without which Prussia would not and could not fight.

In any case, the King and Haugwitz believed that Prussia had only committed itself to armed mediation and negotiation. The convention allowed Prussia four weeks to present terms to Napoleon and get his reply (this at a time when the French were already approaching Vienna); the peace terms themselves were purely Continental in scope, ignoring Britain; and the Prussian generals, fearful that Napoleon would threaten Silesia from Moravia, prepared only slowly and for a limited, largely defensive war. As for war aims, Prussia thought at most of restricting French expansion, making gains for Prussia, and promoting a purely Continental peace in which Austria would remain in existence as a counterweight to France and Russia but not as a partner for Prussia. Hardenberg still mainly aspired to make Prussia the leader of all Germany, and Haugwitz tended to agree with Talleyrand and the

Bavarians that Austria should be pushed south-eastward against Turkey.[76]

In any case, whatever Prussia's intentions might have been, the more than four weeks allowed for a decision (Haugwitz deliberately delayed carrying out his mission) gave Napoleon ample time to finish the war. Even before Austerlitz, Austria had begun to seek an armistice and a general or separate peace. The negotiations between various Austrians and Napoleon and Talleyrand have some interesting features, but the pattern and outcome were predictable. While Napoleon hinted at a reasonable final peace in Europe, he demanded armistice terms designed both to render Austria militarily helpless and to compel it to pay France for continuing the war against its other foes. His territorial demands were also specific and severe: surrender of all Austria's south-west German territories plus some of the hereditary provinces and all of Venetia, including the Adriatic coast. To ask what Napoleon really wanted of Austria and to what extent he was interested in peace with it is to mistake both his character and the nature of the question. Napoleon knew fairly well what he wanted *from* Austria, both at this time and at others; the problem was that he did not know what to do *with* Austria, beyond ending its trouble-making by a harsher peace. He certainly did not want an Austrian alliance against Russia, as Talleyrand did; but neither was he really interested in allying with Russia against Austria or breaking Austria up by revolution, even though he discussed the former possibility with Talleyrand and threatened Vienna with both. Even after being defeated and reduced in size, Austria would be too big to be a convenient satellite, as Bavaria was, or a pliable junior partner, as Prussia still might be; and it would still lie athwart a major target of Napoleon's ambition, the Near East. Hence Napoleon never developed a policy on Austria, at this time or later, except to exploit his victories for the moment and leave all possibilities open for the future.

As for the Austrians, they displayed their usual confusion and unrealism in negotiation after defeat. Until Austerlitz they hoped to save all the hereditary provinces and much of their Italian holdings, thus failing to face facts about Napoleon's character, the dimensions of their defeat, and the loss of their historic role and importance. Accustomed to thinking of the monarchy as the

---

[76] Bitterauf (1914: 486–501); Griewank (1935: 277–90); Thielen (1967: 146–9); Oer (1965: 60–3); Dunan (1961: 188–92); Metternich (1880–4: ii. 59–83); *VPR* (1960–: 1. ii. Nos. 194–200).

linchpin of Europe, they could not envision it now as an ordinary country for which Napoleon might have no real use. But this unrealism did not cost Austria anything, for it had no chances to get a better peace, either by war or diplomacy. Even had Prussia been willing to help, Austria could not have waited for it to come in. The problems of supply and morale among the combined Austro-Russian forces at Olmütz were so bad by mid-November that, according to Czartoryski, the only two options being discussed were to fight one last battle or to let the armies dissolve without fighting. Had the allies refused to offer battle, Napoleon would probably have quartered his army for the winter in Austria at its expense, making its plight worse. He even seriously considered and prepared for an attempt to break up the Habsburg monarchy through a Hungarian national revolution. Austria made another futile effort to win concessions from France in the peace negotiations following Austerlitz, but this did not cause the delay in concluding the Peace of Pressburg until the end of December. The reason was that Napoleon ordered Talleyrand to spin the negotiations out while he settled first with his South German allies and Prussia.[77]

This proved easy and profitable. Napoleon had made ruthlessly efficient use of his satellites and allies during the war;[78] the German troops had fought especially well against Austria. To reward their governments, Napoleon summoned Talleyrand to Munich after Ulm and dictated to him a programme which stood the Strasbourg memorandum on its head. He increased Austria's territorial losses only slightly, but reversed Talleyrand's whole concept by proposing that he ally with Russia against Austria and himself replace Francis as German Emperor. As Talleyrand later worked Napoleon's idea out, Germany would contain three empires, French, Prussian, and Austrian; within the French Empire there would be smaller kingdoms of Saxony, Hanover, Bavaria, Württemberg, and possibly Baden (even the Margrave of Baden, jealous as he was of rival princes, knew that the title 'King of Baden' would be ridiculous). All this was improvisation rather than carefully considered plan, however; Napoleon and Talleyrand cared little about legal niceties. The essential thing was to oust Austria from Germany, satisfy France's German clients with ter-

---

[77] Oer (1965: 66–183); Beer (1877b: 184–94); Rössler (1940: i. 87–91; 1966: i. 212–21); Kosary (1979: 19–37).

[78] For examples of the way he issued orders to other rulers, see Fournier (1930: i. 531–35); Schlossberger (1889: 1–36); Napoleon (1858–70: xi. Nos. 9130, 9157, 9281–2, 9307–8, 9310).

ritory and independence, and ensure Napoleon direct control of Germany, military assets, and hard cash.

This was accomplished by separate treaties of alliance between France and Bavaria, Württemberg, and Baden concluded in Brünn from 10 to 12 December. The treaties rounded out these states with Austrian territory along with the property of the last remaining Imperial knightly order, the German Order; made them independent 'within the German Confederation'; and gave Bavaria and Württemberg the status of kingdoms while Baden became a grand duchy. Bavaria came off far the best territorially, because it was most useful militarily (Napoleon insisted that it must provide him 50,000 men in time of war), because it was the best outpost against Austria, and because Napoleon wanted a dynastic marriage between Eugène de Beauharnais and Princess Augusta.[79]

How little France was concerned about the possibility of Prussian intervention is shown by the fact that Napoleon did not even meet Haugwitz on his mission of armed mediation until 28 November, after Talleyrand had worked out the plans for South Germany, when he already was negotiating with Stadion for peace, and when Austria and Russia had resolved to try one more battle. But then Haugwitz, who had remained in Berlin eleven days after the Potsdam Convention, had let the French know, both there and at Vienna, that Frederick William was unwilling to fight. Napoleon, therefore, had little trouble restraining Haugwitz from even conveying Prussia's conditions. The news of Austerlitz crowned the triumph of the Prussian peace party.

The relief in Berlin over avoiding war was gradually clouded, however, by the realization that Prussia would now have to pay France for Hanover, and not with neutrality but with an alliance. Napoleon, after failing in November to force Austria into a quick peace so as to gain a weapon against Prussia, reversed course. Ordering Talleyrand to spin out the negotiations with Austria, he turned to exploiting Prussia's fears that Napoleon might ally with Austria or offer it Hanover, and thereby succeeded in hustling Haugwitz into an offensive–defensive alliance treaty at Schönbrunn on 15 December. It ceded Prussia Hanover, but at a considerable price: that Prussia guarantee the territories of France, the Ottoman Empire, Italy, and the South German states in whatever form Napoleon gave them at the final peace. In addition, Prussia had to surrender Cleves and Neuchâtel to France and Ansbach to Bavaria, to pay Bavaria for handing over a principality

[79] Oer (1965: 46–57, 131–40); Gmeinwiser (1928: 162–4, 172–7); Dunan (1961: 66–7).

for Napoleon's brother-in-law and cavalry leader Joachim Murat to rule, the Duchy of Berg.[80]

With Prussia harnessed by this humiliatingly unequal treaty, Napoleon finished with Austria at Pressburg on 26 December. It was the first peace treaty to cost Austria heavily in territory. Venetia and the Dalmatian coast down to Cattaro went to France, Tirol, Vorarlberg, and a number of smaller territories to Bavaria, and Austria's scattered South German possessions to Württemberg and Baden. Its only compensation was Salzburg, taken from Grand Duke Ferdinand, who was transferred to the Duchy of Würzburg in central Germany. These losses, plus the require-ment that Austria recognize all the political changes included in Napoleon's treaties with his clients and foreshadowed by them, and in addition pay a 40 million franc indemnity, reduced Austria to political, military, and fiscal impotence. Also in place were Napoleon's usual devices to enable him for long after the peace to hold on to Austrian prisoners of war, occupy Austrian territory, and support large contingents of his army at Austria's expense, insuring that Austria would stay in this condition.

The Battle of Austerlitz and the Peace of Pressburg were not signs, as has been argued, that Napoleon was moving from a basically national course to an all-out imperialist one. All efforts to find some point in Napoleon's career at which he turned wrong or went too far are misguided. His whole character and career were fundamentally wrong; he always went too far. Pressburg was indeed a turning-point of sorts, but only for Austria. Napoleon's earlier peace treaties had taken a little while to become unbearable; this one was so from the outset. Austria either had to become a useful French satellite like Bavaria or ultimately rebel against it.[81]

It would take years, however, for Austria to face up to this. It took Prussia almost no time to learn its fate as Napoleon's junior partner. Austerlitz had converted even Hardenberg, the leading supporter of the coalition in Prussia, into advocating an alliance with France. But that alliance, as it emerged in the form of Haugwitz's unauthorized Treaty of Schönbrunn, met severe criti-cism in Berlin, especially since Talleyrand made it clear that France's demands had merely begun. France would not recognize Prussia's title to Hanover, or turn over the Hanoverian fortress of Hameln which it still occupied, until Prussia had forced the

[80] Bitterauf (1914: 502–15); Oer (1965: 88–92, 151–61); Driault (1912: 254–7); Beer (1877b: 197–206); Bailleu (1881–7: ii. 407–24); Napoleon (1858–70: xi. Nos. 9420–1, 9434).
[81] DeClercq (1880–1917: ii. 145–51); Oer (1965: 184–221); Deutsch (1938: 375–419); Fugier (1954: 200–3).

British, Russians, and Swedes in North Germany to go home, had wiped out all traces of British rule in Hanover, and had turned over Cleves, Neuchâtel, and Ansbach to their future owners. Talleyrand also insisted that Lucchesini be recalled and Hardenberg ousted, accompanying these demands with hints of war.

Haugwitz, defending himself in Berlin by arguing that his treaty laid the basis for a necessary and mutually profitable condominium of France and Prussia over South and North Germany respectively, suggested to Talleyrand that France make the alliance more palatable by helping Prussia acquire Hamburg, Bremen, and possibly Lübeck. The acquisitions would also promote the joint economic war against Britain. But Frederick William, frightened by the treaty, struck the word 'offensive' from it, called for changes in Prussia's guarantee of Italy, and, while insisting that Prussia must immediately occupy Hanover to insure North German neutrality, declined to annex it formally because that would mean war with Britain. As it stood, the King insisted, the treaty was onesidedly favourable to France. Members of both camps in Prussia supported his view, arguing that no one threatened Prussia's possessions, while the treaty required Prussia to guarantee to France conquests of which Europe was jealous.

Haugwitz, sent to Paris to secure the modifications Berlin desired, quickly discovered the folly of trying to maintain such language to Napoleon. Told that, since Prussia had repudiated the alliance it must want war, he was forced to sign a new Treaty of Paris on 15 February which turned Prussia from a junior partner of the French Empire into its chief lackey. In addition to the commitments of the earlier treaty of Schönbrunn, Prussia now had to cede further territory to France, including the key North German fortress of Wesel, immediately occupy Hanover and break relations with Britain, guarantee to France the results of any future war fought with the Kingdom of Naples, and pledge France total support in any war for any French object. Lombard complained bitterly to the French minister at Berlin, Laforest, of how his King felt trapped and betrayed. This was the greedy and gullible businessman complaining to his gangster partner as he sees his firm being taken over: 'I thought you were a gentleman.'[82]

Having smashed Austria, put Russia out of action, and cowed Prussia, Napoleon was understandably confident that he could now impose peace on Britain. The British alliance with Russia was badly strained. Alexander was not Paul, and therefore did

[82] Griewank (1935: 294–9); Fournier (1930: i. 406–7); DeClercq (1880–1917: ii. 143–4, 154–6); Bailleu (1900: 89–96; 1881–7: ii. 424–3).

not repeat Russia's volte-face of 1799–1800. In fact, nothing in
the history of the Third Coalition so became the Tsar as the way
he left it. Unlike some in Russia and many in Britain, he and
Czartoryski did not blame the allied defeats on Austria's 'treachery
and imbecility' (Malmesbury's phrase). He made real if ineffective
efforts to aid Austria, did not object to Austria's seeking peace to
save itself, quickly agreed to pull the shattered Russian army out
of Austria after Austerlitz, and genuinely regretted the disappearance of Austria as an independent factor in the balance (though
Russian fears were soon aroused by Austria's cession of Dalmatia
to France, an obvious threat to Russia in the Near East).

None the less, Anglo-Russian military and political co-operation
in the war had gone badly. The Russian troops landed in Naples,
violating the treaty of neutrality Naples concluded with France
on 22 September, had to be pulled out after Ulm without ac-
complishing anything. A British expedition of 20,000 men to
North Germany met the same fate after Prussia switched sides in
December. Once again, glaring deficiencies showed up in the respective British and Russian military establishments. More serious
in the long term was the friction and suspicion growing between
them over the Near East. Czartoryski complained sharply about
the activities of British agents in the Ionian Isles and the Morea
(Greece south of the isthmus of Corinth), and reports reached
Britain even before the war that Russia was bent on partitioning
Turkey in Europe and dominating Turkey in Asia. The alliance
was undermined most of all simply by the war itself, not only
because it ended in defeat (though Britain had triumphed at sea)
but even more because it destroyed the alliance's basic premises. It
proved that their flank positions did not make Russia and Britain
invulnerable, and proved more decisively than in 1799–1801 that
even when they fully co-operated they were unable to form and
lead a coalition sufficient to defeat Napoleon and give them control
of the destinies of Europe.

Thus 1805 gave Napoleon another great opportunity, better in
most ways than 1802, to make French hegemony secure, this time
in Central as well as Western Europe. The only thing able to stop
him from seizing this opportunity was himself.[83]

[83] On the war, see Mackesy (1957: 78–84); Acton (1956: 514–17); Bartlett
(1966: 52–62). On Anglo-Russian friction, see *VPR* (1960–: i. ii. No. 187), and
various unsigned letters of Mar. 1805 in Canning Papers (Leeds), 57. For some
British reactions to the catastrophe on the Continent, see Malmesbury (1844:
iv. 339); Windham (1913: ii. 246–9, 268–9, 272–7); Grenville (1892–1927: vii.
316–17).

6
From Pressburg to Tilsit,
1806–1807

IF the Revolutionary and Napoleonic Wars are seen in the usual way, as a series of attempts to defeat France and restore a balance of power in Europe, 1806–7 brought nothing new. All that happened essentially was the revival of the Third Coalition in a different form, leading to more battles, another Napoleonic victory, and a further expansion of his empire. But if the real story, as this book argues, is the transformation of international politics during this era; if this change required a long, painful process of learning from hard experience; and if what needed to be learned was less how to defeat France than how to construct a peaceful Europe and a stable international system on a new basis, then this period emerges as an important stage in the learning process, in which there were some set-backs but also some irreversible progress.

Some states had already learned various lessons by 1806. The smaller states directly in France's path, having learned the futility of resisting France and the folly of accepting help from other powers, chose to collaborate with the former. Austria had begun to learn from its repeated defeats not only that military victory, gains in power and territory, and useful great-power alliances were extremely hard to obtain, but also that, even if obtained, they might not solve its security problem. Some Austrians already recognized the need for a broader, more political solution, some sort of guaranteed joint security arrangement for all of Central Europe as an intermediary sphere, in which Prussia should be Austria's partner rather than its enemy and the smaller independent states in Italy and Germany Austria's associates rather than its satellites and victims. Gaining this insight, however, was one thing, implementing it quite another. Prussia, though still trying to play the balance-of-power game between the two sides, had become all too aware of its dangers. Like Austria, it wanted stable partners in an independent European centre, and could not see how to get them. Britain and Russia had so far learned little more than to appreciate somewhat better France's strengths and their

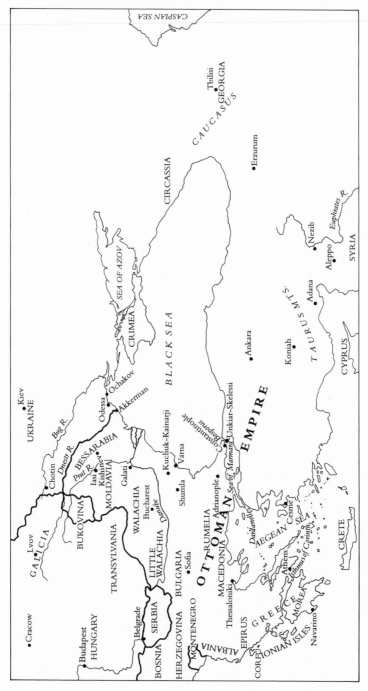

The Balkans and the Black Sea

own limitations, which moderated their war aims without over-throwing their basic assumptions.

I. REORGANIZING THE EMPIRE

Napoleon, on principle, never learned from experience in the sense of admitting defeat and accepting limits, and at this point had no compelling reason to do so. After December 1805 he could have concentrated on the peaceful consolidation of his gains, trying, for example, to reorganize Germany on a permanent basis or pursuing peace talks with Britain and Russia. In fact, his immediate recourse was to try to conquer Naples and Sicily; to create a new state in north-west Germany as a weapon against Prussia; to keep his Grand Army intact in Germany at German expense; to order his son-in-law, Prince Eugène, and Marshal Auguste Marmont to advance further into Istria and Dalmatia and to organize Dalmatia for war; to force Austria to concede him a better military frontier on the Isonzo and a military route through Istria; to exact more contributions from Austria, Venice, Spain, Switzerland, Holland, and other states; to extort tariff privileges for French goods from Spain and Italy; to promote desertion among Austrian prisoners of war so that his German satellites could recruit them; to put Joachim Murat on the throne of the Grand Duchy of Berg and make his brother Louis King of Holland; to establish a new military nobility by granting French generals titles and fiefs in Germany and Italy; to force his satellites to build more warships and his navy minister to wage a more active cruiser warfare against Britain; and to build more forti-fications along the Rhine while he seized new strong points in North Germany. As ever, peace for Napoleon was a continuation of war by other means.[1] The foreign ministry did not try to check him. Talleyrand, though nervous, was more sycophantic and anti-British than ever, and Hauterive had come to believe in security through indefinite expansion.[2]

Victory also offered Napoleon the chance to punish those who had (genuinely or according to his lights) defied him during the war: Naples, which after signing a neutrality pact with France had allied with the Russians and British, and the Pope, who had dared

---

[1] Napoleon (1858–70: xii. Nos. 9951, 9953, 9955, 9871, 10423, 10440, 10448, 10524–6; xiii. 10751–2).

[2] Angot (1913: 497–99); Lacour-Gayet (1928–30: ii. 200–3).

to protest when France occupied Ancona without his consent. The day after Pressburg, Napoleon announced that the Bourbons had ceased to reign at Naples and sent an army to occupy the mainland, a task rendered easy by the retreat of Britain's forces to Sicily and Russia's to Corfu. Napoleon's promise that the French and Neapolitan Crowns would not be united proved as meaningless as his other such promises; Joseph Bonaparte was installed in May as King of the Two Sicilies. The choice was evidence of Napoleon's Corsican family feelings, but not of generosity, either to Joseph or to Naples. He ordered Joseph to make his impoverished kingdom pay not only for itself but also for the occupation army, its armaments, and the conquest of Sicily.

This latter assignment proved difficult. Instead of the French army crossing the Straits of Messina, the British crossed into Calabria and inflicted a stinging defeat on General Jean Reynier's forces at Maida. The battle, the first victory of British line tactics over the French column, was an omen of the future and helped to save Sicily, but failed to shake France's hold on the mainland. The British withdrew again to Sicily, and the French captured the last Neapolitan stronghold at Gaeta in the summer. Though peasant resistance revived and persisted in Calabria, ultimately causing the occupation army losses proportionately as heavy as the French would later experience in Spain, the revolt could not expel the French without foreign help, which the British never dared give. Napoleon, in fact, welcomed the resistance as a good pretext for the salutary terror he always considered necessary before any conquest could be consolidated. None the less, France lost its best chance to take Sicily, and Joseph, despite his attempts to gain popularity, found his regime resting on military force and exploitation.[3]

Pius VII's protests earned him more lessons in Napoleon's doctrine of Church–state relations. According to this, the Pope could exercise the spiritual rights Napoleon had conceded him in the Concordat (which Napoleon arbitrarily extended to all of Napoleonic Italy without the Pope's permission), but only so long as he obeyed Napoleon in temporal affairs like any other vassal prince of the empire. The notion that he and the Pontiff might define spiritual and secular affairs differently simply did not enter Napoleon's mind. Pius resisted demands that the Papal State close its ports to the British, expel British and Russian subjects, and

---

[3] Driault (1912: 296–9); Acton (1956: 520–40); Napoleon (1858–70: xii. Nos. 9936, 10395–6, 10467, 10499, 10522; xiii. Nos. 10573, 10657).

recognize Joseph as King of Naples, abandoning Papal claims to suzerainty there. The French responded to Pius's obstruction by occupying the whole Adriatic and Tyrrhenian coast and devastating papal territory in the march against Naples. Pius could offer no armed resistance and wanted no quarrel; none the less, he refused either to renounce the traditional papal doctrine of the two swords or to join Napoleon's federative system like the Emperor's other crowned prefects in Italy and Germany. He escaped punishment for this temporarily because in midsummer 1806 Napoleon became preoccupied with Prussia. None the less, the *de facto* incorporation of Rome into the Grand Empire began in 1806.[4]

Rome and Naples were punished for resisting Napoleon. Venetia and Dalmatia, which had not, received the same treatment or worse, having to supply even more in the way of costly fiefdoms and sacrificed revenues for Napoleon's new feudal nobility. The Dutch, under threat of annexation if they refused, invited Louis Bonaparte to become their king in April–May 1806. Louis was promptly ordered to form his own multi-national army like Napoleon's. Even the Swiss were threatened with occupation for failing to enrol in the French army in sufficient numbers and for other alleged misdeeds. No higher purpose lay behind the bullying and exploitation. Napoleon's goal may fairly be described (as Pierre Muret and Georges Lefebvre do describe it) as universal domination, and his Empire at this time pictured as more like Rome's than Charlemagne's (following Edouard Driault). But even these characterizations suggest too much purpose to an Empire whose central characteristic was negative, the absence of any idea or purpose beyond centralization and expansion of power.[5]

This verdict seems to fly in the face of one great fact: Napoleon's creation in July 1806 of a Confederation of the Rhine, a permanent league uniting France and sixteen West and South German states, the more important ones being Bavaria, Württemberg, Baden, Berg, and Hesse-Darmstadt, with Napoleon as its Protector. The Rheinbund today is widely hailed by historians, especially in Germany, for clearing the German stream-bed of medieval rubbish, promoting modernization and rationalization in law, ad-

[4] Hales (1961: 178–9, 184–9); Latreille (1935: 460–510); Driault (1912: 326–41); Napoleon (1858–70: xi. Nos. 9655–6; xii. Nos. 10264–7, 10274, 10377, 10434).
[5] Ibid. Nos. 9902, 9904, 9968–70, 9999, 10088, 10113–16, 10503; xiv. Nos. 11344–5, 11460); Schama (1977: 484–5); Driault (1912: 316–21, 345–50); Muret (1913); Sieburg (1971: 144–9). For a valuable general analysis of Napoleon's empire, which appeared too late to be used fully for this book, see Woolf (1991).

ministration, and politics, and even laying the foundation for civil rights and early constitutional liberalism. Napoleonic rule helped to develop modern independent states such as Bavaria, Württemberg, and Baden as potentially valuable alternatives to the Prussian or German nationalist patterns of Germany's development.

All this may be true, and yet confirm rather than contradict a negative verdict on Napoleon's policy toward Germany and Europe, for two closely connected reasons. First, the beneficial long-range results of the Rheinbund for Germany were almost entirely ironic, unintended consequences of Napoleon's policy, and have little or nothing to do with Napoleon's purposes or the objective direction in which these reforms were taking Germany. Second, the reason that these benefits accrued to Germany over the long run at all, as is obvious but often overlooked, is not that the Rheinbund itself endured and produced these consequences, thus proving the value of Napoleon's domination of Germany. The reason instead is precisely the fact that both the Rheinbund and Napoleonic domination were so short-lived that Germany escaped their real, full long-term consequences. Few historians today would deny that Nazi rule had certain modernizing effects on Germany and Austria; fewer still would deny that the Soviet Union transformed and modernized some of the states and societies it dominated in Eastern Europe after 1944. The comparisons illustrate why the regimes and institutions cannot be judged simply by a naïvely empirical account of their apparent consequences in history. The consequences may seem clear and directly traceable to them, but the outcomes always involve a vast web of other causes and circumstances as well, so that often, as here, historical results are unintended and ironic. Therefore to judge regimes and institutions one has to consider other things alongside their actual historical consequences—above all, their essential nature, purpose, and principles, and the results these would have produced had these purposes been carried out, the basic principles sufficiently applied over time. This commonsense principle is constantly used in daily life. A mugger's blow may restore an amnesiac's memory, a lover's betrayal turn a person toward a saintly life of good works. The consequences do not alter the nature of the actions themselves.

Sometimes in history it is relatively easy to judge regimes and institutions by their intrinsic principles and purposes, though these go partly unfulfilled. The Soviet empire in Eastern Europe endured long enough for most of its long-range results to become obvious. The Nazi empire did not, but in its short life it accomplished such terrible things that few observers dispute the character of its overall effects had it endured longer. Napoleon's rule in Germany, overthrown after just seven years, inevitably leaves more room for debate. Enough is clearly known about its fundamental nature and purposes, however, to show that, had it lasted long enough, its long-term results would have been mainly bad. The Rheinbund was essentially designed to enable Napoleon to dominate and control Germany, especially militarily. Its core was a permanent unequal alliance giving him command of the foreign policies, the armies, and ultimately the economic resources of the member states; the most important clauses were those stipulating the contributions of member states to the common army—200,000 men from France, 30,000 from Bavaria, 33,000 from all the rest. True, Napoleon applied some of his undeniable talents and zeal for rational, modern administration to Germany, though only sporadically and inconsistently, and this, combined with the efforts of modernizing leaders and officials in Germany, produced some progressive changes. But from the beginning these were accompanied by changes of a different tendency—the introduction of a new military feudalism, the maintenance and intensifying of certain class and gender distinctions, and the heightening of political repression. Moreover, as will be shown later, Napoleon used the Confederation from 1806 on almost exclusively for war, imperialism, economic exploitation, constant territorial expansion, and increasingly direct interference with local governments by Paris.

The credit, therefore, for whatever ultimate benefits Germany derived from this era and for the survival of the Rheinbund states and princes themselves does not belong to Napoleon, or to its other leaders and statesmen. The ones who deserve it were the allies in 1813–15. They overthrew the Rheinbund before its poisonous fruits could fully ripen, and they allowed most of its progressive results and features to survive. The leaders of the Rheinbund states lived by Napoleon's sword, served under it, and should by Napoleonic and Rheinbund principles have died by it; many in Germany called for this in 1813. Had a Montgelas ruled Austria in 1813–14, he would not have let Bavaria's Montgelas live, and perhaps not Bavaria itself. They and Napoleon's 'reforms' survived, not according to their deserts, but by the grace of the allied coalition.

Besides, in organizing Germany in its fashion the Rheinbund deliberately excluded other, better schemes. The central German problem, dimly sensed even by egocentric state-builders like Montgelas or Frederick of Württemberg, keenly felt by many others, was how to reconcile the independence of individual states with the required amount of overall unity within the Third Germany, through some sort of federalism. The individual states, while each seeking sovereignty and autonomy, also needed and wanted a union for mutual protection and benefits, especially once the Reich was formally dissolved. The Rheinbund did not even attempt to provide this. Instead, it imposed French control from the top down, which, though readily accepted at first, became increasingly resented and unworkable with time. None of the potential federal instruments of the Confederation, such as its College of Princes and its Diet, ever meant anything, nor did other common institutions lead toward federalism. Napoleon's approach to the German problem was retrograde compared to that of 1815 in this respect also.[6]

II. THE FAILURE OF 'PEACE'

Thus Napoleon after victory reorganized his empire in clear preparation for more war rather than peace; but Britain would also help decide whether the war would continue. By early 1806 the British saw peace as desirable, though not absolutely necessary. The Continental war was lost and the coalition shattered, but Britain's economy was still resilient, its industries were either flourishing or stable, popular unrest was under control, and the end of subsidies to allies relieved the government's finances. The losses in trade caused by the break with Prussia were made up by smuggling through the Hanseatic cities and elsewhere (Gibraltar, Portugal, Sicily) plus the growth in normal trade with the rest of Northern Europe, Russia, and the western hemisphere. Pitt's loss was not widely mourned, but neither was there a great public outcry for peace. Once again British insularity, psychological and political as well as geographic, proved an asset. For months

[6] The literature on the effects of Napoleonic domination on Germany, especially the Rheinbund states, is too massive to review here; more attention is given the subject in Ch. 9. On the actual origins of the Rheinbund and the points made here, see Driault (1912: 367–81); Quint (1971: 166–211); Dunan (1942: 28–48, 192–5); Raumer (1952: 160–3); Aretin (1967: ii. 497–504); Jürgens (1976: 99–104, 132–5, 164–7); Huber (1957: 76–84); Hölzle (1931: 3–31); Chroust (1932: 22–153); Schlossberger (1889: 37–54). The Rheinbund treaties are in DeClercq (1880–1917: ii. 171–9, 198–201); a sample of Napoleon's attitude is in Napoleon (1858–70: xii. No. 10298).

after Pitt's death, domestic questions occupied ministers and Parliament—the formation and reshuffling of the new Ministry of All the Talents, Catholic emancipation, the abolition of the slave trade. The new Whig premier, Charles James Fox, nearly despaired at Britain's long-range prospects in the war, but his colleagues Grenville and Windham were indifferent or relatively optimistic.[7]

A decision by Britain to carry on the war involved first of all working out where and how to do so. At first the New World seemed a promising theatre for conquests. Arthur Wellesley, Britain's best general now returned from India, was always sceptical about it, however, and his doubts were soon vindicated. General Popham's unauthorized capture of Buenos Aires in June 1806 at first aroused great enthusiasm, but the British mood changed with the loss of Buenos Aires in August and the disastrous end to a second expedition to the Plata River in mid-1807. Grenville tried rather half-heartedly to use Britain's South American conquests as diplomatic currency in the peace talks of 1806, but after 1807 Britain sought trade, not colonies, in the New World.[8] On the Continent, Britain's direct co-operation with Russia ended when they both evacuated the Neapolitan mainland in January. The expeditionary force under Sir Sidney Smith defended Sicily tenaciously and even won the victory at Maida, but could achieve only defensive successes.[9]

This meant that there was only one important positive reason for staying in the war: to keep Russia from making a separate peace with France. Since Czartoryski also wanted to avoid this, the two powers agreed to stay in secret contact with each other while ostensibly negotiating separately with France. Czartoryski unrealistically hoped that this diplomatic co-operation would lead to a new Mediterranean balance in which Britain and Russia would check France from Malta and Corfu, while two new states, one Slavic and one Greek, would arise in the Balkans, nominally under Turkish suzerainty, actually under Russian protection and

[7] Crouzet (1958: i. 164–84, 192–206); Ziegler (1965: 250–6, 262–9); Glover (1973: 13–20); Anstey (1972; 1975: 35–7, 403–8). On the particular attitudes of Grenville and various of his colleagues, see Grenville (1892–1927: viii. 26–7, 37–8, 72–3, 105–8). His preoccupation with domestic issues shows clearly in his correspondence with the foreign secretary, Lord Howick, later the second Earl Grey (Grey Papers, Durham University), and with his brother Thomas, BL Add. MS 48152.

[8] Watson (1960: 452–7); Crouzet (1958: i. 184–9); Grenville (1892–1927: viii. 321, 358–9, 365–7, 415–21; ix. 39–44, 479–93).

[9] Mackesy (1957: 97–105, 121–53).

serving to defend Russian interests. Fox's goal was simpler and more modest—peace if possible, but continued ties to Russia above all.[10]

Negotiations opened in February with exchanges between Talleyrand and Fox, leading to direct Anglo-French talks conducted by a British prisoner of war released by the French for the purpose, Lord Yarmouth. Yarmouth proved an unorthodox and unreliable negotiator, and had to be first supplemented by Lord Lauderdale and then recalled when London learned of his financial speculations during the negotiations. When Fox fell ill in mid-summer and died in September, Grenville took over, with Lord Howick (later the second Earl Grey) succeeding Fox as foreign secretary. They followed a tougher line, which led to a stalemate and final breakdown in October.

The details of the negotiation are not important, given the obvious reasons for ultimate failure. Napoleon hardly bothered to conceal the fact that the only treaty he wanted was one like Amiens which would exclude Britain from the Continent, keep it from interfering in the Near East, and enable France to prepare for further commercial and ultimate naval war against it, and that he expected to force Britain into this by a separate peace with Russia. Talleyrand, wanting peace in order to save Napoleon from himself, tried to make Napoleon's demands plausible, a test for even his talents at sophistry. An example: Talleyrand first proposed a peace of *uti possedetis* (current possession), which would mean that Joseph Bonaparte would rule the Neapolitan mainland while the Bourbons kept Sicily. After the British took this up and Napoleon then demanded that Britain must recognize Joseph's title to Sicily, Talleyrand explained that the principle of *uti possedetis* meant that a power was entitled not only to the conquests it had already made, but also those which it was in a position to make at any time without meeting serious resistance, so that Sicily really belonged to Joseph already.

Fox, long a friend of France and critic of the war, sought peace without dishonour, which meant that at least Britain must get back Hanover, retain Malta, and secure some compensation to King Ferdinand for surrendering Sicily. Britain's goal of maintaining its ties to Russia seemed lost when Talleyrand succeeded in hustling Oubril, the Russian chargé at Paris, into signing a separate peace in July. Fox's reaction was to try to accommodate Russia's desire

[10] Sherwig (1969: 172–6); Shupp (1931: 86–91); Martens (1874–1905: xi. 126–7); *VPR* (1960–: 1. iii. Nos. 13, 17, 38).

for peace. As he explained to Robert Adair, sent to Vienna as British minister less to deal with the Austrians than to keep contact with Oubril through the Russian ambassador at Vienna Count Andrei Razumovski, 'Except those [terms] in wh[ich] our honour is concerned Hanover + Malta I sh[oul]d be very much inclined to defer almost implicitly to the opinion of Russia herself.'[11] Grenville took a harder anti-French line, urging the Tsar not to ratify Oubril's treaty, insisting on keeping Sicily or exchanging it for Dalmatia, and raising Britain's demands near the end of the talks. But he was as determined as Fox to stick with Russia; his willingness if necessary to give up Sicily so that a Balkan buffer state could be created for Russia in Dalmatia proves it.

In any case, Britain and France never came close to an agreement even with Fox in charge, and had they done so the peace would not have lasted. The most interesting thing about the failed negotiations is once again the kind of peace Britain envisioned at this time: an implicit three-way division of the world, with Britain enjoying naval and colonial supremacy, including a presence in the Mediterranean to guard the route to India; Russia being supreme in Eastern and Northern Europe and the Near East; and France controlling Western, Southern, and Central Europe. Here is still more evidence that the British, far from being steadfastly determined to preserve a balance of power on the Continent, were ready at various times to come to terms with French hegemony. Checking France and keeping it out of the Low Countries remained desiderata, but were not *sine qua non*, and at present they were out of reach. This shows a certain realism in Britain's attitude—and a certain Micawberism as well. Peace was desirable, but if the war had to go on, sooner or later something would turn up.

Most striking in the negotiations and the British concept of peace was, once again, the absence of Central Europe. The British did not contest the fate of Germany and Italy (indeed, hardly mentioned it) because they could do nothing about it, and did not really care. They would concede Continental hegemony, at least for the time, to Napoleon, and concerned themselves with Hanover, Sicily, and to a lesser degree the King of Sardinia and the Hanseatic cities, solely in terms of honor, compensations,

---

[11] Private, 17 June 1806, Holland Papers, BL Add. MS 51549. He gave Yarmouth similar priorities: '1st Honour. 2nd Hanover. 3d A preservation of the Russian alliance.' Private, 16 July, ibid., 51548.

commerce, or British and Russian security in the Mediterranean and Baltic. It annoyed Grenville that the French first concealed the formation of the Rheinbund from Britain and then lied about it, but the question played no role in the negotiations. More important to the British government than the German settlement was the possibility of getting French co-operation to abolish the slave trade. Fox felt sorry for the Austrians and criticized Pitt for contributing to their downfall, but Austria mattered to Britain solely as a possible factor in British ties with Russia. Some British actions—its support of Russia's occupation and retention of Cattaro, which Austria was obligated by treaty to turn over to Napoleon, and encouragement of Russian ideas of a buffer state in Dalmatia—served to increase the pressure and danger from France for Austria. As for Prussia, the British, finally disillusioned, ceased even to pay attention to it. London remained unaware that France and Prussia were on a collision course in 1806 long after this had become obvious to most European observers. Grenville, on finally noting in mid-September that Prussia seemed determined to fight, remarked offhand that he could not understand why.[12]

It serves no purpose to condemn this sort of British thought and attitude—only to re-emphasize a fact vital for analysing the European states system and its collapse, yet widely ignored. Throughout this period, as throughout the eighteenth century, Britain was only marginally a European country. Although the wars were fundamentally the products of Napoleon's ambition and aggressions, Britain's insularity, ignorance of Europe, and indifference to its needs were prominent among the causes of the absence and impossibility of peace. Thirteen years of war had brought no sign of a change for the better—if anything, the reverse.

For Russians, Central Europe was not a far-away country of which they knew nothing. From their standpoint, recent developments in Germany and Italy meant a general French threat to Russia and an immediate danger to its position in the Near East. Even after Austerlitz Czartoryski, fighting for his political life, claimed that Russia's position remained basically sound. The only serious threat lay in the south, and even this one would not become acute unless Napoleon coerced Austria into acting with

[12] Shupp (1931: 94–9, 106–7, 110–13, 120–5); Mackesy (1957: 118–21); Driault (1912: 411–22, 432–8). For documentation, see Grenville (1894–1927: viii. 195–367); Holland Papers, BL, Add. MSS 51457–61.

him in the Balkans. Russia should ward this off by maintaining its ties to Britain and Austria. Other Russians, however, called for peace with Napoleon or a nationalist policy of expansion southward. The State Council, in meetings on 17 and 19 January, took no decisive steps, but urged military precautions against the threat to Turkey and considered asking Prussia to help keep Austria out of Napoleon's arms.[13]

Czartoryski waged a Near Eastern diplomatic offensive from February to May, promoting his scheme for Balkan buffer states, threatening to occupy Moldavia and Wallachia if the Turks drew closer to France, and pressing Austria to arm the Serbian rebels. Alexander ordered the troops withdrawn from Naples to occupy the Ionian Isles and authorized Admiral Siniavin to seize and hold Cattaro (modern Kotor), a key strongpoint on the Dalmatian coast which Austria was pledged by the Treaty of Pressburg to deliver to the French.[14]

This promoted a Russo-French confrontation both at Constantinople, where the French renewed their efforts to pull the Ottoman Empire away from Russia and Britain and to create a Franco-Turkish–Persian bloc, and in the Adriatic. Napoleon hoped to entangle Russia in war with the Ottoman Empire and Austria, but at the moment this was less important than achieving a separate Franco-Russian peace which would let him concentrate on the British in Sicily. Hence he responded to Russia's seizure of Cattaro by occupying nearby Ragusa (modern Dubrovnik) and trying to force Austria to expel the Russians from Cattaro.[15] The confrontation issued in a small war in the Adriatic in the summer and early autumn. The Russians cut France's sea communications but failed to oust the French from Ragusa, while the Montenegrins helped Admiral Siniavin beat off a French attack on Cattaro.[16]

During this conflict Oubril, an inexperienced negotiator charged with a peace mission in France, fell prey to Talleyrand's and Clarke's deceptive tactics, signing an unauthorized treaty *sub spe rati* on 20 July. Oubril had been instructed to seek a general peace

[13] Shupp (1931: 15–18); Driault (1912: 389–95); Mouraviev (1954: 171–4); *Sbornik* (1867–1916: lxxxii. 240–1, 252–85); *VPR* (1960–: 1. iii. pp. 8–35); Vorontsov (1870–95: xv. 359–66).

[14] Shupp (1931: 18–22, 30–1, 46–65); Stanislavskaia (1962: 414–18); Paxton (1982: 54–7); *Sbornik* (1867–1916: lxxxii. Nos. 85–6, 94–5); *VPR* (1960–: 1. iii. Nos. 14–15, 24–6, 31).

[15] Shaw (1971: 334–41); Shupp (1931: 66–77); Driault (1912: 400–5); Napoleon (1858–70: xii. Nos. 10197, 10339, 10346); Vorontsov (1870–95: xx. 309–14).

[16] Stanislavskaia (1962: 418–28); Saul (1970: 202–9); Mouraviev (1954: 152–7); Shupp (1931: 268–77); *VPR* (1960–: 1. iii. No. 110).

in which the French would evacuate Austrian soil, while King Ferdinand would get Dalmatia, Ragusa, and Albania to serve as his compensation for Naples and Sicily and as a buffer state in the Adriatic for Russia. Instead, the treaty Oubril signed required Russia to evacuate Cattaro, acknowledge the independence of the Ionian Isles and restrict the Russian forces there to 4,000 men, and recognize Joseph as King of Sicily, while consigning Ferdinand to the Balearic Isles in the western Mediterranean. For these concessions France promised Russia to evacuate Germany and Ragusa—a promise violated in advance. Just before this treaty Napoleon ordered his chief of staff, General Alexandre Berthier, to station the entire Grand Army between Passau and Linz in Austria if Austria showed any sign of objecting to the Confederation of the Rhine, and simultaneously he instructed General Lauriston to stay in Ragusa regardless of what any treaty might say.[17]

Napoleon was already putting great pressure on Austria by his occupation of Braunau and stationing of his army on Austrian soil; the Russo-French struggle in the Adriatic gave him further leverage. Now, in a sense, he had a right to force Austria to expel the Russians from Cattaro, since the Austrian general in charge there had failed actively to resist the Russian take-over. Austria accepted a whole series of other French demands, granting France a military road through Istria to Dalmatia, swallowing a one-sided exchange of territories along the Isonzo River in Italy, closing its remaining Adriatic ports to British and Russian vessels, quickly surrendering its ancient Imperial crown when Napoleon dissolved the German Empire (this particularly grieved Austrian patriots), and enduring Napoleon's acts of preventive terror on Austrian soil without protest.[18] None of this did any good; the dread prospect loomed that Austria would be forced into war with Russia.

[17] Shupp (1931: 82–6, 100–4); Driault (1912: 422–31); *Sbornik* (1867–1916: lxxxii. Nos. 93, 98, 99, 121–30); DeClercq (1880–1917: ii. 180–2); Napoleon (1858–70: xii. Nos. 10502, 10531). An example of how Napoleon made peace serve the cause of war is provided by his instruction to his brother Joseph, King of Naples, to publicize the still unratified peace with Russia (the Oubril treaty), though not with much fanfare, so as not to wound French pride. The news of the treaty would make the English abandon Sicily. Joseph must then immediately occupy it, arm, and squeeze 100 million f. from Naples and Sicily to help make Napoleon master of the whole Mediterranean. This, said the Emperor, was 'the main and constant goal of my policy. But for this the peoples must pay dearly.' Ibid. No. 10536.

[18] At the same time as the French, in a case that became famous throughout Europe, executed a bookseller named Palm in Nürnberg for selling seditious (i.e. German patriotic) literature, they also executed two Austrian booksellers in Linz.

As always, there were divergent ideas for survival at Vienna. Archduke Carl and Trauttmansdorff urged trying for an alliance with France. The new premier and foreign minister, Prince Stadion, hoped for a purely defensive *entente* with Prussia and Russia, while the new minister to France, Count Metternich, proposed conceding France everything from the mouth of the Weser to the Adriatic and retiring behind this frontier in passive defense. No one, however, least of all the Emperor, contemplated active resistance or even preparations for it.[19]

Austria's obvious wish to appease Napoleon made no difference. He had a simple prescription for Austria's foreign policy: it should have none. As he put it to Berthier in February, 'It is time for Austria to leave me in peace and stay at home.'[20] How an ancient great power situated in the heart of Europe could manage to 'stay at home', avoiding Napoleon's path while he roamed Europe seeking what he might devour, he did not explain. Russia promised to support Austria if it stood firm, but the Austrians knew that this support would be purely verbal and rose from fear of an Austrian alliance with France. The signs Vienna saw from Russia— Czartoryski's resignation in May (though no real friend of Austria, he was always more pro-Austrian and anti-Prussian than most Russians, including Alexander), his replacement by the more militant and expansionist Count Andrei Budberg, and Alexander's rejection of the Oubril treaty—all foreshadowed more trouble. A Russian war council resolved to prepare to occupy Moldavia and Wallachia, directly on Austria's frontiers, and even to go to war with the Ottoman Empire to prevent it from falling into the French camp. Budberg promised Vienna he would hand over Cattaro, but secretly instructed Count Razumovski on how Russia could delay the evacuation.[21]

Just when war seemed likely in the east, it shifted unexpectedly

Rössler (1966: i. 254); Napoleon (1858–70: xiii. Nos. 10593–4, 10597). For the debate in Austria over the surrender of the Imperial Crown, and an eloquent protest against it, see Raumer (1964); Rössler (1966: i. 249–52). Gentz, who in June–July 1806 wrote a long *mémoire* from his exile in Dresden on how to save something from the wreckage of Europe, gave up hope of this after hearing of the Empire's final inglorious demise. Gentz (1867: ii. 1–99).

[19] Beer (1877b: 209–33, 498–9); Botzenhart (1967: 4–5, 30–4, 43–8, 50–5); Rössler (1966: i. 244–9); Rössler (1940: i. 198–207); Shupp (1931: 38–43); Driault (1912: 292–3); Napoleon (1858–70: xii. 9877, 9988, 10016–17, 10213).
[20] Ibid. No. 9810.
[21] Grimsted (1969: 142–52); Shupp (1931: 32–6, 114–19); Puryear (1951: 69–71); *VPR* (1960–: 1. iii. Nos. 28, 76, 87, 96); *Sbornik* (1867–1916: lxxxii. Nos. 81, 117, 136, 140–3).

to central and northern Germany. The questions of cause and responsibility—what caused the war between France and Prussia in 1806 and who was most responsible for it—are more interesting and important in this instance than in most.[22] The answer is at once simple and paradoxical: Napoleon forced Prussia into war, and Prussia brought the war down on its own head.

Napoleon's policy is easy enough to understand. Immediately after his treaty with Haugwitz at Schönbrunn in December 1805, he had begun seeking 'security' and freedom of action vis-à-vis Prussia. It did not matter that Prussia was no threat to him, that he had already turned aside its feeble move to restrain him in his war with Austria and Russia, and that he was able with equal ease to make Prussia his lackey by the Treaty of Paris. To understand Napoleon's reactions, think of how an American gang-leader or a mafioso don would react. Prussia had tried to challenge him, and had to be taught a lesson. Even before the Treaty of Paris he decided to form a new French satellite, the Grand Duchy of Berg in north-west Germany, to push Prussia away from the Rhine. When he decided that peace with Britain might be worth pursuing after Pitt's death, Napoleon found himself hampered by Prussia's annexation of Hanover, which France had guaranteed. Though he himself had insisted on this in order to alienate Prussia from Britain, it quickly provided the ground for a quarrel with Prussia. Prince Murat started it by seizing three abbeys (Essen, Elten, and Werden) to add to his domains in Berg, claiming they belonged to Cleves which Prussia had ceded to France. When Prussia responded by moving in its own troops, Talleyrand backed Murat and insisted that Prussia must evacuate them before France would negotiate. Murat further asked for the county of Mark, suggesting that Prussia, involved in a serious quarrel with Sweden at the time, take Swedish Pomerania as compensation. The usual Napoleonic bullying ensued, with the Prussians told that the Prusso-French alliance was worthless unless they actively joined the war against Britain, guaranteed the Ottoman Empire, and helped expel the Russians from Poland.

More directly menacing to Prussia was the formation of the Rheinbund; with the forces of South Germany under his command, Napoleon completely outflanked Prussia to the south. The Grand Army remained in Germany, despite Napoleon's earlier

[22] For explanations concluding that Prussia went to war out of légèreté, see Fugier (1954: 207–9); Tulard (1977: 186–9); Pierre Muret's explanation in Sieburg (1961: 138–41) is more satisfactory.

promises that it would be pulled back behind the Rhine, and Prussia acquired irrefutable evidence that France had offered to return Hanover to Britain. None the less, Haugwitz, in sole charge of foreign policy since Hardenberg's resignation under French pressure in April, continued his appeasement policy, warned by Lucchesini from Paris that the least sign of resistance might set off a war. Nothing, however, relieved the pressure.

As a last resort, Prussia took up the suggestion Talleyrand had made when he wanted Prussia to accept the Rheinbund: that Prussia form its own North German Confederation for purposes of compensation and balance. But when Prussia tried to do this, it found France working directly to block it, advising the nervous Hansa towns, Saxony, and Hesse-Cassel not to join. Finally, on the eve of war, the French declared that a Prussian move into Saxony (which was absolutely necessary for any Prussian line of defense) would be a *casus belli*. It makes no real difference whether Napoleon specifically wanted war with Prussia (at this moment he doubtless did not—most of his aggressive wars came when he did not want or plan them), or whether Prussia remained loyal to the French alliance (it did until June but not thereafter). The obvious question is what made so constitutionally timorous and irresolute a king as Frederick William III finally resolve on war. Only one explanation is adequate and accords with the facts: that Napoleon confronted Prussia with an overwhelming military threat, forcing it to choose between total dependence or fighting for its life. Napoleon did this not to avert a particular threat or achieve a concrete goal, but simply because it was his style. Talleyrand served here, as usual, as a skilful amanuensis, manoeuvring Prussia into a corner where it had to stand and fight. He was never the bully and criminal in international politics Napoleon was, but he was often contemptible in ways Napoleon was not.[23]

Yet at the same time Prussia brought its fate on itself, choosing to be a lion only after trying long and hard to remain a jackal. The debate at Berlin after Schönbrunn was not one between collaborators and resisters, but between collaborators like Haugwitz driven by fear, and 'resisters' like Hardenberg (partly supported by another reformer, Baron Karl vom Stein) who were willing to collaborate with France if it brought Prussia sufficient gains. Presiding over the debate was a King convinced that any-

[23] Fournier (1903: i. 414–15); Raumer (1952: 198–200); Shupp (1931: 108–9); Lacour-Gayet (1928–30: ii. 186–9); Bailleu (1881–7: ii. 450–61, 476–80, 484, 541–4, 558–61, 564–7); Napoleon (1858–70: xi. No. 9716; xii. No. 9742; xiii. Nos. 10604, 10586–7).

thing Prussia might try would make things worse. Hardenberg presented his programme on 5 February 1806; it called for reconstituting the Reich and aggrandizing Prussia by dividing up Germany with France against Austria. The Treaty of Paris offered him grounds to attack Haugwitz, and the fact that the French attacked him enabled him to resign thereafter with undeserved patriotic laurels, while continuing to work behind Haugwitz's back for a treaty with Russia—also intended to pay off in gains for Prussia.[24]

In negotiating with Russia in the late spring, Prussia tried to balance between France and Russia, at the same time seeking support from Britain, Austria, and other German states. Russia and Prussia each tried to use the other at minimum risk and commitment for itself; this led them to separate Prussian and Russian declarations on 30 June and 24 July, renewing their defensive alliance of 1800. Prussia wanted solely to restrain France, not to challenge it. The declarations were not a violation of the Treaty of Paris, especially since the Oubril peace treaty had just been signed with France and was not yet rejected at St Petersburg. At the same time, Berlin continued to argue at St Petersburg that Prussia needed to expand to meet the threat from France—and at Paris that it would make Prussia a better French ally. In June, Hardenberg tried to persuade the King that if Prussia wanted a permanent partnership with France, it must gain further territory besides Hanover, and suggested Swedish Pomerania as the logical target. The Russians, meanwhile, indicated that the role they could best play should France attack Prussia would be to watch Austria and crush it if it joined France.

Thus the Russo-Prussian entente, intended strictly as a deterrent, was an unconvincing one; so were Prussia's armaments. As for its attempts at a North German Confederation and other alliances, they were feeble in themselves and made more so by the King's hesitations. In the end, Prussia resolved on an offensive strategy out of desperation, believing, as Austria had in 1805, not only that it had to fight now or be strangled, but also that, unless it broke through French encirclement by its own offensive, it would not be able to fight at all.[25]

This negative portrait of Prussian policy, however, is not quite

[24] Griewank (1935: 300–7); Thielen (1967: 152–61); Herre (1973: 114–15); Haussherr (1960a: 273); Raumer (1952: 188–9); VPR (1960–: 1. iii. No. 29).
[25] Driault (1912: 452–4, 458–69, 475–8); Thielen (1967: 165–6); Bailleu (1881–7: vol. ii, pp. lxxiv–lxxx, 462–72, 482–3, 488–95, 506–10, 518–23, 526–38, 552–6, 562–3; 1900: 99–102, 108–11); Martens (1874–1905: vii. 371–85); VPR (1960–: 1. iii. Nos. 54, 56, 57, 60, 75, 90, 95).

the whole picture. The Prussian decision to stand and fight also reflected a patriotic reaction to French threats and humiliation, a reaction connected with the increasingly vocal attacks of Prussian reformers on the reigning system in general. 1806 thus was a war of Prussian (though not German) patriotism. It was also a patriotic war for the Rheinbund states. They had fought well against Austria in 1805, and would fight equally well against Prussia in 1806, not merely because their leaders and governments were afraid of Napoleon and ambitious for themselves, or because soldiers felt a loyalty to their princes, commanders, and units, but also out of a substratum of Third-German patriotism within these states, a desire for their own independence and for a Third Germany free of Austrian and Prussian domination and rivalry. This was not an indication of a lack of German patriotism and national feeling, but of the fact that German patriotism was rooted in local states, dynasties, and tradition, and that the German sense of national identity was cultural more than ethnic or modern nationalist. This was no bad thing. Here, as he so often would do, Napoleon found a development in international politics useful for his purposes, exploited it ruthlessly, and thereby ruined it for France and Europe in the future.[26]

The patriotic fervour in Prussia, real but superficial, lasted only until Napoleon destroyed the main Prussian army at the Battle of Jena-Auerstädt on 14 October. Thereafter Prussian resistance quickly collapsed, one fortress surrendering after another. Napoleon entered Berlin unopposed on 25 October, while the court fled to East Prussia and the protection of Russia. Prussia's military collapse, almost without equal, came as a worse shock to Prussians than the initial defeat. Yet even had the army fought better it would not have changed the outcome; the Imperial coalition was too powerful and Prussia too isolated. Only Saxony had stood by Prussia, and Hesse-Cassel remained neutral, while all of Napoleon's Rheinbund allies joined France. Russia, engaged by this time in war with Turkey, did not even mobilize to help Prussia until the campaign was effectively over, and Britain, which had good grounds for holding aloof, did nothing at all.[27]

[26] Herre (1973: 116–25); Raumer (1952: 175–6); Rosenberg (1968: 190–1, 195–201); Fournier (1930: i. 420–1); Driault (1912: 471–5; 1917: 32–4). A patriotic reaction to the war occurred in Hanover as well—against Prussia. Resentment of Prussian rule led Hanoverians to welcome Prussia's defeat and humiliation at Jena and after. Sieske (1959: 78–98).

[27] Münchow-Pohl (1987: 37–48); Raumer (1952: 214–15, 222–3); Martens (1874–1905: vii. 389–96); VPR (1960–: 1. iii. Nos. 115, 135). When Lord Lauderdale argued that, if Britain wanted a new coalition against France, it had to aid Prussia immediately, Grenville responded that no associations with Prussia

The only reason fighting continued after the fall of Berlin, so that the war turned into another contest between two coalitions, was, as will be seen, that Napoleon decided not to let Prussia have peace. In any case, the importance of the Battle of Jena for the international system is not mainly that it led to a renewed coalition, further war, and still greater French expansion. Nor is it, as patriotic Prusso-German history once held, that out of defeat at Jena Prussia began its long uphill climb toward victory, freedom, and the ultimate leadership of Germany. Whatever mixture of truth and legend this theme contains for Prusso-German history in general, it misses the impact of Jena on international politics entirely. This battle, instead, ended three generations of Prussian attempts, beginning with Frederick II's attack on Austria in 1740, to aggrandize itself into a genuine great power at the expense of its neighbours. After Jena, Prussia stopped trying to be a real, independent great power and leaned instead on Russia for its security, almost totally till 1815, less completely for the following four decades.

The Prussian effort to make peace illustrated the transition. Negotiations with France begun just a week after Jena led to a Truce of Charlottenburg signed with General Duroc on 16 November. Prussians wanted to turn the truce into a peace treaty, even at considerable cost. But Napoleon, after some hesitation, had decided that even a profitable peace with Prussia was not good enough. He already saw the Poles as potentially more useful than Prussia, and wanted to try to force Prussia to bring Russia to terms, preferably by war, so that the whole Continent could be organized against Britain. Certain terms inserted in the armistice agreement and designed to promote this were accepted by the Prussian negotiators, thereby exceeding their instructions. The King's advisers warned him that agreeing to this would bring Prussia war with Russia rather than peace, and that the expulsion of Russian troops from East Prussia as the truce required might lead to revolt in Prussia's Polish provinces. On 21 November the Prussians, therefore, decided not to ratify the truce, and the war continued.[28]

---

could even be discussed without a complete agreement over Hanover and other issues first. Lauderdale to Howick, 5 Oct. 1806, BL Add. MS 51458, fos. 204–7; Grenville to Howick, 18, 21, 27 Sept.; 3, 11 Oct. 1806, Grey Papers, Durham Univ.

[28] Butterfield (1929: 8–15, 224–9); Driault (1917: 39–45); Shupp (1931: 189–92); Bailleu (1881–7: vol. ii, pp. lxxxii–v, 577–9).

Prussia thus threw itself into Russia's arms, just at a time when Russia itself was blundering into a war with the Ottoman Empire. Its ostensible grievance was that the Sultan had violated one of Russia's treaty rights in failing to get Russia's consent before replacing the hospodars of Moldavia and Wallachia with his own nominees. The real reason was Russia's fear of an Ottoman alliance with France, closing the Straits to Russian warships. Neither side wanted war or was ready for it; the Porte backed down on the hospodar issue in the face of a Russian ultimatum supported by Britain. But when the Tsar insisted on further concessions and went ahead with Russia's planned occupation of Moldavia and Wallachia in November, the Turks declared war on 22 December. It was an outcome the Russians would come to regret over the next five years. At the time, however, Alexander and Budberg believed that Russia required a dominant influence at Constantinople in order to defend its interests elsewhere, including the Balkans and Poland. Russia occupied the Principalities not only to bring the Porte to heel, but also to make contact with rebellious Christians in the Balkans, including the Serbs already in revolt, and to mobilize them on Russia's behalf.[29]

The expansion of war in eastern Europe in late 1806, both north and south, was thus partly accidental. Napoleon's escalation of commercial war against Britain was not. On 21 November he issued a decree at Berlin declaring the British Isles under blockade and ordering the arrest of all Englishmen in the Empire and its allied states, a total end to all commercial and postal intercourse with Britain, and the confiscation of all British goods and of all vessels involved in trade with Britain and its colonies.

This Berlin Decree laid the foundations of Napoleon's Continental System. Its importance in the war and in deciding the fate of his empire has prompted wide debate over its origins, nature, and purposes. Was this a new departure or merely an outgrowth of earlier Revolutionary and Napoleonic policies? Was it an essentially defensive response to the British blockade and British industrial competition (Jean Tulard), or a decisive switch to the offensive (François Crouzet)? Was economic warfare against Britain the real *raison d'être* of the Empire after Trafalgar, making the conquest of Northern Europe necessary (Albert Sorel), or

---

[29] Grimsted (1969: 152–63); Puryear (1951: 102–12); Lebel (1955: 114–21); Shupp (1931: 200–11); Shaw (1971: 345–55); Driault (1917: 114–21); Paxton (1982: 58–62); *VPR* (1960–: 1. iii. Nos. 105, 109, 136, 139, 146, 147, 158); *Sbornik* (1867–1916: lxxxii. No. 160).

was this economic warfare actually more an excuse for further Continental conquests (Édouard Driault)? Did the Continental System as originally conceived represent a constructive programme for the industrial development of Europe under France's lead, a programme later spoiled by the war and Napoleon's selfishness (Marcel Dunan), or was it from the beginning a programme for French economic imperialism and exploitation (Evgenii Tarle and others)? These questions and others like them are interesting and useful, and the evidence permits a range of tenable positions. But none of them points to the real meaning of the decree for international politics; in fact, they obscure it.

From the standpoint of international politics, what makes the Berlin Decree significant is that it was less a French declaration of economic war against Britain than a French declaration of political control over the states of Europe, allies and neutrals alike. The most striking thing about it is the matter-of-fact way in which Napoleon legislated for Europe—not simply for France and the Kingdom of Italy, but also for the Rheinbund, for territories Napoleon had occupied in the war and would later absorb, and for Spain, Naples, Holland, and Etruria, who were to be notified but not consulted. The decree directly violated the Convention of Mortefontaine with the United States, and the French knew it; but that was nothing compared to the way solemn guarantees of sovereignty and independence given to every state under French protection were trampled underfoot. Their foreign trade, economic policies, civil and commercial law, and even their postal systems would now be governed by a decree to be enforced, as its text specified, by the French ministers of external relations, war, the navy, finance, police, and the post. Two actions Napoleon took on the same day as the decree vividly illustrate the point. He ordered General Mortier to seize Mecklenburg and the Hanseatic cities in order to enforce the decree, and he told Talleyrand to warn neutral Denmark to cut off its courier and postal contacts with Britain and to reduce its armed forces to 4,000–5,000 men. Denmark, said the Emperor, 'must find its guarantee in its own good conduct and in the friendship of France'.[30]

Only by seeing the Berlin Decree as first and foremost an act of

---

[30] See a good summary of the Decree in Melvin (1949: 6–9); the text in DeClercq (1880–1917: ii. 196–7); Napoleon's further orders in Napoleon (1858–70: xiii. Nos. 11282, 11285). For various explanations of the Decree's purposes, origins, and impact, see Driault (1917: 48–54); Crouzet (1958: i. 142–9, 209–10); Bonnel (1961: 212–15); Dunan (1942: 320–9); Tulard (1977: 205–6).

aggression against the Continent itself can one understand not only what the Continental System was, but also how the decree gave a different turn to the war. To anticipate the story somewhat, the researches of François Crouzet and others have shown that the Continental System and Britain's counter-measures to it, though intensifying the economic warfare they had waged since 1793, did not really change its character or prove decisive; neither side was ever able to cripple its opponent economically or force it to terms. Not only did the Berlin Decree soon prove ineffective, but so did the British response in their Orders in Council of 7 January 1807, banning neutral trade between French ports but not direct colonial trade with France.[31] Later decrees would further escalate the conflict without bringing it closer to a decision. Some reasons for this are obvious. Britain was able largely to evade and penetrate the system in Europe, to compensate for losses in trade by developing other markets, and to manage the fiscal burdens of war better through its superior financial resources, organization, and public credit. France, though unable to enforce the system adequately and suffering somewhat more damage economically and financially from British counter-measures, was better able to transfer the costs of the struggle to others. Moreover, as events would show, at a pinch both Britain and France were able and willing to make deals with each other, restricting their own economic warfare to ensure their survival while continuing the contest against other parties.

Thus the Continental System again demonstrates the real character of the struggles of this era. They were not a contest between the French Revolution and the old regime, or between expansionist France and the rest of Europe, or even between France and Britain as secular rivals, the tiger and the shark, but a conflict between three hegemonic powers as to which, or which combination of them, would control and exploit the countries in between.

In one sense the Berlin Decree continued this struggle; in another, it changed it. Up to 1806, it would have been difficult to say confidently which of the two sides or the three powers had done more damage to the rest of Europe in their struggle over it. France had certainly done more conquest and looting, but until recently, unlike Britain and Russia, it had done most of its own fighting and relied less on proxies, and had succeeded better in protecting its allies and satellites and rewarding some of them.

---

[31] Crouzet (1958: i. 211–47); D. Gray (1963: 168–73).

The same uncertainty prevailed as to which side or power most threatened the independence of other states. France clearly posed the greatest threat for Holland, Prussia, and North Germany; Russia did so for the Poles and the Ottoman Empire. Many Germans and Italians still looked to France to defend them against Austria, and Austrians and Swedes were divided over who most threatened their independence. On the score of commerce, Britain and France looked perhaps equally dangerous to most (though not to the Danes). And if, as was increasingly believed all over the Continent, the independence of intermediary Europe was being destroyed most of all simply by the continuation of war, many Europeans in 1806 blamed Britain and Russia for this as much as France, or more.

The Berlin Decree and succeeding actions changed this in the long run by altering the character of the war. Napoleon's decision to block all European trade with Britain, followed by Britain's determination to cut off all trade between Napoleonic Europe and the rest of the world except on its terms, turned the strategy they had long shared, by which each pursued victory at the expense of the Continent, from a covert, secondary, unsystematic aspect of the war into a primary, central, highly organized one. The blockade became Napoleon's main weapon to force Europe into an all-out struggle against Britain, Britain's Orders in Council and other measures its main means of making Europe rebel against France.

The ultimate result was not, as is readily supposed, to change the minds and hearts of Europeans, convincing them that France was the real threat to their independence and well-being, so that they rallied behind Britain and Russia to overthrow its yoke. Again anticipating the story, that change, in so far as it occurred at all, came very late and had relatively little to do with the outcome of the war. Instead, the ultimate result was to help change the minds and hearts of some Russians and, to a lesser extent, some Britons. To over-simplify, the longer the economic struggle launched by the Berlin Decree went on, the more Napoleon would prove that France intended to fight it to the last European, and the more Russians and Britons would realize that to win they had to become European themselves. Thus what happened in the end was not so much that Europeans joined Russia and Britain to overthrow Napoleon, but that Russia and Britain, in order to defeat France, joined Europe. The Continental System merely developed Napoleon's imperialism; it ultimately made Britain and Russia alter theirs, even partly abandon it.

III. FROM CHARLOTTENBURG TO TILSIT:
NOVEMBER 1806 TO JULY 1807

No change was perceptible at first in the pattern of war. To be sure, Napoleon found a campaign in the mud and snow of a Polish winter far different from those in Italy, south Germany, or Thuringia. The bloody but indecisive battles at Pultusk in December and Eylau in February, the latter his first real set-back, spurred talk of possible peace. Baron vom Stein, taking power in Prussia after Jena, resigned in early January 1807 over the King's resistance to his reforms, leaving foreign policy in the hands of Count Zastrow, who believed that neither Russia nor Britain, once again an ally, could save Prussia.

Zastrow sent General Krusemarck to St Petersburg to persuade the Russians to help Prussia reach peace with Napoleon, as the only way to preserve the Hohenzollern dynasty and some remnants of the state. Expecting to be turned down, Krusemarck discovered to his surprise that Czartoryski and Novosiltsev were urging peace openly, while N. P. Rumiantsev, minister of commerce, denounced the war for ruining Russia's foreign and domestic trade. The Russians also had fears of risings in Poland and elsewhere; and though the Battles of Pultusk and Eylau had proved that the Russian army could stand and fight against the French, they had also cooled its eagerness for battle. After Eylau Napoleon, now in difficulty though not real danger, directed his usual array of vague promises, intimidation, and lies at Prussia. Claiming to want the glory of restoring the Hohenzollerns to their throne at Berlin and of reconstituting Prussia as a *puissance intermédiaire*, he pressed Prussia not to wait for a general peace congress but make a separate peace now.[32]

Napoleon also exploited the opening given him by Russia's war in the south. While the Sultan sent an envoy to France seeking an alliance and immediate French military assistance, Russia chose the limited strategy of seizing and holding the line of the Danube and the Turkish fortresses along its lower course. Rather than drive south on Constantinople, the Russians planned to extend their right wing westward to make contact with the Serbs and, beyond them, with Montenegro, Herzegovina, and the Ionian Isles. The penetration westward was not expected to bring the

---

[32] Butterfield (1929: 54–64); Herre (1973: 132–9); Driault (1917: 84–90); Bailleu (1881–7: ii. 584–99); Napoleon (1858–70: xiv. 11810, 11890); *VPR* (1960–: 1. iii. No. 180; pp. 442–4).

Turks to heel—these territories, remote from Constantinople, were barely under the Sultan's control at the best of times—but designed instead to pre-empt a French advance in the Adriatic and western Balkans. (Once again, this strategy caught Austria in the middle and directly threatened it.) Napoleon, free with promises and advice, offered the Sultan a perpetual alliance between France, Turkey, and Persia against Russia, and suggested plans for the invasion of the Crimea and Georgia. But the only concrete help he proffered was 25,000 men to operate in extreme western Wallachia under Marmont, and six ships of the line to support Turkey in the Straits and the Black Sea. Obviously he wanted Turkey and Persia to divert Russia from the war in the north. At this same time France, Russia, and Britain were all trying to lure the powerful Balkan chieftain Ali Pasha of Janina, engaged in a long-standing struggle against the Porte in Albania and Epirus, into their respective camps. The wily Ali led them all in circles. In February Russia tried to disengage itself by offering the Turks peace, but on terms that only a defeated foe would accept.[33]

Thus neither the French nor the Russians succeeded in waging war in the Near East by proxy. Similar efforts elsewhere also proved inconclusive. Napoleon had only limited success in getting the Poles to rise under the provisional government he organized, while Alexander resisted the pleas of Czartoryski and other Poles to rally the Poles by proclaiming himself King of Poland, fearing the reactions of Austria and Prussia.[34] Russia tried to get Godoy and Spain to switch sides but failed.[35] After intervening in mid-1806 to prevent open war between Prussia and Sweden, the Russians succeeded, with British help, in wooing Gustav IV into an alliance, taking advantage of his anger at France's conquest of northern Germany. However, Gustav again proved more trouble in the campaign than he was worth, even seizing part of the British subsidy being passed through Sweden to Russia as payment for money he claimed Russia had owed Sweden since 1791. As for the Danes, Jena had taught them that Prussia and Russia could not protect them, and they frankly told the Russians so.[36]

[33] Shupp (1931: 192–9, 234–64, 277–89, 295–8, 442–4, 459–72); Puryear (1951: 130–4); Baggally (1938: chs. 1–2); Testa (1864–1911: ii. 288–95); *VPR* (1960–: 1. iii. Nos. 77, 182, 189–92, 201, 209).

[34] Shupp (1931: 303–5); Driault (1917: 80–1); Napoleon (1858–70: xiii. No. 11258).

[35] *VPR* (1960–: 1. iii. Nos. 129, 132, 138, 164, 209).

[36] Butterfield (1929: 42–5); Bailleu (1881–7: ii. 474–5); *Sbornik* (1867–1916: ii. 48–58); *VPR* (1960–: 1. iii. Nos. 48, 61–62, 83–6, 119–23, 149, 216).

These disappointments added force to another reason for Russia's considering getting out of the war: its worsening relations with Britain. Differences emerged even before France invaded Prussia (Russia refused to guarantee the return of Hanover in exchange for British support of Prussia, and the British refused to endorse Prussia's North German Confederation) and widened thereafter. The British agreed to aid Prussia only grudgingly, as a concession to Russia; Grenville regretted committing £100,000 'to so hopeless a speculation'. Russia, convinced that it was bearing an unfair burden in the war, constantly pressed Britain for more subsidies, a massive loan, and British diversions on the Continent, to which the British replied that Russia showed no appreciation for all they were already doing. The allies' military and political co-operation against the Ottoman Empire was hampered by suspicion and cross-purposes. Budberg called for more British diplomatic and naval pressure on the Turks, but Grenville saw no reason for Britain to do more than the alliance called for; many Britons feared that Russia intended to destroy Turkey and ruin British interests. The commander of Russia's Black Sea forces, Admiral Pavel Chichagov, opposed admitting the British into Russia's sphere at all, and St Petersburg sharply rejected a suggestion that a British fleet carry out a preemptive occupation of the Straits. Their trade problems grew worse, with Britain protesting against Russia's continued trade with France and Russia complaining of the British blockade. The Russian government, though aware that its own commerce benefited from British control of the sea, increased its restrictions on British merchants in Russia and demanded changes in the trade treaty in its favour.

Behind this were the suspicions of each that its partner was exploiting it in the war and contemplating a separate peace. British and Russian historians have both blamed the growing alienation mainly on Britain, on plausible grounds. The ministry of all talents proved generally ineffective, especially after Fox's death, and Grenville and Howick displayed a pinchbeck attitude toward Britain's allies. The real source of the growing tension, however, was not particular policies or personalities, but a shift in the burdens and dangers of the war rendering the two powers' positions inherently unequal. The Russians continued to claim that they were invulnerable, were fighting solely for Europe's benefit, and could still withdraw from the war at any time, but both powers knew that this was no longer true. Russia was now caught in the war as Britain was not; French power directly threatened Russia as it could not threaten Britain.

British policy reflected this basic change. Rather than go all-out for a Continental victory now, as its allies needed and demanded, Britain concentrated, naturally enough, on surviving and winning over the long haul. Like Austria earlier, Russia and Prussia now discovered what it meant to face the full might of France with only Britain as an ally. Grenville's stance toward Russia in 1807 was something like Churchill's toward France in May–June 1940—which makes it easier to understand why Britain's relations with Russia would soon become like Britain's with Vichy France.[37]

Meanwhile, with both sides locked in military stalemate and under financial strain,[38] Austria, largely written off in international politics before the war was revived and still treated as a negligible quantity in Near Eastern questions,[39] once again became an important factor. From early 1806 on Austria had tried to accommodate Napoleon and bury the hatchet with Prussia. Neither power paid much attention to it until the Franco-Prussian war grew near. Then Vienna had to cope with desperate Prussian pleas for help and with the usual French switch from crude bullying to crude seduction.[40] Though Austria remained neutral during the war, the French army still occupying Braunau threatened its neutrality, and after Jena Napoleon resumed his bullying. Austria, he claimed, had secretly armed during the war and must disarm. He would welcome a war with Austria now, and was replacing his minister at Vienna Larochefoucauld with General Andréossy in order to end Austria's menaces and enjoy real peace.

The resumption of war with Russia and Prussia in late November brought a return to seduction. The Emperor proposed including Austria in a partition of the Ottoman Empire and, if Austria wished, exchanging Austrian Galicia for Prussian Silesia, to restore

---

[37] On the failings of the ministry, see Emsley (1979: 124–9); Butterfield (1929: 92–101); R. Glover (1973: 20–3); Sherwig (1969: 176–83); Stanislavskaia (1962: 474–87); Martens (1874–1905: xi. 128–35). For particular frictions, see *VPR* (1960–: 1. iii. Nos. 134, 137, 145, 165, 167, 173–4, 179, 183, 200, 210, 215, 220, 224). Grenville's remark about Prussia is in Grenville to Howick, 25 Feb. 1807, Grey Papers, Durham; his suspicions of Russia's policy in Turkey in ibid., 23 Feb.

[38] Napoleon, to be sure, could meet his fiscal problems mainly by extortions from his satellites. See e.g. Napoleon (1858–70: xiv. No. 12091; xv. Nos. 12251–2).

[39] For samples of how Napoleon ignored Austrian interests in the Near East even while he was courting Austria in Europe, see ibid., xiv. Nos. 11669–70, 11729, 11734).

[40] Beer (1877b: 234–55); Shupp (1931: 216–33); Botzenhart (1967: 66–71); Driault (1912: 480–5); Metternich (1880–4: ii. 83–95, 104–5, 114–20); Napoleon (1858–70: xiii. Nos. 10677, 10699, 10809, 10817, 10932).

what Austria had lost in 1740–63. In December Andréossy pressed Vienna for a formal convention on the exchange. This was, of course, merely a counter to British and Russian offers of alliance to Austria, and an attempt to keep Austria inert while Napoleon developed his plans for Poland and the Ottoman Empire and gained time to win the war. At this same time, he ordered Eugène quietly to prepare to attack Austria if necessary.

None the less, the French offer stimulated the usual divergent reactions at Vienna. Stadion, though officially an advocate of neutrality, was tempted to join Russia and Prussia in a bid to regain Austria's independence. Carl continued to urge an alliance with France because Austria could not stand alone and Russia was a more permanent menace to Austria's existence. Metternich more or less agreed with Carl, while the Emperor simply wished to be left in peace. More significant than these differences at Vienna, however, was a consensus on where Austria was most threatened: no longer in Germany and Italy, but in Poland, the Ottoman Empire, and the Adriatic.[41] Thus even after it accepted Napoleon's domination of Central Europe, Austria still found itself caught between two fires, with the Russian one in certain respects hotter.

Unlike Napoleon's deceptive alliance offers, Russia's and Britain's efforts to get Austria to rejoin the coalition were in dead earnest. Napoleon's old Corsican rival, Count Andrea Pozzo di Borgo, now in Russian service, and the British minister, Robert Adair, laid siege to Vienna, using the old arguments of 1799 and 1805. These impressed Austria little; Russia's moves in the Balkans were taken more seriously. When the Serbs captured Belgrade from the Turks in early 1807, Carl, fearing a Russian occupation, proposed that Austria occupy it preemptively until Russia and Turkey made peace. Stadion vetoed the move as too dangerous, likely to promote war and play into Napoleon's hands.[42]

In any case, neither war nor passive neutrality seemed a viable choice. Austria therefore chose to try to mediate a general peace, sending General Vincent to French headquarters in Warsaw in January. Predictably, Austrian mediation efforts had little practical effect. Napoleon used them only to gain time for a military victory, and since Carl objected to military preparations and the

[41] Beer (1877b: 255–69, 500–10); Botzenhart (1967: 91–114); Rössler (1940: i. 249–54); Rössler (1966: i. 259–71); Shupp (1931: 299–324); Napoleon (1858–70: xiii. Nos. 11088, 11172–3, 11194, 11337–9, 11418, 11631); Declercq (1880–1917: ii. 189).

[42] Shupp (1931: 319–22); Butterfield (1929: 118–19); Adair (1844); VPR (1960–: 1. iii. Nos. 151–3, 184, 187–8, 197).

Hungarians refused to mobilize, Stadion could not try armed mediation. The peace proposal sent to Vincent in early March, however, showed a further evolution in Austria's concept of a pacified Europe. It proposed that Napoleon continue to rule over France and much of Italy; that the Rheinbund remain in existence, with its members given more autonomy *vis-à-vis* France; that Prussia be restored to something like its status of 1806; that Dalmatia and Istria be returned to Austria, possibly along with a better Italian frontier; and that an undefined maritime peace be concluded with Britain. The proposal had no importance at the time, but foreshadowed the future. The connection frequently (and, as seen, incorrectly) drawn between the peace settlement of 1813–15 and Pitt's peace plan in 1805 should be made instead between that settlement and the ideas for peace emerging on the Continent in 1807, especially Austria's. Austria here laid out almost exactly the same terms for peace as Metternich would propose when Austria tried to mediate for peace in the spring and summer of 1813, after Napoleon was defeated in Russia and the War of Liberation had begun. In both cases Austria's main goals were the same: to preserve French hegemony in Western Europe as a structural element of the system, while constituting North Germany, Prussia, Austria, part of Italy, and the Ottoman Empire into a great independent European centre separating France and Russia. In 1807, as again in 1813, Napoleon's ambition would frustrate the idea of preserving a limited French hegemony in Western Europe. The most important Austrian goal, however, the creation of an independent intermediary European centre, would emerge as the heart of the new system in 1815.

At this time, unlike 1813, Napoleon did not consider Austria's proposal dangerous enough to resent it; like his own offer of a peace congress to Prussia, it gained him time for military victory. Had Napoleon died of disease or been killed in battle or assassinated, however, which his followers constantly feared, Austria's ideas could have led to something. Talleyrand favoured a Franco-Austrian alliance, conceived of peace along similar lines, and had a secret plan, in case of Napoleon's death, to have Joseph recognized as Emperor and French troops withdrawn behind the Rhine.[43]

While the fighting was stalled by winter in the north, it spread in the south. The British, though irritated at Russia for provoking a war with the Ottoman Empire, decided to send their Mediterranean fleet east to help Russia force Turkey to make peace and join the Anglo-Russian alliance, as well as to strengthen Britain's own position at Constantinople. An attempt by the British in February to force the Straits and bombard the Porte into compliance, however, failed because of unfavourable winds, the British Admiral Duckworth's indecision, and a stubborn Ottoman defence partly organized by the French. The Russians were irritated when the British broke off the venture, and outraged to see the British fleet sail off to attack Alexandria in Egypt. This expedition, also a failure, further convinced the Russians that Britain cared about nothing but its own interests.[44]

Meanwhile the Turks, spurning Russia's renewed offer of peace, began to fight the war along the Danube seriously, and by spring had made some progress.[45] The Russians were equally unsuccessful in ending a war with Persia they had waged fitfully since 1804, arising out of Russia's occupation of Georgia. Worried by French contacts with Persia, St Petersburg ordered the Russian commander, fighting against local opposition as well as the Persians, to seek peace with the Shah, though on terms which would preserve Russia's gains and allow its creeping expansion in the Russo-Persian borderlands to continue.[46] Persia sought help first from London, but Britain, having secured its own position in India by a successful war against the Mahrattas Confederacy in 1803–4, cared more about maintaining its Russian alliance against Napoleon than about Russia's advance against Persia.[47] The Shah therefore turned to France. At Napoleon's headquarters in the Finckenstein Castle in Poland, a Franco-Persian offensive–defensive alliance was signed on 4 May 1807 in which France promised to guarantee Persia's territory, send it military advisers and materiel, maintain its war against Russia, and support a Persian thrust toward India.[48]

The agreement was less ominous for Britain and Russia than it seemed. Napoleon was, as always, free with promises and propaganda, offering the Turks and Persians permanent guarantees of their integrity and claiming to be fighting the war now to

[44] Mackesy (1957: 158–81); Shupp (1931: 353–413); Driault (1917: 121–33).
[45] Shaw (1971: 356–64); *VPR* (1960–: 1. iii. Nos. 213, 223).
[46] Atkin (1980: ch. 7); *VPR* (1960–: 1. iii. Nos. 50, 53, 154, 186; pp. 64, 293, 380).
[47] Yapp (1980: 34–40); Butler (1973: chs. 18–19); Shupp (1931: 524–37).
[48] Puryear (1951: 155–69); Driault (1917: 141–51); Shupp (1931: 434–9); DeClercq (1880–1917: ii. 201–3); Napoleon (1858–70: xv. No. 12563).

save them from Russian encroachments, and displayed his usual skill at concocting projects and luring others into them. But even had he not won the war in Europe soon after the Treaty of Finckenstein, he would not have carried through on such projects as a drive on India or a joint French–Turkish campaign in the Balkans. Nor would the Shah have helped him. The Shah's aim was not to throw Russia out of Georgia or join France, but to secure Britain as an ally against Russia. Once he had a defined and defensible border with Russia, he expected Persia to be a useful buffer state for Britain in the Middle East. The French alliance was intended to make the British take Persia seriously. The British would not do so as long as they considered the alliance with Russia all-important, a stand strengthened when the Tories returned to power with George Canning as foreign secretary in May 1807.[49]

In any case, the war would be decided in northern Europe, not the Middle East. On 26 April Russia and Prussia defined their war aims in the Convention of Bartenstein, based on a plan for reconstructing Germany drawn up by Hardenberg, once again in charge of Prussian policy. The convention has been seen both as more proof of Prussia's incorrigible greed and as a forerunner of the 1815 settlement and the peaceful Austro-Prussian dualism in Germany that followed;[50] one can find some basis for both views. The main and immediate Russo-Prussian aim, however, was to secure Austrian, British, and Swedish help in forcing France back to the Rhine. Hence the convention was most clear in what it promised to Britain (the restoration and expansion of Hanover) and Austria (the Tirol and the Mincio frontier in Italy). Other provisions were more vague. The Rheinbund might be allowed to exist, but no longer be under French influence; Prussia must be restored to the status of 1805 (significantly better than 1806) and given a better military frontier; Germany should be federated under Prussian and Austrian leadership, with a military frontier along the Rhine; and some provisions should be made for the Houses of Orange and Savoy. If Britain and Austria refused to join, the two powers would have to reconsider their options (among which, the Russians warned Vienna, was a separate peace with Napoleon excluding Austria).

Prussian and Russian ambitions were also in evidence at Bartenstein. Hanover, though nominally to be independent and restored to the British royal house, would, with the rest of

Germany, be permanently tied to Prussia for military purposes. This would give Austria an honorary leadership in Germany, Prussia the real power. The Ottoman Empire would also be preserved—under Russia's influence. In the European system indicated by Bartenstein, France would be checked by a Germany led and organized by Prussia, guaranteed by Russia and Britain, and serving along with the Ottoman Empire and Poland as Russia's protective glacis. Austria would be the titular head of Germany and balance France in Italy. The power-political heart of the system would be a permanent, intimate, unequal alliance between Russia and Prussia.

Yet it would be wrong to see nothing but power politics in the treaty; the language about Europe's need for a stable peace, security, independence, and balance was more than window-dressing. Russia and Prussia also recognized, at least dimly, the need for a stable intermediary zone between France and Russia, above all in Germany; they merely continued to pour this new wine into old, rotten wine-skins. Just as Stadion's mediation effort of 1807 anticipated that of Metternich in mid-1813, so Bartenstein, with its unstable mixture of idealism and power-political ambition, anticipated the Russo-Prussian Treaty of Kalisch earlier in 1813.[51]

Bartenstein also had the effect, as Kalisch would, of helping Napoleon continue the war. He dangled the lure of a peace congress at Copenhagen before Frederick William while continuing his siege of the key fortress of Danzig. Austria responded to what it saw as the dangerous and impossible terms of Bartenstein with another mediation proposal, which convinced Russia and Britain that she was worthless and doomed.[52] The coalition suffered new reverses—Danzig fell in late May, the British attack on Alexandria failed, the planned Anglo-Swedish–Russian diversion in North Germany never came together, Russia's hopes for help from the Serbs were disappointed. (This set-back for Russia in the Balkans was outweighed, to be sure, by a palace coup in Constantinople that overthrew Napoleon's ally, Selim III.)[53]

---

[51] Driault (1917: 91–6); Martens (1874–1905: vii. 409–18); *VPR* (1960–: 1. iii. Nos. 220, 231–3; p. 545); Bailleu (1900: 154–5).

[52] Butterfield (1929: 155–61, 174–8, 202–11); Shupp (1931: 447–58); Driault (1917: 97–110); Rössler (1940: i. 269–75); Napoleon (1858–70: XV, Nos. 12464, 12487, 12594); *VPR* (1960–: 1. iii. Nos. 222, 236, p. 577). As so often happened, the only Briton to show much understanding for Austria's position was the minister at Vienna, Robert Adair; see Adair (1844: 386–99). For a more typical British appraisal, see Malmesbury (1844: iv. 388–9).

[53] Shupp (1931: 426–33, 482–501); Shaw (1982); Mackesy (1957: 203–11); Lebel (1955: 129–32); *VPR* (1960–: 1. iii. Nos. 227, 242, 253).

Canning tried feverishly to stop the rot in the Anglo-Russian alliance, blaming everything that had gone wrong on his Whig predecessors. Unfortunately, Britain had neither the money, the men, nor the time to do what Russia demanded, besides which Russia's proposals for a British descent on North Germany or another try at the Straits made no military sense, and Russia's frustration and anger had grown too deep to be appeased in any case.[54]

It was, therefore, not only Napoleon's decisive victory over the Russian army at Friedland in mid-June which forced Alexander to make peace, but also a rising peace movement in Russia, to some degree led by his brother, Grand Duke Constantine.[55] If the Tsar had to conclude some sort of peace to save his army from defeat, revolt, or dissolution, however, it need not have been precisely the peace he actually signed at Tilsit on the Russo-Prussian frontier on 7 July. The Treaty of Tilsit, while leaving Russia intact, reduced Prussia to a thin, indefensible wishbone of territory east of the Elbe, mainly still occupied by Napoleon's troops and surrounded by his satellites old and new. The treaty further required Russia to hand over the Ionian Isles and Cattaro to France, to offer Britain Russo-French peace terms and then to break relations and go to war if Britain rejected them, and to help force Sweden, Denmark, Portugal, and Austria to do the same. The only compensation for Russia, besides hints that it would have a free hand in the North against Sweden, was France's promise to join the war against Turkey if the Turks would not accept French mediation and make peace within three months. In this case the Ottoman Empire would forfeit all its territories in Europe except Rumelia and Constantinople.

The natural explanation for so one-sided a treaty, besides the effect of Napoleon's personality on Alexander, is that the Tsar thought he was obtaining a real if unequal division of Europe into French and Russian spheres, in which France would help Russia aggrandize itself at the expense of Turkey and Sweden. In other words, Alexander fell into a typical Napoleonic trap, exchanging concrete concessions for vague promises. There is something to this, but as an overall explanation it is too easy. It was Hardenberg

[54] Roach (1983); Sherwig (1969: 184–90); Shupp (1931: 509–13); Butterfield (1929: 194–200). Canning was determined to revive Pitt's policy and press the war effort at almost any cost; see PRO 30/22/8/4, fos. 420–5, and various letters of his to cabinet colleagues and envoys in Canning Papers (Leeds), 32, 34, 42, 50.

[55] Butterfield (1929: 184–92); Pienkos (1987: 12–14); VPR (1960–: 1. iii. pp. 593, 611–12, 750–1). For an (unconvincing) opposing argument, see Mouraviev (1954: 272–3).

rather than Alexander who tried to promote a partition of the Ottoman Empire at Tilsit, in a desperate effort to save Prussia. The most puzzling feature of the treaty, moreover, is Alexander's agreement to break with Britain and even go to war if she would not accept Russia's terms. What induced him to agree to a new war with Britain for the sake of France? There lies the key. Alexander did this, not for France, but for himself, Russia, and Europe. The task of imposing peace on Britain, the common enemy of Europe, was not a burden attached to the alliance, but an aim which Alexander adopted in 1807 as his father had done in 1800, and which he had considered for some time. A number of factors entered into this: his concrete grievances against Britain; the conviction that forcing Britain to terms was the only way to achieve a peace which would relieve French pressure on Russia and the Continent; and various psychological and political reasons, including the Tsar's injured self-view and the feeling that Britain had exploited Russia. If Russia were forced to come to terms with Napoleon, so must Britain be. To make Russia's partnership with France a secure and equal one, moreover, Alexander needed to demonstrate that Russian help would be indispensable for bringing Britain to heel, and profitable for excluding Britain from a Russo-French partnership in the Near East. Hegemonic partnerships like that of Tilsit require bonds of mutual opportunity and threat for any sort of durability. The Ottoman Empire provided the necessary area of opportunity, Britain the necessary threat.

An alliance with France against Britain, therefore, seemed to offer Russia certain advantages. There was also little alternative. All the other expedients available to protect Russia's glacis in Eastern Europe and its general influence and security—seizing more territory, urging other powers to fight France, forming coalitions in which it fought as an auxiliary, even doing the main fighting against France itself—had been tried and had ended in bringing the French threat directly to Russia's frontiers. Now Napoleon offered Russia a way out—an alliance to stabilize their respective empires. The two superpowers would guarantee each other's territory, and their respective satellites would form an intermediary zone between them. Metternich as well as Alexander saw this as the essence of the treaty. The alternative, that Russia confront France alone, was unthinkable. (The analogy to Stalin's thinking in the Nazi–Soviet Non-Aggression Pact of August 1939 is obvious.)

The anti-British aspect of Tilsit is, therefore, not really surprising. Alexander's acceptance of such harsh terms for Prussia and Sweden is actually harder to explain. Certainly, the Russians contemplated very different ones before the conference. But Alexander was used to deciding for other states what was good for them, and could say that the treaty at least saved Prussia from extinction, while many Russians felt that Russia had cared too much about other states and not enough about itself. The most remarkable thing about Tilsit is actually the Tsar's acceptance, if not actual encouragement, of Napoleon's creation of a Polish state, the Duchy of Warsaw, to be ruled by the King of Saxony, since December 1806 a subservient ally of France and member of the Rheinbund. The only possible explanation for this lies in the lack of acceptable alternatives. For the Tsar to have taken Prussia's Polish provinces himself, which Napoleon may at one time have offered him, would not only have seemed a cynical betrayal of his ally, but would also have increased the restless Polish minority within Russia and brought Russia into greater direct contact with France. Alexander could still believe, or pretend to believe, Napoleon's assurances that this small Polish state, together with Prussia and Saxony, would constitute a buffer zone between them. Here is another proof of the indispensable importance of intermediary bodies; even dangerous ones turned out to be better than none at all.

In fact, Napoleon did not intend to end his expansion at the Elbe—or rather, he may genuinely have meant his assurances at the time but could be relied on not to carry them out. The actions by which France soon after Tilsit began to threaten Russia in eastern Central Europe belong to a later chapter, as does the Franco-Russian quarrel over the Ottoman Empire. Yet if the roots of their later conflict can be traced back to Tilsit, it was not because Napoleon had a fixed plan or policy in regard to Russia that he was already following—for example, first to use it against Britain and then turn against it in the East. The fact that Napoleon began preparing weapons for possible use against Russia already at Tilsit merely reflects his normal style; he was doing the same thing with Austria and the Ottoman Empire. Nor was it fore-ordained that France and Russia would quickly fall out over the control of Europe or the division of the spoils. At least in the short run, it would have been possible for them mutually to recognize each other's spheres of influence and co-operate against Britain. A good deal of this actually happened, despite the growing friction; there was a considerable fund of Anglophobia in Russia and the Continent for Napoleon to draw on. For this alliance, unequal and unnatural though it may have been, to last a reasonable period of time, Napoleon needed only to let Russia, or at least the Tsar, continue to believe that Britain was the real enemy. Napoleon's instinct for exploiting any weakness, going for the jugular, would not let him do so.[56]

[56] Butterfield (1929: 218–31, 254–62); Driault (1917: 14–24); Vandal (1891–6: i. 86–91); Shupp (1931: 542–7); Schiemann (1904: i. 96–9); Thielen (1967: 195–6); VPR (1960–: 1. iii. Nos. 258–9; p. 621); Sbornik (1867–1916: lxxvii. Nos. 46, 47). For Metternich's interpretation of Tilsit, see Metternich (1880–4: ii. 121–3); Botzenhart (1967: 120–7). For interesting samples of Napoleon's tactics, see Napoleon (1858–70: xv. Nos. 12849, 12851, 12865, 12886–7).

7
Tilsit Undermined, 1807–1809

HESE two years were to see two dramatic developments. Spain would rise against Napoleon's attempted take-over and begin a national war of independence. Austria, fearing the same fate as Spain, would fight one more great war for dynastic independence. Both these stirring events would contribute something to the final outcome of the Napoleonic wars and the transformation of European politics. Both, however, owed their ultimate importance also to two other undramatic developments of these years: that France and Russia never became real allies, and that Britain survived.

I. *BRITANNIA CONTRA MUNDUM*

As will be seen, not everything Napoleon did in reorganizing and expanding his empire after 1807 had the principal aim of bringing Britain down. Almost everything was in some way connected with this effort, however, and the measures taken were thorough and generally effective. First Denmark and Russia were brought actively into the anti-British coalition, then Austria and Prussia. A series of annexations and occupations were carried through in Italy, ostensibly to destroy British trade. The Emperor renewed his demands on his satellites for naval construction and a more vigorous war at sea.[1] He pushed further his plans and preparations for the conquest of Sicily and the development of bases for more war in the east,[2] and he annexed part of his brother Louis's Kingdom of Holland, all supposedly to organize the Continent against the common enemy. The Russo-Swedish war in early 1808 and Napoleon's campaign launched in late 1807 to destroy Portugal and turn Spain into a French province were at least ostensibly designed to bring England down.

[1] For the pre-Tilsit demands, see Napoleon (1958–70: xiii. Nos. 11165, 11237; xiv. Nos. 11377, 11425, 11568; xv. Nos. 11646–7); for some of his actions and plans thereafter, ibid. No. 13039; xvi. Nos. 13109, 13145, 13314, 13327.

[2] It may be, as Desmond Gregory claims (1988: 45, 71), that Napoleon ceased seriously trying to conquer Sicily after Tilsit and concentrated more on Corfu. He certainly did not stop urging Joseph to attack it.

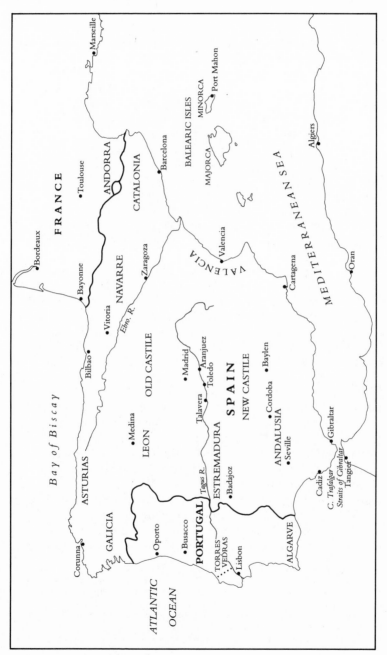

Spain and Portugal

The Edict of Fontainebleau in October 1807 and two Decrees of Milan in November and December expanded the Continental System, declaring all ships and goods which complied with the British Orders in Council fair prize, and all colonial goods and many others subject to confiscation unless their non-English origin could be proved. These measures did not, as Georges Lefebvre supposed, change the system from a fiscal instrument into an instrument of war. That had already happened with the Berlin Decree, and fiscal motives always remained a key factor in Napoleon's actions. Instead, the new edicts made it even more clear that the system, ostensibly intended to protect the Continent's trade and economy against Britain, was really designed to ruin Europe's economy in the hope of thereby bringing Britain down. The impact of Napoleon's decrees on the European states and on the United States must be discussed elsewhere. For Britain, they seemed to make its already grave economic and strategic situation desperate.

Britannia contra mundum thus describes Britain's situation in 1807 even better than in 1781 or 1940. In 1781 only its North American empire, its prestige, and momentarily its control of the sea were seriously at risk; in 1807 its very existence and freedom were on the line. In both twentieth-century world wars Britain could look to its Empire and the New World for financial and military help. This world war it fought alone, surviving in 1807–12 against American hostility and triumphing in 1812–14 against American arms. The year 1807 must therefore rank with 1940 (perhaps surpass it)[3] as Britain's finest hour. Survival would come through unheroic heroism, unspectacular feats of endurance and ingenuity: beating the Continental System through smuggling, bribery, and the development of alternate markets, mobilizing the wealth to sustain the war through taxes and public credit, replacing crucial naval stores cut off by the closing of the Baltic from new colonial sources, scotching every French effort to pose a new naval threat, and wearing France down by long grinding campaigns at sea.[4]

In 1807, however, the prospects for winning or even surviving such a war of attrition looked bleak. There were almost no places

---

[3] Especially if one believes accounts of 1940 like that of Clive Ponting, *1940: Myth and Reality* (London, 1990), stressing British boredom, apathy, and pessimism.

[4] On Britain's political, military, and economic problems, see Lefebvre (1969: ii. 8–11); R. Glover (1973: 28–35); Crouzet (1958: i. 248–83); Mackesy (1957: 210–15); Albion (1926: 327–44). On the Continental System, see Melvin (1949: 29–45); Watson (1960: 462–8). For the text of the Milan Decree, see DeClercq (1880–1917: ii. 242–3).

where commitments could be cut back. Egypt was evacuated and the British thought of abandoning Sicily, but reconsidered in view of its strategic and symbolic importance and renewed the subsidy treaty with King Ferdinand in December. There were even fewer places to strike at France. Robert Stewart, Viscount Castlereagh, the secretary for war, looked first for opportunities for action in South America and the Middle East, then gradually came to advocate all-out commercial war against the Continent; Canning thought something could be done to encourage revolts in France or elsewhere. Everyone saw, however, that Britain's immediate task was to save whatever could be saved in Europe from French control. This basically defensive strategy, surprisingly, led to a bold and highly controversial move after Tilsit: an attack on Denmark.[5]

The story is well known. Britain, fearing that Denmark and its sizeable fleet would fall into French hands, decided in mid-July, while still negotiating with the Danes, to send an expedition to force Denmark to accept a British alliance and surrender its fleet to British custody. When the Danish government refused, Britain landed an army in mid-August to occupy the main island of Zealand and in early September bombarded Copenhagen into submission with its fleet, destroying or confiscating the Danish navy.

The British attack was widely denounced in Europe then and since, with two questions central in the debate. First, how much did the British know about the secret Franco-Russian agreement at Tilsit to force Sweden, Denmark, and other states into a new naval league against Britain? Second, would Denmark have resisted Franco-Russian pressure and welcomed British help against a French attack, so that Britain might have secured the Danish fleet and a new island strong point in Europe without the odium of attacking a small neutral country?

Both questions are somewhat beside the point. The British did not know the exact details of the Franco-Russian agreement at Tilsit, but they knew some things and could guess the rest; and regardless of whether Denmark might have resisted the ultimatum and attack Napoleon was preparing, Britain could not afford to gamble on the outcome. In any case, the British ultimatum to Denmark and subsequent attack did not spring directly from

[5] Shupp (1931: 548–51); Sherwig (1969: 193–6); Bartlett (1966: 66–9); Castlereagh to Canning, 23 Aug., 31 Dec. 1807, Canning Papers (Leeds), 34; Castlereagh to the Duke of Portland and Portland to Castlereagh, both 21 Dec. 1807, Castlereagh Papers, PRONI, D3030/2549–50.

Tilsit, but from long-standing British fears of Danish subservience to France. In the six months since Prussia's defeat, constant Anglo-Danish quarrels over the British blockade and Denmark's measures against it had convinced the British that Denmark was fundamentally hostile and about to go over to the enemy.[6]

Moreover, the expedition had another, bigger target besides Denmark and its fleet—Russia. Canning had sent his close friend, Granville Leveson-Gower, on a special mission to St Petersburg, hoping to save the Russian alliance on which he believed the fate of Europe hung. Even after Tilsit he instructed Gower to 'cultivate him [the Tsar], and him only!', assuring Alexander that Britain would support Russia whether it chose war or peace.[7] Gower's reports, however, were pessimistic, and the evidence mounted of a Franco-Russian agreement at Tilsit to organize the Continent against Britain, which made Russia's proposal to mediate peace between France and Britain into a threat. Gower warned that Britain would soon be at war with the whole Continent unless it either accepted Russia's proposal unconditionally or took some powerful action to mobilize Russian opinion against Tilsit. Most Russian leaders, he said, were hostile to the treaty, and Alexander had only agreed to it out of fear of France.

Canning, seeking to combine concessions and firmness, told Gower that Britain's desire for peace, and even more for good relations with Russia, made it willing to accept Russia's mediation, though he personally considered it shameful, useless, and possibly harmful for Britain. At the same time, 'We must not let Russia think that we are bullied, or that she can bully us'.[8] The naval expedition against Denmark, already launched and expected by Canning to succeed without the actual use of force, now became his means of preserving Britain's tie to Russia without a

[6] The best account of British policy is Ryan (1953). See also D. Gray (1963: 162–5); Vandal (1891–6: i. 148–51); W. Groote (1969: 70–1). For Napoleon's threat to Denmark, see Napoleon (1858–70: xv. Nos. 12962, 12974); Canning's policy emerges most clearly in various letters to Brook Taylor and Francis Jackson at Copenhagen and Henry Pierrepoint at Stockholm, July–Sept. 1807, Canning Papers (Leeds), 42.

[7] 21–2 July 1807, PRO 30/29/8/4, fos. 428–35.

[8] This account is based on Gower's private letters to Canning, 12, 15 July, 1 Aug. 1807, Canning Papers (Leeds), 57, and Canning's to Gower, 22 July, 5, 12, 13, 25 Aug., ibid. 42 and PRO 30/29/8/4/, fos. 438–53. The quotation is from Canning's letter of 13 Aug. Just as striking in this correspondence as Canning's almost sycophantic pursuit of Russia is his contemptuous indifference to Austria, which at this time was seeking to join Russia's mediation for peace and promising to support Britain in it. This attitude was perhaps defensible in 1807; but Canning maintained it all his life.

humiliating British surrender. By bringing its fleet into the Baltic, Britain would prove that it could not be bullied, would strengthen Russian opinion hostile to Tilsit, and would encourage Alexander to resist the French out of fear of a British bombardment of Kronstadt. The same motives applied to the British occupation of Zealand. The British military envoy to Russia, Sir Robert Wilson, argued that a British occupation of the island was crucial for British influence at St Petersburg, and Canning claimed that from Zealand Britain could defend Sweden and help Russia militarily against France.

The Danish expedition was thus, if a crime, even more a blunder—an attempt, not uncommon in international politics, to bludgeon and threaten someone into becoming or (in this case) remaining friendly. The tactic which had seemed to work for Britain in 1801 here had no chance, given Russia's interests and traditions in the Baltic and Alexander's well-known pose as the protector of small states. His angry reaction was predictable, and quickly reported by Gower. It was unwise, further, to suppose that threats of bombarding Kronstadt and seizing Admiral Siniavin's fleet in the Mediterranean would intimidate Russia, particularly when the threat of the French army was so much more immediate, and it was almost absurd for Canning to instruct Gower at the end of September to press for a commercial treaty as a way of restoring good Anglo-Russian relations. To top it all, the government, having occupied Zealand and committed itself to keeping it, then learned from Arthur Wellesley and other military experts that an attempt to hold it against a hostile Danish population and a Continent dominated by France would cost Britain far more than it could possibly be worth, so that it had to be evacuated.[9]

Still, desperate expedients are understandable in desperate times. In any case, the attack on Copenhagen did not really cause Russia subsequently to break with Britain, expel Gower and Wilson, and declare war. All this would have happened anyway, though Copenhagen speeded it up. The same holds for the rise of Anglophobia on the Continent and Denmark's turn toward France. The consequences of Copenhagen did not even serve quickly to disabuse many Britons, including Canning, of their notion that Alexander's anti-British stance was unpopular in Russia and might

---

[9] Butterfield (1929: 294–301); Canning to Gower, 25 Aug., 29 Sept., 1, 2, 10 Oct. 1807, Canning Papers (Leeds), 42; Canning to Castlereagh, 25 Aug., 19, 20 Sept. 1807, and to Lord Hawkesbury, 23 Sept., 5 Nov., ibid. 32; Wellesley to Castlereagh, 25 Sept. 1807, PRONI, D3030/2534/2.

be reversed, or that if he maintained it very long it would bring
him down. That illusion was cured, if at all, only with time.

What Copenhagen mainly did instead was to help the British
and others see what the war had become and what kinds of peace
were possible or impossible—another small, uncertain step on the
long road by which Europe ultimately arrived at a usable collective
definition of peace. Canning put it eloquently to Gower in defending the bombardment of Copenhagen. Had Britain made
peace before doing this, he said,

With a Northern confederacy formed against us, we should have had to
contend with fears at home, as well as with the enmity of all Europe (for
we must not disguise the fact from ourselves—we *are* hated throughout
Europe—and that hate must be cured by *fear* . . . We have now, what we
had had once before and once only in 1800, a maritime war, in our power
— unfettered by any considerations of whom we may annoy, or whom
we may offend—And we have (what would to God poor Pitt had then
resolved to have, instead of going out and leaving Addington to make
peace) determination to carry it through . . . Could any peace settle Europe
now, in a condition in which it could remain? Unquestionably not. But it
would sanction and settle some dozen green and tottering usurpations;
and leave Bonaparte to begin anew . . . But that is not our interest. Our
interest is that *till* there can be a final settlement that shall last, every thing
should remain as unsettled as possible; that no usurper should feel sure of
acknowledgement; no people confident in their new masters; no kingdom
sure of its existence, no spoliater sure of his spoil; and even the plundered
not acquiescent in their loss. All this touches not us: but in the midst of
all this it is our business to shew what England, as England, is: and to
teach the world, and Russia, perhaps more than any other nation in the
world, that while we accept her mediation, and the Austrian mediation,
and the mediation of any other power that pleases to offer it—whenever
the true balance of the world comes to be adjusted, *we* are the natural
mediators for them all, and it is only through us alone that they can look
for secure and effectual tranquillity.[10]

Here was not only a defiant roar from the British lion, but also,
it would seem, an accurate forecast of how the war would be won
and a stable peace be established. Britain would hold out against
French tyranny until the Continent rebelled against it, and then
lead in re-establishing the European balance. Not really. Canning
accurately indicated here, as elsewhere, what kind of war it was—
one which Britain and France both waged against the European
Continent, trying to win by imposing sacrifices upon those caught
in the middle. He also rightly contended that peace now could

[10] 2 Oct. 1807, Canning Papers (Leeds), 42.

only be based on the principle of *uti possedetis*, with Britain consigning the Continent to perdition and keeping the rest of the world, and he was almost certainly right, against many Continental politicians, in believing that no real peace was possible until Napoleon was overthrown.[11] But he was mainly wrong, like a good many historians after him, in believing that his kind of policy would eventually produce victory and peace for Britain and Europe—that Britain's defiance of Napoleon and its leadership of a coalition to defeat and overthrow him represented the efficient cause of peace, rather than simply one necessary condition of peace among many. Britain's greater and more indispensable contribution to European peace would come only after it, like the rest of Europe, changed its thinking about peace; learned as Canning never would to surrender a part of its insular advantages; recognized to a certain degree that, in John Donne's sense, no state, even Britain, was an island.

II. NAPOLEON AND RUSSIA

For all his proud defiance, Canning had also recognized Britain's limits. It would not persist in its efforts to stop France and Russia from dividing Europe, or to break up their alliance, or to make them pay directly for it. In fact, if its interests were fully protected, Britain would consider ending the war and accepting the new order, at least for the time being. In other words, the British government realized that it had to live with the Franco-Russian partnership.

It is not true that France and Russia were never real allies, or that their alliance was ruined by the war against Britain. France and Russia were genuine allies against Britain; their alliance eventually broke down over Europe. Many Russian notables, it is true, were opposed to the French alliance or at least the way Alexander carried it out (Czartoryski, S. Vorontsov, Kochubei, Stroganov, Novosiltsev, General Count Tolstoi, Budberg, and others). The break with England also made many in the merchant class unhappy. But peace itself was popular in Russia, and the alliance had its strong partisans, especially Chancellor N. P. Rumiantsev and Admiral Chichagov, now minister of war. While many diplomats criticized the break with England, the strongest charges against Tilsit derived from Russian nationalism, stressing other humili-

---

[11] Canning to Gower, 5 Nov. 1807, ibid. 42.

ating provisions of the treaty, especially the surrender of the Ionian Isles, its failure to give Russia the peace and security promised, and the impossibility of real peace with Napoleon. Tolstoi, the new ambassador to France and one of the treaty's strongest opponents, insisted that if France evacuated Prussia and Poland so that Russia and France nowhere touched each other, he would gladly endorse the French alliance.[12] The steps Russia took after breaking with Britain—trying to organize a defence of the Baltic with Denmark, forcing Sweden to break with Britain, and destroying British trade and confiscating British property in Russia—represent serious efforts to wage war against Britain jointly with France; all had precedents in Russia's recent past. The commercial measures, the ones most painful for Britain, merely escalated measures Russia had begun in early 1807 while it was still Britain's ally in the war.[13]

Alexander, who finally decided policy, was never totally committed to the French alliance, but he genuinely favoured it and felt a personal attachment to Napoleon which he hoped and believed was mutual and would last. He also anticipated benefits from the alliance: a favourable peace with the Ottoman Empire, i.e. not necessarily a partition of it or territorial gains but a revival of Russia's leading position at Constantinople, and a renewal in some form of the old Northern System in the Baltic and Scandinavia.[14] Rumiantsev and Chichagov entertained much higher hopes.

Within six or eight months these hopes were dashed and the bloom was off the alliance rose even for its partisans in St Petersburg. Personal factors, as always in this era, played a considerable role. Alexander was jealous of every other liaison France had; General A.-L.-M.-R. Savary, the first French envoy, was vain, prickly, and overbearing; French representatives were coldly received in Russian society and did not bother to conceal their disdain for Russia; and Tolstoi at Paris made no secret of his dislike for his assignment and the alliance in general.

A larger reason, however, was that even Alexander's fairly modest expectations in regard to pay-offs in northern and south-

---

[12] Grimsted (1969: 164–79); *VPR* (1960–: 1. iv. Nos. 19, 24–5, 32, 41; pp. 571–4); Vorontsov (1870–95: xv. 425–30); *Sbornik* (1867–1916: lxxxix. 80–1, 84–5); Tolstoi's letter to Rumiantsev, 20 Feb. 1808, ibid. 421.

[13] *VPR* (1960–: 1. iv. Nos. 37–9, 47–8, 50–1, 55, 58); MacMillan (1975: 441–6).

[14] *Sbornik* (1867–1916: lxxxix. 97–113, 132–9 and *passim*); Butterfield (1929: 300–5). For the general effects of Tilsit on Russia's war with Turkey and position in the Mediterranean, see Saul (1970: 220–3).

ern Europe were soon frustrated. Russian proponents of the alliance assumed that Russia would be rewarded for concluding the treaty, changing its system, and breaking with Britain. Napoleon, lavish with promises and hints while negotiations were under way, announced after pocketing his gains that the partnership must start out even and work on the basis of equality—i.e. no Russian gains without corresponding ones for France. The principle was disturbing enough, the way France applied it worse. Napoleon claimed, for example, that his conquest of Portugal was a sacrifice for the alliance, and that Russia must follow suit by invading Sweden. Savary insisted that, besides excluding British goods, Russia must also give monopoly privileges to French firms. Napoleon not only claimed that, if Russia took Moldavia and Wallachia, he must have Prussian Silesia as compensation, but worse still, having earlier lured Russia with the prospect of a partition of the Ottoman Empire, he now decided that no partition could possibly be an equal one. By virtue of geography, Russian gains at Ottoman expense would constitute new provinces, but French acquisitions would be only colonies, and Russian gains would threaten France, but not vice versa. Both at this time and later the French seriously argued that, if France acquired Constantinople and the Straits, this would not menace Odessa because these possessions were far from France, while if Russia acquired them its navy would threaten Toulon.[15]

Tolstoi, purely a soldier and Russian nationalist, immediately saw through Napoleon, and sent his superiors a steady stream of warnings, pleas for armaments, and unvarnished criticism (for example, he urged Rumiantsev to prevent the two Emperors from ever meeting again—Alexander obviously could not stand up to Napoleon). He had two main refrains: first, that Napoleon aimed to take over more of Prussia and Poland, and that this was his reason for pushing Russia into war with Sweden and frustrating and distracting Russia in its war with Turkey; and second, that Napoleon would never stop expanding. He had a huge army, he lived by it, and he had to use it somewhere.[16]

Tolstoi's warnings, though sound, were ineffective, partly be-

---

[15] Documents on Savary's mission to St Petersburg July–Dec. 1807 are in *Sbornik* (1867–1916: lxxxiii); see also ibid. lxxxix. 735–9, 742–5; Vandal (1891–6: i. 165–77, 182–7, 190–203); Romanov (1905–14: i. Nos. 4, 6, 7, 10); Puryear (1951: 234–6, 248–9). For Russian disappointment with the results of Tilsit in the Baltic and north Germany and the reasons for that disappointment, see *Sbornik* (1867–1916: lxxxix. 194–5, 366–8, 407–11, 476–9).

[16] Ibid. *passim*.

cause Alexander was still committed to the alliance and Rumiantsev naively sure that he could make it profitable, partly because even Tolstoi could not suggest a way out of the trap. A Russo-Swedish war which broke out in February 1808 tightened it. Once again the plausible explanations for the war, that Alexander wanted to acquire Finland to justify Tilsit to the Russian people or that he was settling old scores with Sweden and Gustav IV, do not hold up. Finland actually was more useful to Russia in Sweden's hands as a buffer zone and place to put pressure on Stockholm than as a Russian province. Only violent Anglophobes like Rumiantsev and Chichagov considered it worth taking. Gustav IV and the Swedes did not especially want Finland either, coveting Norway instead; the Finns were probably more eager to break away from Sweden than either Russia or Sweden was to have them. As for Sweden's being Russia's 'geographical enemy', this was French propaganda.

The war was actually caused by Gustav, or rather by his reaction to Alexander's attempt, in line with Tilsit, to force Sweden to break with Britain and join the Continental System. Gustav, long hostile to Napoleon, was further outraged when Napoleon seized Stralsund in Swedish Pomerania and the Isle of Rügen in the Baltic at the same time as the British were capturing Zealand in 1807. Alexander's betrayal of Sweden at Tilsit made him even angrier. The Swedish nobility and Diet did not want war and might even have accepted an alliance with Russia, but nothing would move Gustav; in January 1808 he concluded a new alliance and subsidy treaty with Britain. Alexander, fearing further entanglements when he was already at war with the Ottoman Empire, tried to resist French pressure to carry out his promise to bring Sweden into the Continental System. Ultimately, however, his prestige at stake, he issued a long-prepared ultimatum to Sweden in February. When it was ignored, he followed it by war and in March declared Finland, not yet conquered, annexed to Russia, all in the hope of still bringing Gustav to his senses.[17]

At this point, in February 1808, a British move gave Napoleon a chance to seal his partnership with Russia. On his final departure from Britain in January 1808, the Russian ambassador at London, M. M. Alopeus, took with him a statement from Canning directed to France and Russia, indicating that Britain was willing to deal directly with France for peace on the basis of *uti possedetis*. Napoleon reacted to this signal with a show of interest, telling

[17] Driault (1917: 294–7); Käiväräinen (1965: ch. 3); *VPR* (1960–: 1. iv. No. 59; p. 159); *Sbornik* (1867–1916: ii. 69–81).

Alopeus that to get a quick peace he would not only cede Britain a number of lost colonies but also restore Portugal, Hanover, and Swedish Pomerania. Herbert Butterfield has argued that Canning's move was a bluff intended to frighten Russia. It certainly had that impact, saying in effect, in reply to Russian denunciations of British perfidy: 'You claim that we betrayed you as allies. Very well; see how you like it if we really ignore your interests, make peace with Napoleon as you claim to want, and leave you to face him alone.' Yet Canning's private letters show that he seriously contemplated the possibility of an *uti possedetis* peace.[18]

Any such peace, of course, could only have been a truce like Amiens, as Canning knew. The move is significant less for Canning's motives or the French and Russian direct responses to it (they fenced cautiously with each other through March over how to reply) than for how Napoleon used it, especially *vis-à-vis* Russia. Though Canning was not entirely bluffing in proposing peace, Napoleon was certainly bluffing with the Russians in indicating a willingness to accept it. Taking the British peace move, as usual, as a sign that Britain was on its last legs, he intensified preparations for a final push to bring it down. Corfu was reinforced, Joseph ordered again to attack Sicily, Rome occupied; Portugal, already seized (of which more later) was exploited militarily, and more of Spain occupied; Germany, Spain, and even Rome were combed for soldiers, Spain, Holland, and Italy for more ships; the camp at Boulogne was reinforced, the Atlantic coast inspected and made ready. The French tried to bring the United States into the war by the offer of an alliance and the cession of Spanish Florida; the Irish were also expected to rise. Denmark had already been tied tightly to France by treaty in November. For Russia, already at war with Britain and on the brink of war with Sweden, Napoleon's new ambassador at Petersburg, Armand Marquis de Caulaincourt, proposed a new active role: an expedition down the Euphrates toward India. The inducement was to be a partition of the Ottoman Empire between France, Austria, and Russia.[19]

Transparent though Napoleon's ploy was, telling Russia in

[18] Butterfield (1929: 339–55); Martens (1874–1905: xi. 147–52); *VPR* (1960–: 1. iv. Nos. 79, 87).
[19] Vandal (1891–6: i. 240–72, 308–10); Fugier (1930: ii. 376–9); Napoleon (1858–70: xvi. Nos. 13480, 13512, 13516, 13524, 13536–8, 13540, 13573, 13581, 13592, 13636–7). Napoleon's messages to Alexander and Caulaincourt's to Rumiantsev are in ibid. pp. 498–9 and *Sbornik* (1867–1916: lxxxix. 433–4).

effect, 'Either you wage war against Britain more actively through-out the world or I will make peace and concentrate on the Conti-nent', it could conceivably have succeeded temporarily in making Russia more active and cementing the alliance. Rumiantsev was gullible and greedy and Alexander, according to Caulaincourt, would have ignored the continued French occupation of Prussia for the sake of a genuine agreement on Turkey. Russian excep-tionalism worked in Napoleon's favour, making it hard for Russians to believe that the Emperor would put Russia on the same level as Prussia or Austria and be unwilling to pay for something so valuable as Russia's partnership.[20]

Caulaincourt's talks with Rumiantsev and Alexander in late February and March, however, quickly failed. Not merely did Napoleon have no real intention of partitioning the Ottoman Empire with Russia (the dispute over who would get Constan-tinople and the Straits was the ostensible focus of disagreement) but, as the Russians learned through a succession of absurd and demeaning arguments from Talleyrand's successor as foreign min-ister, the pliable mediocrity Jean-Baptiste Champagny, Napoleon was incapable of any fair bargain or commitment. All France's proposals were blinds for continued military activity.[21]

Nothing changed in subsequent French–Russian negotiations. Tolstoi's unwelcome advice to Rumiantsev (he argued for military preparedness, peace with Turkey and Britain, and a secret de-fensive understanding with Austria), combined with Napoleon's complaints against him, finally got him recalled from Paris as he wished (he had gone for months without real instructions anyway). Tolstoi's successor, Kurakin, was soon making the same arguments, as did other Russians.[22] Alexander saw that his role in Europe as France's ally was demeaning, but nothing indicates that

---

[20] *VPR* (1960–: 1. iv. Nos. 72, 89–90). Rumiantsev's correspondence with Tolstoi is full of evidence of his greed and naïvety *vis-à-vis* France (*Sbornik*, 1867–1916: lxxxix. 259–63, 272–4, 278–9, 362–4, 378, 466). Tolstoi's replies were often trenchant; e.g. responding to Rumiantsev's rejoicing over the annex-ation of Finland, he reminded the chancellor that Austria and Prussia had acquired Venetia and Hanover with Napoleon's help, and hoped Russia would not repeat their subsequent experiences. He further noted that Finland was no compensation for Tuscany, Rome, Portugal, Spain, and all the other territory Napoleon was gobbling up (pp. 548–9, 566). But his warnings never did any good.

[21] Documents in Romanov (1905–14: vii. Nos. 1, 3, 5–6 and *passim*); see also Vandal (1891–6: i. 272–307, 343–5); Puryear (1951: 292–3); Driault (1917: 278–91).

[22] *Sbornik* (1867–1916: lxxxix. 520–693; vi. 372–86); *VPR* (1960–: 1. iv. Nos. 60–1, 108); Botzenhart (1967: 180–3); Gritzbach (1974: i. 204–11).

he thought of breaking with it, even after Napoleon got into trouble in Spain.[23]

Not much need be said of the Congress of Erfurt in October 1808, a summit meeting of the two Emperors attended by a host of Napoleon's crowned prefects, because nothing much happened there. Too much has been made of Talleyrand's role (as indeed of his historic importance generally). Though out of office and not in Napoleon's favour, he was brought along to beguile the other princes, instead of which he warned Alexander to resist Napoleon. Whether this was treasonable conduct or an attempt to save Napoleon and France despite themselves depends on one's point of view; it is doubtful that Talleyrand's advice made much difference in any case. By the time the Congress met, the Near Eastern question was in abeyance, overshadowed by the danger of a new Franco-Austrian war. Talleyrand's advice did not hold the Tsar back from joining France in an all-out war on Austria, for the Tsar never intended this. At the same time, the Tsar's policy of helping France keep Austria inert and helpless did not change; in fact, a new treaty signed by the two emperors at Erfurt strengthened it. Nor did the Congress do anything to promote eventual peace, if that was Talleyrand's purpose. Russia and France agreed to make no separate peace or negotiations with Britain, and declared the retention of Finland and Moldavia-Wallachia by Russia and Spain by France *sine qua non* for any settlement. If Napoleon was irritated by Russia's stance at Erfurt, it was because of his own attitude, beautifully epitomized by his words in complaining to Caulaincourt years later about Alexander's conduct: 'He was defiant, and unspeakably obstinate. He wanted to treat with me as between equals.'[24]

III. NAPOLEON AND SPAIN

Something far more important had already developed before Erfurt, serving in time to entrap France without freeing Russia: Napoleon's intervention in Spain.

[23] Caulaincourt was certainly convinced of Alexander's loyalty to the alliance (see his reports in Romanov, 1905-14: i. Nos. 20-160); the fact that Russia accepted everything Napoleon was doing in Italy, Spain, and elsewhere in W. Europe is further evidence that the Tsar was at least making *bonne mine au mauvais jeu*. See *VPR* (1960-: 1. iv.); *Sbornik* (1867-1916: lxxxix); Dodolev (1968).

[24] DeClercq (1864-1911: ii. No. 161); Vandal (1891-6: 392-407, 427-39); Dard (1937: 182-92); Lacour-Gayet (1928-30: ii. 247-53); Lebel (1955: 155-61); *VPR* (1960-: 1. iv. Nos. 158, 160-1, 163-4, 168, 173). The quotation is from Caulaincourt (1935: i. 540).

Like many such moves, it grew out of the Emperor's dissatisfaction with the performance of an ally. Though most Spaniards resented from the start Spain's re-entry into the war in late 1804, Godoy pushed the war effort vigorously, building up the navy and hoping to use it to make various gains (Gibraltar, Jamaica, possibly India, and above all Portugal). Napoleon, however, insisted on making the Spanish fleet serve his plans for an invasion of Britain while delaying the promised break with Portugal. A British violation of Portuguese neutrality then induced Napoleon to agree to Godoy's plans for an assault on Portugal, but Napoleon's Continental campaign of 1805 cancelled them, and Trafalgar wiped out the Spanish fleet. In June–July 1806, Godoy extracted an agreement from Napoleon for the partition of Portugal so that he could rule a principality of his own. While promising this, however, Napoleon also negotiated with Britain and Russia for a general peace, desired by most Spaniards but feared by Godoy, and Spain was excluded from the negotiations. Worse still, Napoleon was willing to make Spain pay the price for peace (for example, he proposed that Spain's Balearic Islands be given to Ferdinand of Naples as compensation for Sicily). When once again Napoleon ignored a British rescue mission to Portugal in August and launched his own war against Prussia, Godoy blew up, issuing a manifesto in October 1806 calling on Spaniards to rise and arm themselves. Godoy did not name the foe, but everyone assumed it to be France.

Godoy beat a hasty retreat after Prussia's collapse, but Napoleon, to punish his insubordination, forced Spain to join the Continental System and recruited 15,000 of Spain's best troops under General La Romana to serve in the Grand Army in northern Germany. The move typically served several Napoleonic purposes—to get these troops out of the Kingdom of Etruria, where they had been stationed and which Napoleon had decided to annex; to weaken Spain; to use the troops himself; and to compromise Spain more deeply with Britain and Russia. He also once more shut Spain out of the peace negotiations at Tilsit.[25]

Shortly thereafter Godoy's hopes revived, when Napoleon demanded that Portugal close its ports to England by 1 September or face a French–Spanish invasion. His delight was short-lived. Though Britain could only offer its old ally ships to take the

---

[25] This account rests primarily on Fugier (1930: i. 22–395; ii. 85–211). For samples of Napoleon's demands on Spain during the Russo-Prussian war, see Napoleon (1858–70: xiv. Nos. 11476, 12169).

government and court to safe refuge in Brazil, Portuguese attempts to appease Napoleon without a full break with England at first seemed successful. But after more delay France finally declared war and invaded Portugal in October. Now the Portuguese full submission to the French ultimatum was too late; Napoleon had conquest in mind and, as the treaty he concluded with Spain at Fontainebleau on 27 October 1807 showed, Portugal was not his only or main target.

The treaty, on its surface a typical eighteenth-century partition scheme, provided that France and Spain jointly conquer Portugal and divide it into three parts, the northern one for the King of Etruria, whose Italian territories France had annexed in May, the centre with the capital, Lisbon, reserved for later disposition, and the south for Godoy. But as Napoleon's instructions to General Jean-Andoche Junot make clear, this partition scheme was a blind to enable him to introduce Junot's troops into Spain. With strategic portions of Spain occupied, Napoleon would be ready to annex northern Spain up to the Ebro and/or seize control of the rest of Spain to galvanize the unsatisfactory Spanish war effort, as well as to conquer Portugal. At the same time as Napoleon was luring Godoy with his own kingdom in southern Portugal and Charles IV with control over the whole Iberian peninsula and the Portuguese New World empire, he also encouraged Charles's son and heir apparent Ferdinand, Prince of the Asturias, to marry a French princess and thus gain French support in his struggle for power against Godoy and his father.

Napoleon's attempt to deceive and manipulate everyone while keeping his own options open soon threatened to unravel. Godoy, seeing how the wind was blowing, now secretly turned against the Treaty of Fontainebleau, and Charles IV arrested Ferdinand for plotting against the Crown.[26] On 30 November Marshal Junot's troops took Lisbon, barely failing to capture the regent, Prince John and the government before they embarked on a British squadron for Brazil. Napoleon ordered Junot to disarm the country, hold all strong points, and generally treat it as conquered territory. This led to the usual confiscations and contributions, seizing of booty, and French take-over of the administration, all disturbing to Spain. More sinister still were orders to Junot to be ready for possible actions to his right (Spain). The operations in

[26] For a detailed exposition of events, see Fugier (1930: ii. 216–345); for a brief survey, Fugier (1954: 244–5). The Treaty of Fontainebleau is in DeClercq (1880–1917: ii. 235–7); on Napoleon's aims, see Napoleon (1858–70: xvi. Nos. 13235, 13237, 13287, 13351, 13353–4).

Portugal could conceivably explain the additional French forces moved into north-western Spain, but not the simultaneous French occupation of Barcelona and Catalonia in north-eastern Spain. Napoleon refused to publish the convention for the partition of Portugal, and called on Spain to help feed Portugal while his army was ordered to live off the country. Godoy's announcement that he was going to be ruler of the Algarves aroused indignation in Spain, and the French occupation of the Basque country in the north began to meet popular resistance.

As usual, resistance drove Napoleon forward. By late February and March 1808 he had definitely decided that Spain must be reorganized for war and incorporated into his Empire, and that in passing he would settle the question of the Spanish Crown, but he still had not decided exactly how he would do so. The series of threatening demands sent to Madrid through the Spanish envoy to France Izquierdo, following up the occupation of northern and north-eastern Spain, make it appear that initially Napoleon envisioned merely forcing Spain to cede its northern territories up to the Ebro in exchange for central Portugal. As for rump Spain, he seemed at first willing to stop with dominating its government, abandoning earlier ideas about replacing Charles with Ferdinand as king and marrying him to a French princess. Yet soon after this he decided to lead 50,000 men himself against Madrid, on the pretext that they were on the way to attack Gibraltar, and to seize the throne of Spain once he was in Madrid. In late March he offered the Crown to his brother Louis, King of Holland.[27]

Even then he may not fully have made up his mind. His uncertainty, however, did not stem from any restraints, moral or prudential, or any fear of resistance. He was already planning how to correlate the take-over of Spain with other moves he had planned or already launched in connection with the Continental System, the naval war, his colonial ambitions, his general campaign against the Bourbons, and his programs for Russia, Italy, Eastern Europe, and Germany. He had specific ideas on how he would use Portuguese troops in Italy and Portuguese and Spanish ships in the war against Britain. The only thing more remarkable than Napoleon's ability to grasp immediate opportunities and exploit them was his ability to ignore deeper problems and deceive himself in doing so. He seems, for example, genuinely to have believed that Spain was a rich country full of potential booty for

---

[27] Fugier (1930: ii. 338–82, 407–17); Napoleon (1858–70: xvi. Nos. 13406, 13409, 13416, 13444, 13446, 13495–6, 13585–9; pp. 500–1 (unnumbered)).

himself and France, and that the Spanish Empire would automatically fall into his hands when he took over at Madrid. These
notions, to be sure, were not his alone; here, as in Egypt, Talleyrand was Napoleon's *âme damnée*.[28]

Napoleon thus undertook the Spanish venture, like many others,
for varied reasons—anti-British, familial and dynastic, economic,
military, and personal. It is useless to debate which was decisive,
and wrong to suppose that a venture which had such profound
effects must have had equally profound causes, or must have
differed in principle from what Napoleon regularly did. It is still
worse, as even good Napoleon scholars do occasionally and his
hero-worshippers do regularly, to look for some special cause
making this venture go terribly wrong.[29] Napoleon spent virtually
his entire career courting disaster; the wonder—a tribute to his
luck and gambler's instincts—is that it took so long to catch up
with him. Owen Connelly has shown this for his military career,
and it is even more true politically. The key to the Spanish
venture is what was missing in Napoleon—any controlling purpose or idea and any sense of limits. An adequate explanation of
the Spanish venture is simply Napoleon's refusal to stop with the
indirect control over Spain he already had and could easily have
maintained. If he could have stopped, he would not have been
Napoleon.

At first Napoleon's confidence that he could get away with
anything at first seemed justified. The initial Spanish reaction to
the French intervention and threat turned mainly against the hated
Godoy and his protectors, Charles IV and Queen Maria Luisa. On
17–19 March, in the so-called Revolution of Aranjuez, a mob of
conspirators backing Ferdinand, supported by widespread pro-
Ferdinand and anti-Godoy feeling in the country, deposed and
arrested Godoy and forced Charles IV to abdicate in favour of his
son. While this was happening, the Spanish minister Izquierdo
arrived in Paris with Spain's answer to the French demands of 24

[28] Fugier (1930: ii. 383–91); Dard (1937: 150–5); Lacour-Gayet (1928–30: ii.
221–9); Napoleon (1858–70: xvi. 13168, 13181, 13622, 13624, 13627, 13629,
13760). For Napoleon's Latin American and world ambitions, see Robertson (1939:
16–39); Gollwitzer (1972: 314–17).

[29] e.g. Jean Tulard, a distinguished Napoleon scholar, gives a correct, if somewhat superficial, explanation of the war in Spain as due to Napoleon's 'folie
dynastique'—following this by asserting that here 'for the first time war was not
born of a European coalition formed against revolutionary France'; Tulard (1977:
304). His discussion of the international consequences and further developments of
the Spanish imbroglio (pp. 307–52) is equally incredible, as is that of Vandal
(1891–6: i. 346, 350–3, 366–8).

February, an offer to make the lands north of the Ebro into a buffer state ruled by the King of Etruria instead of ceding them to France. Napoleon, after brief hesitation, spurned this chance for a new satellite state, in order more fully to exploit the recent events. He refused to recognize Ferdinand as King, but through his special envoys Joachim Murat and Savary he managed to get Ferdinand to leave Madrid in the company of French soldiers. Ferdinand, believing that Napoleon favoured his cause and would meet him in northern Spain, discovered *en route* that Napoleon awaited him on French soil at Bayonne; Marshal Jean-Baptiste Bessières was ordered to bring him there by force if necessary, but did not need to use it. At Bayonne Ferdinand was soon joined by his parents, Charles having already repudiated his earlier abdication and laid his fate in Napoleon's hands.

This enabled the famous comedy to be played out in early May in which Napoleon, as 'mediator' between the Bourbons, got Ferdinand to abdicate in favour of Charles and Charles to assign his throne and all his rights to Napoleon. His brother Louis had already declined the Spanish crown, knowing that if he took it Napoleon would promptly annex his present kingdom, Holland, and Jerome was unenthusiastic about taking it. Napoleon therefore summoned Joseph from Naples to rule at Madrid. In late May a junta of Spanish notables was convened at Bayonne to draw up a Spanish constitution, a task completed by early July. Napoleon meanwhile announced to the Spaniards that he had graciously decided to regenerate their fatherland; Joseph, proclaimed King of Spain by Napoleon, arrived in Madrid on 20 July. The move facilitated a wider game of dynastic musical chairs in which Murat, Napoleon's brother-in-law, who had served temporarily as Lieutenant-General of Spain, was sent to Naples to replace Joseph. This made Murat's Grand Duchy of Berg available as part of a new Kingdom of Westphalia in central Germany for Jerome. As a reward for his generosity Napoleon exacted more men and money from all of them.

By this time, however, the Spanish people had replied to Napoleon's offer to protect and regenerate them. A fierce rising in Madrid on 2 May (the *Dos de Mayo*, immortalized by Goya) led to a general insurrection and regular battles between the French and Spanish armies. Though Bessières was able to clear the way for Joseph's entry into Madrid at the Battle of Medina, on 22 July a French army under General Dupont capitulated at Baylen; this defeat and the general danger compelled Joseph to evacuate Madrid soon after he had occupied it. Napoleon at first did not take the rising seriously; he always believed that some popular resistance followed by bloody suppression and terror was necessary to establish a new regime on a sound basis. His correspondence in June and July was filled not only with orders for organizing and exploiting Continental Spain and Portugal but also with plans for taking control of South America, Havana, Mexico, and even the Philippines, all written in the same matter-of-fact style with which he was simultaneously decreeing the annexations of Tuscany, Parma, and Piacenza or the seizure of the Isle of Cadzand from Holland. The Spanish coup is distinguished from these and other moves only by the particularly odious combination of force, treachery, and swindle involved. In talents, Napoleon was a great military captain; in character and methods, a great capo mafioso.[30]

The Spanish War of Independence—a war partly heroic, mainly tragic, and wholly grim—has many aspects of interest and importance: the social base of the insurrection, which began with an urban mob but struck deep roots in the populace and overwhelmed the élite of Spanish *afrancesados* ready to collaborate with the French for the good of their country; the social, religious, dynastic-monarchic, and popular nationalist sources of resistance, a unique combination with which Napoleon never came to terms and on which his policy ultimately foundered; the character of Spanish guerilla warfare, evolving from the *petite guerre* of absolutist Europe but different from it, unique in some respects to Spain and impossible elsewhere in Europe. For our purposes a few comments will have to do. The Spanish venture turned out differently for Napoleon not because he did anything differently—as usual, he governed through salutary selective terror, making occupied territories pay for their own occupation and for wars he waged elsewhere—but because Spaniards were able, at terrible cost to themselves, to pay him back in his own coin, bleeding France more than France could bleed Spain. There is a further irony: the collapse of the Spanish court, which Napoleon had helped to engineer and then manipulated, promoted a profound national movement in Spain in favour of the monarch and against the French invaders, which contributed to Napoleon's ultimate loss of control.

Yet the Spanish rising took a while to become serious, and was certainly not bound eventually to succeed. The French defeat and

[30] Fugier (1930: ii. 393–455); Wohlfeil (1965: 8–15); M. Glover (1971: 20–5, 44–5). Documents in Napoleon (1858–70: xvi–xvii) illustrating his actions and attitudes are too numerous to list; see Nos. 13733–998. The various treaties are in DeClercq (1880–1917: ii. 246–9, 257–66).

surrender at Baylen was a disgrace rather than a real danger; Napoleon remained confident throughout 1808–9 that the trouble would quickly be over. During the first years the Spanish insurrection (and the anti-French rising in Portugal also, which was almost as important and is often overlooked) barely managed to survive heavy defeats inflicted by the French army and France's general success in occupying the country.[31]

Nor did the Spanish rising at first greatly affect the military and political course of the wider war. The news certainly electrified Britain; within weeks, after a delegation from the Asturian junta came to Britain in early June asking for aid, Arthur Wellesley landed in Portugal with 15,000 men, and soon defeated Junot's army at Vimiero. Much of the effect of this victory, however, was dissipated when Wellesley's nominal superior, the incompetent Sir Harry Burard, overruled Wellesley's proposed advance to Lisbon, and a Convention of Cintra signed on 30 August allowed the French army to be evacuated on British ships with honors of war, carrying their Portuguese loot with them.

The agreement, greeted by a storm of protest in Britain, did mean that Portugal was cleared of the French and that Russia's Mediterranean fleet under Admiral Siniavin, trapped in the Tagus since the outbreak of war between Russia and Britain, fell into British hands. This gave Britain Portugal as a base from which to operate in Spain.[32] But Canning's hopes that revolts would break out in northern Europe or France, the admiralty's similar hopes for southern Italy, and Secretary for War Lord Castlereagh's optimistic plans for operations in Spain were all quickly disappointed. The fleet and expeditionary force based in Sicily, waiting for something to happen in Italy, were unable or unwilling to attack the French in Catalonia. The first British incursion into Spain under Sir John Moore was nearly trapped by a French offensive led by Napoleon himself, and had to be evacuated at Corunna in January 1809 with serious losses, including the death of Moore. Wellesley returned and mounted another offensive into Spain in the summer of 1809, winning a useful victory at Talavera, but once again superior French numbers forced him to retreat into Portugal. Despite fairly massive British aid, Spain caused Britain constant difficulties—a hopelessly divided Spanish government,

[31] Wohlfeil (1965: 16–39; 1968: 106–9, 116–21, 322–7); R. Carr (1966: 72–5, 79–89); Artola (1976); Napoleon (1858–70: xvii. Nos. 14242–5, 14289–304; xvii. Nos. 14537, 14798; xix. Nos. 15848, 15694, 15716, 15933).

[32] For an argument that the real concealed purpose behind the Cintra Convention was achieving British control within Portugal, see Schneer (1980).

profound suspicion of British motives and aims especially in regard to the Spanish Empire, resistance to British commercial penetration of both Spain and the colonies, and constant failures of co-operation between the Anglo-Portuguese and Spanish armed forces. The same problems existed in Portugal, but there the British enjoyed greater control, integrated the armies into one, and were more successful in conciliating the Portuguese by diplomacy.[33]

Meanwhile, the supply and finance of the Peninsular War, where the British had to use specie both to pay their own forces and support the Spaniards, exacerbated Britain's economic problems. Trade already hurt in 1807 by the Russian and Prussian embargoes was further restricted by the American Embargo and Non-Importation Acts, and while the Portuguese and Spanish Continental markets and that of Brazil were opened up to some extent, trade with Spanish America proved more difficult with Spain as an ally than as an enemy. By the end of 1809, even though economic conditions had improved, the British had grave doubts whether Spain could survive, and whether the peninsular expedition was viable or worth the cost.[34]

The immediate effects of the Spanish rising on the rest of Europe were even more disappointing. Canning hoped to recreate a Northern Confederacy against France led by Russia, arguing that Spain would surely wake Alexander up. He even thought in passing of trying to persuade Austria to come back into the war. Nothing came of it. Spain enabled Alexander to take a somewhat more independent stand within the French alliance; it did not tempt him to leave it. Nor did Russia's refusal to react to the Spanish rising (it quickly recognized Joseph's regime) cure the British of their Russophilia, least of all Canning. In Central Europe the Spanish junta had no success in gaining recognition or support, and while the German press and patriotic Prussian and German reform circles reacted to the rising to some degree, the general (and correct) conclusion in Germany was that Spain would not bring Napoleon down, and that Central Europe was no place for a Spanish-type guerilla war. After Austria was crushed in

[33] D. Gray (1963: 178–87); Mackesy (1957: 265–71, 289–96); Sherwig (1969: 196–205, 216–25); Bartlett (1966: 75–80); Severn (1981: 46–131); Fryman (1977). Canning's attacks on the Convention of Cintra and on Sir John Moore and other commanders in Spain are in numerous letters to Castlereagh, Spencer Perceval, and Portland from Sept. to Dec. 1808, Canning Papers (Leeds), 32.

[34] Crouzet (1958: i. 284–403).

1809, moreover, Napoleon and his satellite princes cracked down more drastically on the German press.[35]

All this means that, though the Spanish ulcer ultimately had profound effects on Napoleon's empire, these developed only over the long run and in conjunction with other changes Spain did not and could not produce. The greatest mistake is to suppose that the Spanish rising influenced European governments to change the way they fought Napoleon, harnessing the forces of the masses in a united effort to bring him down. As will be seen, even during the War of Liberation in 1813–14 this happened only to a limited degree, and for reasons that had nothing to do with Spain. The immediate direct effect of the Spanish rising on the European powers in 1808–9 was to encourage them either to continue to appease or co-operate with France as they were doing, or to return to old, failed strategies. Britain was encouraged to try once more to weaken France by diversions in Europe, to restore its alliance with Russia, and to revive a Continental coalition under Anglo-Russian leadership. Russia tried to use the Spanish rising to improve the terms of its alliance with France, so that it could further enhance its security and interests at the expense of Central Europe. Germany remained deeply divided, with the more important parts of it, beneficiaries of Napoleon's empire, remaining loyal, and its victims unable to agree on how to overthrow it. And, as will be seen, Spain indirectly encouraged Austria to try one more time, with disastrous results, to solve its security dilemma by military means.

IV. PRUSSIA AND AUSTRIA BETWEEN THE MILLSTONES

After Tilsit, Prussia's survival seemed to depend on a quick end to the French occupation. In addition to its crushing direct burdens (contributions, deliveries, occupation costs), the occupation diverted the bulk of the state's revenues into the French treasury. Prussia thought it might convince France that, if granted tolerable conditions, it would become more profitable to France as an ally and buffer state. The hope was illusory. The Convention of Königsberg on 12 July 1807 looked promising, providing for

---

[35] Wohlfeil (1965: 41–62, 76–92, 102–5, 150–1). For Canning's hopes, see his letters to Edward Thornton, British minister to Sweden, 10, 30 June 1808, Canning Papers (Leeds), 42, and his letter to Novosilstev, 23 July, 22 Aug., ibid. 57.

Prussian territory to be evacuated in stages ending by 1 November. But evacuation was conditional on Prussia's first paying an unspecified amount of contributions to France, and the convention excluded from the reckoning all the contributions in money and goods France had exacted during the war. Thus, when Intendant General Pierre Daru presented the bill, it turned out not to be the 20 million francs the Prussians expected, but over 150 million, a sum impossible for Prussia to raise. This meant the continued occupation of most of the country; even the eastern provinces which came up with their quota were evacuated only after they had been stripped bare on Napoleon's orders.

The Stein ministry now tried a policy of 'fulfilment' like Cuno's and Rathenau's after the First World War: an attempt, more or less genuine, to pay enough to convince France that Prussia would do what it could but that it was impossible and counter-productive to collect the entire sum, while appealing to Russia to press France for reductions. Twice agreements for a reduced total worked out between the Prussians and Daru were rejected by Napoleon, who simply insisted that Prussia could pay the whole sum if it wanted to, and might begin by disbanding its army. By mid-year Stein's optimistic fulfilment policy was in ruins. He now began to listen to certain army leaders (Gerhard Scharnhorst, August Count Gneisenau, Hermann von Boyen, and Count Götzen) and other liberals calling for a policy of resistance culminating ultimately in a German national rising against Napoleon in partnership with Austria. Stein, however, proved unlucky in conspiracy as well as diplomacy; Napoleon's agents seized his correspondence with another Prussian leader, Prince Wilhelm Wittgenstein, whom Stein was trying to recruit for the plot. When Prussian negotiators brought Napoleon new proposals for a final settlement of the contributions question, accompanied by another offer for a Franco-Prussian alliance (this time deceptive), he confronted them with evidence of Stein's 'treason'.

This gave Stein's opponents in Prussia, including his erstwhile collaborator Hardenberg, the weapons to force him out of office and into exile by the end of 1808. More immediately, it compelled Prussia to accept Napoleon's terms. In the Convention of Paris in September 1808, Prussia obtained a fixed agreement for French evacuation at an enormous price: 140 million francs, payable in cash and mortgages on royal estates; the indefinite occupation of three more fortresses in eastern Prussia, Glogau, Küstrin, and Stettin, largely at Prussia's expense; a system of French military roads throughout Prussia; the cession of the fortress of Magdeburg and a surrounding glacis on the right bank of the Elbe; the restriction of the Prussian army to 42,000 men; an alliance in which Prussia would be obliged to provide 16,000 men for a war against Austria; and the recognition of Joseph as King of Spain and the Indies and of Murat as King of Naples and Sicily. The Convention of Elbing the next month gave France further military routes across Silesia connecting the Duchy of Warsaw and Saxony, along with free transit of all French, Polish, and Saxon goods. This meant that Prussia, having lost most of its foreign trade to the Continental System, now surrendered control of customs and trade on much of its internal frontiers. Perhaps worst of all was that these draconian agreements still left Prussia's future as unclear and menaced as ever. It was not an ally of France, or a satellite and member of the Rheinbund, or a neutral; its fate was subject to Napoleon's whim.[36]

Again, one must not ask what Napoleon's final aim was—to soften Prussia up for destruction, or suck it dry, or forestall Prussian revenge, or use his grip on Prussia to put pressure on Russia and Austria, or take revenge on Prussia for having dared to challenge him. All these purposes and more probably crossed Napoleon's mind, but not as part of some final positive goal, because he had none. Only his negative aims are clear—not what he wanted finally to do with Prussia, but a series of things he would not do or permit. Prussia must not be allowed to recover and rearm, or think of allying with Austria and leading a German rising. Prussia could not be his junior ally and partner, because he had done it too much harm ever to trust it and because this would challenge Russia too overtly. It could not be brought into the Rheinbund because this too would challenge Russia, and unless Prussia was broken up it would still be inconveniently large and remote. Partitioning Prussia, on the other hand, would frighten Austria and Russia and increase the existing dynastic and administrative difficulties of Napoleon's empire; he was already running out of useful and manageable relatives as satraps. In fact, Napoleon had never known what he wanted to do with Prussia, even earlier when he had treated it with contemptuous indulgence. This was

---

[36] The best account is clearly Münchow-Pohl (1987: 49–88); but for particular points see also Ritter (1958: 308–47); Haussherr (1960a: 276–7); Huber (1957: 112–17); Herre (1973: 192–4); Driault (1917: 37–8); DeClercq (1880–1917: ii. 223–30, 270–3). For Napoleon's role, see Napoleon (1858–70: xv. Nos. 12895–7, 12904, 12907, 12909, 12953–4). For a French historian's attempt, written during the Franco-German reparations struggle of the early 1920s, to blame everything on Prussia's evasions and aggressive aims, see Lesage (1924: esp. 4–13).

something new in French politics, another evidence that Napoleon was and remained a Corsican, never part of a real French tradition. Eighteenth-century France had always had a Prussian policy; leaders during the Revolution, whether they were for or against Prussia, had ideas of what it should be, whether ally, opponent, neutral, mediator, or buffer state. But this was because Frenchmen, however they differed on the subject, had always had some general concept of Europe, and Napoleon did not.

The Altenstein–Dohna ministry which succeeded Stein also failed either to appease France or to secure Russian support, which was limited to expressions of platonic sympathy and anodyne diplomatic intercession at Paris. Rumiantsev told the Prussians bluntly that Russia could not propose anything on its behalf which France was unwilling to accept. In reality, Russia had a certain interest in keeping Prussia nominally alive and independent but none in helping Prussia recover, at least so long as Russia was still allied to France; French exploitation of Prussia was even useful in certain ways for Russia. It kept Frederick William subservient to Alexander, and enabled Russia to squeeze its own concessions from Prussia—for example, demands that Prussia let Russia use Prussian ports and territory for its war on Sweden.[37]

Austria's situation after Tilsit resembled Prussia's, except that Napoleon's heel was less firmly on Austria's neck and that Russia threatened Austria almost as much as France did. It is no surprise, then, that Austria also tried to survive by convincing Napoleon that it could be a useful ally. There were the usual differences between Stadion, Carl, and Metternich over how far to go in this, but these nuances hardly affected actual policy, and everyone agreed on what Austria should do if France and Russia decided to partition the Ottoman Empire. Undesirable though it was, if partition became inevitable Austria must join them and get a major share of it. Austria had given up trying to compete with the great flank powers; its goal now was to avoid being ground between the upper and nether millstones, to keep France and Russia as much as possible away from itself and from each other.

For a brief time after Tilsit, Stadion nourished the illusion produced by Napoleon's friendly language during the war that a *rapprochement* was possible.[38] But Napoleon, though satisfied with

---

[37] *VPR* (1960–: 1. iv. Nos. 21, 64, 84, 94; pp. 214, 216–17, 229–30); Martens (1874–1905: vii. 426–8); *Sbornik* (1867–1916: lxxxix. 216–18, 223, 457–8, 463–5).

[38] This is another instance of a phenomenon frequent in this era, though one does not expect it from a Francophobe like Stadion: the belief on the part of Napoleon's victims that somehow *this* time would be different, that they

Austria's behaviour during the war (and lucky to have had it), immediately after Tilsit denounced its conduct as treacherous and aggressive, and use his normal bullying tactics to force Austria to break totally with Britain and give him new concessions on German affairs, the Isonzo border in Italy, and Portugal. Metternich at Paris detected the cooling in Russo-French relations, but took little comfort from it, calling Tolstoi's proposal of a Russo-Austrian alliance to check Napoleon at once necessary and impossible.[39]

He was right, and right also in believing that St Petersburg was not interested in it. Rumiantsev ordered Tolstoi to stop talking about it, while the Austrian ambassador to Russia, Count Merveldt, reported that Napoleon had promised Alexander at Tilsit that Russia could annex the Danubian Principalities—a mortal threat to Austria's one relatively safe frontier. Just as it did with Prussia, Russia exploited France's pressure on Austria for its own purposes. When the war with the Ottoman Empire was renewed after Alexander rejected a truce concluded in the fall of 1807, this cut off the trade on which the Serbs depended for their livelihood. The Russian government therefore tried to get Austria, which took a neutral stance toward both the Russo-Turkish war and the Serb revolt, to supply the Serbs with food and military supplies. At the same time, Russian commanders in the field and their chief agent in the Balkans were instructed to do everything possible to counteract Austrian influence in Serbia.[40]

From Britain Austria had less to fear, but even less to hope. For a brief moment after Tilsit, Canning thought that Austria might somehow help Britain avoid a break with Russia; but the British envoy, Lord Pembroke, reported that Austria was too timid, and that Russia's hatred of Austria was such that Britain would only harm itself by continuing any association with Vienna. On Austria's part, Prince Starhemberg at London went beyond his instructions, earning a rebuke from Stadion, in efforts to avoid a complete break between Austria and Britain. Metternich at Paris

could achieve decent relations with Napoleon. This has often been explained by Napoleon's charm. That may be part of it; but it is more plausible to see the real explanation in that psychology of the victim which leads abused wives and cowed schoolboys time and again to believe that this time the drunkard husband or school-yard bully will not beat them up.

[39] Beer (1877b: 291–332, 510–15); Botzenhart (1967: 129–99); Rössler (1966: i. 280–1); Butterfield (1929: 320–30); Kraehe (1963: 57–9); Metternich (1880–4: ii. 122–77); Napoleon (1858–70: xv. Nos. 12813, 13013, 13022–3, 13086–7; xvi. No. 13146).

[40] Shaw (1971: 388–93); VPR (1960–: 1. iv. Nos. 81, 101; pp. 110, 158).

associated himself with Canning's effort to convey peace terms to Russia and France through the Russian ambassador, Alopeus, on the latter's departure from London. This made no difference when Austria, under French and Russian pressure, broke relations and declared war; Britain reacted with profound contempt more than anger.[41] This was natural and no surprise to Vienna. Not only had Austria willy-nilly joined Britain's enemies; perhaps more important, the European system which Metternich had in mind and which Stadion at least considered, involving a union of France, Russia, and Austria, would have deliberately excluded Britain. In a phrase he would repeat in 1813, Metternich described Britain as being 'outside of this world like the moon'. The British in turn showed none of the understanding for Austria's position that they did for other states forced to bow to French pressure, like Russia, Sweden, Portugal, or even Prussia. This is important again only in showing how throughout this era Britain and Austria were anything but natural allies, bound when conditions were ripe to come together out of mutual interests.[42]

V. AUSTRIA'S RESOLVE AND EUROPE'S REACTION

Austria's and Prussia's situations in early 1808 were bleak but not immediately life-threatening, and neither government wished to prepare for war or felt compelled to do so. Spain changed this for Austria—not the Spain of the Dos de Mayo and Baylen, of heroic resistance to the foreign tyrant, but the Spain of Aranjuez and Bayonne, of an ancient dynasty undermined by popular revolt and overturned by Napoleon. Metternich and Stadion explained to a horrified Francis that the popular rising at Aranjuez was the

---

[41] Canning described Austria as totally hostile to Britain for the last 2 years, and the prime minister, the Duke of Portland, wrote, 'Whether it is to be attributed to the pusillanimity, the debasement, the abandonment of all principle & total absence of all sense of Honour I will not attempt to determine, but the behaviour, the language & intentions of Austria much rather incite my contempt than my anger.'; Portland to Canning, 20 Nov. 1807, and Canning to S. Perceval, 16 Jan. 1808, Canning Papers (Leeds), 33, 32.

[42] Butterfield (1929: 330–8); Botzenhart (1967: 201–7) (Metternich's phrase is quoted on p. 186); Metternich (1880–4: ii. 155–71); Adair (1844: 447–68); Pembroke to Canning, 14, 15 July, 31 August 1807, Canning Papers (Leeds), 50; evidence of Metternich's and Starhemberg's involvement in the Canning–Alopeus peace proposals is in ibid. 57.

result of French intervention and the Spanish government's failure to resist it; this helped induce Francis to accept some of
Stadion's proposed military and political reforms. The comedy at
Bayonne followed, bearing out Metternich's prediction that the
Bourbon dynasty itself would be overthrown, further terrifying
the Emperor, and convincing even Carl that war with France was
inevitable sooner or later. Metternich himself took Bayonne fairly
calmly, insisting that it made no immediate difference to Austria,
which should prepare for trouble but not precipitate it. Meanwhile it should stick with France to ensure its share of the spoils
in Turkey, evidently Napoleon's next target. Everyone agreed,
however, that a policy of further inertia and lying low had become
impossible.

Otherwise the Spanish horrors influenced Austrian decisions
fairly little. The military reforms implemented in the spring and
early summer, beginning with the addition of two reserve battalions to each regiment and culminating in the founding in June
of a reserve army of trained militia (Landwehr), had their roots
in Austrian or general European developments, not Spanish.
Undoubtedly Stadion and his associates drew heavily on the example of the Spanish insurrection in their propaganda campaign
intended to enrol popular forces behind Austria's foreign policy.
The effort to make Austrians consciously identify themselves with
the state and its individual provinces as their homeland, so that
they would willingly fight and sacrifice for God, Emperor, and
country, was, for Austria, a new and fairly radical departure.
Stadion's military proposals seemed doubtful to Carl, his political
ideas dangerous to Francis. But Stadion never proposed to let the
people, or any representatives of them, share in political power or
policy-making, and his goal was the traditional one of preserving
the dynastic state and restoring its independence as a great power.
The movement thus had little to do with liberal nationalism in the
modern sense, in particular German nationalism. Indeed, the one
place where the Austrian 'national' rising would really succeed
was the Tyrol, where the popular motives for insurrection were,
as in Spain, overwhelmingly local and monarchic-dynastic, and
the immediate enemy not the French but the Bavarians, Germans
very close to Tyrolese and other Austrians in tribal origins, dialect,
customs, and religion. Furthermore, the Austrian government in
launching its effort expected Spain soon to succumb, and did not
believe that Spanish methods of fighting could and should be
adopted in Austria. In sum, Napoleon's aggression in Spain did
not arouse or inspire the Austrian government and its peoples to

fight for freedom; it frightened and goaded a dynastic state into a war for its existence.[43]

Napoleon, promptly alerted by his espionage system in Austria, launched a campaign from mid-1808 to force Austria to disarm and keep quiet. Almost no inducements accompanied his threats; compliance would earn Austria only a chance to survive. He demanded that it not only disarm but also enforce the Continental System more rigorously and recognize Joseph and Murat in Spain and Naples unconditionally; he threatened Austria with other armies, especially those of Russia and the Rheinbund, as much as with his own; and he designed his propaganda as much to mobilize them as to warn Austria. Once again, he anticipated and outstripped his opponents in coalition-building.

Yet, like virtually all his wars, this was one he did not want at the time and tried in his way to avoid—though not from fear of Austria's armaments. To the contrary: he had long considered another war with Austria likely, was sure he could win it, and expected that victory would solve his Austrian problem once for all and help him handle others. Nor was he seriously distracted by the Spanish problem. At the time relations with Austria grew most tense, in late 1808 and early 1809, the Spanish threat seemed nearly over. The French army was regularly defeating Spain's, and it would be a long time, if ever, before Napoleon would take Spanish popular resistance and guerilla warfare seriously. Napoleon himself had driven out Moore's army in January, and as for the forces that returned under Wellesley that summer after the Austrian war started, Napoleon assured Joseph with evident conviction that this was a step toward final victory; in the peninsula the British were certain to be beaten. Nor was he worried about strained relations with Russia; from early 1808 these remained fairly stable rather than deteriorating. His main reason for avoiding further war at this time was the fragile personal basis of the Empire. He still had no heir, and even the Empire's strongest supporters and beneficiaries were unsure of its direction and future, so that any danger to his person, inescapable in war, created concern even within France.[44]

---

[43] Wohlfeil (1965: 164–73, 180–203, 218–19); Botzenhart (1967: 212–21, 229–45); Rössler (1940: i. 298–9, 304–7, 315; 1966: i. 290–4); Falk (1962); Rothenberg (1982a); Metternich (1880–4: ii. 172–9); Oncken (1876: ii. 588–97).

[44] Napoleon (1858–70: xvii. Nos. 13912, 14124–5, 14128, 14147, 14230, 14247–8, 14269, 14294, 14302, 14380, 14382; xviii. Nos. 14700, 14706–7, 14710, 14718–25, 14782, 14790–9); Rössler (1966: i. 321); Oncken (1876: ii. 599–605); Whitcomb (1979: 136–8).

Austria, rather than Napoleon, wavered on the road to war. It had armed out of fear that Napoleon might immediately launch a Spanish-style coup against Austria. After a stormy confrontation with Napoleon at his audience of 15 August and a long interview on the 25th, Metternich advised Vienna that this danger was past. Now was the time for Austria to recognize Joseph and Murat, secure an invitation as a full participant to the Erfurt Congress, and safeguard its interests by an attachment to France for some unspecified price.

Stadion declined to follow Metternich's advice about Erfurt, fearing among other things the loss of his tenuous influence with Francis; yet he also hesitated at the prospect of war. Carl returned to opposing it in September, arguing that even a limited victory was unlikely and would give Austria no long-range security against France. An outspoken peace party at Vienna, which included the Empress, pointed out not only the risks of war but the moral and political disadvantages of starting it by a preemptive offensive into Germany. Though by late October 1808 most were resigned to war as unavoidable, the ultimate decision, reached after long debate from 8 to 23 December, clearly rose from desperation and lack of alternatives rather than confidence in victory. Stadion and the war party, which by this time again included Archduke Carl, argued mainly that war could not be avoided in the long run and that Austria could not wait to fight it. Until mid-1809, they calculated, Napoleon would be tied up in Spain; thereafter he was sure to turn on Austria. (Unfortunately for Austria, in early 1809 the drain in Spain was mainly on the wane.) The finance minister, O'Donnel, insisted that Austria's armaments could not be sustained fiscally past March. Thus Austria had only a brief window of opportunity for defeating Napoleon, principally on its own but with some anticipated help from risings in Germany and Prussia (which Stadion also gravely overestimated).

How much Metternich influenced this decision by his reports from Paris and memoranda written while he visited Vienna from late November to January 1809 is not clear. As so often, under his pose of omniscient certainty he seems to have been something of a weather-vane, neither an all-out hawk nor simply an objective reporter of facts. In any case, the impact of Metternich's advice derived not from his optimistic assessments of the resistance in Spain, the unprepared state of the French army, popular apathy and discontent within France, and the possibility that Napoleon might be overthrown by Talleyrand and Fouché if he met defeat. These, like other unrealistic hopes and calculations Austria played with (that Russia would remain neutral, Prussia join the war, and the Germans rise), were not so much reasons for going to war as attempts to argue that, if Austria did, it had some realistic hope of succeeding.[45] Metternich's ultimate recommendation of war, convincing because it came from a long-time advocate of passive resistance, was based on his insistence that Austria had no choice. Recent years had proved that even major powers could not prevent French aggression and preserve their independence either by political resistance and defensive alliances (tried by Austria in 1805) or by neutrality (tried by Prussia in 1806) or by alliance with France (tried by Spain till 1808). Only all-out struggle was left.[46]

Austria's approach to Russia, like its other diplomatic preparations (including bribing Talleyrand), were inspired by the same mixture of desperate hope and gamble as its decision for war. Vienna called on Alexander to join it in saving Europe, but did not expect the appeal to work. The real hope was for Russian neutrality or a merely nominal participation in the war, and the payment offered a high one in Austrian terms: acceptance of Russia's annexation of Moldavia and Wallachia, along with a request that a portion of western Wallachia be ceded to Austria.[47] If, as seems likely, some Austrians believed that they had assurances of Russian neutrality (Metternich even argued that this was better than an alliance because it left Austria's hands free), they were deluded. Russia obviously opposed the war; it could cause complications, promote more French expansion in Russia's direction, and destroy Austria or drive it wholly into France's arms. But Austria, though useful as a buffer state, was certainly not worth Russia's taking any risks. Russian nationalists like Rumiantsev considered Vienna the epitome of the decadent Europe for which Russia had uselessly sacrificed itself in the past.

[45] This illustrates a point of some theoretical importance. Blainey (1977) and some other scholars have argued that miscalculation of relative strengths is a principal cause of war—perhaps the principal one. If states correctly calculated their chances in war, far fewer wars would occur. Yet in this instance, as in others, the calculations made by a state as to its probable success in a possible war are clearly not objective analyses on which the decision for war was really based; they are essentially rationalizations of a decision made, or accepted, on other grounds. Austria did not decide to go to war because it thought it would win; it thought it could win because it believed it had to go to war. Many such cases occur.

[46] Beer (1877b: 516–35); Kraehe (1963: 64–81); Botzenhart (1967: 261–4, 270–84); Rössler (1940: i. 371–85; 1966: i. 307–15); Wohlfeil (1965: 263–4); Metternich (1880–4: ii. Nos. 117, 120, 124–5). Gentz's arguments illustrate some of Austria's desperation and illusions—Gentz (1867: ii. 109–58).

[47] Beer (1877b: 342–62); Botzenhart (1967: 286–91); Rössler (1940: i. 394–7; 1966: i. 306); Metternich (1880–4: ii. Nos. 109, 131).

Just as Napoleon expected Austria to block Russia's path while staying out of his, so Russians expected the same from Austria in reverse. Instead they saw Austria as blocking their way in Serbia, the Danubian Principalities, the Ottoman Empire, Poland, and potentially even Germany.[48] Hence Russia pocketed Austria's offer on the Principalities but gave Austria no assurances, repeatedly warned that if it armed and went to war Russia would be forced to come in on France's side (secretly it was delighted at the check Austria put on Napoleon's ambition), urged Austria to appease Napoleon on Spain and Naples as Russia itself did, and in general exploited Austria's peril to its own advantage.[49]

In any case, Russia had other things to worry about. The war with Sweden, though fought ingloriously, was ended successfully with the aid of Gustav IV's overthrow and assassination by a Swedish conspiracy in March. This enabled Russia to acquire the Grand Duchy of Finland in the Treaty of Friedrichshamm in August. The main stumbling-block was not Finland but Russia's insisting, under French pressure, that Sweden break with Britain and join the Continental System. The war left both empires dissatisfied with the other, Russia because France had given it little help and now dominated Denmark, the French because Russia had fought the war and enforced the Continental System with little vigour.[50]

The southern theatre was much worse for Russia; the war remained stalemated and Russia's occupation of the Principalities proved an economic and political failure. The Russian policy of trying to keep the Serbs fighting, mobilize them for Russia's war effort, and prevent them from turning toward Austria, while at the same time opposing Serbian independence in favour of an autonomous Serb principality under nominal Turkish suzerainty but dependent on Russia, broke down under its internal contradictions. A Serb appeal to France in August 1809 showed it. The Russians blamed the Porte's refusal to make peace on French intrigues, but the real problem was Rumiantsev's imperialist peace terms.[51] They also complained about French policy in Persia and

[48] VPR (1960–: 1. iv. No. 228).

[49] This verdict is based on ibid. Nos. 123–212; see also Martens (1874–1905: iii. 27–33).

[50] Sbornik (1867–1916: ii. 82–94); Käiväräinen (1965: 152–250); VPR (1960–: 1. iv. Nos. 157, 179–80).

[51] Jewsbury (1977: 40–3, 50–3); Vucinich (1982a: 95–129); VPR (1960–: 1. iv. Nos. 66, 73–4, 99, 165, 182; pp. 330, 523); Testa (1864–1911: ii. 331).

the Caucasus, when in fact the Persians had far better reason to complain of French betrayal.[52]

These complaints against France were minor, however, compared to its armed presence in Prussia and Poland, which angered even Rumiantsev. The Continental System was another grievance, compelling Russia not only to submit to it itself but also to reject proposals from old clients like Denmark for a joint return to neutrality. Russian diplomats, especially Kurakin at Paris, arguing from Russia's national and strategic interests or the balance of power, repeatedly called on Alexander to drop out of the system, make peace with Britain, or even unite with Austria against France. At least one of them, Baron Stroganov, who had left his post as minister to Spain under Charles IV at the French take-over and was now ordered to return as Russia's minister to Joseph's court, dared to raise a further argument: that of morality and honour. Reminding Alexander that he had formerly represented him at Madrid as a ruler ready to defend the honour and independence of Europe, and especially of smaller states like Spain, Stroganov continued:

Called to my task to follow the different events of which Spain was the theatre, I have witnessed the evils which have shaken that ancient monarchy and have seen the frightful crimes which have precipitated its fall, unable not to see whose hand sowed disorder and corruption everywhere in order to subjugate it. I have seen, Sire, usurpation and tyranny cover itself with the impostor cloak of disinterested friendship. I have seen the sanctity and good faith of treaties serve as an instrument for cupidity and lies. I have seen the most sacred rights, those by which Your Imperial Majesty governs his vast estates, those which ought to confer upon the throne heredity and the love of its peoples—I have seen these despised and violated in the most outrageous fashion; I have finally seen torrents of blood and tears spread by an insatiable lust for conquest and domination. And I am to go to represent you, Sire, in the midst of a subjugated people, surrounded myself by its tyrants and oppressors? What language could I hold today which would not be entirely opposed to that which up until now Your Imperial Majesty himself authorized? . . . How could I face the meanest Spaniard who would compare my past discourse and conduct with that which I would display now? By what means could I persuade those on whose opinion I would attempt to base my public image [*considération*] that Your Imperial Majesty has remained entirely foreign to all the revolting iniquities that I cannot pretend any longer not to know about? Would I not thus expose myself either to compromising Your Majesty's lofty virtues or passing myself for the vilest of mortals?

[52] *VPR* (1960–: 1. iv. Nos. 49, 187; pp. 52–61, 144, 198–9); Puryear (1951: 344–53, 366–9); DeClercq (1880–1917: ii. 244–5).

No, Sire, of all the sacrifices which I am ready to make for Your
Imperial Majesty's glory and service, that of my honour is the only one
not in my power to offer. . . .[53]

Stroganov's eloquent moral appeal had no effect in 1809;
Rumiantsev's *sacro egoismo* and Alexander's fear of France and
hope for gains were still too strong. But this too would change in
time.[54]

Austria also tried for British help in its coming war; the story
can be summed up in three sentences. Austria began seeking
British financial help only late in 1808, on the brink of its decision
for war, without trying seriously to co-ordinate its strategy or
war aims with those of Britain. The British government, having
earlier encouraged Austria to rise, reacted coolly to the Austrian
request, insisting that Austria must fight on its own with little
or no British help. The British got their way, to the detriment
of their own cause and Austria's. The story, depressing but not
very important, could be dropped there, except for two recurring
myths. The one, dear to some French historians, is that this war
was somehow another Anglo-Austrian attempt to destroy France
and its Revolution.[55] It is not worth discussing. The other, primarily British in origin and marginally more plausible, is that
Britain, sympathetic to Austria's plight and recognizing Austria's
importance, tried to help her; that the British expedition to capture the Dutch isle of Walcheren in particular was planned and intended as a diversion in favour of Austria; but that a combination
of other commitments, concern about Austria's own intentions
and trustworthiness, and military misfortunes kept British aid
from being effective.[56] This story is just as untenable, but somewhat more interesting and important to refute.

As to Britain's actual policy: in late December 1808 Canning
finally replied to the Austrian request he had received more than a
month earlier for aid totalling more than 7 million pounds. He
expressed satisfaction that Austria had come to its senses: Britain

---

[53] 13 Feb. 1809, *VPR* (1960–: 1. iv. No. 219).
[54] This account rests on ibid. Nos. 169–232); for instances of Kurakin's protests,
see Nos. 172, 227; for examples of Rumiantsev's *sacro egoismo*, Nos. 196–8, 221.
The minister of war, Arakcheev, was also anti-Austrian and Russian nationalist—
see No. 184 and p. 461. Romanov (1905–14: iii) is full of French–Russian exchanges over the Austrian threat; vol. iv is dominated by Russian fears and
complaints over the Duchy of Warsaw.
[55] See e.g. Dunan (1961: 304–20, esp. 304–5).
[56] See, e.g. Bartlett (1966: 80–7).

forgave Austria its past misdeeds. But Austria would have to prepare for the war and launch it entirely on its own; only when it was fully engaged would Britain decide what, if anything, it might do to help. In February Canning decided to send a secret envoy, Lord Bathurst, to renew diplomatic relations once war actually broke out, and, in response to an Austrian special embassy on the eve of war, contrived to come up with some money for preparations (£250,000), and transferred more during the war itself to a total of somewhat more than £1 million. No alliance or regular subsidy, however, was ever granted; the British adhered to their basic principle that Austria must fight on its own.

Canning's caution and slowness, according to the standard accounts, derived from his aversion to previous subsidy arrangements, uncertainty as to whether to promote risings in Prussia and North Germany instead of trying to help Austria, and consciousness of Britain's limited resources and far-flung commitments. Of course these factors were present; Canning's correspondence, however, rules them out as the main explanation. Canning, like most Britons, realized that an Austrian rising against Napoleon had a certain instrumental value for Britain. It might help promote a general German rising, could possibly bring Russia back into the field, might conceivably thus help bring France down, and would certainly help as a diversion for the planned British campaigns in Holland and the Iberian peninsula. But to Austria itself, its fate and its role in Europe, Canning was even more indifferent or actively hostile than most Britons, and would be throughout his career. His correspondence with the King and with his colleagues Portland, Perceval, and Castlereagh in 1809 hardly mentions Austria, much less shows any interest in its life-and-death struggle, in the course of which it confronted Napoleon with his most serious military challenge prior to 1812. Like his colleagues and most Britons, Canning considered a host of other countries and areas in Europe and the world more important in 1808–9 than Austria—Russia, Sweden, Portugal, Spain, Hanover, the Ottoman Empire, North Germany, Prussia, India, America, the Mediterranean; all figure more prominently in his policy and his correspondence.

There was one particular respect, and one only, in which Austria's decision to go to war was fairly important to Canning. He used it as an additional weapon in his efforts, launched early in 1809, to oust Castlereagh from the war office and to bring the whole war effort and the government of Britain under his control.

Most of Canning's time and energies throughout the summer of 1809 were absorbed in this campaign for political power.[57]

As for the Walcheren expedition, in the first place the claim that a landing on a Dutch island could help Austria was either strategic nonsense, self-deception, or a flat falsehood. It had even less relation to saving Austria than the British landing at Narvik in 1940 had to saving Norway from the German invaders. Robert Adair, one of the few British with some sense of Austria's European role and importance, sent on a mission to Constantinople in late 1808 and 1809 to promote peace between Russia and the Ottoman Empire, repeatedly and vainly urged the British to take action in the Mediterranean as the only effective way of helping Austria.[58] In fact, the British never seriously thought of the Walcheren expedition, much less planned it, as a diversion for Austria. Exactly the reverse is true; they considered Austria's whole war effort a diversion for Walcheren and their Iberian expedition. The plan, to seize the Isle of Walcheren off the Flushing coast as a base and then descend on Antwerp to open the Scheldt and destroy the French and Dutch fleets, was another and grander Copenhagen devised for purely British military and domestic-political reasons. (Canning wanted especially to erase the shame of the Cintra Convention and the evacuation of Spain at Corunna, and to advance his political ambitions.) In urging the plan on the Duke of Portland, Canning barely mentioned Austria; Lord Mulgrave supported it precisely on the grounds that Spain and Austria were at this time keeping France occupied. The fact that some Britons talked of Walcheren as an aid to Austria, and that in the black night of their despair some Austrians believed them, should not deceive historians. The British made this same sort of claim with every ally for everything they did, however remote and unconnected with the vital theatre it was, throughout every coalition save the last.[59]

---

[57] For Austria's approach to Britain, see Beer (1877b: 336–41, 425–7); Rössler (1966: i. 318–19); for Britain's response, Sherwig (1969: 208–13); Mackesy (1957: 306–11); D. Gray (1963: 338–9); and correspondence in Canning Papers (Leeds), 50. Canning's correspondence with the King and his cabinet colleagues are in ibid. 32, 38, 57. For an interesting contrast between his dealings with Austria and his extraordinary efforts in 1808–9 to save Gustavus IV and Sweden, see Sherwig (1969: 193–6, 206–7); Canning to Perceval, 29 Dec. 1808, Canning Papers (Leeds), 32; and various letters to Edward Thornton, Andrew Merry, and Baron Stedingk, ibid. 42, 57.

[58] Adair (1845: i, 4–9, 127–9, 143–73).

[59] Canning to Portland, 21 Mar., 2 Apr., 5 May 1809 (along with many succeeding letters attacking Castlereagh), Canning Papers (Leeds), 33; Canning to

The purpose of this is not to destroy Canning's reputation,[60] still less to denigrate Britain's overall military performance in this period, and least of all to portray Austria as a victim of British selfishness or perfidy. Britain might possibly have done more for Austria, but it could not have made a serious difference in this war. Canning was indifferent to Austria's fate, but he was also basically right in thinking that Austria, having launched this war on its own, had to fight it in the same way. Moreover, though Stadion and Gentz were pro-British in the sense that they would ally with anyone fighting Napoleon, other leading Austrians like Carl and Metternich were explicitly or implicitly Anglophobe. The justification for this discussion, besides setting the record straight, is to bring out again two points vital to a general understanding of the Napoleonic wars and the 1815 settlement and a particular understanding of 1809. The first point is by now familiar: that Britain was not European in outlook and understanding, and that until it became at least minimally so all its achievements at war, however indispensable they might be to ultimate victory, would not really serve to create peace. Metternich had a point, though he greatly exaggerated, in saying that Britain was outside the European orbit like the moon. It was not a question of sympathy or antipathy toward Austria, or of what one thought of it as a government and a state; it was a question of what statesmen needed to know and understand to develop a workable definition and concept of peace. No government which displayed as little understanding for Austria's position and role in Europe as Canning did (and he was typical rather than exceptional) could understand the problems of eastern or south-eastern Europe or Germany or Italy, or other issues vital to any durable European settlement. It was fortunate for everyone that Britain's leaders learned just enough, just in time, in 1813–15. Canning never did.

The second, more immediate point concerns the interpretation and significance of 1809. It marked for Austria and Europe not the beginning of the end, but the end of the beginning; not another sign that a new national spirit like Spain's was abroad in Europe, which though defeated here would rise again elsewhere to over-

Castlereagh, 21 Mar. 1809, ibid. 34; Canning to Gower, 27 June 1809, PRO 30/29/8/4, fos. 481–8; Mulgrave to Wellesley, 25 Mar. 1809, BL Add. MS 37291, fos. 160–3.

[60] I confess, however, that he often strikes me as a vain, ambitious schoolboy who never quite grew up. For a devastating portrait of him, see Ziegler (1965: 114–15); for a description of his concept of politics and political action, see McQuiston (1971).

throw Napoleonic rule, but instead another crushing failure in the long series of allied, especially Austrian, attempts to achieve peace simply or mainly through military victory over France. The particular lesson Austria would learn from 1809, and needed to learn, was not that British help alone was insufficient to enable Austria to win, and that an all-European coalition was needed. The lesson went much deeper: that Britain and Russia under present conditions were useless, even harmful, for Austria's survival. To survive, Austria had to join France against them, no matter how humiliating and dangerous the union would be. The fact that Austria in 1809 was finally beaten into a humiliating, subservient alliance with France ultimately prepared the ground for tolerable Austrian relations with Britain and Russia; for only their realization that an Austro-French alliance was a genuine possibility prepared them for a decent relationship with Austria.

VI. EUROPE AND AUSTRIA AT WAR

But this has gone ahead of the story. Stadion hoped to win the war partly by enlisting German popular support and minimizing the Rheinbund's participation in the war. Since the strategy had no chance of succeeding, the war aims Austria developed to support it are worth examining only to see what it had learned about building a coalition for victory and peace. In some respects its programme was better than earlier ones. Once again, it genuinely wanted partnership with Prussia, which would be restored to its 1806 status, as Austria would to that of 1805. There would be no restoration of the Empire, and Austrians spoke of reaching out to other German states, guaranteeing their territories or promising them compensations. Austria proposed to regain its Italian losses to the line of the Mincio, but to overthrow only the Napoleonic rulers in Italy, restore despoiled sovereigns, and give the King of Sardinia additional territory besides. And the Austrians were insistent that their only quarrel was with Napoleon and his conquests, not with France.

Yet the programme had plenty of contradictions and weaknesses. The call for popular risings in Germany, which made Emperor Francis nervous, would drive any Rheinbund princes tempted to abandon Napoleon back to him. By hinting at conquests on the left bank of the Rhine, Austria contradicted its claim to be fighting Napoleon but not France. It spoke of guaranteeing only the 'inherited' territories of German princes and of restoring some of the mediatized ones, another red flag to the Rheinbund. Finally, while the Austrians were sincere in speaking of partnership with Prussia and a general German confederation, Stadion remained an old *Reichsritter* and German patriot who wanted to replace French influence in Germany with Austrian—and dared not tell his own stock-Austrian Emperor just how this would be done. The resultant lack of clarity indicated further that Austria still was thinking of military victory first, and then finding solutions to political problems.

If Austria's political goals were hazy, its military strategy was crazy, riddled with confusion, divisions, and rash assumptions. Austria's generals knew they could not count on Prussia's participation, a popular rising in Hesse and elsewhere in the north, and Saxon neutrality; yet they had somehow to devise a strategy that would enable them to take advantage of these hopes if they were realized. At the same time, they had to launch their main offensive in South Germany and meet the likely Polish and Russian interventions. The answer was to launch offensives everywhere to meet every danger and exploit any possibilities. Even worse was the calculation that made Austria's maximum potential of 340,000 men equal or superior to Napoleon's 800,000 because his were scattered about Europe, when obviously if Austria won initial victories this would serve to unite them. Finally, the all-out gambling strategy actually envisioned a limited goal, driving the French to the Rhine. What would Austria do when and if this succeeded?[61]

All this merely reflects the desperate character of Austria's situation and resolve. Other patriots were also swept along in the same current. Stein and his associates (Scharnhorst, Gneisenau, Götzen) had continued to push their plans for war and a popular rising even after Napoleon discovered Stein's activities, but in November and December 1808 Stein was finally driven from office and into exile in Austria, while Götzen failed to get Austria to promise major Austrian support for a Prussian rising. Only after Frederick William decided in early 1809 to try for alliance with France and remain dependent on Russia did Austria make serious efforts to woo Prussia into a joint rising. The war party supported the idea, but the King would have none of it.

This was all too understandable; Stein's plans were riddled with unrealism and contradictions. A fake alliance with France was to pave the way for a real secret alliance with Austria; a revolutionary

[61] Rössler (1940: i. 424–7, 498–546; 1966: i. 322–3; ii. 15–23, 32–42, 46); Metternich (1880–4: ii. Nos. 125, 127–8, 141–4).

insurrection in Germany in behalf of German liberation and constitutional unity was to be launched in the name and under the
lead of a pacific, conservative King; insurrections and guerilla
warfare would be waged by stolid peasants on the North German
plain under the noses of the French. The gulf between plans and
actual preparations, hope and reality was immense. But this, too,
reflected the cruel hopelessness of Prussia's situation.

Hence for our purposes the main question is not how the
Prussian and German patriots hoped to reach their goal, but what
that goal was, and how much they had learned about peace. They
too had clearly learned the necessity of subordinating the Austro-
Prussian rivalry to their common interest. The best proof of this is
the fact that even Frederick William, seeing war approaching and
considering Prussia's destruction as sure to follow hard upon
Austria's, was tempted to come into the war, and tried rather
timidly to get Russia to join him.

Beyond this, however, little had been learned. There was little
understanding of how Napoleon's satellite regimes, the German
people, and potential resistance forces themselves would react to a
summons to rise without serious preparations in advance and military forces ready to support them. Even Austria's and Prussia's
desperate need of each other, moreover, could not keep them
from trying to use one another, getting the other mouse to bell
the cat. The Prussian patriots, for example, wanted Austria to
start the war, win victories, and draw the bulk of Napoleon's
forces upon it, so that then the Prussians could rise and operate in
mainly secondary theatres.[62]

This helped assure that, so far as the Rheinbund and Germany
were concerned, Napoleon had little to fear and Austria nothing
to hope for. The Spanish rising had encouraged some anti-French
sentiment, even in Bavaria, but had not influenced the governments at all. They did not dare defy Napoleon, and Austria gave
them little reason to want to. Bavaria and Württemberg, smelling
victory and loot, positively promoted the war; German patriotism,
especially in the Tyrol, was more dangerous to them than to
Napoleon and the French Empire in general.[63]

Thus the actual war, which began in April 1809 with an Austrian
invasion of Bavaria, appeared anticlimactic for most of its course,

[62] Ibbeken (1970: 116–53); Münchow-Pohl (1987: 132–5); Koch (1987: 141–64);
Wohlfeil (1965: 203–9, 220–3); Herre (1973: 202–5, 214–17); Ritter (1958: 352–3);
Rössler (1940: i. 401–8); Bailleu (1900: 184–97).

[63] Dunan (1942: 226–40); Hölzle (1937: 35–43); Napoleon (1858–70: xviii. Nos.
14901–2).

another routine parade of French victories. Within little more than a month, Archduke Carl had been badly defeated at Eckmühl and driven down the Danube; Vienna fell again in the middle of May. Not only had Napoleon prepared for war militarily and diplomatically far better than Austria, but also the forces of the Rheinbund (including Poles from the Duchy of Warsaw) fought well for Napoleon, while the rest of Germany did not fight for Austria. The risings that did occur, Colonel Dornberg's in Hesse and Major Schill's in Prussia in April and May, were heroic failures, and one that succeeded, Andreas Hofer's in the Tyrol, came too late and against a secondary foe.

No outside miracles intervened to prevent Austria's defeat. The Walcheren expedition, even if it could have helped Austria, was launched far too late, at the end of July; Britain's prosecution of the war in the Mediterranean also gave Austria no help; despite Frederick William's momentary temptation, Prussia remained quiet.[64] As for Russia, contrary to some accounts, it did not help Austria even by passivity. Much has been made of the promises Alexander allegedly made to Austria in April which supposedly emboldened Vienna to undertake the war. Thanks to Soviet scholarship we know how little there was to this—a promise (obvious and worthless) not to pursue a revolutionary policy in Poland, and another (not worth much more) not to prosecute the war too vigorously. Russian public opinion may have been anti-French; the Russian opinion that counted, including the Tsar, was anti-Austrian. The reasons Russia's action against Austria was delayed were partly Alexander's desire to strike a blow against the Turks at the same time, and partly Russian routine and the inertia of its commander Prince Golitsin. Nonetheless, the Russian campaign came at a crucial stage and contributed to Austria's discouragement. The Tsar, who actively encouraged it, did not consider his policy at all disloyal to France. In fact, he rendered France valuable service, both in attacking Austria and in restraining Prussia.[65]

Thus Austria's defeat was the inevitable outcome of an heroic but hopeless gamble. Yet something occurred to prove that contingencies and individual actions may alter history. In the Battle

[64] Dunan (1942: 239–57); Rössler (1940: ii. 30–4); Rothenberg (1982b). For divergent views of the war's impact in Prussia and Germany, see Münchow-Pohl (1987: 136–70); Koch (1987: 215–91); Ibbeken (1970: 154–68). On Britain's efforts, see Mackesy (1957: 318–28, 336–40); Bond (1979).

[65] Kazakov (1969); Kraehe (1963: 84–8); Martens (1874–1905: viii. 7–10); Nikitin and Dostian (1980–3: ii. No. 61). As Dunan (1942: 265–7) shows, Alexander was more interested in preserving Bavaria than Austria.

of Aspern on the Danube in May, Napoleon gambled, under-estimating the fighting power of the Austrian army, and by losing the battle put himself and his army in real peril. At this juncture something unexpected, such as a little more resolve by Frederick William, a little more offensive spirit by Carl, or a different decision by Alexander, might have made a difference. Absent these, the sequel to Aspern in July was Wagram, a French victory won by sheer force of numbers, which finished Austria off. A week later followed the armistice of Znaim; a day thereafter, the British landing on Walcheren.[66]

VII. THE BALANCE SHEET IN 1809

One need not describe how Napoleon prodded Austria into the Treaty of Schönbrunn on 14 October. During the war, and briefly thereafter, he had entertained two radical notions about dealing with Austria. The first was to divide the monarchy into three separate kingdoms of Austria, Hungary, and Bohemia; it was actually signalled by a proclamation in mid-May calling on the Hungarians to rise for independence. The Hungarian feudal no-bility failed to respond, however, and the idea was not seriously pursued. The second, apparently seriously entertained for a brief time, was to leave Austria largely intact but force Francis to abdi-cate in favour of Grand Duke Ferdinand, now Napoleon's obeisant client as Duke of Würzburg. Whether or not this was a mere ploy, it certainly frightened Francis and helped gain Napoleon what he chose to accept: a purely punitive peace paying him with cash and territories, rendering Austria harmless, and helping him take care of certain nascent problems in his own Empire which now con-cerned him more than Austria did. Yet threats of forced abdication or partition were not really necessary to make Austria conform. After Austria's defeat and occupation, Metternich, taking over from the discredited Stadion as foreign minister, made his funda-mental principle that of surviving by attaching Austria limpet-like to France, regardless of the cost in dignity and principle.[67]

The Treaty of Schönbrunn cost Austria heavily in territory (Salzburg, Berchtolsgaden, and a part of Upper Austria went

---

[66] Rauchensteiner (1972: 104–9).

[67] On Napoleon's general peace tactics, see Napoleon (1858–70: xix. Nos. 15683–903); for specific evidence of his considering a more radical solution, see ibid. Nos. 15215, 15816, 15832; Chroust (1932: 314–22); Driault (1917: 464–7); Kosary (1979: 52–89). For Metternich's advice to Francis, see Metternich (1880–4: ii. Nos. 145–6).

to Bavaria, Istria, Carniola, and the Littoral to France, some Bohemian enclaves to Saxony, much of Galicia to the Poles and Russia). It reduced Austria by 3.5 million inhabitants, leaving it landlocked, without outlet for its foreign commerce. Almost worse for its economic and political future was the requirement to pay 200 million francs in contributions and to restrict its army to 150,000 men. Yet Austria's punishment was not as harsh as Prussia's had been, or as Bavaria in its greed and great-power mania wanted it to be. Here again, Napoleon showed his lack of imagination toward Austria; rich in expedients, he lacked a concept. Austria, hobbled and reduced to second- or third-rank status, remained a sizeable state, with no function in Napoleon's system save his absurd one of staying where it was and keeping out of his way.[68]

Meanwhile other business in the Empire had to be transacted, with the usual commissions paid to Napoleon and his friends. Bavaria had fought well against the Austrians but badly against the insurgent Tyroleans (the insurrection under Andreas Hofer was only finally put down in January 1810 by French troops under Prince Eugène). This did not promote Bavaria's dream of replacing Austria as the greatest German power in the south. It had to pay for its acquisitions from Austria by ceding part of Swabia to Württemberg and the South Tyrol to the Kingdom of Italy, which in turn ceded Illyria to France. The Roman question was finally settled during the war by annexation, so that Rome became the second largest city in France. Thinly veiled annexation was also planned for the Hanseatic cities of North Germany, especially Hamburg.[69] The Poles of the Duchy, who had fought hard for Napoleon and themselves, were rewarded with more territory but no more genuine autonomy or freedom from heavy French exactions, and no more attention to their ambitions for a Great Poland.[70] One area in which Napoleon failed to act decisively was Spain. Wellesley had landed again with a British force and defeated the French at Talavera in mid-July (earning him elevation to the peerage as the Duke of Wellington), but had then been forced to retreat into Portugal by the approach of superior French forces. Whether Napoleon took the Anglo-Portuguese

[68] DeClercq (1880–1917: ii. 293–9); Beer (1877b: 445–50); Dunan (1942: 260–3).

[69] Driault (1917: 472–9) (for background and analysis of Napoleon's final actions toward Rome, Latreille, 1935: 587–606); Napoleon (1958–70: xviii. No. 15193; xix. Nos. 15218–19, 15225, 15862, 15908–11, 15917).

[70] Birke (1960: 14–27); Fugier (1954: 164–5); Kosary (1979: 38–41); for background, Handelsmann (1909).

threat too lightly or actually saw more difficulties in Spain than he was ready to admit to Joseph and his marshals is not clear. In any case, while he repeatedly talked of going to Spain again to finish the war, he never did, choosing instead to direct it from a distance, constantly criticizing his subordinates and ignoring the mounting guerilla problem.

All in all, then, 1809 was a normal Napoleonic war with normal imperialist results—certainly no sign of the Empire's coming decline or disintegration. Yet there were small clouds on the horizon. The war deepened the strain in Franco-Russian relations. Napoleon washed his hands of the Tilsit alliance in a letter of 2 June to Caulaincourt, though telling Caulaincourt to conceal the fact; a Russian army of 40,000 men to attack Austria would, he said, at least have sustained 'some illusion about a phantom alliance'. The Russians were bitter that four-fifths of Galicia went to expand the Duchy of Warsaw, especially since the Polish commander, Prince Joseph Poniatowski, had sought to raise a Polish revolt not only in Austrian Galicia but also in Russian Poland. There were further Franco-Russian quarrels over other terms of Schönbrunn and over the concurrent Russo-Swedish peace treaty, which France claimed failed really to fulfil Russia's obligations under Tilsit because it did not make Sweden actually fight Britain. The French charged that Russia had done nothing against Austria (an exaggeration) and that Russia secretly sympathized with Austria (untrue). The pace of Russian military action in this war was no slower than it had been against Sweden and Turkey, and, as the Russians pointed out, they helped France against Austria more than France had helped them against Sweden. Alexander's claim that he distrusted Austria and had never forgiven it for 1805 was sincere. In contrast, Russia had a sound complaint, that France was building up Poland and using it as a cat's-paw against Russia. It made little sense as an accusation, however, because essentially Russia had agreed to this at Tilsit.

Russia's real source of worry and dissatisfaction was one that Alexander and Rumiantsev could not openly admit: its need for buffer states, a need growing with their steady erosion and the increasingly intolerable pressure from France. To admit this would be embarrassing, especially given the vocal criticism of Alexander's policy within Russia, and to try to do anything about it now by reconstituting an independent, intermediary Europe would be suicidal.[71]

[71] Driault (1917: 430–1, 482–3); Romanov (1905–14: iv. Nos. 314, 323, 329); vii. Nos. 65, 75, 81, 83, 87).

The war had also, as a side-effect, impeded the economic war against Britain. Napoleon's attempt to tighten the Continental System without undermining France's own economy and those of its allies could never have succeeded in the long run anyway, but having to mount and wage a new war made the task worse. 1809 became a boom year for British trade and industry, at the same time as the further extension and heavy costs of the system continued to erode the initial European support for it.[72] While British military strategy proved no better in this war (the troops landed on Walcheren had to be evacuated in December after heavy losses by disease), there were other bright spots. Castlereagh reorganized and greatly improved the war office, and Britain retained its footholds in Portugal and Sicily and continued to win the less spectacular but vital naval war in the Mediterranean, the Indian Ocean, and the Far East.[73] Aspern and Wagram showed that, if Napoleon's armies remained superior to other European ones, the gap was narrowing. In the naval war, the gap between Britain and the whole French-led Continent was widening, and Napoleon's own plans and orders prove it. He never ignored the war at sea or abandoned his naval and colonial plans; his victory over Austria, in fact, helped revive them. But these plans became increasingly unreal and crazy, implemented more and more simply by bullying satellites into greater exertions, while Napoleon's own military-political efforts in late 1809 and into 1810 turned unmistakably toward creating a Fortress Europe.[74]

Britain, however, could derive little comfort in late 1809 from these small straws in an uncertain wind. Canning's underhanded campaign against Castlereagh in order to make himself leader of a reorganized ministry ended in September in a cabinet crisis and a duel between the two men, forcing both out of the ministry and leaving them lifelong rivals. The Walcheren fiasco led to a parliamentary inquiry in which the opposition attacked both the ministers and the war itself; even the government itself became discouraged and doubtful about the prospects of carrying it on. Austria's defeat played only a minor, indirect role in this. Widely ignored in Britain and, when noticed, considered almost entirely in terms of its effects on Walcheren or the war in the Iberian

---

[72] Melvin (1949: 48–76); Crouzet (1958: i. 282–3; ii. 421–524); Fugier (1954: 226–33).

[73] D. Gray (1963: 278–81); Schama (1977: 595–8); Mackesy (1957: 340–67, 376–95); Lefebvre (1969: ii. 86–91); R. Glover (1973: 146–7); Syrett (1979).

[74] e.g. Napoleon (1858–70: xix. Nos. 15692, 15868); the evidence of a 'Fortress Europe' mentality becomes much stronger in vol. xx.

peninsula, it merely confirmed British beliefs about the uselessness of Continental allies and the impossibility of doing anything significant on the Continent outside Portugal and Spain, if there.[75]

What made 1809 a turning-point, as noted earlier, was something the British scarcely noticed, and which would only have increased their pessimism had they thought about it. Austria abandoned for the indefinite future any further attempts to resist France. With the brief exception of Russia in early 1807, Austria had been for seventeen years the only formidable foe France had faced on the Continent. With its elimination, Russia and Britain would finally face the full weight of Napoleon's imperialism alone.

[75] D. Gray (1963: 214–53). I have found only a few scattered, unimportant references to Austria's defeat and the Peace of Schönbrunn in the published sources, e.g. Grenville (1892–1927: ix); Windham (1913), and the private papers of Grey, Grenville, Canning, and Castlereagh; but expressions of war-weariness, a defensive mentality, and even defeatism were fairly common.

8
Napoleon's Empire and the International System

NAPOLEON'S Empire reached its zenith in 1809; all his later annexations and campaigns really weakened it. This is therefore the point at which to discuss its nature and its impact on Europe. Both subjects are controversial, and include the question of whether it had any lasting impact at all. Thomas Nipperdey begins his magisterial history of nineteenth-century Germany with the words, 'In the beginning was Napoleon'. With him came Germany's breakthrough to modernity, bourgeois society, and the strong centralized state. But Nipperdey's view has been challenged, and Louis Bergeron's equally authoritative work on French history in the Napoleonic era suggests in its title, *L'Épisode napoléonien*, his belief that Napoleon changed little in the deeper rhythms of French life—demography, social structure, religious, cultural, and intellectual life, and economics. Not only the Empire's overall results, but also the individual aspects of its putative legacy in France and Europe—modernization, centralization, the rationalization of politics and public life, industrialization and economic progress, advances toward social and legal equality, democracy, nationalism, state-building—remain topics of debate.

In contrast, the question of how the Empire affected international politics and the international system has provoked little controversy in recent decades. Historians may differ over the kind of empire it was and the type of imperialism it represented, and on occasion still speculate, as they once commonly did, on how European history might have been altered had the Empire survived instead of collapsing in military defeat. But given the actual course of events, it seems obvious that in international history the Empire was a brief, sensational episode with no lasting consequences; the spectacular rise of a military leader and the state he commanded to unprecedented power and glory, followed by their even swifter fall and a restoration of the old balance-of-power system.

Neither the purpose of this book nor its author's expertise justify any confident judgements about Napoleon's overall legacy.

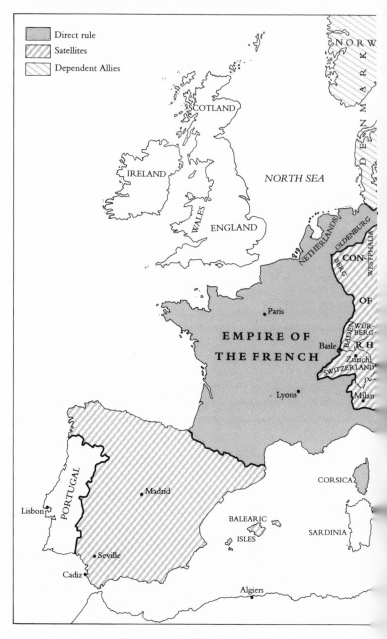

Europe under Napoleon, 1812

What will be attempted is only a brief survey of the Empire's effects on France and Europe, and of the reactions of Frenchmen and Europeans to it. But this overview, when combined with what is known about the international politics of the era, leads to a paradoxical conclusion. At the same time as it may suffice to show why the judgements of experts about Napoleon's general legacy are usually mixed and guarded and often contradictory, it refutes the commonplace consensus on Napoleon's impact on international politics as ephemeral and superficial. It suggests instead that his Empire affected Europe most profoundly and durably precisely in the arena of international politics; that here, as nowhere else, one may speak of a Napoleonic revolution.

I. FRANCE AND ITS COLONIES

What the Empire did to France's political development is in any case clear enough—it stifled it. Napoleonic rule in France was an experiment in enlightened despotism which, as time went on, produced increasingly less enlightenment and more despotism. Its basic features were a further rationalization and centralization of state power and administration in the tradition of the Old Regime and the Revolution, limited only by difficulties in communication and the resistance of local bodies and officials; the growing use of obedient mediocrities rather than powerful ministers to carry out the Emperor's policy; the atrophy of elective bodies in favour of government by decree and administrative fiat; and the rejection of the representative principle, with the Emperor himself and his government constituting the state and representing the people. Civil liberties, especially freedom of the press, were steadily eroded by judicial, administrative, and police action until in the end only freedom of conscience was left, and this did not mean full freedom of religion. Jews gained greater emancipation, though Napoleon was personally hostile to them and mainly interested, as elsewhere, in control. On the whole, Albert Guérard's comment that when it came to civil liberties the restored Bourbons at their worst were better than Napoleon at his best is correct.

Perhaps most striking was the government's ability to exploit social institutions and various elements of public life as instruments of control—the Church and religion, history, art and science, literature, the economy, patriotic sentiment. It was not the circumstances of Napoleon's rise to power and his reign as a usurper that compelled him to use the ruling techniques he did.

His hold on power and over the French people actually gave him a fairly free hand. They derive instead from his basic outlook as an archetypal Machiavellian prince. Almost automatically he reduced politics to techniques of control, and viewed history, art, human nature, religion, and national feeling as instruments to this end. By the same token his actions were not original or impelled by some higher vision and aim—to achieve a new society and a new man, or even a new and greater France. His frequent injunction to his satraps, 'Be French!' meant little more than 'Do what I tell you! Put me first!'

The mass of Frenchmen accepted his rule, with attitudes ranging from apathy to enthusiasm, because it provided order, military glory, and relative prosperity. Taxation and the economic and human costs of war bred discontent and conscription was widely evaded, especially in the latter years, but political repression under Napoleon did not cause major discontent. There were elements of opposition—Royalists, Jacobin republicans, rival generals and disgruntled officials, liberals, especially the so-called *Idéologues* (Destutt de Tracy, Madame de Staël, Benjamin Constant, and others), and Catholics alienated when Pius VII excommunicated Napoleon for annexing Rome in 1809. But opposition activity was confined to occasional conspiracies and inner emigration; the only serious danger to the regime was that Napoleon might die in battle or by assassination. There is nothing odd about the fact that Metternich, allegedly Napoleon's enemy and nemesis, admired his principles of governance and later tried to imitate them. For Napoleon achieved what Metternich regarded as the ideal basis for political authority—a stable, apolitical apathy among the masses. As René Rémond says, Napoleon created a political void in France, and even the renewal of opposition as a result of military defeat and hardship in the last years of the Empire did not serve to fill it.[1]

Politics apart, the remaining results of Napoleonic rule in France are mixed. The great Napoleonic Codes completed and promul-

---

[1] For general accounts, see Lefebvre (1969: ii. 160–71); Bergeron (1972: ii. 100–11); Rémond (1965: 222–41). On conscription, see Forrest (1989); on Napoleon's use of his parliamentary bodies, Collins (1979); on the court and new aristocracy, Mansel (1987: chs. 3–4); Jardin (1985: 172–3). For Napoleon's attitudes and actions on art treasures and archives, see Gould (1965: esp. 42–3); Boyer (1964); Quynn (1945); Napoleon (1858–70: xvi. No. 13692); on religion, education, and the press, Lefebvre (1969: ii. 179–91); Godel (1970); Moran (1981); Schwarzfuchs (1979); Raumer (1952: 247–9); on history, ibid. 238–9; Napoleon (1958–70: xv. Nos. 12416; xx. Nos. 15977, 16053).

gated between 1807 and 1810 (civil, commercial, criminal, and penal) represented a triumph for rational modernization in public, legal, and commercial affairs, as well as for male and bourgeois supremacy. Socially, Napoleon went far toward refeudalizing French society with his new court and his creation of a new service nobility, largely military in make-up and endowed with the plunder of conquered Europe. He went even further toward militarizing French society, placing the army and military glory at the centre of French life, and here also succeeded in making Frenchmen willing partners. Yet he neither wiped out the social changes of the Revolution nor effected a real substitution of elites. The old nobility survived and revived along with the new, the army never became a state within the state, and Frenchmen, though warlike, did not become militarist.[2] In some areas of administration, such as the reorganization and development of the diplomatic service, Napoleon's leadership was initially efficient and progressive, though ultimately his preference for sycophantic mediocrities over independent talent and his prostitution of the service to military ends undid most of the good he had done.[3] In others, such as taxation, fiscal policy, and procurement, his rule has to be called regressive and harmful.[4] But nowhere was he a revolutionary innovator. Even in the military realm, where his impact on logistics, tactics, strategy, and other aspects of warfare was most obvious and would be most closely studied by later practitioners and historians, he built on tradition and precedent.[5]

Napoleon's success in gaining the consent of the populace and of elites to his rule was not confined to old-regime France. In the older annexed territories (Belgium, the Rhineland, Luxemburg, Piedmont, Genoa) his achievement was even more striking. Belgium and Luxemburg had been in active revolt against French rule before Napoleon took power, and the Rhineland was certainly

---

[2] Bergeron (1972: i. 77–85); Lefebvre (1969: ii. 192–8); Best (1982: 112–21); Senkowska-Glück (1970).

[3] Whitcomb (1979).

[4] On Napoleon's fiscal and tax policies, which both were inadequate and constituted a reversion to some of the abuses of the Old Regime, see Bergeron (1972: i. 52–62); Bosher (1970: 314–17); Thuillier (1983: esp. 92–106); on Napoleon's military-authoritarian outlook toward commerce and industry, Viennot (1947: 154–62). Ullmann (1981) credits Napoleon's centralization of power and his exaction of contributions from his conquests with ultimately laying the foundation of later French capital markets. Be that as it may, the Empire itself proved far less capable of mobilizing credit for war than Britain, and Napoleon's crude views on finance and public credit were at least partly responsible.

[5] Rothenberg (1978: 240–5); Nanteuil (1968: 66–75).

not contented. Yet the same acceptance of French rule came to prevail here as in metropolitan France; a good deal of support and collaboration was garnered from local notables, officials, and the middle class, and little nationalist or patriotic resentment and resistance had to be overcome. The defeats and burdens of 1812–14 destroyed all enthusiasm for the regime, to be sure, and its fall was received without regret—but also without active rebellion.[6] If, as some have argued, Napoleon aimed to denationalize the peoples of Western Europe, allowing them to retain their local attachments so long as these did not promote what he considered religious or political fanaticism, one has to conclude that in the short run he largely succeeded.[7]

And not only in Greater France. In the other area most important to his Empire in terms of power and resources, western Germany and Holland, Napoleon achieved overall political and administrative success—political in that he was able to retain control without serious resistance until he was militarily defeated, administrative in that in both areas, especially in Germany, French rule meant permanent modernization and transformation. In Germany the limited scope of his aims helped him succeed. He never really wanted to revive Charlemagne's empire or to make the Rheinbund a genuine confederation uniting Third Germany under his protection; most of his princely allies would have resisted this had he tried. What he wanted from his German satellites on the positive side was men, money, and control of their foreign policy and to some degree their economies, and on the negative side the exclusion from Germany of Austria and, after 1806, of Prussia, leaving the individual states tied exclusively to France.

This programme included winning Germans over through good government and administrative, legal, judicial, and social reforms, but these aims were also supposed to serve purposes of French power and security. German princes, encouraged to expand their power at the expense of their nobles and local authorities, would become more dependent on Napoleon for support. Rationalized and centralized bureaucratic administrations along French lines were supposed to accustom German elites to French leadership, promote the efficient collection of taxes and exploitation of resources, and help unify the system. The introduction of the Napoleonic Codes, along with the abolition of feudal privileges

---

[6] Lefebvre (1969: ii. 202–3); Trausch (1978); Braubach (1976: 333–41); Dufraisse (1973); Faber (1973); Molitor (1980: 176–8).
[7] L'Huillier (1973); Tulard (1977: 310–13).

and the disbanding of guilds or their control by the state, were expected to satisfy the middle classes and (to a lesser degree) the peasants, freeing careers for talents, encouraging private initiative in commerce and agriculture, and promoting economic progress.

Napoleon's reforms were incomplete and inconsistent in application. Only on the left bank and in Baden and Berg was the full *Code Napoléon* introduced, and much legal and judicial reform actually worked to strengthen and preserve the nobility and its privileges rather than promote equality. Napoleon himself helped undermine his own reforms, especially in his 'model kingdom', Westphalia, where his own financial interests and those of the new nobility he had endowed with titles and estates prevented the abolition of feudalism. This was normal; in his scale of priorities men and money always came before reform, and a usable ally before a model state. Yet in much of Germany, especially the west and south, Napoleonic control had the effect of galvanizing political activity rather than stultifying it as in metropolitan France. The fact that state constitutions were encouraged did not mean a direct advance in real constitutional government, in Germany any more than in France; constitutions were intended and used to promote strong centralized government rather than to protect civil liberties or share power and decision-making. None the less, they had the effect of promoting more political participation than before.

Moreover, the German bureaucrats and ministers of state who got their chance at power in the Napoleonic era were often far more radical and genuine reformers than the French. They found French models and French support not only useful for the state-building programmes they had derived from the German cameralist tradition, but also the only models now available for application, slower gradual reforms having been ruled out by the great territorial and internal revolutions of 1803–6. Besides, by adopting French reforms themselves, German states could to some degree deter France from intervening too directly in German affairs. Thus some parts of Germany, especially the core Rheinbund states of Bavaria, Baden, and Württemberg, benefited from French leadership and protection, at least at first, and reacted mainly neither with Francophobia nor with German nationalism, but with a specific Bavarian, Württemberger, and Badenese state consciousness and patriotism.[8]

[8] For general discussions, see Lefebvre (1969: ii. 230–51); Dunan (1942: 368–77); J. Sheehan (1989: 251–74); Wehler (1987: i. 368–401); Fehrenbach (1981: 76–88) (pp. 129–95 give an excellent survey of the controversy and literature). On the

Not all the results were favourable, of course. Certain areas—the Hanseatic towns, the two Mecklenburgs, Oldenburg, and Saxony—felt French rule and innovations as foreign tyranny. Some modernization proved harmful and even reactionary in tendency, promoting princely absolutism, bureaucratic control from above, and the continued domination of old elites in a new form, while stifling useful liberties and autonomy. Mack Walker speaks flatly of 'the failure of centralizing reform' in the Napoleonic era, as administrators discovered that it was impossible to control, regulate, and reform so many local institutions and administrations. The survival of Germany's home towns against state centralization and the conversion of German bureaucrats after Napoleon from cameralist to liberal principles may have been as important to later German development as the original French and Napoleonic reform impulse.[9] Above all, even in relatively favoured states like Bavaria, Baden, Württemberg, Westphalia, Berg, and Würzburg, the good intentions of able princes and administrators grew increasingly futile in the face of Napoleon's wars, expanded military establishments, expensive government, and (as will be seen) French economic imperialism.[10] Yet, despite all this, Napoleonic Germany did provide a model of state-building, socially and economically conservative but politically moderately progressive and enlightened, which persisted into the so-called Restoration period and was a significant alternative to the one offered by Prussia.

In Holland's case the verdict, though still mixed, is more clearly unfavourable. As Simon Schama has shown, the Dutch also made their breakthrough to a modern centralized state in the revolutionary and Napoleonic period, and French rule was a major catalytic agent. But the impulses and sources for genuine reforms in the United Provinces were far more Dutch than French (in particular, Dutch religious humanitarianism), and the cost for modernization was extremely high—the ruin of Dutch trade and finances, the destruction of its navy and loss of its colonies, all

Napoleonic Codes in Germany, see Fehrenbach (1978); on Napoleon's principles for ruling conquered territories, H. Parker (1952). For important contributions on other points, see Berding (1973); Schmitt (1983); Dann (1979); and various essays in Sieburg (1971); Reden-Dohna (1979); Berding and Ullmann (1981); Weis (1984; 1990).

[9] M. Walker (1971: 186–215); Dipper (1980: 68–73).

[10] Besides the literature mentioned in n. 8, see for Bavaria esp. Dunan (1942); for Baden, Gall (1968: 12–17); for Westphalia, Berding (1973; 1982); Connelly (1966: 186–209); Tulard (1973); for Berg, C. Schmidt (1905); and for Würzburg, Chroust (1932).

kinds of Napoleonic exactions far more ruthless than in most of Germany, and the ultimate absorption of Holland into France. Napoleon's brother Louis, who accepted the throne of the Kingdom of Holland and was in turn accepted by the Dutch people in order to defend Holland against what Schama calls Napoleon's protection racket, put up a stubborn resistance, which ultimately cost him his throne but did nothing for Holland.[11] Yet even in Holland, where no moral or popular base for French rule existed (the Francophile sentiment once felt among the Patriot party had long since evaporated), there was no serious resistance. Not until the French fled in 1813 did the Dutch rise for liberation.

Napoleon was more attracted to Italy than to Germany or the Low Countries, but this did not mean that Italians got more respect from him. He considered Italians incapable of self-government, poor fighters, and incurably Francophobe, and treated them accordingly. Surprisingly, then, the overall effects of Napoleonic rule in the Kingdom of Italy, though mixed, are usually seen as favourable. But the achievements pointed to— confiscations of Church and noble land which largely benefited the bourgeoisie, improvements in education, an efficient and generally incorruptible administration, and the awakening of Italians to a sense of nationhood and autonomy—were due mainly to Eugène and servants of his like Melzi and his finance minister, Giorgio Spina. Napoleon's own legacy, having created the state by his conquests, consisted of imposing repeated territorial changes for strategic reasons: grinding taxation; economic subjugation (Italy became an economic colony for French goods, losing control of its own trade); the destruction of foreign trade and the ports that depended on it; political and civil repression; and above all, militarization and war. It was Eugène who strove to make soldiers and officers of Italians through military schools and training; it was Napoleon who constantly demanded more men and supplied the wars to employ them. 142,000 men were drafted from 1805 to 1814. The army grew from 23,000 in 1805 to 44,000 in 1808 to 90,000 in 1813. 30,000 were sent to Spain, of whom 9,000 survived; 27,000 to Russia, with 7,000 surviving; 28,000 more to Germany in 1813, again to suffer huge losses. Yet the system, however exploitative, worked. The army's desertion rate, though high, was only slightly greater than in France; taxes were

---

[11] Schama (1977: 530–53); Connelly (1966: 132–48). For a typical sample of Napoleon's instructions to Louis on how to rule Holland, see Napoleon (1858–70: xvi. No. 13252); for Napoleon's personal stake in extorting cash from the Dutch, DeClercq (1880–1917: ii. 239–42).

collected and state expenses covered until the disasters of 1813–
14; little public discontent emerged until after the Russian and
German campaigns of 1812–13; and the Italians, like so many
others, finally rose against Napoleon only after foreign arms were
already liberating them.[12]

In contrast, Naples suffered less from Napoleonic rule, partly
because Napoleon expected less from the Neapolitans and perhaps
also because they had fewer expectations about what Napoleon or
any other ruler would do for them. Here there was no pretence,
as in northern Italy, about developing an Italian national spirit.
Naples was treated simply as conquered territory. Joseph Bonaparte and later Joachim Murat wore the Neapolitan Crown as a
kind of second hat, Joseph continuing to be Grand Elector of
the Empire and Murat a marshal and commander of Napoleon's
cavalry. Yet both, especially Joseph, proved more effective in
resisting Napoleon's pressure than most of his other crowned
prefects, and both were fairly popular in Naples, Joseph for his
amiability, Murat for his dash and flair. Most of the typical
Napoleonic reforms (a constitution, centralized authoritarian
government, an end to feudalism) had little concrete impact on
Naples, leaving the nobility great landowners as before, only now
in fee simple, and doing little for the peasant masses. The government was less efficient than the Kingdom of Italy's, mainly due to
established Neapolitan traditions and the fact that neither Joseph
and Murat nor their subordinates, with certain exceptions, were as
industrious and dedicated to governing as Eugène and his public
servants. The Continental System hurt, but widespread smuggling alleviated its impact and the encouragement of the production
of colonial goods in southern Italy gave some artificial stimulus
to agriculture. The most important boon to Naples arose from
Napoleon's contempt for Neapolitans as soldiers; he did not even
try to force Naples to raise an army for his use, only a foreign
legion.[13]

As for the Papal State, because of its special polity it could
neither resist Napoleon nor conform to his Empire nor survive by
letting the flood wash over it, and so it disappeared directly into
France's maw; but French occupation and annexation made little
permanent change. Yet even in Italy the long-range impact of
Napoleonic rule was not all bad. Italians were at least awakened

[12] The chief works are Zaghi (1969; 1986), but see also Connelly (1966: 30–57);
Tarle (1928: 26–47); Rath (1941: 14–26); A. Pingaud (1914: i. 240–63).
[13] Connelly (1966: 68–118).

from their political torpor; authoritarian government, arguably regressive in France, was in some ways progressive here; and French rule taught Italians to think of themselves more as Italians and overcome the municipal spirit—or so it is often claimed.[14]

As already noted, Napoleon's Act of Mediation in Switzerland had beneficial results and was well received. He could not keep up a good act long, however; from 1809 to 1813 Franco-Swiss relations steadily deteriorated over a series of issues connected with Napoleon's wars. Many Swiss sympathized with Austria in the war of 1809. Napoleon, who suspected them of complicity in the Tyrolean rising, violated Swiss neutrality during the war. Following it he formally annexed the Valais, still nominally Swiss though under *de facto* French governance, and occupied the Canton of Ticino, threatening to annex it to the Kingdom of Italy as well. French military and economic pressures on Switzerland continued to grow up to and through the Russian campaign, so that by 1813 the Swiss were ready to be liberated, though not to fight for liberation themselves. Yet even this last phase of alienation between the Swiss and the French contributed to a Swiss multiethnic and federal nationalism.[15]

A similar conclusion applies to two outlying areas of the Empire, Poland and Illyria. Napoleon repeatedly held out to the Poles the prospect of their national resurrection and reunification if they proved themselves worthy of it. In no satellite did he exploit national feeling with more deliberate deception. A French-style administration and the introduction of the *Code Napoléon* in the Duchy of Warsaw provided a façade under which a poor country of 2,300,000 inhabitants, whose best lands were given to French and other Imperial *donataires*, had to support a 30,000-man army and a 30,000-man French occupation force, in addition to the economic burdens of the Continental System. Yet no subject people fought harder for Napoleon while he reigned, or did more to perpetuate his legend after he fell. As for Illyria, Napoleon annexed it to France simply because he had strategic reasons for controlling it and saw no other convenient way to do so. French rule was too short-lived and purely military in character to have

[14] O'Dwyer (1985: 56–115); see also Chadwick (1981); Hales (1961); Reinerman (1979). For the emancipatory effect of Napoleonic rule, see Zaghi (1986: 651–81); Lefebvre (1969: ii. 218–25); Ghisalberti (1979). I find it interesting that this defence of Napoleon, driven by strong anticlerical and anti-papal sentiments, was made already by pre-1815 liberal German publicists; see Altgeld (1984: 18–35).

[15] Pfulg (1961: 97–105); Bonjour (1965: i. 146–55); Oechsli (1898: 8–13); Surrateau (1973: 59–66).

much long-range impact. Yet even here, as more obviously in Poland, Napoleonic rule may have done something to arouse Illyrian and South Slav national feeling.[16]

II. BRITAIN AND THE CONTINENTAL SYSTEM

To assess the impact of the Napoleonic Empire on Continental Europe, it is useful to look at the outlier, Great Britain, and see what happened to it in the course of staving off French domination. The contrast to the Napoleonic pattern of revolution from above could hardly be more striking; British society and politics from 1807 to 1812 remained remarkably normal. The war was a great test of strength and will, but it did not dominate British public life or even deflect its development in a major way. If anything, it contributed to the strength and stability of the central government and conservative forces in general. Its fiscal burdens were enormous: annual national expenditures almost quadrupled between 1792 and 1806, the debt trebled, direct taxes rose fivefold and stamp duties more than seven. Despite the public's confidence in the government's credit and in Pitt's sinking fund, and despite the able management of the treasury by Spencer Perceval, chancellor of the exchequer in the Portland ministry, a serious bullion crisis arose in 1810. As for the British economy, the war did not really advance it but caused serious distortions; the best one can say (which none the less says a great deal) is that Britain coped with the pressures of war and the Continental System in terms of its trade, industry, agriculture, and the cost of living far better than its enemies. Nevertheless, serious industrial unrest (of which more later) arose, especially in the industrial midlands and north, and contributed to a general war-weariness and some rise in peace sentiment. Nor were the burdens of war solely economic and fiscal. The navy, the regular army, and the militia, reorganized and greatly expanded in this period, brought to more than 700,000 the number of British men under arms.

Yet the war, depending on its shifting fortunes, aroused sentiments of dogged determination, resignation, or discouragement more than either clamour for peace or patriotic enthusiasm. War no doubt contributed to the defeat or postponement of internal reforms, though it is doubtful that those most often proposed,

---

[16] Schiemann (1904: i. 100–2); Grochulska (1970a); Lefebvre (1969: ii. 226–9); Markov (1979); C. Black (1942–3).

like Catholic emancipation and the reform of Parliament, would
have gone through in its absence. Only one major reform measure
dates from this period, the abolition of the slave trade in 1807, and
though this was an important move backed by strong religious
and humanitarian concerns and effective political organization, it
also happened to be the one reform which would least disturb
the even tenor of British everyday life. It says volumes for the
stability of British politics that in early 1809, at a critical stage of
the war in Spain and with a new one brewing in Central Europe,
Parliament could for two months be primarily engaged in investigating charges of corruption against the Duke of York and looking
into his relations with his mistress. One can understand Napoleon's
rage and frustration. With all his power, he not only could not
bring the British down, he could not even gain their full attention.
The disadvantages for British foreign policy of Britain's insularity
and preoccupation with domestic politics were clear enough—
tunnel vision, an inability even with goodwill to appreciate the
concerns of others, a failure to understand long-range effects or
systemic consequences in international politics. But the long-run
strengths this insularity gave them in remaining British while
fighting Napoleon may well have been greater.

The British experience of this war contained no real equivalent
of what 1806–7 and 1813 meant for Prussia, or 1809 and 1813–14
for Austria, or 1812 for Russia—a profound national crisis and
learning experience, in which overwhelming danger and humiliation produced a great collective effort followed by ultimate triumph and deliverance. Only two battles stood out in the British
public mind, and neither was decisive for the war's outcome.
Trafalgar helped save England but did not win the war, while
Waterloo won the only war the allies were certain to win in any
case. (This is not at all to downgrade Waterloo; it was vital not for
winning a war which might have otherwise have been lost, but
for something more important—preserving a peace which might
otherwise have been lost.) Patriotic Frenchmen after 1815 had
somehow to remember numerous battles and forget the whole
war; patriotic Britons could cheerfully do just the reverse, remem-
bering the war as a whole and the way the whole of Britain had
waged it.[17]

---

[17] For general overviews, see Emsley (1979: 130–46); D. Gray (1963: 188–
213); Christie (1982: 270–315). For particular arguments on how the war period
strengthened conservatism, see Clark (1985: 199–200); Thomis and Holt (1977);
Colley (1984); Deane (1988); and various essays in Dickinson (1989). On the
abolition of the slave trade, Drescher (1977: 1–25, 162–84); on the disastrous

The Continental System needs special attention in any appraisal of the Empire, being rightly regarded as its keystone and Achilles' heel. Here again a distinction must be drawn between the policy and its aims on the one hand and its immediate and long-range results on the other. There is no question about what the Continental System was: an attempt to bring the whole Continent into economic subjugation to France. The rest of Europe was supposed to supply the markets, the raw materials, and the commercial profits for French industry and goods, on French terms. Not only did Napoleon subordinate all the other goals of the Continental System—the defeat of Britain, the creation of a unified Continental economy, the general promotion of industry and trade—to this aim; whenever these other ends conflicted with the central purposes of French economic colonialism in Europe, they were deliberately sacrificed to it. This was especially the case with the supposed aim of winning the war by destroying Britain's economy, as will later be shown. In the crunch, Napoleon preferred to sustain the British economy and destroy that of his own satellites and allies in Europe for the sake of profits for France.[18]

But when it comes to judging the long-range economic results of the Continental System both overall[19] and in individual countries and regions, the experts reach a verdict both mixed and cautious. This is due not only to the inherent complexity of the question and the difficulty of distinguishing the economic effects of the Continental System from those produced by other factors (the war, secular and conjunctural economic trends, other social and political developments), but because the results themselves are simply unclear in many cases.

Nowhere is the verdict more guarded than in the case of France. The Continental System may have promoted industrialization, above all in key industries such as textiles and metal-working; but it undoubtedly hurt shipping and virtually destroyed overseas trade. It probably hurt agriculture, certainly did not help it. It helped promote the building of roads and waterways, though not enough to meet the enormous load of the transfer of commerce from water to land; at the same time it led to the ruin of harbours and maritime industry. In conjunction with other changes during Napoleon's regime, the Continental System preserved and ad-

failure of reform in Ireland, Jenkins (1988: 46–53, 100–1, 299–304); M. Elliott (1989).

[18] Viennot (1947: 33, 40–1); Lefebvre (1969: ii. 254–61); Roosbroeck (1969).

[19] Milward and Saul (1979: 250–381); Crouzet (1989).

vanced some administrative, juridical, and social changes that cleared the way for economic growth and modernization; but it also promoted others (the French addiction to protectionism, the dependence on artificially controlled markets, a tendency to small-scale production at artificially high prices) which retarded or obstructed it. Some areas of metropolitan France clearly benefited on the whole—Alsace, Belgium, the left bank of the Rhine—while others suffered. To what extent the advance in industrialization in these areas was due to pre-Revolutionary foundations, to the peculiar ability of these areas to benefit from the positive features of the system while avoiding its negative ones (the left bank, for example, won some of the benefits of the high French tariff against foreign goods while retaining much of the earlier trade with the right bank by smuggling), and to the fact that with the territorial changes of 1814 the links in some of these areas to the restrictive French protectionist system were broken, cannot be answered here. The one clear judgement possible is that, however France fared in its economic development in absolute terms, relative to its great rival Britain and in its ability to compete in a burgeoning world economy it lost crucial ground. In the late eighteenth century, the gap between British and French industry and commerce in terms of technology and productivity had not been very great, and was if anything closing. By 1815 it had widened decisively, and would remain open throughout the nineteenth century despite France's recovery and economic growth after 1815.[20]

In the Rheinbund on the other hand, a better case, though still an inconclusive one, can be made for long-range economic benefits from the Continental System. The system itself was highly exploitative. Even areas in Germany and Italy annexed by Napoleon directly to France remained subject to French protectionism, while their own markets were forced open to French goods. No matter how loyal they were, allies like Bavaria and dependencies like Berg succumbed to French economic penetration and control. Napoleon, for example, simply cancelled a trade treaty negotiated between Bavaria and the Kingdom of Italy in

---

[20] The literature on this subject is vast; I have relied on O'Brien (1978: ch. 1; pp. 57–63, 186–95); Price (1975: 93–166); Kemp (1971: 88–104); Crouzet (1964); Bergeron (1970); Bouvier (1970); Imbert (1968); Zaghi (1969: 131–68); Pollard (1981: 40–1, 161); and Viennot (1947: esp. 26–7, 214–33, 278–85). For the left bank and Belgium, see Ellis (1981); Dufraisse (1973; 1978); Bergeron (1973). Additional important works on the British economy are Neal (1991: 180–222); Crouzet (1980; 1989); O'Brien (1988; 1989); Hueckel (1985).

1808. French enforcement of prohibitions against British goods was never very effective except for a brief period in 1810, but the measures France took against these goods grew steadily more draconian and expensive (the army of French customs agents spread throughout Europe grew to 27,000), and included widespread arbitrariness and violence (e.g. forcible seizures of suspect goods and attacks by French corsairs in German waters against ships thought to be carrying such goods). Yet an argument can be made that the system helped promote industrial growth in some regions, notably in the right bank of the Rhine and Saxony, where, of course, the Germans were building on earlier foundations. An even better case can be made that Napoleonic domination served to clear the German stream-bed of economic obstacles just as it did territorially, juridically, and politically. This can be seen particularly in the disappearance of internal customs barriers within states such as Bavaria. The German figures on internal and external trade seem to prove that both kinds of trade grew faster there than in France, despite the Continental System.

Against these gains, of course, there were losses—artificial distortions of trade caused by French protectionism and French violations of other states' commercial sovereignty, the artificial division of some naturally integrated economic regions such as the Rhineland, the heavy burdens laid on some economic sectors such as foreign trade, shipping, and agriculture, the huge costs of war, taxes, and large military establishments, and the price paid by consumers in terms of high prices, shortages of goods, and the growth in military at the expense of civilian consumption.[21] Moreover, even this mildly favourable verdict applies only to part of Germany. In some areas occupied and ultimately annexed by France, notably the Hanseatic cities and Mecklenburg, the economic results were almost wholly negative. Hanseatic trade was badly damaged, Mecklenburg's grain exports were ruined, and their weakened economies were saddled with huge new burdens of occupation, contributions, and confiscations.[22]

The same negative verdict holds even more strongly for Prussia, where, as will be seen, the economic burdens grew constantly worse up to and through the Russian campaign of 1812. Only the relatively short duration of the French exploitation accounts for

[21] For general discussions, see Dufraisse (1984; 1989); Bergeron (1973); Berding (1980); Kutz (1980); Ullmann (1982). For the Palatinate, see Dufraisse (1982); for Bavaria, Dunan (1942: 295–303, 334–50); for Berg, C. Schmidt (1905: 278–9, 320–1, 326–54, 406–11).

[22] Mistler (1973); Patemann (1973).

the fact that the vital springs of Prussian economic life were not permanently damaged—this plus the fact that Prussia had indigenous sources of recovery after liberation.[23] As for Austria, never really a part of the French Empire like the Rheinbund or even like conquered Prussia, it suffered by having its nascent trade through its Adriatic ports first damaged by the system and then cut off by territorial losses in 1809. Areas of early industrialization, especially Bohemia, were affected by French prohibitions and protectionism. But the worst blight on the Austrian economy, which did the most to set back some promising eighteenth-century developments in the western and northern portions of the Empire, was the government's desperate fiscal situation and the crushing taxation that arose with it, and this resulted more from lost wars than from the Continental System.[24]

Italy's economic fate paralleled its political one. Areas most faithful to the Empire, especially Venice as part of the Kingdom of Italy, suffered the most; Naples had to endure much less, the reward of its backwardness. Yet the case can be made that agriculture profited more than industry and commerce suffered during the era.[25] For Holland, Denmark, and the Duchy of Warsaw, the economic results were also very negative for obvious reasons—their dependence on seaborne trade and, in Poland's case, on the export of grain.[26] The worst results of the Continental System, whether they were in it as France's allies or fighting it as France's enemies, were felt by Spain and Portugal, and had repercussions down to the twentieth century.[27]

III. THE NATURE AND FATE OF THE EMPIRE

The fact that most scholars have reached a mixed verdict on the long-range political, social, and economic impacts of Napoleon's Empire on Europe, with some arriving at a favourable one, added to the fact that Napoleon's rule encountered surprisingly little resistance or rebellion until it was overthrown by foreign armies, has encouraged historians to speculate on what the Empire might

---

[23] The standard work is now Münchow-Pohl (1987); but see also Herre (1973: 158–9); Ibbeken (1970: 92–5).

[24] Good (1984: 34–7).

[25] Tacel (1961); Tarle (1928: 48–149, 364–73); Dunan (1942: 350–67); A. Grab (1988).

[26] For Holland, see Schama (1977: 494–524, 561–93); for Denmark, W. Carr (1963: 39–42); and Ruppenthal (1943); for Poland, Grochulska (1970b).

[27] For Spain, Payne (1973: i. 417–23).

have led to had it not been destroyed by certain contingent events, above all military defeat. A number of questions are posed, all more or less directly linked to the central one of the Empire's potential for survival. Could the Continental System ultimately have forced the British to come to terms? What if Napoleon had not invaded Russia, or had won that war, or had evacuated his army before the onset of winter? What if he had concentrated on creating a genuinely integrated Continental economy, instead of one so obviously exploitative in favour of France? What if he had gone to Spain himself to drive out the British? What if (the silliest speculation of all) he had not tied himself to Austria by marrying Marie Louise? And among arguments still occasionally advanced is one that, had the Empire survived and been consolidated, Europe might have been united, avoiding the nationalist enmities which destroyed it in the later nineteenth and twentieth centuries.[28]

This speculation is unhelpful because it tries to use counter-factual reasoning to deduce what might have happened rather than to illuminate what actually did; useless further because the arguments themselves are often circular or involve gaps and inconsistencies. Two examples: the thesis that the Continental System could have brought Britain down cites the various crises and dangers experienced by Britain—economic, social, military, fiscal, naval, even revolutionary—as evidence that Britain was vulnerable and that more consistent pressure or one more real push by Napoleon could have been decisive. This overlooks several major considerations:

(1) These crises and dangers in Britain were not simultaneous and mutually reinforcing, building toward collapse, but mainly discrete and serial. The peak period of one danger seldom coincided with that of others. The economic troubles of 1810 were diminishing by the time social unrest hit its peak in 1811, by which time the war was going better; the military discouragement of 1809 coincided with relative economic prosperity; the danger of internal revolution was largely over by 1798, that of naval mutiny and defeat by 1797, and so on.

(2) What these crises really show is, therefore, not the vulnerability but the remarkable resilience and adaptability of the British system. Britain never came close to succumbing to the downward spiral of mutually reinforcing crises.

---

[28] The most clear-cut argument on this point is that of Connelly (1966: 336–45); see also his remarks in *PCRE* (1972: 336–41). For other arguments along this line, see Dunan (1961: 145–7); Tulard (1973; 1980a); Lefebvre (1969: ii. 252–3).

(3) Most important, for Britain to have accepted terms of peace, Napoleon would have had to propose them, or at least have some terms in mind which were at least conceivably acceptable. This he never did, or could do. The British were certainly at times war-weary enough to consider peace; occasionally they tried to do something about it, at least until 1808. The British mood or willingness to entertain peace, however, could make no difference so long as Napoleon persisted in seeking victory without ever defining concretely, even to himself, what a victorious peace with Britain would mean.

Another example of a counterfactual argument which falls apart on closer inspection, because it not only ignores certain facts and draws dubious inferences but also misses the main point at issue, is the notion that the Continental System, had it attempted in a positive way to create an integrated Continental economy, could have had beneficial effects for European economic development as a whole, perhaps alleviating the problems of depression, industrial and commercial backwardness, and dependence on Britain in the post-war world.[29] There are many individual peculiarities about this line of argument. It tends to conflate as 'benefits' of the Napoleonic system both the growth it directly fostered or encouraged in certain areas and economic sectors and the growth which occurred as the result of the ingenuity of producers and merchants who fought it or evaded it. It assumes the value of a protectionist system and cites the growth of industrial and agricultural production which occurred under its wing, while ignoring the great distortions this system entailed and the inevitable stagnation and depression that would come when protected sectors were exposed to competition, as happened after 1815 (or else it blames these results on the British or the Restoration governments). It argues that Napoleonic expansion created larger internal markets, ignoring all the internal and external markets which that expansion destroyed and the new barriers to trade it continued to create as it expanded.

But all these inconsistencies pale beside a central one. The supposition that the system could have led to a beneficial economic integration of Europe had other circumstances obtained (e.g. had it not been for the war, or had someone other than Napoleon run the system) ignores the central fact about the Continental System:

[29] For various arguments tending in this direction, see Bergeron (1973: 552–6); Dunan (1942: 273–6, 288, 290–5); Viennot (1947: 164–73); C. Schmidt (1905: 418–21); Lefebvre (1969: ii. 215–17).

it was anti-economic from the ground up, in spirit and essence. The ancillary absurdities involve trying to separate the war from the Continental System, when war was always its basic purpose and necessary to promote it; or separating Napoleon from it, when he was the only one who could or did enforce it. The central absurdity is that of ignoring the fact that the Continental System at its heart was a grandiose attempt to force economic behaviour to follow other than economic rules, to defy and destroy the market principle, to conduct economic policy on the same command principle as Napoleon used to conduct politics and war, to make producers march like soldiers and merchants function like bureaucrats. The whole enterprise was impossible, irrational; it could never have worked economically, and the longer it was tried, the worse its results would have been.

This indicates the central flaw in all the speculation as to what might have happened had the Empire endured longer. It rests on the premiss that the Empire could conceivably have endured, that it had a possible future, and that it was aborted or ended only by contingent events. That central assumption is demonstrably false.

It is a natural assumption, given the aversion of most historians to what they call 'determinism' and given the reigning belief that the deep currents of history, powerful and relatively difficult to alter, lie in structures of society, economics, and culture, while war and international politics constitute realms of contingency where almost anything can happen and usually does. But Napoleon's Empire, like much else in history, casts doubt on these suppositions. It is possible, at least conceivable, that deep structures governed the evolution of European domestic politics, society, economics, and culture in this era. If so, we cannot say with confidence what effects Napoleon's Empire had upon them, or judge what its hypothetical long-term survival and institutionalization might have done to them. What we can assert with confidence, simply by analysing the character of the Empire within the framework of European international politics, is that the Empire did not have a possible future. To know its character and to understand the inherent structure and limits of international politics is to see that Napoleon's Empire was over the long term a structural impossibility, and could never have endured and been institutionalized.

Why not? Because it represented a vast experiment in colonialism within Europe. Napoleon's overseas colonial plans and ventures were sporadic and peripheral; his quest for colonies in Continental Europe was constant and central. This is an obvious, even commonplace conclusion. The Empire was founded on a typical colonial basis, military conquest, and maintained by typical colonial means, superior military power, economic subjugation, and direct or indirect administrative control by the metropolis. There was no difference between the spirit and principles by which Napoleon ruled Egypt and those by which he controlled Italy and tried to take over Spain. The economic principles and relationships of the Empire were patently colonialist. Politically, Napoleonic France allowed other states to enjoy various kinds of more or less durable relationship, just as Imperial Rome, for example, did—dependent ally, protectorate, satellite, annexed province—but never the normal European international one of equal juridical status in a system of co-ordinate states. The term 'colonialism' serves equally well to describe and explain other aspects of the Empire, including Napoleon's programme of bringing artistic and national monuments and archival and historic treasures from all over Europe to Paris. When art treasures and historic monuments are brought in one era from Egypt or India to London, and in another from Venice, Rome, or Germany to Paris, the kind of political relationship this presupposes is the same.

Historians have usually labelled Napoleon's attempt to make all of Europe into dependencies of France 'imperialism'. The term is not wrong, but inherently ambiguous, an ambiguity made worse by the long-standing debate over what historic model of imperialism (Alexandrine, Roman, Charlemagne's, Byzantine, or other) Napoleon's Empire most resembled and which one most inspired him. This line of inquiry has proved a cul-de-sac. All the great conquerors of history inspired Napoleon; none gave him a specific model or blueprint, much less any sense of limits.

More important, the term 'imperialism' tends to tame and emasculate the Napoleonic Empire, making it one more instance of a generic phenomenon in European international politics, only somewhat worse than hegemony or domination. It thereby denies or obscures the Empire's specific historical character and the claim of that Empire and of Napoleon to historic uniqueness. In the history of international politics, Napoleon does not really resemble Charles V, Philip II, Louis XIV, William II, Stalin, or other real or supposed aspirants to European empire or hegemony. The only one to whom he can be compared (and the comparison must be made, though not pushed too far) is Adolf Hitler. Each, going far beyond normal imperialist drives for hegemony, domination, or even simple conquest, tried to make Europe, long after it had irrevocably developed into independent states and organized its relationships on that basis, into a collection of colonial dependencies under his own country. Hitler did it for the sake of an unbelievably horrible ideal; Napoleon for no underlying purpose at all.

The serious questions to ask about Napoleon's Empire are not the usual ones, in particular why Napoleon did certain things, like attacking Russia, or failed to do others, like stopping French territorial expansion at the natural frontiers, and so undermined his achievement. For one thing, the answers to such questions are, in the last analysis, easy, and come down to saying that Napoleon did what he did because he was Napoleon. More important, simply to ask why Napoleon failed to stabilize his Empire begs the question, for it assumes that Europe in the early nineteenth century might somehow, through different means and measures, have been made into a collection of stable and durable colonies of France—an assumption contradicted by everything in our knowledge of European international politics and in the actual history and development of the Empire itself.

The question that should be asked, because it rests upon historical facts and points us in the right direction, is rather why the efforts of other European states to get along with the Napoleonic Empire and to achieve normal durable relations with France within the European system always failed. It was not Napoleon who tried to make his Empire durable, to institutionalize it within a European framework; except in a personal and dynastic sense, he was not concerned with this. Other Frenchmen—Talleyrand, Hauterive, Caulaincourt, and others—tried in vain to interest him in it.[30] Even more striking, other European leaders repeatedly tried to make the Napoleonic Empire work within the framework of European international politics. It is not an exaggeration to say that the main policy of most European states from about 1803, and of all of them at certain times, was to find a way of getting along with Napoleonic France on some kind of predictable, stable, *international* basis. That last adjective is the key: international. Russia tried to do this from 1807 to 1812, Austria from 1809 to 1813, Prussia from 1807 to 1812, the Rheinbund states until late in 1813, Spain, Portugal, Italy, Denmark, Sweden, the Pope, Britain at various times—even deposed and exiled leaders like William of

---

[30] See e.g. Botzenhart (1967: 248–9); Driault (1917: 68–9); Lacour-Gayet (1928–30: ii. 162–5); Raumer (1952: 340–1). As Gollwitzer (1964: 128–39) and others have pointed out, it was this fundamentally anti-European aspect of Napoleon's imperial policy which gave his opponents their best ammunition.

Orange.[31] They all failed because there was no way to achieve a stabilization of the Napoleonic Empire within the European international system; because the only relationship allowed by Napoleonic France was colonial dependency. The very notion of Napoleon's Empire as a conceivable, potentially durable form of European international politics, or as leading to one, is a contradiction in terms.

This does not clash at all with the mixed, cautious verdicts of historians on the Empire's long-range impact on Europe in domestic politics, society, economics, and culture; it fits with them and helps explain them. Colonialism, under the right circumstances, can have certain beneficial effects—modernization, technology transfer, injection of capital, a salutary shock to entrenched, unproductive elites and patterns of life, widened horizons, a speeding-up of history—always at a certain cost.[32] Colonial rule has always taken diverse forms, some more benign or less exploitative than others; the different varieties of Napoleonic colonialism help explain its diverse effects in Europe.

All this is, however, neither new nor especially profound; others have pointed out that Napoleon's Empire was colonial in nature. Nor is this fact crucial for explaining what happened during and after the Napoleonic era to Europe in society, culture, domestic politics, and economics. It is important only for understanding what really happened in European international politics, and for recognizing that international politics is also 'real' history, an autonomous, systemic, structural factor in human development, which moulds other forms of human experience as much as it is moulded by them. Napoleon's Empire affected Europe as it did, and ended as it did, principally because what he attempted was impossible in terms of international politics. His failure lay in its structure, not merely in those of domestic politics, warfare, or economic and social life. On purely economic grounds, for example, it would have been possible (though very difficult) for Europe to have developed an integrated Continental economy. The task has, to a considerable degree, been accomplished in recent decades. What was impossible, for structural reasons of international politics, was to construct an integrated Continental economy on the basis of a French colonial empire in Europe. Napoleon could never have made this last and work, any more

---

[31] Demoulin (1938: 21).

[32] For remarks on how Napoleon hastened historical change in Europe, see Zaghi (1969: 11–13); for comments on the dangers of precisely such a speed-up, like the effects of taking benzedrine, see Butterfield (1929: 96–7).

than Hitler or the Soviet Union could, or than the United States could have done after the Second World War had it tried.

Hence, without denying some positive long-term benefits in Europe from Napoleon's Empire, one sees again why these should not be ascribed to Napoleon himself or to the Empire as an institution, or, still worse, the statesmen of 1815 condemned for having crushed or stultified them. The only possible way for any long-range benefits of the Empire to survive was for that Empire first to be overthrown early, before its real fruits were ripe, and then be replaced by a stable international system which permitted independent states, if they chose, to consolidate certain changes from the Revolutionary–Napoleonic era and build on them. This is what the post-Napoleonic generation of statesmen did.

Napoleon's role in this process was a crucial though wholly negative one. He was never in the least degree a potential unifier of Europe, but he proved in the end an extremely effective scourge of God. He finally convinced the statesmen of Europe, hard persons to teach, that what was at risk was not merely certain goods in international politics (peace, security, territorial integrity) but the very life principle of European politics which made these goods and others possible, the independence of European states, the existence of a European states system. He made them see that the kind of politics they had hitherto practised themselves had made his rise to power and his colonial rule possible; that to preserve the international system on which they depended from being wholly destroyed and replaced by colonial rule, they would have not only to defeat or curb him but also to abandon their own old politics, and discover or invent something else.

9
Napoleon's War with His Empire, 1810–1812

L ATE 1809 to mid-1812, like late 1939 to early 1940, was an interlude of *Sitzkrieg*, without new military campaigns or critical developments in those under way. Yet most of the era was tense with expectation of a new collision, this time between France and Russia. Many contemporaries believed, as some historians have argued since, that Napoleon brought on this great conflict because of his other failures and omissions. Had he not neglected the Spanish ulcer but seriously worked at ending it himself, or had he given his Continental System enough time to work, he might have won in the peninsula and even defeated Britain, and thereby kept Russia in line or at least had no reason to fight it. Failing to win these campaigns, or even to make an all-out effort to do so, he tried instead to save his Empire and bring Britain down by conquering Russia.

There is an important insight here: the decision to invade Russia did stem from profound problems in Napoleon's Empire and the way he dealt with them. However, his invasion of Russia was not a direct consequence of his failure to win in Spain or defeat Britain. In the first place, as will be seen, the main reasons he lost the contests in Spain and with Britain were not that he neglected good opportunities for victory. There were deeper organic reasons making the Spanish war very difficult for him to win and the one with Britain impossible. Essentially he lost these campaigns, as he ultimately lost half the campaigns he launched in his career, because he lacked the strategy and resources to win them.

In the second place, an invasion of Russia was never a reasonable or even half-plausible solution for Napoleon's difficulties with Spain, Britain, and his Empire. Virtually all Napoleon's advisers knew this and told him so. Even a successful conquest of Russia (something very difficult to imagine) would not have solved his old difficulties and would have created new ones. A comparison of Napoleon's and Hitler's invasions of Russia may help make this clear. In a sense, as Andreas Hillgruber, Klaus Hildebrand, and other scholars have shown, the strategic situation in which Hitler found himself in 1941 called for an attack on the

Soviet Union and made it a plausible solution for his problems of empire, at least in the short and middle run. His quest for *Lebensraum*, his need for Russian raw materials, the growing economic dependence of Germany on Russia under conditions of peacetime trade, Germany's inability to break British resistance and the likelihood that America would soon enter the war, the prospect that Germany would soon lose its current superiority in modern weapons, and the pace of Soviet industrialization and armaments, all added up to the conclusion that to win the war and secure his Continental empire Hitler needed to destroy the USSR, failing which he would soon face a superior coalition and an unwinnable, two-front war. Moreover, given modern technology and Nazi ruthlessness, Germany could expect to control and exploit European Russia after a victory, at least for a good while, just as it already controlled and exploited the rest of Continental Europe.

None of these reasons for an invasion held for Napoleon. Russia's strength was not growing in relation to that of France; it had no territory France wanted or could use; it did not threaten France's Empire; the New World was no factor; France was not becoming dependent on Russia economically; Russia, though alienated, was not in danger of actively defecting and fighting on Britain's side; Napoleon had already gained all the territory and control in Western and Central Europe that France could use. As for the argument that he had to defeat Russia to save the Continental System and thus bring Britain down, it will not do on several grounds. First, as will be seen, defeating Russia would not have saved the system; second, Napoleon could have better preserved the system and used it against Britain by not attacking Russia; and third, well before the invasion of Russia and quite separately from it, Napoleon himself abandoned the attempt to destroy Britain by economic pressure, at least for the short term.

The connections between Napoleon's problems with Spain, Britain, and his Empire and his decision to invade Russia must therefore be rethought, these developments seen as organic and seamlessly interwoven, of a piece, rather than in terms of cause and effect. The invasion of Russia was not a climactic blunder growing out of earlier, lesser blunders; all were parts of one single overall 'blunder', natural, organic developments in an imperial venture that never went wrong, but always was wrong. In understanding this, one also understands 1810–12 differently. It was not a period of *Sitzkrieg* in which the war, so to speak, hibernated, to awake with new fury in June 1812. Instead, it was a period in which the war was really escalated, not simply or primarily against Spain, Britain, or Russia, but first of all against Napoleon's own Empire. In invading Russia, Napoleon was not, in the last analysis, turning away from his campaigns in Spain and against Britain so much as he was expanding his long-standing war against Continental Europe, his own Empire. This war, already stepped up in 1810–12, naturally evolved into a war against Russia. Just how must be made clear.

I. THE CRISIS IN FRANCE AND THE WAR AGAINST EUROPE

The background to the expanded war against Europe was a fairly serious economic crisis in France which developed in late 1809 and reached its height in 1811, with after-effects lasting into 1812. It affected all major aspects of the economy—commerce, banking, industry, agriculture, and food prices. The exact origins and nature of the crisis, in particular the degree to which it resulted from the war and Napoleon's wartime economic and fiscal policies, or was instead a normal conjunctural crisis produced by a cyclical rise in the price of grain and worsened by speculation and bad weather, must be left to the experts. The same holds for its extent—whether it was general and national or whether, with the French economy still largely localized and regionally quasi-autonomous, only certain areas experienced serious distress while others went largely untouched.

In any case, the price of bread rose more than 50 per cent in two years; many businesses failed; unemployment rose, though unevenly; various industries, particularly the cotton industry, were hard hit; centres such as Paris, Lyons, and the textile-producing areas of Normandy, Picardy, Flanders, and the upper Rhine now shared the long-standing distress of the depressed sea-trading coasts; and visible signs of discontent appeared in the form of popular demonstrations and protests. Napoleon, knowing how important prosperity was for his continued popularity at home and even for the loyalty of his troops and officers, responded with various relief measures, including government loans to business, attempts to control the price of grain especially in Paris, public-works projects, and finally soup kitchens. Yet none of the measures was more than a palliative, and the chronic problem of government finances, in part the result of Napoleon's crude views on public finance and credit, prevented larger ones.

The crisis seemed to reveal grave flaws in Napoleon's economic policies. Even France proved not immune to the hardships of economic war and the Continental System. Attempts to promote French industry and to create substitutes for materials cut off by the British blockade (cotton, sugar, natural dyes, etc.) were shown to be inadequate, able to succeed, if at all, only after much time and investment. The Empire was not headed toward economic collapse, nor did the discontent seriously jeopardize Napoleon's hold on power or force him to strengthen it by more victories abroad. As he boasted, France was still more prosperous and its finances far sounder than the rest of the Continent (though it was not better off than Britain, as he claimed). No important challenge to his rule or even any plausible alternative was in sight; the Bourbon pretender, Louis XVIII, if not forgotten within France, was certainly no serious rival. Conscription, which had been meeting growing resistance, went far more smoothly in 1811, due mainly to the use of flying armed columns to enforce it. The crisis meant simply, as the Tsar's aide-de-camp, Colonel Chernishev, reported from Paris, that the war was coming home to France, and especially to those who had hitherto profited from it. The money and loot which had built the Empire and from which Napoleon and his marshals had profited the most (in boasting of France's wealth Napoleon pointed proudly to the 200 million francs in his private treasury) was running short; the current wars in Spain and at sea drained France's coffers rather than filling them. The solution, since times were hard and war outside the Empire unprofitable, was to find more profits of war within it.[1]

Napoleon's extinction of the Kingdom of Holland in 1810 exemplified this policy. It went by stages; first the annexation of Flessingen, then the bullying of King Louis and the Dutch into a treaty in March by which all of Holland south of the Waal was annexed to France. The rump kingdom was still compelled to support 6,000 French and 12,000 Dutch troops as a French occupation army, maintain and expand the Dutch navy, assume the entire former state debt, and allow all goods pronounced by France to be of English origin to be confiscated or destroyed, including all goods imported on American ships since 1809.

In exchange for these extortions, Napoleon gave the remainder

---

[1] Dufraisse (1978); Thuillier (1983: 107–52); Viennot (1947: 247–75); Tulard (1977: 378–81). On conscription, see Woloch (1986: 123); for Chernishev's reports, including samples of Napoleon's bombast, *Sbornik* (1867–1916: cxxi. 51–4, 60–9, 122–3).

of the Kingdom his permanent guarantee. It lasted four months, until in July Louis abdicated in despair (Napoleon could not decide whether Louis had betrayed him or whether he had had to force his brother out because he was a weakling) and France annexed the remainder of the kingdom. As always, multiple purposes were involved, and as usual Napoleon made his victim his accomplice even while he was preparing it for execution. He forced Louis and his Dutch ministers to appeal to Britain to cancel its Orders in Council as the only way to save Holland from extinction. But his most obvious and prominent motives were colonialist and fiscal—to acquire the Dutch navy on the cheap, get direct control of Dutch revenues and goods, and force the Dutch to contribute even more to his war machine without paying for it. Immediately ordering a great new programme of naval construction, he told his Lieutenant-General, Lebrun, 'The lack of money must not hold up either the armaments or constructions', and answered the Dutch protests conveyed by Lebrun with 'Do these Dutchmen take me for the Grand Pensionary Barneveldt? I will do what suits the good of my empire, and the cries of madmen who think they know better excite nothing but my contempt.'[2]

Further annexations and territorial shifts in 1810–11 hit others among Napoleon's relatives and allies. After the Austrian war he gave Bavaria part of the Austrian loot in Bayreuth, Regensburg, and the Inn Quarter, but since he blamed Bavaria for the Tyrolean insurrection, it had to surrender South Tyrol for eventual disposition to Italy, and to sacrifice 170,000 souls in Germany to other Rheinbund states. With Bavaria he made at least a pretence at negotiation; for most other states (Württemberg, Baden, Würzburg, Nassau, Berg, Westphalia, and a host of other principalities and their rulers) Napoleon simply dictated their new frontiers. In every case he also annulled debts France owed other states for earlier annexations or for the 1809 campaign, protected his feudal donations to his marshals and other servants, and extracted further loot. German internal questions were settled in the same way. He decreed the dissolution of the postal service of Thurn and Taxis, ordered Bavaria to grant the Tyrol a constitution, and demanded a different religious policy in Baden in the same way as he ordered the reconstruction of the Louvre in Paris. No promise could be trusted. Jerome, promised all of Hanover for Westphalia, ended up getting less than half, and this burdened

[2] Schama (1977: 600–10); Connelly (1966: 169–75); Bond (1974); DeClercq (1880–1917: ii. 329–30); Napoleon (1858–70: xx. Nos. 16002, 16133, 16352, 16616, 16620, 16660); the quotation is in ibid. xxi. No. 16947.

with dotations; Eugène de Beauharnais, robbed of his hopes for the Italian kingship by Napoleon's remarriage in 1810, was fobbed off with reversionary rights to a Duchy of Frankfurt which Napoleon created for the Prince Primate, because Regensburg was taken from him to be given to Bavaria.[3]

This was the fate of satellites and loyal supporters; that of the Hansa cities and the adjacent territories of North Germany was, naturally, worse. Occupied since 1806, their trade ruined by the Continental System and their accumulated wealth stripped by French exactions, Hamburg and other cities had shown some sympathy in 1809 for the anti-French North German movements led by Major Schill and the Duke of Brunswick-Oels. It was not this hint of rebellion that doomed them, however, but the failure of French customs controls to stop smuggling, along with Napoleon's growing fears for the safety of the North Sea coast from British raids, especially in the event of war with Russia. In December 1810, therefore, Hamburg, Lübeck, and the territory stretching from Lippe on the lower Rhine to Steckenitz on the Elbe was annexed to France, along with Bremen, Lauenburg, and the Duchy of Oldenburg. The division of these territories into three departments of metropolitan France was more than usually arbitrary and meaningless; the reality of French rule was represented by their union into one military district, the 32nd, with final power resting in the hands of the ruthlessly efficient Marshal Davout.[4]

A similar pattern of action in Italy and Switzerland ended in French annexation of the Valais, the occupation of the Italian cantons and their annexation by the Kingdom of Italy, and further expansion of the Kingdom in South Tyrol, central Italy, and Illyria.[5] None of the territorial changes in the Empire made any pretence of being final, and more were contemplated or bruited— the annexation of Hanover by France, the partition of Prussia in favour of Westphalia and Saxony, the annexation of Spain north of the Ebro. New decrees applied to Naples gave a hint of a Roman-Empire type of citizenship for Frenchmen everywhere, who would enjoy citizenship in any 'independent' state in which they lived without losing it in France.[6]

[3] Connelly (1966: 210–14); DeClercq (1880–1917: ii. 311–13, 315–18, 331–49); Napoleon (1858–70: xx. Nos. 16085, 16118, 16236–8, 16339; xxi. Nos. 17197, 17200, 17220).

[4] Vidalenc (1973); Raumer (1952: 256–7); Napoleon (1858–70: xxi. Nos. 16987–8).

[5] Ibid. xx. Nos. 16263–4, 16711; xxi. 17007, 17093–6, 17240.

[6] Lefebvre (1969: ii. 212–13); Napoleon (1858–70: xxi. 16869, 16875, 16877).

The connection of these measures to the war against Britain was more specious than real, even where they were linked with the Continental System, for, as will be seen, the Continental System itself was ceasing to be a measure of war against Britain. Napoleon continued to predict a coming victory over Britain at sea and to try to force others into naval programmes to win it. Perhaps in some sense he still believed in this himself; he had played with dreams so long on this score that they were now playing with him. But even as propaganda his maritime boasts and promises became ever more hollow, like his pledge to build a Baltic–Rhine canal in order to justify his annexations in northern Germany. His main military purpose in these annexations and other territorial changes was defensive, to make Europe a French fortress secure against British raids and internal revolt. Even here the usual fiscal motive was unmistakeable, to force Europe rather than France to pay for these efforts and to keep the Imperial Army quartered on Germany.[7]

Yet the Empire was not a powder-keg ready to explode under Napoleonic oppression, nor did Napoleon have to seek new military laurels and booty abroad to prevent his regime from being undermined within. Napoleon's despotic rule over captive Europe, with every exploitative French step accompanied by a drumbeat of anti-British propaganda,[8] affected the future peace more than the current war, by undermining France's natural hegemony in Western Europe and helping pave the way for Britain's throughout the nineteenth century. As late as 1805 or 1807, Europeans had little reason to believe British propaganda more than French, and not many were inclined to; by 1812 Napoleon had made it unmistakably clear who was the greater threat to Europe's independence. Even staunch allies like the Kings of Bavaria and Württemberg became disillusioned with the Empire, as its political and economic results turned harmful also in regions which it earlier had benefited. Yet this brought no rise in resistance, much less revolt; areas suffering the most, like the Hanseatic cities, reacted with resigned lassitude.[9] The Empire was a manifest

[7] For examples of Napoleon's persistence in naval plans, see ibid. xx. Nos. 16490, 16643, 16663; xxi. Nos. 17434–5, 17452. The evidence of his 'Fortress Europe' preparations in 1810–11 is scattered throughout vol. xxi.

[8] For samples of Napoleon's orders for anti-British propaganda, see ibid. Nos. 17012–16; for Gentz's legal-historical replies, see Nesselrode (1904–12: iv. 143–87, 223–86).

[9] For various German states, see C. Schmidt (1905: 126–9, 363–417); Dunan (1942: 269–71); Weis (1990: 176–8); Schlossberger (1889: 225–45); Jürgens (1976: 204–6); Chroust (1932: 328–30); Pedlow (1988: 85–6). For Holland, see Schama (1977: 611–22); for Naples, Connelly (1966: 118–26).

failure, going nowhere, incapable of development other than senseless, arbitrary expansion, but in no danger of collapse.

Something similar is true of the Continental System, but here the direct connection with the war against Britain seems undeniable. Without doubt Napoleon still wanted to bring Britain down, committed by a passion personal and Corsican more than political and French—hatred of the only rival which had successfully defied him. Moreover, the Continental System apparently enjoyed its best chance ever for success in 1810–11, due to a combination of three main factors: economic and social developments in Britain to be described later; a series of French actions enforcing the system (crack-downs on smuggling following the annexations in Holland and North Germany, pressure on Sweden and Austria to conform more rigorously to it, stronger enforcement in Denmark, the activity of French corsairs in the North Sea and Baltic, confiscations and burning of alleged British goods on the Continent); and the closing of the American market by the Non-Intercourse Act of 1810.

Yet just at this time Napoleon, following a series of earlier measures, issued the Trianon Decree of 5 August 1810, inaugurating a system of government licences to French merchants for trade with Britain. It provided that grain, wine, spirits, and silks would go to Britain in French ships and that British colonial goods (not manufactures) would be brought back, with steep French duties collected for the treasury and with French merchants profiting from the sale of some of these goods to Europe at maximum prices.

It is barely possible to interpret this move, together with the Edict of Fontainebleau two months later decreeing the burning of all British goods on the Continent, as only a temporary modification of the economic war against Britain, intended to combat smuggling, raise revenue, meet France's current economic and fiscal troubles, especially the shortage of raw materials for industry, and drain Britain of specie to pay for grain and other imports. Napoleon's trade policy was never consistent, especially in this period. But the evidence points mainly in a different direction: that Napoleon was tacitly abandoning the alleged central purpose of the Continental System, to destroy Britain's economy by excluding British commerce and goods from Europe, and entering instead into a secret partnership which would allow Britain to supply France and, through France, the Continent with goods, in order that the huge profits of this trade might go to French producers, merchants, shippers, and above all the French treasury, at the expense of France's European colonies. The further development and enforcement of the licensing system fits this interpretation; so does Napoleon's stated policy of destroying industries in other lands (Italian and Swiss textiles, for example) for the benefit of France's; his admission, like that of the author of the scheme, the French minister of commerce, Jean-Pierre Montalivet, that it would benefit Britain but profit France even more; Napoleon's boasting of the revenues the sale of licences brought into the treasury; and his decision secretly to allow British goods into the Continent via Holstein and Hamburg provided the profits for the treasury were high enough.

Clearest of all is a note he dictated to the council of commerce and manufactures in January 1812, in which he proclaimed a further extension and formalizing of this arrangement as marking the final goal and triumph of the Continental System. His new idea was to allow Britain to ship colonial goods anywhere to the Continent under French licences and French tariffs, which would be enforced uniformly throughout the Empire, with satellites like Italy, the Rheinbund states, and even Austria allowed a French-assigned quota of the imports, provided these states drove up the price of these imports by imposing the same tariff as France, stamped out smuggling, and paid a major portion of their customs revenues (two-thirds for the German states, one-third for Austria) into the French treasury. Napoleon specifically conceded here that France's needs for goods supplied by Britain could no longer be met by smuggling and confiscations of contraband, and that the trade would also benefit Britain. He argued, however, that French profits would be three times as great, and that the great boost this would give to France's Continental industry and commerce would eventually force Britain to accept France's economic superiority. Naturally he expected other European governments willingly to join him in exploiting their own peoples for their share of the customs revenues. If they refused, he always had the option of further annexations.[10]

This shows that all the arguments that the Continental System might, if stringently applied, have brought Britain down in the long run, and that Britain was rescued by Napoleon's defeat in Russia, are unhistorical. The question of which power could withstand all-out economic warfare longer, France or Britain, was

---

[10] Crouzet (1958: ii. 591–607); C. Schmidt (1905: 358–9); Roosbroeck (1969: 132–7); Napoleon (1858–70: xxi. Nos. 16810, 16824, 16930, 16984; xxiii. No. 18431).

settled well before the invasion of Russia; France broke off the contest first. Any further arguments that the Continental System could have been made sufficiently watertight to bring Britain to terms, or speculations of what might have happened had Napoleon won in Russia, are equally unhistorical, also clearly answered by events. As will be seen, the attempt to make the Continental System watertight proved impossible and self-defeating, forcing Russia to break with it and helping bring on a war Napoleon never had a chance to win in any meaningful sense. As for speculating about how the Empire might have developed had Napoleon managed to bring Britain and/or Russia to terms, this requires, besides the primary counter-factual assumptions, two additional unhistorical ones: first, that the Empire had a possible future, lines of development open to it had these contests somehow turned out differently, and second, that the phrase, 'bringing Britain and Russia to terms' is meaningful, that Napoleon had some kind of reasonable terms to offer them, places and roles for Russia and Britain to play within his Imperial world after a French military victory. No assumptions could be more gratuitous.

One counter-factual question, however, does make sense in the light of the actual developments of 1810–12. Could France have stopped in 1810 or 1811? That is, could France, given other leadership than Napoleon's or some miraculous change in Napoleon, have tacitly given up trying to destroy Britain by direct economic warfare (as Napoleon actually did), and have silently accepted Russia's defection from the Continental System (which he may briefly have contemplated), and still have maintained the Empire in Europe for an indefinite period? The answer is 'Yes'. The Empire would not have developed into something different and better, would have remained an exploitative colonialist system, but it would not soon have crumbled from within.[11]

Napoleon's dealings with Austria show how much room he still had to manipulate and consolidate his Empire. Metternich is sometimes seen as an implacable enemy of the Revolution and Napoleon, forced for the moment to lie low and feign friendship with Napoleon to survive, but always looking for the chance to restore the European balance and regain Austria's independence. This is Metternich's propaganda; no one excelled him at disguising his uncertainties, concealing his purposes, and covering his tracks. He hated the Revolution, to be sure—and genuinely admired

---

[11] Crouzet (1958: ii. 830–42, 854–61); Tulard (1977: 382–3).

Napoleon for conquering it. Besides, he knew how to separate Austria's interests and the realities of international politics from his horror of revolution. As he and Francis understood well, *war* above all was revolution; the great threat to Austria and its monarchic-aristocratic principles at the present moment was not Jacobin doctrine, but further war and defeat. Metternich's central premiss was, therefore, that Austria's armed struggle against France was over. For the foreseeable future Austria had to survive under France's shadow, exploiting Austria's strategic position to convince France that Austria was its indispensable ally.

In other words (though Metternich would never say so), Austria aspired to be a bigger and better Bavaria, becoming for France the ally *vis-à-vis* Russia which Bavaria had been *vis-à-vis* Austria. Metternich had no illusions as to Napoleon's character or that of his Empire, and only faint hopes of changing either. None the less, fearing Russian expansion and/or an exclusive Franco-Russian partnership as much as he feared French expansion or even more, he sought an alliance with France, not in order to break up the Russo-French alliance or cause them to fight (this would endanger Austria even more), but to join their partnership and influence it, which Austria could only do as France's ally.

Metternich's first chance to try this arose when Napoleon divorced Empress Josephine and Alexander thwarted his marriage to Grand Duchess Anne, as Napoleon would have preferred. Metternich stepped in eagerly, promoting Napoleon's marriage to Francis's daughter Marie Louise in 1810. He and Francis knew that she would be a hostage in Napoleon's hands, but hoped that a French alliance and possible territorial, fiscal, and prestige advantages would accrue to Austria from it. As usual, Napoleon took what was offered and gave nothing in return. A long visit to Paris after the wedding convinced Metternich that Napoleon intended to use the new family tie to control Austria, and that no French guarantees were any good. None the less, in his report to the Emperor in January 1811 on the coming Franco-Russian war, Metternich insisted that, while no good policy was available to Austria, it could not remain neutral if war broke out but must enter it on France's side, selling a minimal Austrian participation in it for the highest possible price.

Equally significant was Metternich's reaction to Napoleon's repeated hints that he would return Illyria to Austria in exchange for Galicia. Austria did not want to see territorial changes and annexations anywhere, especially in Eastern Europe and the Near East; above all, it needed time and peace for recovery (it had gone into state bankruptcy in February 1811). Metternich told Francis, however, that if Austria were compelled to choose between Galicia and Illyria, especially if it had to fight as France's ally in war against Russia, Austria must not merely accept the exchange but insist upon it. Trade and state revenues figured in his argument, but the central reasons were political and strategic—the same ones, in fact, that had made Stadion in 1808–9 draw the opposite conclusion, that Austria must fight France rather than accept this exchange. Austria in ceding Galicia would surrender its last stake in the Polish question, turning the contest in East Central Europe entirely over to France and Russia, with Austria passively supporting France. At the same time, in accepting Illyria Austria would become an active partner, almost a cat's-paw, for France in its confrontation with Russia in the Near East. Metternich knew this. Like Counts Beust and Andrássy after the Franco-Prussian war in 1871, Metternich decided in 1810–11 to accept defeat, surrender Austria's historic roles in Central Europe, and seek a Western alliance against Russia in order to defend Austria's Near Eastern interests.[12]

The Serbian revolt and the Russo-Turkish war played into this policy, heightening Austria's fears about its south-eastern frontier. Some Austrians, especially certain military leaders (Archduke Carl, General Simbschen, and a rising star, General Joseph Radetzky) were tempted by the Serbs' appeals to Austria for help and their requests to be taken into the Habsburg Empire. The government, however, firmly rejected this idea, as well as that of a partition of the Ottoman Empire, urging the Serbs to submit themselves to the Porte in exchange for an Austrian guarantee of their privileges. Austria took a similar stance toward the Russo-Turkish war, repeatedly urging peace on both sides; its advice helped produce a Turkish peace feeler to Russia in 1810. Many reasons motivated this pacific caution: Francis's horror of any rebellion, and especially of the effects of a Serbian revolt on the monarchy's South Slavs; Hungarian fears of Serb nationalism; the desire to preserve the Ottoman Empire as a buffer against a dominant France and an encircling Russia; simple war-weariness and the desire for peace, order, and trade along the Danube. France and Russia were both trying to use Austria, as Metternich knew, but Russia remained the more immediate threat. Hence Austria flatly rejected Russia's

---

[12] Lefebvre (1969: ii. 72–7); Wohlfeil (1965: 179–80); Kraehe (1963: 119–41); Luckwaldt (1898: 4–36); Metternich (1880–4: ii. 367–90, 405–26). The best Metternich biography is Bertier (1986); for this period, see chs. 8–9.

alliance offer in mid-1810 and refused to recognize Russia's annexation of the Principalities, though Napoleon had endorsed it. He even urged that Austria fight Russia if the latter tried to take more Turkish territory south of the Danube, and insisted that if a Russo-French partition of the Ottoman Empire became inevitable, Austria must join them for its share.[13]

Thus Napoleon easily gained the alliance of the one European state besides Russia which still had some independent choice. Prussia enjoyed none; it was a caged beast tormented by its captor. Denouncing the attitude Prussia had shown in the war of 1809, Napoleon demanded that the fortress of Glogau and part of Silesia be ceded to him as payment for arrears of contributions, and, using the fate of the Hansa towns as an example, compelled Prussia to enforce the Continental System even after France had abandoned it for itself. The only way one could recognize that Prussia had once been considered a great power was that Napoleon threatened Prussia with war rather than simple annexation like Mecklenburg. He ordered Davout to prepare for a preventive war, dared the Prussians to try an alliance with Russia, and warned the Russians not even to protest against anything he did. Long before Napoleon made Prussia into his main staging area for the assault on Russia, he treated it as entirely at his disposal.[14]

Prussia is often pictured as responding by a reform movement out of which the War of Liberation eventually emerged; historians ever since have debated the nature of the reforms and their significance for Prussia's and Germany's future, domestic and international. Once again this approach may be valuable for Prussian, German, and European history generally, but for international history it leads us astray. The reform movement certainly was intended to help Prussia survive and recover its independence. Survival and independence, however, could be found in either of two ways: by procuring Prussia a decent place within a French-dominated Europe, or by liberating Prussia and central Europe by armed force. Prussia considered and tried both possibilities, mainly the former. One has to say not merely that its efforts failed, but that by 1812 Prussia had given up both without fighting.

The reform programme Prince Hardenberg developed in 1810–

[13] Vucinich (1982a: 141–51); Turczynski (1982: 175–95); Petrovich (1976: i. 58, 66–8); Metternich (1880–4: ii. Nos. 168–70, 173, 176). For Napoleon's attempts to force Austria to confront Russia in the Balkans, see Napoleon (1858–70: xxi. Nos. 17388, 17518).

[14] Ibid. xx. Nos. 16212, 16242, 16479; xxi. Nos. 17062, 17517; xxii. No. 18241; xxiii. Nos. 18259–60.

11 included various elements: bureaucratic centralization, economic liberalism (moves toward greater equality of taxation, freedom of occupation, and the reduction of feudal privileges and restrictions on economic activity), a limited representative constitution to promote state patriotism and active citizenship, and the attempt to create an independent peasantry without destroying the noble landowning class. It can be argued that the programme as executed did something to strengthen, modernize, and to a limited degree liberalize Prussia, and that it might, if carried through fully, have forged new bonds between the throne, the government, and the people. It could also be argued that the programme was pushed so feebly by Hardenberg and so emasculated by its conservative opponents within and outside the court that it did little more than substitute bureaucratic for royal absolutism. But whatever its potential results for Prussia in the long term, it did not and could not promote Prussia's revival as an independent state, because Napoleon would not let it.

In the crucial area of economics and state finance, for example, the Prussian government depended upon smuggling and secretly encouraged it as a way to revive commerce and manufactures, get vital raw materials, and secure revenues. This clashed with Napoleon's determination to stamp out smuggling and extract every ounce of surplus from what Prussian economic activity still went on. The military reformers (Scharnhorst, Gneisenau, Boyen, Clausewitz, Blücher, and others) developed plans to expand the army, train a militia, and promote popular insurrection against the French. Their ideas and measures, however, were not only expensive, highly controversial among military experts, and considered by many, including the King, a revolutionary danger to the throne, but above all unrealistic, given France's crushing military superiority, its occupation of much of Prussia, and Prussia's lack of allies.

An exchange in August 1811 between the King and the most ardent military reformer, Gneisenau, over the latter's plan for waging an insurrectionary war at Russia's side illustrates the fatal dilemma. To Gneisenau's contention that the people's love of its King and country and its hatred of the foreign oppressor would make a popular militia effective even against a trained foe, the king noted 'Good as poetry'. Gneisenau responded eloquently that no great things were possible in politics without poetry, that everything depended finally on unseen but deeply felt ties between a people and its state and sovereign, and that the security of the throne itself rested on poetry. Both were right—Gneisenau on the fundamental moral and emotional bases of politics, the king on the military and political facts of the Napoleonic Empire. Moreover, the overriding need to liberate Prussia from foreign oppression, far from establishing the case for radical reforms, could just as well enable conservatives like Count von der Marwitz to argue that Prussia had to rely for salvation on its traditional social order and existing loyalties to king, God, and country.[15]

In any case, the policy Prussia actually followed was not to prepare to rise against France at the first opportunity, but to make itself an attractive ally, thereby securing more tolerable conditions under French leadership. This was the initial policy of every ministry from 1807—first Stein, then Dohna–Altenstein, and now Hardenberg. Count Dohna had even proposed ceding parts of Silesia to Napoleon as the price for a genuine alliance. The King, refusing to go this far, then summoned Hardenberg to office, who offered France an alliance in exchange for improved terms on contributions and the occupation. Despite the fact that Napoleon ignored this, maintained his demands on Prussia, and proceeded with his annexations and military build-up in North Germany, Hardenberg renewed the offer in May 1811, and this time met flat rejection.

It was not mainly this rejection, but Napoleon's expansion of his Army of Germany under Davout that temporarily drove the King and Hardenberg into partnership with the military party. In the summer and autumn of 1811, plans and preparations went forward for enlarging the Prussian army, strengthening the fortifications and strong points still in Prussian hands, and reaching agreements with Russia and England. The reformers' hopes for victory rested on maintaining a popular resistance movement in Prussia while the Russian and Prussian armies fought Napoleon in Poland. Meanwhile a people's war like Spain's, aided by British arms, gold, and men, would be waged behind the French lines in North Germany. In the end both Hardenberg and the King backed away from this, partly because of Napoleon's threats and demands that Prussia disarm, mainly because even if (a big if) a new allied coalition was formed and finally defeated Napoleon, long before this happened Prussia would be destroyed. The military convention for Russo-Prussian military co-operation concluded by General Scharnhorst's mission at St Petersburg in

[15] The best discussion is in Münchow-Pohl (1987: 171–227, 322–7); but see also Simon (1955: ch. 5; pp. 105–13); Rosenberg (1968: 202–28); Ibbeken (1970: 230–47, 278–81) (for the Gneisenau–Frederick William exchange, see 238–9); Thielen (1967: 264–77); Sweet (1978: ii. 107–22).

October made it clear that Russia expected Prussia initially to be overrun; the two armies were only to join forces when France reached the Vistula. Contacts with the British demonstrated that, while they were eager to support an uprising, what they could do was strictly limited. Scharnhorst followed up his Russian mission with one to Vienna, but was turned away with polite correctness by Metternich, who advised the Prussians to look to Russia but would give no promises on what Austria would do. Secretly Metternich considered Prussia doomed, and had made up his mind to join France.

The King and his advisers, timid and irresolute, fearful of the war party's revolutionary methods and realistic about the political and military possibilities of resistance, decided under Napoleon's threats first to stop arming and then to conclude a humiliating offensive alliance treaty on 24 February 1812. In it, Napoleon forced Prussia to join in his planned attack on Russia and, still worse, to bear the main burdens of quartering and supplying the Grand Army being readied for the invasion. The war party scattered into exile or went underground. Their policy was heroic but impossible. The prolonged national resistance Gneisenau envisioned required not merely a people more inspired and adapted to it than the Prussians, a terrain different from North Germany, and allies other than Russia and Britain. Even more, it required an enemy with some long-range goals he would be unwilling to destroy for the sake of immediate victory and power; one with some concern for the future, some sense of political and moral limits, and some willingness to stay within them. In short, Prussia needed a different enemy from Napoleon. Since no Prussian policy could have worked, Prussia's decision to enter into a servile alliance with Napoleon was the correct choice, because it was a delayed, slower form of death.[16]

Yet Napoleon's success in extorting what he wanted from Prussia and Austria for almost nothing represented only his usual victories of empty technique and power. How might he have dealt with Austria and Prussia had somehow no war broken out with Russia? We do not know, because Napoleon did not know. They were too big to be comfortable Bavarias, and too remote from France and too rooted in their own state traditions to be easily annexed. If partitioned, they would have had somehow

---

[16] Münchow-Pohl (1987: 316–21, 327–51); Ibbeken (1970: 343–5); Kraehe (1963: 140–2); DeClercq (1880–1917: ii. 354–63). For Napoleon's exploitation of the treaty, see Napoleon (1858–70: xxiii. Nos. 18648, 18661–4, 18728).

to be shared with Russia, making the problems of Franco-Russian coexistence even worse. He bullied them into subservience basically because he did not know anything better to do—essentially the same reason for which he would attack Russia.

II. BRITAIN'S SURVIVAL

Napoleon's conquests within his Empire did not substitute for victory over Britain, and did not bring that victory closer. It has seemed to some that in 1810–12 France was within sight of victory, only to let Britain off the ropes. In reality, France broke off the contest, while Britain, though under serious strain, once again survived, maintained its national life, and even in certain respects grew stronger.

On the surface and at the time, the situation looked grave. A series of intersecting crises seemed to shake the British economy, government, and social order, threatening to paralyse the war effort. Bad harvests in 1808 and 1809 led to a steep rise in the price of grain and serious shortages of food, bringing food riots in 1810 and 1811. Maintaining Wellington's army and supporting the Portuguese and Spanish resistance in the peninsula demanded huge amounts of bullion, acquired only with increasing difficulty in Latin America and elsewhere. This led to specie shortages in Britain, the depreciation of the paper currency, and some flight of capital abroad. More serious were the blows to trade involved in Napoleon's drastic measures against smuggling and the hoarding of British goods on the Continent. These, combined with the American government's Non-Intercourse Act and the saturation of the Latin American market, caught British merchants with large stocks of costly imports and manufactured goods in surplus, leading to a fall in prices, a series of banking and commercial failures, and a general industrial depression in 1810–11, not really surmounted until late 1812 and 1813. Widespread unemployment, especially in the industrial midlands and north, contributed to the suffering and helped produce in 1811–12 the most serious social unrest in England for a generation, the Luddite movement and attendant riots in Nottinghamshire, Yorkshire, and Lancashire. Small wonder that some contemporaries feared a revolution, or that some historians have argued that had Napoleon not sold grain to Britain in 1810 and 1811, or not opened the licensing trade in colonial goods, or not invaded Russia, the British could not have continued the war.

Yet the story is really one of how Britain successfully rode out the storm. None of the crises, singly or in combination, was serious enough to paralyse it or force it to end the war. The grain shortage was less severe than in 1800–1; even without French imports, Britain would not have faced famine. Food riots were not unusual in the late eighteenth and early nineteenth centuries. The shortage of bullion never seriously undermined confidence in the currency. Even the industrial crisis was a normal cyclical phenomenon, made in Britain, though worsened by the war. Moreover, Britain's troubles were rolling and successive more than cumulative; there was always some sign of recovery to counter those of crisis or decline. The worst dissatisfaction with the war effort came in late 1809 and early 1810; by 1811–12, at the height of social unrest, the war was going so much better in the peninsula that Whigs who had earlier condemned it were criticizing the government for not supporting Wellington sufficiently. The worst declines in trade and industry came before the worst social unrest; better harvests in 1811 and especially in 1812 alleviated somewhat the discontent caused by higher unemployment. Some limited gains in Baltic trade in 1811 cushioned the blow of the Non-Intercourse Act, which Americans widely evaded in any case, and Russia's break with the Continental System at the end of 1810, though it did nothing concrete for British trade, brought at least a psychological boost. Even in industry the crisis was not simultaneous, but hit various industries worst at different times, with corresponding different periods of recovery.

The most that one can say is that there was a perceived crisis, possibly the preconditions for a potential revolution, but none of the forces necessary to make it reality, and no revolutionary movement which tried to do so. There was no union between the middle class and workers for radical change; no general breakdown of the economy; no crushing military defeat; no fiscal crisis; no rebellion in the armed forces; no panic or loss of confidence in the ruling élite; no widespread alienation from the country's institutions. Even Luddism was a protest movement rather than one for revolution, directed more against men than machines (manufacturers of fraudulent goods, those who undercut wages with women and child labour). Criticisms of the government were directed against men and policies rather than institutions (taxes, parliamentary corruption, and especially the Orders in Council). As for the war, it was probably an integrating, anti-revolutionary factor rather than the reverse. George III as a symbol of British resistance was now far more popular than he had been earlier in his reign; criticism of the conduct of the war was fairly wide-spread, depending on its course, but total denunciation of it, like wild enthusiasm for it, existed only on the fringes.[17]

The course of British politics demonstrates this essential stability. In the last analysis, a slide into revolution or an acceptance of defeat in war are political phenomena. British political life at the national level showed no sign of either; it was fairly turbulent, but astonishingly normal. There were cabinet and parliamentary crises aplenty, over the death of Portland and formation of the Perceval ministry in 1809, the parliamentary inquiry into Walcheren, the king's madness and resultant regency crisis in late 1810, the Marquis of Wellesley's attempt to gain the premiership in January 1812, and Perceval's assassination in May and the efforts to form the succeeding Liverpool ministry. All were managed by normal political means. The Perceval cabinet, apparently distinguished by its lack of talent, turned out to be more effective than expected. Perceval proved a sound financier whose budgets increased the national debt less than at any other period during the war, and Castlereagh an efficient Secretary of War.[18]

The same unspectacular steadiness characterized the war effort. Quite apart from the main theatre, Spain (to be discussed later), solid successes were gained in the war at sea and in the East. French cruisers continued to plague commerce, but represented no major danger. The capture of Bourbon and Mauritius in the Indian Ocean in 1810 scotched a persistent nest of raiders, and the capture of Java in 1811 effectively ended the colonial-maritime war in the East. Alarms (largely illusory and promoted by men on the spot) were raised over India and the north-west frontier in 1807–8 as a result of the French–Russian and French–Persian alliances, but the British effectively consolidated their territorial control, and whatever damage had been done to Anglo-Persian relations in 1807 was made good by a treaty of alliance in 1812.[19] The war in the Mediterranean was a steady drain on limited British resources, so that they could never do things they wanted or hoped to do from their base in Sicily (e.g. support Wellington with an expedition in Catalonia, or start an insurrectionary war in Italy, or even keep control of the upper Adriatic). Moreover, dealing with the lazy and cowardly King Ferdinand and his terma-

---

[17] Crouzet (1958: ii. 540–808); Emsley (1979: 150–3, 158–61); Gille (1965: i. 46–8); Olson (1963: 60–72); Ziegler (1965: 308–15); Best (1982: 140–3).

[18] Gray (1963: 274–7, 340–454); Ziegler (1965: 284–307); Emsley (1979: 148–9).

[19] Parkinson (1954: 274–8, 300–19, 375–420); Yapp (1980: 40–95); Ingram (1979: 20–9); Alder (1972: 36–44).

gant Queen Maria Carolina was not easy, and not made easier by the British commander Lord William Bentinck's tendency to let his Whig principles get the better of his tact and judgement. But the British held onto the island, throwing back Murat's forces with heavy loss in the one French attempt to invade in September 1810, and by controlling the Mediterranean the British damaged French trade and communications while preserving routes vital to Britain.[20]

As for Britain's policy toward the Continent, effectively it had none and could develop none. The one serious initiative was Robert Adair's mission to Constantinople in 1809–10, to promote peace between Russia and Turkey, and indirectly to promote peace between Britain and Russia. Only its negative aims, to keep Turkey from falling into French–Austrian hands and breaking with Britain, succeeded. The Marquis of Wellesley's private correspondence with his diplomats shows much concern with Spain and some attention to Sicily, the United States, Spanish America, the Indian Ocean, and the possibility of insurrections somewhere in Europe, but that was all. The British, though eager enough for openings on the Continent, could find none and, to a degree, ceased to hope for them.[21]

In contrast to earlier periods, there were no peace talks or feelers between France and Britain at this time. Napoleon not only could not force Britain to the peace table, but having discarded and discredited every concept or basis for peace on which they might conceivably have agreed, had no peace table to bring Britain to. The British knew this and accepted it. Less obvious but more important is the change in Britain's response to Napoleon's success in conquering the Continent, sealing it off, and denying Britain allies. Previously Britain had responded in three ways: by trying for a separate peace with France, attempting to lure or force Continental states into a new coalition, and pursuing maritime and colonial conquests as a way of making its war effort pay. Now it abandoned the first strategy, put the second on hold, and pursued the third with only a minimum of effort and interest. There is a sharp contrast between Britain's often ardent quest for colonial and maritime conquests in the first three coalitions and the relative indifference that greeted its conquests of Java or the Seychelles in 1810–12. Now the British carried on the war as if

---

[20] Mackesy (1957: 219–27, 367–74); Rosselli (1956: 14–17, 23–43).

[21] Adair (1845: i. 258–352; ii. 10–24, 35–45, 72–86). Wellesley's private correspondence is in BL Add. MS 37292.

they had no other choice—which was true. Their leaders had
learned, or were learning, important lessons as to what would
not win the war or make victory worthwhile, and these were
necessary preludes to discovering what would.

III. FRANCE'S BREAK WITH RUSSIA

As everyone knows, the heading could read 'Russia's Break with
France'. On 31 December 1810, Alexander issued a decree (*ukaz*)
taking Russia out of the Continental System. This formalized the
breach in their alliance and led ultimately to war. The decree and
the dispute over the Continental System, however, were only the
formal cause of alienation and conflict. The real roots lay in their
clash over Poland, and here France broke with Russia.

It is risky, to be sure, to designate any one root cause for a
collision with so many causes, all intertwined and interacting: the
Continental System and the diverse questions connected with it,
Near Eastern rivalry, Russia's complaints about France's treatment of Prussia, its fears of a French alliance with Austria, the
failure of Napoleon's suit for a Russian princess and his marriage
to an Austrian archduchess, mutual dissatisfaction with each
other's conduct in the Austrian and Swedish wars, Napoleon's
consent to Marshal Bernadotte's election as heir to the Swedish
throne, Napoleon's moves and annexations in Europe, above all
in Northern Germany, Russia's continued use of *émigrés* in its state
service and Napoleon's enlistment and use of Poles in his Grand
Army, Napoleon's special insult and challenge to Alexander in annexing Oldenburg—the list extends almost indefinitely. Domestic
politics, factional struggles, and economic developments within
both countries, especially Russia, were clearly part of the picture.
It is tempting either to term the collision inevitable, the result of a
host of quarrels creating intolerable insecurity and distrust on
both sides, or, going a little further, to explain it in general by
the inherent expansionism of Napoleon's empire and the typical
inability of two hegemonic powers to remain stable partners and
divide their spheres of influence amicably.

But these answers, though sound enough, give up too easily,
stopping with a penultimate answer. Had one central issue been
settled, as it could have been and nearly was, the clash would have
been postponed for some time; as it was, this issue, exacerbated
over time, made war unavoidable. The issue, as the Marquis de
Caulaincourt, France's ambassador to Russia from 1809 to early

1811, repeatedly said, was Poland. Caulaincourt was perhaps the ablest foreign-policy adviser Napoleon ever had, and clearly the ablest honest and loyal one; he was in the best position to know; and what happened bears him out.

The end of the wars of 1809, with their final success for both French and Russian arms, seemed temporarily to restore the popularity of the French alliance within Russia and to improve Russo-French relations. Napoleon made some conciliatory gestures toward Russia, including an assurance to the Russian ambassador Kurakin that Poland would not be restored. But this was temporary and superficial. Napoleon had armed the Poles under Prince Poniatowski and used them against Austria. The fears this raised in Russia grew when France during the peace negotiations initially demanded that Austria cede all of Galicia to the Duchy of Warsaw; and the terms of the peace, which gave 1,500,000 additional souls to the Duchy and only 400,000 to Russia, turned these fears into a concrete grievance. The Russians did not complain that the Treaty of Schönbrunn had weakened Austria too much. Alexander and Rumiantsev thought Austria deserved its fate; Caulaincourt made no impression at St Petersburg with his argument that Napoleon, in permitting Austria to exist, had made a generous concession to Russia. Nor did the Russians mainly complain that Russia's services in the war were inadequately rewarded. They were angry primarily because Napoleon had strengthened the Duchy and encouraged Polish nationalism.

Rumiantsev, the strongest defender of the French alliance, now demanded a formal Russo-French convention guaranteeing Russia against the restoration of a Polish state, with Austria and Prussia to be drawn into it. This was a defensive version of Russia's old glacis policy; since Russia no longer expected to acquire most Polish territory or control the Polish state, it sought international guarantees that no state recognized as such would exist.

To their mutual relief, Rumiantsev and Caulaincourt were able to agree in early January 1810 on a draft convention banning any restoration of a Polish kingdom. Caulaincourt was confident that he had not exceeded his instructions in doing so. A month later Napoleon rejected it, contending that he could only answer for his own conduct and that it was an insult to demand that he pledge himself to prevent a contingency which might arise from conditions beyond his control. The argument was specious; Napoleon, who was good at finding and taking offence, may even have genuinely believed it. But someone who boasted to St Petersburg, as Napoleon did, that he could end Prussia's and Austria's existence at any moment, or immediately summon 400,000 men to stop Russia from doing anything of which he disapproved, could hardly claim plausibly that he could not guarantee Russia against the restoration of a Polish state. Rumiantsev's willingness to accept a paper promise from Napoleon, backed only by the accession of two powers already under France's thumb, showed his eagerness to sustain the alliance. Napoleon's repudiation of Caulaincourt's draft treaty had to convince even Rumiantsev that Napoleon had a hidden agenda on Poland.

And so Napoleon did. Aware of the potential fighting power of the Poles, he ordered his minister of war, Clarke, in July to have a large quantity of arms kept ready in the Duchy in case he wanted to arm the Polish population. More important in this decision than the Poles' military value was Napoleon's general style. He could no more surrender Poland as a potential weapon against Russia than a blackmailer will voluntarily turn incriminating evidence over to his victim. Nor, in response, could Russia give up the possibility of using the Poles against France; in 1810 Alexander renewed his correspondence with Prince Adam Czartoryski in anticipation of a possible conflict with France.

Caulaincourt constantly warned Napoleon that France's repudiation of this convention had destroyed his usefulness in Russia and was responsible for the rising tension, the increasing stridency of Russian complaints, and the growing expectation of eventual war. An agreement on this issue, he insisted, would make every other problem soluble or manageable; without it, all were becoming worse. The argument made sense. Russia, after all, had accepted Napoleon's actions and claims in Spain, Italy, Sicily, and Switzerland without protest and continued to do so, in glaring contrast to its former stands. It even tolerated many things that harmed Russian interests—France's annexation of Holland, which made peace with Britain, the ostensible goal of the alliance, even more difficult; the election of Marshal Bernadotte as Crown Prince and heir to the throne in Sweden; Napoleon's bullying of Prussia; the French annexations and troop movements in Northern Germany (except for Oldenburg, a special case); and Napoleon's dynastic tie to Austria. Napoleon offered Russia paper concessions and assurances on certain issues in return. He endorsed Russia's acquisitions of Finland and the Danubian Principalities, assured St Petersburg (sincerely enough) that the Austrian marriage meant no French alliance or *rapprochement* with Austria, and insisted (insincerely) that Bernadotte's election was harmless and had occurred despite his wishes. On Poland, he refused even paper assurances.[22]

To emphasize Poland as the root cause of the Franco-Russian break is not to downgrade the Continental System as a factor, but to change the way one looks at it. The French and Russian concepts of the Continental System always diverged somewhat, as they were bound to. Nonetheless, no European leader save the King of Denmark accepted its original anti-British aims more genuinely than Alexander and Rumiantsev. From 1808 to 1810 it was enforced fairly systematically against British shipping and goods, over the protests of many Russian statesmen and most merchants, in an effort not only to force Britain to make peace and surrender its maritime rules but also to pave the way for Russia's own commercial expansion. Rumiantsev was strongly in favour of protecting native industry and commerce against foreign domination, especially British, and rejected the *laissez-faire* arguments of his opponents that competitive advantage made Russia and Britain natural economic partners.

The Russians, however, never accepted the idea that the economic war on Britain obliged them to destroy their own trade with Europe or with neutrals; they especially wanted to develop their trade with the United States and Latin America, in competition with Britain. Still less did they accept that the Continental System should make Russia an economic tributary of France. By mid-1810, these Russian premises, along with the original assumption that Franco-Russian co-operation would quickly bring Britain to a peace settlement, had become untenable. As Caulaincourt reported, Russians believed that France, Russia, and the Continent were all suffering more from the blockade than was Britain, and Russian diplomats abroad confirmed this view. Worse yet, Napoleon had turned the system against Continental trade with neutrals as well as Britain, especially the United States. From mid-1810 on he further made clear, by his annexations of Holland and North Germany and his changes in the Continental System, that he intended to destroy Russia's trade in colonial goods and

---

[22] The best source is Romanov (1905–14: iv, v, and vii (much of the evidence is also summarized in *VPR* (1960–: 1. v). For Napoleon's attitudes, see Napoleon (1858–70: xx. Nos. 15992, 16178–81, 16341, 16629, 16676, 16706); for examples of Rumiantsev's Francophile instructions to Chernishev and the latter's pessimistic reports to Alexander, see *Sbornik* (1867–1916: cxxi. 3–5, 95–6, xxi. 1–21); for Alexander's contacts with Czartoryski, see Alexander (1865: 65–102, 127–35). See also Lefebvre (1969: ii. 78–80); Schiemann (1904: i. 106–9); Fournier (1930: ii. 108–10).

with the rest of the Continent, even if that trade was carried on through neutrals, while France established its own profitable monopoly on trade in colonial goods directly with Britain.

The system was already blamed in Russia for economic disaster. Russia's balance of trade showed a mounting deficit, the prices of its main raw-material exports fell while those of imports rose, the value of the rouble declined to less than 40 per cent of its 1807 value by 1811, and the government's budget deficits grew hugely. Whether these resulted mainly from the system or from other causes like government mismanagement and excessive military expenditures makes no difference; opponents blamed the system, and the government, itself divided on the issue, could not refute them. By mid-1810, with the rift with France over Poland and other issues already hardened, Russia relaxed its enforcement of the System against ships with neutral flags, though the ban on British shipping was retained (it stayed in force, in fact, until well after Napoleon invaded Russia in 1812). This helped British merchants to evade the blockade either by shipping under false flags or by using American vessels.

Thus Russia loosened the system just as Napoleon was imposing his most draconian measures to tighten it. Russia's re-export of colonial goods to Prussia and Austria also competed with the trade in colonial goods Napoleon wanted to monopolize for French licensees and merchants. This divergence simply dramatized a long-standing difference in principle. Russia claimed that free ships made free goods, and that its war against Britain was fought for this principle; that France, not Russia, was abandoning the system as a weapon against Britain; and that British commercial exploitation should not be destroyed in order to erect French exploitation in its place.

In any case, after Napoleon had further challenged Russia by his annexations of the German North Sea and Baltic coasts, including Oldenburg, a duchy tied dynastically to the House of Romanov and specifically guaranteed in the Treaty of Tilsit, Alexander issued his *ukaz* of 31 December. In conformity with Alexander's and Rumiantsev's declarations of loyalty to the war against Britain, it did not open Russia's markets and ports to British goods, but closed them to France, excluding French wines and silks with prohibitive tariffs. The decree, in short, was not pro-British but anti-French, a refusal to allow Napoleon to impose his economic colonialism on Russia.[23]

[23] The basic work is Zlotnikov (1966); but see also Crosby (1965: 100–225); Girnius (1981: 9–20, 81–100); Saul (1991: 42–8, 55–61); Heller (1983: 78–85);

Though the *ukaz* did not mean a *rapprochement* with Britain, it did mark a stage in Anglo-Russian relations and in Alexander's political education. Alexander and Rumiantsev were still basically loyal to the anti-British aims of the Continental System, but had lost faith in its efficacy. As everyone knows, one reason Napoleon invaded Russia was that he could not get at Britain. A lesser-known corollary of this proposition is that one reason Alexander broke with Napoleon was that he had lost Russia's war against Britain, though he refused to admit it. A few years of Russian economic warfare against Britain had left Russia's economy tottering while Britain's survived; Russian vessels rotted in port or in British custody while British warships and merchantmen plied the Baltic unchallenged.

After the *ukaz*, France and Russia in early and mid-1811 seemed to be preparing for war. In fact, both were trying to avoid it by warning and intimidating the other. Russia did so only reluctantly, trying first to persuade France to withdraw from Oldenburg and restore its confiscated treasure, and stressing Russia's honour as the crucial issue rather than its military security. Napoleon rejected the demand; his offer to compensate the Duke of Oldenburg in Thuringia added insult to injury by treating Russia as if it were Austria. The Duke, an agnate of the Romanov house, would thereby become Napoleon's satrap in the heart of his Empire, just like the Habsburg Ferdinand of Würzburg. Only after this did Rumiantsev denounce the seizure strongly and Alexander cut off serious contact with Caulaincourt.

Napoleon answered Russia's complaints of his violation of Tilsit with counter-charges,[24] raised his levy of troops in France, formed three armies of observation on the Elbe, the Rhine, and in Italy, reinforced Davout's forces in North Germany, particularly at Danzig, and put even greater pressure on his satellites for contributions. But this was only intimidation. Naked threats were directed more at his allies and Prussia than at Russia. The King of Württemberg, for example, was warned that his territories would be annexed if he did not do his duty in garrisoning Danzig. Napoleon did not withdraw major forces at this time from Spain, gave even more attention than before to the security of his coasts against Britain, and continued to push his plans for naval building and an eventual invasion, though this may have been mainly for

Viennot (1947: 226–7). For Russian attitudes, see Romanov (1905–14: v. Nos. 460–1, 554–5, 558, 562–3, 577).

[24] Ibid. Nos. 580, 612–15, 624–5, 638; *VPR* (1960–: 1. vi. Nos. 1, 3–4, 22).

purposes of deception and domestic morale. His language to the Tsar's personal aide, Chernishev, and the Russian ambassador, Kurakin, indicates that he was seeking peace through bullying; so does his offer, allegedly inspired by Talleyrand and thrown out to Kurakin in the course of one of Napoleon's public tirades on 15 August, that he would give Russia a guarantee against the restoration of Poland and draw Austria into it. This did not indicate any real willingness of Napoleon to solve the Polish issue—he had made and broken such verbal promises before. It does show that he knew where the crux of the problem lay, and was not eager for war.[25]

The Russians (at least the Tsar, Rumiantsev, and Alexander's liberal adviser, Michael Speranski) were equally reluctant to fight. The Tsar, resisting the war party, sent Chernishev on a special peace mission to Paris, while the foreign ministry sought to form a deterrent coalition. Alexander promised Czartoryski a restored great Polish kingdom in personal union with Russia and offered Austria and Prussia defensive alliances, arguing that the Russo-French alliance was perfectly firm, that they and not Russia needed help, and that they had better join Russia now before it was too late. Besides representing bluff and deception, this reflected the persistent assumption at St Petersburg that Russia could always find defensive allies in Germany, and then use them to make a deal with Napoleon. The mission to Paris of a rising young diplomat, Count Karl von Nesselrode, to gather information, contact Talleyrand, and report secretly to Alexander, also shows this. If anyone favoured an anti-French stand, it was Nesselrode, a cosmopolitan Austrophile conservative and friend of Gentz, who shared his hatred of Napoleon. Yet he assumed at first that Russia, after getting Austria, Prussia, and other states to ally with her in checking French expansion, could then divide Europe with France along the Elbe. When in mid-1811 he recognized that this was impossible, he began urging Alexander to negotiate with Napoleon for peace.[26]

The policies of both powers toward the Ottoman Empire are

---

[25] This is based primarily on Napoleon's correspondence Apr.–Sept. 1811 in Napoleon (1858–70: xxii. Nos. 17136–18143); see also Chernishev's reports to Alexander in *Sbornik* (1867–1916: xxi. 49–65, 101 and *passim*), and Dard (1937: 240–5).

[26] Martens (1874–1905: iii. 34–7, 56–60, 70–9; viii. 11–18); *VPR* (1960–: 1. vi. Nos. 14–16, 18, 20–1, 23, 27, 43, 46); Alexander (1865: 136–68); Bailleu (1900: 206–18); Gritzbach (1974: i. 218–35); Nesselrode (1904–12: iii. 322–5, 327–9); Schiemann (1904: i. 55–91, 519–26); *Sbornik* (1867–1916: xxi. 329–35).

further proof of how neither of them was steering deliberately toward war or bent wholly on preparing for it. Napoleon did threaten Russia with immediate war if it took one inch of territory south of the Danube. But he tried to make others (Austria, Ali Pasha, and the Turks) actually fight Russia, while the French in Illyria and Ragusa took the same Fortress Europe stance *vis-à-vis* Russia as they did elsewhere against Britain.[27] Meanwhile the Tsar and Rumiantsev actually aided Napoleon in his strategy of distracting them from the danger in the north. Resisting strenuous domestic protests and foreign pressure, they insisted that the Turks must cede Russia the Principalities and once again become Russia's dependent ally, perhaps even joining it against Napoleon, before they would agree to end the war with the Ottoman Empire and concentrate on the coming one with France. At the same time, Russia tried to sustain the dying Serbian insurrection and maintain its influence among the Balkan peoples. Trying for everything, Russia gained nothing; the French threat prevented Russia from achieving peace by military victory, and Rumiantsev's refusal to return to the status quo ante prevented one by negotiation.

From May 1811, this policy of retaining the Principalities and waiting the Turks out began to crumble. A peace mission under Fonton marked the first in a series of piecemeal retreats from Russia's earlier demands. A major military victory won over the Turks by Marshal Kutuzov in early 1812 failed to force a decision. As late as February and March 1812, with war against France certain and imminent, the Tsar ordered a military offensive to end the war, and Rumiantsev still threatened the Turks with a settlement imposed by force. Finally Russia managed to escape from the Turkish war by the Peace of Bucharest in May 1812; it gained Bessarabia but not Moldavia and Walachia, and also failed to get the desired alliance with Turkey. Tactically, the Peace of Bucharest came too late to help deter Austria from joining Napoleon or to let Russia transfer troops from the south in time to meet Napoleon's onslaught. Strategically, it did not really mean a new Russian policy toward Turkey and the Balkans, or even a full concentration on defending Russian soil against the French invader. Instead, some leading Russians continued to think that Russia could fight France partly through revolutions and war in the Balkans and southern Europe directed against Austria.[28]

---

[27] Napoleon (1858–70: xxii. Nos. 17468, 17471, 17571, 17923).
[28] The evidence is scattered through *VPR* (1960–: 1. vi. Nos. 1–165 (cf. also pp. 288, 419); for general accounts see Lebel (1955: 157–79); Jewsbury (1977: 32–5); Jelavich (1991: 2–18); Vucinich (1982a: 151–68).

The Tsar and Rumiantsev clung to the anti-British aspect of their policy even more stubbornly than to the anti-Turkish and implicitly anti-Austrian ones. Until his departure from St Petersburg in mid-1811, Caulaincourt regularly insisted that the Russian government had not abandoned the war against Britain, despite its widening rift with France. His successor, General Lauriston, said much the same. As late as April and May 1812, Rumiantsev told the French that Russia had confiscated fifty British ships and their cargoes in the past year—while France was trading openly with Britain.[29] Russia co-operated with Napoleon against the British also in other ways, where it did not directly threaten Russia's security (i.e. Spain, Italy, Holland, most of Germany, Italy), and at the same time competed seriously, if ineffectively, with Britain for trade and influence in North America, Latin America, and the Middle East.[30]

The Russian government's reluctance to abandon the contest with Britain was demonstrated most strikingly in late 1811 and early 1812. With war against France now inevitable, Britain and Spain approached Russia directly to offer peace and an alliance against France. Rumiantsev proposed simply telling the British that Russia would not break with France until forced to do so. Alexander, however, decided to make Britain an indirect counter-offer through his unofficial contact with the Spanish Cortes, Oberhofmeister R. A. Koshelev. If Britain first obtained Russia a peace with Turkey on favourable terms and agreed to assume Russia's debt to Holland (over 87 million silver roubles), Russia would consent to open its ports to British ships (though nothing was said about a trade treaty or reducing the prohibitive Russian tariffs).

Thus Russia, which for five years had worked with France to defeat Britain and subjugate Spain, succeeding only in ruining its own economy in the process, now, facing a life-and-death threat from France, announced that it would graciously accept peace and an alliance from the hands of Britain and Spain, if they paid Russia enough for it. St Petersburg maintained this stance up to the outbreak of war and beyond. Rumiantsev claimed that Russia had saved Britain and Spain: by cooling its relations with France and by transferring some of its troops to its central front, it had

---

[29] Romanov (1905–14: iv. Nos. 431–2, 440–3, 445–58; v. 479–80, 493, 504); VPR (1960–: 1. vi. Nos. 5, 32, 135); Nesselrode (1904–12: iv. 213–22).

[30] Bartley (1978: 43–50, 70–7, 88–91, 96–102); VPR (1960–: 1. vi. Nos. 10, 58, 131, 133).

prevented France from crushing the Anglo-Spanish resistance. In the light of this, if France attacked Russia the Tsar expected Spain to do its duty by carrying the war into France, and Britain by promptly creating diversions for Russia in the Baltic and Mediterranean or in Italy, and by supporting Russia's revolutionary plans in the Balkans. Russia rejected a British offer, conveyed through the new British chargé at Constantinople, Stratford Canning, to mediate its wars with Turkey and Persia, but agreed to let Britain tell the Persians that Russia would accept peace on the basis of *uti possedetis*. St Petersburg further insisted that a peace treaty and alliance with Britain include Sweden first (the procedure actually followed). Rumiantsev even expected the foreign secretary, the Marquis of Wellesley (replaced by Castlereagh in early 1812), to come personally to St Petersburg with full powers to negotiate it.[31]

One has to admire the panache with which Russia, concealing its actual peril and panic, played the role of the courted party; there would be no comparable performance until Stalin's after 1941, and then the Russians could at least claim legitimately that they were bearing by far the greatest burden in the war. Not only was this shrewd tactics; it was also the fruit of Russian exceptionalism, an attitude the British and other Europeans in recent decades had done much to encourage. Once again, the British tolerated Russia's arrogance and presumption well beyond the requirements of a rational coalition policy. British Russophilia was hard to cure.

IV. THE DESCENT INTO WAR, 1811–1812

From mid-October 1811, unmistakable signs appeared of Napoleon's preparations for a great offensive: further reinforcements for Davout, the occupation of Swedish Pomerania in January, the summoning of Marshal Berthier from Spain to be the Grand Army's chief of staff and Murat from Naples to head the Imperial cavalry, and the transfer late in the day of thirty-six battalions from Spain.

More subtle but equally unmistakable was the virtual cessation of international politics. Napoleon had long used France's foreign ministry and diplomatic service as much for military intelligence

[31] Ibid. Nos. 63–4, 104, 108, 111, 127–8, 148–552, 157, pp. 241, 359.

as for diplomacy; now they became little more than an auxiliary commissariat for the Grand Army.[32] Champagny, who like many others advised Napoleon not to invade Russia, was replaced as foreign minister in April 1811 by Hugues Maret, Duke of Bassano, Napoleon's personal cabinet minister. Maret's lack of diplomatic talent (Talleyrand repeatedly made fun of his stupidity) was no handicap. He was the docile functionary Napoleon wanted, and diplomatic skill was not needed in Napoleon's preparations for war. All the satellites were pressed into line, some like Switzerland for contributions far exceeding their alliance obligations. Prussia, as noted, was brought completely under France's control, and Austria signed an offensive–defensive alliance in March, turning away feelers for peace and alliance from Russia, Britain, and the Spanish junta, and desperate pleas from Prussia. Metternich boasted of the difference between the limited alliance he negotiated, in which Austria pledged a corps of 30,000 men under Austrian command to operate on the southern flank of the Grand Army in Russia, and the vassaldom to which Prussia was reduced. The contrast was real enough, but it had little to do with Metternich's skill at negotiation, and indicated no desire or intent on Metternich's part ultimately to break with France. He expected France to win, as almost everyone did, and, while hoping to guard against the unexpected, wished to make the best of a permanent Austro-French connection.[33] Austria's more limited commitments were due mainly to geography. Prussia was the indispensable staging area for the thrust over Smolensk toward Moscow that Napoleon had planned; Austria was needed only to keep the Russians distracted and pinned down in the south.

Besides, Napoleon wanted to win this war with his own Grand Army, using only auxiliary corps from suspect allies like Austria and Prussia. If Austria were given too important a role, it would claim too much at the peace, a potentially embarrassing prospect, since Napoleon had no idea how he would end the war he was determined to start. Some of those trying to dissuade Napoleon from invading Russia suggested other ways to safeguard the Empire. Champagny, for example, proposed partitioning Prussia

[32] The evidence is scattered throughout Napoleon (1858–70: xxii, xxiii); for some of the particular moves made in late 1811, see Nos. 18175–6, 18249, 18300, 18334, 18398, 18442, 18444. For his use of the foreign ministry, see No. 18403 and Whitcomb (1979: 97–9).

[33] Metternich (1880–4: ii. 426–44); DeClercq (1880–1917: ii. 369–72); Kraehe (1963: 136–43); Wohlfeil (1965: 64–6); Oncken (1876: ii. 611–14; Martens (1874–1905: iii. 78–9).

and constructing a large Poland ruled by Saxony, while Caulaincourt called for an Austro-Polish–Swedish buffer zone against Russia. Such suggestions, whether practical or unrealistic, were irrelevant; Napoleon's real concern was not the security of the Empire. Even his own propaganda to his allies reveals the real *casus belli*: that Russia wanted to be independent. All the crimes, insults, and threats of which Napoleon accused St Petersburg were normal actions of independent states in international politics. Russia now presented an obstacle to his will, as Austria and Prussia had done before and Britain still did, and it would have to be removed by military force.[34]

Russia's final passage to war was as hesitant as Napoleon's was direct. The war party, including the Empress Dowager and Alexander's favourite sister, Catherine, continued to grow, while the French party had almost disappeared save for Rumiantsev. But many Russians who had lost all trust in France, including the Tsar, dreaded war enough to want at least to postpone it. Nesselrode, who was appointed state secretary with rights of direct access to the Tsar and was apparently being groomed as Rumiantsev's successor, tried to sell his ideas for peace to the Tsar in late 1811 and early 1812 and prepared for a peace mission to Paris. Though the mission failed to come off, his proposals (a French evacuation of Prussia and Swedish Pomerania and a Russo-Austrian–Prussian defensive coalition to preserve the territorial status quo) contributed to a last-minute peace effort in April 1812, growing out of an exchange of letters between the two Emperors. Russia proposed that France evacuate Prussia and Swedish Pomerania and reduce its garrison in Danzig to its status of early 1811, give some unspecified compensation to the Duke of Oldenburg, and promise to negotiate with Sweden, in exchange for Russia's maintaining a strict prohibition of British goods, agreeing to a system of licences like France's, and modifying the Russian tariff in favour of France.

The proposal, though it had no chance, proves the Russian government's reluctance for war. Poland, France's annexations in North Germany, and even Oldenburg were no longer crucial issues; what counted most was removing Napoleon's immediate military menace and reconstituting some kind of defensive glacis

---

[34] Caulaincourt (1935: i. 94–5); *Sbornik* (1867–1916: xxi. 204–13). For a sample of Napoleon's propaganda, see Napoleon (1858–70: xxiii. No. 18458); for a persuasive psychological explanation of Napoleon's decisions, see H. Parker (1979; 1990).

for Russia (from which even Austria was left out). As a price for this, Russia would partly re-enter the Continental System and continue the commercial war against Britain. Kurakin, another long-time foe of Napoleon who now wanted peace, presented these proposals to Napoleon and Maret. At his meeting with Napoleon he encountered the usual bullying, flattery, evasion, and deception (now that Russia no longer asked for a convention on Poland, Napoleon offered one, only quickly to withdraw the bait as soon as Kurakin began to nibble), followed by two weeks of silence on Kurakin's formal proposal. Kurakin therefore decided in May to demand his passports. Rumiantsev criticized him sharply for doing so and proposed continuing the peace talks through Nesselrode on revised terms, but here Alexander finally broke with Rumiantsev and would make no further effort for peace.[35]

One reason Russia tried to avert war at the last minute was that it had failed to gain any real allies, much less build the great coalition for which some hoped. Many Russians, unlike Alexander, did not regret losing the Poles, but losing Prussia to France after the military convention negotiated with Scharnhorst was a bitter blow, and Austria's defection, though not unexpected, a further one.[36] Peace with Turkey and Persia was reached too late to help, by Russia's own fault; peace and alliances with Britain and Sweden even more so.[37] Yet Russia's diplomatic failures in 1810–11 contributed in a way to its ultimate salvation. Its original strategy had called for carrying the war to Napoleon in Central Europe, raising the Poles, joining the Prussian army in Poland and East Prussia, gaining Austria's alliance or neutrality, and wearing Napoleon down with revolts in Germany, Italy, and even France. As late as early February 1812, the Russian minister of war, General Barclay de Tolly, still favoured promoting insurrections in Central and Western Europe, though not in Poland. But by spring Barclay had turned to a strategy of defending Russia's western borders, and by the eve of war the enormous size of the

[35] Gritzbach (1974: i. 238–45, 255–65); Nesselrode (1904–12: iv. 192–9); Romanov (1905–14: vi. No. 87); *Sbornik* (1867–1916: xxi. 266–304, 338–42, 357–91); *VPR* (1960–: 1. vi. Nos. 38, 155, 161; pp. 307–9, 400).

[36] For the Russian failure with Austria, see ibid. Nos. 87, 101, 137, 153, 158, 181; Martens (1874–1905: iii. 78–87); Oncken (1876: ii. 611–14). On Prussia, *VPR* (1960–: 1. vi. Nos. 76, 106); Bailleu (1900: 225–31, 238–9); Martens (1874–1905: viii. 18–20, 23–37, 40–5).

[37] Russian documents (*VPR*, 1960–: 1. vi; *Sbornik*, 1867–1916: xxi; Nesselrode, 1904–12: iii) show how strongly Chernishev, Kurakin, Nesselrode, Prince Stackelberg, and others in 1810–11 pleaded that Russia make peace with the Ottoman Empire and Britain and conciliate Austria before it was too late.

Grand Army had forced him into the strategy of retreat and avoiding battle which ultimately would save Russia.

A revolutionary strategy, however, was maintained in the south. Alexander and Vice-Admiral Chichagov, military commander and governor in the Principalities, worked out a programme for raising the Balkan Slavs and Hungarians in revolt, hoping thereby to paralyse Austria and pave the way for anti-French risings in southern Europe—Illyria, the Tyrol, Italy, and Switzerland.[38] The plan came to nothing, but not because the Tsar or Chichagov had second thoughts; its intrinsic unrealism and the overwhelming threat of the Grand Army forced Russia to abandon it.

Russia gained one modest political victory, but only because Napoleon pushed Sweden toward Russia and Britain helped Russia pick up the prize. France appeared to enjoy solid influence over Sweden following the Russo-Swedish war in 1809. Napoleon gave the Swedes back Pomerania and the Isle of Rügen in January 1810, and Sweden formally joined the Continental System and declared war on Britain. Napoleon approved an attempt to create a Swedish–Danish–Polish alliance under his protection and agreed, without enthusiasm, to Sweden's election of Marshal Bernadotte as Crown Prince (taking the name Carl Johan) to succeed the childless and senile King Carl. Though Napoleon and Bernadotte were too alike in temperament and ambition to be friends, they both expected Sweden to remain in the French orbit. So did Bernadotte's wife, one of Napoleon's early loves, the Swedes who elected him, and the Russians.

The basic trouble was that Sweden, a poor country dependent on maritime commerce, simply could not carry into practice its formal adherence to the Continental System and war against Britain. An attempt by Bernadotte to do so would have destroyed his hold on the Swedish people. Besides, Sweden, even with France and Russia as allies, could not defend its commerce and coasts against the British fleet, which was now convoying merchant ships in the Baltic against French privateers. Bernadotte constantly told the French this, but Napoleon in 1810–11 simply increased the pressure on Sweden to enforce the system, and Bernadotte's resistance and resentment mounted accordingly. In addition, Bernadotte and the Swedes had ambitions, not to regain Finland from Russia, but to acquire Norway from Denmark. The

[38] For Barclay's advice to Alexander, see *VPR* (1960–: 1. v. p. 379; vi. No. 107; pp. 140, 426). For the Tsar's and Chichagov's plans for the Balkans, ibid. Nos. 144–5, p. 438; Nesselrode (1904–12: iv. 204–7).

French connection, far from advancing this aim as Bernadotte had hoped, obstructed it; Denmark was too loyal and important an ally of France. In calling on Sweden to fight Britain and Russia, and promising to help it reconquer Finland, Napoleon was demanding of the Swedes what they could not do and offering them what they did not want.

The new French occupation of Swedish Pomerania in January 1812 added the final blow, compelling Bernadotte to break with France to avoid political suicide and possible assassination (Sweden's record in dealing with unsatisfactory monarchs was no less impressive than Russia's). Still, Bernadotte had no intention of helping Russia or drawing Napoleon's wrath down on himself. His goal was to do as little as possible against France, and be paid handsomely for it by France's enemies; and he executed this typical small-power policy beautifully.[39]

Russia cooperated with him. The Swedes had sent Russia alliance feelers in late 1811; Rumiantsev wanted to respond only with flattery and vague promises, using the Swedes to obtain British help for Russia without Russian commitments. But Alexander was more forthcoming, and when Sweden answered the French occupation of Swedish Pomerania with a mission to St Petersburg, the Russians, now faced with imminent war, received it eagerly. The Russo-Swedish alliance treaty of 5 April was a typical eighteenth-century instrument for joint aggrandizement, but remarkably favourable to Sweden, considering that it faced the same threat as Russia and was even more vulnerable. It provided for a joint descent on North Germany by 25,000–30,000 Swedes and 15,000–20,000 Russians—to be carried out, however, only *after* Sweden had conquered Norway and, if necessary, made a descent on Zealand to eliminate Denmark as an enemy in its rear. The treaty also guaranteed each partner its potential conquests—in Sweden's case, Norway. Thus Russia committed itself to support a Swedish attack on Denmark and Sweden's acquisition of Norway prior to Sweden's helping Russia. To make things worse, by the time the treaty was signed Russia had already abandoned its original strategy of promoting landings and insurrections in North Germany, and Sweden, as Russia knew, was financially and militarily incapable either of attacking Denmark on its own or of helping defend Russia.

[39] F. Scott (1935: 10–15); Fournier (1930: ii. 172–3); Ryan (1959); DeClercq (1880–1917: ii. 304–6); Napoleon (1858–70: xx. 16313, 16402; xxi. Nos. 17023, 17229; xxii. No. 18233; xxiii. Nos. 18516, 18524; *Sbornik* (1867–1916: xxi. 22–48; cxxi. 113–14); *VPR* (1960–: 1. v. pp. 551, 604).

The first secret clause of the treaty gives Russia's reason, apart from its general desperation, for concluding this fool's deal: a provision that Britain was to be invited to accede to the alliance if war actually broke out with France. The Russian government knew that it had to have peace with Britain and British assistance in the war, especially financial aid, but it hated to approach Britain itself or even to respond directly to British invitations. A Swedish alliance was its means to reach Britain indirectly. The Swedes recognized this fact and exploited it.[40] This was the sole fruit of Russia's efforts at coalition-building, a process described by a leading Napoleonic scholar, with unconscious humour, as follows: 'The Tsar with the support of England had formed the sixth coalition, which included hardly anything but Russia itself.'[41]

V. OLD WAR IN SPAIN, NEW WAR IN AMERICA

While France prepared its Empire to fight Russia, its own forces remained concentrated more in Spain. The main element keeping the Spanish ulcer open and festering, though Wellington's skill and leadership, the discipline and stiffening supplied by the British forces, and massive British material and financial aid were indispensable, was the Spaniards and Portuguese themselves. Despite consistent defeats in open battle, the Spanish army managed to stay in being and open new fronts, forcing the French to divide their forces. Meanwhile guerillas wreaked havoc on French supply lines and communications, inflicting heavy losses especially on the raw French recruits Napoleon sent into Spain, and in general made it impossible for Joseph's regime to become stable and self-sustaining. Portugal supplied half the soldiers for Wellington's army and the base and bastions for his defensive war in 1810–11 and his offensives thereafter into Spain, at great human and economic cost. Ultimately the resistance in the peninsula depended at least as much on moral and psychological factors as on military and material ones. Britain had to maintain its commitment to

---

[40] Roginski (1974); F. Scott (1935: 16–21); *VPR* (1960–: 1. vi. Nos. 97, 119, 130, 171); *Sbornik* (1867–1916: xxi. 421–6).

[41] Tulard (1977: 391). Despite the stark contrast between Russia's hopes for allies in 1811 and its actual situation in 1812, some good historians (e.g. Zaghi, 1969: 257–9; Chandler, 1966: 854–5) still argue that Russia won the diplomatic war against Napoleon.

an enterprise of very uncertain outcome, undertaken with some hesitation in 1808 and nearly abandoned in early 1810; the Spaniards and Portuguese had to remain determined not to become French colonies.[42]

This meant, among other things, that international politics, virtually dormant on most of the Continent, became vital in the peninsula. Sustaining the military resistance required maintaining tolerable political relations between Britain and the Portuguese regency and the Spanish junta respectively—a very difficult task. Wellington, retreating to the lines of Torre Vedras before Lisbon after his victory at Busacco in September 1810, had deliberately devastated the Portuguese countryside in order to starve Masséna's besiegers out. The heavy strain this put on Anglo-Portuguese relations, relieved somewhat when the strategy proved successful in early 1811, was renewed by later British retreats into Portugal.

Portugal at least was Britain's traditional ally, accustomed to lean on Britain against Spain and France. Spain knew Britain only as a deadly imperial and maritime rival, and nothing in its current situation changed the Spanish picture of Britain as the main threat to the Spanish Empire in the New World, the major interloper in its trade, and the captor of several Spanish colonies and aggressor against others. The British even at the time carried on a large-scale illegal trade with Spain's colonies, and constantly pressed for a trade treaty opening the Spanish and American markets to its goods. In 1810 a British general endorsed Venezuela's liberation from the authority of the Spanish junta, and though the British government disavowed him, insisting it only wanted to mediate and help reconcile Spain and its colonies, the incident fed the natural if mistaken Spanish belief that Britain was behind the growing Spanish American independence movement.

The British had at least as many grievances. The junta was fractious and could not control its generals, some of whom hated the British, refused to co-operate, and repeatedly overestimated their own capacities and those of their troops. Wellington, denouncing their incompetence and unreliability, fought for supreme command over the Spanish forces as the only way to co-ordinate operations. Spain's insistence on being paid in bullion for every-

---

[42] As an historian of the French regime in Spain puts it, 'Seen from the internal Spanish situation, one would prefer to explain the [French] defeat on moral grounds, for a regime could hardly be built on greater lies and more shameless use of force, and it was finally moral elements that made the resistance arise and maintained it, despite all the unfavourable external circumstances.' Juretschke (1961: 280).

thing the Anglo-Portuguese forces required in Spain, though understandable in view of the country's poverty, increased the British burden of supporting its own expeditionary force and two other armies in addition, and helped cause its bullion crisis of 1811. The fact that the junta steadfastly refused to open its doors fully to British trade made things worse.

That the Anglo-Portuguese–Spanish coalition held together at all was due in good measure to diplomacy—that of Henry Wellesley and Charles Stuart as ambassadors to Spain and Portugal, of Richard Marquis of Wellesley as foreign secretary (here at least he showed energy), of Castlereagh as secretary for war and various treasury and admiralty officials in maintaining vital supplies and money, and not least of Wellington. His growing reputation and leadership were almost as important in politics as in battle. Britain learned something vital in Spain about how to lead a coalition in war, showing a readiness not only to do everything needed to keep the cause alive rather than seek the maximum foreign effort for the least cost but also to drop impossible political demands and seek a real consensus with its allies on what the war was for.[43]

The corollary to Spanish, Portuguese, and British survival in the peninsula, leading to a turn of the tide in mid-1812 just before Napoleon invaded Russia, was France's failure. This, too, owed as much to political as to military factors, and the chief responsibility lies not with Joseph or the generals but with Napoleon himself. There had once been some basis for a regime in Spain allied to France and influenced by it, as there was in Germany, Italy, and Western Europe generally. The *afrancesados* (a pejorative term applied by Spanish traditionalists indiscriminately to both collaborators and anti-French liberals) who drew up the original Bayonne constitution, and initially worked with Joseph, shared many ideals with the liberals who drew up the constitution of the Cortes in 1812. They wanted a more modern Spain with some restrictions on the Church, an end to the Inquisition, greater equality of status and taxation, and some political representation. Joseph would have made a decent monarch, perhaps a popular one, precisely because he was unmilitary, amiable, and willing to

---

[43] On the war, see Aymes (1973); Esdaile (1988a); Horward (1989); Livermore (1976: 245–57); on the finances, diplomacy, and politics involved, Sherwig (1969: 226–65); Severn (1981: 142–7, 158–83, 191–205, 210–11). The Marquis of Wellesley's papers (BL Add. MSS 37291–2) demonstrate his enterprising, if not always prudent, policy on Spain (including, e.g. various plans for trying to rescue Ferdinand from French captivity).

adapt to Spanish needs and customs. Most of the time after 1808 the French controlled most of Spain, and though the War of Independence was not a Spanish civil war, neither was the nation united in resistance. Spaniards could treat other Spaniards as brutally as the French did, guerilla warfare took a terrible toll on civilian life, and as time went by opportunists and ordinary people trying to survive replenished the ranks of the original collaborators.

In other words, France theoretically had a chance to succeed in Spain—but not under Napoleon. The military strategy and tactics he followed proved as defective as his original political calculations. He refused, at least publicly or to his subordinates, to confront military realities, constantly denying the problem of guerillas (whom he referred to as 'bandits'), ignoring those of communications and supply, and underestimating the British and Wellington. He harried his commanders into unwise offensives, and persisted in a system of recruitment and replacements for Spain leading to needless losses and ultimate breakdown. New recruits were assigned occupation duties which made them easy prey to guerillas, and foreign troops employed that were prone to desert.[44] Above all, Napoleon persisted in trying to make war nourish war in impoverished, mountainous, rebellious Spain, just as he had done in Germany and northern Italy.

His political decisions were even worse. He knew by 1810 that political support for Joseph's regime had disappeared, writing in November to Laforest, French ambassador to Joseph's court, that any town of 4,000 was stronger than all of France's partisans in Spain combined. The conclusion he drew was that the Spaniards' rejection of his benevolent protection absolved him from all obligations and promises and gave him Spain by right of conquest. He was therefore free to make the war pay by any means necessary, and in 1810 he converted the lands north of the Ebro into four military governorships preparatory to annexing them to France. This was the final blow to Joseph's regime; even the most reform-minded and pro-French of his collaborators would not sacrifice Spain's territory and identity to a foreign invader. The

---

[44] As an historian of the French military occupation writes, 'Throughout the Peninsular War Napoleon was bombarded by voluminous testimony from his commanders that their losses were devastating, the replacement procedures inadequate, and the insidious practice of deploying conscript battalions away from their regiments for long periods was ruining the army. But Napoleon clung to the very end to his disastrous methods of responding to each unexpected crisis with a proliferation of new conscript units. He either failed to realize or refused to acknowledge the limited power of his military administration.' D. Alexander (1980: 196).

answer to the common claim that Napoleon could have won the war in Spain had he gone there himself after 1809 is the familiar, almost monotonous one: whatever chances France had in Spain, Napoleon ruined them.[45]

The struggle between France and Britain brought the issue of independence to a head in 1812 also for another power, the United States. Its problem was one of protecting its interests, principles, and honour under circumstances in which its commercial interests led in one direction and its principles and honour in another. Its position as the most important neutral and Britain's major competitor in trade, especially in colonial goods, offered it some leverage and ability to affect the outcome of the war, and it had serious complaints against both sides. The charges against Britain included the impressment of sailors from American vessels as alleged deserters from the British navy, illegal searches and seizures of American cargoes under the Orders in Council, and various questions left over from the Paris Peace Treaty of 1783 (especially British dealings with North American Indians) and the Jay trade treaty of 1794. Against France the complaint was constant raids on American ships by French privateers and cruisers, under the pretext that the ships and goods were really British. Yet the profits of America's wartime trade were such that, even after the Berlin and Milan Decrees and the British Orders in Council, American merchants stood to lose more than to gain by counter-measures, quite apart from the risk that these might involve America in the war.

Nevertheless, the American government tried to force Britain to respect its neutral rights, first with the Non-Importation Act of early 1806. Since this failed to ban the most important British goods from import into the United States and gave the British until November to comply with American demands, the British considered it insulting but impotent. Secretary of State James Madison sent William Pinkney on a special mission in June 1806 to negotiate a treaty ending impressment and ensuring a more liberal treatment of the American re-export trade. Finding the British not frightened by the threat of losing the American market, Pinkney and the regular American ambassador, James Monroe, managed to circumvent Madison's unrealistic instructions and, by hard

[45] On the military side, see Horward (1984: esp. 61–2, 115–16); D. Alexander (1985); on the political aspects, Juretschke (1961: 249–61, 279–81, 285–94); Wohlfeil (1965: 66–76); M. Glover (1971: 166–9, 178–9); Coverdale (1984: 34–9). For samples of Napoleon's views, see Napoleon (1858–70: xx. Nos. 16158, 16175–6, 16650–1; xxi. Nos. 16928, 17111).

bargaining with the Fox and Grenville governments, to reach a treaty in December. Though the British refused formally to renounce the practice of impressment, they promised to reduce it to a minimum, granted important concessions on the re-export trade, and reaffirmed Jay's Treaty. President Thomas Jefferson and Madison rejected the treaty, however, because it failed to satisfy American principles.

As a result, the commercial war escalated, exacerbated by the attack of the British warship *Leopard* on the American *Chesapeake* in June 1807, and created a danger of open war. Jefferson, a 'halfway pacifist' torn between his principles of republican morality, his desire to defend American interests, and his hatred for England, resorted to a policy of passive coercion in the Embargo Act of December 1807, which proscribed all American trade with the belligerents. Meanwhile Napoleon, delighted by the rise in Anglo-American tension, had intensified his war against American shipping at sea and in France's prize courts; American losses mounted.

The Embargo Act hurt Britain enough to cause the Tory cabinet to consider changing the Orders in Council to ease British–American relations, but Canning as foreign secretary successfully resisted this. The Act had even worse effects on the United States. The North-East, dominated by the commercially oriented Federalists, reacted to it with threats to secede from the Union and massive evasions of its provisions. In February 1809, after Madison, another Democrat, had been elected to succeed Jefferson, the embargo was replaced, amidst considerable confusion in the American Congress, by a Non-Intercourse Act which forbade trade with both Britain and Napoleon's Empire and banned their warships from American harbours, but restored American trade with neutral states. Though this act too was widely evaded, its general results benefited Britain more than France. Any good effect of the end of the embargo on Anglo-American relations, however, was negated by the Erskine fiasco of 1809. Canning, hoping to elevate Britain's prestige along with his own, tried to draw the United States into an agreement by which Britain would modify the Orders in Council in America's favour in exchange for humiliating American concessions, including the right of British ships to execute American laws against trade with Napoleonic Europe on the high seas. The British ambassador, David Erskine, exceeding his instructions, concluded an agreement with the United States without these British conditions, and then had it promptly repudiated by the cabinet.

Thus the United States failed to resolve trade issues with either France or Britain in 1809–10. This suited Napoleon perfectly. For while Canning dreamed of gaining American support against France, and British merchants and cabinet ministers yearned to regain the American market, Napoleon aimed to force a break between the United States and Britain. Undeterred by material losses or the needs of French industry for raw materials, especially cotton, he stepped up his campaign of privateering, seizures, prohibitions, and confiscations against American ships, justifying this with the claim that the United States was failing to defend its flag against Britain. In a Trianon Decree of August 1810, he finished what an earlier Rambouillet Decree had far advanced, the simple negation of all American claims against France. In the dispute between the minister of commerce, Montalivet, and the director-general of customs, Collin de Sussy, over whether France should relax its system of prohibitions in order to feed its industry at the cost of weakening the Continental System, Napoleon, though willing to license trade with his enemy Britain, stood firmly with Collin against concessions to the United States.[46]

Precisely at the time when France was expanding its war against American shipping and goods, the United States laid a trap for itself; the French then baited it and the Americans subsequently fell into it. In an effort to escape from the Non-Intercourse Act, a proven failure as originally passed, Congress in early May 1810 passed something called Macon's Bill Number 2, an attempt to combine bribery and surrender. It removed all restrictions on American commerce, but promised to end all intercourse with any power which after a certain interval refused to respect American commerce. The British celebrated this as a triumph; Napoleon saw it as his opportunity. On the same day, 5 August, as he wiped out all American claims against France and instituted the extremely high Trianon tariffs against colonial goods, effectively excluding American exports, the foreign minister, Champagny, Duke of Cadore, sent a letter, commonly called the Cadore letter, to the American minister at Paris promising to revoke the Berlin and Milan Decrees in respect to the United States as of 1 October, provided that the British revoked their Orders in Council or the United States took measures to make its rights respected by Britain.

Napoleon never had the slightest intention of fulfilling this

[46] Perkins (1963: 70–5, 90–4, 108–215); Hickey (1987); Stuart (1978: 17–65); L. Kaplan (1987: 60–113); Bonnel (1961: 226–61); D. Gray (1963: 176–7).

promise, conditional in the first place. At this same time France was announcing its intention to continue the policy of excluding British goods from the Continent (while in fact monopolizing the import of those it wanted); it took its most drastic steps ever in Holland, North Germany, and the Baltic to enforce this policy; it continued to denounce American certificates of origin as forgeries; it made Russia's trade with America a central target of its campaign against Russia; and it continued to confiscate and sell American goods seized on the high seas and the Continent. Yet Madison accepted this letter as sufficient notification of France's intent to conform to America's demands. He did so not because he trusted France but because he hoped to force Britain to yield, giving Britain until 2 February 1811 to alter its policy. The British understandably refused to accept the Cadore letter as worth anything, and the Non-Intercourse Act took effect against Britain.[47]

The step took the United States closer to war, but there was still room to avoid it. All Madison's suppositions were quickly disproved by events—that he could concentrate on only one foe, Britain, that his policy would unite his countrymen behind it, and above all that Napoleon out of self-interest would carry out his promises to the United States. The Emperor, who announced that he would generously refrain from exercising his right to demand an American declaration of war on Britain, devised ways to pretend to grant American ships and goods access to French ports while continuing his *guerre de course* against the United States, especially in the Baltic. Even ardent Anglophobes like John Quincy Adams, the American minister to Russia, saw what the French were doing, and the minister at Paris, Joel Barlow, reported it clearly.

As fate would have it, a rigid, foolish American policy was answered by a rigid, unimaginative British one. More fruitless negotiations ensued in which Britain maintained its position, while British seizures of ships and violations of American waters, troubles with the Indians in the American West, and economic unrest in America caused by low agricultural prices and blamed on the British blockade heightened the tension. Yet there were forces working counter to war. An organized campaign in Britain for changes in the Orders in Council, reinforced by the economic crisis and industrial unrest, climaxed in a major parliamentary struggle from February to June 1812 which compelled the British

[47] Perkins (1963: 223–48); Bonnel (1961: 270–4); Napoleon (1858–70: xx. No. 16589; xxi. No. 16753).

government to abandon its policy—just too late to avoid a final break by the United States.

The decision in America was not the result of popular pressure. The war party was distinctly a minority, New England was solidly against the war and would become mutinous in its course, and Madison's failure to gain any concessions from France made it harder to justify war against Britain for its violations of American rights. Congress did little to prepare the nation militarily or fiscally for the war toward which it was consciously drifting. In the end, the failure to gain British concessions in time and the sense that the national honour was at stake, plus unrealistic hopes of somehow influencing France while fighting Britain, led to Madison's reluctant decision to call on Congress for a declaration of war. Pressure by Western war hawks for territorial expansion was also not a major motive. The attempt to conquer Canada was more the consequence of war than its cause, undertaken less because Canada was a coveted prize than because attacking it was the best way to get at Britain.[48]

Historians are not supposed to act as moral judges; at least they are supposed to disguise it discreetly when they do. Still, that canon has been violated often enough in this book, and some remarks on responsibilities for this war seem justified. The judgements of its leading historians, Bradford Perkins, Donald Hickey, and James Stagg, seem sound: that it came despite Madison rather than because of him, though it reflects badly on his leadership; that national honour was the central issue; that the war resulted from drift rather than clear resolution or warlike spirit on either side; and that from the American standpoint it was probably justified but perhaps unnecessary. Clearly the United States had a real grievance on impressment, though the British could counter it with their own on the American practice of issuing false papers to seamen, and the impressment issue largely dropped out of sight on the eve of war. America's commercial and legal complaints were also justified, though France harmed American trade and property rights at least as much as Britain did, and Americans themselves notoriously evaded their own laws and bent the international rules in their favour. Part of Britain's problem clearly derived from the same insular attitudes and mercantilist principles that plagued their relations with other countries besides America;

[48] Perkins (1963: 249–410); Crouzet (1958: ii. 699–707, 808–29); Bonnel (1961: 289–301).

they learned, but in this instance too late. At the same time Americans had their own prejudices and blinkers, especially in failing to allow for the enormous strains of a world war on their opponents and the inability of a parliamentary regime to match Napoleon's unscrupulous flexibility.

Among the wars in the history of the United States, this one was at least as justified as most; in the world conflict it turned out, fortunately, to make no great difference. But an American historian of European politics may perhaps be permitted to wonder why American historians have made little of the paradox that an infant democratic republic should have entered this titanic world struggle on the side of one of modern history's worst tyrants. Contingent events can explain this, no doubt; but usually something deeper lies behind them. Was it perhaps that one emotion linked Jefferson and Madison, great theorists of democracy, with Napoleon, a great military despot: a visceral hatred of Great Britain?[49]

Events in the New World, in any case, were of little concern to Europe as Napoleon prepared to invade Russia. A teleological view of history may see this as the darkness just before the dawn. Like many teleological views, it contains an important truth, but misses what was central at the time. Europeans in mid-1812 certainly did not expect to be liberated from Napoleonic rule; many did not even hope or long for this. They now knew, to be sure, that Napoleon was in trouble against Britain and in Spain. Nevertheless, even most of those who tried to warn Napoleon against invading Russia believed that he would win the war, and would not have expected a defeat in Russia to lead to his downfall. The message they drew from the prospect of war against Russia was simply that the Empire would not settle down, as they had hoped; the decade of uncertainty, upheaval, and war under Napoleon would continue. This was a correct, unavoidable conclusion. So was the growing recognition that this would happen most of all because Napoleon himself, though more wilful than ever, was not really in control of events, but trapped by them. What ensnared him was not simply opponents he could not destroy or ambitions within himself he could not bridle, but an absence, a vacuum, something missing in his inner and outer worlds, which he could not create or even conceive: an idea and structure of peace.

[49] See above all Perkins (1963; 1962); Hickey (1989); Stagg (1983); Horsman (1962); also Blumenthal (1970: 20–7); D. Gray (1963: 450–3).

Europe was trapped along with him—France and its satellites, vassal states, and unequal allies first and foremost. But so were Napoleon's opponents—Spain and Portugal in wars which were destroying them but which they could not abandon, Russia in a conflict it dreaded but had to face, even Britain in a war it was not losing but for which it could envision no end. The only states not caught in the general quicksand, Sweden and the Ottoman Empire, had only recently escaped, and the escape looked very temporary. All, like Napoleon, were trapped not only in apparently interminable conflict, but also in exhausted alternatives, the absence of a concept of peace.

Europe, in short, was lost. The word may sound melodramatic, but it can apply to politics as well as to psychology, theology, or literature, and only the word 'lost' captures the mood which infected Europe's leaders in 1811–12 and percolated down toward their peoples. Napoleon still probably had as many defenders and followers as secret and open enemies; the masses, as often happens, were mainly trying to endure and survive. But no one, even partisans of the Empire, any longer believed in its permanence or knew what would come next, and few were any longer confident that Napoleon knew. Those outside the Empire were little better off. This condition of profound and pervasive political uncertainty and disorientation was not simply the product of Napoleonic imperialism or revolutionary upheaval or protracted war; it represented the climax of a long historic development. Out of the collision between the amoral, unrestrained international politics of the eighteenth century and the ideologically charged, pseudo-moral international politics of the French Revolution had emerged a wholly lawless Napoleonic politics, not even international but colonial-imperialist in essence. Eighteenth-century and revolutionary rules of international politics had proved not to work for the purpose of ending war and stabilizing the European state system; now, under Napoleon's rules, that very system was being destroyed and nothing durable put in its place. No one knew how to stop this process, or escape it, or put it right. The question of who would win the coming war in Russia was crucial, but not so critical as another: what kind of international system would come out of the war? Would any at all?

PART II

The Construction of the Nineteenth-Century System

10
Beginning and End, 1812–1813

A single continuous theme seems to run through the story from June 1812 to August 1813, starting with the destruction of the Grand Army in Russia and continuing with the formation of a great new coalition to liberate Europe: the beginning of the end of Napoleon's Empire. For purposes of general history and military history this theme serves reasonably well. In international history, however, the dominant note is discontinuity: the story is one of three successive failures and the changes they brought to international politics. Napoleon's defeat in Russia was the first and most spectacular failure, but two others, less well known, also affected the emerging pattern of European politics: the failure of the allied effort to win the war in the spring of 1813, and the failure of an Austrian attempt to negotiate a Continental peace. The period 1812–13 therefore involved not only the beginning of the end for Napoleon's Empire, but also the end of the beginning in the search for a new basis for European international politics, in which two avenues to peace were tried and found wanting.

I. NAPOLEON'S DEFEAT IN RUSSIA

The Grand Army's destruction in Russia is too epic and familiar a story to be retold here, but we need to note its basic causes, for they relate to politics. The Grand Army did not fall prey to winter or bad luck. As David Chandler points out, it was decisively defeated already when it reached Moscow, shrunk by about two-thirds and facing inevitable further decline.[1] Winter weather intensified the army's sufferings, but was not the main cause of its dissolution; in fact, at certain key points the cold actually aided the retreat, and certainly helped Napoleon himself to escape.

Many factors explain the disaster—on the French side, summer heat, the vast distances, the breakdown of Napoleon's elaborate supply system, his gambling, one-shot strategy and his tactical blunders, and above all the fact that even a huge, well-prepared

---

[1] Chandler (1966: 858).

army like this one could not really conquer a vast, remote territory like Russia under early nineteenth-century conditions, much less occupy it, supply itself within it, and maintain its lines of communications. On the Russian side, the factors include a shrewd plan of attrition through strategic withdrawal, scorched-earth warfare, Cossack and partisan attacks and harassment, and, finally, the staying power of the Russian army, which did not cover itself with glory in battle and showed some of the same organizational and leadership deficiencies as earlier, but remained a coherent fighting force despite sufferings only somewhat less harrowing than those of its foe.[2]

But while military causes clearly explain the disaster, they also point up the fundamental political folly of the enterprise: launching such a war without a clear political goal and waging it without an accompanying political strategy. Military historians stress the deterioration of Napoleon's powers of military decision and command in this campaign.[3] There was no deterioration, or even change, in his political style; in 1812 its ultimate consequences merely began catching up to him. It is easy to be dazzled by Napoleon's genius in certain fields and overlook those in which he was incompetent. Conspicuous among these was normal politics—the ability to organize and lead without overt coercion, to achieve and sustain durable co-operative relationships—and that incompetence helped ruin him here. Militarily he made mistakes in this campaign; politically he was simply out of his depth. He debated, for example, whether to use such political weapons against Russia as proclaiming a Polish Kingdom or emancipating the Russian serfs, but decided against it because it would frighten his allies. His fatal indecision and delay in abandoning Moscow in the fall, and his genuine shock and anger at Russia's scorched-earth warfare, especially when it culminated in the burning of Moscow, show his inability to cope with enemies who refused to fight as he expected, or to admit defeat and ask for terms when he considered them beaten.

The most striking proof of his political incompetence came when, having captured Moscow and (he claimed) won the war, he discovered that he could not end it and get out of Russia, because

---

[2] Ibid. *passim*; Kolosov (1985). For other critiques of Napoleonic and Russian tactics, organization, and strategy, see Paret (1966: 196–8, 202–4); Groote and Müller (1968: 240–4); Beyrau (1984: 62–4); Keep (1980). A thorough, admiring account of the Grand Army is Elting (1988). Wellington, writing in 1825, analysed the campaign much as Chandler did; Wellington (1862–80: iii. 1–53).

[3] e.g. H. Parker (1944).

he could not conceive or define peace. His recourse was to send his former ambassador, General Lauriston, uninvited to the Russian commander, Marshal Kutuzov, with hints that his master wished to know the Tsar's ideas on peace. The move got the reception it deserved. Alexander flatly rejected it, exploited it for Russian propaganda, and forbade any more contacts with the French until they were off Russian soil. Napoleon, searching for a way to make Alexander speak to him, next thought of threatening St Petersburg on his way out of Russia. That notion, hopeless in any case, turned absurd as his army's retreat degenerated into desperate flight and dissolution. The normal diplomatic ways of opening contacts with the enemy for peace, mediation by neutrals or pressure from allies, were barred to him, both because he had forced all the states of Europe to fight either with or against him in this war and because he had no ideas to propose.[4]

Thus seen, the Russian campaign becomes in a sense less a normal European international war than a colonial disaster, a failed imperialist venture, like the destruction of the Roman legions in the Teutoberg Forest or Britain's defeat in Afghanistan in 1839–42 on a grander scale. Napoleon's reaction to defeat confirms that impression. Abandoning his army in western Russia to its fate, he fled to Paris to reassert control over his Empire. In his famous 29th Bulletin he blamed the destruction of the Grand Army on bad weather, bad luck, and failures and betrayals by others. Most important, he set out, not to seek peace and a new political relationship with Russia, but to bar it from his fortress empire. He promptly demanded new armies and contributions from his satellites and allies to preserve European civilization, he said, from Tsarist barbarism and revolution and from English tyranny and corruption. His final words in the 29th Bulletin announcing the destruction of the Grand Army, 'The Emperor's health has never been better', indicated not only his egoism and the personal nature of the Empire, but also its Achilles' heel. In October 1812, a conspiracy led by General Claude-François de Malet and two other ex-generals, using a false report of his death, momentarily shook his throne at Paris; news of the Malet affair helped motivate Napoleon's flight home. He conceded now that Russia could not be conquered and that some of Poland might be lost (which the Poles deserved, he claimed, for not fighting as they should have), but he retained his old imperial-colonialist

---

[4] This is based generally on Napoleon (1858–70: xxiv. esp. Nos. 18962, 18971, 18982, 19044, 19213, 19237, 19369–72, 19384) and Caulaincourt (1935: i.); see also Schiemann (1904: i. 110–11); *VPR* (1960–: 1. vi. 576, 587).

outlook and goals, refusing to consider concessions on Danzig, the Oder fortresses, or the Continental System, and proposing to erect a *cordon sanitaire* against Russia in Europe.[5]

The Russians in some ways conducted their wartime politics as skilfully as Napoleon had bungled his. Throughout the war they maintained secret contacts with Prussia and Austria (warm with Berlin, chilly with Vienna), accepting their private assurances that only *force majeure* put them on Napoleon's side (knowing this was not true in Austria's case), and promising not to seek revenge if they defected. Alexander's refusal to talk to Napoleon complemented Russia's popular resistance and its strategy of retreat and scorched-earth warfare. It also suited the Tsar's revived messianic mood, and was necessary if he wished to survive on his throne. With many already blaming him for Russia's dangers and suffering, any negotiation with Napoleon, especially while Russia's confidence in ultimate victory was rising, would have invited a palace revolt or assassination. But political wisdom often involves recognizing necessity and obeying it. This holds also for the decision Russia took in December to pursue the war into Europe. It was not really a controversial or difficult decision to reach, though it involved great risk and sacrifice. Russia would obviously not be secure until France was expelled from Central Europe; even Kutuzov, often considered an opponent of continuing the war, only wanted to wait and rest his troops in Lithuania first.[6]

Thus Russia's strategy was sound, first to drive out the French and then to build a new coalition for Russian and European security. But Russian tactics, though better than Napoleon's, still left something to be desired. The Treaty of Bucharest failed to produce real peace with the Ottoman Empire, much less an alliance, because Chichagov continued to promote revolution among the Balkan Slavs, especially the Serbs, kept the treaty unfulfilled with an eye to renewing the war later, and planned a revolutionary campaign in the south against Austria. Even after this was abandoned, Russia's territorial claims in the Transcaucasus helped induce the Porte to refuse to ratify the treaty. By withdrawing from the Principalities Russia took a step toward better relations with Austria, but its other activities in the Balkans kept Vienna's suspicions and fears as lively as ever. True, Met-

[5] Napoleon (1858–70: xxiv. Nos. 19385, 19424, 19462, 19481, 19488, 19517 and *passim*). For the Malet affair, see Melchior-Bonnet (1962: 203–18).
[6] *VPR* (1960–: 1. vi. Nos. 147, 272–4, 279, 297–8; pp. 597, 600); Gritzbach (1974: i. 268–72); Schmitt (1959); Raeff (1964: 257); Martens (1874–1905: viii. 62–3).

ternich maintained secret contacts with Russia, and the Austrian commander, General Prince Karl Schwarzenberg, did as little fighting in Russia as possible, but both would have done this in any case. In the Convention of Abö in late August 1812, Russia persisted in its plans with Sweden for a landing on the North German coast and a German rising in Napoleon's rear, even though these plans had long become impracticable. The result, since Russia could not give Sweden the promised military aid, was to tie Russia further to Sweden's anti-Danish ambitions and help Carl Johan extract a large loan from Russia while doing nothing concrete for Russia in return. Moreover, the fact that Russia in this treaty claimed the Vistula as its future frontier was bound to give Prussia concerns about East Prussia and Silesia and arouse Austrian and British suspicions of Russian war aims.[7]

These mistakes could be attributed to the pressures of a profound national emergency. Russia's delays in concluding an alliance with Britain were deliberate. Alexander declined to respond to Britain's overtures until after France had formally declared war, and then rebuffed a special mission by Lord Cathcart to promote an alliance, preferring to deal through his own emissary, Count Lieven, not sent to London until late in the year. Meanwhile Russia tried through Sweden to make Britain pay a considerable price for the restoration of peace, trade, and the old alliance. The Russian demands included British accession to the existing Russo-Swedish alliance, a British promise to subsidize Sweden, Russia, and any other states or forces Russia might lead into the coalition, British assumption of Russia's debt to Holland, large quantities of material aid, British support for Sweden's proposed campaign against Zealand, and British diversionary landings in North Germany and Italy. Though Britain was eager for an alliance, these demands slowed the pace of Anglo-Russian reconciliation to a crawl. Formal Anglo-Russian peace was not restored until a month after the invasion, trade relations were opened and permission given to individual Russian merchants to trade with Britain only after the Battle of Borodino, Russian ports were opened to British vessels only after the fall of Moscow, and Russia's steep tariffs on British goods were not abolished at all.[8]

[7] *VPR* (1960–: 1. vi. Nos. 187, 192, 207, 215, 221, 230; pp. 459–60, 603); Chichagov (1909: 383–408); Schiemann (1904: i. 278–9).

[8] *VPR* (1960–: 1. vi. Nos. 169, 175, 182, 193, 199–200, 228; pp. 529, 550, 565, 568); Martens (1874–1905: xi. 155–61); Sherwig (1969: 275–82). For evidence that the Russians knew they needed British aid badly, see *VPR* (1960–: 1. vi. Nos. 269, 289, 295).

On Poland, Russians remained sharply divided. Czartoryski, having earlier refused to join Alexander against Napoleon and the Poles of the Duchy, now urged Alexander to bring all of Poland, including Austria's and Prussia's shares, into permanent union with Russia under Romanov rule. Nesselrode and others warned the Tsar that this would create a permanent revolutionary danger within Russia and alienate Austria forever. Alexander compromised, deciding not to proclaim himself King of Poland openly, but to finesse his way to Russian control of all or most of it, while at the same time luring Austria onto his side against Napoleon.[9] In sum, by early 1813 Russia's military victory had given it a chance both to regain its own independence and security and to help establish that of Europe as a whole. This was in general what the Tsar and many Russians wanted; their goals were not openly or consciously imperialist. But whether Russia's particular aims and tactics would actually help build European peace was another question.

II. PRUSSIA'S RISING AND THE WAR OF LIBERATION

Russia, however, would not decide everything. Just as the rising of the Russian people in 1812 had changed the whole picture, cancelling five years of Russian alliance and collaboration with Napoleon, so a popular rising in Prussia beginning in 1813 seemed to offer a chance not only to rescue Prussia and Germany from the French yoke but to counter the danger to Europe from a too-powerful Russia. Prussians now would prove, as Spaniards, Britons, and Russians already had, that peoples fighting for their lives and liberty were more important in winning the war and creating a new Europe than chanceries and diplomats.

There is some truth to this view. A real rising did occur in Prussia. It was broad and deep enough to be called 'national', and closely connected with the ultimate victory over Napoleon and the European peace settlement in 1814–15, as well as with the rise of German nationalism later in the nineteenth century—so closely connected, in fact, that one cannot see how these developments could have come about without it. But another generalization must accompany this one: the Prussian rising was not basically

---

[9] Ibid. 1. vii. Nos. 40, 138; pp. 11, 28, 179; Alexander (1865: 169–213); Nesselrode (1904–12: iv. 287–320).

German nationalist or any kind of nationalist in the modern sense of the term, and the German nationalism that did arise during the War of Liberation was not an important factor in winning the war and fashioning the peace. In fact, its military and political influence in 1813-15 was, on balance, harmful and counter-productive.

Only the unfolding story can show how these apparently contradictory generalizations fit together; it must start with an examination of the Prussian rising. As already seen, the reform movement in Prussia had preceded the French occupation in 1806 and lasted through it. Except for certain military reforms, however, the movement owed little to French influence, and its aim was not to prepare a rising against France but to secure Prussia a more tolerable existence under French hegemony. Even in this, as we have seen, the movement failed.[10] Up to and even beyond the fall of Moscow, the war in Russia served to tighten France's grip on Prussia and increase its sufferings, but not to evoke a general resistance. As elsewhere in Europe, some in Prussia wanted to resist, some collaborated, and most tried to stay out of trouble and survive. The Prussian government repressed what anti-French conspiracy it found. Until the general collapse of the Grand Army, Prussia's contingent served in it reasonably well. At home, Hardenberg's reform program, far from uniting the nation, kept class divisions and the old civil–military antagonisms alive while fuelling a new conflict between feudal conservatives and bureau-cratic centralizing reformers. This reached a peak in late summer 1812 over Hardenberg's Gendarmerie Edict, an attempt to cen-tralize the local administration of justice.[11]

Though the rising against France which began in early 1813 ultimately spread widely, enthusiasm and popular support for it varied greatly, being strongest in East Prussia and the Mark of Brandenburg, which had been least under the French heel, weaker in Silesia, and weakest of all in Berlin. Moreover, to the extent that Prussians united behind it, they did so not for reform, constitutional liberty, and Prussian and/or German unity, but out of hatred of the foreign invader and a religiously based traditional loyalty to God, king, and country. This puts the Prussian move-ment in the same general category as concurrent ones in Spain,

[10] See (in addition to the discussion in Ch. 9) Herre (1973: 144–9, 184–5); Thielen (1967: 214–15, 234–41); Sieburg (1971: 208–13); Ibbeken (1970: 60–5, 82–5); Huber (1957: i. 118–21).

[11] Ibbeken (1970: 96–319); Münchow-Pohl (1987: 352–71); Siemann (1985: 67–71).

Russia, the Tyrol, and Calabria, as well as other regions which revolted against Napoleon and the French earlier or later. The genuine popular risings were all traditional and backward-looking more than modern and liberal. Even in the army, the arena of most successful reform, the war of liberation tended less to make Prussia's professional army more national and popular than to make the Prussian state and nation more military. The same trend would continue in 1866 and 1870.[12]

As for winning the war, the main contribution the Prussian rising made to this was indirect, though crucial: not to destroy or expel the enemy directly, but to help force Prussia's king and government to switch sides, thereby bringing the regular army into action, and then to support that army in the field. Hardenberg did not want Napoleon to conquer Russia, but he fully expected him to. Only when Moscow went up in flames did Hardenberg recognize that the Emperor was in trouble, and only after he had raced through Germany toward Paris, pausing at Dresden to order Prussia to mobilize another 30,000 men for him, did Hardenberg begin preparing to take Prussia over to Russia's side at the proper moment. He still had to move cautiously, in order to deceive the French who retained most of Prussia in their grip, to gain time for military and diplomatic preparations, to keep the patriotic movement under control, and above all to get his monarch to take a stand.

Thus the government did not welcome the first clear signal of the rising, an unauthorized armistice signed at Tauroggen in East Prussia on 30 December by Russian officers with General Johann Yorck, commander of the Prussian corps operating on the French left flank. The King and Hardenberg promptly condemned and repudiated the convention, the former genuinely, Hardenberg for tactical reasons. The insurrection none the less gained momentum when another Prussian general, von Bülow, though declining to sign a convention like Yorck's, agreed to let the Russians advance to the Oder River as his own forces retired. Accompanying the Russian move into East Prussia and Silesia were Yorck, a leading feudal-conservative opponent of reform, and Baron vom Stein, a leading reformer who since June 1812 had advised the Tsar on German affairs. In late January, Stein organized a meeting of the East Prussian Diet at Königsberg presided over by Yorck, acting

---

[12] Münchow-Pohl (1987: 408–9, 426–9); Ibbeken (1970: 73–6, 385–8); Ritter (1958: 396–8); Rothenberg (1978: 195–6). For recent restatements of the traditional view, see Best (1982: 64–5, 155–7); Koch (1987: 340–65).

as governor-general of the province. Here 13,000 reservists were summoned to the colours, a 20,000-man *Landwehr* (reserve army or national guard) was created, and a *Landsturm* (home guard) was decreed, all in the King's name and with appeals to him to lead the movement.

Soon the same basic drama was repeated at Breslau for Silesia; volunteers from other provinces went east to join the insurgent forces. Hardenberg meanwhile put Scharnhorst back in charge of Prussia's armaments, holding the French off with assurances that Prussia was still loyal to France and only obeying its calls to arms, and warnings that unless the King armed to gain control of the patriotic movement he would be overthrown by it. These arguments were not simply a smokescreen. The King and many of his advisers were deeply averse to more war and fearful of its risks. As late as 4 February Frederick William's adviser, Johann Friedrich Ancillon, drew up a proposal, actually offered to France but rejected, calling for Prussia to mediate between France and Russia for peace, with Prussia to be restored as a middle-sized state between the Elbe and the Vistula while Russia made gains in the east and France retained its grip on the rest of Germany. Even Hardenberg, though he went along with this proposal mainly for tactical reasons, wanted to secure Prussia's gains from war politically before entering it, the gains being generally those he had pursued since 1794—territorial expansion in Germany and political leadership in at least all of North Germany. It took till 20 February, by which time two-thirds of the Prussian army were operating independently of the King's command, to bring Frederick William finally to leave Berlin for Breslau to join the Russians and his people against France.[13]

A series of landmarks in Prussia's insurrection and Germany's war of liberation quickly followed: a Russo-Prussian alliance at Kalisch and Breslau on 27–8 February, Prussia's declaration of war on France in mid-March, and on 19 March a Russo-Prussian convention at Breslau on the liberation and reconstruction of Germany, accompanied by appeals to the Prussian and German people to rise against the enemy. These great steps, however, would lead the allies, not to victory and freedom, but to a dead end.

To understand why, one needs to see first what Russia meant and aimed at in these treaties and proclamations. There were

[13] Münchow-Pohl (1987: 371–83); Thielen (1967: 280–7); Ibbeken (1970: 372–83); *VPR* (1960–: 1. vii. No. 1).

positive sides to its policy. It promised to restore Prussia to its power and status as of 1806, and abandoned certain gains for itself—the designs on East Prussia indicated in the Convention of Abö (which had probably not been seriously entertained, though the idea had cropped up in Russian foreign policy ever since the early eighteenth-century) as well as Czartoryski's ideas of uniting all of Poland with Russia. Prussia would retain enough Polish territory to connect East Prussia and Silesia, and would be compensated for the sacrifice of its other Polish territories from the allies' joint conquests in Germany. To this extent, the agreements represented a better kind of Russian coalition-building than earlier, not as nakedly hegemonic or ready to exploit the rivalries and exposed positions of other states in Central Europe.

Other aspects of Russia's policy, however, remained traditional and worrisome. One reason it proved difficult to negotiate the Treaty of Kalisch was that the Prussian negotiator, the King's aide, Colonel Knesebeck, either misunderstood or deliberately defied Hardenberg's instructions, stubbornly defending Prussia's claim to all its former Polish territory. Knesebeck, an old-fashioned Prussian who cared little for Hardenberg's German plans but much for Prussia's former European great-power position, recognized that Russia was really reviving its old Northern System in an expanded and more dangerous form. By controlling most of Poland, it would threaten Prussia strategically, make it dependent on Russia for its compensations in Germany, and push Sweden and Prussia westward as Russia's buffer states. Alexander's messianic zeal to liberate Prussia and Europe only made this worse. As the Tsar made clear in his initial instructions to his new ambassador to Prussia, Daniel Alopeus, he was willing to welcome Prussia back into the fold, but as a forgiven sinner to be watched, kept on the right path, and not permitted to question his decisions and leadership on vital questions, especially Poland.[14]

The presence of Stein in the Tsar's entourage, along with other fiery German patriots like the poet-publicist E. M. Arndt, did nothing to avert this danger, and appointing Stein as head of a Central Administrative Council for organizing insurrections in Germany and provisionally governing liberated German territories made it worse. Stein and others developed constitutional plans for Germany from September 1812 on, which have been the object of

[14] Martens (1874–1905: viii. 50–2, 74–81, 82–7, 96–9); *VPR* (1960–: 1. vi. No. 23; n. 43, pp. 711–12; vii. No. 56); Bailleu (1900: 246–52); *Sbornik* (1867–1916: cxxxiii. 433–546); Ritter (1958: 428–30).

controversy ever since. Two of the most important responses to
Stein's ideas came at the time from Gneisenau and Count Münster,
the Hanoverian minister and spokesman for Britain and Hanover
on German questions. There were divergences, but in three
respects their plans were alike. First, they would have divided
Germany, not united it. Stein's central aim was to strengthen
Germany against France, and while he often changed his mind on
the best way to do so, his regular means was to divide Germany
along the Main River, make Austria and Prussia partners in
control of their respective halves, and sharply limit the size and
independence of the Rheinbund states. Münster and Gneisenau
opposed this Austro-Prussian dualism, but rather than a united
Germany they favoured an enlarged Hanover in north-west
Germany to limit Prussia's expansion. They saw Austria and
Prussia as European more than German powers, and conceived
the rest of Germany primarily in Third German terms. All the
plans connected the new Germany to areas not strictly German—
i.e. Schleswig-Holstein, which was partly Danish and belonged to
the King of Denmark, Switzerland, and even Holland and part of
Belgium.

Secondly, partly as a result of the extension of Germany into
non-German areas, these schemes would not have banned foreign
influence and intervention from Germany but preserved or increased it. Stein thought of bringing in Russia, Britain, and even
Sweden as guarantors and supervisors of the new Germany;
Münster envisioned tying Britain to it via Hanover and Holland.

A third point, and the most important for international politics,
is that Stein's and other patriots' ideas for creating a great popular
rising against Napoleon not only were unlikely to work (and in
fact did not) but also were regressive rather than progressive in
terms of international politics. They represented an attempt,
under the mantle of a general German patriotism, to make the
governments and peoples of Germany gamble their existence for a
supposed common cause which others would define and lead,
on pain of punishment if they refused. This was to revive the
disastrous attempts of the first three coalitions to coerce governments and peoples of Europe into fighting for a supposed new
European order whether they wanted to or not. Not only would
this not produce a new European order; the belief that such tactics
would work militarily, that the allies could bring about a mass
insurrection by such exhortation and pressure, defied all the
experience of previous wars, including those of 1809 and 1812,
when efforts to organize landings and insurrections behind the

enemy lines had come to nothing. A German Legion formed of prisoners of war and deserters in Russia in 1812 turned out to be small and proved militarily almost worthless. In the campaign of April–May 1813, efforts under Stein's leadership to raise popular armies and promote a general insurrection in Germany were unsuccessful, and aroused the resentment even of princes sympathetic to the Russo-Prussian cause such as the Dukes of Oldenburg and Mecklenburg-Schwerin.[15]

While the Russo-Prussian policy in Germany thus set its course toward failure, Napoleon managed to extract new levies and exertions from his satellites, despite their bitter resentment of his new demands after their losses in Russia, proportionally far worse than those of France. Even the King of Saxony, who signed a neutrality agreement with Austria in April, returned to the fold in May. Napoleon had powerful weapons to hold his vassal states in line: his control of propaganda and information, the threat of force, the fact that many princes owed their political existence to him, and the still-persistent belief in his military genius. But Russia, Prussia, and Stein and Company also provided him a propaganda weapon he exploited to the hilt: that an allied victory would mean revolution in Germany, overthrowing all thrones, undermining the existing order, and destroying the possibility of peace.[16]

Thus political and military factors combined to blight the allies' high hopes for the spring campaign. Napoleon's army, hastily thrown together from veterans and new recruits, drove the Russo-Prussian forces out of Saxony back into Silesia in the battles of Lützen and Bautzen in May. The victories, unlike Napoleon's earlier ones, were won by superior numbers rather than skill, with the French incurring slightly more casualties than they inflicted and being unable to exploit their advantage for lack of cavalry. The allied armies, especially Prussia's raw and ill-equipped forces, proved that they could absorb defeat and remain a fighting force. Yet the defeats cost the allies heavily in morale and control of territory they needed for supplies and recruitment. Though neither came close to being knocked out of the war, General Barclay, who had resumed command of the Russian army on Kutuzov's death, seriously considered withdrawing his forces into Russia to regroup.

[15] Ibid. 404–7, 434–5, 440–5; Ibbeken (1970: 346–58, 364–5, 394–439); Groote (1953: 52–63); Huber (1957: i. 486–993); *VPR* (1960–: 1. vi. No. 54).

[16] Caulaincourt (1935: i. 418–19, 528–31); Chroust (1932: 339–52); Schwarz (1933: 6–12); Dunan (1939: 139–42); Schlossberger (1889: 258–90); Bonjour (1965: i. 165–76); Zaghi (1969: 379–93).

Almost as discouraging was the failure of North Germany to rise and rally to the allied cause. Even at Hamburg, which the allies had liberated and occupied with a Cossack detachment while the French were still demoralized, a combination of factors (the inertia and greed of the Russian commander, General Tettenborn, lack of coordination between the Prussians and Swedes who were supposed to move in to support the occupation, and Swedish–Danish rivalry) enabled Davout, with Danish help, to recapture the city and hold it until the very end of the war. Meanwhile, all allied efforts to lure Austria into the coalition failed. In early June, Metternich arranged a six-weeks' truce which both sides accepted as a welcome breathing-space and a chance to bring Austria over to their side.

Britain provided a ray of light for the hard-pressed allies on 8 June by concluding alliance and subsidy treaties with them at Reichenbach. Once again, Britain was the suitor though Russia was the one in desperate need. To meet its calls for massive financial aid, the British devised a scheme to supplement its direct subsidies (two million pounds, two-thirds of which would go to Russia and one-third to Prussia) with five million pounds in 'federal paper', a special currency to be issued and used by the Russian and Prussian governments for war expenditures, to be backed by the British government's credit and redeemed jointly by the three governments after the war. The British also concluded a generous subsidy alliance with Sweden, partly for Russia's sake. In all this they deliberately overlooked how Russia and Prussia in the Treaty of Kalisch had ignored British interests save for Hanover and aimed at a Continental peace with Napoleon. For Castlereagh and the British government, Russia was still Britain's natural ally; for the Russian government, Britain was still a rival. Russian envoys in the Near East, Italy, and the New World warned St Petersburg about British imperialist aims and urged it to compete with Britain now for world trade and influence. The one move that appeared a friendly gesture, Russia's offer to mediate in the British–American war, was just the opposite—an attempt to save the American fleet as a counterweight to British maritime supremacy and a way of forcing Britain to end its maritime despotism. The fact that a year went by between the time Napoleon invaded Russia and the point at which Russia signed an alliance with Britain was due partly to technical problems, especially in the federal-paper scheme. The basic problem, however, was that Russia really wanted to obtain British aid without having to share leadership in the coalition and the war with Britain. In this sense, in signing a British alliance and pledging itself to no separate peace or negotiations, Russia accepted something of a political defeat.[17]

If the alliance meant a grudging recognition by Russia of its limitations, the unstinting character of British aid in both money and material, coming on top of Britain's efforts in Spain, North America, and the high seas,[18] demonstrated a further change in Britain's outlook toward Europe. One indispensable element in the change was accidental and providential. Castlereagh, rather than Lord Liverpool's first choice, George Canning, became foreign secretary in the Liverpool ministry formed in 1812 on the death of Spencer Perceval.[19] The difference this made to British policy was as important as the difference it made that, in May 1940, Winston Churchill rather than Lord Halifax succeeded Neville Chamberlain. With Halifax in charge instead of Churchill, Britain might have made peace in 1940; with Canning instead of Castlereagh, Britain would still have won the war in 1814–15, but would not have made the contribution it did to a durable peace. Castlereagh came to office believing in all the traditional British aims: to win the war and restore a balance of power against France, free Holland and Antwerp, set up Germany and Italy as barriers against France, restore Hanover, retain Britain's more valuable colonial gains, and maintain its maritime rights and supremacy. What set Castlereagh apart from most of his colleagues and countrymen was his uncommon fund of good sense, his ability and readiness to see other points of view, and his willingness to adapt British policy to the facts and needs of Europe. Liverpool, formerly Lord Hawkesbury, had himself been foreign secretary, and generally supported Castlereagh's efforts to compromise and feel his way toward the goal. On a whole series of issues—relations with Russia and Prussia, the German question, Holland, Hanover, Sicily, and ultimately Austria—Castlereagh showed not only good sense and moderation but also a genuine

---

[17] Martens (1874–1905: xi. 166–76); *VPR* (1960–: 1. vii. Nos. 13–14, 55, 62, 87, 105, 127). On the Russian offer of mediation, see ibid. Nos. 126, 128; Saul (1991: 71–2). For Soviet interpretations of British aid as niggardly, selfish, designed to use Prussia and Austria against Russia, driven by class interests, and forced upon a reluctant British government by the public's enthusiasm at Russia's victories, see Zak (1957); *VPR* (1960–: 1. vii. n. 142, p. 734).

[18] Sherwig (1969: 272–93).

[19] Webster (1921: p. xxx). Canning lost his chance to be foreign secretary by insisting on the leadership of the House of Commons as well. He later bitterly regretted his decision as a set-back to his career, writing to his close friend Granville Leveson-Gower, 'The situation in Europe and in history which I have thrown away is full before my eyes'; 22 Oct. 1813, PRO 30/29/8/5, fos. 660–1.

interest in Europe and a readiness to listen to others and to work with them that one could never expect from Canning or Wellesley.[20]

Britain's generosity toward its allies did not always pay off, especially with Sweden, whose Crown Prince continued to manipulate the great powers for his own purposes. In the Anglo-Swedish alliance of 3 March 1813, Britain promised Sweden a million-pound subsidy for 30,000 men to fight on the Continent, naval support to help compel the Danes to surrender Norway, and the island of Guadeloupe as a possible additional or consolation prize. This amazing alliance ruined the prospects for bringing Denmark's King Frederick VI into the coalition, and made any allied military action in the North hostage to Sweden's ambitions. It bore fruit first in late May when, as already noted, the Swedes failed to prevent the loss of Hamburg to a combined French–Danish army under Davout, and then in July, when Denmark was forced back body and soul into France's camp. The episode demonstrated Britain's persistent tendency to concentrate more on the Baltic and Northern Europe than on Central Europe or Europe as a whole, and to try to gain one small state at the expense of another. In fairness, one must note that Russia launched this policy with Sweden, Britain only inherited it, and Castlereagh never liked it.[21]

III. THE FAILURE OF AUSTRIAN MEDIATION

British policy worked even worse with Austria, but this was mainly because nothing could have brought Austria into the coalition before its own policy had failed. Historians, seeing how complicated and devious Metternich's diplomatic moves were

[20] For Castlereagh's earlier views on war aims and British policy, showing him Pittite in general outlook but unusually perceptive and objective in analysing European points of view, see Bartlett (1966: 48–50) and Castlereagh Papers (Durham), D/Lo/C/3, F/16. For his views in early 1813 on Russia, Prussia, and Germany, see Webster (1921: 1–4); Castlereagh (1850–3: viii. 355–9, 364–5, 374–5; ix. 4–7, 11–14, 21–3); Castlereagh to Stewart, 4 May 1813, PRONI D3030/3478. On British policy on Holland, see Renier (1930: 40–75); additional material on Hanover is in Lange (1956); Ompteda (1869: iii. 74–9); on Sicily and Italy, Rosselli (1956: 44–101); Sherwig (1969: 265–71).

[21] F. Scott (1935: 22–74); Tangeraas (1983: 197–206); Norregard (1954: 13–15); Castlereagh (1850–3: viii. 294–5, 325–31, 344–7, 376–7, 382–5); VPR (1960–: 1. vii. Nos. 8–9, 70, 88, 95; p. 179). The Anglo-Swedish treaty is in Chodzko (1863: i. 2–5); the Franco-Danish in DeClercq (1880–1917: ii. 386–92).

from late 1812 to mid-1813, have sometimes ascribed a similar complexity to his aims and calculations, and have supposed that uncovering his hidden agenda would enable them to explain the outcome. Metternich's tactics were certainly subtle and deceptive. He never told anyone the full truth, even his Emperor or Austria's representatives abroad; he always tried to lure others into commitments while remaining ready himself to change course and cover his tracks in retreat. Much of this is normal in diplomacy, of course, but other factors contributed to his devious flexibility— his personal style, the perils of Austria's situation between France and Russia, its military unpreparedness and the financial weakness that limited its efforts to rearm, a fear of revolution, especially strong in the Emperor, and the existence of a strong party within Austria that was suspicious of Metternich and wanted to lead Austria in another direction.

Yet Metternich's central purpose in 1813 was not a mystery at all. It was simple and consistent; he stated it time and again; and it was clearly distinct from those of the other main players. Napoleon wanted to win the war—indeed, had no other goal but winning. The British wanted to win the war in order to gain a general peace, still defined in traditional British fashion but pursued more flexibly than earlier. The Russians and Prussians wanted to win the war, above all in Germany, so as to achieve their particular version of a Continental peace. Austria (i.e. Metternich and Francis) wanted peace, an end to war, full stop. Behind this quest lay above all their fear of extinction. As Metternich said to the Russian ambassador, Prince Stackelberg, 'All the calculations of Austria and other poor intermediaries must be directed at how not to be *wiped out*' (emphasis in original).[22] But behind it was also the conviction that the war, if pursued to the point of military victory for either side, would ruin the chance for peace that had now emerged.

Not peace on just any terms, of course. Austria had to mediate it; Austria's nightmare was another Peace of Tilsit concluded by France and Russia over the heads of intermediary Europe. Peace also had to bring 'equilibrium and durable tranquillity', as the Treaty of Reichenbach, signed by Austria with Russia and Prussia on 27 June, would stipulate. This was not a mere conventional phrase. It defined a particular kind of settlement which Metternich repeatedly pressed on other powers through his various envoys. Gentz, now his secretary and a secret critic of Metternich's tactics

[22] To Stackelberg, 15 Jan. 1813, Nesselrode (1904–12: v. 11).

but supporter of his overall aim, most clearly expressed what it meant in a memorandum of 6 June, which the Emperor endorsed as a correct exposition of Austria's aims. Peace and durable tranquillity must arise primarily from persuasion and consensus, not force. Austria was arming, to be sure, but to defend itself against pressure from either side and to lend support to its mediation, not to prepare for war or to compel either side to accept its terms. The equilibrium of Europe would likewise have to rest, not on force, but on voluntary agreements and the deliberate acceptance of limits by all parties. Napoleonic France and Russia should both voluntarily retire behind their respective impregnable frontiers, the Rhine and the Vistula, and agree to be separated by an independent intermediary Europe, in which Austria, Prussia, and the rest of Germany would be sufficiently strengthened to remain independent. As Metternich suggested to Napoleon, an independent, neutralized Confederation of the Rhine might form part of this intermediary Europe. He was vague on what would happen to other areas in it (Switzerland, Italy, the Low Countries, Scandinavia), but insisted that Spain was not a European concern at all.

Clearly, two common notions about Metternich's policy in 1813 are hopelessly wide of the mark: that it was a return to eighteenth-century balance-of-power ideas, and that it was shrewd but short-sightedly selfish, concentrating too narrowly on averting revolution and protecting Austrian interests. Austria's vision of a settlement in 1813 broke radically with the old eighteenth- and early nineteenth-century Austrian ambitions for aggrandizement and visions of peace through military victory and power, and broke just as radically with the whole eighteenth-century balance-of-power game still being played by Britain and, in different ways, by Prussia and Russia. The fatal defect of Metternich's policy was not that it was short-sighted and selfish, but that it was visionary and impractical. It depended on persuading the two invulnerable flank powers of Continental Europe voluntarily to retire and allow an independent European centre to separate them, and (an unspoken premiss) on persuading or forcing Britain to go along with this, even while giving Britain's particular war aims in Europe scant attention or actually opposing them.

Yet, improbable as it seems, what Metternich did fits into a pursuit of this goal. He had already extended a peace feeler to Britain in November 1812. He attempted to draw Prussia into joint neutrality in January 1813. He endorsed Prussia's decision to join Russia, because it at least helped prevent another Tilsit and might persuade Napoleon to make peace; but he refused to join the allies and strongly criticized their tactics and aims in Germany. He sent peace missions to all the powers in February and March. He manœuvred carefully to get Austria out of the war and the French alliance and to gain Napoleon's tacit consent to Austria's armed mediation for peace. He tried hard to get Napoleon's German allies to join Austria in neutrality, temporarily succeeding with Saxony and almost doing so with Bavaria. After the allied defeats in May he mediated the armistice of Pleswitz on 4 June, following it by putting pressure on Napoleon to make peace and by negotiating with Russia and Prussia over the peace terms he would offer Napoleon on their behalf.[23]

Metternich continued to pursue this peace offensive, as will be seen, up to Austria's entry into the war in August and even beyond it. Yet it never had much chance of success, nor did it really offer a sound, long-term basis for peace. Metternich's aims and tactics are most important for the reaction they elicited from other powers and the role they played in the learning process ultimately leading Europe to peace. Though Russia never came close to accepting Metternich's version of a European settlement, it did adopt more conciliatory attitudes and tactics toward Austria. The Tsar, initially very angry over Austria's support of Napoleon's invasion, was persuaded by Nesselrode, Gentz's friend and Austria's strongest defender in Russia, to try gradually to pull Austria over to neutrality and then to accept Austrian mediation on condition that Austria enter the war if mediation failed—which, given Napoleon, it no doubt would.

The policy seemed to work. Austria and Russia managed to end the fighting between them and separate their forces, and co-operated in disbanding captured Polish units which had served under Napoleon (a blow to Czartoryski's hopes of reviving a Great Poland within Russia). Russia tacitly helped Austria liberate itself from the French alliance. It became clear fairly soon that Russian views on Germany and the Rheinbund states were not as radical as Stein's. In the Balkans, meanwhile, the Russians found themselves forced to co-operate more closely with Austria

---

[23] The main accounts are Luckwaldt (1898: 187–230, 249–307, 388–407); · Kraehe (1963: 147–80); Bertier (1986: 143–58). For Metternich's dealings with Bavaria, see Schwarz (1933: 11–78); for some Austrian, German, and Prussian reactions to his policy, see Rössler (1940: ii. 162–3; 1966: ii. 80–93); Ompteda (1869: iii. 145–54); Sweet (1978: ii. 128–31); Ritter (1958: 448–51). On Metternich's dealings with Russia, see Luckwaldt (1898: 78–87); Nesselrode (1904–12: v. 83–90); Oncken (1876: ii. 95–7, 101); VPR (1960–: 1. vii. Nos. 30, 59, 92, 96, 106–8, 114; pp. 220, 245).

as a result of the Peace of Bucharest and the abandonment of Chichagov's revolutionary plans during the war. Though Rumiantsev still argued that Russia must support the Balkan Slavs, it was plain that the Serbian insurrection was doomed, and that Russia needed Austrian help to provide humanitarian aid to the Serbs and restrain Turkish policy toward them.

Yet serious obstacles still impeded a *rapprochement*. The Russians blamed Austria for the failure of their spring campaign, and the conventions of Kalisch and Breslau intensified Austrian suspicions of Russia. The price Russia offered Austria for joining the alliance, a restoration of its status of 1805, was vague and less than what Prussia was promised. Austria in 1805 had already lost two great wars; Prussia in 1806 was profiting from ten years of neutrality. Besides this, Russia was committed to fight at Prussia's side to conquer its compensations in Germany; Austria was supposed to gain its prizes in Italy on its own. Poland was not yet a burning issue for Vienna at this time, and Metternich seems to have accepted the idea of Russia's advance to the Vistula. But Russia's failure to offer a clear plan on Germany, the evidence that Russia and Prussia regarded North Germany as their exclusive sphere, and Russia's protests at Austria's efforts to get Bavaria and Saxony out of the war in joint neutrality all suggested that Russia would challenge Austrian influence even in southern Germany. Such a challenge, if successful, would rule out an independent centre for Europe.[24] Yet despite the gap between them, by the armistice of Pleswitz Russia had learned that Austria was indispensable for purposes both of the war and of the future peace, and that was an important insight.

Prussians knew this truth even better. No party in Prussia by early 1813 was still Austrophobe in the traditional sense; all sought Austria's partnership, whether they wanted joint war against France, a defensive alliance, or joint mediation for peace. Before sending Knesebeck to negotiate the alliance with Russia, Frederick William sent him to Vienna first, where he received only noncommittal expressions of Austrian goodwill. But much as Prussians wanted a link with Austria, they had to be wary lest Austria betray or abandon them, or lest a connection with Austria alienate Russia and prematurely challenge France. New issues also arose between them. Prussia resented Metternich's efforts to lure

[24] For Russia's wooing of Austria, see Gritzbach (1974: i. 264–8); Nesselrode (1904–12: v. 12–21, 27–31); *VPR* (1960–: 1. vii. Nos. 6, 12, 17, 27–8, 32, 50–1). For evidence of continued differences and tension, see ibid. Nos. 39, 53, 61, 65–6; Nesselrode (1904–12: v. 81–2).

the Rheinbund princes into neutrality, with good reason. Not only did this clash with Prussia's search for allies, but Metternich specifically promised to protect Saxony and Bavaria against Prussian ambitions. Austrians denounced the revolutionary *Deutschtümelei* promoted by Stein, Arndt, and other Prussian 'Jacobins' in Germany.

Worst of all was a gap in confidence between them, impossible to close and easy to widen. The problem was not simply mistrust of each other's purposes, though there was plenty of that. For example, some argued, as did Count Hardenberg, the Hanoverian minister at Vienna, Prince Hardenberg's cousin, that Metternich was really trying to save Napoleon and prevent the liberation of Europe. But others, like Prussia's minister at Vienna, Prince Wilhelm von Humboldt, answered that Metternich's caution was understandable and that he could eventually be won over. The real difficulty was that, whatever the two governments intended, and however much Austria and Prussia needed each other and knew it, neither could take the initiative in helping the other. They were like two climbers stranded on separate ledges on a mountain face, each unable to reach the other and afraid of being pulled to his death if he threw the other a rope.[25]

Britain, reacting to Austria's efforts at mediation even more coolly than Russia and Prussia, saw Austria as a possible enemy. Even Castlereagh was convinced that Metternich's negotiations could only help Napoleon regain his grip on Europe. Many retained the traditional British view of Austria as slow, timid, incompetent, and untrustworthy, and all feared Austria's family ties to Napoleon. On Austria's side, even old Anglophiles like Prince Stadion, Baron Wessenberg, and Gentz (earlier in British pay) considered the British crude, self-centred, and ignorant in their approach to European politics, half-Europeans at best. But deeper than their mutual dislike and suspicions was the problem of incompatible concepts of peace. Put simply, Britain still wanted the Continent, Central Europe in particular, to help defeat France and hold it in check so that Britain would enjoy a free hand *vis-à-vis* Europe and hegemony in the wider world. Austria's goal now was to get the two Continental hegemons, Russia and France, to pull back and allow an independent European centre to live and breathe, and for its sake was willing to bypass Britain, ignore its special European concerns, and try to make it pay for the general peace with colonial and maritime cessions. A reconciliation be-

---

[25] Luckwaldt (1898: 93–120); Sweet (1978: ii. 122–5).

tween these concepts was still far off. The British gave Baron Wessenberg the cold shoulder on his mission to London in early 1813, and Metternich paid little attention either to Wessenberg or to Britain after his initial mediation proposals were turned down.[26]

In any case, the fate of Austria's mediation depended more on Napoleon's reaction than on that of the allies. It is fairly easy to answer some of the charges levelled against Austrian policy in 1813 at the time and since—cowardice, irresoluteness, pursuit of selfish advantage, willingness to let dynastic and family concerns control Austrian policy. In contrast, the most serious one raised by Metternich's opponents, that he was trying to save Napoleon and his Empire, cannot really be refuted. Metternich later claimed that he always expected his attempts to impose Austria's terms on France to fail, and always intended then to join the allies. This is how he explained his actions to the Russians and Prussians at the time; Napoleon and other Frenchmen chose to believe it for their own reasons, and it has been accepted by some historians as obvious and self-understood. Certain facts make it superficially plausible. Metternich withdrew Austria from the French alliance, lured Napoleon into accepting first Austria's armed neutrality and then its mediation, evaded Napoleon's pressure to join the war as an ally, and tacitly co-operated with Russia against Prince Poniatowski's Polish forces in the spring, a move which momentarily threatened to sever Austro-French relations.

Yet all these moves by Metternich had the obvious purpose of gaining room for manœuvre in preparation for pursuing his goal; they do not define what that goal was. In looking for it, one readily finds evidence that he was suspicious and fearful of Russia, at best indifferent toward Britain, hostile to Prussian schemes for Germany, and even willing to profit from the possible destruction of Prussia (though he did not desire it). The one thing impossible to find is evidence of hostility to Napoleon or a desire to oppose him, much less overthrow him. Napoleon's defeat in Russia, for example, caused Metternich real dismay. The evidence indicates that Metternich saw the best chance for achieving his kind of peace (i.e. an independent European centre) through close ties between Austria and a Napoleonic France which was still the dominant power in Western Europe.

[26] For further evidence of Austrian attitudes, see Luckwaldt (1898: 37–59); Arneth (1898: i. 152–5); Nesselrode (1904–12: v. 14–19, 38–41). For the British, esp. Castlereagh, see Buckland (1932); Castlereagh (1850–3: viii. 276–77, 302–5, 358–9); Castlereagh papers, PRONI D3030/3348, 3411. For the failure of the Wessenberg mission to London, see Luckwaldt (1898: 123–30); Arneth (1898: i. 156–80).

All the Austrian arguments to France fit this thesis. The same proposal was made time and again, by General Count Ferdinand Bubna, sent on special mission to Paris in December 1812, Prince Schwarzenberg, who returned there as regular ambassador in the spring, and Metternich himself, in talks with French envoys at Vienna and with Napoleon: Austria would help preserve him and his dynasty as rulers of a powerful, secure French Empire, if Napoleon would accept an independent neutral European centre between himself and Russia. The inducements Metternich held out to Napoleon—that France could retain the Rhine frontier plus beach-heads beyond it, and that the Rheinbund could be preserved and neutralized with France and Austria as its guarantors—show that he really wanted a powerful France to serve as a counter-weight to Russia. He repeatedly argued that a Continental peace would force Britain to the peace table, where it would have to make concessions to France. He hinted that Austria would help France control Russia and Prussia, and de-emphasized or ignored once-crucial conflicts between France and Austria over Italy and Switzerland. His territorial claims for Austria were relatively small (Illyria, the Inn Quarter, Salzburg) and he dismissed Spain as a question for Britain and France to settle, not Europe. His language to Russia and Prussia, while naturally different in emphasis, did not really contradict these basic themes.[27]

Napoleon responded to all attempts to restrain him, whether by Metternich or others, in his usual way. He had a chance to avoid a break with Prussia when Frederick William sent Prince Hatzfeldt to Paris in January to ask for certain territorial restitutions, and the payment of 90 million francs France owed Prussia for war supplies, as the price for Prussia's remaining loyal to the alliance. Napoleon dismissed Hatzfeldt and ordered Prince Eugène at Berlin to proceed with requisitions as before and to redouble his use of salutary terror. He blamed Eugène for losing control and letting Prussia defect, but he may actually have preferred Prussia to go over to the enemy. The fact that he intended to name one of his more unscrupulous servants, Joseph Fouché, to govern Prussia after its reconquest suggests that he expected to pay off his reluctant German satellites for their efforts in this new war by partitioning Prussia.

With Austria, Napoleon could not use the same tactics. It was

[27] Luckwaldt (1898: 61–78, 110, 153–86); Schwarz (1933: 21–3); Greulich (1931: 16–21). For examples of Metternich's *ex post facto* explanations, see Metternich (1880–4: i. 128–31, 136–7; iv. 113).

too big and important to be as openly bullied, his marriage tie with Austria, which he valued for personal and dynastic reasons, exerted some inhibiting effect on him, and a public break with Austria would promote the defection of Rheinbund states like Bavaria and Saxony. But his policy remained basically the same: to refuse all real concessions and, while claiming to want peace, deliberately to act to make peace impossible. For example, he publicly declared inalienable all the territories France had annexed, which now included most of Italy, all of Belgium and Holland, much of western and northern Germany, and most of Dalmatia. He boasted constantly of his power and victories, and insisted that Austria would not dare desert him. He even tried in early 1813 to order Austrian contingents into line for the coming campaign. His energy was spent preparing for war—not just the current campaign in Germany, but future ones against Britain. No one, not even his minister of police, Savary, was allowed to speak to him of France's own need and desire for peace. He accepted Austria's proposals for an armistice and a subsequent peace congress at Prague only after much wrangling and threats and out of military necessity (he could not afford more Pyrrhic victories like Bautzen), but made clear in his instructions to Caulaincourt for the congress that, if forced to make peace, he would do it directly with Russia and even with Prussia rather than through Austrian mediation. He also ordered Eugène in Italy, Murat in Naples, and King Max of Bavaria to station armies of observation against Austria, 'in order', he told Eugène, 'to have by this means ascendancy over Austria, so that I can menace her and not her me'.[28]

There are two common explanations as to why Napoleon rejected good chances for peace here, as he had often done before and would continue to do until his final downfall. His opponents and even some friends attributed it to his fatalistic ambition. Napoleon himself claimed that, though he wanted peace, he could not make peace after defeat, like other European monarchs secure in tradition and legitimacy, because his popular support depended on military power and glory. The first explanation is true, but incomplete; the second is false. The claim that other leading monarchs of Europe were more secure against overthrow than Napoleon by virtue of their legitimacy, and therefore able to make peace after defeat where Napoleon could not, is nonsense. The opposite is true. The Bourbons were overthrown three times

[28] 12 May 1813, Napoleon (1858–70: xxv. No. 1998).

in France between 1792 and 1830. Frederick William could easily have been overthrown in 1806–7, and faced a potential insurrection and army revolt in 1813. Francis felt his throne totter in 1805 and 1809, and lived in constant fear of overthrow. Paul I was assassinated as his father Peter had been; Alexander faced a possible armed revolt had he tried to continue fighting in 1807 or to stop fighting in 1812. The Bourbon throne in Spain was first shaken by popular insurrection and then subverted by Napoleon; the Swedish throne was overturned in 1792 and again in 1809. The only secure major crown in Europe was that of George III, and it had earlier in his reign more than once looked shaky.

In contrast, Napoleon, a parvenu military despot, lost six of the twelve campaigns he launched, the last four in succession—Egypt, Spain, Russia, Germany in 1813, France in 1814, and Waterloo—in addition to losing his naval and commercial wars against Britain. All these losses were costly to France, some devastating. Yet none of these defeats, not even all of them put together, undermined the popular basis for his rule. After 1804 no serious conspiracy threatened his reign (the Malet affair of October 1812 was an isolated affair which momentarily grew serious because of Napoleon's absence and the confusion among those he left in charge in Paris), and individual assassins were no more a danger to him than to other monarchs. The most unpopular aspect of his reign, conscription, was brought sufficiently under control by draconic means that, even after successive disasters in 1812 and 1813, he could still raise large new armies and keep them in the field.[29] As has been seen, he enjoyed great success in consolidating his reign, legitimating his authority, and amalgamating the old and new élites in France behind it.[30] He was equally successful in getting himself and his dynasty accepted as legitimate in the rest of Europe.

Only one thing threatened his regime, and ultimately destroyed it: war. Had he made peace, he could have ruled indefinitely. Every foreign war raised the danger of his death or capture, as his followers warned, and what finally cost him the allegiance of many civilian and military followers in 1814, as will be seen, was not his military defeats *per se* or the loss of his aura of invincibility, but the simple fact that he was an insuperable obstacle to peace. His followers would have continued to serve him in defeat; they had done so for some time. They finally refused to follow him

---

[29] Isser Woloch (1986) argues that Napoleon's success in solving his conscription problem helped promote his intransigence in 1813–14.

[30] Ponteil (1966).

any longer when he stubbornly refused to admit defeat and make peace in the face of an overwhelming foreign invasion. Napoleon's claim that he had to fight to the bitter end because his throne and Empire could not survive without glory, together with his twin claim that treason and defection among his followers brought him down, were simply self-serving, stab-in-the-back legends of the same order as Ludendorff's after the First World War; the fact that they have retained some credibility even among historians merely proves that Napoleon was one of the most remarkable, persuasive, and impudent liars in history.

The other explanation, stressing his ambition, fatalism, and sense of honour, is, of course, correct. But it needs supplementing, both for purposes of explanation and to show that by emphasizing Napoleon's character and actions one is not necessarily endorsing an individualist, 'great man' view of history and abandoning systemic explanation. Napoleon shows that individual leadership still makes a great difference in international history, and that sometimes character is destiny; but he also demonstrates their limits, showing how man proposes and the system disposes. Napoleon refused to make peace because he did not want to, chose not to—and also because he could not; could not make peace because he was no good at it, but also because, by this time, even if he had had the requisite knowledge and skill, he was probably caught too deeply by his own past to carry it off. What France above all required for peace in early 1813 was a trans-formation of Napoleon's Empire in France and Western Europe into a sphere of stable, tolerable French hegemony. Even at that stage that task was not impossible, though it had become much harder. Many of Napoleon's followers in France and the Empire and some outside it, including Metternich, wanted this change, had ideas for it, and would have collaborated in it. But Napoleon had neither the credibility nor the disposition nor the skill for this task. Gentz, a shrewd observer, defined the hallmark of Napoleon's politics in this period as ineptitude,[31] and events bear Gentz out. Already Napoleon's ruthless disregard of the needs and security of anyone besides himself had helped force Prussia into the hostile coalition against him. Now those attitudes were undermining his own coalition almost as rapidly as he had formed it, and his enemies counted on him to commit the same follies with Austria.[32]

[31] To Nesselrode, 12 Mar. 1813, Nesselrode (1904–12: v. 44–5).

[32] The evidence is scattered throughout Napoleon (1858–70: xxiv–xxv. Nos. 19529–20205); see also Fournier (1903: ii. 258–61); Schlossberger (1889: 291–305).

This ultimately happened. Russia's initial attempts to win Austria over by propaganda and pressure, portraying Lützen as an allied victory and blaming Austria for the defeat at Bautzen, threatening a separate agreement with France, and talking of supporting the anti-French insurrection in the Tyrol which the British had helped raise and Metternich was engaged in suppressing, failed and proved counter-productive. But Nesselrode and Stadion, Austria's envoy to the Tsar's headquarters, agreed on an alternative strategy: to allow Metternich, acting on the allies' behalf, to present Napoleon with his conditions for a preliminary peace, unsatisfactory though they were to the allies, without a binding commitment on their part. Napoleon would undoubtedly reject them, compelling Austria to fight; should he accept them, the allies could raise additional demands at the final peace.[33] At Reichenbach on 27 June, an agreement negotiated by Nesselrode, Hardenberg, and Stadion along these lines was signed by the three powers (its details will be discussed later).

Just the day before, Metternich, who was staying with Francis at nearby Gitschin, had finally managed to obtain an interview with Napoleon at Dresden. Since only the two principals were present, no one knows exactly what took place at this historic meeting in the Marcolini Palace. Metternich's own account, which has him coolly turning aside Napoleon's outbursts of bluster and rage and emerging to pronounce Napoleon a doomed man, is no doubt embroidered; Napoleon's version as dictated to his secretary Baron Fain may well be more accurate on certain details. But both accounts agree on the central point: Napoleon, having agreed to an armistice only to gain time to prepare for more war against Britain as well as the Continent, would not even consider the alliance for peace Metternich offered. In fact, he refused to believe that Metternich himself wanted it. Assuming instead that Austria must be seeking profits from the war, he used threats of war or of another Peace of Tilsit and vague territorial offers, especially of Illyria, to try to extort an Austrian pledge of neutrality from Metternich.

Metternich attempted in every way possible to convince the Emperor that his offer was genuine. He insisted that Austria needed and wanted a durable peace above all; that peace required

Napoleon's arch-chancellor, Jean-Jacques Cambacérès, in charge of the French administration in Napoleon's absence, tried in vain to convince Napoleon of the public's eagerness for peace; Cambacérès (1973: ii. Nos. 1112, 1126, 1145–6, 1224).

[33] *VPR* (1960–: 1. vii. Nos. 78, 80, 83, 97, 102–4).

the existence of independent, secure intermediary bodies separating the great powers; that any territorial redistribution (*repartition des forces*) must serve this end; that Austria only wanted for itself the territories and position necessary to sustain its independence, and that it would not even permit the German Empire or Austria's old position in Germany to be restored. To all this Napoleon responded in effect, 'Stop lying and tell me what you really want!' At Dresden, it has correctly been observed, two different personalities with incompatible world-views faced each other. The confrontation was not, however, between a nineteenth-century romantic hero and an eighteenth-century *grand seigneur*, but between a sixteenth-century Italian *condottiere* and a nineteenth-century conservative European statesman representing a kind of politics the *condottiere* could not understand or even admit as possible. At this stage in their careers, Metternich was abreast of the times and Napoleon centuries behind.[34]

The Dresden interview ended any serious hope that Austria and France together would impose terms on the allies, or that Metternich could reach separate agreements with both sides and then whittle down the differences between them at a peace congress until they were not worth fighting over, though Metternich continued to try for this. Instead, the Reichenbach treaty which Austria signed the next day obliged it to put four minimum peace conditions to Napoleon at the proposed peace congress at Prague: a partition of the Duchy of Warsaw among Russia, Prussia, and Austria, without French participation; the expansion of Prussia in Poland, including Danzig and its environs, and France's evacuation of all the fortresses it still occupied in Prussia and the Duchy of Warsaw; the return of Illyria to Austria; and the restoration of the Hanseatic cities and their old territories, or at least Hamburg and Lübeck, as independent free cities, together with a vague call for 'a possible arrangement tied to the general peace on the cession of other parts of the 32nd Military District' in North Germany. If France failed to accept these terms by 20 July, Austria was committed to join the allies in war, contributing at least 150,000 men (the same as Russia) while Prussia raised at least 80,000. Once the war resumed, moreover, Russia and Prussia were free to demand further conditions, unspecified at Reichenbach but including two they had already agreed on in addition to Austria's four: that Prussia be restored to its full status of 1806, and that the

---

[34] Luckwaldt (1898: 308–38); Napoleon (1858–70: xxv. 20175); Nesselrode (1904–12: v. 108–18).

Rheinbund be dissolved and the French frontier in Germany pushed back to the Rhine.

Each party gained something in this treaty. Besides the promise of regaining Illyria and the assurance that Austria could exercise a veto over any future military operations, Austria obtained the allies' promise to negotiate for peace on a basis so moderate that under enough pressure Napoleon might possibly accept it. Russia basically got its way on Poland. Prussia got some of its demands endorsed by Austria and was allowed to hold its own wider goals and Russia's in reserve. Russia and Prussia seemed to gain a decisive advantage in that Austria was pledged to go to war if Napoleon rejected these terms, while they were not fully committed to peace even if France accepted them. But if they supposed that Metternich was so easily snared, they underestimated his guile. Within three days he had secured a French convention formally agreeing to Austria's armed mediation and the opening of a peace congress on 5 July at Prague. For this purpose, to the rage of the allies, Metternich unilaterally extended the armistice by three weeks, to 10 August. His excuse, that Austria needed the extra time to complete its armaments, was true enough, but his main reason was to give peace a real chance.

The person Metternich was most ensnaring by these manœuvres was Emperor Francis, who was extremely averse to more war and largely indifferent to anything beyond his hereditary domains and Austria's narrower interests. It took repeated pleas and arguments, reaching a climax in Metternich's *Vortrag* of 12 July, for Metternich to get the Emperor to commit himself to enter the war should negotiations prove useless. Even then (a further sign of how much Metternich wanted the negotiations to succeed and how much Francis dreaded war), Metternich gained his permission, if the success of the negotiation required it, to defer Austria's claim to Illyria, the one territorial gain it was promised at Reichenbach, from the preliminary to the general peace.[35]

The question of which of the allies deceived and got the better of whom at Reichenbach and after, however, obscures the real significance of the agreement. Its central importance lies in the fact that all three agreed to make peace with Napoleonic France on the basis of specific, minimal conditions (even the Russo-Prussian additional terms fell far short of real victory), and to seek that peace above all by negotiation rather than military force (even Russia and Prussia, who expected further war, wanted to pursue it

---

[35] Metternich (1880–4: ii. 463–7); Martens (1874–1905: iii. 106–9).

only to a pre-designated point and then stop). This marks a crucial break with the past. From this Treaty of Reichenbach on, Napoleon was the only important leader on the Continent still aiming at military victory for its own sake or insisting on a peace based upon it. Russia's and Prussia's terms, to say nothing of Austria's, would have left France still clearly the strongest military power on the Continent and Napoleon still on his imperial throne. Even his old enemies like Gentz and Nesselrode rejected the idea of pursuing the war beyond the Rhine, and would soon become outspoken opponents of carrying on the war beyond the goals the allies had agreed upon earlier.

Alongside this obvious point (though one frequently ignored) is another, subtler one. Reichenbach represented a further step toward a joint recognition that the allies' main security dilemma— the problem which two of them had already gone to war to solve, while the other was contemplating resorting to it—arose as much from the relations between themselves as from the common threat from France. The Reichenbach agreement presupposed, even more than Kalisch had, that once French power was somewhat reduced and a certain amount of independence and breathing-room gained for Germany, the three Eastern great powers could be secure, *provided they remained united.* If they could solve the problem of their own internal relations, the French threat could be managed.

This shared insight, that a reasonable co-operation between the Eastern powers themselves, especially in Germany, was the key to durable peace, was an immense step in learning, a vital break with their common delusive, destructive past. Since the beginning, the allies had fought the Revolutionary and Napoleonic wars as if France were the only important security threat, so that eliminating that threat would make things right. Most of the powers most of the time knew this was not true; yet the exigencies of politics and war kept them fighting the wars as if it were. Now the grip of this wilful self-deception was finally at least loosened. Abandoning a blind alley, these three allies turned toward the future: a coalition whose central goal and purpose would not be military victory but durable co-operation among its members; a peace settlement which would rest not on defeating France and keeping it restrained under a so-called balance of power (which was never more than a minor and transient aspect of the 1814–15 settlement) but on balancing and pacifying Central and Eastern Europe under the aegis of their own alliance.

In the short run, however, Reichenbach led to more war.

Metternich (to use a figure he applied to his opponent Capodistrias in 1822) writhed like the devil in holy water, but could not escape from the snares of Napoleon's intransigence, Austria's commitment at Reichenbach, and his own conviction that Austria could not remain on the sidelines while its fate and that of Europe was being decided. At Prague, Caulaincourt simply stalled the negotiations as Napoleon had ordered him to do, and Maret, whom Napoleon characterized as useless and whose foreign ministry was still being used mainly for military requisitioning and espionage, tried to make Austria rejoin the French alliance as a condition for negotiations. Only after the congress broke up and Austria declared war on 11 August did the French, while denouncing Austria's treachery, accept part of Austria's terms in order to sow dissent among the allies, proposing that the congress meet and discuss peace while the war went on. Like an ageing courtesan, Napoleon could not believe that his tricks would no longer work.

Metternich postponed the evil day as long as he could and deceived his allies as far as he dared. Even the ultimatum he gave Napoleon on 7 August did not, as he had promised, convey all the allies' additional conditions. But when the time was finally exhausted, Austria entered the war with resolution. As for Metternich, he was not enthusiastic, as he later claimed; he conveyed France's counter-offer to the allies and continued to try to persuade the French to make peace, but he did so without hope. Napoleon, genuinely outraged at Austria, claimed it had betrayed him and sold itself to Russia in order to reconquer Germany; Gentz again thanked God for Napoleon's incompetence or madness that had forced Austria to fight.[36]

A shrewd Russian policy had also helped. Here, as in all the campaigns from 1812, Napoleon's foes were superior to him more in political skill than in military power. The Russians, though livid at Metternich's extension of the armistice, had learned that pressure and threats were counter-productive, and continued to give Metternich enough rope so that Napoleon could hang him. Alexander's instructions to his envoy, I. O. Anstett, for the proposed negotiations at Prague were a model of moderation and prudence. Nesselrode, while warning Austria that France was only trying to break up the coalition, none the less granted Austria six more days beyond 10 August for the notice of termination of the armistice. The Russians and Prussians were not above

[36] Greulich (1931: 30–43, 70–5, 80–104); Chodzko (1863: i. 13–20, 47–9); Napoleon (1858–70: xxv. Nos. 20286–7; xxvi. 20375–6, 20395); Nesselrode (1904–12: v. 122–3).

deceiving Austria themselves, carefully concealing from Vienna Britain's tardy acceptance of Austria's mediation so as not to encourage Metternich's peacemaking efforts. But even the Russian military commander Barclay, though eager to support the Tyrolese insurgents and start other insurrections in southern Europe, recognized that gaining Austria was more important.[37]

Russia and Prussia thus helped bring Austria into the war. Britain did not.[38] Castlereagh and his envoys to Russia and Prussia, Lords Cathcart and Stewart, were aware of the danger that the allies might make a Continental peace at British expense. Castlereagh in particular realized that Britain could not force its allies to continue the war beyond their interests or capacities, but must instead persuade them that a defeat for Britain, which he conceded was possible, would ultimately be worse for them than for Britain itself. He was also flexible on peace terms, defending Britain's interests but emphasizing that Britain's main goal was simply a good, moderate, general peace and that it would give up some colonial conquests for the sake of that goal.[39] But the shrewd and generous flexibility shown Russia, Prussia, and Sweden was not on display toward Austria. Britain rejected Austrian mediation, and when the government finally accepted it reluctantly and with conditions, it conveyed the news, not through Baron Wessenberg, who was still shunned at London, but through Russia and Prussia, so that it never reached Vienna. No British envoy was named to Vienna until August, by which time Austria was already virtually certain to join the war, and then the young, inexperienced Lord Aberdeen was chosen for the delicate task of concluding a formal Anglo-Austrian peace and an alliance. His ultimate success was a piece of undeserved British luck.

The British, of course, correctly suspected that Metternich was working for a Continental peace at Britain's expense. But Austria also had plenty to object to in British ideas and attitudes. Britain

[37] VPR (1960–: vii. Nos. 118, 129–31, 136, 139–40; p. 282).

[38] According to British diplomats at the time and some British historians since, what gave Austria the courage to enter the war was the news of Wellington's decisive victory over the French at Vitoria in northern Spain on 21 June. In fact, Vitoria served to encourage the Russians and Prussians and gave the British new weight in the negotiations, where they had sometimes been treated as outsiders, but Metternich used the news of the victory simply as one more means to persuade Napoleon to negotiate seriously for peace. R. Glover (1973: 26–7); Luckwaldt (1898: 340–1); VPR (1960–: vii. No. 135); Castlereagh (1850–3: viii. 415–16).

[39] Chodzko (1863: i. 21–4); Castlereagh (1850–3: ix. 30–3, 39–41); Castlereagh Papers, PRONI, D/3030/3507, 3523, 3532.

renewed its old tactics of raising European insurrections against France regardless of their consequences for other powers, this time even in Austria's own territory. Besides supporting a national rising in Germany, urging one in Austria as well, and toying with promoting a Bourbon movement within France, Britain actually had its agents help foment a conspiracy and rising in the Tyrol in the spring of 1813, which Metternich allowed to form and then crushed. Once more, as in the past, the British also expected Austria to prepare for a great war with France and to enter it on its own before Britain would provide any subsidies, and then to be satisfied with whatever British help was left over after British, Swedish, Russian, and Prussian needs were met. Moreover, London envisioned Austria's role in the war as essentially an auxiliary one, that of fighting in Italy for particular Austrian goals. Though Castlereagh talked about wanting to see Austria restored to independent great-power status as a bulwark against France, the British ignored vital Austrian concerns in Central Europe. In Germany Britain's favoured ally was once more Prussia; in Europe as a whole, Russia remained its natural partner for war and peace.[40] At London, Lieven boasted that Britain's concessions to Russia would 'serve to throw the balance in favour of Russia' and make the Tsar the arbiter of the coming peace—exactly Metternich's fear.[41]

Thus by late summer two roads to peace apparently open in early 1813—the Anglo-Russian–Prussian route of national rising and liberation and the Austrian one of a mediated compromise peace—were in fact blocked, though not yet abandoned. A coalition with a good chance of defeating Napoleon had finally come together; an alliance to forge a durable peace had not yet emerged.

[40] Webster (1921: 5–10, 16–19, 66–9, 74–5, 94–6); Castlereagh (1850–3: viii. 414–6; ix. 34–7); Bartlett (1966: 114–20).
[41] To Nesselrode, 16 July 1813, *VPR* (1960–: 1. vii. No. 125, p. 306).

11
War Ended, Peace Launched, 1813–1814

PART of the conventional wisdom about the final coalition, that it succeeded because the allies, despite many disagreements, remained united, and that Napoleon's intransigence and Castlereagh's leadership were vital factors in keeping them so, is true. Another part of the conventional view, however, is wrong: that the coalition preserved its unity by putting military victory ahead of the individual interests and divergent aims of its members. First of all, this did not happen. Military victory was never the primary goal for the coalition as a whole, even in the final stages of the war. The allies, though they sometimes differed sharply over terms, always sought a negotiated peace in one form or another and agreed that the war should be ended as soon as the right terms were attained. The reason the war lasted to a military decision, though not total victory, was Napoleon's persistent refusal to negotiate seriously. As soon as a French government agreed to negotiate, the war was ended, though at the time the French army was still capable of fighting and controlled most of France and vital areas outside it as well. Secondly, when, as happened at particular times, certain allied leaders did try to make military victory the primary goal of the alliance, they did so not to hold the coalition together but to promote special purposes of their own, and invariably in so doing they jeopardized allied unity. Pursuit of military victory as the prime goal tended to tear the final coalition apart, just as it had done to earlier ones.

Finally, it was important that the allies generally sought unity and were willing to co-operate in reaching a common goal; but this spirit was only a necessary and not a sufficient condition either for maintaining allied unity or for constructing a satisfactory peace. Maintaining the right spirit was less critical than learning the right ideas. What primarily kept the allies together was not mutual goodwill, but the fact that they achieved, or at least approached, consensus on a sane, practical concept of peace. This was the product of learning, of changing their previous concepts of peace and victory to fit reality.

I. FROM TEPLITZ TO FRANKFURT:
THE LIBERATION OF GERMANY

On 9 September Austria, Russia, and Prussia concluded alliance treaties at Teplitz uniting them for war then and for mutual defence after the peace. Some general goals were set: restoring Austria to its status in power (not its boundaries) of early 1805, abolishing the Rheinbund, making the German states from the Rhine to the Austrian and Prussian frontiers independent, and partitioning the Duchy of Warsaw along lines to be negotiated later. The fact that the treaties failed to specify how these broad aims would be carried out gave Russia important advantages. It had its own gains in Poland already in hand; Prussia and Austria still needed Russian help to secure theirs in Germany and Italy. Austria was now committed to support Russia's and Prussia's main conditions for peace; the uncertainty over Germany's future constitution would provide Russia further opportunities to intervene in German politics; and the alliance itself would help Russia maintain its leadership of the coalition against possible competition from Britain.

The alliance, however, also entangled Russia. Rumiantsev, still trying to retain his post despite his dwindling influence, argued cogently that the treaties would prevent Russia from being the sole arbiter of Europe, because Austria would now spoil Russia's game in Southern Europe as Britain had already done in the North. Unfortunately, Rumiantsev and other Russian nationalists found Alexander's own ideas a kind of obstacle to the notion of an exclusive Russian leadership in Europe. Alexander still intended to promote Russia's national interests, but at the same time he wanted to be the saviour and arbiter of Europe and a loyal member of the European family of states, and had not yet learned that he could not do all three things at once, or decided which goal he would sacrifice if he had to.[1]

If Metternich failed to protect Austria's interests as carefully as he might have at Teplitz, especially in regard to Poland, one reason was that at the time he was mainly bent on winning allies in Germany against Stein and the others he called Prussian Jacobins. The treaty he concluded with Bavaria at Ried on 8 October was his greatest victory in this campaign. Bavaria came over into the coalition as Austria's ally, with Austria guaranteeing

[1] Martens (1874–1905: iii. 111–26); Kraehe (1963: 202–7); Metternich (1880–4: i. 164–5).

Bavaria's sovereignty and independence and promising to compensate it fully in contiguous German territory at the peace for the lands it would have to return to Austria. The treaty came at a critical moment, just when the autumn campaign was heading toward its climax. After a brilliant start, Napoleon's effort to defeat the allied armies in detail and knock Prussia out of the war had failed. Instead, he found himself pressed back in Saxony by a concentric allied offensive. The two armies met at Leipzig on 16-19 October in the so-called Battle of Nations, the greatest single battle in European history to that date, inflicting terrible losses on both sides. Napoleon's forces were compelled to retreat; the defeat turned into a rout when key Saxon contingents defected. Napoleon managed to escape with a remnant of his army over the Rhine, but the disaster was almost as great as that in Russia and even more irreparable; Germany was lost for good.[2]

Bavaria played no part in this battle, and failed to do much for the common cause in its aftermath.[3] But its defection and the Treaty of Ried had far greater political effects than direct military ones. It set the pattern other Napoleonic satellites were eager to follow, especially since, after Leipzig, many Prussian and other German patriots, including some Austrians, called still more loudly for revenge on the Rheinbund states. Frederick of Württemberg abandoned Napoleon on the eve of Leipzig, and the whole confederation collapsed thereafter; even Frederick August of Saxony tried to come over to the allies, but Prussia and Russia prevented it and seized his territory. Ried, and other similar treaties which Metternich quickly concluded with Napoleon's former satellites, not only saved them from German or allied vengeance but also obstructed any ideas of seriously limiting their sovereignty in the interest of unifying Germany. At the same time the treaties preserved the territorial, social, legal, and domestic-political revolutions of 1803-6, and blocked the restoration of territories they had annexed and princes they had mediatized.

All this fitted into Metternich's campaign against Stein and the German patriots, itself part of his overall struggle to keep the war within conservative monarchic bounds compatible with Austrian

---

[2] Koch (1987: 379-98). The deterioration in both Napoleon's position and his strategy is revealed dramatically in his correspondence—Napoleon (1858-70: xxvi. Nos. 20395-830).

[3] The Bavarian general, Wrede, ordered to block Napoleon's escape route with his combined Bavarian-Austrian forces, chose to attack Würzburg first in order to occupy part of Bavaria's future compensations in Germany, and as a result arrived too late athwart Napoleon's path at Hanau and was brushed aside. Chroust (1932: 403-5); Hölzle (1937: 159-60).

interests. He had already suppressed an insurrection against Bavaria in the Tyrol raised by Austrian national patriots, among them the Emperor's younger brother, Archduke John. Besides eliminating some dangerous opponents at home, this action helped Metternich convince Bavaria that Austria was no longer its enemy, and further aided his search for allies in Germany against a potential Prusso-Russian hegemony. Unlike Austro-German patriots and *Reichsritter* like Prince Stadion, Metternich and Francis were ready to abandon Austria's former south-west German territories and Imperial clients for the sake of South German allies.

For Bavaria, facing defeat and allied revenge, the treaty was thus manna from heaven; yet it had to be dragged into it. Montgelas, aware of Bavaria's desperate need for an escape route, none the less instructed his negotiator, General Wrede, to demand incredible terms for an alliance.[4] King Max Joseph was worse. Despite pressure from Austria, the Bavarian army, Bavarian public opinion, Crown Prince Ludwig, Wrede, and Montgelas, strict neutrality was as far as he would go in abandoning France and approaching Austria. Napoleon and Alexander finally broke his stubborn resistance—Napoleon by ignoring his pleas for protection and leaving Bavaria's frontiers exposed to an Austrian invasion, the King's worst fear; the Tsar by rejecting Max Joseph's pleas to save him from Austria and telling him he must come to terms with Vienna and join the common cause. The King's letter to Crown Prince Ludwig announcing his decision to accept the Austrian alliance illustrates how Napoleon had ruined France's influence in South Germany. He could only hope now, Max Joseph wrote, that Austria would not betray Bavaria; 'this would be all the worse because so long as Napoleon exists we cannot count upon France.'[5]

The Treaty of Ried thus had a major impact on the war, the German question, inter-allied diplomacy, and Bavaria's development as a state—all of which is fairly well known. As a signpost of emerging deeper changes in international politics, however, its significance has been overlooked. It effectively ended a secular rivalry between Austria and Bavaria which had just reached its

---

[4] e.g. he asked that Bavaria, after joining the war as Austria's ally, be excused from fighting except to defend its own frontiers, and allowed immediately to occupy the territories in Germany that it was eventually to receive as compensations, while retaining the territory it was to turn over to Austria until the final peace.

[5] 1 Oct. 1813, Schwarz (1933: 135). The motives and feelings of King Frederick of Württemberg in defecting were almost exactly the same; Schlossberger (1889: 311–24).

peak in 1805–9. Of course, the two states did not immediately become close friends or solve all their former problems; some tension and suspicion between them was commonplace in the decades after 1815. But after 1813 they were never outright enemies again. Consider how different history would have been had something like this happened between Austria and Sardinia-Piedmont or Austria and Prussia.

As for the bargain they struck at Ried, it looks like a typical eighteenth-century transaction in which a smaller power switches alliances during a war to avoid defeat and reap a profit. This was undoubtedly Montgelas's intention; while he was a modernizer in administration and state-building, his foreign policy was pure eighteenth-century *sacro egoismo*. But if Bavaria still played by eighteenth-century rules, Austria did not. Eighteenth-century coalition-building, as practised throughout the revolutionary and Napoleonic wars until now, called for the great powers to set the goals of the war and to entice or compel smaller states to fall in line, accepting their decisions on war aims. Austria had always before used bribes and threats of force to win Bavaria over, and, when this failed, opened each campaign by invading or occupying Bavaria. This is what Max Joseph expected and feared. Yet in 1813, with Bavaria almost wholly defenceless, Austria not only refrained even from threatening to use force but actually placed a contingent of its own troops under Wrede's command as a guarantee against an Austrian threat or betrayal. The treaty further specifically guaranteed that none of the territories Bavaria had earlier conquered from Austria as Napoleon's ally, including the Tyrol, which twice had risen in revolt against Bavarian rule, would have to be turned over to Austria until the peace, at which time Bavaria would be fully compensated.

Austria's goals in this alliance are as striking as its methods of achieving it. Previously it had tried to lure Bavaria with a share of the spoils of victory over the common enemy. The Treaty of Ried, in contrast, barely mentioned France, said nothing about military victory, and stated the general goal of the alliance as 'a state of true peace', 'the re-establishment of an order of things in Europe which assures to all their independence and future tranquillity', 'a just redivision of the respective forces of the powers and ... the establishment of their limits on mutually agreeable bases', and for Bavaria in particular, the preservation of 'its present dimensions so as to enable it to find in its own weight guarantees of its political independence'.

Historians have routinely interpreted this sort of language, typical of negotiations and treaties in 1813–15, as indicating the quest for a balance of power. This is mistaken. It demonstrates instead a quest for political equilibrium in the absence of balance of power. This was a treaty between two historic enemies, one of them a great power, the other a neighbour a fraction of its size; it obviously did not and could not rest upon a balance of power. Balance-of-power considerations would have led Bavaria, as it always had, to seek allies *against* Austria—like Prussia or France earlier, Russia or Prussia now. The alliance was designed and intended by Metternich to bring Bavaria into Austria's fold, making it the core of an Austrian-led bloc in South Germany, with Austria replacing France as the hegemonic partner there. The fact that Bavaria's contribution to the joint war effort was to be only one-quarter the size of Austria's underlined the disparity in power. What induced Bavaria to agree to the alliance was a promise that Austria would be restrained and compelled to respect Bavaria's independence and interests, not by countervailing power exerted by Bavaria or other states in Europe, but by a general legal and political system in Europe designed to ensure political equilibrium—meaning a balance in rights, security, and independence—between all states, including Austria and Bavaria, despite the existence of permanent, unavoidable imbalances of power among them. This is what the language of the treaty says and what it meant. Given the persistent confusion over terms, especially this one, one needs to emphasize the point: what this treaty and others promised, what the Vienna system ultimately created, and what made that system work was political equilibrium, not balance of power.

The same point applies to Metternich's success in drawing other smaller states in Germany into alliance with Austria in November, and winning over Murat's Kingdom of Naples in January. This was not balance-of-power politics on a higher level, an Austrian effort to recruit allies to match French and Russian power in the general balance. Stadion, indeed, thought along these lines; for Metternich, this kind of power politics represented at most a desperate last resort. The goal, clearly expressed and genuinely sought, was to achieve a political equilibrium. throughout the system resting primarily not on counterbalanced power but on mutual interests, consensus, and law.[6]

Naturally one can explain this as simply Austria's enlightened

---

[6] Schwarz (1933: 79–107, 127–8, 132–5); Rössler (1940: ii. 154–7, 167–9; 1966: ii. 94–7); Kraehe (1963: 208–14); Martens (1874–1905: viii. 113–15).

way of pursuing its own interests, its security uppermost among them. It had no force to spare to use against Bavaria or other smaller states, and had to find a better way than power politics to solve its security dilemma in Germany and Central Europe. But this condition had prevailed ever since 1790, as Leopold II and Kaunitz had seen; it had not stopped Austria from resorting to force time and again. Here was the point at which Austria changed course, redefined its security interests, and altered the way it pursued them. When enough states, especially great powers, do this, whether it be Austria and other states in 1813–15 or the Soviet Union and others in the 1980s, a different system of politics emerges. It is never easy for a state, especially a great power, to redefine its security and the requirements for it, and it was certainly not easy here, in the midst of a great war. There were costs and risks for Austria involved in conciliating the German middle states. Some opposed it at Vienna; it meant renouncing part of Austria's historic heritage and power base in Germany; the sacrifice reaped no loyalty or gratitude from the middle states and angered smaller ones. The decision by this big fish not to swallow the middle-sized ones left the latter free to digest the lesser fry they had gobbled up earlier, helping explain how it was that the middle-sized states of Europe—Bavaria, Württemberg, Sardinia-Piedmont, Naples, Sweden, the Netherlands—could continue their competitive eighteenth-century brand of politics in 1813–15, while great powers, like Austria here, were working to construct a less dangerous and conflictual international system.[7]

The Treaty of Ried was not the only blow to Stein's plans. Humboldt attacked new proposals of his in August, arguing that Germany was a cultural rather than a political unit and did not need political unity for security, and that expanding Austria and Prussia and separating them from France by a system of independent intermediary states including Holland and Switzerland would suffice. Colonel Schöler, Prussia's military envoy to the Tsar, agreed, telling Alexander that Germans did not even want a common fatherland, only freedom from foreign rule and a return to their traditional dynasties. On 21 October the three main allies agreed to change Stein's Council into a Central Executive

---

[7] For the divergences between Stadion and Metternich, see Rössler (1966: 106–12); Kraehe (1963: 271–2); for further testimony on Metternich's thinking, see Castlereagh (1850–3: ix. 60–7); Gentz (1887: 36–9); for evidence of the continued ambitions of the middle states over against smaller ones, see Chroust (1932: 447–72; 1939–44: i. Nos. 1–11); Hölzle (1937: 156–73).

Department, sharply reducing its powers and functions. This change, in addition to the restoration of the ousted Elector of Hesse to his throne, Austria's signature of the Treaty of Fulda with Württemberg on 2 November, and successive treaties concluded on 20–3 November at Frankfurt between the allies and other smaller German states analogous to the Treaty of Ried, reduced Stein's provisional government to the administration of certain conquered territories supposedly without legitimate rulers (Saxony, Berg, Fulda, and some smaller territories along the Rhine). The German Department, as it was usually called, still played a role in organizing the war effort in some states, but by the end of 1813 any chance that it would reshape Germany had disappeared.[8]

Meanwhile Napoleon, vowing vengeance on the Bavarians and Saxons for his loss of Germany, worked in France to cut his losses and prepare for another come-back. With central Italy equally lost, he liberated Pius VII from his prison in exile at Savona and resigned himself to losing Naples by Murat's defecting to Austria. Making Joseph and his marshals the scapegoats for his defeat in Spain, he concluded a peace treaty with Ferdinand VII in exile at Valençay. By restoring Ferdinand to his throne, he hoped not only to remove Spain from the war but to make the Spaniards expel the victorious British, now preparing to invade southern France, while he removed his own army from Spain for use elsewhere. He insisted, however, on holding onto the Kingdom of Italy, Holland, and the Rhineland, and in the face of growing defeatism and war-weariness in France set out to raise still another army of 500,000, this time all Frenchmen. To justify this, he relied on his regular armoury of lies, anti-British slogans, and appeals to glory, refused to discuss French desires for peace or fears of invasion even with his close associates, and used allied peace moves and offers solely to try to break up the coalition, concentrating on Austria as its weakest link. How profoundly Napoleon could deceive himself in attempting to trick others is shown by his instructing Berthier, a month after Leipzig, to negotiate an arrangement with the allied commander-in-chief,

---

[8] The basic work on Stein and the central administration is Kielmannsegg (1964); but see also Huber (1957: i. 476–87, 498–507). On the disagreements between Stein and other patriots and their critics, see Ritter (1958: 451–60; Rössler (1940: ii. 173–80); Sweet (1978: ii. 140–1, 144–7); Martens (1874–1905: viii. 102–3). On the treaties with Württemberg and other German states, see ibid., 124–53; Huber (1957: i. 494–7); Kraehe (1963: 233–4, 238–42); Facius (1977). For the restoration in Electoral Hesse, see Speitkamp (1986: 53–61); Pedlow (1988: 31–2).

Prince Schwarzenberg, whereby France would hand over the fortresses it still occupied on the Oder and Vistula with the honours of war, the allies transporting their garrisons, artillery, and equipment to France, while France still kept possession of fortresses along the Elbe, also hundreds of miles behind enemy lines. But he was not always or wholly blind to his real position. Along with cries of vengeance ('Munich must burn! And burn it shall!') appeared signs in early 1814 of despair (e.g. orders to destroy his château at Marrasq in case of invasion so that no Englishman should ever sleep in his bed).[9]

II. FROM FRANKFURT TO LANGRES: BRITAIN JOINS EUROPE

Napoleon's intransigence initially created a rift among the allies and then helped heal it. The problem did not exactly arise from divergences in the war aims of the Continental allies, but from the fact that, although the original goal of driving Napoleon across the Rhine was achieved, they still could not end the war. Some wanted to stop the fighting regardless; others called for a new campaign and new goals to accompany it. This problem made an existing one with Britain worse. Through mutual combat and bargaining, the three Continental powers had gradually drawn closer together, but Britain remained essentially apart, with a different concept and programme of peace. Closing this gap would be a major task in late 1813 and early 1814.

There was no real quarrel, as in earlier coalitions, over Britain's financial and material support and its commitment to the war. London improved on its already impressive performance in the autumn of 1813, granting new subsidies ˌto the importunate Swedes, resuming the subsidy payments to Prussia and Russia suspended by the armistice, and assuming sole responsibility for redeeming the federative paper, to be issued on a reduced scale. In what turned out to be a crucial development, Lord Aberdeen, ambassador at Vienna, succeeded in concluding an alliance with Austria on 9 October. Austria's subsidy, £1 million for one year's campaign with 150,000 men, was considerably less generous than

---

[9] The evidence is scattered through Napoleon (1858-70: xxvi. Nos. 20813-21034); the proposal to Berthier is in No. 20918. See also Fournier (1930: ii. 331); A. Pingaud (1927); for the treaty with Ferdinand VII, DeClercq (1880-1917: ii. 392-5); for Napoleon's rejection of pleas for peace, Cambacérès (1973: Nos. 1328, 1345); Melchior-Bonnet (1962: 237-60).

what Russia and Prussia received and niggardly compared to Sweden's. Yet added to other British contributions in money and arms, including obligations to Spain, Portugal, and Sicily, it exceeded everything Britain had done in all the earlier wars combined. Britain's own military effort cost far more than the subsidies and material aid given to its allies; the Napoleonic Wars put a proportionately greater burden on Britain in terms of lives and resources than the First World War would do. Only an upswing in the British economy following the collapse of the Continental System enabled Britain to sustain it, and it could not do so forever—a fact important for peace. The British, though still determined to carry on, were willing to modify their notions of an acceptable victory and peace if necessary. As for the Continental great powers, though they still made unreasonable demands on Britain, they matched its commitment to the war. The power the British most distrusted, Austria, proved more eager once it entered the war to get British arms with which to fight than to increase its subsidy, and above all sought an agreement with Britain on war aims.[10]

There, as noted, lay the key problem. The Continental powers, especially Austria, were willing to accommodate Britain on its special interests like Hanover, but treated Britain's general concerns in Europe as peripheral and expected not only British subsidies to help pay for the war but also British colonial and maritime concessions to help pay for European peace. Austrians (Metternich, Gentz, Wessenberg, even Stadion) frequently complained that Britain wanted to continue the war forever and to create still more chaos in Europe.[11] Russia and Prussia were less obviously indifferent to British interests, but also played fast and loose with them for the sake of a Continental peace.

At the same time, some of Castlereagh's attitudes and ideas worried the Continental allies, especially Austria. He was still preoccupied with Western and Northern Europe, understood little in detail about the German, Italian, or Polish questions, favoured mass risings and revolts in Europe regardless of their effects on Central European politics or on Napoleon's satellites, and looked

---

[10] Sherwig (1969: 294–314, 345–56); Emsley (1979: 161–6, 169–76); Crouzet (1989); Grenville to Grey, 21 Oct. 1813, Grey Papers (Durham). Lieven after the war frankly acknowledged the promptness and generosity of British aid; *VPR* (1960–: 1. vii. No. 275).

[11] Gentz advised Metternich on 5 Nov. 1813 to make peace on the basis of an Austro-Russian agreement, with only the pro forma consent and participation of Britain, Prussia, and others; Gentz (1887: 98–103).

to Russia as Britain's natural ally. Behind the moderate and sensible Castlereagh, moreover, stood a Cabinet, a Prince Regent, a Parliament, and a public whose war aims were to defeat France and strip it of its conquests, overthrow Napoleon, perhaps through a revolution within France, restore the Bourbons and a so-called balance of power, and then leave Europe to its devices. No serious opposition to the war any longer restrained the government. The Whigs were divided and impotent, and one of their leaders, Lord Grenville, after years of denouncing the government's war policy now preached the old anti-French crusade and condemned any compromises in Europe more vigorously than ever.[12] Thus on both sides of the Channel the allies' spirit for war was willing, their mutual understanding of peace was weak.

Some differences between Britain and its allies could be healed by time and Britain's (i.e. Castlereagh's) firmness. The Russians repeatedly offered to mediate its war with America, and various powers suggested at different times that the question of maritime rights should be drawn into the general peace. The British answer on both points was a polite but firm 'Hands off', and that settled it.[13] Problems with Sweden (i.e. with Carl Johan) were finally worked out, though not without great irritation for Castlereagh and more harm to the war effort. The Crown Prince, having tried unsuccessfully to avoid taking any part in the autumn campaign in Germany, used the Prussian contingents under his command to fight the French while sparing his Swedes for use against Norway. After obtaining more subsidies, he then refused to follow the joint allied strategy after Leipzig which required him to help liberate Holland. Instead, he prepared to invade Denmark first, engaging in unauthorized negotiations with Davout for the surrender of Hamburg to facilitate his attack.

Metternich, eager to prove his value to Castlereagh and to woo Britain away from Russia, attempted to mediate a compromise, proposing that Denmark cede Sweden part of Norway now, the Bishopric of Trondheim, leaving the final settlement to the general peace. To foil this, Carl Johan, with Russian assistance, invaded Holstein and forced the Danes to make peace at Kiel in January 1814, Denmark ceding Norway for Swedish Pomerania and Rügen. Even this failed to end the allies' difficulties with Carl

[12] Webster (1921: 166–8, 171–2); Martens (1874–1905: xi. 204–5); Castlereagh Papers, PRONI D3030/3636, 3676, 3679, 3691, 3712–3 and *passim* (letters of Liverpool and Lord Bathurst to Castlereagh); Grenville to Grey, 21 Oct. 1813 to 4 Jan. 1814, Grey Papers (Durham).

[13] Webster (1921: 31–3).

Johan, since the Norwegians resisted the transfer and sought independence. Meanwhile Carl Johan began intriguing with Alexander to exchange his Swedish throne for one in France. The Peace of Kiel did, however, pave the way for Denmark to make peace with Russia and Britain, be accepted into the coalition, and eventually also receive a British subsidy.[14]

In the Low Countries the British had an easier time. The minimum British goal was to liberate Holland and remove Antwerp from French hands, but through much of 1813 Castlereagh proceeded cautiously, for several good reasons. The war was far from won, his allies had a peace programme which included allowing France the Rhine frontier, William VI and other Orangist leaders had expansionist ambitions he was reluctant to encourage, and he was not clear himself on how best to strengthen and protect Holland—whether by expanding it territorially in the direction of France and/or Germany, or by giving Belgium as a buffer state to Austria or Prussia. Leipzig enabled Castlereagh to be bolder. In a memorandum of 5 November to the allies he rejected the Rhine frontier in the Low Countries, pointed out that one major purpose of the war was to establish viable independent smaller states, and demanded that Holland be protected either by an adequate military frontier or by a great power interposed between it and France, hinting that Britain might withdraw its subsidies and retreat to naval warfare if its interests were ignored.

Events played into his hands. Throughout 1813 the French in Holland had been harassed by lower-class riots and a middle-class anti-French movement. In November the French army and military government, hearing reports of the approach of the dreaded Cossacks, broke and fled. In the wake of this scuttle, the Dutch rose. The leader of the anti-French movement, Van Hogendorp, took control, established a provisional government, and invited William VI to return as sovereign of the United Netherlands, which he did in early December. Britain, claiming that the Dutch had liberated themselves (which was formally true, if not entirely true in substance) quickly recognized his government and other states followed suit. By late December, on the eve of his departure for the Continent to deal with the allies in person,

---

[14] Norregaard (1954); F. Scott (1935: 93–148); Tangeraas (1983: 208–11). The treaties are in Chodzko (1863: i. 91–104); for allied pressure on Carl Johan and Austria's attempted mediation, see Gentz (1887: 129–32); Castlereagh (1850–3: ix. 48–59, 103–4, 126–7); *VPR* (1960–: 1. vii. No. 141); Aberdeen to Castlereagh, 9 Nov. 1813, BL Add. MS 43075, fos. 142–3; British minister to Sweden, Edward Thornton, to Castlereagh, 29 Dec. 1813, Castlereagh Papers, PRONI D3030/3631.

Castlereagh still was not committed to any final settlement on the Netherlands; but he was prepared to demand at least the Dutch frontier of 1792 plus Maastricht, Jülich, Antwerp, and some Rhenish territory, and in an excellent position to enforce his demands.[15]

He had certainly achieved Britain's goals: promoting Britain's particular interests and special relationship in the Low Countries, strengthening a barrier against France, and circumventing the natural frontiers, all without straining the coalition. Yet praise for this accomplishment seems somewhat misplaced, for here Castlereagh was pushing at an open door. All the allies recognized Britain's primary interest in the Low Countries; no one actively opposed what it wanted or had a fixed programme on Dutch boundaries, just as Castlereagh had none for the Franco-German frontier. There were conflicting Dutch and Prussian claims in the German Rhineland, but no clash between British and allied aims over Holland and Belgium *per se*. Austria was determined not to get involved in the Netherlands at all, at a time when some Belgians and Britons were interested in establishing her again in Belgium, and if Prussia and Russia hoped to gain influence in the Low Countries, they could do so only by co-operating with Britain and favouring the Dutch cause themselves. Moreover, everyone acknowledged that the Rhine frontier made no sense in the Low Countries. The Continental allies thought of it only in connection with Germany. If some Continental statesmen were still offering France its natural frontiers, it was not because they considered it inherently an ideal frontier, but for the purpose of achieving a quick peace and controlling the aims of their coalition partners; and Napoleon's intransigence made this device increasingly useless.

Castlereagh and Britain thus may deserve less credit than they have been given for successfully defending Dutch and British interests in the Low Countries, but merit higher praise for the manner in which they did so, the limits they observed. They did not push Dutch interests at the expense of the general settlement, they did not persist in unrealistic and dangerous ideas like creating an Austrian or Prussian buffer state in Belgium, and above all they did not try to make the United Netherlands simply a British satellite. This last possibility was real and potentially harmful. The United Netherlands which emerged from Napoleon's rule in 1813–15 was more dependent on Britain for its existence and

[15] Renier (1930: 88–130, 198–212); Sas (1985: 45–50); Schama (1977: 622–45).

support than any small state in Germany, Italy, or East Central Europe was on Austria, Prussia, or Russia. All the other smaller states had at least a possible choice of protectors; the Dutch in practical terms had only Britain. Europeans routinely assumed that the Dutch were simply Britain's clients. Yet the British allowed and encouraged the Netherlands to be an independent intermediary power, at the risk, as actually happened fairly quickly, that the Netherlands would develop political, commercial, and colonial policies contrary to British interests. The difference between the Castlereagh–Liverpool and the Pitt–Grenville policies on the United Netherlands is the difference between benign and predatory hegemony.[16]

Still clearer changes in collective outlook revealed themselves by the end of 1813 in relations between Austria and Britain, only recently far apart and now real allies. Austria, pledged to no separate peace or negotiations, fought the war on two fronts, Italy and Germany, with armed forces that matched or exceeded Russia's and outstripped Prussia's in numbers, with an Austrian general commanding the victorious allied armies. Castlereagh, realizing that Metternich's methods were better suited than Stein's for destroying the Napoleonic coalition, dropped or de-emphasized British ideas about insurrections in France, Italy, or elsewhere. Metternich, eager to prove that Austria was a better ally than Russia, began including British interests in his conditions for peace, proffered his mediation to London in dealing with Sweden and Denmark, and co-operated with Castlereagh in his quest for a general wartime and post-war alliance, while Russia obstructed it. Castlereagh, ready to grant Austria undisputed primacy in Italy and to pay more attention to Austrian views about Germany, endorsed Metternich's deal with Prince Murat taking the Kingdom of Naples out of the war, thereby frustrating the dreams of Lord Bentinck in Sicily.[17]

The *rapprochement* was sorely tested in November, to be sure, when Metternich and Nesselrode, ignoring their Prussian colleagues, sent a captured French diplomat, Baron St Aignan, to Napoleon with an unofficial suggestion of peace on the basis of the natural frontiers, accompanied by the hint that Britain might make some concessions on its maritime code. Aberdeen, consulted on the move, expressly reserved Britain's position on the maritime code but did not try to stop the mission. Napoleon was too busy planning his future campaigns, especially the reconquest of Italy,

[16] Renier (1930: 117–62, 212–25); Sas (1985: 55–79); Colenbrander (1905–22: vii. Nos. 7–8, 13, 446).

[17] Schroeder (1988); Gregory (1988: 97–9, 121–5).

to pay attention to the proposal save for propaganda purposes. In his reply through his new foreign minister, Caulaincourt, he indicated a willingness to accept these so-called Frankfurt Bases, on condition that all nations be accorded their natural limits, that Britain make sacrifices equal to those required of France, and that all sorts and kinds of supremacy on land or sea be terminated.

It was another transparent attempt to split the allies, especially Austria, away from Britain and put the onus of continued war on the British. The mission naturally caused an outcry in Britain, and Castlereagh criticized Aberdeen sharply for letting it appear that Britain would let France keep Antwerp or negotiate about its maritime rights. The affair, though intrinsically unimportant, demonstrated how slippery Metternich could be and how far he and Nesselrode were prepared to go in bypassing the Prussians and trying to lure Britain into their kind of peace. It further illustrated the problems Britain had in co-ordinating its policy on the Continent and making its voice heard. There were three British representatives at allied headquarters in Frankfurt, Cathcart from Russia, Stewart from Prussia, and Aberdeen from Austria, getting in each other's way, while Thornton and Clancarty also put in their oars from Stockholm and the Hague. Castlereagh's main problem, however, lay not in the communication and co-ordination of policy but in the inherent difficulty of his task. He needed to conciliate Britain's allies, hold the coalition together, and dispel the impression on the Continent that Britain was an obstacle to peace, while at the same time securing terms the cabinet and British public would accept as safe and honorable.

The St Aignan affair soon blew over—Metternich was, as usual, quick to disavow a failed manœuvre—and the Austro-British *rapprochement* continued to develop. Metternich now looked to Britain to support his independent Central Europe against Russia, and Aberdeen helped him, urging Britain's views on Metternich and Austria's on Castlereagh with equal vigour. More important, he repeatedly pleaded with Castlereagh to change his 'odious system of Russian preference' and to trust Austria more and Russia less. This advice might have been Aberdeen's biggest contribution to the war effort. The fact that Britain and Austria became friends no doubt helped in conducting the war and establishing the peace; but the fact that Britain and Russia did not become either intimate allies or serious rivals was more important in the long run.[18]

---

[18] See Schroeder (1988: 533–5) and the literature cited there; for Napoleon's response to the St Aignan mission and his plans for the reconquest of Italy, see Napoleon (1858–70: xxvi. Nos. 20956, 20963).

The long-feared crisis within the alliance broke in December over an unexpected issue, Switzerland. The dispute, on the surface at least, resembles a series of concentric circles. It apparently arose over an Austrian-sponsored breach of Swiss neutrality, which violated a promise Austria had given Alexander, on the basis of which he had given assurances to the Swiss. The Austro-Russian quarrel which resulted seems to fit into a larger pattern of conflict between Austria and Russia over allied strategy and their own influence in Switzerland and elsewhere, and this in turn can be seen as part of a general struggle among the great powers in the coalition to control and make pawns of the smaller ones.

The interpretation, though it seems plausible and supported by some facts, is really misleading—above all in suggesting that Switzerland here was a potential or actual victim of great-power conflicts and intrigues. Ever since 1800 Switzerland had been lucky compared to most of Europe; never was it more so than in 1813–15. The main aim both Austria and Russia pursued was to save Switzerland, not control it—and not least to rescue it from its own internal rifts and rivalries.[19]

Despite everything that had happened—Napoleon's territorial seizures, occupations, and violations of Swiss neutrality, the economic losses Switzerland suffered under the Continental System, the heavy military losses it incurred in Russia, and renewed French troop demands in 1813 which compelled some cantons to resort to conscription—most Swiss still did not want to be freed from French domination, much less fight for their liberation. They preferred to be left in peace. Napoleonic hegemony, moreover, had preserved or widened the old Swiss internal divisions (patricians versus democrats, old versus new cantons, city versus forest, Protestants versus Catholics). Patricians with their strongholds in Bern and the Grisons wanted to restore the old Confederation, while a new generation of élites identified Switzerland entirely with France, and the new cantons, especially the Vaud and Aargau, saw their survival and independence linked to the Napoleonic regime. Even after Austria's entry brought the war directly to the Swiss frontiers in the east and south, the Swiss failed to react. Only in November, when Napoleon, now back in France and hoping to use Swiss neutrality to help bar the invading allied armies, evacuated the canton of Ticino which he had earlier

---

[19] The Swiss historian William Martin writes: 'In 1814, it was internal passions which would tear the Confederation apart, while exterior forces would tend to unite and strengthen it' (1931: 12).

seized and renounced his claim to the Swiss contingent (though not his title as Mediator of the Confederation) did the Diet even resolve on neutrality. It aimed further to preserve the existing internal order based on the Act of Mediation, and it called on the European powers to honour it.[20]

The allies were not opposed to Swiss neutrality. It fitted with their main goals in Switzerland, to end French influence and establish it as an independent, neutral barrier state. But to be asked in the midst of a great war to recognize strategically vital Swiss territory as inviolable while the Swiss still clung to their French constitution and connection was something else. What happened was that the allied military problem of carrying the war into France, combined with hesitations and divisions among the Swiss themselves, served to produce a basically accidental Austro-Russian dispute, which in turn became tangled up with Swiss internal quarrels.

Three allied plans were developed in November for invading France, one by Gneisenau, another by Schwarzenberg, and a Russian compromise between them. Each called for moving through a portion of north-west Switzerland into the French plateau of Langres, either as the main allied thrust or as a diversion for a more direct drive on Paris. The allies hoped to get the Swiss to consent to this move, either by bringing Switzerland into the coalition or by persuading it to grant their armies a right of passage. Baron Lebzeltern of Austria and Count Capodistrias of Russia, sent to deal with the Diet and the Swiss *Landamann*, Max von Reinhard, a nervous but stubborn adherent to the Napoleonic system, at first believed that under pressure the Swiss would concede the right of passage. Alexander, eager here as elsewhere to be seen in the role of protector of small, weak states, was especially influenced by Swiss *émigrés* in his entourage, including his former tutor, the Swiss liberal unionist, La Harpe. Though the Tsar reluctantly agreed to allow the allied armies to draw up along the Swiss border, he declined to sanction any use of force. At the same time Schwarzenberg, strongly opposed to a Prusso-Russian proposal for a direct drive across the Rhine on Paris, in late November ordered a move through Switzerland toward Langres, to begin by mid-December.

The allies tried to secure Swiss benevolent neutrality and permission for this move, but failed. Reinhard agreed *de facto* to cancel the French alliance, but clung to the Act of Mediation and

[20] Ibid. 12–29.

rejected any right of passage. At the same time, under advice from the French minister to Switzerland, Count Augustin Talleyrand, a nephew of the Prince, the Swiss failed to arm seriously to defend their neutrality. Metternich argued that the Swiss should be forced to yield, but Alexander, though he had earlier approved a military operation through Switzerland, now promised the Swiss that their territory would not be violated, and got Emperor Francis to pledge to honour his promise. At the same time Metternich's representative at Bern, Count Senfft-Pilsach, was assured by his Swiss patrician friends that the majority of the Swiss really wanted the allies to intervene and would join a rising in their favour led by Bern. There was also evidence that the Swiss commander, General Niklaus Wattwyl, would not resist an allied move, and that Reinhard himself might actually prefer to yield to *force majeure*.

Metternich used these arguments to persuade Francis, after the Emperor had first cancelled Schwarzenberg's orders, to authorize them once again, and the march through Switzerland was launched in late December. It met no Swiss resistance and succeeded militarily, enabling the main allied army to occupy the plain of Langres and outflank the French positions on the upper Rhine. But Alexander was outraged, believing that Metternich had deliberately deceived him and compromised his honour, and his anger grew when the Austrians occupying north-west Switzerland encouraged a Bernese counter-revolution in which Bern tried to reincorporate the breakaway cantons of the Vaud and Aargau. Capodistrias's allegations that Austria was promoting a reactionary revolution in Switzerland in order to dominate it and possibly to annex the Grisons further fuelled Alexander's rage. As a result, by January and February the quarrel between Austria and Russia over Switzerland and personal animosity between the Tsar and Metternich threatened the coalition and the war effort.[21]

The dispute over Switzerland was quickly brought under control. When Metternich learned that Senfft had been deceived by the Bernese and had misled him in turn, he promptly disavowed and recalled him. Lebzeltern, who had always co-operated with Capodistrias in dealing with the central Swiss authorities, convinced Metternich that the Vaud and Aargau had to remain independent of Bern and all the existing cantons be preserved and reconciled. Francis rejected a request for annexation from the Grisons. While Metternich certainly favoured the conservative

---

[21] Ibid. 29–186; Oechsli (1898: 13–42); Bonjour (1965: i. 176–85); Ritter (1958: 468–71); *VPR* (1960–: 1. vii. Nos. 200, 205, 208, 215; pp. 523, 532).

cause in Switzerland and Alexander the liberal-democratic one, Austria had far too much to lose by a general revival of power politics in Europe to want to play that game in Switzerland. The Austrian proclamations accompanying the allied invasion, promising to liberate Switzerland and guarantee its independence and neutrality, proved substantially true.[22]

As for the Swiss, naturally they wanted to avoid becoming a battleground again, as in 1799. But after they had themselves abandoned their neutrality for over eleven years and profited from doing so, their expectation that the allies should now honour that neutrality for Napoleon's benefit, and should liberate and guarantee Switzerland without any Swiss help and without ever touching Swiss soil, was asking too much, and Alexander was wrong to encourage it. But the effects of the quarrel long outlasted its Swiss origins.

III. WINNING UNITY AND PEACE, JANUARY–APRIL 1814

Added to the political strains in the coalition was a military threat which arose in late winter 1814, when Napoleon apparently recovered his youthful boldness and skill. His position appeared so desperate in early February, with Schwarzenberg's army poised at Langres and Blücher's Army of Silesia defeating the French at La Rothière and driving toward Paris, that he gave Caulaincourt virtual *carte blanche* to negotiate for peace with the allies at Châtillon. In mid-February, however, he scored a series of victories over the reckless Blücher, and for a month thereafter was able to hold his own against a numerically superior enemy, bewildering his foes with rapid movements and threatening at times to force them into a retreat like that of 1792. Yet his strategy, brilliant and risky in 1796, was brilliant and hopeless in 1814. Militarily his situation was grave, but not quite desperate. Though his army of raw and ill-equipped recruits was outnumbered and France was war-weary and approaching exhaustion, his enemies were not much better off (Schwarzenberg, for example, claimed that the Austrian army had 50,000 sick), and they had to contend with a hostile population, long lines of communication, and serious divergences in their strategy and

---

[22] Martin (1931: 191–203); Hatze (1949: 44–7). For Aberdeen's defence of Austrian policy, see BL Add. MS 43076, fos. 106–7.

aims. Moreover, other French armies (Davout's in Hamburg, Eugène's in northern Italy, Soult's in southern France) continued to engage sizeable enemy forces and give a good account of themselves. Man for man, except for Wellington's British, the French probably remained better soldiers than their opponents to the very end.

None the less, to have any chance for success Napoleon had to break up the coalition; what made his cause hopeless was his refusal to exploit that chance. Like Ludendorff in 1918, he refused to accompany his military offensive with a meaningful political one, ignoring or denouncing as defeatism and treason the warnings and pleas even of loyal followers like Caulaincourt. As always, he was ready to negotiate while fighting and even to discuss specific peace terms, but only for the purpose of making propaganda, sowing divisions, and winning this war so as to prepare for another. His political position shifted with every military change of fortune. In early January he called for the natural frontiers plus much of Italy; he retreated to the natural frontiers by mid-January; after giving Caulaincourt a free hand early in February, he cancelled these instructions following his string of victories and revived his claims to the natural frontiers plus much of Italy, maintaining these aims until mid-March; and at the end, when everything collapsed about him, he still talked of Antwerp and the Scheldt as the French frontier and a regency for Marie Louise in favour of their son, the King of Rome, while in the back of his mind still counting on one more throw of the dice.

Even tactically his politics made little sense. He knew that Britain and Russia were the foes most bent on overthrowing him, and Austria the one most likely to defect out of fear that an all-out struggle would produce too great an allied victory. His propaganda tried to exploit these Austrian fears and stressed the family connection (though privately he vowed that he would rather see his son strangled than let him fall into Austrian hands). But he never responded seriously to Metternich's repeated peace efforts, and in concrete terms he tacitly conceded most of Britain's and Russia's goals, supremacy on the sea, the loss of Holland, and control of Eastern Europe and Germany, while continuing to challenge Austria directly by his ambitions in Italy.[23]

[23] For the military campaign, see Chandler (1966: esp. 982–3). The evidence on Napoleon's political and military moves is scattered through Napoleon (1858–70: xxvii. Nos. 21062–467); see also Caulaincourt (1935: i. 612–13); Lacour-Gayet (1928–30: ii. 332–4); Dard (1937: 274–81); Fournier (1900: 82–90); Arneth (1898: i. 188–93).

Just as Napoleon's refusal to exploit his political opportunities earlier had helped save the coalition, so did his victories in mid-February, when it seemed ready to collapse from military success. By late January Russia had decided to continue the war to a military victory and overthrow Napoleon. A variety of motives entered in: the belief that Napoleon was finished; the desire to see Russia shine on the world stage; Alexander's personal dream of avenging the destruction of Moscow by capturing Paris, sparing it, and giving ordered liberty to France; his anger at Metternich, dislike of the Bourbons, and notions about putting Bernadotte on the French throne; and Russia's plans for Poland, which could proceed while the world's attention was fixed on France.[24] For other reasons the decision suited some Prussians and most Britons. But many others—Metternich, Gentz, Stadion, Ancillon, Knesebeck, Schöler, Frederick William, Hardenberg, and Nesselrode—considered it dangerous to fight longer than necessary and almost criminal to abandon the terms adopted in earlier treaties. Castlereagh and Metternich had met at Basel and agreed on certain points—that maritime rights would not be discussed and that neither Bernadotte nor a Napoleonic regency would be allowed to rule France—but beneath the agreement divergences lingered. Metternich still hoped somehow to save Napoleon and bring about a negotiated peace, while Castlereagh thought that, since Napoleon was doomed and a regency or Bernadotte excluded, the Bourbons were the only choice left, and wished above all to hold the coalition together until France was ready to make peace.

None the less, the Anglo-Austrian partnership, if it stayed firm, could restrain Alexander and the Prussian military leaders, given Russia's and Prussia's financial dependence on Britain and the vital role of the Austrian army. With the consent of Castlereagh and the Prussian government, Metternich had Francis pose six questions to the Tsar designed to force Russia to hold to the agreed war aims and to negotiate seriously with France at a forthcoming peace congress at Châtillon. Alexander was not easily pinned down. He agreed to negotiate but insisted on continuing the allied offensive, denied that the allies' war aims, which had evolved considerably between Kalisch and Frankfurt, were now complete or immutable, and insisted that the allies could not shape the final peace until the campaign was over, and should not interfere in

[24] Fournier (1900: 27–32, 44–5); *VPR* (1960–: 1. vii. Nos. 242–3; p. 523); *Sbornik* (1867–1916: ix. 431–43, cxxi. 232–4).

French politics by excluding any possibilities on France's future regime in advance.[25]

Thus the negotiations began at Châtillon on 4 February with an uneasy truce among the allies. Metternich yielded a good deal to Britain and Russia on the proposed peace terms. The basis was now to be France's ancient rather than natural frontiers, to be revised by mutual agreement in France's favour. Italy and Germany would be composed of independent intermediary states, with the German ones joined in an alliance (*lien fédératif*). The only lures for France were the promise of compensations from British colonial conquests and a role in the European guarantee of Swiss independence and neutrality. Yet Caulaincourt, desperate to save Napoleon, offered on the 10th to accept the ancient limits as a basis for peace if the allies would grant France an immediate armistice, with French fortresses to be turned over to the allies as a pledge.

Obstacles to progress were now raised initially on the allied side. Castlereagh, the only allied foreign minister at Châtillon alongside three British plenipotentiaries and envoys from the Continental allies, argued that Britain could not specify what colonies she would return to France without being clearer on the whole European settlement. Caulaincourt claimed in turn that France could not make the sacrifices required of her without knowing how they would be disposed of. Both implicitly were calling for an agreement on the general peace now, which meant postponing a preliminary peace or armistice indefinitely. Yet both raised valid concerns. It proved once more that the allies could not first win the war and then construct Europe, but needed to agree on a viable concept of Europe's structure before winning the war.

Russia meanwhile wanted a further military victory before any peace, preliminary or general. The Tsar, from his headquarters at nearby Troyes, first instructed Count Razumovski to delay the negotiations by pleading lack of instructions and then, when France seemed likely to accept the allied terms, ordered him to suspend the negotiations to allow the monarchs to confer. At Châtillon, Prince Stadion, warning that Russia and Prussia seemed bent on abandoning the treaties and going over to a 'system of aggrandizement and conquest', laid out for Castlereagh the dangers this would raise and the claims Austria would have to make for itself in reply. At the same time he insisted to Metternich

[25] Fournier (1900: 62–73); Gritzbach (1974: 284–7); Gentz (1887: 150–75, 211–19); Webster (1921: 136–40); *VPR* (1960–: 1. vii. No. 207; p. 551); Nesselrode (1904–12: v. 152–7).

that, if Austria was forced to acquire compensations in a competitive scramble, these should 'be at least in proportion with and equal in value to those of our modest and honest allies'.[26]

Russia's action in breaking off negotiations threatened to renew the worst problem of earlier coalitions, a revival of the eighteenth-century politics of compensations and indemnities, with the peace terms for France becoming hostage to the Eastern powers' ambitions and rivalries in Poland and Germany. Castlereagh hastened to Troyes for an allied ministers' meeting to head off the threat; Gentz prayed that he was cured of his predilection for Russia.[27]

He was, in fact. Not only did he see the danger in the combination of Alexander's exalted ideas and Russia's power, but it angered him personally that the Tsar had tried to undermine his position at home with Liverpool and the Prince Regent, and irritated him further that the Russians demanded special treatment and recognition as leaders of the coalition—extra subsidies to pay for their superior war effort, British assumption of Russia's debt to Holland, and (most outrageous of all, especially to Britons) the appointment of a Russian military governor when Paris was occupied because Russia had been fighting France the longest. Castlereagh informed Liverpool that the Austrian and Prussian military efforts were at least equal to Russia's, if not superior to it. In tense conferences at Troyes on 11–13 February, Britain, Austria, and Prussia agreed to accept Caulaincourt's offer of peace on the ancient frontiers and to grant France an armistice on the basis of adequate guarantees. Alexander refused to go along with this, agreeing to resume the negotiations at Châtillon, but not to grant an armistice. The allies must drive on Paris, overthrow Napoleon, and allow the French nation to decide its future dynasty through an assembly of leaders summoned on the spot.

Efforts by Castlereagh and Hardenberg to sway the Tsar failed, though Hardenberg offered to allow the peace talks to be moved to Paris after the armistice to give the Tsar his much-desired triumphal entry into the French capital. Metternich then worked out another agreement with Hardenberg, comprising both a draft of the terms to be offered France and a secret convention among the allies. It provided that the war would continue and Schwar-

---

[26] Stadion to Metternich, 9 and 10 Feb. 1814, Fournier (1900: 316–18); the passage quoted is on p. 318.
[27] Nesselrode (1904–12: v. 88–104, 306–7); Rössler (1966: ii. 120–1); Colenbrander (1905–22: vii. No. 40); *VPR* (1960–: 1. vii. No. 219; pp. 560, 565); Aberdeen to Castlereagh (5–7 Feb. 1814, BL Add. MS 43076, fos. 326–50); Gentz (1887: 238–9).

zenberg would come to the aid of Blücher's Army of Silesia, now hard pressed by Napoleon, but that the allies also would seek peace with Napoleon either at Châtillon or at Paris. Moreover, any future victories and conquests the allies might make would not affect the peace bases they had already decided on. If Napoleon fell, the allies would recognize only the Bourbons as rulers of France, and an allied civil commission would administer occupied Paris alongside a Russian governor. Repeated threats by Metternich to pull Austria's army out of the coalition and make a separate peace brought Alexander to accept this compromise on the fourteenth.

The Tsar had prevented an armistice and the other powers had brought Russia back to the peace table at Châtillon, but still no real unity had been achieved. Napoleon's victories over Blücher on 10–14 February reinforced the Russian view that Napoleon was too dangerous to be left on his throne; Castlereagh secretly agreed, Münster and others did so openly. But these same victories confirmed Schwarzenberg's pessimism about the allies' military prospects and intensified the eagerness of others, including Emperor Francis, for peace. Despite the secret convention in favour of the Bourbons, the dynastic question in France remained open and subject to events. To his horror, Gentz found even Metternich wavering on whether peace was possible with Napoleon, and on whether the French people should be allowed a say in determining their future rulers. For Gentz anything, including Napoleonic rule, was better than such concessions to Russia and popular sovereignty.[28]

Once more the irony of history made Castlereagh and Napoleon partners in converting the crisis at Troyes into a solid allied agreement. When the allies now offered Caulaincourt what he had earlier sought, a preliminary peace based on the ancient frontiers with revisions in France's favour, he was forced to stall, knowing that his Emperor would no longer accept it. Then Schwarzenberg, in violation of the Troyes agreement and over Castlereagh's protests, persuaded Frederick William and the Tsar to agree to offer the French an armistice. Napoleon's response was to demand the natural frontiers as the basis for the armistice, insist that the fighting continue during armistice negotiations, and withdraw Caulaincourt's full powers to conclude a peace at Châtillon. Napoleon's military offensive, meanwhile, foiled Alexander's and

[28] Fournier (1900: 105–36, 283–94); Castlereagh (1850–3: ix. 212–13, 266–73, 284–5, 328–9); *VPR* (1960–: 1. vii. Nos. 221–2; p. 571); Gentz (1887: 245–8).

Blücher's dreams of driving directly on Paris, and forced the allies back on Schwarzenberg's 1813-style strategy of avoiding battle with Napoleon while attacking the inferior forces of his marshals. By the beginning of March this strategy had begun to pay off, though the allied operations were no more vigorous or free of friction than before.

Castlereagh's positive contribution to allied unity was even more important than Napoleon's negative one. In reassuring the allies that Britain would not cut off its subsidies or retire from the Continent and retain its colonial conquests, he deftly reminded them of what Britain could do and how they could neither wage war nor make peace without her. He was not willing, like Metternich, to compromise key security issues for a quick peace. (Metternich continued to try to persuade Napoleon, for example, that the allied call for the revised ancient frontier was really no different from the natural frontiers offered earlier, only more detailed.) But neither would he, like some Prussians and Russians and many of his countrymen, sacrifice a satisfactory peace with Napoleon for the sake of military victory or a particular regime in France. His central goal was now to preserve the unity of the alliance during the war and after it. A united Europe would be secure even against Napoleon; a divided one would soon fall into new conflicts, regardless of the kind of victory it won or the terms of peace it imposed. (This was exactly the conviction which had brought the Continental allies together at Reichenbach and Teplitz, which some of them had now forgotten.) This focus helped him first secure agreement on a set of war aims moderate enough to gain the conservatives' assent yet severe enough to prevent a premature, insecure peace. Then, after the period the allies had given Caulaincourt to respond to their terms at Châtillon had expired, Castlereagh finally was able to bring his long-sought general alliance to fruition, he himself, Metternich, Hardenberg, and Nesselrode signing it at Chaumont on 9 March. The treaty, pre-dated 1 March, bound the allies to continue the war for the agreed aims, provided new subsidy arrangements for another year's campaign if necessary, and most important, united them for twenty years in jointly maintaining peace.[29]

Chaumont, it is everywhere recognized, was a special British achievement and laid the foundations for victory, peace, and post-war security. Metternich in Castlereagh's place would have

[29] Fournier (1900: 148–53, 160–83, 297–8, 326–36); Sherwig (1969: 315–21); Webster (1921: 138–61); Castlereagh (1850–3: ix. 290–1, 335–6); Martens (1874–1905: iii. 155–65).

claimed the credit for himself; Castlereagh called it a tribute to Britain's power and indispensability in the coalition. In a further sign of British leadership and another subtle rebuff to Russian pretensions, Britain used certain side-payments (the promise of an arrangement on the Dutch debt and double return pay for the Russian army after the campaign) to induce Russia to accept the same basic subsidy as Prussia and Austria.

Yet beyond recognizing what Chaumont did and who was responsible for it, one needs to look further at what was behind the crisis in the coalition and just how Chaumont surmounted it. A common and plausible interpretation has it that Russia brought on the crisis in an attempt to replace French hegemony in Europe with its own. Much in Russia's aims seems to fit this. A military victory led by Russia, a triumphal Russian entry into Paris, a Russian governor of the city, and deliberations by Frenchmen on their new monarch and constitution under Russian protection would confirm Russia's leadership in Europe and give it a solid base for world rivalry with Britain. Meanwhile Russia could settle the Polish question with the help of its dependent partner, Prussia. Most Austrians and some Prussians and Britons believed this scenario, and the Tsar's adviser on French affairs, Napoleon's old Corsican rival, General Pozzo di Borgo, may have had something like it in mind.

But as a general explanation this ascribes too much coherence and clear purpose to a Russian policy characterized more by inconsistency, uncertainty, and idealism. The Tsar, who had had a religious conversion in 1812 and was still influenced by the mystical ideas of Baroness von Krüdener, wife of one of his diplomats, genuinely wanted to lead France and Europe into a new era of ordered freedom. His idealism, to be sure, had its selfish and inconsistent aspects. At the same time as he promoted the liberal cause in Switzerland and France and protected weaker states in Germany and Italy, he was backsliding on reform in Russia and carefully protecting concrete Russian interests in Poland.[30] But this was natural. Nor was his desire to play the leading role on the world stage a mere personal whim. Russian nationalists like his aide, Colonel Chernishev, saw this as something important to Russia, which the world owed it. Furthermore, not everything Russia proposed or did served Russia's national

---

[30] Grimsted (1969: 39–65); Ley (1975); Schiemann (1904: i. 88–9). For a contrary argument, stressing Alexander's determination to wage a contest for world supremacy with Britain and dominate central Europe, see Griewank (1954: 48–9, 72–5); Pirenne (1946–9: i).

interests; sometimes the opposite is true. Nesselrode, for example, argued for a quick peace with Napoleon, granting him France's natural frontiers on the grounds of Russian national interests. Having the French on the Rhine, he argued, would not endanger Russia but would menace the Germans, Prussians, and Austrians, and force them to seek Russia's protection. Moreover, a prompt peace would enable Russia to settle the Polish and Turkish questions quickly by itself; the longer Russia waited and the more it entangled itself in general European questions, the more difficult this would become. Nesselrode's arguments were sensible from a strictly Russian standpoint, and his forecasts would be borne out by events. The Tsar, however, rejected his advice on general European grounds. Besides, the Russians had reasonable arguments for some of their stands. A France ruled by Napoleon would indeed have been dangerous for European security; making peace with him now, as Count Münster argued, would have enabled him to gather his scattered forces from Germany and Italy back in France; and it was incompatible with general allied principles to impose a particular regime, the Bourbons, on the French without their consent.

None the less, Russia did pose a general danger and Alexander a special one. Castlereagh recognized their source: not greed for land and power, but lack of prudence and consistency, inability to decide what they really wanted. Part of the problem was the tension between liberalism and autocracy deeply rooted in Alexander's personality—his wish, to paraphrase Czartoryski, that the whole world should be free to do what he wanted. But mainly it was a wish to have one's cake and eat it too; to help fashion a harmonious European family of states free of hostility and threats, in which all Russia's wants would automatically be satisfied and it would peacefully arbitrate the desires and claims of all others. This kind of unrealism was not unique to Alexander and Russia. Hardenberg wanted Prussia to dominate north Germany and be free to pursue its German mission while enjoying a friendly alliance and co-operation with Austria, Russia, and Britain. Metternich and Francis, especially the latter, wanted Austria to be able to withdraw within its own borders for peace and recovery while at the same time exercising leadership in Germany and Italy and checking Prussia and Russia with the help of Britain. The British wanted a 'balance of power' which France would peacefully accept, and which would operate by itself or be enforced semi-automatically by the rest of the Continent, and enjoyed and supervised with little effort by Britain. There were no visions of peace in 1814 entirely free of selfish or utopian expectations (usually both simultaneously).

What counts in the last analysis and made Chaumont possible is that no state, even Russia, insisted to the end on its vision come what may, made its best the enemy of the common good. Chaumont was a British triumph, but not a triumph over foes or even over rivals. Everyone in the end compromised and took risks for the sake of allied unity, Castlereagh included. He risked the possibility that a peace would be concluded with Napoleon which the great majority of Britons would have condemned at the time. Austrian and Prussian conservatives risked a prolonged war with potentially dangerous consequences; the Prussian military risked its chance for victory and revenge; Alexander risked his moment of supreme triumph. Even more important, the allies finally united, not on the goal of military victory or an abstract vision of peace, but on a practical concept of Europe: a Europe of independent sovereign states, equal in rights, status, and security, if vastly unequal in power, responsibility, and influence, protected by a balance between power on the one hand and rights, law, morality, and consensus on the other.

Chaumont made fairly sure that the allies would remain together and not lose the war. It could not, however, ensure that if war continued much longer they would not lose control of the outcome. Castlereagh saw this, and suggested to Aberdeen a possible strategy: to declare victory and go home. If Napoleon remained stubborn, the allies, after conquering and organizing the territory needed to carry out their agreed war aims, could offer France peace on the basis of *uti possedetis* and, if this was refused, could evacuate France to the frontiers they agreed on and leave it to itself. This again shows Castlereagh's moderation, and proves that victory *per se* and the destruction of French power were not the allies' main aims. They were still less Metternich's goals; he continued after Chaumont to seek peace with Napoleon. No one wanted this more than Caulaincourt, but when after repeated allied ultimatums he had to present Napoleon's formal counter-proposal on 15 March, it ended the talks at Châtillon. Napoleon claimed, among other things, the natural frontiers for France, the Kingdom of Italy to the Adige plus the Ionian Isles for Eugène, Lucca and Piombino for his sister Elisa, the restoration of the King of Saxony and the Grand Duke of Berg, and the return of all France's colonies and overseas rights as of the Treaty of Amiens; anything less was incompatible with France's honour. Even after this absurd proposal, Metternich kept trying until he learned of

Napoleon's instructions of the nineteenth authorizing Caulaincourt as a last resort to yield Belgium and the German left bank, but with the intent, if the military situation permitted, to retain Antwerp, Mainz, and Alessandria in Piedmont. Forced to stop dealing with Napoleon or be left behind by his allies, Metternich now acted, as he explained to his aide, Baron Hudelist, on his eternal principle 'that events which cannot be prevented must be led'. (For once he told the strict truth; this was the central principle of all his politics.)[31]

With the cessation of talks came an allied military decision to drive on Paris to end the war. No firm decision was yet made, however, to overthrow Napoleon or restore the Bourbons. A Bourbon movement had already taken control of Bordeaux on 12 March, with Wellington looking on, and the allies on 20 March met with a Bourbon representative, the Baron de Vitrolles, and authorized Bourbon activity within France. The aim, however, was still not to force France to surrender or to impose a pro-allied government on it, but to persuade the French leaders and people to stop fighting and rejoin Europe on the terms the allies offered.

Once again Napoleon played into the allies' trump card of peace, helping them and the Bourbon cause alike. He divided his army, taking the best part under his command east toward the upper Marne to cut the allied communications and liberate the French forces trapped in fortresses along the Rhine. The move might have represented his only military chance still to escape defeat, but it demanded in typical Napoleonic fashion that his marshals sacrifice themselves and their armies to aid his coup. He also ordered the regency council at Paris under Joseph, along with Marie Louise and his son, the King of Rome, to retire with the army to the Loire to continue the resistance should Paris fall to the allies. In other words, Napoleon expected the army, the dynasty, the regime and its officials, and Paris itself to go down with him if his desperate military gamble failed.

Talleyrand, invited to the session of the regency council on 28 March called to consider whether it should leave Paris or stay, predictably declined to conform. While others left for Blois, Talleyrand stayed behind (Napoleon's police minister, Savary, making only a feeble attempt to force him to leave) and became the key mediator between the allies seeking to end the war and

[31] Fournier (1900: 198–233, 338–43) (the Metternich quotation is on p. 266); Gentz (1887: 186–93, 275–93); Chodzko (1863: i. 130–3); Kraehe (1963: 297–310); Fournier (1885: 229–41); *VPR* (1960–: 1. vii. No. 240); Castlereagh to Aberdeen, 10 Mar. 1814, BL Add. MS 43077, fos 128–30.

Napoleonic marshals and officials seeking to save themselves and France from further useless sacrifice. On 30 March, after a fierce but indecisive battle between the allied army and that of Marmont and Mortier in the suburbs of Paris, Joseph authorized negotiations with the enemy, which led early the next day to the surrender of Paris. Napoleon, who had hastened back to rescue the capital, arrived too late and retired with his forces to join the army at Fontainebleau.

That same day Alexander, having led the allied army into Paris, accepted Talleyrand's assurance that France would recall the Bourbons to power under a constitution; the allies now excluded Napoleon from the throne and authorized a provisional government. The next day the rump of the Napoleonic senate still in Paris proclaimed a provisional government headed by Talleyrand. On 2 April this government released the army from its oath to Napoleon and called for his deposition. The next day Marmont resolved to withdraw his troops from Napoleon's army, destroying any chance of success for the counter-attack Napoleon planned from Fontainebleau. On the 4th Napoleon, faced with the defection of all his marshals and the deposition voted by the senate and legislative corps, tried to abdicate in favour of his son, but after two more days of tense developments he agreed to abdicate unconditionally, at the same time as the senate adopted a constitution restoring Louis XVIII to the throne of France.[32]

No chronicle of events, least of all a bare-boned one like this, does justice to the uncertainty and tension of those days. Nor did these developments solve the problem of establishing a constitutional basis for the monarchy, persuading Louis XVIII to accept it, and getting the people to accept the monarchy. As things turned out, Louis on his return to France on 24 April rejected the constitution which the senate had drawn up with Alexander's encouragement and under Talleyrand's leadership, because it would have compromised his divine right of kingship. He promised, however, to grant one himself on bases agreed upon with the senate.

Yet contingent as each development in the fall of Napoleon and restoration of the Bourbons was, the final outcome was in a sense inevitable, because there were no viable alternatives. Militarily no other outcome was plausible, not because France was incapable of further resistance—even after Waterloo further resistance was

---

[32] I have relied principally on Bertier (1966: 3–55); but see also Bertier (1948); Jardin and Tudesq (1984: 3–13); Lacour-Gayet (1928–30: ii. 318–19, 394–6); Mansel (1983).

possible—but because even a French military victory, by now impossible, would not secure France the peace it wanted and needed so long as Napoleon ruled. Napoleon's arguments to his marshals that only victory could save France from intolerable allied terms simply demonstrated again his willingness to destroy France rather than accept a tolerable peace.[33] The debate occasionally flaring up since 1945 in Germany over whether the conspirators against Hitler in July 1944 were patriots or traitors is repellent—as if the question could possibly be put that way, or could have more than one answer if it were. The similar minor but persistent debate over whether the French officials and marshals in 1814 acted as traitors is merely ridiculous—as if Napoleon had some right to demand that France and Frenchmen commit national suicide for him.

Louis XVIII was also the only plausible choice as a ruler. Though not popular, he had not really been forgotten within France. In some areas, especially the south, he had a considerable following, and a minority of committed partisans and an active secret organization, the *Chevaliers de la Foi*, worked for his cause. Besides, there were no viable competitors. Napoleon had eliminated himself; a regency under Marie Louise, which Metternich may have favoured, was impossible so long as Napoleon was alive; Bernadotte or the Duke of Orleans were not taken seriously as candidates by anyone besides Alexander and themselves. Moreover, establishing anyone other than a Bourbon would have required an active allied political intervention, which almost everyone, including Alexander, was determined to avoid, and the Bourbons at this juncture were ready for concessions to regain power and promote peace and national reconciliation.

The problem of the regime was thus solved by letting events and the French themselves solve it. Napoleon's fate, unfortunately, could not be settled the same way. Publicly he posed as ready to sacrifice himself for France, while through Caulaincourt he demanded not only suitable pensions and establishments for himself and his family but also a kingdom to rule somewhere on the mainland of Europe, preferably Tuscany. There were good military and political reasons for treating him generously. As Castlereagh pointed out, it was too early to celebrate victory; no formal armistice was yet concluded and French garrisons were still holding out over much of Europe. To punish Napoleon might

---

[33] He argued e.g. that peace would destroy French industry, and that it would do no good to regain France's commercial colonies unless France also had positions of power from which to challenge Britain. Caulaincourt (1935: ii. 166).

further alienate the army; many of its marshals and rank and file were clearly unhappy with the new regime, the Bourbons, and the Bourbon flag, and fearful of their prospects under it. It would also threaten the fragile coexistence between the old Bourbon and new imperial élites. But another motive for generosity was less valid: Alexander's desire to display his personal magnanimity to his fallen foe, and to steal a march on Britain and the others in the competition for influence in post-war France.

The Treaty of Fontainebleau, worked out between the Tsar and Talleyrand on 11 April and accepted only reluctantly and with misgivings by Castlereagh and Metternich, assigned Napoleon the island of Elba to rule. It also pledged the French government to pay a handsome annuity to him and members of his family, allow them to retain their personal property, pay off Napoleon's debts, and make him a grant for presents to his followers. The money pay-offs could be justified, though the Bourbons and their followers were bound to be outraged by the contrast between this treatment of the usurper and their treatment in the long years of exile. But choosing Elba, dangerously close to France and even closer to Tuscany, Italy, and a potential co-conspirator, Murat, at Naples, was an egregious blunder. No one who knew Napoleon could suppose that he would vegetate there till he died.

Still, the treaty did get Napoleon out of France and paved the way to an armistice signed on 23 April by which the allies promised to evacuate France in exchange for the surrender of fortresses the French still held in Europe. The agreement, part of the general allied effort to help the Bourbons establish themselves, ended an allied occupation which the French fiercely resented and which some of the allies, especially the Prussians, had exploited for revenge and loot. It further protected France against any German notions of recovering Alsace. Yet it was attacked in France then, and has often been criticized since, for giving away assets which, if saved for the peace negotiations, might have gained France a better frontier than the one of January 1792 promised at Châtillon and in the armistice. This criticism illustrates the main problem the allies faced in trying to reintegrate France into Europe: too many Frenchmen, rather than the Bourbons, had learned nothing and forgotten nothing. Twenty years of war and a succession of convincing defeats had not destroyed Napoleon's nimbus of glory or the delusions and injured self-view of many in France.[34]

[34] Ibid., 10–11, 136, 156–7, 218–19 and *passim*; DeClercq (1880–1917: ii. 402–5); Bertier (1966: 48–51); Webster (1921: 175–6).

In fact, this armistice helped France on the way to a much better peace than it had any right to expect. In the peace negotiations Talleyrand haggled for souls and strong points in good eighteenth-century fashion, taking advantage of the Tsar's desire for a liberal internal and external settlement with France and the promise he had made on entering Paris that a new French government might expect better terms than those the allies had offered Napoleon. Hardenberg, who had received some Russian support in late January for the idea of taking Alsace, now got none. As a result, the Peace of Paris signed on 30 May 1814 ceded to France border rectifications along all its frontiers except the Pyrenees, adding more than 600,000 inhabitants to the status quo of January 1792. It also restored to France all its lost colonies save Tobago and Santa Lucia in the West Indies and the Seychelles in the Indian Ocean, and settled other questions (an amnesty for supporters of the Revolution and Napoleon, French debts and private property acquired in former conquests, and claims regarding the artistic and historic treasures the French had looted from Europe) on a generous basis. There were limits to this European effort to appease France, in the best sense of that much-abused word. Castlereagh made sure no vital strategic assets were given away, especially *vis-à-vis* Belgium, and France had to accept general territorial provisions regarding Italy, Holland, Germany, and Switzerland, to be worked out in detail at the peace congress supposed to meet at Vienna in two months. All Napoleon's dotations in Europe were cancelled. The allies also intended to exclude France from the most vital European security question, the reorganization of Germany. Nonetheless, France here reaped the benefits of a new kind of European politics which it had not yet learned to practise itself.[35]

IV. PACIFYING THE REST OF EUROPE

The allies had other tasks in the first half of 1814 besides making peace with France. Ending the war and establishing a new consensus and post-war system in Italy actually took longer and proved harder. Austria's campaign against Eugène's army in northern Italy in the autumn and winter of 1813–14 was slow and disappointing, partly for military reasons (the Austrian commanders were indecisive and the two armies evenly matched),

[35] Bertier (1966: 62–5); Griewank (1954: 76–83); Chodzko (1863: i. 161–78); DeClercq (1880–1917: 414–26); Gentz (1887: 314–52); Lacour-Gayet (1928–30: ii. 406–8, 417–19).

even more for political ones. After the French regime in Illyria collapsed and Eugène retreated across the Adige in the wake of the Treaty of Ried and the Battle of Leipzig, Austria tried to win Eugène over by diplomacy, even offering to guarantee him an Italian kingdom up to the Adige. This failed, as did Austrian appeals to the Italians to rise and fight for their freedom. Though the Italians were by this time sick of French conscription, taxes, and economic exploitation, like most other conquered peoples in Europe they wanted to be liberated first before rising. A sizeable liberal and national élite had emerged in the Napoleonic era, moreover, as distrustful of Austria as of France.

Meanwhile Murat, after earlier abandoning Napoleon and then returning to him, finally approached Austria and concluded an alliance on 11 January. Austria paid a high price for his defection, and got little in return. Murat received an Austrian guarantee of Naples, along with Austrian promises to try to persuade the Bourbon King Ferdinand to renounce it formally for compensations elsewhere, to promote peace between Murat and England, and to help him gain 400,000 more souls from the Papal State. Murat, arguing that he deserved to be treated no worse than the allies had treated Bernadotte, now resorted to Bernadotte's tricks. Instead of uniting his 30,000-man army with that of the Austrian commander, Bellegarde, as promised, he stopped in Tuscany to promote his dream of becoming king of a united Italy. Thus he took no part in a bloody battle on the Mincio on 8 February, which, though it badly weakened Eugène's army, also stalled the Austrian advance. Murat then competed with the Austrians and Eugène in summoning the Italians to freedom and independence under his banner.

A fourth British party entered the competition. Lord William Bentinck, commander in Sicily, had on Castlereagh's orders reluctantly made peace with Murat in early February, but clung to his plans for promoting constitutional liberty in Sicily and Italy, as did other British agents and generals. Moving north to combat Murat's intrigues in Tuscany, Bentinck liberated Genoa, proclaimed the old Genoese Republic, and through Generals MacFarlane and Sir Robert Wilson contacted the liberals in Milan, encouraging them to seek British protection. Bentinck's plan, tacitly supported by Castlereagh's under-secretary at the foreign office, William Hamilton, was to create an Italy independent from Austria and open to British liberty, influence, and trade, able to check both France and Austria within the balance of power.

Meanwhile Eugène, who remained loyal until Napoleon accepted the Treaty of Fontainebleau on 11 April, signed an armistice with Austria on 16 April and withdrew his French forces across the Alps. But this left his kingdom and the Italian part of his army still functioning, and opened the field to a host of contending parties—officials and partisans hoping to keep the Kingdom of Italy alive under Eugène or someone else, a Lombard 'nationalist' party with Italian aspirations but a primary interest in Lombard independence, a 'pure Italian' party hoping for Italian unity under Murat or the House of Savoy, an Austrian party promoting Austrian rule, and various secret societies actively promoting both radical and reactionary causes.

A revolution in Milan on 20–3 April, carried through by the combined forces of the Austrians, the 'pure' Italians, and secret societies, overthrew the Kingdom of Italy, and Castlereagh quelled the activity of Bentinck and his subordinates, leaving the further fate of Italy up to the forthcoming congress. In fact, however, the die was already cast. The allies had long since decided on the restoration and expansion of Sardinia-Piedmont, Austrian control of Lombardy and Venetia (which it had conquered), and a general system of independent Italian intermediary states. As Castlereagh told Bentinck, an insurrectionary policy was fine so long as the goal was to weaken Napoleon. But now Italy had to settle down, Austria and Sardinia-Piedmont were the powers with which Britain had to work, and liberal experiments would have to wait.[36]

All this fits the picture of Italy as an arena for the old competitive balance-of-power politics, with its scrambles for territory and advantage and disregard for what the people wanted. This is true to a degree, and foreshadows the unsatisfactory aspects of the final settlement in Italy. But the impression that even in Italy the great powers, Britain and Austria in particular, chose to impose their will arbitrarily on peoples and small states is misleading. Austria had certain territorial aims which it pursued, and both Britain and Austria were determined to exclude France and make Italy an intermediary barrier zone. But beyond that their main interest was Italian stability and peace, and the chief characteristic of Metternich's policy is an almost reckless improvisation in his search for useful allies. Rather than concentrating on Austrian territorial and dynastic gains, he thought, for example,

[36] This is drawn mainly from Rath (1941: 27–175); but see also Rosselli (1956: 136–43); Gregory (1988: 114–25; 1985: 182–3); Lackland (1926). For the Austrian treaty with Murat, see Chodzko (1863: i. 83–7); for Murat's claim to the same treatment as Bernadotte, Aberdeen to Castlereagh, 10 Nov. 1813, BL Add. MS 43075, fos. 152–3.

of giving Tuscany, a former Habsburg secundogeniture, to the King of Württemberg to help provide compensations to Bavaria in Germany. Murat, Bentinck, and the various Italian parties were the real practitioners of the old competitive politics; all the groups claiming to represent the 'people' were actually small interested minorities trying to make the allies fight to realize their particular programs. What the unorganized mass of the Italian people wanted in early 1814 was pretty much what the great powers wanted—a return to peace and stability.

In other words, allied policy in Italy was essentially pragmatic, an attempt to settle Italy down. The same pragmatism helped to put most other European problems on the road toward settlement even in advance of the peace congress. The complications in the Netherlands, as in Italy, came primarily from within. The Dutch people ('these lively turtles', as one Briton termed them), exhausted from occupation and war, had little interest in expansion or power politics, yearned to return to peace and commerce, and had an ingrained aversion to their southern neighbours born of two centuries of religious and political separation. But William VI, now Sovereign Prince and soon to be crowned William I, King of the United Netherlands, was determined to play a major role in Europe and to rule over a kingdom worthy of the name, which meant extensive territorial claims to Belgium and the German Rhineland. The Belgians, however, who unlike the Dutch were united in religion and divided in language, were mainly averse to Orange and Dutch rule, without being able to unite on an alternative. A small, now cowed minority preferred the French connection; others called for independence under some European prince (the Habsburg Archduke Carl was frequently mentioned); and a clerical-aristocratic group wanted a return to Austrian rule to secure their old privileges.

Utopianism was as grave a problem as disunity. William's goal, constructing a middle-sized state capable of pursuing an independent policy in Europe, was impractical and dangerous. What the two peoples wanted was impossible—that each should enjoy peace, security, and privileges within the international system without incurring any obligations or burdens. None of the great powers was eager to take over. Austria, though willing to help ease the transition by accepting the temporary military government of liberated Belgium, flatly rejected any long-range responsibilities in the Low Countries. Russia used the issue of the Dutch frontier to get the Dutch and British to assume its Dutch debt, and Hardenberg tried out his idea of bringing the Netherlands into the prospective German Confederation as another device to help promote Prussian hegemony in Germany. But neither was ready to take responsibility for the defence of the Low Countries or, fortunately, to make much trouble over its frontiers; Prussia especially had too much at stake elsewhere (Poland, Saxony, Mainz, its own Rhenish territories, the whole German question) to antagonize Britain on this critical issue. Hence the settlement for the Low Countries outlined in the Peace of Paris was managed though not imposed by Britain, and gave all the main parties something. The Dutch gained expansion to the Meuse and Luxemburg, and the Belgians the opening of the Scheldt for commerce, with Antwerp to be a purely commercial port (thereby protecting British naval interests); even France gained a rectification of its 1792 Belgian frontier.[37]

Switzerland is another example of how the allies helped smaller states and peoples escape the consequences of their own disunity. In February the confederation fell into near-anarchy. The allies, concerned to promote a new constitution and military frontier that would make Switzerland secure, had to deal with different cantons and factions trying to present the allies with *faits accomplis*. It took an allied decision at Chaumont in early March that either the Swiss must settle their differences peaceably or the allies would intervene to impose a constitution, plus patient diplomacy by Capodistrias and Lebzeltern, to bring the cantons to agree on a new Federal Pact adopted on 31 May. In the process, Austria abandoned the patrician party in Bern it had earlier encouraged, Lebzeltern was attacked as a Jacobin by Swiss and Austrian conservatives, and Capodistrias, the liberal champion of the new and smaller cantons, urged a compromise in the Bern–Aargau dispute that the Argovese themselves were willing to accept, only to have his master Alexander reject it. The allies also encouraged the Swiss to expand at France's expense, and the Swiss chief of staff responded with a military line which would have incorporated a series of strong-points; but the Swiss, whose patriotism was largely cantonal, held back, showing more desire to expand north and east on the German and Austrian borders than to the west. In the end, the confederation retook only territories France had annexed, and brought Geneva into the confederation.

There was, of course, some great-power competition over Swiss issues. Capodistrias, for example, suggested compensating

[37] Renier (1930: 244–9); Sas (1985: 79–95); Colenbrander (1905–22: vii. Nos. 10–12, 42–4, 53–6, 66–7, 76, 88); Castlereagh (1850–3: ix. 306–7, 340–1, 354–6); Martens (1874–1905: xi. 200–1).

Bern for the loss of Vaud and the Aargau by giving it the Fricktal, formerly Austrian territory; Austria had no objection to disposing of it, but not for nothing. Louis XVIII was no sooner back in power than he attempted to reassert French influence in Switzerland. The Austrians occupied the Valtelina in the south to make sure its passes, vital for the defence of northern Italy, did not fall into other hands, and there were signs that Austria's chronic problem in Italy, the failure to co-ordinate policy between its civil and military authorities, also affected its actions in Switzerland. But overall it is clear that the main goal of allied policy was to create a viable neutral and independent Switzerland, and that they co-operated in setting it up.[38]

The way the Swedish–Norwegian question was handled in the spring and summer fits the same pattern of allied attempts to satisfy both rulers and peoples for the sake of stability and peace. By the time the war was over, Bernadotte had alienated everyone except Alexander and the British minister, Thornton, by his persistent refusal to fight and his intrigues for the throne of France. Even more embarrassing for Castlereagh, however, was the Norwegian revolt for independence. Sweden's efforts to crush it by armed force aroused protests in Parliament leading to a vote on a resolution attacking its policy. The ministry easily won, Castlereagh taking the sensible stand that Britain and the allies had to carry through on their agreements and could not punish Sweden for the sins of the Crown Prince. Nonetheless, pressure from him and others led Sweden to grant Norway autonomy under its own constitution, which was accepted by the Norwegians in August.[39]

Along with settling questions or putting them on the road to settlement, the allies also explicitly or tacitly excluded some things from the purview of the coming congress at Vienna. The British, as noted earlier, refused to let anyone interfere in their war in America or their maritime rules, and while they put their colonial conquests on the table for compensations, they did so strictly on their own terms. Russia also exploited its freedom of action *vis-à-vis* Persia and the Ottoman Empire. It made a victorious if unstable peace with Persia at Golestan in December 1813, gaining most of the territory in dispute in the eastern Caucasus and turning the Caspian Sea for naval purposes into a Russian lake, and it continued to press the Ottoman government over its claims in the

[38] Martin (1931: 204–326).
[39] F. Scott (1935: 149–69; 1933); Tangeraas (1983: 214–23); Castlereagh (1950–3: ix. 500–7, 514–20).

western Caucasus and elsewhere, without getting much to show for it.[40]

The freedom of action Russia and Britain enjoyed was significant in several ways. The fact that each could pursue its world interests during the critical last months of the war without harming—indeed, almost without affecting—its war effort or its relations with the other and with other European states illustrated their status as the sole world powers, a fact France's defeat and decline further underlined. Equally clearly, though this has been less noted, it showed that they were not really world rivals. The seeds of rivalry were sown, but had hardly begun to germinate; what rivalry existed was one-sided, perceived more in Russia than in Britain and apparent more in European than in world politics, and represented a dying echo of the genuine struggle for influence they had waged, whether as allies or enemies, for the previous quarter-century. Now Britain could *de facto* claim the western hemisphere as its sphere and worry only about American competition, although Russia had long been active in the western hemisphere. In the Middle East, far from Britain's encouraging Persia's resistance to Russia, as some Soviet scholars have claimed, the British were unwilling to employ against Russia the Persian alliance they had intended to use against France, and so failed to respond to Persia's quest for British support, relying instead on persuasion and appeasement to moderate Russian policy.[41]

This all fits into a general picture of what had been accomplished by mid-1814 in establishing peace. The positive accomplishments— a solid alliance, victory, the ouster of Napoleon and restoration of the Bourbons, a moderate peace with France, the outline of a settlement in the rest of Europe—were important, but no more so than the negative achievements in avoiding pitfalls. Some obvious dangers to peace had been avoided—breakup of the coalition, territorial rivalries among the powers, military failure—but so had other, less obvious ones—attempts to impose 'national' solutions on Italy and Germany, a peace signed with Napoleon, or a fall back into an eighteenth-century scramble for compensations and indemnities. Except for military failure or peace with Napoleon, these potential snares remained, but the worst dangers they presented were probably over.

The main components of the new world order were also

---

[40] Semenev (1963: 16–37); Atkin (1980: 144–5); *VPR* (1960–: 1. vii. Nos. 158, 169, 187, 203).

[41] The Russian commander in the Caucasus acknowledged Britain's help in reaching the peace of Golestan—*VPR* (1960–: 1. vii. p. 426).

emerging more clearly. The system's members would consist of two world powers, more invulnerable than ever; three major Continental powers, distinctly weaker and more vulnerable; and a host of smaller intermediary bodies. This made the most important problem obvious: how to organize intermediary Europe for peace, guaranteeing independence to the smaller states and securing the influence the larger ones would require and demand. Another problem, however, was equally vital and directly connected with it: how to keep British and Russian world hegemony and leadership on the Continent stable, tolerable, and useful rather than dangerously competitive and oppressive.

12
The Congress of Vienna,
1814–1815

THE Congress of Vienna was supposed to be a brief formal meeting to confirm the Paris peace treaty, fill in some gaps, and tie the pieces of the settlement together. Instead it lasted nine months without ever convening officially, and turned into a marathon of difficult negotiations punctuated by crises. Contemporary observers blamed this either on the congress's spending too much time on festivities and too little on work, or on the powers being so divergent in their aims that they were barely able to reach a settlement at all and could easily have fallen back into war.

Both impressions are unsound. By and large the statesmen at the congress worked hard, and to a surprising degree they agreed on basic aims, even on the two most difficult and divisive issues at the congress, the Polish–Saxon and German questions. The other major crisis, created by Napoleon's return from Elba, would demonstrate strikingly how united and committed to the peace settlement they were. The chief obstacles to progress at the congress were not really struggles over territory and power, though these cropped up, but problems of learning. Peace was endangered less by greed and fear than by inconsistency and inconsequence, the belief that ends almost everyone agreed on and wanted could be reached without changing old means and practices. The real danger at the congress was, therefore, not a new general war or a failure to reach any settlement at all, but an unintentional relapse into the old competitive politics.

I. THE ANGLO-RUSSIAN DANGER AND FRANCE'S OPPORTUNITY

Russia was more dangerous in that regard than Britain because its kind of power, essentially military, was closer at hand and easier to exert, it occupied a more decisive position in respect to the great unresolved questions of Poland, Germany, and the Near East, and its ruler was more unpredictable. The summer of 1814 proved less

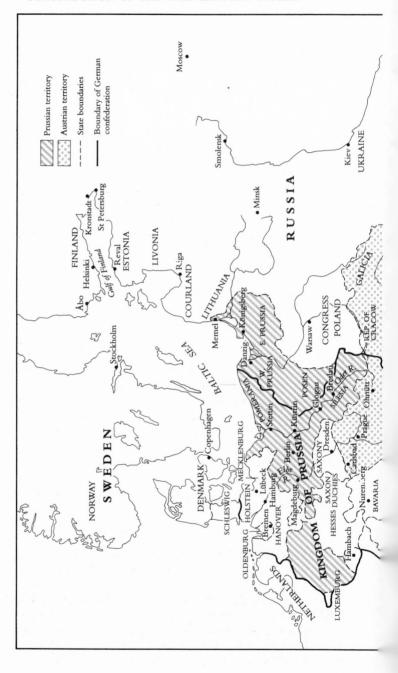

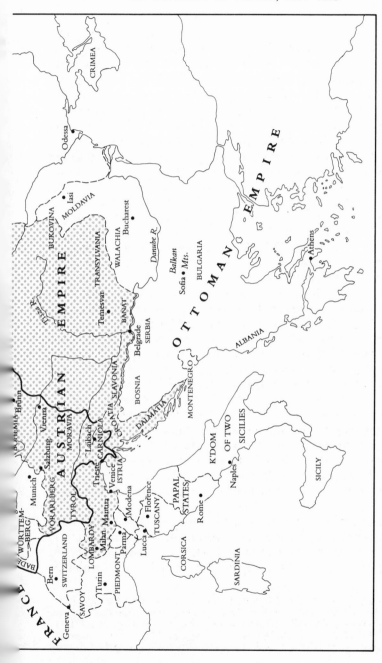

Central and Eastern Europe, 1815

glorious for Alexander than he had anticipated. His state visit to England after the Treaty of Paris was not the public triumph hoped for (on Castlereagh's urging, the ministry worked to restrain popular adulation of the Tsar and to make sure that credit for the victory was shared with the other allies), and Alexander conducted himself in ways that worsened his relations with the government and the Prince Regent. Continental princes continued to appeal to him for help, however, while his subordinates and advisers plied him with sycophantic praise and advice. The programme presented to him by Russia's minister at Stuttgart, Count Iuri Golovkin, at the urging of the Württemberg government, represented potentially the most dangerous brand of Russian power politics in the post-war era. Russia, Golovkin argued, should protect and encourage liberal and national aspirations in Germany and Italy. By so doing it would win the hearts and minds of the peoples, while at the same time it would compel the smaller states to look to Russia for protection against revolution or great-power intervention and revive the old Austro-Prussian rivalry, thus forcing them to compete for Russia's support. Out of this, Russia would emerge the unchallenged arbiter of Europe.

By no means everyone at St Petersburg favoured this. Conservatives like Nesselrode emphasized Russia's need for repose and a stable, peaceful European order, while Capodistrias and La Harpe urged the Tsar to support moderate liberal reforms in Europe, not in order to expand Russia's power and influence, but to establish a real European peace based on harmonious relations between princes and peoples. Alexander used both Nesselrode and Capodistrias as his foreign ministers, a sign of his own oscillation and determination to be his own minister. At least one current of Russian opinion, the nationalism and semi-isolationism represented by Rumiantsev, was out of favour; the question was not whether Russia was part of Europe and should lead it, but where and how.[1]

The British, in contrast, could contemplate an isolation of sorts, once France had been defeated and Western European issues largely settled. The public, Parliament, and much of the cabinet, including even Liverpool and Bathurst, would have preferred to withdraw

---

[1] Grimsted (1969: 32–7). Golovkin's memoir of 3 July 1814 is in *VPR* (1960–: 1. viii. No. 17); for other evidences of a Russian concern to protect peoples from their rulers, especially in the Ottoman Empire, see ibid. vii. Nos. 261, 273; viii. Nos. 7–8, 29, 54; pp. 194–5; Martens (1874–1905: iii. 178–9). For Castlereagh's warnings about the need to 'group' Alexander, see Castlereagh (1850–3: ix. 459–61, 478–80, 491–3).

from an active role in Europe and concentrate on trade, empire, the reduction of debt and taxes, and ending the American war. Only Castlereagh's and Wellington's prestige and influence kept Britain involved in Europe, especially beyond the Rhine.[2]

The uncertainty of Russian policy and the possibility of British withdrawal seemed to offer Louis XVIII and Talleyrand an opportunity to achieve their goal, restoring France to its leading place in Europe. But serious problems at home stood in the way: fiscal strains and economic hardship; an army angered by steep cuts in military expenditure; Protestants, Jews, sceptics, and liberal Catholics alienated by the restoration of a militant Catholicism as the state religion; and discontent over the reimposition of censorship and the retention of unpopular imperial taxes. The constitutional charter the King proclaimed, while emphasizing divine right and royal power, also recognized the representative principle and conceded some legislative powers and wide freedom of debate to a lower house (Chamber of Deputies), elected by wealthy taxpayers from the narrow ranks of even wealthier ones. This combination of monarchic authority with limited concessions to the representative principle proved a recipe for future conflict.

The fact that Louis's regime ran into trouble, however, does not make the first Restoration a failure or its policies a series of blunders. The charter was a deliberate compromise intended to preserve some of the heritage of the Revolution and Empire and show the regime's desire to reconcile France's old and new élites, and on the whole it succeeded. Political life, dormant under the Empire, revived, and civil liberties were broader and better protected. Neither the bureaucracy nor the army was drastically purged. Those who had purchased noble and church property confiscated under the Revolution retained it. Even regicides were not hunted down. The religious conflict that broke out was local and minor compared to the Second Restoration in 1815. The government's fiscal and economic troubles, and some of its political and social ones, arose mainly from a generation of war which had distorted or blighted France's development and ended in defeat. No government inheriting these problems could have handled them without hardship and dissatisfaction. Moreover, in one vital area, international politics, the regime achieved quick success in ending the war and the occupation on moderate terms and protecting French interests in the peace negotiations.

[2] See Webster (1931), and for documents, Castlereagh (1850–3: x); Webster (1921); Castlereagh Papers, PRONI, D3030/3971, 4233, 4234, 4244, 4291.

This points to the most serious difficulty faced by the Bourbon regime: like the Weimar Republic, it suffered from the political immaturity, illusions, and injured self-view of the political nation, and failed to confront the problem. Too many Frenchmen refused to see that France had waged war against Europe for two decades, had lost, and now must face the consequences of defeat; and leaders who knew this, like Talleyrand, declined to try to teach Frenchmen the unpleasant facts. Instead, Frenchmen continued to portray France as *la grande nation*, now cruelly oppressed; clung to the natural frontiers, more as symbol and myth than as concrete goal; denounced the settlement as unjust and humiliating, on no more serious grounds than that France had gained less than its rivals, or that other peoples (Belgians, Italians, Germans, Poles) were deprived of their natural rights; assumed against good evidence that the peoples formerly annexed to France longed to return to her bosom, or that France still enjoyed an inalienable sphere of influence in Germany and Italy, or that the old Austro-Prussian rivalry was still there for France to exploit; and, above all, were obsessed with France's lost glory and prestige.[3] Such attitudes would hurt France's international recovery for decades, above all in 1815.[4]

Yet this is one-sided. France, unlike Germany after 1918, did not take out its illusions and injured self-view on the rest of the world; it harmed itself rather than Europe. And in one way French nationalist pride was useful, frustrating Russian efforts in 1814 to achieve a Russo-French partnership against Britain. Alexander soon discovered how wrong Pozzo di Borgo was to assure him that Frenchmen wanted his patronage.[5] Moreover, the French did learn one vital lesson from their recent past and never forgot it: not to fight Great Britain. Emotionally, Anglophobia in France endured well into the twentieth century, as did Francophobia in

[3] A characteristic incident: the Duke of Noailles, French ambassador to Russia, complained to Talleyrand that by current rules the British ambassador, Lord Cathcart, took diplomatic precedence over him, and protested, 'But how can one acknowledge such an advantage, when one remembers that six hundred years ago our kings received homage from those of England? It is certain that the pretensions of that island's government grow every day.' Instead of telling Noailles to grow up, Talleyrand assured him that Britain did not contest France's pre-eminence—only Austria did—and that the congress would settle the issue of precedence. Polovstsov (1902–7: i. Nos. 98, 109).

[4] Bertier (1966: 66–84); Jardin (1984: 3–17); Mansel (1981: 176–88). For some examples of how French newspapers and publicists made Talleyrand's task more difficult, and his complaints about it, see Jaucourt (1905: 52–3, 75–6, 88, 91, 171–3, 181–2).

[5] Polovtsov (1902–7: i. Nos. 21, 25, 34); Pozzo (1890–7: i. 72–5).

Britain, but not as policy. The historic Anglo-French struggle for supremacy in Europe and overseas effectively ended in 1814, with a brief flare-up but no real revival during the Hundred Days. France instead began in 1814 to seek an *entente* with Britain, hoping to gain support for French interests on the Continent and British consent to a limited renewal of French colonial and maritime activity. London responded to the quest. The Liverpool ministry, without trusting France more than before but counting on the barrier system and the Continental states to check France militarily, also wanted an informal partnership with France, partly to help check Russia, mainly to keep Louis XVIII on the throne and to manage French policy. Thus an informal Anglo-French restraining partnership developed which suited Talleyrand's and Louis's immediate aims perfectly—to oust Murat from Naples and Napoleon from Elba, to loosen the Eastern coalition against France, and to participate as an equal in the general settlement, especially on German and Italian issues. These goals could be reached only with British help, and did not clash with Britain's chief interests.[6]

II. THE POLISH–SAXON QUESTION

The new relationship with Britain paid off quickly for Talleyrand in helping him defeat an attempt to organize the congress in September without France. The four powers, with Castlereagh's reluctant consent, had worked out a compromise by which they would draw up the plans for a German and Italian settlement and submit them to France and Spain for their approval, with all six powers then dealing with the smaller states. Talleyrand's protest, and insistence that all the eight signatories of the Paris Peace Treaty had equal rights and that the smaller powers must also be heard, resulted in negating the proposed four- and six-power directories without making the committee of eight a genuine working body either. As a result, the formal convening of the congress was postponed, first to 1 November and then indefinitely; its real work came to devolve on the five great powers, with special committees dealing with the German question and other issues.[7]

Even without France's protest, four-power control of the con-

---

[6] For evidence of Castlereagh's and Wellington's desire for this restraining partnership, see Webster (1921: 189–91, 195); Castlereagh (1850–3: x. 92–4).

[7] Griewank (1954: 145–54).

gress would soon have broken down. The preliminary meetings in mid-September blew open a long-brewing dispute over Poland and Saxony, and Russia, in promising Prussia on 28 September to turn Saxony over to its administration, showed that it would not wait for the congress to decide it. The quarrel was apparently over territory. Russia, Austria, and Prussia, having agreed at Kalisch, Reichenbach, and Teplitz in 1813 to dissolve the Duchy of Warsaw and to partition it among themselves by future friendly agreement, now had to carry this engagement out. No one thought seriously about restoring an independent Poland, though Metternich, Castlereagh, and Talleyrand all raised the idea for tactical reasons at one time or another. As for Czartoryski's dream of uniting all the Polish lands under the Russian Crown, as Gentz pointed out, it was everyone else's nightmare.

Russia's claim to the Duchy rested on several grounds: conquest and possession, the claim that it represented Russia's only important compensation for its uniquely superior wartime efforts and sacrifices, and the argument that the great bulk of the Duchy, including the capital, Warsaw, had to remain with Russia to satisfy the Poles, preserve the Polish nationality, and prevent further divisions and unrest in Europe. Austria and Prussia had already accepted this principle, the Russians insisted, in agreeing to treaties restoring them to their size and status of 1805 and 1806, but not their particular territories. The gains they would make in Germany and Italy, which Russia's victories had made possible, would amply compensate them for their losses in Poland. In addition, out of loyalty and generosity Russia would concede Posen and the Kulm district to Prussia and the Wieliczka salt-mines and the Podgorze district to Austria. But beyond this, Russia would insist on its rights and, as Alexander later boasted, it had 200,000 men in Poland to back them up.[8]

The challenge to Russia's neighbours and to Europe was a formidable one. This Russian Poland would thrust a salient deep into Central Europe, threatening Prussia and Austria and making Russia's glacis more extensive and impregnable than ever. Almost as dangerous was Russia's style—setting *faits accomplis* before Europe and daring it to try to reverse them, basing its demands on rights of conquest and indemnities, and claiming credit (in defiance of its record of 1807–12 and the military realities of 1813–14) for bestowing victory and peace on everyone. Finally,

---

[8] Grimsted (1969: 222–5); Pienkos (1987: 18–19); Martens (1874–1905: iii. 170–3, 214–17; viii. 158–9); *VPR* (1960–: 1. viii. Nos. 21, 27, 35; pp. 89, 118).

Alexander's insistence that no one had a right to discuss what policies and institutions Russia would implement in Poland—that other powers must trust him as the Poles did—made nonsense of his calls for a new general alliance uniting all the monarchs and peoples of Europe. Yet the arrogance was unconscious rather than calculated. Everything suggests that Alexander and other Russians took it for granted that Russia had superior rights to Poland based on history, the treaties, and the good of Europe. When Alexander called on Europe to trust him and rejected any protests as aspersions on his honour, he was speaking from conviction.

Austria, considered by Nesselrode Russia's only serious opponent, knew how strong Russia's position was. It had on its side military power, possession, treaty claims, moral self-assurance, and the confidence that Europe could not act jointly or effectively against it. Metternich had not helped matters by failing in 1813 to stipulate the lines of a future partition or to demand the return of Austria's main losses in 1809, Cracow and Zamosc, but this was not the real problem. For even the Vistula–San line in Poland, Austria's maximum territorial claim, would still not have made Austria secure against Russia. An independent Polish buffer state restored and backed by Europe, a suggestion Metternich made seriously, though not hopefully, to Prussia in August, would be better but still insufficient. Nor would great-power alliances do the job. The combination Metternich dreamed of, an Anglo-Austrian–Prussian alliance, would be powerful enough to restrain Russia, but would also put Austria on the front line, immobilize it elsewhere, and continue to drain its strength in constant military preparations. Austria, in short, faced the same old dilemma which Kaunitz and Leopold II had confronted, and which Austria had nearly destroyed itself trying to solve by power-political means: its own vulnerbilility in the face of a Russia growing ever more invulnerable, increasingly threatening its survival as an independent great power.

Nor was this simply or mainly an external security threat for Austria, a matter of geography, boundaries, population, and military resources, especially where Poland was concerned. Metternich defended Austria's territorial claims and criticized Russia's on strategic grounds, but he repeatedly emphasized that this was not Austria's main objection to Russia's plans. Far worse was Russia's intention to establish an autonomous constitutional Kingdom of Poland under the Russian Crown. Austria could tolerate a major expansion of Russian power, but not a Polish Kingdom; it would breed Polish nationalism and revolution and make Poland ungovernable for Russia, Austria, and Prussia alike. This suggests that Metternich and Francis feared revolution more than external military threats, which is true in one sense, but misleading in a more important one. In Austria's case, the normal distinction between an internal threat of revolution and its external security dilemma was inapplicable; they were completely intertwined, in Poland and everywhere else. For most European great powers, Russia included, the acquisition of territory at this time still usually meant gaining additional wealth, power, and security; once assimilated, the new territory would yield soldiers, revenues, and resources. Austria, because of its ethnic composition and geographical location, was already in the situation faced by all European powers and most states in the world today: territorial acquisitions would give Austria additional wealth, power, and security *if and only if* other powers, especially Russia, allowed them to. (By the late nineteenth century, to be sure, another key condition would apply: whether the peoples involved would allow them to; but this condition was not yet critical in 1815.) Other states, especially Russia, could if they wished render an Austrian territorial acquisition ungovernable, turning it into a burden rather than an advantage, by exploiting one or another of Austria's vulnerabilities.

This general truth, repeatedly apparent in eighteenth-, nineteenth-, and early twentieth-century history (think of Austria in Belgium in the eighteenth century, in Lombardy-Venetia in the mid-nineteenth, or in Bosnia in the late nineteenth and early twentieth), applied with special force to the Polish–Saxon question and generally in 1814. Russia claimed that Austria would be generously compensated in Italy for its Polish losses. But given the appeals already being made to Russia by Sardinia-Piedmont, the Papal State, and other Italian states to protect them against Austrian domination, Russia could if it chose make Austria's Italian territory a further source of weakness and trouble. The Russians also claimed that the disappearance of the old German Empire in favour of a new confederation strengthened Austria. But however Austria's relationship to the new Germany might develop, appeals to Russia for protection from Baden, Württemberg, Oldenburg, and other states gave Russia opportunities to spoil it. Russians like Rumiantsev and Chichagov took it for granted that Russia could always use its influence over the Balkan peoples, especially the Serbs, to keep Austria in line. On top of this, giving Saxony to Prussia would greatly increase the Prussian internal and external threat to Bohemia, long a serious problem

for Austria, while a Russian Kingdom of Poland would undermine Austria's hold on Galicia.[9]

The point is not to arouse sympathy for Austria and its leaders,
or antipathy to the Russians (or the French, Piedmontese,
Prussians, Germans, Italians, Serbs, Rumanians, and British),
who would exploit this situation at this time or later; it is, rather,
to make clear its implications. The Habsburg monarchy was not a
normal great power, and could not become one by expanding its
military power or reforming itself internally in the directions of
modernization and unity. Either of these kinds of reform might
have been wise for Austria to pursue; no matter how vigorously
pursued, they would not have solved its security dilemma, and
could have made it worse. The only alternatives which could
conceivably have given Austria security and independence were
either imperialist conquest and expansion on a massive scale,
embracing all of Central Europe and beyond—a course impossible and unthinkable, never attempted by any Austrian leader before Hitler—or a European international system which somehow
transcended the limits of normal balance-of-power politics. For
Austria to become independent and secure, Europe as a whole,
and especially the whole European centre, had to become independent and secure.

Naturally, achieving this end involved establishing a certain
distribution of power; should the end prove unattainable, Austria
might have to go back to power politics for security as a *pis aller*.
But as Metternich and other Austrians saw, power politics *per se*
could not construct this kind of security, and too much reliance on
power politics would block it. An independent European centre
had to derive from and rest upon a broad political consensus
in Europe, underpinned by law. The states in the centre would
have to unite against pressure from the too-powerful flanks; some
outside states would have to support this unity and the flank
powers themselves would have to accept it; and institutions would
have to be constructed to sustain that independence, particularly a
confederate organization for Germany.

At the heart of the Polish–Saxon question, therefore, lay the
question of whether there would be an independent centre in
Europe. The concept was unquestionably European in spirit and
Metternich was, at this time at least, a real European statesman,
but not from any abstract idealism. He was a cosmopolitan aristo-

---

[9] Fournier (1918; 1899: 444–67); Griewank (1954: 203–6); Arneth (1898: i.
224–31, 256–60); Gentz (1887: 384–99).

crat working for Austria, inordinately vain, slightly frivolous, above all concerned to preserve his own position, protect his class, and advance his monarch's interests, who happened to understand better than most the connections between his goals and the requirements of a durable European settlement and the only practical way to make these connections, and he was fortunate enough to have most of his useful ideas succeed and his bad ones fail.

His dealings with Prussia called on all his flexibility. Neither the King nor Hardenberg felt as threatened as Austria by the Russian advance in Poland, Hardenberg because his main ambitions lay in Germany, the King because he trusted Alexander and retained some of his old suspicions toward Austria. Besides, Russia had already conceded the most important of Prussia's Polish claims. Hence the primary Prussian goal was to get Austria to agree to the annexation of Saxony. Metternich knew that this concession clashed directly with Austria's strategic and other interests, and that the logical, legal, and moral arguments used by Prussia and Russia in its favour were untenable.[10] Saxony was as important to Austria as an intermediary body vis-à-vis Prussia as Poland had been vis-à-vis Russia, and as the Ottoman Empire still was. Monarchical principle and tradition as well as strategy called for keeping the Saxon King on his throne, and the Saxon government, which had tried to escape the war in early 1813 through a neutrality treaty with Austria, could argue that it was forced to rejoin Napoleon in 1813 because none of the allies would protect Saxony's neutrality. Emperor Francis and other prominent Austrians were pro-Saxon. None of this swayed Metternich. He let the Prussians know, tentatively as early as January 1814 and clearly in late summer, that Austria would co-operate on Saxony if Prussia would join Austria in resisting Russia in Poland and Germany.[11]

Prussian support, however, would not be enough; Britain's partnership was equally vital. Though Metternich was delighted to see Alexander alienate the British government in the summer of

[10] The central Russo-Prussian claim, that Frederick August had forfeited his throne by rejoining Napoleon in mid-1813, would have made most European thrones, including those of Alexander, Frederick William, and Francis, also forfeit. As Talleyrand remarked, treason was a matter of dates (and who would know better than he?). The arguments that Saxon public opinion favoured annexation to Prussia, or that Saxons would prefer being absorbed entirely into Prussia to being divided, were even more disreputable.

[11] Griewank (1940: 250–3; 1954: 197–203); Kohlschmidt (1930: 4–6); Arneth (1898: i. 224–31, 256–60); Sweet (1978: 188–9); Chodzko (1863: i. 194–7).

1814, thus apparently ruling out an Anglo-Russian condominium over Europe, this did not guarantee effective Anglo-Austrian co-operation. Castlereagh believed that the King of Saxony deserved to lose his throne, and, though aware of a Russian threat in Poland, saw it in purely balance-of-power terms and envisioned a mechanical solution—to push the Russian frontier far back and strengthen Prussia in Poland, Saxony, and on the Rhine, thus enabling Austria and Prussia to defend Germany against both France and Russia. He failed to understand what such a power-political confrontation would do to the general post-war alliance, and what so huge an expansion of Prussia would do to the German settlement and the Austro-Prussian partnership. Liverpool for his part admitted that Russia posed a strategic threat, but insisted that any attempt now to compel it to retreat would have revolutionary effects in France and the Low Countries. Better a resumption of the normal sort of wars in Central and Eastern Europe in a few years' time, after the situation in Western Europe had stabilized, than any war now.[12]

If Metternich did not get quite the support from Britain that he wanted, he received more from France than he was ready for. From the outset Talleyrand was the most outspoken opponent of Russia and Prussia at Vienna, particularly on Saxony, and he would later claim credit for having forced them to back down. (More precisely, he would claim to have saved Saxony and checked Prussia himself, and blame Metternich and Castlereagh for losing the fight against Russia.) But there were three distinct aspects of his stand, differing in direction and significance.

The first was an eloquent defence of the King of Saxony's legitimate rights to his throne and territory as essential components of the new European order. Talleyrand's argument for legitimacy was naturally self-interested, as his always were, and loaded with a scarcely veiled Bourbon and French agenda. Defending the legitimate throne in Saxony was a way of preserving and rejuvenating it in France, and a preparatory step for ousting Murat from Naples and Napoleon from Elba. Nevertheless, when Talleyrand contended that the recent generation of violence and usurpation in Europe had resulted above all from the reign of despotism, of rule based on fear, force, and fraud; that this era could only be ended and peace established by restoring law as the basis of international life; that the balance of Europe (*l'équilibre européen*) could not rest

[12] Webster (1921: 195–205, 218–21, 244–7); Castlereagh (1850–3: x. 172–5, 183–5); Chodzko (1863: ii. 265–70, 274–8, 280–6, 291–3); *VPR* (1960–: 1. viii. No. 46).

solely or mainly on power, but depended on mutual trust among states and nations arising from mutual respect for everyone's rights; and that all rights and titles to all kinds of possession and good, including those of individuals, nations, and states, were vitally connected with the rights of rulers to their thrones—when he so argued, Talleyrand not only spoke as sincerely as he ever could, but also expressed a conviction common to European statesmen everywhere. Statesmen at Vienna could argue over the interpretation and application of this doctrine, and did so; unlike statesmen of later generations and many so-called realist historians and political scientists today, they could not ignore the principle, and did not. Hence the great resonance and persuasiveness of Talleyrand's argument. No doubt the doctrine of legitimacy was often restricted, twisted, manipulated, and shunted aside at Vienna, not least by Talleyrand himself. That should surprise no one. But in its real meaning—the rule of law, not the divine right of kings—it was widely believed, followed, and practised at Vienna, and that is far more important.[13]

The second aspect of Talleyrand's campaign, his chief practical goal, was to gain France an equal status and voice among the great powers at Vienna, and to exploit the rifts among the Eastern powers so as to revive French influence in Germany and Italy and pave the way for future concrete gains. Here too Talleyrand made important headway, and would have made more had not Napoleon returned in 1815.

But in its third and most sensational aspect, France's allying itself with Britain and Austria to restrain Russia and impose a Polish–Saxon settlement by force if necessary, Talleyrand's stand arouses scepticism. One has to question first whether France was able to fight. Even if the army was ready and willing, using it would have threatened the regime. Would the French army, moreover, willingly have fought at Britain's side, or worse, at Austria's?[14] Where would France get the money for war? Liverpool was flatly unwilling to subsidize Austria, Britain's ally, for a war against Russia; could he have obtained subsidies from Parliament for France, a few months after defending a peace settlement in Parliament criticized by some as too favourable

---

[13] See Schroeder (1992) and the evidence cited there.

[14] Count Jaucourt, interim foreign minister, told Talleyrand that the French army and public opposed fighting at Austria's side for Poland and Saxony, while Noailles warned from St Petersburg that the Russian army was eager to fight and that the government might welcome a foreign war as a way of maintaining itself fiscally. Jaucourt (1905: 52–3, 75–6); Polovtsov (1902–7: i. No. 113).

to France—one which he promised would return Britain to the carefree security of 1688–1789?[15] Did the allies dare march a French army across Germany to fight Russia and Prussia?

Anyway, France's aims in joining Britain and Austria against Russia and Prussia were all too obvious—to destroy the wartime coalition, overthrow the settlement, shed responsibility for the Revolutionary-Napoleonic era, and perhaps try again for the natural frontiers, certainly for greater influence in the Rhineland and Low Countries. The specific side-payments France demanded or hinted at were disturbing—an immediate overthrow of Murat, the removal of Napoleon from Elba, changes in the Italian settlement, and perhaps an altered Belgian frontier. (As the price for its diplomatic co-operation alone, France tried to get the United Provinces to assume debts made to Dutch contractors for building French warships during Napoleon's rule, and to collect from Hamburg the unpaid portion of contributions levied during the French occupation.)

Most important, the real aim of France's action was not to push back Russia in Poland; it was to revive the old enmity between Prussia and Austria so that France could exploit it in Germany and Italy, and to make France indispensable to Britain in the West. Talleyrand, though he publicly sympathized with the Poles, thought them unfit for self-government and considered a return to the partition lines of 1795 the best solution. Even Britain, if France had its way, would be unable to retire from Europe to enjoy its empire, but committed to holding a line in Central Europe for which it would need France as a partner.[16] Knowing this, Nesselrode reassured a worried Pozzo that France could not and would not really help Austria any more than the British could; ultimately, Vienna would have to yield.[17]

By mid-November Nesselrode's prediction seemed to come true. Out of the war of diplomatic notes came deadlock; neither side's arguments moved the other. Alexander tried again to undermine Castlereagh by getting at Liverpool and the Prince Regent through Lieven.[18] He failed there, but had decisive success with the King of Prussia. On 22 October Metternich had told Hardenberg

[15] Speech of 27 June 1814, Hansard (1814: 369–71).

[16] For general appraisals of Talleyrand's policy, see Lacour-Gayet (1928–30: ii. 424–37); A. Pingaud (1899); Birke (1960: 28–34); Kohlschmidt (1930: 53–4); Hammer (1963: 10–20). For particular documents relevant here, see Talleyrand (1891–2: ii. 373–5, 394–5; iii. 202–5); Castlereagh (1850–3: x. 170–1, 184–5); Polovtsov (1902–7: i. 90–1); Colenbrander (1905–22: vii. Nos. 244–7).

[17] Pozzo (1890–7: i. 82–3).

[18] VPR (1960–: 1. viii. Nos. 50, 63).

he would let Prussia annex Saxony (though he still asked Prussia to allow the Saxon King to retain a kernel of territory around Dresden) in exchange for a joint stand against Russia on Poland. Austria's promise was not unconditional—Prussia had to yield on its claim to the fortress of Mainz, contested with Bavaria—but still constituted a real sacrifice and gamble. Besides the fact that many Austrians objected to it on monarchic, strategic, and general anti-Prussian grounds, it stood to wreck Austria's new reputation as the protector of smaller states against Prussian expansion and domination, and would eliminate an Austrian ally and vital intermediary body in Germany. Worst of all, this agreement threatened to repeat the Cobenzl–Spielmann blunder of 1792 by compensating Prussia in advance for its promise to support Austria in its confrontation with a third power, running the risk that Prussia would defect once it had collected its payment. And it meant a return to the kind of balance-of-power politics Austria least of all could afford.

It shows the depth of Metternich's fear of Russia that he would make such an agreement, and it was lucky in the long run for him, Austria, and Saxony that, under pressure from Alexander, Frederick William repudiated it early in November, ordering Hardenberg not to enter into any agreements directed against Russia. Russia now turned Saxony over to provisional Prussian administration, and Prussia nailed its colours to Russia's mast.[19]

While Metternich, as often in his career, had been saved by the collapse of his own plans, this only made Castlereagh's position more difficult. He now recognized that the real danger for Europe lay not in Poland but in Germany, which Russia could dominate by splitting Austria from Prussia and exploiting their renewed rivalry. Yet Liverpool continued to oppose any active British role in central Europe, and Castlereagh himself believed that, if it came to war, the Russian army could not be stopped short of the Meuse. Meanwhile the French were complicating matters, threatening to break up the congress, pressing for the immediate ousting of Murat from Naples, or proposing a cure for the Russian menace more dangerous than the disease. Louis XVIII's personal representative, Count Blacas, advocated forming a coalition against Russia, initially including Britain, France, Spain, and Holland, which Austria and Prussia would quickly be forced to join.[20]

Castlereagh attempted to persuade Alexander to yield in a pri-

[19] Griewank (1954: 213–29); Kraehe (1983: 205–36); Chodzko (1863: 316–20, 379–81).
[20] Webster (1921: 227–33); Castlereagh (1850–3: x. 200–1).

vate exchange of letters in November. It was a dialogue of the deaf, but interesting in indicating how the leaders of Europe's twin hegemons conceived the new European system. Some Russian arguments in defence of its current claims and actions were preposterous—the claim, for example, that Austria and Prussia now enjoyed more security than Russia, or that Alexander had more than compensated for the change in the power balance created by Russia's acquisition of Finland by permitting Sweden to annex Norway. Others were arrogant, especially the repeated insistence that Russia had saved Europe almost single-handed. Castlereagh had ammunition he could have used had he not been concerned to prevent a total rift. He could have compared Russia's record in the war from 1793 to 1798 and from 1807 to mid-1812 to Britain's, or reminded Alexander how much Russia had depended financially on Britain during the war, and still did in peacetime.[21] Castlereagh did challenge Russia's concept of a proper European balance of power, which called for Russia to be as strong as the rest of the Continent together, and insist that Alexander's character, however noble, was not a sufficient guarantee against a potential abuse of Russia's power.

At the same time, the balance of power Castlereagh proposed in reply (Austria, Prussia, and Germany organized to check Russia in Eastern Europe) was wholly unacceptable to Russia, and dangerous and unworkable in the bargain. Moreover, Alexander's central argument made considerable sense: that Europe needed a 'natural' equilibrium, in which each state possessed the power required for its particular functions and role—the smaller German states enough to play their role in the inner-German balance, Austria and Prussia enough for their broader German and Italian duties, and Russia enough to meet its vast responsibilities in Eastern, Central, and South-Eastern Europe as well as in the Middle East and Asia. And there was no good British reply to the Tsar's observation that Russia, though relatively powerful in Europe, possessed nothing like Britain's total domination of the commercial and colonial worlds, India, and the high seas.

The exchange showed, in short, how much Russia and Britain resembled each other in international politics despite their other

---

[21] At this very moment, the Russians were still working to get the British and the Dutch to assume all or most of Russia's debt to Holland, Lieven was trying unsuccessfully through private parties to induce the British government to guarantee a Russian loan, and the former president of the Russian department of state economy proposed that Russia secure a large, long-term British loan to reform Russia's banking system so that it could revitalize its rural economy. *VPR* (1960–: 1. viii. No. 70; p. 154).

differences. Both were hegemonic powers and determined to remain so; each defined the European balance of power in a way designed to preserve its own hegemony while restraining the other's.[22]

In any case, Castlereagh saw that he could not shake Alexander's position. Metternich, drawing the same conclusion earlier, decided to make the best of defeat, approaching Alexander in mid-November to ensure that if, as now seemed inevitable, Russia both absorbed the lion's share of Poland and kept Prussia as its junior partner, at least Prussia would not get its way in Saxony and Germany. Thus, when Hardenberg tried to get Metternich to carry through on his promise of 22 October regarding Saxony, he received a rude shock. Austria's note of 10 December cut Prussia's gains to a mere fraction of their original size. At the same time, Metternich abandoned his support for Prussia's dualistic programme for Germany, turning to a far looser confederation and to closer co-operation with the middle states. Castlereagh also accepted defeat, writing to Liverpool in mid-December that the Polish question was now virtually settled; only the Saxon and Neapolitan questions remained as serious seeds of conflict.[23]

To this point the Polish–Saxon question had been a typical power-political confrontation, and Russia had won it, facing down both the initial Austro-Prussian and the later Anglo-French challenges. Now Alexander began to be aware of what his victory cost. He had alienated Britain, made Austria lean more toward the Western powers, lost any chance of exercising influence in France, and forfeited his coveted leadership of the general postwar alliance—all for the sake of territorial gains in Poland which Nesselrode opposed and La Harpe thought excessive, and for a benevolent policy toward the Poles which, as Chernishev told him, frightened most Russians, and which many Poles could have told him would not satisfy them. Alexander, having won the contest and still determined to face down allied threats and to undermine Castlereagh's and Metternich's positions, began to seek a compromise.[24]

As in 1807, he was ready to promote one at Prussia's expense. Prussia had already lost considerably by returning to Russia's

[22] Chodzko (1863: ii. 350–5, 398–9, 452–5) (also Webster, 1921: 222–7).
[23] Griewank (1940: 254–61); Quint (1971: 310–11); Chodzko (1863: ii. 485–91, 505–10, 531–35); Metternich (1880–4: ii. 506–7); Castlereagh (1850–3: x. 219); Webster (1921: 261–3).
[24] Martens (1874–1905: xi. 210–16); Gritzbach (1974: i. 294–301); *Sbornik* (1867–1916: cxxi. 280–9); *VPR* (1960–: 1. viii. Nos. 57, 64; p. 139).

side, forfeiting Austria's consent to the annexation of Saxony and undermining Austrian and British support and co-operation in Germany. Now came a worse blow: Berlin found the Russian ground shifting under its feet. By late December and early January, Europe was no longer trying to get Russia to retreat in Poland. Instead, three great powers confronted Prussia, which was only tepidly supported by Russia, to force it to disgorge most of Saxony. Not only would such a humiliating concession gravely damage Prussia's prestige and great-power standing; to allow a Saxon kingdom to survive would also be to create a permanent enemy attached to Austria on its frontiers—the same disastrous mistake, the Prussians argued, which Austria had made in the eighteenth century in allowing Bavaria to survive. (Prussia's role in forcing that 'mistake' on Austria went unmentioned.)

The Prussians resisted desperately. Hardenberg threatened to convert Prussia's provisional administration of Saxony into a permanent one, i.e. *de facto* annexation, and to regard any outside interference as a *casus belli* for Prussia and Russia. This brash threat provoked a brief war scare and prompted Britain, France, and Austria to sign a secret alliance on 3 January committing each to provide 150,000 troops for defence against any attack. But the kind of attack stipulated in the *casus foederis* was highly improbable and the whole war scare artificial. Castlereagh and Liverpool both viewed the alliance, not as a preparation for war, but as an alliance to restrain France, provide for possible Anglo-French armed mediation, and thus prevent hostilities between the Eastern powers, especially Austria and Prussia. Liverpool was especially determined to hold Austria back. The fact that the weakest great power, Prussia, rather than the strongest, Russia, was the target of the alliance was underlined by the three powers' invitations to Bavaria, the United Netherlands, and Hanover to accede to the treaty, which they did.[25]

Berlin could not have held out against this pressure even with full Russian support, and it was missing. On 7 January Alexander, who knew of the existence of the Western alliance but not its details, agreed in principle that Saxony must be divided, and let Prussia know that it would have to yield. Castlereagh, supported by Talleyrand, then took the lead in shaping the Saxon settlement as Alexander had shaped the Polish one. He urged the Austrians to concede Prussia more Saxon territory, especially the fortress

[25] Webster (1921: 252–5, 260–1, 266–73, 277–86); Griewank (1954: 248–51); Chodzko (1863: ii. 556–7, 579–82); DeClercq (1880–1917: ii. 447–50).

of Torgau, and promised Prussia 50,000 additional souls in the Rhineland at the expense of Holland and Hanover if Prussia would give up Leipzig. Alexander helped by ceding Prussia Thorn. Even the Austrians, though their rhetoric was Prussophobe, privately urged Alexander to help Berlin swallow the bitter pill. An agreement concluded on 8 February gave Prussia about half of Saxony's territory but only about two-fifths of its population and neither of its two largest cities.

The final details of the Polish frontier took even longer to work out, with the three powers negotiating the main points into May and the finer points well beyond the congress. As a result of Austro-Russian rivalry a small remnant of Polish independence survived; Alexander, unwilling to let Austria have Cracow, agreed to make it and its environs a free city governed by its own senate under the supervision of the three partitioning powers. Austria and Prussia had to accept Russia's autonomous constitutional Kingdom of Poland; Castlereagh's advice was that they could only counter it by enlightened administration of their own Polish territories.[26]

What had the crisis and its resolution accomplished? In some respects, little or nothing. It certainly had not ended the Russian strategic and political threat to Central Europe; that would persist down to the First World War. It had not saved legitimacy and the rule of law, as Talleyrand claimed he had done.[27] The King of Saxony's rights were compromised, if not destroyed, and Talleyrand went along with the compromise. The crisis did not serve to unite Austria and Prussia in the defence of Germany, but threatened to split them and Germany wide apart. They were fairly soon reconciled, but this resulted from other pressures, circumstances, and needs, and the settlement reached did not stop Prussia's ambitions in Germany, but only delayed them. As Humboldt remarked in accepting the outcome, Prussia could not readily have assimilated more of Saxony at this time, and the rest could be acquired in the next war. And, of course, the settlement perpetuated the Polish problem rather than settling it.[28]

It is therefore far from obvious that the crisis was a salutary one

---

[26] Griewank (1954: 252–7); Chodźko (1863: ii. 602–4, 676–83, 706–24, 737); Webster (1921: 287–8, 292–305); Mauersberg (1966).

[27] For Talleyrand's various claims, see Talleyrand (1891–2: ii. 556–7; iii. 6–7, 18–19, 48–9); Polovtsov (1902–7: i. 146–7).

[28] Zak (1966: ch. 3); Gentz (1887: 504–19); Sweet (1978: ii. 194–5); Bertier (1966: 90–1). For evidence that Humboldt was right about the difficulties Prussia would have had absorbing all of Saxony, given the organizational difficulties it faced with new territories in any case, see Mieck (1989).

or the outcome an achievement. None the less, the crisis did accomplish something very important. What it is often supposed to have done is to have saved the balance of power, and to have proved the efficacy of balance-of-power tactics. It was supposedly a successful exercise of brinksmanship, an example of the game of Chicken analysed by game theorists. Russia's power and expansion threatened the balance strategically and politically, putting the independence and security of Austria, Prussia, and Central Europe at stake. The blocking coalition formed in the crisis supposedly forced Russia to recede from its claims, and apparently achieved a compromise solution enabling an independent centre for Europe to survive.

As has been seen, what really happened was quite different. Balance-of-power tactics were tried and failed. The initial confrontation, which pitted Russia against Austria supported by Britain and France and momentarily by Prussia, was won by Russia hands down, as it forced Prussia back into line and compelled the others to accept its basic territorial and constitutional aims in Poland. (Incidentally, balance-of-power confrontations usually end more or less this way; balance-of-power tactics, like God, favour the *beati possidentes* and the big battalions.) In so far as there was a genuine crisis and danger of war at all, it came, not while the powers were trying to curb the hegemonic threat to the balance, Russia, but while they were imposing defeat and retreat on Prussia, already the weakest and most dependent of the great powers.

In other words, this was not a game of Chicken, or a brinkmanship crisis of the kind analysed by political scientists.[29] It did not preserve a balance of power or demonstrate its utility; it instead proved the possibility and salutary uses of hegemony. A peaceful outcome was achieved and it proved acceptable because one hegemon, Russia, controlled its junior partner and joined the others in imposing the chief costs of the settlement on it, while the other hegemon, Britain, used its restraining alliance with France and Austria to prevent any clash and helped arrange a settlement minimally tolerable to Prussia. The process worked, moreover, because everyone, facing the likely consequences of a return to balance-of-power politics, retreated from it. Alexander, having won on Prussia and Poland, considered the victory too costly in terms of driving Austria to the West and ruining the general alliance of Europe he aspired to lead, and recouped his

[29] e.g. Lebow (1984).

losses by volunteering some Russian concessions and helping force heavier ones from Prussia. Castlereagh, seeing that a true military balance of power in east Central Europe, if possible at all, could be created only by a war which he feared and which his premier and his country considered wholly unacceptable, decided to pursue a different kind of European equilibrium. Austria, France, and Prussia, each in its own way, came to terms with what the hegemons had decided. The outcome, a defeat for balance-of-power politics, was a victory for common sense and peace. (Admittedly, the Poles and Saxons paid the main price for the settlement, as someone almost always must.)

III. THE GERMAN QUESTION

1. The Issues

The German question lacked the drama and crises of the Polish–Saxon one, but was at least as crucial and even more complicated. Two main aspects of it were obviously European in nature: territorial questions (both the territorial disputes between individual states and the issue of what territories and rulers should be included in the proposed German confederation) and the federal issue, i.e. the nature of the German federal constitution. Both involved the most critical aspect of the peace settlement, the security, unity, and power of Germany and thus of Central Europe. But a third major issue, extensively argued but never conclusively settled at the congress, looks like an internal German question rather than a European one: whether to require all member states of the new federation to have constitutions based on their traditional estates (landständische Verfassungen).

It is easy to understand why this issue was hotly disputed. On one side were the sovereign rights of the individual states and the interests of the ruling princes and their bureaucracies, especially in the former Rheinbund states; on the other the call by some patriots for greater German unity and federal power and the interests of the princes, imperial knights, and self-governing cities and towns who had lost out in the German revolution under Napoleon. Religion and Church polity, always critical factors in German history, were involved, particularly over whether the Catholic Church should be organized into state Churches like the Lutheran and Calvinist confessions or into a single German Church. Fundamental constitutional principles were at stake: the right of subjects to have their status and property protected against despotic monarchs and arbitrary bureaucrats, versus the individual state's right to defend its unity and the legal equality of its subjects against old entrenched privilege and power; traditional corporate liberties versus modern individual liberty; representation by estates according to rank versus representation by individuals according to wealth; traditional community versus modern society. Yet vital as these concerns were, they seem to belong to domestic politics, not international affairs and the peace settlement.

None the less, there was a connection. The issue of estate constitutions in Germany, like many other constitutional questions in 1814–15 (France and its Charter, Sweden and Norway, Switzerland and its federal constitution, even Poland) involved the central make-or-break question of the peace settlement: how to temper state power through consensus and law. The widespread recognition at Vienna that the chief cause of a generation of war and disaster had not simply been revolution or Napoleonic imperialism, but the arbitrary, lawless use of power in general, and that this had to be stopped, applied to this issue as well. Naturally, there was no consensus over what law should be established by whom against which tyrants and law-breakers. Stein and many of his fellow *Standesherren* denounced the Rheinbund princes, especially King Frederick of Württemberg, as archetypal despots. These princes and their ministers in turn saw Austria as an old tyrant, Prussia, especially under Stein's influence, as a menacing new one, and the dispossessed princes, knights, and cities as dangerous *frondeurs*. But most agreed on the principle that despotism must be ended in internal as well as international politics and all rights brought under the protection of law; even a rigid conservative like Emperor Francis genuinely believed in the principle that justice was the foundation of kingdoms. Just as the new international order had to rest on law as well as power, so the German confederation, whatever form it took, had to be a *Rechtsordnung* as well as a *Machtordnung*. It needed not only to reconcile and guarantee the sovereign rights of individual states and rulers within the confederation but also to guarantee Germans that each state was a *Rechtsstaat*, each ruler ruling on the basis of constitutional law.

Unfortunately, divergent philosophies as well as conflicting interests kept Germans far apart over the kind of constitution to adopt and the model of the *Rechtstaat* to follow. England, Prussia, enlightened absolutism, the old Imperial constitution, individual state traditions, and the Napoleonic constitutions and reforms all served as examples; none commanded a majority, and no good

compromise emerged. This meant that the issue of estate constitutions added a further dangerous, paradoxical factor to the complications of the German question. Instead of advancing German
unity and harmony, it promoted divisions; part of the quest for
curbs on arbitrary power, it threatened to increase the use of
such power. We cannot know just how German domestic politics
might have developed in the following decades had estate constitutions somehow been imposed on all the members of the German
Confederation in 1814–15. It could arguably have produced progress toward the *Rechtsstaat* ideal or, as some have contended,
could have represented a reaction, the restoration of outworn
privileges, obstruction of legal equality, and silent mediatizing of
the independent middle states.

Regardless of its domestic consequences, however, any such
attempt would surely have had negative results in international
politics. Not only did some leaders of the constitutional movement (e.g. the poet E. M. Arndt, Hans-Christoph von Gagern of
Nassau, Franz von Gärtner) also have dangerous ideas in foreign
policy, about retaking Alsace and bringing the Netherlands and
possibly Switzerland into the Confederation; any such 'reform'
would also have required using Austrian and Prussian power to
coerce some states into it, thereby reviving Prussia's ambitions
and Austria's fears, straining Germany's new federal institutions,
and undermining the very rule of law which constitutional reform
was supposed to advance.[30]

These pitfalls in the constitutional question became apparent
only over time. At first it looked as if Austria and Prussia would
be able to co-operate in settling the German question quickly.
Hardenberg still aimed, as he had since 1794, at Prussian expansion and control in North Germany for now while leaving the
way open for further moves in Germany later. He reversed his
former ideas on allies and opponents, however, with Austria now
to be Prussia's partner and the middle and lesser states its rivals
and targets. As always, Prussian gains were justified in the names
of Germany and Europe. A strong Prussia would help defend
Russia against the West, he told Russia, while pointing out to

[30] In the huge literature on this subject, I have relied chiefly on Kraehe (1983;
1977); Wunder (1978); Vierhaus (1972); Hoff (1913); Press (1980b); Mager (1973).
On particular points see also Huber (1957: i. 410–17); Haussherr (1960a: 284–5);
Rössler (1958: 162–76). For some of the dangerous foreign-policy ideas mentioned,
see ibid. 151–62, 177–9; Dunk (1966: 32–3, 51–74). For a defence of Stein's and
Stadion's actions in favour of the mediatized princes, see Rössler (1940: ii. 200–1);
for an attack on them, see Aretin (1976: 134–41).

others how it would defend the West and Austria against Russia. To take only part of Saxony would constitute aggression and arouse Saxon national feelings; the legal and conciliatory course was, therefore, to take it all. Mainz would be a vital bastion of German and European security against France—but only if Prussia held it. At the same time, the way to guard the middle and lower Rhine against France was not to give Prussia a common frontier with France, but to strengthen Prussia with more territory in the Rhineland so that it could organize and support France's immediate neighbours like Nassau and the Low Countries. Though Hardenberg's ambitions were extensive and his arguments transparent, he seemed to have a good chance of achieving them. The King, though worried about the risks, did not stop him and there was no serious domestic opposition: annexing Saxony was especially popular. Most important, no great power except France stood in his way; Britain and Russia were sympathetic and Austria surprisingly pliable.[31]

This showed again how far Austria had moved away from its eighteenth-century stance toward Prussia and Germany. Though some Austrians like Stadion and Schwarzenberg wanted it to retake and expand its south-west German lands so as to revive Austria's old imperial position and defend Germany on the upper Rhine,[32] Francis and Metternich, though they occasionally wavered, never adopted this notion. The Emperor wanted to rule his hereditary lands in peace, Metternich to win German allies for his independent European centre. Anyway, acquiring more territory or reviving the German Empire would not restore Austria's power base in Germany. Too much had happened, the middle states had acquired too much independence and solidity, too many groups in Austria, especially the Hungarians and Italians, were against the whole idea, and Austria had too many other problems and tasks. Here, as in much of its history, the Habsburg monarchy faced the choice of whether its first priority as a great power should be to defend the Reich against France or to sustain its own power on the Danube. It opted for the latter.[33]

[31] Griewank (1954: 156–9, 174–7; 1942); Born (1957); Rössler (1940: ii. 198–9); Thielen (1967: 300–7); Huber (1957: i. 520–5, 527–30).

[32] Griewank (1954: 160–5); Rössler (1940: ii. 202–3).

[33] Franzel (1970). A treaty with Bavaria Metternich and Wrede signed on 3 June 1814, never ratified, illustrates his priorities. It would have given Bavaria additional territory in Germany simply for immediately handing over to Austria the former Habsburg territories it was already committed to return at the final peace. The text is in Chodzko (1863: i. 178–81); for the reactions from Montgelas, Emperor Francis, and Stadion, see Arneth (1898: i. 198–99); Rössler (1940: ii. 197).

Precisely for this reason, Metternich wanted harmony but not unity in Germany (*Einigkeit ohne Einheit*). He may well have been consistent in this overall goal, and thought in terms of Germany as a whole more steadily than anyone else;[34] he was certainly not consistent in his methods of reaching it, or in the kind of organization of Germany he would accept. Behind the quest for a viable organization for Germany, as for a new European politics and an independent European centre, lay concern for Austria's survival as a great power. This required two things above all: that Germany as a whole be tranquil, and that it support Austria where and when Austria needed that support. Anything that might achieve these ends he would consider, even the great-power dualism sought by Prussia or the Germany of separate sovereign states tied only by special alliances envisioned by Bavaria and Württemberg.[35] This outlook, in addition to the fact that he usually reacted to events rather than controlled them, accounts for the striking flexibility in expedients he displayed and the frequent obscurity of his manœuvres. Perhaps Metternich was, as he believed, the coachman of Europe; if so, his efforts went mainly to keeping the horses under control, the coach upright, the passengers reasonably peaceable, and himself at the reins rather than bringing the coach to his choice of destination.

2. The Breakdown of the Hegemonic Solution

Austria and Prussia, working together, opened the first session of the German Committee on 16 October by presenting the other members, Bavaria, Württemberg, and Hanover, with a constitutional plan for a German Confederation consisting of Twelve Articles, Hardenberg's revision of his earlier plan, now made more acceptable to Austria and the middle states. It was a complicated scheme whose details cannot be elaborated here, but essentially it provided for a fairly strong central authority wherein the real executive power, including control of foreign policy and the powers of alliance and war, would vested in one of the two legislative councils, the council of circle chiefs (heads of the territorial circles or regions into which Germany would be organized). The circle chiefs would consist of the two great powers and three German kingdoms; in this council Austria and Prussia, having two votes each to the others' one each, would form a

---

[34] This is a main thesis in Kraehe (1983).

[35] On Bavaria's and Württemberg's concept of Italy as the model for the organization of Germany, see Aretin (1976: 142–4, 148–52); for a sample of Bavarian arguments for unrestricted middle-state sovereignty, see Chodzko (1863: ii. 326–7).

majority if united, but could also form a majority against the other with the aid of any two of the smaller chiefs. The circle chiefs would also have wide powers over their individual circles, presiding over circle assemblies, controlling the federal military contingents, and settling disputes between individual states along with a federal supreme court. Besides the restraints of the circles and the federal supreme court, the plan limited the sovereignty of individual states also in other ways. All members (except Austria and Prussia as European powers) would renounce the right to make separate alliances or wage war, and would undertake to introduce estate constitutions guaranteeing certain minimum rights to their subjects.

Hardenberg hoped to induce the three kingdoms to accept this strong federation by giving them a share in controlling the lesser states. But Bavaria and Württemberg would have none of it, insisting that the sovereignty of individual states must be explicitly recognized. Metternich, who had promised to do this in the Treaty of Ried and elsewhere, now joined Hardenberg in arguing that the word 'sovereignty', unlike its German synonym, *Landeshoheit*, was a foreign concept incompatible with any federal tie. Had the two great powers remained united, they probably could have broken the south German resistance. The Bavarian representative Wrede was isolated and unpopular within the committee and in Germany generally; Stein waged a fierce campaign against the Rheinbund despots in the press; Bavaria's claims to unrestricted sovereignty, including the right to declare war and peace, were seen as extreme and arrogant; and both states, especially Württemberg, had acquired a reputation for despotic rule during the Napoleonic era. Other great powers added to the pressure on them, Britain and Russia agreeing that no state had the right to negate the proposed Bund or opt out of Germany, while Stein mobilized twenty-nine lesser princes and cities in a petition of 16 November, which denounced the special status accorded the middle kingdoms and demanded equal representation for the smaller states and the introduction or resurrection of estate constitutions everywhere. The French looked on expectantly, hoping for a breach between Vienna and Munich, while Metternich's need for Prussian co-operation against Russia overcame his reluctance to alienate Bavaria.[36]

The South German kingdoms were saved by the rift between Austria and Prussia over Poland and Saxony. The German committee was first suspended by the great powers, and then never

---

[36] Quint (1971: 284–309); Aretin (1976: 170–3); Huber (1957: i. 544–51).

reconvened. The breach over Saxony did not end Metternich's willingness to work with Prussia for a solution of the German question, but it sharply limited the concessions he would make. Austria's change in approach became clear in his note of 10 December to Prussia and in a new plan for Germany revealed on 24 December by the second Austrian delegate to the Congress, Baron Wessenberg. The proposal he presented for a loose confederation of basically sovereign states, a move to regain the South German states as allies, effectively ended the chances for a strong dualist hegemonic constitution in Germany.

It was a blow to Prussian ambitions, but no loss to Germany or Europe. The Prussian plan could conceivably have been imposed by force, but could hardly have worked durably or well. Its obvious internal weaknesses—middle-state resistance, heavy administrative expense, severe problems of coordination between circle assemblies and circle chiefs on one level, and the two-chamber federal assembly as legislature and the council of circle chiefs as executive body on another—meant that it would probably have developed the same clumsiness, paralysis, and internal disputes that had ruined the old Empire. Besides, and more important for our purposes, the plan had a critical weakness for international politics. It demanded close co-operation between Austria and Prussia, but contained nothing to guarantee it (even within the council of circle chiefs they could conspire against each other) and a good deal to make it unlikely. For it offered the two partners very unequal advantages and costs. Basically Germany would be divided into their spheres of influence north and south of the Main. But Prussia was stretched across North Germany, where the other states were mainly small and weak, so that it could easily control the circles in its sphere. Austria, having an eccentric geographical position, less pure German territory than Prussia, and sizeable, headstrong South German states to deal with, could not have controlled its circles, and would have been hard pressed even to manage them. In short, the plan was a recipe for continual strife between different elements within the confederation and for rivalry between the two powers intended to run it. Once again, Metternich's luck had proved better than his foresight.

3. Loose Confederation and Austrian Hegemony

Though the Austro-Prussian conflict over Saxony was substantially settled by early February, their co-operation on the German question took time to revive. Months were required to carry out the agreement over Saxony and Poland, especially to persuade the King of Saxony to accept his losses.[37] Meanwhile Prussia replied to Austria's December proposal with two revisions of its own plan by Humboldt in mid-January, the second of which abandoned the division of Germany into circles but continued to insist on a strong federal military structure, a federal supreme court, and estate constitutions guaranteed by the federal pact. Bavaria, horrified by Humboldt's ideas and encouraged by Metternich's concessions, held out for a simple alliance between sovereign states, and decided to refute Stein's charge of despotism and to prevent any estate constitution from being imposed by the future confederation by announcing that Bavaria intended to proclaim its own modern representative constitution. Württemberg, where King Frederick also decided to follow a similar course on the constitutional question, proposed a purely South German confederation to defend the sovereignty of its member states against great-power encroachment, and offered Bavaria the leadership of it. The Bavarian response showed the unrealism of Montgelas's ambitions and claims to full sovereignty; Bavaria could not accept the offer because it needed the help of the great powers to enforce its own territorial claims against Württemberg and Baden. Stein muddied the waters further by reviving his plan for a reformed Empire under Austria, enlisting the small states and Alexander in its favour. At the end of February the German question seemed as mired down as ever.[38]

Napoleon's return from Elba in March changed things, though not by rallying all Germans against the common enemy. Some states responded readily enough to the great powers' call on 25 March to rejoin the coalition, but Württemberg, Ducal Hesse, and Baden resisted as long as they could, and Bavaria, which outstripped its previous military performances by pledging 60,000 troops, did so for purely Bavarian reasons—to counter the attacks on its Rheinbund record, prove its immunity to Napoleon's appeals, and acquire independent European status and more territorial gains. What Napoleon's return did instead was make it vital to settle the German question quickly, before the congress broke up and the sovereigns and leaders departed for the war, leaving a host of territorial and political arrangements and agreements half-

[37] Chodzko (1863: iii. 1146–74; iv. 1858–83); Arneth (1898: i. 267–8, 275).
[38] Kraehe (1983: 246–51, 299–326); Quint (1971: 311–23, 332–35); Burg (1989: 33–9); Hölzle (1937: 189–95); Ritter (1958: 512–13); Chodzko (1863: ii. 605–11).

concluded and Germany once more prey to internal rivalry and great power intervention.

The emergency helped Metternich wrest a series of concessions from Prussia which led to an Austro-Prussian agreement in mid-May. Bavaria also was slowly turning away from Montgelas's extremist goals and intransigent eighteenth century style, while the more supple Count Rechberg replaced Wrede at Vienna. Still, it took more of Metternich's devious manœuvres to get both Bavaria and Prussia to consider the plan he produced on 14 May. (For example, he inserted the word 'sovereignty' in the version he showed Bavaria and omitted it from the one he showed Prussia.) Then he had to wage more battles with Bavaria from 23 May until 10 June before the Vienna Final Act, pre-dated 8 June, actually could be signed. In this struggle Rechberg not only got Metternich to guarantee the sovereignty of the individual states in Article 1, but also eliminated the federal court and weakened other 'special regulations' in Articles 11–20 of the Federal Act impinging on states' rights. Despite these concessions, Rechberg signed the Act without being authorized by his government to do so, fearing that otherwise Bavaria would be completely excluded from the Bund. The Act provided only the skeleton of a German Con-federation, a permanent defensive league of independent states and free cities; its flesh and organs remained to be developed after 1815.

Meanwhile, territorial compromises had been worked out as well, the most critical of them concerning Mainz. After a heated contest between Prussia and Bavaria, it was finally given terri-torially to Hesse-Darmstadt, with Prussia to command a mixed garrison in its federal fortress. Some territorial quarrels remained unresolved, especially the conflicting claims of Bavaria, Baden, and the two Hesses in the left and right bank of the upper Rhine. Austria was given back its former scattered possessions in south-west Germany for the purpose of using them to help work out a compromise settlement. A number of states also were raised in rank (e.g. from duchy to grand duchy); many lesser princes were as obsessed with their rank and status within the Bund as Bavaria was with its sovereignty, and both issues continued to vex German politics.[39]

Clearly, if the goal at Vienna was to unify Germany and pro-mote its political and commercial development, the results of

[39] Quint (1971: 332–90); Kraehe (1983: 327–99); Huber (1957: i. 551–61, 576–9); Chodzko (1863: iii. 995–6, 1073–5, 1178–9); Chroust (1939–44: i. Nos. 26–8, 30–1).

all this work and struggle were not impressive. The hopes of some for customs unification, constitutional development, military union, and guaranteed civil and political rights in all of Germany were fulfilled only in small part or not at all. The Final Act left the door open for further development in these directions, however. What had been achieved was probably the only practicable outcome in terms of internal politics and, more important, the best possible for purposes of international security and peace. As Humboldt remarked, Germany could not be united in 1815 because the nationalists were numerically too weak, the dynastic states' instinct for self-preservation too strong, and a strong federation impractical so long as two great powers contended for hegemony in it. He might have added, as scholars increasingly emphasize, that any sort of national unification was neither popular nor viable for Germany in 1815. The sense of belonging to a German nation was still too diffuse and confused, loyalties too undefined and overlapping, including local, religious, civic, and dynastic attachments of a bewildering variety. Besides, as has been noted, some of the restorationist aspects of the nationalist movement were actually reactionary, not progressive.[40]

These, moreover, represented only the inner-German obstacles to German unity. The really critical one was European, international. No united Germany, however constituted and ruled, would have been safe and acceptable for Europe. It would worry too many great powers and threaten too many smaller, non-German peoples. Yet at the same time, peaceful coexistence and co-operation in Central Europe were very unlikely without some federal tie between Austria, Prussia, and the rest of Germany. Even if Austria and Prussia buried their rivalry, they would surely be drawn into the many quarrels breaking out between the smaller states, as would Germany's great-power neighbours. In short, Europe could afford neither a strong, united Germany nor a recurrence of the anarchy and rivalries of the dying Empire.

What emerged in June 1815, by luck and compromise more than artful design, was a loose confederation based upon an informal dualism, Austria leading the confederation as a whole while in practice conceding Prussia hegemony in North Germany. This was an ideal outcome for international peace, satisfying both great powers without irrevocably alienating the smaller ones, and compelling Austria and Prussia to co-operate if the confederation was

[40] Gruner (1985: 25–72); Burg (1989: 39–68); Buse (1987); Nipperdey (1983a; 1984); Veit-Brause (1983); Thielen (1967: 322).

to work. Europe had played a role behind the scenes in bringing this about. Castlereagh had put pressure on all the parties to agree while leaving them to work out the details, and had especially pushed Austria, Prussia, and the Netherlands into final territorial compromises in the Rhineland. Alexander, even while watching out for the interests of his particular German client states (Oldenburg, Holstein, Saxe-Weimar, Saxe-Coburg, Württemberg), came to accept and support Austria's leadership in Germany as a whole, and refused to respond to Württemberg's and Bavaria's appeals for help. Though the Tsar did not sacrifice Russian influence or give up the idea of possible intervention in Germany, he kept it in reserve for real trouble. A moderate, limited Austrian hegemony in Germany went well with a moderate Russian hegemony in Europe as a whole.[41]

IV. THE HUNDRED DAYS AND THE SECOND PEACE OF PARIS

One more make-or-break crisis arose at the congress with the return of Napoleon from Elba. Landing in southern France with a handful of men at the end of February 1815, he gathered support as he marched toward Paris, as army units sent to arrest him defected to his side. By late March the Bourbon regime had collapsed, Louis XVIII had fled to Belgium, and Napoleon was back on his imperial throne.

Napoleon had an excuse for this last venture, even some provocation. Louis had violated the Treaty of Fontainebleau, refusing to pay Napoleon's pension and confiscating his property in France, so that Napoleon, though far from penniless, was forced to live off his accumulated capital. He knew, moreover, that the French government, now pressing Britain and Austria to let them throw Murat out of Naples, had in mind the same fate for him.[42] But he also knew, or should have, that the allies, especially Russia, would not have allowed Louis to wreck the peace for purely Bourbon purposes; and in any case this threat was not the real motive for his return.

The reason for the gamble, a wager with the life and future of France even more than his own, was his old fatalistic belief in his star. His attempt to recapture power in France was very bold but

---

[41] VPR (1960–: 1. viii. Nos. 74, 76, 113–14, 169–72, 227; p. 200).
[42] Mackenzie (1982: 156–60, 184–7).

not irrational. He detected the widespread uncertainty and rest-
lessness in France and knew that Louis lacked his charisma, his
ruthlessness, and his lack of scruple about starting a civil war. He
also could expect to find useful supporters once he got control,
not only among old Napoleonic officials and generals but also
among other disaffected groups—former Jacobins, some of whom
did rally to him, or the liberals, whom he actually chose.[43] But
anyone who cared anything about France would know that seizing
power in Paris would solve nothing. His regime and France could
not survive unless it gained at least the passive acquiescence
of Europe.

Nothing Napoleon could have done would have secured this; at
the same time, what he did worked to foil any chance there might
have been. Not only did his lifelong record of lies and aggressions
belie the profuse assurances he gave, after seizing power, that he
wanted peace and friendship with Europe and would honour the
existing treaties and respect the independence of other states.
From the moment he landed in France, his actions constituted
a virtual declaration of war on Europe. His proclamations to
the French army and people, soaked in xenophobic nationalism,
summoned them to follow him to new heights of glory and to
avenge France against the foreign despoilers and domestic traitors
of 1814. He immediately began trying to induce Murat to rise and
join him (though without committing himself to help Murat). He
instructed Caulaincourt, once again his foreign minister, to rally
Switzerland, the small states of Germany and Italy (including
Rome!), and Spain and Portugal to his cause. He ordered Davout
to publish appeals along the French borders to get former foreign
soldiers in the Grand Army to abandon their countries and rejoin
the colours. He planned on a partisan war within France and a
war to nourish war outside it. No one, least of all Napoleon,
could doubt that his return to power in France meant war against
Europe and its new order sooner or later, and that the only
question was whether it would come at Europe's time or his.

This is enough, or should be, to strip away the romantic pathos
and myths that for some still surround Napoleon's last fling; but
more is needed to define its place in history. The Hundred Days
have been seen as a final eruption of French energy and imperialist
expansion, the last explosion of the French Revolution. Not
really.[44] Napoleon's return was not the last act of an epic French

---

[43] Rémond (1965: 241–7).

[44] The Hundred Days did bring a brief revival of French revolutionary fervour,
including radical anticlericalism—but also an even stronger revival of the counter-

and European drama, but the first staging of a third-world melo-drama, later to be played in many backward countries of the world. Karl Marx remarked in a famous phrase that Napoleon's nephew Louis Napoleon, in his *coup d'état* of 1851, turned tragedy into farce. In fact Napoleon, anticipating his nephew, did this himself in the Hundred Days. Everything about this venture, from the initial proclamations through the pseudo-liberal con-stitution and the bungled war down to the mendacious excuses and bathos accompanying his defeat and the propaganda campaign he waged from exile on St Helena, was one great self-serving imposture. The return from Elba, stripped of its false glamour, be-comes simply the first in a long series of nineteenth- and twentieth-century pronunciamentos. An ambitious, unscrupulous Corsican general took advantage of his adopted country's divisions and discontents to seize power—nothing more. Murat followed his example almost immediately, others would adopt it in southern Europe in 1820–1, and a host of generals, dictators, and other political strong men would imitate it to the present day.[45]

Bad theatre though it was, Napoleon's return was a threat to Europe. The real danger, to be sure, was not that Napoleon might win the war and renew his career of conquests. Only total disunity in Europe could have made that possible, and that did not arise. On 13 March the great powers declared Napoleon an outlaw, and on 25 March formally renewed their alliance to overthrow him. The smaller states invited to accede to the alliance began to rally round, some with no enthusiasm but others, like Bavaria, with more fervour than in 1813–14. Even more impressive was the way the congress ignored Napoleon and continued its work. Napoleon's return helped it to settle not only the German question, but also many others less critical but cumulatively important— the navigation of international rivers, Switzerland, various terri-torial questions concerning Saxony, Prussia and Bavaria, the Low Countries, and Italy, the union of Sardinia-Piedmont and Genoa, conventions governing military co-operation and supplies in the coming war, and more. Thus the congress was successfully wound up before fighting actually started in June. Meanwhile, the assets which in 1814 had given Napoleon a slight chance for military

revolution and political Catholicism. See R. S. Alexander (1991); Bertier (1948); Fitzpatrick (1983: 32).

[45] Napoleon (1858–70: xxviii. Nos. 21681–2, 21693, 21739, 21759, 21769, 21777, 21779, 21792, 21809, 21826, 21831, 21836, 21997). Finer (1988: 188) labels the Revolution and Empire 'the true seed plot of military intervention as we know it today' (cf. 188–200).

victory—strong points still held in Europe, exhaustion and divisions among his foes, a populace in north-eastern France aroused by the invasion, the command of an organized army already in the field—were all gone, and royalist rebellion was beginning within parts of France itself.[46]

Just one thing could have saved Napoleon: a British refusal or inability to subsidize its allies. Even Continental powers eager to fight, such as Russia, could not do so without money. Britain instead committed itself to another unprecedented financial effort, pledging £9 million in subsidies, and the Continental powers prepared for war just as seriously, expecting more fighting spirit in France and more revolts or troubles in Europe than they actually encountered. Virtually everyone agreed on the central aim of overthrowing Napoleon.[47]

The actual campaign was, therefore, less exciting and crucial than it seemed. True, Napoleon won the first round at Quatre Bras on 16 June, and Waterloo on 18 June was a major battle and a near thing. But here, as in the whole campaign, Napoleon's entire army, the best he could muster, was pitted against the most makeshift one among the allied forces. Far from shattering the coalition, an allied defeat at Waterloo would have galvanized it. Only part of Britain's and Prussia's forces, a smaller part of Germany's, and none of Austria's or Russia's were yet engaged against France. Prussia was eager to fight and the Russians, especially Alexander, even more so; Austria and the German lesser states did not dare remain behind.[48]

Wellington's victory was therefore crucial, not for averting a possible allied defeat in the war, but for keeping the problems of victory and peace manageable. The dangers were obvious—that with the Bourbons discredited the question of the French regime

[46] Chodzko (1863: iii. 912–13, 980–1, 1110–15 and *passim*); Arneth (1898: i. 271–2); Martens (1874–1905: viii. 177; xi. 216–18).

[47] Castlereagh (1850–3: x. 285–305); Polovtsov (1902–7: i. No. 256). Gentz, often an extremist, was the one exception. He condemned the war and wanted to let Napoleon rule, arguing that once Napoleon was defeated the Russians would promote the revolutionary principle of popular sovereignty by allowing the French to choose their own sovereign. Gentz (1887: 596–626).

[48] McElwee (1975: 5) points out that even a victory at Waterloo would have done Napoleon no good in the long run. For (unconvincing) arguments otherwise, see Fugier (1954: 313); Fournier (1903: ii. 413–14, 430–1). Metternich was not worried about the military outcome, even when Blücher was defeated just before Waterloo; Arneth (1898: ii. 1–2). The only rift the war caused in the allied camp was a mutiny among units of the Saxon army protesting against being integrated into the Prussian army prior to the signature of a Prussian–Saxon peace treaty; Huber (1957: i. 572–5).

would be thrown open, France punished with a harsh peace, and the entire settlement overthrown. Even Castlereagh believed France had to pay for its follies, while Liverpool, formerly an advocate of *entente* with the Bourbons, now wanted major reductions in French territory and power. Public opinion was strongly anti-French in Britain, and even more violent in Prussia, South Germany, the Netherlands, Piedmont, and Spain, where revived territorial ambitions fed the spirit of revenge. German nationalists took up the cry for Alsace, Spain wanted to take Parma away from the King of Rome, the King of the Netherlands wanted a slice of northern France. It was taken for granted that France would now have to surrender art treasures and historic spoils it had retained in 1814, and pay the full costs of the war.

Invaded, occupied, and open to spoliation, France saw not only its territorial integrity and wealth but its political independence at stake. Napoleon had claimed that the allies, having no right to interfere in France's choice of ruler, must accept him as Emperor. The response of the congress, anticipating the later Holy Alliance doctrine of intervention, was that the requirements of international law transcended a nation's right to choose its sovereign; France was not entitled to choose a ruler incapable of living at peace with Europe. Implicit in the doctrine and explicit in the minds of many was the demand for a long-term international supervision of the French government. Besides, it was doubtful whether France in its present divided and demoralized state was capable of choosing its ruler, or whether anyone, including the Bourbons, was capable of governing France.[49]

The greatest risk was to the new international system. Napoleon's adventure had torn open barely closed wounds not only in France but even more in Europe. It ruined the nascent Anglo-French *entente*[50] and revived Russia's messianic conviction that only its power and leadership could save Europe. Nesselrode

---

[49] Webster (1921: 324–36); Chodzko (1863: iii. 1018–20, 1182–5); DeClercq (1880–1917: ii. 485–6); Jaucourt (1905: 248–50); Castlereagh (1850–3: x. 410–13, 422–3, 431–3, 445–7). Louis XVIII seems also to have believed he was unlikely to return. He deposited large sums in francs and pounds sterling in London banks during the Hundred Days and left them there after the second Restoration; Mansel (1981: 270). As for Napoleon, even after Waterloo he made things worse for France, publishing his usual mendacious, self-exculpatory account of his defeat and urging his soldiers still to fight on a week later. Napoleon (1858–70: xxviii. Nos. 22061, 22065).

[50] The dramatic effects it had on British attitudes both toward the Bourbon cause in France and that of Murat in Naples are clear from Webster (1921: 305–8, 314–18).

boasted that Russia, though menaced the least, would again do the most for the common cause by raising 400,000 men, and demanded as much subsidy as all the rest of the coalition put together—and Nesselrode was the most moderate of Russians. Once again, Russia sought to woo Britain away from Austria and Prussia into a close hegemonic partnership over Europe. The fact that Austrians and Germans were horrified at the thought of great Russian armies crossing their soil meant nothing to the Tsar, eager once more to lead his troops into battle and on to Paris.[51] Convinced by the Bourbon collapse that the existing charter was not liberal enough to reconcile throne and people, he proposed that after the war France exercise its inalienable rights to choose its own ruler and constitution under the protection of the European alliance (read 'Russia').[52]

Wellington, in quickly ending the war, performed the inestimable service of keeping these dangers within bounds. Russia's slow mobilization and financial weakness (the minister of finance warned Nesselrode that without British subsidies on a scale far greater than 1814 the war would bankrupt Russia) and Alexander's fear of another European alliance against Russia enabled the British to ignore his rashness and presumption and to turn his ideals to good purpose. While Russia was granted a special subsidy to cover the extra distance between its armies and the theatre of war, Britain basically treated the major allies equally, and after Waterloo Wellington's enormous prestige and Britain's prior presence in France gave the British the deciding voice in policy.[53]

This greatly simplified the problem. Wellington and Castlereagh agreed that the vital thing was to settle France and Europe down as quickly as possible, and that Louis XVIII was still better than any conceivable alternative (Napoleon II, the Duke of Orleans, or a choice made by some French assembly). A Talleyrand–Fouché provisional government was quickly formed, with Fouché arranging the surrender of the remaining French forces and foiling any Bonapartist or Orleanist movement in Paris. Louis XVIII came back from exile on 8 July to a Paris occupied by the British and the Prussians. This settled the question of the regime, though it

[51] *VPR* (1960–: 1. viii. Nos. 87, 104, 134–6, 147–9; pp. 320, 374–6); Pozzo di Borgo (1890–7: 142–3); Arneth (1898: i. 272–3); Sherwig (1969: 332–9); Webster (1921: 309–13).

[52] *Sbornik* (1867–1916: cxii. 207–11); Polovtsov (1902–7: i. Nos. 213–14, 239); Pozzo di Borgo (1890–7: i. 106–9, 125–41).

[53] *VPR* (1960–: 1. viii. Nos. 117, 167; p. 376); *Sbornik* (1867–1916: cxxi. 289–95); Polovtsov (1902–7: i. No. 240).

branded Louis irrevocably with the stigma of returning in the baggage train of foreigners.

The Second Restoration could not restore internal tranquillity to France. A royalist rebellion against Napoleon's usurpation which had simmered in the south and west during the Hundred Days now burst into open flame, leading to a White Terror of Royalists against Bonapartists and Jacobins and of Catholics against Protestants. It also did not spare France an allied occupation in which for the first time the bulk of France suffered what most of Europe had endured for two decades under the Revolution and Napoleon. The allied armies, arriving too late to fight, settled down to live off France; sixty-one departments were occupied by 1,200,000 men, more than half of them Prussians, Austrians, and other Germans. Not all were rapacious; the British were the most correct, the Russians (except for the Cossacks) fairly disciplined, the Prussians the worst. But the enormous cost of the occupation, coming on top of a lost war and the certainty of a heavy indemnity for having caused it, threatened to bankrupt an already shaky French government and destroy an economy already in chaos.

Yet the sufferings and humiliation of the White Terror and the occupation, dilated on by French politicians, publicists, and historians for generations (Clemenceau, for example, included 1815 in his anti-German propaganda campaign in 1919, and a few historians have declared the Royalist terror of 1815 worse than the republican one of 1793–4), have to be seen in proportion. G. de Bertier has aptly compared the royalist risings of 1815 to the rising of the French militia in 1944, something inevitable and understandable, if not salutary. Another analogy is useful, if applied carefully. French charges about the occupation of 1815, like German charges about the Russian occupation of 1945, are true; but one needs to keep in mind what preceded and led to them, and who was finally responsible.[54]

Besides, the sufferings and internal unrest in France had some good side-effects. They failed to make French politicians wiser or its government more flexible in dealing with the allies; the regime was probably too weak to be anything but rigid. Its commission designated to negotiate with the allies used the same stale

[54] Bertier (1966: 105–11, 118–20); Jardin and Tudesq (1984: 20–5). For a sample of the historiography that emphasizes the rapacity of the occupation, ignoring what France had done to bring it on, see Mansel (1981: 242–55, 259, 264–5). For the negative impact of the occupation on the French image of Prussia, see Wenger (1979: 54–9).

arguments and counter-productive tactics as before; Talleyrand exasperated even Castlereagh and Wellington by contesting virtually every allied demand, even some, like the return of art treasures, which he knew did no real harm to France. France's troubles, however, did strengthen the contention that a vengeful peace would only promote more chaos, revolution, and war, while at the same time Castlereagh and Wellington used them to press Louis toward a moderate, non-vengeful domestic policy.[55] Alexander, even while he tried to enlist the Prussians and Austrians in checking Britain's preponderant influence, was forced to work with the British in protecting the Bourbons. His envoy Pozzo di Borgo displayed such zeal in the Bourbon cause that Nesselrode warned him to be more discreet; as Bismarck once said of Gorchakov, he deserved a medal struck with the motto, *Pozzo protège la France*. The Russian jealousy of Britain (the Russian commander, Barclay de Tolly, at first declined even to admit that Waterloo was a British triumph, referring to it in his first proclamation to the French people as a victory of 'the combined army of the North') served to constrain Russia and promote a tolerable peace.[56]

In protecting France from vengeance, Britain and Russia also saved the hotly contested and half-finished German settlement. The Hundred Days revived and strengthened the arguments for German expansion: Napoleon had proved that France was incorrigible, and that Germany had to recover its old territories lost to France in order to defend Europe. Those who advocated this, however, were less interested in weakening France than in over-throwing the Federal Act and realizing their individual ambitions within Germany. The Prussians were the most determined in this regard, the South Germans including the Bavarians the most greedy, and the Austrians, including Metternich, the most uncertain. On 12 June Metternich concluded a secret agreement with Prussia in which, at the price of certain concessions to Prussia and Hesse-Darmstadt in the Rhineland, Metternich gained Prussia's consent to Austria's regaining and, if it chose, permanently retaining its former south-west German territories. Were these possessions rounded out with other possible gains, including Austrian or Austro-Prussian control of the fortress of Mainz, Austria would hold a new position of strength on the German–French border.

[55] Chodzko (1863: iv. 1458–92, 1510–14, 1543–6); Polovtsov (1902–7: i. No. 301); Gentz (1887: 664–98).
[56] *VPR* (1960–: 1. viii. Nos. 170, 179–224, pp. 565, 584); Polovtsov (1902–7: i. Nos. 311, 318–19).

Metternich was probably merely taking out insurance here against a possible failure of the Austro-Bavarian territorial exchange negotiations, in which the Bavarians were proving extremely stubborn. It shows again how improvisation was his middle name. Nevertheless, the agreement raised the possibility that Austria, giving up on Bavaria, would join Prussia in a new dualistic arrangement for Germany. The Prussians, eager for this, urged Austria to add Alsace to its loot.

Russo-British co-operation in defending France's essential territorial integrity ruled out such ideas. Castlereagh instead proposed to reduce France to its frontier of 1790, Alexander forced Prussia to go along with this, and Metternich, seeing how the wind was blowing and reluctant himself to upset the German settlement and let Prussia grow in power, helped arrange the final inter-allied compromise.[57] Talleyrand resigned his post to demonstrate his patriotic opposition to terms he knew would be unpopular in France; for the rest of his life he would make political capital out of the difference between the settlements of 1814, which he had negotiated, and of 1815, which he had refused to accept. His successor was the Duke of Richelieu, an *émigré* whose governmental experience was acquired in administering Russia's newly acquired lands in the south-west (hence Talleyrand's gibe that he was qualified to be premier because of all Frenchmen he best knew Odessa). The terms the allies presented to France on 20 September were fairly severe compared to the first Peace of Paris, but designed to enhance the defensive capacities of France's small neighbours rather than to weaken France in comparison to the other great powers. Richelieu, who quickly proved that he was an able negotiator and not subservient to Russia, managed further to reduce the amount of territory France had to cede, the time of the proposed allied occupation (from seven to five years), and the size of the allied indemnity.

The Second Treaty of Paris signed on 20 November retained the essential features of the first (Bourbon rule, the charter, France's territorial integrity and independence), while strengthening its barrier provisions by ceding key territories and fortresses to France's small neighbours, especially the United Netherlands. France had to accept a five-year occupation of its northern departments at its own expense, subject to review after three years, and pay a 700 million franc war indemnity, part of it dedicated to the

[57] Griewank (1954: 266–71, 305–13, 318–43); Arneth (1898: i. 289–91); Hammer (1963: 20–3).

construction and maintenance of additional fortresses in Germany and Belgium. Most important, the four powers renewed their alliance against France for twenty years, making French aggression or any return of Napoleon or his family an automatic *casus foederis* and calling for consultation in case of a new overthrow of the Bourbons. Article 6 of this alliance provided for future European reunions to promote repose, prosperity, and peace, and thus became the basis for the post-war European Concert and its conferences.[58]

This treaty not only saved France and Europe from the perils created by Napoleon's gamble, but in some ways strengthened the settlement. It did not cure Frenchmen of their desire for glory, but it made them more circumspect in seeking it. French statesmen and publicists still routinely denounced the 1815 system, but those who came to power usually realized that France had more to lose than to gain by destroying it. The 1815 campaign also demonstrated, though no one fully recognized it at the time, that France was no longer a military colossus; and the Richelieu government, by sharply reducing, purging, and strictly controlling the army, further reduced the French threat to Europe while provoking no corresponding threat against France. The military barrier against France, supposedly reinforced by the treaty, turned out to be little stronger than it had been in 1815, when it had proved useless.[59] Neither the United Netherlands nor the German Confederation was eager to build fortifications with the funds supplied them for the purpose. But it was actually less important to strengthen the so-called balance of power against France than to guarantee the independence of the intermediary bodies bordering France, and this was accomplished by the treaty and its accompanying great-power security alliance.

Castlereagh and Wellington were most responsible for this outcome. There was genuine idealism in their stand (for instance, Castlereagh's insistence that the purpose of the alliance was not to gather trophies but to return the world to peaceful habits), but the decisive factor was their sense of practical realities. They recognized that the choice lay between reducing French power drastically and permanently or preserving France much as it was; that even if the former policy were desirable (and Wellington conceded that it might be), it could not be carried out; that the worst policy would be a piecemeal punishment and spoliation of France; that in

---

[58] Chodzko (1863: iv. 1523–7, 1595–1601, 1636–8); Griewank (1954: 350–1).
[59] Renier (1930: 304–6); Colenbrander (1905–22: Nos. 753, 755, 760–1).

any case French power was relative, and might some time be useful against the growing power of other states, especially Russia; and that those who wanted to despoil France now would not be able to hold her down when she recovered.[60]

Yet their good sense would have had a harder time winning out without Alexander's ideals. In September, he and the monarchs of Austria and Prussia signed the famous treaty forming the Holy Alliance. It bound them, along with the other European sovereigns who would later accede to it, to deal with each other and with their peoples on the basis of the Christian Gospel, so that the European alliance would become a fraternal union between rulers and peoples banishing war and conflict from the earth. It is easy to poke fun at this idea, especially the attempt to embody it in a treaty. It is also possible (though finally unconvincing) to see the Holy Alliance as just another of the Tsar's attempts to gain and exercise hegemony over Europe and to flatter his ego. This misjudges both his motives and the practical effects which Alexander's ideals and the Holy Alliance had in Europe. They obviously helped promote another moderate peace treaty for France; it is less obvious but equally true that they helped guard Europe against an active, power-political Russian hegemony.

Those who argue that Alexander was bent on increasing Russian influence and hegemony in Europe ignore how many things he did in 1815 which worked in the other direction. Historically, the pillar of Russia's Northern System had been a close partnership with Prussia. To save the general alliance, Alexander early in 1815 had helped isolate Prussia and force it to give up its expansionist aims, and thereby almost forced Prussia back into Austria's arms. Various German states, especially Bavaria and Württemberg, offered themselves to Russia to help block Austria. Russia regularly backed Austria's claims against Bavaria and ultimately helped force it and Württemberg to join the German Confederation, all for the sake of the general alliance. Historically, Russia had built up its security and its influence in Germany by exploiting intra-German rivalries, especially between Austria and Prussia. Alexander instead promoted peaceful settlements in Germany, and encouraged Austria and Prussia to run Germany as partners. In helping Britain protect France, Alexander strengthened Wellington's hand and encouraged the French to look to Britain rather than Russia for protection.

---

[60] Webster (1921: 339–69); Castlereagh (1850–3: x. 484–91); Castlereagh Papers, PRONI D3030/4586, 4617.

The Holy Alliance itself served to restrain Russia. It had this effect partly because Metternich, before Austria signed the treaty, altered it so that it called, not for a fraternal union between monarchs and their peoples, but for a paternal alliance of monarchs over their peoples. The main restraint, however, lay in the fact that Alexander really believed in his ideals. Metternich and Castlereagh, realists in politics themselves, recognized this and took advantage of it. Just as Alexander's language should not be dismissed as mystical nonsense or a cover for Russian ambitions, Metternich should not be seen as simply manipulating him for Austrian purposes. Metternich also, in his way, believed in the Holy Alliance. Both, like many other statesmen and political theorists of the time, were genuinely convinced that politics had to rest on moral principles, which in turn derived from religious truths. They differed not as a sceptic in religion does from an evangelical preacher, but as a rigidly orthodox churchman does from a mystical enthusiast suspected of heresy and proselytizing.

Castlereagh likewise knew better than to dismiss the Holy Alliance as nonsense. He recognized its absurdity as a working treaty and he characterized Baroness Krüdener, who inspired it in Alexander, as 'an old Fanatick, who has a considerable reputation amongst the few high flyers in Religion that are to be found at Paris'. At the same time he urged Liverpool to persuade the Prince Regent to subscribe to it personally, though without involving the British government. Alexander's mind, he explained, was not quite stable. Last year he seemed bent on conquest, this year on universal peace and benevolence. 'It is at all events wise', he said, 'to profit by this disposition as far as it will carry us. This is peculiarly the feeling of Austria + Prussia, who hope to keep down, now that they are compatriots, much of the spirit of the frontier jealousy wh.[ich] has hitherto embarrassed them.' Castlereagh, in short, saw that the Holy Alliance served to restrain both Russia and the German powers.[61] Unlike some historians and political scientists, he did not ignore the role and value of moral principles in international politics.[62]

[61] On the Holy Alliance generally, see esp. Näf (1928); Bourquin (1954); Ley (1975). For evidence of Russia's self-restraint after Sept. 1815, see *VPR* (1960–: 1. viii. Nos. 233–62). On Metternich's attitude toward it, see Bertier (1960); for Castlereagh's, see Castlereagh (1850–3: x. 384–91); the quotation is from his letter to Liverpool of 28 Sept. 1815, Castlereagh Papers, PRONI, D3030/4716.

[62] Britain, after all, was also carrying on an international moral-religious crusade at Vienna in 1815, its campaign to outlaw the slave trade. Like the Holy Alliance, this was an intrinsically good cause involving genuine idealism, which served

V. THE NETHERLANDS

The first Peace of Paris, though it established the basic structure of the United Netherlands, left various frontier questions open, especially between Prussia and the Dutch. William I, proclaimed King in March 1815, and his son the Prince of Orange both had ambitious dreams, William of a large centralized state that would play an independent role in Europe and justify his royal title, his son of a restored Burgundian kingdom. Along with all the fortresses and alliances possible, both sought German territory on the Rhine as well as Belgium, preferring the former if a choice had to be made. But accepting international obligations for the new state was another matter; William tried to reduce his ties and commitments to the German Confederation as Grand Duke of Luxemburg to the bare minimum.

All this clashed with Prussia's competing claims along the lower Rhine and the Meuse, and with its wish to see the Netherlands expanded in Belgium as the front line against France. While the Prussian notions of possibly bringing all of the Netherlands into the Confederation as part of Prussia's sphere, or even of a Prussian–Dutch political union sometime in the future, were unrealistic, the hope that Prussia might enjoy a sort of shared protectorate with Britain over the Netherlands and thereby acquire Britain as a general partner in Europe made more sense, given British policy in recent decades. The Prussians, however, spoiled whatever chance there might have been for this by their exploitative occupation of Belgium in 1814.[63] France, naturally, was barred from the Low Countries. As for Austria, it rejected any responsibility and wanted to keep Prussia from making gains there or from upsetting the German settlement. Metternich was not indifferent to the fate of the United Netherlands, considering them a vital link in a chain of intermediary bodies which connected Britain and Austria, the two satisfied powers of Europe, and separated France and Russia, the two devouring ones. These purposes made him back British initiatives. As for Russia, its attempts to gain influence in the Netherlands mainly produced irritation all round. Grand Duchess Catherine, touring Europe

indirectly to restrain Britain itself. If Britain wished other states to co-operate in wiping out the slave trade, especially Spain, Portugal, and France, it had to exercise restraint in its control of the seas.

[63] Sas (1985: 96–112); Colenbrander (1905–22: vii. Nos. 103, 123, 153, 160–1, 168, 256, 265–81, 666, 706, 709).

with her brother the Tsar, helped to break up the Dutch Hereditary Prince's engagement to England's Princess Charlotte and to promote his marriage later to her sister Anne. This angered the British but did nothing to bring the Netherlands, as some Russians hoped, into a revived Northern System to counterbalance British maritime and commercial supremacy.[64]

None of these foreign-policy issues, however, were really serious, or the main problem in the Netherlands. As noted, that lay in the differences between the two peoples and their historic aversion or apathy toward each other. Thus their union under the House of Orange at Vienna looks again like an eighteenth-century type of trafficking in souls with no concern for the people involved. This was no more really true here, however, than in the settlement as a whole. The statesmen of that era certainly did not believe in popular sovereignty, and wished to deal with governments rather than peoples (still a useful idea in international politics). At the same time, they knew that popular feelings affected the durability of a settlement, and they tried to discover what these were and to satisfy them where possible. Many territorial exchanges and political compromises at the Congress were designed to meet popular wishes; often territorial settlements had conditions attached to them designed to satisfy local needs (e.g. the Eastern powers' promises to their Polish inhabitants or the conditions governing Piedmont's annexation of Genoa). In the Belgian case, the powers knew the union was unpopular but saw no other way to secure the Low Countries and Europe against France, and no way at all to satisfy the peoples involved. The Belgians were notoriously incapable of organizing, ruling, and defending themselves. Except for a clerical-noble élite who wanted the Austrian Emperor to come back to restore and guarantee their privileges, there was no organized Belgian opinion to deal with. Barring Austrian or Prussian rule, which was impossible, undesired by these powers, and more alien to Belgium than Orange rule, this left only a union of the provinces, which the congress intended as a federal union under one crown, not Dutch rule over the Belgians.[65]

Britain therefore had a delicate task: somehow to balance Dutch demands, Prussian ambitions, and its own special interests without damaging the overall peace. Castlereagh managed it, though not

---

[64] Ibid. Nos. 293–301, 307, 315; Renier (1930: 163–98, 275–6); *VPR* (1960–: 1. viii. Nos. 52, 168).

[65] Dunk (1966: 22–30); Renier (1930: 252–74); Castlereagh (1850–3: x. 31–6).

without fancy footwork. Where the fate of the Dutch colonies was concerned, British commercial and strategic interests prevailed, though not in a rapacious way. The East Indies were restored to the Dutch, but not the Cape, Ceylon, or Demerara, Essequibo, and Berbice in the West Indies. Payments made to the Dutch to construct barrier fortresses served as a fig-leaf to cover Britain's annexations, but London claimed them by right of conquest and compensations, not purchase. Even Java was returned on the assumption that Britain and the Netherlands would be commercial as well as political allies, an assumption events would soon belie.[66]

The problem of the Prussian–Dutch frontier along the lower Rhine and the Meuse proved trickier, since Castlereagh wanted to strengthen both states. At first he approved a proposal from Hardenberg on 28 September, but William I and Lord Clancarty denounced it as unfair to Holland, and Wellington and Liverpool said it gave Bavaria too much responsibility and Prussia too little for Germany's defence against France. Soon Prussian misconduct in Belgium changed Castlereagh's mind about Prussia, and the Polish–Saxon crisis ended all thought of including the Netherlands in the German Confederation as a Burgundian circle. Instead, the Netherlands joined the alliance of 3 January against Prussia. Prussia's retreat over Saxony in February only intensified the Prussian–Dutch conflict over the lower Rhine. The Prussians tried to reverse their defeat over Saxony and to punish the Netherlands by establishing a principality for the King of Saxony on the Rhine, while the Dutch fought stubbornly for more territory and political independence. In the end, an elaborate territorial compromise was worked out. Prussia acquired former Swedish Pomerania and the Isle of Rügen, which Denmark did not want, made certain concessions to Hanover, and gained territory south of the Moselle, while the Dutch retained the Meuse frontier and sovereignty over Luxemburg, whose citadel became a German federal fortress. The solution satisfied no one fully at the time; William especially complained that his state was too small to play the role Europe expected of it. Yet except for changes caused by the Belgian Revolution of 1830, the frontier between the Low Countries and Germany lasted till 1919.[67]

[66] Renier (1930: 317–38); Colenbrander (1905–22: vii. Nos. 121, 125, 130, 132); Robson (1931).

[67] Renier (1930: 276–92); Griewank (1954: 164–72, 258–61); Gruner (1977b: 100–9; 1977a: 308–9); Colenbrander (1905–22: vii. Nos. 154, 156–7, 716–23, 729–30, 732–4, 763); Castlereagh (1850–3: x. 142–5, 166–7).

The Hundred Days threw the Netherlands question open once again, with both the Dutch government and the Belgians showing their readiness to let others fight on their behalf and fearing a rescue by the Prussians almost as much as an invasion by the French. Wellington complained bitterly about their military performance. Yet the episode had its good side. Only a few ambitious and discontented former military officers and officials in Belgium responded to Napoleon's propaganda, and the actual experience of French invasion helped dispel any Belgian nostalgia for French rule and reconcile Belgium somewhat to union with Holland.

After Waterloo, William I made another try for more territory, fortresses, and security, particularly a line of fortresses originally constructed by Vauban in northern France, but in the end defeated his own cause. Austria and Prussia were willing to give the Netherlands more French fortresses if William would cede Luxemburg to Prussia, but he refused. Castlereagh, exasperated in general by the short-sighted greed of the smaller powers, asked him whether he really wanted to add large numbers of French subjects to his other problems, and told the Dutch they simply had to accustom themselves to living in peace with their two powerful neighbours. In the revised settlement the Netherlands acquired four strong points from France, but not the ones it most coveted, Condé and Maubeuge, while Prussia got to command and garrison the fortress of Luxemburg.[68]

The United Netherlands appears the most obvious failure of all the experiments at Vienna, breaking up as it did in civil war after only fifteen years. But at least two observations are in order. The first general one is that the breakup of a federal union does not necessarily prove it a failure. The American Union was broken up by massive secession and saved only by a prolonged, bloody civil war. The United Kingdom was broken up by Irish revolt and independence, and may devolve further. Canada has long been in danger of breakup. None of these unions, or other examples that could be cited, should on this account be labelled a failure overall. The second point is that one needs to specify precisely where and how the United Netherlands 'failed', in which of its intended functions, and to what extent this reflects a failure or error at the congress. Where the Kingdom most clearly failed was as an effective military barrier against France, its primary purpose for many. It was useless for this purpose in 1815 (to be sure, a test

[68] Renier (1930: 306–16, 338–41); Colenbrander (1905–22: vii. Nos. 180, 195, 218–23, 229, 231–2, 234, 237, 777, 791, 794–5, 813, 817).

for which it could hardly have been prepared so early), it broke up in 1830, and it became dispensable for the purpose thereafter. It also 'failed' to reconcile the Dutch and Belgians to living together under the same rule. This was partly because ingrained differences were too deep, partly because William I insisted on a centralized state rather than the federal union the congress intended, and partly because the proposed solution was ahead of its time. It would take another century and two world wars to produce the Benelux of today, remarkably similar to the United Netherlands the congress had in mind. The United Netherlands also failed most conspicuously to be the strong, independent European power William I was determined to erect. But this ran counter to the congress's purposes, and was a 'failure' fortunate for the system. A really strong United Netherlands, such as William wanted, would have run into trouble with both France and Prussia. In some ways (e.g. economic recovery and growth, especially in Belgium) the new state proved its value.

Most important, all these supposed failures obscure the overriding fact that in terms of international politics the creation of a United Netherlands at Vienna was not a failure at all, but an astonishing success. For the first time, after centuries of being the cockpit of Europe, subject to the ambitions and aggressions of one great power after another, the Low Countries were shielded from this destructive balance-of-power competition and transformed, almost despite themselves, into an element of political equilibrium, an intermediary body separating and linking the great powers and forming part of a European centre not dominated by any one power or any combination of them. Britain itself, which had largely created the United Netherlands and could have dominated it, did not try to; no one else, including France, attempted to take it over either; and when the new state broke up from within, Britain would lead and the other powers co-operate in saving and even improving the international status of the Low Countries as an intermediary body. If that is not success in international politics, what is?

VI. ITALY

The Italian settlement was far less satisfactory. Part of the difficulty came from Austria's acquiring Lombardy and Venetia, the largest and in some ways most valuable part of northern Italy. In the case of Venetia, no alternative to Austrian rule was considered. Austria had conquered it in 1813, now occupied it, and chose to keep it on traditional grounds—by right of conquest, as compensation for Belgium, and for arrondissement, revenues, security to the south and south-east, and general leadership in Italy. (Other possible motives for Austria, such as economic development and maritime trade or becoming a naval power in the Adriatic, actually played little role in Austria's decision.) Gaining international sanction for this acquisition was no problem. Except for France, all the other great powers wanted Austria to round itself out in Italy, at least until 1814; no one thought seriously of restoring the Venetian Republic. Austria's take-over was even initially popular with the inhabitants, ruined by war and the Continental System.

Austria failed to win or hold the Venetians' hearts and minds, however; its fairly good intentions were overwhelmed by circumstances and systemic obstacles. Austria's military and civil authorities arrived on the scene instructed to act legally, operate as far as possible within existing institutions, co-operate with the present officials, uphold native customs, and try to make the transition to Austrian rule tolerable. None of this could alter the fact that, instead of bringing the Venetians relief from war and taxation, made worse in 1813 by a bad harvest, Austria had to fight a slow, inglorious, and costly war in northern Italy with Venetia as its base. The initial goodwill evaporated under continued war, taxes, economic distress, and military rule.

In addition, two of Austria's purposes contradicted each other: to conciliate public opinion so as not to arouse Venetian or Italian patriotism, and to govern the province from Vienna like the rest of Francis's centralized patrimonial empire. Had the new regime been efficient, even if remote and 'German', it would have helped, but it proved cumbersome and slow. Yet the seeds of alienation had only begun to sprout by 1815. Venetia never became as discontented as Lombardy, though it was worse governed and much worse off economically.

The question of Lombardy was more complicated. As mentioned earlier, it was not conquered by Austria but surrendered by Eugène after Napoleon's abdication. By that time, as already noted, there were various parties contending for power—Eugène himself, looking for a principality to govern, the old pro-French party, calling for an independent Kingdom of Italy, the so-called 'pure' Italians, the Piedmontese pursuing old Savoyard expansionist ambitions in Lombardy under the guise of preserving a balance of power in Italy, Murat pursuing Italian ambitions from his base in Naples, and even outsiders like Lord Bentinck and other British agents, as well as some Russian ones. Austria was not especially eager to acquire Lombardy. It did not round Austria off or connect with Illyria and Dalmatia as Venetia did, and it brought Austria dangerously close to France. But the need to keep France out of Italy, the impractical character of other solutions, and Francis's conviction that Lombard movements and conspiracies posed a revolutionary danger to his domains, persuaded Austria to take it and the other powers to offer it. A Milanese delegation attempted to make the best of this, urging Francis to expand Lombardy at the expense of Piedmont and the Papal State and to make it an autonomous Kingdom of Italy under an Austrian archduke. Both pleas were ignored.

Many Lombards were initially relieved that the Austrian takeover ended the prevailing uncertainty, though liberals, army officers, and former officials were disgruntled. Unfortunately, Austrian military and civil rule, despite the efforts of General Bellegarde to soften it, proved inefficient, slow, and vexatious, though not tyrannical. Austrian taxation, if less burdensome than in Venetia, was none the less resented, and post-war economic troubles made it worse.

Internationally, Austria's acquisition of Lombardy-Venetia went unchallenged. Even Piedmont concentrated on defending its own territory against Austria and getting Austria's support for its claims against France. Yet Austria's acquisition of Lombardy-Venetia created a deeper problem for the international system. It was defensible from a balance-of-power standpoint, as the only practical way to support and defend Piedmont and keep France out of Italy. But from the standpoint of Italy's general function as an intermediary body between France and Austria, Austria's acquisition of Lombardy-Venetia proved both too much and too little. It virtually forced Austria to lead and organize Italy, yet did not really empower her to do so. Lombardy-Venetia was not big enough as a power base to give Austria control of the whole peninsula, yet too big for the comfort of others, especially Piedmont and the Papal State. Venetia alone might have been a province for Vienna to develop; Lombardy-Venetia became a cow for Vienna to milk, partly to cover the extra military obligations it involved. Owning Lombardy made Austria more rigid in its reaction to all French efforts to regain a foothold in Italy. At the same time it enabled other Italian states, including Piedmont, to push onto Austria most of the burden of their own defence. All this does not prove that the arrangement was a blunder; only that no good arrangement was available in 1815.[69]

To maintain its hegemony in Italy, Austria needed good relations with Sardinia-Piedmont. In some ways the chances for *rapprochement* seemed better here than with Bavaria. Certainly Austro-Piedmontese relations during the wars had been less hostile, and Piedmont clearly needed Austria for protection against France. But given old Piedmontese ambitions and resentments, new Italian-nationalist feelings, and Austrian attitudes, a real reconciliation was very unlikely. Turin's resentment and fear were aroused by Austria's attempt, promoted by military men, to get Piedmont to cede the Angogna district and control of the Simplon pass. Metternich was not responsible for this, but he shared the common Austrian assumption that Italy was Austria's power base and that Piedmont must fall into line, and tried in vain to bring Piedmont into a Lega Italica (an Austrian-led defensive league like the German Confederation), making Alessandria a confederate fortress. King Victor Emmanuel I, in abolishing Napoleonic reforms, restoring the old regime, and hoping to make Piedmont an independent European power, was both more reactionary and more independent than Austria would have liked. The British and Russian agents at Turin, unlike their governments, encouraged Piedmont's anti-Austrian ambitions.[70]

It could conceivably have made a difference if Vienna had tried to co-opt Piedmont as a junior partner in Italy, as it did with Prussia in Germany and wanted to do with Bavaria in south Germany. This would not have solved Austria's problem in the long run but would have made it more manageable. Metternich considered this, but did not seriously pursue the idea and passed up an apparent opportunity to try it during and after the Hundred Days. When Napoleon returned from Elba, Piedmont reacted as other front-line states did, calling for allied protection but failing to mobilize rapidly itself, and seeking British and Russian support against possible Austrian encroachments. Waterloo restored calm at Turin and revived its quest for territorial gains in French Savoy. Had Metternich promised Piedmont strong support for its claims in exchange for Piedmont's joining his proposed Lega Italica, or offered Piedmont joint leadership of the league, Turin might have accepted. But Metternich insisted that Piedmont accept

[69] Rath (1941: 129–37, 182–215; 1969).

[70] *Rel. dipl. Aust.–Sard.* (1964–: 1. i. Nos. 4–5, 15, 18; pp. 457–76); *Rel. dipl. GB–Sard.* (1972–: 1. i. No. 1); *VPR* (1960–: 1. viii. Nos. 10, 15); Zak (1966: ch. 5); Rössler (1966: ii. 129–30); Arneth (1898: 240–1).

Austrian preponderance as a matter of course and did not push the Piedmontese territorial claims. Piedmont ended up with a somewhat improved frontier and Austria without its Lega Italica.[71]

While Austro-Piedmontese relations stayed in the traditional groove, Austro-Papal relations, badly strained since 1780, improved immensely. Pius VII and Francis wanted to join forces against revolution. Metternich and the papal secretary of state, Ercole Cardinal Consalvi, shared not only the same world-view but a similar pragmatic approach to politics and comparable negotiating skills. This did not make the Austro-Papal *rapprochement* easy or automatic. Metternich, having to deal with diverse interests and states and inclined to be and say all things to all men, was often unreliable, while Consalvi cared only for papal interests and, knowing the Papal State's weaknesses, was often rigid in defending them. Both, moreover, faced opposition at home, the Josephist bureaucracy in Vienna, the reactionary *Zelanti* party in the papal *Curia*.

Metternich took the first step in the spring of 1814 by abandoning old Austrian designs on the Papal Legations. This was not a trifling concession; the Tsar at that time wanted Austria to take them, so did some Austrians, and many of the inhabitants would have preferred Austrian to papal rule. Serious problems remained: Austria's continued occupation of the Legations, Murat's occupation of the Papal Marches, and, worst of all, the fact that Rome had learned from Murat about the Austro-Neapolitan treaty of 14 January in which Austria promised to add 400,000 souls to Naples at Rome's expense. Further difficulties arose with Austria's demands, prompted by military leaders, that it annex the part of the city of Ferrara on the left bank of the Po and garrison its fortress and that of Comacchio on the right bank. Austria also insisted that the Pope help the allied cause with either money or men during the Hundred Days.

Despite the haggling, Metternich earned Consalvi's personal confidence in various ways. He defended the Pope's rights to the Legations against other claimants, helped the Pope recover his enclaves of Benevento and Pontecorvo in Naples, and, most important, finally dealt with Murat. Metternich first attempted to promote a compromise between Murat and Rome. When this failed, Metternich, under increasing French pressure, secretly agreed in February to help depose Murat once the congress was

[71] *Rel. dipl. Aust.–Sard.* (1964–: 1. i. Nos. 21, 23–4, 30–41, 59); *Rel. dipl. GB–Sard.* (1972–: 1. i. Nos. 29–31, 38, 42, 45). On Metternich and the Lega Italica, see Bettanini (1939); Grossmann (1931).

over. After Murat brought on his own demise during the Hundred Days, Austria and Rome signed a treaty on 12 June which restored virtually all former papal territory to Rome's control. The Austro-papal reconciliation came just in time to counter a Russian move for increased influence at Rome. Alexander's instructions for General Tuyll, the new Russian minister, show that St Petersburg hoped now to put pressure on Austria in Italy as it formerly had in Germany and the Balkans. Consalvi would have played the Russian card if he had needed to, but he now put his main reliance on Austria.[72]

Austria also ultimately gained hegemony over Naples, though more by luck than by skill. One can defend Metternich's original deal with Murat in January 1814 as useful in helping win the war in Italy and excluding Russia. By sticking with Murat later, while everyone else save Castlereagh turned against him, he at least managed to keep France and Russia out of Italy and the Neapolitan question out of the congress. But Metternich's belief that he could control Murat because he was dependent on Austria proved quite wrong. By early 1815 Metternich was forced to agree to help depose Murat eventually—a concession that both offered France a re-entry into Italian politics and ensured that Murat, given any chance, would try once more to start an Italian revolution.

The Hundred Days gave Murat his chance, and once again rescued Metternich from a failed policy. After Napoleon regained power, Murat summoned Italians to follow him in a 'war of independence' in late March. With the other Italian and European governments backing Austria. Murat's appeal to Italian national-ism fell flat, his invasion of Central Italy got him proclaimed an outlaw like Napoleon, and his army, though larger on paper than Austria's in Italy, dissolved after one battle. Following Murat's fall, the Bourbon King Ferdinand of Sicily, already tied to Austria by a preliminary alliance in late April, returned to reign in Naples under Austrian protection. Happy to be rid of Bentinck's liberal constitution and wanting only to reign in peace and enjoy his fa-vourite sport of hunting, Ferdinand readily entered into an alliance with Austria in June by which Austria guaranteed his throne, while he promised Austria that he would grant no constitution which Vienna did not approve.[73]

France's inability to regain a foothold in Italy after the Second

[72] Reinerman (1979: 7–19); O'Dwyer (1985: 134–7); *VPR* (1960–: 1. viii. Nos. 95–6).

[73] Maturi (1938); Rosselli (1956: ch. 7); Rath (1969: 316–61); Gentz (1887: 525–8, 620–5); Chodzko (1863: iii. 1047–50, 1065–8, 1126–8).

Restoration[74] left Austria in full charge. It controlled Naples, enjoyed good relations with Rome and an alliance with Turin, owned Lombardy-Venetia, and had Habsburg princes reigning in Tuscany, Parma, and Modena. This illustrates an important difference between the German and Italian settlements. Both areas were intermediary zones, and both involved Austrian hegemony, but of two different kinds. Germany was arranged mainly to achieve a good working arrangement among all the German governments and peoples involved, Italy mainly to promote the balance of power and make Austria secure, as much from revolution and conspiratorial secret societies as from war. Prussia and, to some extent, Bavaria were co-opted into the leadership of Germany; France and, to some extent, Piedmont were excluded from it in Italy. Other factors also made the Italian settlement brittle. The Italian regimes, some of them unpopular, most of them weak, all expected Austria to protect them, at the same time as they jealously guarded their sovereignty and rejected Austrian proposals for joint defence, confederation, or administrative reform. Italian nationalism, though not yet a serious force, loomed on the horizon.

Yet the settlement was not all bad or all Austria's fault. Territorially it was reasonable enough; it gave Italy some decades of peace for recovery and economic development; some restorationist proposals were defeated; and there were no good alternatives. Given their respective attitudes, Austria and France could not have shared hegemony in Italy peacefully, and Italy could not have done without a hegemon. Had Austria not taken the role, Russia might have tried to do so. The settlement in Italy suffers mainly when compared to other parts of the Vienna settlement; unlike them, it failed to transcend eighteenth-century politics, was merely a good balance-of-power arrangement.[75]

VII. OTHER ISSUES

Since the Swiss Diet had ratified its new constitution and admitted three new cantons to the Confederation by September 1814, the

[74] This was not for want of trying. Talleyrand reached a secret agreement with Piedmont in Sept. ceding it part of Savoy on condition that Piedmont give no compensations to Austria, but the allies cancelled it as a violation of Piedmont's pledge not to engage in separate negotiations. Chodzko (1863: iii. 1518–19, 1529).

[75] For various provisions of the Italian settlement, some progressive, others not, see Chodzko (1863: ii. 478–85, 516–19; iii. 1045–7); Martens (1874–1905: iii. 302–5). For some of the reactionary protests at what was done, see DeClercq (1880–1917: ii. 554–5, 615–22). On the secret societies, see Rath (1969: 190–242).

Swiss committee at the congress needed to work only on what seemed fairly routine details of drawing the final frontier and preparing the Swiss constitution and its international guarantee for inclusion in the Vienna Final Act. This turned out, however, to be difficult for the same reasons as earlier: not great-power quarrels, though there were some occasions for them,[76] but inertia and divergences within Switzerland itself.

The most difficult territorial disputes involved Geneva, France, and Sardinia-Piedmont and concerned the area around Lake Geneva and North Savoy. The allies were especially eager to improve the Swiss military frontier vis-à-vis France (the Swiss preferred German territory), but France resisted stubbornly. Napoleon's return from Elba helped solve this problem. Needing allied help, the restored Bourbon regime yielded a strip of territory along the lake to connect Swiss territories, while for Switzerland's protection neutrality was also extended to Piedmontese North Savoy. Napoleon's reappearance had also caused other complications, however. Not only had some Swiss sympathizers with Napoleon emerged, especially in the new cantons, but the Diet and many Swiss expected Europe to defend them gratis, considering Swiss neutrality a service to Europe, not a boon conveyed by Europe. It took weeks to negotiate a convention to allow allied troops to cross Switzerland to invade France. The confederation itself was only asked to defend Swiss soil; the small Swiss forces which undertook a brief and inglorious invasion of the French Jura did so on their own to back territorial claims against France.

In the aftermath of Waterloo, the Swiss looked chiefly to Britain for support against France and Piedmont, and ended up somewhat disappointed at the results. Yet Switzerland fared well, getting the French fortress of Hüningen razed and acquiring useful tariff and customs concessions from both France and Piedmont. The Valtelina, Chiavenna, and Bormio fell to Lombardy, partly because their inhabitants feared the Grisons, who were compensated elsewhere.

Swiss and other historians agree that the settlement was a good one, both for Switzerland and for Europe. But some have seen the inclusion of the Swiss federal constitution in the Vienna Final Act as a trap, laying the ground for great-power intervention in Swiss internal affairs. The international guarantee of the constitution,

---

[76] Capodistrias still suspected Austria of nefarious purposes, Humboldt wanted to bring the Swiss cantons into the German Confederation, and Austria had territorial aims regarding the Lombard–Swiss frontier and was determined to prevent political radicalism from taking root in Switzerland and spreading to Italy.

giving the powers the right to preserve it, unquestionably limited Swiss sovereignty and led to incidents of great-power intervention, as will be seen. Rather than being a special snare for the Swiss or restriction on them, however, it expressed the prevailing belief at Vienna that everyone's sovereignty had to be restricted to some degree in the interest of peace and international law. The immediate reason for including the Swiss constitution in the Final Act was to protect cantonal independence and prevent more party strife and civil war such as had destroyed Swiss independence earlier; the wider reason was to help ensure that the confederation would actually fulfil its obligations as a neutral, independent, intermediary body—hold the vital mountain passes, separate Austria and France, not fall under any power's exclusive influence, not harbour revolutionaries or violate international law, and not disintegrate in civil war. Obviously this right of great-power supervision was capable of abuse, and may have been abused in the event; but it also prevented other abuses, including those perpetrated by stronger Swiss cantons and factions on the weaker. The restrictions on Swiss sovereignty were a natural accompaniment of the guarantee of Swiss neutrality, and gave the Swiss little ground to complain.[77]

The Scandinavian settlement at Vienna did in fact take the form the Swiss settlement had been expected to take, a matter of wrapping up final details. In June 1815, the Swedes finally broke the stubborn Norwegian resistance to their rule. With Russia taking the lead, another territorial compromise was worked out in which Denmark accepted the tiny Duchy of Lauenburg in exchange for remote Swedish Pomerania, and Prussia bought Pomerania from the Swedes.[78] No earth-shaking development, of course; but this settlement closed the long-standing Northern Question and began a tradition of Swedish neutrality ultimately as important as that of Switzerland.

The fate of the Ionian Isles was decided in a way that illustrates how great-power rivalry and co-operation intertwined at the congress, with Britain and Russia rivals and joint hegemons at the same time. Russia would have liked to have the islands, but Turkish opposition and British suspicions ruled this out. The British, who had conquered the islands, would have preferred to turn them over to Austria, but this the Russians would not

[77] Martin (1931: 330–421); Hatze (1949: 82–124); Bonjour (1965: i. 193–224); Gentz (1887: 407–20); Chodzko (1863: ii. 528–31).

[78] Höjer (1971: ii. 211–69; 1958); Rosencrantz (1953: 31–98); Chodzko (1863: iii. 1338–40, 1353–6); Höjer (1958).

tolerate, especially Capodistrias, a native Corfiote who suspected a British–Austrian conspiracy to block Russia in the Balkans and to crush the national aspirations of Greeks. Rather than let Austria have the islands, Russia insisted that Britain keep them. They were accordingly neutralized in a four-power treaty of 5 November as the United States of the Ionian Islands, to be governed by a British High Commissioner under a constitution drawn up by an Ionian assembly (another example of moderate liberalism at the Vienna Congress).[79]

The Congress also provided for international control of the navigation of various rivers (the Rhine, Neckar, Moselle, Main, Meuse, and Scheldt were dealt with in special treaties), regulated diplomatic rules and protocol, and outlawed the slave trade. In a move of major symbolic and practical importance, all the various treaties were tied together into one great package, so that while there was no formal guarantee of the whole settlement, the violation of any treaty implicitly threatened them all.[80]

Not every question was settled at Vienna or included in the treaties. Two important areas, each viewed by one of the hegemonic powers as its primary sphere, were deliberately left out. Britain chose to protect its interests in the New World by keeping Europe at bay; Russia tried to advance its interests in the Near East by bringing the European alliance in on its terms. But each pursued an essentially moderate policy, and in both cases the European settlement benefited.

Britain was the first to raise the idea of including the Ottoman Empire under the guarantee of the Vienna treaties; Metternich also entertained the idea, and Gentz thought it vital to Austria's survival. Nesselrode knew that the intent of the proposal was to check Russia's encroachments. In April 1815, therefore, he shrewdly ordered the Russian ambassador at Constantinople, Count A. Ia. Italinski, to propose the idea himself. Given Turkish suspicions of Russia, there was little chance that it would be adopted, especially since Italinski was to make the guarantee conditional on an amicable settlement of the Russo-Turkish disputes over the Caucasian frontier. Yet by offering to guarantee Turkey's integrity and independence, Russia would help dispel the anti-Russian sentiment left over from the Polish–Saxon question, and

[79] Wrigley (1988: 65–70); *VPR* (1960–: 1. viii. Nos. 161–2; p. 379); Webster (1921: 319, 324); Chodzko (1863: iii. 1337–8); DeClercq (1880–1917: ii. 635–7).
[80] Berding (1974); Chodzko (1863: iii. 1372–1433); Martens (1874–1905: iii. 308–13); Gentz (1887: 546–9); Bourquin (1954: 147–50).

would acquire a European lever to use against the Turks. Seeing this, the British and Austrians quickly backed away from the idea.

Still, the Russian offer was not merely a tactical manœuvre. Both the way in which the Russians approached the Turks in their disputes and the manner in which they responded to Austrian concerns over the Serbs and to British concerns about Persia showed a further evolution of Russian policy in the Near and Middle East. Russia still expected to have primary influence, but wanted to enjoy it in moderation, not exploit it.[81]

Britain reached a similar decision in regard to North America, where no European power could interfere. Throughout most of the war of 1812 even the moderates in Britain—Castlereagh, Liverpool, Bathurst—wanted a settlement that would improve on the status quo ante, and expected to get it. Though the military action was not decisive, the United States was clearly on the defensive militarily and diplomatically. Castlereagh's instructions to his team of peace negotiators in July 1814 called for a series of ominously vague concessions from the Americans, and the government seemed in no hurry for peace, expecting commercial pressure and military victories to advance the British cause.

The expected victories, however, failed to materialize or, when they did, like the capture and burning of the city of Washington, proved unproductive. Wellington declined to take command of the forces in America after his victory in Europe in 1814, pointing out that he was needed on the Continent, that Canada was safe, and that territorial cessions from the United States would do Britain no good anyway. As a result, Castlereagh's normal prudence won out. Both sides abandoned their hoped-for gains and passed over the key insoluble issues in silence (impressment, fisheries, the disputed Canadian frontier), concluding an indecisive peace in late December.[82]

It is easy to miss the importance of thus keeping North America excluded from the European settlement.[83] Educated Europeans in the early nineteenth century were quite aware of the future importance of North America; predictions of a time when the United States would rival or overshadow Europe were already

[81] Ibid. 153–4; *VPR* (1960–: 1. viii. Nos. 67, 79–80, 103, 127, 150, 153, 158, 221, 238–9); Rosencrantz (1953: 94–5).

[82] Perkins (1964); Bartlett (1966: 236–41); Castlereagh (1850–3: x. 186–9).

[83] Duchardt (1976: 154–5) notes and explains this feature of the Vienna settlement, but fails, I think, to see its full significance. See the remarks of G. A. Rein in W. Groote (1969: 198–200); Schroeder (1986: 13–17).

common. None the less, or precisely for this reason, separating the New World (and the rest of the world generally) from European politics added importantly to Europe's stability. For centuries since the Age of Discovery, European overseas trade, naval rivalry, and colonial imperialism had formed part of Europe's politics, diplomacy, and war. The French Revolutionary and Napoleonic Wars were in this respect typical, the last and greatest in a series of eighteenth-century world wars (Spanish Succession, Austrian Succession, Seven Years' War, War of American Independence) fought over these issues along with others. The vicious cycle was ended in 1815. The Vienna settlement, in settling European questions and ignoring extra-European ones, shielded Europe, fenced it off from extraneous quarrels. European states and others could continue to trade, expand, compete, and even wage war abroad, and did so. But for sixty years after 1815, European politics and overseas politics were effectively separated, until the so-called new imperialism began to erode the barrier from about 1875, and the Fashoda crisis of 1898 completed its destruction.

One reason this salutary barrier was maintained was the way the British exercised their overseas hegemony, beginning in 1815. Most of the time most European states considered Britain's use of its naval power tolerable, even beneficial. It kept the sea lanes open, encouraged and protected commerce, and, as will be seen, was not used to monopolize overseas expansion for Britain. There were problems over the slave trade and colonies, as will be seen, but not of a serious magnitude. The common impression that Britain promoted peace in the nineteenth century by upholding the European balance of power, but threatened it by its imperialist expansion, may have things just backwards. The British belief that the European system rested on a balance of power, i.e. on natural rivalries between the Continental states which Britain could manipulate and in which it could be the balancer, was a potential danger to peace even when Britain's policies and aims were moderate, as they were most of the time. But the way the British after 1815 ran their formal and informal overseas empire clearly contributed to stability, at least in Europe.

VIII. AN APPRAISAL

The old liberal nationalist charges against the Vienna Congress and system are no longer taken seriously. Historians now commonly praise the settlement for its moderation, prudence, and stability, though still regretting that peoples and territories were shunted about like freight cars in a railway yard, or that the scales were weighted heavily in favour of restoring order and peace at the expense of promoting liberty, justice, and progress.[84] Even these modified charges can be challenged. Much of the congress's alleged trafficking in territories and peoples, as has been shown, did not happen at all, or not in the way and for the reasons supposed. Some of the objectionable outcomes (Sweden-Norway, Lombardy-Venetia, Poland, Belgium) were not really the outcome of decisions and work by the congress, but the product of earlier actions taken to win the war, or the absence of alternatives, or both. As argued earlier, the congress seriously considered popular demands and tried to bring them into harmony with strategic and political realities.

It is less important, however, to examine particular criticisms of the congress's work than to analyse the assumption underlying both praise and blame. That assumption would seem to be that what the settlement needed to do was to meet and balance two main sets of needs and demands: those of governments and ruling élites for a return to order and legality and those of peoples for a greater measure of liberty and natural rights. The congress supposedly met the former requirement well, the latter much less so.

The premiss can be challenged on several grounds. The first is factual: one may seriously doubt that there was at this time any wide popular demand in Europe for freedom, natural rights, and national unity. The claims made at Vienna in the name of liberty and national rights, closely examined, usually turn out to be pleas by particular groups for special privileges, often impractical and restorationist, sometimes reactionary and dangerous. If the people (that dangerous abstraction) called for anything *en masse* in 1815, it was for the same thing most princes and élites wanted, and what the congress gave them—peace and order under their traditional rulers.

The second ground is principial. No international settlement can be expected of itself to promote a better, more just society, or judged primarily on how well it does so. It may require a better society; as will be argued later, any international order depends

---

[84] See e.g. Nipperdey (1983a: 94–101); Dakin (1973: 36); Church (1983: 14–18); Bartlett (1966: 134–5, 138–41, 151). These criticisms of the congress's work were made already by contemporaries, including even Gentz (1887: 496–531, 540–3, 550–5).

for durability on how demands not only for order but also for welfare and legitimacy are satisfied. The question, however, is whether an international settlement can be expected to create the wider societal and cultural conditions necessary to make it durable, and the broad answer is that it cannot. To expect it to do so is not only to ignore the necessary, inescapable priority of the pursuit of order over justice in international affairs,[85] but to demand of an international order what it cannot deliver and what would ruin it for its other central purposes if it tried. Even in the late twentieth century, when a far greater world consensus exists on the desirability of respect for civil rights, democratic processes, and economic co-operation in international affairs, the most an international order can be expected to do is to encourage these among member states, not produce or compel them. The Vienna settlement should therefore be judged primarily not on how well it met the demands and desires of rulers, élites, and the general populace, but on how well it faced and met the permanent, structural problems of international politics. This means asking how well it reconciled great-power demands for influence and control with small-power requirements for independence; how well it succeeded in balancing the needs of the international community against the needs and claims of individual states; how well it secured and legitimized international rights while also allowing room for international change. In this sense, how well did it establish peace?

Judged on this basis, the Vienna system comes out with a remarkably positive balance sheet. This is immediately apparent simply from its handling of the major persistent areas of conflict in Europe. While no solution worked ideally, it solved perennial difficulties in Switzerland, Scandinavia, and the Low Countries in 1815 as much as international questions can ever be permanently solved; it managed the German, French, and Near Eastern questions as well as could reasonably be hoped; and even in areas of comparative failure, like Italy and Poland, though it did not prevent future conflict, it at least controlled it for a good while. No other general peace settlement in European history—1648, 1713–14, 1748, 1763, 1801–2, 1919–20, or 1945—comes anywhere close to this record. Every one failed this test, led almost immediately to new or continued conflict. Only the Vienna settlement got things right; only it genuinely established peace.

This was not the accidental result of favourable circumstances,

---

[85] On this point, see the useful discussion in Bull (1977: 77–99).

war-weariness, ideological uniformity, or other contingent factors. It came by effort and design, resulted from deliberately, consciously confronting structural problems and conflicts—the incompatible security drives and requirements of great powers and small alike, the rights and needs of the international community versus those of individual states, legal and historic rights versus new claims and needs for change—facing these real problems more squarely, persistently, and in concrete detail than other peace congresses have done, and devising creative practical answers. The congress, for example, revived and developed the eighteenth-century idea of intermediary bodies, independent smaller states and areas designed to buffer, separate, and link contending great powers. It worked out rules and understandings for co-operation and concert between the powers, especially the great ones. It found ways of guaranteeing the rights and status of all states while discriminating between their different functions and responsibilities, necessarily conditioned by divergent capacities and interests. It fenced Europe off from extraneous conflicts. It escaped the quest for the *ignis fatuus* of a self-adjusting, peace-enforcing 'balance of power' and achieved something better, a political equilibrium based on the tacit acceptance by smaller powers of a general great-power hegemony so long as their independence and rights were guaranteed, and the acknowledgment by the Continental great powers of Russian and British hegemony in their respective spheres provided it was exercised in a tolerable way.

It is also easy to overlook how the Vienna Congress produced a sea change in international affairs in other ways. It regulated many questions of diplomatic precedent and procedure once troublesome and dangerous, and promoted valuable principles like the abolition of the slave trade and the international regulation and navigation of waterways. The most fertile and unmanageable cause of war in the seventeenth and eighteenth centuries, dynastic succession disputes, ceased after 1815 to be a major international problem. They still cropped up in European politics, both domestically and internationally (one thinks, for example, of Schleswig-Holstein in 1848–9 and 1863–4), but they were no longer the real cause of great crises, subjecting states to attack, partition, or foreign take-over. This was not fortuitous, but part of the development of international law. After 1815, the legitimacy of states, especially new ones, rested not on patrimonial divine right, but on the treaty system and its guarantees, backed by the consent of Europe. The state itself had now become the subject of sovereignty, a kind of moral person, and its prince had become essentially the executive organ of that sovereignty.[86] The principle was explicitly recognized and applied, as Bavaria's dispute after 1815 with Baden, to be discussed later, will illustrate.

After 1815, the old rule that treaties became defunct on the death of a sovereign and had to be renewed ceased to apply; treaties now bound the state, not merely the sovereign. Dynastic marriages, once the essence of international politics, now became only an ornament to it. Patronage, bribes, and corruption, a major element of eighteenth-century politics, declined after 1815, though persisting outside Europe and in semi-colonial areas like the Balkans. Individual statesmen could still occasionally be bought; whole governments like those of Sweden or Poland or armies like that of Hesse-Cassel could not. Trade and economic activity became more important in international affairs than ever; the old calculations of state power strictly on the basis of revenues, population, territory, strategic frontiers, and armed forces expanded to include economic and technological development, commerce, natural resources, and political stability. At the same time, the overt trade wars so common in the seventeenth and eighteenth centuries ceased.

All this adds up to a third objection to the prevalent appraisal of the 1815 settlement, a terminological or conceptual one. Like the whole era that followed it, the Vienna system is constantly referred to as a 'restoration'—restoration of peace, order, monarchy, the balance of power, the old regime, whatever. The term 'restoration' can, within limits, be applied to aspects of the domestic politics and social life of Europe after 1815—though even here, in general, the clock was not turned back. In fact, a powerful argument can be made that 1815 far more than 1789 launched Europe on a century of genuine political, social, and economic progress.[87] But for purposes of international politics, the term 'restoration' simply does not fit the Vienna settlement at all. Of course the statesmen of 1815 drew on history and precedent; they would have been fools not to. Yet the spirit and essence, the fundamental principles and operation, of the international system they devised were anything but backward-looking, were instead progressive, oriented in practical, non-Utopian ways toward the future.

In fact, another term might substitute for 'restoration': revol-

---

[86] T. Schieder (1978: 24–7).

[87] This is the thesis of Johnson (1991); L. Girard (1985) argues convincingly that 1814–15 marks the beginning of the rise of liberalism in France.

ution. It has now become possible, even fashionable, to doubt that the French Revolution revolutionized domestic politics and society in France and Europe. If it remains in the long term the source of liberal and democratic ideals, it may in the short term have set them back. Even graver doubts, as already indicated, can be raised about the revolutionary impact of Napoleonic rule or the War of Liberation. Economic historians still differ on how much revolution there was in the Industrial Revolution, and are near consensus that, if one was under way before 1789, the wars of 1792–1815 slowed it down, even in Britain. Only in one arena in 1789–1815 can one speak unequivocally of progress, break-through, even revolution: in international politics. Here there was unmistakable structural change. A competitive balance-of-power struggle gave way to an international system of political equilibrium based on benign shared hegemony and the mutual recognition of rights underpinned by law.

This book, especially this chapter, has attempted to describe the new system and how it emerged. It remains to add a few comments on how the breakthrough became possible. An indispensable factor was sufficient time. The historian Jacques Bardoux once said of the Peace of Versailles that it was too mild, considering that it was so harsh. His epigram, somewhat altered, could apply to many great wars, especially the two twentieth-century World Wars. For purposes of a durable peace settlement, they were too short, considering that they were so long. That is, while long in terms of the destruction and havoc they created, they were too short in terms of the time they permitted for learning; time for old illusions and new dreams alike to be shattered, for one programme and ideology after another to fail, for the limits of possibility to be tested and perceived and hard realities faced and accepted.

For promoting lasting peace, the revolutionary and Napoleonic wars proved just long enough. It is possible that the statesmen of 1813–1815 were somewhat more sensible and creative than those of 1919 or 1945. They certainly enjoyed better learning opportunities and conditions (though it hardly seemed that way to them). Their wars, though terribly costly (perhaps five million died, proportionally as many as in the Europe of 1914–18), did not destroy the fabric of society or lead to a sweeping over-throw and replacement of élites. The pace of historic change they experienced, though bewildering and shattering enough, was more capable of being mastered. Yet at the same time they experienced so persistent a cycle of recurrent and expanding war, each 'peace' failing more hopelessly than the last, that a single generation of leaders could finally accrue learning experiences which in the twentieth century required two World Wars and a Cold War to provide. Had that learning process been aborted at any point before 1814 by an allied victory, there would have been no stable peace settlement; the old self-destructive international principles and practices would have persisted. The allied programmes of 1793, 1799, or 1805 would have yielded results comparable to those of 1919 and 1945—unenforceable terms imposed upon the defeated enemy, unstable hegemonies quickly producing new rivalries and conflicts, new instability under the guise of balance of power. Time and repeated failure, plus good luck and a certain amount of insight and wisdom, enabled the allies in 1813–15 to do better.

The heart of what the allies learned has already been described. Abandoning the fatal concentration on military victory, the reduction of French power, and the creation of an illusory, undefined, and undefinable 'balance of power' which ruined so many earlier coalitions, they managed to concentrate on creating a political coalition for the purpose of durable peace rather than victory. The vital difference this change made is clear. The old strategy had required them to try to ignore palpable differences in their own aims and interests and deep systemic sources of international conflict, instead identifying and demonizing one threat as the special source of the evil—the Revolution, French power and aggression, Napoleon's ambition, whatever. They were called on to believe, or increasingly to pretend to believe against their better knowledge, that destroying this menace would in itself restore peace, rationality, and stability to international politics, or make them readily attainable. The strategy thereby prevented them from really confronting the task of building peace by a general reconciliation of claims and interests.

The last coalition finally shook off this simplistic outlook. Even during the Hundred Days, when popular propaganda could still portray Jacobins as fiends and Napoleon as the Antichrist, and when the potential rewards of an anti-French crusade looked very seductive, allied leaders resisted the temptation to locate the evil in a single point and destroy it at its root, or to believe that doing so would help. They remained basically in agreement in recognizing limits and doing only what would truly end the war and make peace, even if they disagreed on precisely what that included. Real principles were involved in this, but principles finally non-ideological and pragmatic, focused on the practical requirements of a stable order. The defence of legitimacy meant a recognition of the necessity of norms and law in international affairs. Upholding the European alliance meant respecting the rights of other states and eschewing the use of force in seeking one's own. The call for political equilibrium meant the quest for a balance of rights, satisfactions, and responsibilities. A sense of limits and responsibility lay behind even the conservative, religious language of the Holy Alliance. Even absolute monarchs were not despots, had to respect the law and the rights of their subjects and fellow rulers. That no full consensus on rights and responsibilities in international politics was ever reached at Vienna, that rivalries and suspicions persisted, and that the consensus actually reached was in some respects narrow and time-bound, was sometimes violated in practice, and was destined eventually to become obsolete and tyrannical unless adapted to changed conditions—all this is obvious. That such a consensus should have arisen at all, and come to control the use of power in international politics to a significant degree, was none the less revolutionary.

13
The Congress Era, 1815–1823

THE axiom 'Whatever ceases to grow starts to rot' has often been used in power politics, where it does not really fit. It does not correspond to the facts; durable success in power politics, as Napoleon's career illustrates, depends less on expanding one's power than on knowing where and how to stop and consolidate it. The maxim also suggests a mistaken notion of what power is and how it works. Except in the crudest sense, state power in international politics is not a thing, a definable and measurable entity, which at any particular time must be either growing, declining, or levelling off. It is not even a combination of factors (military capability, industrial capacity, wealth, territory, population, etc.) which add up to such a measurable entity. A state's power in international politics involves above all a relationship between its international needs and goals, its capacity to meet them, and the costs of doing so. The sources of that power or capacity, moreover, lie in a complex network of interwoven factors (domestic-political, foreign-political, economic, social, even cultural and psychological) subject to constant change in different ways at different rates. This makes it virtually certain that any state's power will be simultaneously growing and decaying in different ways at the same time, and probable that any particular action or policy will have that ambiguous result. Again, Napoleon's career or almost any era in history offers examples.[1]

But the maxim quoted above, misleading on power politics, applies well to the kind of politics instituted at Vienna, operating mainly not by the exercise of power but through consensus underpinned by law. Whenever such a system ceases to grow—ceases, that is, to include new rights, deal with new claims, bring in new actors, build new consensus, and adapt to new conditions and problems—it begins to decay. This was the test the Vienna system faced after 1815. The story of how it met the test is

---

[1] For an illustration, see *International History Review*, 12/4 (Nov. 1991), an issue discussing Britain's alleged decline in power in the late nineteenth c. and first half of the twentieth and arguing that it has at least been greatly exaggerated. The essays seem to me really to prove a simultaneous decline and growth in different aspects of British power, from the same causes. Something similar applies to the debate over the rise or decline of American power in the late 20th c.

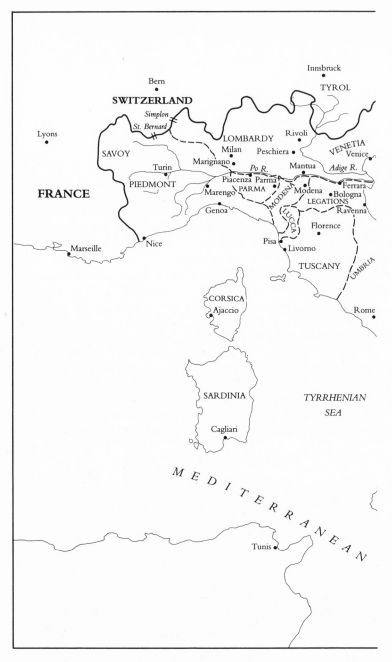

Italy in 1815

outwardly not very dramatic, like most stories of how children learn and develop or fail to do so, but none the less important.

I. RECUPERATION, 1815–1818

One of the objections to calling the post-1815 era 'the Restoration' is that it implies that the governments of that time wanted to restore the old order, even if incompletely.[2] Only a few regimes, and none of the great powers, really wanted or tried to do this. The first few years after 1815 were an 'Age of Recuperation', in which governments were trying to heal the wounds of war and resume normal life, especially through economic recovery and development.[3]

Recuperation dominated the domestic and foreign agenda alike in Britain. Instead of prosperity, peace brought years of industrial depression. While war debts and taxation persisted, foreign markets were quickly saturated with British exports and government and military purchases dried up. The resultant economic distress, besides reviving political radicalism and provoking a wave of domestic political repression which reached its climax in 1819, helped make the cry for cheap government a staple of British politics in subsequent decades.[4] Foreign policy was directly affected. The army was drastically reduced and kept in its Wellingtonian mould for decades. The navy, hit by steep cuts in expenditure, had particular difficulty carrying out its assignments in the Indian Ocean and the Far East. While Britain's interests and its need for representation abroad continued to expand, Parliament tried repeatedly to bring the foreign office and the diplomatic service under its direct control to reduce expenditure and eliminate supposed waste.[5]

[2] For examples of this view, see Best (1982: 194–7, 258–9); Pounds (1979: 307). A much sounder picture is in Contamine (1970: 295–7).

[3] This effort, a natural reaction to wartime devastation and post-war depression, also reflected a growing recognition among Continental statesmen and publicists, learning from Britain, that the new science of political economy was rendering the old German *Kameralwissenschaft* obsolete, and that the national economy constituted a kind of autonomous power complex within the state, needing to be both cultivated and controlled; Huber (1957: i. 788–9); Tribe (1988). On the close co-operation between governments and banks, esp. the Rothschilds, in this effort, see Gille (1965: i. 56–81).

[4] Gash (1978).

[5] R. A. Jones (1983: 54–71); Middleton (1977: 212–17); Graham (1967: 16–23, 444–54); P. Kennedy (1976: ch. 6); McElwee (1975: 23–5). For an argument that the army did not stagnate tactically or technologically despite the rigid economies, see Strachan (1985).

The indirect effects of domestic hard times on foreign policy were even greater: an aversion to foreign adventures, outside involvement, and unnecessary expense of any kind. The British Empire never stopped expanding, its expansion often being driven by local circumstances or men on the spot; but unless an overseas venture quickly succeeded and paid for itself, it risked being repudiated by London. Reform of the old mercantile system came only slowly. A prohibitive Corn Law was passed in 1815, and while Lord Liverpool tried to modify the Navigation Acts in practice, no systematic dismantling began until the latter 1820s. Yet British trade policy changed in emphasis. Unlike previous foreign secretaries, Castlereagh did not try to wrest trade concessions from other states in exchange for alliances or diplomatic cooperation. An equal position for Britain in as open a system as possible was his goal. Though Britain pursued its trade interests actively in the Arab littoral, against the Dutch in the Far East, in India and the Indian Ocean, and in the New World, it no longer did so with the beggar-my-neighbour tactics of the eighteenth century.[6]

Castlereagh's attitude toward Europe clearly showed the connection between economic recovery and fiscal retrenchment at home and a moderate policy abroad. He downplayed British competition with Russia in Asia, especially over Persia, for the sake of good relations in Europe; he declined to respond to alarms others raised over the Russian menace to the Ottoman Empire or Russian influence at Paris; he refused to get excited about German troubles or internal unrest in France and Prussia or Britain's own difficulties with the Dutch and Belgians. All this reflected Castlereagh's usual good sense, his recognition that these were signs of Europe's returning to normalcy, not the build-up to a new conflict, but it went hand in hand with Britain's need for retrenchment and cheap government.[7]

Thus Britain was not really competing for world leadership with Russia after 1815, or Russia with Britain, as some accounts suggest. For one thing, Russia could not afford to compete. For months while Alexander occupied himself with European politics

[6] Tarling (1962); Lowe (1981); Graham (1967: 348–58); Bartlett (1966: 252–8); Ingram (1979: 12–15); Barratt (1983: pp. xi–xii, 5); Sas (1985: 125–62, 171–81). Halstead (1983), though taking a superficial Anglocentric view of the European system (p. 21), is useful on the overall character of the 2nd British Empire.

[7] In general, see Webster (1934); Gruner (1977). For the Great Game in Asia, see Ingram (1979: 32–6). Castlereagh (1850–3: xi) is full of evidence of his calm, sensible advice to alarmists in Britain and elsewhere.

at Paris and Vienna, his ministers pleaded with him to come home to deal with Russia's problems—a devastated economy, disorganized state finances, peasant unrest, an expensive military establishment, discontented army officers, and troublesome new territories, especially Poland and Bessarabia. The reforms the government attempted seldom worked and were usually soon abandoned, but affected Russian foreign policy by discouraging adventures and making Russia seek co-operation from other governments. For example, Russia with Prussia's cooperation tried to promote economic growth, especially in Poland, through tariff reforms in 1816 and 1819. These were abandoned in 1822 when it became obvious that the Poles and Prussians were gaining all the benefits; but Russia still needed Prussia's co-operation to make the transition. Another failure was Alexander's attempt to reduce the economic burden of the army on the state, and to make it an instrument of economic and social development, by founding military settler colonies in underpopulated parts of Russia. After needlessly frightening the rest of Europe and proving costly, the experiment was abandoned.

The worst disappointment was the effort to govern Poland under its constitution and through Polish institutions, especially the Diet (Sejm). The attempt fell between two stools, offering too little to Polish nationalists and too much for Russian ones. Czartoryski was disillusioned by 1816, the Polish viceroy, Grand Prince Constantine, by 1818, and Alexander by 1820. The development of Bessarabia also proved disappointing, if less dangerous. New settlers were brought in from Russia, Bulgaria, and Germany, but living conditions and culture among the native Rumanian peasantry remained very low, and the beginnings of a reaction against Russian rule, though not yet a nationalist one, could be detected.[8]

Russia's domestic troubles, however, were not the sole or even prime factor in Russia's conservative foreign policy. After all, Russia's backwardness compared to Western Europe was an old, endemic problem; earlier rulers, including Alexander himself, had ignored it or compensated for it by seeking foreign adventure and glory. Russia's domestic problems now represented additional but

---

[8] On Russia's economy, see Pintner (1967: 44–7, 68–77); Heller (1983: 103, 111–12); on the army, Keep (1980: 500–5); Blum (1978: 340–1); Beyrau (1984: 72–5); on Poland and Prusso-Polish commercial negotiations, Schiemann (1904: i. 120–78); Pienkos (1987: 157–72); Alexander (1865: 246–79); Black (1981); *VPR* (1960–: 2. i. Nos. 3, 183; 2. iv. Nos. 129, 138–9, 162–3, 181; 2. v.). On Bessarabia, see Jewsbury (1977: 66–76, 94–5; 1979: 287–95).

not decisive reasons for a policy of peace and co-operation within the European alliance which Alexander time and again, at home and abroad, insisted was vital for its own sake. What chiefly motivated him was clearly his role and image as arbiter of the system. In order to help enrol Italian princes in the Holy Alliance (he failed only with the Pope, who did not like religious ties with schismatics or wish to be instructed in how to govern as a Christian prince), he solemnly renounced any special Russian aims in Italy. Trying to mediate in the persistent quarrels between Denmark and Sweden over the Norwegian debt, he assured both sides that the old notion of a Russian-led Northern System was dead.[9]

Russia's supposed world rivalry with Britain had more to do with status and prestige than real interests. (A good example is the effort of Russians, especially Grand Duchess Catherine, to break up the engagement of the Dutch Hereditary Prince to Princess Charlotte of Britain and instead promote his marriage to Grand Duchess Anne—a sensation in court society, essentially meaningless politically.) Neither government paid much attention to the alarmists within its camp or tried seriously to encroach on the other's sphere. Chernishev frequently detected British and Austrian plots against Russia, but was really most concerned with the Tsar's image and incensed that Europeans refused to acknowledge that Alexander had saved them.[10] While Capodistrias and Chernishev encouraged Pozzo's efforts to influence Richelieu and play a leading role at Paris, Nesselrode kept this within bounds, and the very instrument Russia used to enhance its influence at Paris, the allied ambassadorial conference set up to advise Wellington as commander of the occupation army, actually restrained Russia and strengthened Britain's position. The conference could offer Wellington and the French government advice, but only Wellington could fulfil France's requests, so that the French got the benefit of Russia's patronage and shrugged off much of Russia's advice. Besides, Russia would not give the French what they really wanted, an end to the anti-French coalition and a revised peace settlement, any more than other powers would.[11]

[9] VPR (1960–: 2. i. Nos. 13, 44, 53, 81, 127, 144–5, 186, 193). For the Pope's rejection of the Holy Alliance, see O'Dwyer (1985: 156, 195–7). For an interpretation of these initiatives as Russian power politics, see Pirenne (1946–9: ii. 8–106).

[10] Ibid. 43–5, 48–9, 138–9; VPR (1960–: 2. i. Nos. 17, 38, 54, 68, 95, 101–2); Sbornik (1867–1916: cxxi. 339–40, 345, 355–9); Gillard (1977: 18–21).

[11] Polovtsov (1902–7: ii. Nos. 182, 202, 211, 215, 220).

Russia's relations with Prussia, despite some trade friction, were generally cordial; not so with Austria. Their mutual suspicion, however, did no harm in practical terms; Austria and Russia were able to settle concrete issues between them (various Polish questions, the borders of Cracow, payment for wartime deliveries of goods, etc.) with less trouble than in the past, and co-operated in dealing with France. Fears of a possible Austro-British or Austro-Turkish alliance helped moderate Russia's policy toward Germany and Italy.[12]

There was only one area in which Russians seriously maintained their former pretensions, and even here they were more restrained—the Ottoman Empire and Persia. The new Russian ambassador to the Porte, Baron Stroganov, continued to browbeat the Turks over the Asiatic frontier, trade, the straits, and the protection of Christians, while Russia's general consul, A. A. Pini, tried to introduce more Russian agents into the Balkans for the purpose of bringing Rumanians, Greeks, Serbs, and other Christians under Russian protection. Russians tended to resent British or Austrian influence in the area, claiming that only Russia knew how to deal with barbarous peoples like the Turks and Persians, or was entitled to do so. In April 1816 Alexander warned Britain to keep its hands off Asia, especially Russia's negotiations with Persia.

These were dying echoes of the eighteenth century, however, not signs of revived expansionism. Catherine's ambitions were abandoned; new conditions made them unreachable anyway. Russia lost its free hand after 1815, with Britain no longer courting Russia as in the eighteenth century and far more involved itself in the Near East, Austria no longer as dependent and threatened by Prussia or France, and Europe no longer paralyzed by rivalries and war. Russia's power may have been greater; its opportunities were definitely diminished. The idea that nineteenth-century Russia had dangerous expansionist aims in Europe, especially toward the Ottoman Empire, is an old myth, already refuted many times. For most of the century, especially after 1815, the Russian government pursued no such goals. It did not dare use force against the Ottoman Empire without unacceptable consequences and complications, could not bully the Turks into submission, and discovered that for certain purposes (such as dealing with the Barbary pirates or getting better treatment for the Serbs) it needed help from other powers at Constantinople, especially its opponents, Austria and Britain.[13]

Thus a combination of external circumstances and conservative aims made Britain and Russia good stabilizers of the new order. Though no balance-of-power model really suits the new system, if one must be devised, it cannot be one of the usual ones—the jeweller's balance, the chandelier, or the typical Central European model of a solid, immoveable weight in the centre (the ballast in the hold of a ship, Metternich's picture of Austria as an immovable rock in the midst of waves, or Bismarck's of Germany as the stabilizing weight in the base of the punching doll). The only model at all close to the so-called balance prevailing after 1815 is the catamaran—a light, frail, but mobile and buoyant vessel, its vulnerable centre held above the waves by outriggers on both sides, needing constant attention and seamanship to keep it afloat.[14]

The most fragile section of the catamaran's centre seemed to be France. Many observers predicted more revolution there, and they had ominous signs to point to: a throne propped up by foreign bayonets and threatened by secret societies and conspirators; the monarchists, though representing a majority in the country and an even larger majority in the newly elected Chamber of Deputies, deeply split between ministerials and ultra-royalists and attacked by Bonapartists, liberals, and Jacobins; beneath a superficial revival of religion and the union of throne and altar, a persistent anticlericalism and a growing alienation of the urban populace from religious practice; post-war depression and bad harvests; open opposition from important élites, including former army officers and many intellectuals. There was another side to France after 1815, however: steady if painfully slow economic recovery and growth in the small-scale, decentralized French style, and a continuity in administration, the bureaucracy, and institutions counterbalancing the surface turbulence in politics. France's religious and intellectual divisions and quarrels were also signposts of its greater freedom. More groups were integrated into the post-1815 regime than were alienated, though the latter made more

[13] Dostian (1972; 1974: 18–23); Schiemann (1904: i. 280–302); VPR (1960–: 2. i. Nos. 36, 48, 55, 83, 107–9, 131, 142, 150, 180, 187, 198, 200); Martens (1874–1905: xi. 264–5; iv. 66–7). For a brief argument that Russian policy was essentially conservative and law-abiding, see Schroeder (1983); for excellent scholarly surveys, see Jelavich (1984; 1991).

[14] One historian who understands this character of the system is Heinz Gollwitzer (1964; 1972). Even he, however, over-stresses the East–West split (1964: 181–7).

noise; property was more widely distributed, interests better, if still very imperfectly, represented, power more diffused.[15]

In any case, France's internal problems made it safer rather than more dangerous in foreign policy. No regime had more to fear from renewed war or revolution, and while Richelieu hoped to hollow out the Treaty of Paris, split the coalition, and end France's occupation and isolation, he proposed to do so, like some German statesmen after Versailles, by 'fulfilment'. His appeals to the Russians for support were no indication of Russophile sentiment or a desire for a Franco-Russian alliance. In fact, popular Russophobia, founded in France in the Napoleonic era, continued to grow after 1815, though it only became overt later. Those like Metternich who warned that France was about to undergo a new revolution or to ally with Russia usually had self-interested reasons for the claim, and by 1816–17 even Metternich began to change his tune.[16]

Proof that the French danger was manageable came in the orderly way the allies ended their occupation and brought France into the European Concert. The process, culminating in an international conference at Aachen in 1818, naturally involved intrigues, subterranean rivalries, and competition for influence; these can be found in every dog show or bridge tournament, and should not obscure from view the real progress being made in international politics. By 1816 the allies had deflated their war claims against France to one-sixth of their original exorbitant size, with Prussia the main loser. In 1817 they reduced the size of their occupation forces, and at Aachen they granted France's request to end the occupation two years ahead of its original term. France paid off its outstanding indemnity in advance with loans from British bankers, and a compromise was devised bringing France into the European Concert as a full member and participant in future meetings, while at the same time maintaining the Quadruple Alliance against her as a precaution. Europe's statesmen worked this out not because they were fully confident of France's

[15] On economic conditions, see Kemp (1971: 112–31); Caron (1979: 1–34, 118–21); Bertier (1966: 222–35, 254–7). On politics, administration, and government finance, see Jardin and Tudesq (1984: 32–45); Jardin (1985: 210–25, 272–9); Girard (1985); Corciulo (1983); Bertier (1966: 272–82, 298–99); Jacobs (1988); Kieswetter (1982). On religious and intellectual life, see Bertier (1966: 238–9, 302–5, 322–3, 374–84); Fitzpatrick (1983). On the army, see Porch (1974: 1–6); Vidalenc (1983a); Griffith (1989: 6–20). On the sects and conspiratorial activity, see Spitzer (1971).

[16] Bertier (1968–71: i. 42–112); Hammer (1963: 23–39); McNally (1958); Polovtsov (1902–7: i. Nos. 398, 482, 486).

stability—Richelieu himself was far from that—but because everyone, including the Prussians and Austrians, wanted to help keep Louis XVIII and Richelieu in power. Metternich expressed the spirit of the approach (and the important role of intermediary bodies in it) aptly in March 1817:

Internally tranquil, that power [France] will not disturb any other for a long time; but that tranquillity can only be assured to it with the help of its great neighbours. No displaced rivalry can exist today between Austria and France; we have no more contacts, and consequently no more immediate frictions. It depends only on us and the wisdom of our course to prevent the small intermediary bodies between us and France from turning their eyes, as in the past, toward the latter.[17]

Russia and Prussia sent up trial balloons at Aachen in favour of expanding the alliance to guarantee treaties, boundaries, and governments in Europe; one version of the Prussian proposal was secretly supported by Metternich. But the proposals, a shadow of Holy Alliance doctrine to come, were advanced only half-heartedly, especially by Russia, and easily defeated by Castlereagh.[18]

II. REPRESSION IN GERMANY, 1815–1820

Aachen went as smoothly as it did partly because it barely touched the areas where important changes were occurring in 1817–20: Latin America in world politics, Germany in Europe. Much of what happened in Germany can be organized around an obvious theme, political repression. During these years the reform movement was defeated in Prussia, the liberal constitutional movement brought to a halt there and elsewhere in Germany, and the Confederation Diet pushed into decrees against radicalism and dissent which altered the character of the confederation itself and challenged the rights and sovereignty of its member states. But the theme of repression and reaction, important though it is, is too simple to encompass the German question, which also involved how various individual states would develop politically and constitutionally, and how the skeleton of the German federal constitution would be filled out and Germany organized to act within the international system. To understand the complex picture even

---

[17] To Prince Esterházy at London, 26 Mar. 1817, quoted in Bertier (1968–71: i. 147; translation mine).
[18] Bourquin (1954: 211–46); Bertier (1968–71: i. 145–59); Baack (1980: 42–8); Sas (1985: 165–71); Martens (1874–1905: 298–328); DeClercq (1880–1917: iii. 164–8, 172–4).

superficially, one needs to understand something of what was happening to certain actors in it.

Prussia in 1818 was in most ways a progressive state, with its reform movement still alive and apparently moving forward. It had introduced universal military training and a civilian-officered reserve army, the *Landwehr*.[19] The peasants were legally free, the abolition of serfdom having been decreed in 1807 and further implemented after 1815. Prussia enjoyed a fairly progressive legal code, the *Allgemeines Landrecht*, an independent judiciary (though many vestiges of patrimonial jurisdiction survived on noble landed estates), and an educated, efficient bureaucracy. The government had had considerable success in uniting, reorganizing, and administering the country, which had doubled in size since 1812 and now had eight provinces separated into unequal western and eastern portions and spread all over North Germany. The economy, still overwhelmingly agrarian, suffered in the general post-war depression. None the less, the regime deliberately promoted economic liberalism, abolishing or limiting guilds and restrictive rules, advancing industrial freedom, and eliminating internal tariffs by a unified tariff system in 1818. The policy soon began paying economic, fiscal, and political dividends.

As ever, reform did not solve all the old problems, and new ones arose. There was tension between Rhenish and east Elbian Prussia, the new Saxon regions were discontented, some Protestants were incensed at the King's union of the Lutheran and Calvinist confessions in 1817, and the abolition of serfdom provoked continued resistance. But some problems were handled more smoothly in Prussia than elsewhere—for example, relations with the Pope and the Catholic Church, vital for a state now two-fifths Catholic, or the conferring of special status on the Poles in Posen and West Prussia.

Hardenberg intended to cap his reform programme with a representative constitution, which he had persuaded the King to promise to the country in May 1815; but this final step was in jeopardy. Hardenberg had delayed the move dangerously long in order to finish the administrative reorganization of the kingdom first. Humboldt, increasingly his rival, criticized his proposed constitution as too conservative, while many bureaucrats saw

---

[19] As things turned out, these military reforms, unaccompanied by general political reform, ironically contributed to the growth of Prussian militarism in the long run by separating the universal obligation of military service from the universal right of political participation originally connected to it; Huber (1957: i. 224–5).

little need for a representative constitution at all, believing that they already represented the citizens of culture and property (*Bildungsbürger*). Feudal conservatives also opposed any modern representative constitution, and Frederick William was his usual fearful and irresolute self. Yet Hardenberg seemed to have a good chance to push his constitution through in 1819. The public generally favoured it as a reward for the sacrifices of the war, though without being clear on what a representative constitution meant, and even opponents saw their best chance in modifying his plan rather than defeating it.[20]

Austria faced fewer obvious difficulties and felt far less impulse to reform. Except for Lombardy-Venetia, its problems in assimilating new or regained territories were less pressing, and the temptation was greater to rest content with moral leadership in Germany and political hegemony in Italy. None the less, Metternich, bombarded with warnings particularly from military and political authorities in Italy and Illyria, knew that the monarchy needed political and administrative reorganization. He and his aides in 1817–18 worked out plans for reorganizing the Empire, intended to concentrate fundamental policy in Vienna but allow the provinces considerable autonomy in its execution. Like Hardenberg's, Metternich's programme had foreign policy goals in view as well as internal ones—in this case, keeping Austria competitive with Prussia as a standard-bearer of practical progress in Germany.

In economic reform, however, especially commercial and industrial freedom, Austria did not even try to compete, and major obstacles blocked even Metternich's modest programme—the Josephist-centralizing bureaucratic tradition, the resentment of many stock Austrians against Metternich and other Reich aristocrats who dominated Austria's high offices, particular economic interests (Bohemian and Styrian industry and Hungarian agriculture) opposed to moves toward economic liberalism, and the great differences in economic, cultural, and social development between various areas of the monarchy. Most important, Emperor Francis, a rigid conservative jealous of his personal authority, buried Metternich's plans in his bureau drawer, and Metternich, sensing

[20] I have relied heavily on Koselleck (1967: 24–35, 63–78, 144–9, 153–62, 167–215); but see also Koselleck (1978); Berdahl (1988: 144–57, 182–95); Huber (1957: i. 121–7, 442–9, 464–5, 794–5); Büssem (1974: 26–9, 201–28); Vogel (1983: esp. 120–32); Behrens (1985: 194–7); Sweet (1978: ii. 304–7). For a magisterial treatment of the whole German picture from the view of *Gesellschaftsgeschichte*, see Wehler (1987: ii. esp. 297–369). For surprisingly favourable pictures of Prussia's administration of Posen, see Biskup (1983: 12–15); Jablonowski (1972: 274–7).

the futility of a struggle, did not try hard to save them. This failure to reorganize Austria may have been a factor in a shift in Metternich's German stance (one cannot be sure, given Metternich's frequent inconsistencies). Although he was mildly progressive in working for German harmony up to 1815 and at least flexible in his methods for a while thereafter, Metternich's policy from 1819 on became almost solely defensive and repressive, concerned to prevent whatever might disturb Austria.[21]

In the rest of Germany, especially the middle states, the constitutional movement defies brief recapitulation. The central goal for most governments was state-building—to organize a viable state and develop a common state consciousness among its subjects, while wrestling with problems of debt, depression, the need to assimilate new areas and subjects, and the resistance of the old estates, the *Standesherren*, and local authorities defending their traditional autonomy. Sometimes modern representative constitutions were chosen for the purposes of state-building, but more estate constitutions were restored and refurbished than modern ones established. Monarchy was the unchallenged basis of constitutional doctrine and the foundation of political community. The central difference between 'right' and 'left' was not even whether royal authority should be absolute or restricted, but whether the monarch was still to be the traditional *paterfamilias*, the residual legatee of authority in case of need, or the effective head and locus of authority in a modern state with developed means of enforcing its control. Yet pragmatic and self-interested though the motives for constitutionalism mainly were, the movement clearly brought some advance in civil rights and the growth of a civil society.

In international affairs, all the Third German states wanted to gain and preserve their independence, but they tried different ways to do so—Bavaria through acquiring independent European status, Württemberg and certain others through a special league with other middle states to foster their independence and exploit differences between the great powers, others through opting out of high politics or attaching themselves to one of the great powers for protection. Depending on their individual situations and policies, the Bund could be either a safeguard or a threat to their independence.[22]

---

[21] Haas (1963); Radvany (1971); Büssem (1974: 2–3, 12–21); Preradovich (1955: 8–29, 42–5, 78–84); Matsch (1980: 70–1).

[22] Huber (1957: i. 314–19, 329–60); Boldt (1975: 48–53); Weis (1976); Zorn (1962: 114–29); T. Schieder (1978); M. Walker (1971: 260–79); Gruner (1984); Burg (1989: 69–95).

The most important of them, Bavaria, experienced a series of set-backs in 1816–18. First came the Treaty of Munich in April 1816, in which Austria forced it to turn over Salzburg and other territories before it received its promised compensations in the west. The treaty was costly for victor and loser alike, ending Montgelas's hopes that Austria would help Bavaria achieve independent European status, but also badly damaging Metternich's hopes of basing Austria's policy toward Third Germany on close ties with Munich. In addition, it committed Austria to helping Bavaria achieve its extensive claims against Baden, including a territorial corridor along the Main to connect old Bavaria to the Palatinate.[23] Then followed disappointments at Frankfurt. When Bavaria finally entered the Federal Diet at Frankfurt with hopes of taking up Württemberg's proposal for a bloc of purely German states against Austro-Prussian domination, it found territorial disputes among the South German states, especially its own with Baden, an insuperable obstacle to this, and the obstructionist tactics Bavaria followed at the Diet so alienated everyone that it was threatened with expulsion. The new foreign minister, Count Rechberg, repaired some of the damage after Montgelas fell from power in February 1817, but then an Austrian-sponsored compromise in the Bavarian–Badenese territorial dispute broke down over a succession question, Bavaria insisting on its rights to portions of Baden's territory once the current line of the Badenese ruling house died out (as was imminent). Baden defended itself with a House Law in 1817 declaring the territories claimed by Bavaria inalienable. All this was normal eighteenth-century politics, and Bavaria's notable lack of success with it indicated how at least among the great powers it was no longer in style.

Complicating these quarrels over territory and federal politics was the question of estate constitutions, called for in Article 13. The Bavarian government and others saw these as a device to promote Austro-Prussian domination within the Bund and *Standesherren* resistance to royal authority and centralization at home; this was the main reason Bavaria proclaimed a modern representative constitution modelled after the French Charter in May 1818. Baden followed suit with its own centralist modern constitution in August 1818, and William I of Württemberg, who when he took the throne in 1816 inherited his father Frederick's struggle against his estates as well, did the same in 1819. Hesse-Darmstadt

---

[23] Aretin (1976: 179–85); Quint (1971: 405–7); Spindler (1974: 4. i. 60–2); Martens (1874–1905: iv. 251–63); Chroust (1939–42: i. Nos. 41–79).

and Nassau had already taken the same route earlier. By 1819 much of South Germany had liberal-conservative constitutions, useful in defending these states' sovereignty against the Bund and promoting centralization at home, but little help in the short run for domestic political tranquillity and no help to Bavaria in its territorial claims. At Aachen the great powers took Baden's side, declaring its state territory inalienable regardless of competing succession claims.[24] In July 1819, a commission of the four great powers went even further. In a Territorial Recess of Frankfurt which settled various territorial and other problems left over from Vienna, it rejected both Bavaria's reversionary rights in Baden and its demand for a territorial link between old Bavaria and the Palatinate. Though Bavaria denounced this decision as a violation of treaties, rejected the proffered territorial compensation, and maintained its claim against Baden in various forms for more than a decade thereafter, effectively it had lost. Now, like Prussia, it had to govern a Rhenish province which was separated from the heartland both geographically and by the historical experience, customs, and sentiments of its inhabitants.[25]

German nationalists, then and later, viewed these quarrels as baneful evidence of the failure of unification and the success of the small-state sovereignty swindle (to use Bismarck's phrase of the 1860s). Once again, an international viewpoint may detect success where a nationalist one sees failure. The outcome showed the 1815 system to be working and growing. Complex, hotly contested issues of great importance to the parties involved were settled peacefully through compromises brokered by the great powers without the overt use of force, with solutions representing advances in international law and practice. In confirming Baden's territorial integrity against Bavaria's dynastic claims, the powers helped rule out wars of succession, the bane of the eighteenth century, and asserted the concert's right to mediate inter-state quarrels, even as a last resort imposing solutions and revising treaties. Another delicate issue, whether all the great powers as guarantors of the German Confederation were entitled to intervene directly in its affairs, was solved at Aachen in a way that affirmed both the confederation's autonomy and Europe's rights of guarantee. The four powers left the direct guidance of the con-

[24] Quint (1971: 407–53); Aretin (1976: 185–97, 202–15); Huber (1957: i. 323–8, 641–5); Hahn (1984: 28–35); Chroust (1939–42: i. Nos. 136, 141–2, 166–8, 171; 1949–51: 70–86, 105–11).

[25] Arneth (1898: ii. 45–56, 60–73); Büssem (1974: 101–16, 126–7); Huber (1957: i. 580–5); Chodzko (1863: iv. 1688–95, 1769–88).

federation to Austria and Prussia, but issued provisional instructions to their delegates to the Bund at Frankfurt in case it should be paralyzed by internal rivalries.[26]

No such neat solution was available to the Bundestag for filling out the skeleton of the Vienna Final Act, especially on two vital and thorny questions: the Bund's defence system (how to organize and command the federal army and what territories to include within the Bund's defence perimeter), and the execution of Article 13 with its undefined mandate for estate constitutions. The obstacle to progress on both was not Austro-Prussian rivalry or the two powers' determination to suppress dissent and political change; that would come later. With Prussia afraid of the revolutionary and military threat from France and Austria of Russian influence in Germany and the rise of liberal centralized constitutions, they were for the moment partners in a moderately progressive programme. Metternich, as noted, favoured some federalist reform within Austria and was willing to tolerate or encourage something similar within Germany, and neither great power tried for overt or exclusive control of the Bund. Both accepted fewer votes in the two councils of the Diet than their size and power would have justified, and though each thought about putting their particularly vulnerable territories outside the confederation under federal protection (Silesia for Prussia, Galicia for Austria), they agreed to forego this, leaving much of Prussia and most of Austria outside, partly in order not to irritate Russia.[27]

As a result, the lesser states gained much more military security from Austria and Prussia and the federal defence system than they contributed in return. Each German state was supposed to supply contingents to the ten-corps Bundeswehr in rough proportion to their respective resources (three army corps from Austria and Prussia, one from Bavaria, and three from the other states). But since the Bundeswehr would not stay in being but only be mobilized by federal resolution in emergencies, and since the only large standing armies and military organizations were those of Austria and Prussia, the great powers clearly shouldered the real burden of Germany's defense.

All this indicated the intention of Austria and Prussia to exercise their leadership responsibly. Yet from 1816 to 1819 the middle states who stood to benefit from the confederation, especially Bavaria and Württemberg, steadily obstructed all attempts to

[26] DeClercq (1880–1917: iii. 168–72).

[27] Austria did get a small portion of Galicia included in the Bund, and in return gave Prussia its special guarantee against an attack on Silesia.

make it viable, threatening to leave it and appealing to outside powers for help, especially Russia. At the same time, their jealousies and quarrels kept them from forming an effective Third German block to counter the great-power domination they supposedly feared.[28]

One consequence was that no progress was made on the economic unification of Germany, a goal of the Bund according to Article 19 of the Final Act. For the time being this did not seriously concern the German great powers; it left both of them free to follow their respective economic paths.[29] The constitutional issue, however, could not be ignored, especially by Austria. Already territorial disputes had undermined Metternich's hopes of basing his German policy on friendship with Bavaria. Now the most important south German states had proclaimed modern representative constitutions in 1818–19; these became the model for the educated German public of the way Article 13 should be fulfilled. Article 13 thereby ceased to be a useful prophylactic against such constitutions, and instead threatened Austria's leadership in Germany and even its internal stability. Austria could never adopt a modern representative constitution, given its historical and ethnic make-up, but Prussia could and apparently intended to.[30] Though Metternich boasted of Emperor Francis's popularity in Germany, he knew that Austria's following in Germany was shallow.[31] Metternich found his opportunity for a counter-offensive to save Austria's leadership in the radical agitation of the late teens. Much as he hated liberal and radical agitators, the real target of his conservative campaign, in Germany in 1819–20 and in Italy immediately thereafter, was what he considered suicidal actions by weak and foolish governments.

This does not mean that the German radical movement was merely a pretext for political repression. True, it represented no clear revolutionary danger. Political radicals within the patriotic student organizations (*Burschenschaften*) at the Universities of Giessen, Jena, and Tübingen were only a small minority among the dissidents in Germany, and these only a small minority of the po-

[28] Burg (1989: 96–139); Kraehe (1977: 168–75); Huber (1957: i. 609–15); Gruner (1984: 32–5); Seier (1986: 397–409).

[29] H. W. Hahn (1984: 23–8, 58–61); Büssem (1974: 346–50).

[30] Aretin (1976: 224–5, 230–1, 245–67); Quint (1971: 454–92); Aretin (1955: 718–24); Büssem (1974: 34–46); Chroust (1939–42: i. Nos. 157, 160).

[31] Emperor Francis's trip down the Rhine in 1818 attracted enthusiastic crowds, but this meant little. Cheering the Emperor simply enabled the Rhinelanders to express their Catholic feelings and their nostalgia for the good old days while giving one in the eye to their Prussian rulers; Arneth (1898: ii. 59–60).

pulace as a whole. Instead of a viable programme, moreover, they had only a vague, unstable amalgam of notions about recreating the Empire as a German constitutional monarchy and reviving the old estates, religion, and the authentic German folk spirit, inspired by contradictory liberal, national, romantic, religious, and reactionary ideas. The public incidents they created in 1817–19, though inflammatory, did not seriously disturb public order, much less threaten revolution. The main ones were the Wartburg Festival in October 1817, which celebrated the fourth anniversary of the Battle of Leipzig and the 300th anniversary of the Reformation with radical speeches and book-burnings,[32] and the murder in 1819 of a conservative publicist and playwright, August Kotzebue, by a mentally unbalanced theological student named Karl Sand.

Yet the radical movement was not necessarily trivial and harmless. Disturbing elements of Francophobia, xenophobia, anti-Semitism, and German frenzy were connected with it. Sand's teacher, Karl Follen, had forged a genuine small-scale revolutionary conspiracy at Giessen. A large segment of the German public made a hero out of Sand because he supposedly acted out of political conviction. Not even the Grand Duke of Saxe-Weimar, who had protected academic freedom at Jena, could tolerate the liberal nationalist programme; still less could the international community have allowed its ideas to be carried out in practice.[33]

In other words, Metternich did not have to whip up sentiment for repressing student radicalism in Germany; the movement itself invited it, and every German government favoured it. Many other leaders feared revolution more than Metternich did (Gentz, the Prussians, the Bavarians, even the French). It would have been easy to pass appropriate resolutions in the Bundestag to suppress the *Burschenschaften*, control the universities and the popular press, and bring negligent governments into line. Bavaria and Baden, whose troubles with their newly elected representative bodies seemed to confirm Metternich's predictions that modern constitutions and civil rights would destroy any monarchy experimenting with them, would have acquiesced. King Max and Crown Prince Ludwig even thought of revoking Bavaria's new charter.[34]

---

[32] Book-burning in that era, it should be noted, was only a dramatic way of expressing opposition to an author's ideas, not a call for censorship or repression.

[33] Siemann (1989: 88–94, 101–2); Büssem (1974: 47–67); Huber (1957: i. 696–732); Wegert (1978); Faber (1979: 260–1).

[34] Büssem (1974: 159–200); Chroust (1949–51: i. 212–18); Hammer (1963: 67–72). For the Grand Duke of Weimar's fight against Metternich, see Tümmler (1972).

The important point, therefore, is not that Metternich decided on the repression of radicalism and liberalism in Germany. In a sense, he had little choice in the matter. Other German governments wanted it as well, and other European governments, including Britain and France, were taking similar actions. It is that he directed his campaign, not mainly against specific revolutionary or liberal dangers, but against the whole constitutional movement, especially in Prussia, and conducted it in a way which perverted the Bund from its original purposes into an instrument for a repressive, specifically Austrian policy. The charge that Metternich, in defeating the nascent forces of liberalism and nationalism in 1819–20 so as to save Austria's position in Germany, created a road-block in the path of Germany's domestic political development may be true, but it emphasizes the less serious and durable effects of his actions. At best, he won only a limited and temporary victory over liberalism, nationalism, and constitutionalism; he may have slowed and distorted Germany's domestic-political development, but could not fully block it or even delay it long. He did worse and more permanent damage to the structure, purposes, and image of the German Confederation; a road he had himself helped open was now blocked, and remained closed.[35]

Yet ascribing this result to him personally is giving him too much blame and credit. He was feeling his way, he did not foresee and control everything, and he had much help. He met first with Frederick William of Prussia at Teplitz in late July, to draw up an anti-revolutionary programme for Germany, and then got this programme adopted by representatives of ten selected German states brought to Carlsbad in Bohemia in August. In both cases he anticipated more resistance than actually arose. At Teplitz he failed to get what he most wanted, a promise that Prussia would not adopt a constitution, but the King and Hardenberg readily agreed to repressive measures in Germany.[36] At Carlsbad Austria and Prussia met no serious obstacles either to their proposals or to the illegal procedure they were following (having resolutions privately drawn up by the great powers approved by a minority of the Bund's members before being rubber-stamped into federal law by the Diet). The four draft federal laws known as the Carlsbad Decrees provided for preventive press censorship in all

[35] For various appraisals of the Bund and its potential for development, see Büssem (1974: 466–773); Derndarsky (1982: 95–100); Heinz Gollwitzer (1964: 232–5); T. Schieder (1957); Gruner (1985: 73–6).
[36] Büssem (1974: 248–89); Baack (1980: 60–1).

German states, state supervision of university teaching, a federal Central Investigation Commission to co-ordinate information and action against subversives, and provisions to compel Bund members to conform to these decrees regardless of their individual laws or constitutions. Metternich was careful not to draw the bow too tight; Prussia and other states proposed stronger measures in certain areas than he.

But while the decrees went through easily at Carlsbad, Metternich did not succeed in using Article 13 to impose estate constitutions on all German states and to ban modern representative ones. Rechberg co-operated on the decrees despite his fears for Bavaria's sovereignty, but defended Bavaria's constitution (even though his King at that moment was willing to overthrow it) and succeeded in deferring the question to later ministerial conferences at Vienna.[37] After Carlsbad, the decrees were then rammed through the Bundestag without discussion in an illegal ratification process on 20 September, only the Holstein-Oldenburg delegate registering a reservation and the delegate for Württemberg, Baron Wangenheim, voicing a protest against the degradation of the Bundestag. Nor was there much trouble in getting individual states to publish the laws and enforce them. Bavaria, for example, chose to co-operate in substance while registering objections in principle to what it claimed was an extension of the powers of the Bundestag—another evidence that more damage was done to the Bund than to state sovereignty.[38]

The victory Metternich was most eager to win in 1820 was actually handed to him by his conservative allies in Prussia. A split between Hardenberg and the leading reformers, Humboldt and the war minister, Hermann von Boyen, leading to the latters' fall from office, gave dominant influence to conservatives in close touch with Metternich, Johann Ancillon in the foreign office and Prince Wittgenstein as minister of police. Under their pressure Frederick William repudiated his promise to grant a constitution, and Hardenberg accepted the defeat.[39]

Meanwhile, in Vienna, ministerial conferences held from

[37] Büssem (1974: 353–415); Huber (1957: i. 734–49); Quint (1971: 493–502); Burg (1989: 139–45). On the use of secret police for political repression in Germany generally, see Siemann (1985); Liang (1980); for Metternich's particular role in their development and use, see Mayr (1934).

[38] Büssem (1974: 418–51); Chroust (1939–42: i. Nos. 193–5, 214, 218, 233); Chroust (1949–51: i. 229–47).

[39] Koselleck (1967: 208–9, 284–332); Baack (1980: 34–40, 70–2); Büssem (1974: 228–47, 452–65); Simon (1955: 114–42); Sweet (1978: ii. 338–45); Branig (1981: chs. 8–10).

November 1819 to May 1820 produced a new Vienna Final Act of 65 articles, filling out and revised the Bund constitution, later rubber-stamped at Frankfurt like the Carlsbad Decrees. The revision of the Final Act was overall a triumph for the great retrograde movement, as Gentz proudly called it, yet it had its paradoxical aspects; it is easier to say that liberalism lost than to say who won. The Bund's powers over individual states were expanded in various ways for purposes of repression, and more power was concentrated in the narrow federal council of seventeen which Austria and Prussia could more easily dominate. Yet the Final Act also strongly affirmed the rights of member states and sovereigns, making it even more difficult for the Bundestag to develop into a representative German parliament. It reaffirmed every state's obligation to grant estate constitutions (a meaning-less requirement, since Austria and Prussia both ignored it) and guaranteed existing constitutions against change by uncon-stitutional means, while requiring all future constitutions to strengthen royal authority and grant only limited specific rights to assemblies. A Prussian attempt to reform the federal military constitution was defeated, as was Prussia's proposal of a formal defensive alliance between the confederation and Austria and Prussia in their capacity as European powers, intended to protect Prussia's eastern provinces outside the confederation. The federal military arrangements concluded in 1822 provided that no small-state troops would be placed under direct Austrian, Prussian, or Bavarian command, and that at the time of mobilization the Diet would choose the supreme commander—further guarantees for small-state particularism and military inefficiency.

Thus overall the revision tended to produce deadlock and stand-still more than movement backward. The Bund, once intended to develop in different directions, was now strengthened for political repression, blocked for progress, sealed off from the public, and used to carry out the main tenet of Metternich's political philos-ophy from now to the end of his life: that every legally existing thing must be preserved.[40]

A final episode in the resistance of middle states to great-power domination in the confederation, described later in connection with the European revolutions and interventions of 1820–3, provided a justification for renewing the Carlsbad Decrees in 1824. The Central Investigation Committee at Mainz proved inef-

[40] Huber (1957: i. 606–9, 630–83, 752–5); Baack (1980: 91–5); Seier (1986: 409–33); Werner (1977: 18–25, 31–45); Quint (1971: 502–4); Chodzko (1863: iv. 1789–1800).

fective either for investigating revolutionary activity or co-ordinating secret police work, but that made little difference. After 1820 the doldrums of the Biedermeier era characterized German political life.[41] The Bund retained its usefulness in the international system, keeping Germany strong and united enough for mutual defence but too weak and fragmented for offense. There was, in fact, little danger of Russian or French intervention to guard against. Russia was certainly not indifferent to German affairs, but it considered the Bund a valuable part of its buffer zone and of the conservative European alliance, and Austro-Prussian control over it as a good restraining partnership for both of them. Hence it repeatedly turned down appeals to intervene in German affairs, especially from Bavaria and Württemberg, telling these states instead to line up behind Austria and Prussia.[42] As for France, it hardly had a German policy worth the name. Paris ignored opportunities to revive France's political and economic influence in western and southern Germany, sometimes for practical reasons, often in the belief that France was intrinsically so attractive and influential that chances would always be there.[43]

This underscores the irony of this chapter in the history of the Bund. It was set up to protect the independence and security of the middle and small states, yet the middle states obstructed its development in its first years, when Austro-Prussian leadership was fairly moderate and flexible, and did little to save it later when that leadership turned domineering and repressive. Austria, which had helped create the confederation and was dependent on it for general peace and security and its own leadership in Germany, took the lead in undermining its capacity for develop-ment, at a time when the prevailing stability in international politics afforded a fairly safe chance for such development. The real threat for both the middle states and Austria was Prussian ambitions; yet these were precisely what their policies toward the Bund in the long run promoted. The Bund as it emerged in the 1820s helped protect Prussia in its current relative weakness, but was not sufficiently strong or solid to stop Prussia from developing independently of it, or to defend its members against

---

[41] Huber (1957: i. 765–6); Burg (1989: 162–78); Körner (1980: 328–38); Siemann (1980).

[42] Of many relevant documents in *VPR* (1960–: 2. i.), the ones best illustrating these attitudes are Nos. 185 and 199; see also Martens (1874–1905: viii. 218–22, 281–2; xi. 272–4).

[43] I base this verdict on a reading of the documents in Chroust (1935–9: i. 2–271); but see also Hammer (1963).

renewed Prussian expansion in the future, or to supply the general unity, political leadership, and economic progress that Germans increasingly came to want and that Prussia seemed to offer.

III. REVOLUTION IN SPAIN AND ITALY, 1820–1821

The revolutions in Spain, Italy, and the Balkans made more noise than events in Germany, but less difference. With the exception of the revolt in Greece, rather than opening up new possibilities in Europe or closing off existing ones, they merely made some unsatisfactory situations in Europe marginally worse.

In Italy, as Metternich recognized, such revolutionary danger as existed arose not from conspiratorial secret sects on the right and left or from widespread liberal movements, but from weak and inept regimes which failed to provide efficient, orderly government. Unfortunately, in some ways his own government was among them. Austrian rule in Lombardy-Venetia was the best in Italy in respect to legality, order, and concern for education and social welfare. Offsetting this was high taxation, 'Germanization' (meaning rule from Vienna by Austrian laws and officials, not compulsory use of the German language), and a slow, cumbersome administration. Other governments of Italy followed various styles of governing and staying in power. In Piedmont the regime attempted to wipe out the changes of the Napoleonic era, with only partial success. 'Live and let live' was the recipe in Tuscany and Parma. Archduke Francis at Modena was an arch-conservative and an ambitious intriguer; King Ferdinand of Naples followed the rule of *dolce far niente*. No regime was strong and secure.[44]

Nor did Austria, though responsible for defending these regimes, have really close relations with any, even the other Habsburg princes. There were no major quarrels, but plenty of negative attitudes: papal suspicions of Austria; Piedmontese fears and ambitions; a general resistance to Metternich's schemes for Italy (the *Lega Italica*, postal and customs unions, police co-operation and co-ordination against revolution, all designed to enhance Austrian control); and an ingrained dislike of many Italians for

[44] On Austria in Lombardy-Venetia, the basic works are Sandonà (1912); Rath (1969); but see also Rath (1941; 1950); Filipuzzi (1958a). For Italy in general, see Spellanzon (1933–51: ii); Woolf (1979: 226–55); and the literature cited in Schroeder (1962a); for the Papal State, Reinerman (1979: 30–42).

Germans, often cordially reciprocated by the Austrians.[45] Yet none of this meant too much in the international system, so long as France was excluded and Austria's leadership enjoyed the active support of Britain and the passive consent of Russia.

When revolution raised its head in Italy, it came by way of Spain. Here the root cause of revolt was fairly clear: the blighting political, economic, and social legacy of the revolutionary and Napoleonic wars. Spain's real, if limited, economic development in the eighteenth century had been reversed. The American revenues and trade on which both the government and the mainland economy depended were cut off; nascent centres of industry and trade in Catalonia, Valencia, and the Basque provinces ruined; much accumulated wealth carried off or destroyed; and Spanish agriculture undermined. The after-effects of the wars on politics and culture were almost as bad: deep divisions between 'collaborators' and 'patriots', with the reforming and modernizing officials who had promoted progress in the eighteenth century discredited and largely driven from public life; the politics of rhetoric and honour promoted at the expense of interest and consensus; a doctrinaire version of loyalty to God, king, and country made the national creed, with only an equally doctrinaire liberalism to oppose it; army officers seen as the real representatives of the national will, and a tradition of military intervention in politics launched.[46]

Worst of all, Spain after 1813 failed to achieve real peace. Ferdinand VII, though not highly endowed in intellect and character, wanted to heal Spain's wounds and was even willing to make some concessions to the new age and to revive the eighteenth-century tradition of royally inspired reform. The deeper problem was the wide gaps between what he was willing to grant, what some Spaniards wanted, and what his country needed; a more immediate one was that, with Spain's finances still devastated by war, European depression, and the loss of overseas revenues and trade, Ferdinand insisted on trying to reconquer Spain's empire in the Americas. How this effort affected international politics has to be discussed later. Its immediate consequence in January 1820 was a revolt among the troops being readied for another American expedition. The rising, a military coup rather than a broad movement, seemed at first likely to fizzle out. In March, however,

[45] *Rel. dipl. Aust.–Sard.* (1964–: 1. i. 128–541); see also Reinerman (1979: 44–9); O'Dwyer (1985: 199–207).
[46] Vicens Vives (1969: 602–3, 610–13); R. Carr (1966: 22–37, 49–51, 94–115); Coverdale (1984: 12–42); Barbier (1980); Esdaile (1988a: 199–200).

the conspirators gained control of the government. Ferdinand then surrendered to their demands, proclaiming the radical and impractical constitution of 1812, which gave real power to a unicameral, broadly elected Cortes. The revolution thus became an attempt by the military to impose a bourgeois constitutional monarchy on an unwilling sovereign and a backward country without the benefit of mass support or a viable middle class.[47]

The movement initially had little impact on European politics. The Tsar proposed a European conference to discuss what the allies should do about it. Castlereagh answered with a State Paper of 5 May 1820, arguing that any joint intervention was incompatible with the treaties and the purposes of the alliance. Castlereagh's arguments were circularized to the allies but not made public, and not really needed at this time. Other powers also opposed the idea of intervention. Metternich, absorbed in German affairs, expected the spectacle of Spanish radicalism to have a sobering effect on Russia and France, and did not think the revolt would spread.[48]

Unfortunately, it did spread to Naples in July 1820. The Neapolitan revolt was even more superficial than Spain's, the work of members of the secret sect of the Carbonari and army officers, and owed its success mainly to Ferdinand I's laziness and cowardice. The Neapolitan revolutionaries promptly adopted the Spanish Constitution, even more impractical for Naples than Spain, and made the king swear an oath to it.[49] The Two Sicilies were hardly closer to the heart of Europe than Spain and intrinsically less important, but Naples was Austria's satellite and ally. The revolution violated their treaty of June 1815 and endangered the whole labile edifice of Austrian hegemony in Central Europe, threatening to spread revolution and constitutionalism to northern Italy and Germany and raising the spectre of Russian or French intervention in Italy, or both. Metternich later said that had the Austrian army been ready he would have crushed the revolt immediately, consulting no one. This is a typical claim; he seldom showed such boldness, and was usually better off without it. What is true is that he never considered dealing with the revolution otherwise than by overthrowing it with Austrian forces.

---

[47] Coverdale (1984: 45–82); Payne (1973: i. 428–31); Christiansen (1967: 18–27); Martinez and Barker (1988: chs. 3–4).

[48] Webster (1925: 226–46); Bertier (1968–71: ii. 305–12).

[49] The principal documentary source for the Neapolitan revolution is Alberti (1926–41); Alberti's historical account is in vol. iv, pp. vii–cdx. See also Romani (1950); Schroeder (1962b: 30–41); Rath (1964).

He needed to prepare the ground for this, however, first in Italy. He sent a trusted lieutenant, Count Karl Ficquelmont, on a special mission to Piedmont, and checked also with Florence and Rome. Everywhere in Italy, as in Prussia and Germany, he enjoyed support from governments more frightened of the revolution than he, even if Turin and Rome worried that Austria might take advantage of its intervention in Naples for special Austrian purposes. The British government had no objection to Austria's intervening, though for diplomatic and parliamentary reasons Castlereagh could not say this publicly and wanted Austria to act quickly, quietly, unilaterally, and on the basis of its special rights as Naples's ally rather than on general anti-revolutionary grounds. Metternich said that Castlereagh's feelings about Austrian intervention were like those of a music-lover in church; he wished to applaud but dared not.

The difficulties lay with France and Russia. In France, Richelieu and the King's adviser, Count Pierre Blacas, an ultra-royalist, saw a chance here for France to check Austria, restore French influence in Italy, and draw closer to Russia. In addition, Richelieu feared that, if France did nothing while Austria triumphed, his ministry might fall in favour of his mildly liberal rival, Élie Duc Decazes. In Russia, a party led by Capodistrias also saw an opportunity to promote their vaguely liberal ideals in Europe, gain influence over Alexander at Nesselrode's expense, and assert Russian leadership in the alliance. Russia therefore backed France's call in August for a European congress on the Neapolitan revolution. The avowed purpose of the congress would be to support Austria's action, the unavowed one to control it. The proposal dismayed Austria and Britain alike. Metternich tried hard to dissuade the Tsar or get him to accept some substitute for a congress that would not alienate Castlereagh, to no avail.[50]

The Russo-French challenge to Austria's freedom of action was less formidable than it looked, however. The Spanish and Neapolitan revolts cured Alexander of any residual liberalism at the same time as they aroused his interventionist instincts. His instinctive horror at revolts by army officers against their sovereigns was intensified when a minor mutiny broke out in one of the crack guard regiments at St Petersburg in November 1820. Metternich soon saw his chance to exploit Alexander's ideas and impulses for his own counter-revolutionary policy. The French government, meanwhile, was paralyzed by rifts between ultras

[50] Webster (1925); Bertier (1968–71: ii. 320–47); Schroeder (1962b: 41–52).

and ministerials, by the possibility of a revolution or military coup at home (France also had discontented military officers and Carbonari), by distrust of the other four powers, and above all by the fear of being separated from Britain. The only thing the regime feared more than being isolated against the Holy Alliance was becoming aligned with the Holy Alliance against England. Moreover, the result, if France stopped Austria from crushing the Neapolitan revolution, might be that Britain, not France, would gain dominant influence at Naples.[51]

Therefore, while France backed away from its own congress proposal because Britain opposed it, Austria reluctantly accepted it because Russia insisted (another sign of the dual-hegemonic nature of the European system). The resultant conference (not a congress, because Britain and France were represented only by observers) met at Troppau in Austrian Silesia from October to early December, where Metternich could not only preside over it but also keep undesired visitors out and have his agents read everyone's mail. Dealt a strong hand, he played it skilfully. His main concern was to prevent any kind of mediation between Europe and the revolutionary regime at Naples. The French foreign minister, Baron Denis Pasquier, the French ambassador to Russia, Count Pierre-Louis de La Ferronnays, Pozzo di Borgo, and especially Capodistrias made various proposals that the four powers or the Pope mediate between Naples and Europe. The issue raised a storm in some of the conference sessions, but the outcome was never seriously in doubt. Alexander was soon persuaded by Metternich that any mediation or even hint of one would encourage revolution throughout Europe. In any case, there was really no one with whom to mediate at Naples, only craven and/or ferocious absolutists (King Ferdinand, his minister to Vienna, Prince Alvaro Ruffo, and his adviser, the Prince of Canosa) on one side and doctrinaire revolutionaries on the other, with some decent but hapless moderates in between.[52]

Austrian intervention was proclaimed and justified in the Troppau Protocol of 19 November, inspired by Alexander, accepted and exploited by Metternich, and jointly adopted by the three Eastern powers (often called the Holy Allies). It came to have considerable symbolic importance at this time and later. In justifying the intervention in Naples on the basis of a general right to save legitimate sovereigns from revolutions, supposedly

[51] Bertier (1968–71: ii. 347–57); Beyrau (1984: 186–97); Spitzer (1971).
[52] Bertier (1968–71: ii. 358–416); Schroeder (1962b: 52–80).

derived from the European alliance and the Vienna treaties, it laid
the foundation for the Holy Alliance doctrine of intervention and
provoked in return a counter-doctrine of non-intervention. The
doctrinal controversy and propaganda war would last for decades.
Castlereagh, forced to reply, repeated his arguments of May 1820
in a public circular of 21 January 1821, thus producing the first
open break between Britain and the Holy Alliance.

The controversy, however, had more ideological than immediate practical significance. The protocol itself subjected the right of
intervention to various conditions and escape clauses, meaning
in practical terms that the particular circumstances of each case
would decide whether the Holy Alliance powers would intervene
or not. This was as Metternich intended and what Austria always
did. He was eager here and at other times to pin Russia down
to his absolutist principles and to gain Russian support for any
actions Austria wanted, but not to give others, especially Russia,
a general sanction for similar actions. Moreover, the fact that
the sovereign whose rights were violated had to make a formal
request for intervention made the practical meaning and application of the doctrine even more unpredictable.[53]

It became clear that this last condition could pose a practical
difficulty when the conference resumed in January at Laibach
(Llubljana) in Austrian Slovenia. Ferdinand, invited to attend by
the Holy Alliance powers, obtained his captors' permission to
leave Naples by solemnly swearing to defend the Neapolitan
revolution and constitution. Once free, he repudiated his oath and
gladly accepted the first part of Metternich's program, the total
overthrow of the revolution by force. But Metternich also had
serious plans for Naples and Italy, designed both to prevent further
revolutions and to show Alexander and Europe that Austria's
aims were not purely repressive or reactionary. This part of
Metternich's programme called for Ferdinand, once the revolution
was overthrown, promptly to return to Naples to carry out a
series of 'reforms' under allied (i.e. Austrian) supervision, supposed to give sensible Neapolitans all they wanted and needed,
namely, good government and security for their property. The
same reforms would also be extended to all regimes in Italy. The
goal was to make Italy's governments legal and orderly in administration, fiscally sound, and efficient in rooting out subversion,
without concessions to liberalism, constitutionalism, or the repre-

---

[53] Ibid. 80–92; Webster (1925: 294–305); Bertier (1960); text of the protocol in
Martens (1874–1905: iv. 281–6).

sentative principle. Austria would supervise the changes with European backing.

Despite pressure from Metternich, Gentz, Prince Ruffo, and the Tsar, however, Ferdinand refused to promise to return to his kingdom and execute the programme Metternich had worked out for him, partly out of laziness, mainly out of fear for his life. Metternich and Gentz were finally forced to fabricate a series of non-existent conferences at which Ferdinand supposedly accepted the whole programme and authorized Austria to intervene at Naples with armed force. At the same time, Metternich easily defeated some feeble last-minute Russian and French proposals for a mediation between Europe and Naples to save Naples some form of a constitution. The Pope willingly condemned the revolution and the sects behind it, and more reluctantly agreed to allow Austrian troops to cross his territory to overthrow it. To meet the costs of the campaign, which had led Austria's finance minister, Prince Stadion, to oppose the intervention on fiscal grounds, the House of Rothschild loaned Austria the money for the campaign and agreed also to lend the restored Neapolitan government (at ruinous rates of interest) the funds with which to repay Austria for the campaign and the succeeding occupation.[54]

Just when the way seemed clear for Austria to intervene without European control or restrictions, revolt broke out in Piedmont. Metternich had been keeping his eye on Turin, but more to check France and gain support for his future programme in Italy than out of fear of a revolution. Though the Piedmontese government did not object to an Austrian intervention in Naples, the Austrian envoy at Turin and the Austrian commander in Lombardy, Count Ferdinand Bubna, were worried by student clashes with the authorities in Piedmont and Lombardy in January, and especially by Piedmont's using its troops to suppress the disorder.[55] Despite their fears that disaffection would spread to the army, it was a severe shock to Vienna that on 10 March a part of the Piedmontese army rose under one of its generals, Santorre de Santarosa, seized the fortress of Alessandria, and called on King Victor Emmanuel to grant a constitution and lead the country in saving Italy from the Austrians. With panic spreading among royalists and loyal

[54] Schroeder (1962b: 92–111); Bertier (1968–71: ii. 417–73); Reinerman (1979: 77–90; 1968); Gille (1965: i. 88–97); Crawley (1970: 49–51).

[55] The major work on the Piedmontese revolution is Rossi and de Magistris (1927); in it, see Rinieri (1927); Colombo (1927) for the developments discussed here. For a brief account, see Nada (1980: 27–33); for documentation, *Rel. dipl. Aust.–Sard.* (1964–: 1. ii. 93–147); and *Rel. dipl. GB–Sard.* (1972–: 1. i. 305–417).

army leaders, the Turin government immediately appealed to Austria for help.

The danger, however, receded as quickly as it had arisen. In Naples, the revolution the Piedmontese rising was supposed to rescue collapsed ignominiously in the face of the Austrian invasion. At Turin, King Victor Emmanuel decided to abdicate in favour of his brother, Charles Felix, rather than grant a constitution or fight Austria. Much of the Piedmontese army failed to join the rising, and Victor Emmanuel's son and heir, the Duke of Carignan (later King Charles Albert), on whom the insurrectionists counted in his temporary role as regent, proved a broken reed. Neither Metternich nor Count Bubna was keen to intervene in Piedmont, fearing a hostile public reaction in Italy and Europe and a further spread of the revolt. Some diplomatic representatives at Turin were, as usual, more eager for action than their governments were. The Russian minister, Count Mocenigo, urged his government to mediate to forestall an Austrian intervention; the French, Count La Tour du Pin, pleaded with Paris to support the rising. But Russia relieved Metternich's fears by giving Austria such prompt and total support that Metternich suggested (for purely tactical reasons) that Russia intervene in Piedmont rather than Austria. The French silently stood by while loyal Piedmontese troops, aided by an Austrian contingent, quelled the insurrection in early April, with Austrian troops then staying on in a partial occupation. When Austria failed to persuade Victor Emmanuel to withdraw his abdication, his brother took the throne to deal with the aftermath of the revolt. Charles Felix's rigid absolutist principles pleased Metternich; his suspicious and stubbornly independent spirit did not.

One bright spot in this otherwise unedifying picture is that Austria did not revert to some aspects of its late eighteenth-century policy, Neapolitan and Piedmontese fears that it would use its intervention to try to annex territory, or gain control of strong points in Piedmont, or even exclude the Duke of Carignan, badly compromised in the revolt, from eventual succession to the throne all proved groundless. Austria's characteristic post-1815 weaknesses, however, showed up along with its new virtues. Financially precarious itself, it insisted on full payment from both countries for all the expenses of intervention, which Stadion calculated generously and the army inflated, so that ultimately Austria made a profit from intervention. It also tried to supervise the anti-revolutionary reorganization of Piedmont as well as Naples. Haggling over these issues between Vienna and Turin lasted into the late summer of 1821; between Vienna and Naples, to 1827. Meanwhile refugees from both Italian revolutions gathered in Switzerland and elsewhere to keep their cause alive.[56]

This meant that the suppression of the Neapolitan and Piedmontese revolts, while ending the immediate threat to Metternich's system in Italy, left its endemic problems unsolved or marginally worse and did Austria's general reputation no good. Yet this did not mean that Italy rejected Austrian hegemony; the governments were as anti-revolutionary as Austria, besides which the wide acceptance of the primacy of international politics and the need for peace made Austrian leadership seem indispensable. As one German observer remarked, 'Precisely in the middle of Europe there must be states that cannot conquer.'[57]

IV. THE GREEK REVOLT AND
THE RUSSO-TURKISH CRISIS, 1821–1823

Meanwhile a graver challenge to the Holy Alliance, the international system, and the general peace was rising in the East. The uprisings of 1821 in the Danubian (Romanian) Principalities of Moldavia and Wallachia and in Greece grew not so much out of Ottoman misrule in the Balkans as out of non-rule, the condition of pervasive lawlessness and frequent rebellions over the whole region. The Sultan, having little effective control of his far-flung empire, one which in principle had always let non-Muslims largely govern themselves, often dealt with revolts by co-opting certain rebels and using them against others. The Rumanian Principalities were in theory autonomous under Ottoman suzerainty; their traditional privileges were protected under the Russo-Turkish Treaty of Bucharest of 1812. But this did not help the great peasant majority of the population, ground down by large landlords (boyars) and governed and exploited by Phanariot Greek officials (i.e. Greeks from the Phanar or lighthouse district of Constantinople) under Christian hospodars (governors) nominated by the Sultan and approved by Russia.

Turkish rule in Greece, nominally direct, was actually dispersed

---

[56] Bertier (1968–71: 475–509); Schroeder (1962b: 121–63). The main documentary source for Austro-Neapolitan relations after the revolution is Moscati (1937). On Piedmont, see Nada (1980: 33–9); *Rel. dipl. Aust.–Sard.* (1964–: 1. ii. 148–337); *Rel. dipl. GB–Sard.* (1972–: 1. i. 338–417); *VPR* (1960–: 2. iv. Nos. 26, 41, 108); Obermann (1966), for Count Ficquelmont's reports to Metternich.

[57] Altgeld (1984: 36–50) (the quotation is on p. 40).

through local authorities and constantly defied by bandits and chieftains, the most famous and successful being Ali Pasha of Janina, effective ruler for many years of large parts of Epirus and Albania. An economic, cultural, and political renaissance had begun among a minority of Greeks, the effect partly of the Enlightenment and the French Revolution on European-educated Greeks, partly of Greek experience of self-rule under British protection in the Ionian Islands. Along with Jews, Greeks constituted the commercial class of the Ottoman Empire. Among Greeks of the Diaspora, especially in Russia, a small but active nationalist organization called the *Philike Eteria* had grown up since 1814, part cultural and propaganda movement, part secret conspiratorial society. Religion was more important as a source of identity in the Balkans than ethnicity or language. In both Greece and western Anatolia, Orthodox Greek and Muslim lived side by side, deeply divided and hostile, with taxation, landowning, and legal status largely determined by religious community. Even more powerful a factor than religious differences and legal inequality in paving the way to armed revolt was the fact that Greece, especially in the mountains, teemed with armed bands, half bandits, half irregular soldiers (*klephts* and *armatoloi*) led by local chieftains, for whom fighting was a way of life.

Yet a mass revolt was not inevitable. The Orthodox hierarchy under Patriarch Grigorios at Constantinople served the Sultan loyally according to the Byzantine theocratic tradition; Greek Catholics, a substantial minority in the Ionian Islands, were hostile to the Orthodox; many Greeks, including the Phanariots, occupied privileged positions in the Empire; most peasants were too ignorant and downtrodden to rebel; and Greek life was too riddled with factions to unite behind any movement.[58]

It therefore took a combination of conspiracies and accidents, which can only be sketched here, to touch things off. With Sultan Mahmud occupied in trying to destroy Ali Pasha, Aleksandr Ipsilantis, a Russian general and former aide to the Tsar who now led the *Eteria*, saw the chance to launch a revolt somewhere in the Balkans—Serbia, Moldavia and Wallachia, or Greece. Wherever it was started, he hoped from it to produce a war between Turkey and Russia. With the Christian Balkan peoples joining in and Ali acting as a diversion, the war would destroy the Ottoman Empire

---

[58] Clogg (1973), esp. the essays by R. Clogg, G. Frangos, C. Mango, D. Dakin, and P. Sherrard; Jelavich (1984: 21–4); Dakin (1973: 67–79); Frazee (1969: 37–69); Runciman (1968: 408–9); Wrigley (1988: 68–105).

and liberate Greeks everywhere. His plans also reckoned with a rebellion headed by Tudor Vladimirescu, a wealthy-boyar in western Wallachia, though Vladimirescu's movement was not anti-Sultan but directed against corrupt and oppressive boyars and Phanariot Greek officials. Ipsilantis, encouraged by Vladirimescu's movement and hoping to gain Ali Pasha as an ally, dropped the earlier *Eteria* plan to start the rising in the Morea (Greece south of the Isthmus of Corinth). Instead, on 6 March he invaded Moldavia from Bessarabia with a small armed force, proclaiming himself the advance guard of a liberating Russian army and calling on Christians everywhere to rise. He received some initial support in Moldavia, whose hospodar was attached to the *Eteria*, but then everything went wrong. His reception in Wallachia was so cool that he hesitated before occupying it. Then Vladirimescu began negotiating with the Turks, whereupon Ipsilantis had him arrested and executed. The fatal blow fell when the Tsar publicly denounced his movement, cashiered him, and authorized the Porte to send in troops to crush the rising. At Laibach, Capodistrias, strongly pro-Greek but not a member of the *Eteria* and opposed to the conspiracy, had the painful duty of drawing up an allied declaration condemning the revolt. By 10 April the Turks had dispersed the rebel forces; Ipsilantis fled to Austria, where he was interned and ultimately died in exile.

While Ipsilantis's movement went up in smoke, something more profound was breaking out in the Morea—a revolt of the Greek military class, sparked when Christian Souliots rose in the north and Turkish authorities attempted to stamp out plots discovered in the Morea by summary arrests and executions. The revolt spread with elemental fury, the populace joining the *klephts* and *armatoloi* out of a mixture of enthusiasm and fear. By early April, 15,000 of the 40,000 Turks in the Morea had been killed, and some of the Greek islands were also in flames.[59]

Despite the fact that Alexander promptly and publicly condemned the rebels and gave his consent to a Turkish occupation of the Principalities as required by the Treaty of Bucharest, tension between the Ottoman Empire and Russia rose ominously. The Turks, not surprisingly, believed that the Tsar and the Russian government were behind the conspiracy. Capodistrias was innocent on this score, but like most Russians he sympathized with the

---

[59] Clogg (1973), esp. the articles by E. D. Tappe and C. M. Woodhouse; Dakin (1973: 41–69); Koliopoulos (1989); Petropoulos (1976), esp. the essay by D. Skiotis. On the general theme of brigandage and Greek politics, see Petropoulos (1976); Koliopoulos (1987).

Greek cause, and along with Ipsilantis some Russian agents in the Principalities had been complicit in the revolt. The Russian ambassador, Stroganov, and other Russian representatives in Turkey denounced Turkish atrocities while ignoring or minimizing those of the Greeks; even a conservative like Nesselrode treated the Turks as a lesser breed beyond the law.

Ottoman resentment was thus understandable, but the Porte's actions were illegal and bound to intensify the quarrel. After the insurrection was quelled, Turkish troops remained in occupation of the Principalities, while the Sultan refused to nominate new hospodars to replace the old ones compromised in the revolt— violating Russian treaty rights in both instances. Turkey also interfered with Russian trade through the straits, allowed Greek and Russian property to be destroyed at Constantinople, and committed atrocities which, if less extensive than those of the Greeks, were more spectacular—for example, publicly executing the Patriarch of Constantinople in degrading fashion and violating and burning churches in the Morea. The excesses were predictable given the rebels' atrocities, the reactions among Muslims, the support most of the lesser Orthodox clergy in Greece gave the insurrection, and, above all, the Sultan's lack of enough disciplined troops to deal simultaneously with Ali Pasha, the Principalities, and a savage civil war in Greece. But none of this counted as an excuse at St Petersburg; after a barrage of protests and recriminations, Russia broke relations with Turkey in July 1821.[60]

This was by far the worst crisis to hit Europe since 1815. Everyone believed that a Russo-Turkish war would destroy the Ottoman Empire in Europe. Even if war were avoided, a prolonged Near Eastern crisis would endanger a key element of the system, the continued coexistence of Britain and Russia on fairly good but not intimate terms, neither close allies nor open enemies. Already Russian leaders, from Capodistrias down to Russia's consular agents in the Ottoman Empire, were blaming Turkish intransigence on the British, especially the British ambassador at Constantinople, Viscount Strangford, while Strangford and other British opponents of Russia warned London about Russia's encroachments on Turkey. A Near Eastern crisis also created temptations and dangers for France. Richelieu was opposed to more war or revolution, but a strong party headed by the aged King's brother and presumptive heir, the Count of Artois, was

[60] Jelavich (1984: 24–6); Frazee (1969: 21, 40–5, 64); Puryear (1941: 18–21, 25–9); VPR (1960–: 2. iv. Nos. 5–6, 23–4, 31, 42–3, 49, 57–8, 63, 78, 83, 85).

eager for war between Russia and Turkey so that the 1815 settlement could be overthrown, with France gaining something out of
the resultant mêlée. If Richelieu remained inactive or, worse, co-
operated too much with Austria to prevent war, he could easily
find himself overthrown by the Ultras. That Austria was horrified
at the prospect of a Russo-Turkish war goes without saying.[61]

From July 1821 into the spring of 1822 Europe lived in expectation of a war, with many leading Russians looking forward
to it and most Europeans fearing it. Britain and Austria worked
together at St Petersburg and Constantinople to prevent it, but the
arguments and weapons they had at their disposal were limited.
Metternich constantly warned the Turks of inexorable disaster if
they failed to meet their treaty obligations, and even more constantly exhorted Alexander to remember that the Greeks were
part of a universal revolutionary conspiracy centred at Paris, and
that the first shot fired between Russia and Turkey would send
Europe up in flames. But he could not reinforce these admonitions
with even a hint of a break with Russia or open opposition to its
policy. The strongest warning he gave was an intimation that
under certain circumstances Austria might not give Russia its full
moral support. Moreover, he was compelled not merely to admit
but to stress that Russia had the treaties on its side. For his main
argument to restrain Russia was that Russia could legitimately
require the Turks to fulfil their treaty obligations, though it should
allow for the Sultan's difficulties, but that it had no right to go
beyond the treaties and use force for the sake of the Greeks, no
matter how humanitarian its aims.

As for Britain, it had no coercive weapons either, beyond a
refusal to commit itself and hints that it would remain neutral
and maintain relations with the Porte should Russia go to war.
The combination of Austrian pleas and British menacing silence
reminds one of the 'good cop, bad cop' technique familiar to
readers of American crime novels; but neither of the two had
any sanctions to apply, legal or otherwise. Too open an Anglo-
Austrian co-operation against Russia, moreover, could prove
counter-productive. A joint strategy meeting between Castlereagh
and Metternich at Hanover in October prompted Alexander to
resume his old courtship of France, offering or hinting at a Russo-
French alliance that might bring France territorial gains in Belgium
or the Morea. The French ambassador, La Ferronnays, urged his

---

[61] Bertier (1968–71: ii. 511–48); *VPR* (1960–: 2. iv. Nos. 45, 47, 81, 87);
Crawley (1970: 48–9).

government to follow this up. Though Richelieu and Pasquier declined to do so, Richelieu's ministry fell in December in favour of an Ultra one headed by Baron Joseph de Villèle, with Mathieu Viscount Montmorency as foreign minister. As it happened, Villèle's shrewdness and caution and Montmorency's devotion to absolutist principles kept them from entering into partnership with Russia; still, the change added a new uncertainty to the picture.

While the Turks held out stubbornly against concessions to Russia, the insurrection ground on in Greece, its atrocities multiplying. This helped to focus the international crisis not on Turkish treaty violations in the Principalities, where the issues were definable and inherently soluble, but on Greece and the right Russia claimed to protect Greek Christians from Turkish barbarism. This right, claimed by Russia on a dubious and dangerous interpretation of its treaties with the Sultan as well as on general grounds of humanity, created a diplomatic issue without bounds or hope of peaceful solution. Within the Russian government, the opponents of war seemed to be losing. Nesselrode, an opponent of war on conservative European grounds, found his position shaky, and his father-in-law, the finance minister, Count Gurev, who opposed it for fiscal reasons, lost his office, as did others of Nesselrode's associates. The Russians knew that a war would not be child's play—the Balkans were a terrible military theatre logistically—but no Russian feared the final outcome. Worst of all, in contrast to most other Eastern crises, this time the Turks had no real allies or friends in Europe and Russia had little or no international opposition to fear. No government was willing to act against Russia, or really able to; Berlin actually sympathized with its aims. Moreover, the rise of a broad European philhellenic movement with roots in Europe's classical and Christian traditions, predominantly religious-humanitarian in form in Prussia, Germany, and France and more political in Britain, made important segments of the public favour a Russian intervention in support of the Greeks.[62]

The actions and influence of Metternich and Castlereagh certainly helped prevent a Russo-Turkish war in 1821-2, but the real credit belongs to Alexander. Whatever pressures from outside may have contributed to the restraint he displayed, its main source

[62] Driault and Lhéritier (1925: i. 149-73); Dakin (1973: 63-5); Gritzbach (1974: i. 310-16); Bertier (1968-71: ii. 511-60); Heydemann (1989); Stoneman (1984); Nesselrode (1904-12: vi. 113-17, 119-24); Hammer (1963: 106-13); VPR (1960-: 2. iv. Nos. 84, 103, 115, 120, 127, 140, 148).

was his own European principles. Like most Russians, he favoured the Greeks and despised the Turks, but he insisted on getting a European mandate for action like Austria's in Naples, because to act unilaterally would undermine his great achievement, the European alliance. He failed or refused to see (Capodistrias pointed it out to him often enough) that in the Near East the alliance's function was to hold Russia back.

The turning-point came when, in February 1822, the Tsar sent a trusted adviser, Count Dmitri Tatishchev, to Vienna to work out the terms which Austria was to present to the Porte on Russia's behalf, terms which would mean war if rejected or evaded by the Turks. Metternich boasted that this mission and its outcome proved the effectiveness of his propaganda and his personal ascendancy over the Tsar; this had some basis, but was not strictly true. Alexander knew perfectly well what Metternich wanted to do, i.e. tie him up by his own principles. In his instructions to Tatishchev he stuck to Russia's claims and demanded that Europe, or at least Austria and Prussia, support Russia if Turkey's stubbornness compelled Russia to go to war. Tatishchev expected Metternich to cave in, and Gentz feared that he would. But Alexander had left openings in Russia's case for Metternich to exploit. While persisting in all his demands, the Tsar tacitly admitted much of Metternich's case: his distinction between Russia's treaty rights which, if unfulfilled, gave it just cause for war, and Russia's humanitarian demands for the restoration of churches and better treatment of the Sultan's rebellious subjects, which did not constitute a *casus belli* and which Russia could not expect Turkey entirely to fulfil so long as the rebellion continued. Alexander also tacitly conceded his inability to specify just how the Ottoman Empire, supposedly rotten to the core, could be reformed to fulfil Russia's humanitarian demands, and he failed to answer Metternich's argument that no one should dictate to a legitimate sovereign how he must deal with his rebellious subjects.

Metternich, the self-styled coachman of Europe, drove his coach and four through these openings. Out of his struggle with Tatishchev at Vienna and Capodistrias at St Petersburg emerged an Austro-Russian agreement which enabled the Tsar to declare victory and pull back from war. Austria would present Russia's demands at Constantinople that the Sultan fulfil his treaty obligations *vis-à-vis* Russia in the Principalities; if the Sultan continued to refuse this, Russia could go to war and Austria would give its moral support. But if the Sultan complied with these demands within a reasonable time, Russia would renew relations with the

Porte, meanwhile entrusting its humanitarian demands on behalf of the Greeks to Europe, which would enforce them by diplomatic pressure on the Turks. Capodistrias drew the obvious conclusion and took indefinite leave from his office in June 1822, commenting bitterly that with friends like Austria Russia did not need enemies.

Metternich's victory amounted to no more than crisis management and buying time. The Greek issue was only postponed, initially to a Vienna conference in September 1822. Metternich subsequently had to fight just as hard to avert war and restore normal Russo-Turkish relations, and the efforts repeatedly threatened to break down. None the less, the immediate crisis had been managed without overt coercion of the Ottoman Empire and without the use of threats against Russia, even diplomatic ones. This was a remarkable triumph of diplomacy over the use of force. The Tsar was not primarily motivated by fear that the revolution would spread through Europe into Russia, as one might suppose. Metternich, of course, warned of this constantly, but his sermons on this theme irritated even conservatives like Nesselrode in St Petersburg, and his opponents answered by saying that the way to prevent more revolution was to force the Sultan to govern more humanely—a view Alexander once held in regard to Europe in general and still held in regard to the Balkans.

In short, Alexander in 1822 acted mainly to save the European alliance, and for this purpose was willing to forego the likely gains of a legally justified war and to accept the risk that Russia's influence would decline and that of Britain and Austria rise in the Near East. Capodistrias and La Ferronnays criticized his policy precisely on this ground. Believers in power politics (for some reason often called 'realists') sometimes ask rhetorically to be shown an instance where a state has foregone concrete material advantages for the sake of moral principle. There are many answers; but the easiest and simplest is, 'Russia under Alexander I in 1822'.[63]

V. VIENNA, VERONA, AND FRENCH INTERVENTION IN SPAIN, 1822–1823

In retrospect, one sees that the conferences held at Vienna and Verona in the latter part of 1822 did not accomplish much. The

[63] Schroeder (1962b: 185–94); Grimsted (1969: 253–65); *VPR* (1960–: 2. iv. Nos. 153, 157, 159, 164–5, 171, 173, 175, 178–9); Martens (1874–1905: iv. 304–13); Crawley (1970: 52–6).

powers put off one issue, Greece; put the lid back on another, Italy; and temporarily held up action on a third, Spain. Even the French intervention in Spain which followed Verona did little to alter the course of international politics. Yet the meetings had some results worth noting, and they tie into a development which did change the world political scene, the rise of Latin American independence.

The conference at Verona itself developed accidentally out of changes of plan. It had been called originally to deal solely with Italy: to review how Turin, Naples, and the other Italian governments were carrying out the anti-revolutionary 'reforms' Metternich was urging on them. First its venue was changed from Florence in Tuscany, where Metternich claimed dangerous influences would be at work, to Verona, where Austria's secret police could keep them out. Then a preliminary ministerial conference was scheduled for Vienna so that Castlereagh, who refused to discuss Italian affairs, could come to help promote peace between Russia and Turkey in the current Eastern crisis. Castlereagh, however, committed suicide in August. His old rival, George Canning, became foreign secretary and Wellington was appointed chief British delegate to Vienna, with resultant delays that kept him from reaching Vienna until 29 September, by which time the others were impatient to move to Verona.

In the mean time the Vienna conference, supposed to deal with the Russo-Turkish quarrel, became mired in Anglo-Russian wrangling. Strangford failed to persuade the Turks to send plenipotentiaries to deal with Russia on issues concerning the Principalities or to wrest other concessions from them, and had as little success defending the Ottoman position at Vienna. Still, the danger of a Russo-Turkish war grew no worse, and Metternich succeeded in excluding representatives of the Greek cause from Vienna and later from Verona.[64]

Not much more was accomplished on the Italian question when the conference moved to Verona. Metternich's aim, as noted, was to make the governments in Italy more efficient and orderly, especially at Naples and Rome, and to create Austrian-led joint institutions in Italy to combat revolution and liberalism as in Germany. He had already gained considerable control of Italy's postal system and persuaded the Pope publicly to condemn the sects, and now sought a central investigation commission com-

---

[64] Driault and Lhéritier (1925: i. 177–95); Nichols (1971: 48–53); Reinerman (1968); *VPR* (1960–: 2. iv. Nos. 182, 197–8, 202).

parable to the one at Mainz. But the suspicion of Austrian motives prevailing at Naples, Rome, and elsewhere, plus the general lethargy of Italian governments, blocked his campaign for administrative reforms, and opposition from the Papal State and Tuscany, encouraged by France and ultimately joined by Piedmont, killed the idea of a central investigation committee. Verona, therefore, produced only a set of pious declarations by the various governments.[65] Metternich largely abandoned his reform effort now; the revolts of 1830-2 would give him another chance.

Even success in his effort, however, would not have meant much. The remedy Metternich proposed for revolution was not only inadequate and superficial but also self-contradictory. Making Italian governments more efficient by, among other things, bringing the more educated and enlightened subjects of the various princes into the tasks of administration, would also mean ultimately making these governments more independent of Austria and promoting calls among these enlightened citizens for emancipation and representative government, which neither Austria nor the absolutist governments it was protecting could tolerate. Moreover, Austria was unable to make its political leadership in Italy more palatable by providing economic benefits and leadership (for example, a customs union or more free trade). Instead, while insisting on the repayment of every florin of its occupation costs from Turin and more than its due from Naples, Vienna tried to stop Piedmont from developing its trade and communications wherever Lombard interests would be affected. This negative, hold-the-line Austrian stance was even more pronounced in regard to France. Metternich discovered to his surprise during 1822 that the Villèle government in France was more safely conservative than its predecessor, and so began working with France to prevent war and check Russia in the Near East.[66] But in Italy both powers persisted in their sterile competition.

Anyway, it had become clear before the Verona congress convened that Spain rather than Italy would be the real issue. In April 1822 Ferdinand VII appealed to Alexander for a European army to rescue him. The appeal, coming just when the Tsar had agreed to forego action against the Turks for the sake of the alliance, revived his desire for joint European action. Metternich alleged that Pozzo and Capodistrias had incited it to recover their lost influence over

---

[65] Reinerman (1979: 91-113; 1971); Tamborra (1960); Furlani (1948; 1960; 1978); Moscati (1937: vol. i, pp. xviii-xxvii); *Rel. dipl. GB-Sard.* (1972-: 1. ii. Nos. 1-110); *Rel. dipl. Aust.-Sard.* (1964-: 1. ii. Nos. 157-210).

[66] Bertier (1968-71: ii. 560-607).

the Tsar and to make him break with his allies when, as anticipated, these allies once again rejected his plans.[67] This was a
reasonable inference as to the proposal's likely effects, but unfair
to Capodistrias, who in fact was retiring from active office at this
time. Alexander was still his own foreign minister with his own
ideas of what should be done, some of them more dangerous than
those of Capodistrias. For example, he thought that a European
army sent to Spain might prove useful in bringing the political
crisis in France to a boil, so that the incipient revolution could be
crushed there as well.

Besides, Spain did seem to demand attention. After an unsuccessful royalist coup in 1822, the Cortes remained in control of the
central government and the king, but in the north an absolutist-
clerical government was set up at Urgel near the French border,
which declared itself a regency on behalf of Ferdinand and appealed
to France and the other powers for money, arms, and intervention. Volunteers from France slipped across to serve with the
liberal forces while royalists aided the regency at Urgel. Most of
the Ultras, including the foreign minister, Montmorency, and
Monsieur, the Count of Artois, were eager for war, but Villèle
held back and Louis XVIII supported him. Meanwhile Canning
was determined to block any European action in Spain, especially
by France.[68]

Thus there were ample possibilities for trouble, but also good
chances for Metternich's aim and speciality, creating a deadlock
and calling it peace. The French assisted him by sending a badly
divided delegation to Verona. Montmorency wanted Holy Alliance support for a French intervention in Spain. Two other
delegates, however, La Ferronnays and the famous author who
was then ambassador to Britain, the Vicomte de Chateaubriand,
wanted France to act independently to enhance its prestige, while
the ambassador at Vienna, the Marquis de Caraman, agreed with
Metternich that France should not act in Spain because this would
increase the risk of revolution at home.

Villèle had still other ideas. Convinced that Metternich was
trying to lure France into intervention in Spain under Holy Alliance control, he instructed Montmorency to reserve France's full
freedom of action while at the same time securing back-up from
the allies in case France decided to act and Britain tried to stop
her. Montmorency's instructions may have been impossible to

---

[67] Ibid. 596–8.
[68] Schroeder (1962*b*: 195–211); Bertier (1968–71: ii. 614–18).

execute; in any case he disobeyed them, asking the allies to state how they would respond to each of three possible courses of action France might take. This gave Metternich his opening. He played Russia's fears of French instability off against France's fears of Russian intervention, and parried Russia's demand that the Spanish revolution be overthrown with Britain's insistence that Spain be left alone, coming out with a decision that only appeared to represent united action by Europe. The four Continental powers would apply joint moral and diplomatic pressure to bring down the revolutionary regime in Spain without armed intervention, either French or allied. A four-power resolution at Verona called for a simultaneous break in relations with Spain. The Holy Alliance powers pledged that they would support French military action if Spain responded to the break by attacking France, overthrowing the Spanish throne, or attacking the Spanish royal family (all unlikely contingencies). A revived ambassadorial conference at Paris would discuss what action should be taken after the break in relations. Unfortunately for Metternich, while preventing French intervention in Spain by tying up both France and Russia in loud-sounding inaction, he had misled Wellington, the British delegate, into believing that the four powers would take no action at all. The Duke, surprised and embarrassed at the congress resolution, protested strongly against it, and the British government formally broke with the four powers over the issue. Metternich regretted this outcome but considered it unavoidable; Gentz derided Wellington for having let himself be deceived.[69]

Metternich's paper triumph, however, quickly came apart. Villèle was determined that the Holy Alliance must neither push France into action (the opposite of what Metternich was trying to do) nor control whatever action France took (precisely Metternich's intention). Villèle first repudiated Montmorency's action at Verona, insisting that the allies' notes to Spain breaking diplomatic relations be postponed. Metternich would have gone along with the French request rather than let France loose from Holy Alliance control, but Alexander insisted on the three powers' proceeding with the action they had resolved on. Villèle then refused to let France break relations with Spain, and won a decisive contest in late December with Montmorency over the issue; Montmorency resigned.

[69] Ibid. 619–48; Nichols (1971: 84–136); Chateaubriand (1838: i. 111–26); Schroeder (1962b: 211–21). Wellington's correspondence is in Wellington (1862–80: i. 319–611); Temperley (1925a: 72–5) discusses Canning's reaction to the congress.

The victory, however, was a pyrrhic one. Montmorency's successor Chateaubriand, a favourite of the Ultras and Count Artois, was Villèle's rival, ambitious to control French policy and ultimately to take over the ministry. Villèle found himself increasingly isolated. Rumours began to spread of a French invasion of Spain and of liberal plots and Carbonarist conspiracy in the French army; the more the liberals in the Chamber of Deputies condemned intervention and the British opposed it, the more the rightists and the army grew enthusiastic and warlike. The British tried everything to hold the French back, offering to mediate, trying to get the Spaniards to change their constitution, warning France of the dire military and political consequences of war, and attempting, while declaring British neutrality, to rouse French fears of possible British action in Spain or elsewhere. Canning's bluff only played into Chateaubriand's hands, helping him secure ostentatious support from Russia against a phantom menace from Britain. Independently of the Holy Alliance, France in late January and February delivered Spain an ultimatum, broke relations, and declared war, French troops crossing the frontier in late March.[70]

This was a galling but insubstantial defeat for Canning; he would have chances later for revenge. Metternich felt more threatened. He viewed Chateaubriand and Canning as equally dangerous, both of them being capable of setting Europe aflame for the sake of personal popularity and power, and saw real risks in France's action and its resultant quarrel with Britain. As Metternich liked to say, an ambitious France, royalist or not, was a revolutionary France, and he knew that Chateaubriand sought a Franco-Russian alliance against Britain and Austria. The French intervention, besides destroying Metternich's hopes that the Spanish revolution would burn itself out without disturbing Central Europe, also made it very likely that the Anglo-French quarrel would spread from the Iberian peninsula, where Britain's ally Portugal had also undergone a revolution in 1821, to Latin America, where Portugal's colony Brazil had joined the Spanish colonies in revolution. The rest of Europe might be dragged into the struggle.

These dangers, plus the fear that the French would reach a compromise with the revolutionaries and retain a constitution in Spain, explain Metternich's repeated moves through the spring and early summer of 1823 to gain control of France's action in Spain. All were ineffective and some were absurd, the silliest being

[70] Nichols (1971: 286–315); Bertier (1968–71: ii. 660–710); Spitzer (1971: 197–200); Chateaubriand (1838: i. 177–9, 245–73, 289–316, 424–30, 463–77).

his effort to persuade the French government and the Spanish royalists to make Ferdinand of Naples regent of Spain until Ferdinand VII was liberated. The British also attempted to mediate in Spain, with equal futility. The French intervention was a political and military success, overcoming just enough Spanish resistance to give the army and regime some glory and to raise French morale. Moreover, France, unlike Austria, paid for its own military campaign rather than collect the costs from those it liberated. French troubles in Spain arose not from its foes but from its clients, first the regency and other royalists, and then Ferdinand himself. Restored to power, he ignored all French advice, and though the French army stayed in Spain until 1827 it never established secure French influence or control.[71]

Still, the intervention helped to restore France's international position and self-confidence and reconcile the army and people to the Bourbon regime.[72] It is also supposed to have weakened the 1815 system, by deepening the breach between Britain and the Holy Alliance and creating tension between France and Britain, reviving French national ambitions, and generally promoting a renewal of competitive politics and rival national interests. This is true only on the surface. The competition over Spain was superficial and largely meaningless; the elements of joint European co-operation and restraint at work throughout the affair were deeper and more decisive. What really happened, after all, was that France, reasserting one of its historic roles, moved to regain Spain as its natural sphere of influence, and the other European powers, so recently mortal enemies of France, either encouraged this or acquiesced in it, Britain against its will. Then France, having occupied all of Spain, withdrew with nothing permanent to show for it. History did not repeat itself; all the fears entertained at the time proved empty—that the intervention would renew the eighteenth-century Bourbon family compact, revive French revolutionary ambitions and conquests, rekindle the anti-French fanaticism of Spain's war of independence, or touch off a wider war or new revolution. This was not accidental. Both the French government and others knew where the precipices were and carefully avoided them. France understood, as Austria did in Italy, that an indispensable condition for Europe's toleration of French

[71] Bertier (1968–71: ii. 742–803); Schroeder (1962b: 229–36); Temperley (1925a: 78–83).

[72] For different views of the effects on the French army and politics, see Porch (1974: 7–22); Savigneur (1969); Spitzer (1971: 197–200, 264–5); Jardin and Tudesq (1984: 47–56).

action in Spain was that France should not aggrandize itself. The Continental powers accepted a prestige victory for France as the price of keeping the Bourbons in power. Britain disliked it, but did not dream of fighting over it. Beneath the roiled surface of European politics lay a deep, calm sea of restraints, recognized limits, and co-operative purposes.

VI. REVOLUTION AND INDEPENDENCE IN SPANISH AMERICA

If further evidence of such restraint and co-operation is needed, Latin America furnishes it. In Spain, the European Concert provided France, its most suspect member, a harmless outlet in its quest for renewed prestige. In Spanish America, the Continental powers allowed Great Britain and the United States, ideologically their most dangerous foes, to exploit a revolutionary movement for their own interests, concerning themselves mainly with limiting its harmful ideological and political repercussions in Europe.

The Latin American revolutions are clearly important in the international politics of this era, but do not fit easily into its history. In some ways European events served only as a catalyst for them, in other ways they were a driving force. The internal roots of Spain's loss of its colonies go back to the eighteenth century and involve many factors: growing tensions between creoles and peninsulars over positions, status, and authority in the Empire, producing demands for local control; Spain's closed mercantilist system, cutting off the colonies from valuable markets and goods and promoting the cry for more free trade; Spain's late eighteenth-century wars and, after 1796, the progressive destruction of the Spanish navy, further isolating the colonies and worsening already severe problems of administration and communication; the political impact, both attractive and repulsive, of the emergence of United States as an aggressive independent republic; and the even greater impact of British and American goods and trade. Britain abandoned the idea of colonial conquest in South America after 1807, but continued its illegal commerce there and pressed Spain to make it legal; even Napoleon promoted revolution in the colonies for anti-British purposes. All this helped make the idea of freedom through constitutionalism merge within the colonies with the desire for a better commercial system and administrative autonomy. Already by 1804 Charles IV and Godoy saw the writing on the wall, and considered autonomy under the suzerainty of the

Spanish Crown as the best way to retain some links of the colonies to the metropolis.

From this standpoint, the events in Spain from 1808 simply accelerated a more or less inevitable break. But in a certain way they were also the real cause of the revolutions. In the colonies as in Spain, the French Revolution, Spain's experiences as France's ally, Napoleon's take-over, and the Spanish revolt against it all had the effect of strengthening the loyalty of Spain's subjects to the patriarchal Catholic monarchy. Except for La Plata, which was already in revolt before 1808, it is hardly an exaggeration to say that the viceroyalties in the Americas, like the juntas in Spain, rose in revolt out of loyalty to the Crown, in order to remain Spaniards, and that what drove the Americas toward ultimate independence was the dissolution of legitimate authority in Spain, forcing them to govern themselves. The illegitimacy of Joseph's regime, the ineffectiveness of the Junta Central against other juntas, especially the Junta of Seville, the breakup of Spain into decentralized centres of resistance, and the initial encouragement given by the metropolis, especially the Junta of Cadiz, to autonomous juntas abroad, helped push the viceroyalties into filling the vacuum of authority. Spain's defeats in 1809–10 and the French occupation of much of the country led in the same direction.

The Cortes, when it finally managed to gain some unified control of the anti-French forces in Spain, proved to be dominated by commercial interests at Cadiz, which meant that, despite the presence of American representatives, it could not meet American needs and demands. Its reform efforts, real if limited in Spain, proved half-hearted, inconsistent, and even hypocritical in regard to the Americas. It could proclaim equality between creoles and peninsulars but not implement it, and it clung stubbornly to metropolitan control and the old monopolies on trade. Spain's final victory over Napoleon produced a new wave of affection in the Americas for the father-king Ferdinand, but also a tide of expectations he was unwilling or unable to fulfil. Gradually but decisively he returned to absolute rule over Spain and the empire, and by late 1814 and early 1815 set out to repress rebellion in the Americas.[73]

The European powers became involved not because they pushed their way in but because Spain pulled them in. The fact that Spain initially won victories over most of the rebellions, except in La

---

[73] I rely here principally on Anna (1983); Lynch (1973); Humphreys and Lynch (1966); Costeloe (1986); Liss (1983: 172–92, 208–9, 222–41); but see also Bartlett (1966: 70–3); Costeloe (1981).

Plata, where the Portuguese in Brazil were also involved and posed a threat, did not deceive sensible Spaniards. Knowing that they must conciliate the colonials, they sought help especially from Britain in their attempt to square the circle, i.e. to persuade the insurgents to accept reforms which would leave real control of the colonies with Spain.[74] The European powers were not opposed to this, or even seriously divided on the question. They all wanted if possible to promote a reconciliation between Spain and the colonies; if not, to preserve monarchic regimes in Spanish America; and in any case to avoid direct European intervention.

This meant that Spain never came close to getting serious, concrete help from Europe in suppressing the rebellions. It sought it first from Britain in 1815–16, but Britain would not go beyond mediation, and even that was conditional on Spain's opening its colonies to trade. Nor did the Spaniards have better luck with Russia. The one concrete move Russia made, the sale of eight naval vessels to Spain for an American expedition, was financially a swindle, militarily something of a joke, and politically a futile gesture.[75] By 1817, when the subject of European action first arose, the tide was already turning in favour of the insurgents; by late 1818 the only remaining questions were when and how independence would come and which European power would gain most from the transition in terms of trade and influence. Russia and France both believed they had a stake in this contest, Russia because of its North American possessions and its fading dream of expanding its commerce in Latin America, France because of French Guiana, the West Indies, its maritime and colonial traditions, and its traditional ties with Bourbon Spain. But Britain enjoyed such obvious and decisive advantages in the competition that both Russia and France basically sought to lure it into a restraining partnership.[76]

This explains why there were only two semi-serious proposals for European mediation. One came from Russia, and was based on Spain's plea for intervention in the Spanish–Portuguese terri-

[74] Anna (1983: 148–220).

[75] Bartley (1978: 121–27); *VPR* (1960–: 2. i. Nos. 148, 175, 179, 190); Martens (1874–1905: xi. 267–9). Austria also thought of selling Spain part of the fleet it had acquired from the former Kingdom of Italy, but it was more cautious than Russia about the political ramifications; Sondhaus (1989: 44–5).

[76] Martens (1874–1905: xi. 155–64, 197–200; Humphreys and Lynch (1966: 281–6); Bartlett (1966: 242–51); Ferns (1960: 106–8); Völkl (1968: 223–6); Robertson (1939: 105–28, 176–7, 224–8); Nichols (1971: 137–60). For Russia's declining prospects for expansion in the Pacific after 1815, see Barratt (1983: 20); Saul (1991: 88–9).

torial struggle over the Banda Oriental in 1817. The other was a Franco-Russian proposal at Aachen in 1818 to invite Spain to the conference and develop a programme for reconciling Spain and its colonies under European mediation, with a European boycott of Spanish American goods envisioned as a possible sanction against the insurgents. Castlereagh, in retaliation for Alexander's warning Britain off Persia in 1816, warned the Russians off Latin America in 1817, and at Aachen he easily defeated the Franco-Russian proposal with help from Metternich. In any case, the conditions Russia and France proposed and the limits they set on European action (no armed action, commercial freedom for the colonies, wide autonomy, etc.) were close to Britain's own and unacceptable to Ferdinand. All Russia achieved by its proposal was to irritate both Portugal and Spain. The French scheme of establishing independent Bourbon monarchies in the Americas as a way of accepting the inevitable and protecting French trade and influence in the colonies without alienating Spain and Europe was inherently fragile, and broke down on Ferdinand's resistance.[77]

To this question, Austria and Prussia contributed inertia. It was not the case that, though wishing to help Spain defend its empire against revolutionary republicanism, they were stopped by their weaknesses and the revolutionary dangers at home. Instead, recognizing early on that the Spanish empire was doomed, they never wanted to do anything substantial; the aim of their diplomatic activity, such as it was, was to help ensure that the empire would die quietly without causing shocks in Europe. Naturally, Metternich assured the Spaniards that right was on their side and that the revolutions in the Old and the New Worlds were connected. He believed it, but the purpose of this assurance was purely tactical, to support his claim that Austria could not act until the danger in Germany, Italy, and France was over. This excuse for inaction served until the 1820 revolution in Spain itself gave him an even better one. Prussia was more interested than Austria in sharing in the Latin American market, but politically its attitude was no different.[78]

The German powers' inertia helped restrain Russia, but the help

[77] Bourquin (1954: 370–3, 378–98); Robertson (1939: 134–75); Bartley (1978: 104–31); Kossok (1964: 54–7); *VPR* (1960–: 2. i. Nos. 173, 182, 184, 197); Polovtsov (1902–7: ii. No. 223).

[78] Kossok (1964) presents a different thesis, but his evidence all points the other way. Temperley's contention (1925a: 91) that Austria encouraged armed Russian intervention is not backed by evidence. Even the Pope, after condemning the revolutions, came to accept the inevitability of Latin American independence; O'Dwyer (1985: 221–5).

was hardly needed, even in 1820–1 when the Spanish revolt, a similar one in Portugal, and a constitutional coup in Brazil seemed to prove the infectious character of the Spanish American revolutions. While Russian envoys at Madrid and Lisbon urged action of some sort without being able to specify its nature, Nesselrode declined to do anything more than to deplore the revolutions. The constitutional regime in Spain refused to cut its overseas losses just as Ferdinand had, making it still more likely that Britain would take the lead in recognizing the colonies' independence and that then the Continent would have to follow. The Holy Alliance powers and France wanted to avoid this, not because they saw any chance for Spain to regain control of its colonies, but because they feared the political and commercial impact of unilateral British action on Europe and the New World.

Alexander inadvertently increased the danger, however, by issuing a *ukaz* in September 1821 which restricted the commercial activity of other powers in the sphere Russia claimed on the west coast of North America north of the 51st parallel. This aroused the United States, already Britain's chief competitor commercially and politically in Latin America. Hitherto the Americans had held off recognizing Latin American independence until they had induced Spain to hand over Florida (the 1819 treaty ceding it was ratified by Spain in late 1820). In March 1822 President James Monroe announced his intention to recognize five independent Latin American governments, and in May he carried out his decision.[79]

The American action provoked a final flurry of diplomatic activity over Spanish America before, during, and after the Congress of Verona. It contained ironic twists, but produced nothing serious. The Spanish constitutional regime, increasingly dominated by radicals (*exaltados*), appealed to its ideological enemies, the Holy Alliance powers, to help save the Spanish empire from nefarious plots by Britain and France, or at least prevent the Western powers from recognizing the colonies' independence. Meanwhile Ferdinand VII, in secret contact with Russia and the French Ultras through the Russian and French ministers at Madrid, Counts Bulgari and La Garde, was pleading for their help in overthrowing the revolutionary government in Spain. Alexander encouraged France to do something about Spanish America and Montmorency was tempted to try, but Villèle had

[79] Anna (1983: 221–57); *VPR* (1960–: 2. iv. Nos. 3, 19, 38, 51–3, 82, 109, 118, 185–7); Bourquin (1954: 427–9); Nichols (1967); Saul (1991: 96–105).

different ideas. Already in March Montmorency had tried to sound Britain on its intentions in Latin America. Castlereagh had used his inquiry to try to draw France away from the Holy Alliance on the issue and into a joint policy of moving gradually toward recognition, beginning by recognizing ships flying Latin American flags in international commerce. Montmorency drew back out of concern for Spain and the alliance, however, while Villèle decided to use the Spanish American issue at Verona to distract the Holy Alliance from (as he supposed) trying to make France intervene in Spain. He proposed that the congress offer to mediate between Spain and its colonies on terms which meant de facto American independence. If Spain agreed, it would at least prevent the rise of Spanish American republics and enable Spain to send its royal offspring abroad as sovereigns. If it refused, the powers would have an excuse to break with Madrid and recognize the insurgents. In either case, his proposal would give the congress a bone to gnaw on and would keep Britain from acting with a completely free hand.

Throughout this period Castlereagh was the only one who really knew what he wanted and was in a position to go after it. Recognition, he knew, was only a matter of time; Britain had already gone half-way toward it. But Castlereagh wished, without letting the Americans get too far ahead, to stay in touch with Europe, especially the French, and to try to draw them along, or at least not destroy the European Concert. He intended, therefore, to propose at the Vienna ministerial conference that Europe jointly extend de facto recognition to those colonies which had made good their independence, while employing Europe's advice and good offices to help Spain retain ties to those colonies still loyal or in contest. The insurgents in Latin America meanwhile put their own pressure on Europe by threatening to close their ports to governments which denied them recognition.[80]

All the schemes devised by Ferdinand, the exaltados, Villèle, and Castlereagh came to nothing. As a result, the subject of Spanish America arose at Verona only when Wellington declared on 24 November that Britain intended to proceed to de facto recognition in order to protect its commerce and prevent piracy, and invited the other powers to follow Britain's example. The other powers reacted unfavourably but in a guarded way, only Russia flatly refusing to do so. Castlereagh's successor, Canning, maintained

[80] Bourquin (1954: 398–403); Anna (1983: 265–71); Robertson (1939: 205–52); Bertier (1968–71: ii. 629–30).

Castlereagh's basic policy in a different spirit. Where Castlereagh had wanted to draw France along with Britain and at least prepare the Holy Alliance for recognition, Canning wanted to teach France a lesson and prove that Britain was independent of Europe. To what extent he believed at this time and later his claims of French designs on Spain and the colonies, even including a revival of the Bourbon family compact, is unclear. What happened in fact is that he summoned a threat to the New World into existence to redress his defeat in the Old.[81]

In all this manœuvring, Spain hardly counted. Ferdinand's policy after his restoration ruined any chance that Madrid would move toward recognition in order to save monarchic government in the colonies, a policy which Britain also would have preferred. With all Spain's colonies on the mainland making good their independence, the last by 1825, Canning's desire to exploit the situation met little resistance from the Holy Alliance, which was only interested in preserving appearances, or from France, which sought to stay with Britain in some sort of restraining partnership. The real problem came from the United States. Canning was able to defeat French proposals for another congress on the Spanish American question by arguing that the United States must be involved, but could not draw the Americans into a joint policy. The American secretary of state, John Quincy Adams, was as suspicious of Britain as Canning was of France, and was unwilling to give up the advantage of outflanking Britain ideologically on the left just as Britain would not do so *vis-à-vis* the Holy Alliance. The United States responded to Canning's invitations with its Monroe Doctrine, ostensibly a warning to the European monarchies against interfering in the New World, actually a rejection and exploitation of Canning's offer of partnership. Canning meanwhile engaged the French ambassador, Prince Polignac, in an agreement, the Polignac Memorandum, in October 1823 which pledged both of them to territorial non-aggrandizement and the renunciation of the use of force in dealing with Latin America.[82]

Neither the Monroe Doctrine nor the Polignac Memorandum had much practical impact at the time, but they indicate something

[81] Nichols (1971: 137–60); Kossok (1964: 97–108); Bourquin (1954: 404–5). Temperley (1925a), while emphasizing the alleged aggressive purposes of the European powers which Castlereagh and Canning checked, also writes (p. 103): 'In any case, Canning had to win diplomatic prestige over Spanish America as a set-off to his diplomatic defeat in Europe.'

[82] Bourquin (1954: 407–46); Anna (1983: 286–90); Robertson (1939: 267–95); Temperley (1925a: 110–21).

about the European system. There has been some discussion of who helped most to liberate Latin America and protect it from European interference and imperialism, with many American politicians and a few historians pointing to the Monroe Doctrine, British historians on better evidence pointing to Britain and the British navy, and very many historians, Latin American and others, challenging the value and disinterestedness of the alleged 'liberation' and 'protection'. In the process, the most important fact in regard to the Vienna system is overlooked: Latin America did not really need to be saved from Continental Europe. The Continental powers accepted Anglo-American domination of the western hemisphere, and preferred to fence Europe off from the quarrels, troubles, and dangerous ideologies of North and South America. They recognized the importance of the New World, and equally recognized their inability to control or seriously influence it. The denunciations of revolutionary republicanism in the Americas by France and the Holy Alliance were not evidence of a desire to intervene in the western hemisphere, but of their fear of the long-range decline of old Europe, an *Untergang des Abendlandes.*[83]

Thus both the Monroe Doctrine and the Polignac Memorandum really suited Europe's wishes, applying to Latin America the principles of mutual non-aggrandizement and renunciation of force which Europe was practising at home and which helped prevent European competition throughout these years from getting out of hand. Both instruments also fit with other developments of 1815–23 in illustrating how various hegemonies—the overall European and world hegemony of Britain and Russia, Anglo-American hegemony in the New World (still shared uneasily at this time), and local hegemonies on the Continent—were basic to the system. So long as a hegemonic power kept its exercise of hegemony within reasonable bounds, no one was willing to challenge it. There was only one exception to this rule, Russia in the Near East. But Russia's claim to primacy in dealing with the Ottoman Empire was made so moderately, readily conceding the legitimate European voice in Turkey's fate and the paramount need for peace, and challenged so skilfully by Britain and Austria in terms of concert principles, that the outcome actually strengthened the system.

In its adaptation of hegemony and hegemonic techniques of leadership to new conditions, the Vienna system thus met the

[83] Barraclough (1966: 284–5).

challenge of growth or decay in 1815–23 quite well. In other respects the adaptation was less successful and promising for the future. Canning indicated that he intended not to seek different goals for Britain—the existing system favoured British interests too much—but to act in a style different from Castlereagh's, using Britain's invulnerability and leading position to set the Continental powers at odds with each other and take advantage of their rivalry. How long Austria could keep Russia from actively helping the Greeks was a serious question; how long French governments could satisfy Frenchmen with successes purely of prestige, like that in Spain, was another. Most important, the vital systems of intermediary states in Central Europe and the vital hegemonies of Austria–Prussia in Germany and Austria in Italy had developed in ways not viable in the future, for their members, for the great powers, or for the system as a whole.

14
Greece and the Russo-Turkish War, 1823–1829

THE years 1823–9 were the most tranquil of the post-war era. Only one major crisis in international politics developed, over Greece and the Eastern question; and though it was always troublesome and sometimes dangerous, things finally turned out better for the international system than most had anticipated. Other international problem areas either remained quiescent or were managed in fairly routine fashion. The relative tranquillity, however, would end abruptly in 1830, in revolutions much wider and more threatening to the international system than those of the early 1820s. Conservatives like Metternich saw a direct link here: governments in opening the floodgates to liberalism and revolt in the Near East had undermined the dikes against revolution in the rest of Europe. Liberals argued just the opposite: the 1830 revolutions were the result of the repressive policies of most governments in the 1820s. In fact, the connection between the stability of the 1820s and the upheavals of the early 1830s was real, but more indirect and subtle than either side recognized.

I. THE GREEK QUESTION, 1823–1825

Greece remained a danger spot for Europe after 1823 not mainly because of the continued fighting and the strains in Russo-Turkish relations but because of Alexander's growing frustration with his allies. Other powers had used Russia's permission or help, he felt, to win victories and gain prestige in their spheres, Austria in Italy, France in Spain, Britain in Latin America. In Russia's sphere, however, they used the European alliance to stop Russia from intervening to end a brutal conflict, thereby undermining Russia's prestige and rewarding Turkish barbarism and intransigence.

This view was basically right. Metternich, who had devised and led this game of restraining Russia while pretending to be its friend and ally, found his act growing more difficult and transparent with time. Emperor Francis, wanting to gain trade and revenues out of the Greek conflict at Russia's expense, ordered

Metternich to persuade the Ottoman Empire to open its ports to Austrian commerce, even in the Black Sea. Austrian ships took over much of the Turkish carrying trade formerly in Greek hands and, according to the Russians, transported Turkish war materials and even Turkish soldiers within the war zone. At the same time the Greek navy, little more than privateers, wreaked havoc on European shipping, intensifying the pressure for European intervention to end the civil war. Adding to Metternich's difficulties, he now faced enemies in Canning and Chateaubriand at London and Paris instead of his former friends Castlereagh and Montmorency. Yet he continued to predict success for his policy, and it was not blind optimism. The end of the Spanish campaign and Chateaubriand's fall in early 1824 helped revive Austro-French co-operation in the Near East and dispel the threat of Russo-French co-operation. As for Canning, though he hated Metternich and the Holy Alliance, his goal for the moment, to get Russia to restore full diplomatic relations with the Turks, ran parallel to Austria's. Once this was done, Canning believed he could disengage Britain from its peacemaking activity at the Porte and pursue other British interests undisturbed.[1]

By autumn 1823 Alexander had partially restored diplomatic relations with the Ottoman Empire, thus satisfying Europe's demand for an assurance of peace as the prerequisite for the promised mediation of the Turco-Greek conflict. He then persuaded Francis in a meeting at Czernowitz in October to agree to an ambassadorial conference on the Greek question at St Petersburg the following spring, and sent Russia's proposals on Greece to the powers in January. They called on Europe to join Russia in pressing the Sultan to create three autonomous Greek principalities under the protection of the European powers, connected to the Sultan only by the payment of an annual tribute. If European advice and diplomatic pressure failed to persuade Mahmud to accept this solution, the powers would have to consider how to coerce him into it.

The other powers, especially Austria and France, saw immediately that from their standpoint this proposal was a recipe for disaster. It would produce first a Turkish rejection, then coercion, and finally war, and even if the war did not destroy the Ottoman

[1] See Metternich's memoranda (*Vorträge*) of 7 July, 8 Aug., 14, 22 Nov., 13 Dec. 1823, and 11 July, 29 Aug., 29 Nov. 1824, HHStA, *Vorträge* 1823/234–6, 1824/238–9. For Austria's efforts to promote its Levantine trade generally, see Sauer (1971); for a report on Russia's heavy commercial losses, see *VPR* (1960–: 2. v. No. 51). On Canning's Greek policy generally, see Dakin (1973: 150–5).

Empire, it would extend Russian domination, already dangerous in the Principalities and Serbia, to Greece and the Porte itself. Not daring to reject Russia's proposals outright when the Petersburg Conference met in June 1824, the ambassadors engaged in artful dodging, praising the principles and goals of the Russian memorandum but declining to forward it to Constantinople for action, with the plea that they lacked instructions. This merely gained them time; suspending the conference, Nesselrode called for it to meet again in early 1825, with the ambassadors this time to come armed with specific instructions and full powers.[2]

Austria and France now urged Britain to take the lead in restraining Russia. But Canning, rebuking the British ambassador to Russia, Sir Charles Bagot, for even taking part in the original conference, rejected Russia's invitation to another meeting on the grounds that Britain could not participate in any deliberations until Russia had restored full relations with Turkey. Besides, he said, there was little point in discussing proposals which both belligerents had already rejected. Members of the British cabinet disagreed over Canning's move, not from fear of what Russia's proposals would do to Turkey and Europe but because of their personal and political rivalries and divergent attitudes toward the European Concert and international politics in general. Canning, his main opponent, Wellington, and Liverpool, who usually supported Canning, all believed that the Greek conflict would eventually have to be ended by some scheme like Russia's to force the Turks into concessions leading ultimately to virtual Greek independence. Settling the conflict, however, was not the main concern, particularly for Canning, who had little or no interest in solving the Greek question or the Russo-Turkish quarrel at this time, or even in preventing a Russo-Turkish war, so long as it did not harm particular British interests. Other issues interested him far more—Latin America, Spain and Portugal, a dispute with France over fishing rights in the English Channel, and above all his position in the cabinet and with King George IV, under attack by his opponents and Metternich.

So far as the Greek question was concerned, Canning was simply determined not to co-operate with Metternich, whom he hated, or with France, whose victory in Spain he still resented, especially in any policy not initiated and clearly led by Britain. More important still, where Wellington wanted to preserve the

[2] Bertier (1968–71: ii. 848–52); Schiemann (1904: i. 334–9); Driault and Lhéritier (1925: i. 222–32).

European Concert and to use it here to prevent war and to restrain Russia and France, Canning considered the concert an intrinsically bad instrument of the Holy Alliance and wanted to break it up, restoring the old European politics of normal everyday rivalries, to the benefit of Britain's interests and prestige and his own. He therefore wanted to force Austria to restrain Russia on its own without British help, which would sooner or later create an Austro-Russian rift for Britain to exploit. Canning, long celebrated as the liberal opponent of the reactionary Holy Alliance, was really, in a literal sense, reactionary and restorationist, trying to restore the competitive international politics of the eighteenth century.[3]

At first Canning's tactics seemed to backfire on him. Russia promptly broke off communications with Britain on the Eastern question. Threatened with isolation, Canning sent his cousin Stratford Canning, newly appointed as ambassador to the Porte, on a special mission to St Petersburg offering to have Britain mediate between Russia and the Porte separately from Austria and France. The overture merely convinced Nesselrode that Russia's firmness had shaken Canning, and that more of the same would bring the British into line. At the same time the new British ambassador to Russia, Viscount Strangford, hinted that under the right conditions Britain might join Europe in putting pressure on the Sultan. Strongly reprimanded by Canning for this, he resigned not long after.[4]

Canning, however, secured the desired breach between Austria and Russia as a result of the St Petersburg Conference, reconvened from late February to early April 1825. Metternich had lined up France and Prussia in advance behind a proposal, which the

[3] For the specific quarrel over the St Petersburg conference, see Temperley (1925a: 335–7, 342–3); Wellington (1862–80: ii. 203–5, 313–39, 398–406). On the Wellington–Canning rivalry generally, and Metternich's anti-Canning intrigues, see Thompson (1986: 44–7); Wellington (1862–80: ii. 81–6, 89–92, 207–8, 221–6, 232–3, 278–80); on Canning's triumph in 1825, see Temperley (1925a: 246–51). Three fairly recent articles on Canning's Greek policy (Cunningham, 1978; Schwartzberg, 1988; Cowles, 1990), though they differ in interpretation, agree in rejecting the old Whig view. My reading of Canning's correspondence convinces me that he was preoccupied with his own position in office and place in history, and that he certainly had no policy on Greece or interest in it at this time. On taking office, he wrote to Granville Leveson-Gower that he felt little incentive to do so when there was so little opportunity for fame: 'There is nothing in domestick politics to tempt one—and as to foreign politicks—what is there remaining but the husk without the kernel? Ten years have taken away all that was desirable'; 22 Aug. 1822, PRO 30/29/8/6, fos. 727–8.

[4] Martens (1874–1905: xi. 329–32); VPR (1960–: 2. vi. 36, 43–6, 136–7, 142–3, 181–6).

Austrian ambassador, Baron Ludwig Lebzeltern, offered to Russia at the conference as their joint solution to the Greek problem. It argued that Europe could not agree to coercing the Sultan into surrendering his sovereign rights; this would violate fundamental international and monarchic principles. But as a last resort, if all else failed to end the conflict, Austria would consider joining the other powers in recognizing a small independent Greek state and entering into limited commercial and political relations with it. Gentz, one of the authors of this proposal, may have thought of it as a step toward ultimately resolving the Greek question. Metternich's purposes were purely tactical. His proposed 'solution' was bound to be rejected by both belligerents, would therefore not have stopped the conflict, and was intended solely to keep Russia from acting and thereby gaining more influence in the East. The conference, as a result, broke up in failure. Alexander and Nesselrode were then further angered by reports from Pozzo di Borgo of how Metternich had boasted of his policy and its triumph during his visit to Paris in the spring. In August the Tsar ordered his ambassador at Vienna Tatishchev to cease communicating with Austria on the Eastern question, following this with similar action toward France, Turkey, and even Prussia.

Though this seemed to foreshadow a Russian military move against Turkey, Metternich continued to insist that the storm would blow over, and again he had reasons. In the summer of 1825 the army and navy of Mohamed Ali, Pasha of Egypt, the nominal vassal of Sultan Mahmud whom the latter had summoned to help stamp out the Greek insurrection, seemed near that goal. By next spring, the time when Alexander hinted Russia might go to war, there might be no Greek revolt left to fight for. Besides, the Tsar was outraged less by the plight of the Greeks than by the treacherous conduct of his allies, especially Austria. Canning and Metternich both doubted that the Tsar, deprived of overt European support, would attack Turkey simply to defy Europe.[5]

[5] On the St Petersburg conference and the Metternich–Alexander split, see Driault and Lhéritier (1925: i. 359–74); Schiemann (1904: i. 345–50); Grimsted (1969: 284–5); Kiniapina (1952: 194–5); Nesselrode (1904–12: vi. 218–21); *VPR* (1960–: 2. vi. 9–16, 63–7, 82–5, 92–9, 105–8, 130–5, 161–8, 190–5, 229–38, 264–7). On Metternich, Gentz, and the independence proposal, see Bertier (1968–71: iii. 1067–76); Sweet (1941: 253–9). Metternich's optimism shows up constantly in his *Vorträge* to the Emperor and his correspondence in 1825 with Prince Paul Esterházy, ambassador at London, HHStA, *Vorträge* 1825/242–3; *Weisungen Grossbritannien* 227. What is interesting from a systemic point of view is that, while

II. RUSSIA TAKES OVER: THE ROAD TO NAVARINO, 1825–1827

Developments in late 1825, however, tore Metternich's web of restraints to shreds. While the Egyptians advanced relentlessly in Greece, the Russians and others spread reports that the Sultan had promised Greece to Mohamed Ali so that he could depopulate it and colonize it with Africans. This heightened the philhellenic agitation among the educated classes in Europe, especially important for governments sensitive to public opinion like Britain and France. Even in Germany, the fear that the cradle of Western civilization might become Muslim and African made it harder for Metternich to recruit Prussian and Bavarian support for his pro-Turkish policy. In August 1825 the provisional Greek government appealed to the British government to save it, promising to accept any solution Britain could achieve. Canning rejected the appeal, but it gave him new diplomatic leverage. At the same time, Metternich's international coalition to restrain Russia melted away. France made clear to Russia that it would support a general European intervention to end the war and give the Greeks some kind of autonomy, a course Prussia had always favoured if it did not bring war or trouble in Europe.[6]

The decisive development, however, was that Britain and Russia began drawing together in the autumn of 1825. After George Canning had signalled to Russia through Stratford Canning that he was willing to work with it separately from France and Austria, Nesselrode used the Russian ambassador at London, Count Lieven, and his wife Dorothea (Daria), an avidly political socialite and former mistress of Metternich, to let the foreign secretary know that a British approach to Russia would not be rebuffed. In both camps there was opposition to the *rapprochement*. Wellington and Strangford urged Canning not to abandon joint action with Europe. Pozzo, Stroganov, and M. Ia. Minchaki, current chargé at Constantinople and general consul at Bucharest, warned the Tsar against Britain, pleading that Russia should either work with France or act alone. So did Capodistrias from retirement. But in both foreign offices the potential gains were considered worth the

some Russians were urging Alexander to abandon the alliance and return to balance-of-power politics, Metternich believed he could still use concert grouping methods to restrain Russia even if it tried to intervene; see Metternich (1880–4: iv. 180–1).

[6] Dakin (1973: 156–66); Schiemann (1904: i. 604–11, 616–19); Heydemann (1989).

risk. Canning, a Russophile in the Pitt tradition, was delighted to think that all parties (the Greeks, the Continental powers, and now Russia) had appealed to Britain to take the lead; this would mortify Metternich and the French, enhance Britain's prestige, and solidify his position at home. Nesselrode and the Lievens had a more concrete hope and aim: to use a British connection to nullify the European resistance to Russia's plans.

Each side thus expected to gain leadership and a free hand from their partnership, but their ideas on how to secure and exercise that lead differed greatly. Canning entered into co-operation with Russia with no clear idea as to the exact goal and purpose that co-operation would serve. He was unsure, for example, of whether the partnership should remain exclusive or be expanded to include the other European powers. Surprised by Lieven's allegations that the Egyptians planned to depopulate and colonize Greece, he considered using the British navy to enforce an armistice in Greece, acting either unilaterally or in conjunction with Russia and France. Yet at the same time he told Lieven that Britain could not intervene actively until it had first tried to mediate between the Turks and Greeks through Stratford Canning—though he admitted that this would require European support, and that he did not know what terms the Turks and Greeks might be brought to accept. He seems to have hoped that Britain could somehow mediate the Turkish–Greek quarrel at Constantinople, frightening the Turks into concessions to the Greeks by holding the threat of a Russo-Turkish war over their heads, while simultaneously Britain would hold St Petersburg back from actually going to war. Yet he was also convinced that Britain could not really hold Russia back, for, as the Ochakov crisis of 1791 had shown, the British Parliament and public would not support a war against Russia, or even the threat of one, for the sake of the balance of power and the integrity and existence of the Ottoman Empire. The only thing restraining Russia from conquering Turkey any time it wished, according to Canning, was that Alexander did not really want war.

In contrast to Canning's uncertain fumbling, the Russian policy, as laid out in the Nesselrode–Lieven correspondence, was crystal clear. By forging a separate Anglo-Russian partnership, they intended to force the Continental powers to fall into line behind them or be isolated, to entangle Britain in the Turkish–Greek conflict, to lure Britain into supporting Russia's measures against the Turks, and thus to guarantee that Britain would either be allied with Russia or at least remain neutral in a possible Russo-

Turkish war. The Russians also had calculated just how they would entice the British into this partnership and then manipulate them within it. Lieven, who shared the disdain for Canning widespread in Europe, wrote to Nesselrode that he proposed to exploit Canning's ignorance of the East, his vanity and desire for popularity, his contempt for the Continental powers, and his eagerness to lead Europe, in order to make the foreign secretary, in Lieven's words, 'abjure what one may call the credo of England', the defence of the Ottoman Empire.[7]

It was not clear in late 1825 what Canning's opening to Russia would lead to, or if it would lead to anything. France and Prussia were also competing for Russia's favour, while Metternich hoped that some good might arise from the *rapprochement* between Russia and Britain: that it would frighten the Turks into meeting Russia's special grievances, thus preserving peace between them and allowing the Greek revolt to die a natural death. All calculations went out of the window in early December, when Alexander died suddenly and under mysterious circumstances in the Crimea. A period of confusion over the succession was ended only when the older of Alexander's brothers, Constantine, refused the crown and a younger brother, Nicholas, accepted it. A widespread Russian revolutionary conspiracy flared up during the interregnum. Known to history as the Decembrist Movement, it was headed by liberal nobles and army officers, had partly liberal-constitutionalist and partly republican aims, and produced a brief armed revolt against the regime. The revolt, though quickly suppressed, left an indelible mark on Nicholas I, hardening his instinctive hatred and fear of revolution and helping to make him a champion of orthodoxy, autocracy, and Russian nationality at home and the gendarme of Europe abroad, which he remained throughout his thirty-year reign.

Canning, worried about what line the new regime would take and considering Strangford, still at St Petersburg, as too European in outlook to be trusted, decided to send Wellington on a special mission to Russia. Ostensibly Wellington was to congratulate Nicholas on his accession, but his actual charge was to develop the Canning–Lieven conversations into a Russo-British agreement on the Greek problem. Nicholas immediately saw how a visit by Europe's most honoured warrior and statesman could help him restore his own prestige and that of Russia, and shake off Austrian and European restraints. He had a different view of Russia's

[7] Cowles (1990: 701–4); Sinkiewicz (1854: 4–56, 207–38); Martens (1874–1905: xi. 334–6); Canning (1887: i. 313–15, 317–19, 321); Wellington (1862–80: ii. 569–71); *VPR* (1960–: 2. vi. 284–7, 301–5) (the passage quoted is on p. 286).

interests from that of Alexander, however. Where the former had sympathized with the Greeks, though not with Greek nationalism, Nicholas despised the Greeks as rebels and feared that a war might subvert his army and regime. His goals were simply to teach the Turks a lesson, advance purely Russian goals in the Near East, and thereby reassert Russia's leadership in Europe. Other Russians supported these aims.[8]

Even had Canning understood this, it would not have changed his strategy or the instructions he gave Wellington for his mission, or made them more practicable. The contradictions were built into British policy. Wellington was instructed to persuade Russia to support Stratford Canning's efforts at mediation of the Turkish–Greek conflict at Constantinople. But while Stratford's job was to warn the Turks that Russia was preparing for war, thus frightening them into granting the Greeks virtual independence, Wellington was supposed to get the Russians to set aside their special grievances and resume normal peaceful relations with Turkey. Wellington was also to avoid sanctioning any Russian use of force against Turkey or committing Britain to use force in support of Russia's proposals for Greece. Though Wellington was not a clever diplomat, his good sense told him, as it told others like Lord Bathurst, the French foreign minister, Baron Ange Damas, and Metternich, that this strategy would not work. A separate Anglo-Russian partnership would only further antagonize the Porte, encourage the Greeks to raise their demands, and free Russia from European control. Canning, however, learning that a French party was also active in Greece, became even more determined to maintain Britain's supposed lead in the Greek question, and Wellington accepted the mission to St Petersburg as his soldierly duty, telling himself that if he could not restrain Russia from war he might at least confine their war aims to their terms of January 1824. Neither Canning's goal for the mission, to make Russia support Britain's lead in the Greek question and in Europe, nor Wellington's, either to restrain Russia from going to war or to restrain its conduct of it, was attainable by Britain's methods. Wellington, however, at least had a sensible, concrete aim.[9]

At St Petersburg Wellington soon discovered that Nicholas cared nothing for the Greeks, but seemed determined to go to war

[8] Jelavich (1991: 72–5); Lincoln (1978); Pienkos (1987: 79–100); *VPR* (1960–: 2. vi. 328–30, 332, 334–6, 340–2, 344–5, 347–62, 428–33, 439–44). On the Russian army's involvement in the Decembrist movement, see Beyrau (1984: 198–208).

[9] Temperley (1925a: 290–2, 353–6); Wellington (1862–80: iii. 54–96, 104–7, 113–16, 121–6, 142–3); Canning's letters to Granville, Oct. 1825 to April 1826, PRO 30/29/8/9, 10, fos. 1029–1188 (some of these are published in Canning, 1887; i).

unless Turkey promptly satisfied Russia's other grievances. After trying in vain to soften Russia's demands and rejecting a request that Britain guarantee that Turkey accept them, Wellington agreed on 17 March to support a Russian ultimatum to Constantinople. The ultimatum demanded among other things that the Porte send plenipotentiaries to the Russian frontier to settle all of Russia's complaints on the spot.

Except as a step toward ultimately restoring full Russo-Turkish relations, this had little to do with Britain's purposes in the mission. Wellington, rather than the Russians, first raised the Greek question at St Petersburg. But after Lieven arrived from London to take part in the talks, Russia's interest in the fate of the Greeks suddenly revived. Wellington, still trying to prevent a war or to limit Russia's aims if it came, was dragged by hard bargaining into an alarmingly vague agreement known as the St Petersburg Protocol on 4 April. It committed the two powers to settle the Greek conflict by giving Greece full autonomy, with all Turkish property in Greece and the isles to be bought out by the Greeks. The protocol left to be settled later the vital questions of Greece's boundaries and the means for achieving a peaceful settlement, and called for an invitation to the other powers to support the Anglo-Russian move and to join Russia in guaranteeing the new arrangements for Greece, though Britain itself refused to take part in this guarantee. Most important, the agreement specifically authorized Russia, if the Turks rejected these Anglo-Russian proposals, to continue to pursue the goal of Greek autonomy either together with Britain or separately, regardless of the state of Anglo-Turkish relations.

Britain thus not only tied itself to a vague, indefinitely expansible Russian programme which the Turks were sure to reject and the Greeks had already spurned but also, without explicitly sanctioning the use of force against Turkey, expressly authorized Russia to pursue its aims with or without Britain and without limits as to time or means. In addition, Britain pledged to help marshal the rest of Europe behind Russia as the guarantor of the new Greek state, though Britain itself would not participate in the guarantee.[10] Russia secured these concessions from Britain

---

[10] The text of the protocol is in DeClercq (1880–1917: iii. 416–17). For various discussions of the negotiations and their outcome, see Dakin (1973: 178–83); Cowles (1990: 697–710); Schiemann (1904: ii. 126–39); C. Howard (1974: 35–6); Driault and Lhéritier (1925: i. 300–19). Important Russian documents are in *VPR* (1960–: 2. vi. 393–400, 411–25); Wellington's correspondence on his mission is in Wellington (1862–80: iii. 148–296, 302–7).

without giving any counter-concessions, not even a pledge that it would restore full diplomatic relations with Turkey; nor did Russia make any side-payments to the British or change its anti-British stance on other issues. Later in 1826, when long-standing differences led Persia to initiate a war against Russia, Russia brushed aside British offers of mediation, proceeded to win the war, and dictated peace terms to Persia at Turkmanchai in 1828 without British interference. The Russians also continued to criticize Britain at Madrid and elsewhere for having recognized the independence of Spain's American colonies.[11]

Wellington was no match for wily Continental negotiators, as the Verona Congress had already demonstrated. He must bear part of the blame for this diplomatic fiasco. The main responsibility, however, was Canning's. He fashioned the policy, and he sent Wellington on a misconceived, impossible mission. Historians have debated what Canning's aims were, and whether he had any clear Greek policy or any strategy at all—good questions, but not central for explaining either this particular outcome or its aftermath.[12] The decisive fact, whatever Canning's intentions may have been, is that he lost control of events, or gave it away. His initiative put Russia in command of the Eastern question, and from April 1826 Britain would increasingly follow Russia's lead.

The protocol's first dividends fell to Russia in the convention which Russian and Turkish penipotentiaries signed at Akkerman on the Bessarabian frontier on 6 October. Here the Turks accepted Russia's demands regarding their Asian frontier, the Romanian Principalities, and Serbia. This served to restore normal Russo-Turkish relations, both in a technical sense and in Russia's sense of what normal Russo-Turkish relations should be. Count A. I. Ribeaupierre, nominated two years earlier, now went to Constantinople as ambassador, with instructions to assert Russia's ascendancy and seek further concessions from the Porte on executing the Akkerman Convention.

The Ottoman government, along with Metternich, hoped that by satisfying Russia on its special demands the Sultan might gain a breathing space for dealing with the Greeks and his other internal

[11] On Persia, see Fadeev (1958: 126–65); Yapp (1960: 164–71); *VPR* (1960–: 2. vi. 371–3, 386–9, 571–3, 708); Wellington (1862–80: iii. 108–12, 465–7). For other evidences of Russian Anglophobia, see Jelavich (1966: 128–33); Crawley (1970: 71–6, 87–8, 94–103).

[12] Useful discussions are in Dakin (1973: 173–7); Cunningham (1978: esp. 172–7); Schwartzberg (1988); Cowles (1990); an unconvincing conspiratorial interpretation of British policy is in Sabry (1930: 101–7, 110).

enemies. (The most dangerous of the latter were the janissaries, originally an élite military corps recruited from Christian slaves and now degenerated into a rebellious militia centred in Constantinople. The Sultan eliminated them by mass slaughter in mid-1826.) Whether this might have happened without the St Petersburg Protocol cannot be known. The Convention of Akkerman did satisfy Nicholas's main goals, bringing the Turks to heel and elevating his own prestige, and he did not care about the Greeks. But since the protocol guaranteed Russia almost unlimited British co-operation in the Greek question, Russia would have been foolish not to exploit this for other ends as well—luring France and Prussia into its camp, isolating and chastening Austria, and transforming the Holy Alliance from a pact serving to restrain Russia in the East into an instrument for enhancing Russia's general prestige and freedom of action.

The protocol was promptly communicated to the other great powers and leaked for publication to *The Times* of London, probably by Russia. To Continental statesmen dismayed at seeing an Anglo-Russian solution in the Near East being imposed on them over their heads, the Russians replied that it lay in the nature of things that Russia and Britain together could solve the Eastern Question by themselves without consulting anyone else. The other powers should be thankful that Russia had brought Britain into alliance, eliminating the danger that a European war would erupt over the problem if Britain remained outside, in opposition. Europe should be further grateful that Russia was now inviting the other powers to join the partnership. It was not abandoning the general alliance; it had brought Britain back into it. Here the Russians neatly described how the European system operated under Anglo-Russian hegemony (more accurately than many historical accounts have done), and explained why they considered this joint hegemony benign.[13]

Canning, still mainly interested in other questions,[14] ignored repeated warnings from Wellington and Bathurst on how Russia interpreted their partnership and intended to use it in Europe. Like

[13] For Russia's defence of the protocol, see *VPR* (1960–: 2. vi. 459–62, 666–8); for its leaking and exploiting it in Europe and with the Turks, ibid. 465, 473, 491–4, 500–2, 513–16, 576–9, 582–3, 632–42, 645–6, 650–6; Wellington (1862–80: iii. 323, 334–5).

[14] Principally domestic politics, especially his running quarrel with Wellington, and the Spanish–Portuguese conflict and British intervention. On the latter question he was prepared for drastic action, recommending to Liverpool the seizure of Cuba if Britain got into war with Spain: 'It would settle all better than half a dozen Peninsular campaigns'; 6 Oct. 1826, Canning (1887: ii. 144).

the Russians, he was confident that Britain and Russia could either force the other powers to follow their initiative or settle the question without them, and was more anti-Austrian and suspicious of France than the Russians were. Moreover, he could see no alternative to working with Russia. Whether or not Russia's reports of an Egyptian colonization scheme in Greece were true (they proved not to be, though other Turco-Egyptian practices such as taking Christian slaves were bad enough), he now thought the fighting in Greece had to be stopped, which meant somehow persuading the Greeks and forcing the Turks to accept the Anglo-Russian settlement, if possible by means short of open war. Between August and December Lieven used Canning's assumptions to draw him into agreeing that the two powers must demand an immediate armistice in Greece, break relations with Turkey if it was refused, and impose an armistice with the use of their joint naval power. Canning conceded to Lieven that still further coercive measures might be necessary to carry out the protocol, though he declined to specify them now.[15]

Canning's belief that an Anglo-Russian agreement would force the other powers to fall into line proved only partly correct. He enjoyed the sweet revenge he had gained on Metternich, who was shocked by the St Petersburg Protocol into the unprecedented admission that he had been mistaken. The separate Anglo-Russian accord he had considered impossible was now a reality, though (said Metternich) no mortal could possibly have foretold so monumental a British blunder. Further blows to Metternich followed. Despite the Akkerman Convention, Russia continued to push the Greek question; Nicholas, though a realist rather than a romantic like Alexander, proved not to be the safe conservative Metternich had hoped for. Metternich's efforts to unseat Canning not only failed, but backfired. When Liverpool resigned in ill health in February 1827, Canning defeated Wellington in the contest for the premiership, whereupon Wellington, who disapproved of Canning both on general grounds and for his recklessness on the Greek question, resigned from the cabinet, leaving Canning to run foreign policy through Lord Dudley as titular foreign secretary.

All this, however, forced Austria not into line with Britain and Russia but into diplomatic abstention. Vienna rejected British and Russian invitations to join them in coercing the Sultan. Simple prudence as well as monarchic principle dictated this choice. One

[15] Ibid. 59, 153-4; Wellington (1862-80: iii. 349-50, 355-9, 363-5, 373, 394-5, 402-3, 455-7, 459-62, 476-7); *VPR* (1960-: 2. vi. 603-8, 660-2).

reason was obvious (though ignored by many historians): if the two hegemonic powers successfully claimed the right today to force the Ottoman Sultan to make concessions to a rebellious nationality, they could do the same thing to the Austrian Emperor tomorrow. But Austria's refusal had another ground, clear to the Russians and others at the time: the Anglo-Russian initiative in the Near East was always, in purpose and nature, anti-Austrian as well as anti-Turkish.[16] Ever since 1824, Russia's main aim had not been to liberate the Greeks but to force Austria to accept Russian leadership of the Holy Alliance, Russian freedom of action within it, and Russian domination over the Porte and in the Balkans; and Canning, sometimes unthinkingly but usually knowingly, had supported this anti-Austrian aim. As Nesselrode wrote to Lieven, Austria's refusal to join in coercing the Ottoman Empire made it all the more necessary for Russia to do so successfully, or it would lose all the prestige it had gained since Nicholas came to power.[17]

Austria managed to keep Prussia at its side and away from the Anglo-Russian partnership, but could not hold back France. The French government explained to Vienna that, though it deplored the Anglo-Russian union and the threat it posed to the Ottoman Empire and to European peace, it had to join an enterprise where great French and European interests were at stake. This was true, but other, even more powerful motives were also present— Charles X's longing for action and glory, the French desire for a closer link with Russia, the prestige to be gained by helping pacify Greece, and the hope that territorial revisions in the East would promote similar ones on the Rhine.[18] On 6 July 1827, after long negotiations, France, Russia, and Britain signed a Treaty of London committing them jointly to pursue the goals of the St Petersburg Protocol. The sting lay in the secret article. Besides agreeing to open commercial and consular relations with the pro-

[16] One Briton who saw this clearly, and told Wellington so, was Robert Adair; Wellington (1862–80: iv. 294–7).

[17] The best sources for Metternich's thinking are his *Vorträge* to the Emperor, Jan. 1826 to Jan. 1827, HHStA, *Vorträge* 1826/245–6, 1827/248–9; for his arguments against British and Russian policy, see his dispatches to Prince Esterházy in London, Jan.–Apr. 1826, HHStA, *Weisungen Grossbritannien* 230. His admission to Esterházy that for the first time in his career he had to recognize an error in his previous instructions is in ibid., Secret to No. 1, 29 Apr. For Austria's anti-Greek propaganda in the official press, see Dimakis (1975). Interestingly, the Russian ambassador at Vienna, Tatishchev, defended Austria's refusal to join in coercing the Sultan—*VPR* (1960–: 2. vi. 698–700). For Nesselrode's argument, see Wellington (1862–80: iii. 649–50). On the Canning–Wellington struggle in 1827, see ibid. 609–12; Temperley (1925a: 416).

[18] Bertier (1968–71: iii. 1082–1125); Driault and Lhéritier (1925: i. 332–7).

visional Greek government (if it was still in existence when the time came to do so), the three powers also resolved that if within a month Turkey failed to grant the Greeks an armistice or the Greeks refused to accept one, the allies would impose an armistice by a joint use of their Mediterranean naval squadrons.[19]

The Triple Treaty thus made an armed clash between the allies and the Turks more likely and imminent, though not quite inevitable. Canning, ill and beset by other foreign and domestic problems, died on 8 August.[20] Lord Goderich succeeded Canning as prime minister, retained the hapless Dudley as foreign secretary, and continued the British drift in policy. Wellington, rejoining the cabinet, agreed with Bathurst that the liberal Tories and Whigs should be left for a while to stew in their own juice.[21] Meanwhile the Greeks, though still mired in factional disputes and some collaboration with the enemy, managed to achieve a measure of political consolidation. In March British officers, Lord Cochrane and Admiral Church, were engaged to lead the Greek land and sea forces. In April Count Capodistrias, terminating his nominal connection with the Russian government, arrived in Greece and was elected president for a seven-year term by a Greek assembly. He immediately went abroad to seek financial and military help and political recognition from Europe. Though he failed to gain much in concrete terms, his election at least insured that there would be a Greek government for which the allies could intervene at Constantinople and with which they could deal in Greece.[22]

Greek military fortunes did not immediately improve; Athens

[19] Martens (1874–1905: xi. 344–61); Schiemann (1904: ii. 188–95); Driault and Lhéritier (1925: i. 338–44); Temperley (1925a: 394–403); Wellington (1862–80: iv. 56–63). While fighting the emerging triple treaty, Metternich kept up his act of optimistic whistling past the graveyard until June–July 1827, and then gave way to Cassandra cries about how the Triple Alliance menaced Europe with imminent war, revolution, and the destruction of society. See his correspondence with Esterházy and Vorträge to the Emperor, HHStA, Weisungen Grossbritannien 234; Vorträge 1826/246, 1827/247, 249.

[20] Charles K. Webster writes (1951: i. 259) that Canning almost certainly had not decided what to do about Greece before he died, but would surely have acted forcefully to control Russia's actions and protect British interests had he lived. Webster, as always, is sound on the facts; his conjecture may be doubted. I am struck, in contrast, by how often Canning would acknowledge dangers to British interests—e.g. that a war in which Britain sided with the Greeks against the Sultan would endanger British rule over 100 million Muslims in Asia—but go ahead anyway. To Gower, 2 June 1826, PRO 30/29/8/10.

[21] Wellington (1862–80: iv. 80–1).

[22] Dakin (1973: 166–72, 184–220); Schiemann (1904: ii. 139–42); Fleming (1970: 9–17). For Greek internal conditions, see also Koliopoulos (1987: esp. 44–5, 78–9) and various essays in Petropoulos (1976); on Capodistrias, see also Kaldis (1963); Batalden (1979).

fell in the spring of 1827, leaving the Greeks clinging precariously to a few strongholds on the mainland and in the islands. Yet it was still barely possible that the allies in 1827 could have ended the fighting in Greece without touching off a wider conflict between Russia and Turkey. They had virtually no chance to compel the Porte to accept their terms on Greece. Not only did these represent losses for the Sultan as severe as those he could expect from military defeat, but they also took no account of Turkish internal politics; a Sultan who gave way supinely to the dictates of European infidels could easily be overthrown by a palace coup. With the allies either ignoring this or dismissing it as Turkish and Muslim fanaticism, European diplomatic pressure on the Porte failed again in the summer of 1827, though Austria supported it. Neither was there much chance that Canning's death would break up the Triple Alliance, as Metternich hoped. Villèle shared Metternich's satisfaction at Canning's demise, but believed that, with Britain adrift, France needed more than ever to stay in the alliance to check Russia; and the Russians were determined to retain their advantageous position.[23]

The only hope for a peaceful success of the allied strategy would have been to persuade Mohamed Ali to pull his Egyptian forces out and go home, and then to induce the Sultan *de facto* to abandon Greece. Mohamed was ambitious, opportunistic, and ruthless, but he was also a realist. He knew that the territorial and political gains the Sultan had promised him for his help were out of reach now that the European powers had intervened, and he did not wish to fight the French, who had helped him, or the British, whose power he feared and whose patronage he hoped to gain.[24]

That one slight chance disappeared in a four-hour battle on 20 October 1827, when a combined Anglo-French–Russian fleet under the general command of Britain's Admiral Codrington virtually annihilated a Turco-Egyptian fleet in the Bay of Navarino, killing 4,000 men. Historians have discussed at length what caused the battle to break out and who was to blame. The more important questions, however, are whether it could have been avoided, and what it led to. Several means could conceivably have prevented an armed clash; bribing Mohamed Ali to withdraw, perhaps by the guarantee or hint he sought that Britain and France

[23] Bertier (1968–71: ii. 1100–7).
[24] On Mohamed Ali, see Sabry (1930: 62–73, 89–96, 120–9); Cattaui and Cattaui (1950: 78–96); Driault and Lhéritier (1925: i. 293); and esp. Al-Sayyid Marsot (1984).

would not oppose a future bid for Egyptian independence, or preserving the de facto truce which Codrington had concluded with
the Egyptian commander Ibrahim until Ibrahim's final instructions arrived from Egypt, or pressing the demand for suspension
of hostilities as vigorously against the Greeks as against the
Muslims. None of these possibilities was pursued. If Codrington
can be criticized for having precipitated the battle, the root problem lay in the vague instructions he was given and the lack of
clear policy prevailing within the alliance.

III. WAR AND PEACE IN THE NEAR EAST,
1828-1829

Unlike the responsibilities for the battle, the results of Navarino
are beyond dispute. It forced both Mohamed Ali and the Sultan to
give up Greece as a lost cause, making an independent Greece
inevitable. At the same time, it dealt the Sultan so public a blow
and insult as to make it impossible for him to renounce Greece
openly, or even to listen to further European proposals without an
apology and reparations first. Thus it also made a Russo-Turkish
war inevitable. After a sterile exchange of Russo-Turkish demands
and counter-demands in November, Russia insisted that its allies
authorize it to occupy the Danubian Principalities in order to
bring the Porte to its senses. In late December the Sultan summoned his peoples to a holy war.[25]

While the Russians, exuberant over their military successes at
Navarino and in Persia, looked forward to more victories against
the Turks, Metternich, though near despair, still tried to fend
off war. He urged first Goderich and then Wellington, who
succeeded Goderich as premier in January 1828, to adopt his old
plan of immediately recognizing an independent Greek state, so as
to eliminate Russia's excuse for war. But Wellington, though he
deplored Navarino and the drift toward war, insisted that Britain
was committed to the July alliance and could only attempt to hold
France and Russia to its terms. Metternich had even less success at
Paris, where Navarino had aroused enthusiasm for military action
and hopes for territorial revisions in Europe. Villèle, insisting
that France also had to stick with the July treaty, began moving
toward active collaboration with Russia just as the British were

[25] Dakin (1973: 222-9); Temperley (1925a: 403-9); Driault and Lhéritier (1925:
i. 369-95); Schiemann (1904: ii. 214-23). Various documents on the allied ultimatum are in DeClercq (1880-1917: iii. 458-64).

moving away from it. Like the Russians, he began talking about the possible break-up of the Ottoman Empire, with Bosnia and Serbia to be Austria's share. The Austrian ambassador at London, Prince Esterházy, reported to Metternich's dismay that George IV apparently contemplated Egypt as Britain's.[26]

One last-minute proposal in late January and early February 1828 seemed to offer a chance of arresting the slide into war. La Ferronnays, now foreign minister in the new Martignac ministry, suggested that Europe sanction a Russian occupation of the Principalities as a way of putting pressure on the Sultan, while at the same time Britain and France forbade Russia to go further and themselves occupied the Morea. Britain and Austria, however, refused to sanction a Russian occupation of the Principalities, Britain because it involved a dangerous precedent and commitment, Austria because it would mean a grave Russian strategic threat to itself. This last chance of European intervention gone, the Russians, citing Turkish violations of the Convention of Akkerman, demanded in late February that their allies support Russia's coercive measures against Turkey, threatening if denied it to declare themselves absolved of treaty restrictions and free to act according to their own interests and convenience. Wellington reacted angrily to this threat to escape from the restraints of the Triple Treaty and Russia quickly withdrew it, but then proceeded to declare war against the Ottoman Empire at the end of April. Most powers recognized Russia's right to do so, France and Prussia cheerfully, Britain grudgingly; Austria simply announced neutrality. While at the Porte the final decision to accept war was made reluctantly and with significant opposition, Russia went to war in a spirit of buoyant confidence. Its war aims were restricted territorially to small claims on the east coast of the Black Sea, but included other dangerous demands on the Ottoman Empire in regard to the Principalities, Serbia, the mouth of the Danube, and a unilateral right of naval passage for Russia through the straits.[27]

[26] Nesselrode (1904–12: vi. 256–62); Bertier (1968–71: iii. 1107–1111); Martens (1874–1905: iv. 366–75; xi. 362–75); Wellington (1862–80: iv. 136–8, 142–4, 230–52, 278–9, 302–7). For Metternich's arguments, see his dispatches to Esterházy in HHStA, *Weisungen Grossbritannien* 236, especially the secret one of 31 Dec. 1827; for his reaction to Navarino, his *Vortrag* of 5 Nov. 1827, *Vorträge* 1827/252.

[27] Bertier (1968–71: iii. 1168–72, 1194–1200); Wellington (1862–80: iv. 270–1, 274–8, 280–5); Martens (1874–1905: xi. 376–9); Metternich's dispatches to Esterházy, Feb.–Apr. 1828, HHStA, *Weisungen Grossbritannien* 240. Until early April Metternich continued to hope for Russian moderation—see his *Vortrag* of 8 Apr. 1828, HHStA, *Vorträge* 1828/253.

Then the unexpected developed: the war turned out to be a struggle rather than a military promenade. Besides the problems which usually made wars between Russia and Turkey, in Frederick the Great's phrase, fights between the one-eyed and the blind—disease, difficulties of supply and communication, and bad leadership and organization on both sides—there were special reasons for Russia's difficulties. First, it mobilized only 106,000 men instead of its projected 160,000. This too had several causes: Russian inefficiency, Nicholas's desire not to destroy the Ottoman Empire but to preserve it as a weak and dependent buffer, his commitment to Europe not to fight a war of conquest, and his general fear of the revolutionary consequences of all-out war. In addition, Nicholas helped spoil Russia's chances for a quick victory by interfering personally in the conduct of the war effort. Finally, the Russians were aware that in invading the Balkans they dangerously exposed their army and its communications to a thrust from Transylvania by Austria, possibly with Prussian and German support. As a result, though Russia made good progress in 1828 on the Asian front, where its leadership was more vigorous and the danger of European complications less, in the Balkans they managed only to cross the Danube and take the port of Varna, but failed to capture Shumla and faced having to winter in the Balkans and fight a second campaign.[28]

So long as Austria remained neutral, this was militarily embarrassing but not really dangerous. Politically, it threatened to undermine the control over the Eastern question Russia had enjoyed since 1826 and to give Europe an opportunity to force Russia to a premature peace. Signs of Austrian opposition appeared in the form of certain military measures and an insistence on Austria's neutral trading rights under a 1785 treaty. But Metternich's moves were too tentative, Europe was too divided, and Russian diplomacy was too supple to let this grow into a real threat. Instead, France profited from Russia's embarrassment. With at least superficial order established in Greece under the presidency of Capodistria, and with Russia preoccupied with the war and Wellington with reorganizing his government in the spring of 1828 (Lord Aberdeen replacing Dudley as foreign secretary), the French government got its allies to consent to a French occupation of the Morea in July 1828, ostensibly to supervise the evacuation of Egyptian forces. Thus, while Austro-

---

[28] Curtiss (1965); Schiemann (1904: ii. 224–83); Shil'der (1903: i. 515–24, 544–8); Beyrau (1984: 160–2); Heller (1983: 211).

Russian tension grew, France supplanted Russia as the chief defender of Greek interests. When the allied ambassadors to the Porte met in conference on the island of Poros to settle the frontiers of the new Greek state, the French persuaded the British government to concede Greece a better northern frontier. Stratford Canning co-operated at Poros, while Aberdeen secretly favoured the Greek cause at London.[29]

The Russians managed to preserve the Triple Alliance, despite Britain's growing distrust of both Russia and France, by co-operating with their partners on the Greek question, repeating assurances that they were not waging a war of conquest, and agreeing to keep their war effort out of the Mediterranean. At the same time, by accusing Austria of trying to create a four-power coalition against Russia, they forced Metternich to disavow any such attempt. His disclaimer was truthful enough; he dared not try this because he could not count even on Prussian support, much less French and British. What he actually tried was to get the British and French quickly to settle the Greek issue between themselves, restore their relations with the Porte, and then mediate peace between Russia and Turkey, possibly by a congress at Constantinople. This idea, too, got nowhere at London. Wellington and Aberdeen wanted to end the strain in relations with Austria brought on by Canning, but were not interested in close co-operation. They remained committed to the Triple Alliance, knew that by working with Austria they would alienate Russia and France, and had no real confidence in Austria or Metternich. Besides, Wellington's greatest concern was not the Russo-Turkish war but Anglo-French relations (at one point in mid-1829, he feared that extremists on both sides would bring on a war). As he told Aberdeen, Britain's only chance to escape from the Greek affair and prevent France and Russia from doing whatever they wanted was by staying away from Austria and sticking closely to France. Yet though the British would not work with Austria (even Aberdeen by late 1828 complained about Metternich's incessant advice), they continued to count on Austria and Prussia to extract concessions from the Ottoman Empire and, if worst came to worst, to help save it by restraining their ally Russia. The situation again illustrates how the Vienna system

---

[29] Dakin (1973: 238–44, 252–3, 257–64); Fleming (1970: 17–66); Bertier (1968–71: iii. 1200–18); Hammer (1963: 126–9); Driault and Lhéritier (1925: i. 408–32); Baack (1980: 148–61); Schiemann (1904: ii. 294–9); Kiniapina (1952: 204–12); Chamberlain (1989: 79–81); Martens (1874–1905: iii. 495–8, 502–3; iv. 399–403; xi. 383–401).

worked in critical as well as normal times: through divided hegemony, pacts of restraint, allocations of specific managerial tasks, concert rules, and grouping methods—everything, in short, but balance of power. As for Franco-Austrian relations, by the spring of 1829 they had fallen into a deep chill, La Ferronnays having resigned on account of illness and his successor, Portalis, and Metternich being at odds. In early 1829 Metternich, giving up on Britain and France and no longer sure about Prussia, began trying for a *rapprochement* with Russia.[30]

Thus Russia escaped the danger of isolation fairly easily, and the Triple Alliance held together on the Greek question despite British complaints that the French and Russians were encouraging Greek expansion. In March 1829 the London Conference endorsed the decisions reached earlier at Poros on Greece's future frontiers and its form of government (a constitutional monarchy). Capodistrias went along with these decisions even though they fell far short of his territorial hopes and meant that he would soon have to surrender his presidency. The Sultan, though still stubbornly resisting the virtual independence for Greece the allies demanded, eagerly welcomed British and French envoys back to Constantinople to negotiate on how much autonomy and privilege he would concede the Greeks.[31]

None the less, the Russo-Turkish war still hung over Europe, a cloud made darker by growing unrest and liberal opposition to Charles X in France. In August the Martignac ministry fell, and its successor, a highly conservative and unpopular one under Prince Polignac, was widely seen as the prelude to a royal *coup d'état*. The Russians themselves were nervous about their military prospects at the outset of their 1829 campaign. A decisive victory by General Diebitsch over the Turks on 11 June, however, changed everything. The Russian army now crossed the Balkan mountains almost without resistance. Adrianople, key to the defences of Constantinople, fell on 20–1 August, and the Turks,

---

[30] Bertier (1968–71: iii. 1220–45). For additional material on Metternich, I have used his *Vorträge* for 1828, HHStA, *Vorträge* 1828/254–5. On British policy, besides Wellington (1862–80: iv. 495–9, 542–4, 630–1, 639–41; v. 408–11), I have relied on Aberdeen's correspondence with Lords Granville and Stuart at Paris in 1828–9, BL Add. MSS 43080, 43082–3. An early opponent of Russia, the High Tory Lord Ellenborough, president of the board of control for India, also advocated restraining Russia through close partnership with France and using the St Petersburg Protocol and Triple Treaty as tools of restraint; Wellington (1862–80: iv. 164–5; v. 54–7).

[31] Fleming (1970: 76–83); Driault and Lhéritier (1925: i. 433–45); DeClercq (1880–1917: iii. 533–7, 542–6).

who had already conceded everything in the Greek settlement to British and French representatives in hopes of getting European support against the Russians, sued for peace.[32]

Turkey's collapse, though not unexpected, created near-panic in the courts of Europe. Two long-anticipated perils seemed at hand: that the Ottoman Empire would break up from Russian action or the simple weight of defeat, and that a general territorial scramble in the Near East and Europe would result. A signal of the latter danger was the so-called Polignac Project, a proposal sent by France to Russia early in September. It called for an alliance between the two states, joined by the other Continental powers, to partition the Ottoman Empire and redraw the map of Europe. Russia would take the Principalities and part of eastern Asia Minor, pushing Russian expansion in the direction of India and thereby checking Britain; Austria would get Serbia and Bosnia; Prussia would take Saxony and Holland, with the King of Saxony to be compensated with the Prussian Rhineland; France would take Belgium; and Britain would be compensated with Dutch colonies.

The general sense of crisis was understandable. Yet all the dangers, of Turkish collapse, Russian expansion, and French revisionism, were less critical than they seemed. On 16 September the Russian State Council reaffirmed Russia's policy of preserving the Ottoman Empire in its present weak and dependent condition. General Diebitsch had already signed the Peace of Adrianople with Turkey two days earlier, and the treaty conformed to this policy. It restored to the Ottoman Empire all Russia's conquests save a strip of territory on the east coast of the Black Sea and another at the Danube delta. It also compelled the Turks to accept the London Conference's decisions on Greece, and saddled the exhausted Turkish treasury with a huge indemnity for Russia's losses in trade and war costs, with Russia to occupy the Danubian Principalities until it was paid. It was thus not really a soft peace, but rather the maximum which Diebitsch had been instructed to demand; Metternich, long a doomsayer, judged it realistically (and less pessimistically than most) as moderate in the short run but fatal to the Ottoman Empire in the long run. Most dangerous to Austria and damaging to Turkish and European trade was the fact that the treaty gave Russia territorial control of critical portions of the Danube delta where it entered the Black Sea. Yet at least it was not a peace of overt conquest, and gave the Turks

[32] Schiemann (1904: ii. 308–26, 339–50); Bertier (1968–71: iii. 1299–1303).

time to recover and Europe time to do something about the basic problem.[33]

As for the Polignac Memorandum, it was absurd more than dangerous. (Or rather, it was dangerous as a proof of how much old eighteenth-century thinking was still around and how easily it could surface, rather than as a practical scheme likely to be put into effect.) Its authors were certain officials in the foreign ministry; its ideas were those of Charles X. Prince Polignac sent it to St Petersburg in early September in the same mood of panic that inspired other wild notions in Europe on how to keep Russia from swallowing the Ottoman Empire whole. (Wellington, for example, proposed establishing a large Greek kingdom with its capital at Constantinople and a Dutch or Prussian prince as king.) At St Petersburg, where it arrived after the Peace of Adrianople, the memorandum was dropped without even being communicated to Russia by the French ambassador. Had he presented it, every government, including Russia's, would have shot it down.[34]

The fears about Ottoman collapse, Russian conquests in the straits and Balkans, and French revisionist ambitions in Europe were not only exaggerated but somewhat misdirected. The Ottoman Empire was not ready to die; in a sense it was too un-European and unmodern to collapse even after military defeat. Russia was not interested in territorial expansion at this time, at least not in Europe. As for the Polignac Project, it reveals not merely what follies Frenchmen could concoct in their desire to overthrow the 1815 settlement, but also how relatively modest and self-defeating their concrete territorial and power-political aims were. The project would only have given France Belgium, not the more important Rhine frontier in Germany; the territorial gains assigned to both Russia and Prussia were much more valuable than France's. More important still, Russia's, Prussia's, Austria's, and even Britain's gains under the plan would have had considerable strategic value for them, at least in immediate power-political terms. France's gains, in contrast, would have made its strategic position on the Continent worse. The United Netherlands as a buffer state was as valuable for France's security as for that of its neighbours; eliminating it would actually increase France's defensive tasks *vis-à-vis* Prussia and Germany while

---

[33] Schiemann (1904: ii. 362–9); Jelavich (1991: 85–9); Shil'der (1903: ii. 548–51); Dakin (1973: 272–5).

[34] A full discussion of the project from its origins to its aftermath is in Hammer (1963: 130–69); but see also Bertier (1968–71: iii. 1310–15); Driault and Lhéritier (1925: i. 450–1).

making Britain once again a mortal enemy. As sensible Frenchmen like Talleyrand knew, this was the worst thing France could do.

The real European and Near Eastern dangers lay elsewhere and deeper: not that the Ottoman Empire would collapse, but that it would in the future try to survive by dragging Europe into its quarrels with Russia and escalating them into a general war; not that Russia would revive its territorial expansion, but that, over-confident about its hegemony in the East, it would try to exercise it in ways ultimately intolerable to the rest of Europe; not that France would return to revolutionary expansion and Napoleonic imperialism, but that France and Europe would revive the old competitive eighteenth-century politics.

There were signs of these dangers at the time; the Polignac Project was one, as noted. The Russians gloated over Adrianople not so much as a triumph over the Turks but as a victory over Europe, especially Austria. It proved that, when Russia took the lead resolutely in the Near East, Europe could not unite to stop it. Though Russia never seriously entertained the Polignac Project or anything like it, it did think about forming a special Russo-French partnership. Nicholas corresponded with Charles X and encouraged him to take bold action in Algiers in order to raise his prestige. France was not the only power tempted to exploit the Eastern question in order to revise the map of Europe. Sardinia-Piedmont's foreign minister, Count de la Torre, promptly laid claim to the throne of Greece for the House of Savoy, not because he really wanted it but in the hope of gaining Modena and/or Lucca in exchange for surrendering Savoy's rights to the Greek throne.[35] Every one of the concrete advantages Russia gained from the Turks at Adrianople, moreover—the indemnity, the occupation of the Principalities, the navigation of the straits, the control of the mouth of the Danube, territorial gains in the Caucasus—would later cause trouble between Russia and Europe, and most of them affected Austria and Britain as well as the Ottoman Empire. Above all, Russia's success at this juncture in drawing Britain into a hegemonic partnership, enabling it to ignore opposition from the other powers in Europe, had given Russia a dangerous model for its policy in the East. It would try the same tactic again in 1839–41, successfully; once more in the mid-1840s, without doing any harm; and finally before the Crimean War, disastrously.

[35] Schiemann (1904: ii. 210–11, 213–14, 379–80, 383–5, 392–7); Jelavich (1966: 137–46); *Rel. dipl. GB–Sard.* (1972–: 1. ii. Nos. 258, 260).

The episode also demonstrated how difficult it was for other powers to stop Russia from making the Ottoman Empire its exclusive sphere of influence even when they were reasonably united in this aim. Besides the obvious reasons—Russia's geographical, military, and religious-ethnic advantages, Turkish weakness, divisions within Europe—there was a less obvious but fundamental one: the Austro-British partnership vital for the success of any such effort could not be counted on. Once again, in this crisis, their so-called natural alliance proved necessary but unnatural. The best way to check Russia—perhaps the only feasible one—was the one which Austria had been advocating off and on ever since Kaunitz's time, and consistently since 1820: not challenging Russia directly or competing with it for dominant influence at Constantinople, but grouping it, requiring Russia to act *vis-à-vis* Turkey only in concert with Europe. Canning had deliberately spurned this policy and thereby opened the door to war and Russia's gains.

Yet one cannot blame everything on Canning. Even Wellington and Aberdeen, about as pro-Austrian as Britons could be, declined to work with Austria in a general concert. This was not because of ideology. Wellington's High Tory political views hardly differed from Metternich's; one of the monarchs he liked best in Europe was the rigidly absolutist Charles Felix of Sardinia-Piedmont. Nor does Wellington seem to have borne a personal grudge against Metternich for what had happened to him at Verona. Contingent factors made some difference: the British parliamentary system, the general aversion of most Britons to Continental links of any kind, and the particular dislike of many for Catholic, unprogressive Austria. The main reasons for Wellington's determination to work with France and Russia and stay away from Austria, however, were systemic. While Austria and Prussia in certain circumstances could be useful to Britain, they could not be dangerous. France and Russia in different ways were dangerous, and the Triple Treaty and European Concert had to be used to control them, over Austria's and Prussia's heads if necessary. Besides, forming a concert with Austria meant recognizing its special interests and conforming to its rigid brand of conservatism. Here this called for letting the Greek revolt grind on indefinitely or be snuffed out by the Turks and Egyptians; elsewhere, co-operation with Austria meant supporting or tolerating its policies in Italy and Germany. Many British understandably found this too high a price to pay.

This explains why after Adrianople the two governments,

though aware of their common dangers and interests and willing to co-operate, found it as difficult to work together as before. Concrete occasions and suggestions for co-operation arose. Aberdeen proposed Prince Philip of Hesse-Homburg, an Austrian general, for the throne of Greece. Both governments considered having the five powers guarantee Turkey and/or Greece to prevent further Russian encroachments. Metternich urged that the four powers guarantee a loan to the Ottoman Empire so that it could pay off Russia's indemnity and get rid of its occupation forces. But while Metternich insisted that Turkey could still be saved, Aberdeen and Wellington were inclined to give up on it and look to Greece as a barrier against Russia. Metternich wanted the 6 July treaty buried, the British insisted it had to be fulfilled. Each government grew irritated with the other; each knew that it could not really trust the other for support. In a crisis, Austria would lean toward Russia, both to gain security and to restrain Russia, and Britain would do the same with France.[36]

All these potentially dangerous effects of this Eastern crisis showed up only in the longer run, however; its immediate results ranged from tolerable to good. Both Turks and Greeks benefited from ending their savage war. Out of decisions of the London Conference from November 1829 to early February 1830 there emerged a Greek monarchy, independent rather than autonomous, with somewhat expanded frontiers. The new state inevitably became a source of international friction, for a variety of internal and external, economic and political reasons, and has remained so to the present day. The choice of king was an initial bone of contention among the three founding powers, until more serious troubles overtook Europe in the summer of 1830. They finally settled on Prince Leopold of Saxe-Coburg, only to have him first accept and then decline their actual terms. Yet even an unstable Greece was better than continued Ottoman rule, though hardly the great triumph for freedom and progress that has often been portrayed. Moreover, the outcome proved again the strength of the international system. The main alliances of restraint, those between Britain and France and Russia and Austria respectively, though strained or temporarily dissolved, survived the crisis and were quickly reinstated. More important, all the powers observed

---

[36] For Metternich's views, see Bertier (1968–71: iii. 1315–19); on Wellington and Aberdeen, I have relied on Wellington (1862–80: vi) and Aberdeen's private correspondence with Lord Cowley at Vienna and Charles Stuart at Paris, BL Add. MSS 43080, 43083. The most succinct statement of Wellington's policy is in Wellington (1862–80: v. 416–17).

the basic principle of non-aggrandizement embodied in the self-denying clauses of the St Petersburg Protocol and the 6 July treaty. Wellington and Aberdeen would yield grudgingly to their allies on other points, but not this one, and Russia and France never tried to break loose. Charles X and Chateaubriand and Nicholas and Diebitsch never dared implement the dangerous ideas they sometimes entertained. Russia, having put Austria and Turkey in their places, returned to its inactive hegemony in Eastern Europe; Metternich, wanting to be Europe's coachman, resigned himself to the role of brakeman.[37]

It is not easy to say who, if anyone, deserves the credit for Europe's thus avoiding disaster and achieving some good. Certainly not Canning; there is no better example of someone's dying just in time to save his reputation. Clearly Nicholas and Russia won the diplomatic contest, and the fact that the outcome of the war was tolerable owes much to their restraint. But given their abhorrence of revolutionary goals, it is hard to see what Russia gained that was worth the war's considerable effort and risks (a conclusion Barbara Jelavich applies to Russia's Balkan policy throughout the nineteenth century).[38] In this case, Russia fought to help establish a Greek state which would soon be a revolutionary thorn in its own side, and over which Britain and France, as naval and commercial powers active in the Mediterranean where Russia was excluded, were bound to exert a dominant influence. From that standpoint, Russia's success in luring Britain into partnership in Greece over the heads of the Continental powers also had its ironically counter-productive side. So did its successful war with Turkey; more than anything else, this promoted Russophobia in Britain and spurred it to oppose Russia in Asia.[39] As for Metternich, his forecasts of what British and Russian actions would lead to were remarkably accurate, but when it came to practical solutions, he basically had nothing better to propose than letting the Turks and Greeks fight it out indefinitely. The French did reasonably well in exploiting the situation to bolster their prestige, but some of their bolder ideas would have been as disastrous to them as to the system.

This leaves two implausible contenders for the prize of having done most to keep Europe peaceful and on the rails in 1828–30:

[37] Dakin (1973: 276–87, 314); Molden (1913); Martens (1974–5: xi. 415–29); DeClercq (1880–1917: iii. 557–67).

[38] Jelavich (1991). I am grateful to Prof. Jelavich for pointing out the importance of Anglo-French naval supremacy and rivalry in the Mediterranean.

[39] Gleason (1972); Ingram (1979).

Wellington and Aberdeen. Nothing is easier than to criticize them for lacking the energy and decisiveness of Canning and Palmerston, or to poke fun at the dire predictions and complaints they constantly made while they were being dragged along by the French and Russians. Yet to read their correspondence is to recognize that they understood what needed doing, namely, making the best of the bad situation they had inherited, sticking with France, holding back Russia, not falling in with Metternich's schemes, fulfilling Britain's treaty obligations so that others had no excuse to break theirs, and thereby saving both peace and the system.[40] They understood and practised the art of damage control, the use of pacts of restraint, and the wisdom of accepting the inevitable and muddling through.

IV. SPAIN, PORTUGAL, AND AMERICA

The only other international development of note achieved in 1823–9 was Britain's recognition of the independence of Spain's Latin American colonies. (The complications of these years in the Iberian peninsula itself belong to a later chapter.) This was little more than a footnote in the history of international politics, not to be compared with the Eastern question, but it too illustrates the strengths of the system. British policy has been aptly summarized by Charles K. Webster as developing in four stages: 1810–20, mediation; 1820–4, preparation for recognition; 1825, recognition; and after 1825, attempts to reconcile Spain and its former colonies. It was a prudent course, involving more continuity in policy between Castlereagh and Canning than prevailed in Europe. As

---

[40] For evidence of Wellington's sceptical common sense on the Greek question, see Wellington (1862–80: v. 198–9; vi. 491–8). For Aberdeen's prudence, the best source is his correspondence with his brother Robert Gordon, then at Paris. Some samples: on France, 'The French Govt are too bad; their cowardly temporizing conduct is in the highest degree provoking; but we must have patience' (4 June 1829, BL Add. MS 43210, fos. 67–8). In regard to Russia and Austria, Aberdeen was convinced that Nicholas wanted to end the war and be friends with Britain, and regretted that 'There is no making them [Russia and France] believe that we are not in league with Metternich, to some end hostile to them both'. Metternich, Aberdeen correctly suspected, was deliberately promoting this belief (9 July 1829, ibid. fos. 94–5). On Russia and the Ottoman Empire after the war: 'It is to be expected that the Porte should now look to Russia rather than to any other Power; and to this we can have no objection . . .', provided Russia preserved Turkey as it was, which Nicholas would probably do. Britain's interest was solely to keep things quiet and keep the 'crazy machine' going as long as possible (8 May 1830, ibid. fos. 242–3).

already noted, no one tried seriously to thwart British policy or even manage it. By Castlereagh's death in 1822 all governments except Spain's accepted the inevitability of independence. Despite the publicity surrounding it, Canning's policy of promoting a peaceful separation of the colonies where revolution had become irreversible and of trying to preserve monarchic governments in them did not differ in substance from those of France or Austria.

An apparently serious quarrel over the issue in 1824–5 arose from Canning's need to score points against his domestic and foreign opponents and his desire if possible to lure the United States, Britain's only real opponent in Latin America, into a restraining partnership. His first major success, as noted, was the Polignac Memorandum concluded with Prince Polignac as French ambassador in late 1823. Chateaubriand, supported verbally by the Holy Alliance, tried in 1824 to stop Britain from acting unilaterally by luring Britain into a European congress on the recognition question. Canning, easily turning this aside, proceeded to extend recognition unilaterally and with a maximum of publicity in 1825. Alexander's protest was angry and genuine, Metternich's purely tactical, designed to keep Russia and Britain separate and to restrain Russia in the East. None of the Holy Alliance powers had any intention of helping Spain in any concrete way or interfering with Britain's actions. At this same time Russia and Britain came to terms over their respective frontiers in western North America, Russia abandoning its unilateral decree of September 1821.

Here, at least, there is no ground to criticize Canning's policy. He faced little opposition and had a winning hand, but played it skilfully in the interests of Britain and Latin America as well as his own, with no damage to Spain or the European states. The system worked here as it was supposed to, with Britain exercising hegemony in a reasonable if overly ostentatious way, and the Continental powers accepting the inevitable.[41]

[41] The best account is Webster (1938: i. 8–75); but see also Robertson (1939: 253–67, 320–59); Bertier (1968–71: ii. 852–905); Bourquin (1954: 410–11, 448–55); Baack (1980: 141–7); Kossok (1964: 109–37). For arguments that Canning faced serious opposition and dangerous intrigues from France and the Holy Alliance, see Temperley (1925a: 133–7, 152–9, 184–5; 1924a; 1925b). For the Russo-British negotiations over N. America, see Martens (1874–1905: xi. 310–22).

15
Revolutions, Progress, and Standstill, 1830–1833

CONTEMPORARY observers and historians agree, by and large, on the results of the revolutions of 1830–1. In the domestic sphere they produced real and useful political and social change in France, Belgium, Switzerland, and parts of Germany, though in Italy and Poland they failed. In foreign affairs, they led to serious crises and war scares which challenged the Vienna system and weakened it over the long run. Major treaties were overturned, conservative solidarity was eroded, and Europe was divided more clearly into rival ideological camps, portending future trouble.[1]

On the domestic side the verdict is sound. The year 1830 may not compare with 1789 or 1848 in drama, violence, and ideological resonance, but its revolutions arguably produced or paved the way for more solid political, social, and economic progress in Europe than either of them. The Metternich system of internal governance (union of throne and altar, unalloyed monarchic sovereignty, preventive censorship, no representative constitutions, etc.) was clearly weakened, even where it survived outwardly intact. Whether the 1830 revolutions also undermined the international system, however, is another question. The case can be made that the Vienna system emerged from the 1830 challenge unshaken, perhaps in certain ways improved. Once again some of the system's distinctive characteristics—a de-emphasis on balance of power and emphasis on obeying the rules of the game, the use of restraining alliances and *ententes*, and the preservation of intermediary bodies—proved their value.

I. THE JULY REVOLUTION IN FRANCE

The Paris revolution that overthrew Charles X in late July and replaced him with Louis-Philippe, Duc d'Orléans, is a good example of how the same revolution could undermine the Met-

---

[1] Church (1983).

ternich system and strengthen the international system. The revolt grew out of France's domestic problems—the economic troubles of the late 1820s, growing discontent among various élites over the narrow limits on political rights and participation under the charter, and hatred of the reactionary Polignac ministry. The King and Polignac, having lost the parliamentary elections of May 1830 to the liberal opposition, tried to regain control through revising the election laws by decree (the so-called July Ordinances). The attempted royal coup, badly timed, triggered a public reaction in the form of widespread protests leading to an armed revolt in Paris, which caught the government unprepared for trouble it should have foreseen. The small armed forces available to the government in the capital were worn down and defeated in three days of street fighting on 27–9 July. Charles left Paris, abdicated, and fled into exile in England, and Louis-Philippe was installed first as lieutenant-general and then as king in early August.[2]

The fall of the Bourbons was a heavy blow to Metternich and his brand of conservatism. His advice to Charles, as to other constitutional monarchs, had been pretty much in line with what Charles attempted: not to try to overthrow the constitution directly, but to revise it in the direction of expanding his own authority and curbing the press and the opposition. Naturally, he blamed the outcome on the French ministry's ineptitude rather than his own advice. It was little solace to him that Louis-Philippe immediately adopted a conservative stance himself, working with like-minded moderates in France to limit the revolution's political and constitutional changes and prevent any social revolution. From an absolutist point of view, the damage remained. The revolutionary tricolor instead of the Bourbon lily now flew in France; the King ruled by the will of the people as well as the grace of God; the active political class in France, though still narrowly restricted by wealth, was tripled in numbers and changed in character, dominated no longer by landowners and nobles but by industrialists, merchants, and professionals; and the government had to rule through parliament and with its consent. Metternich, Nicholas, and others considered a mongrel regime like this in some ways worse and more dangerous than red revolution. Though Metternich soon came to accept the July monarchy

---

[2] On the origins and course of the revolution generally, see Pinkney (1972); Jardin (1985: 284–93); Jardin and Tudesq (1984: 93–101); Bury and Combs (1986: 26–39). On the role of the French army, see Porch (1974: 26–37); Holroyd (1971: 538–52).

as preferable to any available alternative, he declined to work closely with Louis-Philippe until shortly before 1848, by which time both the Orléans regime and Metternich's were on their last legs. As for the Tsar, he never forgave Louis-Philippe for usurping Charles's throne.

The revolution, however, dealt no such blow to the international system, as on its face it should have. The Quadruple Alliance of November 1815 called for consultation if the Bourbons were overthrown. There was widespread and understandable fear in Europe that the revolt would revive France's revolutionary expansionism and provoke more revolutions elsewhere; the latter concern would be quickly justified by events. Yet no one, including Russia, made a serious move to invoke the *casus foederis* of the alliance. Both the threat from France and the spin-off revolutions in Europe proved manageable without the use of force or overt conflict. The radicals in France, though they made much noise, showed little skill and had little luck in trying to export the revolution, and the new French regime by and large worked to restrain them and preserve peace.

All this is well known. Less commonplace is another proposition: the July Revolution improved the system, by eliminating an existing French threat to it. International politics, though it had not caused the revolution, was involved in its background and development. Charles X's principal ambition and main hope of strengthening and popularizing his rule lay in reviving the glory of France and the Bourbon dynasty by foreign-policy victories. He dreamed constantly of overthrowing the treaties, redrawing the map of Europe, expanding in Belgium and the Rhineland, restoring French influence in Italy, and uniting the Continent against Britain. In foreign policy, Charles at his best was more dangerous by far than Louis-Philippe at his worst, good proof of Metternich's axiom that an ambitious France, whatever its ideology, was a revolutionary France.

Two earlier moves by Charles, the French occupation of the Morea and the Polignac Plan, had failed to produce a conservative *ralliement* round the Bourbon flag. He and his ministers in 1830 therefore turned to something new, a military expedition against the Dey of Algiers. Neither they nor the French people cared much about Algiers for its own sake. Italy, the Levant, the Iberian peninsula, and Latin America were of greater interest; Britain had shown more concern than France to combat piracy and slave-trading by the Barbary states. The government had a long-standing pretext for acting against the Dey, an insult dealt to a French consul in 1827, but it had hitherto tried for satisfaction by diplo-

matic means. In January 1830, however, the ministry decided on a
punitive expedition for prestige reasons.

The expedition, carried out in May, proved a diplomatic and
military success. There was virtually no European opposition;
even Wellington and Aberdeen, secretly urged by Metternich to
stop it, decided to tolerate it to maintain the informal Anglo-
French restraining alliance. The British were less sensitive about
Algiers than about Egypt and the eastern Mediterranean or about
Morocco and the Straits of Gibraltar to the west. By July, Algiers
was in French hands. But at home the coup came too late to
distract public attention from France's domestic troubles.[3] So far
as the revolution was concerned, the expedition meant mainly that
37,000 picked soldiers were in North Africa when Charles needed
them in France.[4]

Charles got away with the Algerian expedition, though all the
powers save Russia disapproved of it, because none of them
wanted to quarrel with France or to increase French domestic
unrest. The same prudence kept them from doing anything for
Charles once he was overthrown. Britain's reaction was the most
important, and it was never in doubt. Wellington followed his
usual principle: the greater the potential danger from France, the
closer Britain should stick to France and the less it should do to
stir France up. He held Charles responsible for his own downfall, first by provoking the revolt and then by abandoning his
throne, and considered Louis-Philippe far better as a ruler than
a Bonapartist or republican would be. Besides, Wellington's
ministry was in great trouble at home. With the Tories divided by
the Catholic Emancipation Act just carried through by the ministry
and under siege by the Whigs and popular demands for parliamentary reform, Wellington dared not intervene against a revolution which many Britons applauded. Behind these practical
grounds for non-intervention lay something broader: the fact that
France was no longer automatically Britain's natural and necessary
enemy. While the old popular antipathies persisted and political
relations were often strained, the social, economic, and cultural
ties between the two countries were growing closer.

[3] One leading opposition journal, however, Adolphe Thiers' *National*, changed
from initial disdain for the venture to nationalist euphoria and Anglophobia, and
the conquest eventually became popular. Charles's strategy was less to blame for
his downfall than his timing; Bury and Combs (1986: 24–5).

[4] Julien (1964: 1–63); Braunstein (1983: 51–6); Bertier (1966: 432–9; 1968–71:
iii. 1339–51). Hammer (1963: 219–22) sees the expedition as part of a broad
French plan for a break with Britain and territorial expansion on the Continent.
For Wellington's and Aberdeen's reactions, see Wellington (1862–80: vi. 576–80);
Aberdeen to Robert Gordon, 1 July 1830, BL Add. MS 43210, fos. 264–5.

As for the Eastern powers, Metternich predictably called for a union of the four powers or, if Britain refused, the three Holy Allies to denounce the revolution—but not in order to do anything about it. His main worries were about Italy and the Near East and his main aim was to make sure of Russian support in those theatres. Though he obtained this, it was not, as he claimed, because Russia had been brought back to the right path by his sermons, preaching that its policy in the Near East had opened the floodgates of revolution in Europe, and that only an intimate Austro-Russian alliance could stop the revolutionary tide now. Nesselrode signed a vague anti-revolutionary declaration with Metternich in August at Carlsbad, but assured the other powers it meant little. As for Nicholas, he needed no prompting from Metternich to denounce the July Revolution. It challenged his legitimist principles, wrecked the Franco-Russian *rapprochement* he had been promoting, encouraged a dangerous Anglo-French liberal *entente* instead, and aroused his fears for Poland. For these reasons, Russia's anti-revolutionary rhetoric and military preparations in response to the July Revolution were stronger than any other power's. Its measures, however, were always intended to stiffen the backbone of Russia's timorous allies more than to prepare for action, and they failed to have even that effect. Prussia feared a spread of the revolution to Germany, particularly the Rhineland, but was also aware that intervention would only increase the danger. Foreign minister Count Bernstorff had little trouble convincing the King that full recognition of Louis-Philippe was the best way to avoid complications. By early October all the great powers, Britain in the lead, had recognized the new government, and even the conservative Italian regimes most afraid of the revolution (Sardinia-Piedmont, Naples, Rome) did the same.[5]

II. THE BELGIAN QUESTION

Thus the July Revolution both got rid of a dangerous international actor and demonstrated once more how systemic restraints and satisfactions worked to promote system-conforming and system-

[5] On Anglo-French relations, see Guyot (1926: 17–51); Beales (1933–4). For Austrian, Prussian, and Russian reactions, see Bertier (1968–71: iii. 1351–65); Seide (1971: 57–9); Molden (1913: 7–9); Martens (1874–1905: xi. 430–7); Baack (1980: 165–77). I have also used Metternich's correspondence with Count Karl Ficquelmont at St Petersburg, HHStA, *Weisungen Varia Russland* 90. Papal and Sardinian reactions are documented in *Rel. dipl. Stat. Pont.–Fr.* (1962–: 2. i. Nos. 10–12, 42–3); *Rel. dipl. GB–Sard.* (1972–: 1. ii. Nos. 261–81); *Rel. dipl. Fr.–Sard.* (1974–: 2. i).

preserving conduct. A much graver challenge, however, was raised by the Belgian revolution. As in France, it had its roots in domestic affairs. A downturn in the Belgian economy in the late 1820s leading to unemployment and worker demonstrations increased and focused the long-standing discontent with Orangist rule in the southern Netherlands. Economic factors, however, were only a temporary catalyst for discontent, not its main cause. Overall, the union of north and south under King William I's enlightened absolutism had benefited the Belgian economy. On paper, in terms of government positions, the Dutch were favoured; but policy seemed increasingly to favour the Belgian half of the kingdom. It was rather the religious, educational, administrative, and fiscal aspects of his centralist rule, coming on top of centuries of antagonism, that had managed both to alienate the Dutch and to drive the rival liberal and aristocratic-Catholic élites in Belgium together into opposition.[6]

But as with Charles X, while domestic factors caused the revolt, international politics lay behind it, proving again that foreign policy can lie at the roots of domestic politics just as well as the reverse. Obviously, one ultimate source of the revolt was the decision at Vienna to unite the Dutch and Belgians under Orange rule in the first place; a larger one, however, was William I's determination to make the United Netherlands into at least a respectable middle-sized power, possibly a major one equalling or surpassing Prussia. To this end he refused to let the United Netherlands be what the Congress of Vienna intended: a peaceful intermediary state serving as a buffer against France, leaning on Britain and Prussia for security, tied to the German Confederation, and respectful of the differences between Dutch and Belgians at home. The very policies which benefited Belgium—economic development, the promotion and protection of industry, opening the Dutch colonies to Belgian goods while closing them to outsiders—were the King's means to an unattainable power-political dream that neither of his peoples shared, especially the Dutch. As will be seen, once the Belgian revolution occurred the great powers quickly recognized that their original scheme would not work, and sought a new way to achieve their ends. William would stubbornly pursue his failed dream for eight more years.[7]

[6] On the general development of the revolt, see Helmreich (1976: 8–14); Lademacher (1971: 37–46); Kossman (1978: 113–60); Dunk (1966: 80–1, 108–15); Gruner (1977a: 327–45); Fishman (1988: 21–6); Omond (1919). On William's economic policies and their impact, see H. Wright (1955: esp. 208–34); Demoulin (1938); Terlinden (1922); Boogman (1968a: 140–3).

Though there was widespread Belgian (and Dutch) discontent with existing conditions, the revolt which broke out in Brussels on 26–7 August was at first a minor matter of worker demonstrations and liberal risings. Soon, however, a civic guard was formed which took control of the city, and the revolt spread to other areas, succeeding in good part because William's control in the southern Netherlands was loose and his response indecisive. A mission to Brussels by William's son and successor, the Prince of Orange, on 31 August neither satisfied nor intimidated the insurgents. William I then invited the four powers who were signatories of the original Eight Articles setting up the United Netherlands (thus barring France) to a conference at the Hague to advise him on the Belgian demands for administrative separation. This invitation received a cool, wait-and-see response from Britain. William next convoked the States General, which granted the Belgians some concessions that failed to conciliate them, and thereafter sent his younger son, Prince Frederick, with 14,000 men to overawe them. When this expedition led to armed conflict ending in a confused retreat by the Dutch forces on 27 September, William's hope of dealing with the revolt unaided was over. The next day he formally invited the four powers to come to his aid with military force.

Meanwhile the Belgians formed a provisional government on 26 September and declared their independence on 4 October. The Prince of Orange, sent to Brussels in mid-October as newly appointed governor-general of the southern Netherlands, compounded the problem by an unauthorized declaration recognizing Belgium as independent under his rule, a solution quickly repudiated by both sides. After he left, the revolution, already in control of most of Belgium and Luxemburg, spread to Antwerp, where the Belgians captured the city but failed to take the citadel. The Dutch responded in early November by blockading the Scheldt.[8]

The revolution was thus a chapter in Belgian and Dutch internal history, not international politics. First the Dutch rejected the kind of unification the King was pushing, as well as the administrative autonomy the Belgians initially demanded; then the Belgians rejected any further connection with the House of Orange or the Dutch. Yet the revolt illustrates a general point

[7] On William's foreign policy, see esp. Sas (1985: 182–298); also Boogman (1955: i. 3–14; 1968a: 144–6; 1966).

[8] Besides the works cited in n. 6 above, see Fishman (1988: 26–34); Gruner (1977a: 346–8).

about the Vienna era and system. The international peace and stability of the era is sometimes ascribed to the ability of the great powers to dominate and manipulate the smaller powers and to repress popular movements and revolutions. When this ability was lost in 1848 and after, international peace went with it. Whatever truth this may hold in some instances, the Belgian revolution and the European response show why it cannot be seen as the general rule. Belgian and other historians, as is natural, have mainly discussed what caused the revolution, and above all whether it was driven by a genuine Belgian nationalism—a legitimate question and debate.[9] But if one asks not what caused the revolt, but what allowed it to happen, the plain answer must be that it arose and succeeded because of the fairly loose character of William's rule, the feeble and hesitant attempts of the government to quell it, and above all the subsequent refusal of the powers to help William do so. The distinguishing characteristic of the post-Vienna era was not the zeal, rigour, and united will with which conservative governments stamped out popular risings. It was instead the lax, inefficient nature of many regimes and the inhibitions almost all monarchs of this era felt about using force against their own citizens or other countries, which constantly permitted risings and conspiracies, often derived from a slender base both in power and popular support, to occur and sometimes let them succeed. This was true of all the risings in the 1820s and 1830s and the initial stages of 1848.

In other words: one of the distinguishing features of the Vienna era, compared to the earlier and later ones, was that it was relatively easy and safe to promote revolution. In Europe from 1848 to 1914, the kind of popular rising so common from 1815 to 1848 remained possible only where regimes remained old-fashioned and inefficient, like the Ottoman Empire, or fell into crisis because of a lost, unpopular war, like Russia in 1905. One can say that many regimes in the Vienna era were unprogressive, illiberal, repressive, inefficient, old-fashioned, and so on—but not that they prevented or crushed popular revolts efficiently and ruthlessly. It took the French Revolution and Napoleon to do this before 1815, and the forces of nationalist revolution, liberalism, industrialism, and the strong bourgeois state to do so after 1848, to produce the June Days, the American Civil War, or the Paris Commune.

[9] See, e.g. Stengers (1950–1; 1981a; 1981b); Willecquet (1974); Witte (1989); Rooney (1982); Bartier (1967).

In any case, the powers were now faced with a quarrel between two small governments and peoples, important because they occupied a strategic location and played a vital role in the international system. Making the struggle intractable were, on one side, a monarch determined to maintain his state and his sovereign rights regardless of what his subjects, both loyal and rebellious, felt about it and, on the other, Belgian leaders now bent on creating as large a Belgian state as possible, regardless of the shaky political, ethnic, linguistic, and strategic foundations on which it would rest. Small-power conflict and great-power co-operation were the hallmarks of the Belgian question from beginning to end. The Belgians and the Dutch caused almost all the trouble; no great power really wanted to intervene unilaterally in their dispute or tried seriously to profit from it at the expense of the others.

The powers had practical reasons for caution, especially initially. Wellington and Aberdeen responded tardily to the revolt out of distraction with domestic troubles, suspicion of France, and a rather surprising insouciance about British interests in the affair.[10] But after declining to co-operate with France early on in preventing or controlling the revolt, they then insisted that France must be included in settling the issue once the revolt had succeeded.[11] The new French government had even stronger incentives for offering its co-operation than Britain had for accepting it. Besides the fact that it wanted international recognition and needed to control its radicals at home, France, more than any other great power, simply could not afford a war over Belgium. A major contingent of its army was in Algeria, a smaller one in Greece, and the remainder, schooled to personal loyalty to Charles X, disorganized and possibly unreliable for combat. War for France in 1830 would have meant 1792 without the *élan* of the original revolution and with the *Feuillants* in charge. While Europe feared a French intervention in Belgium, the French government feared a British or Prussian one even more.[12]

At Berlin a few hotspurs, including the King's brother, Prince William, argued that now might be a good occasion for the war

---

[10] e.g. Aberdeen wrote to Lord Cowley at Vienna on 27 Oct. that, even though King William had lost the southern Netherlands for good, so long as he kept Antwerp and Maastricht Britain could still control the situation; BL Add. MS 43080, fos. 364–5.

[11] See Sas (1985: 299–315); Colenbrander (1905–22: x, pt. 1, Nos. 20–84, esp. No. 72); Aberdeen to Robert Gordon, 20 Sept. 1830, BL Add. MS 43210, fos. 270–3.

[12] Fishman (1988: 43–50); Webster (1951: i. 95–7); Guyot (1926: 52–9); Gruner (1977: 349–51); Demoulin (1960).

with revolutionary France they considered inevitable sooner or later. The government, however, resolutely opposed intervention for various economic, domestic, and foreign-policy reasons, including a fear of the French army as lively as the French one of Prussia's. Besides, some Prussians, including the foreign minister, Bernstorff, saw the revolutionary crisis as a chance for Prussia to loosen its ties to Austria somewhat, strengthen them with Britain, and gain influence in Germany, where all the south German states were in favour of neutrality.[13] Metternich also had good reasons for inaction—concern for Poland, Italy, and Germany, military and fiscal weakness, and a recognition early on that William's cause was lost, and that European intervention in Belgium could cause Louis-Philippe to be overthrown in France. Any possible successor would be worse.[14] The Tsar, outraged by the Belgian revolt, seemed bent on action, ordering mobilization measures, denouncing the French principle of non-intervention, and constantly haranguing his allies. Yet Russians, like everyone else, knew that Russia could only act with and through its allies, and the necessary co-operation was nowhere in sight.[15]

These ordinary, short-range reasons and calculations suffice to explain the great powers' prudent response to the Belgian revolution; but that prudence and moderation had a significance far beyond its immediate causes. It is sometimes supposed or claimed that the conflicting interests and ideologies of the powers probably would have led sooner or later to intervention and war over the Belgian question, had not skilful British leadership prevented it.[16] It could better be argued that, had the rules and restraints operating here been only those of immediate practical interest, the calculations of *raison d'état* and balance of power typical of the eighteenth century, neither Britain's leadership nor anyone else's could have prevented war sooner or later. This was the most strategically vital, fiercely contested theatre in Europe, as it had been for four centuries. The normal, short-run restraints discussed so far were

---

[13] Baack (1980: 177–87); Dunk (1966: 85–91); Gruner (1977a: 351–5). Pertinent documents are in Colenbrander (1905–22: x, pt. 3).

[14] Arneth (1898: ii. 94–6); H. Müller (1980: 7–15); Obermann (1966: 226–38); Shil'der (1903: ii. 506–8); Colenbrander (1905–22: x, pt. 3, Nos. 124–5, 130); Metternich to Ficquelmont, No. 1 and Reserved to No. 1, 21 Oct. 1830, HHStA, *Weisungen Varia Russland* 90.

[15] Schiemann (1904: iii. 1–30, 167–75); Shil'der (1903: ii. 572–9); Martens (1874–1905: xi. 437–43); Leslie (1969: 118–20); Colenbrander (1905–22: x, pt. 3, Nos. 302–20).

[16] See e.g. Fishman (1988: 13–15); Bourne (1982: 333–5); Seton-Watson (1937: 158); or Calmès (1932–57: i. Chs. 4–5).

precisely the kind that fanatical or desperate men often defy, and clever, resolute ones exploit. The situation in Belgium in 1830 offered just the sort of historic opportunity that Frederick the Great, Cavour, Bismarck, and many other power politicians have chosen to seize. Great prizes were at stake, and most other states and leaders were afraid to try for them.

One must conclude, therefore, that in no earlier century, under no other international system than that of Vienna, could the Belgian crisis have been solved peacefully as it would be here. It took something more than normal politics. It required new rules of the game which all the great powers recognized and were willing to obey and enforce; restraining alliances to keep anyone from going off the rails; and, above all, the conviction that only European unity could solve the Belgian problem and others like it, and thereby save Europe itself from destruction. This is exactly the spirit which the crisis evoked immediately and everywhere—as much, for example, in Sir James Mackintosh, a leader of the radical Whig opposition, as in Wellington and Aberdeen on the Tory end of the British political spectrum—and it made a vital difference. Metternich, in appointing Baron Wessenberg to second Prince Esterházy at a London ambassadorial conference on Belgium, as usual blamed everything on the tardiness and foolishness of other powers—and then consigned the affair to 'the wisdom of the conference'. Wessenberg defined his assignment as one of reconciling 'the welfare [bonheur] of peoples with the legitimacy of principles and the general interest of Europe', and took for granted from the outset that this required three simple things: separating Belgium from Holland, making it into a monarchy, and keeping it independent from France.[17] The Prussian attitude was no different, even though, like Britain and unlike Austria, Prussia had major strategic, political, and commercial interests at stake in the Netherlands.

Two great powers allegedly posed a special danger to this European approach and to a peaceful solution. France is supposed to have tried repeatedly to aggrandize itself territorially and gain other special advantages in Belgium, failing in this only because of determined resistance from other powers.[18] The evidence looks convincing, especially at certain times. From late November to February 1831, with the weak Lafitte ministry in power and a

[17] Arneth (1898: ii. 97, 103–6); Colenbrander (1905–22: x, pt. 3, Nos. 136–7).
[18] Besides the works cited in n. 16 above, see Webster (1951: i. 122); Lannoy (1903: 89–96); Colenbrander (1905–22: x, pt. 2, pp. xiii–xxiii); Guyot (1926: 66–7).

former Napoleonic general, Count Sébastiani, as foreign minister, at a time when nationalists in the Chamber and the press were constantly denouncing the regime for betraying the revolution and pursuing peace at any price, French representatives more than once privately suggested partitioning Belgium between France, Holland, and Prussia, with Britain's interest to be safeguarded by special measures regarding Antwerp and the Scheldt. Similar ideas would come up on other occasions. The French also had some notions about forming a dynastic connection with the new Belgian state or a federal structure for Belgium that might hold the door open for French annexation in the future, and certainly tried at various times to make small territorial gains or extract strategic concessions from the Belgian question.

It is one thing, however, to recognize that these things happened, quite another to make them the centre and purpose of French policy. First of all, this confuses means and ends. The main goal of the French government was not territorial gains, but peace and security abroad and stability and popularity at home. The July monarchy was the most peaceful, status quo-orientated regime France had in the whole nineteenth century—perhaps ever. The main foreign-policy instrument it envisioned and pursued for its security and prestige was an alliance with Britain. Naturally French leaders, including the ever-opportunistic Talleyrand, now ambassador to Britain and delegate to the conference, would have accepted territorial prizes if they could get them cheaply. But no responsible leader, especially not Talleyrand, was willing to jeopardize the real goals of peace and a British alliance for their sake.[19] The government knew that any attempt to annex a major part of Belgium would mean war with all of Europe, that even minor territorial gains in Belgium would be hard to obtain, and that, if obtained, they could ruin the real political gains France would harvest from the breakup of the United Netherlands: the overthrow of a major section of the 1815 system directed against France and the forging of a working alliance with Britain. The problem in French foreign policy, as throughout this era, arose

---

[19] Talleyrand (1891a: Nos. 8–89), is full of evidence of this. An analogy to French policy on Belgium here would be Napoleon III's search for territorial gains in the Rhineland in the 1860s, when what he really wanted was not territory *per se*, e.g. the Rhine frontier, but political alliances with Prussia and Italy. The territorial gains were supposed to give him enough prestige and popularity to sustain his alliance policy against opponents at home. The difference is that Napoleon III was willing to risk war and even to promote it, where Louis-Philippe was not. On the regime's foreign policy in general, see Pinkney (1972: 296–313).

from the immaturity and unrealism of the French body politic. As almost always in history, the French government needed to be wiser, less selfish, and more far-sighted than its people, and found it hard to meet the need. A substantial party in France insisted that political gains in the Belgian question were useless, or would be useful only if they led to acquisitions of territory and power, and denounced the government as cowards and traitors for not seeking them. The half-hearted *démarches* of the government were primarily responses to this pressure.

In fact, not only did the French government recognize that it had to accept an independent Belgium as the price of its other goals; it wanted this for its own sake.[20] An independent Belgium would break the strategic ring around France, assist Louis-Philippe in uniting old conservative and new liberal forces in France against the radicals, and help him achieve recognition and good relations with other powers, including Prussia, the state next to Britain in importance to France. The French government was not really trying to deceive the other powers into thinking that it was working for an independent Belgium while it secretly tried to unite Belgium with France, but the opposite: to deceive the French radicals and nationalists while it worked with other powers for an independent Belgium. The policy of conditional non-intervention announced by Louis-Philippe's foreign minister, Count Molé, in early October suited this aim perfectly. It both reassured the other powers and tacitly warned them against an armed intervention in Belgium to which France would be compelled to respond.

A mass of evidence supports this interpretation. French envoys were constantly instructed to work for peace and European unity, and did so at London and Brussels, especially by co-operating with Britain. France proposed ideas unfavourable to particular French interests, such as giving the Belgian throne to the Prince of Orange, and accepted other unfavourable outcomes. French efforts to collect a territorial or political side-payment for their good behaviour, never pushed long or hard, were hastily dropped whenever an initiative encountered opposition or publicity. Some of the reports about dangerous French initiatives, derived from Prussian sources, are suspect. Some of these supposedly dangerous initiatives, moreover, had to do with legitimate French security interests in the Low Countries and concerns about other powers' aims. Many Frenchmen were opposed to French annexation of

[20] Lademacher (1978: 54–7).

Belgium on normal, non-political grounds—merchants and industrialists, for example, afraid of Belgian competition inside the protected French market.

Talleyrand, who is 1 'ost frequently accused of pursuing annexations, seems in fact ι have viewed a partition of Belgium less as a goal than as a *pis alle*. Even when he occasionally suggested it, he knew and said that it would have bad consequences for France—a longer military frontier with Prussia and the return of Britain to the Continent as a special guarantor of Antwerp and the Scheldt, which no Frenchman could want. The central question in 1830–2 for Talleyrand and many others, including some Belgians, was whether any durable Belgian state could be established at all. Talleyrand, like the French representative at Brussels, Charles Count Bresson, sometimes argued that it could not; that an independent Belgium would eventually bring on a European war, while partitioning it by European agreement would preserve peace. This was a bad eighteenth-century idea, of course; Talleyrand had more talent for survival than for statesmanlike vision. But just as not every Russian proposal for an agreed partition of the Ottoman Empire was proof of Russian imperialism, so not every suggestion for partitioning Belgium was a proof of French expansionism.[21]

In other words, France was not really more expansionist than the other powers in the Belgian question; it pursued basically the same sort of ends as they did. This signalled more than a short-range shift in French tactics. Under Louis-Philippe, an idea which Louis XVIII had accepted only partially and *malgré lui*, and which Charles X had tried to reverse, gradually became central to French policy, though many Frenchmen refused to accept it: France would seek its security and greatness, not in overthrowing the 1815 system, but in working within the concert in partnership with its great-power neighbour, Britain.[22]

The other dangerous power in the Belgian question, supposedly, was Russia. As the gendarme of Europe, it allegedly wished to use military force to uphold William's rights, and was stopped from doing so only because revolution broke out in Poland. Actually, the Russian government faced a problem not unlike Louis-

[21] It is worth noting that Talleyrand more than once indicated that he expected all of Belgium eventually to reunite with France (e.g. Colenbrander, 1905–22: x, pt. 2, No. 178). By partitioning it now, France would sacrifice part of its prospective gains.

[22] The foregoing rests principally on the correspondence in Talleyrand (1891a; 1891–2: iii); Colenbrander (1905–22: x, pt. 2, Nos. 17–121); see also Lannoy (1903: 133–5); Guyot (1926: 68–74).

Philippe's. It knew that it could not intervene effectively in the Low Countries, and did not really want to. Russia could best prevent a dangerous Anglo-French liberal alliance and cut its ideological losses through a neutral, independent Belgium under European guarantee. Nesselrode saw this clearly. But for domestic-political and ideological reasons Russians could not proclaim this or openly endorse this outcome. The Tsar was personally committed to the struggle against revolution, and ready to join in using force if others would take the lead. Yet there was the crucial point: Nicholas wanted to join a *European* crusade, not act on his own. When his dream of another anti-revolutionary crusade like that of 1813–14 became hopeless, he gave it up. Other Russians had done so earlier, or never shared it.[23]

Thus even before the ambassadorial conference on the Belgian question convened in London on 4 November, the most important issue had already been decided in principle. The powers would not aid William to recover his domains, but help set up an independent Belgian monarchy. This still left plenty to do—negotiate and enforce an armistice, draw the new frontiers, divide the old state debt, decide on a monarch, and settle questions of international security and commerce. These tasks, difficult in themselves, were complicated by additional problems—the repugnance felt by the Eastern powers at revising treaties for the benefit of rebels, the fact that the conference had supposedly been summoned to mediate on William's behalf rather than force him to accept the loss of more than half his territory and subjects, and above all the stubborn antagonism of the two principals.

None the less, the conference made remarkably smooth and rapid progress. A major factor in its success was vigorous and skilful leadership from Henry Temple, Lord Palmerston, foreign secretary in the Whig cabinet of Lord Grey which took power in late November. Palmerston was just as suspicious of France as Wellington and Aberdeen were, and shared, Canning's feelings about the European Concert and the Eastern powers, but he recognized that Britain could best preserve peace and the balance of power and keep France out of the Low Countries by working with other powers, especially France, for an independent, neutral Belgium. The tactics he used, playing the other powers' rivalries, suspicions, and separate aims against each other and compelling them to follow Britain's lead, were able to succeed precisely because these rivalries were not deep enough to destroy the basic

[23] Fishman (1988: 60–1, 83–7); Colenbrander (1905–22: x, pt. 3, pp. 324–55).

consensus necessary for co-operation. In addition, Palmerston's membership in a ministry ostensibly more pro-French than its Tory predecessor made it easier for France to work with him, while simultaneously frightening the Eastern powers into co-operation by creating the spectre of a liberal Anglo-French alliance. Between 4 November and 27 January the conference called for and enforced an armistice, compelling the Dutch to raise their blockade of the Scheldt and the Belgians their siege of Maastricht; proclaimed the separation of Belgium from the United Netherlands and its permanent neutrality; and laid down the territorial and financial bases for that separation.[24]

The conference seemed to have achieved success when William I in mid-February accepted the Bases of Separation set down in its 27 January protocol. Actually, its problems were just beginning. The four issues still unresolved—the choice of a monarch, division of the state debt, frontier questions, and Luxemburg—were made intractable by a wide gap in aims and principle between William and the Belgians. The King had accepted the Bases of Separation, which were relatively favourable to the Dutch, solely as conditions for an administrative separation of Belgium, silently reserving his legal sovereign rights. The Belgians, claiming the right of self-determination, raised further territorial claims in Limburg, Maastricht, Zeeland Flanders, and Luxemburg, denounced the proposed division of the state debt, and rejected the bases.

The choice of a Belgian king was intrinsically not as troublesome as other issues. The original Anglo-French choice, the Prince of Orange, was unacceptable to most Belgians on religious and political grounds; a French attempt to press this choice at Brussels only spurred the national congress to exclude the House of Orange by law. Various suggestions of sovereigns from Austria, Bavaria, Saxony, or Naples also proved unappealing or unacceptable. Still, the powers were agreed on ruling out any great-power dynastic connection, and the eventual choice, Leopold of Saxe-Coburg, was already in the wings, after declining the Greek throne because his conditions were not met. His candidature was agreeable to the British, and he was ready to marry a French princess so as to be acceptable to France as well.

[24] Webster (1951: i. 104–27); Fishman (1988: 78–93); Lannoy (1903: 100–20); Baack (1980: 206–10); DeClercq (1880–1917): iii. 586–90). For excellent discussions of Palmerston's personality, tactics, principles, and preparation for his task, see Webster (1951: i. 18–59); Bourne (1982). Chamberlain (1989: 70–1) sees Grey as playing a leading role in British policy. If so, it seems to have been primarily in the direction of avoiding war and European involvement, conciliating France, and resisting the snares of the absolutist powers. Smith (1990: 279–80, 283–5).

The dynastic question, however, enabled the Belgians to spring a trap on the French foreign minister, Sébastiani, and foment a quarrel between the great powers, a tactic which both small states repeatedly tried, but at which only the Belgians succeeded. Belgium's agents at Paris, arguing that the 27 January bases made its survival as an independent state impossible, pleaded that France allow it either to unite with France or at least to elect Louis-Philippe's son, the Duc de Nemours, as its king as a sign of French support. Sébastiani, knowing that annexation would mean war with Europe, flatly rejected this option. But whether because of his own nationalism and Napoleonic memories, the pressure he was under from the French left, or his belief that the other powers were trying to impose an anti-French candidate on France (which was true—Palmerston was still trying to promote the Prince of Orange), Sébastiani declined to ratify the 27 January Bases which Talleyrand had signed, and tacitly allowed the National Congress to elect Nemours on 3 February. This provoked a major outcry in Europe, strong warnings from Britain, and much resentment against the Belgians. The famous statement in the London Conference protocol of 19 February that Europe had rights superior to those of individual states, conferred on it by the social order (i.e. the international order, the European family of states), was a direct answer to the Belgians' defiance of Europe's authority and the Belgian 'views of conquest'.[25]

For Europe, the flare-up proved salutary on the whole. Louis-Philippe, having allowed the Nemours candidacy to come up, now vetoed it, faced down his nationalist critics, and replaced the weak Lafitte ministry with one headed by the resolute Count Casimir-Périer, who promptly ratified the 27 January bases. This should logically have led to a united European effort to force the Belgians into line. Two things got in the way of this, one being British and French domestic politics. First, a ministerial crisis distracted France in February and March 1831, and then a parliamentary struggle over electoral reform preoccupied Britain from March to June. The second factor, more fundamental and durable, was the problem of Luxemburg. The Grand Duchy not only was central in the Belgian–Dutch territorial disputes but also involved the German Confederation, and though few took it as seriously, the confederation's role in Europe was at least as important as Belgium's and Holland's. Luxemburg, moreover, was the one

[25] Lannoy (1903: 140–54); Fishman (1988: 105–11); Arneth (1898: ii. 106–9); Calmès (1932–57: ii. 107–8); Sas (1985: 325–30).

issue which seriously divided the Eastern powers, especially
Prussia and Austria, from the West.

William I, granted title to Luxemburg in 1815 with its citadel
becoming a key German federal fortress, had paid little attention
to the Duchy or to his role in the German Confederation. When
the Belgian revolution also swept over Luxemburg, William,
invoking his rights as a confederation prince, appealed for German
help to restore order. But the German states, especially the constitutional ones, wanted no part of a great-power quarrel, while
Prussia also feared war and revolution and was reluctant to compromise itself with the liberals in south-west Germany. Therefore
the confederation did nothing as all of Luxemburg except the city
and the fortress fell into Belgian hands, where, as things turned
out, it remained till 1839. Ignoring local grievances and Luxemburg's desires for independence, the Belgians claimed the whole
Duchy, less for its own sake than to give them leverage for their
demands for Limburg and the left bank of the Meuse. The French,
if they could not get Luxemburg or a piece of it for themselves,
wanted it neutralized along with Belgium. Palmerston, determined
to frustrate any such French schemes, thought of including all of
Belgium along with Luxemburg in the German Confederation
(which would have ruined the confederation's German character
and dangerously provoked France). In general, Palmerston was
inclined to use Luxemburg as material for territorial bargains
without worrying much about German rights and concerns.

Austria and Prussia proposed in December to protect German
interests by mobilizing the 10th Federal army corps (North
Germany and Lower Saxony) as a possible reinforcement of the
Luxemburg garrison. (The fact that the 9th corps, supposed to
include Luxemburg, had never been constituted proved fateful
here.) Even this hesitant measure, however, was blocked by
diplomatic opposition from France and Britain, unrest in central
Germany, especially Hanover, and German neutralist sentiment.
None the less, it was clear that the Belgian–Dutch territorial
quarrels could not be settled without dealing with Luxemburg and
the German rights and security interests there. At the same
time, the longer the Belgians held Luxemburg, the stronger their
position and their claim to a revision of the 27 January bases
would become.[26]

This caused a fairly serious crisis in the summer and autumn,

---

[26] Calmès (1932–57: i. 132–63; ii. 12–82); Huber (1963: 116–23); Baack (1980:
188–92); Boogman (1951: i. 15–27); Gruner (1977a: 360–5); Seier (1986: 421, 436).

growing, oddly enough, out of the fact that Britain and France came to agreement on a king for Belgium. Since the Belgians requested Leopold of Saxe-Coburg as one of their conditions for accepting the bases, the French in mid-April agreed to him in exchange for a promise by the great powers that some of the southern Belgian fortresses would be razed. Leopold's insistence that he could not accept the throne until Belgium's frontiers were settled gave the shrewd secretary-general of the Belgian foreign office, J.-B. Nothomb, the opportunity to seek further concessions to Belgium. The conference could have demanded that Belgium promptly agree to the bases and frontiers already specified, but Britain and France were both reluctant to enforce the deadline of 1 June set for Belgium's acceptance. France wished to enhance its future influence at Brussels, and Palmerston, though he was adamant on saving Limburg for the Dutch, was willing to compromise on Luxemburg if the German Confederation would go along.

This led to the conference's offering concessions to Belgium in late May insufficient to end Belgian resistance but enough to anger the Dutch as a whole and to encourage William and his minister Verstolk to believe that the peace effort was breaking down. When the 1 June deadline passed, the Dutch, as they had warned, withdrew their co-operation, while the Belgians quickly elected Leopold king and called for more negotiations. The conference now tacitly accepted the Belgian stand, amending the original Bases in a pro-Belgian direction into the so-called Eighteen Articles which it proposed as preliminaries for a Dutch–Belgian treaty, to be negotiated by special Dutch and Belgian representatives at London. Meanwhile the status quo (Belgian occupation) would continue in Luxemburg. Hailing this as a victory for the Belgian cause, the National Congress accepted the plan on 9 July. While most of the Dutch did not share William's desire to retain Belgium come what may, this treatment reinforced their existing dislike of the Belgians, resentment of the conference's tactics, and desire to reverse their humiliating defeat of 1830.

Dutch resentment, combined with William's conviction that the Eastern powers were bound to come to his aid in an armed struggle, was thus the proximate cause of the ensuing crisis. The deeper cause, however, lay in the way the conference had responded to Belgium's tactics under Palmerston's leadership, with Palmerston influenced by Grey's fears that the conference would fail and involve Britain in war. Palmerston had warned the Belgians that their resistance put Belgium in acute danger of partition, but both sides knew the warning had little behind it. Palmerston's private conviction was that, so long as the Dutch accepted the bases while the Belgians stubbornly rejected them, there were only three possible courses, two of them unacceptable. The powers could let the two parties fight it out, which was too dangerous. They could coerce Belgium into accepting the conference terms, which would require the use of force and might lead to French annexation, equally impermissible. This left the third alternative: for the conference to come up with a new plan and persuade both sides to accept it. Thus Palmerston let the Belgians get away with being the dog in the manger, meanwhile ignoring repeated warnings from Charles Bagot at the Hague about the dangerous mood building up in Holland and William's threat to use armed force. The conference's actions, abandoning its own terms after the Dutch accepted them, rewarding Belgian resistance with new terms which the Belgians hailed as a victory, and then inviting the Dutch to negotiate on these new pro-Belgian bases, were a prescription for trouble.[27]

It soon came. The British and French, having led in appeasing the Belgians, assigned the Austrian delegate, Baron Wessenberg, the task of making William accept the new package of Eighteen Articles.[28] Wessenberg's arguments and warnings failed. On 2 August the Dutch invaded Belgium, claiming to want to enforce the original Bases of Separation and offering at the same time to negotiate with the powers. Leopold, without consulting his government, immediately called on France for armed aid. On 11 August a large French army began marching into Belgium. The Belgians, quickly regretting their appeal to France, tried to stop the Dutch themselves and were routed.

The Dutch were quickly compelled to withdraw by French and European pressure in mid-August, but then the problem became getting the French to withdraw. French nationalists cried that France's services must be compensated; the government, while

[27] Lannoy (1903: 154–64, 173–94); Sas (1985: 334–7); Fishman (1988: 111–19); Webster (1951: i. 135–7); Guyot (1926: 76–9); Colenbrander (1905–22: x, pt. 1, Nos. 148, 150, 155); x. 2, Nos. 205, 208, 212, 217.

[28] Lannoy (1903: 194–8); Arneth (1898: ii. 119–21). Wessenberg defended his decision to accept this task to Metternich with the Eastern delegates' standard excuse for appeasing Britain: the necessity of keeping it from working exclusively with France. Here lay a weakness Palmerston could and did exploit. Metternich, though he disapproved of Wessenberg's action, accepted his reasoning; for even when the Holy Alliance powers disagreed with British policy, they had to respect Britain's ability to cause them trouble to which they could not reply in kind. For illustrations of this sentiment in Russia, see Colenbrander (1905–22: x, pt. 3, No. 357).

continuing to plead Belgium's cause, tried to negotiate a private deal with Belgium for the destruction of its fortresses; the Belgians were eager to keep at least some French troops in Belgium to defend them and support their claims; and Talleyrand, while urging his government to obey the conference's calls for a swift evacuation, hinted again to his colleagues at London that the Belgians were incorrigible and that partition might be the answer.

By mid-September, however, France had agreed to complete its evacuation by 30 September, and the conference turned to revising the Eighteen Articles into a proposed Belgian–Dutch treaty consisting of twenty-four articles, which the conference adopted on 14–15 October. The so-called Twenty-Four Articles revised the debt settlement in favour of the Dutch, gave the Belgians commercial advantages on Dutch waterways between the Scheldt and the Rhine, and most important, satisfied Dutch claims in Limburg and Maastricht by dividing Luxemburg. The larger western part would go to Belgium, the eastern part with the capital and citadel remain under William's rule and in the German Confederation. This plan again demonstrates something about the London Conference frequently acknowledged in passing, but seldom given its due weight in a literature which has concentrated on showing how the Belgians achieved nationhood or how Palmerston supposedly foiled dangerous French and Holy Alliance schemes and preserved peace. This was the remarkably constructive and cooperative European spirit shown by the Eastern delegates. Wessenberg and the Russian second delegate, Matuszewicz, were the main authors of this plan. The Russians, including Lieven, here urged a joint European guarantee of Belgian neutrality, while the British still hesitated to join out of fear of becoming involved in a future war with France. Wessenberg meanwhile reaffirmed the conference's role as the arbiter rather than the mediator of the Belgian question, and insisted on upholding William's and the Bund's rights in Luxemburg; any German concession on these was to be paired against other provisions as part of a general settlement.[29]

[29] In general, see Fishman (1988: 142–55); Lannoy (1903: 198–247); Baack (1980: 214–17). For evidence of Palmerston's determination not to let France gain any advantage from its occupation, see Colenbrander (1905–22: x, pt. 1, pp. xiv–xxxvi, Nos. 162–3, 169–70); for evidence of the determination of Grey and other Whigs not to alienate France or join with the Eastern powers, see Webster (1951: i. 823–4); Holland (1977: 13–54). On French policy, see Guyot (1926: 80–1); Colenbrander (1905–22: x. 2, Nos. 234–51). For the Luxemburg issue in particular, see Calmès (1932–57: esp. ii. 281–5); Gruner (1977a: 366–77); Dunk (1966: 92–5); Roghe (1971: 43–75).

The new plan, however, seemed to lead only to another stalemate, and in its course the European unity which had been sustained till now temporarily broke down. Though the Belgians opposed some of the Twenty-Four Articles, Leopold persuaded them to accept the proposal, while William held out stubbornly, again proving the Belgian King more sensible than his people, the Dutch King the reverse. William had legitimate complaints about the conference's procedure of negotiating with Belgium and presenting him with *faits accomplis*, and plausible ones on some substantive issues. He argued, for example, that the provisions internationalizing the Netherlands' rivers and canals benefited British trade more than either the Dutch or the Belgians. But the real ground for his refusal to grant more than *de facto* recognition of Belgian independence was his hope to recover Belgium sooner or later when it collapsed or a European war broke out.[30] On 15 November Palmerston and Talleyrand, pulling the other delegates along with them, cut the Gordian knot by signing a treaty with Belgium based on the Twenty-Four Articles which recognized Leopold I as King of Belgium. Britain and France now called on the other three governments to ratify the treaty. When they declined, the Western powers went ahead with their ratifications in January 1832, and Europe was apparently split into two camps.

The division was actually not deep and posed no great danger. The Eastern powers neither objected to the substance of the twenty-four articles nor encouraged William's resistance to the treaty, and knew that ultimately they would have to ratify it. Like William, they resented the conference's procedure—not giving William more time, demanding that he formally recognize Leopold, and (Metternich's particular complaint) having the conference, which was not a government and had no authorization or right under international law to make treaties, conclude one with Belgium rather than issue a joint declaration of its stand. Behind these formal and legal grounds lay the growing anger of the two emperors over the way their own representatives were helping the Western powers flout their principles. Other factors fuelled their resentment—criticism of Austria by some of its allies in Italy and Germany for its weakness over Belgium, Austrian and Prussian concerns over Luxemburg and the German Confederation, Austria's quarrel with France in Italy, and Russia's anger at the West's anti-Russian attitude toward the revolution that had

[30] Webster (1951: i. 140–5); Lannoy (1903: 246–53); Colenbrander (1905–22: x, pt. 3, Nos. 40–2, 175, 177, 365).

broken out in Poland and been suppressed. In other words, the East–West dispute was more about form and feelings than substance, and, where it had substance, was more about other areas in Europe than about Belgium.

The actual policy of the Eastern powers remained what it had been from the beginning: to get an independent Belgium established and the question settled as quickly and quietly and with as little damage to monarchic principles as possible. While Palmerston denounced them for defecting from the conference, they directed their criticism more at their own delegates than against Britain and France and redoubled their efforts to persuade William I to give in. A special mission by Count Orlov to the Hague in early 1832, though it failed to shake William, enabled the Tsar to say that he had done his best and to wash his hands of the affair. In April Prussia and Austria ratified the 15 November treaty and in May Russia followed suit, though still refusing to recognize Leopold formally before William did so.[31]

Meanwhile another minefield had been successfully skirted, the issue of Belgian fortresses. A secret agreement reached by the four powers with the Belgians in April 1831 for razing some Belgian fortresses had been communicated to France as a concession, and was greeted by Frenchmen as a victory over the 1815 system. Actually, however, it represented an attempt by the four powers to maintain the old barrier against France in a new form. They intended to commit Belgium to maintain fortresses in its interior that would help stop an invading French army short of Holland and Germany, while razing those forts on its frontier which France might be able to occupy and use itself at the outset of a war. Prussia even hoped to sustain the old allied right to occupy fortresses in Belgium when war broke out. All this was inconsistent with the proclaimed principles of Belgian neutrality and independence.

When the French tried to seize control over which fortresses would be razed by sending a special envoy to negotiate with Belgium during the French occupation in August and September 1831, the four powers answered by summoning the Belgians to negotiate with them at London. Prolonged four-power negotiations with the Belgian emissary, General Goblet, led to a convention in December committing Belgium to raze the southern

[31] Fishman (1988: 161–87); Arneth (1898: ii. 128–35, 140–3); Schiemann (1904: iii. 176–9); Baack (1980: 220–30); Martens (1874–1905: xi. 443–87); Colenbrander (1905–22: x, pt. 3, Nos. 44–5, 50–1, 166–9, 171, 179–80, 184–5, 203, 209, 212, 369–91).

fortresses France wanted to save while maintaining the others. A storm of protest in France threatened to bring down the government; the French premier, Casimir-Périer, talked of refusing to ratify the 15 November treaty if the convention were not cancelled. As Frenchmen knew and privately admitted, the issue involved *amour propre* rather than genuine interests; but for many Frenchmen and not a few others, *amour propre* was what counted. A joint conference note of 23 January 1832 making the December convention valid only in so far as it respected Belgium's full sovereignty and neutrality calmed the tempest in a teapot. As it turned out, none of the fortresses was actually razed in the 1830s, and most eventually were in the 1860s.

The one who came out of this petty fracas looking most like a statesman was Talleyrand. The Prussians, out of fear of France, had gone after an unnecessary and illegitimate advantage. Palmerston seemed bent on excluding France from any voice in the fortress question, above all to show the French who was boss—an attitude opposed by some of his colleagues in the cabinet. Many Frenchmen exaggerated the insult, or continued to expect other powers to pay them for their good behaviour or to keep their national pride under control. Talleyrand, in contrast, consistently argued that France must not sacrifice the real victories and prizes it had achieved, i.e. the treaty of 15 November, its working alliance with Britain, and the breakup of the 1815 coalition, over a trivial issue which its own intrigues had helped stir up.[32]

But Talleyrand erred in supposing that Britain and France, having signed the November treaty, could now wait for William to give in. The King continued to reject the Twenty-Four Articles, and this left the Dutch still in the fortress of Antwerp, the Belgians in occupation of Limburg and Luxemburg, and trade obstructed on the Scheldt. In late summer 1832, the two Western powers decided that William had to be coerced. This produced a more serious split in European unity, arising first within the Holy Alliance. Austria and Prussia, hoping to stop Britain and France from acting on their own and particularly from sending French troops into Belgium, urged that all five powers use joint financial

---

[32] For the issue in general, see Lannoy (1903: 254–84); Lademacher (1971: 62–7); Dunk (1966: 98–106); on Palmerston's tactics and the British cabinet, see Webster (1951: i. 112–15, 145–7, 826–7); Bullen (1974*a*: 6–10); Holland (1977: 95–102). The account of the London Conference in Bourne (1982: 332–52), is valuable for the roles of Palmerston and the British cabinet but misleading on some other aspects. For Talleyrand and France, see Colenbrander (1905–22: x, pt. 2, Nos. 267, 269, 275–8, 280–4, 286, 291, 295).

pressure to force William to yield. Nicholas, disgusted at his allies' lack of principle, forbade his delegates to go along with this proposal. Palmerston and the Duc de Broglie, foreign minister in the Soult ministry formed after Casimir-Périer's death in May, then concluded a convention on 22 October for joint land and naval action to compel William to surrender Antwerp. Russia pulled out of the conference, Prussia protested, and Austria pleaded for some other form of coercion. Their objections were brushed aside by the Western powers, who tried instead to get Prussia to join them in coercion, taking over Belgian-occupied territories in Limburg.

The entry of French troops into Belgium on 15 November to besiege Antwerp, accompanied by a British blockade of the Scheldt, caused the suspension of the conference and created a war scare more serious than any earlier one. Metternich tried to devise a unified Eastern response or to transfer the conference to another site, without success. The Eastern powers had to watch as William was forced in December to yield Antwerp and in May 1833 to renounce any further use of force and cease obstructing trade on the Scheldt. In the ensuing months, Metternich, eager to see the dispute finished and buried, worked hard to achieve a compromise agreement under which William would accept twenty-one of the Twenty-Four Articles and be promised genuine negotiations on his grievances over the rest. This effort also failed, however, and the Belgian question entered five years of stalemate before a new crisis led to a final settlement.[33]

Meanwhile the status quo proved fairly stable and tolerable. The two rivals were separated, Belgium was on its feet, all danger of war was over. But there were untidy aspects to this interim solution. William, for symbolic reasons, had chosen to retain two small useless outposts at Antwerp, which played into Belgium's hands, allowing it to continue to occupy sizeable territories in Limburg and Luxemburg and store up trouble. The way in which the Luxemburg issue was handled created ill feeling between Belgium and the German Confederation, in some respects natural political and commercial allies, and showed how the great powers

---

[33] In general, see Webster (1951: i. 148–76); Lannoy (1903: 285–312): For further light on Anglo-French policy, see Guyot (1926: 82–7): C. Howard (1974: 44–8); Colenbrander (1905–22: x, pt. 2, Nos. 312–16). The British minister at the Hague repeatedly warned Palmerston that an Anglo-French coercion of Holland ran the risk of provoking a Dutch internal revolt or collapse of the monarchy; ibid. x, pt. 1, Nos. 233, 243–4, 248. On the Eastern powers, see Arneth (1898: ii. 147–69); H. Müller (1980: 30–3); Shil'der (1903: ii. 562–5); Colenbrander (1905–22: x, pt. 3, Nos. 57–61, 88–9, 207, 213, 218–20, 226–8, 231).

were inclined to ignore the Bund and its interests. When one sees how the Anglo-French *entente* arose and operated in Belgium, and in particular how Palmerston used it, it becomes easy to understand why it would later collapse over Spain and the Near East. The Western powers, in simultaneously challenging Prussia by a French occupation of Belgium and making a crude attempt to split Prussia away from its allies, helped Metternich to keep Prussia in the conservative-absolutist camp and oust the semi-liberal pro-Westerners from the Berlin government (of which more later).[34]

Still, the successful management of the Belgian question was clearly a great achievement in international politics. War was averted, treaties were peacefully revised, and a new, more viable intermediary body was substituted for one that had broken down. The Belgian state that emerged proved more viable than anyone could have predicted, and its constitutional development became a model for much of Europe. Holland (though not its King) recovered fairly quickly from the political blow to its morale, though more slowly from the real economic harm done by the separation. Palmerston's hectoring policy of peace had worked. The fact that it worked not by manipulating other powers' rivalries but by exploiting their peaceful, co-operative tendencies, and that he sometimes had to surmount difficulties of his own making, does not diminish his success. In the Low Countries themselves, the rest of the nineteenth century speaks for the wisdom of the 1830 solution; the twentieth century, especially since 1945, suggests that there was something to the Congress of Vienna's ideas after all. And, as Bismarck said about the law and sausages, if one loves small powers and appreciates their importance in international relations, one should not inquire too closely into how they were made.

III. ITALY

Compared to the French, Belgian, German, or Polish movements of 1830, the Italian revolts did not amount to much—small risings in Central Italy produced more by the breakdown of government than by serious revolutionary movements. Yet they caused the most serious international complications outside Belgium, and probably a greater danger of war, though even here Europe

---

[34] Gruner (1977a: 378–97); Dunk (1966: 104–8); Werner (1977: 104–7); Roghe (1971: 76–7).

would never get really close to the brink. At the centre of the trouble was Rome.

Though the Papal State and other Italian regimes survived the initial shock of the French and Belgian revolutions, signs of unrest soon appeared in the Papal Legations and the neighboring central Italian duchies of Parma and Modena. On Austria's urging, the papal regime ordered preventive measures but actually did little to forestall a revolt, counting from the outset on Austrian intervention if needed. This policy became even feebler when Pius VIII died in November 1830 after only a short reign. The interregnum until a conclave finally elected his successor, Gregory XVI, in early February allowed the revolution to brew. Though Gregory was personally friendly to Austria, he chose as his Pro-Secretary of State Cardinal Bernetti, who opposed Austria's idea of combating the revolution by a combination of preventive repression, conciliation, and conservative reform. Bernetti, an opponent of Metternich's ideas of tampering with the old system of clerical rule as ultimately subversive of papal authority, proposed instead to fight back with a kind of reactionary clerical populism, mobilizing the loyal urban and peasant masses against the disaffected middle- and upper-class liberals.

In any case, the new regime had no time to try to prevent a revolution. Immediately after Gregory's election, revolts broke out first in Modena and then in the Papal Legations, spreading from there to the Marches and Umbria. By mid-February most of the papal territories were no longer under the control of Rome. The Pope appealed to Austria to intervene, and Metternich, though not eager, agreed. An Austrian occupation of Modena and the Papal Legations, delayed until March by hesitations of the Austrian commander in Italy, was carried out in easy, almost bloodless fashion.

Austria's action brought to a head the long-standing conflict of aims between itself, France, and the Papal State. Austria was determined to keep France out of Italy and stop the revolution (seen as two sides of the same coin), and to sustain the Pope's temporal sovereignty while strengthening his rule through administrative reforms. The papal government wanted Austria to help it crush the revolts and preserve papal rule, but a large party, the *Zelanti*, rejected any reforms as tending to undermine the regime and opposed any foreign interference in papal affairs, including Austria's. France wished to stop or limit Austrian intervention, or, if that was impossible, to join in intervention so as to break Austria's hegemony and restore French influence. Each government faced internal opposition and restraints, France from the so-called party of movement, Metternich from fearful or restive satellites and Austria's fiscal and military weakness, Rome from within the college of cardinals.

The French government, which had been warning Rome and Vienna against an intervention for months, answered the outcry in France by mobilizing 80,000 men. The action, coming at a time when the Belgian question was at a delicate stage and the Lafitte ministry struggling to survive, made many fear war. Yet it could break out only if Louis-Philippe lost control of French policy; this danger, never imminent, receded when Lafitte fell and Casimir-Périer took power in mid-March. Besides, France's warnings to Austria were always specific and limited: an Austrian intervention in central Italy would strain Austro-French relations, an Austrian intervention in Piedmont would mean war. Austria never intended the latter; even if France invaded Piedmont, Austria planned to declare war but fight a defensive campaign. (To be sure, it was ready to use radical means in fighting a defensive war, such as employing Napoleon's son, the Duke of Reichstadt, in Austrian custody, against the Orleanist regime in France.) Again this shows the importance of intermediary bodies: the existence of a Piedmont separating France and Austria, uncomfortable for the Piedmontese, proved vital for European peace.[35]

The March crisis led to an effort to solve the Roman question by concert action through a five-power ambassadorial conference meeting at Rome from April to July. It was assigned the task of drawing up a programme of reforms to enable the Papal State to prevent further revolution, so that the Austrian occupation could be ended quickly. The conference actually served more to keep the great-power quarrel within bounds. For the French it was a forum for their views, a sop to their injured honor, and a means of pressing Austria to evacuate. Metternich more genuinely welcomed it as a way of avoiding war, deflecting criticism of the Austrian occupation, and, as he often liked to do, defusing a dangerous question by internationalizing it. But most of all he really wanted conservative reforms in Rome's judicial, fiscal, and administrative systems so as to promote stable, orderly papal government. The conference represented his chance to renew his general Italian reform programme of 1822. The papal authorities

---

[35] Reinerman (1989: 1–34); Nada (1953: 15–78); Lemmi (1928: 4–58); Martens (1874–1905: iv. 424–5). For important documents, see *Rel. dipl. Stat. Pont.–Fr.* (1962–: 2. i); *Rel. dipl. Fr.–Sard.* (1974–: 2. i.); also Talleyrand (1891a: No. 46).

resented the conference but had to accept it for the sake of international support against revolution.

For reform purposes, the conference failed. The ambassadors induced the Pope to grant an amnesty and reached agreement among themselves on some laicization and administrative changes, reorganization of the judicial system, and municipal self-government. In June and early July there appeared to be some hope of bridging the gap between papal resistance and French demands for more drastic changes and an immediate Austrian evacuation. Under European pressure, Rome agreed to accept certain reforms and to set an early date for an Austrian withdrawal, provided Europe in return would guarantee the papal territories and consent in advance to a renewed Austrian occupation should revolution broke out again. The French government, however, rejected this compromise, though its own delegate at Rome, Count Saint-Aulaire, had agreed to it; and the conference broke up in failure. Bernetti had his own reasons for preferring to let matters take their course. Under British, French, and Prussian pressure he asked the Austrians to pull out beginning 15 July, and Austria promptly complied.[36]

French domestic politics was the direct cause of the conference's failure; Casimir-Périer consciously sacrificed its programme to his need for victory in the French parliamentary elections. A deeper reason for the failure of reform, however, was that the actors pursued aims which were both incompatible and internally self-contradictory. The French knew that unless the papal government changed its methods of government another revolt, Austrian intervention, renewed crisis, and humiliation for France were almost bound to happen. Yet they refused either to co-operate with Austria for the sake of reforms or give the Pope the assurances required to induce him to accept them. A more general contradiction was France's attempt to undermine papal rule through an international conference called to support it. In Rome, papal officials knew that their regime depended on Austria to survive, that revolution would break out again as soon as the Austrians left, and that only reforms like those proposed by Metternich or the conference could enable the regime to stand on its own. At the same time they resisted any reforms, especially ones imposed by Europe, and resented Austria's assistance as expensive, humiliating, and potentially dangerous, possibly lead-

---

[36] Reinerman (1989: Ch. 2); Nada (1953: 79–141); *Rel. dipl. Fr.–Sard.* (1974–: 2. i. Nos. 60–119); *Rel. dipl. Stat. Pont.–Fr.* (1962–: 2. i. Nos. 130–1, 146, 160, 168).

ing to ultimate Austrian annexation of the Legations. (They had reason to fear this, not because Austria had territorial ambitions, but because the inhabitants preferred Austrian to papal rule.) Hence Bernetti's policy was one of 'the worse the better', rejecting reform, letting the conference fail, hoping then to suppress the ensuing revolution by his reactionary-populist methods, and counting on Austria to rescue the Pope once more if he failed.

Compared to these policies, Metternich's looked sane and moderate, and in some respects it was. Yet it also had internal contradictions. It proposed to internationalize the Roman question in order to preserve Austria's exclusive hegemony in Italy; to reform papal rule without really changing it; to get France to co-operate in perpetuating its exclusion from Italy; and to persuade a liberal government in Britain to support an illiberal regime at Rome. Most central was the contradiction within Metternich's concept of 'reform'. Everywhere by this time, especially in 1830–2, the idea of reform was connected in some way with emancipation, or at least was sure to pave the way for it. Reform at Rome would at a minimum involve enlisting the better-educated classes in the work of running the state; Metternich and other Austrians understood this perfectly and stressed its necessity. But Metternich's reform would never permit any kind of political emancipation to emerge from this activity; everyone was to remain an obedient subject and ward of the state, not aspiring to active citizenship and political participation, no matter how vital his role might be in the operation of the state. That kind of reform could never have worked for long, if at all. Metternich's program, if successful, would in the end have undermined the Papal State and Austria's kind of Italy as surely as its failure did.

The Roman Conference, therefore, shows both the strength and the limits of the Vienna system. The prompt and ready extension of the conference principle to the Roman question proves again how attractive and readily adaptable to new problems the concert ideal was. In a sense, the conference represented a new step forward in international politics, an attempt to anticipate a crisis and solve it in advance by international agreement. The failure of the conference, however, proves that a working, co-operative international system can permit its members to achieve internal progress and reform, perhaps promote it, but not compel it—just as a chamber group cannot produce music if each individual member insists on choosing his own score or uses his instrument to hit another player over the head. The only advantage of maintaining the group may then be that, however bad the cacophony it produces, its members at least are not shooting each other.

The Austrian evacuation made another rising in the Legations inevitable, not because the revolutionary conspirators were eager to try again but because the papal government never regained real control of the province and instead provoked a new rebellion by introducing an untrained and lawless civil guard into it. By December it was plain that only foreign troops could sustain the Pope's regime, his own being too few and too undisciplined. Sébastiani, urged on by the French minister at Turin, Baron Barante, suggested using Piedmontese forces to forestall Austria, but this was both a forlorn hope and a transparent attempt to exploit the desire of some Piedmontese for papal territory. By early January Metternich had secured the two conditions he insisted on for another Austrian intervention, that the papal government formally request it and agree to Austrian control of all military operations, including those of the papal forces.

The other ambassadors at Rome, including Saint-Aulaire, consented to an Austrian intervention. Casimir-Périer, to the dismay of the allied ambassadors at Paris, had already decided not to stop it but to counter it with France's own, an occupation of the papal port of Ancona on the Adriatic coast. Saint-Aulaire, instructed to probe Bernetti's reaction to the idea, reported the cardinal as saying that the Pope was in the habit of resignation. Bernetti meant that his government would not actively resist; the French, though knowing better, took this to say that the Pope did not really object. Hence, after Austrian forces under General Radetzky moved into the Legations in late January (Roman troops having disbanded the civic guard but provoked further popular resistance by their own lawlessness), France sent a force by sea to land at Ancona on 23 February. Though the intervention was supposed to rest on the Pope's consent and serve to uphold his authority, the French raised their own flag at Ancona, seized papal property, encouraged radical agitation, and issued their own anti-Austrian liberal propaganda. Rome, joined by Sardinia and the Holy Alliance powers, immediately denounced the move as an invasion and demanded an immediate French withdrawal. Even Saint-Aulaire, not informed in advance of the action, condemned it. Coming once again at a time when East and West were split over Belgium, the incident seemed to set the stage for war.

Yet once more the danger was less serious than it seemed. Rome, which had legitimate grounds for war, had no intention or means of waging it, while Metternich only wanted to embarrass the French thoroughly. Sardinia, while urging Austria forward against France, wavered itself between joining the crusade and remaining neutral. The affair ended in a Papal-French arrangement, accepted rather grudgingly by Metternich, which allowed the French to stay at Ancona at their own expense as tolerated intruders, but only so long as the Austrians remained in the Legations as invited guests. Metternich now gave his attention wholly to excluding French and British influence from Rome and preventing radical change. His conservative reform programme, though not formally abandoned, gradually became a dead letter.[37]

The real danger point in Italy, as this last flare-up of the Roman crisis showed, lay in Piedmont. Here was where the Austro-French rivalry was most acute and where they could collide militarily as they could not at Rome or elsewhere. The Sardinian government oscillated between wishing to destroy the July monarchy and restore Charles X and preferring just to stay out of trouble, or possibly exploit Italy's troubles and Franco-Austrian rivalry for Piedmontese gains. Its vacillation, plus the fact that it depended on Austria but also feared it, rendered easier Metternich's policy of preserving peace and the status quo. There were challenges to meet. The French minister, Baron Barante, tried to break Piedmont away from its Austrian alliance with threats and territorial bribes, hoping to form a neutral league of Italian states, Switzerland, and constitutional German states under French protection. Austria's minister at Turin, Count Senfft, had to be recalled because he supported Piedmontese calls for an anti-French crusade. French radicals, Piedmontese liberals, and even Giuseppe Mazzini and his fellow exiles on French and Swiss soil looked to Charles Albert, who succeeded Charles Felix as King in April 1831, to lead them against Austria. They were quickly disappointed. One of the King's first moves was to conclude a secret military convention with Austria in July 1831; Vienna obtained it by granting him supreme command of any joint army fighting the French in Piedmont. He also struck out at the secret societies, denounced the concessions made by the Holy Alliance powers in Belgium and Italy, defended the Pope's rights, was ready for war over the Ancona affair, and in the mid-1830s broke relations with constitutional regimes in Spain and Portugal in support of absolutism.

Yet the Austrians never trusted him, or he them. Metternich

---

[37] Reinerman (1989: Chs. 3–4); Nada (1957: 11–28, 143–7); Lemmi (1928: 81–4); Guyot (1926: 98–9); *Rel. dipl. Fr.–Sard.* (1974–: 2. i. No. 158; and 2. ii. Nos. 1–49); *Rel. dipl. Stat. Pont.–Fr.* (1962–: 2. ii. Nos. 53–98); *Rel. dipl. Aust.–Sard.* (1964–: 2. i. Nos. 185–6). Talleyrand also condemned 'the filibustering capture of Ancona' as a danger to peace and the Belgian settlement; Colenbrander (1905–22: x, pt. 2. Nos. 299, 302).

agreed that a war against the revolution might well be inevitable and urged Piedmont to prepare for it, but insisted that conservative powers could only wait for it in a united defensive position. Casimir-Périer and Sébastiani meanwhile told Barante that some day his hopes for an overthrow of the territorial and political settlement in Italy and the restoration of French prestige would be realized, but that France was now isolated and needed peace and consolidation. Even Barante's plans for a general overthrow in Italy could not ignore the concert or dispense with it; he expected that when the upheaval came, Europe would somehow intervene to regulate it and prevent a general war. Clearly Metternich's policy helped everyone, including the French, avoid a useless war. Yet he would get little credit for it from contemporaries or for many decades from historians; even in Germany, Austria and the conservatives were pictured by most publicists as the law-breakers.[38]

In the rest of Italy, notably Naples, the rivalry between Austria and France reminds one of Lewis B. Namier's remark about historic communities regularly being 'dominated by unconscious memory, fixated upon the past, and unable to overcome it'.[39] Every French foreign minister and every minister or chargé at Naples thought in terms of a serious ongoing Austro-French struggle over Italy in general and Naples in particular. Vital French interests would supposedly be destroyed if Austria renewed its treaty of 1815 with Naples or revived its projected Italian league. France itself would be threatened if Naples joined Austria in a war over Rome; on the other hand, France would gain significantly by winning Naples over through a dynastic marriage or luring it into the liberal alliance France concluded with Britain, Spain, and Portugal in 1834, so that it would form part of a general Mediterranean alliance under French leadership. The Austrians were little different. No one seems to have asked himself whether Naples could be 'won' or 'lost' by either side and what it was worth to either.

Yet reality kept breaking through. French diplomats knew and privately stated that Metternich was at least as eager for peace in Italy as they were; that King Ferdinand II of Naples hated and

---

[38] This account rests mainly on the documents in *Rel. dipl. Fr.–Sard.* (1974–: 2. i; ii); *Rel. dipl. Aust.–Sard.* (1964–: 2. i); see also Nada (1980: 38–59); Lemmi (1928: 35–9); Mastellone (1960: i. 54–103). On the propaganda contest in Germany, see Altgeld (1984: 168–81).

[39] 'History', in F. Stern, (ed.), *The Varieties of History* (rev. edn., New York, 1973), 375.

feared Austria, was fiercely independent, and regarded the Austrian alliance as a dead letter; that in case of war with Austria the French navy, unless Britain stopped it, could easily compel Naples to stay neutral, and that it might actually improve France's position if Naples went to war at Austria's side, because this would be the easiest place to attack Austria. Some Frenchmen saw that their differences with Austria over governing principles in Italy had little relevance at Naples. Ousting Austria's influence would not help France make Naples liberal or constitutional, just as excluding France's would not help Austria make Naples reliable or well governed. There was even some French recognition that the real threat to French interests in the Mediterranean might not be Austrian domination but Neapolitan misgovernment, leading to more revolution and the independence of Sicily under British protection. Yet none of this changed the nature of the game, or the way each side played it.

Yet the game, if useless and somewhat stupid, none the less remained within safe limits. Neither side was willing to write Naples off or share it, but both knew better than to try for serious gains. The British attitude on Naples, as on Italy generally, seems more sensible: since change was inevitable, it should be tolerated and promoted by peaceful means, and a certain amount of independence for Italy was better than either Austrian or French domination. But this was easy for the British to recommend. They had nothing to lose and much to gain in Italy, and even their policy showed a latent contradiction beginning in the early 1830's. While they demanded reforms in the Papal State, they also pressed the Pope to instruct his bishops in Ireland to help keep the Irish docile under English rule.[40]

IV. GERMANY

One difference between the Italian and the German movements in 1830–3 is that the German risings were more widespread and had more important and durable effects. The other is that, while Austria and France fought openly in Italy over a prize neither of them could really win or define,[41] Austria and Prussia competed

[40] The main sources are Moscati (1937); *Rel. dipl. Fr.–Sic.* (1966–: 2. i). For the standard account of British policy on Italy in 1830–2, see Webster (1951: i. 200–20); for differing views, see Mooney (1978); Buschkühl (1982: 45–83); on the Protestant crusade in Britain generally, see Wolffe (1991).

[41] Metternich, to be sure, could define the stakes in Italy to his own satisfaction— e.g. to Count Apponyi at Paris on 6 Apr. 1831: 'Our interest [*convenance*] is that

covertly in Germany over stakes that were clear and vital to both, but then still needed each other too much to engage in open rivalry.

The July Revolution had fairly wide and deep repercussions in Germany. In the south-western constitutional states, Bavaria, Württemberg, Baden, Hesse-Darmstadt, and Nassau, it stimulated greater political activity, promoted calls for new constitutional reform, and in time promoted some radical agitation, but, as will be seen, ultimately produced no major change. In northern and central Germany (Brunswick, Hanover, Electoral Hesse, and Saxony) liberal-constitutional and worker-peasant risings occurred, and though the radical aspects of the movements were defeated, they led to compromise conservative-liberal constitutions in these states similar to those elsewhere. Austria and Prussia remained relatively undisturbed by revolution, and ultimately led a successful counter-offensive on the federal level. None the less, 1830–2 dealt the Metternich system another blow, increasing the number of constitutional states, tipping the balance in Germany in their favour, and apparently proving that states with working representative constitutions could handle revolts better than those without. While 1830–2 brought the liberal-conservative struggle to the fore, with democratic radicalism and socialism arising on the fringe of German politics, older particularist forces, such as the German home towns with their insistence on autonomy, remained active, and new conservative ones, including Catholicism as an organized political force, began to emerge. Perhaps most important, the revolutions gave new life to attempts to forge a distinct Third Germany within the Bund free of Austro-Prussian domination.[42]

Metternich, who had long spoken of revolution in France as exhausted and in Germany as dormant, launched his campaign against the German revolution almost immediately after the July days. He used the same tactics as in 1819–22: dire predictions that the social order would be destroyed by the international revolutionary conspiracy centred in Paris, appeals to Russia, cries of alarm at Prussia's turning liberal, efforts to enlist Prussian help

Italy should not belong to the revolution, or what is the same thing, to France; we want each Italian state to belong to itself'; Metternich (1880–4: v. 176). But this was more an ideological stand than a real definition of interests and calculation of gain and loss.

[42] In general, see Huber (1963: 31–91); J. Sheehan (1989: 589–614). For individual themes, see Speitkamp (1986: 593–5); H. A. Schmitt (1977); Werner (1977: 90–103); Huber (1957: 406–9); M. Walker (1971: 310–12). On the Trias movement, see Burg (1989: 185–251).

in manipulating the Bund, and underhanded attempts to overthrow suspect ministers by appeals to their princes directly or through Metternich's conservative friends. This time, however, he did not get full Prussian co-operation and failed on two contested points in Germany, an Austrian resolution at Frankfurt committing Bund members to military intervention against revolutions and a struggle between William of Brunswick and his reactionary brother, Duke Karl, over who should rule the Duchy. This was because to some degree Prussia had changed its stance on revolution. Count Bernstorff, like other moderates in Prussia and Germany, wanted a middle way between all-out repression and a policy of *laissez-faire*, and sought closer political ties between Prussia and some of the middle states.

These same hopes were even stronger in South Germany. Fearing war between Austria and France and wanting to be more independent of Austria, Bavaria and Württemberg began discussing the formation of a South German neutrality league in the fall of 1830. As usual, the proposal ran aground on their own disputes, but the Austro-French war scare over Italy in early 1831 gave it new life. The Prussian chief of staff, General Rühle von Lilienstern, sent on a mission to South Germany, encountered widespread anti-Austrian neutralist sentiment. At Munich he received a plan on how Prussia and the Third Germany could co-operate in keeping the Bund from being involved in a foreign war. It meshed with broader ideas developed by Bernstorff and the Prussian foreign ministry's director of German affairs, Johann Eichhorn, for a programme of conservative political reforms to satisfy the political demands of Germans of education and property, fight revolution, and promote Prussian leadership in Germany. Hand in glove with this programme went a campaign led by Bernstorff and Duke Karl of Mecklenburg to reorganize the confederation militarily, strengthening both its defensive capacity and its ability to decide independently just when and where German interests needed defending. All this came at a time when Austria had virtually conceded the commercial leadership of Germany to Prussia (of which more later), and when Bavaria and other South German states were increasingly leaning toward Prussia for other special reasons. This time the challenge to Austrian leadership was much more real and immediate than in 1819–20.

Yet by the end of 1831 Metternich could boast that he had routed his opponents, and once again the key to victory was winning over their monarchs with the help of conservative allies.

The decision fell at Berlin, when Frederick William forbade Bernstorff to propose more plans for Germany without working them out with Austria first. Though Metternich eventually accepted an anodyne compromise on the technical aspects of federal military reorganization in late 1832, he won on the central issue: Austria and Prussia would maintain their conservative partnership in running the confederation and controlling the lesser states. Bernstorff's resignation as foreign minister and replacement by Ancillon symbolized Metternich's victory.[43]

The renewed Austro-Prussian partnership apparently had a grave threat to deal with: radical agitation in south-west Germany in the spring of 1832, centred in the Bavarian Palatinate, separated from old Bavaria geographically and alienated from it politically and socially by its heritage of French laws and institutions. Already in March the Bavarian government, spurred by Metternich's warnings and its own fears, banned the source of much of the agitation, the Press and Fatherland Society, and began repressing radical newspapers. But it failed to stop a mass public festival held at Hambach on 27–30 May. There, 20,000–30,000 Germans, mainly from the Rhineland, gathered to hear speakers call for a united German democratic republic. The programme was radical, the drive behind it weak. The leaders of the movement fell out over whether to use force to achieve its goals, with the majority favouring legal means, and the festival broke up without taking action.

None the less, the ideas expressed at Hambach and their resonance in much of the Rhineland (though not in Rhenish Prussia) were frightening to many German governments. It required little pressure on Bavaria by Austria and Prussia to make it crack down further on its radicals, or to get the Bund to pass anti-revolutionary decrees. Two sets of repressive measures resulted, first the Six Acts of 28 June, worked out in Metternich's usual way (delegates of individual states first met in secret conferences at Vienna to bypass the regular federal mechanism). These were designed to curb the powers of the liberal state diets to obstruct federal anti-revolutionary laws. The Ten Articles of 5 July then struck at the supposed sources of radicalism, the universities, the press, and free speech and publicity in parliaments, going in some ways beyond the Carlsbad Decrees of 1819. Legislative repression at Frankfurt was followed by military force.

---

[43] Baack (1980: 231–93); Burg (1989: 228–51); Billinger (1991: 50–109); Holzapfel (1987).

When in April 1833 a group of radical students and teachers from Heidelberg attempted to spark a democratic revolution in Germany by seizing a police post in the Free City of Frankfurt, it led, not to a lower-class rising as they had dreamed, but to a federal occupation of Frankfurt lasting until 1842 and a further codification of repressive federal legislation in 1834.[44]

The conservative victory was a convincing one. The Bund by its decrees and actions infringed further on the rights and sovereignty of individual states, and established the very principle the middle states had once vigorously opposed, that federal law overruled state law (*Bundesrecht bricht Landesrecht*). Smaller German governments, including Bavaria, now accepted this principle and the renewed Austro-Prussian condominium in Germany for the sake of protection against revolution. Yet in another sense even the conservatives had not won anything durable. Austria's leadership in Germany was purely negative and repressive, and Prussia lost a chance to offer Germany a different kind of political leadership to match its emerging economic one. Technically, the legal powers of the Confederation were enhanced, but its reputation and capacity for constructive action declined still further, if that was possible. The smaller states lost their feeble bid for greater independence. The moderate liberals failed, the radicals were suppressed.

This happened in the final analysis because no one at this time had a viable programme for Germany's political future. Metternich's policy was realistic from the standpoint of Austria's interests and capacities, but only in the sense of *Après moi le déluge*. Bernstorff's and Eichhorn's programme looks better, but it had a fatal flaw which Metternich detected. They were not prepared, as Frederick the Great had been earlier and Bismarck would be later, to fight Austria to throw it out of Germany. In fact, they still considered France a threat and Austria a necessary partner. Nor were they ready, as Frederick William IV would be in 1848–50, to try to win Austria over to a different kind of partnership in Germany. Basically, like some Prussians and Germans in 1848 and after, Bernstorff and Eichhorn hoped that Austria could be ignored or bypassed; that Prussia and the lesser states could operate within Germany as if Austria were not there.[45] But as Metternich remarked, Austria was there, and most princes and

---

[44] Huber (1963: 126–72); Faber (1976: 384–9); J. Sheehan (1989: 609–15); Billinger (1991: 110–27).

[45] This is one omission in the otherwise perceptive discussion of the consequences of Bernstorff's fall by Baack (1980: 326–41). See also Murphy (1991).

governments in Germany, including Prussia's, still needed her and wanted her to be there as a protection against revolution, France, and war.

As for the liberals and radicals, from the standpoint of international politics what strikes one about their programme, besides the chasm between their ends and their means, is their naïvety, their apparent unawareness of how much international and domestic violence would have resulted from the changes they called for. At Hambach, for example, some speakers endorsed a French annexation of Belgium and actually supposed that France would welcome a united Germany. At the same time the spokesman for a federated republican Europe, Josef Wirth, chose to remind the friends of German liberty in France that Alsace and German Lorraine really belonged to the German fatherland.

Nor were German liberals the only losers in the affair. The British government, or rather Palmerston personally, earned a sharp rebuff from Austria and Prussia for trying to lodge a protest at Frankfurt against the Six Acts.[46] His defeat was trivial beside France's failure to exploit its opportunities in Germany in 1830–2. French envoys in Germany constantly urged Paris to take advantage of its opportunity to loosen the confederation and form a neutral league with the smaller states and Prussia. Nothing came of it. By mid-1832 the French minister at Munich, Baron Mortier, was pining for the original confederation of 1815. Even if it excluded France, he said, it had at least guaranteed each individual state an independence vis-à-vis Austria and Prussia which the present Bund was fast eroding.[47] And while French political efforts to influence developments in Germany failed, her economic policy toward Germany remained as unimaginative and self-centred as before.[48] Much of this was due to France's distraction with domestic-political and other European concerns, of course. But part lay in the dead weight of tradition—France's inability to conceive of a German policy except in terms of either Richelieu or Napoleon, keeping Germany either divided and impotent or under French control.[49] The notion that France might intrinsically benefit from a viable German Confederation as it did from an independent Belgium, that such a Germany could be good for

[46] Webster (1951: i. 221–6, 231–6); Gruner (1977: 115–23).
[47] Roghe (1971: 14–42, 78–83, 90–116); Owsinska (1974: 15–17, 33–7); Burg (1978: 24–30). Chroust (1935–9: ii, iii) is full of the complaints and warnings of French envoys to Munich; the one cited is in iii. 52–8.
[48] Burg (1978: 30–2); Chroust (1935–9: ii. 334–6, 353–5).
[49] For evidence, see Roghe (1971: 84–8); Owsinska (1974: 22–3).

France for its own sake and not just as a means for expanding French influence or combating Austria's, never took hold.

Yet if the Vienna system did not guarantee internal progress or the development of federalism in Germany, here too it made it hard to start a war. The same point emerges from the last main trouble spot in Europe in the early 1830s.

V. THE POLISH REVOLT AND THE EUROPEAN REACTION

The Polish revolt of 1830–1 is full of paradoxes. Its causes lay deeper than those of any other revolt, yet it was the most accidental in terms of outbreak and development. It produced more armed conflict than any other movement, and next to Belgium involved the most important strategic area, yet it exerted the smallest immediate impact on international politics. The rising was more decisively crushed than any other; but in some ways its suppression founded the nineteenth-century Polish national movement rather than ended it.

No other government also did as much to permit an insurrection to happen, almost to ask for it, as Russia did in Poland. By preserving Napoleon's political changes in Poland and adding a separate Polish constitution, diet, administration, and Crown to them, Alexander had helped keep alive the sense of Polish nationality and encouraged some Poles, even former radicals, to hope for more independence and territory from him (just what Austrians had predicted in 1814). Instead, Alexander and his brother, Grand Duke Constantine, Poland's so-called viceroy, actually governed it in an increasingly illiberal spirit, inspiring a radical new left comprised of students, army officers, and intellectuals imbued with the ideals of romantic nationalism. Though contacts were uncovered in 1825 between the Polish Patriotic Society and the Russian Decembrists, the number of actual conspirators was small and Poland remained quiet. Nicholas, restrained by legal and moral scruples and fears of making the situation worse, declined to use in Poland the measures for rooting out traitors he employed in Russia. By 1830 plans for a revolution had revived, and aversion to Russian rule had spread to many more of Poland's élite.

The revolutions in France and Belgium then fanned the hopes of a small group of conspirators at the infantry officers' school at Warsaw. Nicholas's orders to get the army ready to fight France inspired the plotters to strike soon before the army marched west. They had no sound plans for producing the great popular rising they envisioned (one of their hopes, for example, was that Austria would join their fight for Polish independence) and none of the Polish leaders they approached supported the venture. It was not surprising, then, that when a group of officers and cadets rose on 29 November and attempted to seize Constantine, the movement failed badly. What saved it was that Constantine, who had a Polish wife and was genuinely attached to Poland, declined to use the thousands of loyal troops available to him to crush it, instead withdrawing from the city to let responsible Poles deal with the miscreants themselves. This permitted a failed mutiny to grow into a popular rising in which arsenals were seized and some Polish soldiers defected to the rebel side. Conservatives and moderates in Constantine's administrative council, led by Prince Adam Czartoryski, now assumed power in order to negotiate with Russia for concessions that would enable them to restore order. Constantine, however, having met with the council and received its demands, chose instead on 3 December to leave Warsaw for the Lithuanian frontier, taking the Russian troops under his command with him.[50]

The Polish conservatives, left in charge of an unexpected and undesired revolution, now tried to hold back the pressure for independence from the Warsaw patriots and the Polish Diet while they negotiated terms for ending the revolt with Nicholas. Nicholas condemned Constantine's inaction and retreat, but was almost as reluctant as he to shed Polish blood and willing to believe that the Poles as a whole were loyal and would punish their own criminals. None the less, his reply to the Polish petitions was a demand for submission, after which, he said, he would grant anything compatible with the law and his duty and honour as Tsar. This put Czartoryski, negotiating at St Petersburg, and the veteran General Jan Chlopicki, who had assumed dictatorial powers at Warsaw in an effort to contain the revolution, in an impossible position, unable either to win concessions from the Tsar or to destroy the illusions of the Polish left (that Russia would not fight, or that Lithuania or Ukraine or Europe would also rise, or that a united Polish people could win independence

[50] On the general origins and course of the revolt, see Leslie (1969: 96–120); Pienkos (1987: 30–113); Schiemann (1904: iii. 52–9); Seide (1971: 10–19); Skurnowicz (1981: 56–65). For special points on the roots and character of the movement, see Borejza (1979); Zajewski (1980); Skowronek (1982); Zernack (1987), esp. the essays by M. Wawrykova, J. Kosim, and A. F. Grabski.

by themselves). In mid-January, incapable of stemming the radical tide in the diet, Chlopicki resigned for a second and final time. In early February the diet deposed the Romanovs and declared Poland independent, and a Russo-Polish war began.[51]

At first the Polish cause seemed to have a chance of success. The early fighting was indecisive, the Russian army suffered the ravages of cholera, and insurrections were attempted in Lithuania and Ukraine. Yet without foreign intervention the final outcome was hardly in doubt, especially since the government in Warsaw failed to solve the problems of organizing and financing the war, even losing control of Warsaw by late summer. The diet, moreover, refused to try to mobilize the Polish peasantry by agrarian reform. After Field Marshal Paskevich replaced the indecisive General Diebitsch as commander, the Russian army decisively defeated the Polish army in midsummer, took Warsaw in September, and crushed the last resistance by autumn. Now Nicholas imposed the severe measures he had declined to use earlier. An Organic Statute replaced the Polish constitution in February 1832. The diet and the separate Polish army were abolished, the local assemblies of Polish *szlachta* supposed to replace the diet were never convened, Russians were put in control of the central offices of the Polish administration, and large-scale sequestrations and confiscations of the property of insurgents were carried out, especially in western Russia.[52]

Russia thus dealt with the Polish revolution as an internal Russian affair, hardly of more concern to international politics than British actions in India or Ireland. But the European states system was involved and affected all the same. The Polish movement's roots lay in the unstable half-way house built for Poland in 1815. It survived and grew because of the typical reluctance of monarchs in the Vienna era to use force against their own subjects; as Louis-Philippe would remark after his fall, 'Republics are lucky; they can shoot people'. Diplomatic failure, i.e. the inability of Polish negotiators and Nicholas to reach a settlement, led to the war, and the Poles' inability to gain foreign recognition and political and diplomatic support in Europe sealed their fate.

The most important results of the November revolution for international politics were its after-effects among both governments and peoples. It destroyed any remaining credibility for

[51] Leslie (1969: 138–64); Seide (1971: 20–5).
[52] Leslie (1969: 164–267). On the revolt and the peasant question, see Kieniewicz (1969: 70–82).

those Poles hoping to achieve Polish aims through close ties with Russia—Czartoryski's old goal, which Constantine had adopted. But the victors also were embittered. The Tsar wanted to wash his hands of his Polish subjects, proposing in May 1831 that Russia should conquer Poland, punish the rebels, and then pull its frontier back to Warsaw and the line of the Vistula, turning the rest over to Austria and Prussia to govern (again, what Austria had proposed in 1814). His ministers convinced him that this was impractical, but other territorial changes were also proposed,[53] and anti-Polish feeling became an even stronger element in the Russian national consciousness. The revolt also gave Russia further excuses for advancing its economic interests at Poland's expense and turning away from the West.[54]

In Austria some popular enthusiasm arose for the revolt, especially in Galicia and Hungary, and there was some secret *Schadenfreude* over Russia's troubles; but the government always supported Russia, though cautiously, for fear of the reaction in Galicia. The Poles repeatedly tried to obtain Austrian support, offering the Polish Crown to Archduke Carl or to Francis, but Metternich would only advise them to submit. The revolution helped remove the strain on Austro-Russian relations caused by the Eastern question in the 1820s, though it did not change Nicholas's preference for Prussia or his personal dislike of Metternich.[55] Prussia, even more afraid of the revolt's spreading than Austria was, gave Russia more help, closing its frontier and disarming Polish forces crossing it. The Prussians also had a special reason to welcome Russian repression in Poland; the harshness of Russian rule made Prussia's Poles more satisfied with their lot. The official anti-Polish attitude of the governments contrasted strongly with popular feelings in Germany, where a strong pro-Polish current took up where philhellenism had left off.[56]

The most important after-effect was a large emigration of Poles,

---

[53] Shil'der (1903: ii. 582–4); Schiemann (1904: iii. 119–25).

[54] Lincoln (1978: 134–47); Meyendorff (1923: i. 15–21); Brun-zejmis (1980); Pienkos (1987: 116–19). On the impact of the revolt and war on Russia's economic policy, see Pintner (1967: 82–93); Heller (1983: 169–70, 213).

[55] Seide (1971: 30–57); Leslie (1969: 223–5); Molden (1913: 13–17); Deak (1979: 21–2). For Metternich's analysis of the revolt (a military conspiracy with no popular base, like Naples and Piedmont, which Nicholas should use for good conservative ends), see his letters to Ficquelmont Nos. 1 and private, 31 Dec. 1830, HHStA, *Weisungen Varia Russland* 90.

[56] Baack (1980: 194–203); Kolb (1975); Gerecke (1964). However, Gneisenau, once the most radical of Prussian military reformers, strongly supported the Russian army against the Poles. Shil'der (1903: ii. 581).

principally to Paris. Both the *émigré* movement, split into hostile democratic and aristocratic wings, and the underground nationalist movement in Poland attempted to recruit support among governments, peoples, and revolutionary groups in the West. This affected British and French foreign policy little during the revolution or immediately thereafter. Talleyrand suggested to Sébastiani that France try to restore its old barrier against Russia centred on an independent Poland, and a Franco-Polish committee agitated in the press and parliament; but the French government never went beyond secretly suggesting to Britain that the two governments might offer to mediate in the war. The British cabinet declined.

Yet the Polish cause remained alive, and enjoyed a certain popularity among liberals. Palmerston, conservative at home and liberal abroad, used the Polish cause to attack the Holy Alliance and espouse constitutional government in Europe while doing nothing concrete for the Poles. Polish exiles came to provide shock troops for risings and revolutions in Europe. Thus in a way the Polish revolution did not merely deepen the East–West split in Europe, but constituted it. On other European questions (Italy, Spain and Portugal, Belgium, the Near East, even Germany to some extent) the liberal-conservative contest was often artificial and irrelevant. Over Poland it was real, engaging peoples and governments alike, though neither liberals nor conservatives had a solution to the problem.[57]

VI. TWO SIDESHOWS

There were two developments worth noting in international politics in 1830–3 not linked to the revolutions. The government of Louis-Philippe decided to remain in Algeria, not for any long-range purpose but because the venture had become popular, so that liquidating it would have increased the attacks on the government from the left and the threat from the 'dangerous classes' below. The British government, which like others in Europe had expected the French to leave after the announced punitive expedition, accepted this with some grumbling as tacit payment for French co-operation over Belgium. In the short run, France gained nothing from its decision but additional trouble and expense; militarily, the commitment weakened France and

[57] Birke (1960: 60–3); Webster (1951: i. 180, 182–99); Seide (1971: 28–9); Holland (1977: 8–11, 87, 92–3); Brown (1978; 1980); Colenbrander (1905–22: x, pt. 2, Nos. 102–3).

decreased its diplomatic flexibility in Europe. Yet France's hold on Algeria and Britain's toleration of it was useful for the international system and helped keep the Anglo-French *entente* alive. At a time when the British would make no concessions to France on Belgium, were suspicious of its Italian policy, could not reach a working *entente* with France over Spain, the Near East, or Poland, and rejected almost every initiative by Talleyrand for Anglo-French collaboration against the Eastern powers, Algeria represented one place where Louis-Philippe could use his army and gain prestige.[58]

The Greek question was finally wound up between 1830–3, though not without serious clashes among the Greeks themselves and between them and the French forces of occupation. A final border was traced in the north, Prince Otto of Bavaria was elected and crowned King, a constitution was granted at British and French insistence, and a loan to Greece was guaranteed by the three protecting powers so that Otto's government could begin functioning. For Greece itself this was an unsatisfactory outcome in various ways. Otto was a Catholic in a country where Orthodox religion was one of the few unifying factors, his German advisers largely ran the government, and the loan only increased the financial burdens of a small, weak state. But from the standpoint of the international system, it had its advantages. The Wittelsbachs of Bavaria found some harmless solace in Greece for the frustration of their ambitions in Germany. A genuinely independent Greece would immediately have begun trying to fulfil its irredentist goals against Turkey, as it would do every chance it got once it shook off great power control. Greece under great-power protection became an intermediary body over which the protecting states competed for influence, with Britain and France as Mediterranean naval powers quickly predominating and a disgruntled Russia soon finding its position in the eastern Mediterranean not enhanced but worsened by the liberation of Greece.[59]

Algeria and Greece, therefore, are further instances of how the Vienna system, without solving the political and social challenges raised by the revolutions, worked to manage crises, preserve general peace, and maintain a balance of satisfactions among the major actors. The 1830 revolutions undoubtedly raised problems for international peace and stability in certain ways. They renewed

[58] Julien (1964: 64–105); Jardin and Tudesq (1984: 104–10, 158–65); Sullivan (1983: 67).
[59] Dakin (1973: 288–311); Molden (1913: 1–39); Jelavich (1962: 75–9, 92–7, 109–11); Schiemann (1904: iii. 183–7), Webster (1951: i. 270–2, 504–5).

the appeal of revolution and even gave it a certain legitimacy; revealed the deep divergence between peasant and worker concepts of liberty and those of the upper middle class; sharpened the ideological rift between West and East; and highlighted the growing and potentially dangerous gap in economic development between Eastern and Western Europe. But the period also showed that some serious international conflicts could be solved creatively, and others managed without violence. Just as impressive is the fact that none of the many ideas for territorial expansion roused by revolutions and crises among great and smaller powers, liberals, moderates, and conservatives alike, ever got anywhere. The system shut them all down. Martin Luther once remarked about sexual temptations that one could not prevent birds from flying over one's head, but one could keep them from nesting in one's hair. Fear and greed were rife in Europe in 1830–2, so that temptations to territorial aggrandizement flew over many heads; but they did not nest in anyone's hair.[60]

---

[60] For good appraisals of the social-psychological impact of the revolutions (though not of their international dimensions), see Church (1983); Groh (1961: 157–95); Newman (1974; 1975). For the contribution of international finance, esp. the Rothschilds, to peace in 1830–2, see Gille (1965: 205–31). For further examples of schemes of territorial aggrandizement and imperialism by conservatives, see *Rel. dipl. Fr.–Sard.* (1974–: 2. ii. Nos. 88, 91); *Rel. dipl. Stat. Pont.–Fr.* (1962–: 2. ii. No. 19).

16
Deceptive Calm and Storms,
1833–1841

AFTER the 1830 revolutions a general calm settled over most of Europe, broken only by stormy weather at its opposite ends, the Near East and the Iberian peninsula. Both kinds of weather were misleading. The tranquillity, apparently a sign of stability and peace, actually was more an indication of stagnation and frustration. Yet one quiet progressive development came about in central Europe which changed European politics in the long term far more than the violent conflicts did. As for these conflicts, they made Europe appear to be ideologically sharply divided into two camps and threatened by war—likewise misleading impressions. The contests in the Iberian peninsula, which involved some ideological rivalry among the powers, were never a threat to the system or the general peace. The Near Eastern crises did seriously endanger the European equilibrium and the general peace, but they had little to do with ideology, and when the threat of European war arose, the Near East was not the prime issue.

I. GERMANY, BELGIUM, AND ITALY, 1833–1841

In any case, certain European problems were handled during these years with little conflict and almost no danger of war, including the most important international development of the 1830s: the formation and growth of a German Customs Union (*Zollverein*). After fairly long preparation, it was formed and grew with surprising speed. Its roots went back to 1818, when Prussia, seeing that the German Confederation would not attack the question of customs reform on a German-wide basis, integrated its provinces into a reformed and unified customs system, abolishing all internal customs barriers. The rapid fiscal and commercial success of the Prussian measure, the commercial pressure it put on adjoining regimes, and Prussia's success in annexing small adjacent or enclave German principalities into its system produced

India and Central Asia

two reactions. Prussia itself adopted a programme in the mid-1820s to bring other independent German states into its customs system, for both economic and political reasons. Among the South German states, a movement arose to counter this Prussian offensive with a customs union of their own. Two regional customs unions were formed by 1828, Prussia's with Ducal Hesse and Bavaria's with Württemberg. Other states in central and northern Germany formed a loose association, called the Central German Commercial Union, to resist the Prussian union. But when in 1831–2 Electoral Hesse went over from this association to the Prussian union, this helped precipitate the amalgamation of the South German and Prussian systems into a single German *Zollverein* in early 1833. The accession of a number of states followed, bringing the *Zollverein*'s membership by 1836 to 26 million inhabitants, a clear majority in the Bund.

For smaller states, often afraid of revolution, short of revenues, and looking for economic gains that would not cost them their political independence, the *Zollverein* had powerful attractions. By joining it, they could appease discontented burghers with economic rather than political concessions, acquire revenues safe from the control of their state diets, retain control of their own customs administrations, and still defend their particular economic interests within the union. Prussia offered its partners generous terms, deliberately concealing its actual hegemony under a legal structure of political and administrative independence and equality. Prussia's policy in the *Zollverein* was an ideal example of benign hegemony. Though its political goals were as clear and important as its economic ones, it was not aiming at this time to unify Germany under Prussia, or even to pave the way for unification. In the phrase common at the time, it wanted to make moral conquests in Germany: not to destroy or annex the smaller German states, but to get them to follow Prussia's lead; not to throw Austria out of Germany—even liberals in Prussia saw too much danger from France and Russia and had too much German and European feeling for that—but to make Prussia the leader in their partnership. Nonetheless, in the long run the *Zollverein* was a powerful centralizing force in Germany, both because of its economic effects and because it taught officials in German states and in the customs union itself, as well as a wider commercial and educated public, to think and work in broad German terms.[1]

Austria did little to stop the progress of the *Zollverein* beyond futile protests at Frankfurt and verbal encouragement of the Central German Commercial Union. Such economic and political counter-moves as were discussed at Vienna—separate trade agreements with particular German states and reforms of Austria's prohibitive tariffs—were stymied by the resistance of the Austrian *Hofkammer* (finance ministry) and of Bohemian industrialists. The *Zollverein* not only further damaged Austria's political image in Germany but also reduced Austrian exports and increased the smuggling especially of colonial goods along the Austro-German borders. Prussia, less generous in dealing with Austria than with the smaller states, declined to co-operate in stamping it out. A thriving traffic in illegal books and other publications from Germany indicated that Austria was becoming more isolated from

---

[1] This account relies primarily on H.-W. Hahn (1982: 14–170, 217–55; 1984: 9–109); but see also Huber (1963: 284–305); Burg (1989: 274–353); Speitkamp (1986: 586–93).

Germany intellectually and culturally as well as commercially. Only when a new wave of accessions to the *Zollverein* began in 1841, breaching the resistance front in North Germany, did Austria attempt to complete its own customs union with Hungary and launch a commercial reform within the Habsburg domains, and this effort soon broke down. All this is not evidence that Austria was stagnating economically. The 1830s and 1840s were clearly periods of growth and change in Austrian economic life, especially in transportation; some economic historians see these decades as the foundation of its later industrialization. Austria did, however, miss its chance here to be integrated into the wider German economy, and lost leadership in this sphere to Prussia.[2]

Deprived of economic weapons, Metternich continued to play the best card he had, supporting German monarchs threatened by revolution and liberalism. The existing machinery of the Bund for repressing dissent was refurbished in 1833–4. In 1837–9, with Prussia's co-operation, Austria helped King Ernest August of Hanover avoid federal intervention after the King had first violated Hanover's 1830 constitution and then dismissed seven eminent professors at the University of Göttingen for their public protest. Religion was also a useful weapon in Austria's hands. In the 1830s the Prussian government became involved in a bitter dispute with the Archbishop of Cologne over the issue of mixed marriages; Metternich exploited this internal Prussian quarrel to promote anti-Prussian feeling among Germany's increasingly politicized Catholic population. But none of this really helped Austria or hurt Prussia in their subterranean contest for leadership. Prussia's return to strict political conservatism after Bernstorff's fall, while discouraging German liberals, reassured nervous princes in the middle and smaller states and helped Prussia win them into the *Zollverein*. Even Hanover, which more than any other state feared the growth of Prussia's power and influence, regarded it as a model of progress and efficiency.[3]

Considering the general commercial and political importance of the *Zollverein*, its development caused surprisingly little stir in the rest of Europe. Britain, after trying rather feebly to stop its formation, accepted it in the hope that it would promote lower tariffs and more British trade in Germany. This stand gradually

[2] Vomackowa (1963: 109–24); Huber (1963: 287–91). On Austria's economic growth, see Good (1984: 1–10, 38–73); Komlos (1983: ch. 3); H.-H. Brandt (1978: i. ch. 1).
[3] Huber (1963: 70–105, 173–239); Billinger (1991: 142–70); Werner (1977: 134–51, 180–90); Spindler (1974: 195–7, 203); Bartels (1960: 108–11).

paid off, especially after a trade treaty with the *Zollverein* was concluded in 1842. France displayed an economic conservatism and lack of political agility *vis-à-vis* Germany similar to Austria's and ultimately as costly, though France, unlike Austria, was economically advanced enough to have competed with Prussia. For example, France negotiated a trade treaty with Nassau and then failed to ratify it, whereupon Nassau in 1836 joined the *Zollverein*. As the French chargé at Munich wrote Foreign Minister Broglie in mid-1833, whether the *Zollverein* would hurt France commercially, only time would tell; that it would hurt France politically was certain, unless France considered Austria's decline sufficient compensation for Prussia's rise.[4]

Meanwhile the stalemate over Belgium dragged through the mid-1830s. Repeated attempts at a solution were blocked by William I's intransigence and the question of how the German Confederation and King William's agnates in Germany should be compensated for their territorial losses in western Luxemburg. Personal and political rivalries complicated matters; Metternich, who most of the time was eager to terminate the question at almost any cost, became so angry with Palmerston at one point as to suggest that France, Prussia, and Holland partition Belgium (another proof that not every proposal to partition Belgium grew out of territorial ambitions).[5] Meanwhile Belgium's economic and political importance grew, and with them its potential benefits and dangers for Europe. Trade developed rapidly between Belgium and Germany; with Leopold's encouragement, prominent industrialists and merchants, especially in the Prussian Rhineland, planned to connect the two regions by railways and waterways to circumvent Dutch restrictions on the lower Rhine and to promote commercial and political liberalism in both countries. At the same time, a Flemish nationalist movement took root in Belgium in opposition to the now-dominant Francophones, encouraged by Germans with Romantic notions of regaining old Germanic soil for the common German homeland.[6]

This underscored the need to get the Belgian question settled. The chief road-block suddenly disappeared in March 1838 when

[4] Gruner (1977b: 109–15); Burg (1978); Roghe (1971: 149–67); Kemp (1971: 132–5); Chroust (1949–51: ii. 120–3).

[5] Calmès (1932–57: ii. 345–95); Boogman (1951: i. 50–8); Colenbrander (1905–22: x, pt. 1, Nos. 259–65, 276; x, pt. 2, No. 379; x, pt. 3, Nos. 73–4, 230–71). For Metternich's proposal of partition, see Martens (1874–1905: iv. 470–1).

[6] Dunk (1966: 116–69, 183–206). For French fears of too close ties between Belgium and Germany, see Colenbrander (1905–22: x, pt. 2, Nos. 388, 401).

William I, in the midst of a personal crisis that would lead him to abdicate his throne not long thereafter, announced to the Dutch estates that he was ready unconditionally to accept the Twenty-Four Articles of November 1831. The Belgians, whose quarrelling factions were competing with one another in party and nationalist zeal, now predictably denounced the terms they had once hailed as a triumph for Belgium, and launched a campaign to keep the occupied territories in Luxemburg and Limburg, by armed force if necessary. Their only hope lay in support from France and a split or possible war between the powers. In an attempt to appeal to French radicals and provoke the Eastern powers, the government named a Polish *émigré*, General Skrzynecki, to command its army. Once more France had to try simultaneously to destroy Belgium's illusions and avoid its snares while defending its cause in the councils of Europe. The Belgians did manage to gain better terms from the revived London Conference on certain questions, particularly the division of the state debt, but not on the central territorial issue. It took warnings from Prussia and the Bund and threats by Palmerston to allow German troops to occupy Limburg (an example of Palmerston's practice of threatening recalcitrant states with the armed forces of other powers), combined with financial pressure exerted by the House of Rothschild, finally to force Belgium in April 1839 to accept the Twenty-Four Articles and conclude formal peace with the Netherlands.[7]

This terminated the main question (though not Belgian irredentist feelings) and should have removed Belgium from the international spotlight. But Belgium's neutrality and independence, formally guaranteed by great-power treaties in 1839, were promptly put to the test by a new question: could France and Belgium form a customs union? The French, worried by Prussian–Belgian railway negotiations, had first broached the idea in 1836, and Belgium had rejected it. Another Belgian mission to Germany followed in 1839, and in 1840, with an industrial depression making the idea more attractive to Belgium, the Franco-Belgian idea was renewed with support behind the scenes from Louis-Philippe and Leopold. Palmerston reacted strongly, calling on the Eastern powers to condemn it as a violation of Belgium's neutrality and independence and proposing to forbid Belgium to conclude even a commercial treaty with France. Metternich, pleased by the quarrel, used the opportunity to lecture Palmerston

[7] Boogman (1951: i. 50–8); Lannoy (1948: 50–65); Helmreich (1976: 50–62); Gille (1965: 297–9); Colenbrander (1905–22: x, pt. 1, Nos. 377–406; x, pt. 2, Nos. 422–45).

on international law: one could not deny Belgium the right to conclude normal commercial treaties without violating its independence, which all the powers, including Britain, had just guaranteed. In 1841, however, Austria joined Britain and the other powers in warning Belgium against a customs union. This European opposition might have sufficed to kill the plan, but opposition from French industrialists was actually decisive. Under their pressure the French foreign minister, the Duc de Guizot, leader of a ministry nominally headed by Marshal Soult, rejected Belgian offers in 1841 either to conclude a customs union with special protections for Belgian sovereignty or to agree on mutual reductions in tariffs. The idea of a special Franco-Belgian commercial tie was briefly revived again by fears of a special Belgian connection with the *Zollverein*, but died in 1843. For France, or at least for powerful interests in France, the potential economic losses of a union with Belgium always outweighed the possible political benefits; the reverse was true for Belgium. A bolder French government might have gone ahead anyway, but Louis-Philippe's and Guizot's government was fortunately cautious.[8]

The sterile calm of Italian politics also persisted in the 1830s, broken only by one incident which illustrated how Austrian hegemony, though unsatisfactory for Italy, could be useful for European peace. The Swiss Confederation had aroused the suspicions of Austria and Piedmont already during the 1830 revolutions by a movement to reform and liberalize the constitutions of individual cantons. More trouble developed when certain cantons granted asylum to revolutionary *émigrés* from Italy, Germany, and Poland. The most dangerous of these were Giuseppe Mazzini and members of his Young Italy movement, forced to transfer their headquarters in mid-1833 from Marseille to Geneva. Among his many conspiracies, Mazzini and his collaborators developed a plan to use Polish exiles in Switzerland and France to launch an attack on Savoy, the ancestral home of Sardinia-Piedmont's ruling house. This was supposed to touch off revolts in Italy, south Germany, France, and possibly Switzerland, leading to the creation of a great neutral and republican Confederation of the Alps, while the Poles would gain French and Italian help in liberating Poland. Swiss and French authorities learned something of the plot in advance, but failed to warn the Piedmontese or act vigorously to stop it. The actual armed raid launched from Geneva into

[8] Lademacher (1971: 97–122); Deschamps (1956); Ridder (1932: 8–92); Dunk (1966: 211–14); Boogman (1966: 137).

Savoy in late January 1834 was a fiasco; its easy repression by Piedmontese forces temporarily discredited Mazzini and his movement. Understandably, however, Turin was enraged against France and Switzerland for not stopping it. Charles Albert wished to punish the Swiss himself and wanted Austria to deal with the centre of the trouble at Paris.

Once again, good grounds or pretexts were available to anyone who wanted war, but no one outside the court at Turin did. Metternich concentrated on restraining Piedmont while supporting its claims diplomatically. The French government, shaken by domestic agitation within France, including workers' revolts in Lyons and Paris in April which required the army to put down, now took steps at home to repress radical conspiracies and attacks on the regime by both the legitimist and the republican press. These measures, though not enough to satisfy Metternich completely, led him by the mid-1830s to demote Paris to second place behind London as a centre of revolutionary conspiracy. Under international pressure, the Swiss Diet in 1836 also undertook to supervise the refugees more closely, though cantonal independence ensured that the problem would persist. Swiss patriots naturally resented the foreign pressure and supervision and wished to shake it off, yet actually the Swiss cantons could get away with a good deal under the Vienna system. The inconclusive outcome to the affair suited Metternich's purposes fairly well—preventing war while keeping Charles Albert hostile to France and dependent on Austria. But Charles Albert eventually came to see how his absolutist principles and alliance with Austria were leading him into a cul-de-sac, and grew to hate Austria and despise himself for it.[9]

Elsewhere in Italy political stagnation persisted. Reform was dead at Rome; Metternich's main goal was now to get the Pope to condemn liberalism, especially the Abbé de Lamennais and his followers in France and Belgium, with their attacks on the union of throne and altar. He succeeded in this, though forces within the Church were mainly responsible for the condemnation. The Austrian and French occupations of papal territory finally ended in 1838. Ferdinand of Naples, though deeply suspicious of Austria, was even more hostile to France and Britain, except for a brief

---

[9] Biaudet (1941); Bonjour (1965: i. 258–84); Hales (1956: 39–138); Mastellone (1960). The diplomatic side of the incident is fully documented in *Rel. dipl. Aust.–Sard.* (1964–: 2. ii. Nos. 1–153); *Rel. dipl. Fr.–Sard.* (1974–: 2. ii. Nos. 116–209); see also Lemmi (1928).

rapprochement with France in 1840. Thus Austrian hegemony, though unpopular, remained effectively unchallenged.[10]

II. SPAIN, PORTUGAL, AND THE WESTERN POWERS

Two related factors made the internal struggles and eventual civil wars in Spain and Portugal in the 1830s prominent, though never really important, concerns of international politics. First, the civil wars, though the product of struggles for power within the narrow circles of the royal families, their courts, and small ruling élites, also had an ideological tinge, and in time came to engage the sympathies of wider groups in the peninsula and in Europe. This was especially true of Spain, where the Carlist Wars of the 1830s would have some of the symbolic significance in Spain and Europe that the Spanish Civil War had a century later. Second, the contests came to be widely viewed and portrayed as an outgrowth of the fundamental division and clash in Europe between the constitutional West and the autocratic East. As will be shown, this was not really the case. The differences between the contending parties in Spain and Portugal were not mainly ideological, and where ideology was involved the divisions were never neat. The two liberal-constitutional powers actively involved in the peninsula, Britain and France, were both playing a normal, non-ideological game almost entirely with and against each other, while the absolutist Eastern powers were never seriously involved. What really happened in the supposed conflict of principles is that the Holy Alliance powers, who believed in the principle of intervention, did not intervene, and the Western powers, in particular Britain, intervened under the principle of non-intervention.

Both civil wars started with dynastic quarrels over the succession. After John VI of Portugal died in 1826, his son and successor, Dom Pedro, choosing to retain his throne as Emperor of Brazil rather than return to rule Portugal, bestowed a constitutional charter on Portugal and the Portuguese Crown on his seven-year-old daughter, Maria. She was to marry her uncle, Dom Miguel, Pedro's brother, when she came of age, provided Miguel took an oath to maintain the charter. The charter, unpopular in Portugal, split the country into hostile factions and

[10] Reinerman (1989: 244–69, 300–25); Nada (1957: 193–5, 213–19); Gisci (1931); Derré (1963).

alarmed Ferdinand of Spain, who was fighting off challenges from both liberals and ultra-royalists to his own brand of absolutism. In 1826 George Canning sent a British naval force to Lisbon to deter Portuguese *émigrés* in Spain from trying to overthrow Pedro's charter with Spanish help.

In 1828 Dom Miguel, having solemnly sworn to uphold the constitution while in exile at Vienna, returned to assume the regency for Maria. He promptly violated his oath, suspending the constitution and proclaiming himself King. The powers, including the Eastern ones, withdrew their envoys from Lisbon and refused to recognize him, but his coup met no resistance in Portugal. In 1829 Ferdinand of Spain recognized him. Wellington, whose prime concern was preserving Portugal's internal stability and British influence there and who considered the Portuguese *émigré* supporters of Doña Maria's cause in Britain a dangerous nuisance, began preparing to do so as well. The Whig take-over in 1830 changed this. In opposition they had attacked Wellington for tolerating usurpation and tyranny in Portugal; the Grey ministry now refused to recognize Miguel, ruining British influence in both Portugal and Spain.

In 1832, after forces loyal to Dom Pedro had seized the Azores, Pedro returned to Europe seeking British and French help for an expedition against Miguel. His undertaking seemed to offer Britain a chance to retrieve its position in Portugal. France, however, opposed the idea, and the Spanish government, involved ·in its own internal crises, was terrified by it. The British cabinet was divided, with Lord Holland favouring action if France would co-operate, others advocating non-intervention. Palmerston and Grey agreed that Miguel should be overthrown, but Palmerston found an overt intervention difficult to justify and was reluctant to let France into the action. He therefore proposed to the Eastern powers that they help Britain oust Miguel in favour of Maria, in exchange for which the Portuguese constitution would be suspended. When they declined to pull Britain's chestnuts out of the fire, the British government, still claiming to pursue a policy of non-intervention and neutrality, secretly aided Pedro in equipping his expedition. It succeeded in capturing Oporto, but there was bottled up; by 1832 Portugal was involved in a civil war, with the majority siding with Miguel.[11]

[11] Livermore (1976: 268–75); Bullen (1974*b*); Holland (1977: 58–61, 80–1). For Wellington's views on Portugal in 1826–8, see Wellington (1862–80: iii. 375–7, 381–2, 419–21, 431, 583–4; iv. 544–5).

Meanwhile a succession crisis was also building in Spain. The clerical ultra-royalist party (the so-called Apostolicals) expected to gain power soon when Ferdinand, ailing and childless, died and was succeeded by his brother Don Carlos, leader of the party. But in October 1830 Ferdinand's fourth wife, Maria Cristina of Naples, bore him a daughter, Isabella. Before the birth Ferdinand published a Pragmatic Sanction, decreed by his father Charles IV in 1789 but not ratified by the Cortes, which revoked the Salic Law promulgated by Philip V in 1713 and restored the traditional Spanish law of succession through male and female lines alike. After Isabella's birth she was proclaimed Princess of Asturias and heir to the throne. Carlos and the Apostolicals denounced all this as illegal, but Carlos declined to give the signal for an insurrection. In the autumn of 1832, with Ferdinand incapacitated by illness, the Apostolicals at the court compelled Cristina as his regent to revoke the Pragmatic Sanction. Ferdinand, however, unexpectedly recovered, reinstated it, and forced Carlos into exile in Portugal.

In early 1833 Palmerston tried to use the troubles in Spain for his campaign against Miguel, offering to recognize Isabella's rights if the Spanish government would repudiate Miguel and recognize Maria. At first the move backfired; the Spanish premier, Çea Bermudez, and the Queen, approached behind Çea's back, both rejected this as incompatible with Spain's honour. From mid-1833, however, Britain's prospects in the peninsula began to improve. A Tory attack in Parliament on the government's policy was beaten back; Miguel failed to take Oporto; and Pedro's navy, led by a British commander, succeeded in transporting his forces from Oporto to Lisbon in late 1833. Though Miguel still controlled the countryside, once the capital was in the hands of Pedro's forces Britain could openly recognize and support Maria.

More important, the Spanish government now switched sides. Ferdinand's death in late September and Cristina's assumption of power as regent for Isabella II finally touched off an insurrection in Spain in favour of Carlos. Despite the superior organization and training of the government's troops and Carlos's pusillanimous conduct (he declined to come back from exile in Portugal to lead his movement), the insurgency managed to take root in various parts of Spain, especially the Basque provinces to the north, and for several years the guerilla tactics and superior generalship of the Carlist forces gave the government all it could handle. To save the throne for Isabella, Cristina was forced to break with Ferdinand's legitimist policies. She appointed a moderate liberal ministry, granted Spain a limited constitutional charter in early 1834, and signalled Spain's willingness to co-operate with Britain against Miguel and Carlos.[12]

Palmerston saw the Spanish offer as a chance to overthrow Miguel and thereby defeat what he portrayed as a vast Holy Alliance conspiracy against liberalism in the Iberian peninsula and throughout Europe. He was also determined to carry off this coup alone, without interference from France. Since December 1833 Talleyrand and the Duc de Broglie had sought a defensive alliance with Britain to crown Anglo-French co-operation in Belgium. Palmerston, rejecting the French offers and denying that France had any right to be involved in the Iberian peninsula on an equal basis with Britain, first reached agreement with Spain for joint action in Portugal in March 1834, and then proposed that France simply endorse this agreement. By this time Broglie, under fire at home as pro-English, had resigned the foreign ministry over another issue and been replaced by Admiral de Rigny, the French hero of Navarino. Though Rigny also wanted a British alliance, like Talleyrand, French ambassador at London, he insisted on at least nominal equality for France. The resultant compromise worked out between Palmerston and Talleyrand, the Quadruple Alliance of April 1834 (Britain, France, Spain, and Portugal), made France an auxiliary, supposed to come to the aid of Spain and Britain in Portugal if needed. The subsequent Anglo-Spanish intervention in Portugal worked; within a few months both Miguel and Carlos had fled Portugal.[13]

Palmerston proclaimed this a triumph of world-historical dimensions over Miguel, Metternich, the Holy Alliance, and the forces of absolutism and evil generally. The actual results were more modest. Miguel was ousted and British influence restored in Portugal, but Maria's government proved no more able or less arbitrary than Miguel's. The Carlist wars ground on in Spain until 1839–40, the government finally winning with some help from Britain and France. This was doubtless better for Spain than a Carlist victory would have been, but the wars deepened Spain's political divisions and struggles for power, especially between clericals and anticlericals, promoted the dominance of military

[12] Coverdale (1984: 84–165); Bullen (1974*b*).

[13] Guyot (1926: 100–25); Bullen (1977; 1974*a*: 10–13); Webster (1951: i. 386–97). Webster's account of Palmerston's involvement in Spain and Portugal constantly stresses the threat of Holy Alliance intervention; ibid. 237–53, 370–7 and *passim*.

men in politics, and made Spain even more an object of Anglo-French tutelage and rivalry.[14]

Rivalry between the two Western powers was in fact the most important result of the Iberian imbroglio in international politics. There were undoubtedly structural barriers in the way of any durable Anglo-French partnership in the 1830s and 1840s. It lacked a solid economic basis, traditional rivalries and suspicions persisted, there were incidental frictions over issues like the slave trade, France was internally unstable, and the two powers appeared to have somewhat divergent ambitions and interests in the Near East. But there were also important factors promoting a *rapprochement*—considerable sympathy on both sides, similar governing principles and ruling élites in both countries, the experience of effective co-operation in Belgium, and perceived joint interests and common foes elsewhere. The French government consistently tried for an alliance at this time, at considerable political risk. In the event, Broglie fell and Talleyrand retired in disillusionment about achieving any durable Anglo-French tie, characterizing the Quadruple Alliance as an 'alliance Palmerston' rather than an 'alliance anglaise'. Palmerston's attitude and tactics contributed considerably to this outcome. He could not accept an equal partnership or allow France to have its own sphere of influence; everyone had to see that he and Britain were in control.[15]

A real Anglo-French alliance might have constituted the symbolic triumph over absolutism that Palmerston boasted of, and been an effective instrument for promoting liberalism in Europe. The actual Quadruple Alliance proved a damp squib. In the first place, there was no Holy Alliance conspiracy in the peninsula to combat. The dignified enemy for Palmerston and the Whigs in Spain and Portugal was the Holy Alliance; their real rivals were France abroad and their Tory opponents at home, especially Wellington and Aberdeen, and the main problem they had to contend with in the Peninsula, besides Carlist resistance, was the impoverished, chaotic, and unreformable condition of the Spanish and Portuguese governments.

The Eastern powers certainly disliked representative constitutions in the Iberian peninsula, just as they did elsewhere. Metternich and other conservatives denied the legality of Ferdinand

[14] Coverdale (1984: 3–9, 116–307); Hans Gollwitzer (1953); Christiansen (1967: 28–69); Payne (1973: i. 444–9). On the Anglo-French struggle, see below, nn. 15–16.

[15] Bullen (1974c: 14–17); Guyot (1926: 90–1, 105–15, 126–63); Webster (1951: i. 414–15, 494–5); Bury and Combs (1986: 56–9); Jennings (1980).

VII's changes in the Spanish law of succession, denounced British policy as dangerous and illegal (as did Wellington, Aberdeen, and the Tories, which according to Palmerston made them part of the reactionary conspiracy), and gave the Carlist cause some moral and financial encouragement. But Metternich's policy was strictly a defensive one. Here, as so often, he combined a rigid dogmatism in principle with great caution and inertia in practice. The Eastern governments never even recognized Miguel, much less intervened in the civil wars; Metternich's protests against British policy were ineffective even when Wellington and Aberdeen returned to office during the brief Tory ministry in 1834–5. Just as in the Eastern crisis in 1828–9, Wellington insisted that Britain was willy-nilly committed to the alliance with France. The one time Austria could have caused Britain embarrassment, by taking up the French premier Adolphe Thiers's bid for a *rapprochement* with France in 1836, Metternich carefully avoided doing so, partly because one of his main goals was to regain Britain's co-operation in the Near East. The British, including Palmerston, knew all this.[16]

Russia and Prussia were no different from Austria; Prussia wanted better relations with Britain, as did Nesselrode, and Nicholas wished to separate Britain and France, not drive them

---

[16] Hans Gollwitzer (1953: 386–7); Webster (1951: i. 381). For British party politics in Iberian foreign policy, see Bullen (1978). For Wellington's and Aberdeen's ideas on Iberian issues and the Quadruple Alliance and their reactions to Metternich's complaints, see Wellington (1975: 70–9, 118, 400–2, 540–2, 639–42, 652–3, 663–4, 674–5; 1986: 64–5, 249–50, 376–8). There is convincing evidence that Palmerston himself did not take the Holy Alliance threat seriously in his correspondence with the British ambassador to Spain in 1833–7, Sir George Villiers (later the 4th Earl of Clarendon, foreign secretary during the Crimean War), as published in Palmerston (1985). From the beginning Villiers reported 'the complete nullity of Holy Alliance influence here' (No. 30, 28 Jan. 1834). Palmerston repeatedly derided the 'Unholy Allies' for the ineptitude of their efforts, was delighted that they declined to recognize Isabella, and used the Quadruple Alliance and Spain as offensive weapons in his cold war against Metternich and Nicholas in Europe (see e.g. Nos. 19, 32, 36). Even when he later charged Austria and Russia with sending Carlos money (Nos. 142, 158, 250): he knew and said that this was not what Carlos needed. The most striking proof of how little Palmerston and Villiers really believed their own propaganda came at the end of 1837. Villiers, in despair at Britain's inability to end the Carlist war, reform Spain, save the Quadruple Alliance, and stop the rise of French influence, suggested as a remedy that Queen Isabella (then 5 years old) be married to an Austrian Archduke. According to Villiers, this would frustrate Louis-Philippe, promote the balance of power, delight the Russians, please the Spaniards, and promote peace by reconciling Spain with the Northern Powers and giving it what it most needed, a marriage alliance with Austria. Palmerston rejected the plan because Austrian influence was incompatible with constitutional liberty, but not because this would have meant surrendering Spain to the enemy; Nos. 392–3, 395.

together. The Eastern powers therefore exerted no impact on peninsular affairs worth talking about. At the same time, as will be seen, the Quadruple Alliance had no effects, or only counterproductive ones, in Germany, Italy, Poland, or the Near East. The ideological confrontation between the two camps was sound and fury, signifying nothing. Metternich and Palmerston hated each other, needed each other as enemies, and played off each other for propaganda and prestige purposes. One might well feel that they deserved each other. But they were not seriously fighting one another; each was bent on protecting and consolidating his own turf; and each ignored ideological differences when it suited him.

III.   THE FIRST EASTERN CRISIS, OVER OTTOMAN SURVIVAL

The Near Eastern crises of the 1830s seemed like those in Spain and Portugal: the product of a civil war within the Ottoman Empire, complicated by great-power contests for influence in it. Any resemblance was superficial; the differences were profound. Nothing of major importance for the international system was at stake in Portugal and Spain. In the Ottoman Empire, a reforming Ottoman Sultan trying to keep his empire going confronted an ambitious modernizing vassal determined either to take that empire over or to carve his own empire out of it. This put both the Ottoman Empire and the European equilibrium at risk. For the first time, moreover, the two leading powers, Russia and Britain, confronted each other directly in this critical area, marking a new stage in the Eastern question and the Great Game in Asia.

The Pasha of Egypt, Mohamed Ali, had by the 1820s achieved a great part of his ambition to develop Egypt into a modern state, building it economically, expanding it territorially, and gaining its political independence. He had extended his domains into the Sudan and Arabia, created a European-style army and navy, and was beginning to modernize Egypt's agriculture, communications, public works, and trade. He welcomed and encouraged the Greek revolt in the 1820s in the hope that his jealous overlord, Sultan Mahmud II, would need his help. When Mahmud's appeal came, Mohamed complied in the expectation of gaining territorial and political rewards, but hoping at the same time not to challenge France, which had helped him modernize, or Britain, which he wished to appease. Though he accepted the Pashalic of the Morea offered by the Sultan, not with an eye to resettling it but to expanding Egyptian trade, the real prize he coveted was Syria.

After the Battle of Navarino forced him to pull out of Greece, he continued to cultivate France and woo Britain, with which he had commercial ties, and he expected the Sultan to pay him with territory for Egypt's losses. Mahmud reluctantly granted him Cyprus as an apanage, but refused to hand over Syria. In October 1831, having picked a quarrel with the Pasha of Syria over Egyptian refugees, Mohamed sent in his army under his son and ablest general, Ibrahim, whose ambitions exceeded even those of his father. Six months of hard battles and sieges gained Egypt all of Syria, but Mohamed and Ibrahim were stripped of their titles and ranks and proclaimed rebels by the Sultan. After waiting several months to see whether Europe would support the Turks, Mohamed ordered Ibrahim to attack the Ottoman army in southern Anatolia to force the Sultan to renew his titles and cede him his new conquests. Successfully crossing the Taurus mountains, Ibrahim met the main Ottoman army at Koniah on 21 December 1832 and virtually destroyed it. Ibrahim urged that his army drive on Constantinople, now almost defenseless, and depose the Sultan, but Mohamed held back.[17]

Despite repeated Turkish appeals, Europe had failed to react to this long-developing threat, partly because of distractions elsewhere but mainly because Britain could not decide what to do. The British had various offers of help in the Near East. The French, eager to cement their partnership with Britain, rescue the Ottoman Empire, and preserve their influence in Egypt, urged that Britain and France join to mediate a Turco-Egyptian peace before Russia did so. Metternich, determined to stick close to the Russians to restrain them and hoping to split Britain and France, offered his co-operation to London, warning the British that France was behind Mohamed's conquests and wanted to turn the eastern Mediterranean into a French lake. But the British cabinet, as usual, was divided and distracted. Grey was convinced that Turkey was beyond saving, and Palmerston was only slowly groping toward an Eastern policy. Henry Ellis at the Board of Control for India argued that Britain's aim should be to preserve the Ottoman Empire as a unified state along with Persia as buffers for India, not trying to reform Turkey or establish a protectorate over it but simply keeping any other power out. Eventually this

[17] Al-Sayyid Marsot (1984: 194–226); Sabry (1930: 187–230); Puryear (1941: 43–6); Rodkey (1933).

would become Britain's main policy, though never consistently so; Palmerston already considered Russia's influence at Constantinople as more dangerous than France's. But Ellis's programme was not yet ripe. When Palmerston proposed to offer the Sultan naval support in November 1832, arguing that with British help Mahmud could reform his empire, the cabinet found this unconvincing. Besides, the fleet was needed elsewhere.[18]

Russia, unlike Britain, did not hesitate. It had achieved the dominant influence at Constantinople it wanted in 1829, and had no hesitations about condemning Mohamed Ali as a rebel or shutting France out of the Near East. Nicholas wanted unity in the Holy Alliance and did not want more Ottoman territory. He was convinced that any further acquisitions would be a *damnosa possessio* like Poland (though he did float to Metternich the dangerous idea of a Greek kingdom at Constantinople under King Otto); to gain more influence at Constantinople, he was ready to return the strategically valuable Danubian Principalities Russia had occupied and governed since 1829. The instructions General N. N. Muraviev took with him on his special mission to Constantinople in December 1832 were therefore a genuine offer to the Sultan of Russia's help and friendship.

Despite his peril, the Sultan at first declined the offer, fearing Russia and feeling the pressure of the French envoy, Vice-Admiral Baron de Roussin. France and Russia now competed in an effort to gain Mahmud the peace and respite he craved. Muraviev left for Alexandria, where he persuaded Mohamed Ali to issue orders stopping Ibrahim's advance in Anatolia. But when delays in the transmission of these orders and the dispatch of an Ottoman peace mission gave Ibrahim an excuse to continue his advance, the Sultan in panic called on Russia for help. Nicholas responded with orders to his army and Black Sea fleet the day the appeal reached him. Mahmud meanwhile changed his mind under Roussin's pressure, but not before the Russian envoy at Istanbul had summoned the Russian fleet. It arrived before Constantinople on 20 February and insisted on staying.[19]

This shocked Europe, France most of all. From February to July British, French, and Austrian diplomats worked frantically to put together an Ottoman–Egyptian settlement that would satisfy

[18] Ingram (1979: 218–43); Vereté (1952); Webster (1951: i. 82, 832).

[19] Schiemann (1904: iii. 210–18) (on Nicholas's conservative disposition, fears over Poland, and desire for Holy Alliance unity, pp. 187–208); Georgiev (1975: 5–18); Eremeeva (1956); Martens (1874–1905: iv. 438–45).

Egypt and reassure the Sultan so that he would send the Russians home. The complex European diplomatic efforts at Constantinople and Alexandria basically came to nothing. Instead, the Sultan and the Egyptians on their own reached an agreement at Kutahia in May of such a nature that no one but the Russians could be satisfied with it. In restoring Mohamed to his former ranks and titles and giving him the temporary governorship of all of Syria plus Cyprus and the Adana district in southern Anatolia, the Sultan temporarily surrendered to Mohamed more than he could permanently sacrifice. At the same time the concessions fell short of Mohamed's ambitions, to say nothing of Ibrahim's, and blocked his hope for a junior partnership with one or both of the Western powers in the Levant. Meanwhile Russia had tightened its hold over Turkey. In March Mahmud, frightened by the near-breakdown of negotiations and Ibrahim's renewed advance on Istanbul, had invited a Russian army to his capital along with the fleet. The truce of Kutahia therefore left the Porte just where St Petersburg wanted it, insecure and dependent on further Russian support.[20]

The detailed reasons why European diplomacy failed in dealing with Turkey and Egypt are complex, but the basic explanation is simple enough. France and Britain could not get the Sultan to believe their promises and warnings or make Mohamed fear their threats of naval coercion, and Roussin could not control Egypt's terms as he had supposed he could. This failure in negotiation was more than matched by the inability of Britain, France, and Austria to co-operate against what they all recognized as the main danger, Russia and its dominant position at the Porte. France and Austria both sought Britain's co-operation. Metternich, promising that Austria would fight Russia if it tried to destroy or partition the Ottoman Empire, proposed a grouping coalition. Russia should be confined within a five-power concert binding it to act jointly with Europe in the Near East, the concert to be effected through a mutual self-denying agreement and a conference or centre for action at Vienna. France proposed a blocking coalition instead. By detaching Austria from Russia, the Western powers could confront Russia with a superior alliance, thereby forcing it to internationalize its protection of the Sultan. Meanwhile Britain and France could support the Ottoman Empire with a show of naval force and, if necessary, coerce Mohamed into offering the

[20] Schiemann (1904: iii. 218–22); Sabry (1930: 221–49); Al-Sayyid Marsot (1984: 226–31).

Sultan acceptable terms. Since Russia was actually not bent on expansion or exclusive control (as Metternich constantly insisted), either approach could well have worked, though the French one was more dangerous and harmful for the system. But Britain could not be won for either. Though Palmerston shared Metternich's goal of preserving the Ottoman Empire just as it was, he rejected Austria's proposals, agreeing to a conference only in forms he knew the Eastern Powers could not accept (e.g. proposing to revive the London Conference on Belgium and expand its agenda to cover the Near East). He also declined to work closely with France.

This gave a free hand to Russia's special envoy, Count Orlov, sent to Constantinople to help the Sultan conclude peace with Egypt and to negotiate an alliance. He accomplished little on the first goal, but succeeded in the second, signing on 8 July 1833 a defensive Russo-Turkish alliance at Unkiar-Skelessi. A secret clause in the treaty unilaterally absolved the Sultan of the obligation to come to Russia's aid in case of war, in exchange for his promise to close the Straits to warships in time of peace.[21]

Europe was again shocked, this time Britain in particular. For the next seven years Palmerston would work to break the Treaty of Unkiar-Skelessi. This was not because he thought, as others did, that it gave Russia special privileges in the straits. He knew better than this, but considered the treaty dangerous because it reinforced and sanctioned Russia's special position as protector of the Ottoman Empire. Metternich felt just the same way; this makes the question of why they did not co-operate then or later even more pressing. The obvious answer, that the British distrusted Austria for its intimacy with Russia and its anti-liberal policies elsewhere, including Western Europe, is true, but nothing like the whole or main answer. For one thing, as has been seen, Austria posed no serious obstacle to British policy in Western Europe; even where Metternich disliked what Britain did, he preferred to yield or abstain rather than to invite useless trouble or lose British co-operation elsewhere, especially in the Near East. Whenever British leaders, Palmerston included, wanted or needed

[21] Molden (1913: 39–79); Webster (1951: i. 280–4, 290–301, 802–4); Kiniapina (1958); Puryear (1941); Testa (1864–1911: ii. 355–73). Sabry (1930) claims on the basis of British documents that the Austrian nuncio to the Porte, Baron Prokesch, for anti-British reasons, urged Mohamed Ali to build an Arab empire by expanding into Mesopotamia (pp. 270–2). If so, this was in flat contradiction to Metternich's instructions to Prokesch, to urge the Sultan to yield as little territory as possible to Mohamed while securing Mohamed's formal submission to the Sultan's authority; Metternich (1880–4: v. 495–500).

to badly enough, they could readily ignore Austria's political sins. The real source of Britain's inaction in the Near East in 1832–3, as already seen, was internal divisions and distractions. British distrust of Austria, as well as of France, was the dignified reason for doing nothing and preserving Britain's options. For Palmerston, the ability to blame an unsatisfactory outcome in the Near East on a Holy Alliance conspiracy had a further functional utility. It prepared the ground for either confronting Russia or attempting to detach Austria from Russia, while at the same time he could use his accusations against Austria over its Near Eastern policy to force it to co-operate on questions closer to home and more popular with the British public, like Belgium or Spain.

This was how the British reacted to the Convention of Münchengrätz, signed by Austria and Russia at a summit conference in mid-September. In it the emperors and their ministers affirmed their solidarity in opposition to revolutions and the subversive principle of non-intervention, particularly in regard to Poland. They were united on this score, but not on the Near East. Since January Nicholas had been pressing Austria not only to endorse Russia's special protection of the Ottoman Empire enshrined in Unkiar-Skelessi, but to reach an agreement in advance on what the two powers would do if and when an Ottoman collapse could not be avoided. Nicholas and Nesselrode did not want to partition the Empire; the Tsar was genuinely convinced that its survival as a weak dependent state was in Russia's interests. But Nicholas, beneath his pose as the strong man of Europe, was dominated by pessimism and fears. He saw the collapse of the Ottoman Empire as inevitable and probably imminent, dreaded the possible results, and wanted to make sure in advance that Russia would control the disposition of the spoils and that Austria would not defect to the West.

Metternich and Francis dreaded Turkey's collapse even more than Nicholas did, and had even less interest in acquiring Turkish territory. Austria's dangers and Metternich's fears, however, pulled in contradictory directions. Austria's problems in Central Europe called for a close alliance with Russia; the Near Eastern problem called for joining the other powers in restraining Russia. At Münchengrätz Austria attempted to do both at the same time. Metternich tried not to reply to Nicholas's probes about the fate of the Ottoman Empire at all, knowing that by reaching any agreement with the Tsar he would encourage the very Russian penetration of the Ottoman Empire he wanted to stop. When forced to propose something, he suggested what he knew Russia did not want, just as he had over Greece ten years earlier: the creation of fully independent states in the Balkans. Both powers, as always, used their alliance as a pact of restraint in the East, Russia to ensure that Austria would not defect if Russia chose to act, Austria to keep Russia from acting at all.

The agreement at Münchengrätz was thus a compromise and stalemate. In the public treaty the two powers pledged to co-operate in sustaining the Ottoman Empire under its present dynasty against any threat to the Sultan's authority. In separate secret clauses they applied this pledge especially to Mohamed Ali, ruling out any extension of his authority to the Sultan's European provinces, and promised to co-operate if, contrary to their wishes and actions, the Sultan's authority or dynasty should be overthrown.

The existence and general tenor of the convention quickly became known; Metternich wished to publish it, but the Tsar refused. The British, especially Palmerston, chose to view it as a Russian plot for the slow undermining and ultimate partition of the Ottoman Empire, in which Austria was a real if reluctant partner. Palmerston claimed that, since the convention did not guarantee the Ottoman Empire's territorial integrity, but only its existence and current dynasty, this indicated hidden Austro-Russian territorial designs.

The suspicion was baseless. At this time, talk of guaranteeing the territorial integrity of the Ottoman Empire was almost meaningless. Legally, the Sultan's authority over much of his domains consisted of a vague suzerainty rather than Western-style sovereignty, and practically it often did not extend even to that. Portions of the empire (Algiers and the Danubian Principalities) were occupied by foreign powers, and the current territorial issues between Mahmud and Mohamed had only been postponed rather than settled. It was even worse to read the language of Münchengrätz to mean that Austria was not serious about stopping further Russian territorial encroachments on Turkey. Austria had far stronger reasons than Britain to want to do so, and over the last forty years a far better record of trying. At this very moment some British ministers, including the prime minister, Grey, were ready to write off the Ottoman Empire as doomed. In the 1840s the British government would reach an agreement with Russia to preserve the Ottoman Empire using precisely the same terms as Münchengrätz. The British reading of the agreement not only grossly exaggerated its dangers but ignored its salutary possibilities. Metternich had secured something useful, Russia's commitment to act toward the Ottoman Empire only in conjunction with Austria, and now aimed to bring Prussia into the agreement (which he succeeded in doing in October) to be followed by Britain and France, so that Russia would be constrained to act only as part of a five-power concert.[22]

Britain's real trouble was that, although it had finally learned to recognize certain dangers to British interests in the Near East, it still had to determine just what and where these threats were before deciding how to meet them, if (as Grey doubted) they could be met at all. Did the danger lie at Constantinople, in the decadence of the Ottoman Empire and/or the Sultan's weakness and dependence on Russia? Palmerston, Grey, and Lord Melbourne, Grey's successor as premier in 1834, more or less agreed on this. Or was it Russia's fixed determination to partition Turkey or expand at its expense, as Lord Ponsonby, the ambassador at Constantinople, and the influential publicist and Member of Parliament, David Urquhart, both contended? Or in opportunistic Russian expansionism, as Palmerston thought? Was Russia a threat in the Black Sea? If so, why—because of the defensive security it enjoyed, or the offensive capacity it was building up, or its gradual penetration into Circassia, or its pressure on Persia and Central Asia? Did Mohamed Ali's growing power in the Arab world make him a threat, and if so where—in the region of the Red Sea, or the Persian Gulf and Mesopotamia? What should Britain be most concerned to protect, the straits and Constantinople, the whole Levant, the routes to India, or its trade with and through the Near and Middle East? Was the Ottoman Empire vital for the established balance of power against Russia in Europe, or for an Asian balance of power to defend India, yet to be established?

Even if the Russian threat could be defined and located, how to meet it remained unclear. War with Russia would be dangerous, expensive, and impractical, especially in the Black Sea and Circassia. A direct Anglo-Turkish alliance would be provocative and compromising, one with France difficult, one with Austria unpopular and probably ineffective, a restraining alliance with Russia even more unpopular. Could Mohamed Ali be used to revive the Ottoman Empire or control the Levant, as some businessmen

[22] For the text of the Münchengrätz Convention, see Martens (1874–1905: iv. 446–9); for various accounts of its origins and significance, Molden (1913: 79–123); Schiemann (1904: iii. 232–45); Puryear (1931: 20–4); H. Müller (1980: 50–61). For the British reaction, see Ingram (1979: 245–64); Webster (1951: i. 307–15, 820, 837–8); and Bourne (1982: 377–87).

active in the East suggested? Could the problem be met by the fleet, or armed aid to Turkey, or opening Turkey to trade and Western influences, or forcing Turkey to reform?

It was thus understandable that other powers could have policies apparently simple and consistent compared to Britain's. They were not world powers, with a far-flung, vulnerable empire to defend on the cheap, many potential threats to consider, and cabinet, parliamentary, and popular pressures to complicate any decision. Nor did it make British decisions easier that every power interested in the Near East, including Russia, courted Britain and wanted to be its partner.[23]

One choice, in any case, was easy: to reject Metternich's idea of turning the Münchengrätz Convention into a general treaty in support of the Ottoman Empire. Not only did most British leaders share Palmerston's distrust of Austria, but joining a European *entente* led by Metternich would not have achieved what Palmerston wanted. He insisted on controlling any combination Britain joined, wanted Austria to oppose Russia outright, and expected to achieve this once Metternich died or was overthrown.[24] More important still, Metternich's solution of grouping Russia within the concert would have defeated Palmerston's main purpose, by giving defensive security to Russia as well as to the Ottoman Empire in the Near East. Not only did Palmerston deny that any such concert would restrain Russia, insisting that the only alternative to appeasement and surrender was a blocking coalition and potential confrontation;[25] besides this, a concert 'solution', by

[23] In addition to Ingram, Webster, and Bourne (n. 22 above), see also Dodwell (1931); Kelly (1965); Bartle (1964); Rodkey (1933); Marston (1961: 45–55, 60–3); Lambi (1981); Bailey (1940); Crawley (1929).

[24] Webster (1951: ii. 814–15, 841–3). Characteristically, at the same time as Palmerston wanted Austria to join an Anglo-French combination against Russia in the Near East, he was thinking of extending the liberal Quadruple Alliance into the Mediterranean to include Naples, so as to weaken Austria's grip on Italy; Howard (1974: 54–5).

[25] Ingram (1979: 276–7, 298–9). It may be useful to state clearly where I differ with Charles K. Webster in his view of Palmerston's policy, still followed by some British scholars, though not all. It is not important that Webster is too favourable to Palmerston and Britain or too hard on Metternich and Austria. Here a scholar, especially a great one like Webster, is entitled to his opinion, and many of his strictures on Metternich and Austria are justified. Nor is the main point (though this is more serious) that Webster tended to overlook or excuse Palmerston's abrasive tactics, double standards, and provocative actions on the grounds that he was successful in advancing British interests, without giving much attention to the long-range systemic effects of Palmerston's success (e.g. Webster, 1951: i. 301–2; ii. 525–7). The real issue is Webster's acceptance of Palmerston's view that the only real alternative to his tactics of confrontation and vigorous assertion of British

protecting both Turkey and Russia, potentially freed Russia for action against Britain's position elsewhere in Asia. It was partly for this reason that Ponsonby, who was much more hawkish than Palmerston, urged having nothing to do with Austria at all, but instead confronting Russia directly with an Anglo-Turkish alliance and possibly sending a British fleet into the Black Sea.[26]

Britain's negative response was actually useful for Nicholas, enabling him to keep Austria in tow and to fend off Metternich's efforts to get the Münchengrätz agreement communicated officially to the Western powers. Russian policy was not hostile to Britain, nor was it opposed to all reform of the Ottoman Empire. It was just like Austria's in Italy—in favour of certain kinds of reform and international co-operation, so long as its own leading position was not undermined. Satisfied with the gains it had won, Russia held its ground; in 1836 Nesselrode began seeking an *entente* with Britain, for the sake of general peace and Russia's economic development.[27]

His feelers were ignored at London. Instead, from 1834 to 1838 Palmerston considered various ideas for shoring up the Ottoman Empire against Russia. He thought of a separate Western alliance with Turkey, British instructors to train the Turkish army, the expansion of British trade and influence in Serbia to make it a barrier to Russian expansion, or a European agreement that, if Mohamed Ali declared his independence, the powers would defend the Sultan, with Austria to supply the troops and Britain and France the navy. None of the proposals was even potentially effective against Russia; some directly threatened Austrian interests (e.g. in Serbia) or were designed to create an Austro-Russian confrontation. One idea Palmerston refused to entertain, though Louis-Philippe endorsed it, was a conference at Vienna on the Eastern question; Austria was too subservient to Russia. Metternich pointed out that it was British policy on Greece in the 1820s which had made Russia dominant at the Porte in the first place, and suggested, somewhat more helpfully, that both sides were too suspicious of the other and that Austria would work with both to preserve the status quo.[28]

interests was appeasement and surrender (e.g. ibid. ii. 558). This assumption seems to me incorrect in theory and dangerous in practice. There are other possibilities.

[26] Bolsover (1934–5; 1936*a*; 1936*b*); Webster (1951: i. 338–45; 1947); Ingram (1979: 274–99).

[27] Ingle (1976: 35–8, 57–63); Georgiev (1975: 69–80); Todorova (1977); Martens (1874–1905: iv. 468–9).

[28] Webster (1951: ii. 545–6, 570–9, 582–90); Sabry (1930: 416–17, 430–1).

IV. THE SECOND EASTERN CRISIS, OVER EUROPEAN HEGEMONY

Despite all the talk, when the Turco-Egyptian crisis flared up again in 1838, it caught Britain and Europe unready. In May Mohamed announced his intention to declare Egypt and Syria independent, offering to buy out the Sultan's rights. France, Britain, and Austria protested and called for a European conference, but this led to nothing, partly because London and Vienna could not agree on its venue. Instead, the British responded by offering Turkey a commercial agreement. In the Convention of Balta-Liman signed that summer, the Sultan agreed to abolish commercial monopolies within the Ottoman Empire and switch to a system of low uniform tariffs. Britain expected the agreement to do a number of things—weaken Mohamed financially (he was already under fiscal and economic strain and his mercantilist policies were causing him trouble in Syria); revitalize and modernize the Ottoman Empire through British trade and influence; and above all, replace Russia's influence at Constantinople with Britain's. Balta-Liman was not supposed to do what it actually did—encourage the Sultan to go to war believing that Britain would stand behind him.[29]

Defying British and Russian warnings, Mahmud sent his army across the Euphrates on 21 April 1839. Britain and France promptly agreed that they must save the Sultan, limit and end the fighting, and prevent Russia from coming to Turkey's rescue alone. But once again they differed on how to do it. Palmerston, terming the Sultan's attack on Mohamed a case of legitimate self-defence against a rebel, proposed a joint Anglo-French fleet action along the coast of Syria to try to prevent either side from gaining an advantage and to force Mohamed to evacuate Syria and retire to Egypt. If the Turks once more invited a Russian army to come to Constantinople and Russia sent it, Austria must be forced to join the Western powers in demanding that Russia share its protection of the Sultan with them. Furthermore, the Anglo-French fleets would have to sail to Constantinople, as Russia's friends if possible, its enemies if necessary.

France's policy, as developed by the French premier, Marshal Soult, and the political director of the foreign ministry, Desages, was more cautious. Desages remarked that Palmerston's legitimist

[29] Webster (1951: ii. 548–57, 590–617); Webster (1934); Al-Sayyid Marsot (1984: 232–9); Sabry (1930: 433).

views on the relationship between the Sultan and Mohamed would be more appropriate at Vienna than London, and doubted that Russia would send an expedition to Constantinople, especially since the *casus foederis* of Unkiar-Skelessi did not apply. The Western powers should concentrate on the real dangers and main goals: to save the Ottoman Empire by ending the war, and to break Russian domination of the Porte by accustoming Russia to act within the confines of the European Concert. For these purposes, they should postpone the terms of the Turco-Egyptian settlement till later, and they must bring Austria in to group Russia, preferably by a European conference at Vienna.

France, in other words, adopted Austria's long-standing policy of grouping Russia. Palmerston was brought round by French persuasion, exercised particularly by the able chargé at London, Baron Bourqueney, and by a succession of catastrophic events. On 23 June Ibrahim destroyed the Turkish army at Nezib, leaving the way open to Constantinople. A few days later Mahmud died, leaving the throne to a sickly sixteen-year-old successor, Abdul-Mejid. Finally the Turkish fleet, sent out to fight the Egyptians, went over to the enemy and came into port at Alexandria. In a few weeks the Ottoman Empire had lost its army, its navy, and its ruler.

The gales battering the Ottoman Empire filled Metternich's sails. By late July France had persuaded Palmerston to accept a conference at Vienna; Metternich was aglow at the prospect of guiding Europe in the tasks of rescuing the Ottoman Empire and containing Russia. Nicholas knew it, and knew just what a European Concert organized and led by Austria would do: tie Russia down and undermine its leading position at the Porte. Ever since February Russia, partly to avoid this, had tried to hold back both parties and prevent a Turco-Egyptian war. It had some success with the Egyptians, who adopted a defensive position against the Turkish offensive, but none at Constantinople. But Nesselrode, often underrated as a diplomat, had worked out well before the crisis how to stop Austria from forming a concert to contain and manage Russia. He would form a separate partnership with Britain over the heads of the Continental powers. His aim, as he told Nicholas, was to lure Palmerston into this now as he had lured Canning fourteen years earlier. The only obstacle was the Treaty of Unkiar-Skelessi, due to lapse in two years and useless in the present crisis. Russia could best achieve its purposes, to close the Black Sea and prevent Europe from controlling Russia at the Porte, by sacrificing Unkiar-Skelessi in order to gain an

Anglo-Russian alliance at Austria's and France's expense. By May 1839 Nicholas had accepted this strategy.[30]

This meant that Metternich's delight at the first fruits of concert unity under Austria's leadership, a five-power note of July 27 sent to the new Sultan forbidding him to make peace with Mohamed except with the consent of Europe, was short-lived. Even though Russia had been encouraging direct Turkish–Egyptian talks, the Tsar accepted the joint note and its principle that Europe must control the negotiations. Allowing Metternich to lead in working out the settlement was something else again. Believing Metternich had violated Münchengrätz by failing to consult with Russia in advance, and becoming even angrier when Austria appeared to support the French idea of sending Western naval vessels into the Dardanelles to help protect Turkey, Nicholas flatly refused to let his ambassador take part in a conference at Vienna. The blow helped send Metternich to his sick-bed for weeks; his lieutenant and temporary substitute, Count Ficquelmont, moved quickly to placate Russia.

Metternich's shock at Nicholas's torpedoing of the Vienna conference was almost equalled by Britain's surprise and delight when Russia joined the Western powers in putting pressure on the Porte to stop its direct negotiations with Egypt. At the same time Russia adroitly inserted itself into a gap widening between Britain and France over the terms for peace. Palmerston wanted to punish Mohamed Ali by forcing him to disgorge all his earlier gains including Syria, and proposed sending the Western fleets to Alexandria to compel Mohamed to return the Turkish fleet. Soult was unwilling to do so, both because this would destroy France's influence with Mohamed, who was lionized in France as a French protégé, and because the main threat to the Ottoman Empire was not Mohamed but Russia. Taking Britain's side in this dispute, Russia sent Count Brunnov on a special mission to London, offering Britain Russia's direct co-operation in supporting the Sultan and imposing terms on Egypt by means of an ambassadorial conference to be held at London.[31]

Like Lieven's in 1825, the Brunnov mission found fertile soil in Britain. Already in early August, with signs of Anglo-French disagreement appearing, Palmerston had downgraded Russia's

---

[30] Webster (1951: ii. 629–36, 888–9); Testa (1864–1911: ii. 418–57); Schiemann (1904: iii. 378–83); Georgiev (1975: 78–99).

[31] Webster (1951: ii. 636–45); Schiemann (1904: iii. 384–91); Georgiev (1975: 100–11); Martens (1874–1905: 478–83); Testa (1864–1911: ii. 466–9, 475–7).

predominance at Constantinople to a temporary evil which a joint European guarantee could overcome, reversing his former stand. By mid-August he welcomed the idea of Russian soldiers going to the Bosporus to help defend the Sultan, an even more startling reversal, and by mid-September he discussed how Britain and Russia could force France into line, with or without the help of the German powers, just as in June and July he had spoken about an Anglo-French or Anglo-French–Austrian coalition to stop Russia. Some members of the cabinet, especially Lords Melbourne, Holland, and Clarendon, were reluctant to join Russia and break with France, especially for the sake of overthrowing Mohamed or forcing him back to Egypt. Palmerston, however, welcomed the Brunnov mission, confident that with it he could bring the French 'captive to our measures'.[32]

Palmerston's decision to work with Russia rather than France affected European high politics in some obvious ways. It marked the beginning of a dramatically successful Anglo-Russian collaboration, a serious Anglo-French quarrel, and the most dangerous European war scare since 1815, a crisis which, even though surmounted, continued to affect Anglo-French relations and European politics in general through the 1840s and even beyond. It also led to a settlement of this phase of the Eastern question and an advance in its internationalization. Another change effected by Palmerston's decision is not as obvious and more debatable, but perhaps as important. Here is where the main issue in 1839–41 ceased mainly to concern the Eastern question, i.e. what would happen to the Ottoman Empire, and began primarily to concern European alliances and alignments, the question of who would control the European system, how, and for what ends.

The original issues had been the basic, perennial problems in the Near East: how to save the Ottoman Empire, promote a stable peace in the region, and (for other powers besides Russia) replace Russia's preponderance at the Porte with joint European influence. By the time Britain decided to collaborate with Russia, the first two aspects of the problem were essentially solved. All the powers had agreed on a joint European effort to rescue the Ottoman Empire. Whatever differences already existed or would arise later over the modalities of this effort or the distribution

---

[32] Webster (1951: ii. 646–52); Palmerston to Lord Beauvale, 1 Aug., 10, 14 Sept. 1839, Palmerston Papers (Broadlands), GC/BE/519. (The phrase quoted is from the letter of 14 Sept.) The intra-cabinet struggle over policy throughout the summer and autumn of 1840 into 1841 is detailed in Bourne (1982: 575–620).

of tasks and responsibilities in it, there was no change in the unanimous European consensus on this point. Certain differences would arise between France and the other powers, especially Britain, regarding the precise terms of the peace settlement to be imposed on Turkey and Egypt, centred on Syria. Yet this gap was not unbridgeable, nor was either side originally intransigent on the matter; there would be repeated chances and proposals for a compromise throughout the crisis. More important, the differences over Ottoman–Egyptian peace terms did not really cause the breach between Britain and France, but the other way round. In any case, the difference separating France from Britain and the other powers over what territories Mohamed should be allowed to retain was never a critical factor for the rescue and guarantee of the Ottoman Empire. (What it might have had to do with saving the British Empire is another question.)

As for the issue long central to the Near Eastern problem, how to end Russia's dominant influence at the Porte and substitute a joint European influence for it, Anglo-Russian collaboration simply removed it from the table. Russia chose this collaboration in order to preserve its own dominant influence and prevent a joint European one; Britain did so to accomplish other British purposes, choosing to treat Russian influence as benign so long as it served them. All these facts were clear at the time, and became even clearer as the crisis developed.

In other words, the Near Eastern crisis of 1839–41 was, like the Crimean War fifteen years later, not really about the independence and integrity of the Ottoman Empire, but about the structure and alignments of European politics. Britain's response to the Brunnov mission showed again how the two hegemonic powers, facing challenges from their respective junior partners, preferred to work together so that each could maintain leadership in its own sphere. The crisis was created and shaped by the reactions of their respective junior partners, and their responses in return.

Russia won its hegemonic game immediately. Metternich, resuming office in October, swallowed his humiliation and accepted the Anglo-Russian lead, partly because, like Palmerston, he wanted to treat Mohamed as a rebel, partly because, like Nicholas, he wanted to separate Britain and France, but mainly because Austria was not capable of resisting Anglo-Russian pressure.

The French believed they could and must resist. Their initial miscalculation in 1839 was to think that they could use their supposed assets—the strength of Mohamed's position, their own influence in Egypt, the fact that Austria and France were on the same side in the East, and above all their conviction that Britain wanted and needed French help to break Russia's influence at Constantinople—to win France an equal partnership with Britain. This was the long-standing goal of Frenchmen, at least the moderate ones in the government, and it would give Louis-Philippe's regime the stability and prestige it sorely needed. They knew Palmerston would be an obstacle, but supposed that, with friends in the British cabinet sharing their aim, Clarendon and Holland above all, Palmerston would accept it in order to defeat Russia. They underestimated Russia's skill and flexibility, Austria's weakness, and Palmerston's determination.

Yet even had the French recognized the danger of pressing their luck (and they were warned by Bourqueney and Sébastiani, now ambassador at London), after September they could not have caved in unresisting like Austria. Though French governments regularly laid too much stress on France's honour, no regime, even one more stable and prestigious than Louis-Philippe's, could have meekly accepted Britain's deliberate choice of Russia over France as a partner. Not only was it too obvious an insult, easy for opponents of the ministry and the regime to exploit; it also revived memories of the four-power coalition of 1814–15 against France, and threatened important French interests in North Africa and the Levant. Besides (a point historians repeatedly ignore, often operating with an ethics of success which blames losers for their failure), even if the French had created their own troubles by miscalculation and made them worse out of national pride, on the original and central issue of this Eastern crisis they knew they were right and Palmerston was wrong. If the main danger in the East was Russian domination of the Ottoman Empire, as Palmerston himself had long insisted, then the only real, durable answer to that danger was an Anglo-French partnership with Austria to contain Russia, compelling it to act toward Turkey only in conjunction with the rest of Europe. When this solution was within reach in 1839, Palmerston chose to discard it, thereby virtually guaranteeing that, whatever else would be gained, the main problem would persist and rise again in the future.

From September to its fall in February 1840, the Soult ministry struggled to bring Britain back to France's side. Palmerston was not rigid on the Ottoman–Egyptian peace terms. He reluctantly conceded Mohamed hereditary rule in Egypt, and even a life tenure of the pashalic of Acre without Acre itself. But he rejected all the main French arguments—that Mohamed would fight rather than yield Syria, that his army might invade Mesopotamia, that it would require Russian troops to throw it out; and that therefore the defeat of Mohamed would leave the Ottoman Empire still weaker and more tied to Russia. Efforts to reach an Anglo-French commercial agreement failed simultaneously with the political disagreement.

Nicholas deftly widened the breach by concessions to Britain, offering to allow Western ships into the straits to help defend Turkey, agreeing to a convention on the means of defending Turkey and coercing Mohamed, and supporting Palmerston by putting the issue of dealing with Mohamed ahead of the settlement of the straits question, against the views of Metternich, the French, and some British cabinet members. By January the Anglo-French dialogue had degenerated into sharp charges and counter-charges, with the French accusing Britain of joining the Holy Alliance in isolating and humiliating France, and the British accusing France of seeking to control the eastern Mediterranean. When the Duc de Guizot, named ambassador to Britain by Soult in a last-gasp effort to break the deadlock, asked Palmerston in early March why Britain was so intent on bringing down the seventy-two-year-old Mohamed, Palmerston replied that under his son Ibrahim Egypt could become an independent powerful state, and through it France would control North Africa from Morocco to Alexandretta. To what extent Palmerston believed this scenario is hard to say; it fitted his normal pattern of painting a supposed threat in its darkest colours, so as to justify scotching it in its infancy. Yet he probably genuinely feared Egyptian domination of the Arab world and French influence in it, as threats to the route to India.[33]

The journalist-politician-historian Adolphe Thiers, who in opposition had blamed the Soult regime for ruining the Anglo-French alliance, promised to put things right when he took over as premier in early March 1840. Unfortunately, the nationalist foreign policy he adopted for purposes of satisfying his centre-left constituency, countering republican propaganda, and distracting attention from France's current economic woes could only make things worse with London. Guizot warned Thiers that the four powers might act without France in the Near East if she refused to co-operate. Thiers also knew from France's consul-general in Egypt that Mohamed's ability and will to resist European pressure were limited; he himself urged Mohamed to make concessions to

---

[33] Webster (1951: ii. 653–71); Guyot (1926: 161–87); Charles-Roux (1951: 7–30); Testa (1864–1911: ii. 458–529).

the Turks and their European supporters. But Thiers stubbornly refused to join in coercing Mohamed, determined to show that the other powers could not act without France and hopeful that direct Turco-Egyptian negotiations would produce a settlement without European intervention. He even rejected an Austro-Prussian proposal in April to let Mohamed have south Syria and Palestine for life.

As a result, European diplomacy bogged down till early July. At that point various developments—an insurrection in Lebanon against Egyptian rule, the Sultan's dismissal of his pro-Russian grand vizier, and a special peace mission sent by Mohamed to Constantinople—made Mohamed's regime seem vulnerable on the one hand and raised the danger on the other of an Ottoman–Egyptian peace treaty reached under French auspices against the wishes of Europe. Up to this point Metternich, worried by the close co-operation between Britain and Russia, the breakup of five-power unity, and the danger of war, had been encouraging the Turks and Egyptians to negotiate and resisting Palmerston's pressure for military measures. Now he finally agreed to join in coercing Mohamed, if necessary without France's participation. Since Russia had been urging this for months and criticizing Palmerston for hesitating, and the Prussian envoy, Bülow, also favoured four-power action, Metternich's change of mind cleared the last obstacle at the London Conference. It also aided Palmerston, who had pushed Metternich hard for moral and material support, in other ways as well, by helping assure Russia's moderation and most important, helping him once more defeat his opponents within the cabinet.[34]

Having won his victory there, Palmerston met with the three Eastern envoys on 15 July and signed a treaty committing the four powers jointly to imposing peace terms on Mohamed. The pasha would be granted hereditary rule of Egypt and rule over southern Syria for life if he submitted within ten days after receiving the Sultan's ultimatum. Failing that, he would also lose Syria, and after a further ten days he would risk losing Egypt as well. On 17 July France was informed of the treaty and invited to join in the action. A wave of bellicose rage swept over France, carrying even

[34] Bury and Combs (1986: 60–9); Charles-Roux (1951: 31–89); Pouthas (1938); Deschamps (1956: 58–62); Sabry (1930: 481–2, 491–3, 497–9); Guizot (1858: v. 36–72); Webster (1951: ii. 672–94, 876); Nesselrode (1904–12: viii. 1–32); Testa (1864–1911: ii. 531–8). For examples of Palmerston's calls for Austrian support, see his letters to Beauvale at Vienna, 20 Mar., 12 May 1840, Palmerston Papers (Broadlands), GC/BE/528.

Louis-Philippe along. There was an obvious irrational side to it. France had been warned of this by Britain, the other powers, and its own envoys. Thiers and Desages themselves had seen it coming; France's dog-in-the-manger stance had helped bring it on. But in other ways the outcry was understandable. To inform France two days after the fact that a secret four-power agreement directed against her had been signed and to ask her to accept it was insulting. The terms offered Mohamed were relatively severe, and the powers' intent to deal with him by ultimatums and threats was even more so. Worst of all was the blow to France's status and honour. The 15 July treaty excluded France from the concert, broke the prevailing rule of great-power unanimity on international questions, among which the Near East was the most prominent, and revived the coalition of 1814–15. Louis-Philippe and his supporters saw this as their reward for a decade of co-operating with Britain for peace; nationalist Frenchmen took it as the consequence of France's twenty-five years of tamely accepting the Vienna system.

Thiers, therefore, had little choice but to resist. His policy of gamble and bluff, always risky, now became desperate and incoherent. The powers brushed aside his counter-proposal, that they join in guaranteeing the status quo while France mediated between Mohamed and the Sultan on their behalf. His intelligence from Egypt through regular channels and his special emissary to Mohamed, Count Alexandre Walewski, told him that Mohamed's position was vulnerable, especially in Syria. Thiers himself warned Mohamed off the only strategy that could have given him any chance of victory, an offensive into Anatolia. Mohamed therefore yielded to allied pressure. Within twelve days of receiving the allied ultimatum on 16 August, he offered to accept hereditary rule in Egypt and to rely on the Sultan's generosity for anything beyond it. Thus the last substantive issue, whether Egypt would retreat and how far, was settled; the only question left was how Egypt's retreat would be effected. The Sultan, bent on revenge and encouraged by the British ambassador, Ponsonby, to seek it, rejected Mohamed's offer and shortly thereafter formally deposed him. Meanwhile, Palmerston would not let France foil the intervention he was orchestrating and the victory over Mohamed, France, and his Cabinet rivals he saw ahead. This got under way in September with a British naval bombardment of Beirut and the landing of a Turkish force stiffened with British and Austrian marines to co-operate with Lebanese rebels. While Beirut fell, the revolt spread. Ibrahim's army was defeated in mid-October, Acre fell in early November, and on 27 November Mohamed, his forces broken and driven back to Egypt, signed a convention with the British commander, Sir Charles Napier, accepting hereditary rule in Egypt without Syria.[35]

This ended whatever threat Mohamed may have presented to the Ottoman Empire and to Britain's routes to India over Mesopotamia and the Persian Gulf. But it made the real crisis in Europe momentarily worse. Thiers's hope had been that, while Egyptian resistance stymied the coalition in the East, his programme of French armaments would threaten its weaker members, Austria and Prussia, with war on the Rhine and in Italy, forcing the four powers to invite France back into the concert and a leading role in the settlement. Mohamed's collapse ruined one pillar of this strategy; visible divergences within France threatened to undermine the other. The King soon repented of his earlier belligerence; Soult, Broglie, and Desages all at least wanted France's armaments to be less overt and its posture less bellicose. Guizot went further, warning Thiers that France could not make Syria a *casus belli*. The only real French complaint against Europe was that the powers had paid too little attention to France's voice, and against Britain that it valued France's friendship and alliance too little.

Thiers, while enlisting Leopold of Belgium in his efforts at some sort of mediation (Palmerston also thrust Leopold's approach aside), pressed on for the sake of political survival. On 8 October he issued a veiled threat of war if the powers allowed the Sultan to depose Mohamed, but this was a futile gesture. The powers had no intention of allowing the Sultan to do this, and Palmerston quickly countered it by confirming their offer of hereditary rule in Egypt. Britain's and Russia's actual conduct in victory, coupled with Palmerston's immoderate language, only served to deepen the French sense of impotent humiliation.[36]

At home, Palmerston stood off the persistent attacks of opponents on his policy, with support from Ponsonby at Constantinople and Henry Bulwer, who as secretary of the Paris embassy often acted for the Francophile but aged and sickly Lord Granville. His growing success in the East gained him the support

---

[35] Charles-Roux (1951: 90–238); Guyot (1926: 188–92); Seton-Watson (1937: 200–9); Sabry (1930: 513–24).

[36] Guyot (1926: 193–211); Deschamps (1956: 65–74); Schiemann (1904: iii. 400–1); Charles-Roux (1951: 186–9); Testa (1864–1911: ii. 546–53, 584–604); Webster (1951: ii. 890–3).

of Melbourne, now his brother-in-law, and Lord John Russell.[37] France could neither justify a war nor fight one. As Thiers knew, even if France were able to exploit Austria's and Prussia's fears and weakness (which proved not feasible) and France's supposed popular support in Germany and Italy (largely non-existent) actually emerged, it still could not win against Britain at sea, or do anything against Russia on land. The French army, lacking an offensive strategy, was afraid of war. Yet for a time, in September and October 1840, it seemed possible that France would go to war as it would in 1870, out of wounded national pride. Even as sensible a thinker as Alexis de Tocqueville thought war preferable to dishonour, though he anticipated defeat. The attack on Beirut, the tide of French armaments and agitation, French fears that the British would end up controlling Syria, and Palmerston's threat that war would mean the loss of all France's colonies including Algeria poured oil on the flames.[38]

Third parties, with Leopold I of Belgium, Metternich, and Prussia's new King, Frederick William IV in the lead, tried to build golden bridges over which France could retreat (another proof of the value of intermediaries). Metternich wanted most to save Louis-Philippe from Thiers's radicalism, Leopold to prevent a worse clash between Belgium's three great neighbours, Prussia to avoid war and stay out of the Near Eastern imbroglio where it had no important interests. Both Austria and Prussia proposed bringing France back into the Concert by transforming the 15 July treaty into a general alliance on behalf of Turkey which France could join, and both proposed to include the German Confederation in that alliance, to protect it from the threat posed by France's armaments. Both, in other words, were aware of vital European concerns and trying to advance them while France, Britain, and Russia ignored them. The house of Rothschild, now turning away from its former ties to the German powers and toward the liberal West, also used its international financial power for peace.[39]

Palmerston swept Metternich's proposals aside as evidence of

[37] Besides ibid. 695–737 and Bourne (1982), see Middleton (1977; 1981: 409–21); R. A. Jones (1983: 74–81); Ziegler (1976: 319–29).

[38] Deschamps (1956: 77–81); Charles-Roux (1951: 199–211, 218–31, 260–3); Cox (1987); Sullivan (1983: 60–3); Jardin (1984: 319). A good survey of the impact of the whole crisis on France is in Collingham (1988: ch. 17).

[39] Veit-Brause (1967: 36–47); Testa (1864–1911: ii. 604–5); Nesselrode (1904–12: viii. 51–3); Gille (1965: 302–4, 486–93); Guizot (1858: v. 269–83). Melbourne and Prince Albert, Queen Victoria's consort, both favoured Metternich's approach, but this made no difference to Palmerston's policy. Webster (1951: ii. 840).

backsliding, and Nesselrode, for special Russian reasons, supported him. Praising Palmerston's firmness and criticizing Austrian weakness, he insisted that the confederation and the French threat to Germany had nothing to do with the Eastern question, and urged Austria to mobilize its army against France rather than concoct useless plans to conciliate her. Nicholas and Nesselrode did not want general war, and were not indifferent to Austro-Prussian and German fears and pleas, as Palmerston was. They were both determined, however, to forestall any European coalition that might be used to restrain Russia, and while Nicholas wanted a European alliance isolating France, Nesselrode insisted that his approach of direct Russian co-operation with Britain was the best way of preserving the European Concert and forcing France back into it.[40]

This policy triumphed in late October. Thiers, failing to get the King's support for his programme of continued armaments and threats in support of France's negotiating position, resigned, and was replaced by a Soult–Guizot ministry. This ended the danger of a war by France against Britain over the Near East, the only threat noticed by the British at the time and by some historians since. It did nothing about the new danger revealed and to an extent created by this crisis: a clash between French and German nationalism on the Rhine. Both the Near Eastern and the Franco-German crises had their roots in French pride. But where one arose from too much sensitivity to France's interests in the Levant, honour in Europe, and status relative to Britain, the other derived from too little French awareness of similar feelings among the Germans. During the 1830s, except for a failed attempt at *rapprochement* with Austria in 1836, France had pursued no initiatives in Germany, and the government had paid little heed to reports from French representatives and observers about the rise of a potentially dangerous romantic German nationalism directed against France.[41] Both main wings of French opinion, governmental-conservative and opposition-liberal, preferred to see Germany through rose-colored French glasses. Conservatives still thought in terms of France's old-regime ascendancy, liberals in terms of the French as leaders in the cause of international liberalism and

---

[40] Nesselrode (1904–12: viii. 36–7, 40–1, 48–51, 55–60); Georgiev (1975: ch. 3). A good discussion of Russian policy throughout the crisis is Ingle (1976: 113–47).

[41] Roghe (1971: 117–35, 168–96); Mastellone (1957: 17–28). Warnings of the rise of German nationalism are scattered throughout Chroust (1935–9: iii; iv).

nationalism, looked to by Germans for help in liberating themselves from their reactionary rulers. One leading intellectual, the
democratic republican historian Edgar Quinet, saw the danger
clearly—that a basically despotic Prussia would lead Germany to
national unification and power—and advocated the worst possible
policy to meet it, a French seizure of the Rhineland.

Yet the government's German policy, if unrealistic and in-
attentive, was at least peaceful and unprovocative. That changed
when a wave of chauvinism arose in the French press and
parliament in early 1840 and swelled to huge proportions after
15 July. It was the natural product of a generation of French
self-delusion and myths; but Thiers and Louis-Philippe had unwittingly helped promote it by deliberately encouraging the
Napoleonic legend for domestic political purposes. Not only
Germans felt threatened by it. There was some French talk of
Belgium which worried Belgians, though the French government
never considered a move against the Low Countries. Thiers
himself thought of Italy as the best place to attack Austria. The
symbol round which the French rallied, however, was the Rhine
frontier.[42]

They were unprepared for Germany's reaction. The official
response was moderate and defensive. The South German governments directly threatened took up the ideas and proposals of
1830–2, calling for German unity and neutrality in any great-
power quarrel over the Near East and demanding that the German
great powers, especially Prussia, take the lead in reorganizing the
confederation's defences. Prussia, impressed by the furore in
Germany and aware of the political opportunity it presented,
proposed a sweeping reorganization of the federal military system
under Prussian leadership. This South German–Prussian defensive
reaction, had it got out of hand, might have helped set the stage
for war, but Metternich made sure this would not happen. In one
of his masterly diversionary manœuvres, through moves too
complex to recount here, he managed to get the South Germans
and Prussians to resume the military negotiations stalled in
1831–2, out of which he gained a guarantee from Prussia and the
Bund against a French attack in northern Italy, as well as a
disposition of federal forces in south Germany more favourable to

---

[42] Bury and Combs (1986: 70–6); Owsinska (1974: 41–3, 64–100); Deschamps
(1956: 52–8, 74–7, 89); Veit-Brause (1967: 10–21, 26–33, 86–7); Silva (1917:
270–5); Dunk (1966: 219–22); Thomas (1983: 72–82). On Thiers's and Louis-
Philippe's role in exploiting the Napoleon legend, see Jardin and Tudesq (1984:
123–7); Sieburg (1969).

Austria. Meanwhile he avoided anything provocative of France and let Prussia's proposals for a genuine federal military reorganization run aground. It was a typical Metternichian victory. Austria's interests were protected, peace was preserved, and a potential crisis was defused; but the fundamental problem (in this case, making the Bund a more effective instrument of Germany's defence without endangering its neighbours or upsetting the delicate German equilibrium) was not solved or even confronted.[43]

Thus the German powers handled the French threat diplomatically with skill and prudence, at least in the short run. But alongside the official response was a widespread and violent German popular reaction to French claims, of which the enormous success of Nikolaus Becker's poem, 'Der deutsche Rhein', was the most visible symbol. The agitation in Germany made three things ominously clear, as Baron Paul de Bourgoing, minister to Bavaria and France's ablest diplomat in Germany, reported. First, German nationalists from now on would reply to French demands for the Rhineland with German demands for Alsace-Lorraine. Second, France had lost whatever ideological and popular sympathies it had ever enjoyed in Germany, and would now have to work with governments, not peoples, to defend its interests. Third, German governments, including Prussia, could now at any time raise a hue and cry against France in order to rally the masses behind them, defuse popular discontent, or defer reform.[44]

Bourgoing was an even better prophet than he knew. The momentary Franco-German nationalist agitation subsided, with no government really nourishing or exploiting it and some, like Prussia and Austria, trying to dampen it. But the integral German nationalism accurately described by Bourgoing, who called it the most important development of the nineteenth century, continued to rise. Like French nationalism, it menaced other states besides its immediate target in France—Switzerland, the Low Countries, and especially the smaller German states and Austria as a multi-national empire. Vienna knew this all too well. Partly for this reason it had helped preserve peace and checked Prussia's ambitions for military leadership in Germany. The crisis had revealed once again how much Austria itself needed support, however, thus further weakening its position and strengthening Prussia's in Bavaria and

[43] Veit-Brause (1967: 47–77); Werner (1977: 190–201); Chroust (1949–51: iii. 173–210).

[44] Veit-Brause (1967: 124–35, 148–51, 188–93); Chroust (1935–9: iv. 218–21, 262–3, 268–9, and esp. 256–7).

elsewhere.[45] As for France, the crisis shook some of its illusions as to Germany, but encouraged others in their place: that Belgium might be a better field for French penetration than Germany, or that France could befriend and lead the German and Italian national causes, and profit thereby.[46]

While the British, especially Palmerston, celebrated their victory in the Eastern question, winding it up proved a protracted and messy business. Thiers, who had surrendered the reins graciously to Soult and Guizot in October, decided to defend his policy publicly when Guizot portrayed himself as struggling to salvage France's status and honour in Europe from the disasters caused by his predecessor. One of the classic foreign-policy debates of the nineteenth century was fought out between Thiers and Guizot in the French Chamber in November. Guizot won the debate, in votes and overall in argument, but the contest rendered impossible the traditional left-centre compromises which had hitherto kept the regime going, and split the political nation hopelessly between left and right.[47]

Though Guizot's aims and policy were defensible, the Eastern Question would ultimately compromise and weaken him almost as much as it had Thiers. He needed to make his peaceful, European, basically pro-British approach pay off quickly by restoring France's honour and place in the concert. This the British, enthusiastically supported by Russia, helped prevent. Palmerston employed the arguments devised for Thiers against Guizot as well, and promptly rejected Guizot's first initiative for regaining France a place in Near Eastern questions, a plan (impractical, it is true) to make Jerusalem an enclave for Christians in the Ottoman Empire.[48] Already by January 1841 France had indicated that it would accept the terms that actually went into the final settlement, and in February Guizot proposed attaching a European guarantee of the Ottoman Empire to the preamble of a proposed five-power convention governing the status of the straits. Yet it took till July to conclude a four-power protocol on the cloture of the straits and a five-power Straits Convention which France signed. This convention failed to guarantee Turkey

[45] I gain this impression from the correspondence in Chroust (1949–51: iii, esp. 114–15, 160–1) and Meyendorff (1923: i. 70–200).

[46] Deschamps (1956: 86–95); Birke (1960: 107–12); Wenger (1979: 74–5, 98–9, 111–27).

[47] D. Johnson (1963: 155–75); Charles-Roux (1951: 264–91); Bury and Combs (1986: 77–9); Collingham (1988: 237–8, 289–93).

[48] D. Johnson (1963: 176–89); Vereté (1978).

as France had proposed, and France was readmitted to the concert too late and grudgingly to help Guizot or Louis-Philippe. The main cause of delay was the Sultan's stubborn refusal to conclude peace with Mohamed on the basis the allies had promised; Ponsonby often encouraged his resistance. Meanwhile Austria and Prussia were working to restore France to the concert and end Turkish resistance. Austria once again played a key role in breaking the deadlock by threatening to leave the concert if the Sultan did not give in. Russia did its best to keep France isolated, and Britain made sure the French gained no advantage and the Sultan lost none.[49]

Meanwhile little was done about the root problem, the weakness of the Ottoman Empire. By this time even Palmerston recognized that the efforts he and others advocated to reform and strengthen it through trade, political reform (the Sultan had issued the reform Edict of Gulhanë in November 1839), military reform and assistance, and religious reforms in favour of Jews and Protestants would have only marginal effects and would not enable Turkey to stand up against Russia. In fact, Palmerston expected the Empire to break up sooner or later, but with his usual optimism expected to meet this danger and any renewed Russian threat deriving from it when they arose.[50]

How much Palmerston's victory in 1840–1 was therefore worth has always been debatable. His defenders, while admitting some faults, stress his skill and nerve in defeating his domestic and foreign rivals, manipulating the balance of power, and achieving his goals without war and at minimal cost to Britain. His critics, acknowledging much of this, stress the ephemeral nature of his achievements, his abrasive tactics, the serious risks he ran, and the long-range costs of the victory in terms of strained Anglo-French relations.[51] The critics have the better case, especially if other factors often overlooked are brought in: that if serious risks and dangers were not incurred by Britain, they were by Germany and Italy, bystanders in the quarrel; that the most serious and enduring

---

[49] Webster (1951: ii. 753–76); Mastellone (1957: 12–15); Guyot (1926: 211–19); Charles-Roux (1951: 311–16); Meyendorff (1923: i. 173–4); Nesselrode (1904–12: 73–5, 102–3, 117–19, 131–6).

[50] Rodkey (1929); Webster (1951: ii. 765–9); Bourne (1982: 621–2); Pamuk (1987: 11–12, 18–20). To be sure, if Palmerston's goal was not to preserve the Ottoman Empire but to weaken Egypt and retard its development, here he had some success; Al-Sayyid Marsot (1984: 258–63).

[51] The 2 sides are represented by C. K. Webster and Kenneth Bourne, and R. W. Seton-Watson, Roger Bullen, and Muriel Chamberlain respectively.

result of the crisis was not Anglo-French tension but Franco-German national hostility; and that the crisis had side-effects which clearly did not benefit Britain, the Ottoman Empire, or European peace. It promoted insurrections in the Balkans more dangerous for the Ottoman Empire in the long run than Mohamed's rebellion had been. It made the French government, though unable to advance its pacification of Algeria during the crisis, more determined than ever to retain it. For the first time since 1815, it promoted a significant and permanent build-up of the French army. Likewise, for the first time since 1815 it promoted a great German nationalism directed not merely against France but also toward Italy, with Germans now proclaiming that Austria must keep Lombardy-Venetia and its Adriatic ports for defence against France and the development of German commerce as a whole. It left Britain badly over-extended in 1841, with a war in China, an Afghan expedition going sour (of which more later), strained relations with France, and serious trouble with the United States over borders in North America, especially Maine-New Brunswick. Finally, it encouraged Russia to believe it could act more boldly in the Caucasus and Central Asia because it had a partnership with Britain.[52]

Yet the debate is bound to be inconclusive, for two reasons. First, the verdict on whether the British victory was worth the cost and risks depends heavily on one's initial assumptions about the nature of the international system and the best way to conduct international politics. A defender of Palmerston, for example, could reply that all these were normal, predictable results of the inevitable revival of competition and conflict in international affairs, and that he did a good job of managing the crises and protecting British interests. Second, and more important, the assumption that Britain won at all begs the question and obscures the meaning of the crisis for the European system.

Palmerston certainly won a personal victory over his opponents in Britain and in France, but that is hardly the main point. A distinctive feature of this crisis, as argued earlier, was that both hegemons simultaneously faced twin challenges—directly to their respective vital interests in the Near East, and indirectly to their European positions, the latter challenges posed by junior partners who wanted to use the Eastern crisis to control their policy and gain greater status and equality for themselves. To answer the

---

[52] Julien (1964: 155–63); Djordjevic and Fischer-Galati (1981: 91–7); Chamberlain (1989: 84–5); Altgeld (1984: 228–31); Vierhaus (1985: 360–1).

question of who won in 1840-1, even on a basis of pure cost—benefit analysis, one must therefore ask: given the overall position of each hegemon in early 1839 and the general and particular problems it faced; the means each had at its disposal; the goals it set for itself; the obstacles and dangers it met in trying to achieve them; and the results it had achieved by late 1841, which of the two hegemons won, in the sense of defending and advancing its interests more skilfully and successfully?

This question answers itself: Russia. Consider its situation in 1839. It faced grave and worsening internal problems—chronic fiscal shortages, economic distress, worsening technological and industrial backwardness in comparison to Western and Central Europe, serious agrarian problems, an unreformed and unreformable servile system, latent revolution in Poland, and the rise of an alienated, revolutionary intelligentsia. Its image in Europe was very negative (the Marquis de Custine's famous book, *Voyage in Russia*, with its harrowing picture of Russian conditions, was published in 1839) and its general influence was in decline. In the Near East it had assumed responsibility for defending a weak, threatened ally and then lost control both of that ally and of the general situation, so that its policy and position were at the mercy of events. In Europe it had only one faithful ally, Prussia, the weakest and most timorous of the powers and the one most determined to stay out of trouble in the East. Its other ally, Austria, wanted to control Russia within a five-power concert led by itself, and might be drawn over to the West if Russia refused. The Treaty of Unkiar-Skelessi, already proved useless as a means of controlling the Ottoman Empire, now was worse than useless as a means of saving it, for the *casus foederis* did not apply and any attempt by Russia to use it unilaterally would unite Europe against it. At the same time, the treaty's existence and the general suspicion and fear of Russia it helped engender had driven its two most formidable potential foes, Britain and France, into an alliance and toward an anti-Russian intervention in the East, and were pulling Austria and even Prussia toward their camp.

A comparison of Russia's position at this time with that of late 1814 illustrates how much worse it was now. Then it faced the possibility of a Western coalition, but over a Poland which Russia occupied and controlled, with Prussia firmly in Russia's camp, Austria already back-pedalling, France still highly suspect as a partner against Russia, and Britain bent on peace and led by the cautious Castlereagh. Now it faced a potential Western coalition over a crisis in which the Ottoman Empire was on the brink of collapse, Russia was unable either to control or defend it, Prussia was wavering, Austria was already in the opposed camp, France was rehabilitated, and Palmerston was leading the coalition.

Now see where Russia stood by mid-1841. In exchange for renouncing Unkiar-Skelessi, which it had already decided to discard as a dangerous handicap before the crisis ever ripened, it had (a) forced Austria back into line as its junior partner, inflicting a humiliating defeat on the latter's attempt to confine Russia within the European Concert; (b) split its rivals Britain and France wide apart and left them in enduring rivalry and tension; (c) helped rescue the Ottoman Empire at minimum cost to itself, while keeping it unreformed, vulnerable, and essentially dependent on Russia's goodwill; (d) changed its reputation in European chanceries, especially in London, from the chief menace to the Ottoman Empire to one of its loyal and co-operative supporters, and from a target of the European Concert to its central pillar; (e) gained what it most wanted in the Near East, defensive security in the Black Sea through an international sanction of the cloture of the straits, while avoiding what it did not want, an international guarantee of Ottoman territorial integrity; and (f) proved once again to its potentially restive Eastern partners and to France that if they tried to resist Russia, it could always combine with Britain over their heads and force them to conform. By early 1841 both German powers and even France were seeking a special alliance with Russia.[53] For all this, Russia sacrificed exactly nothing.

Much luck as well as diplomatic skill went into this astounding victory; but it could not have been won without Palmerston's help. Regardless of what reasons, foreign-political, domestic, or personal, were uppermost in his decision to solve the Eastern question with Russia over the heads of the Continental powers, especially France; whether the decisive considerations were the Ottoman Empire, the British Empire, Egypt, Arabia, the Persian Gulf, Mesopotamia, the routes to India, the old Anglo-French rivalry now centred in the Levant,[54] or simply his personal position and combative instincts; in any case, his decision handed Russia the keys to victory.

Consider, in contrast, the results for Britain. It entered the crisis with almost everything in its favour. It was approaching the zenith of its world-wide commercial, industrial, and maritime

[53] For evidence of Nesselrode's satisfaction and confidence, see Ingle (1976: 140–7); Gritzbach (1974: i. 336–8, 344–5); Nesselrode (1904–12: viii. 83–7, 147–50, 157–9).

[54] Marlowe (1971: 9–10, 291 and *passim*).

supremacy; it enjoyed unmatched political influence and ideological attractiveness in Europe; if part of its empire was in principle vulnerable, no power at this time was able or willing to exploit the weakness; indeed, everyone involved in the crisis, including Russia, France, Austria, Prussia, the Turks, and Mohamed himself, wanted to work with Britain.

Yet Britain emerged from this crisis with none of its problems durably solved—not the Russian threat, nor the decay of the Ottoman Empire, nor the threatened routes to India, nor even the potential Franco-Egyptian challenge in the Levant (in the next decade Palmerston would be struggling to keep France from helping Mohamed's successor build a Suez Canal). The chief accomplishment of British policy had been to alienate the most pacific, pro-British regime in French history, making it determined to strengthen its armed forces and to seek prestige victories and imperial conquests so as to reverse its defeat and prove to Britain that, if there were to be any further Anglo-French *entente*, it had to rest on equality and pay attention to French feelings and honour. If this is victory, one wonders what would constitute defeat.

Of course, diplomatic victories, even brilliant ones like Russia's here, often mean little in the long run. This one did not arrest Russia's relative decline, just as Britain's loss (for so it was—a durable concert to control Russia and preserve the Ottoman Empire in the East was sacrificed for an empty prestige triumph over France) did not prevent Britain's continued rise. But recognizing who really won sheds light on the more important question of how the European system worked, and what Palmerston really was doing in, with, and to it.

There is an unmistakable pattern to Palmerston's career in foreign policy—one of general success in leading Europe and controlling the outcomes of crises and problems from 1830 to 1852, followed by a progressive loss of control and mounting failures from the Crimean War to 1865. As always, one can easily account for this shift by contingent factors—more difficult problems, tougher and more determined opponents, divisions within Britain and a changed public mood, perhaps even a decline in Palmerston's powers. But this is to ignore the fundamental systemic factor. Palmerston led Europe and won victories, we are told, by knowing how to manipulate the European balance of power, use the rival ambitions of other powers to neutralize each other and achieve Britain's goals. Not so. He won victories, whether genuine and useful ones, as in Belgium or over the

Schleswig-Holstein question in 1848–52, or showy but insubstantial ones, as in the Iberian peninsula and the Near East here, by manipulating the European Concert, taking advantage of the peaceful co-operation of other powers. His bold tactics and brinkmanship worked when there was a fundamental European consensus which he could exploit and strong systemic restraints binding his partners on which he could rely. When, partly by his doing, that concert broke down after 1853 and serious European rivalries and ambitions emerged—when, in other words, Europe as a whole largely reverted to his kind of balance-of-power politics—the same Palmerstonian tactics and skill that had usually worked in the 1830s and 1840s proved useless, or positively harmful.

V. THE GREAT GAME IN ASIA TO 1842

All this applies to Europe. The Great Game in Asia was separate from Europe though linked to it: an Anglo-Russian competition over the whole area from the Bosporus to India, including Turkey, Egypt, other Arab lands, Persia and the Persian Gulf, Afghanistan, Central Asia, and north-west India. The foci of competition ranged widely, including trade, military relations, and high politics, and displayed no clear pattern or constant theme; but in this decade Persia and Afghanistan formed their centre.[55]

Though some officials in India had begun warning of a Russian threat around the turn of the century, the idea became widespread in Britain only after Turkey's defeat by Russia in 1829. Even then it took time for London to see the Ottoman Empire in a Eurasian rather than simply a European context.[56] Canning's indifference in 1825–7 to Britain's treaty obligations and Persia's fate had meanwhile helped Russia defeat Persia as well. The Russians used the Peace of Turkmanchai as they did that of Adrianople, to achieve dominant influence at Teheran.

---

[55] I omit discussions of other major developments in British imperial history in this era, such as the 1st Anglo-Chinese War, 1839–42 (the so-called Opium War) or events in S. Africa, because they have little or no connection to European politics. For the Anglo-Chinese War, see Fay (1975); Greenberg (1951); Costin (1937); Graham (1979); Inglis (1976). On S. Africa, see Galbraith (1963). Two important works on British overseas expansion in general are Semmel (1970); Graham (1972).

[56] Ingram (1979: 74–117); Gillard (1977: 26–31, 34–5, 46–53); Norris (1967: 22–47); Alder (1974: 186–90).

Russia's ascendancy and Persia's weakness raised several possible dangers for Britain, again only gradually perceived and distinguished. The least likely and immediate one was further Russian territorial expansion in Persia and Central Asia; the more serious ones were that Persia, encouraged by Russia, might pursue its own territorial ambitions eastward against Herat in Afghanistan, or that the Persian state, breaking up from internal strife and bankruptcy, might fall by default into Russia's arms. An expedition led by the son of the reigning Shah, Fath Ali, against Khurasan in 1831 exemplified the former danger, a succession crisis and struggle in Persia in 1833 the latter.

With Russia's co-operation, Britain managed to defeat both dangers. None the less, Persia and Afghanistan remained a source of worry. The problem was not mainly Russia's policy (certain Russian agents, especially its minister to Persia, Colonel Simonich, caused trouble as ambitious men on the spot often do, but the government at St Petersburg tried to control them in the interest of good relations with Britain) but rather Britain's own position. Edward Ingram puts it well: 'To control Persia's relations with Russia was to turn Persia into a protectorate, and the British could not protect Persia.'[57] Something similar held for the British position in India itself, where the central difficulty Britain faced was how to maintain an ill-defined paramountcy over a vast area at little or no cost to the metropolis, once any internal or external challenge to that paramountcy was perceived. Although the East India Company now controlled extensive territories directly, most of India remained under the direct rule of native princes. The chief problem for Britain in India was not so much to keep the maritime links with Britain secure or invaders out as to keep its restive inhabitants quiet inside; the north-west frontier, as Malcolm Yapp observes, needed to serve less as a fortress wall than as a ring-fence (Americans would say, a corral).

The strategy the British preferred resembled its stance toward Turkey in the 1830s: to preserve a broad buffer for India by substituting British for Russian influence in Persia. Two missions to Persia in 1835–6 and 1836–7, in search of a commercial treaty and a revised political treaty, were unsuccessful. The set-backs seemed less important, however, when a Persian expedition against Turcoman tribes north of Afghanistan failed; this convinced the British minister at Teheran, John McNeill, that Persia

[57] (1979: 254); in general, see ibid. 249–55, 279–92, 308–9, 318–9; Yapp (1960; 1980, 113–16, 121–4); Alder (1974: 190–2). For Russia's policy, see Schiemann (1904: iii. 296–301); Yapp (1980: 234–5); Davis (1926: 227–9); Ingle (1976: 57–86).

was no threat. McNeill's optimism was undermined, however, when the Persian–Afghan dispute over Herat revived in 1837. McNeill was unable to mediate it, and Persia, with encouragement from Simonich (later repudiated and recalled by his government because of it), conquered Herat. This pushed the British toward their alternate strategy: to make Afghanistan a secure buffer state for India against Persia and Russia.[58]

The strategy was not new or simply a fall-back one. The British had already tried unsuccessfully to make Afghanistan into a solid, British-backed state by supporting a particular candidate for the Afghan throne in 1809–10 and 1833–4. Afghanistan figured in two broad, interrelated schemes for the security of north-west India, one involving possible British territorial expansion and political and commercial penetration into the adjacent regions of Sind and the Panjab, the other involving the construction of a balance of power both north-west of India (Afghanistan, Sind, and the Panjab) and in South-West Asia as a whole. The British conceived of a system of stable independent states with recognized and inviolable frontiers under general British paramountcy (once again, the British notion of a 'balance of power' as something formed from other units for Britain to control and use). While this stance was in general a defensive one, some already were thinking of wider uses for a British-controlled Afghanistan—preventing Russia from penetrating Central Asia and introducing British goods and influence there.[59]

The actual British decision to intervene directly in Afghan tribal and dynastic politics, as it evolved in 1837–8 in India and Britain, was in any case a response to the perceived Russo-Persian threat from Herat. It led the governor-general in India, Lord Auckland, reluctantly to abandon his previous reliance on commercial penetration of Afghanistan in favour of a plan urged by his political secretary, William MacNaghten. MacNaghten proposed to replace the reigning Khan at Kabul, Dost Muhammad, with a British-backed claimant, Shah Shuja, but without any large-scale British action. The Sikhs of the Panjab would provide the necessary military effort, with political support from the amirs of Sind. By the time the British were ready to intervene in 1839, however, much had changed. Auckland now was eager for the project; originally intended to be mainly Sikh and Sindi, it had become overwhelmingly British; and Auckland, by already achieving

---

[58] Yapp (1980: 129–50); Norris (1967: 82–4). For the basic reasons why the Herat strategy for defending India was not viable, see Alder (1974: 300–7).

[59] Yapp (1980: 160–72, 192–240); Ingram (1979: 124–78); Huttenback (1962).

British domination of Sind, had brought British India closer to the Indus frontier and directly provided the security on the north-west frontier which the move on Afghanistan was supposed to promote indirectly. The Afghanistan project, in the words of its leading historian, was being transformed from a *pis aller* into a cornucopia.[60]

The same change of attitude was occurring at London. Palmerston, afraid of fighting Russia over Persia where Russia's position was strong and Britain's weak, had rejected any action to save Herat beyond sanctioning Auckland's sending an expedition to occupy the isle of Kharg in the Persian Gulf. But in mid-1838 he decided finally to break with Persia and adopt Auckland's plan for intervention in Afghanistan, where he believed Britain's position was strong and Russia's weak. The move would not only stop Persia and save Herat, he thought, but also check Russia and strengthen Britain in Central Asia, the Ottoman Empire, Europe, and even America. With enthusiastic support from the president of the Board of Control for India, J. C. Hobhouse, Palmerston gained the approval of the cabinet in early October, over the misgivings of several members. Shortly thereafter he confronted Nesselrode with the evidence of Russian intrigues in Persia and Afghanistan. Nesselrode, genuinely dismayed, recalled the offending envoys, put pressure on Persia to withdraw and apologize to Britain, and urged that Britain and Russia co-operate in Asia, reaching an agreement on frontiers and spheres of influence. Palmerston declined.

Despite Russia's back-down and Persia's withdrawal from Herat with a grudging apology, the British plan went forward, its aim as clearly anti-Russian as before. Since a Russo-British confrontation over Asia (according to Hobhouse and others, a Russo-British war) was inevitable sooner or later, now was the time and ground for it. A judicious editing of documents presented to Parliament, combined with indecisive opposition from Tories worried about opposing a national cause and being denounced as soft on Tsarism, assured the plan's passage through Parliament. Russophobe chauvinism in the press, especially *The Times*, also helped. An originally defensive move had turned into a great leap forward.[61]

The story of the Afghan expedition is one of hubris followed by nemesis, or (more soberly put) failure caused by overreaching.

[60] Yapp (1980: 290).
[61] Ibid. 241–301; Webster (1951: ii. 738–52); Ingle (1976: 82–95, 150–3).

Launched in April 1839, it enjoyed an easy, almost bloodless success. By early autumn Dost Muhammad had been overthrown, Shah Shuja was installed at Kabul, and the British were in control of the country by treaty and in fact, with attendant gains in prestige in surrounding areas. But the foundations of British paramountcy were shaky. Trying to control the whole country from the far north at Kabul was a mistake. Even more fundamental problems were those of poverty, tribal conflict, Shuja's unpopularity, and the weakness and unreliability of his armed forces. McNaghten's personal flaws as resident, the impractical efforts of his subordinates in Qandahar and elsewhere to carry through a social and political revolution in Afghanistan, and the dreams of other Britons for expansion beyond Afghanistan only compounded them. Meanwhile Auckland and McNaghten were trying to limit Britain's control, expenditures, and responsibility, and to avoid being sucked into the maw of Afghan tribal politics. By 1841 it was clear to them that the venture had failed; maintaining Afghanistan as a buffer state was not worth its cost. Yet unlike their military advisers they could not urge withdrawal because of the general effects this would have on British prestige. Since annexation was no viable option either, all that was left was to hang on.[62]

The fact of failure was even harder to accept in London, especially for Palmerston, for whom a British-controlled Afghanistan represented, among other things, the foundation for a more effective British policy toward Russia in Central Asia. True, Britain took over Afghanistan precisely during the time when Russia was cordially co-operating with Britain in the Near East. But this made no difference—or rather, it reinforced Palmerston's desire to consolidate Britain's hold on Afghanistan, for two purposes: it would help him control Russian policy in Europe and make sure that Britain would not become dependent on Russian help there, and it would counter a Russian expedition against Khiva in Central Asia, launched in 1839 to punish the Uzbeks for taking slaves in their raids on Russian caravans. The expedition proved a failure and was withdrawn in 1840, but once again Palmerston rejected Nesselrode's proposal of a general understanding with Russia on Central Asia, convinced that any agreement would only be a stepping-stone to future Russian advances. This was not based on a misreading of Russian purposes, but on Palmerston's fundamental rejection of Nesselrode's argument that the main

[62] Yapp (1980: 267–71, 308–61).

goal of British and Russian foreign policy should be reconciliation between themselves for the sake of general European harmony. Thus the circle of negatives dominating British policy was completed—Auckland's refusal to go forward from Afghanistan into Central Asia, Palmerston's refusal to make a deal with Russia, and the refusal of both to withdraw.[63]

A rising in Kabul in late 1841 began the disaster; it soon expanded into a national insurrection of tribal chiefs against the British and Shuja. A temporary agreement was reached allowing the British to withdraw from Kabul, but then the truce was broken and the Kabul garrison massacred in the course of its retreat in January 1842. By this time the Tories had taken over in Britain, Aberdeen and Ellenborough supplanting Palmerston and Auckland. Ellenborough restored British prestige by a successful, if brutal, punitive expedition in the summer of 1842, and then completed the evacuation, leaving Dost Muhammad once again ruling an eventually unified Afghanistan.[64]

In the aftermath, Sind and the Panjab suffered the consequences of Britain's defeat. Motives of prestige and military strategy led Britain to a series of wars, culminating in the annexation of Sind in 1843 and the Panjab in 1849. Meanwhile, the Peel ministry which had succeeded Melbourne's decided to let sleeping dogs lie in Central Asia. This added the final ironic touch to the story. A strategy was conceived to defend the British empire in India against a largely imaginary Russian expansionism. It grew into an aggressive scheme for British expansion in Afghanistan and Central Asia. Its spectacular failure in Afghanistan promoted a major expansion of the British Empire in India itself and a marked improvement in Britain's relations with Russia over Central Asia, based on a tacit Anglo-Russian agreement to co-operate for peace in Europe and to leave the other's sphere alone in Asia—a policy which made good sense, which Russia had proposed, and which was what the government in India had always wanted.[65]

It is not enough, however, to view the Great Game in Asia and its connection with European politics solely from the standpoint of the British Empire. Two other perspectives are important as well: Russia's and the rest of Europe's. Not all Russians agreed with Nesselrode's policy of restraint in Central Asia in the interest of partnership with Britain, and few shared his optimism that the

---

[63] Ibid. 378–418.

[64] Ibid. 340–7, 419–39; Norris (1967: 364–416). On Russia's Khivan expedition, see G. Morgan (1981: 43–50).

[65] Yapp (1980: 482–591).

co-operation could last. But there was no real dispute, as in Britain, over which sphere was more important for Russia, Europe or Asia. During this period Europe had a clear priority.[66] Moreover, Russia's perception of opportunities and dangers was the converse of Britain's. The British generally felt secure about Europe, vulnerable in India. The Russians, though generally not eager to expand, felt reasonably safe on their Asiatic periphery, increasingly unsure about Europe. The Ottoman Empire and Persia were safe neighbours so long as other powers did not interfere, and Central Asia, China, and the Far East areas of potential future growth. But at home and in adjacent Europe the Russian government feared instability and revolution, possibly promoted by European developments—a liberal Western alliance in support of the Poles, growing liberalism in Germany, the potential defection of Prussia, and the growing weakness and unreliability of Austria.

This means that, even if one thinks that Palmerston's confrontational style and competitive balance-of-power assumptions were appropriate in dealing with Russia in this period, the place he chose to have the confrontation, in Asia, was surely misguided. If Russia had an Asian stick to use against Britain, as some Britons feared, it showed no desire to use it, and, as events proved, Britain had no Asian stick to use against Russia. But in Europe it had at least two possible weapons, a liberal partnership with France and a conservative partnership with Austria. Russia's fear of these weapons in Britain's hands helps explain its cautious policy in Asia and co-operative policy in Europe. It also underlines again how strange a choice it was for Britain in 1839–41 to discard both, and choose partnership with Russia in Europe instead.

While the two world powers were playing their respective European and Asian games, each concerned to link them for its own interest, the Continental powers, great and small alike, had the opposite goal: to keep the two games separate and not to be dragged too deeply into either. France had a Medium-Sized Game in the Mediterranean and North Africa, and a Small Game overseas; the other two great powers and the lesser powers of Europe had no game outside it, and wanted none. As earlier noted, the

---

[66] This held also for the Far East, to which Russia was fairly indifferent through the 1st half of the nineteenth c.; see Lensen (1959: 466–8). Such facts raise grave doubts about the idea of a persistent Anglo-Russian world rivalry throughout the nineteenth c.—e.g. Heinz Gollwitzer (1972: 426–9). This became important only after the Crimean War, in good part as a result of it, and even then was far from a consistent or dominant part of world politics.

1815 system depended for its stability partly on shielding Europe from the effects of extra-European conflicts. The kind of linkage Russia established between its two Great Games, exercising caution in its expansion outside Europe in order to help preserve stability within it, basically conformed to the desires of the other states and the needs of the system. Palmerston's kind of linkage did not. Russia not only was a more skilful hegemon in this particular period, but also (in its conduct of international affairs, not in its domestic politics and commercial policy) a more benign and tolerable one. It is just possible to see Palmerston's policy as a clever way to manipulate the balance of power; impossible to view it as a good way to preserve the European equilibrium.

17
The Shadow of Revolution,
1841–1848

DOMESTIC affairs dominated Europe in the 1840s. Until the 1848 revolutions and the international conflicts they spawned, there appeared to be few, if any, major developments in international relations. Those that occurred seem important only in portending and setting the stage for these revolutions, representing, as it were, creaks and groans in an ageing building at the first tremors of a coming earthquake.

The generalization is sound, but like most it can be taken too far. Some international developments, though unsensational, had important effects. A small revolt and civil war in Switzerland effected a permanent change in Switzerland's constitution and its international position. Britain and France, after some improvement in their relations, became opponents over an apparently trivial issue and remained so at a time when co-operation between them could have made a real difference both for them and for Europe. The joint suppression of a small Polish revolt by the Holy Alliance powers preserved their alliance at a time when it might have split apart without endangering European peace, as its breakdown would do later. Some developments of the 1840s, in international commerce, for example, pointed not towards trouble and revolution but towards peace and progress.

Yet the generalization holds: not much happened in international politics before 1848, and what did happen looks like a prologue to the main revolutionary drama. A further comment may be useful, however. The international developments of the 1840s were significant, not because they signalled that revolutions were on the way or indicated why they would occur. On these scores they are largely redundant; no revolutions were more widely foreseen or are more readily explained than those of 1848. They were and still are significant instead in giving clues as to why the 1848 revolutions had the results they did, particularly in international politics. To be more specific, the international events of the 1840s help us understand why the revolutions, which attacked the Metternich system and the Vienna system with equal force, would succeed in bringing the Metternich system down, yet leave the Vienna system in some important respects intact.

I. THE ANGLO-FRENCH *ENTENTE* 1841–1846

In 1841, the new Tory ministry under Sir Robert Peel shared the desire of Guizot's ministry in France to renew the liberal partnership wrecked in 1839–40. Yet the proposed *entente cordiale* never took root; sometimes the *entente*'s only real advocates were the two foreign ministers, Guizot and Aberdeen, and the monarchs, Victoria and Louis-Philippe. This was not because either power lacked reasons or motives for a *rapprochement*. Both governments wanted it for domestic as well as foreign-policy purposes, to help them face difficulties growing out of what historians have called the mid-century crisis—the economic distress and political agitation of the hungry forties. For Britain, less affected by these problems and the first to recover, the main dangers were the Chartist movement in England and a devastating famine and incipient revolt in Ireland. In France, Guizot faced growing discontent with the whole system on the part of the masses and élites alike.

Yet traditional obstacles to Anglo-French co-operation, reinforced by the resentment and distrust on both sides left over from 1840, proved too much to overcome. Guizot, much as he wanted good relations, dared not appear to give anything away to the British until the stain on France's honour had been removed. Louis-Philippe, on Thiers's suggestion, had promoted the French appetite for symbolic satisfaction by bringing Napoleon's remains back from St Helena to the Hôtel des Invalides in Paris. Instead of appeasing nationalist feelings, this promoted a wave of Anglophobic chauvinism. On the British side, even Aberdeen grew tired of Guizot's appeals for help in appeasing the French opposition, while most Tory leaders, including Peel and Wellington, held views about France close to those of Palmerston. Francophile sentiments declined even in the Whig party, and fears of a potential French naval threat rose.[1]

This explains why the *entente* never became cordial, but does not quite account for why it broke down completely as a re-

---

[1] Cunningham (1957); Bullen (1974a: 36–41); Gash (1976: 505–25). On the 'mid-century crisis' and the threat of revolution, see G. S. Jones (1983); Traugott (1983); Stearns (1965); Thomis and Holt (1977). For Wellington's alarm about the French naval threat, see N. Thompson (1986: 218–21, 232–4).

straining alliance, which was systemically more important. After all, Anglo-French differences were less profound than Austro-Prussian or Austro-Russian ones. Britons and Frenchmen had their historic memories and traditions of enmity, of course, and were apt to take their current rivalries in Spain, Greece, North Africa, the Indian Ocean, or the Pacific seriously, but their core interests were not actually in conflict or at stake in these areas in the way Austria's and Prussia's were in Germany or Austria's and Russia's in the Near East. Yet the Eastern powers, despite their profound clashes of interest, remained tied together in the Holy Alliance. What made that kind of pact of restraint impossible for Britain and France was a series of quarrels over specific minor issues culminating in an open break over the pettiest of all.

The first issue, substantively the most important, concerned the projected Franco-Belgian customs union already discussed. In retrospect, it is easy to agree with Metternich's verdict that the project was always hopeless because Europe would not permit it and particular interest groups in both Belgium and France would never agree on any version of it. But that was not clear at the time, in 1841–2, and Aberdeen objected to the proposal as strongly as Palmerston had done (he had to, given Palmerston's constant attacks upon him in Parliament). He invited the other powers to take the lead in stopping it; Metternich politely declined to bell the cat, and Aberdeen in response politely accepted Metternich's advice on the problem and then ignored it. Guizot decided on his own to drop the idea, the proposal was interred in 1843, and Belgium concluded normal trade treaties with the Zollverein in 1844 and France in 1845. The affair created additional irritation and suspicion, however, with the British convinced anew that the French were duplicitous and the French noting that Britain reacted far more strongly to Belgian links with France than with Prussia or Germany.[2]

The baneful after-effects of 1840 also showed up clearly in the slave trade issue. Abolition of the slave trade had long been a goal of the British anti-slavery movement, which in 1833 had pushed through the abolition of slavery throughout the British Empire. Throughout the Bourbon Restoration, France resisted British naval action against the trade, despite the fact that the Vienna Congress had condemned it, claiming that British visits and searches of suspect vessels at sea violated other nations' rights and

[2] Ridder (1932: 103–429); Deschamps (1956: 220–59); Mastellone (1957: 47–61); Dunk (1966: 222–9).

promoted Britain's domination of commerce and the high seas. The Orléans monarchy took a more co-operative stand, agreeing in November 1831 to a treaty granting both navies a mutual right of search on both coasts of Africa. The 1840 crisis ended that kind of French co-operation (one of its numerous hidden costs). To teach Palmerston a lesson, Guizot rejected his proposal to renew the treaty on a five-power basis in 1841, but concluded an agreement in December with Aberdeen on a similar five-power treaty. Guizot failed to anticipate the opposition in the French Chambers, however; the treaty was overwhelmingly rejected as a surrender to British hypocrisy and greed. The United States also objected to it, while the main culprits in the trade, Spain, Portugal, and Brazil, enjoyed the quarrel from the sidelines. Guizot persuaded Aberdeen to withdraw the treaty and continued to seek another form of settlement, but it was not until France had gained satisfaction for the humiliation of 1840 by prestige gains in the South Seas and elsewhere, and the British themselves had become disappointed with the results of their previous anti-slave-trade tactics, that a new agreement for naval co-operation was reached in 1845.[3]

The slave trade issue was irritating, but raised no danger of conflict. Others did, in particular a long-brewing one in 1842–4 over the Society Islands in the South Pacific, another illustration of how zealous men on the spot cause international crises. In this case, a French rear-admiral, Dupetit-Thouars, acting without instructions, took the islands under French protection in 1842, allegedly to forestall an imminent British take-over. The British consul in Tahiti, George Pritchard, concurrently chose to ignore his instructions to be conciliatory toward the French in his determination to protect Protestant missionaries. The British government accepted France's protectorate, and even agreed to recall Pritchard after he resigned in protest at a more direct French take-over in 1843, but Britain then exploded in official and public fury when Pritchard in March 1844 was arrested on the unauthorized initiative of a French captain. After much negotiation and some talk of war, France agreed to restore its original protectorate and make reparations.[4]

Similar troubles plagued Anglo-French relations in Greece, where the two ministers, Lord Lyons and Théobald Piscatory, engaged in a running battle over which party, British or French,

[3] Jennings (1977; 1980; 1988: 144–9, 204–7); Mathieson (1929: 15–16, 72–3); Graham (1967: 95–109).
[4] Baldwin (1938); Jardin and Tudesq (1984: 166–7); Ward (1976: chs. 7–8, esp. pp. 76–8).

should control Greek politics. A dispute developed over Morocco in 1844–5, when French troops under Marshal Bugéaud and the French navy under Admiral Joinville carried their war against resistance to French rule in Algeria, led by the native leader Abd-el Kader, into Morocco and bombarded Tangier. Even when the British and French collaborated in Madagascar to suppress the slave trade, it produced less co-operation than rivalry for influence over the native tribes and government.[5]

None of these colonial and semi-colonial quarrels was really important in itself, nor, taken all together, did they mean that the centuries-old Anglo-French rivalry over colonies and trade was heating up again. That would happen only after 1870, partly as France's response to its defeat by Germany, and even then the French believed that they could compete with Britain abroad, especially in Africa, and still maintain good relations in Europe. In the 1840s French merchants and industrialists were even less interested in colonies than they would be later, and Guizot had no wish to rival Britain on the seas or to expand the French Empire, except in Algeria. He mainly wanted *points de relâche*, way stations that would help France protect its trade and its scattered possessions. The problem was political and perceptual more than commercial, naval, or imperial. Guizot envisioned France as Britain's partner in Europe and overseas, inferior in terms of power but equal in rights and status, and able to profit from the partnership in terms of commerce and prestige. In exchange for French co-operation in Europe and elsewhere, Britain was supposed to allow France to advance its interests where these did not hurt British ones. Aberdeen did not object to this idea, but most other Britons did. They would concede France only just enough to avoid war and gain French co-operation in Europe, while remaining determined to keep France from going too far.[6]

This helps explain how one of the most stupefyingly incon-

[5] For the ongoing Anglo-French rivalry in Greece, see Petropoulos (1968); for their clash in 1843–4 over the Greek revolution, despite Guizot's and Aberdeen's efforts to avoid it, see McLean (1981); Seton-Watson (1937: 234–8). On Morocco, see Julien (1964: 164–209); Sullivan (1983: 743–6); on Madagascar, Graham (1967: 58–95).

[6] Mastellone (1957: 152–61); P. Johnson (1957: 78–87); Guyot (1926: 269–83). A letter of Sir Robert Gordon, British ambassador at Vienna, to his brother Lord Aberdeen, 16 Aug. 1844, illustrates how it was difficult even for British moderates to concede equality in status to France. Urging the importance of re-establishing an unquestioned British naval supremacy in the Mediterranean, Gordon wrote: 'The whole world should be taught to look to England as to an armed Mediator, the Arbiter of Peace, having the power to uphold her own supremacy at all hazards'; BL Add. Ms 43211 (II), fos. 462–4.

sequential affairs in European diplomatic history, the Spanish Marriages question, ended in open hostility between the two powers. The question itself arose from an ongoing struggle between the two main parties in Spain, the Progresistas and the Moderados. The contest was a serious one, involving the court, the Cortes, the bureaucracy, and especially the army. What made it serious, however, was not marked differences between the two parties in principle or in policy (both were nominally liberal) but the fact that exclusive power and control of patronage in Spain was the prize of victory. The struggle in Spain, as one historian notes, was not between military and civilian government or liberalism and authoritarianism, but between two bloated, ill-paid bureaucracies fighting for survival.[7] With the Progresistas leaning toward Britain and the Moderados toward France, the British and French ministers at Madrid competed strenuously for influence, as they long had done; but the factions in Spain used Britain and France more than they were controlled by them.

The French, resentful of Palmerston's efforts to exclude them from influence in Spain during the 1830s, expected the Tories on their return to power to change things. Instead they found the Progresista General Espartero retaining control and Aberdeen apparently (though not really) continuing Palmerston's anti-French stance, arguing that the Spaniards should be left to manage their own affairs. Guizot none the less followed a cautious policy in the face of strong criticism in the French Chambers. It seemed to pay off in 1843–4, when accumulated discontent in Spain led to Espartero's overthrow and departure, the accession of a Moderado ministry under General Narvaez, and the return of Queen Isabella's mother, Cristina, from exile in Paris to act as regent for her thirteen-year-old daughter. Cristina set out to secure her daughter's throne and her own position by arranging speedy and glorious marriages for Isabella and her younger sister, the Infanta Luisa. Guizot now saw this marriage question, already alive in Spain, as a way to cement French influence in Spain and to enhance Louis-Philippe's image in France and Europe.

He wanted to achieve this in co-operation with Britain, however. This would have been impossible with Palmerston; it was difficult even with Aberdeen. Where Palmerston's aim had always been to exclude France from Spain and open it to British influence and trade, Aberdeen considered Spain's independence a British national interest, but viewed questions of the control of the parties

[7] Christiansen (1967: 105–6).

in Spain, its constitution, the marriage question, and even trade as secondary issues. For his part, Guizot conceived of the Anglo-French *entente* in the peninsula in terms of a balance in which France would have an exclusive lead in Spain and Britain the same lead in Portugal. (Once again, divergent notions of 'balance' would cause trouble.) But by 1843 Guizot seemed to be making his concept of the Iberian balance a reality. He brought Aberdeen to agree in general terms to a Bourbon spouse for Isabella, provided that this was Spain's choice and that Louis-Philippe's sons were excluded.[8]

From late 1843 on Guizot tried to marry Isabella to Count Trapani, the brother of King Ferdinand II of Naples. This shows how mistaken it is to see this affair simply in terms of Anglo-French rivalry, for Guizot's motives were anti-Austrian, not anti-British. He had certain goals *vis-à-vis* Britain—to gain ascendancy in Spain, confirm the *entente*, and preserve a balance in the Peninsula; but his main aim in arranging the Spanish marriages was to win Naples away from Austria, establish a French-led league of constitutional governments in the Mediterranean, and undermine Austrian influence in Italy. It was a doctrinaire and artificial scheme, as many of Guizot's constructions tended to be, but serious in intent and neither anti-British nor anti-constitutional. It also explains why, while Aberdeen neither aided nor hindered Guizot's efforts on behalf of Trapani, Metternich fought them directly.[9]

Trapani's unpopularity in Spain and Cristina's impatience to hurry the marriage question along proved major obstacles to his candidacy. Though still favouring it, Guizot was willing if necessary to accept a Spanish Bourbon for Isabella, his choice being Don Francisco, the Duke of Cadiz. He would not accept the candidacy of Prince Leopold of Saxe-Coburg, a relative of Victoria's consort, Prince Albert, and of the King of Belgium, who was favoured by Victoria and Albert for family reasons, by Cristina for prestige reasons, and by the British minister at Madrid, Henry Bulwer, as a weapon in his duel with the French minister, Count Bresson. In a meeting of monarchs and ministers at Louis-Philippe's Chateau d'Eu in September 1845, Guizot promised Aberdeen that in exchange for Britain's accepting a Bourbon consort for Isabella and dropping the Coburg candidacy, France

---

[8] Bullen (1974*b*); Parry (1936: 7–16, 23–46, 88–91); Christiansen (1967: 48–51, 69–115). For a good statement of a typical French claim to exclusive leadership in Spain, see Chroust (1935–9: iv. 284–7).

[9] Bullen (1974*c*: 82–7); Parry (1936: 127–89); Mastellone (1957: 99–152).

would delay a proposed marriage between the Infanta Luisa and Louis-Philippe's son, the Duc de Montpensier, until after Queen Isabella had married and borne children, thus securing the succession to the Spanish throne against any dynastic connection between Spain and France. (All this must seem more like comic opera than high politics, but diplomacy is sometimes ridiculous, and one must plough through the petty events in order to understand the results.)

Guizot's and Aberdeen's hopes that this arrangement would allay Peel's suspicions, solidify the *entente*, and speed up a resolution of the question were quickly disappointed. Guizot, growing impatient with Aberdeen's wait-and-see policy and believing correctly that Bulwer was still conspiring with Cristina to promote a Coburg marriage, gave Aberdeen a veiled warning in March 1846 that if France acquired evidence that a Coburg or other non-Bourbon marriage for Isabella was imminent, this would nullify the promise he had made at Eu in September. Thus by the time that the Tory ministry and party, split over repeal of the Corn Laws, tottered to its fall in June 1846, the Anglo-French agreement over the marriages was already in tatters, while all that remained of the *entente cordiale* was personal friendship between Aberdeen and Guizot, and even that had been shaken.[10]

Palmerston's return to office in 1846 brought a change in policy as well as personalities. He had attacked Aberdeen mercilessly while in opposition and was committed to a tougher line with France (he had even used an Austrian agent, Georg Klindworth, to try to find out what was going on between Aberdeen and Guizot). He now set out to promote marriages between Isabella and Don Enrique, Duke of Seville, a favourite of the Progresistas, and between the Infanta and Leopold of Coburg. This meant moving from the behind-the-scenes anti-French manœuvres of Bulwer at Madrid to an open assault on the French position, and threatening the positions of the reigning Moderados and Cristina as well. Guizot and Bresson, with Louis-Philippe's reluctant consent, responded to Palmerston's offensive by pushing through their own scheme to wed Isabella to Cadiz and Luisa to Montpensier. To overcome Cristina's and Isabella's distaste for Cadiz, Guizot agreed to quick simultaneous marriages, thus violating the promise he had made a year earlier to Aberdeen. Both leaders were destroying the *entente* by their tactics, intending to undermine the

---

[10] Ibid. 169-96; Parry (1936: 236-9, 262-5); Bullen (1974c: 42-9); Christiansen (1967: 116-35); Guizot (1858: vii. 238-9; 1963: iii. 204-6).

other's position; yet neither exactly intended to cause an open breach, much less war. Guizot expected the prime minister, Lord John Russell, and other Francophiles in the cabinet to restrain Palmerston; Palmerston, as always, counted on making the French back down by a show of strength, even considering sending out the fleet for purposes of intimidation.

Both ended up paying for their tactics. Palmerston suffered a diplomatic defeat: his threats against the marriages France had arranged and his attempts to mobilize European opinion against them served only to speed up the announcement of the marriages and their consummation in October. This evoked a storm of British denunciation of Guizot; even Aberdeen condemned him for sharp practice.[11]

A kind of cold war then ensued between Guizot and Palmerston and their respective governments, lasting until Louis-Philippe fell from power in February 1848. Guizot won the European duel over the marriage question. All he needed from other powers was neutrality, while Palmerston had to convince them that the marriages must be overturned because they implicitly renewed the eighteenth-century Bourbon family compact and dangerously shifted the balance of power—an argument extreme even by Palmerstonian standards. Guizot also won the Anglo-French contest for influence in Spain, maintaining France's ascendancy in Madrid until Bulwer was finally expelled in May 1848. For a time the rivalry threatened to involve Portugal as well, but here the British retained their hold. The most ironic consequence of the breach was that it drove Guizot into a *rapprochement* with Austria and a certain amount of co-operation with Metternich to maintain the status quo in Italy, the exact reverse of the original aims of his Spanish policy.

Yet Guizot's victories were Pyrrhic. His quarrel with Britain, though it did not directly undermine the Orléans monarchy, combined with France's approach to Austria to deepen his personal unpopularity and that of the regime, and in that sense contributed to its downfall in 1848. Not a few Britons welcomed this as just what the regime deserved for its treachery over Spain.[12]

It is easy, and not unfair, to dismiss this affair as absurd sound and fury over an empty question of prestige. The prize in dispute, Spain, was not really available for either power to win, and hardly worth winning had it been. But to do so is to miss some

---

[11] Bullen (1974c: 52–147); Parry (1936: 319–35); Bullen (1974b); Palmerston Papers (Broadlands), GC/KL/1–2, 4.

[12] Bullen (1974c: 148–331); Mastellone (1957: 198–205).

points about the European system already made but worth re-emphasizing, and one or two new ones. The affair shows again how ill the balance-of-power paradigm fits the Vienna system and how unsuitable and dangerous balance-of-power methods were to its maintenance and operation. Palmerston's claim that the balance of power was at stake in Spain was wholly implausible, and his balance-of-power tactics proved both impotent and self-defeating. The quarrel in Spain was really about political equilibrium, not the balance of power. The government of Guizot and Louis-Philippe was more ready than any French government had ever been before to accept Britain's superiority in power; its goal was equality in status, rank, honour, and satisfactions. The quarrel resulted from the inability of Britain and France to reach this more important kind of equilibrium, either generally or in the Iberian peninsula. Even in dealing with Aberdeen, Guizot made Anglo-French equilibrium difficult by claiming ascendancy in Spain. With Palmerston there was no chance for political equilibrium at all; he would never concede to France any area where he thought Britain could, if it wished, make its own influence prevail.

The affair also illustrates once more how differently the two European hegemons managed their respective spheres and junior partners. Russia knew how to protect its special interests, especially in the Near East. Yet it had no problem conceding control of Italy to Austria, of north Germany to Prussia, and of the whole of Germany to both of them together. A comparison of Britain's dealings with France over the Spanish Marriages with Russia's treatment of Austria and Prussia over Poland and Cracow in 1846 (of which more later) again proves that the Russians understood how to manage their hegemonic sphere and preserve their leadership in it better than the British did.

The main reason for paying some attention to the Spanish Marriages question, however, is that it illustrates the likely fate of statesmen who, becoming aware of long-term changes in international politics, try to adapt themselves and their countries to the new emerging reality. That fate may well be political defeat in their lifetime and posthumous execution by historians thereafter.

The early nineteenth century was not the first time that war has been recognized as counter-productive, an ineffective and self-defeating instrument of international politics. It was, however, the first time in which this conviction made any durable difference in international politics, contributing substantially as it did to the breakthrough to a new system in 1813–15. Aberdeen had become an early convert to this view of war, on both political and religious grounds, from the time he visited Leipzig after the Battle of Nations. He has repeatedly been criticized as too honorable and decent to succeed in international politics—a verdict fair enough in particular instances, but unjust overall. He should be seen and judged, not as an unskilled and irresolute version of Palmerston, but as an alternative to Palmerston and his aims, methods, and values. In regard to Spain, he argued that the petty war between ministers for paramountcy at Madrid was useless; that Britain and France were each strong enough to ruin Spain, but that only their co-operation could help it prosper. In Europe he was more concerned about general peace and maintaining the system than about the so-called balance of power, and convinced that this made the Anglo-French *entente* worth saving even if France proved unreliable and difficult and some minor British interests and prestige were sacrificed in the process. The fact that Britain was the leading power made prudence and forbearance on its part even more important. He did not gain full reciprocity even from Guizot, he could not put across his viewpoint to the public or even to the cabinet, and he could not control his subordinates, especially Bulwer—hence he failed. But Aberdeen's 'failure' derives also in part from his being ahead of his time and of most of his countrymen.[13]

The other change beginning to emerge in the nineteenth century was even more durable and important than this genuine, but dim and transitory, recognition of the futility and ultimate obsolescence of war as an instrument of policy. It consisted of a slow shift in the very foundations, purpose, and functions of states, from their being made by and for war in the sixteenth to the eighteenth centuries, to their being made by and for trade. Historians and political economists have often noted that nineteenth-century Britain led the way in this epochal change in the main function and purpose of states.[14] But the process was also at work in France and elsewhere at this same time, and among the politicians of his era Guizot understood this process best, and tried hardest to apply it to domestic and international politics. He wanted to lead Frenchmen beyond their sterile struggles over revolution at home and the frustrated quest for power abroad;

---

[13] For Aberdeen's reaction to the Battle of Leipzig, see Chamberlain (1983: 134–5); for his policy in 1843–46, ibid. 357–89; on Wellington and Aberdeen as alternatives to Palmerstonian politics, see Chamberlain (1989: 77–91). Bullen's conclusions (1974c: 332–8) are also very useful. For a clear expression of Aberdeen's attitude on Spain, see Guizot (1858: viii. 160–1).

[14] See e.g. Rosecrance (1986); Gilpin (1987); Gruner (1980).

to get them to concentrate upon prosperity rather than power ('Enrichissez-vous!'), upon trade rather than territorial conquest, influence and co-operation rather than domination and conflict.[15] Unlike many of his predecessors and successors in France, he sought not to overthrow but to preserve and improve the 1815 system, remedying its main defect by gaining for France equal standing in the concert and a sphere of influence of its own. The equal standing he envisioned called in any case for partnership rather than rivalry with Britain, and a French sphere of influence which did not rival Britain's or infringe on it. Everywhere his policy demonstrates this: in Spain, the Mediterranean, Italy, North Africa, France's overseas empire, and South America. His commercial rival was not Britain but the Prusso-German *Zollverein*; his political rivals were not the British but Austria and Russia. He failed in part because of his own shortcomings; his support was narrowly based, he lectured better than he persuaded or led, and he lacked charisma. But, like Aberdeen, he failed also because he saw deeper and further than many of his contemporaries, and tried to follow his vision.[16]

II. AUSTRIA AND ITALY

Two of the chronic Italian themes in post-1815 European politics continued basically unchanged in the 1840s: the decline of Austrian leadership and the growth of the Risorgimento (resurrection), the broad, inchoate movement toward independence and some form of national unity in Italy. One old stand-by, Austro-French rivalry, temporarily disappeared, too late to do the Austrian or French governments any good.

[15] Writing to Princess Lieven on the approach of revolution in Germany, Guizot expressed his satisfaction that he and France, having gone through the revolution, were in the post-revolutionary age of progress: 'I detest these great chimerical and deceived hopes, these pleasures that end in storms and abysses. I love order in great affairs, and that regular movement of ascent which keeps all its promises'; 13 Aug. 1845, Guizot (1963: 187).

[16] On Guizot's international philosophy and its applications, see esp. D. Johnson (1957: 62–5, 74–7); Mastellone (1957: 63–8, 74–89); a good appraisal of its role in French economic and other progress in the 1840s is in Pinkney (1986: ch. 7). Rosanvallon (1985) provides a convincing exposition of Guizot's key role in nineteenth-c. classical liberalism, but surprisingly does not connect his liberal world-view with his foreign policy, despite obvious links (e.g. with Guizot's ideas on legitimacy, pp. 186–9). On Guizot's Latin American and colonial policies, see Braunstein (1983: 224–5, 261–76); I. Morgan (1978; 1983). For some evidence that his free-trade ideas were making progress in France, though not enough to win out, see Deschamps (1956: 338–48).

Austria's problems in Italy were part of a general decline which was more political than economic or cultural in nature. True, Austria overall lagged behind Western Europe and much of Germany economically, and suffered from great divergences in development within the monarchy. Yet it remained well ahead of Russia, south-eastern Europe, and much of Italy, and substantial economic growth, innovation, and change occurred in the 1840s, encouraged and promoted by the government, especially in the areas of trade and transportation. Economic change gave new prominence to the Austrian middle class and gained its members wider entry into a state machine once dominated by aristocrats, though without satisfying middle-class discontent or relieving the intense competition for bureaucratic positions.[17] The monarchy's nationalities problems, though they were not being solved and were growing slowly worse, were not yet acute. Only two nationalities, the Italians and the Hungarians, were in a position to cause serious trouble or inclined to do so. Polish and Serb nationalism represented a greater potential danger outside the monarchy than within it. The Germans were still attached to the monarchy and the other ethnic groups were still quiescent. An energetic and capable government could have found opportunity in meeting their needs for development.[18]

There was the rub. Austria's biggest problem in the 1840s was governmental paralysis. In Hungary, Count Stepan Széchényi devoted great energy and a considerable portion of his fortune to trying to overcome Hungary's feudal backwardness and tie it more closely to Vienna. But his plans for liberal-conservative reforms and economic and social development, exploited rather than supported by Metternich, ended in failure. So did Metternich's attempts after 1839 to find a workable compromise between the demands of Hungarian nationalists and Vienna's insistence on control. In Hungary as elsewhere, Metternich stood pat too long and gave way too late. As a result, the radical Lajos Kossuth gained the lead in Hungarian politics, even though, as Széchényi had seen, neither the Hungarian nation (i.e. the nobility and gentry) nor Hungarian liberalism were mature enough for his programme.[19] This was not simply Metternich's fault, but the result

---

[17] Good (1984: 45–73, 94–5); Coons (1975; 1977). The new definitive work on the Austrian bureaucracy is Heindl (1991).

[18] On Serb nationalism within and outside the monarchy, see Adler (1979); Hehn (1975). Major studies of the nationalities question are Kann (1950), still a classic, and the *Austrian History Yearbook*, iii (1967), pts. 1–3.

[19] Andics (1973); Deak (1979: 24–61); Barany (1968); Miskolczy (1959).

of a paralysis of governmental authority and decision-making at the top. The stagnation, already apparent in Francis's reign, grew worse when he died in 1835 and his dim-witted son Ferdinand succeeded him. Actual power was vested in a triumvirate consisting of Metternich, his rival the finance minister, Count Franz Anton Kolowrat, and Archduke Ludwig, who did little to resolve the stalemate between the other two. Viennese wit had it that thirty men ruled Austria: Metternich, Kolowrat, and Ludwig being three, Ferdinand zero.[20] By 1848 a friendly observer, the Saxon envoy, Count Vitzthum von Eckstädt, thought that only a great war could galvanize the Empire.[21]

In Italy, Austria's great handicap remained its inability to promote useful change itself or let others do so. Metternich, for example, feared the subversive side-effects of an Italian customs union, and therefore obstructed one even if it were to be led by Austria. He did the same with development of steamship trade with France. Even where Austria promoted progress (for example, building railways in Lombardy-Venetia), this helped little because Austria was determined to maintain the political divisions in Italy which economic union and improved communications would undermine.[22]

Relations between Austria and Sardinia-Piedmont, once superficially intimate, deteriorated sharply in the 1840's. King Charles Albert, while still holding to absolutism, became an innovator out of personal ambition and anti-Austrian feelings. By encouraging economic, educational and cultural, ecclesiastical, and legal-administrative reforms in Piedmont, he unwittingly promoted a moderate liberal movement as well. Metternich, viewing the difference between this movement and Mazzinianism as the difference between slow poison and murder in broad daylight, tried to fight it from 1843 to 1847 in a series of minor but acrid disputes with Sardinia over tariffs, railways, and the trade in salt with the Swiss canton of Ticino. The main effect was to harden Charles Albert's opposition. When a Papal–Austrian clash arose over Ferrara (described below), the King adopted the papal cause and even briefly considered war against Austria. Finally, with revol-

---

[20] Another, crueller version of Viennese wit changed the Emperor's appellation 'Ferdinand der Gütige' (Ferdinand the Kindly) into 'Gutinand der Fertige' (Gutinand the Washed-Up).

[21] Vitzthum (1886: 62–3, 70).

[22] Schroeder (1962a); Bortolotti (1945). However, for a persuasive argument that economic progress and modernization were not the motive, cause, and driving force of the Risorgimento, but its consequence, see Ullrich (1978).

utionary ferment in Italy nearing a climax in early 1848 and a revolution already under way in Naples, Charles Albert, yielding to strong liberal pressure, promised a constitution in February and actually promulgated it a few days after the February revolution in France. Metternich immediately predicted that Piedmont would next attack Austria; he was proved right in less than a month.[23]

Naples had also escaped Austria's control by 1848, but for different reasons. King Ferdinand II (later known as King Bomba for the methods he would use to overthrow the revolution) regarded Austria with the same fiercely isolationist and suspicious attitude as as he did other powers. Metternich at first called him a 'young fool' and a 'wild madman'. But by 1847 Ferdinand saw that Austrian support was his only hope against the coming revolution and appealed for Austrian intervention. The Austrian minister, Prince Felix Schwarzenberg, nephew of the commander of the allied armies in 1813–14 and future strong man of Austria, also urged it. Metternich refused, though he still warned the King not to grant constitutional concessions. Naples was too far away for Austria to act; Metternich's plan was to wait for the revolutionary onslaught to reach central and northern Italy and then crush it with help from France. Austria therefore did nothing when Naples became the first state to fall to revolution in late January 1848.[24]

In central Italy Austria had managed by late 1847 to shore up its position slightly. Tuscany, ruled mildly by the Habsburg Grand Duke Leopold II, remained loyal to Vienna, while Parma and Modena became virtual satellites, granting Austria extensive rights of intervention and occupation in alliances in December 1847. But these gains, such as they were, meant little beside the open break which developed between Austria and the Papal State. The trouble began in 1846 when Cardinal Mastai-Feretti, a man of genuine piety and vague goodwill but limited intelligence, was elected as Pius IX to succeed Pope Gregory XVI. Pius craved popularity, wanted to rule benevolently, and sympathized with Italian national sentiment. Metternich, remarking privately that he was prepared for anything except a liberal Pope, warned Pius repeatedly against making concessions to revolutionaries who would only use him in order eventually to turn on him and overthrow him. The French minister, Paolo Rossi, gave Pius opposite advice, however, and

[23] Nada (1980: 62–169); Austensen (1969: 57–183); Metternich (1880–4; vii. 403).
[24] Moscati (1947: 47–125); Bortolotti (1942); Berkeley and Berkeley (1932–40: iii. 63–5); Gisci (1931: 405).

the Pope followed it and his own instincts. As a result, for a brief time 'Viva Pio Nono' became a rallying cry of the Italian pre-revolution.

By mid-1847, with popular pressure forcing him to authorize a civil guard at Rome and revolutionary passions heightened by the discovery and suppression of a counter-revolutionary conspiracy at Rome, Pius began to realize that Metternich was right. At that juncture in July and August 1847, however, the commander of the Austrian army in northern Italy, Marshal Joseph Radetzky of War of Liberation fame, helped put the fat in the fire. Austria had been granted the right in the 1815 treaties to garrison the citadel of Ferrara on the papal side of the Po; Radetzky extended this to an occupation and patrol of the whole town. The move was arguably legal but clearly provocative, and the Pope, prodded by Italian sentiment, denounced it, thereby becoming a hero to most Italians and much of Europe. Austria, supported by its Holy Alliance partners and assisted by the Prussian minister at Rome, managed to settle the incident peacefully in December. The Pope's condemnation and protest, however, further damaged Austria's moral and legal standing in Italy, encouraged the revolutionaries, and made Pius still more reluctant to call on Austria for help and Austria more unwilling to grant it.[25]

Though Austria's problems with other Italian states were serious and worsening, they paled beside the dangers and vulnerability it faced in its own province of Lombardy. Everywhere else in Italy Austria confronted the approaching revolution in an essentially defensive, even passive stance. In Lombardy it launched a flurry of preventive activity in 1847 and early 1848. Diplomatic missions, military reinforcements, and special commissioners, first Count Ficquelmont and then Baron Joseph Alexander Hübner, were dispatched to reorganize the government, quell the mounting campaign of civil disobedience, and co-ordinate civil and military action against the revolution. None of this did much good; even the army's reinforcements fell far short of what was planned. Leading Austrians had expected this outcome; no one denounced Austria's governmental paralysis more than Metternich.

Thus even on its own territory Austria stood waiting for the revolution in Italy, hoping when it emerged to crush it by armed force with the co-operation of France. Metternich went so far as to propose to the Emperor a preemptive occupation of the Swiss

[25] Engel-Janosi (1958; 1952); Sked (1979b: 96–9); Berkeley and Berkeley (1932–40: ii. 201–3); Obermann (1966: 239–47); Filipuzzi (1958a); Metternich (1880–4: vii. 246–52, 333–41, 392–3, 404, 433–6).

canton of Ticino, as a move either to warn off the Piedmontese and Lombard revolutionaries or provoke them into an attack.[26] This proves the exhaustion of Metternichian conservatism as clearly as one could ask; he and other legalistic conservatives now were ready to rely on force, even preemptive violence, to meet the political challenges of civic disobedience and unrest. But it also proves that, if the Metternich system was finished, the international one was not. Had seventeenth- or eighteenth-century-style international politics still been in vogue, Austria in 1848 would have been surrounded by powers ready to take advantage of the crisis, as Maria Theresa's Austria was in 1740 and Joseph II's in 1790. Before the 1848 revolution, no government tried to exploit Austria's troubles for purposes of changing the territorial settlement, promoting revolution, or upsetting the general equilibrium, and only Sardinia-Piedmont, driven by revolutionary nationalist aims and pressure, did so after the revolution broke out.

In fact, the reverse happened; other powers either refrained from interfering or supported Austria. This attitude might not be surprising from its Eastern partners, though help could certainly not be automatically expected from Prussia and Frederick William IV. Yet even in helping Austria against revolution, the Eastern powers adhered to the rules of concert diplomacy. Prussia urged the formation of a league of Italian princes including Austria to help stave off revolt. In one of his last actions before he fell from power in March, Metternich proposed an international conference at Vienna to co-ordinate anti-revolutionary policy. More unexpected was France's co-operation with Austria to maintain the status quo in Italy. True, Guizot to some extent needed to approach Austria because of his break with Britain, and wanted more to prevent an anti-French coalition than to help Austria, so that their co-operation amounted to little in concrete terms. Guizot, while assuring Metternich that he supported the status quo against revolution, argued for reform at Rome and non-intervention in Italy to preserve the equilibrium of Europe. Metternich urged Guizot to forget about reforms in Italy and join Austria in the defence of European civilization, meanwhile assuring Britain that in Austria's eyes it was still Austria's natural ally. But this is normal in a restraining partnership. The striking thing is

[26] Sked (1979b: 100–31); Engel-Janosi (1933: 47–51); Obermann (1966: 248–63); Taylor (1934: 57); Berkeley and Berkeley (1932–40: ii. 324); Great Britain (1847–9: i passim); Metternich (1880–4: vii. 571–83); Schmidt-Brentano (1982: 237–8).

that by 1846–8 Austria was no longer trying to keep France out of Italy or France trying to throw Austria out.[27]

Palmerston's resumption of the office of foreign secretary in mid-1846 guaranteed that Britain would oppose Austria in Italy on ideological grounds. Other British leaders felt as strongly on the subject as he, or more so: Prince Albert was probably more Austrophobe than Palmerston was, though more interested in the German than the Italian national cause; and Lord John Russell, the prime minister, was the most Italophile of all. But Palmerston was in charge of Britain's foreign policy, and it was his hostility and suspicions Vienna felt, both directly from London and through ministers like Lord Normanby at Paris and Lord Abercromby at Turin. Lord Ponsonby, however, underwent something of a conversion on his transfer from Constantinople to Vienna, as happened to many nineteenth-century British envoys. He defended Metternich repeatedly if unsuccessfully, warning Palmerston that Austria would fight if pressed too hard and that Britain had no substitute for Austria as a stabilizing force in Europe.

Particularly galling to Vienna was the mission undertaken by Sir Gilbert Minto, Russell's father-in-law, in late 1847 to various Italian courts, especially Rome and Florence. Palmerston's instructions were moderate enough: to report on conditions in Italy, urge governments to grant constitutional reforms as the *via media* between revolution and reaction, and advise them against attacking Austria. Minto was also instructed to enlist the Pope in restoring order and civil obedience among the peasants in Ireland. This was for some, especially Lord Clarendon, governor-general of Ireland, the real goal of Minto's mission: to make the Pope and his bishops assist an anti-papal English regime and a rabidly anti-Catholic English public in keeping the Irish obedient to British authority during a famine and mass emigration of 1846–8 which was the worst in modern European history—at the same time as the British government condemned the Pope for the way he ruled his own domains.

Minto, incautious and Italophile, obeyed the letter of his instructions, but managed also to convey the impression to Italian liberals that if they rose and shook off Austria's yoke, Britain would support them. They were badly mistaken. Palmerston, growing more cautious as revolution approached, never proposed to give the Italians more than advice, for which Britain would

[27] Silva (1936; 1917: 322–31); Mastellone (1957: 166–7); Bullen (1974a: 293–5); Taylor (1934: 50–1); Metternich (1880–4: vii. 20–1, 49–50, 67–9, 324–5, 327, 394–5).

accept no responsibility. The advice, moreover, urged moderate constitutional reform as opposed to revolution, and while Palmerston in principle favoured freeing Italy from Austrian control, he was also against Italian nationalism and unity, wanted peace, and was more anxious to exclude French influence from Italy than to eliminate Austria's. The general advice he gave may well have been sensible; giving advice at all at this critical juncture was probably not prudent. It only increased Austria's determination to retain her position and encouraged the ambitions of Italian nationalists and Piedmontese expansionists to throw her out, while Britain itself had neither the means nor the will to manage the outcome.[28]

III. GERMANY AND CENTRAL EUROPE, 1841–1848

Revolution loomed ahead as clearly in Germany as in Italy in the 1840s. The difference is that in Italy revolution was more likely to cause an international war; in Germany revolution was more likely to undermine the international system. A revolution in Germany was less likely to lead to major war for two reasons: first, here Austria was less able and willing to fight for its leadership than in Italy, and still eager to preserve its conservative partnership with Prussia; and second, German nationalism presented Europe with a different kind of problem from that arising from Italian nationalism. Few Germans inside the Bund lived under foreign rule, and where they did, principally in Schleswig-Holstein under the King of Denmark, they enjoyed superior privileges and status. The many Prussian and Austrian Germans who lived intermingled with Slavic and other non-German peoples both inside and outside the confederation (Posen, West and East Prussia, Silesia, Bohemia-Moravia, Carinthia and Slovenia, Hungary and Transylvania) were all ruled by German princes and were in most places the dominant nationality. Germans in general had plenty of economic, social, and political reasons for discontent in the 1840s—bad harvests and steeply rising food prices, rapid population growth insufficiently relieved by emigration and

[28] British policy and the Minto mission are thoroughly documented in *Rel. dipl. GB–Sard.* (1972–: 3. i); *GB-Ital.-Minto* (1970: i–ii); Great Britain (1847–9: i–ii). See also Taylor (1934); Horvath (1926). For a sample of Ponsonby's arguments to Palmerston, see his letters of 6 Apr. and 5 May 1847, Palmerston Papers (Broadlands), GC/PO/544.

industrialization, economic depression and unemployment, the dislocations of urban growth and nascent large-scale industry, liberal frustrations at the lack of political freedoms and participation in government, some civil–military tension especially in Prussia, and political systems still mired in absolutism in some states or stuck in a stand-off between princes, bureaucrats, and representative chambers in others. Nonetheless, the revolutionary factor most dangerous for international peace and central in Italian nationalism was almost absent from German—rebellion against foreign rule.

Yet this same factor that made the coming German revolution less immediately dangerous in international politics went together with certain others to make it potentially even more dangerous in the longer run. The main goal of Italian nationalism, at least to this point, was not unification but liberation from Austrian rule and/or domination, and even this goal was far from universally shared. Moreover, even the united Italy Mazzini dreamed of, if somehow achieved, would not revolutionize the whole European system as a united Germany would. The fact that there was no urgent need or overwhelming demand in Germany before 1848 for unification was therefore a hopeful sign. Though pre-revolutionary German propaganda contained certain nationalist themes—denunciations of the confederation, demands for a national representation, calls for unification to make Germany more prosperous and powerful—the main foci of German discontent were local, and the remedies proposed for Germany's ills (constitutional reform, civil liberties, and state action on social problems so as to control the restive masses and prevent social revolution) could be achieved best through changes in the governments of individual states, especially the larger ones. This meant that German nationalism had a chance to develop gradually as part of the general European movement for reform and emancipation, rather than as a means of making Germany stronger for European power politics.

There also lay the danger, however. The main question for European international politics was not what character a German national state would have—whether it would be liberal-constitutional and democratic or conservative-authoritarian, peaceful or militarist. Whatever its character, any united Germany would almost automatically be too powerful for the rest of Europe. The long-standing debate in Germany over the primacy of foreign policy versus the primacy of domestic policy has always to some extent missed the point; the primacy governing the German question is and always has been the primacy of the international system as a whole. The central question was never what kind of Germany Germans wanted or needed, but what kind of Germany would be possible and tolerable within Europe.[29] Any united Germany represented a potential threat not only to other great powers, but to smaller states (the Low Countries, Scandinavia, Switzerland, northern Italy) and most of all to the smaller stateless peoples living among and in proximity to the Germans (Poles, Czechs, Slovaks, Hungarians, south Slavs).[30] There were certain ways in which greater German unity might be tolerable, even beneficial to Europe: commercial union, common weights and measures, a common legal code, unified transportation and communications systems, freedom of movement and immigration, and reforms in the confederation, including a national representative body and a more effective organization for joint defense. The Vienna Final Act had opened the door for some of these measures; the Germans themselves, especially conservatives led by Metternich, had failed to use most of them or closed them off.

The view once commonly held, that the rest of Europe somehow opposed German unification and blocked it, is now discredited. Europe had not blocked the *Zollverein*, for example. But sooner or later the other European powers were bound to react to the rise of a united German state organized for purposes of power politics. The fact that most Germans in the 1840s did not need such a state or have great aspirations for power was a good thing, but no guarantee against this danger. Some did want it; others stood to gain by diverting the broad national movement away from reform and emancipation and toward power. Observers saw this danger already in the 1840's, and the history of international politics in 1848 and after would bear out their fears.[31]

Prussia and Bavaria illustrate in different ways the Janus-faced potential of revolution in Germany. In Prussia, popular discontent

[29] The point is emphasized by Gruner (1985; 1989).

[30] For attention to this problem within the context of Austro-Prussian rivalry, see Lutz (1979; 1985).

[31] Obviously, no survey of the enormous literature on German liberalism and nationalism in the *Vormärz* is possible here. I have relied in general on Nipperdey (1983a); Wehler (1987); J. Sheehan (1978: 12–57; (1989)); Faber (1966); Gall (1968); Langewiesche (1974); and various essays in Conze (1978) and Schulze (1987). For useful particular themes and arguments, see Graf (1978: 165–73); Nipperdey (1983b); M. Müller (1981); Hans Gollwitzer (1972: 250–8); Obermann (1979). An example of the views disputed here is Huber (1963: 311–17). For evidence of how the dangerous power-political potential of German nationalism manifested itself in 1848–9, see Wollstein (1977).

grew out of serious internal problems caused by uneven development and accelerating economic and social change. The changes resulted in part from governmental policies which were liberal and modernizing in certain economic and social sectors, highly conservative on other socio-economic questions and in politics generally. Prussia pursued a *laissez-faire* commercial and industrial policy, developed an efficient professional bureaucracy, promoted primary and higher education, pioneered in science, technology, and practical arts, and fostered improvements in communications, especially railways—all progressive trends. At the same time the government worked to preserve Junker landed estates, and defended their dominant position in the army officer corps and higher state offices. Politically it remained a bureaucratic service state, nominally absolutist, actually oligarchic, resting on law yet not constituting a *Rechtsstaat*. For bridging the resulting gap between Prussia's economic and social dynamism and political backwardness, the élites had only a limited and inadequate range of reform models from which to choose: an Old Whig mixed constitution like eighteenth-century England, an old absolutist one looking back to Frederick the Great, and some vague neo-feudal ideals envisioned by the new King, Frederick William IV (1840–61), and his adviser, Joseph Maria von Radowitz.

Meanwhile, economic progress, while it strengthened the middle class and created new demands for political reform, also led, especially in the 1840s, to economic dislocation and poverty. The urban and rural proletariats grew, many artisans were driven down to the laboring class while others rose to be employers, and social pressures from below increased generally. Attitudes among the public toward government and the state reflected similar contradictions. The once lively tensions between the Rhine provinces and Berlin diminished somewhat as a result of the French threat in 1840, the legality and relative efficiency of the Prussian government, and the celebration of the completion of the Cologne cathedral. But meanwhile the Polish problem in the east grew worse, and other Church–state conflicts and a growing political awareness on the part of Catholics raised new difficulties for the authorities.

Frederick William IV, who had raised hopes of a new era at his accession in 1840, was serious about wanting to heal the divisions within Prussia, though without giving up his dynasty's historic rights and power. After long deliberation he decided on a way to allay the discontent. To meet his predecessor's unfulfilled promise of a constitution, he summoned the eight provincial diets to a

special united diet in 1847; to unite Prussians in a common enterprise, he called on the diet to approve funding for a railway
connecting east Prussia with the rest of the kingdom. It was too
little too late. The liberals, though fundamentally loyal and ready
to compromise, wanted the diet to meet periodically and have a
permanent organization; the King refused; and the diet broke up
in failure.

This brought revolution one step closer, but did not make it
inevitable. Prussia was not on an irrevocable course towards either
violent revolt or expansion through power politics. The former
danger, however, was obvious and the latter beginning to emerge.
Already liberals were calling for a new pro-Western, pro-Polish,
and anti-Russian foreign policy which would put Prussia at the
head of a more united Germany; and some conservatives, among
them the young Otto von Bismarck, thought the best way to
fight the revolution was for the government to seize Frederick the
Great's sword and put it to use inside and outside Prussia.[32]

In Bavaria the revolutionary pressures were far less profound.
Constitutional government since 1818, though it did not work
smoothly, helped defuse political discontent, and less rapid economic development and modernization meant less social change
and stress. Protestant–Catholic tensions and Church–state problems, though serious, were less severe than in Prussia, and while
King Ludwig I had dynastic ambitions, his earlier territorial claims
were now largely forgotten in his zeal to promote art and culture
and protect the Wittelsbach throne in Greece.

In fact, a less lofty drive of Ludwig's paved the way to revolution, his attachment to an Irish-born adventuress taking the
name of Lola Montez. First he made her his mistress and Countess
of Landsberg, then he allowed her to interfere in politics, and
finally he proposed to marry her and bring her into the court. The
affair discredited the monarch among the public, alienated his
own conservative advisers, and awakened passions in the most
explosive area in Bavarian politics, religion. Bavaria was divided
between Ultramontanes and Lolamontanes. The scandal paralyzed
the government, providing an opportunity for students, workers,
liberal burghers, and other restless groups to try in 1848 to bring
the government down. The *bon mot* about Berlin and Vienna in
1917 might apply in early 1848: in Berlin the situation was serious
but not hopeless, in Munich hopeless but not serious.

[32] The main work is Obenaus (1984: 521–729); but see also Koselleck (1967:
616–37); Gillis (1968); Berdahl (1988: 311–73); Gall (1980: 64–7); Dunk (1966:
352–5); Sperber (1984); Lill (1974).

Yet in Bavaria, as elsewhere, there was a potentially danger-ous split in German sentiment between a movement for liberal-constitutional reform, in which the notion of national unity was included but not dominant and which cast Bavaria as leader of a Third German or south German bloc, and a conservative-monarchic Teutonic nationalism directed mainly against Germany's supposed foreign enemies. Ludwig himself represented the latter trend.[33]

One area in Germany, Schleswig-Holstein, gave clear signs by 1848 of what German nationalism could lead to. The German population in Schleswig was about half the total; Holstein was wholly German. Though ruled by the King of Denmark, the Germans enjoyed secure rights and privileges and a superior socio-economic and educational position. The German language pre-dominated in the schools, church, and administration, and the two Duchies were united under their traditional constitution which separated them administratively from Denmark proper. The first expressions of German national feeling after 1815 therefore took the form, as elsewhere, of local patriotism, in this case, attach-ment to Schleswig. Germans looked forward to the inevitable triumph of the German language and culture over Danish, just as German was expected to supplant Czech in Bohemia or as French would surely conquer Flemish in Belgium and English Welsh and Irish in the United Kingdom. From 1830, however, this local patriotism was increasingly overtaken by a more modern and fervid liberal-constitutional German nationalist agitation, led by intellectuals and students. A similar Danish counter-movement arose; these tended to squeeze out the factions of local Schleswig patriots, both Danish and German.

In the late 1830s, conflict within the Schleswig estates centred on the use of Danish in lower schools and courts, though both sides remained loyal to the Danish state and the union of Schleswig and Holstein. But when King Christian VIII in May 1840 pre-scribed Danish instead of German for legal and administrative purposes wherever Danish was used in churches and schools (i.e. especially in north Schleswig), this brought German opposition to parity for the Danes into the open and broke the bonds of loyalty to their common province. German leaders began demanding that Schleswig be separated from Denmark and incorporated in a new German federation, while Danes called for incorporating it into a

---

[33] Zorn (1962); Spindler (1974: 198–215). For the impact of the affair on foreign observers and regimes, see Chroust (1935–9: v; 1949–51: iii–iv *passim*).

united Denmark. The death of Christian VIII and accession of Frederick VII in January 1848 added a succession question to the quarrel, Germans denying the Danish Crown's rights to the Duchies. Thus the stage was set for the German revolt against Danish rule in 1848, and the succeeding military and diplomatic conflicts from 1848 to 1864.

The Danes, especially the romantic nationalists among them and above all the students among these, were not innocent bystanders or victims in all this, and Danish dreams of a pan-Scandinavian union were as utopian as any in Europe. Yet the growing clash in Schleswig primarily illustrated the dangers German integral nationalism held for Europe: the refusal to recognize equal rights for smaller nations, the assumption of cultural superiority, the marshalling of history, law, and linguistic science in support of territorial claims, the drive to recover 'lost' areas of the German fatherland, the disregard of European rights and needs.[34]

Europe in general had to worry about German nationalism; Austria in particular had to worry that Prussia would lead it. The subterranean Austro-Prussian rivalry continued in the 1840s, with Prussians pleased at the decline in Austria's influence in south Germany and the harm done to Austria's image by the uprising in Austrian Galicia and Austria's annexation of Cracow in 1846 (of which more later). But there was no open confrontation. Frederick William IV considered himself a loyal supporter of Habsburg leadership in Germany, and his minister, Joseph Maria von Radowitz, hid his anti-Austrian aims under the cloak of plans to reform the Bund so as to give Prussia a greater military and political role in Germany and Germany a stronger voice in Europe. Metternich, well aware of the power-political aims and consequences of such reform, preached his old gospel to Frederick William: the European equilibrium and the social order could be saved from revolution only by preserving the treaties and the federal structure of Germany just as they were. Yet as usual, under pressure Metternich gave way and tried to save what he could. In early 1848 he agreed to meet with Radowitz to discuss his plans for federal reform. This was doubtless Metternich's usual delaying game, yet it indicates that under pressure even he would consider federal reform and still wanted a partnership with Prussia against German nationalism. In any case, the outbreak of revolution in March forestalled the meeting.[35]

[34] W. Carr (1963: 21–164); Wollstein (1977: 23–35); H. Kuhn (1988).
[35] Obermann (1970); Derndarsky (1982: 104–5); Chroust (1949–51: 145–6, 157–61, 163–4, 168–73, 234–64); Metternich (1880–4: 368–71).

Greater change occurred in France's stance on the German question in the 1840s than in Austria's. Though illusions about Germany persisted among French liberals and intellectuals, Guizot and the Quai d'Orsay learned to distinguish between a liberal-constitutional German 'nationalism' not dangerous to France and a monarchic-conservative ethnic nationalism that was. Baron Bourgoing at Munich constantly warned that 'Teutonism' threatened the Bund, the individual German states, France, and the other peoples of Europe. At the same time he defended the existing confederation as valuable to France, and warned that the only way France could regain the friends and influence it had lost in Germany was to earn a reputation for reliability and love of peace. In a particularly acute memorandum of 19 November 1844, Bourgoing argued that those working for the unification of Germany were actually undermining its independence. By challenging powerful interests within Germany itself, they would end up throwing Germany back into the old system of appeals to foreign powers and foreign interventions. He then continued:

In our time, Germany must adopt another role: placed in the centre of Europe and divided as it is, but formed into an indissoluble confederation, it must by its immobile power, its force, inert yet indispensable in the general political system, serve as a counter-weight to the numerous causes of rupture which the great powers find in the rest of Europe.[36]

Bourgoing, a Frenchman, here defined Germany's role in the equilibrium of Europe like a good Central European. His concept was essentially Bismarck's 'Bleigewicht im Stehaufmännchen Europas', Germany as the solid lead weight in the base of the punching doll of Europe, serving to pull it erect after every blow. The 1815 confederation Bourgoing here defended, stultified and maimed though it had been till then, could still in principle have been developed to serve this function in international politics. The united Germany which nationalists dreamed of and Bismarck ultimately created, as events would prove, was too powerful, restless, and dynamic for such a role.[37]

The French change of attitude toward Germany, to be sure, bore no fruit, not only because the revolution overthrew the July monarchy and brought in different actors, but also because, even had France wanted to do something useful in Germany, it had no partners to work with. Though Metternich noted the change at Paris and tried to exploit it, there was too much ingrained Austro-

---

[36] Chroust (1935–9: v. 90; the whole *mémoire* is in pp. 82–93).
[37] Owsinska (1974: 58–63); Poidevin and Sieburg (1978: 3–11); Chroust (1935–9: v. 222–7).

French distrust for their co-operation in Germany to succeed. Russia was still less available as a partner to France. Nicholas remained hostile and leaned more than ever toward Prussia in German affairs, though disapproving of Frederick William's flirtation with constitutionalism, just as in Europe and the Far East he looked to Britain as Russia's partner while disapproving mildly of Palmerston. As for Austria, the Tsar still supported it in Italy, consulted it on the Ottoman Empire, and was determined to sustain it as a barrier against revolution, but increasingly dismissed it as a force in Germany or Europe.[38]

All this has a melancholy air of inevitability about it. Yet something that was not inevitable, the fact that the Anglo-French *entente* broke down in the late 1840s, made a difference, especially to developments in Germany. Here above all was where Western, especially British, ideas about moderate constitutional reform as the middle way between reaction and revolution to promote peace and progress were sound. Palmerston was right in principle: the way to save the federal principle in Germany and prevent revolution was to apply generally the liberal constitutional example set by the south German states and the liberal economic one set by Prussia. Most British leaders, with the exception of the German-born Prince Albert, did not favour German unification. Even the Whigs wanted the confederation reformed, not abolished, with Prussia leading it on paths of economic, political, and religious progress.

The Tories, though more cautious, did not disagree. Historians have noted that leading Tories like Peel and Wellington shared Palmerston's suspicions of France and the July monarchy; less noticed is the fact that they substantially shared his views on Austria and the German question as well. Aberdeen, as pro-Austrian and friendly to Metternich as a British statesman could be, felt a mild regret at Austria's decline. He knew that Austria, despite its protectionism, was a useful partner to Britain in commerce, stood on Britain's side on most international issues, and represented no threat to British security whatsoever. His actual policy toward Austria in the 1840s, however, was that of every other nineteenth-century foreign secretary: to demand Austria's active support for a whole series of British interests (trade, navigation, Spain, the Ottoman Empire, Serbia, Russia, a Protestant Bishopric in Jerusalem, conformist Catholic bishops in Ireland,

---

[38] Gritzbach (1974: ii. 348–51); Meyendorff (1923: i. 206–404; ii. 3–53); Nesselrode (1904–12: viii. 183–287); Winter (1961); Andics (1963: 19–37).

and more), all for nothing—or rather, solely for the sake of British 'friendship'. No service was too demeaning to demand of Austria. The point on which Aberdeen nagged Metternich the longest and hardest, because Victoria was constantly nagging him, was procuring her uncle, Prince Ferdinand of Saxe-Coburg, the Grand Ducal title and honours he coveted. Metternich and Aberdeen's brother, Robert Gordon, minister to Austria, repeatedly explained, in vain, that this could be done only through the confederation, where it would arouse endless trouble and jealousy among the other petty princes of the Bund. Aberdeen, goaded by Victoria, continued the pressure, accompanying it with repeated complaints of Metternich's and Austria's weakness, slipperiness, unfriendliness, deceit, timidity, and general worthlessness. The Habsburg monarchy, Aberdeen said more than once, was becoming like Turkey (a country he despised) and would ultimately share its fate; Russia, France, and Prussia were the important powers to deal with on major questions.[39]

There is no point in denouncing the British attitude. Britain was under no obligation to support Austria, though the question raised by Ponsonby, Gordon, and other British ambassadors at Vienna, as Aberdeen himself had done earlier, remained apropos: how would Britain manage its problems and interests in the Near East, the Mediterranean, and Central Europe if Austria were not there? Nor is it important once more to refute the myth about Anglo-Austrian friendship in the nineteenth century, remarkable and persistent though that myth is.[40] The only point worth making is that Britain's pro-Prussian, anti-Austrian leanings were not the basis for any actual *policy* toward Germany, as they could have been. At no time in the nineteenth century was Britain's prestige and attractiveness as a model higher in Europe than in the 1840s, especially in Germany. But two things prevented Britain from

[39] The Aberdeen–Gordon correspondence is in BL Add. MSS 43211 (I–II), 43222; Metternich's private correspondence with the Austrian charge in London, Philip Neumann, is in ibid. 43128. For Palmerston's views on German unification, see Gillessen (1961: 10–11). On Austro-British commercial relations, see Pavelka (1968).

[40] It takes such forms as giving serious weight to Palmerston's public statements in 1848–9 that he was a friend of Austria north of the Alps; or believing that Britain during the First World War really wanted to save the Austrian Empire, when the promises Britain gave Serbia, Italy, Russia, and Rumania made Austria's future existence impossible. The only thing more remarkable than the British belief in this myth is the Austrian acceptance of it—the conviction of numerous Austrian envoys and publicists that somehow Britain's unfriendly actions were the result of misunderstanding or accident. For a good example of this in 1848–9, see Filipuzzi (1985a: 196–208).

actively encouraging the evolution of Germany along British constitutional lines in co-operation with Prussia. One was the British tendency, like the United States through much of the twentieth century, to prefer giving advice and exerting influence without taking responsibility for it. The other was British rivalry with France, and the impossibility of liberal Anglo-French co-operation on the Continent as a result of the quarrels already described.

The growing conflict between radical and conservative forces was illustrated in two other places in Central Europe. Poland showed where the Holy Alliance could still be effective, Switzerland where it could not.

The limited self-rule under its own senate granted the free city of Cracow under the Vienna Treaties had always been threatened by its supervisors, the three partitioning powers. Metternich delivered the first blow to Cracow's autonomy in 1820 by including its university in the repressive measures carried through in Germany. After the 1830–1 revolution in Russian Poland, with Cracow one centre of the conspiracy, Nicholas decided that Austria must eventually annex it. At Münchengrätz in 1833 and Berlin in 1835, the Holy Alliance agreed to snuff out Cracow's independence the next time it became the foyer of revolution. Fears of how the Western powers would react, however, plus a slight turn toward liberalism in Prussia after 1840 and the growth of Prussian trade with and through the free city, led Prussia and Russia to oppose Metternich's suggestion to carry out the decision in 1842.

Meanwhile, from the late 1830s a new Polish revolt was being planned by the democratic wings of the Polish movement in Poland and abroad, with an *émigré* at Paris, Ludwig Mieroslawski, returning to lead it. The conspiracy called for the movement to start in February 1846 in Posen and Cracow-Galicia and spread from there to Congress Poland. The movement, badly prepared, riddled with factional strife, and lacking much support in large sections of the population, including both the nobles and the peasants, would have had little chance of success even had it remained undiscovered. Instead, the Eastern powers learned of it well in advance. Prussian authorities arrested Mieroslawski and snuffed the movement out quickly in Posen in early 1846. Frightened, the Cracow senate invited the Austrian forces in Galicia to occupy the city. The Austrians did so, but on meeting sporadic resistance they timidly retreated, thus allowing an actual revolt in Cracow to break out. It lasted ten days until the forces of all three powers moved in to restore order. Events took a far bloodier course in Galicia: a part of the Polish landed nobility trying to raise the standard of revolution instead provoked a murderous rising by Ruthenian peasants against their Polish landlords. The Austrian authorities did not actively encourage the jacquerie, as many believed at the time and since, but did passively tolerate it.

These events of February and March 1846 sealed the fate of Cracow. Nonetheless, it took till early November for the three powers to work out their differences over how to dispose of the free city. Prussia was reluctant to see Austria annex it and was determined to protect its economic interests there, and Metternich himself disliked annexing it for fear of the international repercussions. Russia, however, insisted on final action. The announcement of the three powers' decision that Austria would annex Cracow, coming at the height of the Anglo-French quarrel over the Spanish Marriages, evoked pious condemnations and some public outcry from the Western powers, but no real opposition. Aberdeen, still in office during the rising, took the free city's demise for granted and would have passed over the annexation in silence. Palmerston, who had taken office by the time it was announced, used the affair as a stick to beat the absolutists with, but really cared little about Poland and was more concerned about not driving Austria and France together. Thus Austria and the Holy Alliance got away with it easily, yet the move cost them something. Austria's critics cited the affair as one more proof that Austria was too reactionary, incompetent, and un-German to be Germany's leader, and Metternich knew as well as anyone that when a legalist-conservative state violates treaties it helps undermine its own foundations.[41]

While the Polish rising, planned as a progressive national revolution, led to a bloody anti-Polish jacquerie and another defeat for Polish nationalism (though the cause remained alive), the Swiss Sonderbund War, which began as a domestic civil-religious conflict, ended up promoting greater international independence for Switzerland. The conflict grew out of the Swiss version of the *Kulturkampf*, the nineteenth-century religious-political struggle waged throughout Germany over control of education, Church–state relations, and cultural values in general.

[41] Gill (1974); Kieniewicz (1947–8); Martens (1874–1905: iv. 454–62, 472–4, 525–36); Huber (1963: 468–71). For some German reactions, see Vitzthum (1886: 11–12, 19); Chroust (1949–51: iv. 210–11). For Metternich's and Ponsonby's defence of the annexations, see Metternich (1880–4: vii. 354–8), Ponsonby to Palmerston, 4 Dec. 1846, Palmerston Papers (Broadlands), GC/PO/541.

In Switzerland as elsewhere, it was not simply a contest between Protestants and Catholics, but joined liberal and radical Protestants with liberal and Josephist Catholics against traditional Catholicism. The traditional Catholic forces, however, now included popular-democratic as well as clerical-ultramontane ones, with Catholics in Switzerland gradually awakening politically just as they were doing in Germany.[42]

In 1834–6 the Catholic resistance succeeded in defeating proposals for creating a more national Swiss Catholic Church and giving the state supervision of seminaries and safeguards against papal intervention. A decisive factor in this victory was that France and Austria intervened in the dispute, taking the legally sound view that the change would violate the principle of cantonal sovereignty established and guaranteed under the Vienna treaties. In the early 1840s a more serious struggle began, when the Protestants in the Aargau took advantage of their slim control of the cantonal government to overthrow the existing parity of confessions and force through the secularization of all the cloisters in the canton. This violated article 12 of the federal constitution, so that again the question became an international one, with both France and Austria condemning the action. This time the radicals triumphed, because Guizot and Louis-Philippe were unwilling to intervene and Austrian policy was indecisive.

The secularization, which marked another stage in the breakdown of the 1815 Swiss constitution, led to two Catholic initiatives. Seven Catholic cantons formed a Separate League (Sonderbund) for defence, a clearly unconstitutional step, and Lucerne, followed by three other cantons, invited the Jesuits to work in their systems of education. The radicals' direct response to this invitation, attacks by armed bands on Lucerne, proved unsuccessful. Nonetheless, the Catholic cantons felt beleaguered. All the current trends seemed arrayed against them—the growth of Swiss industry and commerce, hard times in the countryside, Protestant domination of higher education, and the rise of Swiss national feeling. The danger to the Catholic cause became acute with the triumph of radicals in Bern and their adoption of a new radical constitution, a similar radical victory in Geneva, and worker unrest in Basel. If the radicals gained one more canton, they would control the Swiss Diet and could not only vote to expel the Jesuits and to outlaw the Sonderbund but also change the Swiss constitution, limiting cantonal sovereignty.

[42] Stadler (1984: 42–71). On the awakening of political Catholicism in Germany, see Graf (1978); Sperber (1984).

To this point, in late 1846, Metternich had responded to Catholic appeals only with limited financial aid, while Guizot, preoccupied with the Spanish Marriages affair, had supplied the Sonderbund small quantities of arms free or on credit. The threat of radical control of the diet finally galvanized Guizot into massing 10,000 troops on the frontiers of Geneva, the Valais, and Basel. The way seemed open for Austria and France to co-operate against the Swiss radicals on the basis of the great powers' rights under the Vienna treaties to uphold the existing Swiss constitution and defend cantonal sovereignty.[43] The South German states, Prussia, and Russia either had no objection to Austro-French co-operation or actually called for it. With the two great powers each trying to make the other take the lead, however, the intervention never materialized. Metternich's normal caution, now reinforced by age, a general sense of Austria's weakness and vulnerability, and fear of the international reaction held him back. In France, Louis-Philippe, a religious sceptic sympathetic to the Protestant cause, helped deter Guizot, a strong Protestant, from supporting the Catholic side. Guizot also feared the domestic impact of intervention in France, besides which he did not really want joint action with Austria, only the appearance of it to intimidate the Swiss radicals. His real aim was a five-power European action in which France would mediate a compromise solution between the Swiss parties and act as the bridge between Britain and the Holy Alliance within the European Concert (much like what Metternich had always wanted in the Near East).

Whatever Guizot's intent, the result was to hand victory to the Protestants in Switzerland and to Palmerston in international politics. The Swiss radicals, once they gained their twelfth vote within the diet in St Gall, could move against the Sonderbund without fear of foreign intervention, because Guizot's insistence on five-power action enabled Palmerston to delay any European action until after the Protestants had triumphed. Metternich had produced a plan for diplomatic intervention in September 1846, but failed to gain the support of France; a similar initiative by Guizot the following February was greeted coolly by Metternich. A new French envoy, Bois-le-Comte, went to Switzerland in mid-1847, but despite energetic efforts failed to rally the conservatives or intimidate the radicals. Metternich tried to get French support for a four-power declaration in favour of cantonal sovereignty in June. Guizot, however, insisted on a five-power declar-

[43] Stadler (1984: 72-81); Sutz (1976: 15-55). Thorough studies of Metternich's policy are provided in Winkler (1927; 1933).

ation, and Palmerston rejected this on the ground that it would lead to forcible intervention, which was unacceptable. Besides, Palmerston believed that the Jesuits should be expelled.

This left the Swiss Diet free under its radical leadership to condemn the Sonderbund in July and decree the expulsion of the Jesuits in September. Both sides mobilized, but the Sonderbund was hopelessly inferior militarily. Its call for an Austro-French military demonstration, which the French minister had incautiously promised, was turned down by Guizot. Metternich lapsed into apathetic inactivity; French plans for the secret dispatch of weapons to the Catholic forces broke down. Isolated, the Sonderbund in desperation tried a preemptive attack before their Protestant foes mobilized, and failed. A month's easy campaign in November gave the Protestants a military victory; the Sonderbund dissolved and many of its leaders went into exile.

Only then did Metternich and Guizot launch a flurry of diplomatic activity to try to curb the radical victory. These efforts also were frustrated by Palmerston. Though he now worried that the radicals were going too far, he confined concert action to an anodyne offer of mediation, useless now that the fighting was over. Giving up on Palmerston, Guizot joined in a four-power note to the Swiss Diet in January 1848; but, as the four powers expected, the diet firmly rejected it. The outbreak of revolutions in France and Europe in February and March made any further action against Switzerland impossible.

While the 1848 revolutions were overthrowing Guizot and Metternich and occupying Europe with bigger concerns, the diet proceeded, from February to June 1848, to revise the Swiss constitution. No dramatic political, religious, or cultural changes were made. Switzerland maintained its confessional division, as well as its toleration of only two recognized confessions. Most political life in Switzerland remained centred in the cantons; only in foreign policy, customs, coinage, and certain other aspects did it become a more unitary state. Internationally, however, the affair emancipated Switzerland from European intervention in its internal constitutional affairs, without weakening the European guarantee of Swiss neutrality.[44]

[44] Sutz (1976: 57–199); Bullen (1974a: 302–15; 1971); Imlah (1966); Stadler (1984: 82–3). For the Swiss patriotic view, see Bonjour (1965: 284–99). There is considerable correspondence on the crisis in Chroust (1935–9: v. 292–346) and Metternich (1880–4: vii). For Palmerston's efforts both to restrain the Protestant victory in Switzerland and to exploit it to get papal help in regard to Ireland, see Palmerston Papers (Broadlands), GC/MI/584, GC/CA/263–4.

This was on the whole a good outcome for both Switzerland and Europe, if not quite the unalloyed triumph for progress and justice that Whigs and Swiss nationalists proclaimed. The explanation for it, however, has to include something beyond the boldness and skill of the Swiss radicals, British diplomacy, and the weakness and disunity displayed on the conservative side. The changes were also made possible by the Vienna system's built-in legal and moral restraints against the use of force, in this case to the benefit of radicals who were themselves breaking the Vienna rules. Metternich failed to intervene, and suffered a political defeat, not solely because Austria was weak and afraid of the international repercussions, but also because he understood that the use of force tended to undermine an international system vital for Austria's existence. Where he felt he had no choice, in Poland and Italy, he used force as a last resort; where he had a choice, in Switzerland and Germany, he chose not to. As he remarked in December 1847, in a pregnant and revealing aside, only Britain and Russia in their invulnerable positions could still think of war as the *ultima ratio regum*. As for France, it was Guizot's determination to have a five-power solution or none, and his hope somehow to revive the *entente* with Britain, that gave Palmerston the chance to take his revenge for Spain in Switzerland.[45]

IV. THE OUTLOOK IN 1848

Cracow proved that the international system could still serve to repress revolution. Switzerland showed that it could also still permit fairly radical change. Other areas of Europe proved that under this system governments had a chance to solve their problems, manage them, or ignore them, as they preferred. Two such were the Low Countries and Greece. The final divorce between Belgium and the Netherlands in 1839 did not lead to smooth relations between them. Problems arose over trade, communications, languages, and nationalism; the two states pursued parallel but competitive policies toward Prussia, the *Zollverein* and the German Bund. Both countries suffered hard times economically (for the Netherlands, partition meant actual economic decline);

[45] Obermann (1966: 248–53); Baxa (1973); Bullen (1974a: 298–301, 315–21). For evidence of how scruples about international legality and the maintenance of the system inhibited both Metternich and Aberdeen over Switzerland, see Gordon to Aberdeen, No. 25, 17 Apr. 1845, BL Add. MS 43222, fos. 28–9, and Aberdeen to Gordon, 20 June, ibid. 43211 (II), fos. 533–4.

both had religious divisions to wrestle with; in both states there were serious problems of identity and doubts about the viability of the regime. For neither state, however, were these difficulties multiplied by threats or challenges from without. Instead the great powers, including France, recognized the importance of their independence as intermediary bodies and watched each other to make sure no one tried to exploit them. This would have been unthinkable in any earlier era.[46] As for Greece, the 1840s did not end Anglo-French rivalry (Russia had ceased to be a major competitor some time earlier), but the Greek government did consolidate itself internally and gain more freedom from foreign domination.[47]

International peace also enabled Russia to ignore its grave internal problems, or try to. While most other states, despite the hardships of the so-called hungry forties, were developing economically, Russia stagnated or actually declined. The government's unusual passivity in economic affairs, connected with Nicholas's preoccupation with the danger of revolution, went along with a generally inactive foreign policy as well. Much as the Tsar disliked the renewal of the Anglo-French *entente* in the 1840s, Russia did not try either to break it up while it lasted or to exploit the rift when it occurred. In fact, Nicholas worried that the breach would prompt Palmerston to promote revolution in Italy. Nesselrode continued to seek a special partnership with Britain. In 1844 Nicholas and Nesselrode reached a gentleman's agreement with Peel and Aberdeen calling for Anglo-Russian co-operation to preserve the Ottoman Empire, a close parallel to the Russo-Austrian agreement at Münchengrätz in 1833. Aberdeen, though putting less store by this agreement than the Russians did, considered it useful as a supplement to the *entente* with France and a substitute for the old British partnership with Austria. The Tsar and Nesselrode overestimated its value, but it helped Russia mask its relative decline in safety.[48] At the same time it helped Britain keep up its active policies in north-west India and Central and North America with little or no impact on European politics.[49] The

[46] Kossman (1978: 179–205); Boogman (1955: i. 72–84, 90–6); Boogman (1968a); Dunk (1966: 229–333); Gooch (1963).

[47] Petropoulos (1968); Djordjevic and Fischer-Galati (1981: 102–4).

[48] For Russia's economic decline, see Pintner (1967: 250–5); Lincoln (1978: 180–1); for the weakness and backwardness of the Russian army, Curtiss (1965: 110–12, 157–9); Beyrau (1984). For the depressant effect of Tsarist censorship, see Choldin (1985).

[49] For an account of Peel's policies in India and N. America, see Gash (1976: 482–504); on Palmerston's in Central America, Alstyne (1936). For important

divided Anglo-Russian hegemony in European and world affairs established in 1813–15 remained intact to 1848.

The best proof that the Vienna system by 1848 was neither a worn-out cloak nor a rigid straitjacket preventing change was its role in the origins of the 1848 revolutions: it let them happen. International problems were clearly not the dominant factors in bringing on the revolutions, except possibly in Italy (or in Poland, where the revolution had come in 1846); economic, social, cultural-ideological, and domestic political factors predominated. But international factors were not absent from the equation. Some of the ingredients and catalysts in the revolutionary ferment were unquestionably international: discontent at Paris with France's conservative foreign policy and its inglorious European position,[50] the nationalist spirit of active minorities in the Germanies and Italy, Austria's loss of international prestige and credibility, Prussian and Piedmontese expansionist ambitions, Italian and Hungarian resentment of 'foreign' rule, and the nationalist discontents of Poles, Serbs, and Rumanians.

The important fact, however, is not that a certain amount of international discontent and conflict had built up under the Vienna system, and that this added some combustible material to the revolutionary bonfire. This will happen under any system, during any peace. The idea that if the right kind of international politics and conditions prevail, no state or group will be so dissatisfied as to resort to violence, or that all problems will be solved by negotiation and compromise, is wildly utopian. The important fact is that the Vienna system, in a literal sense, *allowed* revolutions to happen. The main reason revolution could sweep like wildfire through most of Europe in February and March 1848 was that Europe's governments were mainly conservative, legalistic, and peaceful, restrained by treaties and the rules of the essentially co-operative, consensual game they had learned to play. They were inhibited from using force against their own peoples or each other. No regime in Europe, therefore, adopted preemptive war or violence as an anti-revolutionary strategy in 1848; Austria actively considered it, but thought better of it in the end. Nor did

developments in colonial self-government in this period, esp. in Canada, see Burroughs (1984).

[50] D. Johnson (1963: 200–3). For general accounts of the background to the February Revolution, see ibid. 189–262; Jardin and Tudesq (1984: 191–204). For a convincing argument that the 1840s were actually decisive years of change and progress in France, see Pinkney (1986).

any government try to solve its internal troubles by mobilizing the masses against foreign enemies through hyper-nationalism and imperialism—the solution the French revolutionary government had more or less consciously chosen to solve its internal conflicts in 1792, and one which regimes of various stripes have frequently resorted to down to our own time.

These attitudes on the part of Europe's leaders were no secret, least of all to the revolutionaries. It is striking to see how much the radical leaders in 1848 expected governments to remain the passive targets of their attacks; when governments stopped playing this role and began fighting back, the revolutions were quickly over. A good part of this initial passivity and restraint derived from governments having lived for thirty-three years under an international system dedicated to general peace and bounded by legalistic rules and restraints.

This indicates for what ends the Vienna system and its prevailing rules, norms, procedures, and practices were still useful in 1848. True, under certain circumstances they could still be used to enforce the Metternich system of internal governance (for instance, Cracow). But in this respect the system was becoming increasingly obsolescent and unusable. Well before the main revolutions broke out in 1848, it had broken down as a way of mobilizing international action to repress revolts in Italy, Germany, or Switzerland. In 1848, initially at least, it failed for this purpose everywhere. Yet as a way of preserving a political balance in Europe, i.e. a way of maintaining the independence, vital interests, and status of essential actors, balancing their rights and satisfactions with their various roles and obligations, and enabling them to pursue their individual ends within the European community without violent collisions, the 1815 system was in 1848 still as necessary and effective as it had ever been.

The revolutions themselves would prove it. Without trying here to describe them and their international consequences,[51] one can say what they reveal about the 1815 system. In 1848 the old absolutist and conservative regimes would collapse almost without a fight, and be quickly followed in that collapse by a good number of liberal and nationalist ministries that succeeded them. The upheaval would produce political and social conflict, uncertainty, and revolutionary violence more extensive than that of 1789 and after. Major civil and international struggles would

---

[51] That subject belongs to another volume in this series, Taylor (1954)—a masterly work, though starting from premises different from my own.

break out in France, Germany, Italy, Austria, and the Balkans. Every important European question would be thrown up in one form or another, every major power and many lesser ones would risk being drawn into war. Several important states (Austria, Prussia, Russia, Sardinia-Piedmont, Denmark) would actually become involved in international conflict.

Yet no war between major powers would occur; in fact, except for a brief showdown between Austria and Prussia in 1850 after the revolutions were over, no serious threat of major war would ever arise. The lesser conflicts would be settled quickly, most of them peacefully. All the issues, including thorny ones like those in Schleswig-Holstein, northern Italy, Hungary, and the Near East, would be settled in a way that left the international system still intact—every treaty still in force, every state boundary unchanged. This astounding, almost inexplicable outcome would occur, moreover, after thirty-three years of general peace, long after the war-weariness and conservative monarchic solidarity to which many scholars attribute the tranquillity and stability of post-1815 Europe had vanished. Such an outcome would have been inconceivable in any other era of European history.

Along with this, the 1848 revolutions show that the Vienna system, though a strong web, was only a web. Like any international regime, it could be cut all at once, or frayed and snapped a strand at a time. Every force and movement hostile to the Vienna system came to the fore in 1848 or fairly soon thereafter: revolutionary democratic utopianism, integral romantic nationalism, and above all, traditional power politics in various ideological guises, liberal, pseudo-liberal, neo-absolutist, and opportunist.

These diverse trends undermining the Vienna system shared a basic feature, older than 1848 and still current today. It was the belief, or rather the unexamined assumption, that an international system and its constituent rules and practices are in themselves not of intrinsic value. Systems and rules, attitudes and assumptions, norms and principles, are only instrumental—artificial, manipulable, replaceable, existing for the particular ends of particular states, leaders, groups, causes, peoples. International regimes come and go; the game of international power politics goes on indefinitely. This was, and is, the heart of 'realism'.

This outlook, coming to the fore in 1848, shared to a large degree by right, centre, and left alike, represented a subtle but decisive shift from the collective mentality of the generation of 1815 and after. The statesmen of that era had supposedly pursued peace out of fear of revolution, promoting international harmony so as to preserve the domestic political, social, and economic order on which they and their class depended. As this book has argued, this is one of those near-misses in history often more harmful than plain falsehoods or gross distortions because they are just true enough to get in the way of deeper truths and insights and keep enquirers from digging further. The statesmen of the Vienna generation, to repeat, did not so much fear war because they thought it would bring revolution as because they had learned from bitter experience that war *was* revolution. Certainly they worried about the internal vulnerability of their governments, societies, and economies. But they had learned as well that something else even more fundamental to the existence of ordered society as they knew it was vulnerable and could be overthrown: the existence of any international order at all, the very possibility of their states' coexisting as independent members of a European family of nations. This was the main incentive for the construction of peace in 1813–15, and remained the great deterrent to international violence and war even under revolutionary circumstances in 1848. When someone like Metternich said, as he did at every turn in every crisis, that the existence of the social order was at stake, he meant first and foremost this international order. Like many others, he understood it in a narrow, aristocratic way and used it in a repressive one, and thereby helped to stultify its development and ultimately undermine it. Yet he and many of his generation also understood that an international order is not simply an instrument for the foreign policy of individual states, and must finally not be made into one. Beyond a certain point it cannot be manipulated for particular ends; nor, if destroyed, can it readily be replaced or a new one contrived. Existing to make foreign policy possible, the international order must to a considerable degree control and limit it; the central question the statesman must ask is not how he can use the international system to achieve his goals, but what kind of goals a workable international system allows him to pursue.

This sense of inherent limits, acceptance of mutual rules and restraints, common responsibility to certain standards of conduct, and loyalty to something beyond the aims of one's own state distinguished early nineteenth-century politics from what had preceded and would follow it. It made a different international politics, a different system, and a more stable, peaceful era possible.

It could not last forever, and did not. The élites which supported it and profited from it were too narrow in their outlook and limited in their social base. The system they set up, despite its undeniable improvements over previous systems, contained a number of unjust and unworkable features. The capacity of this system for absorbing and facilitating change and meeting new problems and challenges, though far greater than that of previous ones, was limited from the outset, and was stunted in important ways later on. Above all, the international order established in 1815 was too closely linked in the public mind, justly or unjustly, with a domestic political and social order already past its peak when this system was created, certain to be superseded or overthrown, and widely perceived as oppressive and stifling.

Thus the Vienna system, though not really in decay or obsolete *per se*, was no longer by 1848 functioning as it needed to or providing some of the goods it had to provide. As Edward Kolodziej contends, any international system, if it is to endure, must meet certain general demands for order, legitimacy, and welfare.[52] Order here means rules and procedures to keep relations among international actors from becoming a pure war of all against all; legitimacy means accepted criteria and procedures to legitimate the authority of governments both to act in international politics and to rule over their citizens; and welfare means at least the minimal satisfaction by those governments of the wants and needs of those governed, so that the international order will not be or seem to too many of them intolerably unjust and illegitimate. The Vienna system in 1848 continued to meet the demand for order; its rules for managing and containing conflict were still widely accepted and worked well. But it was ceasing to meet the requirements of legitimacy and welfare in the face of nationalism, liberalism, and accelerating economic change, and was therefore to some extent bound to the same ultimate fate as the Metternich system which had accompanied and burdened it.

Yet it left behind real accomplishments and lessons: the uses and importance of intermediary bodies, the values of concert and grouping methods, the management functions of restraining alliances and *ententes*, and more. Above all, this era proved that a political equilibrium in international affairs is possible without a balance of power, and more easily attained without balance-of-power methods, and that international politics, even if they remain structurally anarchic, involving relations between juridically coordinate states rather than superordinate and subordinate ones, can none the less be restrained by consensus and bounded by law.

[52] 'The Cold War as Cooperation', in Kanet and Kolodziej (1991: 3–30). Kolodziej's scheme is a refinement of the 3 requirements Hedley Bull (1977) lists: order, protection of property, and sanctity of contract.

The light that thus began to shine in international politics in 1815 was brief, fitful, and wintry. It would be followed by a long twilight and an even longer, bitterly cold night. Let there be no mistake, however: 1815 was not a false dawn. It marked a new day, and it helps make other new days thinkable.

Bibliography

Aberdeen, George Hamilton-Gordon, 4th Earl of (1938–9). *The Correspondence of Lord Aberdeen and Princess Lieven, 1832–1854*, ed. E. J. Parry. 2 vols., London.

Actes (1973). *Actes du colloque: patriotisme et nationalisme en Europe à l'époque de la révolution française et de Napoléon*. Paris.

Acton, H. (1956). *The Bourbons of Naples*. London.

Adair, Sir R. (1844). *Historical Memoir of a Mission to the Court of Vienna in 1806*. London.

—— (1845). *The Negotiations for the Peace of the Dardanelles in 1808–9*. 2 vols., London.

Adler, P. (1979). 'Nation and Nationalism among the Serbs of Hungary 1790–1870', *EEQ* 13: 271–85.

Adler-Bresse, M. (1976). *Siéyès et le monde allemand*. 2 vols., Paris.

Aengeneyndt, G. (1922). 'Die Okkupation des Kurfürstentums Hannover durch die Franzosen 1803', *Zeitschrift des historischen Vereins Niedersachsens*, 87: 1–79.

Agulhon, M. (1981). *Marianne into Battle: Republican Imagery and Symbolism in France, 1789–1880*. New York.

Alberti, A. (ed.) (1926–41). *Atti del parlamento delle Due Sicilie, 1820–1821*. 6 vols., Bologna.

Albion, R. G. (1926). *Forests and Sea Power: The Timber Problem of the Royal Navy, 1652–1862*. Cambridge, Mass.

Alder, G. H. (1972). 'Britain and the Defence of India: The Origins of the Problem, 1798–1815', *JAH* 6: 14–44.

—— (1974). 'The Key to India? Britain and the Herat Problem, 1830–1863', *MES* 10: 186–209, 287–311.

Alexander I, Tsar of Russia (1865). *Alexandre Ier et le prince Czartoryski, 1801–1823*, ed. L. Czartoryski. Paris.

Alexander, D. W. (1980). 'French Replacement Methods during the Peninsular War', *Military Affairs*, 44: 192–6.

—— (1985). *Rod of Iron: French Counterinsurgency Policy in Aragon during the Peninsular War*. Wilmington, Del.

Alexander, R. S. (1991). *Bonapartism and Revolutionary Tradition in France: The Féderés of 1815*. Cambridge.

Allardt von Nostitz, F. (1976). *Der Westfeldzug Suvorovs in der öffentlichen Meinung Englands*. Wiesbaden.

Allmayer-Beck, J. C. von (1968). 'Das Nachwirken Napoleons als Feldherr', in Groote and Müller (1968: 223–39).

Al-Sayyid Marsot, A. L. (1984). *Egypt in the Reign of Muhammad Ali.* New York.

Alstyne, R. W. (1936). 'The Central American Policy of Lord Palmerston, 1846–1848', *Hispanic American Historical Review*, 16: 339–59.

Altbauer, D. (1980). 'The Diplomats of Peter the Great', *JGO* 28: 1–16.

Alter, P. (1985). *Nationalismus.* Frankfurt.

Altgeld, W. (1984). *Das politische Italienbild der Deutschen zwischen Aufklärung und europäischer Revolution von 1848.* Tübingen.

Anderson, M. S. (1954). 'Great Britain and the Russo-Turkish War of 1768–1774', *EHR* 69: 39–58.

—— (1956). 'Great Britain and the Growth of the Russian Navy in the eighteenth Century', *Mariner's Mirror*, 42: 132–46.

—— (1958). 'The Great Powers and the Russian Annexation of the Crimea', *SEER* 38: 17–42.

—— (1959). *Britain's Discovery of Russia, 1553–1815.* New York.

—— (1966). *The Eastern Question 1774–1923.* London.

—— (1970). 'Eighteenth-Century Theories of the Balance of Power', in Hatton and Anderson (1970: 183–98).

Anderson, R. C. (1952). *Naval War in the Levant, 1557–1853.* Princeton, NJ.

Andics, E. (1963). *Das Bündnis Habsburg–Romanow.* Budapest.

—— (1973). *Metternich und die Frage Ungarns.* Budapest.

—— (1975). 'Szechenyi and Metternich', *Études historiques hongroises*, 1: 469–99.

Andreas, W. (1956). 'Carl August v. Weimar und das Angebot der ungarischen Königskrone', *MIOG*, 64: 291–311.

Angot, E. (1913). 'Talleyrand et le comte d'Hauterive', *Revue des questions historiques*, 93: 485–500.

Anna, T. E. (1983). *Spain and the Loss of America.* Lincoln, Nebr.

Anstey, R. (1972). 'A Re-interpretation of the Abolition of the British Slave Trade, 1806–1807', *EHR* 87: 304–32.

—— (1975). *The Atlantic Slave Trade and British Abolition 1760–1810.* London.

Applewhite, H. B. (1978). 'Political Legitimacy in Revolutionary France, 1788–91', *JIH* 9: 245–73.

Ardant, G. (1975). 'Financial Policy and Economic Infrastructure of Modern States and Nations', in C. Tilly (ed.), *The Formation of States in Western Europe*, 164–242. Princeton, NJ.

Arese, F. (1950). 'La Lombardia e la politica dell'Austria: un colloquio inedito del Metternich nel 1832', *Archivio storico lombardo*, 77: 5–57.

Aretin, K. O. F. von (1955). 'Metternichs Verfassungspläne 1817/1818', *Historisches Jahrbuch*, 74: 718–27.

—— (1958). 'Die Konfessionen als politische Kräfte am Ausgang des alten Reiches', in *Festgabe Joseph Lortz*, ii. 181–241. Baden-Baden.

—— (1967). *Heiliges Römisches Reich 1776–1806: Reichsverfassung und Staatssouveränität.* 2 vols., Wiesbaden.

—— (ed.) (1974). *Der aufgeklärte Absolutismus.* Cologne.

—— (1980). *Vom Deutschen Reich zum Deutschen Bund*. Göttingen.

—— (1981). 'Tausch, Teilung und Länderschacher als Folgen des Gleichgewichtssystem der europäischen Grossmächte', *JGMOD* 30: 53–68.

—— (1976). *Bayerns Weg zum souveränen Staat: Landstände und konstitutionelle Monarchie 1714–1818*. Munich.

Arneth, A. (1886). 'Graf Philipp Cobenzl und seine Memoiren', *Archiv für österreichische Geschichte*, 67: 1–181.

—— (1898). *Johann Freiherr von Wessenberg*. 2 vols., Vienna.

Arsh, G. L. (1976). *I. Kapodistria i grecheskoe natsional'no-osvoboditel'noe dvizhenie 1809–1822 gg*. Moscow.

Arthur, C. B. (1986). *The Remaking of the English Navy by Admiral St Vincent*. Lanham, Md.

Artola, M. (1976). *Los Afrancesados*. Madrid.

Artz, F. B. (1934). *Reaction and Revolution 1814–1832*. New York.

Askenasy, S. (1925). *Napoléon et la Pologne*. Brussels.

Atkin, M. (1979). 'The Pragmatic Diplomacy of Paul I: Russia's Relations with Asia, 1796–1801', *SR* 60–74.

—— (1980). *Russia and Iran, 1780–1828*. Minneapolis, Minn.

Aubert, R. (1967). 'Kirche und Staat in Belgien im 19. Jahrhundert', in Conze (1967: 5–25).

Auckland, W. E., 1st Lord (1861). *The Journal and Correspondence of William Lord Auckland*. 2 vols., London.

Aulard, A. (1902). 'La Diplomatie du premier comité de salut public', in *Études et leçons sur la révolution française*, 3rd ser., 51–240. Paris.

Austensen, R. A. (1969). 'The Early Career of Count Buol, 1837–1852', diss., Univ. of Illinois, Urbana.

—— (1986). 'Metternich and Charles Albert: Salt, Tariffs, and the Sardinian Challenge, 1844–1848', *PCRE* 16: 384–94.

Aymes, J. R. (1973). *La Guerre d'indépendance espagnole (1808–1814)*. Paris.

Baack, L. J. (1980). *Christian Bernstorff and Prussia, 1818–1832*. New Brunswick, NJ.

Baggally, J. W. (1938). *Ali Pasha and Great Britain*. Oxford.

Bailey, F. E. (1940). 'The Economics of British Foreign Policy, 1825–1850', *JMH* 12: 449–84.

—— (1942). *British Policy and the Turkish Reform Movement, 1826–1853*. London.

Bailleu, P. (ed.) (1881–7). *Preussen und Frankreich von 1795 bis 1807: Diplomatische Correspondenzen*. 2 vols., Leipzig.

—— (1900). *Friedrich Wilhelm III: Briefwechsel König Friedrich Wilhelms III und der Königin Luise mit Kaiser Alexander I*. Leipzig.

Baker, K. M. (ed.) (1987–9). *The French Revolution and the Creation of Modern Political Culture*. 3 vols., New York.

—— (1990). *Inventing the French Revolution*. New York.

Bakshi, S. R. (1971). *British Diplomacy and Administration in India, 1807–13*. New Delhi.

Baldwin, J. R. (1938). 'England and the French Seizure of the Society Islands', *JMH* 10: 212–31.

Bamford, P. W. (1956). *Forests and French Sea Power 1660–1789*. Toronto.

Barany, G. (1960). 'The Szechenyi Problem', *JCEA* 20: 251–69.

—— (1968). *Stephen Szechenyi and the Awakening of Hungarian Nationalism, 1791–1841*. Princeton, NJ.

Barbier, J. A. (1980). 'Peninsular Finance and Colonial Trade: The Dilemma of Charles IV's Spain', *Journal of Latin American Studies*, 12: 21–37.

—— and Klein, H. S. (1981). 'Revolutionary Wars and Public Finances: The Madrid Treasury, 1784–1807', *JEH* 41: 315–39.

Barnett, R. B. (1980). *North India between Empires: Ahwad, the Mughals and the British, 1720–1801*. Berkeley, Calif.

Barraclough, G. (1963). *European Unity in Thought and Action*. Oxford.

—— (1966). 'Europa, Amerika und Russland in Vorstellung und Denken des 19. Jahrhunderts', *HZ* 203: 280–315.

Barratt, G. (1983). *Russian Shadows on the British Northwest Coast of North America, 1810–1890*. Vancouver, BC.

Bartels, G. (1960). *Preussen im Urteil Hannovers 1815–1851*. Hildesheim, 1960.

Bartier, J. (1967). 'Politische Parteien und soziale Klassen in Belgien', in Conze (1967: 93–146).

Bartle, G. F. (1964). 'Bowring and the Near Eastern Crisis of 1838–1840', *EHR* 79: 761–74.

Bartlett, C. J. (1963). *Great Britain and Sea Power, 1815–1853*. Oxford.

—— (1966). *Castlereagh*. London.

Bartley, R. H. (1978). *Imperial Russia and the Struggle for Latin American Independence, 1808–1828*. Austin, Tex.

Barton, H. A. (1967). 'The Origins of the Brunswick Manifesto', *FHS* 5: 146–69.

—— (1975). *Count Hans Axel von Fersen*. Boston.

—— (1976). 'Gustav III of Sweden and the East Baltic 1771–1792', *Journal of Baltic Studies*, 7: 13–30.

—— (1986). *Scandinavia in the Revolutionary Era, 1760–1815*. Minneapolis, Minn.

Batalden, S. K. (1979). 'John Kapodistrias and the Structure of Greek Society on the Eve of the War of Independence', *EEQ* 13: 297–314.

Baugh, D. A. (1988). 'Great Britain's Blue-Water Policy, 1689–1815', *IHR* 10: 33–58.

—— (1988). 'Why Did Britain Lose Command of the Sea During the War for America?' in Black and Woodfine (1988: 149–69).

Baxa, J. (1973). 'Radetzky und der Sonderbund', *Schweizerische Zeitschrift für Geschichte*, 23: 510–26.

Bayley, C. A. (1989). *Imperial Meridian: The British Empire and the World 1780–1830*. London.

Beales, A. C. F. (1933–4). 'Wellington and Louis-Philippe, 1830', *History* 17: 352–6.

Beales, D. (1987). *Joseph II*, i. Cambridge.

Bearce, G. D. (1961). *British Attitudes toward India, 1784–1858*. Oxford.

Beaucour, F. (1982). 'Le Grand projet napoléonien d'expédition en Angleterre: mythe ou réalité', *PCRE*, 225–45.

Beer, A. (1872). 'Denkschriften des Fursten Wenzel Kaunitz–Rittberg', *AOG* 48: 3–162.

—— (1875). 'Zur Geschichte der österreichischen Politik in den Jahren 1801 und 1802', *AOG* 52: 475–540.

—— (1877a). *Die Finanzen Oesterreichs im XIX Jahrhundert*. Prague.

—— (1877b). *Zehn Jahre österreichischer Politik 1801–1810*. Leipzig.

—— (1883). *Die orientalische Politik Österreichs seit 1774*. Prague.

Behnen, M. (1986). 'Der gerechte und der notwendige Krieg', in Kunisch and Stollberg-Rillinger (1986: 43–106).

Behrens, C. B. A. (1985). *Society, Government, and the Enlightenment: The Experiences of Eighteenth-Century France and Prussia*. London.

Bell, H. F. C. (1936). *Lord Palmerston*. 2 vols., London.

Bennigsen, A. (1974). 'Peter the Great, the Ottoman Empire, and the Caucasus', *CASS* 8: 311–18.

Berce, Y.-M. (1987). *Revolt and Revolution in Early Modern Europe*. New York.

Berdahl, R. M. (1988). *The Politics of the Prussian Nobility*. Princeton, NJ.

Berding, H. (1973). *Napoleonische Herrschafts- und Gesellschaftspolitik im Königreich Westfalen 1807–1813*. Göttingen.

—— (1974). 'Die Ächtung des Sklavenhandels auf dem Wiener Kongress 1814/15', *HZ* 219: 265–89.

—— (1980). 'Die Reform des Zollwesens in Deutschland unter dem Einfluss der napoleonischen Herrschaft', *GG* 6: 523–37.

—— (1982). 'Le Royaume de Westphalie, état-modèle', *Francia*, 10: 345–58.

—— (1991). 'Französische Reformpolitik aus revolutionärem Anspruch in später preussischen Gebieten 1794 bis 1814', in Büsch and Neugebauer-Wölk (1991: 331–44).

—— François, E., and Ullmann, H.-P. (eds.) (1989). *Deutschland und Frankreich im Zeitalter der Französischen Revolution*. Frankfurt.

—— and Ullmann, H.-P. (eds.) (1981). *Deutschland zwischen Revolution und Restauration*. Düsseldorf.

Bergeron, L. (1970). 'Problèmes économiques de la France napoléonienne', *RHMC* 17: 469–505.

—— (1972). *L'Épisode napoléonien: aspects intérieurs, 1799–1815*. 2 vols., Paris.

—— (1973). 'Remarques sur les conditions du développement industriel en Europe occidentale à l'époque napoléonienne', *Francia*, 1: 537–56.

Berkeley, G. F. H., and Berkeley, J. (1932–40). *Italy in the Making, 1815–1848*. 3 vols., Cambridge.

Berl, E. (1971). 'Denn wie Karthago muss auch England zerstört werden', in Sieburg (1971: 161–70).

Bernard, H. (1965). *Guerre totale et guerre révolutionnaire*. 3 vols., Brussels.

Bernard, P. (1965). *Joseph II and Bavaria: Two Eighteenth Century Attempts at German Unification*. The Hague.

Bertaud, J.-P. (1972). *Bonaparte et le duc d'Enghien*. Paris.

—— (1983). 'Les Officiers de carrière et l'armée nationale à l'époque de la révolution française', *International Review of Military History*, 55: 71–80.

—— (1988). *The Army of the French Revolution*. Princeton, NJ.

Bertier, G. de (1948). *Le Comte Ferdinand de Bertier et l'énigme de la congrégation*. Paris.

—— (1958). *France and the European Alliance, 1816–1821: The Private Correspondence between Metternich and Richelieu*. Notre Dame, Ind.

—— (1959). *Metternich et son temps*. Paris.

—— (1960). 'Sainte-Alliance et alliance dans les conceptions de Metternich', *RH* 223: 249–74.

—— (1966). *The Bourbon Restoration*. Philadelphia.

—— (1968–71). *Metternich et la France après le Congrès de Vienne*. 3 vols., Paris.

—— (1981). 'The Bourbon Restoration: One Century of French Historiography', *FHS* 12: 41–67.

—— (1986). *Metternich*. Paris.

Best, G. (1980). *Humanity in Warfare*. New York.

—— (1982). *War and Society in Revolutionary Europe, 1770–1870*. New York.

Bethell, L. M. (1965). 'Britain and the Suppression of the Brazilian Slave Trade', *EHR* 80: 761–84.

Betley, J. A. (1960). *Belgium and Poland in International Relations 1830–1831*. The Hague.

Bettanini, A. M. (1939). 'Un disegno de confederazione italiana nella politica internazionale della restaurazione', in *Studi di storia dei trattati e politica internazionale*, 3–50. Padua.

Beyrau, D. (1984). *Militär und Gesellschaft im vorrevolutionären Russland*. Cologne.

Biaudet, J. C. (1941). *La Suisse et la monarchie de juillet, 1830–1838*. Lausanne.

Bien, D. (1979). 'The Army in the French Enlightenment: Reform, Reaction, and Revolution', *PP* 85: 68–98.

Bilger, F. (1931). '"Grossdeutsche" Politik im Lager Radetzkys', *Historische Blätter*, 4: 3–36.

Billinger, R. D. Jr. (1976). 'The War Scare of 1831 and Prussian–South German Plans for the End of Austrian Dominance in Germany', *CEH* 9: 203–19.

—— (1991). *Metternich and the German Question: States' Rights and Federal Duties, 1820–1834*. Newark, Del.

Bindoff, S. T. (1935). 'The Unreformed Diplomatic Service, 1812–60', *TRHS*, 4th ser., 18: 143–72.

Birke, A. (1960). *Frankreich und Ostmitteleuropa im 19. Jahrhundert*. Cologne.

Biro, S. S. (1957). *The German Policy of Revolutionary France*. 2 vols., Cambridge, Mass.

Biskup, M. (1983). 'Preussen und Polen. Grundlinien und Reflexionen', *JGO* 31: 1–27.

Bissing, W. von (1967). *Friedrich Wilhelm II*. Berlin.

Bitterauf, T. (1905). *Geschichte des Rheinbundes*. Munich.

—— (1914). 'Studien zur preussischen Politik im Jahre 1805', *FBPG* 27: 431–515.

Blaas, R. (1972). 'Metternich, Mazzini und die Gründung der Giovine Italia', *MOS* 25: 595–616.

Black, C. E. (1942–43). 'Fouché in Illyria: 1813', *JCEA* 2: 386–95.

Black, J. (1984). 'The Marquis of Carmarthen and Relations with France, 1784–1787', *Francia*, 12: 283–304.

—— (1986). *Natural and Necessary Enemies*. London.

—— (1987a). 'Anglo-French Relations in the Age of the French Revolution 1787–1793', *Francia*, 15: 407–33.

—— (ed.) (1987b). *The Origins of War in Early Modern Europe*. Edinburgh.

—— (1988). 'England's Foreign Alliances in the Eighteenth Century', *Albion*, 20: 573–602.

—— (1990). *The Rise of the European Powers, 1679–1793*. London.

—— and Woodfine, P. S. (eds.) (1988). *The British Navy and the Use of Naval Power in the eighteenth Century*. Leicester.

Black, J. L. (1981). 'Nicholas Karamzin's "Opinion" on Poland: 1819', *IHR* 3: 1–19.

Blainey, G. (1977). *The Causes of Wars*. Melbourne.

Blanning, T. C. W. (1974). *Reform and Revolution in Mainz, 1743–1803*. New York.

—— (1977). 'George III and the Fürstenbund', *HJ* 20: 311–44.

—— (1980). 'German Jacobins and the French Revolution', *HJ* 23: 985–1002.

—— (1983). *The French Revolution in Germany. Occupation and Resistance in the Rhineland 1792–1802*. Oxford.

—— (1986). *The Origins of the French Revolutionary Wars*. London.

—— (1988). 'Die französischen Revolutionsarmeen in Deutschland: der Feldzug von 1796', in Melville (1988: 489–504).

—— (1991). 'The French Revolution and Europe', in C. Lucas (ed.), *Rewriting the French Revolution*, 183–206. Oxford.

Blum, J. (1978). *The End of the Old Order in Rural Europe*. Princeton, NJ.

Blumenthal, H. (1970). *France and the United States: Their Diplomatic Relations, 1789–1914*. Chapel Hill, NC.

Boldt, H. (1975). *Deutsche Staatslehre im Vormärz*. Düsseldorf.

Bolkhovitinov, N. N. (1975). *The Beginnings of Russian–American Relations, 1775–1815*. Cambridge, Mass.

Bolsover, G. H. (1934–5). 'Lord Ponsonby and the Eastern Question (1833–1839)', *Slavonic Review*, 13: 98–118.

—— (1936a). 'Palmerston, Metternich and the Eastern Question in 1834', *EHR* 51: 237–56.

—— (1936b). 'David Urquhart and the Eastern Question in 1833–37', *JMH* 8: 444–67.

Bolsover, G. H. (1948). 'Nicholas I and the Partition of Turkey', *Slavonic Review*, 27: 115–45.

Bond, G. C. (1974). 'Louis Bonaparte and the Collapse of the Kingdom of Holland', *PCRE*, 141–53.

—— (1979). *The Grand Expedition: The British Invasion of Holland in 1809.* Athens, Ga.

Bonjour, E. (1956). 'Die Idee des europäischen Gleichgewichts bei Johannes von Muller', *HZ* 182: 527–48.

—— (1958). *Die Schweiz und Europa.* Basle.

—— (1965). *Geschichte der schweizerischen Neutralität.* 2 vols., Basle.

Bonnel, U. (1961). *La France, les États-Unis et la guerre de course, 1797– 1815.* Paris.

Boogman, J. C. (1955). *Nederland en de Duitse Bond, 1815–1851.* 2 vols., Groningen.

—— (1966). 'Background and General Tendencies of the Foreign Policies of the Netherlands and Belgium in the Middle of the Nineteenth Century', *Acta Historiae Neerlandica*, 1: 132–58.

—— (1968a). 'The Netherlands in the European Scene', in Bromley and Kossman (1968: 138–59).

—— (1968b). *Die Suche nach der nationalen Identität: Die Niederlande 1813– 1848.* Wiesbaden.

Borejza, J. (1979). 'Porträt eines polnischen Revolutionärs—eine vergleichende Studie', in Conze *et al.* (1979: 93–112).

Born, K. E. (1957). 'Hardenbergs Pläne und Versuche einer Neuordnung Europas und Deutschlands 1813–15', *GWU* 8: 550–64.

Bortolotti, S. (1942). 'Austria e Francia a Napoli negli anni 1846–47', *NRS* 27: 439–53.

—— (1945). *Metternich e l'Italia nel 1846.* Turin.

Bosher, J. F. (1970). *French Finances 1770–1795. From Business to Bureaucracy.* Cambridge.

Botzenhart, M. (1967). *Metternichs Pariser Botschafterzeit.* Münster.

Bouloiseau, M. (1984). *The Jacobin Republic, 1792–1794.* Cambridge.

Bourel, D. (1991). 'Zwischen Abwehr und Neutralität: Preussen und die Französische Revolution 1789 bis 1795/1795 bis 1803/1806', in Büsch and Neugebauer-Wölk (1991: 43–57).

Bourne, K. (1970). *The Foreign Policy of Victorian England, 1830–1902.* Oxford.

—— (1982). *Palmerston: The Early Years, 1784–1841.* New York.

Bourquin, M. (1954). *Histoire de la sainte alliance.* Geneva.

Bouvier, J. (1970). 'À propos de la crise dite de 1805: les crises économiques sous l'empire', *RHMC* 17: 506–13.

Boyer, F. (1964). 'Les Résponsabilités de Napoléon dans le transfert à Paris des œuvres d'art de l'étranger', *RHMC* 11: 241–62.

Brandt, H.-H. (1978). *Der österreichische Neoabsolutismus: Staatsfinanzen und Politik 1848–1860.* 2 vols., Göttingen.

Brandt, O. (1929). 'Das Problem der "Ruhe des Nordens" im 18. Jahrhundert', *HZ* 140: 550–64.

Branig, H. (1981). *Fürst Wittgenstein: Ein preussischer Staatsmann der Restaurationszeit.* Cologne.

Braubach, M. (1976). 'Vom Westfälischen Frieden bis zum Wiener Kongress (1648–1815)', in F. Petri and G. Droege (eds.), *Rheinische Geschichte*, ii. 219–365. Düsseldorf.

Brauer, K., and Wright, W. E. (eds.) (1990). *Austria in the Age of the French Revolution, 1789–1815.* Minneapolis.

Braun, R. (1975). 'Taxation, Sociopolitical Structure, and State-Building: Great Britain and Brandenburg-Prussia', in Tilly (1975: 243–327).

Braunstein, D. (1983). *Französische Kolonialpolitik 1830–1852.* Wiesbaden.

Brewer, J. (1988). 'The English State and Fiscal Appropriation, 1688–1789', *Politics and Society*, 16: 335–85.

—— (1989). *The Sinews of Power: War, Money and the English State, 1688–1783.* New York.

Bridge, F. R. (1979). 'Allied Diplomacy in Peacetime: The Failure of the Congress "System"', in Sked (1979a: 34–53).

—— (1990). *The Habsburg Monarchy among the Great Powers, 1815–1914.* New York.

Broadus, J. R. (1981). 'Soviet Historians and the Eastern Question of the Eighteenth Century', *EEQ* 15: 357–75.

Brogan, H. (1971). 'Alexis de Tocqueville and the Liberal Movement', *HJ* 14: 289–303.

Bromley, J. S. (1981). 'Britain and Europe in the Eighteenth Century', *History*, 66: 394–412.

—— and Kossman, E. H. (eds.) (1968). *Britain and the Netherlands in Europe and Asia.* London.

Brown, M. L. (1978). 'The Comité Franco-Polonais and the French Reaction to the Polish Uprising of November 1830', *EHR* 93: 774–93.

—— (1980). 'The Polish Question and Public Opinion in France, 1830–1846', *Antemurale*, 24: 77–299.

Bruguière, M. (1973). 'Remarques sur les rapports financiers entre la France et l'Allemagne du nord a l'époque napoléonienne: Hambourg et "le parti de la paix"', *Francia*, 1: 467–81.

Brunner, O. (1968). 'Vom Gottesgnadentum zum monarchischen Prinzip: Der Weg der europäischen Monarchie seit dem hohen Mittelalter', in *Neue Wege der Verfassungs- und Sozialgeschichte*, 2nd edn., 160–86. Göttingen.

Brun-zejmis, J. (1980). 'The "Russian Idea" and the "Polish Question": Some Russian Views on the Polish Insurrection of 1830', *EEQ* 14: 315–26.

Brusatti, A. (ed.) (1973). *Die Wirtschaftliche Entwicklung*, i: *Die Habsburgermonarchie 1848–1918*, ed. A. Wandruszka and P. Urbanitsch. Vienna.

Buckland, C. S. B. (1932). *Metternich and the British Government from 1809 to 1813.* London.

Büsch, O. (1962). *Militärsystem und Sozialleben im alten Preussen, 1713–1807.* Berlin.

Büsch, O. and Neugebauer-Wölk, M. (eds.) (1991). *Preussen und die revolutionäre Herausforderung seit 1789*. Berlin.

Büssem, E. (1974). *Die Karlsbader Beschlüsse von 1819*. Hildesheim.

Bull, H. (1977). *The Anarchical Society*. New York.

Bullen, R. (1971). 'Guizot and the "Sonderbund" Crisis, 1846–1848', *EHR* 86: 497–526.

—— (1974a). 'Anglo-French Rivalry and Spanish Politics, 1846–1848', *EHR* 89: 25–47.

—— (1974b). 'England, Spain and the Portuguese Question in 1833', *European Studies Review*, 4: 1–22.

—— (1974c). *Palmerston, Guizot and the Collapse of the Entente Cordiale*. London.

—— (1977). 'France and the Problem of Intervention in Spain, 1834–1836', *HJ* 20: 363–94.

—— (1978). 'Party Politics and Foreign Policy: Whigs, Tories, and Iberian Affairs 1830–6', *Bulletin of the Institute of Historical Research* (Univ. of London), 51: 37–59.

—— (ed.) (1982). *The Foreign Office, 1782–1982*. Frederick, Md.

Burg, P. (1978). 'Die französische Politik gegenüber Föderationen und Föderationsplänen deutscher Klein- und Mittelstaaten 1830–1833', in Poidevin and Sieburg (1978: 17–45).

—— (1984). *Der Wiener Kongress: Der Deutsche Bund im europäischen Staatensystem*. Munich.

—— (1989). *Der deutsche Trias in Idee und Wirklichkeit: Vom alten Reich zum Deutschen Zollverein*. Wiesbaden.

Burgos, M. E. (1988). 'The Spanish Army during the Crisis of the Old Regime', in R. Martinez and T. Barker (eds.), *Armed Forces and Society in Spain Past and Present*, 81–103. New York.

Burroughs, P. (1984). 'Colonial Self-Government', in Eldridge (1984: 34–64).

Bury, J. P. T., and Combs, R. T. (1986). *Thiers, 1797–1877*. London.

Buschkühl, M. (1982). *Great Britain and the Holy See, 1746–1870*. Dublin.

Buse, D. (1987). 'Lower-Class German Nationalism in Bremen in 1815: Some Preliminary Observations', *Canadian Review of Studies in Nationalism*, 14: 93–103.

Butler, I. (1973). *The Eldest Brother: The Marquess Wellesley, the Duke of Wellington's Eldest Brother*. London.

Butterfield, H. (1929). *The Peace Tactics of Napoleon, 1806–1808*. Cambridge.

Cabanis, A. (1985). *La Presse sous le Consulat et l'Empire (1799–1814)*. Paris.

Cahen, L. (1939). 'Une nouvelle interprétation du traité franco-anglaise de 1786–7', *RH* 185: 257–85.

Calder, A. (1981). *Revolutionary Empire: The Rise of the English-Speaking Empires from the Fifteenth Century to the 1780's*. New York.

Calmès, A. (1932–57). *Histoire contemporaine du Grand-Duché de Luxembourg*. 5 vols., Brussels.

Cambacérès, J. J. de (1973). *Lettres inédites à Napoleon, 1802–1814*, ed. J. Tulard. 2 vols., Paris.

Canning, G. (1887). *Some Official Correspondence of George Canning*, ed. E. Stapleton. 2 vols., London.

Cantù, C. (1884). *Corrispondenze di Diplomatici della Repubblica e del Regno d'Italia 1796–1814*. Milan.

Caron, F. (1979). *An Economic History of Modern France*. New York.

Carr, R. (1966). *Spain: 1808–1939*. Oxford.

Carr, W. (1963). *Schleswig-Holstein, 1815–48: A Study in Conflict*. Manchester.

Carter, A. C. (1968). 'Britain as a European Power from Her Glorious Revolution to the French Revolution', in Bromley and Kossman (1968: 110–37).

—— (1975). *Neutrality and Commitment: The Evolution of Dutch Foreign Policy, 1667–1795*. London.

Castillon du Perron, M. (1984). *Louis-Philippe et la Révolution française*. Paris.

Castlereagh: Londonderry, R. Stewart, 2nd Marquess of (1850–53). *Memoirs and Correspondence of Viscount Castlereagh, Second Marquess of Londonderry*, ed. C. V. Stewart, 3rd Marquess of Londonderry. 12 vols., London.

Cattaui, R., and Cattaui, G. (1950). *Mohamed-Aly et l'Europe*. Paris.

Caulaincourt, A.-A.-L. (1935). *Memoirs*. 2 vols., London.

Cegielski, T. (1982). 'Preussische Deutschland- und Polenpolitik in dem Zeitraum 1740–1792', in Zernack (1982: 21–7).

—— (1988). *Das alte Reich und die erste Teilung Polens 1768–1774*. Stuttgart.

Cernovodeanu, P. (1976). 'British Economic Interests in the Lower Danube and the Balkan Shore of the Black Sea between 1803 and 1829', *Journal of European Economic History*, 5: 105–20.

Chadwick, O. (1981). *The Popes and European Revolution*. Oxford.

Chamberlain, M. E. (1983). *Lord Aberdeen: A Political Biography*. London.

—— (1989). *'Pax Britannica'? British Foreign Policy 1789–1914*. London.

Chandler, D. G. (1966). *The Campaigns of Napoleon*. New York.

Charles-Roux, F. (1951). *Thiers et Méhémet-Ali*. Paris.

Chateaubriand, F. Vicomte de (1838). *Congrès de Vérone; Guerre d'Espagne; Négociations; Colonies espagnoles*. 2 vols., Paris.

Chaumié, J. (1965). *Le Réseau d'Antraigues et le contre-révolution (1791–93)*. Paris.

Chichagov, P. V. (1909). *Mémoires de l'amiral Pavel Tchitchagov*. Paris.

Childs, J. (1982). *Armies and Warfare in Europe, 1648–1789*. New York.

Chodzko, L. J. B. (pseud. le Comte d'Angeberg) (ed.) (1863). *Le Congrès de Vienne et les traités de 1815*. 4 vols., Paris.

Choldin, M. T. (1985). *Fence around the Empire: Russian Censorship of Western Ideas under the Tsars*. Durham, NC.

Christiansen, E. (1967). *The Origins of Military Power in Spain, 1800–1854*. London.

Christie, I. R. (1982). *Wars and Revolutions: Britain 1760–1815*. London.

Christie, I. R. (1984). *Stress and Stability in Late Eighteenth Century Britain.* New York.

Chroust, A. (1932). *Geschichte des Grossherzogtums Würzburg (1806–1814).* Würzburg.

—— (ed.) (1935–9). *Gesandschaftsberichte aus München,* Abteilung 1: *Die Berichte des französischen Gesandten (1816–1848).* 5 vols., Munich.

—— (ed.) (1939–42). *Gesandtschaftsberichte aus München,* Abteilung 2: *Die Berichte des österreichischen Gesandten.* 4 vols., Munich.

—— (ed.) (1949–51). *Gesandschaftsberichte aus München,* Abteilung 3: *Die Berichte des preussischen Gesandten.* 5 vols., Munich.

Church, C. H. (1981). *Revolution and Red Tape: The French Ministerial Bureaucracy, 1770–1850.* New York.

—— (1983). *Europe in 1830: Revolution and Political Change.* Boston.

Ciachir, N. (1979). 'The Adrianople Treaty (1829) and its European Implications', *RESEE* 17: 695–714.

Ciragan, E. O. (1952). *La Politique ottomane pendant les guerres de Napoléon Ier.* Aurillac.

Clark, J. C. D. (1985). *English Society 1688–1832.* Cambridge.

Clayton, G. D. (1971). *Britain and the Eastern Question: Missolonghi to Gallipoli.* London.

Cleyet-Michaud, R. (1972). 'Un Diplomate de la révolution: François Cacault et ses plans de conquête de l'Italie (1793–1796)', *RHD* 86: 308–32.

Clogg, R. (1969). 'The "Dhidhaskalia Patriki" 1798: An Orthodox Reaction to French Revolutionary Propaganda', *MES* 5: 87–115.

—— (ed.) (1973). *The Struggle for Greek Independence.* Hamden, Conn.

Cobb, R. (1972). *Reactions to the French Revolution.* New York.

—— (1987). *The People's Armies.* New Haven, Conn.

Cobban, A. (1954). *Ambassadors and Secret Agents: The Diplomacy of the First Earl of Malmesbury at the Hague.* London.

—— (1968). *Aspects of the French Revolution.* New York.

Cole, H. (1971). *Fouché: The Unprincipled Patriot.* London.

—— (1972). *The Betrayers: Joachim and Caroline Murat.* London.

Colenbrander, H. T. (ed.) (1905–22). *Gedenkstukken van der algemeene Geschiedenis van Nederland van 1795 tot 1840.* 22 vols., The Hague.

Colley, L. (1984). 'The Apotheosis of George III: Loyalty, Royalty and the British Nation 1760–1820', *PP* 102: 94–129.

Collingham, H. A. C.; with Alexander, R. S. (1988). *The July Monarchy: A Political History of France, 1830–1848.* London.

Collins, I. (1959). *The Government and the Newspaper Press in France, 1814–1881.* Oxford.

—— (1979). *Napoleon and his Parliaments, 1800–1815.* New York.

Colloque Guizot (1976). *Actes du colloque François Guizot, Paris, 22–25 Octobre 1974.* Paris.

Colombo, A. (1927). 'La rivoluzione piemontese secondo fonti austriache', in Rossi and de Magistris (1927: ii. 636–741).

—— (1932). 'Carlo Alberto e la vertenza Austro-Sarda nel 1846', *Il Risorgimento Italiano*, 25: 1–75.

Connelly, O. (1966). *Napoleon's Satellite Kingdoms*. New York.

—— (1987). *Blundering to Glory: Napoleon's Military Campaigns*. Wilmington, Del.

Contamine, H. (1970). *Diplomatie et diplomates sous la Restauration, 1814–1830*. Paris.

Conze, W. (1964). 'Nation und Gesellschaft: Zwei Grundbegriffe der revolutionären Epoche', *HZ* 198: 1–16.

—— (ed.) (1967). *Beiträge zur deutschen und belgischen Verfassungsgeschichte im 19. Jahrhundert*. Stuttgart.

—— (ed.) (1978). *Staat und Gesellschaft im deutschen Vormärz, 1815–1848*. Stuttgart.

—— Schramm, G., and Zernack, K. (eds.) (1979). *Modernisierung und nationale Gesellschaft im ausgehenden 18. und im 19. Jahrhundert*. Berlin.

Cook, W. L. (1973). *Flood Tide of Empire: Spain and the Pacific Northwest, 1543–1819*. New Haven, Conn.

Cookson, J. E. (1982). *The Friends of Peace: Anti-War Liberalism in England, 1793–1815*. Cambridge.

Coons, R. E. (1975). *Steamships, Statesmen, and Bureaucrats: Austrian Policy toward the Steam Navigation Company of the Austrian Lloyd 1836–1848*. Wiesbaden.

—— (1977). 'Metternich and the Lloyd Austriaco', *MOS* 30: 49–66.

Cooper, R. (1982). 'William Pitt, Taxation, and the Needs of War', *JBS* 22: 94–103.

Coppa, F. (1969). '"Realpolitik" and Conviction in the Conflict between Piedmont and the Papacy during the Risorgimento', *CHR* 54: 579–612.

Corciulo, M. S. (1983). 'Les Élections à la "chambre introuvable" en áout 1815', *Parliament, Estates and Representation*, 3: 123–34.

Corvisier, A. (1979). *Armies and Societies in Europe, 1494–1789*. Bloomington, Ind.

Costeloe, M. P. (1981). 'Spain and the Latin American Wars of Independence: The Free Trade Controversy, 1810–1820', *Hispanic American Historical Review*, 61: 209–34.

—— (1986). *Response to Revolution: Imperial Spain and the Spanish American Revolutions, 1810–1840*. Cambridge.

Costin, W. C. (1937). *Great Britain and China, 1833–1860*. Oxford.

Coverdale, J. F. (1984). *The Basque Phase of Spain's First Carlist War*. Princeton, NJ.

Coville, A., and Temperley, H. W. V. (eds.) (1935). *Studies in Anglo-French History during the Eighteenth, Nineteenth, and Twentieth Centuries*. Cambridge.

Cowles, L. (1990). 'The Failure to Restrain Russia: Canning, Nesselrode, and the Greek Question, 1825–1827', *IHR* 12: 688–720.

Cox, G. P. (1987). 'The Crisis of 1840 in the Continuum of French Strategic Planning', *PCRE* 17: 561–72.

Crafts, N. F. R. (1984). 'Economic Growth in France and Britain, 1830–1910: A Review of the Evidence', *JEH* 44: 49–68.

Craig, G. A. (1956). *The Politics of the Prussian Army, 1640–1945*. New York.

Crawley, C. W. (1929). 'Anglo-Russian Relations, 1815–1840', *Cambridge Historical Journal*, 3: 47–73.

—— (1930). *The Question of Greek Independence: A Study of British Policy in the Near East, 1821–1833*. Cambridge.

—— (ed.) (1970). *John Capodistrias: Some Unpublished Documents*. Thessaloniki.

Craybecxx, J. (1968). 'Les Débuts de la révolution industrielle en Belgique et la statistiques de la fin de l'empire', in *Mélanges offerts à G. Jacquemyns*, 115–44. Brussels.

Crimmins, P. (1988). 'The Royal Navy and the Levant Trade, *c.*1795–*c.*1805', in Black and Woodfine (1988: 221–36).

Criste, O. (1912). *Erzherzog Carl von Österreich*. 3 vols., Vienna.

Crook, M. H. (1980). 'Federalism and the French Revolution: The Revolt of Toulon in 1793', *History*, 65: 583–97.

Crosby, A. W. Jr. (1965). *America, Russia, Hemp, and Napoleon: American Trade with Russia and the Baltic, 1783–1812*. Columbus, OH.

Cross, A. G. (ed.) (1979). *Great Britain and Russia in the Eighteenth Century: Contacts and Comparisons*. Newtonville, Mass.

—— (1983). 'Russian Perceptions of England, and Russian National Awareness at the End of the Eighteenth and the Beginning of the Nineteenth Centuries', *SEER* 61: 89–106.

Crout, R. R. (1983). 'In Search of a "Just and Lasting Peace": The Treaty of 1783, Louis XVI, Vergennes, and the Regeneration of the Realm', *IHR* 5: 364–98.

Crouzet, F. (1958). *L'Économie britannique et le blocus continental (1803–1813)*. 2 vols., Paris.

—— (1964). 'Wars, Blockades and Economic Change in Europe, 1792–1815', *JEH* 24: 567–88.

—— (1980). 'Toward an Export Economy: British Exports during the Industrial Revolution', *Explorations in Economic History*, 17: 48–93.

—— (1989). 'The Impact of the French Wars on the British Economy', in Dickinson (1989: 189–210).

Cunningham, A. B. (1957). 'Peel, Aberdeen and the Entente Cordiale', *BIHR* 30: 189–206.

—— (1964–5). 'The Oczakov Debate', *MES* 1: 209–37.

—— (1978). 'The Philhellenes, Canning and Greek Independence', *MES* 14: 151–81.

Curtiss, J. S. (1965). *The Russian Army under Nicholas I, 1825–1855*. Durham, NC.

Czartoryski, A. J. (1988). *Memoirs of Prince Adam Czartoryski and his Correspondence with Alexander I*, ed. A. Gielgud. 2 vols., London.

Dakin, D. (1973). *The Greek Struggle for Independence, 1821–1833*. Berkeley, Calif.

Dann, O. (ed.) (1978). *Nationalismus und sozialer Wandel in Deutschland.* Hamburg.

—— (1979). 'Der politische Strukturwandel und das Problem der Nationsbildung in Deutschland um die Wende des 18. Jahrhunderts', in Conze (1979: 48–58).

—— (ed.) (1986). *Nationalismus in vorindustrieller Zeit.* Munich.

Danziger, R. (1977). *Abdal-Qadir and the Algerians: Resistance to the French and Internal Consolidation.* New York.

Dard, E. (1937). *Napoleon and Talleyrand.* New York.

Darmstadt, R. (1971). *Der deutsche Bund in der zeitgenössischen Publizistik.* Berne.

Davies, N. (1982). *God's Playground: A History of Poland.* 2 vols., New York.

Davis, H. W. C. (1926). 'The Great Game in Asia, 1800–44', *Proceedings of the British Academy,* 12: 227–56.

Davis, J. A. (1982). 'Palmerston and the Sicilian Sulphur Crisis of 1840: An Episode in the Imperialism of Free Trade', *Risorgimento,* 3: 5–24.

Davis, W. W. (1974). *Joseph II: An Imperial Reformer for the Austrian Netherlands.* The Hague.

Davison, R. H. (1976). ' "Russian Skill and Turkish Imbecility": The Treaty of Kuchuk Kainardij [*sic*] Reconsidered', *SR* 35: 463–83.

Deak, I. (1979). *The Lawful Revolution: Louis Kossuth and the Hungarians, 1848–1849.* New York.

Deane, S. (1988). *The French Revolution and Enlightenment in England 1789–1832.* Cambridge, Mass.

Dechamps, J. (1949). *Entre la guerre et la paix: les îles britanniques et la révolution française (1798–1803).* Brussels.

DeClercq, A. (ed.) (1880–1917). *Recueil des traités de la France.* 23 vols., Paris.

De Conde, A. (1966). *The Quasi-War: The Politics and Diplomacy of the Undeclared Naval War with France, 1797–1801.* New York.

Dehio, L. (1948). *Gleichgewicht oder Hegemonie.* Krefeld.

Demel, W. (1983). *Der bayerische Staatsabsolutismus, 1806/08–1817: Staats- und gesellschaftspolitische Motivationen und Hintergründe der Reformära in der ersten Phase des Königreichs Bayern.* Munich.

Demelitsch, F. (1898). *Metternich und seine auswartige Politik.* Stuttgart.

Demoulin, R. (1938). *Guillaume Ier et la transformation économique des provinces belges (1815–1930).* Liège.

—— (1960). 'L'Influence française sur la naissance de l'état belge', *RH* 223: 13–28.

Derndarsky, M. (1982). 'Österreich und der deutsche Bund 1815–1866', in Lutz and Rumpler (1982: 92–116).

Derré, J.-R. (1963). *Metternich et Lamennais.* Paris.

Derry, J. W.(1972). *Charles James Fox.* London.

—— (1976). *Castlereagh.* New York.

—— (1990). *Politics in the Age of Fox, Pitt and Liverpool: Continuity and Transformation.* New York.

Deschamps, H.-T. (1956). *La Belgique devant la France de juillet: l'opinion et l'attitude françaises de 1839 à 1848.* Paris.

Deutsch, H. C. (1938). *The Genesis of Napoleonic Imperialism.* Cambridge, Mass.

Diamandouros, N. P. et al. (eds.) (1986). *Hellenism and the First Greek War of Liberation (1821–1830): Continuity and Change.* Thessaloniki.

Dickinson, H. T. (1985). *British Radicalism and the French Revolution, 1789–1815.* Oxford.

—— (ed.) (1989). *Britain and the French Revolution 1789–1815.* New York.

Dickmann, F. (1971). *Friedensrecht und Friedenssicherung: Studien zum Friedensproblem in der Geschichte.* Göttingen.

Dimakis, J. (1975). 'La Presse de Vienne et la question d'Orient 1821–1827', *Balkan Studies,* 16: 35–43.

Dippel, H. (1977). *Germany and the American Revolution, 1770–1800.* Chapel Hill, NC.

Dipper, C. (1980). *Die Bauernbefreiung in Detuschland, 1790–1850.* Stuttgart.

—— (1984). 'Die Reichsritterschaft in napoleonischer Zeit', in Weis (1984: 53–73).

Djordjevic, D., and Fischer-Galati, S. (1981). *The Balkan Revolutionary Tradition.* New York.

Dlugoborski, W. (1991). 'Volksbewegungen im preussisch–polnischen Grenzraum während der französischen Revolution 1789 bis 1794', in Büsch and Neugebauer-Wölk (1991: 145–211).

Dodolev, M. A. (1968). 'Franko-russkii soiuz 1807 g. i Sitsiliia (k istorii razriva diplomaticheskikh otnoshenii mezhdu Rossieii i Sitsiliei v 1808 g.)', in S. A. Skazkin (ed.), *Rossiia i Italiia,* 77–94. Moscow.

Dodwell, H. H. (1931). *The Founder of Modern Egypt: A Study of Muhammad 'Ali.* Cambridge.

Doeberl, M. (1931). *Entwicklungsgeschichte Bayerns,* iii: *1825–1871.* Munich.

Donaghay, M. (1978). 'Calonne and the Anglo-French Commercial Treaty of 1786', *JMH* 50, On Demand Article No. 1J00038, pp. D1157–84.

—— (1984). 'The Best Laid Plans: French Execution of the Anglo-French Commercial Treaty of 1786', *EHQ* 14: 401–22.

Donner, H. (1939). *Deux adversaires de Napoleon à Vienne (1802–1806).* Helsinki.

Dorda, U. (1969). 'Johann Aloys Joseph Reichsfreiherr von Hugel', diss., Univ. of Würzburg.

Dostian, I. S. (1972). *Rossiia i balkanskii vopros: Iz istorii russko-balkanskikh sviazei v pervoi treti xix v.* Moscow.

—— (1974). 'Osnovye etapy i osobennosti politiki Rossii na Balkanakh s poslednei treti XVIII do 1830 g.', in *Mezhdunarodnye Otnosheniia na Balkanakh,* 5–38. Moscow.

Doyle, W. (1976). 'Was There an Aristocratic Reaction in Pre-Revolutionary France?' in D. Johnson (1976: 3–28).

—— (1980). *Origins of the French Revolution*. New York.

Drescher, S. (1977). *Econocide: British Slavery in the Era of Abolition.* Pittsburgh, Pa.

Dreyfus, F.-G. (1981). 'Die deutsche Wirtschaft um 1815', in Berding and Ullmann (1981: 353–82).

Driault, E. (1910). *Napoléon et l'Europe: la politique extérieure du premier consul, 1800–1803.* Paris.

—— (1912). *Napoléon et l'Europe: Austerlitz. La fin du saint-empire (1804–1806).* Paris.

—— (1917). *Napoléon et l'Europe: Tilsit. France et Russie sous le premier empire. La question de Pologne (1806–1809).* Paris.

—— (1924). *Napoléon et l'Europe: le grand empire (1809–1812).* Paris.

—— (1927). *Napoléon et l'Europe: la chute de l'empire. La légende de Napoléon (1812–1815).* Paris.

—— and Lhéritier, M. (1925). *Histoire diplomatique de la Grèce de 1821 à nos jours.* 5 vols., Paris.

Droz, J. (1949). *L'Allemagne et la révolution française.* Paris.

—— (1960). *L'Europe centrale: évolution historique de l'idée de 'Mitteleuropa'.* Paris.

—— (1983). 'Les Anti-Jacobins en Allemagne (autour de la revue *Eudaemonia*)', in Voss (1983: 149–53).

Drozdowski, M. (1981). 'Eighteenth Century Sources of Polish–Prussian Antagonism', *Polish Western Affairs*, 22: 40–55.

Duchhardt, H. (1976). *Gleichgewicht der Kräfte, Convenance, europäisches Konzert: Friedenskongresse und Friedensschlüsse vom Zeitalter Ludwigs XIV bis zum Wiener Kongress.* Darmstadt.

Duffy, C. (1981). *Russia's Military Way to the West.* Boston.

—— (1985). *Frederick the Great: A Military Life.* London.

Duffy, M. (1971). 'British War Policy: The Austrian Alliance 1793–1801', diss., Univ. of Oxford.

—— (1976). '"A Particular Service": The British Government and the Dunkirk Expedition of 1793', *EHR* 91: 529–54.

—— (1980). *The Military Revolution and the State 1500–1800.* Exeter.

—— (1983). 'British Policy in the war against Revolutionary France', in C. Jones (1983: 11–26).

—— (1987). *Soldiers, Sugar, and Seapower: The British Expeditions to the West Indies and the War against Revolutionary France.* Oxford.

—— (1989). 'British Diplomacy and the French Wars 1789–1815', in Dickinson (1989: 127–45).

Dufraisse, R. (1964). 'Les Populations de la rive gauche du Rhin et le service militaire à la fin de l'Ancien Régime et à l'époque révolutionnaire', *RH* 231: 103–40.

—— (1973). 'La Contrebande dans les départements réunis de la rive gauche du Rhin à l'époque napoléonienne', *Francia*, 1: 508–36.

—— (1978). 'La Crise économique de 1810–1812 en pays annexé: l'exemple de la rive gauche du Rhin', *Francia*, 6: 407–40.

Dufraisse, R. (1980). 'Das napoleonische Deutschland: Stand und Probleme der Forschung unter besonderer Berücksichtigung der linksrheinischen Gebiete', *GG* 6: 468–83.

—— (1981). 'Französische Zollpolitik, Kontinentalsperre und Kontinentalsystem im Deutschland der napoleonischen Zeit', in Berding and Ullmann (1981: 328–52).

—— (1982). 'Industrie et commerce dans le palatinat a l'époque française (1797–1813)', *Geschichtliche Landeskunde*, 22: 104–31.

—— (1983a). 'Les Relations économiques entre la France révolutionnaire et l'Allemagne', in Voss (1983: 214–48).

—— (1983b). 'De la Révolution à la patrie: la rive gauche du Rhin à l'époque française', in *Actes* (1983), 103–41.

—— (1984). 'L'Influence de la politique économique napoléonienne sur l'économie des états du Rheinbund', in Weis (1984: 75–95).

Duhamel, J. (1951). *Louis-Philippe et la première entente cordiale.* Paris.

Dull, J. R. (1983). 'Benjamin Franklin and the Nature of American Diplomacy', *IHR* 5: 346–65.

Dumont, F. (1978). 'Liberté und Libertät: Dokumente deutsch-französischer Beziehungen im Jahre 1792/93', *Francia*, 6: 367–406.

—— (1982). 'Mainzer Republik und Donnersbergdepartement: Gemeinsamkeiten und Unterschiede', *Geschichtliche Landeskunde*, 22: 45–75.

—— (1983). 'Mainz und die französische Revolution', *Francia Beihefte*, 12: 132–48.

Dunan, M. (ed.) (1939). 'Nouveaux documents sur l'Allemagne napoléonienne: lettres du roi de Bavière au maréchal Berthier (1806–1813)', *RH* 186: 112–43.

—— (1942). *Napoléon et l'Allemagne: le système continental et les débuts du royaume de Bavière.* Paris.

—— (1946). 'Napoléon et le système continental en 1810', *RHD* 60: 71–98.

—— (ed.) (1961). *Napoléon et l'Europe.* Paris.

Dunant, E. (ed.) (1901). *Les Relations diplomatiques de la France et de la république helvétique 1798–1803.* Basle.

Dunk, H. von der (1966). *Der deutsche Vormärz und Belgien, 1830/48.* Wiesbaden.

Dupre, H. (1940). *Lazare Carnot.* New York.

Duverger, M. (ed.) (1980). *Le Concept de l'empire.* Paris.

Dyck, H. L. (1980). 'Pondering the Russian Fact: Kaunitz and the Catherinian Empire in the 1770's', *Canadian Slavonic Papers*, 22: 451–69.

—— (1981). 'New Serbia and the Origins of the Eastern Question, 1751–55: A Habsburg Perspective', *Russian Review*, 40: 1–19.

Eade, J. C. (ed.) (1983). *Romantic Nationalism in Europe.* Melbourne.

Easum, C. V. (1942). *Prince Henry of Prussia, Brother of Frederick the Great.* Madison, Wis.

Echeverria, D. (1985). *The Maupeou Revolution—A Study in the History of Libertarianism: France, 1770–1774.* Baton Rouge, La.

Egan, C. L. (1983). *Neither Peace nor War: Franco-American Relations, 1803–1812*. Baton Rouge, La.

Egret, J. (1978). *The French Pre-Revolution*. Chicago.

Ehrman, J. (1962). *The British Government and Commercial Negotiations with Europe, 1783–1793*. Cambridge.

—— (1969). *The Younger Pitt, i: The Years of Acclaim*. New York.

—— (1983). *The Younger Pitt, ii: The Reluctant Transition*. Stanford, Calif.

Eich, U. (1986). *Russland und Europa: Studien zur russischen Deutschlandpolitik in der Zeit des Wiener Kongresses*. Cologne and Vienna.

Eisenstein, E. R. (1965–6). 'Who Intervened in 1788?' *AHR* 71: 77–103.

Eldridge, C. C. (ed.) (1984). *British Imperialism in the Nineteenth Century*. New York.

Elliot, D. C. (1954). 'The Grenville Mission to Berlin, 1799', *Huntington Library Quarterly*, 18: 129–46.

Elliott, G., 1st Earl of Minto (1874). *Life and Letters, from 1751 to 1806*, ed. Countess of Minto. 3 vols., London.

Elliott, M. (1982). *Partners in Revolution: The United Irishmen and France*. New Haven, Conn.

—— (1989). 'Ireland and the French Revolution', in Dickinson (1989: 83–101).

Ellis, G. (1981). *Napoleon's Continental Blockade: The Case of Alsace*. Oxford.

Elting, J. R. (1988). *Swords around a Throne: Napoleon's Grande Armée*. New York.

Eltis, D. (1987). *Economic Growth and the Ending of the Transatlantic Slave Trade*. New York.

Emsley, C. (1979). *British Society and the French Wars 1793–1815*. London.

—— (1981). 'An Aspect of Pitt's "Terror": Prosecutions for Seditions during the 1790s', *Social History*, 6: 155–84.

Engel-Janosi, F. (1933). *Der Freiherr von Hübner, 1811–1892*. Innsbruck.

—— (1952). 'French and Austrian Political Advice to Pius IX 1846–1848', *CHR* 38: 1–20.

—— (1958). *Österreich und der Vatikan, i*. Graz.

—— (1963). *Geschichte auf dem Ballhausplatz: Essays zur österreichischen Aussenpolitik 1830–1945*. Graz.

—— Klingenstein, G., and Lutz, H. (eds.) (1975). *Fürst, Bürger, Mensch, ii: Wiener Beitrage zur Geschichte der Neuzeit*. Munich.

Epstein, K. (1966). *The Genesis of German Conservatism*. Princeton, NJ.

Erdmann, K. D. (1981). 'Der Begriff der Freiheit in der französischen Revolution', *GWU* 8: 455–68.

Eremeeva, T. V. (1956). 'Zakliuchitel'nyi etap' egipetskogo krizisa 1831–33 gg. i velikie derzhavy', *Ucheniye Zapiski po Novoi Istorii*, 2: 475–518.

Ernouf, A. A. (1878). *Maret, duc de Bassano*. Paris.

Ernstberger, A. (1932). *Österreich–Preussen von Basel bis Campoformio 1795–97, i*. Prague.

—— (1955). *Eine deutsche Untergrundbewegung gegen Napoleon 1806/1807*. Munich.

Esdaile, C. J. (1988a). *The Spanish Army in the Peninsular War*. Manchester.

—— (1988b). 'War and Politics in Spain, 1808–1814', *HJ* 31: 295–317.

Evans, E. J. (1983). *The Forging of the Modern State: Early Industrial Britain, 1783–1870*. London.

Eyck, F. G. (1986). *Loyal Rebels: Andreas Hofer and the Tyrolean Uprising of 1809*. Lanham, Md.

Faber, K.-G. (1966). *Die Rheinlande zwischen Restauration und Revolution*. Wiesbaden.

—— (1973). 'Die Rheinländer und Napoleon', *Francia*, 1: 374–94.

—— (1976). 'Die südlichen Rheinlande von 1816 bis 1956', in Petri and Droege (1976: 367–474).

—— (1979). *Deutsche Geschichte im 19. Jahrhundert*. Wiesbaden.

—— (1981). 'Politisches Denken in der Restaurationszeit', in Berding and Ullmann (1981: 258–80).

Facius, F. (1977). 'Zwischen Souveränität und Mediatisierung: Das Existenzproblem der thüringischen Kleinstaaten von 1806 bis 1813', in P. Berglar (ed.), *Staat und Gesellschaft im Zeitalter Goethes. Festschrift fur Hans Tümmler*, 163–205. Cologne and Vienna.

Fadeev, A. V. (1958). *Rossiia i vostochnyi krizis 20-x godov xix veka*. Moscow.

Fagniez, G. (1922). 'La Politique de Vergennes et la diplomatie de Breteuil (1774–1787)', *RH* 140: 161–207.

Fairbank, J. K. (1953). *Trade and Diplomacy on the China Coast: The Opening of the Treaty Ports 1842–1854*. 2 vols. in 1, Cambridge, Mass.

Falk, M. A. (1962). 'Stadion, adversaire de Napoléon (1806–1809)', *AHRF* 34: 288–305.

Fay, P. W. (1975). *The Opium War, 1840–1842*. Chapel Hill, NC.

Fedorowicz, J. K. (ed.) (1982). *Republic of Nobles: Studies in Polish History to 1864*. New York.

Fehér, F. (1987). *The Frozen Revolution: An Essay on Jacobinism*. Cambridge.

Fehrenbach, E. (1976). 'Deutschland und die Französische Revolution', *GG* 2: 232–53.

—— (1978). *Traditionelle Gesellschaft und revolutionäres Recht: Die Einführung des Code Napoleon in den Rheinbundstaaten*. Göttingen.

—— (1979a). 'Der Einfluss des napoleonischen Frankreich auf das Rechts- und Verwaltungssystem Deutschlands', in Reden-Dohna (1979: 23–40).

—— (1979b). 'Verfassungs- und sozialpolitische Reformen und Reformprojekte in Deutschland unter dem Einfluss des napoleonischen Frankreich', *HZ* 228: 288–316.

—— (1981). *Vom Ancien Regime zum Wiener Kongress*. Göttingen.

—— (1989). 'Die Ideologisierung des Krieges und die Radikalisierung der Französischen Revolution', in Langewiesche (1989: 57–66).

Feldbaek, O. (1978). 'The Anglo-Russian Rapprochement of 1801: A Prelude to the Peace of Amiens', *Scandinavian Journal of History*, 3: 208–27.

—— (1980). *Denmark and the Armed Neutrality 1800–1801*. Copenhagen.

—— (1982). 'The Foreign Policy of Tsar Paul I, 1800–1801: An Interpretation', *JGO* 30: 16–35.

Ferns, H. S. (1960). *Britain and Argentina in the Nineteenth Century.* Oxford.

Ferrero, G. (1941). *The Reconstruction of Europe.* New York.

—— (1961). *The Gamble: Napoleon in Italy, 1796–1797.* London.

—— (1968). *The Two French Revolutions, 1789–1796.* New York.

Fieldhouse, D. K. (1963). 'British Imperialism in the Late Eighteenth Century: Defence or Opulence?' in F. Madden and K. Robinson (eds.), *Essays in Imperial Government Presented to Margery Perham,* 23–45. Oxford.

Filipuzzi, A. (1937–8). 'La rivoluzione di Grecia e la diplomazia europea fino al congresso di Verona', *Annali della R. Università degli studi economici e commerciali di Trieste,* 9: 90–143.

—— (1940). 'La restaurazione nel Regno delle Due Sicilie dopo il congresso di Lubiana', *Annali triestini di diritto economia e politica,* 11: 161–206, 230–82.

—— (1958a). *Pio IX e la politica austriaca in Italia dal 1814 al 1848.* Florence.

—— (1958b). 'Die Restauration in Italien im Lichte der neueren Historiographie', *MIOG* 66: 81–92.

Findlay, C. V. (1980). *Bureaucratic Reform in the Ottoman Empire: The Sublime Porte, 1789–1922.* Princeton, NJ.

Finer, S. E. (1975). 'State and Nation-Building in Europe: The Role of the Military', in Tilly (1975: 84–163).

—— (1988). *The Man on Horseback: The Role of the Military in Politics,* 2nd edn. Boulder, Colo.

Fink, G.-L. (1983). 'La Littérature allemande face à la révolution française', in Voss (1983: 249–300).

Fischer, A. (1933). *Napoléon et Anvers, 1801–1811.* Antwerp.

Fisher, A. W. (1970). *The Russian Annexation of the Crimea, 1772–1783.* Cambridge.

Fishman, J. S. (1988). *Diplomacy and Revolution: The London Conference of 1830 and the Belgian Revolt.* Amsterdam.

Fitzpatrick, B. (1983). *Catholic Royalism in the Department of the Gard, 1814–1852.* London.

Fleming, D. C. (1970). *John Capodistrias and the Conference of London (1828–1831).* Thessaloniki.

Flockerzie, L. J. (1990). 'Saxony, Austria, and the German Question after the Congress of Vienna, 1815–1816', *IHR* 12: 661–87.

Flournoy, F. R. (1935). *British Policy toward Morocco in the Age of Palmerston.* Baltimore, Md.

Förster, S. (1988). 'Weltkrieg und Imperialismus: Der Einfluss der Revolutionskriege auf den Beginn des britischen Expansion in Indien 1798/99', in Melville (1988: i. 505–21).

Forrest, A. I. (1989). *Conscripts and Deserters: The Army and Society during the Revolution and Empire.* New York.

—— (1990). *The Soldiers of the French Revolution.* Durham, NC.

Forsyth, M. (1980). 'The Old European States System: Gentz versus Hauterive', *HJ* 23: 521–38.

Fortescue, W. (1988). *Revolution and Counterrevolution in France, 1815–1952*. Oxford.

Fournier, A. (1880). *Gentz und Cobenzl: Geschichte der österreichischen Diplomatie in den Jahren 1801–1805*. Vienna.

—— (1885). *Historische Studien und Skizzen*. Prague.

—— (1899). 'Zur Geschichte der polnischen Frage 1814 und 1815', *MIOG* 20: 444–75.

—— (1900). *Der Congress von Châtillon: Die Politik im Kriege von 1814*. Vienna.

—— (1918). 'Londoner Präludien zum Wiener Kongress (Geheime Berichte Metternichs an Kaiser Franz)', *Deutsche Revue*, 43: i. 125–36, 205–19; ii. 24–33.

—— (1930). *Napoleon the First*. 2 vols., New York.

Fox, F. (1971). 'Negotiating with the Russians: Ambassador Ségur's Mission to Saint-Petersburg, 1784–1789', *FHS* 7: 47–71.

France: Recueil: France, Commission des archives diplomatiques (1884). *Recueil des instructions données aux ambassadeurs et ministres de France depuis les traités de Westphalie jusqu'à la révolution française*, i: *Autriche*, comp. A. Sorel. Paris.

Franzel, E. (1970). 'Österreichs Rhein- und Donaupolitik zur Zeit Napoleons', *Donauraum*, 15: 203–15.

Frazee, C. A. (1969). *The Orthodox Church and Independent Greece*. Cambridge.

—— (1979). 'The Greek Catholic Islanders and the Revolution of 1821', *EEQ* 13: 315–26.

Fryer, W. R. (1965). *Republic or Restoration in France, 1794 to 1797*. Manchester.

—— (1979–80). 'The Mirage of Restoration: Louis XVIII and Lord MacArtney, 1795–1796', *Bulletin of the John Rylands Library*, 62: i. 87–114; ii. 388–422.

Fryman, M. (1977). 'Charles Stuart and the "Common Cause": Anglo-Portuguese Diplomatic Relations 1810–1814', *PCRE*, 105–15.

Fugier, A. (1930). *Napoléon et l'Espagne, 1799–1808*. 2 vols., Paris.

—— (1947). *Napoléon et l'Italie*. Dijon.

—— (1954). *La Révolution française et l'empire napoléonien*. Paris.

Furber, H. (1976). *Rival Empires of Trade in the Orient, 1600–1800*. London.

Furet, F. (1978). *Penser la révolution française*. Paris.

Furlani, S. (1948). 'La questione postale italiana al congresso di Verona', *NRS* 22: 36–49.

—— (1955–6). 'La Santa Sede e il congresso di Verona', *NRS* 39: 465–91; 40: 14–47.

—— (1960). 'L'Austria e la questione Carignano alla vigilia del congresso de Verona', *Bollettino storico-bibliografico subalpino*, 58: 116–51.

—— (1978). 'Metternichs Plan einer italienischen Zentral-Untersuchungskommission auf dem Kongress von Verona', *MOS* 31: 181–95.

Gagliardo, J. C. (1980). *Reich and Nation: The Holy Roman Empire as Idea and Reality, 1763–1806.* Bloomington, Ind.

Galasso, G. (1979). 'Das italienische Staatensystem in der Politik Napoleons', in Reden-Dohna (1979: 81–90).

Galbraith, J. S. (1961). 'Myths of the "Little England" Era', *AHR* 67: 34–48.

—— (1963). *Reluctant Empire: British Policy on the South African Frontier, 1834–1854.* Berkeley, Calif.

Gall, L. (1968). *Der Liberalismus als regierende Partei: Das Grossherzogtum Baden zwischen Restauration und Reichsgründung.* Wiesbaden.

—— (1980). *Bismarck der Weisse Revolutionär.* Frankfurt.

—— (1987). ' "Ich wünschte ein Burger zu sein": Zum Selbstverständnis des deutschen Bürgertums im 19. Jahrhundert', *HZ* 245: 601–23.

Galpin, W. F. (1925). *The Grain Supply of England during the Napoleonic Period.* New York.

Gash, N. (1976). *Sir Robert Peel,* 2nd edn. London

—— (1978). 'After Waterloo: British Society and the Legacy of the Napoleonic Wars', *TRHS* 28: 145–57.

—— (1979). *Aristocracy and People: Britain, 1815–1885.* Cambridge, Mass.

—— (1984). *Lord Liverpool: The Life and Political Career of Robert Jenkinson, Second Earl of Liverpool, 1770–1828.* London.

—— (1990a). 'The Duke of Wellington and the Prime Ministership, 1824–1830', in Gash (1990b: 117–38).

—— (ed.) (1990b). *Wellington: Studies in the Military and Political Career of the First Duke of Wellington.* New York.

Gasser, A. (1969). 'Die Nationen und Napoleon: Tradition und National-gefühl', in Groote (1969: 59–84).

Gates, D. (1986). *The Spanish Ulcer: A History of the Peninsular War.* London, 1986.

GB–Ital.–Minto: ISIEMC (1970). *Gran Bretagna e Italia nei documenti della missione Minto,* ed. F. Curato. 2 vols., Rome.

Geggus, D. (1981). 'The British Government and the Saint Domingue Slave Revolt, 1791–1793', *EHR* 96: 285–305.

—— (1982). *Slavery, War, and Revolution: The British Occupation of Saint Domingue 1793–98.* Oxford.

—— (1983). 'The Anglo-French Conflict in the Caribbean in the 1790s', in C. Jones (1983: 27–39).

Gembruch, W. (1968). 'Zur Discussion um Heeresverfassung und Krieg-führung in der Zeit vor der Französischen Revolution', in Groote and Müller (1968: 9–28).

—— (1986). 'Zum Verhältnis von Staat und Heer im Zeitalter der grossen Französischen Revolution', in Kunisch and Stollberg-Rillinger (1986: 377–95).

—— (1988). 'Prinz Heinrich von Preussen, Bruder Friedrichs des Grossen', in Kunisch (1988b: 89–120).

Gentz, F. von (1867). *Aus dem Nachlasse Friedrichs von Gentz.* 2 vols., Vienna.

Gentz, F. von (1876–7). *Dépêches inédites du chevalier de Gentz aux hospodars de Valachie pour servir à l'histoire de la politique européenne (1813 à 1828)*, ed. Graf A. Prokesch von Osten. 3 vols., Paris.

—— (1887). *Oesterreichs Theilnahme an den Befreiungskriegen*, ed. A. Klinkowström. Vienna.

Georgiev, V. A. (1975). *Vneshniaia Politika Rossii na Blizhnem Vostoke v kontse 30—nachale 40-x godov XIXv.* Moscow.

Gerecke, A. (1964). *Das deutsche Echo auf die polnische Erhebung von 1830.* Wiesbaden.

Gerhard, D. (1932–3). 'Kontinentalpolitik und Kolonialpolitik im Frankreich des ausgehenden ancien regime', *HZ* 147: 21–31.

—— (1933). *England und der Aufstieg Russlands.* Munich.

—— (1970). 'Regionalism and Corporate Order as a Basic Theme of European History', in Hatton and Anderson (1970: 155–82).

Geyl, P. (1967). *Napoleon, For and Against.* New Haven, Conn.

Ghisalberti, C. (1979). 'Der Einfluss des napoleonischen Frankreich auf das italienische Rechts- und Verwaltungssystem', in Reden-Dohna (1979: 41–56).

Ghurbal, M. S. (1977). *The Beginnings of the Egyptian Question and the Rise of Mehemet Ali.* New York.

Gill, A. (1974). *Die polnische Revolution 1846.* Munich.

Gillard, D. (1977). *The Struggle for Asia, 1828–1914.* London.

Gille, B. (1965). *Histoire de la maison Rothschild*, i: *Des origines à 1848.* Geneva.

Gillessen, G. (1961). *Lord Palmerston und die Einigung Deutschlands.* Lübeck.

Gillis, J. (1968). 'Aristocracy and Bureaucracy in Nineteenth Century Prussia', *PP* 41: 105–29.

Gilpin, R. (1987). *The Political Economy of International Relations.* Princeton, NJ.

Girard, L. (1985). *Les Libéraux français.* Paris.

Girnius, S. A. (1981). 'Russia and the Continental Blockade', diss., Univ. of Chicago.

Gisci, M. (1931). 'Un episodio dell' rivalità franco-austriaca nello Stato Pontificio', *RSR* 17: 365–447.

Glassl, H. (1969). 'Pläne zur Lösung der Orientalischen Frage nach dem Siebenjährigen Krieg', *Saeculum*, 20: 69–81.

Gleason, J. H. (1972). *The Genesis of Russophobia in Great Britain.* New York.

Glover, M. (1971). *Legacy of Glory: The Bonaparte Kingdom of Spain 1808–1813.* New York.

Glover, R. (1957). 'Arms and the British Diplomat in the French Revolutionary Era', *JMH* 29: 199–212.

—— (1973). *Britain at Bay: Defence against Bonaparte, 1803–14.* London.

Gmeinwiser, J. (1928). *Die bayrische Politik im Jahre 1805.* Munich.

Godechot, J. (1937). *Les Commissaires aux armées sous le directoire.* 2 vols., Paris.

—— (1949–50). 'Le Directoire vu de Londres', *AHRF* 21: 311–36; 22: 1–27.

—— (1956). *La Grande nation: l'expansion révolutionnaire de la France dans le monde de 1789 à 1799*. 2 vols., Paris.

—— (1981). *The Counter Revolution: Doctrine and Action, 1789–1804*. Princeton, NJ.

Godel, J. (1970). 'L'Église selon Napoléon', *RHMC* 17: 837–45.

Goetz-Bernstein, H. A. (1912). *La Politique extérieure de Brissot et des Girondins*. Paris.

Gollwitzer, Hans (1953). 'Der erste Karlistenkrieg und das Problem der internationalen Parteigängerschaft', *HZ* 176: 479–520.

Gollwitzer, Heinz (1964). *Europabild und Europagedanke*, 2nd edn. Munich.

—— (1972). *Geschichte des weltpolitischen Denkens*, i. Göttingen.

Gooch, B. D. (1963). *Belgium and the February Revolution*. The Hague.

Good, D. F. (1984). *The Economic Rise of the Habsburg Empire, 1750–1914*. Berkeley, Calif.

Goodwin, A. (1979). *The Friends of Liberty: The English Democratic Movement in the Age of the French Revolution*. Cambridge, Mass.

Gordon, N. M. (1969). 'Britain and the Zollverein Iron Duties, 1842–5', *Economic History Review*, ser. 2, 22: 75–87.

Gossman, N. (1969). 'British Aid to Polish, Italian, and Hungarian Exiles 1830–1870', *South Atlantic Quarterly*, 63: 231–45.

Gottfried, P. (1979). *Conservative Millenarians: The Romantic Experience in Bavaria*. New York.

Gough, H., and Dickson, D. (eds.) (1990). *Ireland and the French Revolution*. Dublin.

Gould, C. (1965). *Trophy of Conquest: The Musée Napoléon and the Creation of the Louvre*. London.

Grab, A. (1985). 'The Politics of Subsistence: The Liberalization of Grain Commerce in Austrian Lombardy under Enlightened Despotism', *JMH* 57: 185–210.

—— (1988). 'The Kingdom of Italy and Napoleon's Continental Blockade', *PCRE* 18: 587–604.

Grab, W. (1979). 'Der deutsche Jakobinismus', in Reden-Dohna (1979: 1–22).

—— (1967). *Norddeutsche Jakobiner: Demokratische Bestrebungen zur Zeit der Französischen Revolution*. Frankfurt.

Graf, F. W. (1978). *Die Politisierung des religiösen Bewusstseins: Die bürgerlichen Religionsparteien im deutschen Vormärz—das Beispiel des Deutschkatholizismus*. Stuttgart.

Graham, G. S. (1979). *The China Station: War and Diplomacy 1830–1860*. Oxford.

—— (1967). *Great Britain in the Indian Ocean: A Study of Maritime Enterprise, 1810–1850*. Oxford.

—— (1972). *Tides of Empire: Discursions on the Expansion of Britain Overseas*. Montreal.

Gray, D. (1963). *Spencer Perceval: The Evangelical Prime Minister, 1762–1812*. Manchester.

Gray, D. S. (1980). 'The French Invasion of Hanover in 1803 and the Origins of the King's German Legion', *PCRE*, pt. 1: 198–211.

Great Britain, Foreign Office (1847–9). *Correspondence Respecting the Affairs of Italy, 1846–1849*. 4 vols. in 2, London.

Greenberg, M. (1951). *British Trade and the Opening of China 1800–1842*. Cambridge.

Gregory, D. (1985). *The Ungovernable Rock: A History of the Anglo-Corsican Kingdom and its Role in Britain's Mediterranean Strategy*. Rutherford, NJ.

—— (1988). *Sicily—The Insecure Base: A History of the British Occupation of Sicily, 1806–1815*. London.

Grenville, W. W. Grenville, Baron (1892–1927). *The Manuscripts of J. B. Fortescue, esq., preserved at Dropmore*. 10 vols., London.

Greppi, G. M., Conte (1859). *Révélations diplomatiques sur les relations de la Sardaigne avec l'Autriche et la Russie pendant la première et la deuxième coalition*. Paris.

Greulich, A. (1931). *Österreichs Beitritt zur Koalition im Jahre 1813*. Borna.

Griewank, K. (1935). 'Hardenberg und die preussische Politik 1804–1806', *FBPG*, ser. 2, 47: 227–308.

—— (1940). 'Preussen und die Neuordnung Deutschlands 1813–1815', *FBPG*, ser. 2, 52: 234–79.

—— (1942). 'Preussens Neuordnungspläne für Mitteleuropa aus dem Jahre 1814', *Deutsches Archiv für Landes- und Volksforschung*, 6: 342–60.

—— (1954). *Der Wiener Kongress und die europäische Restauration*, 2nd edn. Leipzig.

Griffith, P. (1989). *Military Thought in the French Army, 1815–1851*. Manchester.

Griffiths, D. M. (1967). 'Russian Court Politics and the Question of an Expansionist Foreign Policy under Catherine II, 1762–1783', diss., Cornell Univ.

—— (1970). 'The Rise and Fall of the Northern System: Court Politics and Foreign Policy in the First Half of Catherine II's Reign', *CASS* 4: 547–69.

—— (1973). 'Catherine II: The Republican Empress', *JGO* 21: 323–44.

—— (1979). 'Catherine the Great, George III, and the British Opposition', in Cross (1979: 306–20).

Griffiths, R. T. (1979). *Industrial Retardation in the Netherlands, 1830–1850*. The Hague.

Grimsted, P. K. (1969). *The Foreign Ministers of Alexander I: Political Attitudes and the Conduct of Russian Diplomacy 1801–1825*. Berkeley, Calif.

—— (1970). 'Czartoryski's System for Russian Foreign Policy, 1803', *California Slavic Studies*, 5: 19–91.

Gritzbach, H. (1974). 'Der russiche Reichskanzler Graf Nesselrode (1780–1862)', 2 vols., diss., Univ. of Nürnberg.

Grochulska, B. (1970a). 'La Conjoncture du blocus continental en Europe centrale', *Acta Poloniae Historica*, 21: 123–39.

—— (1970b). 'L'Économie polonaise et le renversement de la conjoncture (1805–1815)', *RHMC* 17: 620–30.

Groh, D. (1961). *Russland und das Selbstverständnis Europas*. Neuwied.

Groote, W. von (1953). *Die Entstehung des Nationalbewusstseins in Norddeutschland 1790–1830*. Göttingen.

—— (ed.) (1969). *Napoleon I und die Staatenwelt seiner Zeit*. Freiburg.

—— and Müller, K.-J. (eds.) (1968). *Napoleon I und das Militärwesen seiner Zeit*. Freiburg.

Gross, H. (1974). 'The Holy Roman Empire in Modern Times: Constitutional Reality and Legal Theory', in S. Rowan and J. Vann (eds.), *The Old Reich: Essays on German Political Institutions, 1495–1806*. Brussels.

Grossman, K. (1931). 'Metternichs Plan eines italienischen Bundes', *Historische Blätter*, 4: 37–76.

Gruder, V. R. (1984). 'A Mutation in Elite Political Culture: The French Notables and the Defense of Property and Participation, 1787', *JMH* 56: 598–634.

Gruner, W. D. (1977a). 'Die belgisch-luxemburgische Frage im Spannungsfeld europäischer Politik 1830–1839', *Francia*, 5: 299–398.

—— (1977b). 'Europäischer Friede als nationales Interesse: Die Rolle des Deutschen Bundes in der britischen Politik 1814–1832', *Bohemia: Jahrbuch des Collegium Carolinum*, 18: 96–128.

—— (1980). 'The British Political, Social and Economic System and the Decision for Peace and War: Reflections on Anglo-German Relations 1800–1939', *British Journal of International Studies*, 6: 189–218.

—— (1982). 'Grossbritannien und die Julirevolution von 1830', *Francia*, 9: 369–410.

—— (1983). 'The Revolution of July and Southern Germany', *PCRE*, 509–46.

—— (1984). 'Die deutschen Einzelstaaten und der deutsche Bund', in A. Kraus (ed.), *Land und Reich, Stamm und Nation. Probleme und Perspektive bayerischer Geschichte*, iii. 19–36. Munich.

—— (1985). *Die deutsche Frage*. Munich.

—— (1989). 'Föderatives Denken und bündische Formen deutscher Staatlichkeit', *Politik und Kultur*, 16: 11–28.

Guibert, F.-A., Comte de (1977). *Écrits militaires 1772–1790*, ed J. E. Ménard. Paris.

Guillon, E. L. M. (1910). *Napoléon et les suisses, 1803–1815*. Paris.

Guizot, F. P. Duc de (1858). *Mémoires pour servir à l'histoire de mon temps*. 8 vols., Paris.

—— (1963). *Lettres de François Guizot et la princesse de Lieven*. 3 vols., Paris.

Gulick, E. V. (1955). *Europe's Classical Balance of Power*. Ithaca, NY.

Guyot, R. (1912). *Le Directoire et la paix de l'Europe*. Paris.

—— (1926). *La Première entente cordiale*. Paris.

Haas, A. G. (1963). *Metternich, Reorganization and Nationality 1813–1818*. Wiesbaden.

Häusser, L. (1869). *Deutsche Geschichte vom Tode Friedrichs des Grossen bis zur Gründung des Deutschen Bundes*. 4 vols., Berlin.

Hagen, W. W. (1976). 'The Partitions of Poland and the Crisis of the Old Regime in Prussia, 1772–1806', *CEH* 9: 115–28.

Hahn, H.-H. (1987). 'Polen im Horizont preussischer und deutscher Politik im neunzehnten Jahrhundert', in Zernack (1987: 1–19).

Hahn, H.-W. (1982). *Wirtschaftliche Integration im 19. Jahrhundert: die hessischen Staaten und der Deutsche Zollverein*. Göttingen.

—— (1984). *Geschichte des Deutschen Zollvereins*. Göttingen.

Hales, E. E. Y. (1954). *Pio Nono*. New York.

—— (1956). *Mazzini and the Secret Societies*. London.

—— (1961). *The Emperor and the Pope: The Story of Napoleon and Pius VII*. New York.

—— (1966). *Revolution and Papacy, 1769–1846*. Notre Dame, Ind.

Hall, C. D. (1988). 'Addington at War: Unspectacular but Not Unsuccessful', *Historical Research*, 61: 306–15.

Hall, J. (1912). *England and the Orleans Monarchy*. New York.

Halstead, J. P. (1983). *The Second British Empire: Trade, Philanthropy and Good Government, 1820–1890*. Westport, Conn.

Hammen, O. J. (1946–7). 'The Failure of an Attempted Franco-German Liberal Rapprochement, 1830–1840', *AHR* 52: 54–67.

Hammer, K. (1963). *Die französische Diplomatie der Restauration und Deutschland, 1814–1830*. Stuttgart.

—— and Hartmann, P. C. (eds.) (1977). *Le bonapartisme: phénomène historique et mythe politique*. Munich.

Hampson, N. (1988). *Prelude to Terror: The Constituent Assembly and the Failure of Consensus, 1789–1791*. Oxford.

Handelsman, M. (1909). *Napoléon et la Pologne, 1806–1807*. Paris.

—— (1934). *Czartoryski, Nicholas I et le proche orient*. Paris.

Hansard (1814). Great Britain, House of Commons, *Parliamentary Debates*, 28.

Hardenberg, K. A., Fürst von (1877). *Denkwürdigkeiten des Staatskanzlers Fürsten von Hardenberg*, ed. L. von Ranke. 5 vols., Leipzig.

Hargreaves-Mawdsley, W. (1979). *Eighteenth-Century Spain, 1700–1788: A Political, Diplomatic, and Institutional History*. Totowa, NJ.

Harlow, V. T. (1952–64). *The Founding of the Second British Empire, 1763–1793*. 2 vols., London and New York.

Harris, R. D. (1976). 'French Finances and the American War, 1777–1783', *JMH* 48: 233–58.

—— (1979). *Necker, Reform Statesman of the Ancien Regime*. Berkeley, Calif.

—— (1986). *Necker and the Revolution of 1789*. Lanham, Md.

Harrison, B. H. (1982). *Peaceable Kingdom*. Oxford.

Hartmann, O. (1892). *Der Antheil der Russen am Feldzug von 1799 in der Schweiz*. Zurich.

Harvey, A. D. (1978a). *Britain in the Early Nineteenth Century*. New York.

—— (1978b). 'European Attitudes to Britain during the French Revolutionary and Napoleonic Era', *History*, 63: 356–65.

Hase, A. von (1970). 'Friedrich (v.) Gentz: Vom Übergang nach Wien bis zu den "Fragmenten des Gleichgewichts" (1802–1806)', *HZ* 211: 589–615.

—— (1978). 'Das konservative Europa in Bedrängnis: zur Krise des Gleichgewichtspublizisten Friedrich von Gentz (1805–1809)', *Saeculum*, 29: 385–405.

Hatton, R., and Anderson, M. S. (eds.) (1970). *Studies in Diplomatic History*. London.

Hatze, M. (1949). *Die diplomatisch-politischen Beziehungen zwischen England und der Schweiz im Zeitalter der Restauration*. Basle.

Haupt, H.-G. (1977). 'Bourgeoisie und Rheingrenze im Frankreich der Restaurationszeit', *GG* 3: 5–30.

Hauser, C. (1990). *Anfänge bürgerlicher Organisation: Philhellenismus und Frühliberalismus in Südwestdeutschland*. Göttingen.

Hausman, W. J. (1990). 'The British Economy in Transition, 1742–1789', in J. Black (ed.), *British Politics and Society from Walpole to Pitt 1742–1789*, 53–79. New York.

Haussherr, H. (1957). 'Hardenberg und der Friede von Basel', *HZ* 184: 292–335.

—— (1960a). 'Russland und Europa in der Epoche des Wiener Kongresses', *JGO* 8: 10–31.

—— (1960b). 'Stein und Hardenberg', *HZ* 190:267–89.

Hearder, H. (1983). *Italy in the Age of the Risorgimento, 1790–1870*. New York.

Heckscher, E. F. (1922). *The Continental System*. Oxford.

Heer, F. (1967). *Das Heilige Römische Reich*. Munich.

Hehn, P. N. (1963). 'Prince Adam Czartoryski and the South Slavs', *Polish Review*, 8: 76–86.

—— (1975). 'The Origins of Modern Pan-Serbism—The 1844 Nacertanije of Ilija Garasanin: An Analysis and Translation', *EEQ* 9: 153–71.

Heigel, K. T. von (1899–1911). *Deutsche Geschichte vom Tode Friedrichs des Grossen bis zur Auflösung des alten Reiches*. 2 vols., Stuttgart.

Heindl, W. (1991). *Gehorsame Rebellen: Bürokratie und Beamte in Österreich 1780 bis 1848*. Vienna.

Heit, S. (1980). 'German Romanticism: An Ideological Response to Napoleon', *PCRE* 1: 187–97.

Helleiner, K. F. (1965). *The Imperial Loans: A Study in Financial and Diplomatic History*. Oxford.

Heller, K. (1983). *Die Geld- und Kreditpolitik des russischen Reiches in der Zeit der Assignaten, 1768–1839/43*. Wiesbaden.

Helmreich, J. (1976). *Belgium and Europe: A Study in Small Power Diplomacy*. The Hague.

Henderson, W. O. (1939). *The Zollverein*. Cambridge.

Henderson, W. O. (1957). 'The Anglo-French Treaty of Commerce of 1786', *Economic History Review*, 10: 104–12.

—— (1981). 'The German Zollverein and the European Economic Integration', *Zeitschrift für die gesamte Staatswissenschaft*, 137: 491–507.

Heppner, H. (1982). 'Die personelle Entwicklung des österreichischen Balkandiplomatie in der 2. Hälfte des 18. und zu Beginn des 19. Jahrhunderts', *Österreichische Osthefte*, 24: 21–32.

Hermann, C. H. (1984). *Deutsche Militärgeschichte*. Frankfurt.

Herr, R. (1958). *The Eighteenth-Century Revolution in Spain*. Princeton, NJ.

Herre, F. (1973). *Freiherr vom Stein: Sein Leben, seine Zeit*. Cologne.

Herrmann, A. (1912). *Der Aufstieg Napoleons: Krieg und Diplomatie von Brumaire bis Lunéville*. Berlin.

Herrmann, E. (ed.) (1867). *Diplomatische Korrespondenzen aus der Revolutionszeit, 1791–1797*. Gotha.

Herz, J. (1950). 'Idealist Internationalism and the Security Dilemma', *WP* 2: 157–80.

Heuvel, G. van der (1988). *Der Freiheitsbegriff der Französischen Revolution: Studien zur Revolutionsideologie*. Göttingen.

Heydemann, G. (1989). 'Philhellenismus in Deutschland und Grossbritannien', in A. Birke and G. Heydemann (eds.), *Die Herausforderung des europäischen Staatensystems*, 31–60. Göttingen.

Hickey, D. R. (1987). 'The Monroe–Pinkney Treaty of 1806: A Reappraisal', *William and Mary Quarterly*, 35: 65–88.

—— (1989). *The War of 1812: A Forgotten Conflict*. Urbana, Ill.

Higonnet, P. (1981). *Class, Ideology, and the Rights of Nobles during the French Revolution*. New York.

Hinsley, F. H. (1963). *Power and the Pursuit of Peace: Theory and Practice in the History of Relations between States*. Cambridge.

Hintze, O. (1970). *Staat und Verfassung: Gesammelte Abhandlungen zur allgemeinen Verfassungsgeschichte*, 3rd edn. Göttingen.

Historical Dictionary: Napoleon (1985). *Historical Dictionary of Napoleonic France, 1799–1815*, ed. O. Connelly. Westport, Conn.

Historical Dictionary: Revolution (1985). *Historical Dictionary of the French Revolution, 1789–1799*, ed. S. F. Scott and B. Rothaus. 2 vols., Westport, Conn.

Hitchins, K. (1987). *L'Idée de nation chez les roumains de Transylvanie (1691–1849)*. Bucharest.

Höjer, T. T. (1958). 'Die Genesis der schwedischen Neutralität', *HZ* 186: 65–79.

—— (1971). *Bernadotte, maréchal de France, roi de Suède*. 2 vols., Paris.

Hölzle, E. (1931). *Das alte Recht und die Revolution*. Munich.

—— (1933). 'Das napoleonische Staatssystem in Deutschland', *HZ* 148: 277–93.

—— (1937). *Württemberg im Zeitalter Napoleons und der deutschen Erhebung*. Stuttgart.

—— (1969). 'Napoleon und die Randmächte in macht- und ideengeschichtlicher Sicht', in Groote (1969: 99–111).

Hoensch, J. K. (1973). *Sozialverfassung und politische Reform: Polen im vorrevolutionären Zeitalter*. Cologne.

Hösch, E. (1964). 'Das sogenannte "griechische Projekt" Katherinas II', *JGO* 12: 168–206.

—— (1967). 'Zar Paul I (1796–1801) und die russische Mittelmeerpolitik am Ausgang des 18. Jahrhunderts', *Saeculum*, 18: 294–315.

Hoff, J. F. (1913). *Die Mediasiertenfrage in den Jahren 1813–1815*. Berlin.

Hoffman, F. L. (1967). 'Metternich and the July Revolution', *EEQ* 1: 143–54.

Hoke, R. (1983). 'Österreichs Verwaltung in Vormärz', in *Deutsche Verwaltungsgeschichte*, ii. *Vom Reichsdeputationshauptschluss bis zur Auflösung des Deutschen Bundes*, ed. K. G. A. Jeserich *et al.*, 345–98. Stuttgart.

Holbraad, C. (1970). *The Concert of Europe*. London.

—— (1984). *Middle Powers in International Politics*. London.

Holland, H. R. V. Fox, 3rd Lord (1977). *The Holland House Diaries, 1831–1840*, ed. A. D. Kriegel. London.

Holmes, S. (1985). *Benjamin Constant and the Making of Modern Liberalism*. New Haven, Conn.

Holroyd, R. (1971). 'The Bourbon Army, 1815–1830', *HJ* 14: 529–52.

Holt, E. (1971). *The Making of Italy 1815–1870*. New York.

Holzapfel, K. (1977). 'Intervention oder Koexistenz: Preussens Stellung zu Frankreich, 1789–1792', *ZGW* 25: 787–802.

—— (1984). 'La Prusse avant la paix de Bâle: le torpillage du traité de subsidés de la Haye par le "parti prussien de paix" (1794–1795)', *AHRF* 56: 228–39.

—— (1987). 'Die "europäische Friedenspartei" von 1830: Motive und Argumente', *ZGW* 35: 116–27.

Homan, G. D. (1971). *Jean-François Reubell: French Revolutionary, Patriot, and Director, 1747–1807*. The Hague.

Horn, D. B. (1945). *British Public Opinion and the First Partition of Poland*. Edinburgh.

—— (1961). *The British Diplomatic Service, 1689–1789*. Oxford.

—— (1967). *Great Britain and Europe in the Eighteenth Century*. Oxford.

Horsman, R. (1962). *The Causes of the War of 1812*. Philadelphia.

Horvath, J. (1926). 'Le Prince Metternich et Lord Palmerston: les débuts de la rivalité anglo-russe dans l'Europe centrale', *Nouvelle revue de Hongrie*, 34: 22–35, 61–9, 147–54.

Horward, D. D. (1981). 'Portugal and the Anglo-Russian Naval Crisis (1808)', *Naval War College Review*, 34: 48–74.

—— (1984). *Napoleon and Iberia: the Twin Sieges of Ciudad Rodrigo and Almeida, 1810*. Gainesville, Fla.

—— (1989). 'Wellington and the Defence of Portugal', *IHR* 11: 39–54.

Houlding, J. A. (1981). *Fit for Service: The Training of the British Army, 1715–1795*. Oxford.

Howard, C. (1974). *Britain and the Casus Belli*. London.

Howard, J. E. (ed.) (1961). *Letters and Documents of Napoleon*, i. *The Rise to Power*. London.

Howard, M. (1976). *War in European History*. Oxford.

Howe, P. (1986). 'Belgian Influence on French Policy, 1789–1793', *PCRE* 16: 213–22.

Howell, R. C. (1987). *The Royal Navy and the Slave Trade*. London.

Hubatsch, W. (1977*a*). *Der Freiherr vom Stein und England*. Cologne.

—— (1977*b*). *Die Stein–Hardenbergschen Reformen*. Darmstadt.

Huber, E. R. (1957). *Deutsche Verfassungsgeschichte seit 1789*, i: *Reform und Restauration 1798 bis 1830*. Stuttgart.

—— (1963). *Deutsche Verfassungsgeschichte seit 1789*, ii. *Der Kampf um Einheit und Freiheit, 1830–1850*. Stuttgart.

Huck, J. (1984). *Das Ende der Franzosenzeit in Hamburg: Quellen und Studien zur Belagerung und Befreiung von Hamburg 1813–1814*. Hamburg.

Hübner, J. A. Graf von (1891). *Une année de ma vie, 1848–1849*. Paris.

Hueckel, G. R. (1985). *The Napoleonic Wars and their Impact on Factor Returns and Output Growth in England, 1793–1895*. New York.

Hüffer, H. (1868). *Oestreich und Preussen gegenüber der französischen Revolution bis zum Abschluss des Friedens von Campo Formio*. Bonn.

—— (ed.) (1868–79). *Diplomatischen Verhandlungen aus der Zeit der französischen Revolution*. 3 vols., Bonn.

—— (1869). *Die Politik der deutschen Mächte im Revolutionskrieg bis zum Abschluss des Friedens von Campo Formio*. Münster.

—— (1900–1). *Quellen zur Geschichte der Kriege von 1799 und 1800*. 2 vols., Leipzig.

—— (1904). *Der Krieg des Jahres 1799 und die zweite Kalition*. 2 vols., Gotha.

—— and Luckwaldt, F. (1907). *Der Frieden von Campo Formio: Urkunden und Aktenstücke zur Geschichte der Beziehungen zwischen Österreich und Frankreich in den Jahren 1795–1797*. Innsbruck.

Huisman, M. (1934). 'Quelque dessous de la conférence de Londres: Talleyrand a-t-il trafiqué de son influence?' *RHMC*, n.s., 9: 297–316.

Hull, A. (1980). *Charles III and the Revival of Spain*. Washington, DC.

Humphreys, R. A., and Lynch, J. (eds.) (1966). *The Origins of the Latin American Revolutions, 1808–1826*. New York.

Hunt, L. A. (1984). *Politics, Culture and Class in the French Revolution*. Berkeley, Calif.

—— Lansky, D., and Hanson, P. (1979). 'The Failure of the Liberal Republic in France, 1795–1799: The Road to Brumaire', *JMH* 51: 734–59.

Hunter, F. R. (1984). *Egypt under the Khedives, 1805–1879*. Pittsburgh, Penn.

Hutt, M. (1983). *Chouannerie and Counter-Revolution*. 2 vols., New York.

Huttenback, R. A. (1961). 'The French Threat to India and British Relations with Sind, 1799–1809', *EHR* 76: 590–99.

—— (1962). *British Relations with Sind 1799–1843: An Anatomy of Imperialism*. Berkeley, Calif.

Hyam, R. (1975). 'The Peace of Paris (1963)', in R. Hyam and G. Martin, *Reappraisals in British Imperial History*, 21–43. Basingstoke, Hants.

Hyslop, B. F. (1934). *French Nationalism in 1789 According to the General Cahiers*. New York.

—— (1950). 'French Jacobin Nationalism and Spain', in E. M. Earle (ed.), *Nationalism and Internationalism*, 190–240. New York.

Ibbeken, R. (1970). *Preussen 1807–13: Staat und Volk als Idee und in Wirklichkeit*. Cologne.

Iiams, T. M. (1979). *Peacemaking from Vergennes to Napoleon: French Foreign Relations in the Revolutionary Era, 1774–1814*. Huntington, NY.

Imbert, J. (1968). 'Économie et guerre: les "militaires aux armées" en 1806', in *Mélanges offerts a G. Jacquemyns*, 447–60. Brussels.

Imlah, A. H. (1958). *Economic Elements in the Pax Britannica*. Cambridge, Mass.

Imlah, A. G. (1966). *Britain and Switzerland 1845–60*. Hamden, Conn.

Ingle, H. N. (1976). *Nesselrode and the Russian Rapprochement with Britain, 1836–1843*. Berkeley, Calif.

Inglis, B. (1976). *The Opium War*. London.

Ingram, E. (1970–1). 'The Defence of British India', *Journal of Indian History*, 48: 565–84; 49: 57–78.

—— (1973). 'An Aspiring Buffer State: Anglo-Persian Relations in the Third Coalition, 1804–1807', *HJ* 16: 509–33.

—— (1978). 'From Trade to Empire in the Near East, III: The Uses of the Residency at Bagdad, 1794–1804', *MES* 14: 278–306.

—— (1979). *The Beginning of the Great Game in Asia, 1828–1834*. New York.

—— (1981). *Commitment to Empire: Prophecies of the Great Game in Asia, 1797–1800*. New York.

—— (1984). *In Defence of British India: Great Britain in the Middle East, 1775–1842*. London.

Isenburg, W. (1968). *Das Staatsdenken des Freiherrn vom Stein*. Bonn.

Israel, F. L. (ed.) (1967). *Major Peace Treaties of Modern History, 1648–1947*. 4 vols., New York.

Jablonowski, H. (1972). *Russland, Polen und Deutschland. Gesammelte Aufsätze*. Cologne.

Jacobs, L. (1988). ' "Le Moment Libéral": The Distinctive Character of Restoration Liberalism', *HJ* 31: 479–91.

Jardin, A. (1984). *Alexis de Tocqueville*. Paris.

—— (1985). *Histoire du libéralisme politique: de la crise de l'absolutisme à la constitution de 1875*. Paris.

—— and Tudesq, A.-J. (1984). *Restoration and Reaction, 1815–1848*. New York.

Jarrett, D. (1973). *The Begetters of Revolution: England's Involvement with France, 1759–1789*. Totowa, NJ.

Jaucourt, A. F. Comte de (1905). *Correspondance du comte de Jaucourt, ministre intérimaire des affaires étrangères, avec le prince de Talleyrand pendant le Congrès de Vienne*. Paris.

Jelavich, B. (1962). *Russia and Greece during the Regency of Kong Othon, 1832–1835: Russian Documents on the First Years of Greek Independence*. Thessaloniki.

—— (1966). *Russia and the Greek Revolution of 1843*. Munich.

—— (1968). 'The Balkan Nations and the Greek War of Independence', in Petropoulos (1968: 157–69).

—— (1984). *Russia and the Formation of the Romanian National State, 1821–1878*. New York.

——(1991). *Russia's Balkan Entanglements, 1806–1914*. Cambridge.

Jenkins, B. (1988). *Era of Emancipation: British Government of Ireland, 1812–1830*. Montreal.

Jennings, L. C. (1973). *France and Europe in 1848*. New York.

—— (1977). 'France, Great Britain, and the Repression of the Slave Trade, 1841–1845', *FHS* 10: 101–25.

—— (1980). 'The French Press and Great Britain's Campaign against the Slave Trade', *Revue française d'histoire d'outre-mer*, 67: 5–24.

—— (1988). *French Reaction to British Slave Emancipation*. Baton Rouge, La.

Jervis, R. (1970). *The Logic of Images in International Relations*. New York.

—— (1976). *Perception and Misperception in International Politics*. Princeton, NJ.

—— (1978). 'Co-operation under the Security Dilemma', *WP* 30: 167–214.

—— (1992). 'A Political Science Perspective on the Balance of Power and the Concert', *AHR* 92: 716–24.

—— Lebow, R. N., and Stein, J. G. (eds.) (1985). *Psychology and Deterrence*. Baltimore, Md.

Jewsbury, G. F. (1977). *The Russian Annexation of Bessarabia, 1774–1828*. New York.

—— (1979). 'Nationalism in the Danubian Principalities, 1800–1825: A Reconsideration', *EEQ* 13: 287–96.

John, W. (ed.) (1913). *Erzherzog Carl*. Vienna.

Johnson, D. (1957). 'The Foreign Policy of Guizot, 1840–1848', *Univ. of Birmingham Historical Journal*, 6: 62–87.

—— (1963). *Guizot: Aspects of French History, 1787–1874*. London.

—— (ed.) (1976). *French Society and the Revolution*. New York.

—— Crouzet, F., and Bédarida, F. (eds.) (1980). *Britain and France: Ten Centuries*. Folkestone, Kent.

Johnson, P. (1991). *Birth of the Modern World Society, 1815–1830*. New York.

Johnston, O. W. (1986). 'British Pounds and Prussian Patriots', *PCRE* 16: 294–305.

—— (1987). 'British Espionage and Prussian Politics in the Age of Napoleon', *Intelligence and National Security*, 2: 230–44.

Jones, C. (ed.) (1983). *Britain and Revolutionary France: Conflict, Subversion and Propaganda*. Exeter.

Jones, G. S. (1983). 'The Mid-Century Crisis and the 1848 Revolution: A Critical Comment', *Theory and Society*, 12: 505–19.

Jones, P. (1988). *The Peasantry in the French Revolution*. Cambridge.

Jones, R. A. (1971). *The Nineteenth Century Foreign Office: An Administrative History*. London.

—— (1983). *The British Diplomatic Service, 1815–1914*. Gerrards Cross, Bucks.

Jones, R. E. (1984). 'Opposition to War and Expansion in Late Eighteenth Century Russia', *JGO* 32: 34–51.

Joseph II, Emperor of Austria (1869). *Joseph II und Katharina von Russland: Ihr Briefwechsel*, ed. A von Arneth. Vienna.

—— (1871). *Correspondances intimes de l'empereur Joseph II avec . . . le comte de Cobenzl et . . . le prince de Kaunitz*, ed. S. Brunner. Mainz.

—— (1872). *Joseph II und Leopold von Toscana: Ihr Briefwechsel von 1781 bis 1790*, ed. A. von Arneth. 2 vols., Vienna.

—— (1873). *Joseph II, Leopold II, und Kaunitz: Ihr Briefwechsel*, ed. A. Beer. Vienna.

—— (1901). *Joseph II und Graf Ludwig Cobenzl: Ihr Briefwechsel*, ed. A. Beer and J. von Fiedler. 2 vols., Vienna.

—— (1902). *Geheime Correspondenz Josefs II mit seinem Minister in den österreichischen Niederlanden, Ferdinand Grafen Trauttmansdorff, 1787–1789*, ed. H. Schlitter. Vienna.

Jouvenel, B. de (1942). *Napoléon et l'économie dirigée: le blocus continental*. Paris and Brussels.

Julien, C.-A. (1964). *Histoire de l'Algérie contemporaine*. Paris.

Jupp, P. (1985). *Lord Grenville, 1759–1834*. Oxford.

Jürgens, A. (1976). *Emmerich von Dalberg zwischen Deutschland und Frankreich: Seine politische Gestalt und Wirksamkeit 1803–1810*. Stuttgart.

Juretschke, H. (1961). 'Die Franzosenpartie im spanischen Unabhängigkeitskrieg: Ihr Entstehen, ihre Entwicklung, und ihre historische Folgen', in *Gesammelte Aufsätze zur Kulturgeschichte Spaniens*, xviii. 221–309. Münster.

Justi, J. H. G. von (1760–1). *Historische und juristische Schriften*. 2 vols., Frankfurt.

—— (1763). *La Chimère de l'équilibre du commerce et de la navigation . . .* Copenhagen.

Kaiser, D. (1990). *Politics and War: European Conflict from Philip II to Hitler*. Cambridge, Mass.

Kaiser, F., and Stasiewski, B. (eds.) (1974). *Die erste polnische Teilung 1772*. Cologne.

Käiväräinen, I. I. (1965). *Mezhdunarodnye otnosheniia na severe evropy v nachale xix veka i prisoedinenie Finlandii k Rossii v 1809 godu*. Petrozavodsk.

Kaldis, W. P. (1963). *John Capodistrias and the Modern Greek State*. Madison, Wis.

Kampel, B. (1961). 'Die Beziehungen Österreichs zu Spanien in den Jahren 1830–1839', diss., Univ. of Vienna.

Kann, R. A. (1950). *The Multi-National Empire*. 2 vols., New York.

Kaplan, H. H. (1962). *The First Partition of Poland*. New York.

—— (1981). 'Russia's Impact on the Industrial Revolution in Great Britain during the Second Half of the Eighteenth Century: The Significance of International Commerce', *Forschungen zur osteuropäischen Geschichte*, 29: 7–59.

Kaplan, L. S. (ed.) (1977). *The American Revolution and 'A Candid World'*. Kent, OH.

—— (1979). 'The American Revolution in International Perspective: Views from International Symposia', *IHR* 1: 408–26.

—— (1987). *Entangling Alliance with None: American Foreign Policy in the Age of Jefferson*. Kent, OH.

Kaplan, M. A. (1957). *System and Process in International Politics*. New York.

Karal, E. Z. (1982). 'The Ottoman Empire and the Serbian Uprising, 1807–1812', in Vucinich (1982a: 207–26).

Kauffmann, W. W. (1951). *British Policy and the Independence of Latin America, 1804–1828*. New Haven, Conn.

Kaunitz-Rietberg, W. A. Fürst (1899). *Kaunitz, Philipp Cobenzl, und Spielmann: Briefwechsel (1779–1792)*, ed. H. Schlitter. Vienna.

Kazakov, N. I. (1969). 'Taina russkoi strategii v austro-frantsuzkoi voine 1809', *Istoriia SSSR*, 6: 63–80.

Keep, J. H. L. (1979). 'Paul I and the Militarization of Government', in Ragsdale (1979a: 91–103).

—— (1980). 'The Russian Army's Response to the French Revolution', *JGO* 28: 500–23.

—— (1985). *Soldiers of the Tsar: Army and Society in Russia, 1462–1874*. Oxford.

Kelly, G. A. (1980). 'Conceptual Sources of the Terror', *Eighteenth-Century Studies*, 14: 18–36.

—— (1981). 'From Lèse-Majesté to Lèse-Nation: Treason in Eighteenth-Century France', *Journal of the History of Ideas*, 42: 269–86.

Kelly, J. B. (1965). 'Mehemet Ali's Expedition to the Persian Gulf 1837–1840', *MES* 1: 350–81; 2: 31–65.

—— (1968). *Britain and the Persian Gulf, 1795–1890*. Oxford.

Kemp, T. (1971). *Economic Forces in French History*. London.

Kennedy, M. L. (1982). *The Jacobin Clubs in the French Revolution: The First Years*. Princeton, NJ.

—— (1988). *The Jacobin Clubs in the French Revolution: the Middle Years*. Princeton, NJ.

Kennedy, P. (1976). *The Rise and Fall of British Naval Mastery*. London.

—— (1987). *The Rise and Fall of the Great Powers*. New York.

Kennedy, W. B. (1972). ' "Without any Guarantee on Our Part": The French Directory's Irish Policy', *PCRE*, 50–64.

Kenney, J. L. (1979). 'The Politics of Assassination', in Ragsdale (1979a: 125–46).

Keohane, R. O. (1989). *International Institutions and State Power*. Boulder, Colo.

Kerautret, M. (1991). 'L'Image de la France en France pendant la révolution française: changement et continuité', in Büsch and Neugebauer-Wölk (1991: 267–300).

Kielmannsegg, P. Graf von (1964). *Stein und die Zentralverwaltung 1813/14*. Stuttgart.

Kieniewicz, S. (1947–8). 'The Free City of Cracow, 1815–1846', *SEER* 26: 69–89.

—— (1969). *The Emancipation of the Polish Peasantry*. Chicago.

Kieswetter, J. K. (1972). 'Metternich and the Bourbon Succession 1819–1820', *EEQ* 6: 363–75.

—— (1982). 'The Imperial Restoration: Continuity in Personnel and Policy under Napoleon I and Louis XVIII', *Historian*, 95: 31–46.

Kiniapina, I. S. (1952). 'Russko-austriiskie protivorechiia nakunene i vo vremia russko-turetskoi voiny 1828–29 godov', *Uchenye Zapiski Moskovsogo Gosudarstvenogo Universiteta*, 156: 194–224.

—— (1958). 'Unkiar-Iskelessiikii dogovor 1833 g', *Nauchnye Doklady Vysshei Shkoly: Istoricheskie Nauki*, 2: 30–49.

Kissinger, H. A. (1957). *A World Restored: Metternich, Castlereagh, and the Problems of Peace, 1812–1822*. Boston.

Kleinmann, H.-O. (1967). 'Die Politik des Wiener Hofes gegenüber der spanischen Monarchie unter Karl III', diss., Univ. of Cologne.

Klingenstein, G. (1977). 'Institutionelle Aspekte der österreichischen Aussenpolitik im 18. Jahrhundert', in Zöllner (1977: 74–93).

Klueting, H. (1981). 'Die Folgen der Säkularisation: Zur Diskussion der wirtschaftlichen und sozialen Auswirkungen der Vermögenssäkularisation in Deutschland', in Berding and Ullmann (1981: 184–207).

—— (1986). *Die Lehre von der Macht der Staaten*. Berlin.

—— (1988). 'Ewald Friedrich von Hertzberg: preussischer Kabinettsminister unter Friedrich dem Grossen und Friedrich Wilhelm II', in Kunisch (1988b: 135–52).

Klug, E. (1987). 'Das "asiatische" Russland: über die Entstehung eines europäischen Vorurteils', *HZ* 245: 265–89.

Knick, H. C. (1982). 'British Industrialization before 1841: Evidence of Slower Growth during the Industrial Revolution', *JEH* 42: 267–89.

Koch, H. W. (1987). *Die Befreiungskriege 1807/1815. Napoleon gegen Deutschland und Europa*. Berg.

Körner, H. (1980). 'Die "Oppositionspartei" der Mittelstaaten bei der deutschen Bundesversammlung in Frankfurt am Main aus der sicht der sächsischen Höfe und Diplomaten', in *Stadtverfassung, Verfassungsstaat, Pressepolitik: Festschrift fur Eberhard Naujoks*, 318–38. Sigmaringen.

Kohler, A. (1975). 'Das Reich im Spannungsfeld des preussisch-österreichischen Gegensatzes: die Fürstenbundbestrebungen 1783–1785', in Engel-Janosi *et al.* (1975: 71–96).

Kohlschmidt, W. (1930). *Die sächsische Frage auf dem Wiener Kongress und die sächsische Diplomatie dieser Zeit*. Dresden.

Kolb, E. (1975). 'Polenbild und Polenfreundschaft der deutschen Frühliberalen: Zur Motivation und Funktion aussenpolitischen Parteinahme im Vormärz', *Saeculum*, 26: 111–27.

Koliopoulos, J. S. (1987). *Brigands with a Cause: Brigandage and Irredentism in Modern Greece*. Oxford.

—— (1989). 'Brigandage and Irredentism in Nineteenth-Century Greece', *European History Quarterly*, 19: 193–228.

Kolodziej, E. A. (1991). 'The Cold War as Co-operation', in R. Kanet and E. A. Kolodziej (eds.), *The Cold War as Co-operation*, 3–30. Baltimore.

Kolosov, N. A. (1985). 'Der vaterländische Krieg 1812', *Revue internationale d'histoire militaire*, 59: 289–98.

Komlos, J. (1983). *The Habsburg Monarchy as a Customs Union: Economic Development in Austria-Hungary in the Nineteenth Century*. Princeton, NJ.

Konetzke, R. (1929). *Die Politik des Grafen Aranda*. Berlin.

Kopitzsch, F. (ed.) (1976). *Aufklärung, Absolutismus und Bürgertum in Deutschland*. Munich.

Korisis, H. S. (1966). *Die politischen Parteien Griechenlands: Ein neuer Staat auf dem Wege zur Demokratie, 1821–1910*. Herbruck.

Kosáry, D. (1979). *Napoléon et la Hongrie*. Budapest.

Koselleck, R. (1967). *Preussen zwischen Reform und Revolution: Allgemeines Landrecht, Verwaltung und soziale Bewegung von 1791 bis 1848*. Stuttgart.

—— (1978). 'Staat und Gesellschaft in Preussen 1815–1848', in Conze (1978: 79–112).

Kossman, E. H. (1978). *The Low Countries, 1780–1940*. Oxford.

Kossok, M. (1964). *Im Schatten der Heiligen Allianz: Deutschland und Lateinamerika, 1815–1830*. Berlin.

Koumoulides, J. (1971). *Cyprus and the War of Greek Independence, 1821–1829*. Athens.

Kraehe, E. E. (1963). *Metternich's German Policy*, i: *The Contest with Napoleon 1799–1814*. Princeton, NJ.

—— (1966). 'Raison d'état et idéologie dans la politique allemande de Metternich (1809–1820)', *RHMC* 13: 181–94.

—— (1977). 'From Rheinbund to Deutscher Bund: The Road to European Equilibrium', *PCRE* 4: 163–75.

—— (1983). *Metternich's German Policy*, ii: *The Congress of Vienna, 1814–1815*. Princeton, NJ.

Kraft, H. (1953). *Die Württemberger in den napoleonischen Kriegen*. Stuttgart.

Kramer, G. F., and McGrew, R. E. (1974). 'Potemkin, the Porte, and the Road to Tsargrad: The Shumla Negotiations, 1789–1790', *CASS* 8: 467–88.

Krasner, S. D. (ed.) (1983). *International Regimes*. Ithaca, NY.

Krauel, R. (1914). 'Die Beteiligung Preussens an der zweiten Bewaffneten Neutralität von Dezember 1801 [*sic*]', *FBPG* 27: 189–245.

Krautheim, H.-J. (1977). *Öffentliche Meinung und imperiale Politik: Das britische Russlandbild, 1815–1854.* Berlin.

Krüger-Löwenstein, U. (1972). *Russland, Frankreich und das Reich 1801– 1803.* Wiesbaden.

Kuhn, H. (1988). 'Romantic Myths, Student Agitation and International Politics: The Danish Intellectuals and Slesvig-Holsten', *Scandinavica*, 27: 5–19.

Kuhn, O. (ed.) (1974). *Grossbritannien und Deutschland: europäische Aspekte der politisch-kulturellen Beziehungen beider Lander in Geschichte und Gegenwart.* Munich.

Kukiel, M. (1955). *Czartoryski and European Unity, 1770–1861.* Princeton, NJ.

Kunisch, J. (1979). *Staatsverfassung und Mächtepolitik: Zur Genese von Staatenkonflikten im Zeitalter des Absolutismus.* Berlin.

—— (1978). *Das Mirakel des Hauses Brandenburg: Studien zum Verhältnis von Kabinettspolitik und Kriegführung im Zeitalter des Siebenjährigen Krieges.* Munich.

—— (1988a). 'Friedrich der Grosse, Friedrich Wilhelm II und das Problem der dynastischen Kontinuität im Hause Hohenzollern', in Kunisch (1988b: 1–27).

—— (ed.) (1988b). *Persönlichkeiten im Umkreis Friedrichs des Grossen.* Cologne.

—— and Stollberg-Rillinger, B. (eds.) (1986). *Staatsverfassung und Heeresverfassung in der europäischen Geschichte der frühen Neuzeit.* Berlin.

Kunstler, C. (1947). *Fersen et son secret.* Paris.

Kutz, M. (1980). 'Die Entwicklung des Aussenhandels Mitteleuropas zwischen Französischer Revolution und Wiener Kongress', *GG* 6: 538–58.

Lackland, H. M. (1926). 'The Failure of the Constitutional Experiment in Sicily, 1813–14', *EHR* 41: 210–35.

—— (1927). 'Lord William Bentinck in Sicily, 1811–12', *EHR* 42: 371–96.

Lacour-Gayet, G. (1928–30). *Talleyrand, 1754–1838.* 4 vols., Paris.

Lademacher, H. (1971). *Die belgische Neutralität als Problem der europäischen Politik, 1830–1914.* Bonn.

—— (1978). 'Frankreich, Preussen und die belgische Frage in der Juli-Monarchie', in Poidevin and Sieburg (1978: 47–62).

Lambi, M. (1981). 'The Making of a Russophobe: David Urquhart—The Formative Years, 1825–1835', *IHR* 3: 330–57.

Lang, D. M. (1957). *The Last Years of the Georgian Monarchy, 1658–1832.* New York.

Langbein, J. H. (1983). 'Albion's Fatal Flaws', *PP* 98: 96–120.

Lange, G. (1956). 'Die Rolle England bei der Wiederherstellung und Vergrösserung Hannovers 1813–1815', *Niedersächsisches Jahrbuch für Landesgeschichte*, 28: 144–63.

Langer, W. L. (1969). *Political and Social Upheaval, 1832–1852.* New York.

Langewiesche, D. (1974). *Liberalismus und Demokratie in Württemberg zwischen Revolution und Reichsgründung.* Dusseldorf.

—— (1980). 'Republik, konstitutionelle Monarchie und "soziale Frage": Grundprobleme der deutschen Revolution von 1848/49', *HZ* 230: 529–48.

—— (ed.) (1989). *Revolution und Krieg.* Paderborn.

Langford, P. (1976). *The Eighteenth Century, 1688–1815.* New York.

Langsam, W. C. (1930). *The Napoleonic Wars and German Nationalism in Austria.* New York.

Lannoy, F. de (1903). *Les Origines diplomatiques de l'indépendance belge: la Conférence de Londres (1830–1831).* Louvain.

—— (1930). *Histoire diplomatique de l'indépendance belge.* Brussels.

—— (1948). *Histoire diplomatique . . . belge, 1830–1839.* 2nd edn., Brussels.

Latreille, A. (1935). *Napoléon et la Saint-Siège, 1801–1808: L'Ambassade du Cardinal Fesch à Rome.* Paris.

Lauren, P. G. (1979a). 'Crisis Management: History and Theory in International Conflict', *IHR* 1: 542–56.

—— (ed.) (1979b). *Diplomacy: New Approaches in History, Theory, and Policy.* New York.

Lawson, F. H. (1983). 'International Regimes and Commercial Hegemony: Control of the Arabian Littoral, 1800–1905', *IHR* 5: 84–112.

Lean, E. T. (1970). *The Napoleonists: A Study in Political Disaffection, 1760–1960.* Oxford.

Lebel, G. (1955). *La France et les principautés danubiennes (du xvie siècle à la chute de Napoléon Ier).* Paris.

Lebow, R. N. (1984). *Between Peace and War: The Nature of International Crisis.* Baltimore.

Lechner, S. (1977). *Gelehrte Kritik und Restauration: Metternichs Wissenschafts-und Pressepolitik und die Wiener 'Jahrbücher der Literatur', 1818–1849.* Tübingen.

LeDonne, J. P. (1984). *Ruling Russia: Politics and Administration in the Age of Absolutism, 1762–1796.* Princeton, NJ.

Leeb, I. L. (1973). *The Ideological Origins of the Batavian Revolution: History and Politics in the Dutch Republic, 1747–1780.* The Hague.

Lefebvre, G. (1962–4). *The French Revolution.* 2 vols., New York.

—— (1969). *Napoleon.* 2 vols., New York.

Le Goff, T. J. A., and Sutherland, D. G. (1983). 'The Social Origins of Counter-Revolution in Western France', *PP* 99: 65–87.

Lemmi, F. (1928). *La politica estera de Carlo Alberto nei suoi primi anni de regno.* Florence.

Lensen, G. A. (1959). *The Russian Push toward Japan: Russo-Japanese Relations, 1697–1875.* Princeton, NJ.

Leonard, E. G. (1958). *L'Armée et ses problèmes au xviiie siècle.* Paris.

Lesage, C. (1924). *Napoleon Ier, créancier de la Prusse, 1807–1814.* Paris.

Leslie, R. F. (1969). *Polish Politics and the Revolution of November 1830.* Westport, Conn.

Lettner, G. (1988). *Das Rückzugsgefecht der Aufklärung in Wien 1790–1792.* Frankfurt.

Leveson Gower, G., 1st Earl Granville (1916). *Lord Granville Leveson Gower: Private Correspondence 1781 to 1821,* ed. Castalia Countess Granville. 2 vols., London.

Levy, J. S. (1983). *War in the Modern Great Power System, 1495–1975.* Lexington, Ky.

—— (1985). 'Theories of General War', *WP* 38: 344–74.

—— (1987). 'Declining Power and the Preventive Motivation for War', *WP* 40: 82–107.

Levy, M. J. (1988). *Governance and Grievance: Habsburg Policy and Italian Tyrol in the Eighteenth Century.* West Lafayette, Ind.

Lewis, M. (1960). *A Social History of the Navy 1793–1815.* London.

Ley, F. (1975). *Alexandre Ier et sa Sainte-Alliance.* Paris.

L'Huillier, F. (1973). 'Note sur Napoléon et les peuples de l'Europe d'après la correspondance de l'Empereur', *Francia,* 1: 369–73.

Liang, H.-H. (1980). 'International Co-operation of Political Police in Europe, 1815–1914', *MOS* 33: 193–217.

Lill, R. (1974). 'Kirche und Revolution', *Archiv für Sozialgeschichte,* 14: 419–54.

—— (1979). 'Die Säkularisation und die Auswirkungen des napoleonischen Konkordats in Deutschland', in Reden-Dohna (1979: 91–104).

Lincoln, W. B. (1978). *Nicholas I: Emperor and Autocrat of all the Russias.* Bloomington, Ind.

Liponski, W. (1978). *Polska a Brytania 1801–1830.* Poznan.

Liss, P. K. (1983). *Atlantic Empires: The Network of Trade and Revolution, 1713–1826.* Baltimore, Md.

Livermore, H. V. (1976). *A New History of Portugal.* Cambridge.

Livet, G. (1976). *L'Équilibre européen de la fin du XVe à la fin du XVIIIe siècle.* Paris.

Lojek, J. (1970). 'Catharine's Armed Intervention in Poland: Origins of the Political Decisions at the Russian Court in 1791 and 1792', *CASS* 4: 570–93.

—— (ed.) (1974). 'La Politique de la Russie envers la Pologne pendant le premier partage d'après un document secret de la cour russe de 1772', *CASS* 8: 116–36.

—— (1975). 'The International Crisis of 1791: Poland between the Triple Alliance and Russia', *East Central Europe,* 2: 1–63.

Lokke, C. L. (1932). *France and the Colonial Question.* New York.

Long, R. M. (1980). 'The End of Tuscan Neutrality: 1798', *PCRE* 1: 293–302.

Longford, E. (1969–72). *Wellington.* 2 vols., London.

Longworth, P. (1965). *The Art of Victory: The Life and Achievements of Generalissimo Suvorov.* London.

Lord, R. H. (1915). *The Second Partition of Poland.* Cambridge, Mass.

Losch, P. (1922). *Geschichte des Kurfürstentums Hessen 1803–1866.* Kassel.

Lovett, C. M. (1982). *The Democratic Movement in Italy, 1830–1876*. Cambridge, Mass.

Lovett, G. H. (1965). *Napoleon and the Birth of Modern Spain*. 2 vols., New York.

Lowe, P. (1981). *Britain in the Far East: A Survey from 1819 to the Present*. New York.

Lucas, C. (1976). 'Nobles, Bourgeois, and the Origins of the French Revolution', in D. Johnson (1976: 88–131).

—— (1978). 'The Directory and the Rule of Law', *FHS* 10: 231–60.

—— (ed.) (1991). *Rewriting the French Revolution*. Oxford.

Lucas-Dubreton, J. (1959). *Le Culte de Napoléon, 1815–1848*. Paris.

Luckwaldt, F. (1898). *Österreich und die Anfänge des Befreiungskrieges von 1813*. Berlin.

Ludtke, W. (1929). 'Preussen und Frankreich vom Bastillesturm bis Reichenbach (1789–1790)', *FBPG* 42: 230–62.

Lukowski, J. T. (1990). *Liberty's Folly: The Polish–Lithuanian Commonwealth 1697–1795*. London.

Lutostanski, K. (1918). *Les Partages de la Pologne et la lutte pour l'indépendance*. Lausanne.

Lutz, H. (1979). *Österreich-Ungarn und die Gründung des Deutschen Reiches*. Frankfurt.

—— (1985). *Zwischen Habsburg und Preussen: Das Ringen um die Vormacht in Deutschland 1815–1866*. Berlin.

—— and Helmut Rumpler, H. (eds.) (1982). *Österreich und die deutsche Frage im 19. und 20. Jahrhundert*. Munich.

Lynch, J. (1973). *The Spanish American Revolutions, 1808–1826*. New York.

Lynn, J. A. (1984). *The Bayonets of the Republic: Motivation and Tactics in the Army of Revolutionary France, 1791–94*. Urbana, Ill.

Lyon, E. W. (1934). *Louisiana in French Diplomacy, 1759–1804*. Norman, Okla.

Lyons, M. (1975). *France under the Directory*. Cambridge.

McConnell, A. (1969). 'Alexander I's Hundred Days: The Politics of a Paternalistic Reformer', *SR* 28: 373–93.

McDowell, R. B. (1979). *Ireland in the Age of Imperialism and Revolution, 1760–1801*. New York.

McElwee, W. (1975). *The Art of War: Waterloo to Mons*. Bloomington, Ind.

McErlean, J. P. (ed.) (1975). 'Autour de la guerre de 1812', *CASS* 9: 542–89.

McFee, W. (1950). *The Law of the Sea*. Philadelphia.

McGill, W. (1971). 'The Roots of Policy: Kaunitz in Vienna and Versailles, 1749–1753', *JMH* 43: 228–44.

—— (1980). 'Kaunitz: The Personality of Political Algebra', *Topic* 34: 29–42.

McGrew, R. E. (1970). 'A Political Portrait of Paul I from the Austrian and English Diplomatic Archives', *JGO* 18: 503–29.

—— (1979). 'Paul I and the Knights of Malta', in Ragsdale (1979a: 44–75).

McGrew, W. W. (1976). 'The Land Issue in the Greek War of Independence', in Petropoulos et al. (1976: 111–29).

McKay, D., and Scott, H. M. (1982). The Rise of the Great Powers, 1648–1815. London.

MacKenzie, N. (1982). Escape from Elba: The Fall and Flight of Napoleon, 1814–1815. New York.

Mackesy, P. (1957). The War in the Mediterranean, 1803–1810. Cambridge, Mass.

—— (1974). Statesmen at War: The Strategy of Overthrow, 1798–1799. London.

—— (1976). Could the British Have Won the War of Independence? Worcester, Mass.

—— (1978). 'Problems of an Amphibious Power: Britain against France, 1793–1815', Naval War College Review, 30: 16–25.

—— (1984). War without Victory: The Downfall of Pitt, 1799–1802. Oxford.

McKnight, J. L. (1965). 'Admiral Ushakov and the Ionian Republic: The Genesis of Russia's First Balkan Satellite', diss., Univ. of Chicago.

McLean, D. (1981). 'The Greek Revolution and the Anglo-French Entente 1843–4', EHR 96: 117–29.

MacMillan, D. S. (1973). 'Paul's "Retributive Measures" of 1800 Against Britain: The Final Turning-Point in British Commercial Attitudes towards Russia', CASS 7: 68–77.

—— (1975). 'Russo-British Trade Relations under Alexander I', CASS 9: 437–48.

McNally, R. T. (1958). 'The Origins of Russophobia in France: 1812–1830', American Slavic and East European Review, 17: 173–89.

McNeill, W. H. (1982). The Pursuit of Power. Chicago.

McQuiston, J. R. (1971). 'Rose and Canning in Opposition, 1806–1807', HJ 14: 503–27.

Madariaga, I. de (1959). 'The Secret Austro-Russian Treaty of 1781', SEER 38: 114–45.

—— (1962). Britain, Russia and the Armed Neutrality of 1780. New Haven, Conn.

—— (1981). Russia in the Age of Catherine the Great. New Haven, Conn.

Männer, L. (1927). Bayern vor und in der französischen Revolution. Stuttgart.

Mager, W. (1973). 'Das Problem der landständischen Verfassungen auf dem Wiener Kongress 1814/15', HZ 217: 293–346.

Malmesbury, J. H., 1st Earl (1844). Diaries and Correspondence, ed. 3rd Earl of Malmesbury. 4 vols., London.

Mandrou, R. (1977). L'Europe 'absolutiste': raison et raison d'état, 1649–1750. Paris.

Manfred, A. Z. (1971). 'Poiski soiuza s Rossiei (1800–1801g.)', Istoria SSSR, 4: 38–59.

Mann, G. (1946). Secretary of Europe. New Haven, Conn.

Mansel, P. (1981). Louis XVIII. London.

Mansel, P. (1983). 'How Forgotten Were the Bourbons in France between 1812 and 1814?' *European Studies Review*, 13: 13–38.

—— (1987). *The Eagle in Splendour: Napoleon I and his Court*. London.

Marcum, J. W. (1973). 'Vorontsov and Pitt: The Russian Assessment of a British Statesman, 1785–1792', *Rocky Mountain Social Science Journal*, 10: 49–56.

—— (1974). 'Catherine II and the French Revolution: A Reappraisal', *Canadian Slavonic Papers*, 16: 187–202.

Margerison, K. (1983). 'P.-L. Roederer: Political Thought and Practice during the French Revolution', *Transactions of the American Philosophical Society*, 1: 1–164.

Maria Carolina, Queen of Naples and Sicily (1911). *Correspondance inédite de Marie Caroline avec le Marquis de Gallo*. 2 vols., Paris.

Markov, W. (1979). 'Zum Stellenwert des napoleonischen Illyriens', *RESEE* 17: 269–82.

Marlowe, J. (1971). *Perfidious Albion: The Origins of Anglo-French Rivalry in the Levant*. London.

Marshall-Cornwall, J. (1965). *Marshal Massena*. Oxford.

Marston, T. E. (1961). *Britain's Imperial Role in the Red Sea Area, 1800–1878*. Hamdon, Conn.

Martens, F. F. (ed.) (1874–1905). *Recueil des traités et conventions, conclus par la Russie avec les puissances étrangères*. 14 vols., St Petersburg.

Martin, G. (1982). 'Confederation Rejected: The British Debate on Canada, 1837–1840', *Journal of Imperial and Commonwealth History*, 11: 33–57.

Martin, W. (1931). *La Suisse et l'Europe, 1813–1814*. Lausanne.

Martinez, R. B., and Barker, T. M. (eds.) (1988). *Armed Forces and Society in Spain*. New York.

Masson, F. (1903). *Le Département des affaires étrangères pendant la révolution, 1787–1804*. Paris.

Mastellone, S. (1957). *La politica estera del Guizot (1840 a 1847)*. Florence.

—— (1960). *Mazzini e la 'giovine Italia', 1831–1834*. 2 vols., Pisa.

Mather, F. C. (1990). 'Achilles or Nestor? The Duke of Wellington in British Politics, 1832–1846', in Gash (1990*b*: 170–95).

Mathias, P., and O'Brien, P. K. (1976). 'Taxation in Britain and France, 1715–1810', *Journal of European Economic History*, 5: 601–50.

—— (1989). 'The Impact of the Revolutionary and Napoleonic Wars, 1793–1815, on the Long-Run Growth of the British Economy', *Review* (Fernand Braudel Centre, Paris), 12: 335–83.

Mathieson, W. L. (1929). *Great Britain and the Slave Trade, 1839–1865*. London.

Matsch, E. (1980). *Geschichte des auswärtigen Dienstes von Österreich-Ungarn 1720–1920*. Cologne.

Maturi, W. (1938). 'Il congresso di Vienna e la restaurazione dei Borboni a Napoli', *RSI*, n.s., 3: 32–72; 4: 1–61.

—— (1939). 'La politica estera napoletana dal 1815 al 1820', *RSI*, n.s., 4: 226–272.

Mauersberg, H. (1966). 'Rekonstructionsprojekte deutscher Staaten auf dem Wiener Kongress', in W. Abel (ed.), *Wirtschaft, Geschichte und Wirtschaftsgeschichte*, 266–83. Stuttgart.

Mayr, J. K. (1934). *Metternichs geheimer Briefdienst. Postlogen und Postkurse*. Vienna.

—— (1935). *Die österreichische Staatskanzlei im Zeitalter des Fürsten Metternichs*. Vienna.

Mediger, W. (1952). *Moskaus Weg nach Europa: Der Aufstieg Russlands zum europäischen Machtstaat im Zeitalter Friedrichs des Grossen*. Braunschweig.

Meinecke, F. (1957). *Das Zeitalter der deutschen Erhebung, 1795–1815*, 6th edn. Leipzig.

Mélanges (1968). *Mélanges offerts à G. Jacquemyns*. Brussels.

Melchior-Bonnet, B. (1962). *Un policier dans l'ombre de Napoléon: Savary, duc de Rovigo*. Paris.

—— (1965). *Dictionnaire de la révolution et de l'empire*. Paris.

Mellon, S. (1979). 'Nineteenth-Century Perceptions of Revolution', in H. T. Parker (ed.), *Problems in European History*, 59–71. Durham, NC.

Melville, R., et al. (eds.) (1988). *Deutschland und Europa in der Neuzeit*. 2 vols., Stuttgart.

Melvin, F. E. (1949). *Napoleon's Navigation System: A Study of Trade Control during the Continental Blockade*. New York.

Mercy-Argenteau, F. Comte de (1889). *Correspondance secrète du comte de Mercy-Argenteau avec l'Empereur Josef II et le Prince de Kaunitz*, ed. A. von Arneth and J. Flammermont. 2 vols. in 1, Paris.

Meriage, L. P. (1978). 'The First Serbian Uprising (1804–1813) and the Nineteenth-Century Origins of the Eastern Question', *SR* 37: 421–39.

Merriman, J. M. (ed.) (1975). *1830 in France*. New York.

Metternich-Winneburg, C. L. W. Fürst (1880–4). *Aus Metternichs nachgelassenen Papieren*, ed. Prince R. Metternich-Winneburg. 8 vols., Vienna.

—— (1909). *Lettres du prince de Metternich à la comtesse de Lieven, 1818–1819*, ed. J. Hanoteau. Paris.

—— (1966). *Clemens Metternich–Wilhelmina von Sagan: ein Briefwechsel, 1813–1815*, ed. M. Ullrichova. Graz.

Meyendorff, P. K. Baron (1923). *Peter von Meyendorff, ein russischer Diplomat an den Höfen von Berlin und Wien: politischer und privater Briefwechsel, 1826–1863*, ed. O. Hoetzsch. 3 vols., Berlin.

Meyer, H. C. (1955). *Mitteleuropa in German Thought and Action, 1815–1945*. The Hague.

Meyer, J. (1980). 'The Second Hundred Years' War (1689–1815)', in Johnson et al. (1980: 139–63).

Michailowski-Danilevsky, A., and Miliutin, D. A. (1856–58). *Geschichte des Krieges Russlands mit Frankreich unter der Regierung Kaiser Pauls I im Jahre 1799*. 5 vols., Munich.

Michalski, J. (1980). 'Polen und Preussen in der Epoche der Teilungen', *JGMOD* 30: 35–52.

—— and Senkowska-Glück, M. (1981). 'L'Historiographie polonaise de la révolution française et de l'époque napoléonienne', *AHRF* 53: 608–15.

Michon, G. (1941). *Le Rôle de la presse en 1791–1792: la déclaration de Pillnitz et la guerre.* Paris.

Middleton, C. R. (1977). *The Administration of British Foreign Policy, 1782–1846.* Durham, NC.

—— (1981). 'Palmerston, Ponsonby, and Mehemet Ali: Some Observations on Ambassadorial Independence in the East, 1838–1840', *EEQ* 15: 409–24.

Mieck, I. (1991). 'Die Integration preussischer Landesteile französischen Rechts nach 1814/15', in Büsch and Neugebauer-Wölk (1991: 345–62).

Milward, A. S., and Saul, S. B. (1979). *The Economic Development of Continental Europe, 1780–1870.* Winchester, Mass.

Miraflores, M. P. F. (1836). *Essais historiques et critiques pour servir à l'histoire d'Espagne de 1820 à 1823.* 2 vols., Paris.

Miskolczy, J. (1959). 'Metternich und die ungarischen Stände', *MOS* 12: 240–56.

Misra, G. S. (1963). *British Foreign Policy and Indian Affairs, 1783–1815.* Bombay.

Mistler, J. (ed.) (1969). *Napoléon et l'empire.* 2 vols., Paris.

—— (1973). 'Hambourg sous l'occupation française: observations au sujet du blocus continental', *Francia,* 1: 451–66.

Mitchell, H. (1965). *The Underground War against France: The Missions of William Wickham, 1794–1800.* Oxford.

—— (1968). 'The Vendée and Counterrevolution: A Review Essay', *FHS* 5: 405–29.

—— (1974). 'Resistance to the Revolution in Western France', *PP* 63: 94–131.

Mitchell, L. G. (1971). *Charles James Fox and the Disintegration of the Whig Party, 1782–1794.* New York.

Mitchison, R. (ed.) (1980). *The Roots of Nationalism: Studies in Northern Europe.* Edinburgh.

Möller, H. (1983). 'Primat der Aussenpolitik: Preussen und die Französische Revolution, 1789–1795', *Francia Beihefte,* 12: 65–81.

—— (1991). 'Preussische Aufklärungsgesellschaften und Revolutionserfahrung', in Büsch and Neugebauer-Wölk (1991: 103–17).

Molden, E. (1913). *Die Orientpolitik des Fürsten Metternich, 1829–1833.* Vienna.

Molitor, H. (1980). *Vom Untertan zum Administré: Studien zur französischen Herrschaft und zum Verhalten der Bevölkerung im Rhein-Mosel-Raum von den Revolutionskriegen bis zum Ende der Napoleonischen Zeit.* Wiesbaden.

—— (1982). 'Zensur, Propaganda und Überwachung zwischen 1780 und 1815 im mittleren Rheinland', *Geschichtliche Landeskunde,* 22: 28–44.

Moloney, B. (1968). 'Anglo-Florentine Diplomatic Relations and the French Revolution', *English Miscellany,* 11: 273–93.

Mooney, G. (1978). 'British Diplomatic Relations with the Holy See, 1793–1830', *Recusant History,* 14: 193–210.

Moran, D. J. (1981). 'Goethe and Napoleon: The French Pursuit of the Allgemeine Zeitung', *CEH* 14: 91–109.

Morgan, G. (1981). *Anglo-Russian Rivalry in Central Asia: 1810–1895*. London.

Morgan, I. (1978). 'French Policy in Latin America, 1830–1848', *Journal of Latin American Studies*, 10: 309–28.

—— (1983). 'Orleanist Diplomacy and the French Colony in Uruguay', *IHR* 5: 201–28.

Morgenthau, H. J. (1967). *Politics Among Nations*. 4th edn., New York.

Moritz, E. (1968). *Preussen und der Kosciusko- Aufstand, 1794: zur preussischen Polenpolitik in der Zeit der Französischen Revolution*. Berlin.

Morley, C. (1951–2). 'The European Significance of the November Rising', *JCEA* 2: 407–16.

Morrell, W. P. (1930). *British Colonial Policy in the Age of Peel and Russell*. Oxford.

Moscati, R. (ed.) (1937). *Il regno delle Due Sicilie e l'Austria: documenti dal marzo 1821 al novembre 1830*. 2 vols., Naples.

—— (1939). 'I rapporti austro-napoletane nei primi anni del regno di Ferdinando II', *Archivio storico per le province napoletane*, n.s., 25: 138–200.

—— (1947). *Ferdinando II de Borbone nei documenti diplomatici austriaci*. Naples.

Mouraviev, B. (1954). *L'Alliance russe–turque au milieu des guerres napoléoniennes*. Paris.

Müller, H. (1976). 'Die Krise des Interventionsprinzips der Heiligen Allianz: zur Aussenpolitik Österreichs und Preussens nach der Julirevolution von 1830', *JB* 14: 9–56.

—— (1980). 'Der Weg nach Münchengrätz: Voraussetzungen, Bedingungen, und Grenzen der Reaktivierung des reaktionären Bündnisses der Habsburger und Hohenzollern mit den Romanows im Herbst 1833', *JB* 21: 7–62.

—— (1989). 'Deutscher Bund und Deutsche Nationalbewegung', *HZ* 248: 51–78.

Müller, M. G. (1980). 'Russland und der Siebenjährige Krieg: Beitrag zu einer Kontroverse', *JGO* 28: 198–219.

—— (1981). 'Deutsche und polnische Nation im Vormärz', *JGO* 30: 69–95.

—— (1983). *Polen zwischen Preussen und Russland: Souveranitätskrise und Reformpolitik 1736–1752*. Berlin.

—— (1984). *Die Teilungen Polens: 1772, 1793, 1795*. Munich.

—— (1986). 'Staat und Heer in der Adelsrepublik Polen im 18. Jahrhundert', in Kunisch and Stollberg-Rillinger (1986: 279–95).

Münchow-Pohl, B. von (1987). *Zwischen Reform und Krieg: Untersuchungen zur Bewusstseinslage in Preussen 1809–1812*. Göttingen.

Murat, I. (1981). *Napoleon and the American Dream*. Baton Rouge, La.

Muret, P. (1913). 'Une nouvelle conception de la politique étrangère de Napoléon', *RHMC* 18: 177–200, 353–80.

—— (1971). 'Zur Aussenpolitik Napoleons', in Sieburg (1971: 113–56).

Murphy, O. T. (1981). 'The Conservatism of Charles Gravier, Comte de Vergennes', *PCRE* 119–30.

—— (1982). *Charles Gravier, Comte de Vergennes: French Diplomacy in the Age of Revolution, 1719–1787*. Albany, NY.

—— (1986). 'Louis XVI and the Pattern and Costs of a Policy Dilemma: Russia and the Eastern Question, 1787–1788', *PCRE* 16: 264–74.

Murphy, D. T. (1991). 'Prussian Aims for the Zollverein, 1828–33', *Historian*, 53: 285–302.

Nabonne, B. (1951). *La Diplomatie du directoire et Bonaparte, d'après les papiers inédits de Reubell*. Paris.

Nada, N. (1953). *L'Austria e la questione romana dalla rivoluzione di luglio all fine della conferenza diplomatica romana (agosto 1830–luglio 1831)*. Turin.

—— (1955). 'La polemica fra Palmerston e Metternich sulla questione romana nel 1832', *Bollettino storico bibliografico subalpino*, 53: 35–78.

—— (1957). *Metternich e le reforme nello stato pontificio: la missione Sebregondi a Roma (1832–1836)*. Turin.

—— (1980). *Dalla stato assoluto allo stato costituzionale: storia del regno di Carlo Alberto dal 1831 al 1848*. Turin.

Näf, W. (1928). *Zur Geschichte der Heiligen Allianz*. Bern.

Naff, T. (1960). *Ottoman Diplomacy and the Great European Powers, 1797–1802*. London.

Nanteuil, H. de (1968). 'Logistische Probleme der napoleonischen Kriegführung', in Groote and Müller (1968: 65–78).

Napoleon (1858–1870): Bonaparte, Napoleon, *Correspondance de Napoléon Ier: publiée par ordre de l'Empereur Napoléon III*, ed. A. du Casse. 32 vols., Paris.

Narochnitskii, A. L., and Kazakov, N. I. (1969). 'K istorii vostochnogo voprosa (o tseliakh Rossii i Frantsii na Balkanakh v 1807–1808 gg.)', *Novaia i noveishaia istoriia*, 6: 52–66.

Nathan, J. S. (1980). 'The Heyday of the Balance of Power: Frederick the Great and the Decline of the Old Regime', *US Naval War College Review*, 33: 53–67.

Neal, L. (1991). *The Rise of Financial Capitalism: International Capital Markets in the Age of Reason*. Cambridge.

Nesselrode, K. R. Count (1904–12). *Lettres et papiers du chancelier comte de Nesselrode, 1760–1850 [sic*—actually 1856], ed. Count A. de Nesselrode. 11 vols., Paris.

Neugebauer-Wölk, M. (1991). 'Preussen und die Revolution in Lüttich: Zur Politik des Christian Wilhelm von Dohm', in Büsch and Neugebauer-Wölk (1991: 59–76).

Neuhaus, H. (1986). 'Das Problem der militärischen Executive in der Spätphase des alten Reiches', in Kunisch and Stollberg-Rillinger (1986: 297–346).

Newman, E. (1974). 'The Popular Idea of Liberty in the French Revolution of 1830', *PCRE*, 103–12.

—— (1975). 'La Blouse et la redingote: l'alliance du peuple et de la bourgeoisie à la fin de la restauration', *AHRF* 47: 513–35.

Nichols, I. C. Jr. (1967). 'The Russian Ukase and the Monroe Doctrine: A Re-Evaluation', *Pacific Historical Review*, 36: 13–26.

—— (1971). *The European Pentarchy and the Congress of Verona, 1822*. The Hague.

—— (1982). 'Tsar Alexander I: Pacifist, Aggressor, or Vacillator?' *EEQ* 16: 33–44.

Nicolson, H. (1946). *The Congress of Vienna: A Study in Allied Unity, 1812–1822*. London.

Niedhart, G. (1979). 'Aufgeklärter Absolutismus oder Rationalisierung der Herrschaft', *Zeitschrift für historische Forschung*, 6: 199–211.

Nikitin, S. A., Dostian, I. S., et al. (eds.) (1980–3). *Pervoe serbskoe vosstanie 1803–1813 i Rossiia*. 2 vols., Moscow.

Nipperdey, T. (1983*a*). *Deutsche Geschichte 1800–1866: Burgerwelt und Starker Staat*. Munich.

—— (1983*b*). 'In Search of Identity: Romantic Nationalism, its Intellectual, Political and Social Background', in Eade (1983: 1–15).

—— (1984). 'Der deutsche Föderalismus zwischen 1815 und 1866 im Rückblick', in A. Kraus (ed.), *Land und Reich: Stamm und Nation. Probleme und Perspektiven bayerischer Geschichte*, iii. 1–18. 3 vols., Munich.

Noël, J.-F. (1966). 'Les Problèmes de frontières entre la France et l'empire dans la seconde moitié du XVIIIe siècle', *RH* 235: 333–46.

—— (1968). 'Traditions universalistes et aspects nationaux dans la notion de Saint-Empire au XVIIIe siècle', *RHD* 82: 193–212.

—— (1976). *Le Saint Empire*. Paris.

Nolde, B. (1952–3). *La Formation de l'empire russe*. 2 vols., Paris.

Nordmann, C. (1971). *Grandeur et liberté de la Suède (1660–1792)*. Paris.

Norregaard, G. (1954). *Freden i Kiel, 1814*. Copenhagen.

Norris, J. A. (1955). 'The Policy of the British Cabinet in the Nootka Crisis', *EHR* 70: 562–80.

—— (1967). *The First Afghan War 1838–1842*. Cambridge.

Oakeshott, M. (1972). *On Human Conduct*. Chicago.

Oakley, S. (1970). 'Gustavus III's Plans for War with Denmark in 1783–84', in Hatton and Anderson (1970: 268–86).

Obenaus, H. (1984). *Anfänge des Parlamentarismus in Preussen bis 1848*. Düsseldorf.

Obermann, K. (1966). 'Unveröffentlichte Materialien zur Diplomatie Metternichs 1821–1848', *MOS* 19: 210–63.

—— (1970). 'Unveröffentlichte Schriftstücke Metternichs vom Sommer 1845 über deutsche Angelegenheiten', *MOS* 23: 388–97.

—— (1979). 'Zur politischen Haltung der gemässigten Liberalen am Vorabend und in der deutschen Märzrevolution 1848', *ZGW* 27: 209–25.

O'Brien, P. (1978). *Economic Growth in Britain and France 1780–1914: Two Paths to the Twentieth Century*. London.

—— (1988). 'The Political Economy of British Taxation', *Economic History Review*, 41: 1–32.

O'Brien, P. (1989). 'Public Finance in the Wars with France 1793–1815', in Dickinson (1989: 165–88).

O'Dwyer, M. M. (1985). *The Papacy in the Age of Napoleon and the Restoration: Pius VII, 1800–1823*. Lanham, Md.

Oechsli, W. (1898). *Die Verbündeten und die schweizer Neutralität im Jahre 1813*. Zurich.

—— (1903–13). *Geschichte der Schweiz im XIX. Jahrhundert*. 2 vols., Leipzig.

Oer, R. von (1965). *Der Friede von Pressburg*. Münster.

—— (ed.) (1970). *Die Säkularisation 1803*. Göttingen.

Oestreich, G. (1969). *Geist und Gestalt des frühmodernen Staates*. Berlin.

Oliva, L. J. (1964). *Misalliance: A Study of French Policy in Russia during the Seven Years' War*. New York.

Olson, M. Jr. (1963). *The Economics of the Wartime Shortage: A History of British Food Supplies in the Napoleonic War and in World Wars I and II*. Durham, NC.

Omond, G. W. T. (1919). 'The Question of the Netherlands in 1829–1830', *TRHS*, 4th ser., 2: 150–71.

Ompteda, C. L. von (1869). *Politischer Nachlass des hannoverschen Staats- und Cabinets-Ministers Ludwig von Ompteda aus den Jahren 1804 bis 1813*, ed. F. Ompteda. 3 vols., Jena.

Oncken, W. (1876). *Oesterreich und Preussen im Befreiungskriege*. 2 vols., Berlin.

Orieux, J. (1970). *Talleyrand; ou, le sphinx incompris*. Paris.

Otruba, G. (1965). 'Englands Finanzhilfe fur Österreich in den Koalition-skriegen und im Kampf gegen Napoleon', *OGL*, ser. 3, 9: 84–98.

—— (1971). 'Der Deutsche Zollverein und Österreich', *OGL*, ser. 3, 15: 121–34.

Owsinska, A. (1974). *La Politique de la France envers l'Allemagne à l'époque de la monarchie de juillet, 1830–1848*. Wroclaw.

Oye, K. A. (ed.) (1986). *Co-operation under Anarchy*. Princeton, NJ.

Ozouf, M. (1984). 'War and Terror in French Revolutionary Discourse (1792–1794)', *JMH* 56: 579–97.

Palmer, A. W. (1972). *Metternich*. New York.

—— (1974). *Alexander I: Tsar of War and Peace*. New York.

—— (1983). *The Chancelleries of Europe*. London.

Palmer, R. R. (1959–64). *The Age of the Democratic Revolution*. 2 vols., Princeton, NJ.

Palmer, S. H. (1988). *Police and Protest in England and Ireland, 1780–1850*. New York.

Palmerston, H. T., Viscount (1985). *Palmerston, i: Private Correspondence with Sir George Villiers (afterwards fourth Earl of Clarendon) as Minister to Spain 1833–1837*, ed. R. Bullen and F. Strong. London.

Pamuk, S. (1987). *The Ottoman Empire and European Capitalism, 1820–1913*. Cambridge.

Panin, N. P. Count (1888–92). *Materialy dlia zhizhneopisaniia Grafa Nikity Petrovicha Panina (1770–1837)*, ed. A. Brückner. 6 vols., St Petersburg.

Paret, P. (1966). *Yorck and the Era of Prussian Reform, 1807–1815*. Princeton, NJ.

—— Craig, G., and Gilbert, F. (eds.) (1986). *Makers of Modern Strategy*. Princeton, NJ.

Parker, G. (1988). *The Military Revolution: Military Innovation and the Rise of the West, 1500–1800*. Cambridge.

Parker, H. T. (1944). *Three Napoleonic Battles*. Durham, NC.

—— (1952). 'Napoleon's Philosophy of Governing Conquered Territories, 1805–1807', *South Atlantic Quarterly*, 51: 70–84.

—— (ed.) (1979). *Problems in European History*. Durham, NC.

—— (1990). 'Why Did Napoleon Invade Russia? A Study in Motivation and the Interrelations of Personality and Social Structure', *Journal of Military History*, 54: 131–46.

Parkinson, C. N. (1954). *War in the Eastern Seas, 1793–1815*. London.

Parry, E. J. (1936). *The Spanish Marriages*. London.

Parry, V. J., and Yapp, M. E. (eds.) (1975). *War, Technology and Society in the Middle East*. London.

Partridge, M. S. (1989). *Military Planning for the Defense of the United Kingdom, 1814–1870*. New York.

Patemann, R. (1973). 'Die Beziehungen Bremens zu Frankreich bis zum Ende der französischen Herrschaft 1813', *Francia*, 1: 482–507.

Patrick, A. (1972). *The Men of the First French Republic*. Baltimore, Md.

Pavelka, H. (1968). *Englisch–österreichische Wirtschaftsbeziehungen in der ersten Hälfte des 19. Jahrhunderts*. Graz.

Pavlowitch, S. K. (1961). *Anglo-Russian Rivalry in Serbia, 1837–1839*. Paris.

Paxton, R. V. (1982). 'Russian Foreign Policy and the First Serbian Uprising: Alliances, Apprehensions and Autonomy, 1804–1807', in Vucinich (1982a: 41–70).

Payne, S. G. (1973). *A History of Spain and Portugal*. 2 vols., Madison, Wis.

Peball, K. (1968). 'Zum Kriegsbild der österreichischen Armee und seine geschichtliche Bedeutung in den Kriegen gegen die französische Revolution und Napoleon I in den Jahren von 1792 bis 1815', in Groote and Müller (1968: 129–75).

Pedlow, G. W. (1988). *The Survival of the Hessian Nobility, 1770–1870*. Princeton, NJ.

Perkins, B. (1955). *The First Rapprochement: England and the United States, 1795–1805*. Philadelphia.

—— (ed.) (1962). *The Causes of the War of 1812: National Honor or National Interest?* Huntington, NY.

—— (1963). *Prologue to War: England and the United States, 1805–1812*. Berkeley, Calif.

—— (1964). *Castlereagh and Adams*. Berkeley, Calif.

Petitfrère, C. (1983). 'Le Peuple contre la révolution française', *Histoire*, 53: 34–43.

Petraccone, C. (1985). 'La rivoluzione napoletana del 1799', *Studi storici*, 26: 929–36.

Petri, F., and Droege, G. (eds.) (1976). *Rheinische Geschichte*, ii. Düsseldorf.

Petropoulos, J. A. (1968). *Politics and Statecraft in the Kingdom of Greece, 1833–1843*. Princeton, NJ.

—— (1976). 'Forms of Collaboration with the Enemy during the First Greek War of Liberation', in Petropoulos *et al.* (1976: 131–43).

—— *et al.* (eds.) (1976). *Hellenism and the First Greek War of Liberation (1821–1830)*. Thessaloniki.

Petrovich, M. B. (1976). *A History of Modern Serbia, 1804–1918*. 2 vols., New York.

—— (1982). 'The Role of the Serbian Orthodox Church in the First Serbian Uprising, 1804–1813', in Vucinich (1982a: 259–302).

Pfulg, G. (1961). 'Napoléon et la Suisse', in Dunan (1961: 79–105).

Piechowiak, A. B. (1962–3). 'The Anglo-Russian Expedition to Holland in 1799', *SEER* 41: 182–95.

Pienkos, A. T. (1987). *The Imperfect Autocrat: Grand Duke Constantine Pavlovich and the Polish Congress Kingdom*. Boulder, Colo.

Pingaud, A. (1899). 'Le Congrès de Vienne et la politique de Talleyrand', *RH* 70: 1–52.

—— (1914). *La Domination française dans l'Italie du nord (1796–1805): Bonaparte président del la république italienne*. 2 vols., Paris.

—— (1927). 'La Politique italienne de Napoléon Ier', *RH* 54: 20–33.

Pingaud, L. (1894). *Un agent secret sous la révolution et l'empire: le comte d'Antraigues*, 2nd edn. Paris.

Pinkney, D. H. (1972). *The French Revolution of 1830*. Princeton, NJ.

—— (1986). *Decisive Years in France, 1840–47*. Princeton, NJ.

Pintner, W. M. (1967). *Russian Economic Policy under Nicholas I*. Ithaca, NY.

Pirenne, J.-H. (1946–9). *La Sainte-Alliance, organization européenne de la paix mondiale*. 2 vols., Neuchâtel.

Plaschka, R. (1975). 'Austrian Policy toward the Balkans in the Second Half of the Eighteenth Century: Maria Theresia and Josef II', *EEQ* 9: 471–8.

Plumb, J. H. (1966). *The Growth of Political Stability in England, 1685–1725*. London.

Poidevin, R. (1978). 'Aspects économiques des relations franco-allemandes 1834–1848', in Poidevin and Sieburg (1978: 63–71).

—— and Bariéty, J. (1977). *Les Relations franco-allemandes 1815–1975*. Paris.

—— and Sieburg, H.-O. (eds.) (1978). *Aspects des relations franco-allemandes 1830–1848*. Metz.

Polasky, J. L. (1984). 'Traditionalists, Democrats, and Jacobins in Revolutionary Brussels', *JMH* 56: 227–62.

—— (1987). *Revolution in Brussels, 1787–1793*. Hanover, NH.

Pollard, S. (1981). *Peaceful Conquest: The Industrialization of Europe, 1760–1970*. New York.

Polovtsov, A. A. (ed.) (1902–7). *Correspondance diplomatique des ambassadeurs et ministres de Russie en France et de France en Russie avec leur gouvernements de 1814 à 1830*. 3 vols., St Petersburg.

Ponteil, F. (1966). *Napoléon Ier et l'organisation autoritaire de la France*. Paris.

Popov, N. A. (1869). *Rossiia e Serbiia: Istoricheskii ocherk' russkogo pokrovitelst'va Serbii s 1806 do 1856 god*. 2 vols., Moscow.

Porch, D. (1974). *Army and Revolution: France 1815–1848*. London.

Pounds, N. J. G. (1979). *An Historical Geography of Europe, 1500–1840*. Cambridge.

Pouthas, C.-H. (1938). 'La Politique de Thiers pendant la crise orientale de 1840', *RH* 182: 72–96.

Pozzo di Borgo, C. A. Comte (1890–7). *Correspondance diplomatique du comte Pozzo di Borgo*. 2 vols., Paris.

Pradt, D. G. F. de (1817). *Antidote au congrès de Rastadt 1798, suivi de La Prusse et sa neutralité 1799*. Paris.

Pratt, M. (1978). *Britain's Greek Empire*. Totawa, NJ.

Preradovich, N. von (1955). *Die Führungsschichten in Österreich und Preussen (1804–1918)*. Wiesbaden.

Press, V. (1980*a*). 'Das "Droit d'Épaves" des Kaisers von Österreich: Finanzkrise und Stabilisierungspolitik zwischen Luneviller und Pressburger Frieden', *GG* 6: 559–73.

—— (1980*b*). 'Landtage im alten Reich und im Deutschen Bund', *Zeitschrift für Württembergische Landesgeschichte*, 39: 100–40.

—— (1989). 'Warum gab es keine deutsche Revolution? Deutschland und das revolutionäre Frankreich 1789–1815', in Langewiesche (1989: 67–86).

Price, R. A. (1975). *The Economic Modernization of France, 1730–1880*. New York.

—— (1981). *An Economic History of Modern France, 1730–1914*. New York.

Prignitz, C. (1981). *Vaterlandsliebe und Freiheit: Deutscher Patriotismus von 1750 bis 1850*. Wiesbaden.

Psomiades, H. J. (1976). 'The Character of the New Greek State', in Petropoulos *et al.* (1976: 147–55).

Puryear, V. J. (1938). 'L'Opposition de l'Angleterre et de la France au traité d'Unkiar-Iskelessi en 1833', *RH* 182: 283–310.

—— (1931). *England, Russia and the Straits Question, 1844–1856*. Berkeley, Calif.

—— (1941). *France and the Levant: From the Bourbon Restoration to the Peace of Kutiah*. Berkeley, Calif.

—— (1951). *Napoleon and the Dardanelles*. Berkeley, Calif.

Quint, W. (1971). *Souveränitätsbegriff und Souveränitätspolitik in Bayern: von der Mitte des 17. bis zur ersten Hälfte des 19. Jahrhunderts*. Berlin.

Quynn, D. M. (1945). 'The Art Confiscations of the Napoleonic Wars', *AHR* 50: 437–60.

Radvany, E. (1971). *Metternich's Projects for Reform in Austria*. The Hague.

Raeff, M. (1964). 'The 150th Anniversary of the Campaign of 1812 in Soviet Historical Writing', *JGO* 12: 247–60.

Raeff, M. (ed.) (1966). *Plans for Political Reform in Imperial Russia, 1730–1905*. Englewood Cliffs, NJ.

—— (ed.) (1972). *Catherine the Great: A Profile*. New York.

—— (1983). *The Well-Ordered Police State: Social and Institutional Change through Law in the Germanies and Russia, 1600–1800*. New Haven, Conn.

Ragsdale, H. (1968). 'Russian Influence at Lunéville', *FHS* 5: 274–84.

—— (1970). 'A Continental System in 1801: Paul I and Bonaparte', *JMH* 42: 70–89.

—— (ed.) (1979*a*). *Paul I: A Reassessment of His Life and Reign*. Pittsburgh, Pa.

—— (1979*b*). 'Was Paul Bonaparte's Fool? The Evidence of Neglected Archives', in Ragsdale (1979*a*: 76–90).

—— (1980). *Detente in the Napoleonic Era*. Lawrence, Kan.

—— (1983). 'Russia, Prussia, and Europe in the Policy of Paul I', *JGO* 31: 81–118.

—— (1988*a*). 'Evaluating the Traditions of Russian Aggression: Catherine II and the Greek Project', *SEER* 66: 91–117.

—— (1988*b*). *Tsar Paul and the Question of Madness*. Westport, Conn.

Rahbek-Schmidt, K. (1957). 'Wie ist Panins Plan zu einem Nordischen System entstanden?' *Zeitschrift für Slawistik*, 2: 406–22.

Rain, P. (1950). *La Diplomatie française*, ii: *1789–1800*. Paris.

Ranke, L. von (1875). *Die deutschen Mächte und der Fürstenbund*, 2nd edn. Leipzig.

—— (1879). *Ursprung und Beginn der Revolutionskriege 1791 und 1792*, 2nd edn. Leipzig.

Ransel, D. L. (1975). *The Politics of Catherinian Russia: The Panin Party*. New Haven, Conn.

—— (1979). 'An Ambivalent Legacy: The Education of Grand Duke Paul', in Ragsdale (1979*a*: 1–16).

Rath, R. J. (1941). *The Fall of the Napoleonic Kingdom of Italy (1814)*. New York.

—— (1950). 'The Habsburgs and Public Opinion in Lombardy-Venetia, 1814–1815', in E. M. Earle (ed.), *Nationalism and Internationalism*, 303–5. New York.

—— (1964). 'The Carbonari: Their Origins, Initiation, Rites, and Aims', *AHR* 69: 353–70.

—— (1969). *The Provisional Austrian Regime in Lombardy-Venetia, 1814–1815*. Austin, Tex.

Rauchensteiner, M. (1988). 'Erzherzog Carl und der begrenzte Krieg', *Österreichische Militärische Zeitschrift*, 26: 337–43.

—— (1972). *Kaiser Franz und Erzherzog Carl: Dynastie und Heerwesen in Österreich, 1796–1809*. Munich.

Raumer, K. von (1957). 'Absoluter Staat, korporative Libertät, persönliche Freiheit', *HZ* 183: 55–96.

—— (1952). *Deutschland um 1800: Krise und Neugestaltung*, vol. iii, s. 1 of L. Just (ed.), *Handbuch der Deutschen Geschichte*. Konstanz.

—— (1961*a*). *Freiherr vom Stein*. Munich.

—— (1961*b*). 'Politiker des Masses? Talleyrands Strassburger Friedensplan (17. Oktober 1805)', *HZ* 193: 286–368

—— (1964). 'Hugel's Gutachten zur Frage der Niederlegung der deutschen Kaiserkrone (17. Mai 1806)', *ZBLG* 27: 390–408.

Real, W. (1951–2). 'Der Friede von Basel', *Baseler Zeitschrift für Geschichte und Altertumskunde*, 50: 27–112; 51: 115–228.

—— (1958). *Von Potsdam nach Basel: Studien zur Geschichte der Beziehungen Preussens zu den europaischen Mächten 1786–1795*. Basle.

Reden-Dohna, A. (ed.) (1979). *Deutschland und Italien im Zeitalter Napoleons*. Wiesbaden.

Regele, O. (1957). *Feldmarschall Radetzky: Leben, Leistung, Erbe*. Vienna.

Reichardt, R. (1983). 'Die französische Revolution als Masstab des deutschen Sonderweges', in Voss (1983: 323–8).

Reif, H. (1979). *Westfälischer Adel, 1770–1860: vom Herrschaftsstand zur regionalen Elite*. Göttingen.

Rein, G. A. (1970). *Der Deutsche und die Politik*. Göttingen.

—— (1927). 'Über die Bedeutung der überseeischen Ausdehnung fur das europäische Staaten-System', *HZ* 137: 28–90.

Reinalter, H. (1983). 'Einwirkungen der französischen Revolution auf die Innen- und Aussenpolitik des Kaiserhofes in Wien', in Voss (1983: 49–64).

Reinerman, A. J. (1968). 'Metternich and the Papal Condemnation of the Carbonari, 1821', *CHR* 54: 55–69.

—— (1971). 'Metternich, Italy, and the Congress of Verona, 1821–1822', *HJ* 14: 263–87.

—— (1974). 'Metternich, Alexander I, and the Russian Challenge in Italy, 1815–20', *JMH* 46: 262–76.

—— (1979). *Austria and the Papacy in the Age of Metternich*, i: *1809–1830*. Washington, DC.

—— (1989). *Austria and the Papacy in the Age of Metternich*, ii: *1830–1838*. Washington, DC.

—— (1990). 'The Papacy, Austria, and the Anti-French Struggle in Italy, 1792–97', in Brauer and Wright (1990: 47–68).

Reinhard, M. (1950–2). *Le Grand Carnot*. 2 vols., Paris.

—— (1953). 'La Guerre et la paix à la fin de 1793: un interview inédit de Danton', *AHFR* 2: 97–103.

Reinhard, W. (1986). 'Staat und Heer in England im Zeitalter der Revolutionen', in Kunisch and Stollberg-Rillinger (1986: 173–212).

Rel. dipl. Aust.–Sard. (1964–). ISIEMC, *Le relazioni diplomatiche fra l'Austria e il regno di Sardegna*, ed. N. Nada. 1st ser.: 1815–30; 2nd ser.: 1830–48. Rome.

Rel. dipl. Fr.–Sard. (1974–). ISIEMC, *Le relazioni diplomatiche fra la Francia e il regno di Sardegna*, ed. A. Saitta. 2nd ser.: 1830–48. Rome.

Rel. dipl. Fr.–Sic. (1966). ISIEMC, *Le relazioni diplomatiche fra la Francia e il regno delle Due Sicilie*, ed. A. Saitta. 2nd ser.: 1830–48. Rome.

Rel. dipl. GB–Sard. (1972–). ISIEMC, *Le relazioni diplomatiche fra la Gran*

Bretagna e il regno di Sardegna, ed. F. Curato. 1st ser.: 1814–30; 2nd ser.: 1830–48; 3rd ser.: 1848–61. Rome.

Rel. dipl. Stat. Pont.–Fr. (1962–). ISIEMC, *Le relazioni diplomatiche fra lo Stato Pontificio e la Francia.* 2nd ser.: 1830–48, ed. G. Procacci; 3rd ser.: 1848–60, ed. M. Fatica. Rome.

Rel. fr.–belg. (1975). *Les Relations franco-belges de 1830 à 1934: actes du colloque de Metz, 15–16 novembre 1974.* Metz.

Rémond, R. (1965). *La Vie politique en France*, i: *1789–1848.* Paris.

Renier, G. J. (1930). *Great Britain and the Establishment of the Kingdom of the Netherlands, 1813–1815.* London.

Renn, E. M. (1974). 'England Faces Invasion: The Land Forces, 1803–1805', *PCRE*, 129–40.

Riasanovsky, N. (1967). *Nicholas I and Official Nationality in Russia.* Berkeley, Calif.

Rice, G. W. (1980). 'Great Britain, the Manila Ransom, and the First Falkland Islands Dispute with Spain, 1766', *IHR* 2: 386–409.

Richardson, L. (1960). *Statistics of Deadly Quarrels.* Pittsburgh, Pa.

Ridder, A. de (1932). *Les Projets d'union douanière franco-belge et les puissanees européennes (1836–1843).* Brussels.

Riley, J. C. (1986). *The Seven Years' War and the Old Regime in France: The Economic and Financial Toll.* Princeton, NJ.

Rinieri, I. (1927). 'La rivoluzione in Germania, le società segrete, l'Austria e il principe di Carignano', in Rossi and De Magistris (1927: i. 542–660).

Ritcheson, C. R. (1969). *Aftermath of Revolution: British Policy toward the United States, 1783–1795.* Dallas, Tex.

—— (1980). 'Thomas Pinckney's London Mission, 1792–1796, and the Impressment Issue', *IHR* 2: 523–41.

—— (1983). 'The Earl of Shelbourne and Peace with America, 1782–1783: Vision and Reality', *IHR* 5: 322–45.

Ritter, G. (1958). *Stein: eine politische Biographie*, 3rd edn. Stuttgart.

Roach, E. E. (1983). 'Anglo-Russian Relations from Austerlitz to Tilsit', *IHR* 5: 181–200.

Roberts, M. (1964). 'Great Britain and the Swedish Revolution, 1772–3', *HJ* 7: 1–46.

—— (1970). 'Great Britain, Denmark, and Russia, 1763–70', in Hatton and Anderson (1970: 236–67).

—— (1980). *British Diplomacy and Swedish Politics, 1758–1773.* Minneapolis, Minn.

—— (1986). *The Age of Liberty: Sweden 1719–1772.* Cambridge.

Roberts, W. L. H. (1901). 'The Negotiations Preceding the Peace of Lunéville', *TRHS* 15: 47–130.

Robertson, W. S. (1939). *France and Latin-American Independence.* Baltimore, Md.

Robinson, J. M. (1987). *Cardinal Consalvi, 1757–1824.* New York.

Robson, W. H. (1931). 'New Light on Lord Castlereagh's Diplomacy', *JMH* 3: 198–218.

Rodger, A. B. (1964). *The War of the Second Coalition, 1798–1801.* Oxford.

Rodkey, F. S. (1929). 'Lord Palmerston's Policy for the Rejuvenation of Turkey, 1830–41', *TRHS* 12: 163–92.

—— (1933). 'The Attempts of Briggs and Company to Guide British Policy in the Levant in the Interest of Mehemet Ali Pasha, 1821–1841', *JMH* 5: 324–51.

Rodolico, N. (1936). *Carlo Alberto negli anni di regno 1831–1843.* Florence.

Rönnebeck, W. (1968). *Die diplomatischen Beziehungen zwischen Russland und England vom Regierungsantritt Alexanders I bis zur Begründung der Dritten Koalition.* Hamburg.

Rössler, H. (1940). *Österreichs Kampf um Deutschlands Befreiung.* 2 vols., Hamburg.

—— (1958). *Zwischen Revolution und Reaktion.* Göttingen.

—— (1966). *Graf Johann Philipp Stadion: Napoleons deutscher Gegenspieler.* 2 vols., Vienna.

Roghe, D. (1971). *Die französische Deutschland-Politik während der ersten zehn Jahre der Julimonarchie (1830–1840).* Frankfurt.

Roginski, V. V. (1974). 'Soiuz Rossii i Shvetsii pered Otechestvennoi voinoi 1812g', *Novaia i Noveishaia Istoria,* 3: 160–8.

Rohden, P. R. (1939). *Die klassische Diplomatie von Kaunitz bis Metternich.* Leipzig.

Roider, K. A. Jr. (1976). 'Kaunitz, Josef II, and the Turkish War', *SEER* 54: 538–56.

—— (1980). 'The Oriental Academy in the *Theresienzeit*', *Topic,* 34: 19–28.

—— (1982). *Austria's Eastern Question, 1700–1790.* Princeton, NJ.

—— (1987). *Baron Thugut and Austria's Response to the French Revolution.* Princeton, NJ.

—— (1990): 'Austria's Road to Austerlitz', in Brauer and Wright (1990: 11–23).

Rolo, P. J. V. (1965). *George Canning.* London.

Roloff, G. (1902). 'Zur Napoleonischen Politik von 1803–1805', *Historische Vierteljahrsschrift,* 5: 487–503.

Romani, G. T. (1950). *The Neapolitan Revolution of 1820–1821.* Evanston, Ill.

Romanov, Grand Prince Nikolai Mikhailovitch (ed.) (1905–14). *Diplomaticheskie snosheniia Rossii i Frantsii po doneseniam poslov imperatorov Aleksandra i Napoleona, 1808–1812.* 7 vols., St Petersburg.

Rooney, J. W. Jr. (1982). *Revolt in the Netherlands: Brussels—Eighteen-Thirty.* Lawrence, Kan.

Roosbroeck, R. von (1969). 'Betrachtungen uber Ziel und Wirkungen der Kontinentalsperre', in Groote (1969: 119–42).

Rosanvallon, P. (1985). *Le Moment Guizot.* Paris.

Rose, J. H. (1903). 'France and the First Coalition Before the Campaign of 1796', *EHR* 18: 287–302.

—— (1906). 'Canning and the Spanish Patriots in 1808', *AHR* 12: 39–52.

Rose, J. H. (1911). *William Pitt and the Great War*. London.

—— (1912). *William Pitt and National Revival*. London.

Rosecrance, R. (1962). *Action and Reaction in World Politics*. Boston.

—— (1986). *The Rise of the Trading State*. New York.

Rosenberg, H. (1968). *Bureaucracy, Aristocracy and Autocracy*. Cambridge, Mass.

Rosenkrantz, N. (1953). *Journal du congrès de Vienne, 1814–1815*. Copenhagen.

Ross, S. T. (1967). 'The Military Strategy of the Directory: The Campaigns of 1799', *FHS* 5: 170–87.

—— (1969). *European Diplomatic History, 1789–1815*. Garden City, NY.

—— (1973). *Quest for Victory: French Military Strategy, 1792–99*. New York.

—— (1984). *French Military History, 1661–1799*. New York.

Rosselli, J. (1956). *Lord William Bentinck and the British Occupation of Sicily*. Cambridge.

Rossi, T., and de Magistris, C. P. (eds.) (1927). *La rivoluzione piemontese del 1821*. 2 vols., Turin.

Rothenberg, G. (1978). *The Art of Warfare in the Age of Napoleon*. Bloomington, Ind.

—— (1982*a*). 'Archduke Charles and the Question of Popular Participation in War', *PCRE*, 214–24, 263–8.

—— (1982*b*). *Napoleon's Great Adversaries: The Archduke Charles and the Austrian Army, 1792–1814*. Bloomington, Ind.

Roulet, L.-E. (1961). 'Le Visage de Napoléon Ier dans l'opinion suisse du régime de médiation', in Dunan (1961: 109–17).

Rowen, H. H. (1988). *The Princes of Orange: The Stadholders in the Dutch Republic*. New York.

Ruiz, A. (1983). 'Agents de la propagande révolutionnaire en Allemagne de 1789 à 1792: les voyageurs et leur récits sur la France', in Voss (1983: 82–97).

Rumpler, H. (1972). *Die deutsche Politik des Freiherrn von Beust 1848 bis 1850*. Vienna.

—— (ed.) (1990). *Deutscher Bund und deutsche Frage 1815–1866*. Vienna.

Runciman, S. (1968). *The Great Church in Captivity: A Study of the Patriarchate of Constantinople from the Eve of the Turkish Conquest to the Greek War of Independence*. Cambridge.

Runciman, W. G. (1983). 'Unnecessary Revolution: The Case of France', *Archives européennes de sociologie*, 24: 291–318.

Ruppenthal, R. (1943). 'Denmark and the Continental System', *JMH* 15: 7–23.

Russocki, S. (1979). 'Modernisierung oder Reform? Die "Einstimmigkeit" der polnischen Reichstagsbeschlüsse und ihr Wandel im 18. Jahrhundert', in De Conze (1979: 28–33).

Ryan, A. (1953). 'The Causes of the British Attack upon Copenhagen in 1807', *EHR* 68: 37–55.

—— (1959). 'The Defence of British Trade with the Baltic, 1808–1813', *EHR* 74: 443–66.

—— (1988). 'An Ambassador Afloat: Vice-Admiral Sir James Samaurez and the Swedish Court, 1808–1812', in Black and Woodfine (1988: 237–58).

Sabry, M. (1930). *L'Empire égyptien sous Mohamed Ali et la question d'orient (1811–1849)*. Paris.

Sack, J. J. (1979). *The Grenvillites, 1801–1829: Party Politics and Factionalism in the Age of Pitt and Liverpool*. Urbana, Ill.

Sahlins, P. (1990). 'Natural Frontiers Revisited: France's Boundaries since the Seventeenth Century', *AHR* 95: 1423–51.

St Clair, W. (1972). *That Greece Might Still Be Free: The Philhellenes in the War of Independence*. New York.

Sallett, R. (1953). *Der diplomatische Dienst: Seine Geschichte und Organisation in Frankreich, Grossbritannien und den Vereinigten Staaten*. Stuttgart.

Samsonowicz, H., and Bogucka, M. (eds.) (1982). *A Republic of Nobles*. Cambridge.

Sandonà, A. (1912). *Il regno lombardo veneto, 1814–1859*. Milan.

Sas, N. C. F. van (1985). *Onze Natuurlijkste Bondgenoot: Nederland, Engeland en Europa, 1813–1831*. Groningen.

Sauer, M. (1971). 'Österreich und die Levante 1814–1838', diss., Univ. of Vienna.

Saul, N. E. (1970). *Russia and the Mediterranean, 1797–1807*. Chicago.

—— (1979). 'The Objectives of Paul's Italian Policy', in Ragsdale (1979*a*: 31–43).

—— (1991). *Distant Friends: The United States and Russia, 1763–1867*. Lawrence, Kan.

Saunier, C. (1902). *Les Conquêtes artistiques de la révolution et de l'Empire*. Paris.

Savigneur, P. (1969). 'Carbonarism and the French Army, 1815–1824', *History*, 54: 198–211.

Sbornik (1867–1916). Imperatorskoe Russkogo Istoricheskoe Obshchestvo, *Sbornik Russkogo Istoricheskogo Obshchestva*. 148 vols., St Petersburg.

Schaeder, H. (1934). *Die dritte Koalition und die Heilige Allianz*. Königsberg.

Schama, S. (1977). *Patriots and Liberators: Revolution in the Netherlands, 1780–1813*. New York.

—— (1989). *Citizens: A Chronicle of the French Revolution*. New York.

Schenk, H. G. (1947). *The Aftermath of the Napoleonic Wars*. New York.

Schieder, T. (1957). 'Idee und Gestalt des übernationalen Staates seit dem 19. Jahrhundert', *HZ* 184: 336–66.

Schieder (1969). *Zum Problem des Staatenpluralismus in der modernen Welt*. Cologne.

—— (1978). 'Partikularismus und nationales Bewusstsein im Denken des Vormärz', in Conze (1978: 9–38).

Schieder and Alter, P. (eds.) (1974). *Staatsgründung und Nationalitätsprinzip.* Vienna.

Schieder, W. (ed.) (1983). *Liberalismus in der Gesellschaft des deutschen Vormärz.* Göttingen.

Schiemann, T. (1904). *Die Geschichte Russlands unter Kaiser Nikolaus I.* 4 vols., Berlin.

Schlitter, H. (1907). 'Die Sendung Birkenstocks nach Berlin und der "grosse Plan" Hertzbergs', *Beiträge zur Neueren Geschichte Österreichs,* 2: 24–79.

Schlossberger, A. von (ed.) (1889). *Politische und militarische Korrespondenz König Friedrichs von Württemberg mit Kaiser Napoleon I, 1805–1813.* Stuttgart.

Schmidt, C. (1905). *Le Grand-Duché de Berg (1806–1813).* Paris.

Schmidt, H. (1984). 'Die Verteidigung des Oberrheins und die Sicherung Süddeutschlands im Zeitalter des Absolutismus und der Französischen Revolution', *Historisches Jahrbuch,* 104: 46–62.

Schmidt-Brentano, A. (1982). 'Die österreichische beziehungsweise österreichisch-ungarische Armee von Erzherzog Carl bis Conrad von Hötzendorf', in Lutz and Rumpler (1982: 231–55).

Schmitt, H. A. (1959). '1812: Stein, Alexander I and the Crusade against Napoleon', *JMH* 31: 325–8.

—— (1977). 'Revolution and Revolts in the Germanies: Goals and Accomplishments during the 1830s', *PCRE,* 54–66.

—— (1983). 'Germany without Prussia: A Closer Look at the Confederation of the Rhine', *German Studies Review,* 6: 9–39.

Schmitt, H. P. (1971). 'Ursprung und Untergang der ersten immerwährenden Neutralität: Malta', *Österreichische Zeitschrift für öffentliches Recht* 22: 57–72.

Schneer, R. M. (1980). 'Arthur Wellesley and the Cintra Convention: A New Look at an Old Puzzle', *JBS* 19: 93–119.

Schneider, E. (1980). 'Revolutionserlebnis und Frankreichbild zur Zeit des ersten Koalitionskrieges (1792–1795)', *Francia,* 8: 277–394.

Schoeps, H.-J. (1967). 'Metternichs Kampf gegen die Revolution', *HZ* 205: 529–65.

Schroeder, P. W. (1962*a*). 'Austria as an Obstacle to Italian Unification and Freedom, 1814–1861', *Austrian History Newsletter,* 2: 1–32.

—— (1962*b*). *Metternich's Diplomacy at its Zenith, 1820–1823.* Austin, Tex.

—— (1976). 'Alliances, 1815–1945: Weapons of Power and Tools of Management', in K. Knorr (ed.), *Historical Problems of National Security,* 247–86. Lawrence, Kan.

—— (1983). 'Containment Nineteenth-Century Style: How Russia was Restrained', *South Atlantic Quarterly,* 82: 1–18.

—— (1986). 'The Nineteenth Century International System: Changes in the Structure', *WP* 39: 1–26.

—— (1987). 'The Collapse of the Second Coalition', *JMH* 59: 244–90.

—— (1988). 'An Unnatural "Natural Alliance"': Castlereagh, Metternich, and Aberdeen in 1813', *IHR* 10: 522–40.

—— (1989). 'The Nineteenth Century System: Balance of Power or Political Equilibrium?' *Review of International Studies*, 15: 135–53.

—— (1990). 'Napoleon's Foreign Policy: A Criminal Enterprise', *Journal of Military History*, 54: 147–61.

—— (1992). 'Did the Vienna System Rest upon a Balance of Power?' *AHR* 97: 683–706.

Schulze, H. (ed.) (1987). *Nation-Building in Central Europe*. New York.

Schumpeter, E., and Ashton, T. S. (1960). *English Overseas Trade Statistics, 1697–1808*. Oxford.

Schwartzberg, S. (1988). 'The Lion and the Phoenix: British Policy Toward the "Greek Question", 1821–1832', *MES* 24: 139–77, 287–311.

Schwarz, H. W. (1933). *Die Vorgeschichte des Vertrages von Ried*. Munich.

Schwarzfuchs, S. (1979). *Napoleon, the Jews and the Sanhedrin*. Boston.

Scott, F. D. (1933). 'Bernadotte and the Throne of France, 1814', *JMH* 5: 465–78.

—— (1935). *Bernadotte and the Fall of Napoleon*. Cambridge, Mass.

Scott, H. M. (1975). 'France and the Polish Throne: 1763–64', *SEER* 53: 370–88.

—— (1975–6). 'Great Britain, Poland, and the Russian Alliance, 1763–1767', *HJ* 19: 729–38; 20: 53–74.

—— (1977). 'Frederick II, the Ottoman Empire and the Origins of the Russo-Prussian Alliance of April 1764', *European Studies Review*, 7: 153–75.

—— (1979). 'The Importance of Bourbon Naval Reconstruction to the Strategy of Choiseul after the Seven Years' War', *IHR* 1: 17–35.

—— (1990). *British Foreign Policy in the Age of the American Revolution*. Oxford.

Scott, I. (1972). 'Counter-Revolutionary Diplomacy and the Demise of Anglo-Austrian Co-operation, 1820–1823', *Historian*, 34: 465–84.

Scott, S. F. (1973). *The Response of the Royal Army to the French Revolution*. Oxford.

Seide, G. (1971). *Regierungspolitik und öffentliche Meinung im Kaisertum Österreich anlässlich der polnischen Novemberrevolution*. Wiesbaden.

Seier, H. (1986). 'Zur Frage der militärischen Exekutive in der Konzeption des Deutschen Bundes', in Kunisch and Stollberg-Rillinger (1986: 397–445).

Semenev, L. S. (1959). 'Russko-persidskie diplomaticheskie otnosheniia posle Giulistanskogo mira 1813–26', *Uchenye Zapiski Leningradskogo Universiteta*, 270: 83–117.

—— (1963). *Rossiia i mezhdunarodnye otnosheniia na Srednem Vostoke v 20-e gody xix v.* Leningrad.

Semmel, B. (1961). 'The Philosophic Radicals and Colonialism', *JEH* 21: 513–25.

—— (1970). *The Rise of Free Trade Imperialism*. New York.

Semmel, B. (1986). *Liberalism and Naval Strategy*. London.

Senkowska-Glück, M. (1970). 'Les Donataires de Napoléon', *RHMC* 17: 680–93.

Seton-Watson, R. W. (1937). *Britain in Europe, 1789–1914*. New York.

Severn, J. K. (1981). *A Wellesley Affair: Richard Marquess Wellesley and the Conduct of Anglo-Spanish Diplomacy, 1809–1812*. Gainesville, Fla.

Shapiro, A. L. (1956). 'Sredizemnomorskie problemy vneshnei politiki Rossii v nachale XIX v.', *Istoricheskie Zapiski*, 55: 53–89.

Shaw, S. J. (1971). *Between Old and New: The Ottoman Empire under Sultan Selim III, 1798–1807*. Cambridge, Mass.

—— (1976). *History of the Ottoman Empire and Modern Turkey*. Cambridge, Mass.

—— (1982). 'The Ottoman Empire and the Serbian Uprising, 1804–1807', in Vucinich (1982a: 71–94).

Sheehan, J. (1978). *German Liberalism in the Nineteenth Century*. Chicago.

—— (1989). *German History, 1770–1866*. Oxford.

Sheehan, M. (1988). 'The Development of British Theory and Practice of the Balance of Power before 1714', *History*, 73: 24–37.

Sherwig, J. M. (1962). 'Lord Grenville's Plan for a Concert of Europe, 1797–1799', *JMH* 34: 284–93.

—— (1969). *Guineas and Gunpowder: British Foreign Aid in the Wars with France, 1793–1815*. Cambridge, Mass.

Shil'der, N. K. (1903). *Imperator Nikolai Pervyi: Ego Zhizn i Tsarstvovanie*. 2 vols., St Petersburg.

Shneidman, J. L. (1957). 'The Proposed Invasion of India by Russia and France in 1801', *Journal of Indian History*, 35: 167–75.

Showalter, D. E. (1978). 'Weapons Technology and the Military in Metternich's Germany: A Study in Stagnation?' *Australian Journal of Politics and History*, 24: 227–38.

Shparo, O. B. (1965). *Ozvobozhdenie Gretsii i Rossiia (1821–1829)*. Moscow.

Shupp, P. F. (1931). *The European Powers and the Near Eastern Question, 1806–1807*. New York.

Shur, L. A. (1964). *Rossiia i Latinska Amerika*. Moscow.

Sieburg, H.-O. (1969). 'Napoleon, Napoleon-Legende, und politische Gruppenbildung', in Groote (1969: 151–67).

—— (1970). 'Napoléon et la transformation des institutions en Allemagne', *RHMC* 17: 897–912.

—— (ed.) (1971). *Napoleon und Europa*. Cologne.

—— (1978). 'Nationales Selbstverständnis und Gegensatzbewusstsein in der Ära der Julimonarchie und des Vormärz: diplomatie- und geistesgeschichtlicher Aufriss', in Poidevin and Sieburg (1978: 1–16).

Siemann, W. (1980). 'Die Protokolle der Mainzer Zentraluntersuchungskommission von 1819 bis 1828', in *Stadtverfassung, Verfassungsstaat, Pressepolitik: Festschrift für Eberhard Naujoks*. Sigmaringen.

—— (1985). *'Deutschlands Ruhe, Sicherheit und Ordnung': Die Anfänge der politischen Polizei, 1806–1866*. Tübingen.

—— (1989). 'Heere, Freischaren, Barrikaden. Die bewaffnete Macht als Instrument der Innenpolitik in Europa 1815–1847', in Langewiesche (1989: 87–102).

Sieske, G. (1959). *Preussen im Urteil Hannovers 1795–1806*. Hildesheim.

Silagi, D. (1961). *Ungarn und der geheime Mitarbeiterkreis Kaiser Leopolds II*. Munich.

—— (1967). *Der grösste Ungar*. Vienna.

Silva, P. (1917). *La monarchia di luglio e l'Italia*. Turin.

—— (1936). 'La politica francese nell'epoca delle riforme (1846–1848) e l'accordo Metternich–Guizot', *Revue des études italiennes*, 1: 275–95.

Silvera, A. (1974). 'The Origins of the French Expedition to Egypt in 1798', *Islamic Quarterly*, 18: 21–30.

Simon, W. M. (1955). *The Failure of the Prussian Reform Movement*. Ithaca, NY.

Sinkiewicz, C. (ed.) (1854). *Recueil des documents relatifs à la Russie pour la plupart secrets et inédits, utiles à consulter dans la crise actuelle*. Paris.

Sirotkin, V. G. (1960). 'Iz istorii vneshnei politiki Rossii v Sredizemnomore v nachale XIX v.', *Istoricheskie Zapiski*, 67: 213–33.

Sked, A. (ed.) (1979a). *Europe's Balance of Power, 1815–1848*. New York.

—— (1979b). *The Survival of the Habsburg Empire: Radetzky, the Imperial Army and the Class War, 1848*. London.

Skiotis, D. N. (1975). 'Mountain Warriors and the Greek Revolution', in Parry and Yapp (1975: 308–29).

—— (1976). 'The Greek Revolution: Ali Pasha's Last Gamble', in Petropoulos *et al.* (1976: 98–109).

Skocpol, T. (1979). *States and Social Revolutions*. Cambridge.

Skowronek, J. (1982). 'The Direction of Political Change in the Era of National Insurrection', in Samsonowicz and Bogucka (1982: 258–81).

Skurnowicz, J. S. (1981). *Romantic Nationalism and Liberalism: Joachim Lelewel and the Polish National Idea*. New York.

Slezkin, L. Iu. (1964). *Rossiia i voina za nezavisimost v Ispanskoi Amerike*. Moscow.

Sloane, W. M. (1899). 'Napoleon's Plans for a Colonial System', *AHR* 4: 439–55.

Smith, E. A. (1990). *Lord Grey, 1764–1845*. Oxford.

Snyder, G. H., and Diesing, P. (1977). *Conflict Among Nations*. Princeton, NJ.

Sondhaus, L. (1989). *The Habsburg Empire and the Sea: Austrian Naval Policy, 1797–1866*. West Lafayette, Ind.

Sorel, A. (1881–2). 'La Diplomatie française et le comité de salut public', in 4 pts.: 'L'Autriche et le comité de salut public', *RH* 17: 25–63; 'Le Neutralité du nord de l'Allemagne en 1795', ibid. 257–302; 'Les Frontières constitutionelles en 1795', ibid. 18: 21–59; and 'Le Comité de salut public et la question de la rive gauche du Rhin en 1795', ibid. 273–322.

—— (1893–1912). *L'Europe et la révolution française*. 8 vols., Paris.

—— (1898). *The Eastern Question in the Eighteenth Century*. New York.

Sorel, A. (1969). *Europe and the French Revolution*. London.

Sorkin, D. (1987). *The Transformation of German Jewry, 1780–1840*. New York.

Speitkamp, W. (1986). *Restauration als Transformation: Untersuchungen zur kurhessischen Verfassungsgeschichte 1813–1830*. Darmstadt.

Spellanzon, C. (1933–51). *Storia del risorgimento e dell'unitá d'Italia*. 5 vols., Milan.

Sperber, J. (1984). *Popular Catholicism in Nineteenth-Century Germany*. Princeton, NJ.

Spindler, M. (1974). *Handbuch der bayerischen Geschichte*, vi. 1: *Das neue Bayern 1800–1970*. Munich.

Spitzer, A. B. (1971). *Old Hatreds and Young Hopes: The French Carbonari Against the Bourbon Restoration*. Cambridge, Mass.

Sprunck, A. (1951). 'Les Belges et les tentatives de réconciliation de l'Autriche au début de l'année 1790', *RBPH* 29: 93–111.

Squire, P. S. (1967a). 'Metternich and Benckendorff, 1807–1834', *SEER* 45: 135–62.

—— (1967b). 'The Metternich–Benckendorff Letters, 1835–1842', *SEER* 45: 368–90.

Srbik, H., Ritter von (1925–54). *Metternich der Staatsmann und der Mensch*. 3 vols., Munich.

—— (1936–42). *Deutsche Einheit: Idee und Wirklichkeit vom Heiligen Reich bis Königgrätz*. 4 vols., Munich.

Stadler, P. (1955). 'Politik und Geschichtsschreibung in der französischen Restauration, 1814–1830', *HZ* 180: 265–96.

—— (1984). *Der Kulturkampf in der Schweiz*. Frauenfeld.

Stagg, J. C. A. (1983). *Mr Madison's War*. Princeton, NJ.

Stanislavskaia, A. M. (1962). *Russko-angliiskie otnosheniia i problemy Sredizemnomoria*. Moscow.

—— (1976). *Rossiia i Gretsiia v kontse XVIII-nachale XIX veka: Politika Rossii v Ionicheskoi Respublike, 1798–1807 gg*. Moscow.

Stearns, P. (1965). 'British Industry Through the Eyes of French Industrialists (1820–1848)', *JMH* 37: 50–61.

Stefanovic-Vilovsky, T. von (1909). 'Belgrad während des Krieges Osterreichs und Russlands gegen die Pforte, 1787–1792', *Beiträge zur neueren Geschichte Österreichs*, 4: 137–9.

Steffens, W. (1943–52). 'Rheingrenze und territoriale Entschädigungsfrage in der preussischen Politik der Jahre 1795–98', *Westfälische Forschungen*, B. VII. C: 149–81.

Stein, R. (1983). 'The State of French Colonial Commerce on the Eve of the Revolution', *Journal of European Economic History*, 12: 105–17.

Stengers J. (1950–1). 'Sentiment national, sentiment orangiste et sentiment français à l'aube de notre indépendance', *RBPH* 28: 993–1029; 29: 63–92.

—— (1981a). 'La Belgique de 1830, une "nationalité de convention"?' *Revue de l'université de Bruxelles*, 1–2: 7–19.

—— (1981b). 'Le Mythe des dominations étrangères dans l'historiographie belge', *RBPH* 59: 382–401.

Stinchcombe, W. C. (1969). *The American Revolution and the French Alliance*. Syracuse, NY.

—— (1977). 'The Diplomacy of the WXYZ Affair', *William and Mary Quarterly*, 34: 590–617.

Stine, J. E. (1980). 'Frederick William II and the Decline of the Prussian Army, 1786–1797', diss., Univ. of South Carolina.

Stone, D. (1976). *Polish Politics and National Reform, 1775–1788*. Boulder, Colo.

Stoneman, R. (1984). 'The Origins of European Philhellenism', *History Today*, 34: 21–7.

Strachan, H. (1983). *European Armies and the Conduct of War*. Winchester, Mass.

—— (1984). *Wellington's Legacy: The Reform of the British Army, 1830–1854*. Manchester.

—— (1985). *From Waterloo to Balaclava: Tactics, Technology, and the British Army, 1815–1854*. Cambridge.

Stribrny, W. (1966). *Die Russland-Politik Friedrichs des Grossen 1764–1786*. Würzburg.

Strong, J. W. (1965). 'Russia's Plans for an Invasion of India in 1801', *CASS* 7: 114–26.

Stuart, R. (1978). *The Half-Way Pacifist: Thomas Jefferson's View of War*. Buffalo, NY.

Sullivan, A. T. (1983). *Thomas-Robert Bugeaud: France and Algeria, 1784–1849*. Hamden, Conn.

Surrateau, J.-R. (1973). 'Un paradoxe: l'échec de l'unité nationale suisse et le développement du nationalisme helvétique (1792–1815)', in *Actes* (1973: 53–84).

Sutherland, D. M. G. (1986). *France 1789–1815: Revolution and Counterrevolution*. Oxford.

Sutz, C. (1976). *Frankreichs Politik in der Sonderbundskrise*. Berne.

Sweet, P. R. (1941). *Friedrich von Gentz: Defender of the Old Order*. Madison, Wis.

—— (1978). *Wilhelm von Humboldt: A Biography*. 2 vols., Columbus, OH.

Sybel, H. von (1878–9). *Geschichte der Revolutionszeit von 1789 bis 1800*. 5 vols., Stuttgart.

Sydenham, M. J. (1974). *The First French Republic, 1792–1804*. Berkeley, Calif.

Syrett, D. (1979). 'The Role of the Royal Navy in the Napoleonic Wars after Trafalgar, 1805–1814', *US Naval War College Review*, 32: 71–83.

Szabo, F. A. J. (1979). 'Prince Kaunitz and the Balance of Power', *IHR* 1: 399–408.

Tacel, M. (1961). 'La Place de l'Italie dans l'économie impériale de 1806 à 1814', in Dunan (1961: 21–39).

Talleyrand-Périgord, C.-M. de (1891a). *Ambassade de Talleyrand à Londres, 1830–1834*, ed. G. Pallain. Paris.

—— (1891b). *Le Ministère de Talleyrand sous le directoire*, ed. G. Pallain. Paris.

—— (1891c). *Mission à Londres 1792*, ed. G. Pallain. Paris.

—— (1891–2). *Mémoires du prince de Talleyrand*, ed. Duc de Broglie. 5 vols., Paris.

—— (1967). *Lettres de Talleyrand à Napoléon, d'après les origineaux conservés aux archives des affaires étrangères*. Paris.

—— (1987). *Talleyrand und der Herzog von Dalberg*, ed. E. Ernst. Frankfurt.

Tamborra, A. (1960). 'I congressi della santa alleanza di Lubiana e di Verona e la politica della santa sede (1821–1822)', *Archivio storico italiano*, 118: 190–211.

Tan, C. (1978). *China and the Brave New World: A Study of the Origins of the Opium War (1840–42)*. Durham, NC.

Tangeraas, L. (1983). 'Castlereagh, Bernadotte and Norway', *Scandinavian Journal of History*, 8: 193–223.

Tarle, E. (1928). *Le Blocus continental et le royaume d'Italie*. Paris.

—— (1942). *Napoleon's Invasion of Russia*. New York.

Tarling, N. (1962). *Anglo-Dutch Rivalry in the Malay World, 1780–1824*. New York and London.

—— (1969). *British Policy in the Malay Peninsula and Archipelago, 1824–1871*, 2nd edn. Kuala Lumpur.

—— (1975). *Imperial Britain in South-East Asia*. New York.

Tassier, S. (1934). *Histoire de la Belgique sous l'occupation française*. Brussels.

Tatistcheff, S. S. (1891). *Alexandre Ier et Napoléon d'après leur correspondance inédite (1801–1812)*. Paris.

Taylor, A. J. P. (1934). *The Italian Problem in European Diplomacy, 1847–1849*. Manchester.

—— (1952). *Rumours of Wars*. London.

—— (1954). *The Struggle for Mastery in Europe, 1848–1918*. Oxford.

Te Brake, W. P. (1985). 'Popular Politics and the Dutch Patriot Revolution', *Theory and Society*, 14: 199–222.

Temperley, H. W. V. (1924a). 'Canning and the Conferences of the Four Allied Governments at Paris, 1823–1826', *AHR* 30: 16–43.

—— (1924b). 'Princess Lieven and the Protocol of 4 April 1826', *EHR* 39: 55–78.

—— (1925a). *The Foreign Policy of Canning, 1822–1827*. London.

—— (1925b). 'French Designs on Spanish America, 1820–5', *EHR* 40: 34–53.

—— (1936). *England and the Near East: The Crimea*. London.

Terlinden, C. (1922). 'La Politique économique de Guillaume Ier, roi des Pays-Bas, en Belgique, 1814–30', *RH* 139: 1–39.

Testa, I. Freiherr von, *et al.* (eds.) (1864–1911). *Recueil des traités de la Porte ottoman avec les puissances étrangères . . .* 11 vols., Paris.

Thaden, E. C. (1984). *Russia's Western Borderlands, 1710–1870*. Princeton, NJ.

Thielen, P. G. (1967). *Karl August von Hardenberg 1750 bis 1822: Eine Biographie*. Cologne.

Thomas, D. H. (1983). *The Guarantee of Belgian Neutrality in European Diplomacy, 1830s–1930s*. Kingston, RI.

Thomis, M., and Holt, P. (1977). *Threats of Revolution in Britain, 1789–1848*. Hamden, Conn.

Thompson, J. M. (1988). *Napoleon Bonaparte*. Oxford.

Thompson, N. (1986). *Wellington After Waterloo*. New York.

Thugut, J. A., Freiherr von (1872). *Vertrauliche Briefe des Freiherrn von Thugut*, ed. A. von Vivenot. 2 vols., Vienna.

Thuillier, G. (1983). *La Monnaie en France au début du XIXe siècle*. Geneva.

Tilly, C. (ed.) (1975). *The Formation of National States in Western Europe*. Princeton, NJ.

Todorova, M. (1977). 'British and Russian Policy toward the Reform Movement in the Ottoman Empire (30-ies–50-ies of the nineteenth C.)', *études balkaniques*, 3: 17–41.

—— (1983). *Angliia, Rossiia i Tanzimat*. Moscow.

Topolski, J. (1973). 'Reflections on the First Partition of Poland', *Acta Poloniae Historica*, 27: 89–104.

—— (1981). 'The Development of the Absolute Polish State and Prussia's Role in the Partitions of Poland', *Polish Western Affairs*, 22: 24–39.

Traugott, M. (1983). 'The Mid-Nineteenth-Century Crisis in France and England', *Theory and Society*, 12: 455–68.

Trausch, G. (1978). 'Les Luxembourgeois devant la révolution française', in R. Poidevin and G. Trausch (eds.), *Les Relations franco-luxembourgeoises de Louis XIV à Robert Schuman*, 79–117. Metz.

Tribe, K. (1984). 'Cameralism and the Science of Government', *JMH* 56: 263–84.

—— (1988). *Governing Economy: The Reformation of German Economic Discourse, 1750–1840*. New York.

Troisi, G. (1979). 'L'espansionismo cisalpino ed il conflitto territoriale con la repubblica romana', *RSR* 66: 131–44.

Tschirch, O. (1933–4). *Geschichte der öffentlichen Meinung in Preussen vom Baseler Frieden bis zum Zusammenbruch des Staates 1795–1806*. 2 vols., Weimar.

Tucker, R. W. (1982). *Fall of the First British Empire: Origins of the War of American Independence*. Baltimore, Md.

—— and Hendrickson, D. C. (1990). *Empire of Liberty: The Statecraft of Thomas Jefferson*. Oxford.

Tümmler, H. (1972). 'Wartburg, Weimar und Wien', *HZ* 215: 49–106.

Tulard, J. (1971). *Bibliographie critique des mémoires sur le consulat et l'empire*. Paris.

—— (1973). 'Siméon et l'organisation du royaume de Westphalie (1807–1813)', *Francia*, 1: 557–68.

—— (1977). *Napoléon ou le mythe du sauveur*. Paris.

Tulard, J. (1980a). 'Der "Domaine extraordinaire" als Finanzierungsinstrument Napoleonischer Expansion', GG 6: 490–99.

—— (1980b). 'L'Empire napoléonien', in M. Duverger (ed.), Le Concept d'Empire, 279–300. Paris.

Turczynski, E. (1982). 'Austro-Serb Relations, 1804–1813', in Vucinich (1982a: 175–206).

Turner, E. H. (1963). 'The Russian Squadron with Admiral Duncan's North Sea Fleet, 1795–1800', Mariner's Mirror, 49: 212–22.

Turner, M. L. (1980). 'French Art Confiscations in the Roman Republic, 1798', PCRE 2: 43–51.

Ullmann, H.-P. (1981). 'Überlegungen zur Entstehung des öffentlichen, verfassungsmässigen Kredits in den Rheinbundstaaten (Bayern, Württemberg und Baden)', in Berding and Ullmann (1981: 108–32).

—— (1982). 'Der Staatskredit im Rheinbund: Bayern, Württemberg und Baden im Vergleich', Francia, 10: 327–43.

Ullrich, H. (1978). 'Bürgertum und nationale Bewegung im Italien des Risorgimento', in Dann (1978: 129–56).

Valsecchi, F. (1974). 'Der aufgeklärte Absolutismus (Italien)', in Aretin (1974: 205–33).

Van Creveld, M. (1977). Supplying War. Cambridge.

Vandal, A. (1891–6). Napoléon et Alexandre Ier. 3 vols., Paris.

Veit-Brause, I. (1967). Die deutsch–französische Krise von 1840. Cologne.

—— (1983), 'Particularism: A Paradox of Cultural Nationalism?' in Eade (1983: 33–46).

Venturi, F. (1989). The End of the Old Regime in Europe, 1768–1776. Princeton, NJ.

—— (1991). The End of the Old Regime in Europe, 1776–1789. 2 vols., Princeton, NJ.

Vereté, M. (1952). 'Palmerston and the Levant Crisis, 1832', JMH 24: 143–51.

—— (1978). 'A Plan for the Internationalization of Jerusalem, 1840–1841', Asian and African Studies, 12: 13–31.

Verhaegen, P. (1929). La Belgique sous la domination française, 1792–1814. 5 vols., Brussels.

Vicens Vives, J. (1969). An Economic History of Spain. Princeton, NJ.

Vidalenc, J. (1963). Les Émigrés français, 1789–1825. Caen.

—— (1973). 'Les "Départements hanséatiques" et l'administration napoléonienne', Francia, 1: 414–50.

—— (1983a). 'Les Conditions d'exercice du métier militaire en France: une tentative de retour à l'armée de métier (1815–1818)', Revue internationale d'histoire militaire, 55: 103–28.

—— (1983b). 'Les Émigrés français dans les pays allemands pendant la révolution', Francia Beihefte, 12: 154–67.

Viennot, O. (1947). Napoléon et l'industrie française: la crise de 1810–1811. Paris.

Vierhaus, R. (1972). 'Eigentumsrecht und Mediatisierung: Der Kampf um die Rechte der Reichsritterschaft 1803–1815', in R. Vierhaus (ed.), *Eigentum und Verfassung*, 229–57. Göttingen.

—— (1981). 'Politisches Bewusstsein in Deutschland vor 1789', in Berding and Ullmann (1981: 161–83).

—— (1983). '"Sie und nicht Wir": Deutsche Urteile über den Ausbruch der französischen Revolution', in Voss (1983: 1–15).

—— (1984). 'Aufklärung und Reformzeit: Kontinuitäten und Neuansätze in der deutschen Politik des späten 18. und beginnenden 19. Jahrhunderts', in Weis (1984: 287–301).

—— (1985). '"Vormärz": ökonomische und soziale Krisen, ideologische und politische Gegensätze', *Francia*, 13: 355–68.

Vilar, P. (1973). 'Patrie et nation dans le vocabulaire de la guerre d'indépendance espagnole', in *Actes* (1973: 167–202).

Villefosse, L. de, and Bouissonouse, J. (1969). *L'Opposition à Napoléon*. Paris.

Vitzthum von Eckstädt, C. F. (1886). *Berlin und Wien in den Jahren 1845–1852: Politische Privatbriefe*, 2nd edn. Stuttgart.

Vivenot, A., Ritter von (1870). 'Thugut und sein politisches System', *Archiv für österreichische Geschichte*, 42: 363–492; 43: 103–97.

—— and Zeissberg, H. (eds.) (1873–90). *Quellen zur Geschichte der deutschen Kaiserpolitik Osterreichs während der französischen Revolutionskriege, 1790–1801*. 5 vols., Vienna.

Völkl, E. (1968). *Russland und Lateinamerika 1741–1841*. Wiesbaden.

—— (1970). 'Die russische Atlantik-Politik unter Alexander I (1801–1814)', *Saeculum*, 21: 41–56.

Vogel, B. (1983). *Allgemeine Gewerbefreiheit: Die Reformpolitik des preussischen Staatskanzlers Hardenberg, 1810–1820*. Göttingen.

Vomackowa, V. (1963). 'Oesterreich und der deutsche Zollverein', *Historica*, 5: 109–46.

Vorontsov (1870–95). *Arkhiv kniazia Vorontsova*, ed. P. I. Bartenev. 40 vols. in 54 pts., Moscow.

Voss, J. (ed.) (1983). *Deutschland und die Französische Revolution*. (Suppl. 13 of *Francia*.) Munich.

VPR (1960–). Russia, Ministerstvo inostrannykh del. *Vneshniaia Politika Rossii XIX i nachala XX veka; dokumenti rossiiskogo Ministersva inostrannykh del*. 1st ser.: 1801–15; 2nd ser.: 1815–30. Moscow.

Vucinich, W. S. (ed.) (1982a). *The First Serbian Uprising, 1804–1813*. Boulder, Colo.

—— (1982b). 'Russia and the First Serbian Uprising, 1806–1809', in Vucinich (1982a: 95–139).

Waliszewski, K. (1913). *Paul the First of Russia*. London.

Walker, F. A. (1967). 'The Rejection of Stratford Canning by Nicholas I', *BIHR* 40: 50–64.

Walker, M. (1971). *German Home Towns: Community, State, and General Estate, 1648–1871*. Ithaca, NY.

—— (1981). *Johann Jakob Moser and the Holy Roman Empire of the German Nation*. Chapel Hill, NC.

Waltz, K. N. (1979). *Theory of International Politics*. Reading, Mass.

Wandruszka, A. (1963–5). *Leopold II*. 2 vols., Vienna.

Wandycz, P. S. (1974). *The Lands of Partitioned Poland, 1795–1918*. Seattle, Washington.

Wangermann, E. (1982). 'Deutscher Patriotismus und österreichischer Reformabsolutismus im Zeitalter Josephs II', in Lutz and Rumpler (1982: 60–72).

—— (1991). 'Preussen und die revolutionären Bewegungen in Ungarn und den österreichischen Niederlanden zur Zeit der Französischen Revolution', in Büsch and Neugebauer-Wölk (1991: 77–85).

Warburton, R. T. (1980). 'The Rise of Nationalism in Switzerland', *Canadian Review of Studies of Nationalism*, 7: 274–98.

Ward, J. M. (1976). *British Policy in the South Pacific (1786–1843)*. Westport, Conn.

Warner, R. H. (1977). 'The Political Opposition to Tsar Paul I', diss., New York Univ.

Watson, J. S. (1960). *The Reign of George III 1760–1815*. Oxford.

Webb, P. L. C. (1980). 'Sea Power in the Ochakov Affair of 1791', *IHR* 2: 13–33.

Webster, C. K. (1919). *The Congress of Vienna, 1814–1815*. New York.

—— (ed.) (1921). *British Diplomacy, 1813–1815*. London.

—— (1925). *The Foreign Policy of Castlereagh, 1815–1822*. London.

—— (1931). *The Foreign Policy of Castlereagh, 1812–1815*. London.

—— (1934). 'Palmerston, Metternich, and the European System 1830–1841', *Proceedings of the British Academy*, 20: 125–58.

—— (1938). *Britain and the Independence of Latin America, 1812–1830*. 2 vols., London.

—— (1947). 'Urquhart, Ponsonby, and Palmerston', *EHR* 62: 327–51.

—— (1951). *The Foreign Policy of Palmerston, 1830–1841*. 2 vols., London.

Wegert, K. H. (1978). 'Restoration Radicals and "Organic Liberalism": Einheit-Freiheit Reconsidered', *Canadian Journal of History*, 12: 299–323.

—— (1981). 'Patrimonial Rule, Popular Self-Interest, and Jacobinism in Germany, 1763–1800', *JMH* 53: 440–67.

—— (1987). 'Political Engagement and the German Intelligentsia, 1789–1800', *Canadian Journal of History*, 22: 297–320.

Wehler, H.-U. (1987). *Deutsche Gesellschaftsgeschichte*. 2 vols., 1700–1849. Munich.

Weis, E. (1971). *Montgelas, 1759–1799*. Munich.

—— (1973). 'Der Einfluss der französischen Revolution und des Empire auf die Reformen in den süddeutschen Staaten', *Francia*, 1: 569–83.

—— (1975). 'Révoltes paysannes et citadines dans les états allemands sur la rive gauche du Rhin, de 1789 à 1792', *Francia*, 3: 346–58.

—— (1976). 'Zur Entstehungsgeschichte der bayerischen Verfassung von 1818', *ZBLG* 39: 413–44.

—— (1979). 'Napoleon und der Rheinbund', in Reden-Dohna (1979: 57–80).

—— (1981). 'Reich und Territorien in den letzten Jahrzehnten des 18. Jahrhunderts', in Berding and Ullmann (1981: 43–64).

—— (1983). 'Bayern und Frankreich in der Zeit des Konsulats und des Ersten Empire (1799–1815)', *HZ* 237: 559–95.

—— (ed.) (1984). *Reformen im Rheinbündischen Deutschland*. Munich.

—— (1988). 'Das Konzert der europäischen Machte in der Sicht Friedrichs des Grossen', in Melville *et al.* (1988: i. 315–24).

—— (1990). *Deutschland und Frankreich um 1800*. Munich.

—— (1991). 'Preussen–Frankreich–Amerika: Revolutionen und Reformen', in Büsch and Neugebauer-Wölk (1991: 3–20).

Weisser, H. (1971). 'Chartist Internationalism, 1845–1848', *HJ* 14: 49–66.

Weller, K. (1963). *Württembergische Geschichte*, 5th edn. Stuttgart.

Wellesley, F. A. (ed.) (1930). *The Diary and Correspondence of Henry Wellesley, First Lord Cowley, 1790–1846*. London.

Wellington, A. Wellesley, Duke of (1862–80). *Despatches, Correspondence and Memoranda*. 8 vols., London.

—— (1975). *The Prime Ministers' Papers Series: Wellington, Political Correspondence*, i: *1833–November 1834*, ed. J. Brooke and J. Gandy. London.

—— (1986). *The Prime Ministers' Papers Series: Wellington*, ii: *Political Correspondence November 1834–April 1835*, ed. R. J. Olney and J. Melvin. London.

Wenger, K. (1979). *Preussen in der öffentlichen Meinung Frankreichs, 1815–1870*. Göttingen.

Werner, G. (1977). *Bavaria in the German Confederation: 1820–1848*. Rutherford, NJ.

Whaley, J. (1985). *Religious Toleration and Social Change in Hamburg, 1529–1819*. Cambridge.

Whitcomb, E. A. (1979). *Napoleon's Diplomatic Service*. Durham, NC.

Whitworth, C., Earl (1887). *England and Napoleon in 1803; Being the Despatches of Lord Whitworth and Others*, ed. O. Browning. London.

Wickham, W. (1870). *The Correspondence of the Right Honourable William Wickham from the Year 1794*, ed. William Wickham. London.

Wickwire, F. B., and Wickwire, M. B. (1980). *Cornwallis: The Imperial Years*. Chapel Hill, NC.

Willecquet, J. (1974). 'Belgischer Nationalismus?' in Schieder and Alter (1974: 47–56).

—— (ed.) (1983). *Aspects des relations de la Belgique, du grand-duché de Luxembourg, et des Pays-Bas avec l'Italie*. Brussels.

Willms, J. (1983). *Nationalismus ohne Nation: Deutsche Geschichte von 1789 bis 1914*. Düsseldorf.

Windham, W. (1866). *The Diary of the Right Honourable William Windham, 1784–1810*, ed. Mrs H. Baring. London.

—— (1913). *The Windham Papers: Life and Correspondence of the Right Hon. William Windham, 1750–1810*. 2 vols., London.

Winkler, A. (1927). 'Metternich und die Schweiz', *Zeitschrift für Schweizerische Geschichte*, 7: 60–116, 127–63.

Winkler, A. (1933). *Österrreich und die Klosteraufhebung im Aargau*. 2 vols., Aarau.

Winkler-Seraphim, B. (1955–6). 'Das Verhältnis der preussischen Ostprovinzen, insbesondere Ostpreussens zum Deutschen Bund im 19. Jahrhundert', *Zeitschrift für Ostforschung*, 4: 321–50; 5: 1–33.

Winter, E. (1961). 'Eine bedeutsame Unterredung zwischen Zar Nikolaus I und Metternich am Neujahrstag, 1846', *ZGW* 9: 1861–70.

Witte, E. (1989). 'The Formation of a Centre in Belgium: The Role of Brussels in the Formative Stage of the Belgian State (1830–1840)', *European History Quarterly*, 19: 435–68.

Wittichen, P. (1899). *Die polnische Politik Preussens 1788–1790*. Göttingen.

Wittichen, F. K. (1905). *Preussen und die Revolutionen in Belgien und Lüttich 1789–90*. Göttingen.

Wittram, R. (1959). 'Das russische Imperium und sein Gestaltwandel', *HZ* 187: 568–93.

Wohlfeil, R. (1964). *Vom stehenden Heer des Absolutismus zur allgemeinen Wehrpflicht (1789–1814)*, pt. ii: H. Meier-Welcker *et al.* (eds.), *Handbuch zur deutschen Militärgeschichte 1648–1939*. Frankfurt.

—— (1965). *Spanien und die deutsche Erhebung, 1808–1814*. Wiesbaden.

—— (1968). 'Der Volkskrieg im Zeitalter Napoleons', in Groote and Müller (1968: 105–22).

—— (1969). 'Napoleonische Modellstaaten', in Groote (1969: 33–53).

Wolf, G. (1985). 'Le Marquis Scipion de Chambonas, ministre des affaires étrangères de Louis XVI (juin–juillet 1792)', *AHRF* 57: 25–45.

Wolffe, J. (1991). *The Protestant Crusade in Great Britain, 1829–1860*. Oxford.

Wollstein, G. (1977). *Das Grossdeutschland der Paulskirche*. Düsseldorf.

—— (1978). 'Scharnhorst und die Französische Revolution', *HZ* 227: 325–52.

Woloch, I. (1979). *The French Veteran from the Revolution to the Restoration*. Chapel Hill, NC.

—— (1986). 'Napoleonic Conscription: State Power and Civil Society', *PP* 111: 101–29.

Woodhouse, C. M. (1952). *The Greek War of Independence: Its Historical Setting*. London.

Woolf, S. (1979). *A History of Italy 1700–1860: The Social Constraints of Political Change*. London.

—— (1991). *Napoleon's Integration of Europe*. London.

Woronoff, D. (1984). *The Thermidorean Regime and the Directory, 1794–1799*. New York.

Wright, D. (1977). *The English Amongst the Persians during the Qajar Period 1787–1921*. London.

Wright, H. R. C. (1955). *Free Trade and Protection in the Netherlands, 1816–1830*. Cambridge.

Wright, Q. (1963). *A Study of War*, 2nd edn. Chicago.

Wrigley, W. D. (1988). *The Diplomatic Significance of Ionian Neutrality, 1821–31*. New York.

Wunder, B. (1978). 'Landstände und Rechtsstaat. Zur Entstehung und Verwirklichung des Art. 13 DBA', *Zeitschrift für Historische Forschung*, 5: 139–85.

Yakshich, G. (1906). 'La Russie et la Porte ottomane de 1812 à 1826', *RH* 91: 281–306.

Yapp, M. E. (1960). 'The Control of the Persian Mission, 1822–1836', *Univ. of Birmingham Historical Journal*, 7: 162–79.

—— (1980). *Strategies of British India: Britain, Iran and Afghanistan, 1798–1850*. Oxford.

—— (1956). *Bonaparte e il direttorio dopo Campoformio: il problema italiano nella diplomazia europea, 1797–1798*. Naples.

Zaghi, C. (1966). *La rivoluzione francese e l'Italia*. Naples.

—— (1969). *Napoleone e l'Europa*. Naples.

—— (1986). *L'Italia di Napoleone dalla cisalpino al regno*. Turin.

Zajewski, W. (1980). 'L'Influence de la révolution de juillet 1830 sur les évènements de la nuit du 29 novembre en Pologne', *Kwartalnik Historyczny*, 87: 621–34.

Zak, L. A. (1957). 'Iz istorii angliiskoi politiki v otnoshenii Germanii v poslednii period napoleonovskikh voin (1812–13)', *Ucheniye Zapiski po Novoi i Noveishei Istorii* 3: 467–529.

—— (1966). *Monarkhi protiv narodov: Diplomaticheskaia borba na razvalinakh napoleonovskoi imperii*. Moscow.

Zeller, G. (1933). 'La Monarchie d'ancien régime et les frontières naturelles', *Revue d'histoire moderne*, 8: 305–33.

—— (1936). 'Histoire d'une idée fausse', *Revue de synthèse*, 3rd ser., 11: 115–31.

—— (1953–5). *Les Temps modernes*. 2 vols., Paris.

—— (1956). 'Le Principe de l'équilibre dans la politique internationale avant 1789', *RH* 215: 25–37.

—— (1964). *Aspects de la politique française sous l'ancien régime*. Paris.

Zernack, K. (1967). 'Stanislaw August Poniatowski: Probleme einer politischen Biographie', *JGO* 15: 371–92.

—— (1974a). 'Negative Polenpolitik als Grundlage deutsch–russischer Diplomatie in der Mächtepolitik des 18. Jahrhunderts', in U. Liszkonski (ed.), *Russland und Deutschland: Festschrift für Georg von Rauch*, 144–59. Stuttgart.

—— (1974b). 'Das Zeitalter der nordischen Kriege von 1558 bis 1809 als frühneuzeitliche Geschichtsepoche', *Zeitschrift für historische Forschung*, 1: 55–79.

—— (ed.) (1979). *Modernisierung und nationale Gesellschaft im ausgehenden 18. und 19. Jahrhundert*. Berlin.

—— (ed.) (1982). *Polen und die polnische Frage in der Geschichte der Hohenzollernmonarchie, 1701–1871*. Berlin.

—— (1983). 'Die Geschichte Preussens und das Problem der deutsch-polnischen Beziehungen', *JGO* 31: 28–49.

—— (ed.) (1987). *Zum Verständnis der polnischen Frage in Preussen und Deutschland 1772–1871*. Berlin.

Zernack, K. (1991). 'Preussen–Frankreich–Polen. Revolution und Teilung', in Büsch and Neugebauer-Wölk (1991: 21–42).

Ziegler, P. (1965). *Addington*. New York.

—— (1976). *Melbourne*. New York.

Zimmermann, J. (1965). *Militär und Heeresaufbringung in Österreich bis 1806*, vol. iii of *Handbuch der deutschen Militärgeschichte 1648–1939*, 2nd edn. Frankfurt.

Zinkeisen, J. W. (1840–63). *Geschichte des Osmanischen Reiches in Europa*. 7 vols., Gotha.

Zlotnikov, M. F. (1966). *Kontinentalnaia blokada e Rossiia*. Moscow.

Zöllner, E. (ed.) (1977). *Diplomatie und Aussenpolitik Österreichs*. Vienna.

Zorn, W. (1962). 'Gesellschaft und Staat im Bayern des Vormärz', in Conze (1962: 113–42).

Zorsi, A. (1986). *Venezia Austriaca, 1798–1866*. Bari.

Zubow, Graf V. (1963). *Zar Paul I: Mensch und Schicksal*. Stuttgart.

Zwehl, H. K. von (1937). *Der Kampf um Bayern 1805*. Munich.

INDEX